SECOND

MANAGEMENT

SECOND EDITION

MANAGEMENT

RICHARD L. DAFT
VANDERBILT UNIVERSITY

THE DRYDEN PRESS
Chicago Fort Worth San Francisco Philadelphia
Montreal Toronto London Sydney Tokyo

Acquisitions Editor: Robert Gemin
Developmental Editor: Jan Richardson
Project Editor: Karen Steib
Design Director: Jeanne Calabrese
Production Manager: Robert Lange
Permissions Editor: Doris Milligan
Director of Editing, Design, and Production: Jane Perkins

Copy Editor: Kathy Pruno
Indexer: Sheila Ary
Compositor: York Graphic Services
Text Type: 10/12 New Caledonia

Library of Congress Cataloging-in-Publication Data
Daft, Richard L.
Management/Richard L. Daft.—2nd ed.
p. cm.
Includes bibliographical references (p.) and indexes.
ISBN 0-03-033092-0
1. Industrial management. I. Title.
HD31.D134 1991
658—dc20 90-3351
CIP

Printed in the United States of America
012-032-987654321

Address orders:
The Dryden Press
Orlando, FL 32887

Address editorial correspondence:
The Dryden Press
908 N. Elm Street
Hinsdale, IL 60521

The Dryden Press
Holt, Rinehart and Winston
Saunders College Publishing

Cover Source: Morgan Russell, *Cosmic Synchromy,* oil on canvas, 1913–1914, 16¼ × 13⅛ in. Munson-Williams-Proctor Institute Museum of Art, Utica, New York.

To Nancy Lee Moudry

True friendship is the merging of souls.

The Dryden Press Series in Management

Bartlett
Cases in Strategic Management for Business

Bedeian
Management, *Second Edition*

Bedeian and Zammuto
Organizations: Theory and Design

Boone and Kurtz
Contemporary Business, *Sixth Edition*

Bowman and Branchaw
Business Report Writing, *Second Edition*

Bracker, Montanari, and Morgan
Cases in Strategic Management

Cullinan
Business English for Industry and the Professions

Czinkota, Rivoli, and Ronkainen
International Business

Daft
Management, *Second Edition*

Efendioglu and Montanari
The Advantage Ski Company: A Strategic Simulation

Gaither
Production and Operations Management: A Problem-Solving and Decision-Making Approach, *Fourth Edition*

Foegen
Business Plan Guidebook with Financial Spreadsheets

Forgionne
Quantitative Management

Gatewood and Feild
Human Resource Selection, *Second Edition*

Greenhaus
Career Management

Higgins
Strategy: Formulation, Implementation, and Control

Higgins and Vincze
Strategic Management: Text and Cases, *Fourth Edition*

Hills
Compensation Decision Making

Hodgetts
Modern Human Relations at Work, *Fourth Edition*

Holley and Jennings
The Labor Relations Process, *Fourth Edition*

Huseman, Lahiff, and Penrose
Business Communication: Strategies and Skills, *Fourth Edition*

Jauch, Coltrin, and Bedeian
The Managerial Experience: Cases, Exercises, and Readings, *Fifth Edition*

Kemper
Experiencing Strategic Management

Kuehl and Lambing
Small Business: Planning and Management, *Second Edition*

Kuratko and Hodgetts
Entrepreneurship: A Contemporary Approach

Lee
Introduction to Management Science, *Second Edition*

Luthans and Hodgetts
Business

Montanari, Morgan, and Bracker
Strategic Management: A Choice Approach

Northcraft and Neale
Organizational Behavior: A Management Challenge

Tombari
Business and Society: Strategies for the Environment and Public Policy

Varner
Contemporary Business Report Writing, *Second Edition*

Vecchio
Organizational Behavior, *Second Edition*

Wolters and Holley
Labor Relations: An Experiential and Case Approach

Zikmund
Business Research Methods, *Third Edition*

PREFACE

My vision for the second edition of *Management* remains the same as for the first edition — to create a better kind of management text that conveys to students both the contemporary application of management ideas and the intellectual enjoyment of management research. As before, The Dryden Press has challenged me to develop a higher-quality text than is currently available to capture the value, excitement, frustration, and adventure of organizational management.

For my part, I wrote every word in the text, including chapter content, photo captions, boxed items, and in-text examples, with the single desire of being true to theoretical concepts while making them interesting to students. Then I rewrote the chapters as often as needed to make the language smooth and the ideas appealing. While being faithful to management theories and research, I also identified and discussed emerging management trends. For example, the press of *global competition* receives major attention throughout the text, as do the issues of *ethics* and *entrepreneurship*. New material in the book also reflects:

- the increased importance of teamwork in organizations
- horizontal coordination rather than vertical control
- the use of leadership to empower lower employees, time-based competition
- the need for quality in both products and services
- the impact of new information and production technologies
- new network and team-based organization structures
- workforce diversity
- motivational approaches such as gain-sharing and executive information systems
- the new role of product design for simplicity
- small business incubators and spin-offs

For its part, Dryden provided the resources necessary to support this endeavor, creating a team of experts to create and coordinate color photographs, video cases, artwork, and ancillary materials to fulfill our shared dream of what a management book could be. New to this edition are ancillaries such as video cases and a computer simulation, providing the teaching aids necessary to give this text maximum learning impact.

Continuing with the theme of the first edition, we have expanded the use of photo essays. Photos add a visual dimension that carry students into the real world of management. Well-chosen photographs are unrivaled in their ability to convey vivid descriptions of management scenes, events, and people. The photos are combined with written descriptions that portray how management looks and feels and offer intimate glimpses into management life. Some photographs are pleasant, some are disarming, and some are surprising, but all are immensely valuable in helping students penetrate the often abstract and distant world of management.

ORGANIZATION

The chapter sequence in *Management* is organized around the management functions of planning, organizing, leading, and controlling. These four functions effectively encompass both management research and characteristics of the manager's job.

Part One introduces the world of management, including the nature of the manager's job, historical perspectives on management, and the influence of the larger environment on organizations and management. A new chapter on managerial ethics and social responsibility has been added because these issues are making up an increasingly important part of the manager's world.

Part Two presents four chapters on planning. The first two chapters describe goal setting, planning, strategy formulation, and strategy implementation. The next two chapters describe both qualitative and quantitative approaches to making decisions associated with planning.

Part Three focuses on organizing processes. These chapters describe the dimensions of structural design, the design alternatives managers can use to achieve strategic objectives, structural designs for promoting innovation and change, and the design and use of the human resource function.

Part Four is devoted to leadership. This section begins with a description of leadership and paves the way for the subsequent topics of employee motivation, communication, and management of teams.

Part Five describes the controlling function of management, including basic principles of organization control, the design of control systems, management information systems, and techniques for control of operations management.

Part Six describes two significant management issues — international management and entrepreneurship. The international chapter provides a comprehensive introduction to the strategies, structure, control systems, and leadership qualities used to manage organizations in the face of global competition. The new entrepreneurship chapter describes fundamental concepts for launching and managing a new business. The career appendix describes both individual and organizational strategies for managing careers.

SPECIAL FEATURES

One major goal of this book is to offer better ways of using the textbook medium to convey management knowledge to the reader. To this end, the book includes several special features:

VIDEO CASES. One innovation in this edition is the inclusion of six video cases. A written case is provided at the end of each part and is accompanied by a video for the instructor to show students in class. The videos greatly enhance class discussion because students can see the company and more directly apply management concepts. Additional video segments are provided for each chapter from the *Growing a Business* and The Dryden Press series of videos. A detailed description of each video, classroom introductions, video assignments, and discussion questions and answers are provided in the *Video Instructor's Manual.*

Photo Essays. Another innovative feature of the book is the use of photographs accompanied by detailed captions that describe management events and how they relate to chapter material. The photo essays cover a rich assortment of organizations and management events. Many of the photos are beautiful to look at, and all of them convey the vividness, immediacy, and concreteness of management events.

Chapter Outline and Objectives. Each chapter begins with a clear statement of learning objectives and an outline of its contents. These devices provide an overview of what is to come and can also be used by students to see whether they understand and have retained important points.

Management Problem/Solution. The text portion of each chapter begins with a real-life problem faced by organization managers. The problem pertains to the topic of the chapter and will heighten students' interest in chapter concepts. The problem is resolved at the end of the chapter, where chapter concepts guiding the management's actions are highlighted.

Contemporary Examples. Every chapter of the text contains a large number of written examples of management incidents. These are placed at strategic points in the chapter and are designed to demonstrate the application of concepts to specific companies. The examples include well-known companies such as IBM, Hewlett-Packard, Toyota, Motorola, Procter & Gamble, General Motors, Coca-Cola, and Marriott, as well as less well-known companies and not-for-profit organizations such as Huffy Corporation, New York City Transit Authority, Columbia Gas Systems, Crane Plastics, Parsons Pine Products, Troxel Manufacturing, North American Tool & Die, and Whisler Manufacturing. They put students in immediate touch with the real world of organizations so that they can appreciate the value of management concepts.

Winning Moves. This new boxed feature explores how companies, when faced with new challenges, use innovative ideas to compete in both the domestic and global marketplace.

Manager's Shoptalk. These boxed items contain issues of special interest to management students. They may describe a contemporary topic or problem that is relevant to chapter content or may contain a diagnostic questionnaire or a special example of how managers handle a problem. These boxes will heighten student interest in the subject matter and provide an auxiliary view of management issues not typically available in textbooks.

Focus Boxes. These boxed items pertain to ethics, global competition, and entrepreneurship. Their purpose is to help students integrate these topics with other concepts in the book. Too often such topics are presented in separate, discrete chapters that have no connection with other materials. Yet concepts in almost every chapter have implications for ethics, global competition, and entrepreneurship. The focus boxes are referenced in the chapter to help students understand the relevance of the chapter material for these important management topics.

Glossaries. Learning the management vocabulary is essential to understanding contemporary management. This is facilitated in three ways. First, key concepts are boldfaced and completely defined where they first appear in the text. Second, brief definitions are set out in the margin for easy review and follow-up. Third, a glossary summarizing all key terms and definitions appears at the end of the book for handy reference.

Artwork. Many aspects of management are research based, and some concepts tend to be abstract and theoretical. To enhance students' awareness and understanding of these concepts, many exhibits have been included throughout the book. These exhibits consolidate key points, indicate relationships among variables, and visually illustrate concepts. They also make effective use of color to enhance their imagery and appeal.

Management in Practice Exercises. New to the second edition are end-of-chapter exercises called either *Management in Practice: Experiential Exercise* or *Management in Practice: Ethical Dilemma.* These exercises provide a self-test for students and an opportunity to experience management issues in a personal way. Many exercises also provide an opportunity for students to work in teams.

Chapter Summary and Discussion Questions. Each chapter closes with a summary of key points to be retained. The discussion questions are a complementary learning tool that will enable students to check their understanding of key issues, to think beyond basic concepts, and to determine areas that require further study. The summary and discussion questions help students discriminate between main and supporting points and provide mechanisms for self-teaching.

Cases for Analysis. Each chapter ends with two brief but substantive cases for student analysis and class discussion. Approximately half the cases are about companies whose names students will recognize. The others are based on real management events but disguise the identities of the companies and managers. These cases provide an opportunity for students to apply concepts to real events and to sharpen their diagnostic skills for management problem solving.

Supplementary Materials

Dryden has spared no expense to make *Management* the premier text in the market today. Many instructors face large classes with limited resources, and supplementary materials provide a way to expand and improve the students' learning experience. The learning package provided with *Management* was specifically designed to meet the needs of instructors facing a variety of teaching conditions.

Test Bank. The most important part of the teaching package is the *Test Bank.* The *Test Bank* was given special attention during the preparation of the second edition because instructors desire test questions that accurately and fairly assess student competence in subject material. Prepared by Judith Bulin, Monroe Community College, and Allen K. Gulezian, Central Washington University, the *Test Bank* provides 2,500 multiple-choice, true/false, matching, and essay test items. New multiple-choice questions based on self-contained mini-cases are a great time-saving substitute for essay questions, combining the comprehensive testing of concepts and applications with the ease of an objective test.

The test items have been reviewed and class tested by four professors to ensure the highest quality. Each question is keyed to chapter learning objectives, has been rated for level of difficulty, and is designated either as factual or application so that instructors can provide a balanced set of questions for student exams.

Computerized Test Bank. A *Computerized Test Bank* with versions for IBM, Apple, and Macintosh computers is available free to adopters. The *Computerized Test Bank* allows instructors to select and edit test items from the printed *Test Bank* as well as add an unlimited number of their own questions. Up to 99 versions of each test can be custom printed.

Instructor's Manual. A completely re-organized *Instructor's Manual* has been prepared to provide fundamental support to new professors teaching the course and innovative new materials for experienced professors. The manual features detailed *Lecture Outlines* that include additional information and examples not found in the text. *International Perspectives* provide additional international examples and material for each chapter with suggestions on where to integrate the information. *Class Starter* suggestions are included for each chapter, as well as a *Lecture Example File* that includes three to five additional management examples to integrate into class lectures.

The manual also contains annotated learning objectives, changes to the second edition, answers to chapter discussion questions, teaching notes for the end-of-chapter experiential exercises, ethical incidents, and cases. Answers for the end-of-part video cases are also provided.

The *Instructor's Manual* was prepared by a talented group of authors: Cliff Barbee of Houston Baptist University, Stephen Hiatt of Catawba College, Andrea Licari of St. John's University (New York), and Mel Schnake of Valdosta State College.

Computerized Instructor's Manual. A disk will be available to instructors that contains most elements of the *Instructor's Manual.* Teachers can electronically cut and paste together the parts of the manual they desire for customized lecture outlines.

Video Instructor's Manual. This manual contains video cases and teaching notes for each chapter and part of the text. It lists the title, running time, teaching objectives, and a detailed outline for each video case. It also provides page references for chapter concepts to be observed in the videos, video warm-ups, answers to case questions, video recap discussion questions, and coordinated experiential exercises for the videos. A multiple-choice test is also available for each video. The manual was developed by William Schulte of George Mason University.

Study Guide. This guide is invaluable for helping students master management concepts. Prepared by Stephen Hiatt, Catawba College, the *Study Guide* provides a summary and completion exercise for each chapter, a chapter review with multiple-choice, true/false, and short answer questions, and a minicase with multiple-choice questions. Each chapter also contains management applications and an experiential exercise that can be assigned as homework or used in class. The *Career Management Guide*, written by Jeffrey H. Greenhaus of Drexel University, challenges students to manage their careers with self-assessment and career planning exercises.

Computerized Study Guide. The easy-to-use software builds student competency using original questions not found in the *Test Bank* or printed *Study Guide*. The program is available for IBM computers.

Transparency Masters and Acetates. More than 150 transparency masters from text art and 100 all-new color acetates are available to adopters. Masters and acetates are accompanied by detailed teaching notes that include summaries of key concepts and discussion questions for in-class use. The transparencies and teaching notes were developed by Calvin Kellogg of the University of Mississippi and Dale Konicek of Houston Community College.

Computer Simulation. This management simulation, written by Eugene Calvasina of Auburn University-Montgomery, places students in the manager's role and requires them to make decisions about key areas of the business. This is an interactive simulation designed to offer students the opportunity to learn how decisions affect an organization.

Supplemental Modules. Supplemental written modules in the areas of organizational behavior, operations management, and management applications are available. These are designed to supplement text coverage and to address the needs of schools whose management principles courses emphasize any of these areas.

Experiential Exercises and Teaching Notes. This booklet, developed by Mel Schnake, contains additional experiential exercises with complete teaching notes.

Annual Ancillary Update. This unique volume provides updates of chapter material, figures, and new examples to keep classroom lectures up-to-date. New test items, transparencies, and video teaching materials are also included.

ACKNOWLEDGMENTS

A gratifying experience for me was working with the dedicated team of professionals at The Dryden Press who were determined to produce the best management book ever. I am grateful to Butch Gemin, whose enthusiasm and perspective kept the book's spirit alive. I also thank Jan Richardson for her excellent coordination of materials and her suggestions for improvement, and Karen Steib for her superb project coordination. Jeanne Calabrese created an elegant design, Doris Milligan pursued permissions enthusiastically, and Kathy Pruno provided skilled copyediting. Bob Lange and Rose Hepburn helped overcome many obstacles along the way. Thanks also to Bill Schoof and Jane Perkins for their overwhelming support of this book and for putting the Dryden team together. It's not possible to say enough about the caring and commitment of these people. I thank each of you very much.

Here at Vanderbilt I want to extend special appreciation to Rita Carswell. Rita helped me make the transition to Vanderbilt and without her typing and secretarial skills, this book could not have been completed. Phyllis Washburn, Texas A&M, and Sandra Lane here at Vanderbilt also pitched in when needed. Rebecca DeMars, my research assistant, made one creative suggestion after another that helped me when I needed it most. Also here at Vanderbilt, thanks to Jeanne Plas for devoting many hours to this book in her own special way. I also want to acknowledge an intellectual debt to my previous colleagues at Texas A&M and to my new colleagues, Diana Deadrick and Tom Mahoney, here at Vanderbilt. Thanks also to Marty Geisel, Dean, who supported this project fully and maintained a positive scholarly atmosphere here at the Owen School.

Another group of people who made a major contribution to this text were the management experts who provided advice, reviews, answers to questions, and suggestions for changes, insertions, and clarifications. I want to thank each of these colleagues for their valuable feedback and suggestions:

Robert J. Ash
Rancho Santiago College

Hal Babson
Columbus State Community College

Robert W. Baker
Metro Community College

McRae C. Banks II
Mississippi State University

Allen Bluedorn
University of Missouri — Columbia

Eugene Calvasina
Auburn University at Montgomery

Thomas Carey
Western Michigan University

James Cashman
University of Alabama

Herchel Chait
Indiana State University

Sharon Clinebell
University of Northern Colorado

Daniel S. Cochran
Mississippi State University

Raymond L. Cook
The University of Texas

Roy A. Cook
Fort Lewis College

L. A. Digman
University of Nebraska

Vernon Dorweiler
Michigan Technological School of Business

John W. Eastman
Kent State University

Tom Edwards
York Technical College

Judson Faurer
Metro State College

Janice M. Feldbauer
Austin Community College

William Fitzpatrick
Villanova University

Charles Flaherty
University of Minnesota

Steven W. Floyd
University of Massachusetts

Patricia A. Greenfield
University of Massachusetts

Allen Gulezian
Central Washington University

Fred C. House
Northern Arizona University

Charles W. Hubbard
Southwest Texas State University

Edmund Hunter
Delaware County Community College

Robert Insley
University of North Texas

Jackie Lynn Jankovich
Colorado State University

Bradley R. Johnson
University of Nebraska at Omaha

R. Sitk. Karahan
Montana State University

Alan Kardoff
University of Wisconsin — Superior

Ronald A. Klocke
Mankato State University

Don Lytle
University of Oregon

Albert H. Mahrer
Front Range Community College

Robert Marx
University of Massachusetts

Daniel McAllister
University of Nevada — Las Vegas

Bruce Meglino
University of South Carolina

Carolyn Patton Nickeson
Del Mar College

Leah R. Pietron
University of Nebraska at Omaha

Clinton H. Richards
University of Nevada — Las Vegas

Jane Preston Rose
Hiram College

Richard Saavedra
University of Minnesota

Nick Sarantakes
Austin Community College

Karen Schenkenfelder
Oak Park, Illinois

S. R. Siegel
Drexel University

Ray Sifrit
Del Mar College

James O. Smith
East Carolina University

William Soukup
University of San Diego

Richard L. Sutton
University of Nevada — Las Vegas

John Todd
University of Arkansas

Linda Trevino
Pennsylvania State University

Trudy Verser
Western Michigan University

Stephen I. Winter
Orange County Community College

I also want to acknowledge those people who contributed to the first edition, because their impact is still felt in the second edition.

Michael Abelson
Texas A&M University

Paul Babrowski
University of Oregon

Jay Barney
Texas A&M University

Gerald Bassford
Arizona State University

Bruce Blaylock
Eastern Kentucky University

Art Bell
University of Southern California

Van Clouse
University of Louisville

Richard Cuba
University of Baltimore

Barbara Deaux
Santa Fe State University

Fran Emory
Northern Virginia Community College — Woodbridge

J.E. Estes
University of South Carolina

Phyllis Fowler
Macomb Community College

Jeff Heyl
University of Colorado at Denver

Jim Higgins
Rollins College

Chuck Kuehl
University of Missouri at St. Louis

Peggy Lambing
University of Missouri at St. Louis

Janina Latack
Ohio State University

Marcia Miceli
Ohio State University

Thomas Miller
Memphis State University

Van Miller
Baylor University

Marilyn Morgan
University of Virginia

David Nagao
Georgia Tech University

Glen Oddou
San Jose State University

Nikki Paahana
DeVry Institute of Technology

Floyd Paulk
Central State University

Carole Saunders
Texas Christian University

Charles Shrader
Iowa State University

Susan Smith
Central Michigan University

William Smith
Hofstra University

Robert Sullivan
University of Texas — Austin

Eugene Szwajkowski
University of Illinois at Chicago

Mary Thibodeaux
North Texas State University

David Van Fleet
Texas A&M University

Jim Weekly
University of Toledo

Lewis Welshofer
Miami of Ohio University

Daniel Wren
University of Oklahoma

Marlin C. Young
Southwest Texas State University

I would like to extend a personal word of thanks to the many dedicated authors who contributed to the ancillary package for the second edition. Judy Bulin and Allen Gulezian have written a wonderful *Test Bank.* Cliff Barbee, Andrea Licari, Steve Hiatt, and Mel Schnake have made the *Instructor's Manual* a valuable teaching tool with innovative new features. Bill Schulte has developed a *Video Instructor's Manual* second to none. Gene Calvasina and Jim Barton have added a much needed management simulation, and Cal Kellogg and Dale Konicek have done a terrific job revising the transparency package to accompany the text. Steve Hiatt has worked hard to ensure that the *Study Guide* reflects the chapter material in the textbook, and Jeff Greenhaus has added a valuable career management supplement to the *Study Guide.* These people are truly dedicated to improving the classroom experience of management instructors.

I also want to acknowledge my daughters, Danielle and Amy, for their love and support this past year. We no longer live in the same city, but we have reached a new understanding and appreciation for one another, and for what Dad does for a living. Thanks also to B.J. for his warmth, silliness, and laughter that brightened my life during the hectic writing schedule.

Finally, I'd like to pay special tribute to Nancy Moudry, who has made an exceptional contribution to this book since the inception of the first edition. Nancy believed absolutely that students' learning could be enriched and deepened through the use of photo essays, and she spent endless hours searching for just the right photographs. Her photographs convey powerful images and insights and are linked directly to theoretical concepts in the text. Even more important, Nancy's unwavering belief in this book and its author has been especially significant to me. Nancy's friendship, optimism, and encouragement pulled me through some difficult and frustrating days. Thanks to Nancy, I have learned about intellectual and emotional sharing, and have achieved a healthier balance in my life. True friendship is a powerful force, especially when accompanied by caring and selflessness. Nancy, thanks for the emotional support, thanks for the discussions, thanks for the personal growth, thanks for keeping the faith. I am proud to dedicate this book to you.

Richard L. Daft
Nashville, Tennessee
November 1990

About the Author

Richard L. Daft, Ph.D., holds the Ralph Owen Chair in Management at Vanderbilt University, where he specializes in the study of organization theory and management. Dr. Daft is a Fellow of the Academy of Management and has served on the editorial boards of *Academy of Management Journal* and *Administrative Science Quarterly*. He is the Co-Editor-in-Chief of *Organization Science* and served for three years as associate editor of *Administrative Science Quarterly*.

Professor Daft has authored or co-authored six books including *Organization Theory and Design* (West Publishing, 1989) and *What to Study: Generating and Developing Research Questions* (Sage, 1982). He has also authored dozens of scholarly articles, papers, and chapters. His work has been published in *Administrative Science Quarterly, Academy of Management Journal, Academy of Management Review, Strategic Management Journal, Journal of Management, Accounting Organizations and Society, Management Science, MIS Quarterly, California Management Review*, and *Organizational Behavior Teaching Review.* Professor Daft has been awarded several government research grants to pursue studies of organization design, organizational innovation and change, strategy implementation, and organizational information processing.

Dr. Daft also is an active teacher and consultant. He has taught management, organizational change, organizational behavior, organizational theory, and strategic management. He has been actively involved in management development and consulting for many companies and government organizations including the American Banking Association, Bell Canada, NL Baroid, Tenneco, and the United States Air Force.

Brief Contents

CONTENTS

PART 1
INTRODUCTION TO MANAGEMENT 1

PART 1

Introduction to Management

The Southwestern Bell Corporation has a strong commitment to fostering cultural activities in the United States. Through its corporate art collection the company hopes to help ensure the future of American art by encouraging young talent and maintaining the heritage of established modern masters, such as Roy Lichtenstein. In addition, Southwestern Bell believes the collection plays a vital roll in enhancing the employee work environment. This goal is nurtured by the regular tours and lectures that are provided for the employees, as well as an active loan program of artwork to exhibits nation wide.

Roy Lichtenstein, *View from the Window*, 1985, mixed media print. Southwestern Bell Corporation Collection, St. Louis, MO.

C H A P T E R 1

The Nature of Management

Chapter Outline

The Definition of Management

The Four Management Functions

Planning
Organizing
Leading
Controlling

Organizational Performance

Management Types

Vertical Differences
Horizontal Differences

Management Skills

Conceptual Skills
Human Skills
Technical Skills
Making the Transition

What Is It Like to Be a Manager?

Manager Activities
Manager Roles
Small Business

Managing for the Future

Learning Management Skills
Management Success and Failure
Preparing for the Year 2000

Learning Objectives

After studying this chapter, you should be able to:

- Define management and give examples of successful managers.
- Describe the four management functions and the type of management activity associated with each.
- Explain the difference between efficiency and effectiveness and their importance for organizational performance.
- Describe differences in management functions by hierarchical level.
- Define functional, general, and project managers.
- Describe conceptual, human, and technical skills and their relevance for managers and nonmanagers.
- Define ten roles that managers perform in organizations.
- Describe characteristics of managerial success and the issues managers must prepare for in the future.

Management Problem

ReBecca K. Roloff, barely 30, was made manager of Pillsbury Company's distribution department, which handled shipping and freight expediting for Pillsbury's products. Known as the "elephant's graveyard," the distribution department was considered corporate oblivion for managers. Employees did little more than take orders, assign shipments to standard routes, and shuffle invoices. Roloff had a business degree and experience as a grain trader and purchasing agent, and she also had headed a task force to deal with the pesticide-contamination crisis in the food industry. Her job was to manage 450 mostly uninspired employees performing bureaucratic tasks. Her challenge was to transform this graveyard into a lively department making a strong contribution to corporate effectiveness and profits.[1]

If you were in Roloff's position, how would you proceed? What management techniques would you use to reform a large department of uninspired employees?

Few students have heard of ReBecca Roloff or the distribution department. Most are unfamiliar with the management actions needed to create a department that is thriving, inspired, and productive. The management problem at Pillsbury represents a situation that is repeated daily for managers in hundreds of organizations. Successful departments and successful organizations do not just happen — they are managed to be that way. Every organization has problems and dead-end departments, and every organization needs skilled management.

Managers like ReBecca Roloff have the opportunity to make a difference. Lee Iacocca made a difference at Chrysler Corporation when he rescued it from bankruptcy by reducing internal costs, developing new products, and gaining concessions from lenders, the union, and government. Iacocca is today transforming Chrysler again by implementing a strategy for developing a new generation of cars that will appear through 1992.[2] General William Creech made a difference to the huge Tactical Air Command of the U.S. Air Force

Why is Shirley Spoor cleaning windows at 7 A.M. in Little Rock, Arkansas? Because she is top manager of the Hampton Inn and does everything in her power to make a *difference* to the hotel's performance. Spoor sands doors, motivates employees, and promotes new weekend rates; she also added new signs and placed her hotel on the housing list at the local Air Force base. Shirley's enthusiasm, planning, and leadership abilities have increased hotel occupancy in a declining market, exceeding budgeted occupancy and profit. The winner of management awards from her community and Holiday Corporation, Shirley Spoor makes a difference.

when he reversed a sortie rate (number of flights flown with tactical aircraft) that had been declining 7.8 percent a year. Within a year of his appointment as TAC commander, the sortie rate increased 11.2 percent and continued to rise at that rate for five years with no additional people or resources. Kelly Johnson of Lockheed made a difference to an ailing satellite program. Launch effectiveness had been running 12.5 percent, was way behind schedule and over budget, and, as Johnson discovered, one subcontractor was using 1,271 inspectors. Within a year the program was back on schedule, launch effectiveness had improved to 98 percent, and the number of inspectors had been reduced to 35. William Donald Schaefer, mayor of Baltimore (now governor of Maryland), made a difference. He saw a city of dirty parks, housing violations, abandoned cars, dead trees, and uncollected trash. He motivated city workers to clean up the mess and involved citizens in an ownership program that helped pay for and maintain city services.[3]

These managers are not unusual. Every day managers solve difficult problems, turn organizations around, and achieve astonishing performance. Every organization needs skilled managers to be successful. And managers can make a difference in a negative direction. Poor judgment, personal vanity, or greed can cause corporate disaster. For example, Harding Lawrence of Braniff Airlines was responsible for a misguided strategy of rapid national and international expansion, and he alienated executives and employees with his domineering, bullying behavior. His influence launched Braniff on a flight path to bankruptcy.[4] Robert Fomon gained absolute power at E. F. Hutton. Acting like a feudal lord he banished traditional organization structure, budgets, and planning, thereby initiating the lingering death of an old-line brokerage firm.[5] BankAmerica's loss of nearly $1 billion in 1987 was attributed to decisions made by Tom Clausen and Sam Armacost in their succeeding tours as chief executives.[6]

This book introduces and explains the process of management. By analyzing examples of successful and not-so-successful managers and reviewing studies of management techniques and styles, you will learn the fundamentals of management. The problems ReBecca Roloff faced at Pillsbury's distribution department are not unusual for middle managers. By the end of this chapter, you will already understand the approach Roloff took to get her department back on track. By the end of this book, you will understand fundamental management skills for planning, organizing, leading, and controlling a department or an entire organization. In the remainder of this chapter, we will define management and look at the roles and activities of managers in today's organizations.

THE DEFINITION OF MANAGEMENT

What do managers like Lee Iacocca, General Creech, and Kelly Johnson have in common? They get things done through their organizations. One early management scholar, Mary Parker Follett, described management as "the art of getting things done through people."[7] Peter Drucker, a noted management theorist, says that managers give direction to their organizations, provide leadership, and decide how to use organizational resources to accomplish goals.[8] Getting things done through people and other resources and providing direction and leadership are what managers do. These activities apply not only to top executives such as Lee Iacocca or General Creech, but also to a new lieutenant in charge of a TAC maintenance squadron, a supervisor in the Ontario plant that makes Plymouth minivans, and ReBecca Roloff as manager of Pillsbury's distribution department. Moreover, management often is considered universal because it uses organizational resources to accomplish goals and attain high performance in all types of profit and not-for-profit organizations. Thus, our definition of management is as follows:

> **Management** is the attainment of organizational goals in an effective and efficient manner through planning, organizing, leading, and controlling organizational resources.

management The attainment of organizational goals in an effective and efficient manner through planning, organizing, leading, and controlling organizational resources.

There are two important ideas in this definition: (1) the four functions of planning, organizing, leading, and controlling and (2) the attainment of organizational goals in an effective and efficient manner. The management process of using resources to attain goals is illustrated in Exhibit 1.1. Although some management theorists identify additional management functions, such as staffing, communicating, or decision making, those additional functions will be discussed as subsets of the four primary functions in Exhibit 1.1. Chapters of the book are devoted to the multiple activities and skills associated with each function, as well as to the environment, global competitiveness, and ethics, which influence how managers perform these functions. The next section begins with a brief overview of the four functions.

EXHIBIT 1.1
The Process of Management

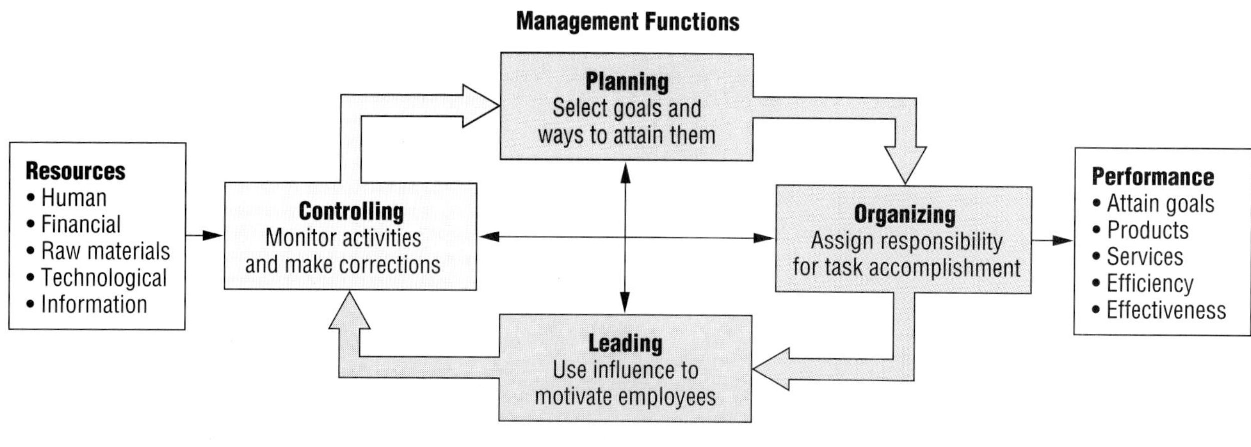

THE FOUR MANAGEMENT FUNCTIONS

PLANNING

planning The management function concerned with defining goals for future organizational performance and deciding on the tasks and resource use needed to attain them.

Planning defines where the organization wants to be in the future and how to get there. **Planning** means defining goals for future organizational performance and deciding on the tasks and use of resources needed to attain them. Senior managers at Bausch & Lomb defined a specific plan: to capture at least 50 percent of every segment of the contact lens market even if prices had to be cut and profits reduced to maintain market share. Senior managers at Chase Manhattan Bank decided to make it the number one service-quality bank in the world and, through extensive planning, to develop a worldwide network of branch banks, implement a sophisticated foreign exchange system, and offer a state-of-the-art electronic funds transfer system. General Creech successfully turned around the Tactical Air Command because he had a specific plan including targets for improved sortie rates and techniques for achieving the new rates.

A lack of planning — or poor planning — can hurt an organization's performance. For example, Tom Clausen was accused of poor planning when he insisted that BankAmerica increase loans 10 percent a year and that profits increase as well. To get new loans, BankAmerica's offices gradually reduced loan quality. To keep boosting profit, Clausen delayed investing in computers, scrimped on bank control systems, failed to modernize the branches, and kept salaries low. The absence of a detailed plan for achieving growth and efficiency in several areas led to loan failures and huge losses in subsequent years.[9]

ORGANIZING

Organizing typically follows planning and reflects how the organization tries to accomplish the plan. **Organizing** involves the assignment of tasks, the grouping of tasks into departments, and the allocation of resources to departments. For example, Hewlett-Packard, Sears, Roebuck, Xerox, and Digital Equipment have all undergone recent structural reorganizations to accommodate their changing plans. General Creech accomplished his plan for TAC's improved sortie rate largely through decentralization and the development of small, independent maintenance units — a drastic departure from the traditional structure that had encouraged centralization and consolidation of Air Force resources. Kelly Johnson of Lockheed used organizing wizardry to reduce the number of subcontractor inspectors from 1,271 to 35 and still achieve the objective of improved launch effectiveness. Indeed, his organizing was so good that the Air Force insisted that a competitor be allowed to visit Johnson's team. The competitor used 3,750 people to perform a similar task and was years behind and way over budget. Johnson's organization was on schedule and under budget — and with only 126 people.[10] Honeywell managers reorganized new product development into "tiger teams" consisting of marketing, design, and engineering employees. The new structural design reduced the time to produce a new thermostat from 4 years to 12 months.[11]

organizing The management function concerned with assigning tasks, grouping tasks into departments, and allocating resources to departments.

Likewise, weak organizing facilitated the destruction of Braniff Airlines under Harding Lawrence. Braniff did not have enough departments and offices to handle passengers and airplanes for the new national and international routes Lawrence grabbed during deregulation of the airline industry. Braniff needed an enormous amount of money to set up a structure to fit its strategy. Even before its expansion Braniff lacked a strong internal structure with clearly defined roles for accomplishing tasks. The structure produced a group of "yes men" who deferred to Lawrence's every decision.[12]

LEADING

The third management function is to provide leadership for employees. **Leading** is the use of influence to motivate employees to achieve organizational goals. Leading means communicating goals to employees throughout the organization and infusing them with the desire to perform at a high level. Leading involves motivating entire departments and divisions as well as those individuals working immediately with the manager.

leading The management function that involves the use of influence to motivate employees to achieve the organization's goals.

Managers such as Lee Iacocca are exceptional leaders. They are able to communicate their vision throughout the organization and energize employees into action. General Creech was a leader when he improved the motivation of aircraft maintenance technicians in hundreds of maintenance squadrons. Maintenance people previously had been neglected in favor of pilots. Creech set up highly visible bulletin boards displaying pictures of the maintenance crew chiefs, improved their living quarters, and established decent maintenance facilities, complete with paintings and wall murals. He introduced competition among the newly independent maintenance squadrons. He created

Leadership and *control* at Tyson Foods, Inc., is illustrated by Jay Benham's (right) discussion with a Quality Review Team (QRT). Tyson's goal is to produce the best quality for each of its more than 1,000 poultry products. Each Tyson plant has its own QRT, a rotating group of employees drawn from all departments, who keep an eye on plant sanitation, employee hygiene, and product quality. Benham's leadership helps motivate these employees to achieve quality goals.

trophy rooms to hold plaques and other prizes won in maintenance competitions. This prominent display of concern for maintenance specialists greatly increased their motivation to keep the planes flying.

When William Schaefer was mayor of Baltimore, he used a number of techniques to motivate city employees. He sent them action memos that were blunt and direct: "Get the trash off East Lombard Street," "Broken pavement at 1700 Carey," "Abandoned car at 2900 Remington." One action memo said, "There is an abandoned car . . . but I'm not telling you where it is." City crews ran around for a week and towed several hundred cars.[13]

Leadership has a negative side, too. Again consider Harding Lawrence. His leadership of Braniff was said to contribute to employees' *demotivation.* Lawrence won notoriety on Braniff's Flight 6, which he took weekly to visit his wife, who worked in New York City:

> His tantrums on Flight 6 are legend. On one flight a stewardess served him an entire selection of condiments with his meal instead of asking him which one he preferred. He slammed his fist into the plate, splattering food on the surrounding seats of the first-class cabin. "Don't you ever assume what I want!" he screamed.
>
> "On several occasions flight attendants came to me in tears, fearful of losing their jobs," says Ed Clements, former director of flight attendant services at Braniff. "I was sickened by what he was doing to the employees."
>
> Lawrence's appearance on an aircraft was likely to arouse two emotions in the crew: fear and hatred.[14]

Inevitably, dissatisfied employees led to dissatisfied customers. Marketing surveys indicated that Braniff was unpopular with many of its passengers. Without a loyal customer base, successful expansion and high performance proved impossible.[15] The Manager's Shoptalk box highlights several leadership problems and possible solutions.

MANAGER'S SHOPTALK

THE TRUST GAP

Fortune magazine reports that top managers in many American companies are not providing leadership. David Sirota, chairman of the polling firm Sirota Alper & Pafu found that "CEOs say, 'We're a team, we're all in this together, rah, rah, rah.' But employees look at the difference between their pay and the CEO's. They see top management's perks—oak dining rooms and heated garages versus cafeterias for the hourly guys and parking spaces half a mile from the plant. And they wonder: 'Is this togetherness?' "

Other polling firms have found similar results.

Item. Management assumes job security to be of prime importance to employees, while employees want their leaders to provide respect, higher ethical standards, recognition of employee contributions, and close, honest communication.

Item. Some 82 percent of Fortune 500 executives believe their corporate strategy is properly communicated, while surveys show that less than one-third of employees say their management provides clear goals and direction.

Item. A ten-year survey shows that attitudes of middle managers and professionals toward the workplace have dropped sharply, approaching those of hourly workers, traditionally the most disaffected group.

Item. Top managements' compensation packages are going out of sight compared with those for the rest of employees. Some CEOs now make over 100 times the average employee's pay, compared with European and Japanese top management pay that runs about 15 times that of the average employee's pay.

What can a new generation of leaders do to bring middle managers, professionals, hourly workers, and themselves closer together? Some advice from well-respected CEOs includes:

- Tie the financial interest of *everyone* in the firm to risk and profit. Nucor's managers took a much bigger pay cut than workers when the steel company experienced difficulty.
- Consider profit sharing, gain sharing, or other programs to let employees share in profits from improved company performance.
- Consider the negative effects that excessive management perks have on other employees.
- Restructure office space so that employees feel important. Union Carbide gave everyone the same amount of space and amenities, increasing productivity at all levels.
- Communicate with employees, and the more personal the better. Rubbermaid CEO Stanley Gault came to his office at 5:00 A.M. to listen to an employee who was just finishing his shift.
- Have top management spend time in the trenches to increase respect for the people on the line.

Source: Based on Alan Farnham, "The Trust Gap," *Fortune,* December 4, 1989, 56–78.

CONTROLLING

Controlling is the fourth function in the management process. **Controlling** means monitoring employees' activities, determining whether the organization is on target toward its goals, and making corrections as necessary. Managers must ensure that the organization is moving toward its goals. Controlling often involves using an information system to advise managers on performance and a reward system for recognizing employees who make progress toward goals. For example, at Domino's Pizza Distribution Company over 1,200 franchises are measured weekly. A phone survey of customers determines the quality of service at each franchise, which is reported to management. Compensation for all employees is based on the results. Expected performance levels are reviewed every six months and set slightly higher for the next six months. The control system then monitors whether employees achieve the higher targets.

controlling The management function concerned with monitoring employees' activities, keeping the organization on track toward its goals, and making corrections as needed.

One reason for organization failure is that managers are not serious about control or lack control information. Robert Fomon, longtime autocratic chief executive of E. F. Hutton, refused to set up control systems because he wanted to personally supervise senior management. At one time he reviewed the salaries and bonuses of more than 1,000 employees, but eventually Hutton grew too big for his personal supervision. To achieve profit goals managers got involved in an undetected check-kiting scheme, and the firm pleaded guilty to 2,000 counts of mail and wire fraud. Other undetected behaviors were the $900,000 in travel and entertainment expenses for one executive in one year and the listing of party girls from escort services as temporary secretarial help. The lack of control led to Fomon's demise. E. F. Hutton has never fully recovered.[16]

ORGANIZATIONAL PERFORMANCE

The other part of our definition of management is the attainment of organizational goals in an efficient and effective manner. One reason management is so important is that organizations are so important. In an industrialized society where complex technologies dominate, organizations bring together knowledge, people, and raw materials to perform tasks no individual could do alone. Without organizations how could 15,000 flights a day be accomplished without an accident, electricity produced from large dams or nuclear power generators, millions of automobiles manufactured, or hundreds of films, videos, and records made available for our entertainment? Organizations pervade our society. Most college students will work in an organization — perhaps Hospital Corporation of America, Federated Department Stores, Boise Cascade, or Standard Oil. College students already are members of several organizations, such as a university, junior college, YMCA, church, fraternity, or sorority. College students also deal with organizations every day: to renew a driver's license, be treated in a hospital emergency room, buy food from a supermarket, eat in a restaurant, or buy new clothes. Managers are responsible for these organizations and for seeing that resources are used wisely to attain organizational goals.

organization A social entity that is goal directed and deliberately structured.

Our formal definition of an **organization** is a social entity that is goal directed and deliberately structured. *Social entity* means being made up of two or more people. *Goal directed* means designed to achieve some outcome, such as make a profit (Boeing, Mack Trucks), win pay increases for members (AFL-CIO), meet spiritual needs (Methodist church), or provide social satisfaction (college sorority). *Deliberately structured* means that tasks are divided and responsibility for their performance assigned to organization members. This definition applies to all organizations, including both profit and not-for-profit. Vickery Stoughton runs Toronto General Hospital and manages a $200 million budget. He endures intense public scrutiny, heavy government regulation, and daily crises of life and death. Hamilton Jordan, formerly President Carter's chief of staff, created a new organization called the Association of Tennis Professionals that will take control of the professional tennis circuit. John and Marie Bouchard launched a small business called Wild Things that sells goods for outdoor activities. Small, offbeat, and not-for-profit organizations are more numerous than large, visible corporations — and just as important to society.

Based on our definition of management, the manager's responsibility is to coordinate resources in an effective and efficient manner to accomplish the

Union Pacific has made giant strides in efficiency and effectiveness. Here a giant "piggypacker" loads a container aboard a double-stack train. Union Pacific is the industry leader in double-stack shipments. The increased *efficiency* is illustrated in the doubling of revenue ton-miles per employee since 1984. *Effectiveness* is revealed in increased traffic and marketshare gains. New technology and the consolidation of dispatching and crew management saved the company nearly $17 million in 1988.

organization's goals. Organizational **effectiveness** is the degree to which the organization achieves a stated objective. It means that the organization succeeds in accomplishing what it tries to do. Organizational effectiveness means providing a product or service that customers value. Organizational **efficiency** refers to the amount of resources used to achieve an organizational goal. It is based on how much raw materials, money, and people are necessary for producing a given volume of output. Efficiency can be calculated as the amount of resources used to produce a product or service.

effectiveness The degree to which the organization achieves a stated objective.

efficiency The use of minimal resources — raw materials, money, and people — to produce a desired volume of output.

Efficiency and effectiveness can both be high in the same organization. Consider the impact of Dick Dauch, vice-president of manufacturing at Chrysler. His leadership has allowed a startling increase in efficiency. Chrysler now can build 8,000 cars and trucks a day compared with 4,500 a few years ago. The number of worker-hours per vehicle has shrunk from 175 to 102. Resources are used more efficiently: Worker absenteeism is down sharply. New technology has transformed the assembly line. The manufacturing improvements have also boosted effectiveness. Chrysler cars are now first quality, rated nearer the top in reliability, durability, and fit-and-finish.[17]

Managers in other organizations, especially service firms, are improving efficiency, too. Labor shortages in the Midwest and northeastern United States have prompted managers to find labor-saving tricks. Burger King and Kentucky Fried Chicken restaurants let customers serve themselves drinks. Sleep Inn hotels have a washer and dryer installed behind the desk so that clerks can launder sheets and towels while waiting on customers. McDonald's is experimenting with a grill that cooks hamburgers on both sides at once, eliminating the need for an employee to flip them.[18]

The ultimate responsibility of managers, then, is to achieve high **performance,** which is the attainment of organizational goals by using resources in an efficient and effective manner. Whether managers are responsible for the organization as a whole, such as Robert Stempel at General Motors, or for a single

performance The organization's ability to attain its goals by using resources in an efficient and effective manner.

department, such as ReBecca Roloff at Pillsbury, their ultimate responsibility is performance. Harold Geneen, a legendary manager who transformed ITT into one of the world's largest and best-run corporations, explained it this way:

> I think it is an immutable law in business that words are words, explanations are explanations, promises are promises — but only performance is reality. Performance alone is the best measure of your confidence, competence, and courage. Only performance gives you the freedom to grow as yourself.
>
> Just remember that: *performance is your reality.* Forget everything else. That is why my definition of a manager is what it is: one who turns in the performance. No alibis to others or to one's self will change that. And when you have performed well, the world will remember it, when everything else is forgotten. And most importantly, so will you.[19]

Management Types

The four management functions must be performed in all organizations. But not all managers' jobs are the same. Managers are responsible for different departments, work at different levels in the hierarchy, and meet different requirements for achieving high performance. For example, Gary Smith, age 21, runs a team of 13 assemblers at Honda's Marysville, Ohio, plant. Charles Strang is chief executive officer for Outboard Marine, a manufacturer of outboard motors. Both are managers, and both must contribute to planning, organizing, leading, and controlling their organizations — but in different amounts and ways.

Vertical Differences

top manager A manager who is at the top of the organizational hierarchy and responsible for the entire organization.

An important determinant of the manager's job is hierarchical level. Three levels in the hierarchy are illustrated in Exhibit 1.2. **Top managers** are at the top of the hierarchy and are responsible for the entire organization. They have such titles as president, chairperson, executive director, chief executive officer (CEO), and executive vice-president. Top managers are responsible for setting organizational goals, defining strategies for achieving them, monitoring and interpreting the external environment, and making decisions that affect the entire organization. They look to the long-term future and concern themselves with general environmental trends and the organization's overall success. They also influence internal corporate culture.

middle manager A manager who works at the middle levels of the organization and is responsible for major departments.

Middle managers work at middle levels of the organization and are responsible for business units and major departments. Examples of middle managers are department head, division head, manager of quality control, and director of the research lab. Middle managers typically have two or more management levels beneath them. They are responsible for implementing the overall strategies and policies defined by top managers. Middle managers are concerned with the near future, are expected to establish good relationships with peers around the organization, encourage teamwork, and resolve conflicts.

Recent trends in corporate restructuring and downsizing have made the middle manager's job difficult. Companies that become lean and efficient often do so by laying off middle managers, both line and staff. New electronic technologies have reduced the need for middle level supervision. Middle managers

Exhibit 1.2
Management Levels in the Organizational Hierarchy

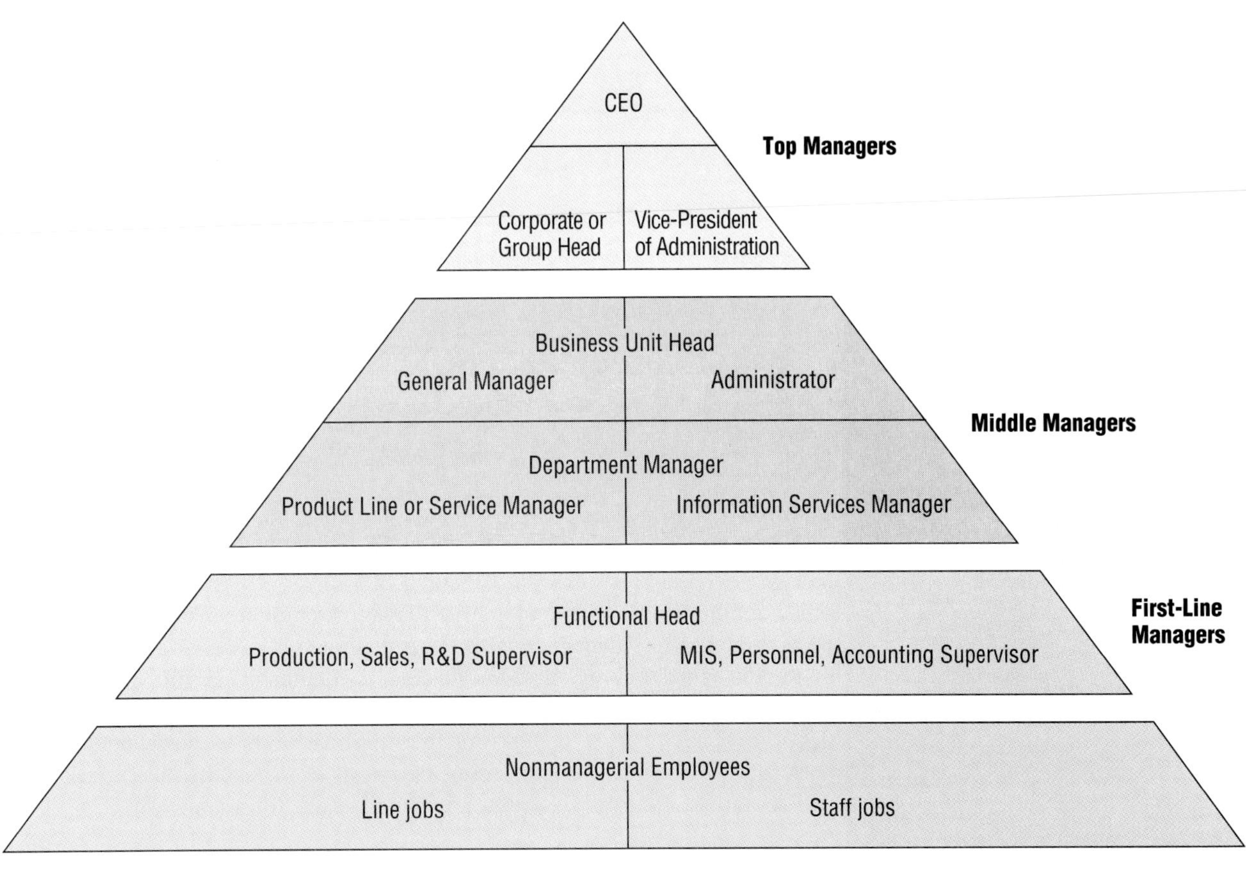

Source: Adapted from Thomas V. Bonoma and Joseph C. Lawler, "Chutes and Ladders: Growing the General Manager," *Sloan Management Review* (Spring 1989), 27–37.

have been cut by 17 percent at Mobil, 15 percent at DuPont, and 35 percent in the Medical Systems Group at General Electric. One estimate is that over one million middle management positions have been removed in the last few years. These cutbacks make organizations efficient, but a recent survey found middle managers restless and dissatisfied. They seem to be at the mercy of top management, and their loyalty to the organization is not always reciprocated. One disgruntled middle manager proclaimed, "The way things are going my company will consist of the CEO at the top, a computer in the middle, and a bunch of workers at the bottom."[20]

First-line managers are directly responsible for the production of goods and services. They are the first or second level of management and have such titles as supervisor, line manager, section chief, and office manager. They are responsible for groups of nonmanagement employees. Their primary concern is the application of rules and procedures to achieve efficient production, provide technical assistance, and motivate subordinates. The time horizon at this level is short, with the emphasis on accomplishing day-to-day objectives.

first-line manager A manager who is at the first or second management level and directly responsible for the production of goods and services.

EXHIBIT 1.3
Percentage of Time Spent on Functional Activities by Organizational Level

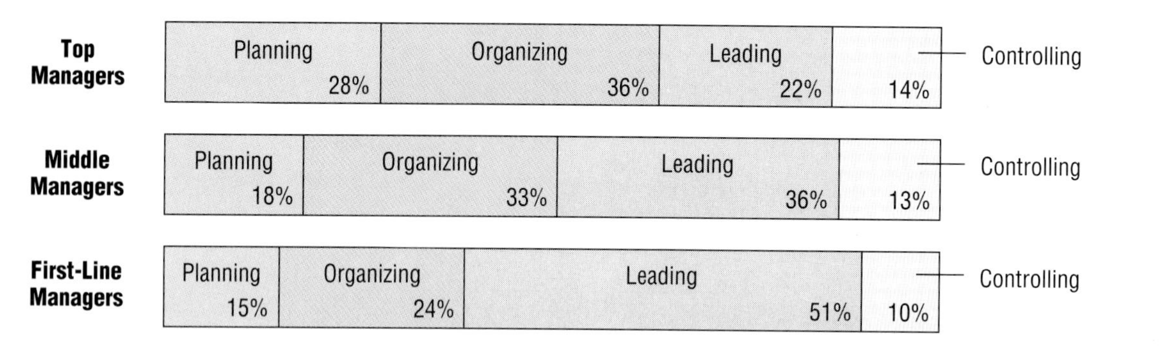

Source: Based on T. A. Mahoney, T. H. Jerdee, and S. J. Carroll, "The Job(s) of Management," *Industrial Relations*, vol. 4, no. 2 (1965), 103. A similar pattern of activity was reported in Luis Gomez-Mejia, Joseph E. McCann, and Ronald C. Page, "The Structure of Managerial Behaviors and Rewards," *Industrial Relations* 24 (1985), 147–154.

An illustration of how the four functional activities differ for the three management levels is shown in Exhibit 1.3. Managers at all levels perform all four functions, but in different amounts. Planning and organizing are primarily the province of top managers, with the time devoted to these tasks decreasing for middle managers and first-line managers. Leading, in contrast, is highest for first-line managers, with the time spent on this function decreasing at higher levels. A primary concern of first-line managers is the leadership and motivation of technical employees. Controlling is similar for all three levels, with somewhat more time devoted by middle and top managers.

HORIZONTAL DIFFERENCES

functional manager A manager who is responsible for a department that performs a single functional task and has employees with similar training and skills.

The other major difference in management jobs occurs horizontally across the organization. **Functional managers** are responsible for departments that perform a single functional task and have employees with similar training and skills. Functional departments include advertising, sales, finance, personnel, manufacturing, and accounting. Line managers are responsible for the line departments that make or sell the product. Staff managers are in charge of departments such as finance and personnel that support line departments.

general manager A manager who is responsible for several departments that perform different functions.

project manager A manager who coordinates people across several departments to accomplish a specific project.

General managers are responsible for several departments that perform different functions. A general manager is responsible for a self-contained division, such as a Dillard's department store, and for all of the functional departments within it. **Project managers** also have general management responsibility, because they coordinate people across several departments to accomplish a specific project. Companies as diverse as consumer products and aerospace firms, for example, use project managers to coordinate across marketing, manufacturing, finance, and production when a new product — breakfast cereal, guidance system — is developed. General managers require human skills because they coordinate a variety of people to attain project or division goals.

Exhibit 1.4
Relationship of Conceptual, Human, and Technical Skills to Management Level

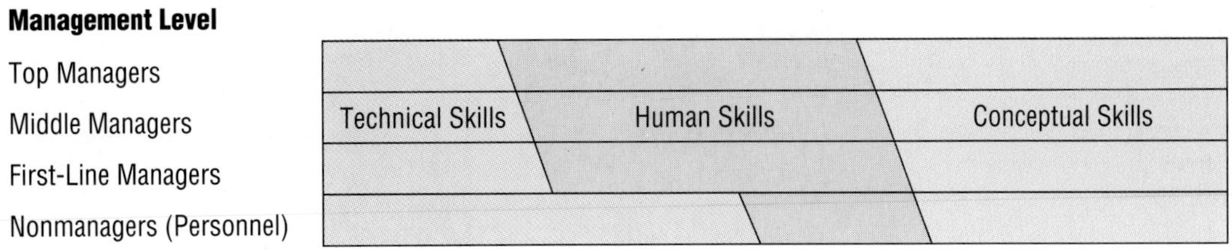

Management Level			
Top Managers			
Middle Managers	Technical Skills	Human Skills	Conceptual Skills
First-Line Managers			
Nonmanagers (Personnel)			

Management Skills

A manager's job is diverse and complex and, as we shall see throughout this book, requires a range of skills. Although some management theorists propose a long list of skills, the necessary skills for planning, organizing, leading, and controlling can be summarized in three categories that are especially important: conceptual, human, and technical.[21] As illustrated in Exhibit 1.4, all managers need each skill, but the amounts differ by hierarchical level.

Conceptual Skills

conceptual skill The cognitive ability to see the organization as a whole and the relationship among its parts.

Conceptual skill is the cognitive ability to see the organization as a whole and the relationship among its parts. Conceptual skill involves the manager's thinking and planning abilities. It involves knowing where one's department fits into the total organization and how the organization fits into the industry and the community. It means the ability to think "strategically"—to take the broad, long-term view.

Conceptual skills are needed by all managers, but are especially important for managers at the top. They must perceive significant elements in a situation and broad, conceptual patterns. For example, Robert Lutz, a senior operating executive at Chrysler, is spearheading development of the Dodge Viper, a sports car with neck-snapping acceleration. He has to conceptualize development of a car that can be produced quickly with costs low enough to make a profit on fewer than 10,000 cars a year sold at less than $30,000 apiece. Lutz helps conceptualize design, supply, and manufacturing problems because he understands how these significant elements fit together.[22]

As managers move up the hierarchy, they must develop conceptual skills or their promotability will be limited. A senior engineering manager who is mired in technical matters rather than thinking strategically will not perform well at the top of the organization. Many of the responsibilities of top managers, such as decision making, resource allocation, and innovation, require a broad view.

Diane Koury, general manager of Parkers' Lighthouse in Long Beach, California, previews the day with her staff. This Stouffer restaurant, a part of Nestlé Enterprises, thrives on the excitement and enthusiasm Koury creates in her team. She is a cheerleader, facilitator, nurturer, while taking charge of scores of daily details. These *human skills* enable Diane Koury's restaurant to excel over the competition.

HUMAN SKILLS

human skill The ability to work with and through other people and to work effectively as a group member.

Human skill is the manager's ability to work with and through other people and to work effectively as a group member. This skill is demonstrated in the way a manager relates to other people, including the ability to motivate, facilitate, coordinate, lead, communicate, and resolve conflicts. A manager with human skills allows subordinates to express themselves without fear of ridicule and encourages participation. A manager with human skills likes other people and is liked by them. Barry Merkin, chairman of Dresher Inc., the largest U.S. manufacturer of brass beds, is a cheerleader for his employees. He visits the plant floor and uses humor and hoopla to motivate them. Employees may have buckets of fried chicken served to them by supervisors wearing chef's hats.

Managers who lack human skills often are abrupt, critical, and unsympathetic toward others. Harding Lawrence of Braniff, described earlier, did not excel in human skills. Another example is the executive who walked into a subordinate's office and insisted on talking to him. When the subordinate tried to explain that he was occupied, the manager snarled, "I don't give a damn. I said I wanted to see you now."[23] Managers without human skills are insensitive and arrogant. They often make other people feel stupid and resentful.

In recent years, the awareness of human skills has increased. Books such as *In Search of Excellence* and *A Passion for Excellence* stress the need for managers to take care of the human side of the organization. Excellent companies and excellent managers do not take people for granted. When Robert Carlson took over United Technologies, he used human skills to induce teamwork among senior executives. His willingness to listen to problems and suggestions and to inspire cooperation helped United Technologies rebound after the stewardship of Harry Gray, who did not use people skills as a part of his management style.[24] Effective managers are cheerleaders, facilitators, coaches, and nurturers. They build through people. Effective human skills enable managers to unleash subordinates' energy and help them grow as future managers.

Technical Skills

Technical skill is the understanding of and proficiency in the performance of specific tasks. Technical skill includes mastery of the methods, techniques, and equipment involved in specific functions such as engineering, manufacturing, or finance. Technical skill also includes specialized knowledge, analytical ability, and the competent use of tools and techniques to solve problems in that specific discipline. One reason ReBecca Roloff, described at the beginning of this chapter, was promoted to department manager at Pillsbury was her technical understanding of freight and distribution.

technical skill The understanding of and proficiency in the performance of specific tasks.

Technical skills are most important at lower organizational levels. Many managers get promoted into their first management jobs by having excellent technical skills. However, technical skills are less important than human and conceptual skills as managers move up the hierarchy.

Making the Transition

As illustrated in Exhibit 1.4, the major difference between nonmanagers and managers is the shift from reliance on technical skills to focus on human skills. This is a difficult transition, because high achievement in the technical area may have been the basis for promotion to a supervisory position. New managers often mistakenly continue to rely on technical skills rather than concentrate on working with others, motivating employees, and building a team. Indeed, some people fail to become managers at all because they let technical skills take precedence over human skills.

Consider Pete Martin, who has a bachelor's degree and has worked for five years as a computer programmer for an oil company. In four short years, he has more new software programs to his credit than anyone else in the department. He is highly creative and widely respected. However, Pete is impulsive and has little tolerance for those whose work is less creative. Pete does not offer to help coworkers, and they are reluctant to ask because he often "puts them down." Pete is also slow to cooperate with other departments in meeting their needs, because he works primarily to enhance his own software writing ability. He spends evenings and weekends working on his programs. Pete is a hardworking technical employee, but he sees little need to worry about other people.

Pete received high merit raises but was passed over for promotion and does not understand why. His lack of interpersonal skills, inconsideration for coworkers, and failure to cooperate with other departments severely limit his potential as a supervisor. Pete has great technical skills, but his human skills simply are inadequate for making the transition from worker to supervisor. Until Pete is ready to work on human skills, he has little chance of being promoted.

What Is It Like to Be a Manager?

So far we have described how managers perform four basic functions that help ensure that organizational resources are used to attain high levels of performance. These tasks require conceptual, human, and technical skills. Unless

The *variety* of *manager activities* is illustrated by these Kellogg top executives sampling several bowls of cereal with concern for "mouth feel" and "bowl life." They discuss appearance, texture, and for Rice Krispies, the snap, crackle, and pop. These hands-on experiences by senior executives keep Kellogg at the forefront of the breakfast cereal industry.

someone has actually performed managerial work, it is hard to understand exactly what managers do on an hour-by-hour, day-by-day basis. The manager's job is so diverse that a number of studies have been undertaken in an attempt to describe exactly what happens. The question of what managers actually do to plan, organize, lead, and control was answered by Henry Mintzberg, who followed managers around and recorded all of their activities.[25] He developed a description of managerial work that included three general characteristics and ten roles. These characteristics and roles have been supported in subsequent research.[26]

Manager Activities

One of the most interesting findings about managerial activities is how busy managers are and how hectic the average workday can be.

Managerial Activity Is Characterized by Variety, Fragmentation, and Brevity.[27] The manager's involvements are so widespread and voluminous that there is little time for quiet reflection. The average time spent on any one activity is less than nine minutes. Managers shift gears quickly. Significant crises are interspersed with trivial events in no predictable sequence. One example of the morning activities for a typical general manager, Janet Howard, follows. Note the frequent interruptions, brevity, and variety.

7:30 A.M. Janet arrives at work, unpacks her briefcase, and begins to plan her day.

7:37 A.M. A subordinate, Morgan Cook, arrives and stops in Janet's office to discuss a dinner party the previous night.

7:45 A.M. Janet's secretary, Pat, motions for Janet to pick up the telephone. "Janet, they had serious water damage at the downtown office last night. A pipe broke, causing about $50,000 damage. Everything will be back in shape in three days. Thought you should know."

8:00 A.M. Another subordinate, Tim Birdwell, stops by. They chat about the water damage. Tim tells a joke. Tim and Morgan both leave, laughing at the story.

8:10 A.M. Pat brings in the mail. She also asks instructions for typing a report Janet gave her yesterday.

8:30 A.M. Janet gets a phone call from the accounting manager, who is returning a call from the day before. They talk about an accounting report.

8:45 A.M. Janet leaves early to attend a regular 9:00 A.M. meeting in her boss's office. She tours the office area and informally chats with people before the meeting starts.

9:45 A.M. Janet arrives back at her office, and a Mr. Nance is ushered in. Mr. Nance complains that a sales manager mistreats his employees and something must be done. Janet rearranges her schedule to investigate this claim.

10:05 A.M. Janet begins to read the mail. One letter is from an irate customer who is unhappy with the product and feels the sales engineer was unresponsive. Janet dictates a helpful, restrained reply.

10:20 A.M. Pat brings in phone messages. Janet makes two phone calls and receives one. She goes back to the mail and papers on her desk.

10:35 A.M. Another subordinate stops by with a question about how to complete forms requesting a maternity leave.

10:45 A.M. Janet receives an urgent phone call from Larry Baldwin. They go back and forth talking about lost business, unhappy subordinates, a potential promotion, and what should be done. It is a long conversation, with much exchange of both official information and gossip.

11:15 A.M. Janet decides to skip lunch, preferring to eat an apple in her office so she will have some time to plan divisional goals for the next six months.[28]

THE MANAGER PERFORMS A GREAT DEAL OF WORK AT AN UNRELENTING PACE.[29] Managers' work is fast paced and requires great energy. The managers observed by Mintzberg processed 36 pieces of mail each day, attended 8 meetings, and took a tour through the building or plant. As soon as a manager's daily calendar is set, unexpected disturbances erupt. New meetings are required. During time away from the office, executives catch up on work-related reading and paperwork.

Sloan Wilson, author of *The Man in the Gray Flannel Suit,* had an opportunity to work with top managers from several companies. He tried to understand how these people had become so famous, rich, and successful. They had no special advantages or influence, because each was a self-made person.

> So what was the secret? As I attempted to work around the clock on the many projects they undertook in addition to their real jobs, one simple answer came to me: raw energy. Super-abundant, inexhaustible energy—that was the one thing all these very successful men had.
>
> They were people who enthusiastically could undertake the fifth rewriting of a speech on education at three in the morning when they were up against a deadline, fly across the continent to deliver it and fly back again, working out of a briefcase on a plane all the time. And when they got to their offices, they were fresh and eager to see what their engagement calendar had to offer for the day and evening ahead. I never understood how they did it, and I was never able to keep up with them.[30]

EXHIBIT 1.5
Ten Manager Roles

Source: Adapted from Henry Mintzberg, *The Nature of Managerial Work* (New York: Harper & Row, 1973), 92–93, and Henry Mintzberg, "Managerial Work: Analysis from Observation," *Management Science* 18 (1971), B97–B110.

Category	Role	Activity
Interpersonal	Figurehead	Perform ceremonial and symbolic duties such as greeting visitors, signing legal documents.
	Leader	Direct and motivate subordinates; training, counseling, and communicating with subordinates.
	Liaison	Maintain information links both inside and outside organization; use mail, phone calls, meetings.
Informational	Monitor	Seek and receive information, scan periodicals and reports, maintain personal contacts.
	Disseminator	Forward information to other organization members; send memos and reports, make phone calls.
	Spokesperson	Transmit information to outsiders through speeches, reports, memos.
Decisional	Entrepreneur	Initiate improvement projects; identify new ideas, delegate idea responsibility to others.
	Disturbance handler	Take corrective action during disputes or crises; resolve conflicts among subordinates; adapt to environmental crises.
	Resource allocator	Decide who gets resources; scheduling, budgeting, setting priorities.
	Negotiator	Represent department during negotiation of union contracts, sales, purchases, budgets; represent departmental interests.

MANAGER ROLES

role A set of expectations for one's behavior.

Mintzberg's observations and subsequent research indicate that diverse manager activities can be organized into ten roles.[31] A **role** is a set of expectations for a manager's behavior. The ten roles are divided into three categories: interpersonal, informational, and decisional. Each role represents activities that managers undertake to ultimately accomplish the functions of planning, organizing, leading, and controlling. The ten roles and brief examples are provided in Exhibit 1.5.

INTERPERSONAL ROLES. Interpersonal roles pertain to relationships with others and are related to the human skills described earlier. The *figurehead* role involves handling ceremonial and symbolic activities for the department or organization. The manager represents the organization in his or her formal managerial capacity as the head of the unit. The presentation of employee awards by a division manager at Taco Bell is an example of the figurehead role. The *leader* role encompasses relationships with subordinates, including motivation, communication, and influence. The *liaison* role pertains to the development of information sources both inside and outside the organization. An ex-

Chairman Harry E. Figgie, Jr. (left) performed the *spokesperson role* when he presented Ohio Governor Richard F. Celeste with a giant-size bat. The presentation was during a press conference announcing the return of Figgie International's headquarters to Cleveland. Figgie's divisions include Rawlings Sporting Goods, the makers of baseball bats. This presentation transmitted information to outsiders about Figgie's plans.

ample is a face-to-face discussion between a controller and plant supervisor to resolve a misunderstanding about the budget.

Informational Roles. Informational roles describe the activities used to maintain and develop an information network. The *monitor* role involves seeking current information from many sources. The manager acquires information from others and scans written materials to stay well informed. The *disseminator* role is just the opposite: The manager transmits current information to others, both inside and outside the organization, who can use it. Managers do not hoard information; they pass it around to others. The *spokesperson* role pertains to official statements to people outside the organization about company policies, actions, or plans. For example, Robert Krandall, CEO of American Airlines, recently testified before Congress three times; delivered keynote speeches to groups in Washington, D.C., Dallas, and Chicago; and appeared on television's "Meet the Press" to champion changes in the airline system.[32]

Decisional Roles. Decisional roles pertain to those events about which the manager must make a choice. These roles often require conceptual as well as human skills. The *entrepreneur* role involves the initiation of change. Managers become aware of problems and search for improvement projects that will correct them. One manager studied by Mintzberg had 50 improvement projects going simultaneously. The *disturbance handler* role involves resolving conflicts among subordinates or between the manager's department and other departments. For example, the division manager for a large furniture manufacturer got involved in a personal dispute between two section heads. One section head was let go because he did not fit the team. The *resource allocator* role pertains to decisions about how to allocate people, time, equipment, budget, and other resources to attain desired outcomes. The manager must decide which projects receive budget allocations, which of several customer complaints receive priority, and even how to spend his or her own time. The *negotiator* role involves formal negotiations and bargaining to attain outcomes for the manager's unit of responsibility. For example, the manager meets and formally negotiates with others — a supplier about a late delivery, the controller about the need for additional budget resources, or the union about a worker grievance during the normal workday.

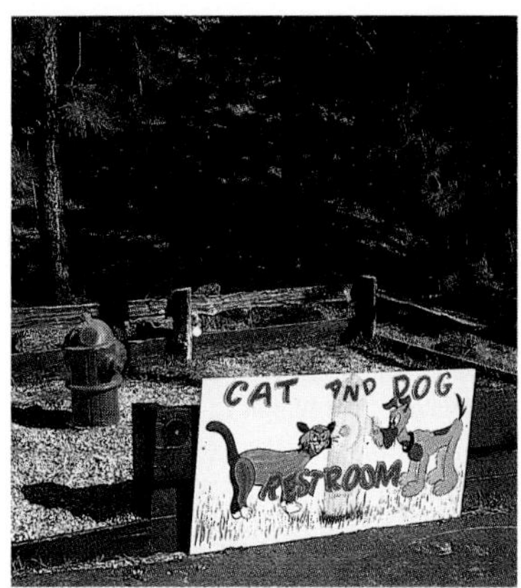

Small-business manager Fred Anderson beats competitors with creative ideas such as this cat and dog restroom at his Chevron station in California. His ability to perform the *entrepreneurial role* has made his station number one in the region, with sales increasing from 300 to 1,000 gallons of gasoline a day.

Small Business

One interesting finding is that managers in small businesses tend to emphasize different roles than managers in large corporations. In small firms, the most important role is spokesperson, because managers must promote the small, growing company to the outside world. The entrepreneur role is also very important in small businesses, because managers must be creative and help their organizations develop new ideas to be competitive. Small-business managers tend to rate lower on the leader role and on information processing roles compared with counterparts in large corporations. In large firms, the most important role is resource allocator and the least important is entrepreneur.[33]

Managing for the Future

One final question: How do you learn to be a manager for the year 2000 in an uncertain and rapidly changing world? More specifically, how does a course in management or a college degree in business prepare you to become a manager ready to face the challenges of the next ten years?

Learning Management Skills

Management is both an art and a science. It is an art because many skills cannot be learned from a textbook. Management takes practice, just like golf, tennis, or volleyball. Studying a book helps, but that is not enough. Many skills, especially the human and, to some extent, the conceptual skills, and roles such as leader, spokesperson, disturbance handler, and negotiator, take practice. These skills are learned through experience.

Management is also a science because a growing body of knowledge and objective facts describes management and how to attain organizational performance. The knowledge is acquired through systematic research and can be conveyed through teaching and textbooks. Systematic knowledge about planning, organizing, and control system design, for example, helps managers understand the skills they need, the types of roles they must perform, and the techniques needed to manage organizations. Harding Lawrence of Braniff and Robert Fomon of E. F. Hutton relied solely on their experience and intuition, and they made grave mistakes.

Becoming a successful manager requires a blend of formal learning and practice, of science and art. Practice alone used to be enough to learn how to manage, but no longer. Formal coursework in management can help a manager become more competent and be prepared for the challenges of the future. The study of management enables people to see and understand things about organizations that others cannot. Training that helps one acquire the conceptual, human, and technical skills necessary for management will be an asset.

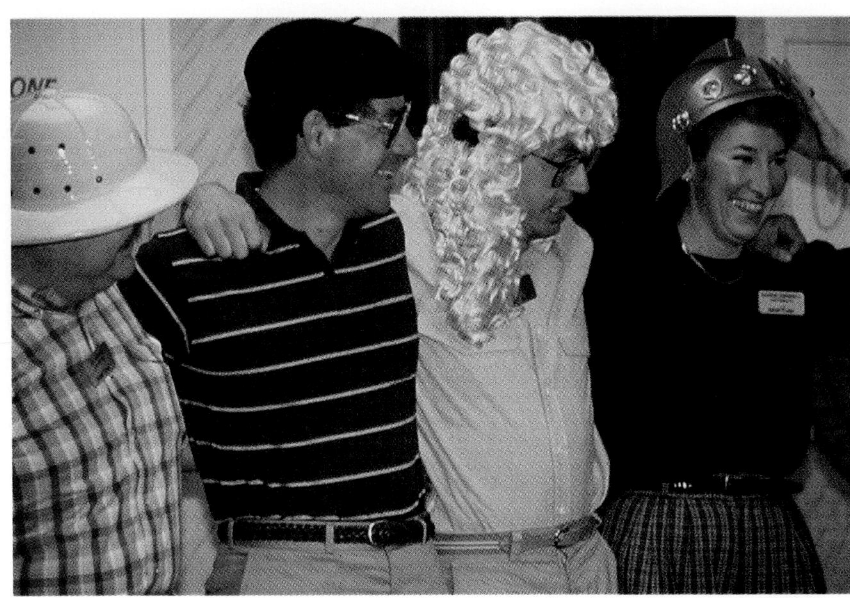

How do people at BANK ONE learn *management skills?* One way is through this workshop to stimulate innovation and creativity. At BANK ONE College, participants look at problem solving through the eyes of a judge, warrior, artist, and explorer, and then put on the hats of the characters as they role-play problem-solving scenarios. Other training sessions focus on leadership, collaboration, and communication, all adding to each manager's store of management knowledge and skill.

Management Success and Failure

A few clues about the importance of acquiring management skills were uncovered by the Center for Creative Leadership in Greensboro, North Carolina.[34] This study compared 21 derailed executives with 20 executives who had arrived at the top of the company. The derailed executives were successful people who had been expected to go far but reached a plateau, were fired, or were forced to retire early. Successful and derailed managers were similar in many ways. They were bright and excelled in a technical area such as accounting or engineering. They worked hard, made sacrifices in order to achieve, and established good track records.

Those who arrived at the top, however, had more diverse track records—they did not rely on a single functional skill. Moreover, they had excellent interpersonal skills. They maintained composure under stress, were able to laugh at themselves, and handled mistakes with poise and grace. They also were conceptually strong and could focus on problems and solve them.

In the managers who had derailed, the single biggest flaw was insensitivity to others. Often this characteristic was associated with other negative personal qualities, such as abrasiveness, aloofness, and arrogance. These managers also failed to display conceptual skills and were unable to think strategically, that is, take a broad, long-term view. One manager was a superb engineer who had advanced rapidly in the early years but could go no further. He tended to analyze problems to death and get bogged down in the details. The successful managers were superb negotiators and could confront people and problems without offending anyone. They did not blame things on others, and if they made a mistake, they did not dwell on it and kept their sense of humor. Because they readily took responsibility for mistakes, their errors were never fatal.

The ability to use human skills was the most striking difference between the two groups. Only 25 percent of the derailed group were described as having good ability with people, whereas 75 percent of those who had arrived at the top did. Some managers had been able to improve their human skills.

At Gannett Corporation, *work-force diversity* includes the disabled. Here Lisa Martinez takes classified advertising at the Reno (Nev.) Gazette-Journal. Gannett's commitment to nourishing a diversified work force is well known and well publicized, especially in its efforts to hire and promote minorities and women. Because of an anticipated labor force shortage in the 1990s, Gannett is working hard to find new sources of employees.

One manager had been cold and arrogant and, once he realized these limits to his career, changed almost overnight. He made a genuine effort to develop better human skills — and succeeded.

PREPARING FOR THE YEAR 2000

Over the next ten years, new forces are going to shape managerial careers. Managers will have to rely heavily on human skills and conceptual skills, but they will apply them in new ways. Major changes on the horizon for which managers must prepare are as follows:

MANAGING DIVERSITY. The increasing diversity of people within organizations is reflected in several ways. The number of male students going into business education has been stable since the mid-1970s. The increase of students has been accounted for by women, who now constitute 45 percent of all bachelor's degrees in business. By the year 2000, most new hires will be women or black, Hispanic, or Asian men. Managers must learn to motivate and lead different types of people and to attract the best people from these groups. U.S.-born white males will make up only about 15 percent of the new entrants into the labor force.[35]

FLEXIBILITY. Speed and flexibility will become dominant competitive issues. For example, The Limited retail chain rushes new fashions into its stores in less than 60 days, compared with 6 months for most competitors. Ford is cutting the time to develop a new car from five years to three, which has already been accomplished by Honda and Toyota. Product and service must be delivered faster to be competitive, which requires new forms of organizing and motivating. Moreover, companies will have to respond with products that fit hot market segments, the preferences of ethnic groups, and fast-growing regions. Speed and responsiveness will be far more important than the organizational stability and reliability of the old days.[36]

MERGERS AND ACQUISITIONS. Mergers and acquisitions have a major impact on managerial careers and will continue through the 1990s. Between 1983 and 1987, nearly 10,000 companies changed hands, and over 2 million people saw their jobs disappear. Mergers and reorganizations are seen as an opportunity for companies to become more efficient, but they require new management responses. Managers have to be flexible enough to work for different bosses within new corporate cultures. Lifetime loyalty to a single firm may be a thing of the past. Downsizing middle management ranks requires managers to produce in ways that are highly visible and guarantee job mobility.[37]

GLOBALIZATION. Managers will need to think globally because companies will be enmeshed with foreign competitors, suppliers, and customers. By one estimate, industrial countries on average will import nearly 40 percent of the parts used in domestic manufacturing. Foreign companies will have strong influence in the United States and Canada, with many citizens working for foreign employers. Even small companies will be affected by globalization and should consider establishing footholds overseas.[38] Some experts feel that glo-

Focus on Global Competition

THE GREAT STUDENT IMPORT

Foreign students are flocking to U.S. business schools. Fully one in five students enrolled in elite business schools come from foreign countries: Japanese students alone account for more than 5 percent of enrollments at top schools. Why? Japanese employers pay students' expenses, not because they are enamored of American business practices, but because they are enamored of American markets. These students go to school in America to learn about America. They hone their English language skills and grasp American culture. These students are learning about their future competitors and plan to run Japanese plants in the United States some day. To them, an M.B.A. means Mastering Being in America.

Naoki Yamamori is a typical foreign student at the Sloan School of Management at M.I.T., where 12 percent of the student body is Japanese. A former bank branch manager in Tokyo, he came to America to understand "how they think." He will use his cultural knowledge after graduation to communicate with branch managers of Mitsubishi's U.S. subsidiaries.

American business schools greet foreign students with open arms in order to globalize their campuses. Globalization is the rage, and international perspectives provoke stimulating case discussions in class. The presence of foreign students enriches the educational experience of American students.

But what about U.S. student exports? Few American students are willing to invest in learning a foreign language and attending school in a foreign country. Stanford and the Tuck School have cooperative programs with Japan, but student participation is modest. As yet, American students do not see the global marketplace or the intensity of global competition within U.S. borders. They do not see non-Americans climbing high in U.S. companies. Experienced managers in both large and small companies are trying to think internationally, but American companies may fall further behind their competitors because future managers are not investing in an international education. It is no surprise that Tokyo has replaced Detroit as the city with the most companies on the list of the world's 100 biggest industrial companies.

Sources: Todd Barrett, "Mastering Being in America," *Newsweek,* February 5, 1990, 64; Susan E. Kuhn and David J. Morrow, "The New Shape of Global Business," *Fortune,* July 31, 1989, 280–283.

balization presents a gloomy picture because the United States is losing worldwide market share in important product areas. One reason is described in the Focus on Global Competition box. Managers of the future will have to lead organizations to greater competitiveness on a global scale.[39]

In 1992, the 12 nations of the European Economic Community will reduce long-standing barriers to the transfer of goods, financing, and people across their borders. This true common market will be substantially larger than the United States, allowing European companies to grow large and powerful and to become more competitive on the global stage. U.S. companies are trying to get a foothold in Europe now to avoid potential barriers in the future. In addition, the U.S.–Canada Trade Agreement reduces trade barriers in North America, creating another common market. These rapid developments are changing the global picture, forcing managers to think internationally.[40]

Summary

This chapter introduced a number of important concepts about management. High performance requires the efficient and effective use of organizational resources through the four management functions of planning, organizing, leading, and controlling. Their importance differs somewhat by hierarchical level. Top and middle managers are most concerned with planning and place greater emphasis on organizing and controlling. First-line managers focus more on leading. To perform the four functions, managers need three skills — conceptual, human, and technical. Conceptual skills are more important at the top of the hierarchy; human skills are important at all levels; and technical skills are most important for first-line managers.

Two characteristics of managerial work were explained: (1) Managerial activities involve variety, fragmentation, and brevity and (2) managers perform a great deal of work at an unrelenting pace. Managers also are expected to perform activities associated with ten roles: the interpersonal roles of figurehead, leader, and liaison; the informational roles of monitor, disseminator, and spokesperson; and the decisional roles of entrepreneur, disturbance handler, resource allocator, and negotiator. Learning these roles and the skills required for management can be accomplished through both formal training and experience. The study of manager success and failure by the Center for Creative Leadership found that the biggest reason for manager failure was the inability to deal with people. Managers who succeeded had excellent human skills. Managers in the future will need even greater human skills as well as conceptual skills to deal with the pressing issues of diversity, flexibility, mergers, and globalization.

Management Solution

ReBecca Roloff took over Pillsbury's distribution department, which consisted of 450 mostly uninspired employees and was considered corporate oblivion for careers. Roloff infused new life into the department through *leadership,* relying heavily on both human and conceptual skills. She transformed employees into a gung-ho group by overwhelming them with recognition. Employees learned to catch each other in the act of excellence, thereby earning special recognition. Winners got plaques and treatment at headquarters as king or queen for a day. Roloff believes her human skills set her apart from her contemporaries and accounted for her success. She believes that taking care of her people means they took care of her, too. Roloff's conceptual skills also were important. She discovered that 25 percent of company sales were tied to decisions about distribution, such as timely shipping. She conceptualized new customer service objectives so her people directly affected sales gains, thereby providing a strategic mission for the department, a far cry from bureaucratic, routine tasks of previous years. By emphasizing human skills and leadership, Roloff made an impact that led to her promotion as Pillsbury's first female marketing director.[41]

Discussion Questions

1. Assume you are a research engineer at a petrochemical company, collaborating with a marketing manager on a major product modification. You notice that every memo you receive from her has been copied to senior management. At every company function she spends time talking to the big shots. You are also aware that sometimes when you are slaving away over the project she is playing golf with senior managers. What is your evaluation of her behavior?

2. What similarities do you see among the four management functions of planning, organizing, leading, and controlling? Do you think these functions are related — that is, is a manager who performs well in one function likely to perform well in the others?
3. Why did a top manager like Harding Lawrence at Braniff fail while a top manager like General Creech of Tactical Air Command succeed? Which of the four management functions best explains this difference? Discuss.
4. What is the difference between efficiency and effectiveness? Which is more important for performance? Can an organization succeed in both simultaneously?
5. What changes in management functions and skills occur as one is promoted from a nonmanagement to a management position? How can managers acquire the new skills?
6. If managerial work is characterized by variety, fragmentation, and brevity, how do managers perform basic management functions such as planning, which would seem to require reflection and analysis?
7. A college professor told her students, "The purpose of a management course is to teach students *about* management, not to teach them to be managers." Do you agree or disagree with this statement? Discuss.
8. What does it mean to say that management is both an art and a science? Discuss.
9. In the Center for Creative Leadership study, many managers made it to the middle and upper levels of the organization before derailing. How do you think managers got so far if they had flaws that prevented them from reaching the top?
10. How should the teaching of management change to prepare future managers to deal with work-force diversity? Do you think diversity will have a more substantial impact on organizations than globalization?

Management in Practice: Experiential Exercise

Test Your Human Skills

The 60 questions that follow will help you evaluate your human skills compared with those of current managers. Be honest in your responses. Your instructor will provide you with information about the meaning of your responses.

Circle the letter, as illustrated below, that represents your acceptance or rejection of the statements that follow.

Strongly disagree:	(D)	d	?	a	A
Moderately disagree:	D	(d)	?	a	A
Sometimes yes/no:	D	d	(?)	a	A
Moderately agree:	D	d	?	(a)	A
Strongly agree:	D	d	?	a	(A)

1. You have been elected or promoted to several leadership positions in your school/work/community/church involvements.	D	d	?	a	A
2. You have impeccably good manners, and people comment on your courteous behavior time and again.	D	d	?	a	A
3. You feel comfortable and at ease when others make you the center of attention.	D	d	?	a	A
4. It irritates you when others treat life as nothing more than a game.	D	d	?	a	A
5. You love old things, poetry, going out to the country, and being alone.	D	d	?	a	A

6. You would love to make a citizen's arrest of someone honking his or her horn needlessly or disturbing the peace.	D	d	?	a	A
7. You are good at praising others and give credit readily when credit is due.	D	d	?	a	A
8. When you deal with people, you tread softly and give them the "kid glove" treatment.	D	d	?	a	A
9. You allow people to manipulate and boss you around too much.	D	d	?	a	A
10. In the end, with every liaison established primarily for ambition's sake, you have to give away a bit of your "soul."	D	d	?	a	A
11. You have a knack for harmonizing the seemingly irreconcilable.	D	d	?	a	A
12. You believe that nothing gets done properly unless you do it yourself.	D	d	?	a	A
13. You seem to possess a natural charm and easily win people over.	D	d	?	a	A
14. In large or new social situations you are poised, relaxed, and self-assured.	D	d	?	a	A
15. You have a real capacity for selling yourself to others.	D	d	?	a	A
16. You really dislike others teasing or making fun of you.	D	d	?	a	A
17. You feel a natural and real warmth toward all people.	D	d	?	a	A
18. You have little patience for human ignorance and incompetence.	D	d	?	a	A
19. You will usually give others the benefit of the doubt rather than argue openly with them.	D	d	?	a	A
20. You seldom (or never) say anything to others without considering how they may receive it.	D	d	?	a	A
21. When friends ask you out, you usually go, even when you would prefer your privacy.	D	d	?	a	A
22. You stay on the lookout for people who can promote your advancement.	D	d	?	a	A
23. You have a talent for diffusing tension and anger when situations are strained.	D	d	?	a	A
24. You usually end up doing other people's jobs in addition to your own.	D	d	?	a	A
25. You go out of your way to introduce yourself and start up conversation with strangers.	D	d	?	a	A
26. You have a special magnetism that attracts people to you.	D	d	?	a	A
27. You go out of your way to make sure other people recognize your accomplishments.	D	d	?	a	A
28. You have an ability to see humor in situations many people overlook.	D	d	?	a	A
29. If people are not doing a good job, you believe they should be fired.	D	d	?	a	A
30. There are a lot of things you would change about people if you had your way.	D	d	?	a	A
31. Others find you very easy to get along with and easy to work with.	D	d	?	a	A
32. You freely tell others what you think is wrong with them.	D	d	?	a	A
33. You dislike having to deal with conflict situations requiring confrontation.	D	d	?	a	A
34. You realize you have to compete for promotions as much on the basis of politics as on merit.	D	d	?	a	A
35. If invited to venture an opinion around a hot issue, you usually seek a conciliatory or middle position.	D	d	?	a	A
36. The average person avoids responsibilities and must be strongly directed to work effectively.	D	d	?	a	A
37. You are an all-around type who can "hit it off" with just about anyone.	D	d	?	a	A
38. You go out of your way to create a lasting first impression when meeting new people.	D	d	?	a	A
39. You pretend to be shy or quiet to avoid attention.	D	d	?	a	A
40. It is very hard to "ruffle your feathers" or "get your back up."	D	d	?	a	A
41. Until you get to know people, you tend to act distant or aloof.	D	d	?	a	A
42. You have little patience for people who ask irrelevant and elementary questions.	D	d	?	a	A

43. You find it easy to seek the advice and counsel of others, as opposed to doing something all on your own.	D	d	?	a	A
44. You are quick to criticize and discount the foolish opinions and actions of people you cannot stand.	D	d	?	a	A
45. You will usually wait for someone else to complain about something that displeases you.	D	d	?	a	A
46. You accept that cultivating your coworkers and bosses is often necessary in getting ahead.	D	d	?	a	A
47. You are a masterful strategist at deftly maneuvering others toward your views.	D	d	?	a	A
48. You prefer to make all the important decisions and then expect others to carry them out.	D	d	?	a	A
49. You avoid superficial "cocktail" talk whenever possible.	D	d	?	a	A
50. Others find you exciting and are swept along by your personal manner.	D	d	?	a	A
51. You are really worried about making people jealous or envious of your accomplishments.	D	d	?	a	A
52. You exude an optimistic appreciation of life that says "all is well."	D	d	?	a	A
53. You have little sympathy for the "dumb messes" people get themselves into.	D	d	?	a	A
54. When dealing with others, you have a very easygoing, "laid-back" style.	D	d	?	a	A
55. You usually have no difficulty collaborating or going along with the majority opinion.	D	d	?	a	A
56. Head-on, direct, "tell it as it is" confrontation is your style of relating to people.	D	d	?	a	A
57. When a quarrel takes place between yourself and others, you usually give in first.	D	d	?	a	A
58. You are a person who is particularly adept at currying special favors when you want something.	D	d	?	a	A
59. You have a facility for altering your opinions and viewpoints and adopting new value standards.	D	d	?	a	A
60. If there are ten ways of correctly doing a job, you would press to have it done your way.	D	d	?	a	A

Cases for Analysis

COMPUTER SPECIALISTS INC.

Computer Specialists Inc. (CSI), a real company, achieved sales of about $3 million by providing computer programmers and system designers under contract to clients. The major client is a well-known bank in western Pennsylvania for whom CSI writes programs for their MasterCard and VISA applications.

While on vacation, Warren Rodgers, CEO of CSI, learned that a star programmer entered the wrong set of instructions into the bank's computer. The mistake caused roughly 500,000 credit cards to be wrongly invalidated, and several thousand cards were quickly confiscated by automatic teller machines. Bank officers were furious, evicting the programmer from the premises and going to the press with the story. The story appeared on the evening news and in the morning newspaper, with the blame placed on CSI.

Two senior managers at CSI, the director of human resources and the marketing director, did not get involved in solving the problem because they had little technical grounding in the bank's data-processing system and no desire to step into this mess. The star programmer was sent home, where she was getting the cold shoulder from CSI managers and the bank. The bank blamed CSI for the fiasco and started demands for financial concessions. CSI's chief competitors were running CSI's name into the ground. They were telling other clients that CSI was totally responsible for the problem.

Before reading on, think for a moment about what you would do if you were Warren Rodgers returning from vacation. Rodgers's response went something like this: (1) Call the star employee at home to let her know that he was behind her 100 percent. This sent the right signal to other programmers and to the bank about her value. (2) Rectifying this problem was made the top management priority for the next few weeks. All available employees were at that bank making amends. Everyone — bank managers, secretaries — was taken to lunch. If any CSI employee was in the area, he or she walked through the bank to show a presence so that bank officials would know the problem was not being avoided. (3) Rodgers did not make a financial settlement with the bank. Instead he offered a reduced rate for programmers, thereby increasing the number of CSI programmers at the bank. This effectively scuttled the rumor that CSI caused the problem. (4) The managers who failed to take immediate action are no longer with CSI. Managers are now promoted from within, and everyone must have some data-processing experience and be willing to get involved with customers in a proactive mode.

Questions

1. How would you evaluate Rodgers's response to the crisis? Do you consider him a good manager?
2. How would you rate Rodgers on conceptual, human, and technical skills?
3. Do the managerial roles revealed in this case seem consistent with the small-business managers described in the text?

Source: Based on Warren Rodgers, "My Terrible Vacation," *INC.*, February 1988, 116–117.

PRO LINE COMPANY

It was almost 6 P.M. and Sally Benson was still at her desk trying to tie up some loose ends with the hope that tomorrow might be a more productive day.

Sally is the western regional sales director, a middle management position, in the Pro Line Company, a manufacturer of a well-known line of sporting goods. As she reads the mail she still has to answer and stacks the phone messages she still has to return, she wonders if being a middle manager is really her kind of job. Selling products, traveling, and meeting with clients seemed much more to her liking than the routine of her present job.

Take today, for example. Sally had come to the office early so she could call Ted Lomax, the eastern regional sales director, to confer on a joint sales forecast they are trying to prepare. Working with Ted isn't the easiest of tasks. Compromise just isn't a word in Ted's vocabulary. She also needs to call the production managers of two of the company's eastern plants to find out what is causing the delay in the receipt of the new product lines. Those production people don't seem to realize that a large inventory is needed to keep sales up. The new product lines were promised two weeks ago and still aren't here. The phone calls took longer than expected, but by midmorning Sally is finally able to get settled into the major project she has planned for the day. After several days of perusing sales reports of the past several years, she concluded that total sales, as well as productivity of individual salespersons, can be improved if the region is redesigned and the territories of each salesperson adjusted. This is a major project and she needs to have a preliminary proposal ready to present to her district sales managers at her monthly meeting tomorrow afternoon.

Lunch keeps Sally away from the office a little longer than expected, and when she returns she finds a half dozen phone messages, including an urgent call from the corporate vice president of personnel, Bill Finley. She returns Finley's call and much to her dismay, she finds she is going to have to allocate a good portion of tomorrow's sales managers' meeting to presenting the company's new benefits program. Bill assured her all the materials she needs will arrive late this afternoon and stressed the need for its immediate dissemination and explanation. After trying unsuccessfully to return several of the other phone calls, she returns to the territory redesign project. She finishes that project just before the 3 P.M. appointment she has with a candidate for a district sales manager position that will open up next week. Sally spends over an hour with the candidate and is impressed enough with him to immediately make some follow-up phone calls to validate the accuracy of some of the information she received.

When 5 P.M. arrives, Sally realizes she won't have much luck with further phone calls. The whole day seems to have gotten away from her, and she still has the materials from Finley to review and she has to prepare the agenda for tomorrow's meeting. She just has to figure a way to motivate better performance from those sales managers. The redesign of the territory was only a partial solution. Sally wonders what else she can do.

Questions

1. Compare Sally's present job to what you think her previous job as a salesperson might have been. How are they similar? How are they different?
2. What major manager roles are depicted in this case?
3. Why do you think Sally might be disenchanted with her present job?

Source: "A Day in the Life of a Middle Manager — Sally Benson," *The Managerial Experience: Cases, Exercises, and Readings,* Fourth Edition, 24–25, by Lawrence R. Jauch, Sally A. Coltrin, Arthur G. Bedeian, and William F. Glueck.

CHAPTER 2

FOUNDATIONS OF MANAGEMENT UNDERSTANDING

CHAPTER OUTLINE

LEARNING OBJECTIVES

After studying this chapter, you should be able to:

- Understand how historical forces in society have influenced the practice of management.
- Identify and explain major developments in the history of management thought.
- Describe the major components of the classical management perspective.
- Describe the major components of the human resource management perspective.
- Discuss the quantitative management perspective.
- Explain the major components of systems theory.
- Discuss the basic concepts underlying contingency views.
- Describe the recent influences of global competition on management in North America.

Management Problem

With drive-in theaters closing and the cost of making movies escalating, would you risk your savings to finance low-budget films? Two Los Angeles lawyers, Lawrence Kuppin and Harry Evans Sloan, bought New World Pictures specifically to make B movies. The movie industry is noted for turning out big-budget losers in pursuit of a single smash hit. Three large competing B-movie companies — Filmways, Avco Embassy, and American International Pictures — have abandoned low-budget films for classier, big-budget productions. New World makes films for an average of $2 million to $4 million, compared with an average of $15 million for a Hollywood film. New World got off to a rocky start, losing almost $5 million its first year. Investment analysts were wary, believing there was little future for schlock movies. Kuppin and Sloan bet $2 million of their own money plus money borrowed from private investors in the belief they could profit by fighting the trend toward big-budget films.[1]

Do you think Kuppin and Sloan made a wise investment by going into the B-movie business? What historical patterns will influence the success or failure of this venture?

Why should history matter to corporate managers? Kuppin and Sloan bought New World Pictures because they were betting on the historical success of B movies, which have had a following since the 1940s. A historical perspective matters to executives because it is a way of thinking, a way of searching for patterns and determining whether they recur across time periods. A historical perspective provides a context or environment in which to interpret problems. Only then does a major problem take on real meaning, reveal its severity, and point the way toward management actions.[2]

A study of the past contributes to understanding both the present and the future. It is a way of learning: learning from others' mistakes so as not to repeat them; learning from others' successes so as to repeat them in the appropriate situation; and, most of all, learning to understand why things happen to improve things in the future.

Going back in *history* to find its future, the Santa Fe railroad's 63 new GM locomotives delivered in 1990 will be painted in the red warbonnet style that graced Santa Fe's famous "Chiefs" passenger trains in the 1940s and 1950s. Linking the old with the new is top management's way of honoring Santa Fe's past with this symbol of commitment to speed and quality of service. Reawakening Santa Fe's history of super service to rail travelers encourages today's employees to show a new generation of customers the same strong, consistent performance with today's modern equipment.

For example, such companies as Polaroid, AT&T, International Harvester, Consolidated Edison, and Wells Fargo Bank have all asked historians to research their pasts. Managers want to know their corporate roots. Polaroid's W-3 plant in Waltham, Massachusetts, started out as a model of efficiency, but over the years productivity dropped and relations with workers soured. A corporate historian was hired to interview employees and examine old records. He pieced together how managers had imposed ever tighter controls over the years that lowered workers' morale.[3] Or consider the signing of Randy Travis, now a country music superstar, by Warner Brothers. Country music had been invaded by pop music influence, and industry managers wanted more pop in the country sound to appeal to younger audiences. Martha Sharp, a vice-president for Warner Brothers, loved Travis's voice and used a cycle-of-history argument on her bosses. She argued that based on historical patterns, a traditional country sound would reemerge, and Travis would be in the forefront. Her argument won, Travis was signed, and he led a resurgence in country music.[4]

This chapter provides an overview of how managers' philosophies have changed over the years. This foundation of management understanding illustrates that the value of studying management lies not in learning current facts and research but in developing a perspective that will facilitate the broad, long-term view needed for management success.

HISTORICAL FORCES SHAPING MANAGEMENT

Studying history does not mean merely arranging events in chronological order; it means developing an understanding of the impact of societal forces on organizations. Studying history is a way to achieve strategic thinking, see the big picture, and improve conceptual skills. We will start by examining how

Lewis Hine's famous 1911 "Breaker Boys" photograph helped promote passage of laws forbidding child labor. These boys picked stone impurities from coal in a bent over position 12 to 14 hours a day, 6 days a week, suffering cut fingers and aching backs, breathing coal dust, for $.75 a day. Public outrage became a strong *social force* against child labor. *Political forces* prompted Congress to outlaw the employment of children. *Economic forces* reallocated resources to materials-handling machinery, which reduced the need for children to do this unpleasant task.

social, political, and economic forces have influenced organizations and the practice of management.[5]

Social forces refer to those aspects of a culture that guide and influence relationships among people. What do people value? What do people need? What are the standards of behavior among people? These forces shape what is known as the *social contract*, which refers to the unwritten, common rules and perceptions about relationships among people and between employees and management. Expressions such as "a man's as good as his word" and "a day's work for a day's pay" convey such perceptions.

Political forces refer to the influence of political and legal institutions on people and organizations. Political forces include basic assumptions underlying the political system, such as the desirability of self-government, property rights, contract rights, the definition of justice, and the determination of innocence or guilt of a crime. Further, political forces determine managers' rights relative to those of owners, customers, suppliers, and workers as well as other publics with whom the organization must interact. For example, deregulation is a political force that has influenced the way of doing business in the banking and airlines industries. Managers can understand deregulation by studying the regulations' original impact on corporations and how new regulations changed the market.

social forces The aspects of a culture that guide and influence relationships among people — their values, needs, and standards of behavior.

political forces The influence of political and legal institutions on people and organizations.

FOCUS ON ETHICS

"IF IT'S HOOTIN', I'M SHOOTIN' "

The historical clash between environmentalists and industry is being played out right now in the great Northwest. The spotted owl endangers the Northwest lumber industry, and vice versa.

Typical of the logging firms is Gregory Forest Products, purchased by William Gregory in Glendale, Oregon, so he could run his own business. Gregory invested heavily in new technology, enabling his lumber mill to recover 20 percent more from each log. Efficiency combined with increased prices produced healthy profits in 1989, yet Gregory is now investing in employee training to help them find jobs elsewhere.

What's the problem? Powerful political and economic forces. Gregory's mill may be forced to close because of a court injunction against harvesting old-growth timber. The spotted owl nests in the tops of the 200-year-old trees. Environmentalists want to protect old-growth forests because they harbor thousands of animals and plants. Because of the injunction, Gregory has eliminated his swing shift, and other mills are cutting back as well. If current bans are made permanent, 25,000 jobs may be lost. Gloom has settled over the area. The local school district cancelled extracurricular activities because of reduced tax income. Yellow ribbons flutter from car antennas, and 1,100 logging trucks streamed through Grants Pass in protest. Bumper stickers sum up the feeling of unemployed residents toward the owl: "If It's Hootin', I'm Shootin'."

Somehow management decisions must strike a balance between the spotted owl and old-growth forest, between environmental protection and the livelihood of lumber industry employees. At this point environmentalists are winning, but lumber industry people feel that harvesting the timber is a legitimate thing to do. Without legislation from Congress to protect the logging industry, Gregory says, "We will be down the tube in a year."

Source: Based on Jonathan B. Levine, "The Spotted Owl Could Wipe Us Out," *Business Week*, September 18, 1989, 94–99.

The Focus on Ethics box gives an example of how social and political forces affect one industry.

economic forces Forces that affect the availability, production, and distribution of a society's resources among competing users.

Economic forces pertain to the availability, production, and distribution of resources in a society. Governments, military agencies, churches, schools, and business organizations in every society require resources to achieve their objectives, and economic forces influence the allocation of scarce resources. Resources may be human or material, fabricated or natural, physical or conceptual, but over time they are scarce and must be allocated among competing users. Economic scarcity is often the stimulus for technological innovation with which to increase resource availability. The perfection of the moving assembly line at Ford in 1913 cut the number of worker-hours needed for assembling a Model T from 12 to 1.5. Ford doubled its daily pay rate to $5, shortened working hours, and cut the price of Model Ts until its market share reached 57 percent in 1923.

CLASSICAL PERSPECTIVE

The practice of management is quite ancient, but the formal study of management is relatively recent.[6] The practice of management can be traced to 3000 B.C. to the first government organizations developed by the Sumerians and Egyptians. The early study of management as we know it today began with what is now called the classical perspective.

The **classical perspective** on management emerged during the nineteenth and early twentieth centuries. It was grounded in management experiences from manufacturing, transportation, and communication industries, which were heavily staffed by engineers. Firms tended to be small or composed of departments or divisions consisting of small groups. Most organizations produced only one line of product or service. Further, major educational, social, and cultural differences existed among owners, managers, and workers.

The factory system that began to appear in the 1800s posed managerial problems that earlier organizations had not encountered. Large numbers of workers were needed, and machines began performing skilled operations. Managers had to cope with large organization size, retrain workers, and schedule complex manufacturing operations. Managers who solved these problems developed the ideas that were the forerunners of modern management thinking.[7] The thrust of the classical perspective was to make organizations efficient operating machines. This perspective contained three subfields, each with a slightly different emphasis: scientific management, administrative principles, and bureaucratic organizations.

Frederick Winslow Taylor (1856–1915)
Taylor's theory that labor productivity could be improved by scientifically determined management practices earned him the status of "father of scientific management."

Scientific Management

Organizations' somewhat limited success in achieving improvements in labor productivity led a young engineer to suggest that the problem lay more in poor management practices than in labor. Frederick Winslow Taylor (1856–1915) insisted that management itself would have to change and, further, that the manner of change could be determined only by scientific study; hence, the label **scientific management** emerged. Taylor suggested that decisions based on rules of thumb and tradition be replaced with precise procedures developed after careful study of individual situations.

classical perspective
A management perspective that emerged during the nineteenth and early twentieth centuries that emphasized a rational, scientific approach to the study of management and sought to make organizations efficient operating machines.

scientific management
A subfield of the classical management perspective that emphasized scientifically determined changes in management practices as the solution to improving labor productivity.

While working at the Midvale Steel Company in Philadelphia, Taylor began experimenting with management methods, procedures, and practices. Taylor wrote frequently, had others write under his name, and consulted with businesses to encourage utilization of his ideas.[8] However, it was after the Eastern Railroad Rate Case hearings before the House of Representatives that his work really caught on. The attorney for the shippers, Louis D. Brandeis, used the term *scientific management* and successfully argued the shippers' side of the issue for using these techniques. The popular press picked up the term, and Taylor and his ideas became heralded as the way to prosperity for the United States.[9]

Taylor's approach is illustrated by the unloading of iron from rail cars and reloading finished steel for the Bethlehem Steel plant in 1898. Taylor calculated that with correct movements, tools, and sequencing, each man was capable of loading 47.5 tons per day instead of the typical 12.5 tons. He also worked out an incentive system that paid each man $1.85 a day for meeting the new standard, an increase from the previous rate of $1.15. Productivity at Bethlehem Steel shot up overnight.

Although known as the "father of scientific management," Taylor was not alone in this area. Two other important pioneers in this area were the husband-and-wife team of Frank B. and Lillian M. Gilbreth. Frank B. Gilbreth (1868–1924) pioneered time and motion study and arrived at many of his manage-

Frederick Taylor's *scientific management* hit Detroit about 1910, where time and motion techniques became the norm. Henry Ford took the concept one step further by replacing workers with machines and having machines do all heavy lifting and moving. One of the first applications of the moving assembly line was the Magneto assembly operation (top) at Ford's Highland Park plant in 1913. Magnetos were pushed from one worker to the next, reducing production time by about one-half. The same principle was applied to total-car assembly, in which stationary workers performed minuscule tasks. The assembly process became so efficient that the worker-hours required to produce a Model-T Ford were cut to fewer than two. A Ford came off the assembly line every ten seconds, creating a huge daily output (bottom).

ment techniques independently of Taylor. He stressed efficiency and was known for his quest for the "one best way" to do work. Although he is known for his early work with bricklayers, his work had great impact on medical surgery by drastically reducing the time patients spent on the operating table. Surgeons were able to save countless lives through the application of time and motion study. Lillian M. Gilbreth (1878–1972) was more interested in the human aspect of work. When her husband died at the age of 46, she had 12 children ages 2 to 19. The undaunted "first lady of management" went right on with her work. She presented a paper in place of her late husband, continued their seminars and consulting, lectured, and eventually became a professor at Purdue University.[10] She pioneered in the field of industrial psychology and made substantial contributions to personnel management.

The basic ideas of scientific management are shown in Exhibit 2.1. To use this approach, managers should develop standard methods for doing each job,

EXHIBIT 2.1
Characteristics of Scientific Management

General Approach
- Developed standard method for performing each job.
- Selected workers with appropriate abilities for each job.
- Trained workers in standard method.
- Supported workers by planning their work and eliminating interruptions.
- Provided wage incentives to workers for increased output.

Contributions
- Demonstrated the importance of compensation for performance.
- Initiated the careful study of tasks and jobs.
- Demonstrated the importance of personnel selection and training.

Criticisms
- Did not appreciate the social context of work and higher needs of workers.
- Did not acknowledge variance among individuals.
- Tended to regard workers as uninformed and ignored their ideas and suggestions.

select workers with the appropriate abilities, train workers in the standard methods, support the workers, and provide wage incentives.

Although scientific management improved productivity, its failure to deal with the social context and workers' needs led to increased conflict between managers and employees. Under this system, workers often felt exploited. This was in sharp contrast to the harmony and cooperation that Taylor and his followers had envisioned.

administrative principles
A subfield of the classical management perspective that focused on the total organization rather than the individual worker, delineating the management functions of planning, organizing, commanding, coordinating, and controlling.

ADMINISTRATIVE PRINCIPLES

The second major subfield within the classical perspective is known as the **administrative principles** approach. Whereas scientific management focused on the productivity of the individual worker, the administrative principles approach focused on the total organization. The contributors to this approach included Henri Fayol, Mary Parker Follett, and Chester I. Barnard.

Henri Fayol (1841–1925) was a French mining engineer who worked his way up to the head of a major mining group known as Comambault. Comambault survives today as part of Le Creusot-Loire, the largest mining and metallurgical group in central France. In his later years Fayol, based largely on his own management experiences, wrote down his concepts on administration.[11]

In his most significant work, *General and Industrial Management,* Fayol discussed 14 general principles of management, several of which are part of management philosophy today. For example:

- *Unity of command.* Each subordinate receives orders from one — and only one — superior.
- *Division of work.* Managerial and technical work are amenable to specialization to produce more and better work with the same amount of effort.
- *Unity of direction.* Similar activities in an organization should be grouped together under one manager.
- *Scalar chain.* A chain of authority extends from the top to the bottom of the organization and should include every employee.

Lillian M. Gilbreth (1878–1972) and Frank B. Gilbreth (1868–1924). This husband-and-wife team contributed to the principles of scientific management. His development of time and motion studies and her work in industrial psychology pioneered many of today's management and human resource techniques.

Mary Parker Follett (1868–1933)
Follett was a major contributor to the *administrative principles* approach to management. Her emphasis on shared goals among managers was embraced by many businesspeople of her day.

Fayol felt that these principles could be applied in any organizational setting. He also identified five basic functions or elements of management: planning, organizing, commanding, coordinating, and controlling. These functions underlie much of the general approach to today's management theory.

Mary Parker Follett (1868–1933) was trained in philosophy and political science at what today is Radcliffe College. She applied herself in many fields, including social psychology and management. She wrote of the importance of common superordinate goals for reducing conflict in organizations.[12] Her work was popular with businesspeople of her day but was often overlooked by management scholars.[13]

Chester I. Barnard (1886–1961) studied economics at Harvard but failed to receive a degree because he lacked a course in laboratory science. He went to work in the statistical department of AT&T and in 1927 became president of New Jersey Bell. One of Barnard's significant contributions was the concept of the informal organization. The *informal organization* occurs in all formal organizations and includes cliques and naturally occurring social groupings. Barnard argued that organizations are not machines and informal relationships are powerful forces that can help the organization if properly managed. Another significant contribution was the *acceptance theory of authority,* which states that people have free will and can choose whether to follow management orders. People typically follow orders because they perceive positive benefit to themselves, but they do have a choice, and their acceptance of authority may be critical to organization success in important situations.[14]

BUREAUCRATIC ORGANIZATIONS

The final subfield within the classical perspective is that of **bureaucratic organizations.** Max Weber (1864–1920), a German theorist, introduced most of the concepts on bureaucratic organizations.[15]

This 1914 photograph shows the initiation of a new arrival at a Nebraska planting camp. This initiation was not part of the formal rules and illustrates the significance of the *informal organization* described by Barnard. Social values and behaviors were powerful forces that could help or hurt the planting organization depending on how they were managed.

During the late 1800s, many European organizations were managed on a "personal," family-like basis. Employees were loyal to a single individual rather than to the organization or its mission. The dysfunctional consequence of this management practice was that resources were used to realize individual desires rather than organizational goals. Employees in effect owned the organization and used resources for their own gain rather than to serve clients. Weber envisioned organizations that would be managed on an impersonal, rational basis. This form of organization was called a *bureaucracy.* Exhibit 2.2 summarizes the six characteristics of bureaucracy as specified by Weber.

Weber believed that an organization based on rational authority would be more efficient and adaptable to change because continuity is related to formal structure and positions rather than to a particular person, who may leave or die. To Weber, rationality in organizations meant employee selection and advancement based on competence rather than on "whom you know." The organization relies on rules and written records for continuity. The manager depends not on his or her personality for successfully giving orders but on the legal power invested in the managerial position.

The term *bureaucracy* has taken on a negative meaning in today's organizations and is associated with endless rules and red tape. We have all been frustrated by waiting in long lines or following seemingly silly procedures. On the other hand, rules and other bureaucratic procedures provide a standard

Elements of Bureaucracy:

1. Labor is divided with clear definitions of authority and responsibility that are legitimized as official duties.
2. Positions are organized in a hierarchy of authority, with each position under the authority of a higher one.
3. All personnel are selected and promoted based on technical qualifications, which are assessed by examination or according to training and experience.
4. Administrative acts and decisions are recorded in writing. Recordkeeping provides organizational memory and continuity over time.
5. Management is separate from the ownership of the organization.
6. Managers are subject to rules and procedures that will insure reliable, predictable behavior. Rules are impersonal and uniformly applied to all employees.

Exhibit 2.2
Characteristics of Weberian Bureaucracy

Source: Adapted from A. M. Henderson and Talcott Parsons, eds. and trans., Max Weber, *The Theory of Social and Economic Organizations* (New York: Free Press, 1947), 328–337.

way of dealing with employees. Everyone gets equal treatment, and everyone knows what the rules are. This has enabled many organizations to become extremely efficient. Consider United Parcel Service, also called the "Brown Giant" for the color of the packages it delivers.

bureaucratic organizations
A subfield of the classical management perspective that emphasized management on an impersonal, rational basis through elements such as clearly defined authority and responsibility, formal recordkeeping, and separation of management and ownership.

United Parcel Service • United Parcel Service took on the U.S. Postal Service at its own game — and won. UPS specializes in the delivery of small packages. Why has the Brown Giant been so successful? One important reason is the concept of bureaucracy. UPS is bound up in rules and regulations. There are safety rules for drivers, loaders, clerks, and managers. Strict dress codes are enforced — no beards; hair cannot touch the collar; mustaches must be trimmed evenly; and no sideburns. Rules specify cleanliness standards for buildings and other properties. Every manager is given bound copies of policy books and expected to use them regularly.

UPS also has a well-defined division of labor. Each plant consists of specialized drivers, loaders, clerks, washers, sorters, and maintenance personnel. UPS thrives on written records. Daily worksheets specify performance goals and work output. Daily employee quotas and achievements are recorded on a weekly and monthly basis.

Technical qualification is the criterion for hiring and promotion. The UPS policy book says the leader is expected to have the knowledge and capacity to justify the position of leadership. Favoritism is forbidden. The bureaucratic model works just fine at UPS.[16]

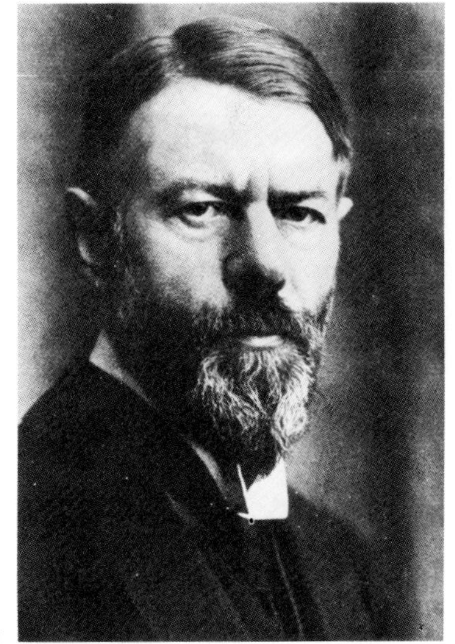

Max Weber
(1864–1920)
The German theorist's concepts on *bureaucratic organizations* have contributed to the efficiency of many of today's corporations.

Human Resource Perspective

America has always had a spirit of human equality. However, this spirit has not always been translated into practice when it comes to power sharing between managers and workers. The **human resource perspective** has recognized and directly responded to social pressures for enlightened treatment of employees. The early work on industrial psychology and personnel selection

human resource perspective A management perspective that emerged around the late nineteenth century that emphasized enlightened treatment of workers and power sharing between managers and employees.

received little attention because of the prominence of scientific management. Then a series of studies at a Chicago electric company changed all that.

The Hawthorne Studies

Beginning about 1895, a struggle developed between manufacturers of gas and electric lighting fixtures for control of the residential and industrial market.[17] By 1909 electric lighting had begun to win, but the increasingly efficient electric fixtures used less total power. The electric companies began a campaign to convince industrial users that they needed more light to get more productivity. When advertising did not work, the industry began using experimental tests to demonstrate their argument. Managers were skeptical about the results, so the Committee on Industrial Lighting (CIL) was set up to run the tests. To further add to the tests' credibility, Thomas Edison was made honorary chairman of the CIL. In one test location — the Hawthorne plant of the Western Electric Company — some interesting events occurred. These and subsequent experiments have come to be known as the **Hawthorne studies.**

Hawthorne studies A series of experiments on worker productivity begun in 1924 at the Hawthorne plant of Western Electric Company in Illinois; attributed employees' increased output to managers' better treatment of them during the study.

The major part of this work involved four experimental and three control groups. In all, five different "tests" were conducted. These pointed to the importance of factors *other* than illumination in affecting productivity. To more carefully examine these factors, numerous other experiments were conducted.[18] These were the first Relay Assembly Test Room, the second Relay Assembly Group, the Mica Splitting Group, the Typewriting Group, and the Bank Wiring Observation Room. The results of the most famous study, the first Relay Assembly Test Room (RATR) experiment, were extremely controversial. Under the guidance of two Harvard professors, Elton Mayo and Fritz Roethlisberger, the RATR studies lasted nearly six years (May 10, 1927, to May 4, 1933) and involved 24 separate experimental periods. So many factors were changed and so many unforeseen factors uncontrolled that scholars disagree on the factors that truly contributed to the general increase in performance over that period. Most early interpretations, however, agreed on one thing: Money was not the cause of the increased output.[19] Recent analyses of the experiments, however, suggest that money may well have been the single most important factor.[20] An interview with one of the original participants revealed that just getting into the experimental group had meant a huge increase in income.[21]

These new data clearly show that money mattered a great deal at Hawthorne, but it was not recognized at the time of the experiments. Then it was felt that the factor that best explained increased output was "human relations." Employees' output increased sharply when managers treated them in a positive manner. These findings were published and started a revolution in worker treatment for improving organizational productivity. To be historically accurate, money was probably the best explanation for increases in output, but at that time experimenters believed the explanation was human relations. Despite the inaccurate interpretation of the data, the findings provided the impetus for the human relations movement. That movement shaped management theory and practice for well over a quarter-century, and the belief that human relations is the best approach for increasing productivity persists today. The Manager's Shoptalk box lists a number of management theories that have been popular over the years.

This is the Relay Room of the Western Electric Hawthorne, Illinois, plant in 1927. Six women worked in this *relay assembly test room* during the controversial experiments on employee productivity. Professors Mayo and Roethlisberger evaluated conditions such as rest breaks and workday length, physical health, amount of sleep, and diet. Experimental changes were fully discussed with the women and were abandoned if they disapproved. Gradually the researchers began to realize they had created a change in supervisory style and human relations, which they believed was the true cause of the increased productivity.

THE HUMAN RELATIONS MOVEMENT

One reason that "human relations" interpretation may have been so readily attached to the Hawthorne studies was the Great Depression. An unprecedented number of people were out of work. Emerging social forces supported people's humanitarian efforts to help one another. The **human relations movement** initially espoused a "dairy farm" view of management—contented cows give more milk, so satisfied workers will give more work. Gradually, views with deeper content began to emerge. Two of the best-known contributors to the human relations movement were Abraham Maslow and Douglas McGregor.

human relations movement
A movement in management thinking and practice that emphasized satisfaction of employees' basic needs as the key to increased worker productivity.

Abraham Maslow (1908–1970), a practicing psychologist, observed that his patients' problems usually stemmed from an inability to satisfy their needs. Thus, he generalized his work and suggested a hierarchy of needs. Maslow's hierarchy started with physiological needs and progressed to safety, belongingness, esteem, and, finally, self-actualization needs. Chapter 14 discusses his ideas in more detail.

Douglas McGregor (1906–1964) had become frustrated with the early simplistic human relations notions while president of Antioch College in Ohio. He challenged both the classical perspective and the early human relations assumptions about human behavior. Based on his experiences as a manager and consultant, his training as a psychologist, and the work of Maslow, McGregor formulated his Theory X and Theory Y, which are explained in Exhibit 2.3.[22] McGregor believed that the classical perspective was based on Theory X assumptions about workers. He also felt that a slightly modified version of Theory X fit early human relations ideas. In other words, human relations ideas

MANAGER'S SHOPTALK

DO YOU KNOW WHEN?

Over the past 40 years a number of management fashions and fads have appeared. Critics argue that managers adopt quick fixes and that new techniques do not represent permanent solutions. Others feel that managers simply are working toward continuous improvement in a highly uncertain world.

The 15 items below represent management ideas that have been popular over the last 40 years. Each of these concepts will be discussed somewhere in this textbook. Can you identify the decade each came into the management repertoire?

1. *Management by Walking Around (MBWA).* Leave the office to walk around instead of relying on written reports.
2. *Matrix Management.* A structure in which some employees report to two or more bosses.
3. *Theory Z.* A hybrid management style using Japanese management methods.
4. *Quantitative Methods.* Trust the numbers and run the business as a science.
5. *Portfolio Management.* Identify and obtain a group of businesses with different cash flows including cash cows, stars, and even some dogs.
6. *Quality Circles.* Workers and managers sit around tables finding ways to solve problems with productivity and quality.
7. *Managerial Grid.* Is a manager's chief concern people, production, or both?
8. *Downsizing.* Trimming the work force, especially middle management and corporate staff.
9. *Management by Objectives (MBO).* Set goals through negotiation between superior and subordinate.
10. *Conglomeration.* Forming disparate businesses under a single corporate umbrella.
11. *Corporate Culture.* The values, rituals, and heroes that typify a company's style.
12. *Zero-based Budgeting.* Start from scratch with this year's budget based on each department's contribution to the company.
13. *Theory Y.* All employees have knowledge and ability to contribute to their work.
14. *Intrapreneuring.* Encourage entrepreneurial projects within the corporation.
15. *Transformational Leader.* Managers with the ability to fundamentally change the company's values, goals, and activities.

Answers

1950s: 4, 9, 13
1960s: 2, 10
1970s: 5, 7, 12
1980s: 1, 3, 6, 8, 11, 14, 15

Based on John Case, "Why 'Fixes' Fail," *INC.*, January 1989, 25–26, and John A. Byrne, "Business Fads: What's In — and Out," *Business Week*, January 20, 1986, 52–61.

did not go far enough. McGregor proposed Theory Y as a more realistic view of workers for guiding management thinking.

The point of Theory Y is that organizations can take advantage of the imagination and intellect of all its employees. Employees will exercise self-control and will contribute to organizational objectives when given the opportunity. Some companies today use Theory X management, but one of the greatest success stories has practiced Theory Y from the beginning.

COMPAQ COMPUTER CORPORATION • Compaq president, Rod Canion, backed out of a merger with Tandy Corporation, refused to build a low-priced "Fox" brand computer in Taiwan, and was years late to market with Compaq's first laptop computer. Why? Compaq's "process" — an endless participative management system — requires inputs from across the company. Unless all players agree, a

EXHIBIT 2.3
Theory X and Theory Y

Assumptions of Theory X

- The average human being has an inherent dislike of work and will avoid it if he can. . . .
- Because of the human characteristic of dislike for work, most people must be coerced, controlled, directed, or threatened with punishment to get them to put forth adequate effort toward the achievement of organizational objectives. . . .
- The average human being prefers to be directed, wishes to avoid responsibility, has relatively little ambition, wants security above all.

Assumptions of Theory Y

- The expenditure of physical and mental effort in work is as natural as play or rest. The average human being does not inherently dislike work. . . .
- External control and the threat of punishment are not the only means for bringing about effort toward organizational objectives. Man will exercise self-direction and self-control in the service of objectives to which he is committed. . . .
- The average human being learns, under proper conditions, not only to accept but to seek responsibility. . . .
- The capacity to exercise a relatively high degree of imagination, ingenuity, and creativity in the solution of organizational problems is widely, not narrowly, distributed in the population.
- Under the conditions of modern industrial life, the intellectual potentialities of the average human being are only partially utilized.

Source: Douglas McGregor, *The Human Side of Enterprise* (New York: McGraw-Hill, 1960), 33–48.

decision is no go. The bride was at the altar in the Tandy merger, but a few managers resisted the idea because Tandy's Radio Shack image might diminish Compaq's premium-brand reputation. Even Compaq's chairman cannot railroad an idea through in top-down Theory X fashion. The cheap Fox computer died when dealers rejected the idea. Compaq's first laptop, the 286-SLT, came out in October 1988, well after Zenith, Toshiba, and NEC were established. Compaq's decision process takes time, and it rejected the first three laptop prototypes. But the final outcome was sensational, and Compaq immediately grabbed 34 percent of all laptop sales through dealers.

The incredibly participative process accumulates ideas and information from throughout Compaq and ensures that issues are fully discussed. The results are just plain astonishing. Compaq's revenues jumped fivefold in three years from 1986 to 1989. Compaq also jumped into the top 50 list of America's exporters, showing the largest sales increase of all companies. The only drawback is that consensus building takes time, and everyone is working long hours. But the impact on the bottom line is so striking that Compaq will stick to its Theory Y philosophy no matter how much time is required.[23]

BEHAVIORAL SCIENCES APPROACH

behavioral sciences approach A subfield of the human resource management perspective that applied social science in an organizational context, drawing from economics, psychology, sociology, and other disciplines.

The word *science* is the keyword in the **behavioral sciences approach** (see Exhibit 2.4). Systematic research is the basis for theory development and testing, and its results form the basis for practical applications. The behavioral sciences approach can be seen in practically every organization. When General Electric conducts research to determine the best set of tests, interviews, and

EXHIBIT 2.4
The Behavioral Sciences Approach

General Approach
- Social science applied in an organizational context.
- Drew from an interdisciplinary research base, including anthropology, economics, psychology, and sociology.

Contributions
- Improved our understanding of and practical applications for organizational processes such as motivation, communication, leadership, and group processes.
- Regards members of organizations as full human beings, not as tools.

Criticisms
- Because findings are increasingly complex, practical applications often are tried incorrectly or not at all.
- Some concepts run counter to common sense, thus inviting managers' rejection.

employee profiles to use when selecting new employees, it is employing behavioral science techniques. Emery Air Freight has utilized reinforcement theory to improve the incentives given to workers and increase the performance of many of its operations. When Westinghouse trains new managers in the techniques of employee motivation, most of the theories and findings are rooted in behavioral science research.

In the behavioral sciences, economics and sociology have significantly influenced the way today's managers approach organizational strategy and structure. Psychology has influenced management approaches to motivation, communication, leadership, and the overall field of personnel management. The conclusions from the tremendous body of behavioral science research are much like those derived from the natural sciences. Although we understand more, that understanding is not simple. Scholars have learned much about the behavior of people at work, but they have also learned that organizational processes are astonishingly complex. All of the remaining chapters of this book contain research findings and applications that can be attributed to the behavioral sciences approach to the study of organizations and management.

MANAGEMENT SCIENCE PERSPECTIVE

World War II caused many management changes. The massive and complicated problems associated with modern global warfare presented managerial decision makers with the need for more sophisticated tools than ever before. The **management science perspective** emerged to treat those problems. This view is distinguished for its application of mathematics, statistics, and other quantitative techniques to management decision making and problem solving. During World War II groups of mathematicians, physicists, and other scientists were formed to solve military problems. Because those problems frequently involved moving massive amounts of materials and large numbers of people quickly and efficiently, the techniques had obvious applications to large-scale business firms.[24]

management science perspective
A management perspective that emerged after World War II and applied mathematics, statistics, and other quantitative techniques to managerial problems.

Operations research grew directly out of the World War II groups (called *operational research teams* in Great Britain and *operations research teams* in

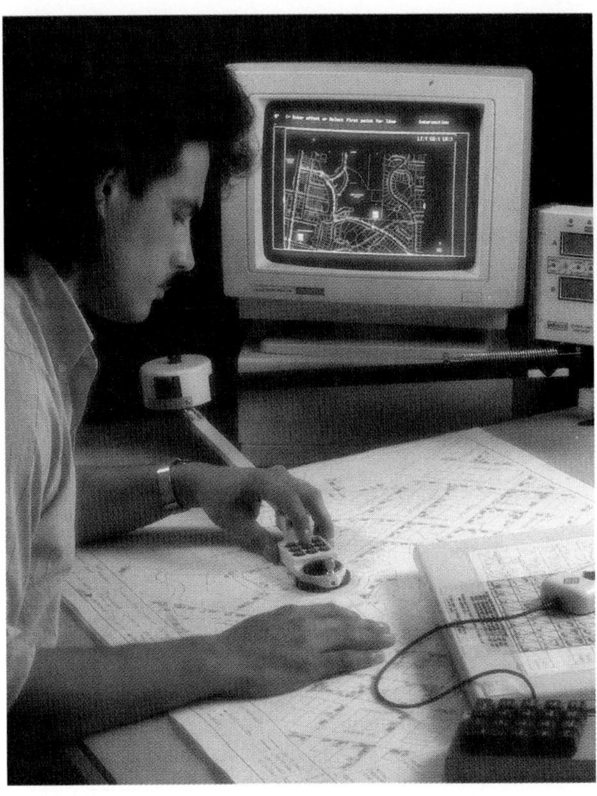

Management information systems, a subfield of management science, uses computers to assist managerial and technical decision making. WestMarc Communications, Inc., a subsidiary of Tele-Communications, Inc., the nation's largest cable company, serves communities in the Midwest and eastern United States. Here Marv Altman uses an in-house computer-aided design technology to precisely calculate each facet of cable installation. The computer illustrates community layout and can calculate relevant variables to predict the actual signal level that will enter each home, thereby providing the most efficient cable layout while minimizing signal leakage.

the United States).[25] It consists of mathematical model building and other applications of quantitative techniques to managerial problems.

Operations management refers to the field of management that specializes in the physical production of goods or services. Operations management specialists use quantitative techniques to solve manufacturing problems. Some of the commonly used methods are forecasting, inventory modeling, linear and nonlinear programming, queuing theory, scheduling, simulation, and break-even analysis.

Management information systems (MIS) is the most recent subfield of the management science perspective. These systems are designed to provide relevant information to managers in a timely and cost-efficient manner. The advent of the high-speed digital computer opened up the full potential of this area for management.

Many of today's organizations have departments of management science specialists to help solve quantitatively based problems. When Sears used computer models to minimize its inventory costs, it was applying a quantitative approach to management. When AT&T performed network analysis to speed up and control the construction of new facilities and switching systems, it was employing another management science tool.

One specific technique used in many organizations is queuing theory. *Queuing theory* uses mathematics to calculate how to provide services that will minimize the waiting time of customers. Queuing theory has been used to analyze the traffic flow through the Lincoln Tunnel and to determine the number of toll booths and traffic officers for a toll road. Queuing theory was used to develop the single waiting line for tellers used in many banks. Wesley Long

EXHIBIT 2.5
The Systems View of Organizations

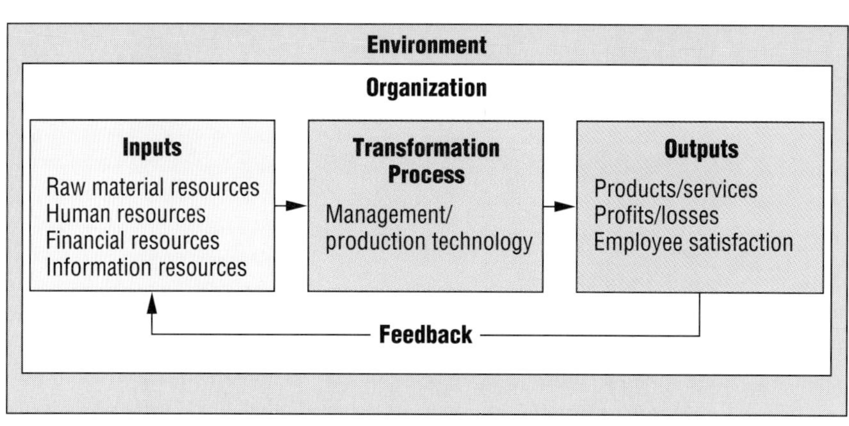

Community Hospital in Greensboro, North Carolina, used queuing theory to analyze the telemetry system used in wireless cardiac monitors. The analysis helped the hospital acquire the precise number of telemetry units needed to safely monitor all patients without overspending scarce resources.[26]

CONTEMPORARY EXTENSIONS

Each of the three major management perspectives is still in use today. The most prevalent is the human resource perspective, but even it has been undergoing change in recent years. Two major contemporary extensions of this perspective are systems theory and the contingency view. Examination of each will allow a fuller appreciation of the state of management thinking today.

SYSTEMS THEORY

system A set of interrelated parts that function as a whole to achieve a common purpose.

systems theory An extension of the human resources perspective that describes organizations as open systems that are characterized by entropy, synergy, and subsystem interdependence.

A **system** is a set of interrelated parts that function as a whole to achieve a common purpose.[27] A system functions by acquiring inputs from the external environment, transforming them in some way, and discharging outputs back to the environment. Exhibit 2.5 shows the basic **systems theory** of organizations. Here there are five components: inputs, a transformation process, outputs, feedback, and the environment. *Inputs* are the material, human, financial, or information resources used to produce goods or services. The *transformation process* is management's use of production technology to change the inputs into outputs. *Outputs* include the organization's products and services. *Feedback* is knowledge of the results that influence the selection of inputs during the next cycle of the process. The *environment* surrounding the organization includes the social, political, and economic forces noted earlier in this chapter.

Some ideas in systems theory have had substantial impact on management thinking. These include open and closed systems, entropy, synergy, and subsystem interdependencies.[28]

Open systems must interact with the environment to survive; **closed systems** need not. In the classical and management science perspectives, organizations were frequently thought of as closed systems. In the management science perspective, closed system assumptions — the absence of external disturbances — are sometimes used to simplify problems. In reality, however, all organizations are open systems and the cost of ignoring the environment may be failure. A prison tries to seal itself off from its environment; yet it must receive prisoners from the environment, obtain supplies from the environment, recruit employees from the environment, and ultimately release prisoners back to the environment.

open system A system that interacts with the external environment.

closed system A system that does not interact with the external environment.

Entropy is a universal property of systems and refers to their tendency to run down and die. If a system does not receive fresh inputs and energy from its environment, it will eventually cease to exist. Organizations must monitor their environments, adjust to changes, and continuously bring in new inputs in order to survive and prosper. Managers try to design the organization/environment interfaces to reduce entropy.

entropy The tendency for a system to run down and die.

Synergy means that the whole is greater than the sum of its parts. When an organization is formed, something new comes into the world. Management, coordination, and production that did not exist before are now present. Organizational units working together can accomplish more than those same units working alone. The sales department depends on production, and vice versa.

synergy The concept that the whole is greater than the sum of its parts.

Subsystems are parts of a system that depend on one another. Changes in one part of the organization affect other parts. The organization must be managed as a coordinated whole. Managers who understand subsystem interdependence are reluctant to make changes that do not recognize subsystem impact on the organization as a whole. Consider the management decision to remove time clocks from the Alcan Plant in Canada.

subsystems Parts of a system that depend on one another for their functioning.

ALCAN ALUMINUM LTD. • A personnel specialist proposed that time clocks be removed from the shop floor. The shop managers agreed but after a few months, several problems emerged. A few workers began to show up late, or leave early, or stay away too long at lunch.

Supervisors had new demands placed on them to observe and record when workers came and left. They were responsible for reprimanding workers, which led to antagonistic relationships between supervisors and employees. As a consequence, the plant manager found it necessary to reduce the supervisors' span of control. Supervisors were unable to manage as many people because of the additional responsibility.

As Alcan managers discovered, the simple time clock was interdependent with many other parts of the organization system. The time clock influenced worker tardiness and absenteeism, closeness of supervision, the quality of the relationship between supervisors and workers, and span of management. The organization system was more complex than the personnel specialist had realized when he proposed the idea of removing time clocks.[29]

EXHIBIT 2.6
The Contingency View of Management

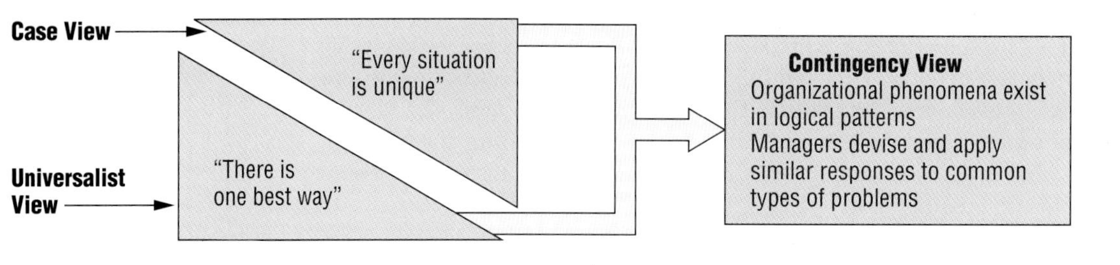

CONTINGENCY VIEW

The second contemporary extension to management thinking is the contingency view. The classical perspective assumed a *universalist* view. Management concepts were thought to be universal, that is, whatever worked — leader style, bureaucratic structure — in one organization would work in another. It proposed the discovery of "one-best-way" management principles that applied the same techniques to every organization. In business education, however, an alternative view exists. This is the *case* view, in which each situation is believed to be unique. There are no universal principles to be found, and one learns about management by experiencing a large number of case problem situations. Managers face the task of determining what will work in every new situation.

contingency view An extension of the human resource perspective in which the successful resolution of organizational problems is thought to depend on managers' identification of key variables in the situation at hand.

To integrate these views the **contingency view** has emerged, as illustrated in Exhibit 2.6.[30] Here neither of the above views is seen as entirely correct. Instead, certain contingencies, or variables, exist for helping management identify and understand situations. The contingency view means that a manager's response depends on identifying key contingencies in an organizational situation. For example, a consultant may mistakenly recommend the same management-by-objectives (MBO) system for a manufacturing firm that was successful in a school system. A central government agency may impose the same rules on a welfare agency that it did in a worker's compensation office. A large corporation may take over a chain of restaurants and impose the same organizational charts and financial systems that are used in a banking division. The contingency view tells us that what works in one setting may not work in another. Management's job is to search for important contingencies. When managers learn to identify important patterns and characteristics of their organizations, they can then fit solutions to those characteristics.

Industry is one important contingency. Management practice in a rapidly changing industry will be very different from that in a stable one. Other important contingencies that managers must understand are manufacturing technology and international cultures. For example, Citicorp and Manufacturers Hanover Corporation both misunderstood the nature of making loans to developing countries. As these big banks raised loan-loss reserves to cope with the prospect of bad international loans, their balance sheet was weakened to the extent that they had to stop expansion into new regions and new business activities. Having been through this experience, managers in the future will know how to handle this contingency in the international financial environment.[31]

RECENT HISTORICAL TRENDS

The historical forces that influence management perspectives continue to change and influence the practice of management. The most striking change now affecting management is international competition. This important trend has social, political, and economic consequences for organizations.

INDUSTRIAL GLOBALIZATION

The domain of business now covers the entire planet, where Reebok's, stock markets, fax machines, television, and T-shirts intermingle across national boundaries. The world of commerce is becoming wired like an integrated circuit, with no nation left out of the loop.

The impact on firms in the United States and Canada has been severe. International competition has raised the standard of performance in quality, cost, productivity, and response times.[32] As a result, the United States and Canada have seen a decline in worldwide market share in traditional products. Moreover, as recently as 1975, the U.S. balance of payments was close to zero. In recent years it has been hundreds of billions of dollars in the red.[33] On the horizon is Europe 1992, when the common market will drop internal economic boundaries to become one large market. This means a new set of opportunities and upheavals for companies that strive to meet global competitive standards.

Globalization causes the need for innovation and new levels of customer service. Companies must shorten the time for developing new products, and new products must account for a larger percentage of total income because international competitors are relentless innovators.[34] Winning companies in the 1990s must provide extraordinary service. The CEO of one home electronics retailer is gearing up to provide international service through computerized files. If someone has a problem, he or she just calls the company and a computer screen shows the product's serial number, warranty information, whether parts are in stock, and when it can be repaired.[35]

Although managers have tried many techniques and ideas in recent years, two management trends that seem significant in response to international competition are the adoption of Japanese management practices and the renewed efforts to achieve excellence in product and service quality.

GTE Electrical Products, an operating group of GTE that manufactures lighting and precision materials, confronted global challenges by setting a goal: to meet the needs of customers with error-free products and service. Management committed itself to changing a traditional, individualistic organizational culture and management style into an approach called Total Quality, characterized by employee involvement and teamwork. The results have been impressive. The Total Quality team called WATTS Express, shown here, solved the problem of occasionally shipping the wrong mix of products from a certain plant. Using a team method, WATTS Express found a solution: color-coded labels that immediately reduced shipping errors to zero, saving thousands of dollars a month. GTE Electrical Products now has hundreds of active Total Quality teams worldwide to enhance its global competitiveness.

JAPANESE MANAGEMENT PRACTICES

In recent years Japanese management practices have been thought to create more efficient and more effective companies. Japanese products — whether motorcycles, automobiles, or VCRs — have been low priced and of high quality. The problem was dramatized by the reaction of executives of General Motors' Buick division who had visited Japan and a Buick car dealership:

> The operation appeared to be a massive repair facility, so they asked how he had built up such a large service business. He explained with some embarrassment that this was not a repair facility at all but rather a reassembly operation where newly delivered cars were disassembled and rebuilt to Japanese standards. While many Japanese admire the American automobile, they would never accept the low quality with which they are put together.[36]

Exhibit 2.7
Characteristics of Theory Z Management

Source: Adapted from William G. Ouchi and Alfred M. Jaeger, "Type Z Organizations: Stability in the Midst of Mobility," *Academy of Management Review* 3 (1978), 308–314.

Type A (American)	Type Z (Modified American)	Type J (Japanese)
Short-term employment	Long-term employment	Lifetime employment
Individual decision making	Consensual decision making	Consensual decision making
Individual responsibility	Individual responsibility	Collective responsibility
Rapid evaluation and promotion	Slow evaluation and promotion	Slow evaluation and promotion
Explicit, formalized control	Implicit, informal control with explicit, formalized measures	Implicit, informal control
Specialized career path	Moderately specialized career path	Nonspecialized career path
Segmented concern	Holistic concern, including family	Holistic concern

How was American management expected to compete with NEC, Nissan, Sanyo, Sony, Toyota, and Kawasaki? Answers have been suggested in William Ouchi's *Theory* Z and Richard Pascale and Anthony Athos' *The Art of Japanese Management*.[37] The success of Japanese firms is often attributed to their group orientation. The Japanese culture focuses on trust and intimacy within the group and family. In North America, in contrast, the basic cultural orientation is toward individual rights and achievements. These differences in the two societies are reflected in how companies are managed.

Exhibit 2.7 illustrates differences in the management approaches used in America and Japan. American organizations are called Type A and Japanese organizations Type J. However, it is impractical to take a management approach based on the culture of one country and apply it directly to that of another country. **Theory Z** proposes a hybrid form of management that incorporates techniques from both Japanese and North American management practices. Type Z is a blend of American and Japanese characteristics that can be used to revitalize and strengthen corporate cultures in North America.[38]

Theory Z A management perspective that incorporates techniques from both Japanese and North American management practices.

As illustrated in Exhibit 2.7, the Type Z organization uses the Japanese characteristic of long-term employment, which means that employees become familiar with the organization and are committed to and fully integrated into it. The Theory Z hybrid also adopts the Japanese approach of slow evaluation and promotion for employees. Likewise, the highly specialized American convention of a narrow career path is modified to reflect career training in multiple departments and functions.

In the Theory Z approach, control over employees combines the U.S. preference for explicit and precise performance measures and the Japanese approach to control based on social values. The Theory Z hybrid also encourages the Japanese characteristic of consensual decision making — that is, managers discuss decisions among themselves and with subordinates until everyone is in agreement. Responsibility for outcomes, however, is based on the American approach of rewarding individuals. Finally, Theory Z adopts the Japanese holistic concern for employees' total personal lives.[39]

ACHIEVING EXCELLENCE

Spurred by ideas from Japanese management and global competition, American managers have reawakened an interest in attaining high-quality products through human resource management. The most notable publication in this area is *In Search of Excellence* by Peters and Waterman.[40] The book reported a study of U.S. companies, including Digital Equipment, 3M, Bechtel, Dow, Johnson & Johnson, Disney, Fluor, Caterpillar, Procter & Gamble, and McDonald's. These companies showed above-average performance for several years, and Peters and Waterman's research sought to uncover why. The findings revealed eight **excellence characteristics** that reflected these companies' management values and corporate culture.

excellence characteristics
A group of eight features found to typify the highest-performing U.S. companies.

1. **Bias toward Action.** Successful companies value action, doing, and implementation. They do not talk problems to death or spend all their time creating exotic solutions. The CEO of a computer peripherals company put it this way: "We tell our people to make at least 10 mistakes a day. If you are not making 10 mistakes a day, you are not trying hard enough."[41] H. Ross Perot, after selling his company, EDS, to General Motors and serving on GM's board, remarked on the action differences between the two companies: "The first EDSer to see a snake kills it. At GM, the first thing you do is organize a committee on snakes. Then you bring in a consultant who knows a lot about snakes. The third thing you do is talk about it for a year."[42]
2. **Closeness to the Customer.** Successful companies are customer driven. A dominant value is customer need satisfaction, whether through excellent service or through product innovation. Managers often call customers directly and learn their needs. Successful companies value sales and service overkill. J. Willard Marriott, Sr., read every single customer complaint card — raw and unsummarized.
3. **Autonomy and Entrepreneurship.** Organization structure in excellent corporations is designed to encourage innovation and change. Technical people are located near marketing people so that they can lunch together. Organizational units are kept small to create a sense of belonging and adaptability. W. L. Gore & Associates will not let a plant grow larger than about 150 employees. Companies such as IBM, 3M, and Hewlett-Packard give freedom to idea champions and venture groups to generate creative new products.
4. **Productivity through People.** Rank-and-file employees are considered the roots of quality and productivity. People are encouraged to participate in production, marketing, and new-product decisions. Conflicting ideas are encouraged rather than suppressed. The ability to move ahead by consensus preserves trust and a sense of family, increases motivation, and facilitates both innovation and efficiency.

5. **Hands On, Value Driven.** Excellent companies are clear about their value system. Managers and employees alike know what the company stands for. Leaders provide a vision of what can be accomplished and give employees a sense of purpose and meaning. Leaders are willing to roll up their sleeves and become involved in problems at all levels.
6. **Sticking to the Knitting.** Successful firms stay close to the business they know and understand. Successful firms are highly focused. For example, IBM, Boeing, Intel, and Genentech confine themselves to a single product line of computer products, commercial aircraft, integrated circuits, and genetic engineering, respectively. Successful companies do what they know best.
7. **Simple Form, Lean Staff.** The underlying structural form and systems of excellent companies are elegantly simple, and few personnel are employed in staff positions. Large companies are subdivided into small divisions that allow each to do its job. For example, when Jack Reichert took over Brunswick Corporation, the headquarters' staff was reduced from 560 to 230 people. The vertical hierarchy was reduced to only five layers of management.[43]
8. **Simultaneous Loose-Tight Properties.** This may seem like a paradox, but excellent companies use tight controls in some areas and loose controls in others. Tight, centralized control is used for the firm's core values. At McDonald's, no exceptions are made to the core values of quality, service, cleanliness, and value. At IBM, top management will tolerate no disagreement with the cultural value of respect for the individual. Yet in other areas employees are free to experiment, to be flexible, to innovate, and to take risks in ways that will help the organization achieve its goals.

In Peters and Waterman's original study and subsequent research not every company scored high on all eight values, but a preponderance of these values was often part of their management culture. One company that displays many characteristics of excellence is PepsiCo Inc.

PEPSICO INC. • PepsiCo is on a roll. Pepsi-Cola is now the best-selling soft drink in supermarkets, and its new lemon-lime Slice is selling like mad.

What makes Pepsi excel is a fast-moving, risk-oriented management philosophy. As president D. Wayne Calloway puts it, the underlying philosophy is "ready, fire, aim." Pepsi is biased toward action rather than toward studying things to death.

Decentralization and autonomy create a highly charged atmosphere that pressures people to perform. High performers are well compensated. Low performers are fired. Calloway also believes that senior managers must look, listen, and learn. "Walk through the hallway at Pepsi, and you hear a lot of conversations about what's going on at the supermarket, what the competition is doing," which reflects the customer orientation.

Pepsi rewards autonomy and risk taking. It made a quick decision to purchase 7-Up Company in order to compete with Coca-Cola's Sprite brand, but the merger was not approved. Pepsi also got the jump on Coca-Cola by being

Exhibit 2.8
Management Perspectives over Time

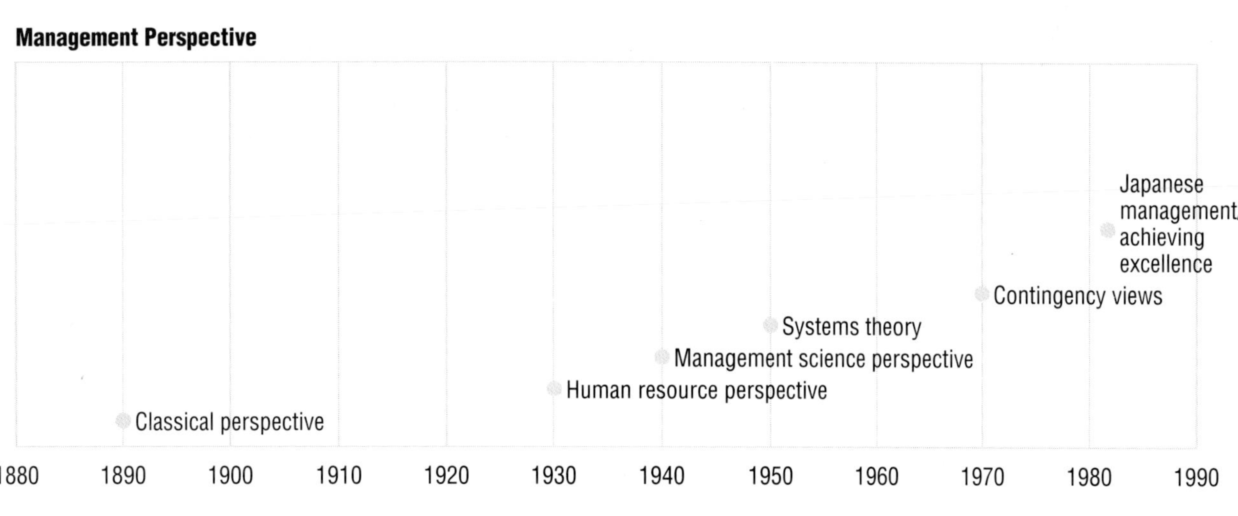

the first to introduce a 100 percent Nutrasweet formula in 1984. To avoid tipping off Coca-Cola, Pepsi didn't test the product in advance. Diet Pepsi's sales volume soared 25 percent to $1.2 billion. As one manager says, "We believe it's more important to do something than sit around and worry about it."[44]

Excellence guidelines and Japanese management practices are not a panacea for all companies. Indeed, some of the high-performance companies originally studied are no longer performing well.[45] But the general approach seems more than a passing fad. These ideas reflect management's response to international competitive forces that have increased the need to fully utilize all employees. They represent a major new trend in the international environment.

Summary

The practice of management has changed in response to historical conditions. The importance of this chapter is to outline the evolution of management so that present and future managers can understand where we are now and continue to progress toward better management. The evolution of management perspectives is summarized in Exhibit 2.8.

Three major forces that affect management are social, political, and economic. These forces have influenced management from ancient times to the present. The three major perspectives on management that have evolved since the late 1800s are the classical perspective, the human resource perspective, and the management science perspective. Each perspective has several specialized subfields.

Two recent extensions of management perspectives are systems theory and contingency views. The most recent historical force affecting management is industrial globalization. The higher standards of quality, productivity, and responsiveness have caused a renewed concern for the full participation of people within organizations. The most recent trend in management has been to adopt Japanese management practices and to create the widespread desire for achieving excellence in North American organizations.

MANAGEMENT SOLUTION

Lawrence Kuppin and Harry Evans Sloan took a risk by purchasing New World Pictures to produce B movies when other movie companies were abandoning the B-movie market. But the risk was not so great, because Kuppin and Sloan were tuned to economic and social forces in the external environment and aware of the historical place of B movies in the industry. B movies have always had a market because a large percentage of the population — youngsters, twin-bill theaters — like low-budget films. Even more important has been the increase in videocassette sales. The films are aimed at 12- to 24-year-olds, who find titles such as *Fraternity Vacation* and *Return to Horror High* appealing. New World Pictures became so successful that it is now New World Entertainment Ltd., with the profits from movies financing the company's move into videocassettes, television programs, comic books, and toys. Kuppin and Sloan understood larger historical patterns and succeeded in what may have seemed a volatile market.[46]

DISCUSSION QUESTIONS

1. Why is it important to understand the different perspectives and approaches to management theory that have evolved throughout the history of organizations?
2. A recent article in *Fortune* magazine commented about the death of socialism around the world and the resurgence of capitalist economies. What impact will the trend away from socialism in other countries have on management in North America?
3. How do societal forces influence the practice and theory of management? Do you think management techniques are a response to these forces?
4. What change in management emphasis has been illustrated by the interest in "Japanese management" and "achieving excellence"?
5. What is the behavioral science approach? How does it differ from earlier approaches to management?
6. Explain the basic idea underlying the contingency view and provide an example.
7. Contrast open and closed systems. Can you give an example of each? Can a closed system survive?
8. Why can an event such as the Hawthorne studies be a major turning point in the history of management even if the idea is later shown to be in error? Discuss.

9. Identify the major components of systems theory. Is this perspective primarily internal or external?
10. Which approach to management thought is most appealing to you? Why?
11. Do you think management theory will ever be as precise as theories in the fields of physics, chemistry, or experimental psychology? Why or why not?

MANAGEMENT IN PRACTICE: EXPERIENTIAL EXERCISE

Are You Cosmopolitan?

One historical shift occurring in employee attitudes is the extent to which their allegiance is to their organization or to their profession. In recent years, salaried professionals, such as engineers, accountants, and lawyers, work within organizations, but express more loyalty to professional standards than to organizational rules and norms. To identify your own work orientation, answer the eight questions below. Use a scale 1 to 5, with 1 representing "strongly disagree"; 2, "somewhat disagree"; 3, "neutral"; 4, "somewhat agree"; and 5, "strongly agree."

_____ 1. You believe it is the right of the professional to make his or her own decisions about what is to be done on the job.

_____ 2. You believe a professional should stay in an individual staff role regardless of the income sacrifice.

_____ 3. You have no interest in moving up to a top administrative post.

_____ 4. You believe that professionals are better evaluated by professional colleagues than by management.

_____ 5. Your friends tend to be members of your profession.

_____ 6. You would rather be known or get credit for your work outside rather than inside the company.

_____ 7. You would feel better making a contribution to society than to your organization.

_____ 8. Managers have no right to place time and cost schedules on professional contributors.

This scale indicates the extent to which your work orientation is that of a "cosmopolitan" or a "local." A cosmopolitan identifies with the career profession, and a local identifies with the employing organization. A score between 30 and 40 indicates a cosmopolitan work orientation, between 10 and 20 is a local orientation, and between 20 and 30 represents a mixed orientation.

Discuss the pros and cons of each orientation for organizations and employees. What conflicts are likely to occur when "cosmopolitan" professions work for a company?

Source: Joseph A. Raelin, *The Clash of Cultures, Managers and Professionals* (Harvard Business School Press, 1986). Used by permission.

CASES FOR ANALYSIS

EASTERN AIR LINES INC.

Were the wings of man broken overnight? The 1989 shrinkage and gradual decline of Eastern Air Lines can be blamed on deregulation according to some legislators in Washington. Deregulation encouraged too many airlines to engage in predatory pricing. Another explanation is that Frank Lorenzo, chairman of Texas Air—the parent of Eastern—tried too hard to squeeze concessions from Eastern's unions, and hence created a long labor strike. But these explanations skim over the history of Frank Lorenzo and Eastern Air Lines.

Frank Lorenzo is often considered a visionary airline builder. Lorenzo is an expert at finance and makes decisions largely on the numbers. Financial and legal arguments typically win the day. He purchased tiny Texas

International in 1972 and built it up to include Continental Airlines in 1982. Continental achieved low-cost status after Lorenzo hired nonunion workers at low wages. In 1986, Texas Air acquired Eastern, and Lorenzo was expected to be tough on unions. After months of fruitless talk, machinists and pilots finally struck. Eastern declared bankruptcy.

Perhaps it was a mistake for Lorenzo to acquire Eastern. Going back to the 1950s, chairman Eddie Rickenbacker, the World War I ace, ran the airline with extraordinary frugality. He lectured employees to save pennies. He scheduled maintenance and aircraft usage to save money rather than for the convenience of passengers. An order of jet-propelled DC-8s was cancelled because prop-driven planes were cheaper.

After Rickenbacker departed, management spent huge sums, often on lavish perks, but did not fix a fundamental strategic problem — the dependence on North-South tourist traffic. By 1976 when ex-astronaut Frank Borman became chairman, Eastern had become a high-cost, low-yield airline with the same lousy service reputation and militant unions. Borman tried to win concessions and to establish East-West routes, but without major success. Frustrated by the repeated refusals of unions to take pay cuts, Eastern's management accepted a low bid from Frank Lorenzo. By 1989 Lorenzo, labor, and management were no longer dealing rationally. It became a grudge match between management and unions. For the unions, the wage struggle was a holy war against Lorenzo the infidel.

Lorenzo insisted that he was an airline builder not a union buster. But the strike by 8,500 machinists and 3,800 pilots left little of Eastern Air Lines.

The comparison with Delta Airlines is striking. It, too, started out as a North-South carrier, but it built an East-West network. Delta also established a tradition of quality service, it took care of its workers, and management eschewed lavish perks. Delta refuses to lay off employees, who are treated as family, even during an economic downturn.

Questions

1. If Frank Lorenzo had carefully examined the history of employee relations at Eastern, could he have predicted the disastrous strike?
2. Which management perspective described in the chapter would best describe Lorenzo's management of Eastern Air Lines?
3. What historical forces are affecting airline companies today? What management approaches should be used in response to these forces?

Source: Based on Pete Engardio and Christopher Power, "The Wings of Man Weren't Broken Overnight," *Business Week,* March 27, 1989, 31; Todd Volgel, Gail DeGeorge, and Pete Engardio, "Texas Air: Empire in Jeopardy," *Business Week,* March 27, 1989, 28–30; "Delta: The World's Most Profitable Airline," *Business Week,* August 31, 1981, 68–71; Charles Perrow, *Organizational Analysis: A Sociological View* (Belmont, Calif.: Wadsworth, 1970).

SOCIAL SERVICE AGENCY

Charlotte Hines had been employed for 17 years in a social service agency in a mid-sized city in Illinois. In 1984, she had a rare opportunity to become a supervising clerk in charge of about 20 employees in the typing room, mail room, and security areas. She worked hard at being a good supervisor, paid attention to the human aspects of employee problems, and introduced modern management techniques.

In 1988, the state Civil Service Board required that a promotional exam be taken to find a permanent placement for the supervising clerk position. For the sake of fairness, the exam was an open competition — that is, anyone, even a new employee, could sign up to take it. The person with the highest score would get the job.

More than 50 candidates took the test. Charlotte was devastated. "After I accepted the provisional opening and proved myself on the job, the entire clerical force was deemed qualified to take the same test. My experience counted for nothing."

Charlotte placed twelfth in the field of candidates, and one of her clerks placed first. Now she must forfeit her job to a virtual beginner with no on-the-job supervisory experience.

Questions

1. What management perspective is reflected in the way the Civil Service Board selected people for su-

pervisory jobs? Would another perspective be better for this type of organization?

2. Why did the Civil Service Board pick a permanent supervisor strictly by test results? Is this fair to employees who have supervisory experience? Is it fair to select a supervisor based only on job experience?

3. If you were Charlotte Hines, what would you do? What options would you explore in order to make the best of the situation?

Source: Based on Betty Harrigan, "Career Advice," *Working Woman,* July 1986, 22–24.

CHAPTER 3

THE ENVIRONMENT AND CORPORATE CULTURE

CHAPTER OUTLINE

The International Environment

The External Environment

Task Environment
General Environment

The Organization-Environment Relationship

Adapting to the Environment
Influencing the Environment

The Internal Environment: Corporate Culture

Symbols
Stories
Heroes
Slogans
Ceremonies

Environment and Culture

Tough-Guy, Macho Culture
Work Hard/Play Hard Culture
Bet-Your-Company Culture
Process Culture

Changing and Merging Corporate Cultures

Symbolic Management

LEARNING OBJECTIVES

After studying this chapter, you should be able to:

- Describe the task and general environments and the dimensions of each.
- Explain how organizations adapt to an uncertain environment and identify techniques managers use to influence and control the external environment.
- Define corporate culture and give organizational examples.
- Explain organizational symbols, stories, heroes, slogans, and ceremonies and how they relate to corporate culture.
- Describe how corporate culture relates to the environment.
- Define a symbolic manager and explain the tools a symbolic manager uses to change corporate culture.

Management Problem

George S. Kachajian sold products to the semiconductor industry for 18 years, then used his personal savings to start his own company. Silicon Technology Corporation (STC) produced a new type of saw for cutting silicon into thin wafers, the first step in creating semiconductors. The saw was highly successful, capturing 80 percent of the domestic market in wafering saws. International demand was also good, with orders of 53 saws from the Soviet Union and 4 from Poland. Then the U. S. government denied an export license application, claiming the saws benefited the Soviet military. Shortly thereafter, a new competitor, Meyer & Burger A.G. from Switzerland, started selling wafering saws in the United States for less than STC's cost of production. Kachajian figured out that the Swiss firm was selling saws to the East bloc at very high prices and dumping saws in the United States at below cost in order to build market share at STC's expense. STC's corporate values would not allow deviation from U.S. export regulations, even though the rules seemed silly in this case. A small, healthy company doing about $10 million in business was suddenly in danger of being killed by government red tape and international competition.[1]

If you were George Kachajian, how would you respond? What steps would you take to correct these problems in STC's environment?

Silicon Technology Corporation faced a crisis brought on by seemingly unpredictable and uncontrollable events in the external environment. The environment surprises many companies. Johnson & Johnson faced a crisis when cyanide was found in Tylenol capsules. Union Carbide was stunned by the gas leak that killed more than 2,000 people in Bhopal, India. So were managers at the Kansas City Hyatt Regency Hotel when two skywalks collapsed, killing and injuring guests and employees. Administrators of rural hospitals suddenly find their hospitals in danger of failing because of changes in Medicare payments and the high cost of treating patients. Each of these situations has a common theme — the events were unexpected, originated in the external environment, and were severe enough to seriously harm the company.

Although few companies experience the crisis of cyanide-laced capsules or a Bhopal tragedy, every organization must cope with changes in the external environment. During the early 1980s, for example, high inflation allowed managers to cover up their mistakes with respect to excess inventory and labor costs. Disinflation and mounting competition in the mid-1980s required a new set of organizational actions. Managers at companies such as H. J. Heinz, TRW, Dow Chemical, and General Electric's Medical Systems Group had to discard weak product lines, trim work forces, modernize plants, and keep tight controls on costs, wages, and inventories.[2] Without these internal changes, the companies would no longer have fitted with the reality of the new external environment.

The study of management traditionally has focused on factors within the organization — a closed systems view — such as leading, motivating, and controlling employees. The classical, behavioral, and management science schools described in Chapter 2 focused on internal aspects of organizations over which managers have direct control. These views are accurate but incomplete. Most events that affect the organization originate in the external environment. To be effective, managers must monitor and respond to the environment — an open systems view. Contemporary approaches to management acknowledge the impact of the external environment, whose magnitude and complexity can influence the organization in unexpected ways.

This chapter explores in detail components of the external environment and how they affect the organization. We will also examine a major part of the organization's internal environment — corporate culture. Corporate culture is shaped by the external environment and is an important part of the context within which managers do their jobs.

THE INTERNATIONAL ENVIRONMENT

The most startling environmental change affecting American managers is the intrusion of global competition. The world of business is changing dramatically because suddenly national boundaries are meaningless constraints. One study identified 136 U.S. industries that have to compete on a global basis or disappear. The industries include automobiles, accounting services, entertainment, publishing, pharmaceuticals, travel services, consumer electronics, banking, and washing machines. Even the largest companies in the biggest countries cannot survive on domestic markets alone. For example, developing a drug costs about $250 million and only a world market can generate enough sales to earn a profit.[3] Small companies also must expand their niche globally because foreign competitors will try to best them in U.S. markets.

On another front, foreign firms are spending over $300 billion a year to purchase U.S. companies, many of which are rejuvenated under foreign ownership. Japan alone purchased 174 American firms in 1989.[4] When Japan's Kao Corporation acquired Andrew Jergens Company, maker of soaps and hand lotions, it immediately increased the marketing and research budgets and added new facilities. Those investments have made Jergens more competitive, but the foreign owner gets the profits. The leverage of foreign companies spills over into government affairs. Japan alone spends $50 million dollars lobbying in Washington and another $45 million on public relations and image making. Lawmakers at the state level have been persuaded to change many laws in the hope of obtaining Japanese investment.

While reading the following discussion on the external environment, remember that international developments are changing the once level domestic playing field for U.S. companies. One example is Toyo Toki, a Japanese manufacturer of plumbing fixtures, which is beginning to offer new products to the American market.

TOYO TOKI • Toyo Toki (translated as Orient Ceramic) is Japan's leading maker of toilets and bathtubs. Toto, as the company is often called, also produces modular kitchens, prefab bathrooms, and microcomputer-controlled hot water heaters.

Having won 95 percent of the Japanese market, Toto is searching for global opportunities for growth. It already has joint ventures in Indonesia, Korea, Thailand, Taiwan, France, and West Germany. Now Toto has targeted the U.S. market, aiming first at the Japanese communities on the West Coast.

Toto plans to offer products not produced by American manufacturers. The Washlet is an electronically-controlled toilet and bidet combined into one unit. Another product is a low-flow toilet, that uses 1.6 gallons of water compared to the American standard of 3.5 gallons and is in demand in U.S. cities with water shortages. Even more competitive is a line of battery-powered hands-free toilet fixtures designed for public lavatories. These products save water, are more sanitary than American-made fixtures, and use cheap infra-red sensors instead of the electric wiring used in U.S. products.

American companies are worried about the competition. Emmanuel Kompouris, chief executive of American Standard says, "I would rank them as our number one threat in the future. We have to hurry."

If American companies do not hurry, this may be another industry that gets beaten by international competition. Future generations of American children may be potty trained on a Toto.[5]

THE EXTERNAL ENVIRONMENT

The environment is important to managers because it creates uncertainty. Uncertainty will be discussed in detail in Chapter 7, but for our purposes uncertainty means that managers lack accurate information about external events and thus cannot predict environment changes that will affect attainment of organizational goals. When uncertainty is low, managers know what to expect. Disruptions in the environment make it difficult for managers such as George Kachajian to achieve the goals of growth and profitability.

The **organizational environment** includes all elements existing outside the boundary of the organization that have the potential to affect the organization.[6] The environment includes competitors, resources, technology, and economic conditions that influence the organization. It does not include those events so far removed from the organization that their impact is not perceived.

The organizational environment can be further conceptualized as having two layers: task and general environments.[7] The **task environment** is closer to

organizational environment All elements existing outside the organization's boundaries that have the potential to affect the organization.

task environment The layer of the external environment that directly influences the organization's operations and performance.

Deregulation in the legal-political sector of the *general environment* has led to competitive changes in the railroad and trucking industries. The Motor Carrier Act and Staggers Rail Act allowed these industries to negotiate rates and services without government interference. The Southern Pacific and Rio Grande railroads responded to the environment by merging operations to provide better service and shipping flexibility to customers throughout the middle and western United States. Managers grabbed at the opportunity presented by deregulation to build a stronger, more competitive railroad system.

the organization and includes the sectors that conduct day-to-day transactions with the organization and directly influence its basic operations and performance. It is generally considered to include competitors, suppliers, and customers. The **general environment** is the outer layer that is more widely dispersed and affects organizations indirectly. It includes social, demographic, and economic factors that influence all organizations about equally. Increases in the inflation rate or the percentage of dual-career couples in the work force are part of the organization's general environment. These events do not directly change day-to-day operations, but they do affect all organizations eventually. The organization also has an **internal environment,** which includes the elements within the organization's boundaries. The internal environment is composed of current employees, production technology, organization structure, physical facilities, and especially corporate culture.

general environment The layer of the external environment that affects the organization indirectly.

internal environment The environment within the organization's boundaries.

Exhibit 3.1 illustrates the relationship among the task, general, and internal environments. As an open system, the organization draws resources from the external environment and releases goods and service back to it. We will now discuss the two layers of the external environment in more detail. Then we will discuss corporate culture, a key element in the internal environment. Other aspects of the internal environment such as employees, structure, and technology will be covered in Parts 3 and 4 of this book.

TASK ENVIRONMENT

As described above, the task environment includes those sectors that have a direct working relationship with the organization, among them customers, competitors, suppliers, and the labor supply.

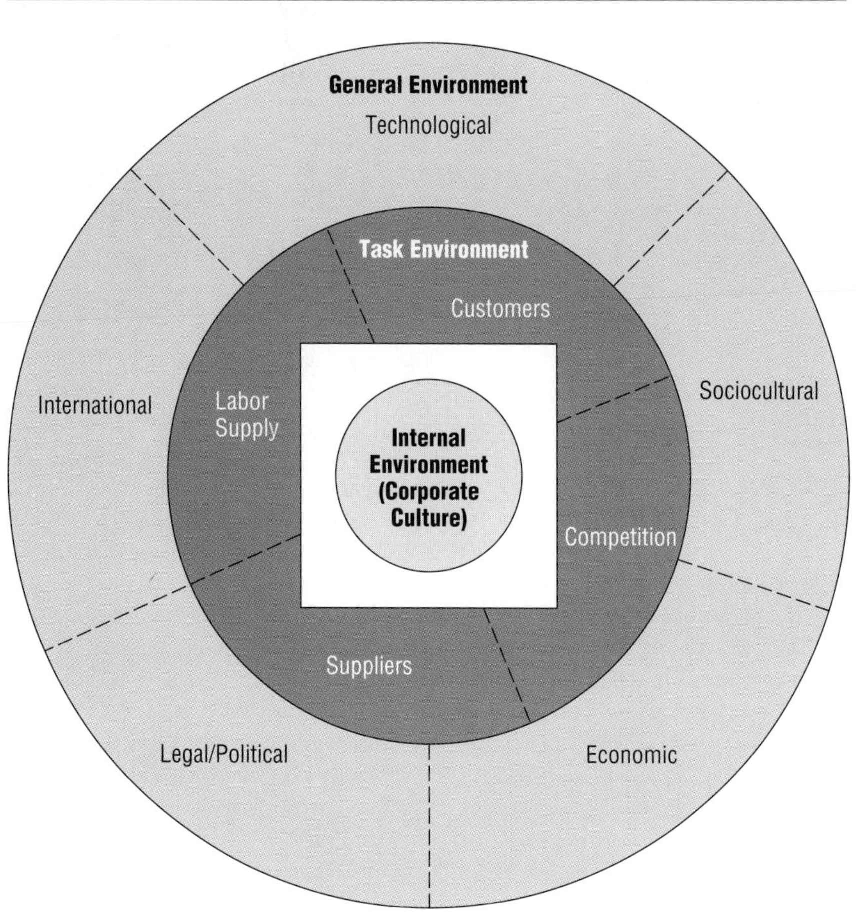

EXHIBIT 3.1
Location of the General, Task, and Internal Environments

CUSTOMERS. Those people and organizations in the environment who acquire goods or services from the organization are **customers.** As recipients of the organization's output, customers are important because they determine the organization's success. Patients are the customers of hospitals, students the customers of schools, and travelers the customers of airlines. Companies such as AT&T, General Foods, and Beecham Products have all designed special programs and advertising campaigns to court their older customers, who are becoming a larger percentage of their market.[8] Overbuilding in the hotel industry forced companies such as Hyatt and Marriott to spend additional money on advertising, direct mail, giveaways, and expansion into new markets to improve customer demand.

customers People and organizations in the environment who acquire goods or services from the organization.

COMPETITORS. Other organizations in the same industry or type of business that provide goods or services to the same set of customers are referred to as **competitors.** Each industry is characterized by specific competitive issues. The recording industry differs from the steel industry and the pharmaceutical industry. Competition in the steel industry, especially from international producers, has caused some companies to go bankrupt. Companies in the pharmaceutical industry are highly profitable because it is difficult for new firms to

competitors Other organizations in the same industry or type of business that provide goods or services to the same set of customers.

Arby's used the highly successful "Burger Boycott" campaign in the competitive fast-food industry. The creative advertising approach combined with new menu items enabled Arby's to increase sales 18 percent in 1988 while the fast-food industry was stagnant. Arby's defines its *competitors* in the *task environment* as the top three burger chains — McDonald's, Burger King, and Wendy's. Residents of Hope, Indiana, participated in the filming of Arby's commercials and agreed to boycott burgers for two weeks.

enter it. Apple, IBM, and Compaq are locked in a titanic power struggle in the personal computer industry.[9] Sometimes industry actions can stir up hot competition in a sleepy industry, such as disposable diapers. The aggressive campaign of Kimberly-Clark increased market share for its Huggies brand disposable diapers but drew a strong response from Procter & Gamble's Pampers. The resulting price war drove Johnson & Johnson and Scott Paper Company out of the business and reduced profits for both P&G and Kimberly-Clark.[10]

suppliers People and organizations who provide the raw materials the organization uses to produce its output.

Suppliers. The raw materials the organization uses to produce its output are provided by **suppliers.** A steel mill requires iron ore, machines, and financial resources. A small, private university may utilize hundreds of suppliers for paper, pencils, cafeteria food, computers, trucks, fuel, electricity, and textbooks. Large companies such as General Motors, Westinghouse, and Exxon depend on as many as 5,000 suppliers. The Big Three automakers have decided to acquire a larger share of parts from fewer suppliers by the early 1990s. They are trying to build a good relationship with these suppliers so that they will receive high-quality parts as well as low prices. Organizations also depend on banks for capital with which to finance new equipment and buildings.

labor supply The people available for hire by the organization.

Labor Supply. The **labor supply** represents the people who can be hired to work for the organization. Every organization needs a supply of trained, qualified personnel. Unions, employee associations, and the availability of certain classes of employees can influence the organization's labor supply. Mary Kay Cosmetics stopped growing when fewer homemakers became available for selling cosmetics door to door due to their entry into the work force as full-time employees. Two current labor supply trends having an impact on organizations are (1) the increasing shortage of workers, especially skilled workers, and (2) the desire by unionized employees to have larger wage settlements than in the past.[11] The strong economy in North America has outstripped the supply of labor. More jobs require education and technical skills, and there are not sufficient people to handle unskilled jobs either. The strength of the economy during the 1980s has prompted union members to want bigger pay increases, and more strikes may occur in the next few years.

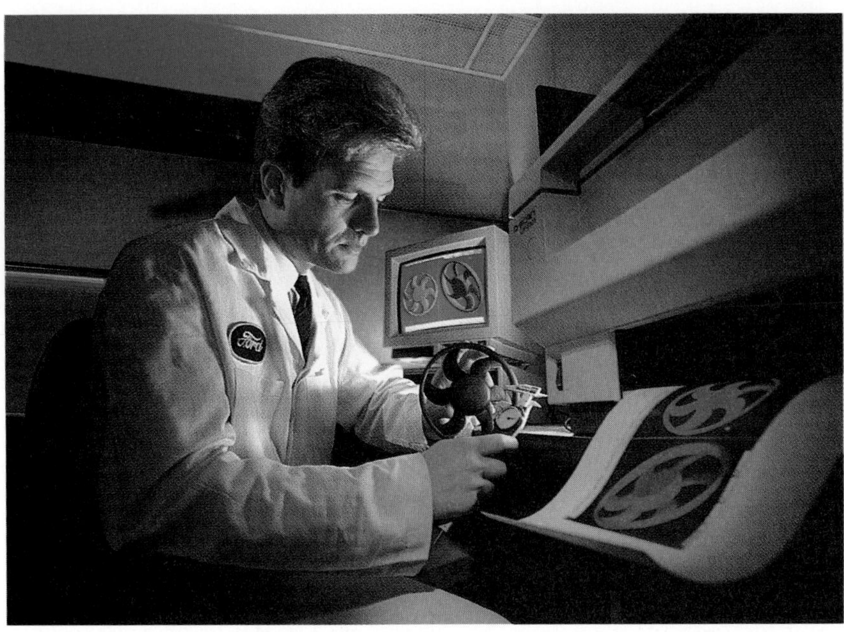

From banks to boutiques, hospitals to hotels, small businesses to large corporations, personal computers are changing the *technology sector* of the environment. In this breathtaking application, Ford Motor Company uses a COMPAQ DESKPRO 386/20 for a new technology called stereo lithography. After a part such as this scale model of a Ford Taurus engine fan is designed on the PC, a laser beam fabricates the part in a vat of liquid plastic. Within a few hours the part is ready for examination without having been touched by human hands.

General Environment

The general environment represents the outer layer of the environment. These dimensions influence the organization over time but often are not involved in day-to-day transactions with it. The dimensions of the general environment include technological, sociocultural, economic, legal-political, and international.

Technological. The **technological dimension** includes scientific and technological advancements in a specific industry as well as in society at large. In recent years, the most striking advances have been in the computer industry. Supercomputers have astonishing power, and many companies are incorporating computerized systems such as automated offices, robotics, and computer-controlled machines. High-definition television promises to revolutionize the worldwide electronics industry. Smart composite materials that think for themselves may revolutionize the aircraft and defense industries. Fiber-optic sensors can be imbedded in aircraft surface materials that can feel the weight of ice or the "touch" of enemy radar.[12] A technological development that may affect companies associated with beverage consumption is the self-chilling can. Opening the can releases a carbon dioxide capsule, and the beverage is chilled to 30°F within 90 seconds. These and other technological advances can change the rules of the game; thus, every organization must be ready to respond.

technological dimension The dimension of the general environment that includes scientific and technological advancements in the industry and society at large.

Sociocultural. The **sociocultural dimension** of the general environment represents the demographic characteristics as well as the norms, customs, and values of the general population. Important sociocultural characteristics are geographical distribution and population density, age, and educational levels. Also important are the society's norms and values. For example, the Playboy enterprises thrived in the 1960s and 1970s by advocating

sociocultural dimension The dimension of the general environment representing the demographic characteristics, norms, customs, and values of the population within which the organization operates.

Sara Lee Corporation's Jimmy Dean biscuit sandwiches reflect changing demographics in the *sociocultural* dimension of the general environment. The breakfast sandwiches, like other of Sara Lee's products, are individually wrapped, microwaveable, and good tasting. This fits the demographics of consumers with on-the-go life-styles and the demographic trend of smaller households, including singles, widowed, and divorced people. Sara Lee's sales have grown rapidly as the result of tailoring products to changing demographics.

new values. *Playboy* magazine and Playboy clubs were highly popular. But changes in the population's values during the 1980s reduced the demand for Playboy products. Magazine sales were off 40 percent, and Playboy clubs were closed. Other recent sociocultural trends that are affecting many companies include the trend toward no smoking, the anti-cholesterol fever, the greater purchasing power of young children, and the increased diversity of consumers, with specialized markets for groups such as Hispanics and women over 30.

ECONOMIC. The **economic dimension** represents the general economic health of the country or region in which the organization operates. Consumer purchasing power, unemployment rate, and interest rates are part of an organization's economic environment. Not-for-profit organizations such as the Red Cross and the Salvation Army find a greater demand for their services during economic decline but receive smaller contributions. They must adapt to these changes in economic conditions. The most significant recent trend in the economic environment is the frequency of mergers and acquisitions. The corporate landscape is being altered and the impact on employees is enormous. In 1989 one of the hottest deals was the merger of Time, the nation's biggest publisher, with Warner Communications, an entertainment conglomerate. In the media industry alone, Sony purchased CBS Records to guarantee control over a supply of music for its Walkman customers. News Corporation acquired both Fox TV and Triangle, publisher of *TV Guide.* Bertelsmann acquired both Doubleday Publishers and RCA Records. The impact of these deals on employees can be overwhelming, creating uncertainty about future job security. The deal is just the beginning of employee uncertainty, because about half of the acquired companies are resold.[13]

economic dimension The dimension of the general environment representing the overall economic health of the country or region in which the organization functions.

legal-political dimension The dimension of the general environment that includes federal, state, and local government regulations and political activities designed to control company behavior.

LEGAL-POLITICAL. The **legal-political dimension** includes government regulations at the local, state, and federal levels as well as political activities designed to influence company behavior. The U.S. political system encourages capitalism, and the government tries not to overregulate business. However, government laws do specify rules of the game. The federal government influences organizations through the Occupational Safety and Health Administration (OSHA), Environmental Protection Agency (EPA), fair trade practices, libel statutes allowing lawsuits against business, consumer protection legislation, product safety requirements, import and export restrictions, and information and labeling requirements. At the state level, in any given year up to 250,000 bills to control some aspects of organizations will be introduced. Of these, about 50,000 will become law. An additional 50,000 regulations will be proposed, of which about 35,000 will be adopted.[14] A recent court decision in Illinois opens businesses up to criminal charges based on hazards to employees or to employees' health. Senior executives have been given jail terms.[15]

INTERNATIONAL. The **international dimension** of the external environment represents events originating in foreign countries as well as opportunities for American companies in other countries. The high-quality, low-priced automobiles from Japan and Korea have created a permanent change in the American automobile industry. Other industries that are deeply affected are illustrated in the Focus on Global Competition box. In addition, many companies have adopted the strategy of having parts manufactured and assembled in other countries (called outsourcing), such as Mexico, because of the low price

FOCUS ON GLOBAL COMPETITION

MANAGING IN A GLOBAL ENVIRONMENT

Today's environment pays no respect to national borders. Managers must learn new rules to cope with goods, services, and ideas circulating around the globe. What is the environment of the new global village like?

- Products and services exist in a one-world market. Build a better machine in Oklahoma City and buyers will be there from Europe and Asia.
- Competitors in the global village hail from all over. As a manager, even if you do not export, you are going to run into competitors in your own marketplace, including some from Third World countries.
- Sharp companies treat the world as a source of supply as well as a market. New products such as liquid Tide are composed of materials and ideas from around the world.
- Smart companies seek common cause with foreign competitors. Business partners are the smart way to work in multiple markets. Consider General Motors, Toyota, and Whirlpool that have joint ventures with foreign partners in several countries.
- You may end up working for a foreign company. If your competitors cannot beat your company, they may buy it. Half of American chemical employees toil for foreign owners. So do Bruce Springsteen and Michael Jackson, because Sony owns CBS Records.
- People in the United States do not know best. A hard lesson to learn, but U.S. decision makers know little about issues and competition in foreign countries. U.S. arrogance is a shortcut to failure. To counter this, Pall Corporation keeps a team of Ph.D.s traveling around the world gathering current information.
- Companies must incorporate a planetary mindset. The new corporate culture emphasizes an international business mission and a gut-level realization that international thinking is vital.
- Smart companies also think standardizing and customizing at the same time. Standardizing products across countries saves money, such as when Nissan reduced the number of car models from 48 to 18. Customizing is essential for tailoring products to local needs, without which even toothpaste will not sell well. Moreover, the temperature has to be turned up to match product quality of international competitors on a global level.
- The global environment represents an uneven playing field compared with the domestic environment. Companies that are not already on board are too late. The global train has already left the station.

Source: Richard I. Kirkland Jr., "Entering a New Age of Boundless Competition," *Fortune*, March 14, 1988, 40–48; Kenichin Ohmae, "Managing in a Borderless World," *Harvard Business Review* (May/June 1989), 152–161; George Rabstejnek, "Let's Get Back to the Basics of Global Strategy," *The Journal of Business Strategy* (September/October 1989), 32–35.

of labor. Changes in the foreign exchange rate can increase or decrease the value of U.S. products overseas as well as the competitiveness of foreign products within the United States. International competition as well as government regulation of export licenses created George Kachajian's failure to sell wafering saws to Eastern bloc countries. The international dimension has become so important to the management of U.S. and Canadian companies that Chapter 21 is devoted to this topic. IBM has a complex environment that includes international as well as the other sectors discussed above.

international dimension The dimension of the general environment representing events that originate in foreign countries and opportunities for American firms abroad.

IBM • The external environment for International Business Machines is illustrated in Exhibit 3.2. IBM is known for its good treatment of employees and hence has few problems in the labor force sector. Sales growth and profits slipped in recent years, and IBM is planning a rebound by providing more attention to customers. Many of IBM's external problems have come from competitors and new technology. Competitors such as Compaq developed cheaper machines, and Digital Equipment beat IBM to the punch with computer networks. IBM's strategy has been to follow new developments rather than be the first to introduce a new product. Current

EXHIBIT 3.2
The External Environment for IBM

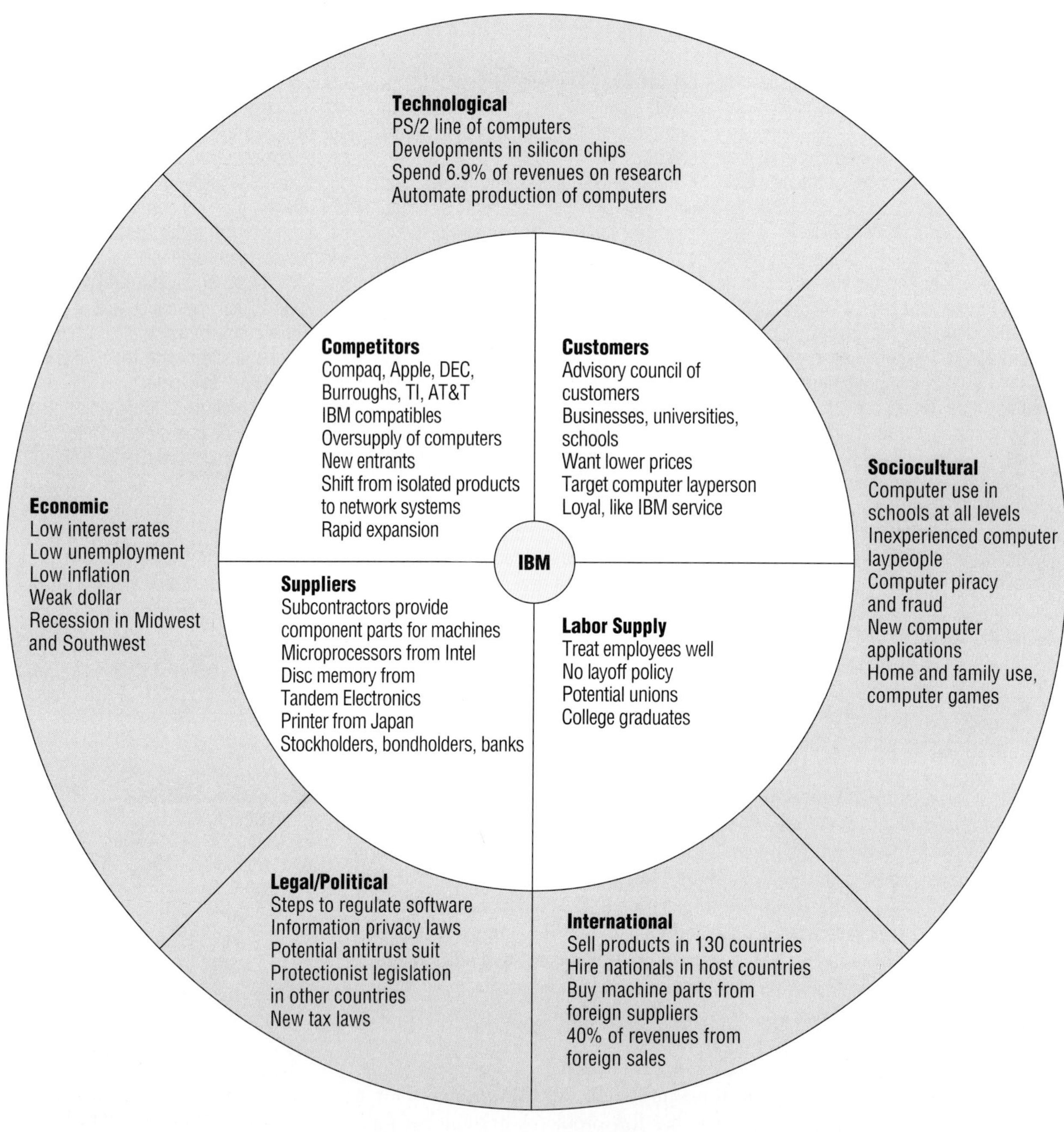

Source: Based on Robert Durand, Teri Fogle, and Matt Stump, "International Business Machines" (Unpublished manuscript, Texas A&M University, December 1985).

economic conditions, such as low interest rates, low unemployment, and reduced inflation, have enhanced the demand for computers. The government has not been a major force in the computer industry, although it has taken steps to regulate software and guarantee information privacy.

IBM spends about 7 percent of revenues on research and development and uses technology to automate production as a way to cut costs. In the international domain, IBM sells its products in over 130 countries. IBM managers try to integrate operations with the culture of the host country by hiring nationals. IBM also acquires many parts from foreign producers for machines that sell in the United States.[16]

A major responsibility of IBM managers is to scan and monitor environmental events and direct internal operations to fit environmental needs. By monitoring customers, competitors, suppliers, economic conditions, technology, and government regulation, managers can either help IBM adapt to the environment or use the organization's resources to attempt to change it.

We now turn to techniques managers use for managing the organization's relationship with the environment.

THE ORGANIZATION-ENVIRONMENT RELATIONSHIP

How does the environment influence an organization? As we discussed earlier, the environment creates uncertainty for organization members. Uncertainty typically pertains to information or resources. Two basic strategies for coping with environmental uncertainty are to adapt the organization to changes in the environment or to control the environment to make it more compatible with organizational needs.

ADAPTING TO THE ENVIRONMENT

If the organization faces increased uncertainty with respect to competition, customers, suppliers, or government regulation, managers can use several strategies to adapt to these changes, including boundary-spanning roles, increased planning and forecasting, a flexible structure, and mergers or joint ventures.

BOUNDARY-SPANNING ROLES. Departments and **boundary-spanning roles** link and coordinate the organization with key elements in the external environment. Boundary spanners serve two purposes for the organization: They detect and process information about changes in the environment, and they represent the organization's interest to the environment.[17] People in departments such as marketing and purchasing span the boundary to work with customers and suppliers, both face to face and through market research. Perhaps the largest growth area in boundary spanning is competitive analysis, also known as snooping and spying. McDonnell Douglas used competitive intelligence to get the jump on Boeing with its new prop-fan airliner. Coors used competitive intelligence to avoid getting behind in wine coolers. Xerox buys

boundary-spanning roles Roles assumed by people and/or departments that link and coordinate the organization with key elements in the external environment.

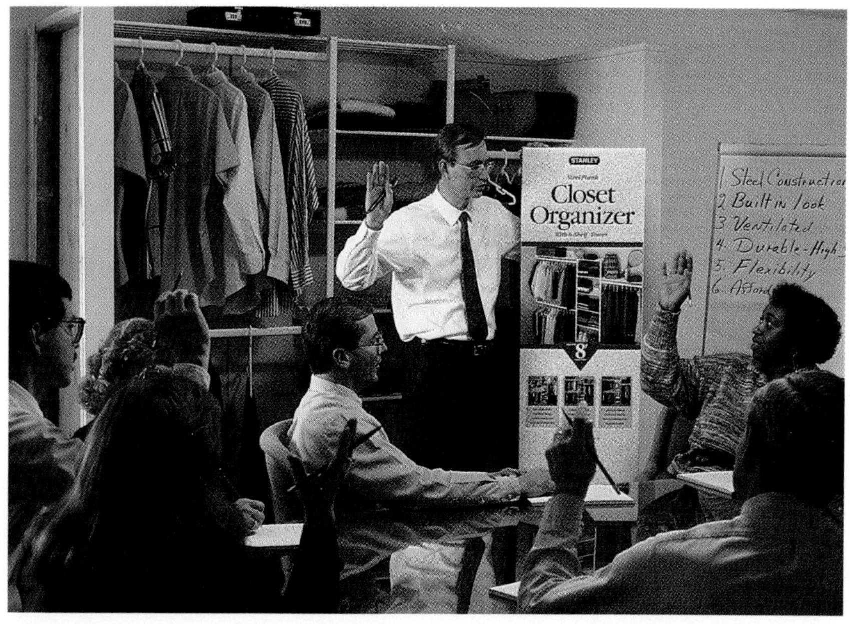

Stanley Hardware Vice-President of Marketing Scott Bannell (seated center) carefully notes responses from a consumer focus group about the Stanley Closet Organizer. Bannell and market researcher Larry Dostal (standing) act as *boundary spanners* to test reactions to a new product and assess whether it meets customer needs. Boundary spanning to potential customers provided competitive intelligence that the closet organizer was clearly preferred over other products for its design and sturdy construction.

rival copiers for its engineers, who take them apart and design a better product component by component. Eighty percent of the Fortune 1000 companies maintain in-house snoops, also known as competitor intelligence professionals. Most of their work is strictly legal, relying on commercial data bases, news clippings, help-wanted advertisements, trade publications, product literature, and personal contacts.[18]

FORECASTING AND PLANNING. Forecasting and planning for environmental changes are major activities in many corporations. Planning departments often are created when uncertainty is high.[19] Forecasting is an effort to spot trends that enable managers to predict future events. Forecasting techniques range from quantitative economic models of environmental business activity to newspaper clipping services. One of these services, called Burrelle's Information Services Inc., monitors 16,000 newspapers and magazines and predicts future trends. Chase investors used information about rapidly multiplying television channels in Western Europe to invest in MCA Inc., which had a valuable film library.

Control Data, Heinz, United Airlines, and Waste Management Inc. have devised specific management plans for handling crises. Whether the crisis is a hostile takeover attempt or product tampering, an organization that does not have a plan will make mistakes. Planning can soften the adverse effect of rapid shifts in the environment.

organic structure An organizational structure that is free flowing, has few rules and regulations, encourages employee teamwork, and decentralizes decision making to employees doing the job.

FLEXIBLE STRUCTURE. An organization's structure should enable it to effectively respond to external shifts. Research has found that a loose, flexible structure works best in an uncertain environment and a tight structure is most effective in a certain environment.[20] The term **organic structure** characterizes an organization that is free flowing, has few rules and regulations, encourages teamwork among employees, and decentralizes decision making to employees doing the job. This type of structure works best when the environment

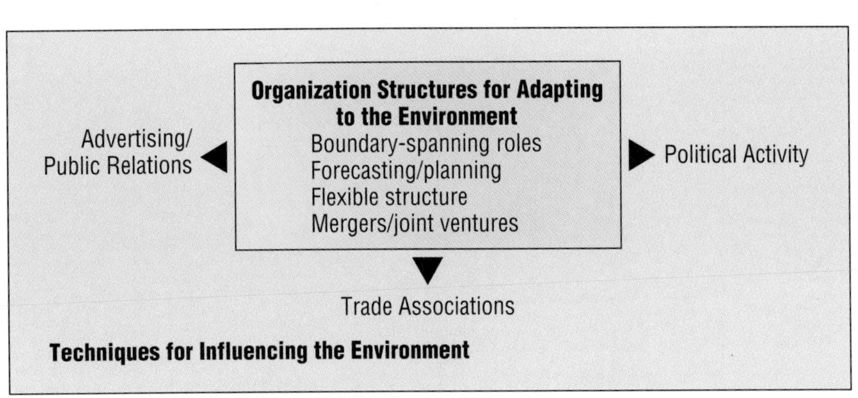

Exhibit 3.3
Organizational Responses to Environmental Changes

changes rapidly. A **mechanistic structure** is just the opposite, characterized by rigidly defined tasks, many rules and regulations, little teamwork, and centralization of decision making. This is fine for a stable environment. Dow Chemical and Star-Kist Foods have set up "SWAT" teams that can swing into action if an unexpected disaster strikes. These teams include members from multiple departments who can provide the expertise needed for solving an immediate problem, such as a plant explosion. Organic organizations create many teams to handle changes in raw materials, new products, government regulations, or marketing.

mechanistic structure An organizational structure characterized by rigidly defined tasks, many rules and regulations, little teamwork, and centralized decision making.

Mergers and Joint Ventures. As we discussed, mergers are a major factor in a company's external environment. A merger is also a way to reduce uncertainty. A **merger** occurs when two or more organizations combine to become one. For example, General Host acquired Hickory Farms, a retail chain, to become an outlet for General Host's meat products, thereby reducing uncertainty in the customer sector.

merger The combination of two or more organizations into one.

A **joint venture** involves a strategic alliance or program by two or more organizations. This typically occurs when the project is too complex, expensive, or uncertain for one firm to do alone. Oil companies have used joint ventures to explore for oil on the continental shelf or in inaccessible regions of Alaska and Canada. Many small businesses are turning to joint ventures with large firms or with international partners.[21] A larger partner can provide sales staff, distribution channels, financial resources, or a research staff. Small businesses seldom have the expertise to deal internationally, so a company such as Nypro Inc., a plastic injection-molding manufacturer in Clinton, Massachusetts, joins with overseas experts who are familiar with the local rules. Nypro now does business in four countries.

joint venture A strategic alliance or program by two or more organizations.

Influencing the Environment

The other major strategy for handling environmental uncertainty is to reach out and change those elements causing problems. Widely used techniques for changing the environment include advertising and public relations, political activity, and trade associations. Exhibit 3.3 summarizes the techniques organizations can use to adapt to and influence the external environment.

"Look, Mom—no cavities!" The introduction by Procter & Gamble in 1955 of Crest toothpaste with this advertising campaign changed the way consumers viewed toothpaste. P&G influenced the American Dental Association to recognize Crest and allow the use of its name in consumer ads. P&G also informed dentists about Crest and fluoride. Over 500 fluoride compounds were tested to develop an effective anticavity toothpaste. This campaign so influenced P&G's *external environment* that toothpaste is now considered a therapeutic product that prevents dental disease.

ADVERTISING AND PUBLIC RELATIONS. Advertising has become a highly successful way to manage demand for a company's products. Companies spend large amounts of money to influence consumer tastes. Hospitals have begun to advertise through billboards, newspapers, and radio commercials to promote special services. Increased competitiveness among CPA firms and law firms has caused them to start advertising for clients, a practice unheard of a few years ago. Advertising is an important way to reduce uncertainty about clients.

Public relations is similar to advertising except that its goal is to change public opinion about the company itself. Most companies care a great deal about their public image. Each year *Fortune* rates over 300 companies to see which are the most and least admired in each of 32 industries.[22] Public relations and a good public image is accomplished through advertising as well as speeches and press reports. In the 1960s and 1970s, Dow Chemical became infamous for supplying napalm and Agent Orange to the military for use in Vietnam. Even when it stopped making these products the image persisted. Dow started a new advertising campaign—"Dow Lets You Do Great Things"—and used other external communications that emphasized the humanitarian use of its products. As a service to reporters, Dow set up a free, 24-hour hotline to answer questions about the chemical industry. Dow also helped its image by putting up most of the money for a new program to train writers at the University of Missouri School of Journalism.[23]

Political Activity. **Political activity** represents organizational attempts to influence government legislation and regulation. Corporations pay lobbyists to express their views to federal and state legislators. At politically savvy companies, senior executives, including the CEO, actively influence legislators. For example, Federal Express flew two members of the House of Representatives to Washington, D.C., for a meeting of the House Ways & Means Committee. By working hard, Federal Express was able to influence a tax law provision worth $3 million a year. The semiconductor industry is another example of how to be extremely successful in Washington. Although a small industry, it has influenced blocks of legislation because companies present a united front, CEOs get personally involved, and the industry treats the government as an ally against unfair competition.[24]

political activity Organizational attempts, such as lobbying, to influence government legislation and regulation.

Trade Associations. Most organizations join with others having similar interests; the result is a **trade association.** In this way they work together to influence the environment, including federal legislation and regulation. Most manufacturing companies are part of the National Association of Manufacturers. The National Rifle Association has thousands of individual and corporate members whose interests are served by the freedom to use guns. One of the most influential trade associations in past years was the U.S. League of Savings Institutions, which virtually controlled government regulations pertaining to the savings and loan industry. Federal Home Loan Bank Board officials admit they took many actions and changed regulations to suit the League. That kind of influence over the years may have contributed to the current mess in the savings and loan industry, which was partially caused by lack of close and effective regulation.[25]

trade association An association made up of organizations with similar interests for the purpose of influencing the environment.

The Internal Environment: Corporate Culture

The internal environment within which managers work includes corporate culture, production technology, organization structure, and physical facilities. Of these, corporate culture has surfaced as extremely important to competitive advantage. The internal culture must fit the needs of the external environment and company strategy. When this happens, highly committed employees create a high-performance organization that is tough to beat.[26]

Culture can be defined as the set of key values, beliefs, understandings, and norms shared by members of an organization.[27] Culture represents the unwritten, informal norms that bind organization members together. Culture can be analyzed at two organizational levels, as illustrated in Exhibit 3.4.[28] At the surface level are visible artifacts, which include manners of dress, stories, physical symbols, organizational ceremonies, and office layout. The surface level represents the cultural patterns observable within an organization. At a deeper level are the values and norms that govern behavior. Values cannot be observed directly, but they can be interpreted from the stories, language, and symbols that represent them. These values are held by organization members who jointly understand their importance.

culture The set of key values, beliefs, understandings, and norms that members of an organization share.

EXHIBIT 3.4
Two Levels of Corporate Culture

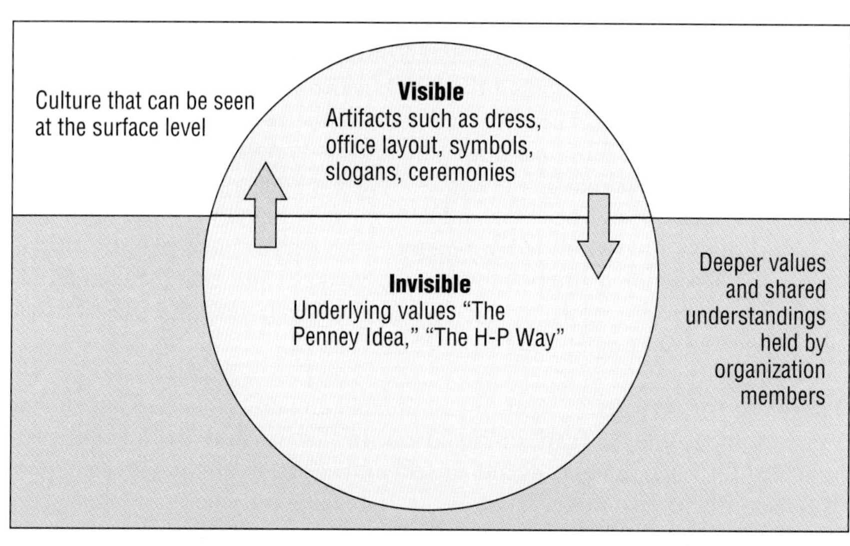

One organization with a strong culture is J. C. Penney Company. James Cash Penney believed in the golden rule: Treat employees and customers as you would like to be treated. He shunned the term *employee,* preferring to call workers *associates* because they were treated as partners. The dominant values in Penney's corporate culture are customer satisfaction and happy associates. Mr. Penney wrote down the underlying values in seven guiding principles called "The Penney Idea" that guide employee behavior. One store manager was reprimanded for making too much profit at customers' expense. Layoffs are avoided at all costs.[29]

Some companies put underlying values in writing so they can be passed on to new generations of employees. Hewlett-Packard created a list of cultural concepts called "The H-P Way." At 3M Company, two fundamental values are the 25 percent rule, which requires that a quarter of sales come from products introduced within the past five years, and the 15 percent rule, which allows any employee to spend up to 15 percent of the workweek on anything he or she prefers, so long as it is product related.[30] At The Limited, a rather sassy retailer, the fundamental principle is "To offer the absolute best customer shopping experience anywhere — the best store — the best merchandise — the best merchandise presentation — the best customer service — the best 'everything' that a customer sees and experiences."[31]

The fundamental underlying values that characterize cultures at J. C. Penney, The Limited, and Hewlett-Packard can be understood through the visible manifestations of symbols, stories, heroes, slogans, and ceremonies. Any company's culture can be interpreted by observing these factors.

SYMBOLS

symbol An object, act, or event that conveys meaning to others.

A **symbol** is an object, act, or event that conveys meaning to others. Symbols associated with corporate culture convey the organization's important values. For example, John Thomas, CEO of a mechanical contractor in Andover, Mas-

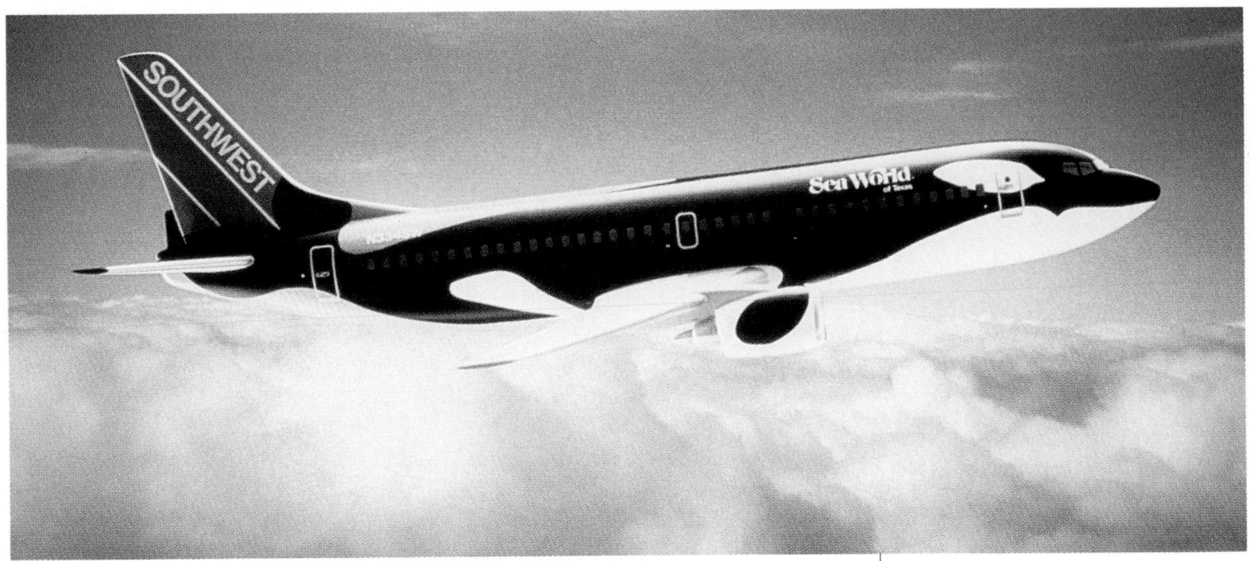

This whale of a symbol signals Southwest Airlines' corporate philosophy of fun. This is the world's first and only flying killer whale, Shamu® One. Southwest's chairman Herb Kelleher captured the company's *culture* when he said, "We take our competition seriously, but we don't take ourselves too seriously." From the early days of attendants wearing hot pants, Southwest has prospered with low fares, lots of flights, and loads of fun.

sachusetts, wanted to imprint the value of allowing mistakes and risk taking. He pulled a $450 mistake out of the dumpster, mounted it on a plaque, and named it the "No-Nuts Award," for the missing parts. The award is presented annually and symbolizes the freedom to make mistakes but not to make the same mistake twice.[32] At Federal Express, Bravo Zulu awards symbolize unusual performance in customer service, such as when an employee spent all day Saturday flying with an aircraft so that freight would get to a customer on time. Sequint Computers Systems Inc. developed the symbol of red buttons worn by people who performed tasks critical to the production of hardware that was behind schedule yet essential to company survival. The red buttons symbolized the gravity of the situation, and all Sequint employees were expected to pitch in and help anybody wearing one.[33]

STORIES

A **story** is a narrative based on true events that is repeated frequently and shared among organizational employees. Stories are told to new employees to keep the organization's primary values alive. At Nordstrom Inc., management does not deny the story about a customer who got his money back on a tire. Nordstrom does not sell tires. The story reinforces the store's no-questions-asked return policy. A story at Dayton Hudson about Ken Macke, CEO, tells how he gave a woman a new washing machine because she complained about wanting a broken belt replaced. The story still serves to improve complaint handling at the lowest company levels. A popular story at Hewlett-Packard communicates the values of the founders, David Packard and Bill Hewlett. Bill Hewlett is said to have gone to a plant one Saturday and found a lab stockroom door locked. He cut the padlock and left a note saying, "Don't ever lock this door again. Thanks, Bill." Hewlett wanted engineers to have free access to components — even take them home — to stimulate the creativity that was part of "The H-P Way." Stories in these companies are widely told; every employee knows them and the values they represent.[34]

story A narrative based on true events that is repeated frequently and shared by organizational employees.

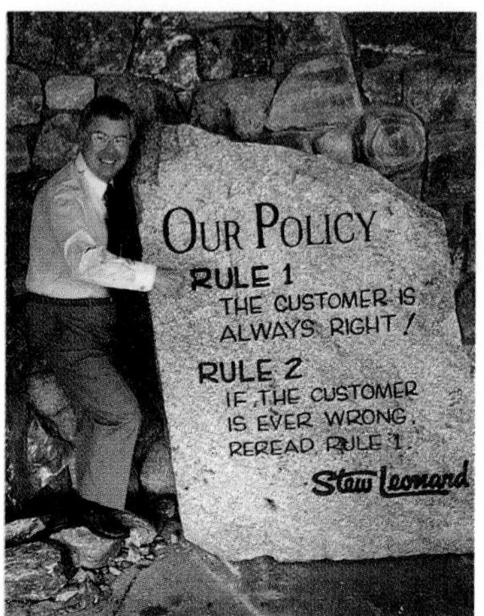

Stew Leonard points to the *slogan* chiseled into a 6,000-pound rock next to the front door of his dairy store—the world's largest. Shortly after he opened his small store in 1969, Leonard disagreed with a customer who wanted to return sour eggnog, telling her that 300 other customers had not complained. He won the argument and as the customer left the store, she said, "I'm never coming back to this store again!" Later that night Leonard realized he had insulted his customer, losing all her family's future business. Hence the policy of extraordinary customer service was born. The small dairy store now does annual sales of $100 million. Both the slogan and the eggnog story are visible manifestations of the company's culture.

HEROES

A **hero** is a figure who exemplifies the deeds, character, and attributes of a strong culture. Heroes are role models for employees to follow. Sometimes heroes are real, such as Lee Iacocca, and sometimes they are symbolic, such as the mythical sales representative at Robinson Jewelers who delivered a wedding ring directly to the church because the ring had been ordered late. The deeds of heroes are out of the ordinary but not so far out as to be unattainable by other employees. Heroes show how to do the right thing in the organization. Companies with strong cultures take advantage of achievements to define heroes who uphold key values.

At Minnesota Mining and Manufacturing (3M), top managers keep alive the heroes who developed projects that were killed by top management. One hero was a vice-president who was fired earlier in his career for persisting at a new product even after his boss had told him, "That's a stupid idea. Stop!" After the worker was fired, he would not leave. He stayed in an unused office, working without a salary on the new product idea. Eventually he was rehired, the idea succeeded, and he was promoted to vice-president. The lesson of this hero as a major element in 3M's culture is: Persist at what you believe in.[35]

SLOGANS

A **slogan** is a phrase or sentence that succinctly expresses a key corporate value. Many companies use a slogan or saying to convey special meaning to employees. H. Ross Perot of Electronic Data Systems established the philosophy of hiring the best people he could find and noted how difficult it was to find them. His motto was "Eagles don't flock. You gather them one at a time." A variation used at PepsiCo to describe the value of turning bright young people into strong managers is "We take eagles and teach them to fly in formation." The slogan chiseled into a 6,000-pound granite slab next to the front door of Stew Leonard's dairy store is "Rule 1—The customer is always right! Rule 2—If the customer is ever wrong, reread Rule 1."[36]

CEREMONIES

A **ceremony** is a planned activity that makes up a special event and is conducted for the benefit of an audience. Managers hold ceremonies to provide dramatic examples of company values. Ceremonies are special occasions that reinforce valued accomplishments, create a bond among people by allowing them to share an important event, and anoint and celebrate heroes.[37]

The value of a ceremony can be illustrated by the presentation of a major award. The award can be bestowed secretly by mailing it to the employee's home or, if a check, by depositing it in a bank. But such procedures would not make the bestowal of rewards a significant organizational event and would be less meaningful to the employee. For example, an important annual event at McDonald's Corporation is its nationwide contest to determine the best hamburger cooking team in the country. The ceremony is highly visible, and McDonald's makes sure all employees know about it. The ceremony communicates to all employees the value of hamburger quality.[38]

hero A figure who exemplifies the deeds, character, and attributes of a corporate culture.

slogan A phrase or sentence that succinctly expresses a key corporate value.

ceremony A planned activity that makes up a special event and is conducted for the benefit of an audience.

A joyous moment during a great day for these Quaker State Minit-Lube National All Star champions. Quaker State Minit-Lube, Inc., uses the annual contest and winner's ceremony to symbolize the importance of speed and quality service for customers. Fourteen jobs associated with an oil change must be performed perfectly in eight minutes. The *ceremony* includes contestant arrival in a white stretch limo, walking on a red carpet through a cheering crowd, and a jazz band. This contest is consistent with Quaker State's Big Q symbol that has always stood for quality.

In summary, organizational culture represents the values and understandings that employees share, and these values are signified by symbols, stories, heroes, slogans, and ceremonies. Managers help define important symbols, stories, and heroes to shape the culture. An example of how such symbols are used to create an ethical culture is found in the Focus on Ethics box.

ENVIRONMENT AND CULTURE

A big influence on shaping corporate culture is the external environment. Corporate culture should embody what it takes to succeed in the environment. If the external environment requires extraordinary customer service, the culture should encourage good service; if it calls for careful technical decision making, cultural values should reinforce managerial decision making.

Deal and Kennedy, two researchers and consultants on corporate culture, have proposed that the relationship between environment and internal culture leads to four cultural categories, which are illustrated in Exhibit 3.5.[39] These categories are based on two strategic factors: (1) the degree of environmental uncertainty associated with the company's strategic decisions and (2) the speed with which the company receives feedback from the environment about the decision's success. The four cultural types associated with these strategic differences are the tough-guy, macho culture, the work hard/play hard culture, the bet-your-company culture, and the process culture.

TOUGH-GUY, MACHO CULTURE

tough-guy, macho culture A type of corporate culture that emerges in an environmental situation characterized by high-risk decision making, rapid feedback, and large-scale projects.

The **tough-guy, macho culture** emerges in an environmental situation with high-risk decision making and fast feedback. Decision makers quickly learn whether their risk taking was right or wrong. This culture often exists in organizations involved with large construction projects, cosmetics, movie production,

FOCUS ON ETHICS

GENERAL MILLS

Not only has General Mills been astonishingly successful, riding the trend toward oat breakfast cereals and giving larger competitor Kellogg's all it can handle, but it has done so while maintaining the highest ethical standards. The continuity of ethical intention has been virtually an unbroken cultural value for more than 50 years. Ethics is a fundamental part of General Mills' corporate culture, thanks to heroes, stories, and symbols.

The hero founder is James Ford Bell, who emphasized the slogan, "Clean and fine" to describe General Mills's record. The founder's values have been kept alive by six subsequent CEOs, who uniformly believed ethics to be a top-down process, requiring their active leadership.

Stories shared among employees reinforce these cultural values. One is about Parker Brothers, a subsidiary of General Mills, which manufactured an extremely successful toy called Riveton. When a child strangled on a rivet, a government investigation concluded that Riveton was safe. When a second strangulation occurred, however, top management removed the product from retail stores at the peak of the holiday sales season. Investigations showed that the problem was product misuse by consumers, but the company went ahead with the recall, absorbing an initial cost of $8.3 million. This story is widely quoted in company folklore to illustrate corporate ethical values.

Another story is about a manager who faked children's test responses to a new toy because of test problems. The manager was later able to verify the results of the test but this did not reduce his punishment for misrepresentation. Managers are dismissed for small discrepancies regardless of motive or position.

An important symbol is General Mills' "Statement of Corporate Values" and "Business Ethics and Conduct." Written statements were not even drafted until the appointment of the present CEO, and no one uses them as the bases for ethical values. However, they do symbolize the importance top management places on these values. Meanwhile, the company culture defines shared values, while the documents reinforce them and instruct new employees.

Recruiting at General Mills is focused on new graduates rather than on employees from other companies, so recruits can be shaped into the company's character. When General Mills wants to acquire a company, the target company's management is carefully scrutinized for cultural fit. The success of General Mills in achieving ethical resolutions of its strategic and operating challenges is attributed to the excellence and judgment of all its employees.

Source: Kenneth R. Andrews, "Ethics in Policy and Practice at General Mills," *Corporate Ethics: A Prime Business Assess* (New York: The Business Roundtable, February 1988), 43–52.

venture capital, and advertising. Financial stakes are high. Managers bet their own futures on a multimillion dollar movie project, a risky construction project in South America, or a new advertising campaign for a major customer. For example, movies at Paramount Pictures cost upward of $30 million (e.g., "Crocodile Dundee II"). These industries move rapidly, and feedback on a new movie's or Broadway show's success is quick to come.

One example of a tough-guy, macho culture is the Crescent Engineering Company in Houston. Crescent provides construction and maintenance of pipelines and refineries around the world. This may seem a rather safe endeavor, but each new project is high risk. Many unknowns influence the cost of providing these services in foreign countries. A serious mistake can ruin the company, and managers quickly learn if they have under- or overbid on a project.

work hard/play hard culture A form of corporate culture characterized by low-risk decision making, rapid feedback, and many small-scale decisions.

WORK HARD/PLAY HARD CULTURE

The **work hard/play hard culture** is also characterized by rapid feedback, but decisions are low risk. Managers make many small decisions rather than a few big ones. This creates an internal culture in which fun, action, and fast pace

Exhibit 3.5
Relationship of Environment to Corporate Culture

		Feedback from Environment	
		Fast	Slow
Environmental Uncertainty	High Risk Decisions	**Tough-Guy, Macho Culture** Construction, cosmetics, movies, advertising	**Bet-Your-Company Culture** Aerospace, new ventures, research and development, capital-intensive projects
	Low Risk Decisions	**Work Hard/Play Hard Culture** Fashion, marketing, consumer goods, electronics	**Process Culture** Government, utilities, insurance, financial services

Source: Based on Terrence E. Deal and Allan A. Kennedy, *Corporate Cultures: The Rites and Rituals of Corporate Life* (Reading, Mass.: Addison-Wesley, 1982), 107–108.

dominate. The culture encourages people to be creative and to undertake a high level of activity and decision making.

Work hard/play hard values often arise in marketing-oriented firms and sales organizations. Mary Kay Cosmetics, Frito-Lay, PepsiCo, retail stores, and many computer manufacturers exist in this environment. The people in these companies make frequent decisions, each one fairly low risk, but the pace is exciting and feedback is immediate. The new line of merchandise either sells or it doesn't. The salesperson either makes his or her quota or not. Cultural values reinforce the fast pace and serving customer needs. Management decisions often pertain to finding a customer need and filling it. Because the environment changes, a stream of new products and services are required. The company must never stand still.

One example of a work hard/play hard culture is Jay Jacobs Stores in Seattle. J. J. is a fashion store, and employees dress the "Jay Jacobs way." The dominant value is: The customer is number one. The emphasis is on thinking and looking young, hard work, creativity, and staying ahead of the crowd in the fast-moving fashion industry. Fashions change at a dizzying speed. Sales ability and fashion savvy are more important than seniority, age, and seasoning. Employees promote new lines of merchandise and then do it all over again.[40]

Bet-Your-Company Culture

The **bet-your-company culture** is characterized by decisions that involve big stakes and several years before decision makers know whether they were correct. This is a high-risk, slow-feedback environment. Companies involved in multimillion-dollar investments that take years to develop have this culture. Boeing Aircraft spent hundreds of millions of dollars to build the Boeing 757 and Boeing 767. Aerospace firms invest millions of dollars in new weapon systems in the hope of successful government and private sector sales. Companies in the capital-goods industry, such as Caterpillar Tractor, and mining companies, such as Alcoa, must invest millions in new products or new mining

bet-your-company culture A form of corporate culture characterized by a high-risk, high-stake, slow-feedback environment.

This cast of managers performed "Rock Around the Clock" during Quad/Graphics, Inc's annual bash to celebrate the year's success. Quad/Graphics has a *work hard/play hard* culture. New employees are expected to throw themselves into their work and train on their own time. Each employee agrees to accept company values. Quad/Graphics' managers think small to keep the culture personal and warm. At the annual party, managers and employees, led by founder Larry Quadracci, twist, calypso, and jump as participants in a fast-paced, energetic show of favorite fifties tunes.

ventures, and knowledge of results is slow to come. A new biotechnology research company developed a bet-your-company culture because it was created without a single product. The company spent years doing research to produce a successful product before the money ran out.

Process Culture

process culture A type of corporate culture characterized by low-risk decision making, little or no feedback, and low-stake decisions.

The **process culture** is characterized by low-risk decisions and little or no feedback to employees about decision effectiveness. Outcomes are hard to measure; hence, employees concentrate on how decisions are made and how work is accomplished. An important value here is that of following the procedures that management believes will get the job done. Low-risk, slow-feedback companies often include government organizations, insurance companies, and heavily regulated industries such as utilities. The financial stakes are low, and decision makers get little feedback concerning their impact.

One example of a process culture is Safeco Insurance Company. Safeco is stuffy and regimented, and working there is a lot like being in the Army. All employees take their coffee breaks at an assigned time (10 to 10:15 a.m. and 3 to 3:15 p.m.). The dress code specifies white shirts and suits for men and no beards. But the starchy culture is just what management wants: The company must be trusted to deliver on insurance policies. Reliability counts. No fads or fashions here; nonconformists need not apply. However, people go home at 4:30 and are expected to work no more. Employees like the culture and feel that it is appropriate for the insurance industry, although it radically differs from cultures that exist in tough-guy, macho, work hard/play hard, and bet-your-company organizations.[41]

The Manager's Shoptalk box lists steps for cultural socialization that any type of organization may follow.

Manager's Shoptalk

KEEPING CULTURE STRONG

A strong corporate culture enables people to feel good about what they do. They are committed to a higher purpose and are likely to work harder. Being able to say "I'm with Morgan Guaranty Trust" rather than "I work at a bank" is important. An often overlooked way to strengthen corporate culture is through the selection and socialization of new employees. Recruits need to understand what makes their company's culture tick. Great American companies that pass a strong culture from one generation to the next include Delta Air Lines, Procter & Gamble, and Morgan Guaranty Trust.

Seven steps for cultural socialization are as follows:

1. *Subject employment candidates to a selection process so rigorous that it seems designed to discourage rather than encourage individuals to take the job.* Recruits should not be oversold. They should be grilled and told the bad as well as the good side of the job. At P&G, recruits are interviewed twice by line managers and must pass a test of general knowledge. Survivors go through additional interviews at headquarters. Morgan Stanley, a New York investment banking house, encourages people to discuss with family and friends the demands of working 100 hours a week.
2. *Subject newly hired individuals to experiences calculated to induce humility and to make them question prior behavior, beliefs, and values.* New recruits get little glory and work long hours at mundane tasks. At Procter & Gamble, a recruit might color in a map of sales territories. Morgan Stanley associates work 12- to 14-hour days and most weekends, and lunches are 30 minutes long in a very unplush cafeteria.
3. *Send newly humbled recruits into the trenches, pushing them to master one of the core disciplines of the company's business.* It takes 6 years to become an IBM marketing representative, 12 years to become a controller. There is no quick way to jump ranks and reach the top. Progress is slow and based on performance.
4. *At every stage of new managers' careers, measure the operating results they have achieved and reward them accordingly.* At P&G, new professionals are measured on three factors: building volume, building profits, and conducting plant change. At IBM, managers track adherence to the core value of respecting the decency of the individual. Climate surveys and open-door procedures let IBM management know whether new employees are on the right track.
5. *Repeatedly promote adherence to the company's transcendent values—those overarching purposes that rise above the day-to-day imperative to make a buck.* The important thing at Delta is the "Delta family feeling." New employees hear about the sacrifices required. Managers take a pay cut during lean times, and senior flight attendants and pilots voluntarily work fewer hours to avoid laying off junior people. Before AT&T's divestiture, new employees learned about the transcendent value of guaranteeing phone service through any emergency.
6. *Constantly harp on watershed events in the organization's history that reaffirm the importance of your firm's culture.* Folklore and stories reinforce key values and the code of conduct for "how we do things around here." Stories have a moral that teach employees about key values. One story at Procter & Gamble concerns how the top brand manager was fired for overstating the product's features. The point is that honesty comes ahead of making money.
7. *Supply role models.* Exemplary individuals—the heroes—convey the traits the culture values most. Role models can be current employees, recognized as winners, whom the new employees can imitate. McDonald's has an obsessive concern for quality control, IBM for customer service, and 3M for innovation. Role models demonstrate these values for aspiring professionals. Role models are the most powerful culture training program available.

Source: Richard Pascale, "Fitting New Employees into the Company Culture," *Fortune,* May 28, 1984, 28–39; Richard Pascale, "The Paradox of 'Corporate Culture': Reconciling Ourselves to Socialization," *California Management Review* 27 (Winter 1985), 26–41.

Changing and Merging Corporate Cultures

A corporation's culture may not always be in alignment with its needs and environment. Cultural values may reflect what worked in the past. The difference between desired cultural norms and values and actual norms and values is called the **culture gap.**[42]

culture gap The difference between an organization's desired cultural norms and values and actual norms and values.

Banc One Corporation, headquartered in Columbus, Ohio, uses *symbolic management* to integrate 20 former Texas MCORP banks into its corporate system. To facilitate the merger, senior managers stress symbols of oneness such as the wearing of Bank One T-shirts. Here, Dallas employees join John B. McCoy, chairman of Banc One Corporation (front right) in a "welcome" wave. To smooth the merger, Banc One managers conduct orientation sessions for every employee, provide newsletters and welcome packets, and attend question-and-answer sessions so Texas employees will learn about Banc One's caring culture.

Culture gaps can be immense, especially in mergers and acquisitions.[43] Despite the popularity of mergers and acquisitions as a corporate strategy, many fail. Almost one-half of acquired companies get sold off within five years, and some experts claim that 90 percent of mergers never live up to expectations.[44] One reason for failure is that although managers are able to integrate the acquired firm's financial systems and production technologies, they typically are unable to integrate the unwritten norms and values that have an even greater impact on a company's success.[45] A merger or acquisition exacts an enormous toll in employee anxiety, fear, and tension. After all, most mergers produce some redefinition of pay, benefits, tasks, and other forms of employee security. Approximately one-third of mergers and acquisitions result in layoffs.[46] These factors create a breakdown in communication, reduced commitment, attempts at self-preservation, and resistance to change. Corporate culture becomes a negative force in which norms and values impede success.

What can managers do to change norms and values toward what is needed for the external environment or for smooth cultural integration during a merger? The answer is symbolic management.

SYMBOLIC MANAGEMENT

To change corporate culture, managers can use cultural artifacts of symbols, stories, slogans, and ceremonies. Managers literally must overcommunicate to ensure that employees understand the new cultural values, and they must signal these values in actions as well as words. A **symbolic manager** defines and uses signals and symbols to influence corporate culture. Symbolic managers influence culture in the following manner:

symbolic manager A manager who defines and uses signals and symbols to influence corporate culture.

1. *The symbolic manager articulates a vision for the organizational change that generates excitement and that employees can believe in.* This means

the manager defines and communicates central values that employees believe in and will rally around.

2. *The symbolic manager heeds the day-to-day activities that reinforce the vision.* The symbolic manager makes sure that symbols, ceremonies, and slogans match the new values. Even more important, actions speak louder than words. Symbolic managers "walk their talk."[47]

The reason symbolic management works is that executives are watched by employees. Employees attempt to read signals from what executives do, not just from what they say. For example, a senior manager told a story of how employees always knew in advance when someone was to be laid off in his company. He finally picked up the pattern. Employees noticed that he always dressed in his favorite pink shirt and matching tie when layoffs were to be announced. When Walter Williams, CEO of Bethlehem Steel, wanted to make substantive cultural changes, he first articulated the new vision of quality and constant improvement, and then acted accordingly. He answers his own phone and meets with 50 customers a year to sound out complaints, thereby providing a symbolic model of how employees should act. He gets his feet dirty in the plant giving sermons on the importance of the new values. He also formed teams of hourly and salaried employees who worked directly with customers so they could solve quality problems.[48] Jack Welch transformed General Electric — a huge corporation — by defining a new type of senior manager. His demand was for symbolic managers, which he described as follows: "Somebody who can develop a vision of what he or she wants their . . . activity to do and be. Somebody who is able to articulate what the business is, and gain through a sharing of the discussion — listening and talking — an acceptance of the vision. And someone who then can relentlessly drive implementation of that vision to a successful conclusion."[49]

Symbolic managers search for opportunities. They make public statements, including both oral and written communications to the organization as a whole. After articulating a vision, managers change corporate culture through hundreds of small deeds, actions, statements, and ceremonies. A strong leader who articulated a clear vision accounted for the extraordinary success of Dana, Wang, Wal-Mart, Disney, McDonald's, and Levi-Strauss. Harold Geneen captured his new corporate value in a few words, "Search for the unshakeable facts." Roy Ash signaled the new culture for AM International by removing copying machines, making his own calls, and encouraging people to drop by and discuss problems face-to-face. His behavior broke the pattern of bureaucracy and centralized decision making.[50]

One famous story used by Mars's executives to illustrate the company's concern for employees relates Mr. Mars's mid-summer visit to a chocolate factory:

> He went up to the third floor, where the biggest chocolate machines were placed. It was hotter than the hinges of hell. He asked the factory manager, "How come you don't have air conditioning up here?" The factory manager replied that it wasn't in his budget, and he darn well had to make the budget. While Mr. Mars allowed that was a fact, he nonetheless went over to the nearby phone and dialed the maintenance people downstairs and asked them to come up immediately. He said, "While we (he and the factory manager) stand here, would you please go downstairs and get all (the factory manager's) furniture and other things from his office and bring them up here? Sit them down next to the big chocolate machine up here, if you don't mind." Mr. Mars told him that once the factory had been air conditioned, he could move back to his office any time he wanted.[51]

Stories such as these can be found in most companies and used to enhance the desired culture. The value of stories depends not on whether they are precisely true but whether they are repeated frequently and convey the correct values.

To summarize, symbolic managers can bring about cultural change through the use of public statements, ceremonies, stories, heroes, symbols, and slogans. To change culture, executives must learn ceremonial skills and how to use speech, symbols, and stories to influence company values. Executives do not drive trucks or run machines. To change culture, they must act like evangelists rather than accountants.[52] Symbolic activities provide information about what counts in the company.

Summary

This chapter discussed several important ideas about internal and external organizational environments. Events in the external environment are considered important influences on organizational behavior and performance. The external environment consists of two layers: the task environment and the general environment. The task environment includes customers, competitors, suppliers, and labor supply. The general environment includes technological, sociocultural, economic, legal-political, and international dimensions. Management techniques for helping the organization adapt to the environment include boundary-spanning roles, forecasting and planning, a flexible structure, and mergers and joint ventures. Techniques managers can use to influence the external environment include advertising and public relations, political activities, and trade associations.

Corporate culture, a major element of the internal environment, includes the key values, beliefs, understandings, and norms that organization members share. Organizational activities that illustrate corporate culture include symbols, stories, heroes, slogans, and ceremonies. For the organization to be effective, corporate culture should be aligned with the needs of the external environment. Four types of culture are the tough-guy, macho culture, the work hard/play hard culture, the bet-your-company culture, and the process culture. Symbolic managers can change corporate culture by (1) communicating a vision to employees and (2) reinforcing the vision with day-to-day public statements, ceremonies, slogans, symbols, and stories.

Management Solution

The inability to get an export license and the dumping of wafering saws in the United States by Meyer & Burger A.G. nearly bankrupted Silicon Technology Corporation (STC). George Kachajian's company was overwhelmed by foreign competition and government red tape. His response was political activity on a large scale. After all, STC's corporate culture valued high ethical standards, so Kachajian would not consider contravention of U.S. export laws, even though the laws seemed wrong in this case. Kachajian had half a dozen meetings with defense department officials explaining that his saws did not contain technology that was a threat to national security because Eastern bloc countries could get as many saws as they wanted from the Swiss. He also peppered the Commerce Department with information and stumped the Office of Foreign Availability (OFA). Kachajian enlisted the help of other CEOs, including prominent customers, and redoubled his lobbying efforts by enlisting New Jersey's two senators and one representative to directly pressure the Commerce secretary. He continued pressure with telephone calls, visits, and a letter campaign that involved all 45 employees of his company. Finally, the Commerce Department adopted the position that STC's saws should be decontrolled for sale internationally, although some restrictions are still placed on Eastern bloc countries. The lesson here is that even small companies can develop political clout if they are willing to reach out and control the external environment.[53]

Discussion Questions

1. Some scientists predict major changes in the earth's climate, including a temperature rise of 8°F over the next 60 years. Should any companies be paying attention to this long-range environmental trend? Explain.
2. Would the task environment for a bank contain the same elements as that for a government welfare agency? Discuss.
3. What forces influence organizational uncertainty? Would such forces typically originate in the task environment or the general environment?
4. *In Search of Excellence*, described in Chapter 2, argued that customers were the most important element in the external environment. Are there company situations for which this may not be true?
5. Caterpillar Corporation was thriving until the mid-1980s, when low oil prices, high interest rates, a worldwide recession, a soaring U.S. dollar, and Japanese competition stunned the giant equipment builder. Discuss the type of response Caterpillar's management might take.
6. Define corporate culture and explain its importance for managers.
7. Why are symbols important to a corporate culture? Do stories, heroes, slogans, and ceremonies also have symbolic value? Discuss.
8. Describe the cultural values of a company for which you have worked. Did those values fit the needs of the external environment? Of employees?
9. What type of environmental situation is associated with a tough-guy, macho culture? How does this culture differ from the work hard/play hard culture?
10. Do you think a corporate culture with strong values is better for organizational effectiveness than a culture with weak values? Are there times when a strong culture might reduce effectiveness?

Management in Practice: Ethical Dilemma

The $10,000 Lunch

Rich has decision responsibility for a $5 million, five-year budget to install a communications network in his company's headquarters building. Suppliers are competitively vying to win contracts for providing the necessary hardware and systems equipment.

Rich is having lunch with his favorite salesperson, Scott. Near the end of lunch Scott says, "Rich, listen, the end of the quarter is next week, and I am about $100,000 in sales short to get a big $10,000 bonus. If you could sign the purchase agreement on that computer network now instead of in three months, I've got tickets to the Super Bowl. How about it?"

Rich responded, "I've got to think about this. I'll call you tomorrow." Rich wanted desperately to attend the Super Bowl because his favorite team was playing, and his wife wanted to visit family in New Orleans. Back at the office Rich thought about the company tradition of purchasing agents and others accepting small favors from suppliers. He also knew that Scott put a lot of effort into bidding for the contract, and his company's bid looked better than any other. Rich also remembered that a newly issued company policy states, "Program managers are prohibited from excepting gifts of any size or form from vendors."

What Do You Do?

1. Sign the contract and accept the tickets. After all, Scott deserved it and would have won the bidding anyway.
2. Ask the support of coworkers. After all, company tradition and cultural values are more important for defining behavior than are written policies.
3. Do not sign the contract or accept the tickets. Breaking company policy is inappropriate.

CASES FOR ANALYSIS

FLORSHEIM SHOE PLANT

The Florsheim Shoe Plant in Hermann, Missouri, is owned by Interco Inc. In 1989, the Rales brothers, takeover artists, decided to acquire Interco, consistent with the merger mania of the 1980s. The Rales brothers believed Interco would be worth more broken up and sold off in pieces.

This was a hostile takeover, leading to a battle that left many outside the ring bloody and dazed. Interco's management responded to the takeover bid with drastic measures to make Interco unattractive. Interco's managers did not want to be taken over, because they would probably be fired; if they were not fired, they would lose discretionary control over Interco. The company made itself prohibitively expensive by assigning $16 million in damages to senior executives if control of the company changed. Interco also borrowed $1.9 billion, paying an extraordinary $65 million in fees and commissions to banks, lawyers, financiers, and accountants.

In addition to the big debt, Interco executives tried to protect themselves by selling off and closing plants. One cost-cutting measure was to close the Florsheim plant in Hermann and a second factory in Paducah, Kentucky. The work of these plants was transferred elsewhere for greater efficiency. Interco also sold Londontown Corporation, maker of London Fog outerwear, and other prestigious names to help offset its giant debt.

Now that the plant is closed, people such as Linda Eikel, a $5-an-hour worker, catch the fallout through the loss of their jobs. "Woody" Wesselschmidt, plant manager in Hermann, lost his job, too. Some 650 jobs were lost in the two closed Florsheim plants. Analysts in the financial community say the changes are worth it. The important thing to them is to have the stock price of Interco as high as possible. Cutting jobs is an important way to increase efficiency and enhance financial value.

But the employees are devastated, paying the ultimate price of merger mania. The big winners are the Rales brothers, who ultimately lost the takeover bid, but sold the stock they acquired for a $50 million profit. The lawyers, accountants, and others who shared the $65 million in fees also made lots of money. Loyal employees worked for years believing that quality was the number-one value. They established a strong culture and an excellent quality reputation for Florsheim shoes and cannot understand the unfairness of losing their jobs anyway.

Questions

1. What aspects of the external environment are having an impact on Interco and the Florsheim Shoe Plant?
2. How do you think the attempted takeover has affected the corporate culture in the remaining divisions of Interco?
3. Is the financial bottom line a more important basis for decision making than corporate culture and employee jobs?

Source: Based on Sharon Cohen, "Workers, the Casualties in Takeover War," *Chicago Tribune*, April 10, 1989, section 4, 3–4.

SOCIETY OF EQUALS

Ted Shelby doesn't make very many mistakes, but . . .

"Hey, Stanley," said Ted Shelby, leaning in through the door, "you got a minute? I've just restructured my office. Come on and take a look. I've been implementing some great new concepts!"

Stanley is always interested in Ted Shelby's new ideas. For if there is anyone Stanley wants to do as well as, it is Edward W. Shelby IV. Stanley follows Ted back to his office and stops, nonplussed.

Restructured is right! Gone are Ted's size B (Junior Exec.) walnut veneer desk and furniture, and his telephone table. In fact, the room is practically empty save for a large, round, stark white cafeteria table and the half-dozen padded vinyl swivel chairs that surround it.

"Isn't it a beauty! As far as I know, I'm the first executive in the plant to innovate this. The shape is the crucial factor here — no front or rear, no status problems. We can all sit there and communicate more effectively."

We? Communicate? Effectively? Well, it seems that Ted has been attending a series of Executive Development Seminars given by Dr. Faust. The theme of the seminars was — you guessed it — "participative management." Edward W. Shelby IV has always liked to think of himself as a truly democratic person.

"You see, Stanley," says Ted, managing his best sincere/intense attitude, "the main thing wrong with current mainstream management practice is that the principal communication channel is down-the-line oriented. We on the top send our messages down to you people, but we neglect the feedback potential. But just because we have more status and responsibility doesn't mean that we are necessarily (Stanley duly noted the word, "necessarily") better than the people below us. So, as I see the situation, what is needed is a two-way communication network: down-the-line and up-the-line.

"That's what the cafeteria table is for?" Stanley says.

"Yes!" says Ted. "We management people don't have all the answers, and I don't know why I never realized it before that seminar. Why . . . let's take an extreme example . . . the folks who run those machines out there. I'll bet that any one of them knows a thing or two that I've never thought of. So I've transformed my office into a full-feedback communication net."

"That certainly is an innovation around here," says Stanley.

A few days later Stanley passed by Ted Shelby's office and was surprised that Ted's desk, furniture, and telephone table were back where they used to be.

Stanley, curious about the unrestructuring, went to Bonnie for enlightenment. "What," he asked, "happened to Shelby's round table?"

"That table we were supposed to sit around and input things?" she said. "All I know is, about two days after he had it put in, Mr. Drake came walking through here. He looked in that office, and then he sort of stopped and went back — and he looked in there for a long time. Then he came over to me, and you know how his face sort of gets red when he's really mad? Well, this time he was so mad that his face was absolutely white. And when he talked to me, I don't think he actually opened his mouth; and I could barely hear him, he was talking so low. And he said, 'Have that removed. Now. Have Mr. Shelby's furniture put back in his office. Have Mr. Shelby see me.' "

My, my. You would think Ted would have known better, wouldn't you? But then, by now you should have a pretty firm idea of just why it is those offices are set up as they are.

Questions

1. How would you characterize the culture in this company? What are the dominant values?
2. Why did Ted Shelby's change experiment fail? To what extent did Ted use the appropriate change tools to increase employee communication and participation?
3. What would you recommend Ted do to change his relationship with subordinates? Is it possible for a manager to change cultural values if the rest of the organization, especially top management, does not agree?

Source: R. Richard Ritti and G. Ray Funkhouser, *The Ropes to Skip & The Ropes to Know*, 3d. (New York: Wiley, 1987), 176–177. Reprinted by permission of John Wiley & Sons, Inc.

C H A P T E R 4

Managerial Ethics and Corporate Social Responsibility

Chapter Outline

Learning Objectives

After studying this chapter, you should be able to:

- Define ethics and explain how ethical behavior relates to behavior governed by law and free choice.
- Explain the utilitarian, individualism, moral-rights, and justice approaches for evaluating ethical behavior.
- Describe how both individual and organizational factors shape ethical decision making.
- Define corporate social responsibility and how to evaluate it along economic, legal, ethical, and discretionary criteria.
- Describe four corporate responses to social demands.
- Explain the concept of stakeholder and identify important stakeholders for organizations.
- Describe structures managers can use to improve their organizations' ethics and social responsiveness.

Management Problem

General Dynamics' ethics crisis struck with little warning. An executive vice-president of this defense contractor was indicted in a $1.3 million kickback scheme. Then charges of overbilling, unethical gifts, conflict of interest, time card cheating, and fraud surfaced. During one year, eight different investigations were proceeding against General Dynamics, and it was suspended from naval contracts. As soon as the company was reinstated, it was suspended again when four current or former executives were charged with defrauding the government through contract charges and violations. Executives billed the government for such things as kenneling their dogs. Enter Chairman Stanley C. Pace, who was expected to clean things up and set the company on a strong ethical footing.[1]

If you were Chairman Pace, how would you respond to this mess, and how would you implement a higher ethical standard within General Dynamics?

Everyone associated with the General Dynamics scandal was surprised—surprised at the intensity of the public backlash, surprised that basically honest people would deceive the government, surprised at the loss of respect for the company and its management. The outcry against General Dynamics symbolizes the rising importance of the need to discuss ethics and social responsibility. Some experts claim that the 1990s is the decade when such issues as ethics and social responsibility will come to the forefront. Corporations are rushing to adopt codes of ethics. Ethics consultants are doing a land-office business. Unfortunately, the trend is necessary.[2]

Hertz Corporation overcharged consumers and insurers some $13 million for repairs to damaged rental cars. Bolar Pharmaceutical Company submitted another company's brand name drug for testing as its own generic drug to get FDA approval. United Brands Company admitted paying huge bribes to foreign government officials to achieve favorable legislation. Ocean Spray Cranberries Inc. was indicted for pollution in Middleboro, Massachusetts. These instances of fraud, price gauging, and pollution illustrate the negative side of the ethics issue.

A *positive ethical approach* to the environment is illustrated in Chevron's work to preserve the habitat of the El Segundo Blue Butterfly. Chevron has a structured program that goes beyond mere compliance to achieve the spirit of laws concerning environmental protection and employee health and safety. Chevron received the "Outstanding Industry Conservationist Award" for its program to protect buckwheat plants, the only source of food for the blue butterfly.

There is also positive news to report.[3] McDonald's has become one of North America's leading crusaders for paper and plastic recycling. Pacific Gas & Electric now teams up with environmental groups it used to fight to do joint projects such as a $10 million study of energy efficiency. United Airlines invests time and money in Chicago schools and provides opportunities for graduates to get jobs. MasterCard is raising $3 million for six charities. Companies such as Hertz and Bolar Pharmaceuticals are embarrassed about their ethical mistakes and are working overtime to prevent future problems.

This chapter expands on the ideas about environment and culture discussed in Chapter 3. In this chapter we will focus on specific cultural values concerning managers' ethical behavior and corporations' social responsibility to the environment. The topic of ethics is hot, but it should be approached as more than a fad. There are fundamental approaches to ethics that help managers think through ethical issues. Understanding ethical approaches helps managers build a solid foundation on which to base future decision making.

WHAT IS MANAGERIAL ETHICS?

ethics The code of moral principles and values that govern the behaviors of a person or group with respect to what is right or wrong.

Ethics is difficult to define in a precise way. In a general sense, **ethics** is the code of moral principles and values that govern the behaviors of a person or group with respect to what is right or wrong. Ethics sets standards as to what is good or bad in conduct and decision making.[4]

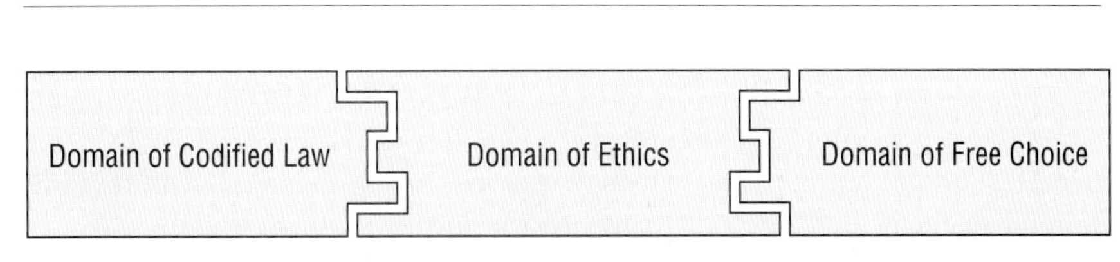

Exhibit 4.1
Three Domains of Human Action

Ethics can be more clearly understood when compared with behaviors governed by laws and by free choice. Exhibit 4.1 illustrates that human behavior falls into three categories. The first is codified law, in which values and standards are written into the legal system and enforceable in the courts. In this area lawmakers have ruled that people and corporations must behave in a certain way, such as obtaining licenses for cars or paying corporate taxes. The domain of free choice is at the opposite end of the scale and pertains to behavior about which law has no say and for which an individual or organization enjoys complete freedom. An individual's choice of a marriage partner or religion or a corporation's choice of the number of dishwashers to manufacture are examples of free choice.

Between these domains lies the area of ethics. This domain has no specific laws, yet it does have standards of conduct based on shared principles and values about moral conduct that guide an individual or company. In the domain of free choice, obedience is strictly to oneself. In the domain of codified law, obedience is to laws prescribed by the legal system. In the domain of ethical behavior, obedience is to unenforceable norms and standards about which the individual or company is aware.

Many companies and individuals get into trouble with the simplified view that choices are governed by either law or free choice. It leads people to mistakenly assume that "If it's not illegal, it must be ethical," as if there were no third domain.[5] A better option is to recognize the domain of ethics and accept moral values as a powerful force for good that can regulate behaviors both inside and outside corporations. As principles of ethics and social responsibility are more widely recognized, companies can use codes of ethics and their corporate cultures to govern behavior, thereby eliminating the need for additional laws and avoiding the problems of unfettered choice.

Because ethical standards are not codified, disagreements and dilemmas about proper behavior often occur. An **ethical dilemma** arises in a situation when each alternative choice or behavior is undesirable because of potentially negative ethical consequences. Right or wrong cannot be clearly identified. Consider the following:

ethical dilemma A situation that arises when all alternative choices or behaviors have been deemed undesirable because of potentially negative ethical consequences, making it difficult to distinguish right from wrong.

Shareholders demand that your company pull out of South Africa. If you pull out, you believe your black South African employees will be hurt. If you stay, your company will be indirectly supporting an oppressive government.

You have been asked to fire a marketing supervisor for cheating the company out of $500 on an inflated expense account. You are aware that a manufacturing supervisor allows thousands of dollars of waste because of poor work habits.

Your company has been asked to pay a gratuity in India to speed the processing of an import permit. This is standard procedure, and your company

Union Carbide has faced an *ethical dilemma* about operating its affiliates in South Africa. At the EMSA affiliate, shown here, production foreman Ishmael Mohlamme (center) discusses graphite electrode pin placement with assistants. Employees are hired, trained, paid, and promoted without regard to race. Union Carbide created a trust, funded by its share of the profits from the operations of its South African affiliates, to benefit victims of apartheid. Its affiliates have adopted schools, made loans to employees to purchase homes, and contributed to legal assistance for blacks and efforts to mount a legal challenge to apartheid. Affiliates also have made their abhorrence of apartheid known to the South African government and have pledged an active role in achieving reform.

will suffer if you do not pay the gratuity. Is this different from tipping a maitre d' in a nice restaurant?

You are the accounting manager of a division that is $15,000 below profit targets. Approximately $20,000 of office supplies were delivered on December 21. The accounting rule is to pay expenses when incurred. The division general manager asks you not to record the invoice until February.

Your boss says he cannot give you a raise this year because of budget constraints, but he will look the other way if your expense accounts come in a little high because of your good work this past year.

These are the kinds dilemmas and issues with which managers must deal that fall squarely in the domain of ethics. Now let's turn to approaches to ethical decision making that provide criteria for understanding and resolving these difficult issues.

CRITERIA FOR ETHICAL DECISION MAKING

Managers faced with ethical choices may benefit from a normative approach — one based on norms and values — to guide their decision making. Normative ethics uses several approaches to describe values for guiding ethical decision making. Four of these that are relevant to managers are: utilitarian approach, individualism approach, moral-rights approach, and justice approach.[6]

UTILITARIAN APPROACH

utilitarian approach The ethical concept that moral behaviors produce the greatest good for the greatest number.

The **utilitarian approach** holds that moral behaviors produce the greatest good for the greatest number. In this approach, a decision maker is expected to consider the effect of each decision alternative on all parties and select the one that optimizes the satisfaction for the greatest number of people. Because actual computations can be very complex, simplifying them is considered appropriate. For example, a simple economic frame of reference could be used by calculating dollar costs and dollar benefits. Also, a decision could be made that considers only the people who are directly affected by the decision and not those who are indirectly affected. When Kimberly-Clark laid off hundreds of employees, the decision was morally justified by the greater good for the larger corporation. The utilitarian ethic was the basis for the state of Oregon's decision to extend Medicaid to 400,000 previously ineligible recipients by refusing to pay for high-cost, high-risk procedures such as liver transplants and bone-marrow transplants. Although a few people needing these procedures have died because the state would not pay, many people have benefited from medical services they would otherwise have had to go without.[7]

INDIVIDUALISM APPROACH

individualism approach The ethical concept that acts are moral when they promote the individual's best long-term interests, which ultimately leads to the greater good.

The **individualism approach,** also called *egoism,* contends that acts are moral when they promote the individual's best long-term interests. Individuals calculate the best long-term advantage to themselves as a measure of a decision's goodness. The action that is intended to produce a greater ratio of good to bad for the individual compared with other alternatives is the right one to perform. With everyone pursuing self-interest, the greater good is ultimately served because people learn to accommodate each other in their own long-term interest. Individualism is believed to lead to honesty and integrity because that works best in the long run. Lying and cheating for immediate self-interest just causes business associates to lie and cheat in return. Thus, individualism ultimately leads to behavior toward others that fits standards of behavior people want toward themselves.[8] One value of understanding this approach is to recognize short-term variations if they are proposed. People might argue for short-term self-interest based on individualism, but that misses the point. Because individualism is easily misinterpreted to support immediate self-gain, it is not popular in the highly organized and group-oriented society of today. Individualism is closest to the domain of free choice described in Exhibit 4.1.

Ben Cohen (left) and Jerry Greenfield, co-founders of Ben and Jerry's Homemade, Inc., use the *distributive justice* approach in managing their ice cream company. Guided by standards of equity and fairness, they established a five-to-one salary ratio policy that limits the top salary of executives to five times that of the lowest-paid employee. This policy recognizes the important role of the workers who actually make the ice cream. Ben and Jerry believe all employees should share in the company's prosperity.

Moral-Rights Approach

The **moral-rights approach** asserts that human beings have fundamental rights and liberties that cannot be taken away by an individual's decision. Thus an ethically correct decision is one that best maintains the rights of those people affected by it.

Moral rights that could be considered during decision making are:

1. The right of free consent — individuals are to be treated only as they knowingly and freely consent to be treated.
2. The right to privacy — individuals can choose to do as they please away from work and have control of information about their private life.
3. The right of freedom of conscience — individuals may refrain from carrying out any order that violates their moral or religious norms.
4. The right of free speech — individuals may criticize truthfully the ethics or legality of actions of others.
5. The right to due process — individuals have a right to an impartial hearing and fair treatment.
6. The right to life and safety — individuals have a right to live without endangerment or violation of their health and safety.

To make ethical decisions, managers need to avoid interfering with the fundamental rights of others. Thus a decision to eavesdrop on employees violates the right to privacy. Sexual harassment would be considered unethical because it violates the right to freedom of conscience. The right of free speech would support whistle-blowers who call attention to illegal or inappropriate action within a company.

moral-rights approach The ethical concept that moral decisions are those that best maintain the rights of those people affected by them.

justice approach The ethical concept that moral decisions must be based on standards of equity, fairness, and impartiality.

distributive justice The concept that different treatment of people should not be based on arbitrary characteristics. In the case of substantive differences, people should be treated differently in proportion to the differences between them.

Justice Approach

The **justice approach** holds that moral decisions must be based on standards of equity, fairness, and impartiality. Three types of justice are of concern to managers. **Distributive justice** requires that different treatment of people not be based on arbitrary characteristics. Individuals who are similar in respects relevant to a decision should be treated similarly. Thus men and women should not receive different salaries if they are performing the same job. However, people who differ in a substantive way, such as job skills or job responsibility, can be treated differently in proportion to the differences in skills or responsibility between them. This difference should have a clear relationship to organizational goals and tasks.

procedural justice The concept that rules should be clearly stated and consistently and impartially enforced.

compensatory justice The concept that individuals should be compensated for the cost of their injuries by the party responsible and also that individuals should not be held responsible for matters over which they have no control.

Procedural justice requires that rules be administered fairly. Rules should be clearly stated and be consistently and impartially enforced. **Compensatory justice** argues that individuals should be compensated for the cost of their injuries by the party responsible. Moreover, individuals should not be held responsible for matters over which they have no control.

The justice approach is closest to the thinking underlying the domain of law in Exhibit 4.1, because it assumes that justice is applied through rules and regulations. This theory does not require complex calculations such as demanded by a utilitarian approach, nor does it justify self-interest as the individualism approach does. Managers are expected to define attributes on which different treatment of employees is acceptable. Questions such as how minority workers should be compensated for past discrimination are extremely difficult. However, this approach does justify as ethical behavior efforts to correct past wrongs, playing fair under the rules, and insisting on job-relevant differences as the basis for different levels of pay or promotion opportunities. Most of the laws guiding human resource management (Chapter 12) are based on the justice approach.

The challenge of applying these ethical approaches is illustrated by decisions facing companies in the tobacco industry.

BROWN & WILLIAMSON

• Brown & Williamson, RJR Nabisco, and other tobacco companies are working hard to increase cigarette exports. Japan, Taiwan, and South Korea are lucrative markets because people are heavy smokers. U.S. trade representatives negotiated freer access to foreign markets on behalf of U.S. companies.

Former U.S. Surgeon General Koop thinks U.S. cigarette exports are like Latin American cocaine. He believes it is the height of hypocrisy to export tobacco. Tobacco companies respond that their brands are actually beneficial. For example, Taiwan's most successful brand with 90 percent of the market has double the nicotine and tar of Marlboro. Because Asians are heavy smokers, they are better off with American cigarettes.[9]

Consider for a moment how the ethics approaches support and refute cigarette companies' actions.

FACTORS AFFECTING ETHICAL CHOICES

When managers are accused of lying, cheating, or stealing, the blame is usually placed on the individual or on the company situation. Most people believe that individuals make ethical choices because of individual integrity, which is true, but it is not the whole story. The values held in the larger organization also shape ethical behavior.[10] Let's examine how both the manager and the organization shape ethical decision making.

Exhibit 4.2
Three Levels of Personal Moral Development

Stage	What Is Considered To Be Right
Level one: Preconventional	Follow rules to avoid physical punishment. Act in one's immediate interest. Obedience for its own sake.
Level two: Conventional	Good behavior is living up to what is expected by others. Fulfills duties and obligations of social system. Upholds laws.
Level three: Principled	Aware that people hold different values. Uphold values and rights regardless of majority opinion. Follows self-chosen ethical principles of justice and rights.

Source: Based on L. Kohlberg, "Moral Stages and Moralization: The Cognitive-Developmental Approach," in *Moral Development and Behavior: Theory, Research, and Social Issues*, ed. T. Lickona (New York: Holt, Rhinehart, and Winston, 1976).

The Manager

Managers bring specific personality and behavioral traits to the job. Personal needs, family influence, and religious background all shape a manager's value system. Specific personality characteristics, such as ego strength, self-confidence, and a strong sense of independence may enable managers to make ethical decisions.

One important personal trait is the stage of moral development.[11] A simplified version of one model of personal moral development is shown in Exhibit 4.2. At the *preconventional level* a manager is concerned with the external rewards and punishment and the concrete personal consequences. At level two, called the *conventional level,* people learn to conform to the expectations of good behavior as defined by colleagues, friends, family, and society. People at the conventional level respect external expectations. At level three, called the *principled level,* individuals develop an internal set of standards and values. The individual will even disobey laws that violate these principles. Internal values are more important than expectations of significant others.

The great majority of managers operate at level two. A few have not advanced beyond level one. Only about 20 percent of American adults reach the level three stage of moral development. People at level three are able to act in an independent, ethical manner regardless of expectations from others inside or outside the organization. Managers at level three of moral development will make ethical decisions whatever the organizational consequences for them. The Manager's Shoptalk box lists some general guidelines to follow for making ethical decisions.

Donald Sheelen acted at the *preconventional level* of personal moral development when he acted in his own immediate interests as CEO of Regina Company. Sheelen had an enormous drive to succeed and committed fraud rather than accept failure. Thousands of Regina vacuums were returned due to poor quality. The returns were not recorded and records were falsified to show profits. Sheelen pled guilty to falsifying company financial records and served a one-year sentence.

The Organization

The values adopted within the organization are important, especially when we understand that most people are at the level two stage of moral development, which means they believe their duty is to fulfill obligations and expectations of

EXHIBIT 4.3
Questions for Analyzing a Company's Cultural Impact on Ethics

Source: Linda Klebe Trevino, "A Cultural Perspective on Changing and Developing Organizational Ethics," in *Research in Organizational Change and Development,* eds. R. Woodman and W. Pasmore (Greenwich, Conn.: JAI Press, 1990), 4: in press.

1. Identify the organization's heroes. What values do they represent? Given an ambiguous ethical dilemma, what decision would they make and why?
2. What are some important organizational rituals? How do they encourage or discourage ethical behavior? Who gets the awards, people of integrity or individuals who use unethical methods to attain success?
3. What are the ethical messages sent to new entrants into the organization — must they obey authority at all costs, or is questioning authority acceptable or even desirable?
4. Does analysis of organizational stories and myths reveal individuals who stand up for what's right, or is conformity the valued characteristic? Do people get fired or promoted in these stories?
5. Does language exist for discussing ethical concerns? Is this language routinely incorporated and encouraged in business decision making?
6. What informal socialization processes exist and what norms for ethical/unethical behavior do they promote?

others. As discussed in Chapter 3, corporate culture can exert a powerful influence on behavior in organizations. For example, an investigation of thefts and kickbacks in the oil business found that the cause was the historical acceptance of thefts and kickbacks. Employees were socialized into those values and adopted them as appropriate. In most companies, employees believe that if they do not go along with the ethical values expressed, their jobs will be in jeopardy or they will not fit in.[12]

Culture can be examined to see the kinds of ethical signals given to employees. Exhibit 4.3 indicates questions to ask to understand the cultural system. Heroes provide role models that can either support or refute ethical decision making. Founder Tom Watson stood for integrity at IBM and his values are still very much alive. With respect to company rituals, high ethical standards are affirmed and communicated through public awards and ceremonies. Myths and stories can reinforce heroic ethical behavior. For example, a story at Johnson & Johnson describes its reaction to the cyanide poisoning of Tylenol capsules. After seven people in Chicago died, the capsules were removed from the market voluntarily, costing the company over $100 million. This action was taken against the advice of external agencies — FBI and FDA — but was necessary because of Johnson & Johnson's ethical standards.

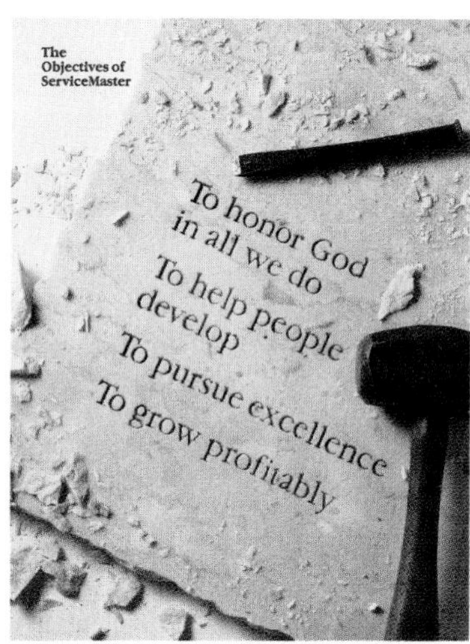

At ServiceMaster, *corporate culture* exerts a powerful force for ethical behavior. These are the four official goals displayed at the company's headquarters in Illinois. Employees honor these values while performing jobs as mundane as polishing floors and cleaning carpets for customers. ServiceMaster achieves extraordinary responsiveness and quality because every manager worries not only about ServiceMaster employees, but about its customer's employees too. Not surprisingly, ServiceMaster is one of the most admired companies in the United States.

Culture is not the only aspect of an organization that influences ethics, but it is a major force because it defines company values. Other aspects of the organization such as explicit rules and policies, the reward system, the extent to which the company cares for its people, the selection system, emphasis on legal and professional standards, and leadership and decision processes can also all have an impact on ethical values and manager decision making.[13]

WHAT IS SOCIAL RESPONSIBILITY?

Now let's turn to the issue of social responsibility. In one sense, the concept of corporate social responsibility, like ethics, is easy to understand: it means distinguishing right from wrong and doing right. It means being a good corporate citizen. The formal definition of **social responsibility** is management's obliga-

MANAGER'S SHOPTALK

GUIDELINES FOR ETHICAL DECISION MAKING

Below is a list of guidelines that you, the future manager, can apply to difficult social problems and ethical dilemmas you almost surely will face one day. The guidelines will not tell you exactly what to do, but taken in the context of the text discussion they will help you evaluate the situation more clearly by examining your own values and those of your organization. The answers to these questions will force you to think hard about the social and ethical consequences of your behavior.

1. Is the problem/dilemma really what it appears to be? If you are not sure, *find out.*
2. Is the action you are considering legal? Ethical? If you are not sure, *find out.*
3. Do you understand the position of those who oppose the action you are considering? Is it reasonable?
4. Whom does the action benefit? Harm? How much? How long?
5. Would you be willing to allow everyone to do what you are considering doing?
6. Have you sought the opinion of others who are knowledgeable on the subject and who would be objective?
7. Would your action be embarrassing to you if it were made known to your family, friends, coworkers, or superiors? Would you be comfortable defending your actions to an investigative reporter on the evening news?

There are no correct answers to these questions in an absolute sense. Yet, if you determine that an action is potentially harmful to someone, would be embarrassing to you, or if you do not know the ethical or legal consequences, these guidelines will help you clarify whether the action is socially responsible.

Source: Anthony M. Pagano and Jo Ann Verdin, *The External Environment of Business* (New York: Wiley, 1988), Chapter 5.

tion to make choices and take actions that will contribute to the welfare and interests of society as well as to the organization's.[14]

social responsibility
The obligation of organization management to make decisions and take actions that will enhance the welfare and interests of society as well as the organization's.

As straightforward as this definition seems, social responsibility can be a difficult concept to grasp, because different people have different beliefs as to which actions improve society's welfare.[15] To make matters worse, social responsibility covers a range of issues, many of which are ambiguous with respect to right or wrong. For example, if a bank deposits the money from a trust fund into a low-interest account for 90 days, from which it makes a substantial profit, has it been unethical? How about two companies' engaging in intense competition, such as that between *The Plain Dealer* and *The Cleveland Press*? Is it socially responsible for the stronger corporation to drive the weaker one into bankruptcy? Or consider companies such as A. H. Robins, maker of the Dalkon shield, Manville Corporation, maker of asbestos, Eastern Airlines, or Texaco, the oil company, all of which declared bankruptcy — which is perfectly legal — to avoid mounting financial obligations to suppliers, labor unions, or competitors. These examples contain moral, legal, and economic considerations that make socially responsible behavior hard to define. Environmental impact is another socially responsible behavior that must be taken into consideration, as illustrated in the Focus on Global Competition box.

ORGANIZATIONAL STAKEHOLDERS

One reason for the difficulty understanding social responsibility is that managers must confront the question "responsibility to whom?" Recall from Chapter 3 that the organization's environment consists of several sectors in both the task

FOCUS ON GLOBAL COMPETITION

EUROPE'S GREEN MOVEMENT

Europe 1992 is going to be full of surprises for American companies. The European Community (EC) is supposed to be ruled in the spirit of free trade. But in an EC suit against Denmark, Denmark was found innocent of restraint of trade. The restraint in question? A ban on all disposable cans for beer, mineral water, and soft drinks.

Denmark's ban is only one example of the European changes resulting from a consumer movement to protect its environment. The so-called Green Movement in Western Europe is driven by consumers who want ecologically safe products, and they are willing to pay higher taxes and utility bills for stricter legislation.

The massive shift in environmental awareness is going to create losers and winners among American companies. The winners are those that can adapt products to the new environmental standards at low cost. For example, both Ford and General Motors are losers because they will spend about $7 billion a year until 1993 to install antipollution equipment in cars sold in Europe. However, GM is in a better position than Ford, because GM used the antipollution technology required by U.S. standards. Ford spent heavily on an alternative engine technology for its European fleet, but the EC ruled that U.S. standards be met on European cars by 1993.

Other winners and losers will be in the soft-drink industry. One of the Greens' main targets is plastic disposable containers. Governmental restrictions such as Denmark's and West Germany's limit plastic bottling and force bottlers to resort to high-cost packaging and recycling in a market in which small price increases greatly reduce volume and profit. The aluminum industry stands to be the winner in this situation, because aluminum cans are lighter than glass and 100 percent recyclable. Plastic is out.

Managers of companies wishing to do business in Europe have to pay attention to the environment. Laws are stricter than in the United States because of quality-of-life demands by consumers.

Source: Based on Shawn Tulley, "What the 'Greens' Mean for Business," *Fortune,* October 23, 1989, 159–164.

and general environment. From a social responsibility perspective, enlightened organizations view the internal and external environment as a variety of stakeholders.

stakeholder Any group within or outside the organization that has a stake in the organization's performance.

A **stakeholder** is any group within or outside the organization that has a stake in the organization's performance. Each stakeholder has a different criterion of responsiveness because it has a different interest in the organization.[16]

Exhibit 4.4 illustrates important stakeholders, including employees, customers, owners, creditors, suppliers, and investors. Investors', owners', and suppliers' interests are served by managerial efficiency, that is, use of resources to achieve profits. Employees expect work satisfaction, pay, and good supervision. Customers are concerned with decisions about the quality and availability of goods and services.

Other important stakeholders are the government and the community. Most corporations exist only under the proper charter and licenses and operate within the limits of safety laws, environmental protection requirements, and other laws and regulations in the government sector. The community includes local government, the natural and physical environments, and the quality of life provided for residents. Special-interest groups, still another stakeholder, may include trade associations, political action committees, professional associations, and consumerists. Organizations that are socially responsible pay attention to all stakeholders that are affected by its actions. In the 1990s, special-interest groups will be one of the largest stakeholder concerns that companies face. The Winning Moves box shows how one company is responding with socially responsible solutions to the problem of excess garbage.

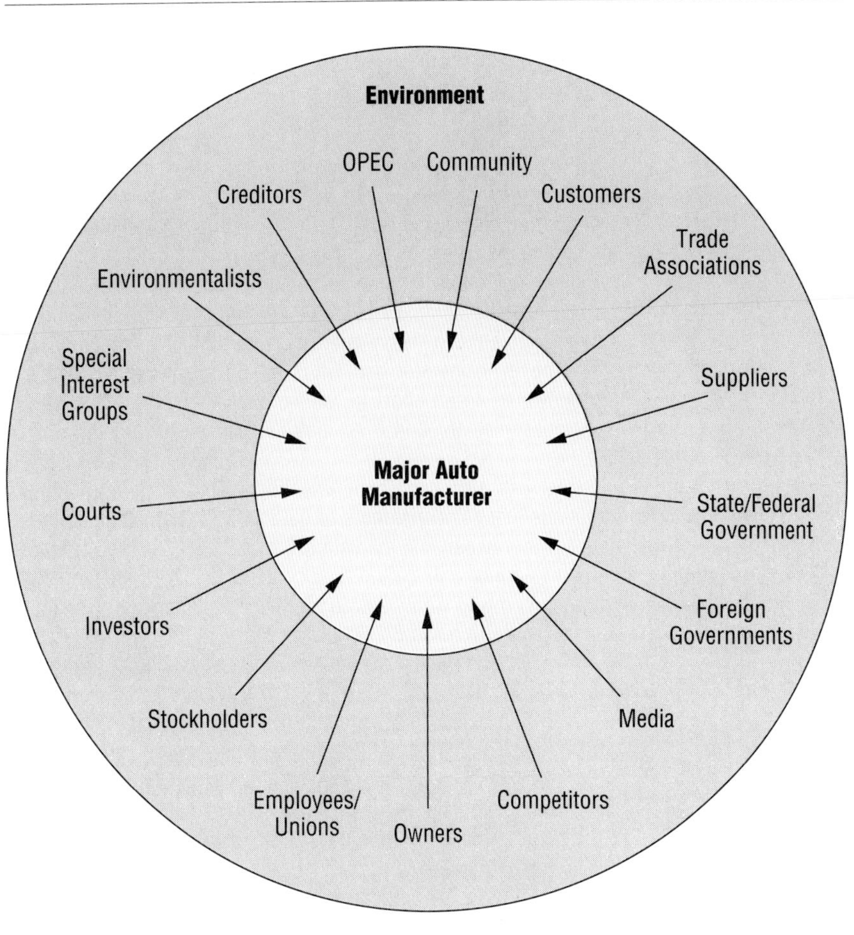

Exhibit 4.4
Stakeholders Relevant to an Auto Manufacturer

Source: Based on Nancy C. Roberts and Paula J. King, "The Stakeholder Audit Goes Public," *Organizational Dynamics* (Winter 1989), 63–79.

In Chicago, Stephen Wolf, CEO of United Airlines, has his company involved in upgrading schools and encouraging students to finish high school.[17] In New York, Alexander's Department Stores, American Express, Citibank, and IBM are all involved with high schools, either offering courses, providing realistic previews of job demands, or simply taking teenagers to Yankee Stadium if they have good school attendance records.[18] These companies are acting in a socially responsible way by helping stakeholders. The company has an interest in stakeholders and visa versa; the company helps stakeholders because they are employees of the future.

Well-meaning companies sometimes run afoul of stakeholders. For example, local communities gave Disney a great deal with respect to low taxes and fees to persuade it to build Disneyworld in Orlando, Florida. Disney is now building hotels, convention centers, and shopping centers, and making large profits. The community wants Disney to defray the costs of all the community services it uses. Disney is negotiating a new agreement in the interest of both itself and its local stakeholders.[19]

Winning Moves

ENVIRONMENTALISM AT PROCTER & GAMBLE

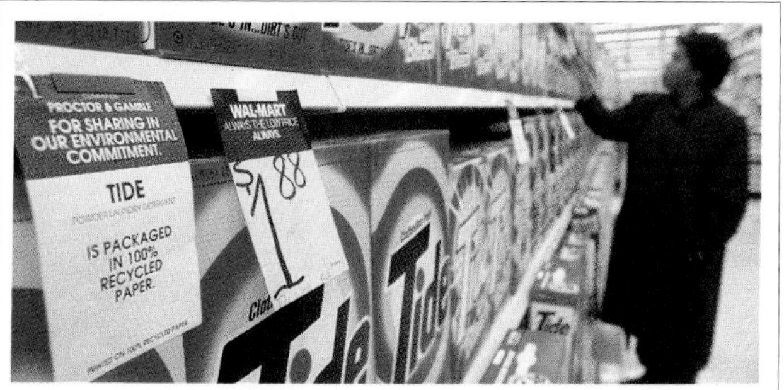

On Earth Day, 1990, millions of people from all walks of life turned out to express their concern about the quality of our environment. No longer the special interest of a few nature lovers, environmentalism has become a worldwide cause. In the United States the courts have been getting tougher about federal pollution laws. For example, in Los Angeles over the last two years at least a dozen businesspeople have faced jail sentences for violations. Recent polls show that 62 percent of all Americans call pollution a very serious problem. Of these, 75 percent believe that businesses should take active steps to handle environmental problems. Public policy expert Gary Miller claims that "In the nineties environmentalism will be the cutting edge of reform and absolutely the most important issue for business."

How are top level executives responding to this? Procter & Gamble, one of America's biggest corporate names, is starting the decade with serious aspirations to help clean up. With $21 billion a year in sales of household products from toothpaste to laundry detergent, P&G packaging is certainly a contributor to the nation's overflowing landfills. Says new chairman Ed Artzt, "We want to be among the leaders in dealing with this problem . . . to make our products environmentally friendly."

Procter & Gamble is at the forefront of research to improve the environmental impact of its packaging. Rather than appointing a special task force, P&G handed over the job to its operating managers, who have been instructed to treat the problem as if it were any other consumer demand that needed to be met. The company has already stopped using inks and colors that contain heavy metals because these sometimes show up in incinerator ash which in turn may contaminate groundwater. In an effort to reduce packaging, the company has redesigned its Crisco Oil bottles to use 28 percent less plastic.

P&G has also been experimenting with some innovative solutions that ask consumers to get involved. For example, in late 1989, it began test marketing Downy Refill fabric softener in a 21½-ounce milk carton type container. This concentrated solution is mixed with water in a previously purchased plastic Downy bottle to make 64 ounces of fabric softener. The refill carton is labeled "better for the environment . . . less packaging to throw away."

On the recycling front, the company that purchases nearly 200 million pounds of plastic a year for packaging is about to begin selling some sizes of household cleaners and laundry detergents in containers made of recycled polyethylene. Spic'n Span Pine cleaner will be sold in bottles made entirely from recycled glass. In the controversial area of disposable diapers, P&G is supporting research into ways to recycle the diapers as drywall backing and compost.

Can one company's socially responsible behavior make a difference? P&G hopes so. Beyond their own contribution to a cleaner environment, top managers hope to see other companies following their lead in cleaning up the global environment.

Sources: Based on Stratford P. Sherman, "Trashing A $150 Billion Business," *Fortune*, August 28, 1989, 90–98; David Kirkpatrick "Environmentalism," *Fortune*, February 12, 1990, 44–51; Emily T. Smith, "The Greening of Corporate America," *BusinessWeek*, April 23, 1990, 96–103.

Criteria for Evaluating Corporate Social Performance

Once a company is aware of its stakeholders, what criteria can be used to evaluate social performance? One model for evaluating corporate social performance is presented in Exhibit 4.5. The model indicates that total corporate social responsibility can be subdivided into four criteria — economic, legal, ethical, and discretionary responsibilities.[20] The responsibilities are ordered from bottom to top based on their relative magnitude and the frequency with which managers deal with each issue.

Note the similarity between the categories in Exhibit 4.5 and those in Exhibit 4.1. In both cases, ethical issues are located between the areas of legal and freely discretionary responsibilities. Exhibit 4.5 also has an economic category because profits are a major reason for corporations' existence.

Exhibit 4.5
Criteria of Corporate Social Performance

Total Corporate Social Responsibility

Discretionary Responsibility
Ethical Responsibility
Legal Responsibility
Economic Responsibility

Source: Archie B. Carroll, "A Three-Dimensional Conceptual Model of Corporate Performance," *Academy of Management Review* 4 (1979), 499.

Economic Responsibilities

The first criterion of social responsibility is *economic responsibility*. The business institution is, above all, the basic economic unit of society. Its responsibility is to produce the goods and services that society wants and to maximize profits for its owners and shareholders. Economic responsibility, carried to the extreme, is called the *profit-maximizing view*, advocated by Nobel economist Milton Friedman. This view argues that the corporation should be operated on a profit-oriented basis, with its sole mission to increase its profits so long as it stays within the rules of the game.[21]

The purely profit-maximizing view is no longer considered an adequate criterion of performance in Canada, the United States, and Europe. This approach means that economic benefit is the only social responsibility, but it can lead companies into trouble. A notorious example was E. F. Hutton managers' attempt to maximize cash returns from bank deposits. They generated overdrafts in astronomical amounts among hundreds of banks — sometimes totaling more than $1 billion — that in effect created interest-free loans by using checking accounts as sources of loans without the banks' agreement.[22]

Legal Responsibilities

All modern societies lay down ground rules, laws, and regulations that businesses are expected to follow. *Legal responsibility* defines what society deems as important with respect to appropriate corporate behavior.[23] Businesses are expected to fulfill their economic goals within the legal framework. Legal requirements are imposed by local town councils, state legislators, and federal regulatory agencies.

Organizations that knowingly break the law are poor performers in this category. Intentionally manufacturing defective goods or billing a client for work not done is illegal. An example of the punishment given to one company that broke the law is shown in Exhibit 4.6.

Ethical Responsibilities

Ethical responsibility includes behaviors that are not necessarily codified into law and may not serve the corporation's direct economic interests. As described earlier in this chapter, to be *ethical*, organization decision makers should act with equity, fairness, and impartiality, respect the rights of individuals, and provide different treatment of individuals only when relevant to the organization's goals and tasks.[24] *Unethical* behavior occurs when decisions enable an individual or company to gain at the expense of society.

EXHIBIT 4.6
One Company's Punishment for Breaking the Law

Source: Barry C. Groveman and John L. Segal, "Pollution Police Pursue Chemical Criminals," *Business and Society Review* 55 (Fall 1985), 41.

February 12, 1985

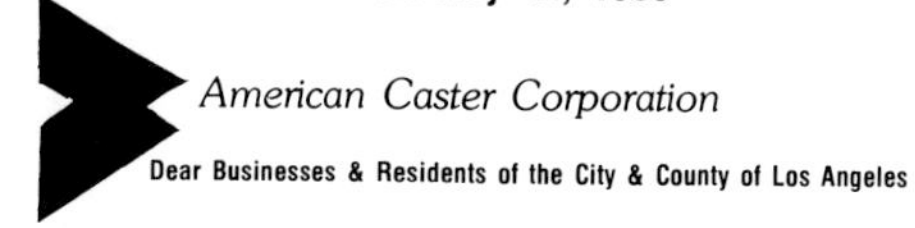

American Caster Corporation
Dear Businesses & Residents of the City & County of Los Angeles

Pollution of our environment has become a crisis.

Intentional clandestine acts of illegal disposal of hazardous waste, or "midnight dumping" are violent crimes against the community.

Over the past 2 years almost a dozen Chief Executive Officers of both large and small corporations have been sent to jail by the L.A. Toxic Waste Strike Force.

They have also been required to pay huge fines; pay for cleanups; speak in public about their misdeeds; and in some cases place ads publicizing their crime and punishment.

THE RISKS OF BEING CAUGHT ARE TOO HIGH—
AND THE CONSEQUENCES IF CAUGHT ARE NOT WORTH IT!

We are paying the price. *TODAY,* while you read this ad our President and Vice President are serving time in *JAIL* and we were forced to place this ad.

PLEASE TAKE THE LEGAL ALTERNATIVE AND PROTECT OUR ENVIRONMENT.

Very Truly Yours,

American Caster Corporation
141 WEST AVENUE 34
LOS ANGELES, CA 90031

When Control Data took a chance by building a plant in Minneapolis' inner city, it performed an ethical act because top management wanted to provide equal opportunity for the disadvantaged. Other businesses had built in the ghetto and failed. Chairman Norris insisted that the plant attempt to be profitable, but the company also wanted to provide jobs to inner-city residents. In this case the ethical goals were compatible with the economic goals, and the company achieved both.[25]

DISCRETIONARY RESPONSIBILITIES

discretionary responsibility Organizational responsibility that is voluntary and guided by the organization's desire to make social contributions not mandated by economics, law, or ethics.

Discretionary responsibility is purely voluntary and guided by a company's desire to make social contributions not mandated by economics, law, or ethics. Discretionary activities include generous philanthropic contributions that offer no payback to the company and are not expected. An example of discretionary behavior occurred when Pittsburgh Brewing Company helped laid-off steelworkers by establishing and contributing to food banks in the Pittsburgh area. It also started a fund-raising program in which people could drink beer with members of the Pittsburgh Steelers for a $5 contribution to their local food

The big heart of Merck & Company is illustrated by giving free supplies of a new drug called Ivermectin to people in Africa, South America, and the Middle East. Ivermectin prevents river blindness, a parasitic infection that affects up to 15 percent of the population of Third World villages. The program could wipe out river blindness in a few years, creating enormous social benefits, but costing Merck millions in lost profits. Merck's *discretionary responsibility* is voluntary and guided by its desire to make social contributions.

bank. Discretionary responsibility is the highest criterion of social responsibility, because it goes beyond societal expectations to contribute to the community's welfare.

Corporate Actions Toward Social Demands

Confronted with a specific social responsibility decision, how might a corporation respond? If a stakeholder such as the local government places a demand on the company, what types of corporate action might be taken? Management scholars have developed a scale of response actions that companies use when a social issue confronts them.[26] These actions are obstructive, defensive, accommodative, and proactive and are illustrated on the continuum in Exhibit 4.7.

Obstructive. Companies that adopt **obstructive responses** deny all responsibility, claim that evidence of wrongdoing is misleading or distorted, and place obstacles to delay investigation. During the Watergate years, such obstruction was labeled *stonewalling*. A. H. Robins Company reportedly used obstructive actions when it received warnings about its Dalkon shield, an intrauterine device. The company built a wall around itself. It stood against all evidence and insisted to the public that the product was safe and effective. The company spared no effort to resist investigation. As word about injuries caused

obstructive response A response to social demands in which the organization denies responsibility, claims that evidence of misconduct is misleading or distorted, and attempts to obstruct investigation.

EXHIBIT 4.7
Corporate Responses to Social Demands

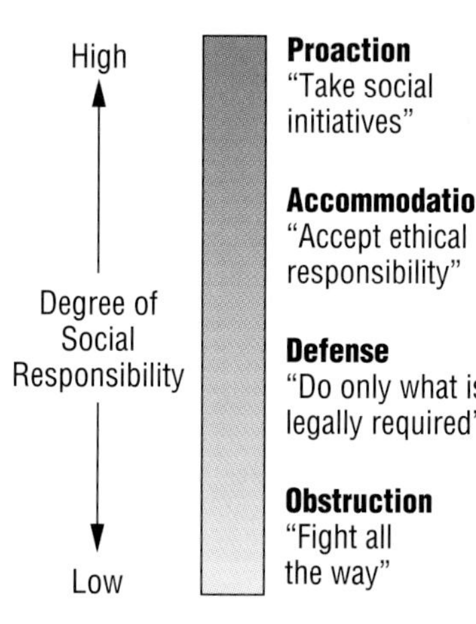

by the Dalkon shield kept pouring in, one attorney was told to search the files and destroy all papers pertaining to the product.[27]

DEFENSIVE. The **defensive response** means that the company admits to some errors of omission or commission. The company cuts its losses by defending itself but is not obstructive. Defensive managers generally believe that "these things happen, but they are nobody's fault." Goodyear adopted a defensive strategy by deciding to keep its South Africa plants open and provided an intelligent argument for why that was the proper action.

ACCOMMODATIVE. An **accommodative response** means that the company accepts social responsibility for its actions, although it may do so in response to external pressure. Firms that adopt this action try to meet economic, legal, and ethical responsibilities. If outside forces apply pressure, managers agree to curtail ethically questionable activities. Exxon's decision to clean up the oil spill in Prince William Sound was an accommodative decision based largely on the public's outcry.

PROACTIVE. The **proactive response** means that firms take the lead in social issues. They seek to learn what is in the public interest and respond without coaxing or pressure from stakeholders. One example of proactive behavior is the Potlatch Corporation. Potlatch makes milk cartons and came up with the idea of printing photographs of missing children on them. The company reported that within days after the Alta-Dena Dairy of Los Angeles placed a missing-kids carton in grocery stores, one of the youngsters returned home.[28] Another proactive response is corporate philanthropy. Many companies, including Miller Brewing, Coca-Cola, and Westinghouse, make generous donations to universities, United Way, and other charitable groups as a way of reaching out and improving society.

These four categories of action are similar to the scale of social performance described in Exhibit 4.5. Obstructiveness tends to occur in firms whose actions are based solely on economic considerations. Defensive organizations are willing to work within the letter of the law. Accommodative organizations respond to ethical pressures. Proactive organizations use discretionary responsibilities to enhance community welfare.

Beech-Nut Nutrition Corporation recently was accused of unethical and socially irresponsible behavior. How would you evaluate its response?

defensive response A response to social demands in which the organization admits to some errors of commission or omission but does not act obstructively.

accommodative response A response to social demands in which the organization accepts—often under pressure—social responsibility for its actions to comply with the public interest.

proactive response A response to social demands in which the organization seeks to learn what is in its constituencies' interest and to respond without pressure from them.

BEECH-NUT NUTRITION CORPORATION • To Beech-Nut feeding babies is a sacred trust. Bottles of fruit juice say, "100% fruit juice." Yet despite these feelings, Beech-Nut was found to have adulterated its best-selling line of apple juice products. Gerome LiCari became suspicious that the concentrate acquired from suppliers was diluted and alerted management, who resisted his information. The top managers were not hardened criminals trying to swindle customers. They were honest and well respected, but under great financial pressure. The cheap concentrate from the new supplier saved millions of dollars and managers simply did not want to recognize that they were receiving a poor

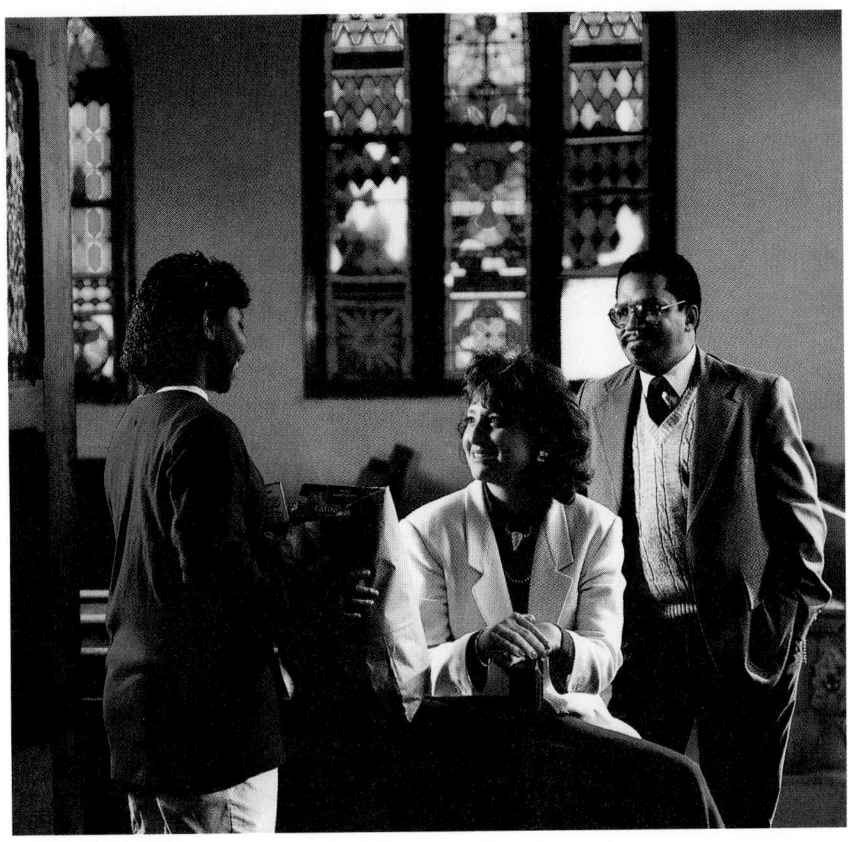

Xerox's *proactive response* to the environment is reflected in its social service leave program, enabling people like Sarah Lampard (center) to deliver truckloads of food to churches that help feed poverty-stricken families. Every Friday, Lampard drops off food to Pastor Robert Woolfork and his assistant LaShawn Marshal, whose church feeds the working poor in Denver's inner-city. Xerox leave-takers receive full pay and benefits, and get their old or equivalent jobs back when they return. Lampard says that her six-month leave from her job as a Xerox account manager to work for a nonprofit food bank cooperative changed her personal values, prompting her to care less for material things and more about helping others.

product. Beech-Nut was running on a shoestring, and enormous financial pressure forced managers to stay with the low-cost supplier.

As suspicions began to circulate, state and federal agencies started investigating. Had Beech-Nut admitted its error, it would have paid a fine and the issue would have been over. But management stonewalled, and this became the issue. So the case changed from civil to criminal, and it became a nightmare. Beech-Nut's strategy was to avoid publicity and stall investigations until it could unload its tainted apple juice products. The case ended with Beech-Nut's two top executives and its concentrate supplier indicted for conspiring to defraud the public. The executives are awaiting trial in New York, and the company paid a record $2 million fine. LiCari testified that the top executives knew about the adulteration problem, but they are pleading innocent.[29]

Managing Company Ethics and Social Responsibility

Many managers are concerned about how to improve the ethical climate and social responsiveness of their companies. They do not want to be surprised or be forced into an obstructionist or defensive position. As one expert on the topic of ethics said, "Management is responsible for creating and sustaining conditions in which people are likely to behave themselves."[30] Managers must take active steps to ensure that the company stays on an ethical footing. Management methods for helping organizations be more responsive include leadership by example, codes of ethics, ethical structures, and supporting whistle-blowers.

LEADERSHIP BY EXAMPLE. The Business Roundtable, an association of chief executives from 250 large corporations, issued a report on ethics policy and practice in companies such as Boeing, Chemical Bank, General Mills, GTE, Xerox, Johnson & Johnson, and Hewlett-Packard.[31] The report concluded that no point emerged more clearly than the crucial role of top management. The chief executive officer and senior managers need to be openly and strongly committed to ethical conduct. They must give constant leadership in renewing the ethical values of the organization. They must be active in communicating that commitment in speeches, directives, company publications, and especially in actions. They must set the tone of the organization by the example of their behavior.

code of ethics A formal statement of the organization's values regarding ethics and social issues.

CODE OF ETHICS. A **code of ethics** is a formal statement of the company's values concerning ethics and social issues; it communicates to employees what the company stands for. Codes of ethics tend to exist in two types: principle-based statements and policy-based statements. *Principle-based statements* are designed to affect corporate culture, define fundamental values, and contain general language about company responsibilities, quality of products, and treatment of employees. General statements of principle are often called corporate credos. Examples are GTE's "Vision and Values," Johnson & Johnson's "The Credo," and Hewlett-Packard's "The HP Way."[32]

Policy-based statements generally outline the procedures to be used in specific ethical situations. These situations include marketing practice, conflicts of interest, observance of laws, proprietary information, political gifts, and equal opportunities. Examples of policy-based statements are Boeing's "Business Conduct Guidelines," Chemical Bank's "Code of Ethics," GTE's "Code of Business Ethics" and "Anti-Trust and Conflict of Interest Guidelines," and Norton's "Norton Policy on Business Ethics."[33]

Codes of ethics state the values or behaviors that are expected and those that will not be tolerated, backed up by management's action. Without top management support, there is little insurance that the code will be followed. Caterpillar's code of ethics covers worldwide business conduct.

CATERPILLAR INC.

• Caterpillar Inc. published A Code of Worldwide Business Conduct and Operating Principles that begins with a clear statement of corporate values. The code is fourteen pages long and covers human relationships, disposal of waste, privacy of information about employees, product quality, sharing of technology, public responsibility, observance of local laws, and inside information. The initial statement of "Business Ethics," quoted below, indicates that Caterpillar expects its employees to display ethical behavior well above that required by law.

> The law is a floor. Ethical business conduct should normally exist at a level well above the minimum required by law.
>
> One of a company's most valuable assets is a reputation for integrity. If that be tarnished, customers, investors, suppliers, employees, and those who sell our products will seek affiliation with other, more attractive companies. We intend to hold a single high standard of integrity everywhere. We will keep our word. We won't promise more than we can reasonably expect to deliver; nor will we make commitments we don't intend to keep.
>
> The goal of corporate communication is the truth—well and persuasively told. In our advertising and other public communications, we will avoid not only untruths, but also exaggeration and overstatement. Caterpillar employees shall not accept costly entertainment or gifts (excepting mementos and novelties of nominal value) from dealers, suppliers, and others with whom we do business. And we don't tolerate circumstances that produce, or reasonably appear to produce, conflict between personal interests of an employee and interests of the company.
>
> We seek long-lasting relationships—based on integrity—with all whose activities touch upon our own.
>
> The ethical performance of the enterprise is the sum of the ethics of the men and women who work here. Thus, we are all expected to adhere to high standards of personal integrity. For example, perjury or any other illegal act ostensibly taken to 'protect' the company is wrong. A sale made because of deception is wrong. A production quota achieved through questionable means or figures is wrong. The end doesn't justify the means.[34]

ETHICAL STRUCTURES. Ethical structures represent the various systems, positions, and programs a company can undertake to implement ethical behavior. An **ethics committee** is a group of executives appointed to oversee company ethics. The committee provides rulings on questionable ethical issues. The ethics committee assumes responsibility for disciplining wrongdoers, which is essential if the organization is to directly influence employee behavior. An **ethical ombudsman** is an official given the responsibility of corporate conscience who hears and investigates ethical complaints and points out potential ethical failures to top management. For example, Boeing has an ethics committee of senior managers that reports directly to the board of directors. Xerox has an ethics ombudsman who reports directly to the CEO.

ethics committee A group of executives assigned to oversee the organization's ethics by ruling on questionable issues and disciplining violators.

ethical ombudsman An official given the responsibility of corporate conscience who hears and investigates ethical complaints and points out potential ethical failures to top management.

Other structures are ethics training programs and hot lines. For example, Chemical Bank has extensive education programs. All new employees attend an orientation session at which they read and sign off on Chemical's code of ethics. Another part of the program provides vice-presidents with training in ethical decision making.[35] The bank has several other seminars, and the CEO is personally involved by stating his commitment to ethical behavior. A hot line is a toll-free number to which employees can report questionable behavior as well as possible fraud, waste, or abuse. For example, Boeing has a toll-free number for employees to report any kind of ethical violation. The LTV Corporation uses a hot line to supplement existing procedures for reporting violations. No reprisals will be taken against anyone using it.

WHISTLE-BLOWING. Employee disclosure of illegal, immoral, or illegitimate practices on the employer's part is called **whistle-blowing.**[36] Anyone in the organization can blow the whistle if he or she detects illegal or immoral organizational activities. Whistle-blowers often report wrongdoings to outsiders, such as regulatory agencies, senators, representatives, or newspaper reporters. In enlightened companies, whistle-blowers can also report to an ethics advocate or ethics committee.

whistle-blowing The disclosure by an employee of illegal, immoral, or illegitimate practices by the organization.

Whistle-blowers must be protected if this is to be an effective ethical safeguard; otherwise, they will suffer and the company may continue its unethical or illegal activity. Helen Guercil noticed something peculiar when she went to work as a secretary to the bankruptcy court of Detroit. The multimillion-dollar cases seemed to be heard by the same judge and handled by the same attorneys. She discovered that one lawyer had been awarded $400,000 in bankruptcy fees from this judge. She blew the whistle when she discovered evidence of special favors bought with lavish trips, expensive gifts, and on-the-job sex. An investigation led to the retirement of two judges, the indictment of the chief clerk, and the conviction of the attorney who had been awarded all the money. However, Helen Guercil received a lot of pressure on the job and was eventually fired.[37]

Do Good Citizens Finish First?

The relationship of a corporation's social responsibility to its financial performance concerns both managers and management scholars and has generated a lively debate.[38] One concern of managers is whether good citizenship will hurt performance — after all, ethics programs cost money. A number of studies have been undertaken to determine whether heightened ethical and social responsiveness increases or decreases financial performance. Studies have provided varying results but generally have found that there is a small positive relationship between social responsibility and financial performance.[39] These findings are very encouraging, because they mean that use of resources for the social good does not hurt the company.

A related finding is that firms founded on spiritual values usually perform very well. These firms succeed because they have a clear mission, employees seldom have alcohol and drug problems, and a strong family orientation exists. One of the largest and most successful companies is Chick-fil-A Inc., which refuses to open on Sunday. The Sunday closing costs some sales and has gotten the chain frozen out of some shopping malls, but the policy helps attract excellent workers that offset any disadvantages.[40]

The important point is that being ethical and socially responsible does not hurt a firm. Enlightened firms can use their discretion to contribute to society's welfare and, in so doing, improve performance.

Summary

Ethics and social responsibility are hot topics for managers in the 1990s. The ethical domain of behavior pertains to values of right and wrong. Ethical decisions and behavior are typically guided by a value system. Four value-based approaches that serve as criteria for ethical decision making are utilitarian, individualism, moral rights, and justice. For an individual manager, the ability to make correct ethical choices will depend on both individual and organizational characteristics. An important individual characteristic is level of moral development. Corporate culture is an organizational characteristic that influences ethical behavior.

Corporate social responsibility concerns a company's values toward society. How can organizations be good corporate citizens? The model for evaluating social performance uses four criteria: economic, legal, ethical, and discretionary. Organizations may use four types of response to specific social pressures: obstructive, defensive, accommodative, and proactive. Evaluating corporate social behavior often requires assessing its impact on organizational stakeholders. Techniques for improving social responsiveness include leadership, codes of ethics, ethical structures, and whistle-blowing. Finally, research suggests that socially responsible organizations perform as well as — and often better than — organizations that are not socially responsible.

MANAGEMENT SOLUTION

General Dynamics' ethics crisis led to a complete reappraisal of its approach to ethics and social responsibility. Chairman Stanley C. Pace started several ethics initiatives. He hired Kent Druyvesteyn as vice-president for ethics. In addition, 39 individuals throughout the company were assigned responsibilities either full time or part time as ethics program directors. Ethics standards were developed and distributed to 103,000 employees. All recipients were asked to sign an acknowledgment card that they had the read the standards and understood that they represented company policy. General Dynamics also developed a 20-page Blue Book that prohibits such things as bribery and kickbacks, and even prescribes who can be bought a meal; it also states that employees cannot accept even a free calendar or pen. To further deepen ethical awareness, training programs entitled "Ethics Awareness Workshops" were held for all employees. Further, 80,000 employees were trained in the specifics of properly filling out time cards and 30,000 employees in travel and business expense reporting. Finally, the corporation established 29 hot lines at various locations, including an 800 number to the corporate office. General Dynamics used all the right techniques, and its forceful ethics program has successfully prevented further trouble.[41]

DISCUSSION QUESTIONS

1. Dr. Martin Luther King, Jr., said, "As long as there is poverty in the world, I can never be rich . . . As long as diseases are rampant, I can never be healthy . . . I can never be what I ought to be until you are what you ought to be." Discuss this quote with respect to the material in this chapter. Would this be true for corporations, too?
2. Environmentalists are trying to pass laws for oil spills that would remove all liability limits for the oil companies. This would punish corporations financially. Is this the best way to influence companies to be socially responsible?
3. Compare and contrast the utilitarian approach with the moral-rights approach to ethical decision making. Which do you believe is the best for managers to follow? Why?
4. Imagine yourself in a situation of being encouraged to inflate your expense account. Do you think your choice would be most affected by your individual moral development or by the cultural values of the company for which you worked? Explain.

5. Is it socially responsible for organizations to undertake political activity or join with others in a trade association to influence the government? Discuss.
6. The criteria of corporate social responsibility suggests that economic responsibilities are of the greatest magnitude, followed by legal, ethical, and discretionary responsibilities. How do these four types of responsibility relate to corporate responses to social demands? Discuss.
7. From where do managers derive ethical values? What can managers do to help define ethical standards for the corporation?
8. Have you ever experienced an ethical dilemma? Evaluate the dilemma with respect to its impact on other people.
9. Lincoln Electric considers customers and employees to be more important stakeholders than shareholders. Is it appropriate for management to define some stakeholders as more important than others? Should all stakeholders be considered equal?
10. Do you think a code of ethics combined with an ethics committee would be more effective than leadership for implementing ethical behavior? Discuss.

MANAGEMENT IN PRACTICE: EXPERIENTIAL EXERCISE

Ethical Work Climates

Answer the following questions by circling the number that best describes an organization for which you have worked.

Add up your score. These questions measure the dimensions of an organization's ethical climate. Questions 1 and 2 measure caring for people, questions 3 and 4 measure lawfulness, questions 5 and 6 measure rules adherence, questions 7 and 8 measure emphasis on financial and company performance, and questions 9 and 10 measure individual independence. Questions 7 and 8 are reversed scored. A total score above 40 indicates a very positive ethical climate. A score from 30 to 40 indicates above-average ethical climate. A score from 20 to 30 indicates a below-average ethical climate, and a score below 20 indicates a very poor ethical climate.

Go back over the questions and think about changes that you could have made to improve the ethical climate in the organization. Discuss with other students what you could do as a manager to improve ethics in future companies you work for.

Source: Based on Bart Victor and John B. Cullen, "The Organizational Bases of Ethical Work Climates," *Administrative Science Quarterly* 33 (1988), 101–125.

	Disagree				Agree
1. What is the best for everyone in the company is the major consideration here.	1	2	3	4	5
2. Our major concern is always what is best for the other person.	1	2	3	4	5
3. People are expected to comply with the law and professional standards over and above other considerations.	1	2	3	4	5
4. In this company, the first consideration is whether a decision violates any law.	1	2	3	4	5
5. It is very important to follow the company's rules and procedures here.	1	2	3	4	5

	Disagree				Agree
6. People in this company strictly obey the company policies.	1	2	3	4	5
7. In this company, people are mostly out for themselves.	5	4	3	2	1
8. People are expected to do anything to further the company's interests, regardless of the consequences.	5	4	3	2	1
9. In this company people are guided by their own personal ethics.	1	2	3	4	5
10. Each person in this company decides for themselves what is right and wrong.	1	2	3	4	5
			Total Score		________

Cases for Analysis

PHILIP MORRIS

The people attending the opening night gala for the Alvin Ailey American Dance Theatre in Washington's Kennedy Center did not breath a word about smoking. They mingled through the invitations-only crowd consisting of politicians, art lovers, and the media, munching on strawberries and salmon, listening to the steel band, and enjoying the show. Except for the free packs of cigarettes being offered, an unknowing observer would never guess that the bash was funded entirely by Philip Morris, the makers of Virginia Slims, Merit, Marlboro, and other cigarette brands.

Philip Morris spends about $13 million a year on art events. It is widely praised for its contributions to smaller arts organizations, often without publicity. It supports institutions such as Carnegie Hall and the Joffrey Ballet.

Those who accept invitations to these events politely refrain from using the occasion to debate smoking. The object is not the promotion of smoking. Philip Morris is selling itself. Philip Morris achieves access to presidents, prime ministers, and the rich and powerful for "the calculated business of portraying themselves as good citizens — and indeed they are not killers," says Charles Simon, a Whitney Museum trustee.

Arts sponsorship by Philip Morris has sparked debate, however. Some people cannot ignore 300,000 deaths in the United States each year attributed to smoking. Nor can they ignore Philip Morris' proclivity toward minority sponsorships where smoking levels are high. But the money-hungry art world does not have many qualms. It does not care where the cash comes from, so long as it keeps flowing. Some claim the art community is prostituting itself with cigarette sponsorship. Others respond by arguing that Philip Morris sells products other than cigarettes. It owns Miller Brewing Company and General Foods Corporation. However, 80 percent of Philip Morris' profits are from cigarette sales. Peter Brown of the Alvin Ailey American Dance Theatre, which received more than $420,000 from Philip Morris in two years, does not seem to mind. He said, "We would accept money from the Mafia if they offered it."

Questions

1. Is Philip Morris acting in a socially responsible way? What criteria of social responsibility are they following?
2. Are art organizations acting in a socially responsible way by accepting this money? Should they take a symbolic stand against cigarette smoking?
3. Do you think this money is well spent by Philip Morris? Does its image improve sufficiently to justify the cost?

Source: Based on Alix M. Freedman, "Tobacco Firms, Pariahs to Many People, Still Are Angels to the Arts," *The Wall Street Journal*, June 8, 1988, 112.

WHAT IS RIGHT?

It is often hard for a manager to determine what is "right" and even more difficult to put ethical behavior into practice. A manager's ethical orientation often brings him or her into conflict with people, policies, customers, or bosses. Consider the following examples:

1. Bob Jones is vice-president of an unprofitable division for a major defense contractor. If the division does not land a major defense contract soon, Bob will be fired and many employees and executives laid off. A close friend of Bob's goes to work for a prosperous defense contractor and gains access to proprietary and confidential information. Bob receives an envelope marked "confidential and personal" that contains cost figures for an air-to-air missile contract on which the competitor is bidding. Bob's division is preparing its own bid, and these data could be enormously valuable. Bob suspects that the envelope is from his friend, because he has helped her a number of times in her career. Bob calls in three subordinates to discuss the issue. The marketing vice-president insists that the data should be used because the industry is so competitive; everyone tries to obtain good information on competitors' plans. The engineering executive insists that the data should not be used; it would certainly be immoral because the government assumes the bids will be made independently, and this could amount to collusion. The personnel executive can go either way but is concerned about the enormous human costs if the division lays off employees. What should Bob do?

2. Jane Smith is president of a $650 million steakhouse chain. This chain, with 650 outlets, is the worst performer among major fast-food restaurants. Jane has been president for 12 years, having gotten this role during a management shakeup following the company's bankruptcy. The steakhouse chain has not kept pace with the environment due to Americans' dietary interest in fish and poultry. McDonald's and other restaurants have taken most of the breakfast business available to fast-food chains. The company is doing so poorly that its stock price is low, and there is a threat of a takeover by U.S.A. Cafes. Jane has gotten the board to approve a golden parachute worth approximately $11 million in case the company is taken over. Five other executives have golden parachutes worth a total of $3 million. Jane's annual salary is $750,000—quite good considering the company's poor performance. The directors, who have been generous with the golden parachutes, are also well compensated. They earn $30,000 a year in their positions ($10,000 more than IBM's directors), and they can retire after 10 years and receive their $30,000 for life. Jane says she deserves the compensation and the golden parachute as CEO of a large corporation. She plans to open new restaurants and change restaurants to be in tune with consumer demand. Is Jane's management of the steakhouse chain ethical?

3. Junior Bolton drives a truck for a local petroleum plant during the summer. He is between his junior and senior years in college. He was lucky to get the job, because few are available in the depressed Southwest. The job pays well, so he will be able to return to college and finish his degree in business administration. As he was filling out the paperwork after his first delivery, the supervisor said, "Be sure you bill the large companies an extra 5 percent for overhead costs." "What do you mean?" Junior asked. "We don't have a charge for overhead." The supervisor responded, "It's been the practice of this company for years. It's the way business is done. It's not illegal, and it helps us make enough profit to stay in business during these hard times." Junior wondered whether he should blow the whistle on what he considered an unethical practice. What should he do?

Questions

1. Use the guidelines described in Manager's Shoptalk: Guidelines for Ethical Decision Making to determine the appropriate behavior in these cases. Do you have all the information you need to make an ethical decision? How would family or friends react to each alternative if you were in these situations?
2. Which approach to ethical decision making—utilitarian, individualism, justice, or moral rights—seems most appropriate for handling these situations?
3. What are the likely consequences for stakeholders if the most ethical option is followed? Does the impact on stakeholders influence the socially desirable response?

Source: The incidents reported in this case are based on Clinton L. Oaks, "David Kingsbury: Employee vs. Employer Problems and Responsibilities," distributed by HBS Case Services; Alan L. Otten, "Ethics on the Job: Companies Alert Employees to Potential Dilemmas," *The Wall Street Journal,* July 14, 1986, 17; Ruth Simon, "Charred Meat," *Forbes,* April 21, 1986, 93; Steve Buckman, "Doing What's Right," *Management Solutions* (June 1986), 24–25.

Video Case

Wal-Mart Stores Inc.

Founded by folksy Sam Walton, Wal-Mart stores has increased sales more than 36 percent per year over the past ten years, reaching $26 billion in 1989. Experts estimate that Wal-Mart will overtake its larger competitors, K mart and Sears, in the next few years. Wal-Mart has yet to enter 23 states and is expected to double the number of stores in its existing territories.

What is the Wal-Mart secret? Nothing more than hard work, clear thinking, and basic values. Sam Walton's original vision was to keep costs at a bare-bones level to be a genuine discounter. In the late 1950s, working with five-and-dime stores, Walton learned that large stores would do well in small communities. People in Berryville, Arkansas, thought a 25,000-square-foot store was huge, and they would drive a distance to shop there. Today Wal-Mart strives to implement the strategy Walton has stressed from the beginning: the "everyday low price" concept. People want value, and Walton is happy to make profits through volume sales rather than high markups.

In 1962, when the first Wal-Mart store opened in Arkansas, the trend in retailing was to shopping centers in cities and suburbs. Small towns were left out. In addition to seeing this opportunity, Walton learned from and observed other companies. He heard of two stores in Minnesota that were self-service, so he took a bus to Worthington, Minnesota, to see how the stores were organized. He adopted the idea and it succeeded. Cutting costs is almost a religion at Wal-Mart, and self-service provided another way to sell retail goods more cheaply. The cost-cutting concept is so popular that Wal-Mart has begun to build rings of stores around major metropolitan areas such as Denver and Dallas.

Wal-Mart's performance is illustrated in key figures. Profitability is 4.1 percent of sales, compared with 2.8 percent at K mart. Each Wal-Mart employee averages $103,000 in sales versus K mart's $82,000. Wal-Mart gets $238 per square foot of sales space versus only $183 at K mart. Fanatic cost cutting enables Wal-Mart to sell a microwave table at $34.94, compared with $89.00 at K mart. The Wal-Mart juggernaut is so powerful that Sears recently adopted a new tactic: lower pricing on some 50,000 items. But Sears cannot reduce its costs anywhere near the level of Wal-Mart.

One Wal-Mart efficiency trick is to do things in-house. Instead of hiring a local electrician to run a security cable through the store during construction, each store manager is taught to run that cable, saving contracting charges. Periodic changes of store locks are performed by in-store personnel instead of hiring outside locksmiths.

Sam Walton provides the leadership spark that makes Wal-Mart go. Considered the wealthiest man in America, he visits stores three days a week. He has no limousine, no guards, no executive parking privileges. His office is unpretentious. He drives to a store and parks in an ordinary customer spot. Walton's personal magnetism sets off employees wherever he goes. When he talks to employees, they cheer and shout after every sentence. He makes employees feel good and gives them pride. He instills a near-religious fervor in his people to produce, be efficient, and most of all, make customers happy. Walton's management team motivates employees with profit sharing, stock ownership, and promotion from within.

Decisions are decentralized to the lowest possible level. The store-within-a-store organizing concept makes the 34 department managers in a store responsible for their own areas. All managers get complete financial information, and departments are ranked by performance. Efficient organizing is also seen in the distribution system, with 150 stores clustered around a distribution center and no store more than a few hours drive away.

Wal-Mart uses up-to-date technology and has automated the flow of merchandise from manufacturers to warehouses to stores. Computers also are used to plan new stores, and stores are being linked into an electronic communication system.

Wal-Mart is forward looking, constantly building on its chain of 1,258 Wal-Mart discount stores across 27 states. By the year 2000, Sam Walton predicts the company will quintuple its sales to approximately $125 billion while doubling the number of stores to about 3,000. While building stores at a rapid pace, plans are to add significantly to the 105 Sam's Wholesale Clubs and the new Supercenter concept.

The wholesale club is half again as large as a typical Wal-Mart, but carries only 3,000 basic items versus 70,000 in a typical store. The Supercenter concept adds groceries to the Wal-Mart store and is attracting lots of business. Walton also introduced Hypermart from Europe, a huge store as big as five football fields. These stores have been so massive that while profitable, they are not meeting expectations and will not be expanded in the future.

Another plan at Wal-Mart is strict buyer-vendor relationships. The buyers are professional and keep vendors at arms length. Buyers are not allowed to have lunch or dinner with vendors unless the buyer pays for it. Moreover, it is a general policy that Wal-Mart does not deal with sales reps, only with the president or sales manager from the company, thereby reducing purchasing costs.

Everyone learns the value of "LTC," company shorthand for low threshold for change. The company listens to all ideas. For example, a marketing student at the University of Florida worked at Wal-Mart one summer. In a distribution center, items were packed by store department, with sporting goods in one box, hardware in another. The student believed this was inefficient because of partially filled boxes, which crushed more easily and wasted boxes. The student proposed mixing materials from different departments to fill boxes headed for a store. The plan went into effect companywide and reduced the number of boxes used by 10 percent, which at Wal-Mart means an annual savings of $600,000.

In the mid-1980s Sam Walton was bothered by the torrent of imports sold through Wal-Mart. He wanted his corporation to start buying merchandise in the United States, provided Wal-Mart could stay competitive. About that time the governor of Arkansas asked for help in saving Farris Fashions, a struggling shirt company in eastern Arkansas. That started Walton's management team thinking about whether they could seek out U.S. manufacturers as suppliers. A few weeks later Wal-Mart ordered 240,000 printed flannel shirts from Farris Fashions that had been previously purchased in the Far East. Farris's payroll has since tripled, and it now provides 75 percent of the flannel shirts sold by Wal-Mart. The company has a close relationship with Wal-Mart, passing along cost savings from the arrangement. Walton has since sent an open letter to U.S. manufacturers inviting them to take part in Wal-Mart's "Buy American" program. Wal-Mart learned that it could affect the cost of goods by giving U.S. manufacturers an opportunity; providing them a commitment; working with them on specifications, quality, and timing; and paying quickly. In many cases the goods cost less than those previously acquired overseas.

The major complaint leveled against Wal-Mart has come from newspapers and Chambers of Commerce in small towns where Wal-Mart has located. The Wal-Mart store is so competitive that downtown hardware stores, drugstores, clothing stores, and the like often go out of business. The decay in the downtown core and the loss of jobs and income destroys the community hub. New Wal-Mart jobs are fewer than those lost. Wal-Mart has not responded to requests from towns not to build a store there, believing that good merchandise provided efficiently is best for everyone.

Wal-Mart sees itself in a partnership with manufacturers, workers, and customers. Manufacturers have a ready outlet, workers get to share in the profits, and customers get goods at inexpensive prices.

Discussion Questions

1. To what extent are the four management functions illustrated at Wal-Mart? What about the concepts of efficiency and effectiveness? Discuss.
2. What historical trends and forces have contributed to Wal-Mart's success? What management perspectives are illustrated in this case?
3. Is Wal-Mart a socially responsible company? What about the loss of jobs and businesses in cities where it locates?
4. How would you characterize the corporate culture of Wal-Mart? Is Sam Walton a symbolic manager? Discuss.

Source: Kevin Kelly, "Wal-Mart Gets Lost in the Vegetable Aisle," *Business Week*, May 28, 1990, 48; "Great News: A Recession," *Forbes*, January 8, 1990, 194; Sharon Reier, "CEO of the Decade," *Financial World*, April 4, 1989, 56–62; "Wal-Mart Rolls Out its Supercenters," *Chain Store Age Executive*, December 1988, 18–19; Michael Barrier, "Walton's Mountain," *Nation's Business*, April 1988, 18–25; David Wilson, *The Wall Street Journal*, June 5, 1990.

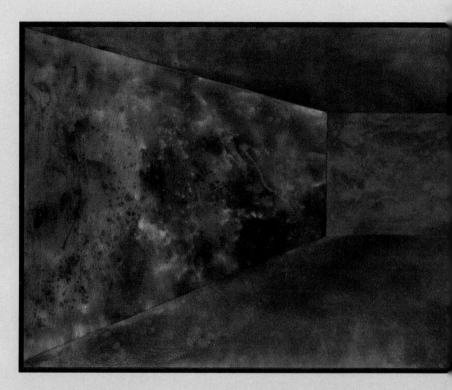

Ron Davis, *Two Deep Rectangles,* 1971, epoxy on fiberglass, 56 × 138 in. (142.2 × 350.5 cm). Security Pacific Corporation Collection.

PART 2

PLANNING

Begun in 1970 and containing over 12,000 works of art, the Security Pacific corporate collection is one of the finest in the nation. Approximately half of the pieces in the collection are by artists from California, Security Pacific's home base. The rest of the collection comprises contemporary works in all media by national and international artists with a selection of historical tapestries. Security Pacific displays its collection in its administrative and banking offices worldwide.

CHAPTER 5

Organizational Goal Setting and Planning

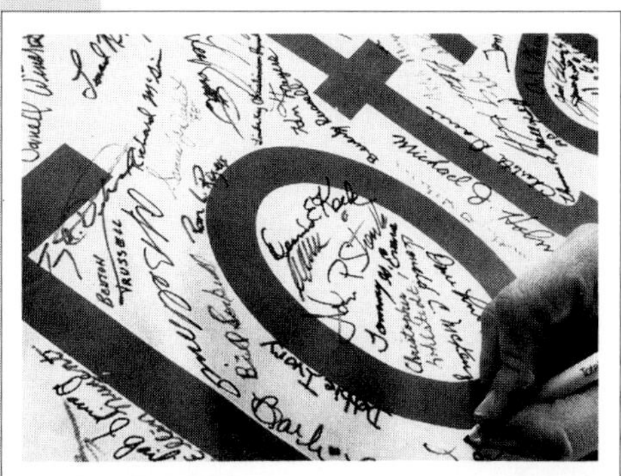

Chapter Outline

Learning Objectives

After studying this chapter, you should be able to:

- Define goals and plans and explain the relationship between them.
- Explain the concept of organizational mission and how it influences goal setting and planning.
- Describe the types of goals an organization should have and why they resemble a hierarchy.
- Define the characteristics of effective goals.
- Explain the behavioral approaches to handling multiple and conflicting goals.
- Explain the difference between single-use plans and standing plans.
- Describe how responsibility can be allocated to accomplish planning and goal setting.
- Examine the barriers to the organization's planning process.

Management Problem

A few years ago, when the price of oil was $28 a barrel and rising, the planning group for the Royal Dutch/Shell companies faced the prospect of planning for bad times. No manager at Shell believed that oil prices could possibly decline, nor did managers wish to consider negative scenarios or contingencies. After all, Shell was prospering. The planning group, on the other hand, felt a responsibility to make managers consider, "What will we do if it happens?" for both higher and lower oil prices. The planning group believed senior managers should start learning about a world of $15 oil as well as $30 oil. Planning for these possibilities would facilitate Shell's learning and adaptation by anticipating new environmental conditions.[1]

If you were a member of the planning group at Shell, how would you engage senior executives in the planning process? How would you get them to anticipate and plan responses to a world of $15 oil?

The senior managers at Shell are not unusual. They do not want to spend time contemplating unlikely future events and developing responses to them. Yet one of the responsibilities of management is to decide where they want the organization to be in the future and how to get it there.

In some organizations, typically small ones, planning is informal. In others, managers follow a well-defined planning framework. The company establishes a basic mission and develops formal goals and strategic plans for carrying it out. Each year organizations such as Shell, IBM, Royal LaPaige, Mazda, and United Way undertake a strategic planning exercise — reviewing their missions, goals, and plans to meet environmental changes or the expectations of important stakeholders such as the community, owners, or stockholders.

Of the four management functions — planning, organizing, leading, and controlling — described in Chapter 1, planning is considered the most important. Everything else stems from planning. Yet planning is also the most controversial management function. Planning cannot read an uncertain future. Planning cannot tame a turbulent environment. Consider the following comment by a noted authority on planning:

> Most corporate planning is like a ritual rain dance: it has no effect on the weather that follows, but it makes those who engage in it feel that they are in control. Most discussions of the role of models in planning are directed at improving the dancing, not the weather.[2]

In this chapter, we are going to explore the process of planning and whether it can help bring needed rain.

Special attention is given to goals and goal setting, for that is where planning starts. Then the types of plans organizations can use to achieve those goals are discussed. In Chapter 6, we examine a special type of planning — strategic planning — and a number of strategic options managers can use in a competitive environment. In Chapters 7 and 8, we look at management decision making. Proper decision-making techniques are crucial to selecting the organization's goals, plans, and strategic options.

OVERVIEW OF GOALS AND PLANS

goal A desired future state that the organization attempts to realize.

plan A blueprint specifying the resource allocations, schedules, and other actions necessary for attaining goals.

planning The act of determining the organization's goals and the means for achieving them.

Goals and plans have become general concepts in our society. A **goal** is a desired future state that the organization attempts to realize.[3] Goals are important because organizations exist for a purpose and goals define and state that purpose. A **plan** is a blueprint for goal achievement and specifies the necessary resource allocations, schedules, tasks, and other actions. Goals specify future ends; plans specify today's means. The term **planning** usually incorporates both ideas; it means determining the organization's goals and defining the means for achieving them. Consider PPG (formerly Pittsburgh Plate & Glass Company). In 1984, PPG's return on equity was 15.7 percent. Chairman Vincent A. Sarni and his senior executives established goals for 1994 of a return on equity of 18 percent, combined with annual sales of $10 billion. Their plan for achieving these goals was to obtain two-thirds of the company's sales from high-profit products. Low-profit operations were put on the sales block. Another part of the plan was to raise R&D spending from 3.5 percent of sales to 4.8 percent. The ten-year goals are ambitious, designed to make PPG one of the most profitable corporations in America, but senior management has a plan it believes will succeed.[4]

objective A specific short-term target for which measurable results can be obtained.

Exhibit 5.1 illustrates the relationship between organizational goals and plans. The planning process starts with a formal mission that defines the basic purpose of the organization. Then companywide strategic goals are determined and form the basis for the organization's lower-level objectives. The term **objective** is often used interchangeably with *goal* but usually refers to specific short-term targets for which measurable results can be obtained. The organization's goals and plans exist at three levels: the strategic (company) level, the tactical (divisional) level, and the operational (department) level.[5] Strategic goals influence the tactical objectives, which in turn influence operational objectives because goals and objectives must support one another.

THE IMPORTANCE OF GOALS AND PLANS[6]

Developing explicit goals and plans provides several important benefits for an organization.

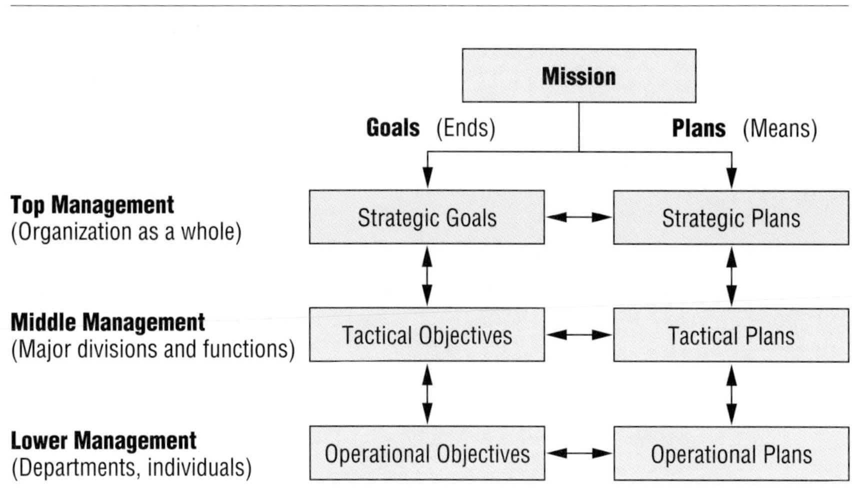

EXHIBIT 5.1
Relationship between Goals and Plans in the Organizational Planning Process

SOURCE OF MOTIVATION AND COMMITMENT. A goal statement describes the purpose of the organization or subunit to employees. A goal provides the "why" of an organization's or subunit's existence. A plan tells employees what actions to undertake. A plan tells "how" to achieve the goal. Goals and plans facilitate employees' identification with the organization and help motivate them by reducing uncertainty and clarifying what they should accomplish.

GUIDES TO ACTION. Goals and plans provide a sense of direction. They focus attention on specific targets and direct employee efforts toward important outcomes.

RATIONALE FOR DECISIONS. Through goal setting and planning, managers learn what the organization is trying to accomplish. They can make decisions to ensure that internal policies, roles, performance, structure, products, and expenditures will be made in accordance with desired outcomes. Decisions throughout the organization will be in alignment with the plan.

STANDARD OF PERFORMANCE. Because goals define desired outcomes for the organization, they also serve as performance criteria. They provide a standard of assessment. If an organization wishes to grow by 15 percent, and actual growth is 17 percent, managers will have exceeded their prescribed standard. If PPG achieves a return on equity of 17 percent and sales of $9 billion in 1994, Chairman Sarni's standard will not be met.

The overall planning process prevents managers from thinking merely in terms of day-to-day activities. When organizations drift away from goals and plans, they typically get into trouble. This occurred at the New York City Transit Authority. But new management was able to implement a strong planning system, illustrating the power of planning to improve organizational performance.

The *goal* of quality is a source of motivation and commitment for the 14,000 Northrop men and women working on the B-2 Stealth Advanced Technology bomber program. The B-2 is the most sophisticated aircraft weapon system ever conceived requiring a ten-year development program. This photo shows a detail of a giant two-story-high scroll bearing the signature of every employee on the B-2 team. It hangs above the B-2 assembly line to symbolize the goal of total commitment to quality. The slogan on the pen reads "Total Quality on the B-2 Begins with Me."

NEW YORK CITY TRANSIT AUTHORITY • A short time ago, the New York City Transit Authority was plagued by track fires, the failure of the Flexible Model 870 bus fleet, and the widespread perception of rampant subway crime. The transit authority was trapped in a straitjacket of civil service regulations and union requirements that affected nearly 95 percent of its 5,000 supervisors and 50,000 employees.

When Robert Kiley took over as chairman of the New York City Transit Authority's parent — the Metropolitan Transit Authority — his initial steps were to define several goals. The transit authority's mission was clear: Provide transportation services for New York City. Within that overall mission, Kiley charted a course for the New York City Transit Authority in terms of three strategic goals:

1. A sustained rate of capital investment that would get the transit systems into good repair and keep them there.
2. A predictable, assured source of operating revenue.
3. An emphasis on recruiting, training, and rewarding good managers and workers and a commitment to shed the anachronistic, demoralizing work practices of the past.

David L. Gunn assumed the presidency of the New York City Transit Authority. He and his new management team developed a system of tactical and operational objectives. They committed themselves to accomplishing more than 340 tactical objectives by the end of the year, including

1. 1,720 (28 percent) of the 6,125 subway cars cleaned, graffiti free, and kept that way.
2. 1,169 (31 percent) of the 3,835 buses free of graffiti and body damage and kept that way.
3. Working lights and loudspeakers, climate control, accurate destination signs, and readable maps on 90 percent of the subway fleet.
4. 450 subway cars overhauled.
5. Over 95 percent of requests for replacement parts filled promptly.
6. Twice-weekly inspections of all 706 miles of subway track and 126 miles of yard track.

The system of goals and objectives paved the way for new plans. One plan was to create positions that would be exempt from union and civil service protection. Plans were made to hire up to 1,200 exempt management personnel to meet strategic goal 3. With the influx of new managerial personnel, plans were implemented to decentralize decision making so that managers have the authority to meet their objectives. Plans were also made to increase training funds by 27 percent and employee training time by 29 percent.

These goals and plans laid the foundation for rapid operating improvements in the New York City Transit Authority. Planning gave new direction to supervisors and employees. A demoralized, reluctant work force was transformed into one that had a place to go and knew how to get there.[7]

GOALS IN ORGANIZATIONS

Setting goals starts with top managers. The overall planning process begins with a mission statement and strategic goals for the organization as a whole.

ORGANIZATIONAL MISSION

As Exhibit 5.1 illustrated, at the top of the goal hierarchy is the **mission** — the organization's reason for existence. The mission describes the organization's values, aspirations, and reason for being. The formal **mission statement** is a broadly stated definition of basic business scope and operations that distinguishes the organization from others of a similar type.[8] The content of a mission statement often focuses on the market and customers and identifies desired fields of endeavor. Some mission statements describe company characteristics such as corporate values, product quality, location of facilities, and attitude toward employees. Mission statements often reveal the company's philosophy as well as purpose. The mission statement for a British company called BBA Group is presented in Exhibit 5.2. BBA builds industrial textile products and automobile components, employs 25,000 people, and enjoys $1.6 billion sales. The colorful language and imagery leaves no doubt about

mission The organization's reason for existence.

mission statement A broadly stated definition of the organization's basic business scope and operations that distinguish it from similar types of organizations.

EXHIBIT 5.2
BBA GROUP MISSION STATEMENT

BBA — A CORPORATE PHILOSOPHY

The inertia of history is a powerful influence on corporate philosophy. BBA in its 103 years of existence has strayed little from:
i. Yorkshire paternalism
ii. Weaving of heavy textiles
iii. Friction technology via woven or pressed resin media
The philosophy of BBA for the next few years will be to adapt rather than abandon the inert.

MANAGEMENT
(a) Grit and gumption are preferable to inertia and intellect.
(b) The Victorian work ethic is not an antique.
(c) One man can only serve one master, to whom he is responsible for a minimum number of succinctly defined tasks.
(d) Most companies owned or yet to be acquired possess adequate people waiting to be transformed by dedicated leadership.
(e) The effectiveness of an organization is in inverse proportion to the number of hierarchical layers.

MARKETS
We shall concentrate in markets where:
(a) The products are in a state of maturity or decline, "Sunset Industries."
(b) The scale of our presence in a market segment will allow price leadership.
(c) The capital cost of market entry is high.
(d) Fragmentation of ownership on the supply side facilitates rapid earnings growth by acquisition of contribution flows.

MONEY
(a) The longer run belongs to Oscar Wilde, who is dead.
(b) The key macro and micro variables of our business are so dynamic that poker becomes more predictable than planning and reactivity more profitable than rumination.
(c) Budgets are personal commitments made by management to their superiors, subordinates, shareholders and their self respect.
(d) The cheapest producer will win.
(e) The investment of money on average return of less than three points above market should be restricted to Ascot.
(f) Gearing should not exceed 40%. The location from which funds emanate should be matched to the location from which the profit stream permits their service.
(g) We are not currency speculators, even when we win.
(h) Tax is a direct cost to the business and, accordingly, should be eschewed.
(i) Victorian thrift is not an antique.
(j) Nothing comes free, cheap assets are often expensive utilities.

MONDAY
Our tactic is to:
i. Increase the metabolic rate of BBA through directed endeavour.
ii. To increase profit margins by drastic cost reduction.
iii. To massage and thereby extend the life cycle of the products in which we are engaged.
iv. To become market dominant in our market niches by:
  (a) outproducing the competition.
  (b) transforming general markets where we are nobody to market niches where we are somebody.
  (c) buying competitors.
v. Use less money in total and keep more money away from the tax man and the usurer.
vi. Avoid the belief that dealing is preferable to working.
vii. Go home tired.

MAYBE
(a) The replication of our day to day tactic provides long term growth.
(b) We need to address 'Monday' this week and what our reaction will be to what may be on 'Monday' for the next three years.
(c) Three years is, in the current environment, the limit of man's comprehension of what may be.
(d) Long term growth necessitates:
  i. Resource — notably men and money.
  ii. Sustained performance rather than superficial genius.

Source: Reproduced by permission of the BBA Group PLC, the diversified multinational group serving automotive, industrial, and aviation markets.

EXHIBIT 5.3
Eight Types of Strategic Goals

- **Market standing:** Objectives indicating where a company wants to be relative to its competitors with respect to market share and competitive niche.
- **Innovation:** Objectives indicating management's commitment to the development of new methods of operation and new products.
- **Productivity:** Objectives outlining targeted levels of production efficiency.
- **Physical and financial resources:** Objectives pertaining to use, acquisition, and maintenance of capital and monetary resources.
- **Profitability:** Objectives specifying the level of profit and other indicators of financial performance.
- **Managerial performance and development:** Objectives specifying rates and levels of managerial productivity and growth.
- **Worker performance and attitude:** Objectives delineating expected rates of workers' productivity and positive attitudes.
- **Public responsibility:** Objectives indicating the company's responsibilities to its customers and society.

Source: Based on Peter F. Drucker, *The Practice of Management* (New York: Harper & Brothers, 1954), 65–83.

BBA's market niche, work ethic, and preference for doing rather than contemplating.

Many companies' mission statements are short and straightforward, describing basic business activities and purposes. An example of this type of mission statement is that of Columbia Gas System, a gas transmission and distribution company:

> Columbia Gas System, through its subsidiaries, is active in pursuing opportunities in all segments of the natural gas industry and in related energy resource development. Exemplified by Columbia's three-star symbol, the separately managed companies work to benefit: *system stockholders* — through competitive return on their investment; *customers* — through efficient, safe, reliable service; and *employees* — through challenging and rewarding careers.[9]

Because of mission statements such as BBA's and Columbia's, employees, as well as customers, suppliers, and stockholders, know the company's stated purpose.

TYPES OF GOALS

Within the organization there are three levels of goals — strategic goals, tactical objectives, and operational objectives — as described in Exhibit 5.1.[10]

STRATEGIC GOALS. Broad statements of where the organization wants to be in the future are called **strategic goals.** They pertain to the organization as a whole rather than to specific divisions or departments. Strategic goals sometimes are called *official goals,* because they are the stated intentions of what the organization wants to achieve.

strategic goals Broad statements of where the organization wants to be in the future; pertain to the organization as a whole rather than to specific divisions or departments.

What do strategic goals cover? Peter Drucker suggests that business organizations' goals should encompass more than profits, because profits alone lead to short-term thinking. He suggests that organizations focus on eight content areas: market standing; innovation; productivity; physical and financial resources; profitability; managerial performance and development; worker performance and attitude; and public responsibility.[11] A description of each goal is given in Exhibit 5.3.

Ted Henry has good reason to celebrate. He and his 346 coworkers have boosted throughput by over 25,000 barrels a day in this Texaco refinery as part of a massive quality improvement program. Texaco's strategic goals of *innovation, productivity,* and *worker performance and attitude,* are reflected in this 33 percent increase in volume in the Puget Sound Plant. Every employee was asked to try any reasonable idea to improve job results, surpassing the goal of 100,000 barrels a day production. Achieving these strategic goals enables Texaco to achieve its mission of being the "best company in the business, and one of the most admired."

Drucker's first five goal areas relate to the tangible, measurable aspect of the organization and its operations. The last three are more subjective and personal. Most organizations have explicit strategic goals in some but not all of these areas. For example, Columbia Gas System set the following four strategic goals for the 1986 to 1990 period to fit the mission described earlier:

1. Meet stockholders' expectations as to total return.
2. Have access to reasonable amounts of capital at reasonable costs at all times.
3. Provide for efficient management of and planned growth in stockholders' equity.
4. Insure the orderly succession of System officers, and enhance employee performance.[12]

These goals pertain to profitability and stockholders' return, efficient management, the acquisition of financial resources, and manager/employee performance and development.

TACTICAL OBJECTIVES. The results that major divisions and departments within the organization intend to achieve are defined as **tactical objectives.** These objectives apply to middle management and describe what major subunits must do in order for the organization to achieve its overall goals. For example, one tactical objective for Columbia Gas was to "regain a long-term debt rating by the end of 1988." This tactical objective pertains to strategic goal 2 regarding access to reasonable amounts of capital. Achieving this objective will increase the organization's ability to borrow money at a reasonable rate. The Winning Moves box tells how Timex used strategic goals and tactical objectives to reassert itself in the wristwatch market.

OPERATIONAL OBJECTIVES. The specific results expected from departments, work groups, and individuals are the **operational objectives.** They are precise and measurable. "Process 150 sales applications each week," "achieve 90 percent of deliveries on time," "reduce overtime by 10 percent next month," and "develop two new elective courses in accounting" are examples of operational objectives.

tactical objectives Objectives that define the outcomes that major divisions and departments must achieve in order for the organization to reach its overall goals.

operational objectives Specific, measurable results expected from departments, work groups, and individuals within the organization.

HIERARCHY OF OBJECTIVES

Effectively designed organizational goals and objectives fit into a hierarchy; that is, the achievement of objectives at lower levels permits the attainment of higher-level goals. This is called a *means-ends chain* because lower-level objectives lead to accomplishment of higher-level goals. Operational objectives lead to the achievement of tactical objectives, which in turn lead to the attainment of strategic goals. Strategic goals typically are the responsibility of top management, tactical objectives that of middle management, and operational objectives that of first-line supervisors and workers.

An example of a goal hierarchy is illustrated in Exhibit 5.4. Note how the strategic goal of "excellent service to customers" translates into "open one new sales office" and "respond to customer inquiries within 2 hours" at lower management levels.

EXHIBIT 5.4
Hierarchy of Objectives for a Manufacturing Organization

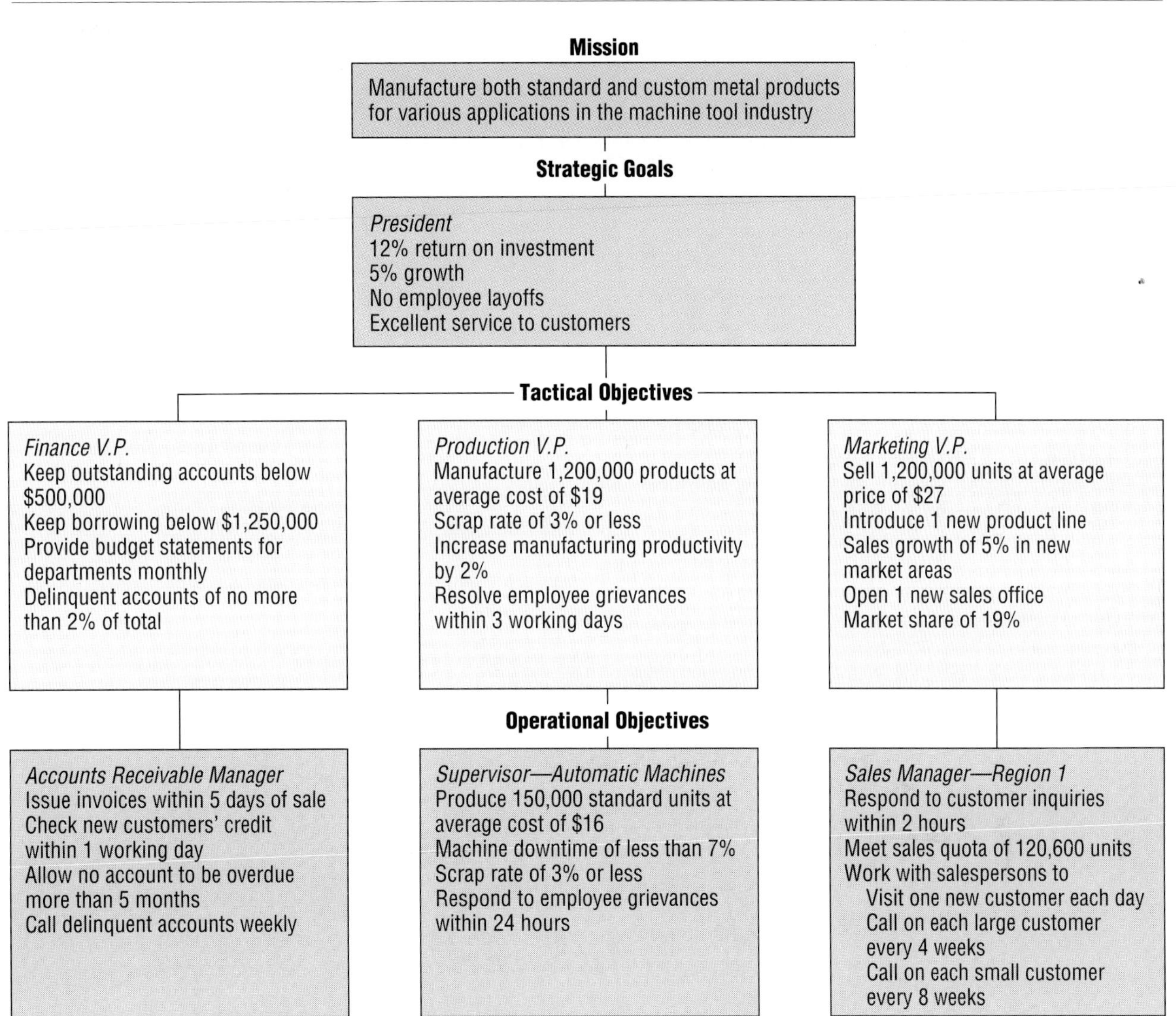

CRITERIA FOR EFFECTIVE GOALS

To insure goal-setting benefits for the organization, certain characteristics and guidelines should be adopted. The characteristics of both goals and the goal-setting process are listed in Exhibit 5.5.

WINNING MOVES

TIMEX

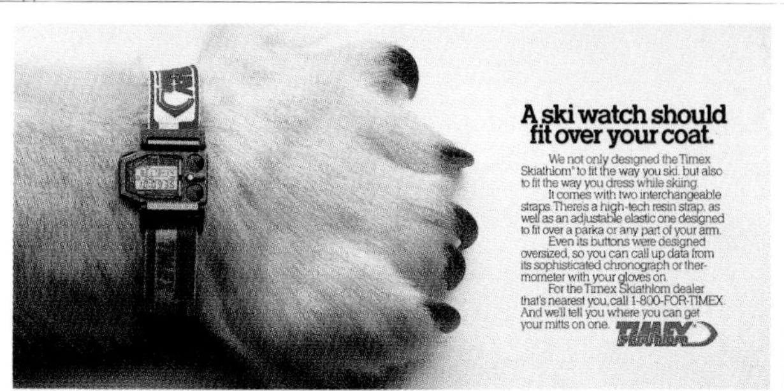

A ski watch should fit over your coat.
We not only designed the Timex Skiathlom® to fit the way you ski, but also to fit the way you dress while skiing.
It comes with two interchangeable straps. There's a high-tech resin strap, as well as an adjustable elastic one designed to fit over a parka or any part of your arm.
Even its buttons were designed oversized, so you can call up data from its sophisticated chronograph or thermometer with your gloves on.
For the Timex Skiathlom dealer that's nearest you, call 1-800-FOR-TIMEX. And we'll tell you where you can get your mitts on one.
TIMEX

In the late 1970s Timex was running down. Timex pushed durability in cheap watches, but consumers became more interested in style. Timex's claim that its watches "take a lickin' and keep on tickin'" did not mean much to consumers in 1990.

Then Timex defined a bold strategic plan. Its strategic goal was to recapture lost market share. Its strategic plan was to appeal to young customers, many of whom were health nuts and who purchased zippy watches from competitors that had hot colors and striking designs.

Timex's tactical objective was to target amateur athletes. Says the marketing vice-president, "We asked athletes exactly what they wanted on a watch, and then we gave it to them." The operational plan was to bring out the Triathlon watch that could clock swimming, bicycle riding, and running. The watch sold 400,000 units its first year. That was exciting because there are only some 300,000 triathletes in the United States. Without realizing it, Timex had caught the wave of sports chic. Most people cannot do a triathlon, but they want to look as if they can by sporting the triathlon watch.

Timex lost no time exploiting this idea. It developed a watch for skiers that measures temperature, a watch for aerobics fanatics that takes the wearer's pulse rate, and a Victory watch aimed at sailors. Coming up are a fisherman's watch and a biker's model.

Timex's advertising is as chic as its watches. The ad for *Ski* magazine shows a polar bear's wrist sporting the ski watch, illustrating how it will fit over any sleeve. Timex's remarkably successful goal achievement can be traced directly to its clear mission and planning. Timex is not selling a timepiece, it is selling fun and fitness, which is what consumers want.

Source: Based on Christie Brown, "Sweat Chic," *Forbes*, September 5, 1988, 96–101.

GOAL CHARACTERISTICS

The following characteristics pertain to organizational goals at the strategic, tactical, and operational levels.

EXHIBIT 5.5
Characteristics of Effective Goal Setting

Goal Characteristics
- Specific and measurable
- Cover key result areas
- Challenging but realistic
- Defined time period
- Linked to rewards

Goal-Setting Behavior
- Coalition building
- Participation

SPECIFIC AND MEASURABLE. When possible, goals should be expressed in quantitative terms, such as increasing profits by 2 percent, decreasing scrap by 1 percent, or increasing average teacher effectiveness ratings from 3.5 to 3.7. Not all goals can be expressed in numerical terms, but vague goals and objectives have little motivating power for employees. At the top of the organization, goals often are qualitative as well as quantitative. John Reed, CEO of Citicorp, has defined both quantitative and qualitative goals for his organization, including:

- Trim work force from 20,000 to 17,000.
- Clean up loan portfolio; reduce writeoffs.
- Wire 90 trading rooms around the globe.
- Build a merger and acquisition finance group.[13]

Each goal is precisely defined and allows for measurable progress.

COVER KEY RESULT AREAS. Goals cannot be set for every aspect of employee behavior or organizational performance; if they were, their sheer number would render them meaningless. Instead, managers should identify a few key result areas — perhaps up to four or five for any organizational department or job. Key result areas are those activities that contribute most to company performance.[14] For example, Rospatch Corporation makes garment labels, and senior managers have specified four goals for financial key results: 5 percent return on sales, 10 percent return on assets, 15 percent return on equity, and 20 percent compound annual growth rate.[15] The marketing department at ALLTEL, a telephone company covering several regions in the United States, identified the following key result areas for which goals were specified: identify emerging areas of service opportunities, assist regions with meaningful information to support current marketing programs, improve marketing of existing products, and develop a strategic market plan based on customer needs, competitive studies, and market trends.[16]

The employees of Indiana National Corporation demonstrated their dedication by generating $112 million in new deposits during the ten-week "You Make the Difference" campaign, an employee incentive program for generating deposits. The overall goal was to raise more than $50 million in new deposits. This program included all five goal characteristics — *specific and measurable, cover key result areas, challenging but realistic, defined time period,* and *linked to rewards.*

CHALLENGING BUT REALISTIC. Goals should be challenging but not unreasonably difficult. One value of limiting operational goals to key result areas is that these offer important challenges to employees. If a goal is too difficult, employees may give up; if too easy, employees may not feel motivated.[17] Managers should also ensure that goals are set within the existing resource base and not beyond departments' time, equipment, and financial resources.

DEFINED TIME PERIOD. Goals and objectives should specify the time period over which they will be achieved. A time period is a deadline specifying the date on which goal attainment will be measured. A goal of revising a company's job classification system could have a deadline such as June 30, 1992. If a strategic goal involves a two-to-three-year time horizon, specific dates for achieving parts of it can be set up. For example, strategic sales goals could be established on a three-year time horizon, with a $100 million target in year 1, a $129 million target in year 2, and a $165 million target in year 3.

LINKED TO REWARDS. The ultimate impact of goals depends on the extent to which salary increases, promotions, and awards are based on goal achievement. People who attain goals should be rewarded. Rewards give meaning and significance to goals and help commit employees to achieving goals. Failure to attain goals often is due to factors outside employees' control. Failure to achieve a financial goal may be associated with a drop in market demand due to industry recession; thus, an employee could not be expected to reach it. Nevertheless, a positive reward may be appropriate if the employee partially achieved goals under difficult circumstances.[18]

GOAL-SETTING BEHAVIOR

In April 1986, President Reagan and the White House staff had decided to retaliate against terrorists in Libya. The specifics of the strike took two to three weeks to hammer out because of major disagreements among cabinet and staff members on which targets to bomb and how to carry out the mission.[19] Although the overall purpose and mission were defined, establishing strategic goals and tactical objectives was both a political and a social process.

Conflict often occurs during goal setting because key managers disagree over objectives. Yet for goals to be effective, commitment is essential. Two techniques for achieving commitment to goals are coalition building and participation.

coalition An informal alliance among managers who support a specific goal.

COALITION BUILDING. An informal alliance among managers who support a specific goal is called a **coalition.** *Coalition building* is the process of forming alliances among managers. In other words, a manager who supports a specific goal, such as increasing the corporation's growth by acquiring another company, talks informally to other executives and tries to persuade them to support the goal. Coalition building involves negotiation and bargaining. Without a coalition, a powerful individual or group could derail the goal-setting process. Coalition building gives managers an opportunity to contribute to the goal-setting process, enhancing their commitment to the goals that are finally adopted.[20]

Coalition building occurs most often at the upper levels of the organization, where uncertainty is high. For example, Compaq Computer Corporation, described as a Theory Y company in Chapter 2, specializes in coalition building. Compaq was slow to develop a laptop computer, because designs were turned down three times because one or more managers did not agree with the prototype. But when the 286-SLT laptop was finally accepted by consensus, it was perfect for the market and was an immediate smash. Robert Forsberg, president of Mupac Corporation, facilitates coalition building through ever-widening circles of managers. He starts with senior managers who set strategic goals and then broadens the circle of participation to include department managers. Moreover, the entire management team participates in brainstorming sessions to plan how to achieve the targets in Mupac's five-year plan. The final action plans are adopted by consensus.[21]

PARTICIPATION. At lower levels of the organization, managers and supervisors try to adopt objectives that are consistent with strategic goals. However, if operational objectives are prescribed in a one-way top-down fashion, supervisors and employees may not adopt the goals as their own. A more effective process is to encourage subordinates to participate in the goal-setting process. Managers can describe the organization's goals and act as counselors by helping subordinates sort out various goal options, discussing whether the objectives are realistic and specific, and determining whether objectives are congruent with organizational goals. Goal discussions between superior and subordinate take into consideration the subordinate's interests and abilities.[22] For example, Joseph Romanowski, CEO of Machinery Systems Inc., personally talks to everyone within his 85-employee organization to ask them to set operational objectives consistent with long-term strategic goals. He found that employees simply are not committed to goals he imposes on them.[23]

DEVELOPING PLANS FOR ATTAINING GOALS

Defining organizational goals and objectives is the first step in the planning process. The second step — which is equally important — is to define plans for meeting objectives. Targets mean little if managers do not map out the path-

One of Alcan Aluminum Limited's significant goals is to support high standards of safety and occupational health. Alcan's desire to facilitate worker *participation* and compliance is illustrated by these maintenance operators at Alcan Brazil's Ouro Preto plant. This daily discussion of safety objectives is part of the plant's accident prevention program.

ways to them. Managers often find the development of plans difficult. One study found that seven out of ten companies did not carry strategy formulation much beyond general statements of objectives.[24] Managers found it difficult to specify how to reach future targets. Yet detailed planning is an important component of future performance.

In developing plans for attaining goals, managers have several types of plans at their disposal, including strategic plans, tactical plans, operational plans, single-use plans, standing plans, and contingency plans.

Strategic Plans

strategic plans The action steps by which an organization intends to attain its strategic goals.

Strategic plans define the action steps by which a company intends to attain strategic goals. The strategic plan is the blueprint that defines the organizational activities and resource allocations — in the form of cash, personnel, space, and facilities — required for meeting those targets.[25]

Strategic planning tends to be long term and may define organizational action steps from two to five years into the future. The purpose of the strategic plan is to turn organizational goals into realities over that time period. For example, Bob Wright, new CEO of NBC, adopted a goal of expansion in an industry where costs have been cut to the bone and growth is slow. The plan NBC's executives adopted involves three parts: buy stations, such as WTVJ-TV in Miami, and perhaps two UHF outlets; expand the audience through cable TV, such as offering sports or entertainment cable channels; and have NBC produce more of the programs it airs, thereby profiting from the production of

These products illustrate the goals and plans of Campbell Soup Company. The *strategic goal* for the organization as a whole is to maximize profitability and shareholder value and to be a leader in each product category. The *strategic plan* for achieving this goal is to enhance the core business, which is soup, by internal growth and acquisition. The *tactical plan* is new-product introductions, such as the launch of "Special Request," "Noodle Nest," "Campbell's Cup," and "Souper Combo." The success of the tactical plan has enabled the Campbell Soup Company to achieve its major strategic goals.

hit shows.[26] As another example, a small company wanted to improve its market share from 15 to 20 percent over the next three years. This objective was pursued through the following strategic plans: (1) allocate resources for the development of new, competitive products with high growth potential; (2) improve production methods to achieve higher output at lower costs; and (3) conduct research to develop alternative uses for current products and services.[27]

TACTICAL PLANS

tactical plans Plans designed to help execute major strategic plans and to accomplish a specific part of the organization's strategy.

Tactical plans are designed to help execute major strategic plans and to accomplish a specific part of the company's strategy.[28] Tactical plans typically have a shorter time horizon than strategic plans — over the next year or so. The term *tactical* derives from the military. For example, strategic weapon systems, such as Intercontinental Ballistic Missiles or the B1 bomber, are designed to deliver major blows to the enemy. Strategic weapon systems reflect the country's overall strategic plans. Tactical weapon systems, such as fighter airplanes, are used to achieve just one part of the overall strategic plan.

Tactical plans define what the major departments and organizational subunits will do to implement the overall strategic plan. Normally it is the middle manager's job to take the broad strategic plan and identify specific tactical actions. For example, Jolt Cola, introduced in 1986, had a strategic plan that called for high levels of sugar and caffeine to appeal to a specific niche in the marketplace for soft drinks. Packaging the product to accommodate this market segment was an important part of the tactical plan. The package had a yellow lightning bolt flashing through a red and white logo. The label looked like something out of a comic book, but its chief tactical purpose was to convey the product's image — a jolt — and this it did.[29]

OPERATIONAL PLANS

operational plans Plans developed at the organization's lower levels that specify action steps toward achieving operational goals and support tactical planning activities.

Operational plans are developed at the lower levels of the organization to specify action steps toward achieving operational goals and to support tactical plans. The operational plan is the department manager's tool for daily and weekly operations. Objectives are stated in quantitative terms, and the department plan describes how objectives will be achieved. Operational planning

MANAGER'S SHOPTALK

TEN STEPS TO EFFECTIVE PLANNING

Step 1.
Establish a Planning Structure
- Line managers are responsible for designing the plan.
- The CEO provides direction and purpose.
- Staff planners provide assistance and legwork.
- Include provision for long-term corporate plan and shorter term operational plan.

Step 2.
Define the Organization's Current Situation
- Where are we now?
- Define the company's mission and purpose.
- Analyze economic and competitive situation, and internal resources.

Step 3.
Set Specific Organizational Goals
- Where do we want to go?
- Define measurable goals for desired results in areas such as profitability, market share, productivity, innovation, financial resources, employee development, growth, and environmental responsibility.

Step 4.
Devise Possible Courses of Action
- Project current trends into the future.
- Analyze basic planning assumptions.
- Develop scenarios for alternative courses of action.

Step 5.
Formulate Strategies
- What will we do to achieve goals?
- Set priorities for strategic alternatives.
- Define specific plans.
- Allocate responsibilities, time, and resource requirements.

Step 6.
Analyze Risks and Resources
- Match resources with plan requirements.
- Identify risks associated with products, markets, competition, and employees.

Step 7.
Set Timetables
- When will goals be met?
- Define schedules and time frames for key accomplishments.

Step 8.
Develop Operational Goals and Plans
- Define short-term objectives in key performance areas.
- Line managers devise short-term action plans.
- Assign responsibilities and schedules.

Step 9.
Finalize Strategic Plan
- Reanalyze resources in light of completed plans.
- Consider financing, manpower, facilities, production schedules.
- Involve entire management team.
- Consider contingency plans in case of changes.

Step 10.
Implementation and Control
- Coordinate strategic planning system with budgets and other control systems to support managerial actions.
- Schedule periodic reviews.
- Link to rewards and management by objectives systems.

Source: Adapted from "Strategic Planning: Part Three," *Small Business Report* (April 1983), 21–24. *Small Business Report* is a monthly management magazine published for top executives in small and mid-size companies by Business Research & Communications, 203 Calle del Oaks, Monterey, CA 93940.

specifies plans for supervisors, department managers, and individual employees. For example, Du Pont has a program called Individual Career Management that involves a series of discussions that define what each manager's new goals should be and whether last year's operational goals were met. At Du Pont the goals are set as high as possible to stretch the employee to insure continued improvement. These year-end discussions also provide the basis for rewards to those who have excelled.[30]

Schedules are an important component of operational planning. Schedules define precise time frames for the completion of each objective required for the organization's tactical and strategic goals. Operational planning also must be coordinated with the budget, because resources must be allocated for desired activities. For example, Apogee Enterprises, a window and glass fabricator with 150 small divisions, is fanatical about operational planning and budgeting. Committees are set up that require inter- as well as intra-divisional review

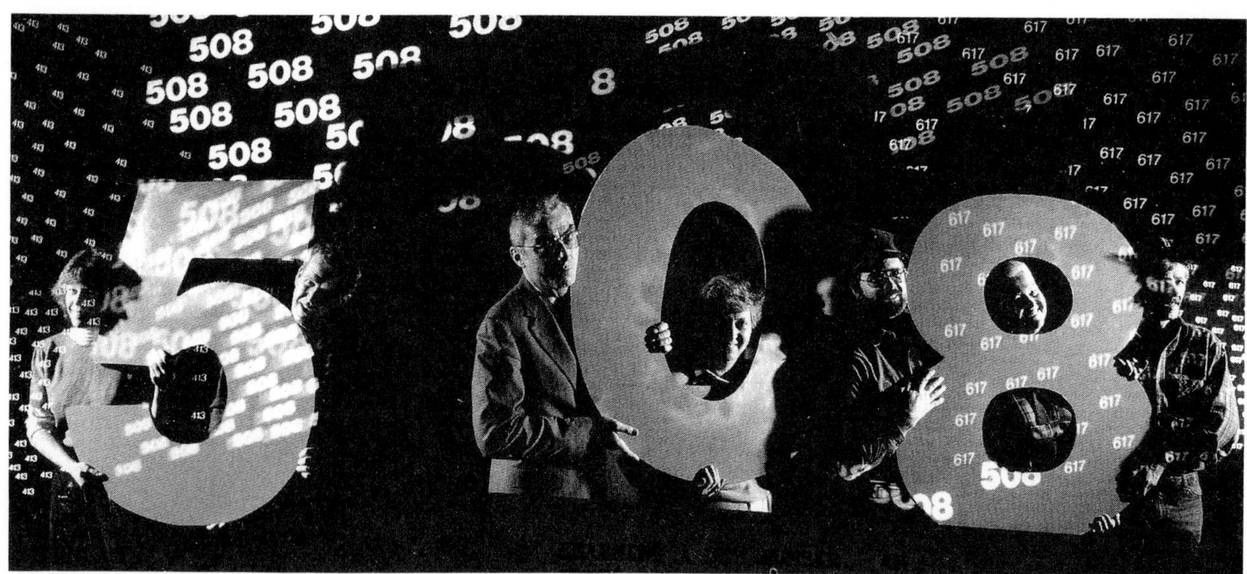

A major *program* was undertaken by New England Telephone to introduce a new area code — 508 — to eastern Massachusetts. This change affected over 1 million customers and 190 communities and took two years to complete. The program required coordination of New England Telephone, the NYNEX Service Company, and NYNEX Information Resources Company. The massive customer campaign informed users of the change and smoothed the transition.

and challenge of budgets, profit plans, and proposed capital expenditures. Assigning the dollars makes the operational plan work for everything from hiring new salespeople to increasing travel expenses.

Single-Use Plans

single-use plans Plans that are developed to achieve a set of objectives that are unlikely to be repeated in the future.

Single-use plans are developed to achieve a set of objectives that are not likely to be repeated in the future. Single-use plans typically include both programs and projects.

program A complex set of objectives and plans for achieving an important, one-time organizational goal.

Program. A **program** is a complex set of objectives and plans for attaining an important, one-time organizational goal. The program is designed to carry out a major course of action for the organization. An example of such a program is the Pershing missile program at Martin Marietta. Others include the development of the space shuttle for NASA, the Boeing 767 aircraft, and the System 360 computer by IBM. Programs are major undertakings, may take several years to complete, and often require the creation of a separate organization. Programs are large in scope and may be associated with several projects.

project A set of relatively short-term, narrow objectives and plans for achieving a major, one-time organizational goal.

Project. A **project** is also a set of objectives and plans designed to achieve a one-time goal but generally is smaller in scope and complexity than a program. It normally has a shorter time horizon and requires fewer resources.

A project is often one part of a program. Thus, when NASA works to complete its space station program, it will have one project for a rocket booster, one for the environment inside the space station, and one for the station's external shell. A specific project is defined for each major component of the overall program. Within business corporations, projects often are undertaken to perform a specific activity that is not part of the normal production process.

For example, the name change from U.S. Steel to USX Corporation was a project. Hundreds of worker-hours and millions of dollars were spent researching a name that would characterize the corporation's new mission. Another project at USX evolved from the decision to close some of its steel plants. A project team was created to study the steel plants and decide which ones to close.

TRW • An excellent example of a single-use plan was a culture program launched by TRW called "TRW and the 80s." This program had four fundamental objectives:

1. The highest standards of conduct for all employees
2. Superior performance as an economic unit, with emphasis on product quality
3. High-quality internal operations, with emphasis on employees and the quality of work life
4. Continued expansion of social contributions and community involvement by employees and company units

These objectives were followed up with specific plans that helped make the culture program a success. The strategy included action plans for product design, organizational innovation, capital expenditures, job design, and productivity improvement. A productivity college was set up for managers, along with regular productivity workshops for all employees. These action steps helped implement the new culture values within the organization. A further step was to appoint a vice-president for productivity, but this position was eliminated once the program succeeded and the employees adopted the new values. The formal culture program was disbanded.[31]

Standing Plans

Standing plans are ongoing plans that are used to provide guidance for tasks performed repeatedly within the organization. The major standing plans are organizational policies, procedures, and rules. These plans pertain to matters such as employee illness, absences, smoking, discipline, hiring, and dismissal.

standing plans Ongoing plans that are used as guidance for tasks performed repeatedly within the organization.

Policies. A **policy** is a general guide to action. It is a general statement based on the organization's overall goals and strategic plans that provides directions for people within the organization. It may define boundaries within which to make decisions. For example, the graduate program of a business school may adopt the goal of increasing the quality of students admitted. It may issue a policy statement requiring applicants to have a minimum general aptitude test score of 500. Many companies have adopted smoking policies. These range from restricting smoking in meeting rooms, reception areas, office areas, or cafeterias, all the way to dismissing employees unless they stop smoking totally, which is the case at USG Acoustical Products Company.

policy A general statement based on the organization's overall goals and strategic plans that provides directions for individuals within the company.

Perhaps the most difficult new policy issue is the handling of employees with AIDS. In 1983, a manager at Bank of America discussed an employee's illness with coworkers, thereby violating the worker's privacy. A policy was

Southern Pacific's *policy* for affirmative action and equal employment opportunity is spelled out in this poster. This policy has been posted at work locations throughout the Southern Pacific system. The policy covers the internal information complaint procedure, guidelines for persons with handicaps, and guidelines that cover sexual harassment and sex discrimination.

adopted that so long as employees with AIDS are able to meet acceptable performance standards, and their condition is not a threat to themselves or others, they should be treated like other employees. Bank of America also has a policy of making reasonable accommodations, such as flexible work hours, whenever possible to help the AIDS victim. The policy is so well adhered to that an employee not wishing to work with an ill colleague had to resign. Bank of America's policy is to protect AIDS patients at all costs.[32]

PROCEDURES. A **procedure,** sometimes called a *standard operating procedure,* defines a precise series of steps to be used in achieving certain objectives. Procedures are very specific and typically apply to individual jobs. For example, in a hospital the nurse in the orthopedic ward must follow strict procedures when treating a patient with a broken leg or one who has just had surgery. These might include having the patient wiggle his or her toes and checking blood pressure and temperature every three hours. Procedures describe how to perform recurring tasks.

RULES. A **rule** describes how a specific action is to be performed. Rules often apply to specific settings, such as a no-smoking rule in areas of the plant where hazardous materials are stored. Universities often have rules pertaining to the receipt of an "incomplete" grade. Such a rule specifies the conditions under which a student can be given an incomplete and requires that the grade be removed within one semester or an F will be given.

procedure A specific series of steps to be used in achieving certain objectives; usually applies to individual jobs.

rule A statement describing how a specific action is to be performed.

Rules and procedures play a similar role in organizations. Both are narrow in scope and prescribe desired activities. The key difference is that procedures normally describe a series of steps or activities, while rules pertain to one specific action. For example, refraining from smoking in a hazardous area is a single action, but the on-duty nurse in the orthopedic ward follows a procedure involving several steps.

Standing plans are used often in large companies, but small businesses can use these management tools, also. Consider a small food market in Texas.

WHOLE FOODS MARKET

• Whole Foods Market, headquartered in Austin, Texas, is said to have "the best little handbook in Texas." Although many small-business owners dismiss employee handbooks as bureaucratic jibberish, founder and CEO John Mackey believes the handbook is a tool for showing people how the business works. The handbook compiles important policies, procedures, rules, and philosophy. After his business grew to more than 80 employees, he found that a frequently updated handbook could substitute for frequent meetings with each employee. There are sections on the company's history and plans for expansion. There is a mission statement that underlines the importance of customer satisfaction. The handbook describes how employees are considered "team members" who must be given the opportunity for personal growth. Company rules and procedures are included, and so are explanations of what lies behind them. For example, employees are not allowed to park in store parking lots, because parking is scarce. The dress code explains the need not to shock or put off customers. The tone of the handbook is warm and engaging and meets Whole Foods' need for standing plans.[33]

EXHIBIT 5.6
Planning Time Horizon

Today	1 Year	2 Years	3 Years	4 Years	5 Years and Beyond
Short-Term Planning (Operational objectives)	**Intermediate-Term Planning** (Tactical objectives)	**Long-Term Planning** (Strategic goals)			

CONTINGENCY PLANS

Contingency plans define company responses to be taken in the case of emergencies or setbacks. To develop contingency plans, planners identify uncontrollable factors, such as recession, inflation, technological developments, or safety accidents. To minimize the impact of these potential factors, a planning team can forecast the worst-case scenarios. For example, if sales fall 20 percent and prices drop 8 percent, what will the company do? Contingency plans can then be defined for possible layoffs, emergency budgets, and sales efforts.[34] Contingency planning was used at Shell as described at the beginning of this chapter for dealing with a potential drop in oil prices that could be catastrophic.

contingency plans Plans that define company responses to specific situations such as emergencies or setbacks.

PLANNING TIME HORIZON

Organizational goals and plans are associated with specific time horizons. The time horizons are long term, intermediate term, and short term, as illustrated in Exhibit 5.6. *Long-term planning* includes strategic goals and plans and may extend as far as five years into the future. *Intermediate-term planning* includes tactical objectives and has a time horizon of from one to two years. *Short-term planning* includes operational objectives for specific departments and individuals and has a time horizon of one year or less.

One of the major problems in companies today is the emphasis on *short-term results.* Long-term planning is difficult because the world is so uncertain. Moreover, the financial community, including stock analysts and mutual funds managers, push companies for strong financial results in the short-term. This pressure fits the natural inclination of many result-oriented managers, who are concerned with outcomes for today and next week, not next year and for sure not five years out. These pressures tend to reward short-term performance and undercut long-range planning. For example, a Tennessee manufacturer of temperature control devices badly needed new plant and facilities that required massive expenditures. The managers' bonuses were calculated on profits for a one-year period. In this case, the pressures for short-term results took precedence, and the managers did not invest money in new facilities because short-term profits would suffer.

Managers at Delmarva Power Company take a *long-term* view. One big challenge facing the company is to provide energy for the next decade. Delmarva developed a plan called Challenge 2000, a combination of peak period conservation programs and new energy sources. This giant disc collects global weather observations for the National Oceanic and Atmospheric Administration, which helped launch Delmarva's Peak Management Program. Without *long-term planning,* Delmarva would not be able to provide electricity in ten years at the lowest reasonable cost.

Many well-managed companies, however, resist short-term pressures. Matsushita Electric of Japan, the world's leading producer of consumer electronics, VCRs, color televisions, and video cameras, has succeeded by taking a long-term view. Senior executives are redirecting the company into four areas where future growth is expected: semiconductors, factory automation, office automation, and audiovisual products. These products generate only 13 percent of sales, but are expected to do well in the twenty-first century and so today are receiving 70 percent of the company's research expenditures.[35] Another company already planning for the twenty-first century is Ford. CEO Donald Petersen spearheaded a move to completely redesign this company to meet needs ten years and more in the future. Ford's general approach is to create centers of excellence, each located in a different country, and each responsible for a key component for cars (engines, undercarriages). Each center will develop its component for all cars worldwide, hence reducing duplication of effort. Projects already underway are replacements for the popular Escort and Tempo/Topaz models. This strategy is designed to work in a future world where competitors can spring up in any country and where something as simple as exchange rates can wipe out a cost advantage in any country overnight.[36]

Organizational Responsibility for Planning

Who should do organizational planning? Chief executive officers and other line managers have primary responsibility for planning. Line managers are responsible for setting goals and objectives and devising plans for achieving them. However, not all line managers have the expertise or skills for doing the analy-

EXHIBIT 5.7
Structural Location of Centralized Planning Department

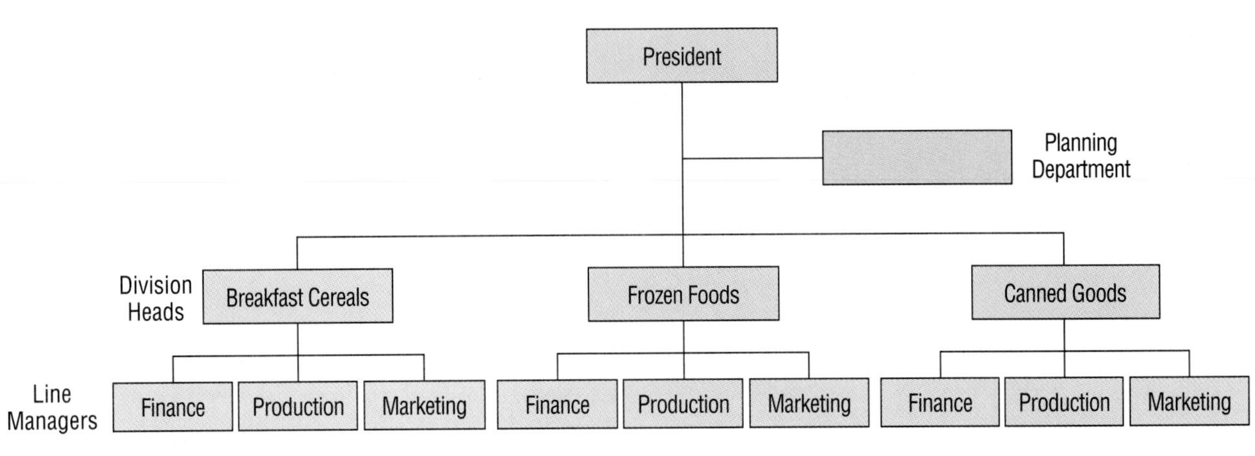

sis required for detailed planning. Thus, three different approaches are used to structure the planning function: central planning departments, decentralized planning staff, and planning task forces.

CENTRAL PLANNING DEPARTMENT

The traditional approach to corporate planning was to have a **central planning department** report to the president or chief executive officer, as illustrated in Exhibit 5.7. This approach became popular during the 1960s and 1970s. Planning specialists were hired to gather data and develop detailed strategic plans for the corporation as a whole. This planning approach was centralized and top down because objectives and plans were assigned to major divisions and departments from the planning department after approval by the president.

central planning department A group of planning specialists who develop plans for the organization as a whole and its major divisions and departments and typically report to the president or CEO.

This approach is still used and works well in many applications. For example, the Columbia Gas System, described earlier in this chapter, has a Corporate Planning Department with eight full-time specialists. The department has two sections. The Operations Analysis Section is responsible for acquiring and analyzing economic and other data for use in the strategic planning process. The Planning Section prepares the strategic plan for the system and also provides guidance to subsidiary companies for strategic planning activities.[37]

The central planning department has run into trouble in some companies. Conflicts have arisen because centralized planning people did not have detailed knowledge of the major operating units' activities. In some companies, line managers have rebelled against the dictates of strategic planners. Those at GE's Major Appliance Business Group became downright hostile to corporate planners. The planners made mistakes because they had relied on abstract data rather than learning the markets and production processes within GE divisions. In one case, GE's corporate planners analyzed data showing that houses and families were shrinking and concluded that small appliances were the wave of the future. But the planners did not realize that working women wanted *big* refrigerators in order to cut down on trips to the supermarket. GE wasted a lot of time designing smaller appliances because the planning group had failed to have contact with customers.[38] Problems such as these have caused many companies to decentralize planning to divisional line managers.

Decentralized Planning Staff

decentralized planning staff A group of planning specialists assigned to major departments and divisions to help managers develop their own strategic plans.

The **decentralized planning staff** evolved when planning experts were assigned to major departments and divisions to help managers develop their own strategic plans, as indicated in Exhibit 5.8. Corporate planners no longer wrote the plans themselves. This change helped resolve some of the conflicts between planners and staff, as did the improved strategic planning training of line managers. By the 1980s, business school graduates understood the basics of strategic planning and were able to take on more planning responsibility.

Sonat Inc. started with a system in which planners from headquarters wrote the blueprint for each subsidiary and presented it to the subsidiary's managers. The planning function has since been reorganized such that staff members have been assigned to the operating units to provide a support function for line managers. A centralized strategic staff was introduced at General Motors in 1971. Several years later, planners were assigned to each business unit to act as catalysts for change and provide support for line managers. General Motors has a small staff at headquarters as well as within each division, and their stated goal is to put themselves out of business by teaching line managers to do the planning. At Borg-Warner, the central planning staff has been reduced from ten to three people; these now serve as consultants to business units, giving advice and helping managers write their own plans.[39]

Planning Task Force

planning task force A temporary group consisting of line managers responsible for developing strategic plans.

The third approach to strategic planning has been the use of planning task forces. A **planning task force** is a temporary group of line managers who have the responsibility of developing a strategic plan. A group of line managers thus takes over responsibility for planning. In one study of corporate planning practices, approximately one-third of the companies used an interdepartmental task force to study and make plans for achieving strategic goals. Each team identified and analyzed alternatives for reaching a specific objective and then outlined the major action steps necessary for achieving it. Several teams can be created, one for each major objective. Each task force must deal with the time horizon, the allocation of responsibility to specific individuals and departments, resource requirements, measuring devices to see whether objectives are being met, and possible contingencies and competitor reactions.[40]

Millipore Corporation, a maker of high-tech filtration systems, uses neither centralized nor decentralized corporate planners. Its planning staff of six was fired and replaced by task forces of operating managers. These meet every 18 months to brainstorm; they pool ideas on current market events and those likely to occur over the next five years. They set long-term and intermediate-

Exhibit 5.8
Structural Location of Decentralized Planning Staff

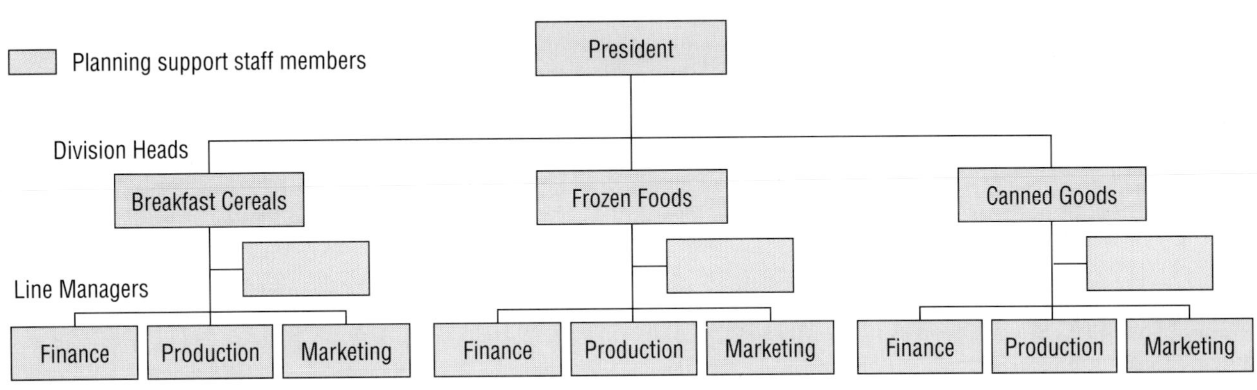

term objectives and hammer out action plans for meeting them. Millipore executives claim this approach has helped make the company a leader in the industry because its plans are based on market realities and operational-level activities.[41]

Barriers to Organizational Planning

Although planning is the primary management function, it does not happen automatically. Planning is difficult because it deals with complex environments and must look toward an uncertain future.

Specific Barriers

Several barriers can interfere with the organizational planning process. Managers can try to remove these barriers to facilitate planning.

Delegation to Staff Specialists. Line managers must be involved. When the goal-setting and planning functions are assigned to planning specialists, negative things can happen. First, strategic planning may put too much emphasis on numbers. Strategic planners collect large amounts of data, conduct statistical analyses, and create a paper product that may be unused in line managers' bottom drawers. Second, lack of involvement by line managers may mean that the strategic plan is too abstract and inapplicable to the organization's operational and market needs. Third, this approach may result in overemphasis on planning techniques. Although the latest methods may be used, the substance of the plan may not be what the organization needs.

Little Top Management Support. Top-level managers must provide the direction, scope, and statement of purpose for the strategic plan. They

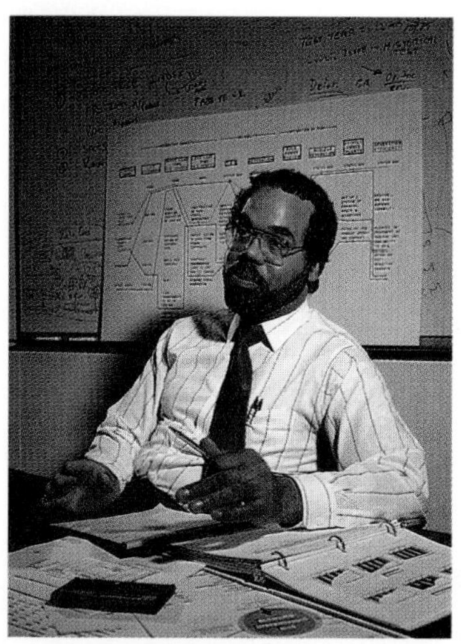

"We're facilitators," says Glenn Rogers, manager of strategic planning for Public Service Enterprise Group Incorporated. "We work closely with the other business units to advise and counsel them with their planning and development efforts." The Strategic Planning Group acts as a *planning support staff* to overcome planning barriers by analyzing key competitive issues and providing financial analyses, thereby helping managers make difficult financial decisions necessary to produce excellent results. Line managers are responsible for final planning decisions.

must support the idea of strategic planning, become involved themselves, and encourage the involvement of line managers at middle and lower levels. Sometimes top managers disagree about strategic objectives. They must build a coalition around a specific set of objectives toward which the organization will move. Without top management support, middle management will not allocate time and energy to planning activities.

Limited Line Management Expertise. Strategic planning requires knowledge of markets and other sectors in the external environment and a thorough understanding of internal operations. Many managers have little expertise in interpreting complex, changing environments or gathering and analyzing data. Managers may feel intimidated by the skills and education associated with planning techniques. Line managers must collaborate with corporate planning specialists who are good with techniques but do not understand the substance of the company.

Overcoming Barriers

The above barriers are not insurmountable. The following techniques can be used to overcome them.

Start Planning at the Top. Effective planning must have the explicit support and involvement of top managers. If top managers take the time to plan and involve other line managers in the planning process, many of the barriers will be overcome. Top managers can remove emphasis on short-term results, help increase middle management's faith in planning, and perhaps even provide training opportunities for line managers.

Use Planning Support Staff. Planning experts who work in an advisory or consulting capacity can help overcome line managers' lack of expertise. Support staff can gather data, perform statistical analyses, use sophisticated scheduling systems, and do other specialized tasks. However, these people perform a support role and do not decide on the substance of goals or plans. Support staff in a consulting role can facilitate line management planning.

Line Management Participation. Many companies are realizing that planning comes alive for the organization when line managers participate. Managers can have scheduled training sessions — perhaps a two-to-three-day retreat — to discuss the future or create a task force to define goals and plans. Line management participation in planning deemphasizes techniques such as data analysis and increases the importance of substantive planning issues. It also increases management's faith in planning outcomes.

SUMMARY

This chapter described several important ideas about organizational planning. Organizational planning involves defining goals/objectives and developing a plan with which to achieve them. An organization exists for a single, overriding purpose known as its mission — the basis for strategic goals and plans. Goals within the organization are defined in a hierarchical fashion, beginning with strategic goals followed by tactical and operational objectives. Plans are defined similarly, with strategic, tactical, and operational plans used to achieve the objectives. Other goal concepts include characteristics of effective goals and goal-setting behavior.

Several types of plans were described, including strategic, tactical, operational, single-use, and standing plans. Long-term, intermediate-term, and short-term plans have time horizons of from five years down to six months. Organizational responsibility for planning typically includes one of three options: a centralized planning department, a decentralized planning staff, or an interdepartmental task force composed of line managers.

MANAGEMENT SOLUTION

The planning group at Shell was faced with the task of planning for a sudden drop in oil prices when the likelihood seemed small. Senior executives wanted to know when the price of oil would fall and by how much before they would take planning seriously. No one can read the future, so the planning group developed a written case — called a scenario — showing one of many ways by which the price of oil could fall. This seemed like a game, but executives agreed to participate. Instead of answering the question, "What will happen?" they explored the question, "What will we do if it happens?" This involved contingency planning for the intermediate term. Managers took the work seriously and began to consider responses to the possibility of lower-priced oil. As it happened, the price of oil fell from $28 to $15 a few months later, and Shell executives were ready. The planning shaped Shell's response, preparing the company for the rapid oil price changes that followed.[42]

DISCUSSION QUESTIONS

1. What types of planning would have helped Exxon respond more quickly to the oil spill from the Exxon Valdez near Alaska?
2. Write a brief mission statement for a local business. Can the purpose and values of a small organization be captured in a written statement?
3. What strategies could the college or university at which you are taking this management course adopt to compete for students in the marketplace? Would these strategies depend on the school's goals?

4. Consider an organization for which you have worked and evaluate the strategic goals in each of the eight areas identified by Drucker. Were the objectives in each area made explicit or left implicit? Can you infer goals from the organization's behavior?
5. A new business venture has to develop a comprehensive business plan to borrow money to get started. Companies such as Federal Express, Nike, and Rolm Corporation say they did not follow the original plan very closely. Does that mean that developing the plan was a waste of time for these eventually successful companies?
6. A famous management theorist proposed that the time horizons for all strategic plans are becoming shorter because of the rapid changes in organizations' external environments. Do you agree? Would the planning time horizon for IBM or Ford Motor Company be shorter than it was 20 years ago?
7. How do managers handle conflicting strategic goals?
8. What are the characteristics of effective goals? Would it be better to have no goals at all than to have goals that do not meet these criteria?
9. What do you think are the advantages and disadvantages of having a central planning department to do an organization's planning compared with having decentralized planning groups provide planning support to line managers?
10. Assume Southern University decides to (1) raise its admission standards and (2) initiate a business fair to which local townspeople will be invited. What types of plans would it use to carry out these two activities?

Management in Practice: Experiential Exercise

Company Crime Wave

Senior managers in your organization are concerned about internal theft. Your department has been assigned the task of writing an ethics policy that defines employee theft and prescribes penalties. Stealing goods is easily classified as theft, but other activities are more ambiguous. Before writing the policy, go through the following list and decide which behaviors should be defined as stealing and whether penalties should apply. Discuss the items with your department members until agreement is reached. Classify each item as an example of (1) theft, (2) acceptable behavior, or (3) in between with respect to written policy. Is it theft when an employee

- Gets paid for overtime not worked?
- Takes a longer lunch or coffee break than authorized?
- Punches a time card for another?
- Comes in late or leaves early?
- Fakes injury to receive worker's compensation?
- Takes care of personal business on company time?
- Occasionally uses company copying machines or makes long-distance telephone calls for personal purposes?
- Takes a few stamps, pens, or other supplies for personal use?
- Takes money from the petty cash drawer?
- Uses company vehicles or tools for own purposes, but returns them?
- Damages merchandise so a cohort can purchase it at a discount?
- Accepts a gift from a supplier?

Now consider those items rated "in between." Do these items represent ethical issues as defined in Chapter 4? How should these items be handled in the company's written policy?

CASES FOR ANALYSIS

A. J. CANFIELD COMPANY

On a cold January day a few years ago, Bob Greene, columnist for the *Chicago Tribune,* wrote lovingly about Canfield's Diet Chocolate Fudge soda. He wrote that "Taking a sip of the stuff is like biting into a hot fudge sundae." Canfield's Diet Chocolate Fudge had been a stable but unimpressive performer, selling 60,000 cases every year for 13 years straight.

Suddenly, all over Chicago people were craving the fudge soda. Canfield's phone lines went crazy. In the following nine days, more Diet Chocolate Fudge was sold than in the entire previous year. Three months later, Canfield was shipping 20,000 cases a day, 100 times the normal amount. What impact did this have on A. J. Canfield Company? It was like shaking a can of pop and then pulling the tab.

Television crews visited the company for stories. Actors such as Mickey Rooney and Burt Reynolds called for soda. The Chicago factory operated on two 10-hour shifts for weeks, and everyone was exhausted. The machinery was not maintained. Warm bodies were hired as new recruits, with no time for training. One senior employee walked into the vice-president of manufacturing's office and said, "I can't take it anymore." He had missed his winter vacation, his home life was a wreck, and he had been in the factory for 29 days straight. Tempers were flaring all over the place. Orders could not be filled. Good customers were deserting out of anger. Canfield Company seemed to be alienating everyone.

The company reached the point where it could not stretch its production and distribution systems any further. Top managers had to plan for more capacity. They had to anticipate whether the increased sales of Diet Chocolate Fudge were permanent or temporary.

One plan was to build a new plant, which would cost about $10 million and must produce about 20,000 cases a day to break even. Would demand hold up to justify that investment? Another possibility was to let other bottlers make, distribute, and promote the beverage outside of the Midwest. Canfield could sell franchises to the highest bidders and make millions from the high franchise price tag plus a cut of all soda sold.

Canfield's executives finally decided on a plan— they would *give* franchises away to bottlers they trusted. This would guarantee high quality while bringing other companies into the production process. Franchisees would pay for the concentrate which would be Canfield's source of revenue. Within 3 months, 11 bottlers were under contract to cover all 50 states and 3 foreign countries. The craze lasted longer than expected, with about $80 million of Diet Chocolate Fudge sold in the two years after Greene's column appeared. But sales have gradually dropped off. Canfield's employees, who once worked 10-, 12-, 16-hour shifts, now do 8-hour stints. Looking back, the CEO admits that Canfield might have made big money by taking the soda national itself or by selling rather than giving away franchises. If Canfield had a staff of 25 more key people, it would have had the management capacity to handle the growth. Executives are very happy with the outcome, but wonder if they might have done better.

Questions

1. Can a company that experiences dramatic growth from a hot product be expected to plan for this outcome?
2. Did Canfield executives handle this explosive growth in the right way? Do you think the final plan was consistent with Canfield's mission and corporate values?
3. What kinds of planning would you recommend for Canfield and other small regional companies of this type? Should a company like this plan for a highly unlikely contingency, or should managers plan strictly for expected changes?

Source: Based on Joshua Hyatt, "Too Hot to Handle," *INC.*, March 1987, 52–58.

H.I.D.

Dave Collins, president of H.I.D., sat down at the conference table with his management team members, Karen Setz, Tony Briggs, Dave King, and Art Johnson. H.I.D. owns ten Holiday Inns in Georgia, eight hotels of different types in Canada, and one property in the Caribbean. It also owns two Quality Inns in Georgia. Dave Collins and his managers got together to define their mission, goals, and objectives and to set strategic plans. As they began their strategic planning session, the consultant they had hired suggested that each describe what he or she wanted for the company's domestic operations in the next ten years — how many hotels it should own, where to locate them, and who the target market was. Another question he asked them to consider was what the driving force of the company should be — that is, the single characteristic that would separate H.I.D. from other companies.

The team members wrote their answers on flipcharts, and the consultant summarized the results. Dave Collins' goal included 50 hotels in ten years, with the number increasing to 26 or 27 in five years. All the other members saw no more than 20 hotels in ten years and a maximum of 15 or 16 within five years. Clearly there was disagreement among the top managers about long-term goals and desirable growth rate.

With the consultant's direction, the team members began to critique their growth objectives. Dave King, director of operations and development, observed, "We just can't build that many hotels in that time period, certainly not given our current staffing or any reasonable staffing we could afford. I don't see how we could achieve that goal." Art Johnson, the accountant, agreed. Karen Setz then asked, "Could we build them all in Georgia? You know we've centered on the medium-priced hotel in smaller towns. Do we need to move to bigger towns now, such as Jacksonville, or add another to the one we have in Atlanta?" Dave Collins responded, "We have an opportunity out in California, we may have one in New Jersey, and we are looking at the possibility of going to Jacksonville."

The consultant attempted to refocus the discussion: "Well, how does this all fit with your mission? Where are you willing to locate geographically? Most of your operation is in Georgia. Can you adequately support a national building effort?"

Tony Briggs responded, "Well, you know we have always looked at the smaller-town hotels as being our niche, although we deviated from that for the hotel in Atlanta. But we generally stay in smaller towns where we don't have much competition. Now we are talking about an expensive hotel in California."

Dave Collins suggested, "Maybe it's time we changed our target market, changed our pricing strategy, and went for larger hotels in urban areas across the whole country. Maybe we need to change a lot of factors about our company."

Questions

1. What is H.I.D.'s mission at the present time? How may this mission change?
2. What do you think H.I.D.'s mission, strategic goals, and strategic plans are likely to be at the end of this planning session? Why?
3. What goal-setting behavior is being used here to reach agreement among H.I.D.'s managers? Do managers typically disagree about the direction of their organization?

Source: This case was provided by James Higgins.

CHAPTER 6

Strategy Formulation and Implementation

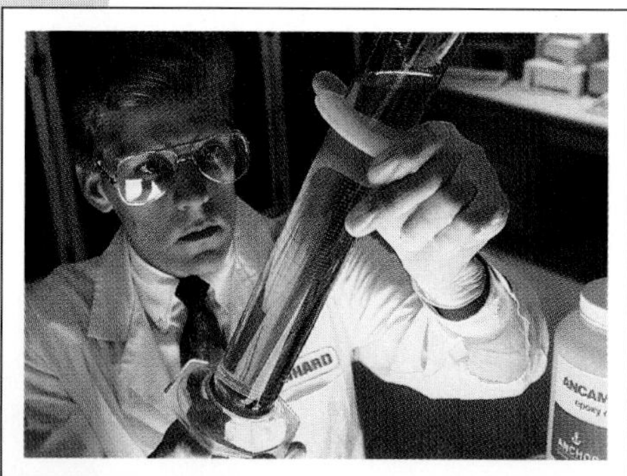

Chapter Outline

Thinking Strategically

What Is Strategic Management?
Levels of Strategy
Strategy Formulation versus Implementation

The Strategic Management Process

Situation Analysis

Formulating Corporate-Level Strategy

Grand Strategy
Portfolio Strategy

Formulating Business-Level Strategy

Miles and Snow's Strategy Typology
Porter's Competitive Strategies
Product Life Cycle

Formulating Functional-Level Strategy

Putting Strategy into Action

Leadership
Structural Design
Information and Control Systems
Human Resources

Learning Objectives

After studying this chapter, you should be able to:

- Define the components of strategic management.
- Describe the strategic planning process and SWOT analysis.
- Define corporate-level strategies and explain the portfolio approach.
- Describe business-level strategies, including strategy typology, competitive strategies, and product life cycle.
- Explain the major considerations in formulating functional strategies.
- Enumerate the organizational dimensions used for implementing strategy.

MANAGEMENT PROBLEM

When CEO David Johnson was recruited to take over Gerber Products Company in October 1987, here is what he found: Gerber's share of the baby food market dropped to 52 percent from 67 percent, due to weak marketing and reports of glass fragments found in baby food jars. Beech-Nut, Heinz, and Nestlé all made inroads into Gerber's market share in the United States and abroad with new products and effective advertising. Gerber's nonfood businesses had a dismal record, dragging down the already meager earnings from the baby food business. Gerber was slipping so badly that some industry experts believed the end was in sight, expecting a takeover and turnaround by another corporation. Johnson's challenge was to develop, formulate, and implement a new strategy, one that would fit the market and satisfy shareholders.[1]

If you were David Johnson, what would you do now? What strategy would you adopt to fend off the competition and regain market share and profitability?

Gerber Products Company was suddenly confronted with the urgent need for strategic planning. The previous strategy of diversifying into nonfood areas was failing, and the baby food business itself was in trouble. Because of intense competition, the strategy was slowly causing Gerber to go broke. Now is the time for a careful analysis of the competitive situation to formulate a strategy that will suit Gerber's strengths and the changing competitive environment.

Every organization is concerned with strategy. Hershey developed a new strategy after losing its number-one candy bar status to Mars. Hershey's new strategy in the bar wars was to be a fierce product innovator. New products included Take Five, Symphony, and the Big Block line of Hershey's standard chocolate bars.[2] The Roman Catholic church in the United States is faced with the need to reevaluate strategy. Its 115,000 nuns, now with a median age of over 60, have no satisfactory retirement benefits and a depressing medical situation. Major air carriers such as American Airlines and Continental Airlines have purchased commuter airlines to gain control of regional markets. Many large corporations engage in acquisitions or divestments as part of a strategic plan. Philip Morris Inc. purchased General Foods Corporation for $5.7 billion. Procter & Gamble acquired Richardson-Vicks, Nestlé acquired Carnation, and R. J. Reynolds spent almost $5 billion to purchase Nabisco Brands. Going in the other direction, National Distillers & Chemical Corporation sold off its liquor division, including Old Grand Dad Bourbon and Gilbey's Gin, and used the money to expand plastics and propane gas.[3]

All of these organizations are involved in strategic management — the topic of this chapter. They are finding ways to respond to competitors, cope with difficult environmental changes, and effectively use available resources. In this chapter, we focus on the topic of strategic management. First we define components of strategic management and then discuss a model of the strategic management process. Next we examine several models of strategy formulation. Finally, we discuss the tools managers use to implement their strategic plans.

THINKING STRATEGICALLY

Chapter 5 provided an overview of the types of goals and plans that organizations use. In this chapter, we will explore strategic management, which is considered one specific type of planning. This planning typically takes place in for-profit business organizations and pertains to competitive actions in the marketplace. Although some companies hire strategic planning experts, the responsibility for strategic planning rests with line managers. Senior executives at companies such as General Electric, Westinghouse, and Delta want middle- and lower-level line managers to think strategically. Strategic thinking means to take the long-term view and to see the big picture, including the organization and the competitive environment and how they fit together. Understanding the strategy concept, the levels of strategy, and strategy formulation versus implementation is an important start toward strategic thinking.

WHAT IS STRATEGIC MANAGEMENT?

strategic management The set of decisions and actions used to formulate and implement strategies that will provide a competitively superior fit between the organization and its environment so as to achieve organizational objectives.

strategy The plan of action that prescribes resource allocation and other activities for dealing with the environment and helping the organization attain its goals.

scope The number of businesses, products, or services that defines the size of the domain within which the organization deals with the environment.

Strategic management is the set of decisions and actions used to formulate and implement strategies that will provide a competitively superior fit between the organization and its environment so as to achieve organizational objectives.[4] Strategic management is a process used to help managers answer strategic questions such as "Where is the organization now? Where does the organization want to be? What changes and trends are occurring in the competitive environment? What courses of action will help us achieve our goals?"

Through the process of strategic management executives define an explicit **strategy,** which is the plan of action that describes resource allocation and activities for dealing with the environment and attaining the organization's goals. A strategy has four components: scope, resource deployment, distinctive competence, and synergy.[5]

SCOPE. The number of businesses, products, or services that defines the size of the domain within which the organization deals with the environment is considered its **scope.** General Electric increased its scope and product line by

Tonka Corporation's strategy for competing in the toy industry was to broaden its *scope* with the acquisition of Kenner Parker Toys and a leading Italian toy company, Polistil. As shown here, Tonka's range of toys now includes popular board games, toy vehicles, action figures, character pets, and creative toys. Broader scope protects Tonka against fashion changes in individual product categories. The new scope also enables Tonka to achieve stable growth and to penetrate foreign markets.

acquiring RCA Corporation. United Airlines Inc. redefined its scope by selling Westin Hotel Company, Hertz Rental Cars, and Hilton International. Selling these businesses allowed United Airlines Inc. to define itself strictly as an airline and to concentrate on providing airline service to the best of its ability. The trend of mergers, acquisitions, and divestments in North America and now spreading to Europe is an exercise in redefining business scope.

RESOURCE DEPLOYMENT. The level and pattern of the organization's distribution of physical, financial, and human resources for achieving its strategic goals is its **resource deployment.** For example, one newspaper had to change all employees' work schedules and buy new equipment to follow its strategy of shifting from an evening to a morning paper. Taco Bell allocated $200 million to remodeling existing stores, testing new products, and increasing its marketing emphasis to become more competitive in the fast-food industry. Owens-Corning redeployed resources away from research and development. Some 480 of the 970 research employees were let go to fit the new strategy of short-term profits instead of developing products for ten years in the future.

resource deployment The level and pattern of the organization's distribution of physical, financial, and human resources for achieving its strategic goals.

DISTINCTIVE COMPETENCE. An organization's **distinctive competence** is the unique position it develops vis-à-vis its competitors through its decisions concerning resource deployments or scope. For example, James River Corporation invested in state-of-the-art automation that has given it the distinctive competence of being able to produce paper towels and tissues more cheaply than Scott Paper Company and Procter & Gamble. Perdue Farms has achieved

distinctive competence The unique position the organization achieves with respect to competitors through its decisions concerning resource deployments, scope, and synergy.

EXHIBIT 6.1
Three Levels of Strategy in Organizations

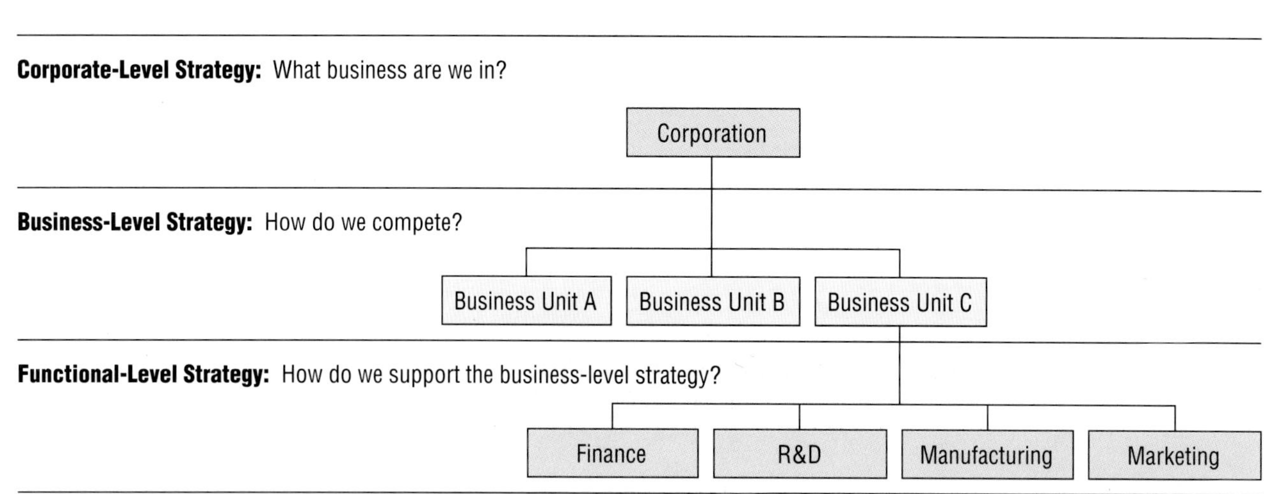

a competitive advantage by limiting its scope to chickens and by investing resources to guarantee the highest-quality chickens available in supermarkets. This distinctive competence allows Perdue to charge a higher price for its chickens. Briggs & Stratton enjoys a distinctive competence because it has concentrated on keeping costs lower than the Japanese and thus is producing more small motors than anyone else.

synergy The condition that exists when the organization's parts interact to produce a joint effect that is greater than the sum of the parts acting alone.

SYNERGY. When organizational parts interact to produce a joint effect that is greater than the sum of the parts acting alone, **synergy** occurs. The organization may attain a special advantage with respect to cost, market power, technology, or management skill. American Express achieves its synergy among its divisions by cross-selling. American Express's two life insurance companies have sold billions worth of life policies by mail to cardholders. Shearson Lehman and IDS Financial Services also sell to customers of other divisions. Through synergy American Express gets more total business than individual divisions could achieve alone. Bob Guccione, the controversial publisher of *Penthouse,* is trying to achieve synergy through the acquisition of *Saturday Review* and other magazines. The synergy comes from arranging package deals with advertisers for space in several magazines. Management skills and new technology can be shared among magazines, thereby increasing productivity for all magazines beyond what they could do alone.[6]

LEVELS OF STRATEGY

Another aspect of strategic management concerns the organizational level to which strategic issues apply. Strategic managers normally think in terms of three levels of strategy — corporate, business, and functional — as illustrated in Exhibit 6.1.[7]

CORPORATE-LEVEL STRATEGY. The question: *What business are we in?* concerns **corporate-level strategy.** Corporate-level strategy pertains to the organization as a whole and the combination of business units and product lines that make up the corporate entity. Strategic actions at this level usually relate to the acquisition of new businesses; additions or divestments of business units, plants, or product lines; and joint ventures with other corporations in new areas. An example of corporate-level strategic management occurred when General Electric purchased Kidder Peabody & Company, the New York securities firm, RCA Corporation, and Employer's Reinsurance Corporation. During the same period General Electric divested its housewares division to Black & Decker, sold its natural resources division, and unloaded its family financial services. Thus, GE redefined its business away from appliances, resources, and family finance toward financial securities, electronics, broadcasting, and insurance. In the meantime, Black & Decker's acquisition of GE's housewares division and then Emhart Corporation redefined it from a power tools producer to a company that also provides household appliances and products for home improvement.[8]

Domino's Pizza answers the question "How do we compete?" by using corporate licensing to help stores sell more pizza pies. One way to get Domino's Pizza logo into every household is with the bubble gum product shown here, which comes in the shape of a pie in a tiny pizza box. This *business-level strategy* helps Domino's succeed in the "pizza wars" being fought in the fast-food industry. Norm Nickin, director of corporate licensing, invented the product.

BUSINESS-LEVEL STRATEGY. The question: *How do we compete?* concerns **business-level strategy.** Business-level strategy pertains to each business unit or product line. It focuses on how the business unit competes within its industry for customers. Strategic decisions at the business level concern amount of advertising, direction and extent of research and development, product changes, new-product development, equipment and facilities, and expansion or contraction of product lines. For example, Food Lion Inc., one of the fastest-growing grocery chains in the nation, has a business-level strategy of cost reduction. Food Lion's economizing allows it to sell cheaper than rivals, yet maintain a higher profit margin. Jostens, Inc., a Minneapolis producer of high-school rings, has a business-level strategy of competing through product innovation. Although students have become less interested in buying class rings over the years, Jostens now offers 23 different stones and 16,000 ring permutations to fit every student's needs. Salespeople visit high schools personally to beat competitors to the student's door.[9]

corporate-level strategy The level of strategy concerned with the question: "What business are we in?" Pertains to the organization as a whole and the combination of business units and product lines that make it up.

business-level strategy The level of strategy concerned with the question: "How do we compete?" Pertains to each business unit or product line within the organization.

FUNCTIONAL-LEVEL STRATEGY. The question: *How do we support the business-level competitive strategy?* concerns **functional-level strategy.** It pertains to the major functional departments within the business unit. Functional strategies involve all of the major functions, including finance, research and development, marketing, manufacturing, and finance. For Hershey to compete on the basis of new-product innovation, its research department adopted a functional strategy for developing new products. The functional strategy for the marketing department at Jim Beam has been to spend $10 million on magazine ads depicting yuppie couples on boats, in bars, and in elegant apartments. This strategy has helped Jim Beam compete in a market where youthful drinkers are turning to white wine and other light beverages.

functional-level strategy The level of strategy concerned with the question: "How do we support the business-level strategy?" Pertains to all of the organization's major departments.

STRATEGY FORMULATION VERSUS IMPLEMENTATION

The final aspect of strategic management is the stages of formulation and implementation. **Strategy formulation** includes the planning and decision making that lead to the establishment of the firm's goals and the development

strategy formulation The stage of strategic management that involves the planning and decision making that lead to the establishment of the organization's goals and of a specific strategic plan.

EXHIBIT 6.2
The Strategic Management Process

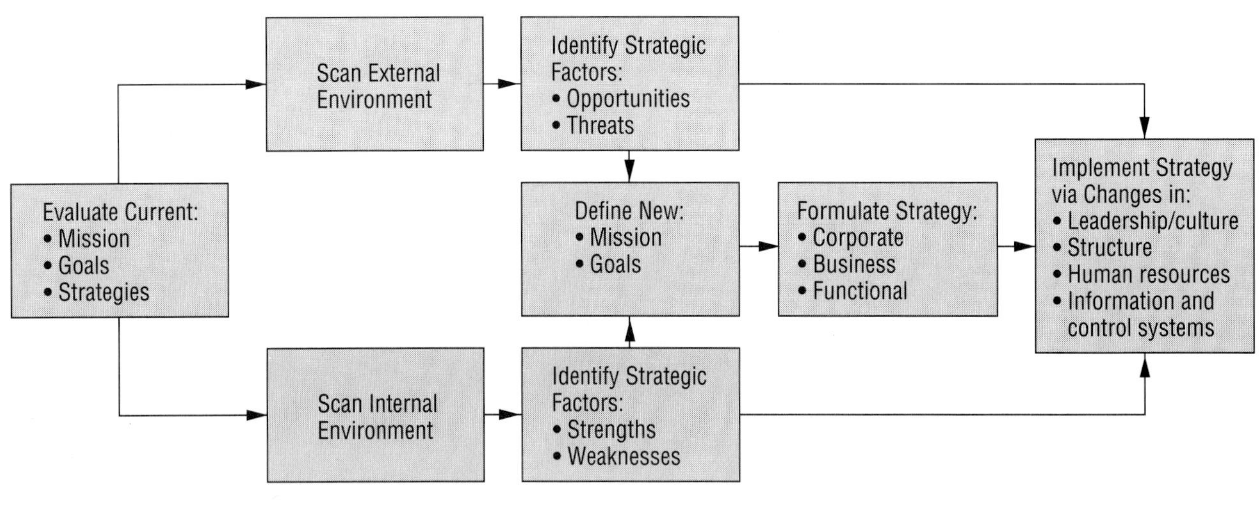

of a specific strategic plan.[10] Strategy formulation may include assessing the external environment and internal problems and integrating the results into goals and strategy. This is in contrast to **strategy implementation,** which is the use of managerial and organizational tools to direct resources toward accomplishing strategic results.[11] Strategy implementation is the administration and execution of the strategic plan. Managers may use persuasion, new equipment, changes in organization structure, or a reward system to ensure that employees and resources are used to make formulated strategy a reality.

strategy implementation The stage of strategic management that involves the use of managerial and organizational tools to direct resources toward achieving strategic outcomes.

THE STRATEGIC MANAGEMENT PROCESS

The overall strategic management process is illustrated in Exhibit 6.2. It begins when executives evaluate their current position with respect to mission, goals, and strategies. They then scan the organization's internal and external environments and identify strategic factors that may require change. Internal or external events may indicate a need to redefine the mission or goals or to formulate a new strategy at either the corporate, business, or functional level. Once a new strategy is selected, it is implemented through changes in leadership, structure, human resources, or information and control systems.

SITUATION ANALYSIS

situation analysis Analysis of the strengths, weaknesses, opportunities, and threats (SWOT) that affect organizational performance.

Situation analysis typically includes a search for SWOT—*s*trengths, *w*eaknesses, *o*pportunities, and *t*hreats that affect organizational performance. External information about opportunities and threats may be obtained from a variety of sources, including customers, government reports, professional jour-

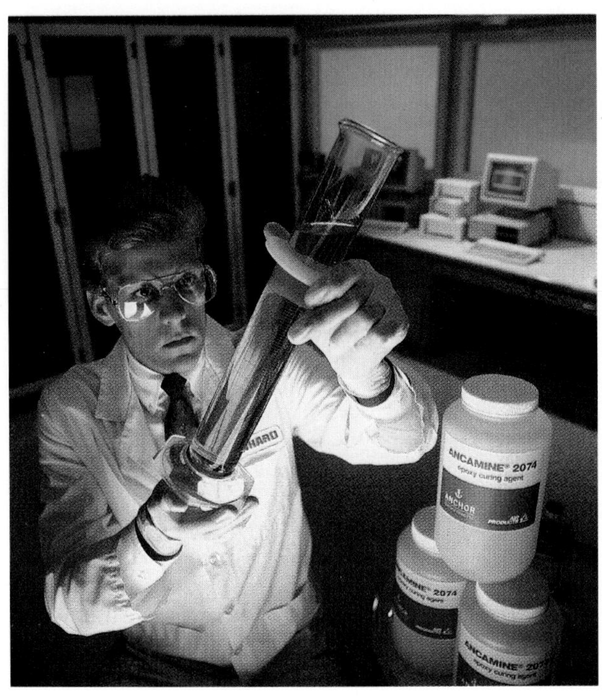

Situation analysis at Air Products and Chemicals, Inc. revealed major strengths to be industrial gases and chemical products, new-product innovation, and the ability to transfer technology to and from international affiliates. Moreover, significant opportunities exist in the environmental and energy markets. Based on this analysis, Air Products formulated the strategy of developing new businesses in the areas of waste-to-energy, cogeneration, and flue gas cleanup. Air Products' strength in technology transfer of chemical products is illustrated by this epoxy curative application where the technology originated in the United Kingdom.

nals, suppliers, bankers, friends in other organizations, consultants, or association meetings. Many firms hire special scanning organizations to provide them with newspaper clippings and analyses of relevant trends. Some firms use more subtle techniques to learn about competitors, such as asking potential recruits about their visits to other companies, hiring people away from competitors, debriefing former employees of competitors or customers, taking plant tours posing as "innocent" visitors, and even buying competitors' garbage.[12]

Executives acquire information about internal strengths and weaknesses from a variety of reports, including budgets, financial ratios, profit and loss statements, and surveys of employee attitudes and satisfaction. Managers spend 80 percent of their time giving and receiving information from others. Through frequent face-to-face discussions and meetings with people at all levels of the hierarchy, executives build an understanding of the company's internal strengths and weaknesses.

External Opportunities and Threats. *Threats* are characteristics of the external environment that may prevent the organization from achieving its strategic goals. *Opportunities* are characteristics of the external environment that have the potential to help the organization achieve or exceed its strategic goals. Executives evaluate the external environment with information about the nine sectors described in Chapter 3. The task environment sectors are the most relevant to strategic behavior and include the behavior of competitors, customers, suppliers, and the labor supply. The general environment contains those sectors that have an indirect influence on the organization but nevertheless must be understood and incorporated into strategic behavior. The general environment includes technological developments, the economy, legal-political and international events, and sociocultural changes. Additional areas that

EXHIBIT 6.3
Checklist for Analyzing Organizational Strengths and Weaknesses

Management and Organization	Marketing	Human Resources
Management quality	Distribution channels	Employee age, education
Staff quality	Market share	Union status
Degree of centralization	Advertising efficiency	Turnover, absenteeism
Organization charts	Customer satisfaction	Work satisfaction
Planning, information, control systems	Product quality	Grievances
	Service reputation	
	Sales force turnover	
Finance	**Production**	**Research and Development**
Profit margin	Plant location	Basic applied research
Debt-equity ratio	Machinery obsolescence	Laboratory capabilities
Inventory ratio	Purchasing system	Research programs
Return on investment	Quality control	New-product innovations
Credit rating	Productivity/efficiency	Technology innovations

Source: Based on Howard H. Stevenson, "Defining Corporate Strengths and Weaknesses," *Sloan Management Review* 17 (Spring 1976), 51–68; M. L. Kastens, *Long-Range Planning for Your Business* (New York: American Management Association, 1976).

might reveal opportunities or threats include pressure groups, interest groups, creditors, natural resources, and potentially competitive industries.

An example of how external analysis can uncover a threat occurred in the Post cereal business of General Foods. Scanning the environment indicated that Kellogg had increased its market share from 38 to 40 percent while Post's share had dropped from 16 to 14 percent. Information from the competitor and customer sectors indicated that Kellogg had stepped up advertising and new-product introductions. This threat to Post was the basis for a strategic response. The first step was to throw additional dollars into cents-off coupons and discounts to grocery stores. The next step was to develop new cereals, such as the successful Fruit & Fibre.[13]

INTERNAL STRENGTHS AND WEAKNESSES. *Strengths* are positive internal characteristics that the organization can exploit to achieve its strategic performance goals. *Weaknesses* are internal characteristics that may inhibit or restrict the organization's performance. Some examples of what executives evaluate to interpret strengths and weaknesses are given in Exhibit 6.3. The information sought typically pertains to specific functions such as marketing, finance, production, and R&D. Internal analysis also examines overall organization structure, management competence and quality, and human resource characteristics. Based on their understanding of these areas, managers can determine their strengths or weaknesses vis-à-vis other companies. For example, Marriott Corporation has been able to grow rapidly because of its financial strength. It has a strong financial base, enjoys an excellent reputation with creditors, and has always been able to acquire financing needed to support its strategy of constructing hotels in new locations.[14]

The value of situation analysis in helping to formulate the correct strategy is illustrated by Federal Express.

FEDERAL EXPRESS CORP.

• Federal Express dominates the overnight delivery business, but things are changing in the industry. Federal Express is considering new strategic directions, which can be understood with SWOT analyses. Federal Express has enormous *strengths*, including a well-trained, loyal, and committed work force; amazing technology that allows it to track every package from pickup to delivery; a huge warehousing, truck, and airplane system; and a strong corporate culture that supports the best on-time delivery in the industry. Since its inception in 1973, Federal Express has displayed no obvious *weaknesses*, leading to its continuing dominance of the industry. One potential weakness is the saturation of the delivery industry, which is slowing growth and profits for Federal Express and its competitors.

The biggest *threat* facing Federal Express is a combination of United Parcel Service and new technology. UPS within just five years has closed in on Federal Express's industry dominance in overnight delivery. UPS is cheap and has an excellent reputation. Another threat is the legions of loyal customers who find it cheaper and more convenient to transmit documents with fax machines or electronic mail. These cheap alternatives reduce market potential for Federal's overnight business. *Opportunities* in the external environment are to play on Federal Express's superb reputation for quality to move into related delivery areas. One target is box hauling from warehouses, which has a higher profit potential and takes Federal Express into territory dominated by UPS. Another opportunity is expansion into foreign markets.

What does SWOT analysis suggest for Federal Express's future strategy? Capitalize on its strengths and pursue its opportunities. With fax machines potentially cutting overnight delivery by 30 percent, Federal Express is entering box delivery to maintain growth and profits. It also is investing in delivery to foreign markets, a business that is growing 60 percent annually. It is also continuing extraordinary service in overnight delivery, which is its major business. Federal Express may lower prices in the near future as one way to drive out weaker air-express companies, leaving more of the market to itself and UPS. Federal Express's new strategy fits the environmental situation, and its employees are relishing the battle with UPS, which they expect to win.[15]

FORMULATING CORPORATE-LEVEL STRATEGY

Corporate-level strategy typically concerns the mix and utilization of business divisions called **strategic business units (SBUs).** An SBU has a unique business mission, product line, competitors, and markets relative to other SBUs in the corporation.[16] Executives in charge of the entire corporation generally define an overall strategic direction—called a *grand strategy*—and then bring together a portfolio of strategic business units to carry it out.

strategic business unit (SBU) A division of the organization that has a unique business mission, product line, competitors, and markets relative to other SBUs in the same corporation.

GRAND STRATEGY

Grand strategy is the general plan of major action by which a firm intends to achieve its long-term objectives.[17] Grand strategies fall into three general categories: growth, stability, and retrenchment.

grand strategy The general plan of major action by which an organization intends to achieve its long-term objectives.

FOCUS ON GLOBAL COMPETITION

PARTNERSHIP STRATEGIES

How do companies — big and small — strategically position themselves to compete internationally? Without experience, an international strategy may turn into disaster. Why not team up with companies abroad?

Consider the strategy employed by Whirlpool Corporation, the huge appliance manufacturer. Senior executives realized they could not simply defend domestic boundaries and continue to prosper. Brainstorming new strategies pointed to globalization. Unfortunately, big American refrigerators do not fit into small Japanese kitchens. Europeans tend not to buy dishwashers.

A Whirlpool strength was a strong position in Canada and Mexico. Europe seemed like the next big market so Whirlpool acquired a ready-made distribution system and manufacturing operation by purchasing 53 percent of Holland's Philips N. V.'s $2 billion appliance business.

Philips and Whirlpool streamlined the two companies, giving them enormous buying clout that will lower cost for materials and components. This streamlining puts Whirlpool in a position of being a low-cost producer in both North America and Europe, a powerful strategic advantage. Whirlpool also achieves an international synergy by using its worldwide distribution network to market products from both American and European plants.

At Nypro, Inc., a small plastic injection-molding and industrial components manufacturer in Clinton, Massachusetts, President Gordon Lankton found the local rules and customs of other countries too complex to fathom from the United States. So he found partners in Ireland, France, and Hong Kong, but his initial efforts failed because he did not understand the other companies or their goals. Finally, Nypro hit it off with partner companies in Switzerland and Singapore. Trial and error worked, and sharing technology has been a big plus, helping both sides.

Nypro has a presence in six countries now and four joint venture plants in the United States. Disputes over quality, management techniques, and strategy still occur but joint ventures account for 25 percent of revenues. More important, Nypro overcame limitations on markets, technology, knowledge, and people. The expended horizon was only possible with partners. And employees love it — they cannot wait for the next foreign adventure.

Source: Claudia H. Deutsch, "Whirlpool is Gathering a Global Momentum," *The New York Times*, April 23, 1989, sec. 3, 10, and Joshua Hyatt, "The Partnership Route," *Inc.*, December 1988, 145–148.

GROWTH. Growth can be promoted internally by investing in the expansion of specific SBUs or externally by acquiring additional business divisions. Internal growth can include development of new or changed products, such as Goodyear's development of the Eagle tire, or expansion of current products into new markets, such as Coors' expansion into the Northeast. External growth typically involves *diversification,* which means the acquisition of businesses that are related to current product lines or that take the corporation into new areas. Sometimes expansion involves acquiring competitors, such as Northwest Airlines' acquisition of Republic, or suppliers or distributors, such as Alcan's acquisition of Bauxite mines. One strategy for international growth is the formation of a joint venture, as described in the Focus on Global Competition box.

STABILITY. *Stability,* sometimes called a *pause strategy,* means that the organization wants to remain the same size or grow slowly and in a controlled fashion. The corporation wants to stay in its current business, such as Allied Tire Stores, whose motto is "We just sell tires." After organizations have undergone a turbulent period of rapid growth, executives often focus on a stability strategy to integrate strategic business units and ensure that the organization is working efficiently.

The BFGoodrich Company used a *grand strategy* of retrenchment when it divested its tire business. BFGoodrich sold its interest in the tire business to concentrate on its polyvinyl chloride business and to rapidly expand its aerospace and specialty chemicals businesses. The divestment provided cash to invest in these core businesses and produced an almost immediate increase in company profits. Through this divestiture, BFGoodrich now begins a new era as a chemical and aerospace company.

RETRENCHMENT. *Retrenchment* means that the organization goes through a period of forced decline by either shrinking current business units or selling off or liquidating entire businesses. The organization may have experienced a precipitous drop in demand for its products, prompting managers to order across-the-board cuts in personnel and expenditures. Apple Computer did so in 1985, and AT&T cut over 20,000 jobs in 1987. *Liquidation* means selling off a business unit for the cash value of the assets, thus terminating its existence. An example is the liquidation of Minnie Pearl fried chicken. *Divestiture* involves the selling off of businesses that no longer seem central to the corporation. When ITT sold 115 of 200 business divisions and when General Electric sold its family financial services and housewares divisions, both corporations were going through periods of retrenchment, also called *downsizing*.

PORTFOLIO STRATEGY

Portfolio strategy pertains to the mix of business units and product lines that fit together in a logical way to provide synergy and competitive advantage for the corporation. For example, an individual may wish to diversify in an investment portfolio, with some high-risk stocks, some low-risk stocks, some growth stocks, and perhaps a few income bonds. In much the same way, corporations like to have a balanced mix of SBUs. Two possible ways to think about portfolio strategy are the BCG matrix and the GE business screen.

portfolio strategy A type of corporate-level strategy that pertains to the organization's mix of SBUs and product lines that fit together in such a way as to provide the corporation with synergy and competitive advantage.

THE BCG MATRIX. The BCG (for Boston Consulting Group) matrix is illustrated in Exhibit 6.4. The **BCG matrix** organizes businesses along two dimensions — business growth rate and market share.[18] *Business growth rate* pertains to how rapidly the entire industry is increasing. *Market share* defines whether a business unit has a larger or smaller share than competitors. The combinations of high and low market share and high and low business growth provide four categories for a corporate portfolio.

BCG matrix A concept developed by the Boston Consulting Group that evaluates SBUs with respect to the dimensions of business growth rate and market share.

EXHIBIT 6.4
The BCG Matrix

Market Share

Business Growth Rate	High (Market Share)	Low (Market Share)
High	**Stars** Rapid growth and expansion.	**Question Marks** New ventures. Risky—a few become stars, others divested.
Low	**Cash Cows** Milk to finance question marks and stars.	**Dogs** No investment. Keep if profit. Consider divestment.

Hasbro Inc. has adopted a portfolio strategy for its many product lines, which include Milton Bradley board games and puzzles, Playskool® infant and preschool products, and Hasbro's traditional toys such as G.I. Joe®, Cabbage Patch, and My Little Pony. Hasbro's diversified portfolio includes products that cover the full spectrum of toy users from infants to adults, as well as products in different stages of the product life cycle. For example, games for older children such as Chutes & Ladders are balanced with innovations such as Playskool's Sandwich-Board Aprons for toddlers shown here.

The *star* has a large market share in a rapidly growing industry. The star is important because it has additional growth potential, and profits should be plowed into this business as investment for future growth and profits. The star is visible and attractive and will generate profits and a positive cash flow even as the industry matures and market growth slows.

The *cash cow* exists in a mature, slow-growth industry but is a dominant business in the industry, with a large market share. Because heavy investments in advertising and plant expansion are no longer required, the corporation earns a positive cash flow. It can milk the cash cow to invest in other, riskier businesses.

The *question mark* exists in a new, rapidly growing industry but has only a small market share. The question mark is risky: It could become a star, but it could also fail. The corporation can invest the cash earned from cash cows in question marks with the goal of nurturing them into future stars.

The *dog* is a poor performer. It has only a small share of a slow-growth market. The dog provides little profit for the corporation and may be targeted for divestment or liquidation if turnaround is not possible.

The circles in Exhibit 6.4 represent the business portfolio for a hypothetical corporation. Circle size represents the relative size of each business in the company's portfolio. Most organizations, like Gillette, have businesses in more than one quadrant, thereby representing different market shares and growth rates.

GILLETTE COMPANY

• Gillette has several cash cows in its corporate portfolio. The most famous is the shaving division, which accounts for two-thirds of the company's total profits and holds a large share of a stable market. This division sells Atra, Trac II,

EXHIBIT 6.5
GE's Nine-Cell Business Screen

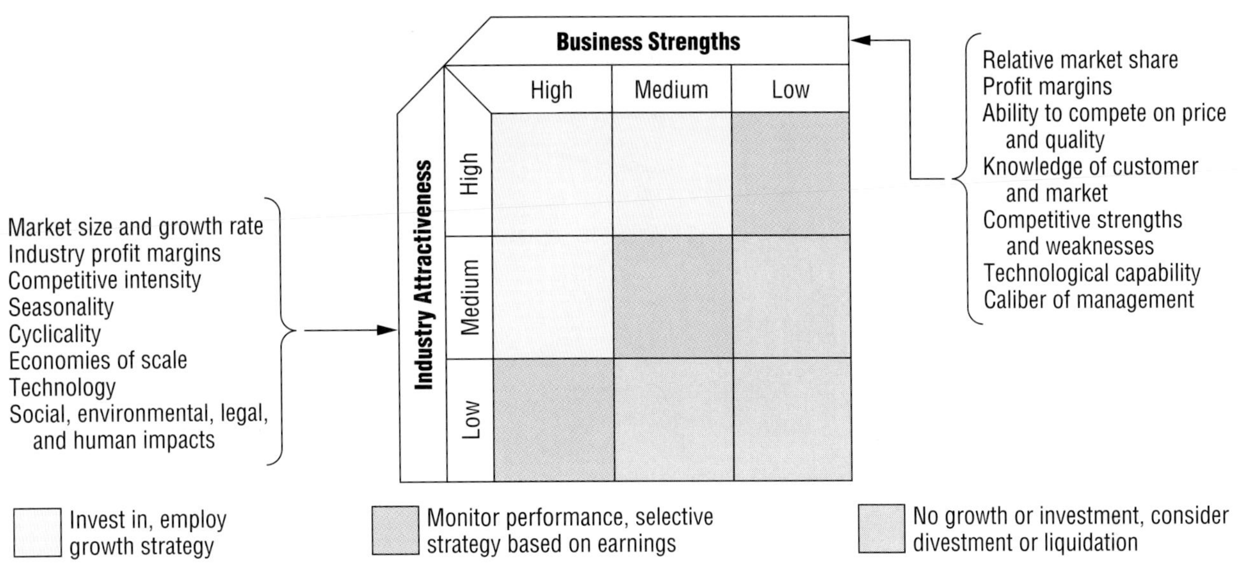

Source: Based on James H. Higgins and Julian W. Vineze, *Strategic Management and Organizational Policy*, 3d ed. (Hinsdale, Ill.: Dryden Press, 1986).

the new Sensor shaving system, and Good News disposables. The Oral-B laboratories division is also a cash cow with its steady sales of toothbrushes and other dental hygiene products. The stationery products division has star status. It has become the world's largest marketer of writing instruments, including Paper Mate, Flair, Erasermate, and Waterman, and it shows potential for rapid growth overseas. Gillette's question marks are in the personal care division, which includes the Silkience line of shampoos and conditioners, Mink Difference, and Aapri Facial Scrub. Aapri has done well, but Mink Difference and Silkience hair conditioners are struggling for a reasonable market share. Without improvement, they may be assigned to the dog category, to which the Cricket line of disposable lighters was relegated. Bic disposable lighters dominated the Cricket line so completely that Cricket became a dog and was eventually put out of its misery through liquidation. Gillette continues to experiment with new products and question marks to ensure that its portfolio will include stars and cash cows in the future.[19]

GE BUSINESS SCREEN. General Electric Company pioneered the development of a more sophisticated portfolio matrix, which is illustrated in Exhibit 6.5. The **GE screen** is used by senior executives to evaluate business units within GE's portfolio to determine whether financial investments should be made to expand the business unit or the unit should be left alone or divested. This matrix is also used to evaluate potential business acquisitions.

GE screen A portfolio matrix developed by General Electric Company that evaluates business units along the dimensions of industry attractiveness and business strength.

The business screen has nine categories based on two dimensions: industry attractiveness and business strength. The advantage of the GE matrix is that it provides a list of criteria for evaluating both. Industry attractiveness includes such dimensions as market size and growth rate, industry profit margins,

Bausch & Lomb uses an *analyzer strategy* with its Ray-Ban brand of quality sunglasses. Bausch & Lomb's market share is approximately five times its nearest competitor, and its strategy is to maintain this stable business while innovating on the periphery with designer sunglasses. Donna Karan (second from left) is involved in the development of sunglasses that have the same status and elegance as designer clothes. This innovation will yield new profits from sophisticated, high-quality, fashion sunglasses.

seasonality, and economies of scale. Business strength is evaluated according to such factors as relative market share, profit margins, and technological capability.

By examining the scores on the two lists of criteria for each business unit, investment and divestment decisions can be made. Business units that fall into the taupe cells of Exhibit 6.5 are considered candidates for divestment, because they rank low in both industry attractiveness and business strength. These SBUs also can be liquidated, or the corporation could find some way to utilize assets but not invest for growth. The three cells in the yellow section of the exhibit are just the opposite: strong businesses in attractive industries. The corporation should invest in these businesses and encourage market and product development. The blue cells along the diagonal should be handled selectively and investment decisions made with respect to the earning characteristics of each business unit. These businesses normally are kept within the portfolio with the expectation of improved performance, but if they do poorly they may be divested.

FORMULATING BUSINESS-LEVEL STRATEGY

Now we turn to strategy formulation within the strategic business unit, in which the concern is how to compete. The same three generic strategies — growth, stability, and retrenchment — apply at the business level, but they are accomplished through competitive actions rather than the acquisition or divestment of business divisions. The three frameworks in which business units formulate strategy are Miles and Snow's strategy typology, Porter's competitive strategies, and the product life cycle. Each provides a framework for business unit competitive action.

EXHIBIT 6.6
Miles and Snow's Strategy Typology

	Strategy	Environment	Organizational Characteristics
Prospector	Innovate. Find new market opportunities. Grow. Take risks.	Dynamic, growing	Creative, innovative, flexible, decentralized
Defender	Protect turf. Retrench, hold current market.	Stable	Tight control, centralized, production efficiency, low overhead
Analyzer	Maintain current market plus moderate innovation	Moderate change	Tight control and flexibility, efficient production, creativity
Reactor	No clear strategy. React to specific conditions. Drift.	Any condition	No clear organizational approach; depends on current needs

Source: Based on Raymond E. Miles, Charles C. Snow, Alan D. Meyer, and Henry L. Coleman, Jr., "Organizational Strategy, Structure, and Process," *Academy of Management Review* 3 (1978), 546–562.

MILES AND SNOW'S STRATEGY TYPOLOGY

A business-level strategy typology was developed from the study of business strategies by Raymond Miles and Charles Snow.[20] The basic idea is that business-level managers seek to formulate strategies that will be congruent with the external environment. Organizations strive to achieve a fit among internal characteristics, strategy, and environmental characteristics. The four strategies that can be adopted based on the environment are the prospector, defender, analyzer, and reactor strategies. These strategies, their environments, and their internal characteristics are summarized in Exhibit 6.6.

PROSPECTOR. The *prospector* strategy is to innovate, seek out new opportunities, take risks, and grow. The prospector strategy is suited to a dynamic, growing environment. In such an environment, creativity is more important than efficiency. The internal organization is flexible and decentralized to facilitate innovation. One example of a prospector strategy is Federal Express Corporation, described earlier, which innovates in both services and production techniques in the rapidly changing overnight mail industry. Another example occurred in the chocolate chip cookie industry: Mrs. Field's Cookies and David's Cookies were both aggressive prospectors that opened many stores, franchised nationally, and attempted to be the dominant producer in the industry.

DEFENDER. The defender strategy is almost the opposite of the prospector: It is concerned with stability or even retrenchment. The *defender* strategy seeks to maintain current market share—that is, hold on to current customers—but it neither innovates nor seeks to grow. The defender is concerned with internal efficiency and control to produce reliable products for steady customers. Defenders can be successful, especially when they exist in a declining industry or a stable environment.[21] For example, big advertising agencies such as Ogilvy & Mather and Foote, Cone & Belding Communications Inc. shifted to a defender strategy when the advertising industry started to shrink. Growth in ad spending declined sharply; thus, the agencies began cost cutting, which meant leaving open positions unfilled, giving fewer bonuses, and trying to retain current customers.[22]

Wendy's International, Inc., has chosen a *differentiation strategy* to compete in the fast-food industry. One point of differentiation is new products such as the Superbar, baked potatoes, and hamburger refinements. By differentiating itself with these products, Wendy's can achieve its business goals of increasing sales volume, offering best value for best price, and insuring consistent dining experiences for customers.

ANALYZER. Analyzers are considered to lie midway between prospectors and defenders. The *analyzer* strategy is to maintain a stable business while innovating on the periphery. Some products are targeted toward stable environments, in which an efficiency strategy designed to retain current customers is employed. Others are targeted toward new, more dynamic environments, where growth is possible. The analyzer attempts to balance efficient production for current lines along with the creative development of new product lines. One example is Anheuser-Busch, with its stable beer line and innovation of snack foods as a complementary line. Another is Frito-Lay Inc. Frito-Lay's overall environment is changing moderately. It maintains market share with such stable products as Fritos, Doritos, and Tostitos. However, Frito-Lay also innovates on the periphery to open new markets and has expanded its total product line with O'Grady's Potato Chips and Grandma's Cookies.[23]

REACTOR. The *reactor* has no strategy at all. Rather than defining a strategy to suit a specific environment, reactors respond to environmental threats and opportunities in ad hoc fashion. Reactors take whatever actions seem likely to meet their immediate needs and have no long-term plan for congruence with the external environment. A reactor strategy seems almost random, because top management has not defined a plan or given the organization an explicit direction. Failed companies often are the result of reactor strategies. Schlitz Brewing Company went through a period in which it dropped from first to seventh in the brewing industry due to poor strategic decisions. W. T. Grant, a large retailer, eventually went bankrupt because executives failed to adopt a strategy consistent with the trend toward discount retail stores.

PORTER'S COMPETITIVE STRATEGIES

Michael E. Porter studied a number of business organizations and proposed three effective business-level strategies: differentiation, cost leadership, and focus.[24] The organizational characteristics associated with each strategy are summarized in Exhibit 6.7.

DIFFERENTIATION. The **differentiation** strategy involves an attempt to distinguish the firm's products or services from others in the industry. The organization may use advertising, distinctive product features, exceptional service, or new technology to achieve a product perceived as unique. The differentiation strategy can be profitable because customers are loyal and will pay high prices for the product. Examples of products that have benefited from a differentiation strategy include Mercedes-Benz automobiles, Maytag appliances, and Tylenol, all of which are perceived as distinctive in their markets. Companies that pursue a differentiation strategy typically need strong marketing abilities, a creative flair, and a reputation for leadership.[25]

COST LEADERSHIP. Another strategy, **cost leadership,** occurs when the organization aggressively seeks efficient facilities, pursues cost reductions, and uses tight cost controls to produce products more efficiently than competitors. A low-cost position means that the company can undercut competitors' prices and still offer comparable quality and earn a reasonable profit. Scottish Inns

Strategy	Commonly Required Skills and Resources
Differentiation	Strong marketing abilities
	Strong coordination among functional departments
	Creative flair
	Strong capability in basic research
	Corporate reputation for quality or technological leadership
Overall cost leadership	Tight cost control
	Process engineering skills
	Intense supervision of labor
	Products designed for ease in manufacture
	Frequent, detailed control reports
Focus	Combination of the above policies directed at the particular strategic target

EXHIBIT 6.7
Organizational Characteristics for Porter's Competitive Strategies

Source: Reprinted with permission of The Free Press, a Division of Macmillan, Inc., from *Competitive Strategy:* Techniques for Analyzing Industries and Competitors by Michael E. Porter. Copyright © 1980 by The Free Press.

and Motel 6 are low-priced alternatives to Holiday Inn and Ramada Inn. The Food Lion Inc. grocery chain is a superb example of cost leadership. The company's credo is to do "1,000 things 100% better." Food Lion builds distribution warehouses close to its stores, recycles banana crates as bins for cosmetics, and even uses waste heat from refrigerator units to warm the stores. With the lowest costs and lowest prices in the industry, Food Lion is still highly profitable.[26]

FOCUS. In the **focus** strategy, the organization concentrates its strategy on a specific regional market or buyer group. The company will use either a differentiation or low-cost approach, but only for a narrow target market. One example of focus strategy is the brokerage firm of Edward D. Jones & Company. It focused on the investment needs of rural America, moving into small towns where Merrill Lynch representatives would not even stop for gas. In this ignored market niche, Jones has opened 1,300 offices and now serves over 1 million customers with its conservative investment philosophy.[27]

Porter found that some businesses did not consciously adopt one of these three strategies and were stuck with no strategic advantage. Without a strategic advantage, businesses earned below-average profits compared with those that used differentiation, cost leadership, or focus strategies. Note the similarity between Porter's strategies and Miles and Snow's typology. The differentiation strategy is similar to the prospector, the low-cost strategy is similar to the defender, and the focus strategy is similar to the analyzer, which adopts a focus strategy appropriate for each product line. The reactor strategy, which is really not a strategy at all, is similar to organizations that Porter found were unable to attain a competitive advantage.

differentiation A type of competitive strategy with which the organization seeks to distinguish its products or services from competitors'.

cost leadership A type of competitive strategy with which the organization aggressively seeks efficient facilities, cuts costs, and employs tight cost controls to be more efficient than competitors.

focus A type of competitive strategy that emphasizes concentration on a specific regional market or buyer group.

PRODUCT LIFE CYCLE

The **product life cycle** is a series of stages that a product goes through in its market acceptance, as illustrated in Exhibit 6.8. First, a product is developed within the laboratories of selected companies and then introduced into the

product life cycle The stages through which a product or service goes: (1) development and introduction into the marketplace, (2) growth, (3) maturity, and (4) decline.

EXHIBIT 6.8
Strategies and Stages of Product Life Cycle

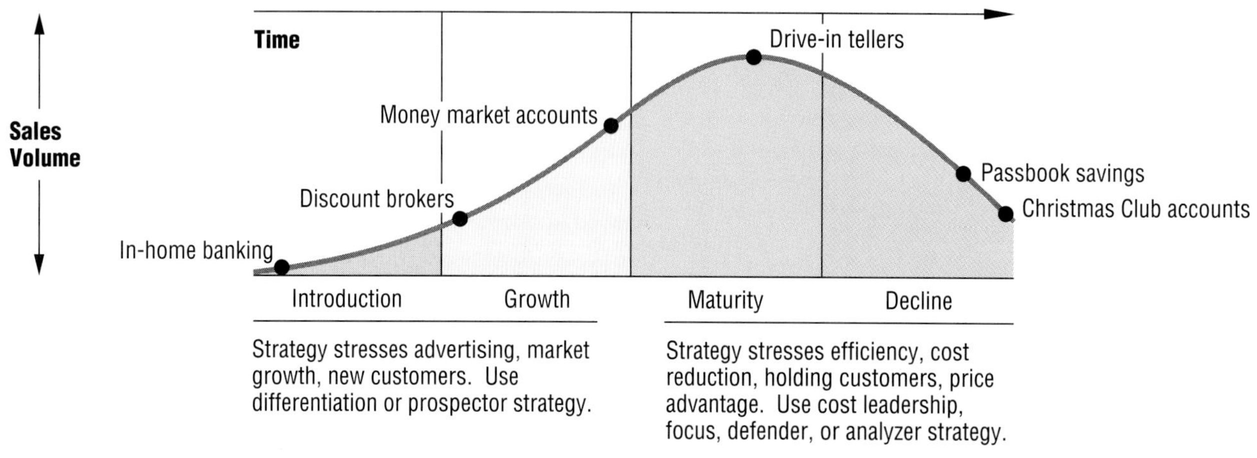

marketplace. If the product succeeds, it enjoys rapid growth as consumers accept it. Next is the maturity stage, in which widespread product acceptance occurs but growth peaks. Gradually the product grows out of favor or fashion and enters the decline stage.[28]

The life cycle concept also applies to services, as the banking example in Exhibit 6.8 shows. In-home banking is a new product, and discount broker services is in the rapid growth stage. Money market accounts have been around for a while and are approaching maturity, which is where drive-in tellers are. Passbook savings accounts are in decline, being replaced by money market accounts and certificates of deposit. The Christmas Club accounts are in serious decline and are available at only a few banks.

Banks and other organizations can tailor strategy to product life cycle stage.[29] During the introduction and growth stages, prospector and differentiation strategies are appropriate, because they stress advertising, attracting new customers, and market growth. After the product reaches maturity, a defender or low-cost strategy is important, because competitors will have developed products that look and perform similarly. Company strategy should stress efficiency, reduce overhead costs, and seek a price advantage over competitors.

To summarize, the three models that describe business-level strategies contain similarities. One company that uses these strategies is H. J. Heinz Company.

H. J. HEINZ COMPANY

• Heinz produces a number of mature products in the consumer food industry and is striving to become the low-cost producer in ketchup, french fries, cat food, tuna, baby food, and soup. At a management get-together, called the Low-Cost Operator Conference, chief executive Tony O'Reilly admonished managers to cut costs even further. One technique was to procure cheap raw materials. Another was to hold down manufacturing costs. In five years, Heinz eliminated $4 million in expenses each year with such ideas as removing the back label from large bottles. Consolidation of factories and renegotiation of work rules eliminated 2,000 jobs. The next step was an automated facility. Heinz will continue cutting costs wherever possible. To keep managers on their toes, O'Reilly plans to eliminate one layer of management if costs cannot be cut in other ways.

Heinz has reduced advertising costs by using 15- versus 30-second television commercials. But Heinz is also working to introduce a few new products. The Weight Watchers frozen entree and dessert lines are doing well, as is a new line of dried instant baby food. Heinz is using the cost savings made in mature product areas to increase advertising and development for the new product lines.[30]

Heinz is using a low-cost strategy for mature product lines, and it is working. Market share and profits are increasing. Heinz also is an analyzer because it is innovating on the periphery. Products in the early stages of the life cycle receive heavy advertising and promotion, which is appropriate during the growth stage in order to gain market share.

FORMULATING FUNCTIONAL-LEVEL STRATEGY

Functional-level strategies are the action plans adopted by major departments to support the execution of business-level strategy. Major organizational functions include marketing, production, finance, personnel, and research and development. Senior managers in these departments adopt strategies that are coordinated with the business-level strategy to achieve the organization's strategic goals.[31]

For example, consider a company that has adopted a prospector strategy and is introducing new products that are expected to experience rapid growth in the early stages of the life cycle. The personnel department should adopt a strategy appropriate for growth, which would mean recruiting additional personnel and training middle managers for movement into new positions. The marketing department should undertake test marketing, aggressive advertising campaigns, and consumer product trials. The finance department should adopt plans to borrow money, handle large cash investments, and authorize construction of new production facilities.

A company with mature products or an analyzer strategy will have different functional strategies. The personnel department should develop strategies for retaining and developing a stable work force, including transfers, advancements, and incentives for efficiency and safety. Marketing should stress brand loyalty and the development of established, reliable distribution channels. Production should maintain long production runs, routinization, and cost reduction. Finance should focus on net cash flows and positive cash balances.

EXHIBIT 6.9
Tools for Putting Strategy into Action

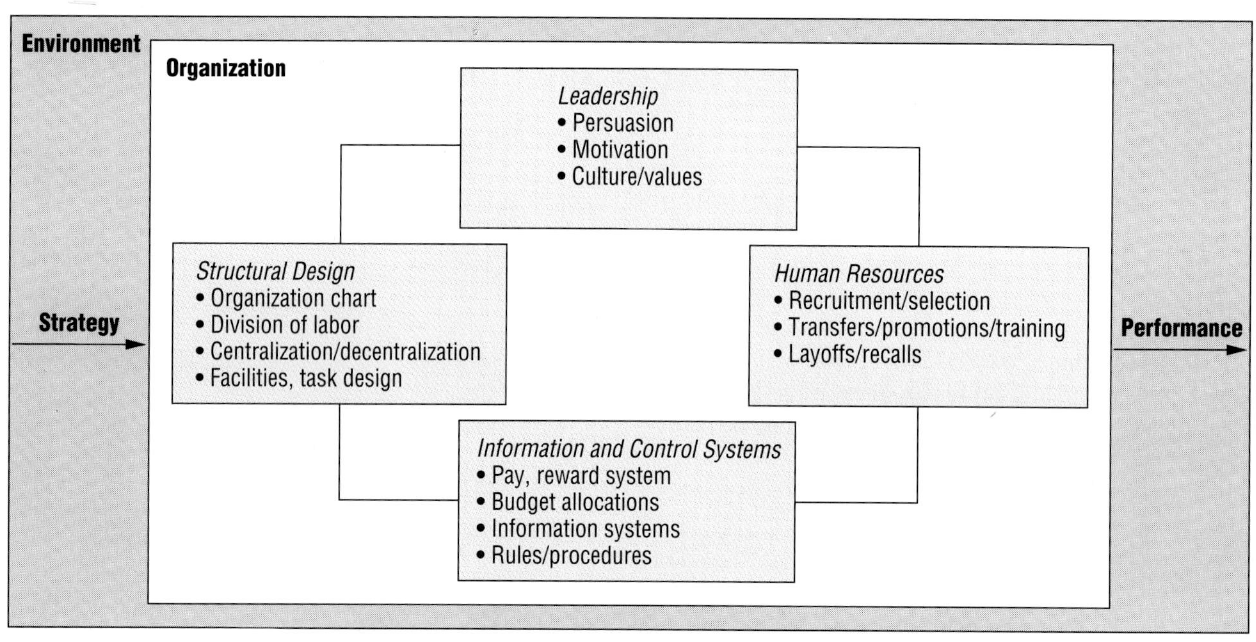

Source: Adapted from Jay R.Galbraith and Robert K. Kazanjian, *Strategy Implementation: Structure, Systems and Process*, 2d ed. (St. Paul, Minn.: West, 1986), 115. Used with permission.

PUTTING STRATEGY INTO ACTION

The final step in the strategic management process is implementation — which is how strategy is put into action. Some people argue that strategy implementation is the most difficult and important part of strategic management.[32] No matter how creative the formulated strategy, the organization will not benefit if it is incorrectly implemented. Implementation involves several tools — parts of the firm that can be changed — as illustrated in Exhibit 6.9. It requires changes in the organization's behavior, which can be brought about by changing management's leadership approach, structural design, information and control systems, and human resources.[33]

LEADERSHIP

Leadership is the ability to influence organization members to adopt the behaviors needed for strategy implementation. Leadership includes persuasion, motivation, and changes in corporate values and culture. Managers seeking to implement a new strategy may make speeches to employees, issue edicts, build coalitions, and persuade middle managers to go along with their vision for the corporation. If leaders let other managers participate during strategy formula-

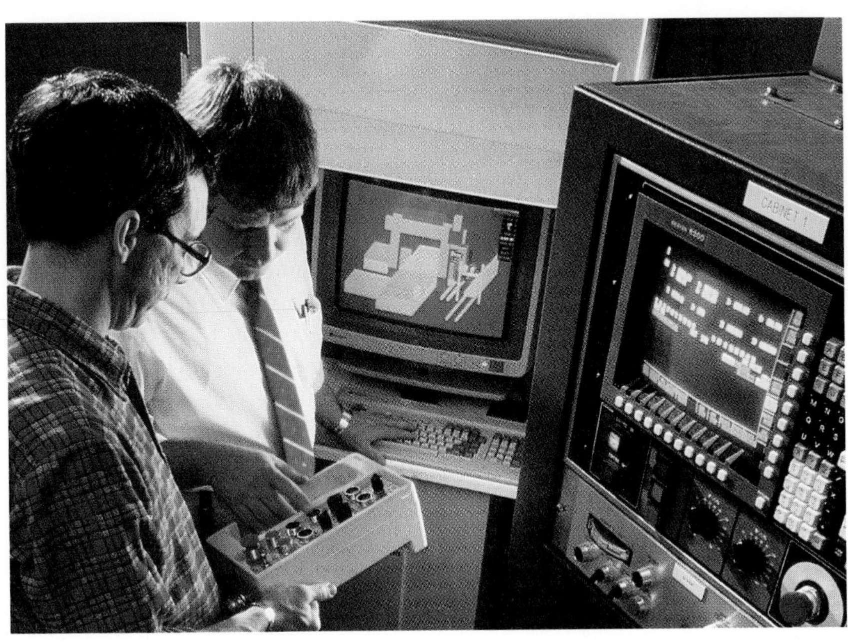

Caterpillar Inc. puts its competitive strategy into action with new factory technology, restructuring of its worldwide manufacturing base, and computer coordination of manufacturing activities. Another implementation technique is the Employee Satisfaction Process in which 2,000 people on more than 200 teams have redesigned their work areas for increased efficiency. Caterpillar also launched a training program, shown here, that uses exciting new technology to simulate production operations. Successful *implementation* of its strategy has reduced Caterpillar's cost 35 percent.

tion, implementation will be easier because managers and employees will already understand and be committed to the new strategy. In essence, leadership is used to motivate employees to adopt new behaviors and, for some strategies, to infuse new values and attitudes.

For example, Linda Koslow, manager of Marshall Field's department store in Oak Brook, Illinois, uses leadership to meet holiday sales targets by pumping up morale, encouraging aggressive selling, and being accessible to employees.[34] As another example, Q. T. Wiles purchases failing electronics manufacturers and turns them around. His emphasis is on strategy implementation. He uses an almost autocratic leadership style to reinforce a new way of thinking and new values within a firm. To this end, each manager must memorize a 12-item list of "Q. T. disciplines" and the organization's official charter.[35]

STRUCTURAL DESIGN

Structural design typically begins with the organization chart. It pertains to managers' responsibilities, their degree of authority, and the consolidation of facilities, departments, and divisions. Structure also pertains to the degree of decentralization, task design, and production technology. (Structure will be described in Chapter 10.)

Q. T. Wiles used structural changes to implement strategy in electronic companies. At MiniScribe Corporation he reorganized the work force into small groups, each responsible for a single product, a single customer, or some other narrowly defined target. Each group was an autonomous structural unit with skills and functions necessary to achieve its goals.[36] The strategy of merging Uniroyal and Goodrich was unprofitable for the first two years because of implementation problems concerning structural design. Such simple things as the tire molds in the two companies' plants being incompatible prevented consolidation of equipment and facilities. Blending the marketing and the accounting departments of the two companies proved difficult because of different philosophies and cost accounting systems.[37]

Information and Control Systems

Information and control systems include reward systems, pay incentives, budgets for allocating resources, information systems, and the organization's rules, policies, and procedures. Changes in these systems represent major tools for putting strategy into action. For example, resources can be reassigned from R&D to marketing if a new strategy requires increased advertising but no product changes. Managers and employees must be rewarded for adhering to the new strategy and making it a success.[38]

Jim Bernstein, CEO of General Health Inc., set the strategy of sales growth of 50 percent in one year. He used a pay incentive by promising every employee an extra month's pay if the company hit the sales target. The strategy worked almost too well, creating a greater increase in sales than the company could handle, which shows the impact of pay incentives for strategy implementation. As another example, John Hancock Mutual Life Insurance Company sold whole-life policies that were out of fashion in the wave of new financial instruments and insurance policies that occurred during the 1980s. President John McElwee's strategy was to change Hancock into a financial supermarket, offering banking and investment opportunities along with insurance products. But because insurance agents received bigger commissions from the traditional insurance policies, McElwee had to increase the commissions for selling noninsurance products. Implementing McElwee's strategy also required changes in information systems, because new reports had to be developed showing whether agents were meeting their goals in new-product areas.[39]

Human Resources

The organization's *human resources* are its employees. The human resource function recruits, selects, trains, transfers, promotes, and lays off employees to achieve strategic goals. For example, training employees can help them understand the purpose and importance of a new strategy or help them develop the necessary specific skills and behaviors. Sometimes employees may have to be let go and replaced with new people. One newspaper shifted its strategy from an evening to a morning paper to compete with a large newspaper from a nearby city. The new strategy fostered resentment and resistance among department heads. In order to implement it, 80 percent of the department heads had to be let go because they refused to cooperate. New people were recruited and placed in those positions, and the morning newspaper strategy was a resounding success.[40]

Since the poison gas disaster at a Union Carbide plant in Bhopal, India, many chemical companies have implemented a strategy of increased safety. American Cyanamid requires workers to attend safety classes. The company had four safety incidents and wants no more. The training consists of 40 hours in the classroom, including courses in basic chemistry to help workers understand plant processes and how to cope with chemical reactions.[41]

In summary, strategy implementation is essential for effective strategic management. Managers implement strategy through the tools of leadership, structural design, information and control systems, and human resources. Without implementation, even the most creative strategy will fail.

Summary

This chapter described several important concepts of strategic management. Strategic management begins with an evaluation of the organization's current mission, goals, and strategy. This is followed by situation analysis (sometimes called SWOT analysis), which examines opportunities and threats in the external environment as well as strengths and weaknesses within the organization. Situation analysis leads to the formulation of explicit strategic plans, which then must be implemented.

Strategy formulation takes place at three levels: corporate, business, and functional. Corporate grand strategies include growth, stability, and retrenchment. Frameworks for accomplishing them include the BCG matrix and the GE business screen. Business-level strategies include Miles and Snow's strategy typology, Porter's competitive strategies, and the product life cycle. Once business strategies have been formulated, functional strategies for supporting them can be developed.

Even the most creative strategies have no value if they cannot be translated into action. Four organizational tools used for strategy implementation are leadership, structural design, information and control systems, and human resources.

Management Solution

When David Johnson took over as CEO of Gerber Products Company, the company was in bad shape, with red ink flowing and takeover threats surfacing. His response reflected sensitivity for both strategy formulation and implementation. After studying the company firsthand, he adopted a growth strategy through aggressive introduction of new products in the baby foods division. To implement this strategy he sold off money-losing subsidiaries such as those that made plush children's toys and baby furniture. Five other children's divisions were merged into a single entity with anticipated savings through consolidation of production, marketing, and distribution facilities. In the baby food division, a new product called First Foods was introduced, generating about $30 million sales in its first year. Other new products such as Fruit Classics and microwave feeding dishes were introduced. The growth strategy also includes an international component. Gerber is developing separate baby foods for each country because kids eat different things. The strategy is to make baby food similar to what is already eaten in a country and then add vitamins and protein supplements. The implementation of the new strategy has been so successful that Gerber is already in the black, winning the praise of food industry experts.[42]

Discussion Questions

1. Assume you are the general manager of a large hotel and have formulated a strategy of renting banquet facilities to corporations for big events. At a monthly management meeting, your sales manager informed the head of food operations that a big reception in one week will require converting a large hall from a meeting room to a banquet facility in only 60 minutes — a difficult but doable operation that will require precise planning and extra help. The food operations manager is furious at just finding out. What is wrong here?
2. Which is more important — strategy formulation or strategy implementation? Do they depend on each other? Is it possible for strategy implementation to occur first?
3. If an organization has hired strategic management professionals, during which part of the strategic management process would they play the largest role?
4. Perform a situation (SWOT) analysis for the university you attend. Do you think university administrators consider these factors when devising their strategy?
5. What is meant by the scope and synergy components of strategy? Give examples.
6. Using Porter's competitive strategies and Miles and Snow's strategy typology, how would you describe the strategies of Wal-Mart, Bloomingdale's, and Kmart?
7. Walt Disney Company has four major strategic business units: movies (Touchstone), theme parks, consumer products, and television (primarily cable). Place each of these SBUs on the BCG matrix and GE business screen based on your knowledge of them.
8. As administrator for a medium-size hospital, you and the board of directors have decided to change to a drug dependency hospital from a short-term, acute-care facility. Which organizational dimensions would you use to implement this strategy?
9. How would functional strategies in marketing, research and development, and production departments differ if a business changed from a prospector to a defender strategy?
10. Compare and contrast the strategy typology of Miles and Snow with Porter's competitive strategies. What are the similarities and differences? Which do you think better describes business-level strategies?

Management in Practice: Experiential Exercise

Developing Strategy for a Small Business

Instructions: Your instructor may ask you to do this exercise individually or as part of a group. Select a local business with which you (or group members) are familiar. Complete the following activities.

ACTIVITY 1 Perform a SWOT analysis for the business.

Strengths: ____________________

____

____

____

____

Opportunities: ____________________

____

____

____

____

Weaknesses: ____________________

____

____

____

____

Threats: ____________________

____

____

____

____

ACTIVITY 2 Write a statement of the business's current strategy.

ACTIVITY 3 Decide on a goal you would like the business to achieve in two years, and write a statement of proposed strategy for achieveing that goal.

ACTIVITY 4 Write a statement describing how the proposed strategy will be implemented.

ACTIVITY 5 What have you learned from this exercise?

CASES FOR ANALYSIS

BETHLEHEM STEEL CORPORATION

Bethlehem Steel, like other companies in the industry, grew fat and happy during the 1960s and 1970s, believing it was impregnable. At Bethlehem, the old days were characterized by perks for executives, including limos, jets, and company-supported country clubs, which bred complacency, poor quality, and poor service. Then in the 1980s, international steel competitors, especially the Japanese, outclassed U.S. steel companies, driving them into recession. When Walter Williams took over as chief executive of Bethlehem, he smoked three packs of cigarettes a day and avoided going out for fear of meeting laid-off friends. Industry experts believed that Bethlehem's failure was imminent.

Williams, however, rolled up his sleeves and started a personal campaign to instill a strategy of increased quality, productivity, and responsiveness to customers. Calling the strategy "Operation Bootstrap," Williams worked 12-hour days and most weekends. He answered his own phone and met with 50 steel customers each year to hear complaints. He regularly visited mills and gave his sermon on quality and constant improvement to whoever would listen. Bethlehem formed teams of hourly and salaried employees who contacted customers directly to learn about and solve quality problems. Bethlehem has invested millions in modern steel-making equipment and motivates the work force by new incentives that tie pay to profits.

Now even the Japanese are impressed. Bethlehem has cut the number of hours to make a ton of steel in half, while becoming more productive and responding quickly to customers. Williams has replaced many of his traditional plant supervisors, preferring instead younger, adaptable people who respond to customer needs. The quality improvement is illustrated in deliveries to Ford Motor Company, for which the rejection rate dropped from 8 percent in 1982 to less than 1 percent today. The huge productivity gains and quality record is equal to or better than Japanese competitors.

Bethlehem Steel has truly reformed itself. The shock of Bethlehem's near failure "will prevent us from becoming complacent again," says Williams. Although not complacent, Williams has relaxed enough to kick his three-pack-a-day smoking habit.

Questions

1. What business-level strategy would you say Bethlehem adopted?
2. Analyze the techniques Williams used for implementation. Why were they effective?

Source: Based on Gregory L. Miles, "Forging the New Bethlehem," *Business Week*, June 5, 1989, 108–110.

EASTMAN KODAK

A few years ago, a marketing consultant working for Kodak commented, "Kodak is a rudderless company, drifting from project to project with little coherent direction." This strategic drift was reflected in declining profits and sales. Kodak became infamous for bringing new products to market too late to take advantage of opportunities. Kodak failed in instant photography when the courts ruled Kodak infringed on Polaroid's patents, and its Disc camera did poorly against improved 35 mm cameras by Canon and other manufacturers. Fuji Film made serious inroads in film sales where Kodak owned the market for years. Kodak's environment is so competitive with new and changing products that it simply must innovate faster and more effectively to succeed.

Kodak's great strength is its technological and research capabilities. To build on this strength, Kodak recently purchased Sterling Drug Inc., maker of Lysol and Bayer aspirin, to build a life sciences business based on Kodak's chemical expertise. To get the life science business off the ground, Kodak hired executives from drug giants such as Ciba-Geigy Corporation and Merck. Kodak also will use Sterling's highly regarded sales force to sell its other products, such as blood analyzers, to hospitals.

Kodak has also moved to reduce the number of employees by 25,000, even trimming top management by 25 percent. The leaner Kodak has stopped its market share loss to Fuji, partly with a new line of film that matches Fuji's brighter colors. Kodak is also moving into electronic photography, with a system that thermally prints a color photo on identity cards. As video cameras become more popular, the demand for Kodak's traditional paper-based film products will decline, so Kodak is developing an electronic camera to prepare for a paperless future. Other new products are a color copier and a machine that allows people to make their own enlargements at photo shops.

Kodak retains its excellent visibility and reputation in film. It has a powerful distribution network and huge financial resources, allowing it to undertake the basic research necessary for new products. So despite its past failures, Kodak is optimistic about the future. Many new ideas are bubbling up within the system, including an optical storage disk that has 1,000 times the capacity of a floppy disk. It is also moving into batteries and expects a whole new line of research in the drug business from the researchers at Sterling. Senior executives are providing leadership to change Kodak's internal culture. The new values of innovation and timely reaction to market opportunities will take precedence over the previous value of lifetime employment.

Questions

1. What strengths, weaknesses, opportunities, and threats characterize Kodak? What are its current mission and strategy?
2. What strategy would you recommend for Kodak? Why?
3. What techniques are Kodak's senior managers using for strategy implementation? What else might they do?

Source: Leslie Helm, "Has Kodak Set Itself up for a Fall?" *Business Week,* February 22, 1988, 134–138; Leslie Helm, "Why Kodak is Starting to Click Again," *Business Week,* February 23, 1987; Subrata N. Chakravarty and Ruth Simon, "Has the World Passed Kodak By?" *Forbes,* November 5, 1984, 184–192.

CHAPTER 7

MANAGERIAL DECISION MAKING

CHAPTER OUTLINE

Types of Decisions and Problems

Programmed and Nonprogrammed Decisions

Certainty, Risk, Uncertainty, and Ambiguity

Decision-Making Models

Classical Model

Administrative Model

Decision-Making Steps

Recognition of Decision Requirement

Diagnosis and Analysis of Causes

Development of Alternatives

Selection of Desired Alternative

Implementation of Chosen Alternative

Evaluation and Feedback

Group Approaches to Decision Making

Vroom-Yetton Model

Group Decision Formats

Advantages and Disadvantages of Group Decision Making

Improving Decision-Making Effectiveness

LEARNING OBJECTIVES

After studying this chapter, you should be able to:

- Explain why decision making is an important component of good management.
- Explain the difference between programmed and nonprogrammed decisions and the decision characteristics of risk, uncertainty, and ambiguity.
- Describe the classical and administrative models of decision making and their applications.
- Identify the six steps used in managerial decision making.
- Discuss the advantages and disadvantages of using groups to make decisions.
- Identify guidelines for improving decision-making effectiveness in organizations.

Management Problem

What if you owned a retail business that does most of its business in four hours each day, but must remain open 24 hours. What decision do you make about the dead time? This problem is real for Tony Andrade, who owns six Dunkin' Donuts franchises. The business is terrific between 6 o'clock and 10 o'clock in the morning when over 50 percent of the coffee and doughnuts are sold. But doughnuts must be replaced every five hours, causing lots of waste the rest of the day. Even worse, the fast-food franchises — Burger King, Wendy's, practically everyone — and supermarket bakeries are throwing themselves into the breakfast competition. Andrade's franchises are still profitable, but between dead time and competition, things are bound to get worse.[1]

If you were Tony Andrade, would you make a decision about dead time? What alternatives would you consider, and what course of action would you select?

The Dunkin' Donuts franchises are not in trouble yet, but Tony Andrade and other franchise owners may need to use their decision-making skills to make important decisions that will affect the future of their businesses. Organizations grow, prosper, or fail as a result of decisions by their managers. Managers often are referred to as *decision makers.* Although many of their important decisions are strategic, managers also make decisions about every other aspect of an organization, including structure, control systems, responses to the environment, and human resources. Managers scout for problems, make decisions for solving them, and monitor the consequences to see whether further decisions are required. Good decision making is a vital part of good management because decisions determine how the organization solves its problems, allocates resources, and accomplishes its objectives.

Decision making is not easy. It must be done amid ever-changing factors, unclear information, and conflicting points of view. For example, when Chairman Patrick Hayes of Waterford Glass tried to cut costs by offering early retirement to the highly paid work force that makes Waterford crystal, too many experienced glassblowers opted for retirement. The remaining workers have not been able to achieve enough output, hence crystal operations have lost money for two years straight. John Sculley, chairman of Apple Computer, bet on a shortage of memory chips, the personal computer's most common component. Apple acquired a big inventory of high-priced chips, and when the shortage alleviated a few months later, Apple was forced to lower the price of its expensive Apple products. Kay Koplovitz worked her way up to president of USA Network and is now betting the company's future to finance 24 original movies and other television programming over the next two years. This is a nail-biting gamble, but she prefers risk taking to playing it safe, despite the incredible consequences if she bets wrong.[2]

Chapters 5 and 6 described strategic planning. This chapter explores the decision process that underlies strategic planning. Plans and strategies are arrived at through decision making; the better the decision making, the better the strategic planning. First we will examine decision characteristics. Then we will look at decision-making models and the steps executives should take when making important decisions. We will also examine how groups of managers make decisions. Finally, we will discuss techniques for improving decision making in organizations.

TYPES OF DECISIONS AND PROBLEMS

decision A choice made from available alternatives.

A **decision** is a choice made from available alternatives. For example, an accounting manager's selection among Bill, Nancy, and Joan for the position of junior auditor is a decision. Many people assume that making a choice is the major part of decision making, but it is only a part.

decision making The process of identifying problems and opportunities and then resolving them.

Decision making is the process of identifying problems and opportunities and then resolving them.[3] Decision making involves effort both prior to and after the actual choice. Thus, the decision as to whether to select Bill, Nancy, or Joan requires the accounting manager to ascertain whether a new junior auditor is needed, determine the availability of potential job candidates, interview candidates to acquire necessary information, select one candidate, and follow up with the socialization of the new employee into the organization to insure the decision's success.

PROGRAMMED AND NONPROGRAMMED DECISIONS

programmed decision A decision made in response to a situation that has occurred often enough to enable decision rules to be developed and applied in the future.

Management decisions typically fall into one of two categories: programmed and nonprogrammed. **Programmed decisions** involve situations that have occurred often enough to enable decision rules to be developed and applied in the future.[4] Programmed decisions are made in response to recurring organizational problems. The decision to reorder paper and other office supplies when inventories drop to a certain level is a programmed decision. Other programmed decisions concern the types of skills required to fill certain jobs, the reorder point for manufacturing inventory, exception reporting for expendi-

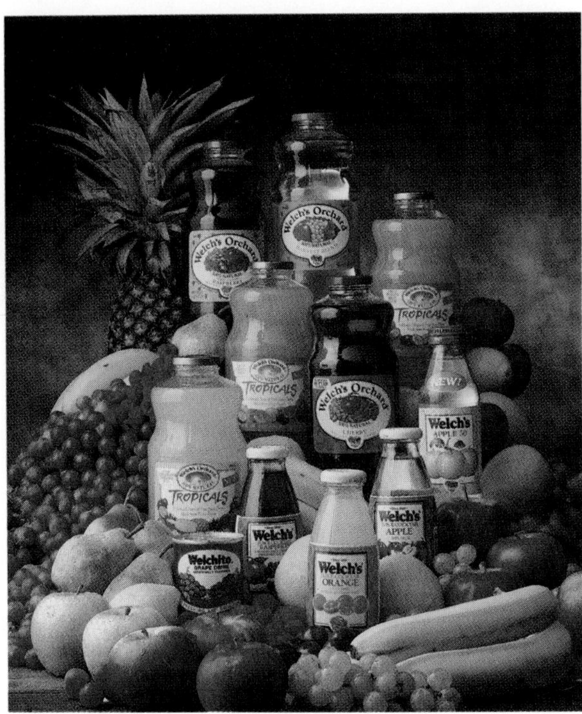

The introduction of Welch's Orchard line of fruit juices was a *nonprogrammed decision.* A strategic decision was made to reshape the image of Welch away from that of a producer of just Concord grape juice and jelly. Most recently, Orchard Tropicals were added to the line. It took five years and executives experienced many doubts, but the decision outcome has been an enormous success. The decision involved product areas about which Welch executives had no experience. Welch is now the number-one marketer of frozen noncitrus juices and has record sales, earnings, and market share, indicating its enhanced presence in the marketplace.

tures 10 percent or more over budget, and selection of freight routes for product deliveries. Once managers formulate decision rules, subordinates and others can make the decision, freeing managers for other tasks.

Nonprogrammed decisions are made in response to situations that are unique, are poorly defined and largely unstructured, and have important consequences for the organization. Nonprogrammed decisions often involve strategic planning, because uncertainty is great and decisions are complex. Nonprogrammed decisions would include decisions to build a new factory, develop a new product or service, enter a new geographical market, or relocate headquarters to a new city. The decision facing Dunkin' Donuts franchisees described at the beginning of this chapter is an example of a nonprogrammed decision. Routine decision rules or techniques for solving this problem do not exist. Tony Andrade will spend long hours analyzing the problems, developing alternatives, and making a choice.

nonprogrammed decision
A decision made in response to a situation that is unique, is poorly defined and largely unstructured, and has important consequences for the organization.

CERTAINTY, RISK, UNCERTAINTY, AND AMBIGUITY

In a perfect world, managers would have all the information necessary for making decisions. In reality, however, some things are unknowable; thus, some decisions will fail to solve the problem or attain the desired outcome. Managers try to obtain information about decision alternatives that will reduce decision uncertainty. Every decision situation can be organized on a scale according to the availability of information and the possibility of failure. The four positions

EXHIBIT 7.1
Conditions That Affect the Possibility of Decision Failure

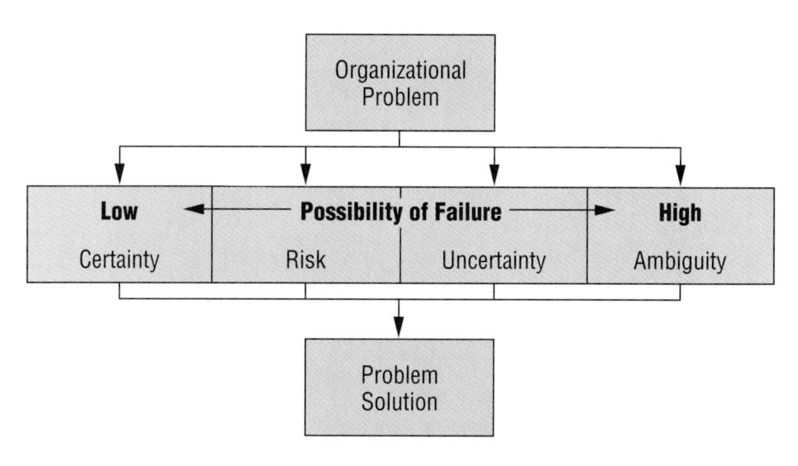

Talk about *uncertainty!* Peter Price (seated) and editor-in-chief Frank Deford are introducing the first all-sports national news daily, called "The National." Many experts question whether sports fans desire their own daily paper or even care about quality writing about sports events. Most sports fans seem stuck to the television. Price and Deford have hired the best talent in the business and believe they have a formula that will work—superb writing, color photographs, and bold graphics. They are genuine risk takers, because no one can say whether their objective of a national sports newspaper is achievable.

on the scale are certainty, risk, uncertainty, and ambiguity, as illustrated in Exhibit 7.1.

CERTAINTY. *Certainty* means that all the information the decision maker needs is fully available.[5] Managers have information on operating conditions, resource costs or constraints, and each course of action and possible outcome. For example, if a company considers a $10,000 investment in new equipment that it knows for certain will yield $4,000 in cost savings per year over the next five years, managers can calculate a before-tax rate of return of about 40 percent. If managers compare this investment with one that will yield only $3,000 per year in cost savings, they can confidently select the 40 percent return. However, few decisions are certain in the real world. Most contain risk or uncertainty.

RISK. *Risk* means that a decision has clear-cut objectives and good information is available but the future outcomes associated with each alternative are subject to chance. However, enough information is available to allow the probability of a successful outcome for each alternative to be estimated.[6] Statistical analysis might be used to calculate the probabilities of success or failure. The measure of risk captures the possibility that future events will render the alternative unsuccessful. For example, a petroleum executive may bid to sell 10,000 barrels of a petroleum distillate, knowing that there is an 80 percent chance of success with a $5 per barrel price and a 50 percent chance with a $4.20 price. When Sears introduced its "everyday low pricing" strategy, managers felt that they had better than a 80 percent chance of succeeding. Using probabilities, managers can determine which alternative is most desirable for their company.

UNCERTAINTY. *Uncertainty* means that managers know which objective they wish to achieve but information about alternatives and future events is incomplete.[7] Managers do not have enough information to be clear about alternatives or to estimate their risk. Factors that may affect a decision, such as price,

FOCUS ON ENTREPRENEURSHIP

RISKY BUSINESS, BIG REWARDS

Welcoming risk and uncertainty is part of small business decision making. David Paschal, president of the highly successful Paschal Petroleum Inc., describes his attitude toward risk taking.

"People looked at me quizzically when I started an oil company in Texas in 1983. . . . Despite the oil industry's downturn, I believed big profits could still be made from Texas' black gold. Since I had only a rudimentary education in the oil business, I decided to learn the industry from the bottom, with a job as a landman — a title researcher — and all-purpose gofer.

"It was 1980, and there I was — 26, no job, a mortgage, a wife, and a child. I called every oil company in the Dallas Yellow Pages. I even called Bunker Hunt, the Texas oil millionaire, at home; I had found his number in the White Pages. I told him I wanted to get into the oil business and asked him for five minutes of his time; he had me come to his office, and he gave me maybe 10 or 15 minutes. Meeting Bunker Hunt at this point in my life really gave me fire. He sent me to a company geologist, which led to my next job, as a landman at Spindletop Oil & Gas Co. For three years I got my hands dirty learning every aspect of the oil business. In 1983, I was ready to go out on my own, ready to generate profits for myself as owner of Paschal Petroleum Inc.

"I cajoled my banker into giving me a $10,000 signature loan to buy an oil lease in an unproven area in Knox County, Texas. I personally raised $70,000, enough to drill the well. It blew in 1984, spewing sizable profits for me and my investors. We have drilled many more wells, whose in-ground reserves total about $35 million.

"I attribute my success to two things. I'm not afraid of taking risks — big risks. In fact, I prefer to take big risks because that's the only way to score big returns. And I'm not afraid of failure. I know that if I make the wrong decision and lose everything in some venture, I still could find another opportunity and become just as successful as I have been in the oil business.

"One reason I enjoy risk is that I believe in my instincts. They are based on detailed observation of the marketplace, which is my second secret of success . . . I read many periodicals and get an overview of developments and directions in business. I can spot brewing trends and devise plans to take advantage of the opportunities they present.

"Season that with a lot of hard work, and you have the formula for my success."

Source: David Paschal, "Risky Business, Big Rewards," *Nation's Business,* March 1990, 6. Reprinted by permission. Copyright 1990, U.S. Chamber of Commerce.

production costs, volume, or future interest rates, are difficult to analyze and predict. Managers may have to make assumptions from which to forge the decision even though the decision will be wrong if the assumptions are incorrect. Managers may have to come up with creative approaches to alternatives and use personal judgment to determine which alternative is best.

For example, Time Inc.'s decision to launch a new magazine called *TV–Cable Week* was made under uncertainty. Time was unable to get good data on critical variables; thus, it assumed that the magazine would capture a 60 percent market penetration among cable subscribers and that Time would reach distribution agreements with 250 cable systems. These assumptions turned out to be wildly unrealistic, and the magazine launch was a failure.[8] Many decisions made under uncertainty do not work out as desired, but sometimes managers must be risk takers. Risk taking is especially important when starting a new business, as illustrated in the Focus on Entrepreneurship box.

AMBIGUITY. Ambiguity is by far the most difficult decision situation. *Ambiguity* means that the objectives to be achieved or the problem to be solved are unclear, alternatives are difficult to define, and information about outcomes is unavailable.[9] Ambiguity is what students would feel if an instructor created student groups, told each group to write a paper, but gave the groups no topic, direction, or guidelines whatsoever. Ambiguity has been called a "wicked" decision problem. Managers have a difficult time coming to grips with the issues. Wicked problems are associated with manager conflicts over objectives and decision alternatives, rapidly changing circumstances, fuzzy information, and unclear linkages among decision elements.[10] Fortunately, most decisions are not characterized by ambiguity. But when they are, managers must conjure up objectives and develop reasonable scenarios for decision alternatives in the absence of information. One example of an ambiguous decision was the marketing department assignment to develop an advertising campaign for a birth control device. Managers were unclear about advertising norms, to whom the ad should be targeted (men, women, marrieds, singles), ad content, or media. The entire approach had to be worked out without precedent.

Another example is the movie industry—one of the most difficult in which to make decisions, because so many new movies are flops. Studio decision makers, however, are seeking new ways to reduce risk and uncertainty.

WARNER BROTHERS

• Warner Brothers had a megahit in *Batman,* and it is no accident that they lead the industry in market share with 45 percent of the box office in 1989. Warner Brothers' executives reduce risk by maintaining a special relationship with stars who have drawing power. Studio executives build personal relationships with these stars so they will want to do pictures with Warner. Warner Brothers also spends lavishly to insure the comfort of top stars, providing them with jets and making them feel appreciated.

Another approach to reduce risk of huge losses is to provide stars with a percentage of gross revenues rather than a huge salary. For *Batman,* Jack Nicholson may receive up to 15 percent of the studio take, and Michael Keaton 8 percent. Nicholson and Keaton stand to make millions because *Batman* was so successful, but they would have made little if it failed. Columbia pictures used a similar deal for *Ghostbusters II.* Bill Murray, Dan Aykroyd, and other stars received only $25,000 to $125,000 salary, but each stands to make up to 15 percent of the take. This arrangement may not leave much for the studio, but a small profit is better than a huge loss. Senior studio executives have learned to manage risks.[11]

The approach of Warner Brothers is becoming more common because the movie industry is so uncertain and volatile. By getting the commitment of stars and sharing the profit, movies have a higher probability of succeeding and less chance of financial losses.

DECISION-MAKING MODELS

The approach managers use to make decisions usually falls into one of two types—the classical model or the administrative model. The choice of model depends on the manager's personal preference, whether the decision is pro-

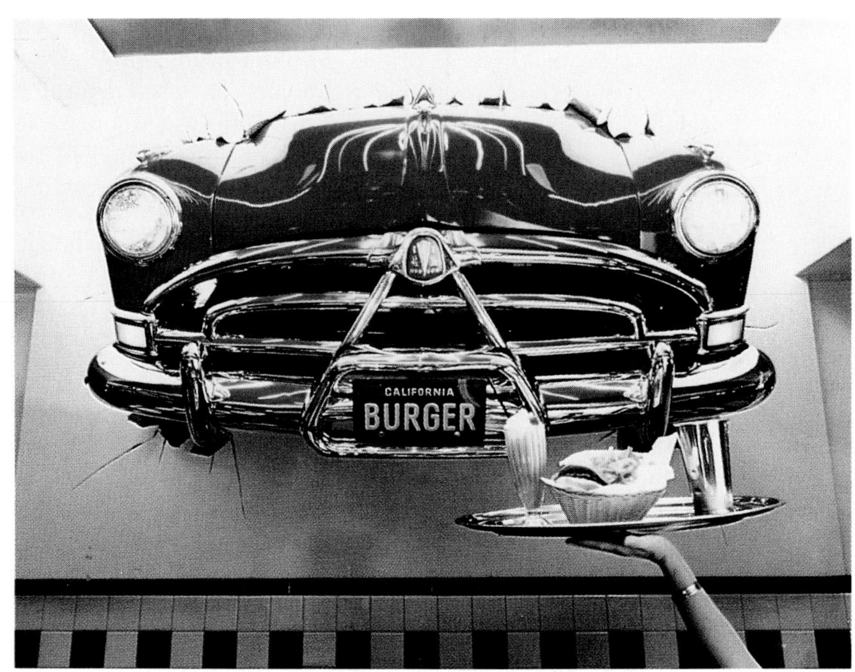

American Restaurants Corporation used the *classical model* of decision making when expanding the eleven-restaurant chain of Hudson Grill restaurants. Senior management decided that the concept of the automobile grille seemingly bursting into the dining area can be franchised nationally. This decision was based on surveys of consumer preferences for upgraded fast food, two-income families, 1950s nostalgia, and excellent per-store volume. Five openings are scheduled during 1990, and eight in 1991, as the first stage of the carefully planned national expansion.

grammed or nonprogrammed, and the extent to which the decision is characterized by risk, uncertainty, or ambiguity.

Classical Model

The **classical model** of decision making is based on economic assumptions. This model has arisen within the management literature because managers are expected to make decisions that are economically sensible and in the organization's best economic interests. The assumptions underlying this model are as follows:

classical model A decision-making model based on the assumption that managers should make logical decisions that will be in the organization's best economic interests.

1. The decision maker operates to accomplish objectives that are known and agreed upon. Problems are precisely formulated and defined.
2. The decision maker strives for conditions of certainty, gathering complete information. All alternatives and the potential results of each are calculated.
3. Criteria for evaluating alternatives are known. The decision maker selects the alternative that will maximize the economic return to the organization.
4. The decision maker is rational and uses logic to assign values, order preferences, evaluate alternatives, and make the decision that will maximize the attainment of organizational objectives.

The classical model of decision making is considered to be **normative,** which means it defines how a decision maker *should* make decisions. It does not describe how managers actually make decisions so much as it provides guidelines on how to reach an ideal outcome for the organization. The value of the classical model has been its ability to help decision makers be more rational. For example, many senior managers rely solely on intuition and personal

normative An approach that defines how a decision maker should make decisions and provides guidelines for reaching an ideal outcome for the organization.

preferences for making decisions.[12] In recent years, the classical approach has been given wider application because of the growth of quantitative decision techniques that use computers. Quantitative techniques (discussed in detail in Chapter 8) include such things as decision trees, pay-off matrices, breakeven analysis, linear programming, forecasting, and operations research models. The use of computerized information systems and data bases has increased the power of the classical approach.

In many respects, the classical model represents an "ideal" model of decision making that is often unattainable by real people in real organizations. It is most valuable when applied to programmed decisions and to decisions characterized by certainty or risk, because relevant information is available and probabilities can be calculated. One example of the classical approach is the decision model developed by Weyerhauser Company for converting a timber harvest into end products. It starts with the description of a tree — size and shape — and evaluates such factors as harvesting costs, hauling, mill location, facility operations, expected end products (plywood, dried trim, fiber, lumber), and customer demand. The model helps managers evaluate hundreds of possibilities for moving lumber through the production process to the consumer and choose the most economically efficient alternatives.[13]

Administrative Model

administrative model A decision-making model that describes how managers actually make decisions in situations characterized by nonprogrammed decisions, uncertainty, and ambiguity.

The **administrative model** of decision making describes how managers actually make decisions in difficult situations, such as those characterized by nonprogrammed decisions, uncertainty, and ambiguity. Many management decisions are not sufficiently programmable to lend themselves to any degree of quantification. Managers are unable to make economically rational decisions even if they want to.[14]

bounded rationality The concept that people have the time and cognitive ability to process only a limited amount of information on which to base decisions.

satisfice To choose the first solution alternative that satisfies minimal decision criteria regardless of whether better solutions are presumed to exist.

Bounded Rationality and Satisficing. The administrative model of decision making is based on the work of Herbert A. Simon. Simon proposed two concepts that were instrumental in shaping the administrative model: bounded rationality and satisficing. **Bounded rationality** means that people have limits, or boundaries, on how rational they can be. The organization is incredibly complex, and managers have the time and ability to process only a limited amount of information with which to make decisions.[15] Because managers do not have the time or cognitive ability to process complete information about complex decisions, they must satisfice. **Satisficing** means that decision makers choose the first solution alternative that satisfies minimal decision criteria. Rather than pursuing all alternatives to identify the single solution that will maximize economic returns, managers will opt for the first solution that appears to solve the problem, even if better solutions are presumed to exist. The decision maker cannot justify the time and expense of obtaining complete information.[16]

An example of both bounded rationality and satisficing occurs when a junior executive on a business trip stains her blouse just prior to an important meeting. She will run to a nearby clothing store and buy the first satisfactory replacement she finds. Having neither the time nor the opportunity to explore all the blouses in town, she satisfices by choosing a blouse that will solve the immediate problem. In a similar fashion, managers generate alternatives for complex problems only until they find one they believe will work. For example, a few years ago Disney chairman Ray Watson and chief operating officer Ron Miller attempted to thwart takeover attempts, but they had limited options. They satisficed with a quick decision to acquire Arivda Realty and Gibson Court Company. The acquisition of these companies had the potential to solve the problem at hand; thus, they looked no further for possibly better alternatives.[17]

The administrative model relies on assumptions different from those of the classical model and focuses on organizational factors that influence individual decisions. It is more realistic than the classical model for complex, nonprogrammed decisions. According to the administrative model,

1. Decision objectives often are vague, conflicting, and lack consensus among managers. Managers often are unaware of problems or opportunities that exist in the organization.
2. Rational procedures are not always used, and when they are, they are confined to a simplistic view of the problem that does not capture the complexity of real organizational events.
3. Managers' search for alternatives is limited because of human, information, and resource constraints.
4. Most managers settle for a satisficing rather than a maximizing solution. This is partly because they have limited information and partly because they have only vague criteria for what constitutes a maximizing solution.

The administrative model is considered to be **descriptive,** meaning that it describes how managers actually make decisions in complex situations rather than dictating how they *should* make decisions according to a theoretical ideal. The administrative model recognizes the human and environmental limitations that affect the degree to which managers can pursue a rational decision-making process.

INTUITION. Another aspect of administrative decision making is intuition. **Intuition** represents a quick apprehension of a decision situation based on past experience but without conscious thought.[18] Intuitive decision making is not arbitrary or irrational, because it is based on years of practice and hands-on experience that enable managers to quickly identify solutions without going through painstaking computations. Managers rely on intuition to determine when a problem exists and to synthesize isolated bits of data and experience into an integrated picture. They also use their intuitive understanding to check the results of rational analysis. If the rational analysis does not agree with their intuition, managers may dig further before accepting a proposed alternative.[19]

Intuition helps managers understand situations characterized by uncertainty and ambiguity that have proven impervious to rational analysis. For example, virtually every major studio in Hollywood turned down the *Star Wars* concept except 20th Century Fox. George Lucas, the creator of *Star Wars,* had attempted to sell the concept to 12 major studios before going to Fox. In each case, the concept had been rejected. All 13 studios saw the same numbers, but only Alan Ladd and his associates at Fox had the right "feel" for the decision. Their intuition told them that *Star Wars* would be a success. In addition,

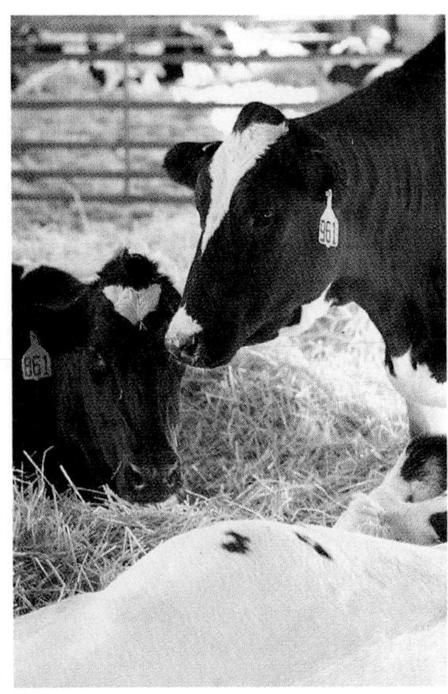

Richard J. Mahoney, CEO of Monsanto, uses gut instinct to make decisions following the *administrative model.* His biggest decision was to redirect the chemical giant away from old-line commodity chemical products into biotechnology. The research budget has been doubled, with more effort devoted to pure research. The first product from this program is bovine somatotropin, a protein that increases the efficiency of milk production in diary cows, lowering costs for dairy farmers. This nonprogrammed decision commits the company to the long term with the potential for launching a technological revolution with a huge profit stream. Or the results may be disappointing. Only time will tell.

descriptive An approach that describes how managers actually make decisions rather than how they should.

intuition The immediate comprehension of a decision situation based on past experience but without conscious thought.

EXHIBIT 7.2
Characteristics of Classical and Administrative Decision-Making Models

Classical Model	Administrative Model
Clear-cut problem and objectives	Vague problem and objectives
Condition of certainty	Condition of uncertainty
Full information about alternatives and their outcomes	Limited information about alternatives and their outcomes
Rational choice for maximizing outcomes	Satisficing choice for resolving problem

George Lucas was told by many experts that the title *Star Wars* would turn away crowds at the box office. His intuition said the title would work. The rest is history.[20]

The key dimensions of the classical and administrative models are listed in Exhibit 7.2. Recent research into decision-making procedures have found rational, classical procedures to be associated with high performance for organizations in stable environments. However, administrative decision-making procedures and intuition have been associated with high performance in unstable environments, in which decisions must be made rapidly and under more difficult conditions.[21]

DECISION-MAKING STEPS

Whether a decision is programmed or nonprogrammed and regardless of managers' choice of the classical or administrative model of decision making, six steps typically are associated with effective decision processes. These are summarized in Exhibit 7.3.

RECOGNITION OF DECISION REQUIREMENT

problem A situation in which organizational accomplishments have failed to meet established objectives.

opportunity A situation in which managers see potential organizational accomplishments that exceed current objectives.

Managers confront a decision requirement in the form of either a problem or an opportunity. A **problem** occurs when organizational accomplishment is less than established objectives. Some aspect of performance is unsatisfactory. An **opportunity** exists when managers see potential accomplishment that exceeds specified current objectives. Managers see the possibility of enhancing performance beyond current levels.

Awareness of a problem or opportunity is the first step in the decision sequence and requires surveillance of the internal and external environment for issues that merit executive attention.[22] This resembles the military concept of gathering intelligence. Managers scan the world around them to determine whether the organization is satisfactorily progressing toward its goals. For example, managers at Wells Fargo & Company in San Francisco survey employees to detect potential human resource problems. The survey covers effectiveness of company advertising, product quality, and responsibility to the community, as well as employee satisfaction and organizational climate.[23]

Exhibit 7.3
Six Steps in the Managerial Decision-Making Process

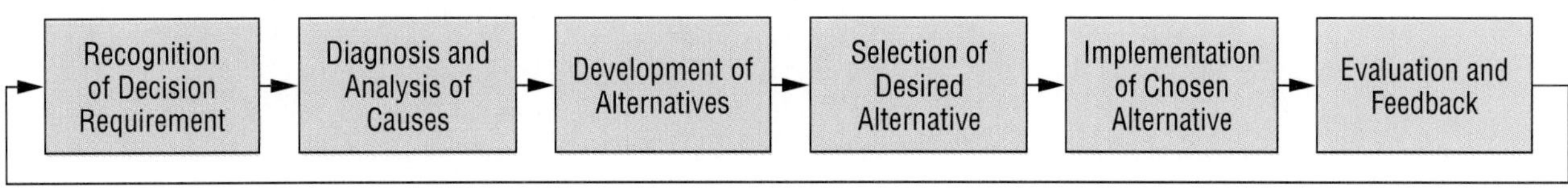

Some information comes from periodic accounting reports, MIS reports, and other sources that are designed to discover problems before they become too serious. Managers also take advantage of informal sources. They talk to other managers, gather opinions on how things are going, and seek advice on which problems should be tackled or which opportunities embraced.[24]

Recognizing decision requirements is difficult, because it often means integrating bits and pieces of information in novel ways. For example, Worlds of Wonder, Inc., developed the first animated talking toy, called Teddy Ruxpin, and Lazer Tag. The astonishing success of these products was due to the pulse taking of customers. Worlds of Wonder works regularly with 1,000 families chosen at random to learn about problems and opportunities in the marketplace for toys. This early recognition contributed directly to the success of Lazer Tag, a toy geared for the young-adult market.[25]

Diagnosis and Analysis of Causes

Once a problem or opportunity has come to a manager's attention, the understanding of the situation should be refined. **Diagnosis** is the step in the decision-making process in which managers analyze underlying causal factors associated with the decision situation. Managers make a mistake here if they jump right into generating alternatives without first exploring the cause of the problem more deeply.

diagnosis The step in the decision-making process in which managers analyze underlying causal factors associated with the decision situation.

Kepner and Tregoe, who have conducted extensive studies of manager decision making, recommend that managers ask a series of questions to specify underlying causes, including:

- What is the state of disequilibrium affecting us?
- When did it occur?
- Where did it occur?
- How did it occur?
- To whom did it occur?
- What is the urgency of the problem?
- What is the interconnectedness of events?
- What result came from which activity?[26]

Such questions help specify what actually happened and why. Toyota asked questions like these when diagnosing the need for a new luxury car.

Now Flying Tigers Delivers 40 Years
Of Worldwide Experience To Federal Express. Overnight.
Federal Express has long been the best way to ship your packages over here.
And now we're also the best way to ship your packages over there. To Europe. Asia. Just about anywhere.
Because we've just acquired even more overseas experience, overseas routes and overseas know-how.
How?
By acquiring the pioneer of overseas delivery.
Flying Tigers.
And that makes Federal Express the largest, most experienced international air express company in the free world.
By far.
Just one phone call to Federal Express and you'll be talking to somebody who's flown more tons of overseas freight and more miles than anybody.
You'll be shipping your package with an air express company that has more planes, flying to more international destinations, than anybody.
And our thousands of local Federal Express employees help your package fly through customs as smoothly as it flies through the air.
In fact, from now on, you can ship virtually any size package to any major country in the free world. And be confident it'll get there—to the next country or the next continent.
So whether it's going over here or over there, ship it with the company that's got it over everyone.
FEDERAL EXPRESS
The Best Way To Ship It Over There.

Recognizing a *decision requirement* is the first step in a decision process. The acquisition of Tiger International enabled Federal Express to expand internationally almost in an instant. Federal Express executives saw the need for global package delivery in the global environment where time savings is important to many companies. The purchase of Tiger, as this advertisement points out, gives Federal Express a commanding presence on the global stage, staying ahead of the competition and meeting the global needs of its customers.

TOYOTA • Toyota's most popular car in North America is the inexpensive Camry, the car targeted at the lower end of the market. Based on informal information from sales records and competitor sales, Toyota executives, especially Chairman Toyoda, perceived a need to move into the luxury car market. The people who for years bought Camrys were moving up in life and wanting more expensive cars, such as the BMW, Mercedes, Porsche, and Cadillac.

To fully define the decision requirements, Toyota dispatched 20 designers to the United States to study what customers wanted. They visited dealers, buttonholed car buyers, and organized focus groups. They learned that the need was for a luxury car that would suit younger buyers who wanted to buy European cars but could not yet afford them. Because the United States was the major market, a small team stayed in California designing clay models. In the meantime, the U.S. subsidiary, Toyota Motor Sales USA Inc., staged expensive consumer research and discovered that the average sales prospect was a 43-year-old male with a household income of $100,000. A separate dealer network to handle the luxury car was also recommended.

After all this information was pulled together, the Lexus was born. Now Toyota and the rest of the automobile industry is waiting to see whether the problem was properly diagnosed and whether the new automobile will provide the conspicuous consumption that affluent Americans love.[27]

Sea water projected into the Arctic sky instantly freezes into cascading ice crystals. This has created a temporary island in the Beaufort Sea off the northern coast of Alaska. For the drilling of a test well, Amoco executives developed several *decision alternatives:* Use a drill ship, build an offshore platform, a concrete island, a gravel island, or the temporary island of ice. They selected the ice island alternative because the cost of drilling a test well would be one-third to one-half of that for a gravel island. This alternative would also turn Alaska's forbidding winter into an advantage. Come summer, the ice island will revert to its natural state.

Development of Alternatives

Once the problem or opportunity has been recognized and analyzed, decision makers begin to consider taking action. The next stage is to generate possible alternative solutions that will respond to the needs of the situation and correct the underlying causes.

For a programmed decision, feasible alternatives are easy to identify and in fact usually are already available within the organization's rules and procedures. Nonprogrammed decisions, however, require developing new courses of action that will meet the company's needs. For decisions made under conditions of high uncertainty, managers may develop only one or two custom solutions that will satisfice for handling the problem.

Decision alternatives can be thought of as the tools for reducing the difference between the organization's current and desired performance. Consider how Chrysler Corporation handled a problem of too little production capacity.

Chrysler Corporation

• After the turnaround led by Lee Iacocca, Chrysler found itself with greater demand for cars in both American and European markets than it could provide. Chrysler executives considered three alternatives, including building new plants, having employees work nights and weekends in existing plants, and renting additional production capacity on a temporary basis. If Chrysler built new plants, it might get stuck with high overhead and excess capacity, and because current plants were working full tilt, additional labor hours would not produce many additional cars. The third alternative represented a creative solution. Chrysler executives rented an American Motors plant in Kenosha, Wisconsin, to build Chrysler automobiles. The AMC workers avoided a layoff,

EXHIBIT 7.4
Decision Alternatives with Different Levels of Risk

For each of the following decisions, which alternative would you choose?

1. In the final seconds of a game with the college's traditional rival, the coach of a college football team may choose a play that has a 95 percent chance of producing a tie score or one with a 30 percent chance of leading to victory or to sure defeat if it fails.
2. The president of a Canadian company must decide whether to build a new plant within Canada that has a 90 percent chance of producing a modest return on investment or to build it in a foreign country with an unstable political history. The latter alternative has a 40 percent chance of failing, but the returns would be enormous if it succeeded.
3. A college senior with considerable acting talent must choose a career. She has the opportunity to go on to medical school and become a physician, a career in which she is 80 percent likely to succeed. She would rather be an actress but realizes that the opportunity for success is only 20 percent.

and Chrysler fulfilled its requirement of greater short-run production capacity. Developing decision alternatives led to a creative idea that helped Chrysler stay efficient and at the same time sell more cars.[28]

SELECTION OF DESIRED ALTERNATIVE

Once feasible alternatives have been developed, one must be selected. The decision choice is the selection of the most promising of several alternative courses of action. Managers' goal is to make the choice with the least amount of risk and uncertainty. Because some risk is inherent for most nonprogrammed decisions, managers try to gauge prospects for success. Under conditions of uncertainty, they may have to rely on their intuition and experience to estimate whether a given course of action is likely to succeed.

risk propensity The willingness to undertake risk with the opportunity of gaining an increased payoff.

Making choices depends on managers' personality factors and willingness to accept risk and uncertainty. For example, **risk propensity** is the willingness to undertake risk with the opportunity of gaining an increased payoff. The level of risk a manager is willing to accept will influence the analysis of cost and benefits to be derived from any decision. Consider the situations in Exhibit 7.4. In each situation, which alternative would you choose? A person with a low risk propensity would tend to take assured moderate returns by going for a tie score, building a domestic plant, or pursuing a career as physician. A risk taker would go for the victory, build a plant in a foreign country, or embark on an acting career. The Manager's Shoptalk describes biases to avoid when selecting the desired alternative.

IMPLEMENTATION OF CHOSEN ALTERNATIVE

implementation The step in the decision-making process that involves the employment of managerial, administrative, and persuasive abilities to translate the chosen alternative into action.

The **implementation** stage involves the use of managerial, administrative, and persuasive abilities to ensure that the chosen alternative is carried out. This is similar to the idea of strategic implementation described in Chapter 6. The ultimate success of the chosen alternative depends on whether it can be translated into action. Sometimes an alternative never becomes reality because

Manager's Shoptalk

DECISION BIASES TO AVOID

At a time when decision making is so important, many corporate executives do not know how to make a good choice among alternatives. They may rely on computer analyses or personal intuition without realizing that their own cognitive biases affect their judgment. The complexities of modern corporate life make good judgment more critical than ever.

Many errors in judgment originate in the human mind's limited capacity and in the natural biases most executives display during decision making. Awareness of the six biases below can help managers make more enlightened choices:

1. *Ignoring the laws of randomness.* Randomness means that the outcome of one event has nothing to do with the outcome of another. Managers often ignore this principle in making business decisions. For example, even though retail sales should be expected to fluctuate each month, a businessperson decides that a slight sales dip is the beginning of a downward trend and takes significant action, such as increasing the advertising budget. If sales rise the following month—which would be expected even without a change in advertising—the executive attributes it to the new advertising strategy. Trends should not be interpreted from a single, random event.
2. *Hindsight bias.* Hindsight bias means that people tend to overestimate after the fact the degree to which they could have predicted an event. This is sometimes called the "I-knew-it-all-along effect." One example occurs when you are traveling in an unfamiliar area with your spouse behind the wheel. You reach an unmarked fork in the road, and your spouse decides to turn left. Twenty minutes later you are hopelessly lost, and you exclaim, "I knew you should have turned right at the fork!" Research on hindsight demonstrates that people are not very good at recalling or reconstructing how an uncertain situation appeared beforehand. Managers should be cautious about evaluating decision errors made by themselves and subordinates, because uncertainty may have been greater before the decision than they recall.
3. *Giving too much weight to readily available information.* Decisions often are based on information that is easily available to certain executives, which precludes their digging for additional information that may provide a more balanced view. For example, geologists at a major oil company were asked to estimate the potential yield at several drilling sites. To do so, they relied on geological features similar to those of existing oil fields. The results were probably flawed because the geologists failed to consider unproductive fields that had features similar to those of the new sites.
4. *Being influenced by problem framing.* The decision response of a manager can be influenced by the mere wording of a problem. For example, consider whether a new product decision is framed to emphasize job savings or job losses. If managers are given the option of approving (A) a modified product that will mean a 100 percent chance of saving 200 manufacturing jobs or (B) a new product that has a one-third chance of saving 600 positions and a two-thirds chance of saving zero positions, most managers choose option A. The same problem with a negative frame would give managers the choice of selecting (C) a modified product that had a 100 percent chance of losing 400 jobs, or (D) a totally new product that had a one-third chance of losing 600 jobs and a two-thirds chance of losing zero jobs. With this negative frame, most managers choose D. Because both problems are identical, the difference in decision choice is accountable strictly by how the problem is framed.
5. *Misconception of chance.* When a series of similar events occur, managers may incorrectly gauge the probability of their future recurrence. For example, a manager who is hiring the fifth sales director in two years may feel that the person should work out well. After all, the first four did not work out, and the odds against five failures is small. In truth, the four people who failed have no bearing on the potential performance of the fifth. Each failure was a random event, and the chance of success on the fifth try should not be overestimated.
6. *Overconfidence.* One of the interesting research findings on decision-making biases is that most people overestimate their ability to predict uncertain outcomes. Before making a decision, managers have unrealistic expectations of their ability to understand the risk and make the right choice. Overconfidence is greatest when answering questions of moderate to extreme difficulty. For example, when a group of people were asked to define quantities about which they had little direct knowledge ("What was the dollar value of Canadian lumber exports in 1977?" "What was the amount of taxes collected by the U.S. Internal Revenue Service in 1970?"), they overestimated their accuracy. Evidence of overconfidence is illustrated in cases where subjects were so certain of an answer that they assigned odds of 1,000 to 1 of being correct but in fact were correct only about 85 percent of the time. These findings are especially important for strategic decision making, in which uncertainty is high because managers may unrealistically expect that they can successfully predict outcomes and hence select the wrong alternative.

Source: Based on David E. Vell, Howard Raiffa, and Amos Tversky, *Decision Making* (Cambridge University Press, 1988); John McCormick, "The Wisdom of Solomon," *Newsweek*, August 17, 1987, 62–63; Max H. Bazerman, *Judgment in Managerial Decision Making* (New York: Wiley, 1986).

Safe T. Bernard, a company-created character, appears at a Wetterau Incorporated plant as part of *decision implementation*. The decision to have a safety program was spurred by concern for the welfare of employees and the escalating costs of worker's compensation insurance. Implementation of the safety program decision has been so successful that within the first 12 months, accidents were reduced by 41 percent.

managers lack the resources or energy needed to make things happen. Implementation may require discussion with people affected by the decision. Communication, motivation, and leadership skills must be used to see that the decision is carried out.

One reason Lee Iacocca succeeded in turning Chrysler around was his ability to implement decisions. Iacocca personally hired people from Ford to develop new auto models. He hired people who shared his vision and were eager to carry out his decisions. By contrast, Tandy Corporation's decision to become a major supplier to businesses by setting up 386 computer centers to support a new direct sales force floundered. Tandy has great success selling to consumers through its Radio Shack stores, but simply did not know how to sell computers to businesses. The results were disappointing, and many of the computer centers had to be closed. Tandy lacked the ability to implement the decision to go after business customers.[29]

Evaluation and Feedback

In the evaluation stage of the decision process, decision makers gather information that tells them how well the decision was implemented and whether it was effective in achieving its objectives. For example, Tandy executives' evaluation of and feedback on the decision to open computer centers revealed poor sales performance. Feedback indicated that implementation was unsuccessful, so computer centers were closed and another approach was tried.

Feedback is important because decision making is a continuous, never-ending process. Decision making is not completed when an executive or board of directors votes yes or no. Feedback provides decision makers with information that can precipitate a new decision cycle. The decision may fail, thus generating a new analysis of the problem, evaluation of alternatives, and selection of a new alternative. Many big problems are solved by trying several alternatives in sequence, each providing modest improvement. Feedback is the part of monitoring that assesses whether a new decision needs to be made.

An illustration of the overall decision-making process, including evaluation and feedback, was Coca-Cola's decision to introduce a "new" Coke flavor.

Coca-Cola Company

• "Dear Chief Dodo: What ignoramus decided to change the formula of Coke?" This was one of thousands of letters sent to Coca-Cola chairman Roberto Goizueta after the introduction of the new Coke flavor in 1985. Coca-Cola had made its decision via a cautious, rational decision process. The problem leading to the decision was clear: Pepsi was increasing market share at Coke's expense through supermarket sales. Pepsi was slightly sweeter and tended to beat Coke in blind taste tests. And the enormous success of Diet Coke — sweeter than regular Coke — reinforced the idea of changing the Coke formula.

The problem led to diagnosis and the development of several alternatives. Coca-Cola spent $4 million to taste-test the new flavor on nearly 200,000 consumers in 30 cities. Coca-Cola identified the flavor people most preferred: 55 percent chose the new Coke over the old, and 52 percent chose it over Pepsi.

Yet within three months after the decision was implemented, old Coke was back in the supermarkets. Why? Because feedback revealed that brand loyalty is an elusive quality that cannot be measured. People had an emotional attachment to the original Coca-Cola from childhood. Millions of advertising dollars could not swing enough people to the new Coke flavor.

Why did the decision fail? It was a bold decision — and bold decisions are inherently risky. Coca-Cola could not measure intangible emotional attachments. On the other hand, thanks to evaluation and feedback, the decision should not be considered a total failure. After the old Coke was reintroduced under the name "Coca-Cola Classic," there were two Coke brands with which to battle Pepsi. As chairman Goizueta commented, "Had I known in April what I know today, I definitely would have introduced the new Coke. Then I would have said I planned the whole thing."[30]

Coca-Cola's decision to introduce a new flavor illustrates all the decision steps, and the process ultimately ended in success. Strategic decisions always contain some risk. In this case, feedback and follow-up decisions got Coke back on track with two brands instead of one.

GROUP APPROACHES TO DECISION MAKING

Decision making is something that individual managers often do, but decision makers in the business world also operate as part of a group. Decisions may be made through a committee, a task group, departmental participation, or informal coalitions. Beginning with the Vroom-Yetton model, here are some ideas for including groups in decision making.

VROOM-YETTON MODEL

Some situations call for group rather than individual decision making. Vroom and Yetton developed a model of participation in decision making that provides guidance for practicing managers.[31] The **Vroom-Yetton model** helps the manager gauge the appropriate amount of participation for subordinates. It has three major components: leader participation styles, a set of diagnostic questions with which to analyze a decision situation, and a series of decision rules.

Vroom-Yetton model A model designed to help managers gauge the amount of subordinate participation in decision making.

LEADER PARTICIPATION STYLES. The model employs five levels of subordinate participation in decision making ranging from highly autocratic to highly democratic, as illustrated in Exhibit 7.5. Autocratic leadership styles are represented by AI and AII, consulting style by CI and CII, and a group decision by GII. The five styles fall along a continuum, and the manager should select one depending on the situation. If the situation warrants, the manager could make

EXHIBIT 7.5
Five Leader Decision Styles

	Decision Style	Description
Highly Autocratic	AI	You solve the problem or make the decision yourself using information available to you at that time.
↑	AII	You obtain the necessary information from your subordinates, then decide on the solution to the problem yourself.
	CI	You share the problem with relevant subordinates individually, getting their ideas and suggestions without bringing them together as a group. Then you make the decision.
↓	CII	You share the problem with your subordinates as a group, collectively obtaining their ideas and suggestions. Then you make the decision.
Highly Democratic	GII	You share a problem with your subordinates as a group. Your role is much like that of chairman. You do not try to influence the group to adopt "your" solution, and you are willing to accept and implement any solution that has the support of the entire group.

Note: A = autocratic; C = consultative; G = group.
Source: Reprinted by permission of the publisher, from "A New Look at Managerial Decision-Making," by Victor H. Vroom, *Organizational Dynamics,* Spring 1973, pp. 67, 70.

the decision alone (AI), share the problem with subordinates individually (CI), or let group members make the decision (GII).

DIAGNOSTIC QUESTIONS. How does a manager decide which of the five decision styles to use? The appropriate degree of decision participation depends on the responses to seven diagnostic questions. These questions deal with the problem, the required level of decision quality, and the importance of having subordinates accept the decision. Each should be given a yes or no answer:

1. *Does the problem possess a decision requirement for high quality?* If a high-quality decision is important for group performance, the leader has to be actively involved.
2. *Do I have enough information to make a high-quality decision?* If the leader does not have sufficient information or expertise, the leader should involve subordinates to obtain that information.
3. *Is the decision problem well structured?* If the problem is ambiguous and poorly structured, the leader will need to interact with subordinates to clarify the problem and identify possible solutions.
4. *Is acceptance of the decision by subordinates important for effective implementation?* If implementation requires that subordinates agree with the decision, leaders should involve the subordinates in the decision process.
5. *If I were to make the decision by myself, is it reasonably certain that it would be accepted by my subordinates?* If subordinates typically go along with whatever the leader decides, their involvement in the decision process will be less important.

These employees discuss improvements to bar tips in the Oregon Cutting Systems Division of Blount, Inc. Managers in this plant use a *GII group decision-making approach* (Vroom-Yetton model) by involving workers in decisions to develop and bring innovative products to market. This style is especially effective when a manager lacks sufficient information, the decision problem is poorly structured, and subordinates share organizational goals.

6. *Do subordinates share the organizational goals to be attained in solving this problem?* If subordinates do not share the goals of the organization, the leader should not allow the group to make the decision alone.
7. *Is conflict over preferred solutions likely to occur among subordinates?* Disagreement among subordinates can be resolved by allowing their participation and discussion.

These questions seem detailed, but they quickly narrow the options available to managers and point to the appropriate level of group participation in the decision.

Selecting a Decision Style. The decision flowchart in Exhibit 7.6 allows a leader to adopt a participation style by answering the questions in sequence. The leader begins at the left side of the chart with question A: Does the problem possess a quality requirement? If the answer is yes, the leader proceeds to question B. If the answer to question A is no, the leader proceeds to question D, because questions B and C are irrelevant if quality is a requirement. Managers can quickly learn to use the basic model to adapt their leader styles to fit the decision problem and the situation.

Several decision styles are equally acceptable in many situations. When this happens, Vroom and Yetton recommend using the most autocratic style because this will save time without reducing decision quality or acceptance.

Although the Vroom-Yetton model has been criticized as being less than perfect,[32] it is useful to decision makers, and the body of supportive research is growing.[33] Managers make timely, high-quality decisions when following the model. One application of the model occurred at Barouh-Eaton Allen Corporation.

EXHIBIT 7.6
Decision Tree for Determining Participation in Decision Making

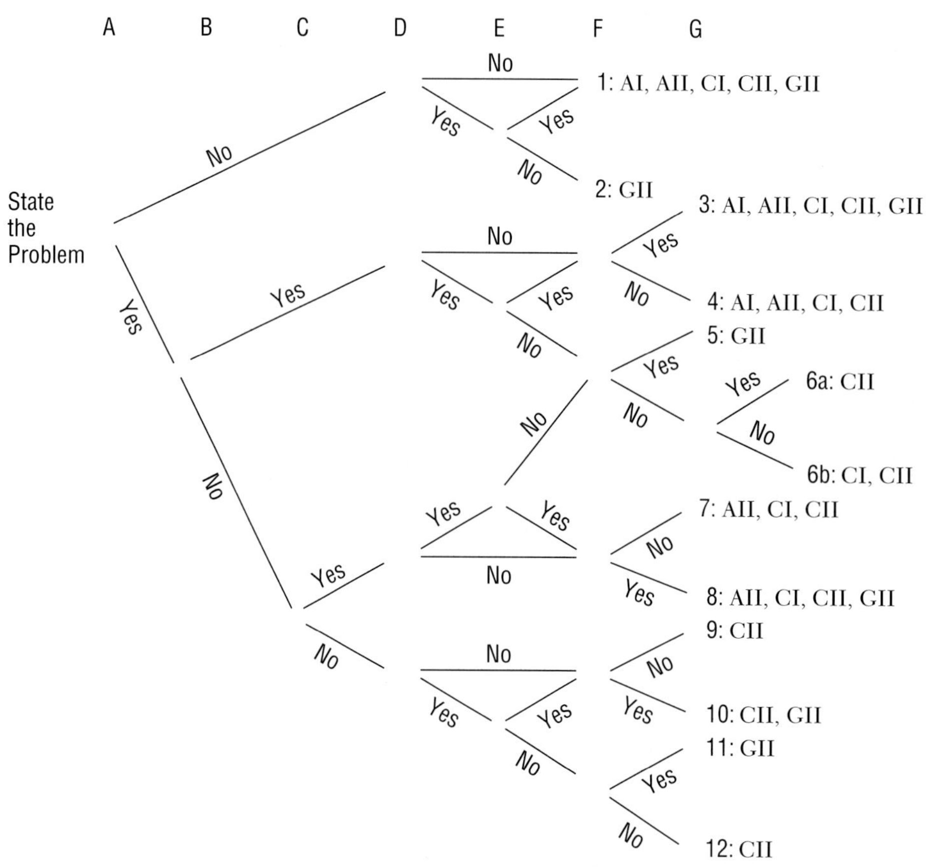

A. Does the problem possess a quality requirement? Does it matter what the answer is?
B. Do I have sufficient information to make a high-quality decision?
C. Is the problem structured? Do I know what information I need and where it is located?
D. Is acceptance of the decision by subordinates important for effective implementation?
E. If I were to make the decision by myself, am I reasonably certain that it would be accepted by my subordinates?
F. Do subordinates share the organizational goals to be attained in solving this problem?
G. Is conflict among subordinates likely in preferred solutions?

Source: Reprinted, by permission of the publisher, from "A New Look at Managerial Decision-Making," by Victor H. Vroom, *Organizational Dynamics,* Spring 1973, pp. 67, 70. © 1973 AMACOM, a division of American Management Association, New York. All rights reserved.

KO-REC-TYPE • Barouh-Eaton Allen started prospering when owner Vic Barouh noticed that a typist kept a piece of white chalk by her machine. To erase an error, she would lightly rub over it with the chalk. It took several passes, but the correction was neatly made. Barouh's company already made carbon paper, so he tried rubbing chalk on one side of a sheet of paper, putting the paper between the error and typewriter, and striking the same key. Most of the error disappeared under a thin coating of chalk dust. Thus, Ko-Rec-Type was born. Demand for the product was enormous, and the company prospered.

Then IBM invented the self-correcting typewriter. Within two days after IBM's announcement, nearly 40 people told Barouh that the company was in trouble. Nobody was going to buy Ko-Rec-Type again.

Barouh bought a self-correcting typewriter, took it to the plant, called everybody together, and told them what they had to do. To survive, the company had to learn to make this ribbon. They also had to learn to make the cartridge that held the ribbon, because cartridges could not be purchased on the market. They also had to learn to make the spools that held the tape. They had to learn to make the ink, the machine that puts on ink, injection-molding to make the spools, and so on. It was an enormous challenge. Barouh got everyone involved regardless of position or education.

To everyone's astonishment, Ko-Rec-Type produced the first self-correcting ribbon in only six months. Moreover, it was the only company in the world to produce that product. Barouh later learned that it took IBM six years to make the self-correcting ribbon. With the new product, Ko-Rec-Type's sales remained high and the company avoided disaster.[34]

The Vroom-Yetton model shows that Vic Barouh used the correct decision style. Moving from left to right in Exhibit 7.6, the questions and answers are as follows. (A) *Did the problem possess a quality requirement?* Definitely yes. (B) *Did Barouh have sufficient information to make a high-quality decision?* Definitely no. (C) *Was the problem well structured?* Definitely no. (D) *Was the acceptance of the decision by subordinates important for effective implementation?* Probably not, because subordinates had a great deal of respect for Barouh and would do whatever he asked. Question E is not relevant. (F) *Did subordinates share the organizational goals?* Yes. Thus, the decision tree leads to alternative 10: Use either CII or GII decision styles. Barouh should have used a participative style — and did.

Group Decision Formats

The Vroom-Yetton model illustrates that managers can select the amount of group participation in decision making. They can also select decision format. Three formats generally can be used: the interactive group, the nominal group, and the Delphi group. Each format has unique characteristics that make it more suitable for certain decisions. Most task forces, committees, and work groups fall into the category of interactive groups. Nominal and Delphi groups normally are convened for the purpose of increasing creativity during group decision making.

Interactive Groups. Research on the Vroom-Yetton model indicates that having subordinates meet as an interactive group leads to more effective decisions than having the group leader meet with each member individually.[35] An

The task force shown here conducted the study and implemented the decision to make the most fundamental change in the history of Northwestern National Life Insurance Company (NWNL). NWNL switched from being a stock and mutual insurance company to a completely shareholder-owned company. The task force provided the advantages of group decision making by providing a *broad perspective*, *diverse knowledge*, and *support* for implementing the final decision.

interactive group simply means that members are brought together face to face and have a specific agenda and decision objectives. Interactive groups typically begin with a group leader stating a problem and asking for inputs from members. Discussion is unorganized. The group may meander through problem identification and may require some problem redefinition. Alternatives are generated and evaluated. Eventually participants will vote or perhaps discuss alternatives until they reach a consensus on a desired solution. A staff meeting or departmental meeting formed to discuss next year's goals is a good example of interactive group decision making. Interactive groups will be described in more detail in Chapter 15.

NOMINAL GROUPS. Because some participants may talk more and dominate group discussions in interactive groups, the **nominal group** technique was developed to ensure that every group participant has equal input in the decision-making process.[36] The nominal group is structured in a series of steps to equalize participation:

1. Each participant writes down his or her ideas on the problem to be discussed. These ideas usually are suggestions for a solution.
2. A round robin in which each group member presents his or her ideas to the group is set up. The ideas are written down on a blackboard for all members to see. No discussion of the ideas occurs until every person's ideas have been presented and written down for general viewing.
3. After all ideas have been presented, there is an open discussion of the ideas for the purpose of clarification and evaluation. This part of the discussion tends to be spontaneous and unstructured.
4. After the discussion, a secret ballot is taken in which each group member votes for preferred solutions. The adopted decision is the one that receives the most votes.

interactive group A group decision-making format in which group members are brought together face to face and have a specific agenda and decision objectives.

nominal group A group decision-making format that emphasizes equal participation in the decision process by all group members.

Delphi group A group decision-making format that involves the circulation among participants of questionnaires on the selected problem, sharing of answers, and continuous recirculation/refinement of questionnaires until a consensus has been obtained.

DELPHI GROUPS. Developed by the Rand Corporation, the **Delphi group** technique is used to combine expert opinions from different perspectives about an ambiguous problem.[37] Unlike interactive and nominal groups, Delphi group participants do not meet face to face — in fact, they never see one another. This technique calls for a group leader to solicit and collate written, expert opinions on a topic through the use of questionnaires. After the answers are received, a summary of the opinions is developed and distributed to participants. Then a new questionnaire on the same problem is circulated. In this second round, participants have the benefit of knowing other people's opinions and can change their suggested answers to reflect this new information. The process of sending out questionnaires and then sharing the results continues until a consensus is reached.

ADVANTAGES AND DISADVANTAGES OF GROUP DECISION MAKING

Whatever group techniques managers use for decision making, there are clear advantages and disadvantages compared with individual decision making.[38] Because managers often have a choice between making a decision by them-

EXHIBIT 7.7
Advantages and Disadvantages of Group Decision Making

Advantages	Disadvantages
1. Broader perspective for problem definition and analysis.	1. Time consuming.
2. More knowledge, facts, and alternatives can be evaluated.	2. Compromise decisions may satisfy no one.
3. Discussion clarifies ambiguous problems and reduces uncertainty about alternatives.	3. Groupthink: Group norms may reduce dissent and opinion diversity.
4. Participation fosters member satisfaction and support for decision.	4. Knowledge overkill and wasted resources if used for programmed decisions
	5. No clear focus for dec. ion responsibility.

selves or including others, they should understand the advantages and disadvantages of group decision making, which are summarized in Exhibit 7.7.

ADVANTAGES. Groups have an advantage over individuals because they bring together a broader perspective for defining the problem and diagnosing underlying causes and effects. In addition to enriching problem diagnosis, groups offer more knowledge and facts with which to identify potential solutions and produce more decision alternatives. Moreover, people who participate in decision making are more satisfied with the decision and more likely to support it, thereby facilitating implementation. Group discussion also can help reduce uncertainty for decision makers who may be unwilling to undertake a big risk by themselves. Finally, group discussion enhances member satisfaction and produces support for a possibly risky decision.

DISADVANTAGES. Group decisions tend to be time consuming. People must be consulted, and they jointly diagnose problems and discuss solutions. Moreover, groups may reach a compromise solution that is less than optimal for the organization. Another problem is groupthink. **Groupthink** is a "mode of thinking that people engage in when they are deeply involved in a cohesive in-group, and when the members' strivings for unanimity override their motivation to realistically appraise alternative courses of action."[39] Groupthink means that people are so committed to the group that they are reluctant to disagree with one another; thus, the group loses the diversity of opinions essential to effective decision making. Another problem — particularly when groups are used for programmed decisions — is decision overkill due to the task's lack of challenge for group members. Finally, there is no clear focus of decision responsibility because the group rather than any single individual makes the decision.

groupthink A phenomenon in which group members are so committed to the group that they are reluctant to express contrary opinions.

One example of the disadvantage of group decision making occurred when a coalition at Citibank refused to change the practice of "parking" — the bogus transfer of foreign exchange deposits to shift bank profits to countries with low tax rates. The line between illegal and legal activities was hazy, and groupthink appeared so people were unwilling to disagree with the current practice because group norms supported high profits and reduced taxes. Group members were willing to compromise their values, groupthink reduced dissent, and there was no clear focus of responsibility because everyone had agreed to the potentially illegal practice.[40]

IMPROVING DECISION-MAKING EFFECTIVENESS

How can managers overcome groupthink and other disadvantages to avoid costly mistakes? A number of techniques have been developed to help individual managers and groups arrive at better decisions.

devil's advocate A decision-making technique in which an individual is assigned the role of challenging the assumptions and assertions made by the group to prevent premature consensus.

A **devil's advocate** is assigned the role of challenging the assumptions and assertions made by the group.[41] The devil's advocate forces the group to rethink its approach to the problem and to avoid reaching premature consensus or making unreasonable assumptions before proceeding with problem solutions.

multiple advocacy A decision-making technique that involves several advocates and presentation of multiple points of view, including minority and unpopular opinions.

Multiple advocacy is similar to a devil's advocate except that more advocates and points of view are presented. Minority opinions and unpopular viewpoints are assigned to forceful representatives, who then debate before the decision makers. President Bush is renowned for using multiple advocacy in his decision making. The proposal for clean-air legislation in 1989 was a textbook case, because White House aides staged debates they called "Scheduled Train Wrecks" to help Bush think through the issue. These were live scrimmages with Bush asking questions back and forth during the debate. The result was a decision based on solid argument and understanding of all perspectives.[42]

brainstorming A decision-making technique in which group members present spontaneous suggestions for problem solution, regardless of their likelihood of implementation, in order to promote freer, more creative thinking within the group.

Brainstorming uses a face-to-face, interactive group to spontaneously suggest ideas for problem solution.[43] Brainstorming is perhaps the best-known decision aid; its primary role is to supply additional, creative solutions. Group members are invited to suggest alternatives regardless of their likelihood of being implemented. No critical comments of any kind are allowed until all suggestions have been listed. Members are encouraged to brainstorm possible solutions out loud, and freewheeling is welcomed. The more novel and unusual the idea, the better. The object of brainstorming is to promote freer, more flexible thinking and to enable group members to build on one another's creativity. The typical session begins with a warmup wherein definitional issues are settled, proceeds through the freewheeling idea-generation stage, and concludes with an evaluation of feasible ideas.[44]

SUMMARY

This chapter made several important points about the process of organizational decision making. The study of decision making is important because it describes how managers make successful strategic and operational decisions. Managers must confront many types of decisions, including programmed and nonprogrammed, and decisions differ according to the amount of risk, uncertainty, and ambiguity in the environment.

Two decision-making approaches were described: the classical model and the administrative model. The classical model explains how managers should make decisions so as to maximize economic efficiency. The administrative model describes how managers actually make nonprogrammed, uncertain decisions. Decision making should involve six basic steps: problem recognition, diagnosis of causes, development of alternatives, choice of an alternative, implementation of alternative, and feedback and evaluation.

In organizations, groups make decisions as well as individuals. The Vroom-Yetton model specifies decision characteristics that indicate when groups should participate in decision making. The types of groups managers may use include interactive groups, nominal groups, and Delphi groups. Groups offer a number of advantages and disadvantages compared with individuals. Techniques for improving decision-making quality include devil's advocate, multiple advocacy, and brainstorming. These techniques help managers define problems and develop more creative solutions.

MANAGEMENT SOLUTION

Tony Andrade faced decisions about how to fully utilize the 24-hour day in his six Dunkin' Donuts shops in Boston. Half of the coffee and doughnuts were sold between 6 o'clock and 10 o'clock in the morning, leaving shops little used the rest of the time. The same problem faced Robert Rosenberg, chief executive of the chain's 1,539 shops. After analyzing this problem, Dunkin' Donuts considered four alternatives: First, expand the menu in hopes of luring the lunch and dinner crowds. The expanded menu could include sandwiches, muffins, soft drinks, and soup. Second, shorten operating hours. Third, remodel the shops, putting in booths and tables to appeal to a lunch and dinner crowd. Fourth, experiment with novel doughnut outlets, such as gas stations and turnpike restaurants. After evaluating these alternatives, Dunkin' Donuts decided to build its image as a sit-down restaurant staying open 24 hours by broadening the menu and remodeling stores. So far the decision is working, with earnings amounting to 18 percent on equity.[45]

DISCUSSION QUESTIONS

1. You are a busy partner in a legal firm, and an experienced secretary complains of continued headaches, drowsiness, dry throat, and occasional spells of fatigue and flu. She tells you she believes air quality in the building is bad and would like something done. How would you respond?
2. Why is decision making considered a fundamental part of management effectiveness?
3. Explain the difference between risk and ambiguity. How might decision making differ for each situation?
4. Analyze three decisions you made over the last six months. Which of these are programmed and which are nonprogrammed?
5. Why are many decisions made by groups rather than by individuals?

6. The Vroom-Yetton model describes five decision styles. How should a manager go about choosing which style to use?
7. What are three types of decision-making groups? How might each be used to help managers make a decision to market a product in a new geographical territory?
8. What is meant by satisficing and bounded rationality? Why do managers not strive to find the economically best solution for many organizational decisions?
9. What techniques could you use to improve your own creativity and effectiveness in decision making?
10. Which of the six steps in the decision-making process do you think is most likely to be ignored by a manager? Explain.

Management in Practice: Experiential Exercise

The Desert Survival Situation

The situation described in this exercise is based on over 2,000 actual cases in which men and women lived or died depending on the survival decisions they made. Your "life" or "death" will depend on how well your group can share its present knowledge of a relatively unfamiliar problem so that the team can make decisions that will lead to your survival.

This exercise will challenge your ability to take advantage of a group approach to decision making and to apply decision steps such as developing alternatives and selecting the correct alternative. When instructed, read about the situation and do Step 1 without discussing it with the rest of the group.

The Situation It is approximately 10:00 A.M. in mid-August, and you have just crash landed in the Sonora Desert in southwestern United States. The light twin-engine plane, containing the bodies of the pilot and the copilot, has completely burned. Only the air frame remains. None of the rest of you has been injured.

The pilot was unable to notify anyone of your position before the crash. However, he had indicated before impact that you were 70 miles south-southwest from a mining camp that is the nearest known habitation and that you were approximately 65 miles off the course that was filed in your VFR Flight Plan.

The immediate area is quite flat and except for occasional barrel and saguaro cacti appears to be rather barren. The last weather report indicated the temperature would reach 110° that day, which means that the temperature at ground level will be 130°. You are dressed in lightweight clothing: short-sleeved shirts, pants, socks, and street shoes. Everyone has a handkerchief. Collectively, your pockets contain $2.83 in change, $85.00 in bills, a pack of cigarettes, and a ballpoint pen.

Your Task Before the plane caught fire your group was able to salvage the 15 items listed in the following table. Your task is to rank these items according to their importance to your survival, starting with "1," the most important to "15," the least important.

You may assume the following:

1. The number of survivors is the same as the number on your team.
2. You are the actual people in the situation.
3. The team has agreed to stick together.
4. All items are in good condition.

Step 1 Each member of the team is to individually rank each item. Do not discuss the situation or problem until each member has finished the individual ranking.

Step 2 After everyone has finished the individual ranking, rank order the 15 items as a team. Once discussion begins do not change your individual ranking. Your instructor will inform you how much time you have to complete this step.

Items	Step 1: Your Individual Ranking	Step 2: The Team's Ranking	Step 3: Survival Expert's Ranking	Step 4: Difference between Step 1 and Step 3	Step 5: Difference between Step 2 and Step 3
Flashlight (4-battery size)	___	___	___	___	___
Jackknife	___	___	___	___	___
Sectional air map of the area	___	___	___	___	___
Plastic raincoat (large size)	___	___	___	___	___
Magnetic compass	___	___	___	___	___
Compress kit with gauze	___	___	___	___	___
.45 caliber pistol (loaded)	___	___	___	___	___
Parachute (red and white)	___	___	___	___	___
Bottle of salt tablets (1,000 tablets)	___	___	___	___	___
1 quart of water per person	___	___	___	___	___
A book entitled *Edible Animals of the Desert*	___	___	___	___	___
A pair of sunglasses per person	___	___	___	___	___
2 quarts of 180 proof vodka	___	___	___	___	___
1 top coat per person	___	___	___	___	___
A cosmetic mirror	___	___	___	___	___
		Totals (the lower the score, the better)		___ Your Score, Step 4	___ Team Score, Step 5

Please complete the following steps and insert the scores under your team's number.	Team Number 1	2	3	4	5	6
Step 6: Average Individual Score Add up all the individual scores (Step 4) on the team and divide by the number on the team.	___	___	___	___	___	___
Step 7: Team Score	___	___	___	___	___	___
Step 8: Gain Score The difference between the Team Score and the Average Individual Score. If the Team Score is lower than Average Individual Score, then gain is "+." If Team Score is higher than Average Individual Score, then gain is "−."	___	___	___	___	___	___
Step 9: Lowest Individual Score on the Team	___	___	___	___	___	___
Step 10: Number of Individual Scores Lower Than the Team Score	___	___	___	___	___	___

Source: J. Clayton Lafferty, Patrick M. Eady, and Alonzo W. Pond, "The Desert Survival Situation: A Group Decision Making Experience for Examining and Increasing Individual and Team Effectiveness," 8th ed. Copyright © 1974 by Experiential Learning Methods, Inc., 14539 Harbor Island, Detroit, MI 48215, (313) 823-4400.

CASES FOR ANALYSIS

GENERAL MILLS

Starting a new restaurant is as risky as starting a Broadway play. Some 65 percent of new restaurants fail within two years. Aware of the odds, senior managers in General Mills' restaurant division decided to develop a restaurant chain from scratch. The restaurant division's performance had been unsteady, relying heavily on its flagship Red Lobster chain for current profits. Something new was required to propel future growth.

General Mills settled on an Italian chain after its problem analysis indicated that Italian food was ranked the most popular ethnic meal by a survey of adults. Moreover, managers found Italian restaurants were only one-third the number of Mexican or Oriental restaurants nationwide. The research produced three prototype finalists: an Italian restaurant that had great appeal for yuppies, a cozy farmhouse with fireplaces, an olive garden with large windows and a fern bar atmosphere. Managers chose the olive garden motif.

The next step was to build a single restaurant in Florida as a pilot. Different recipes were tried, many gained from surveys of restaurants and customers. Some parts of the experiment bombed, including an authentic Italian breakfast and Italian opera music.

Eighty different spaghetti sauce recipes were tried before one was finally picked. But after a year, the Olive Garden restaurant turned a profit, drawing more than 800 customers a day. This justified seven more locations. The bosses worried about possible failure, but decided to go with inexperienced supervisors to keep a fresh approach to operations. The seven new Olive Gardens did well. Success is contagious, and General Mills is now rapidly progressing toward its goal of 500 restaurants. The long-term success looks bright except for competitors, who are now designing their own Italian restaurants. General Mills beat uncertainty with its solid decision approach, but today's success does not guarantee future business. The risk is that customers can be lured away by impulse and competitor advertising.

Questions

1. Which decision-making steps are evident in the Olive Garden decision? Explain.
2. What was the role of evaluation and feedback in this case?
3. Was the decision characterized by risk, uncertainty, or ambiguity? Did this change over time?

Source: Based on Robert Johnson, "General Mills Risked Millions Starting Chain of Italian Restaurants," *The Wall Street Journal*, September 21, 1987, 18.

GUARDIAN ENGINEERING

Lew Calderone, engineering manager, was beside himself. The problem he faced was complex and highly personal in nature. Joey Stark had been an employee of Guardian Engineering for 15 years and had a record of reliable, consistent work. Joey had reported to Lew for two years. However, his performance recently had become so poor that Lew felt Joey must be fired. For one thing, Joey was frequently absent on Mondays despite the company's policy against excessive absences. Once or twice Lew had smelled alcohol on Joey's breath while at work, and he suspected that alcohol was the problem. A couple of other employees had commented on Joey's drinking, but Lew had never personally witnessed Joey drinking excessively.

Lew had talked with Joey twice about his absences and declining performance. He had asked Joey about his family life, personal life, and working conditions to learn whether any of these were causing the problem. Joey had simply said everything was all right. After the second conversation, Lew wrote a short memorandum specifying his concerns, and the memo went into Joey's personnel file. Joey improved his performance for a couple of weeks, but nothing seemed to have changed permanently.

If alcoholism was Joey's problem, Lew was thinking about alternative solutions. One would be to fire Joey, because Lew had read that alcoholics lose their jobs and their families before they become motivated to change their behavior. Another would be to confront Joey and accuse him of alcoholism to let him know the company was aware of his drinking problem. A third would be to refer Joey to a private counselor or physician for possible rehabilitation. A fourth would be to give Joey one more warning, making it clear that the next absence or lapse in performance would cost him his job.

Complicating the problem was Lew's feeling that Joey was a friend as well as a senior employee. However, Lew felt he had to proceed with whatever was best for the company. The company had no clearly defined policy on alcoholism, which made choosing a solution somewhat more difficult. Lew wondered whether he should talk to other senior managers about the problem and seek their guidance and agreement. He also wondered if there were some way he could gather more information about the true nature of the problem before deciding on a solution. Frankly, Lew realized he needed to take action, but he just was not sure what to do.

Questions

1. Is the decision facing Lew Calderone considered programmed or nonprogrammed?
2. How should Lew proceed to make the decision? Should he investigate the nature of the problem? Should he make a decision among the available alternatives?
3. What would you do in this situation? Why?

CHAPTER 8

MANAGEMENT SCIENCE AIDS FOR PLANNING AND DECISION MAKING

CHAPTER OUTLINE

LEARNING OBJECTIVES

After studying this chapter, you should be able to:

- Define management science and the types of management decisions and problems to which management science techniques apply.
- Identify three quantitative methods and three qualitative methods of forecasting future events.
- Describe breakeven analysis and explain how it can be used for organizational decisions.
- Describe the purpose and application of linear programming.
- Discuss the use of PERT in project scheduling and define critical path.
- Describe the payoff matrix and decision tree and explain the difference between them.
- Discuss the advantages and disadvantages of using management science techniques for planning and decision making.

Management Problem

The streets of New York City were filthy; almost half were considered unacceptable. The Department of Sanitation faced numerous problems in trying to keep streets clean. A fiscal crisis left only 800 street cleaners compared with 2,500 only five years before. Employee morale was low because of constant abuse from the public and media blaming them for the city's condition. Sanitation managers hardly knew where to start. They did not understand which factors — waste cans, traffic, parking — influenced street cleanliness or the relationship between the number of street cleaners and cleanliness levels. There was no coordination with other city departments, and the city council had rejected a Department of Sanitation proposal to expand the cleaning force.[1]

If you were a senior manager in New York City's Department of Sanitation, what decisions would you make for improving street cleanliness with available resources? What information would you gather, and what techniques would you use to make the necessary decisions?

The problem of dirty streets in New York City demonstrates that solving a complex problem often requires more than a general, intuitive approach. Solid information was not readily available, and the factors influencing street cleanliness were overwhelming.

In previous chapters we have seen how good managers are distinguished from poor ones by how effectively they set goals, develop plans with which to meet those goals, and make the necessary decisions. This chapter introduces quantitative techniques that can serve as valuable decision aids and planning tools. Management science techniques are especially effective when many factors affect a problem, when problems can be quantified, when relationships among factors can be defined, and when the decision maker can control the key factors affecting performance outcomes.[2] This chapter describes some of the more common management science techniques that are applicable to managerial planning and decision making. It discusses quantitative approaches to forecasting, breakeven analysis, linear programming, PERT charting, and the

Management science uses quantitatively based models to assist managerial decision makers. Employees at Church & Dwight Co., Inc., makers of Arm & Hammer® products, used management science techniques to launch PET FRESH, developed to combat pet odors. A tracking service keyed to grocery store scanning systems provided quantitative data on consumer purchase behavior. Analysis of these data helped managers identify the need for a new product and the advertising strategy.

decision aids of payoff matrix and decision tree. These techniques are not covered in depth; managers only need to understand the basic approach and be able to communicate with management science experts. Understanding management science techniques enabled New York City's Department of Sanitation to formulate solutions to the staggering problem of dirty streets.

The Nature and Role of Management Science

Management science techniques are designed to supplement managerial planning and decision making. For many decisions, management science leads to better answers. For example, in today's organizations it is not uncommon to find experts who use mathematical and statistical analyses to help managers make capital budgeting decisions; decide whether to open a new factory; predict economic trends or customer demands; determine whether to rent or buy a new computer system; schedule trucks, ships, or aircraft; decide among several proposals for research and development projects; and assess whether a new-product introduction is likely to be profitable.

EXHIBIT 8.1
Management Problems and Applicable Management Science Tools

Management Problem	Applicable Management Science Tool
Production mix	Linear programming
Scheduling and sequencing	PERT network
Distribution	Simulation
New-product decisions	Payoff matrix Decision tree
Pricing decisions	Payoff matrix Decision tree
Sales force assignment	Assignment models
Forecasting	Time series Regression analysis Econometric models

Management science is defined as a set of quantitatively based decision models used to assist management decision makers. There are three key components in this definition.

management science A set of quantitatively based decision models used to assist management decision makers.

First, management science is a set of quantitative tools. Mathematically based procedures impart a systematic rigor to the decision process. Certain types of data must be gathered, put into a specific format, and analyzed according to stringent mathematical rules.

Second, management science uses decision models. A *model* is a simplified representation of a real-life situation. For example, small-scale physical models were constructed for every set in the movie *Raiders of the Lost Ark* to diagnose filming problems before constructing the real sets. In a mathematical model, key elements are represented by numbers. Mathematical models are difficult for many students and managers because they use a language that is abstract and unfamiliar. However, outcomes from mathematical models can still aid in decision making.

Third, quantitative models *assist* decision makers; they cannot substitute for or replace a manager.[3] Management science models are simply one of many tools in a manager's tool kit. The manager's role is to provide information for use in the models, interpret the information they provide, and carry out the final plan of action.

Sometimes proponents of management science techniques oversell their value for managerial decision making. Conversely, managers who are unfamiliar with mathematics may resist the use of management science techniques and hence fail to take advantage of a powerful tool. The best management approach is to attempt to understand the types of problems to which management science aids apply and then work with specialists to formulate the necessary data and analytical procedures. For example, a nursing administrator at Grant Hospital of Chicago used a linear programming software package developed for personal computers to arrange monthly schedules for 300 nurses. This management science approach saved the hospital approximately $80,000 per month.[4]

Exhibit 8.1 lists some of the more common management problems and applicable management science techniques. These techniques apply to problems in production, product distribution, new-product decisions, and sales force assignment. Scores of management science techniques are available. The remainder of this chapter will describe some of the most important management science tools and illustrate their use in managerial planning and decision making.

FORECASTING

Managers look into the future through forecasts. *Forecasts* are predictions about future organizational and environmental circumstances that will influence plans, decisions, and goal attainment. Forecasts are a basic part of the SWOT analysis described in Chapter 6. Virtually every planning decision depends on assumptions about future conditions.

Four types of forecasts are frequently used by managers:

sales forecast A forecast of future company sales based on projected customer demand for products or services.

1. *Sales forecasts.* **Sales forecasts** predict future company sales. Sales forecasting is critical, because it defines customers' demands for products or services. Sales forecasts determine production levels for three months, six months, or one year into the future. Managers use them to hire necessary personnel, buy needed raw materials, making plans to finance an expansion, and arrange needed transportation services. Medium- and large-size companies such as Sound Warehouse, Paychex, Wallace Computer Services, and Monsanto use sales forecasts to plan production activities.

technological forecast A forecast of the occurrence of technological changes that could affect an organization's way of doing business.

2. *Technological forecasts.* **Technological forecasts** attempt to predict the advent of technological changes, especially major technological breakthroughs that could alter an organization's way of doing business. Companies forecast technological changes to avoid building plants or acquiring equipment that are out of date and noncompetitive. General Motors has been forecasting the use of robotics in automobile manufacturing so as to remain competitive with other American and Japanese automobile producers. Watch manufacturers are eyeing developments from a company called AT&E Corporation that has found a high-tech way to transform a standard wristwatch into a paging device.

demographic forecast A forecast of societal characteristics such as birthrates, educational levels, marriage rates, and diseases.

3. *Demographic forecasts.* **Demographic forecasts** pertain to the characteristics of society, including birthrates, educational levels, marriage rates, and diseases. For example, the baby bust of the late 1960s and early 1970s has meant a labor shortage in many parts of the country in the 1990s, which is a particular concern of labor-intensive companies. However, the baby boom of the 1980s will permit managers in schools and companies that make children's clothing and toys to plan for increased product demand in the near future.

human resources forecast A forecast of the organization's future personnel needs.

4. *Human resources forecasts.* **Human resources forecasts** predict the organization's future personnel needs.[5] AT&T is predicting a decrease of several thousand employees during the late 1980s. This means that its human resources department must arrange for early retirements and help displaced employees find jobs elsewhere. Companies in rapidly growing high-tech industries forecast hiring a large number of additional employees. Thus, senior managers must make arrangements for employee recruit-

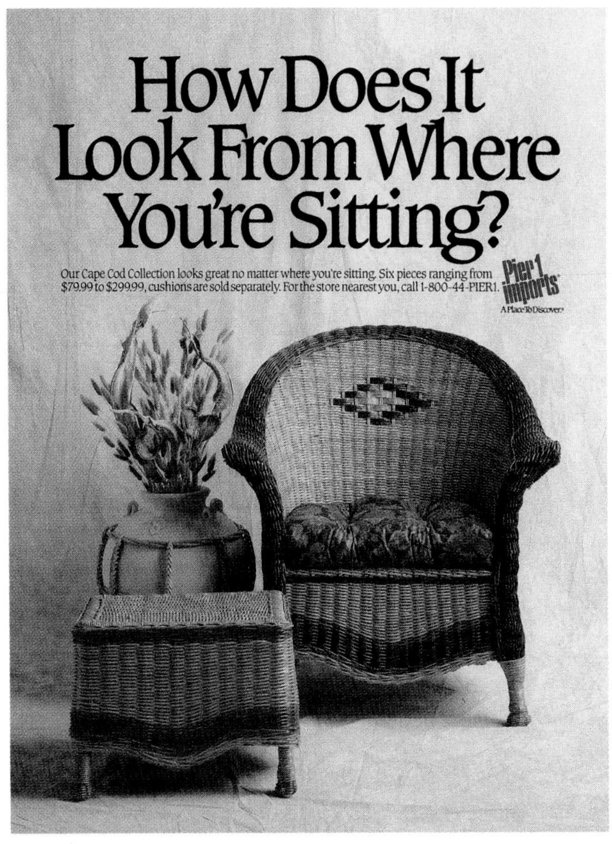

From where Pier 1 Imports is sitting, favorable *demographic forecasts* indicate a bright future for this leading retailer. Understanding the demographic makeup of its customer base is important, because Pier 1 obtains merchandise from 44 countries for its 500+ stores. Pier 1 managers plot customer demographics using data obtained from a 1,000-member customer advisory panel, customer exit interviews, focus groups, and major surveys. Pier 1 offers unique products for its demographically desirable customer base, with household income over $38,000, 72 percent college educated, and 70 percent women.

ment programs and perhaps locate new plants in areas where employees are available.

Forecasts provide information that reduces uncertainty in decision making. Several specific techniques, both quantitative and qualitative, help managers derive forecasts for use in their planning and decision making. Exhibit 8.2 illustrates some of the forecasting techniques, their possible applications, and their degree of accuracy.

Let us now examine both the quantitative and qualitative techniques more closely.

QUANTITATIVE FORECASTING TECHNIQUES

Quantitative forecasts start with a series of past data values and then use a set of mathematical rules with which to predict future values.[6] Quantitative techniques have become widely used by managers for two reasons. First, the techniques have repeatedly demonstrated accuracy, especially in the short and intermediate term, thus earning managers' confidence as a planning aid. Second, improvements in computer hardware and software have increased the efficiency and decreased the expense of using quantitative techniques. A large

quantitative forecast A forecast that begins with a series of past data values and then applies a set of mathematical rules with which to predict future values.

EXHIBIT 8.2
Forecasting Techniques Used by Organizations

		Accuracy		
Quantitative Techniques	**Sample Application**	**Short Term**	**Intermediate Term**	**Long Term**
Time series analysis	Sales, earnings, inventory control	Excellent	Good	Good
Regression analysis	Sales, earnings	Excellent	Excellent	Fair
Econometric models	GNP, sales, demographics, economic shifts	Excellent	Good	Fair
Qualitative Techniques				
Delphi	Product development, technological predictions	Good	Good	Good
Sales force composite	Sales projections, future customer demand	Fair	Fair	Poor
Jury of opinion	Sales, new-product development, earnings	Good	Fair	Poor

Source: Adapted from J. Chambers, S. Mullick, and D. Smith, "How to Choose the Right Forecasting Technique," *Harvard Business Review* (July/August 1971), 55–64.

number of variables can be incorporated into the analysis, and statistical refinements have improved the techniques' ability to meet the forecasting needs of company managers.

Quantitative forecasting techniques can be subdivided into two categories: time series analysis and causal models. Time series analysis project past behavior into the future. Causal modeling attempts to unearth past causes of behavior as a way of projecting into the future.[7]

time series analysis
A forecasting technique that examines the patterns of movement in historical data.

TIME SERIES ANALYSIS. The forecasting technique called **time series analysis** examines the patterns of movement in historical data. It defines patterns in terms of one of four categories:

1. Secular trends
2. Cyclic patterns
3. Seasonal variation
4. Random variation

A *secular trend* is the general behavior of a variable over a long period of time. Panel (a) of Exhibit 8.3 shows a set of data with an upward trend in unit sales each year. The demand for this company's sales is growing regularly, and managers will project sales for 1993 based on this growth.

A *cyclic pattern* involves a recurring up-and-down movement that is periodic in nature. The pattern extends over several years and cannot always be counted on to repeat with precise regularity. Cyclic patterns are related to general business cycles of growth and recession, which managers find extremely valuable to predict. Panel (b) of Exhibit 8.3 shows units sold over a typical business cycle of several years.

Seasonal variation is a regular variation in behavior that recurs within a period of one year or less. Climatic, social, and religious customs can cause seasonal variation. For example, heating sales increase during the winter and decrease during the summer, whereas sales of window air conditioners perform in reverse. Bicycle sales normally peak in November and December—

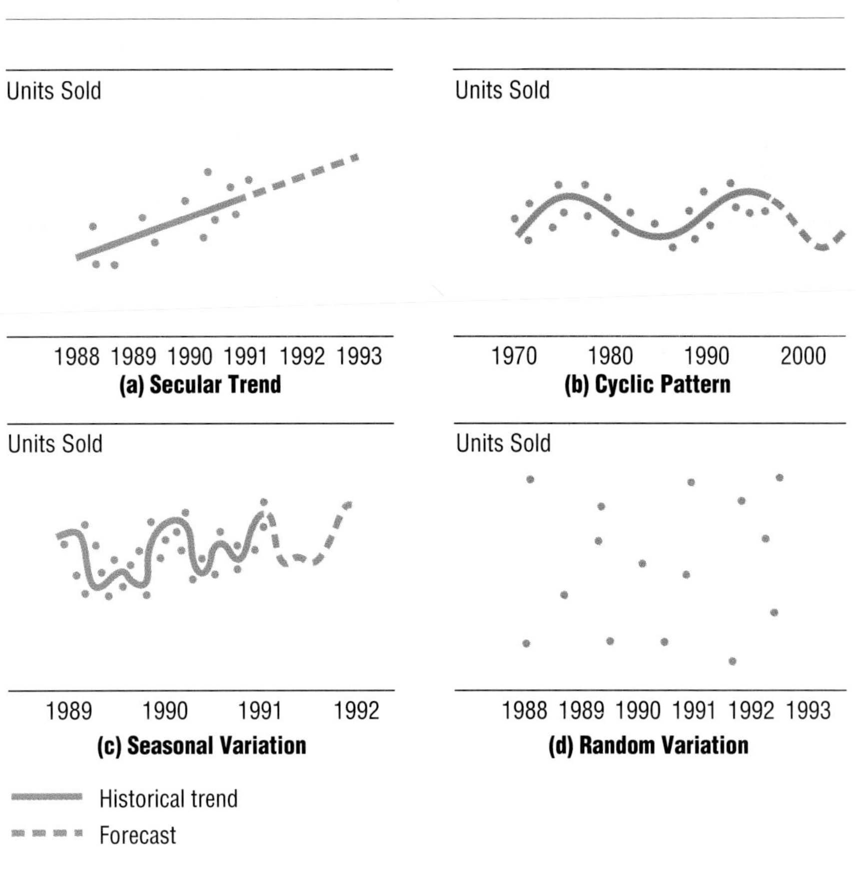

EXHIBIT 8.3
Examples of Time Series Forecasting Patterns

prior to Christmas — decline in the winter months, rise in the spring and summer, and decline again in the fall. Panel (c) of Exhibit 8.3 shows a seasonal pattern of units sold that would help a manager predict future sales.

The fourth category, random variation, is not a pattern at all. *Random variation* means that there are changes in units sold, but they are unpredictable. These movements might be caused by random factors, such as a strike, natural disaster, or changes in government regulations. Panel (d) of Exhibit 8.3 shows data that have random variation. Managers are unable to use random variation to predict the future.

Time series analysis is used to predict both short-term and intermediate-term behavior. Its power is its ability to account for seasonal changes as well as long-run trends. Time series analysis works best when the business environment is relatively stable, that is, when the past is a good indicator of the future. In environments in which consumer tastes change radically or random occurrences have a great impact on sales, time series models tend to be inaccurate and of little value.

One company that was able to take advantage of time series forecasting is Huffy Corporation.

Carnation Company uses *quantitative forecasting techniques* to manage manufacturing materials. The Carnation Data Center, shown here, is a command post for coordinating data to develop a sales forecast. The first step is to review historical data about how much each product sold in the past. Marketing is consulted about the effect of special promotions, and sales offices give further estimates. The forecast is used to buy and schedule the staggering 2 million tons of material a year for Carnation's 24 manufacturing plants.

HUFFY CORPORATION

• Huffy Corporation is the largest U.S. producer of bicycles. In the early 1980s, Huffy's plants were producing at maximum capacity in several of its product lines. Huffy executives were concerned about whether they should undertake plans to increase future capacity. Because a major corporate goal was 100 percent customer satisfaction, managers realized that an accurate sales forecasting system was important.

The internal accounting and financial group was commissioned to develop a forecasting system that would have the following characteristics:

1. Usable by managers responsible for all product lines and divisions
2. Use data from the current management information system data base
3. Cost efficient
4. Easily maintained and readily understood by nontechnical managers
5. Forecasts based on available sales data
6. Forecasts accurate within ±5 percent for divisions, ±10 percent for each product, and ±10 percent for each brand

After studying many forecasting techniques, Huffy's managers selected a time series model. They found it easy to use because it avoided complex statistics. The final model predicted future sales based on both cyclical and seasonal variation projected from six months of sales history. The time series model was easy to understand and accurate, meeting Huffy's forecasting objective.[8]

causal modeling A forecasting technique that attempts to predict behavior (the dependent variable) by analyzing its causes (independent variables).

CAUSAL FORECASTING MODELS. The forecasting technique called **causal modeling** attempts to predict behavior, called the *dependent variable,* by analyzing its causes, called *independent variables.* Thus, causal modeling may attempt to predict sales (the dependent variable) by examining those factors that cause sales to increase or decrease including amount of advertising expenditure, unit price, competitors' prices, and the overall inflation rate (independent variables). This technique differs from that of simply projecting future sales based on past sales.

Causal modeling is based on the use of statistical regression analysis. **Regression analysis** is a statistical tool for predicting the value of a dependent variable based on the known values of independent variables.

The general model for a regression equation is

$$Y = aX_1 + bX_2 + cX_3 + d,$$

where

Y = dependent variable being forecasted (units sold)
X_1, X_2, and X_3 = independent variables
a, b, and c = calculated coefficients of independent variables
d = a constant

regression analysis A statistical tool for predicting the value of a dependent variable based on the known values of independent variables.

econometric model A system of regression equations that are solved simultaneously to capture the interaction between economic conditions and the organization's activities.

A regression analysis could be performed to predict a company's sales based on the causal factors of advertising expenditure, unit price, and competitors' prices. The statistical computations would produce the following equation:

$$Y = -24.50 + 1.35X_1 - 0.75X_2 + 0.25X_3,$$

where

Y = sales in hundreds of units
X_1 = advertising expenditure in thousands of dollars
X_2 = product price
X_3 = competitors' average price

From this equation a manager can explore the causal relationships among sales, advertising, product price, and competitors' prices. For example, a $1,000 budget increase for advertising expenditure would cause a 135-unit increase in sales, or a $1 decrease in price would cause a 75-unit increase in sales. These relationships can be used to predict future sales and to influence causal variables that can increase sales.

Many companies use simple regression models. For example, the vice-president of marketing for Pitney Bowes' Data Documents Division has been able to predict sales of business forms based on the growth of the gross national product. Retailers such as Carter Hawley Hale predict future retail sales based on disposable personal income. The producers of big yachts predict sales based on stock market performance, and Mercury Marine predicts outboard motor sales based on the monthly Consumer Confidence Index published by the Conference Board.[9] Each of these companies has identified factors that cause unit sales to increase or decrease, and watching these factors helps managers forecast sales using a causal model.

Another causal modeling technique is an econometric model. An **econometric model** is a system of regression equations solved simultaneously to take into account the interaction between economic conditions and organizational activities. Econometric models are a complex extension of regression models. When managers need to use econometric models to make forecasts, they should hire a consulting firm that specializes in mathematics and economics to construct them.

This can of Glidden Spred Satin® came from a high-speed line that fills thousands of cans an hour. In the past Glidden has used *causal forecasting models* to predict the demand for its paint and stain products. The independent variables that predict Glidden paint sales are gross national product and disposable personal income. One logical independent variable — new housing starts — has surprisingly little correlation with Glidden's paint sales. The reason is that most Glidden paint is sold through 10,000 retail outlets for use in existing homes and structures.

When choosing between time series predictions and causal modeling, managers should consider that time series predictions are better at describing seasonal sales variations and predicting changes in sales direction, and causal models provide better information on how to influence a dependent variable such as units sold. Both time series and causal forecasting approaches can produce reliable forecasts if they start with proper data and assumptions. Managers using causal or time series models may wish to work closely with management science experts for maximum benefit.

QUALITATIVE FORECASTING TECHNIQUES

qualitative forecast A forecast based on the opinions of experts in the absence of precise historical data.

Qualitative techniques are used when quantitative historical data are unavailable. **Qualitative forecasts** rely on experts' judgment. Three useful forms of qualitative forecasting are the Delphi technique, sales force composite, and jury of opinion.

Delphi technique A qualitative forecasting method in which experts reach consensus about future events through a series of continuously refined questionnaires rather than through face-to-face discussion.

DELPHI TECHNIQUE. A process whereby experts come to a consensus about future events without face-to-face discussion is called the **Delphi technique.**[10] The Delphi procedure was described in Chapter 7 as a means of group decision making. It is especially effective for technological forecasts, because precise data for predicting technological breakthroughs are not available. Technological experts fill out a questionnaire about future events, and the responses are summarized and returned to participants. They then complete a new questionnaire based on their own previous responses and the estimates of other experts. The process continues until a consensus is reached. The Delphi technique promotes independent thought and precludes direct confrontations and participants' defensiveness about their ideas. Its biggest advantage is that experts with widely different opinions can share information with one another and reach agreement about future predictions.[11]

sales force composite A type of qualitative forecasting that relies on the combined expert opinions of field sales personnel.

SALES FORCE COMPOSITE. Another technique called the **sales force composite,** relies on the combined expert judgments of field sales personnel. Experienced salespeople know their customers and generally sense fluctuations in customers' needs and buying patterns before these changes are reflected in quantitative data. Salespeople are polled about their customers' expected purchases in the coming time period. Each estimate is reviewed by a district or regional sales manager, who combines these estimates and makes adjustments for expected changes in economic conditions. Findings by Dun and Bradstreet suggest that businesspeople are good forecasters except in times of unexpected or deep recession. During especially bad periods, both managers and salespeople tend to be overly optimistic about the future.[12]

jury of opinion A method of qualitative forecasting based on the average opinions of managers from various company divisions and departments.

JURY OF OPINION. The technique using the average opinion of managers from various company divisions and departments is considered a **jury of opinion.** It is similar to a Delphi procedure in that jury members need not meet face to face. Because opinions come from several people, the forecast is less risky than it would be if conducted by a single individual. The method is quick and inexpensive and does not require elaborate statistical analysis. It takes advantage of management's knowledge of the environment based on past experience and good judgment. Jury of opinion was used to forecast the 1990s glut

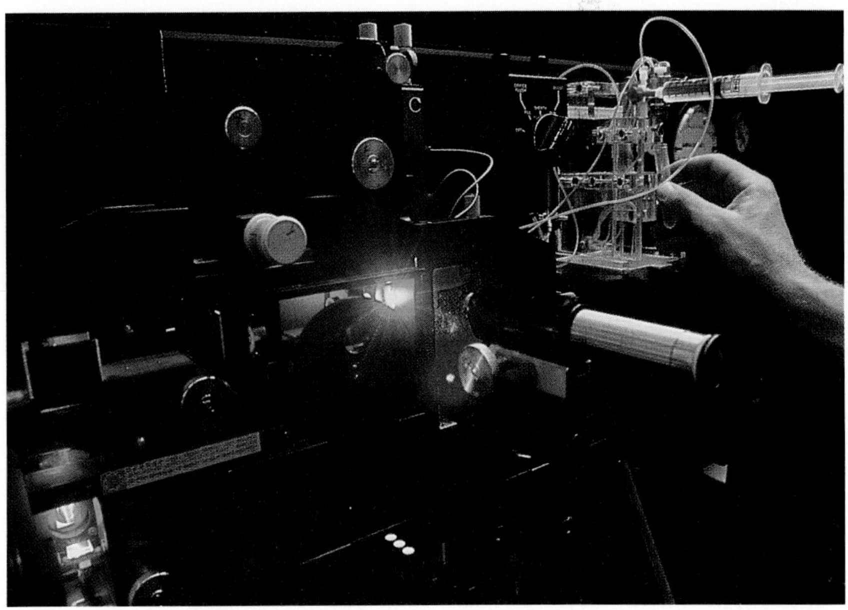

Bristol-Myers Squibb Company interviewed 220 prominent research scientists to examine priorities and promising areas of medical research in the next century. These world scientific leaders formed a *jury of opinion* indicating that diseases will be attacked at their roots. This means treating diseases such as cancer at the level of individual cells rather than treating symptoms. In response to this qualitative forecasting, Bristol-Myers developed the fluorescence-activated cell sorter shown here that uses lasers and computers to target antibodies to individual tumor cells in the body.

of new automobiles. Experts saw that new plants built in the United States by Japanese and American carmakers would lead to overcapacity by 6 million units. Based on this forecast, some companies curtailed expansion plans.[13]

All forecasting is based on historical patterns, and qualitative techniques are used when precise, historical data are unavailable. If managers feel that experts' biases are affecting forecast accuracy, they can correct future forecasts through instructional feedback. As managers or other experts see that their forecasts are too high or too low, they learn to forecast more accurately in future periods.[14]

QUANTITATIVE APPROACHES TO PLANNING

Once a sales forecast is developed, managers incorporate that information into their planning for the firm's future actions. Many quantitative techniques are available to help managers plan. Three of these techniques tell managers how many units must be sold before a product is profitable (breakeven analysis), which combination of products can minimize costs (linear programming), and how to schedule complex projects to be completed in the shortest amount of time (PERT). The following discussion illustrates how these techniques assist planning in some situations.

BREAKEVEN ANALYSIS

breakeven analysis
A quantitative technique that helps managers determine the level of sales at which total revenues equal total costs.

Breakeven analysis is a quantitative technique that helps managers determine the level of sales at which total revenues equal total costs and, hence, the firm breaks even.[15] Breakeven analysis portrays the relationships among units

EXHIBIT 8.4
Breakeven Model

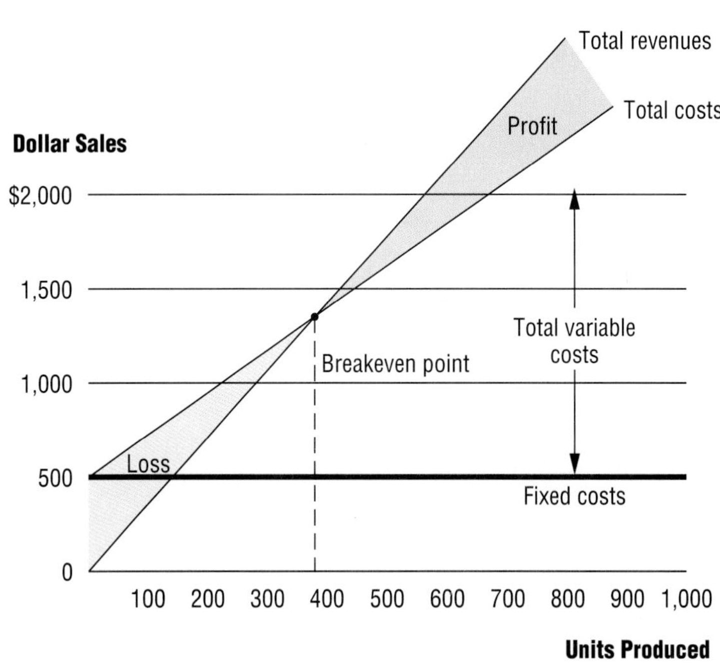

of output, sales revenue, and costs, as illustrated in Exhibit 8.4. This analysis is an important tool for small business and can answer such questions as: What would happen to sales volume and profits if fixed costs rise 10 percent and prices are held constant? What can we do if our competitor cuts prices 10 percent and our sales volume drops 5 percent? What increase in sales volume must be gained to justify a 15 percent increase in the advertising budget? At what point should company operations simply be shut down?[16] These questions can be answered using the following variables of breakeven analysis:

1. *Fixed costs:* Costs that remain the same regardless of the level of production, such as the payment on the building's mortgage. Fixed costs, represented by the horizontal line in Exhibit 8.4, remain at $500 whether production is low or high.
2. *Variable costs:* Costs that vary with the number of units produced, such as the cost of raw material. These costs increase as production increases and are the difference between total costs and fixed costs in Exhibit 8.4.
3. *Total costs:* The sum of fixed and variable costs, illustrated by the diagonal line in Exhibit 8.4.
4. *Total revenues:* Total revenue dollars for a given unit of production, as illustrated by the steep diagonal line in Exhibit 8.4. Total revenues are calculated as units sold times unit price.
5. *Breakeven point:* The production volume at which total revenues equal total costs, illustrated by the crossover of the two diagonal lines in Exhibit 8.4. As the dashed line indicates, the breakeven point in this particular case is about 380 units.

Manager's Shoptalk

ARE YOU A RISK TAKER?

Management science techniques are designed to help managers organize information to reduce risk. As a decision maker, do you tend to steer clear of risky situations, or do you find them tantalizing and invigorating? For example, if you had saved $20,000, would you keep it in the bank or invest it in a friend's new business venture? This quiz, designed by psychologist Frank Farley, measures how likely you are to take risks with finances and your career. Answer true or false for each question.

1. I'd rather start my own business than work for someone else.
   True False
2. I would never take a job that requires lots of traveling.
   True False
3. If I were to gamble, I would be a high roller.
   True False
4. I like to improve on ideas.
   True False
5. I would never give up my job before I was certain I had another one.
   True False
6. I'd never invest in highly speculative stocks.
   True False
7. I'd be willing to take risks just to broaden my horizons.
   True False
8. Thinking about investing in stocks doesn't excite me.
   True False
9. I'd consider working strictly on a commission basis.
   True False
10. Knowing that any new business can fail, I'd always avoid investing in one — even if the potential payoff was high.
    True False
11. I would like to experience as much of life as possible.
    True False
12. I don't feel that I have a strong need for excitement.
    True False
13. I have a lot of energy.
    True False
14. I can easily generate lots of money-making ideas.
    True False
15. I'd never bet more money than I had at the time.
    True False
16. I enjoy proposing new ideas or concepts when the reactions of others — my boss, for example — are unknown or uncertain.
    True False
17. I have never written checks without having enough money in the bank to cover them.
    True False
18. A less secure job with a large income is more to my liking than a more secure job with an average income.
    True False
19. I'm not very independent-minded.
    True False

Give yourself one point for each time you answered true to items 1, 3, 4, 7, 9, 11, 13, 14, 16, and 18, and one point for each time you answered false to items 2, 5, 6, 8, 10, 12, 15, 17, and 19. The more points you have, the more willing you are to take risks with your money and career.

Source: Frank Farley, 1025 West Johnson Street, University of Wisconsin, Madison, WI 53706. Copyright 1986 by Frank Farley.

6. *Profit:* The amount by which total revenues exceed total costs. In Exhibit 8.4, profit occurs at a production volume greater than the breakeven point.
7. *Loss:* The amount by which total costs exceed total revenues, which occurs at a production volume less than the breakeven point in Exhibit 8.4.

The application of these concepts to an organizational situation can be illustrated by the computation of the breakeven point for CCC Bakeries, a small business in California.

CCC Bakeries • The cookie wars have gotten hot in Canada and the United States because profits are terrific. Cookie shops are small and normally have one of the highest sales per square foot of any kind of retail shop. Companies such as the Original Great

EXHIBIT 8.5
Breakeven Analysis for Chocolate Chip Cookies Bakeries

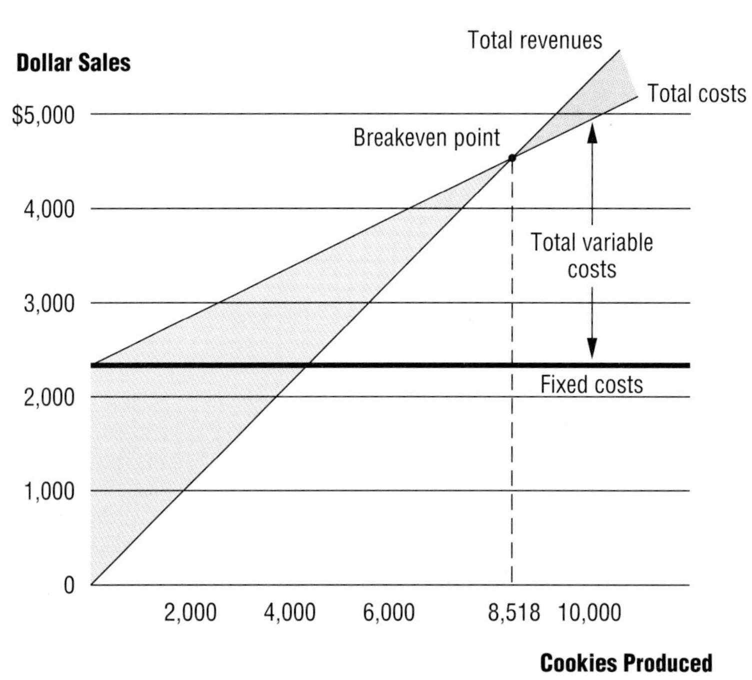

American Chocolate Chip Cookie Company in Atlanta, Mrs. Fields' Cookies, which originated in Park City, Utah, David's Cookies in New York City, and the Original Cookie Company in Cleveland are four rapidly expanding cookie chains.[17]

Jan Smith started the Chocolate Chip Cookies Bakeries in northern California. She has two shops and is considering a third in a San Francisco mall. Before opening the shop, she wants to calculate the cost of the operation and the sales volume required for profitability. She has contacted the owners of the San Francisco mall about the cost of rent and equipment rental, and she has a good idea from her other two shops about salary and raw materials costs. Following are her figures:

Fixed costs:	
Rent	$1,000
Salaries:	
Manager	1,000
Part-timers	500
Equipment Rental	800
Total fixed costs	$2,300
Variable costs:	
Cookie mixture	$0.25/cookie
Paper bags and tissue	0.01/cookie
Total variable costs	$0.26/cookie
Estimated revenue	$0.53/cookie

Linear programming can be used to allocate organizational resources in the most efficient manner. For example, AT&T developed the KORBX System to solve notoriously complex linear programming problems. For Delta Air Lines, AT&T used KORBX to dramatically streamline the planning of pilot flying time. The new linear programming system also has solved many of AT&T's own problems many times faster than conventional methods.

Exhibit 8.5 shows the breakeven analysis for the proposed cookie store. The horizontal line reflects the fixed costs of $2,300. The total cost line is computed by adding the variable costs to the fixed costs. The total revenue line reflects the $0.53 income per cookie. The analysis shows that Jan must sell 8,518 cookies to break even. At this point, Jan's revenue and costs both will be approximately $4,515. If Jan can sell 10,000 cookies a month, she will make a profit of $400. The cookie business has high fixed costs relative to variable costs. Exhibit 8.5 shows that once the breakeven point is reached, profits will increase rapidly. High profits can be earned as volume increases to a high level.

LINEAR PROGRAMMING

Linear programming applies to such planning problems as allocating resources across competing demands or mixing things together efficiently. Farmers want to blend the cheapest feeds to provide enough nutrition to fatten chickens. Oil companies must decide whether to make more jet fuel or heating oil at a refinery depending on the costs of crude oil and market prices. Airlines must decide what mix of planes to put on routes depending on fuel costs and passenger loads. Manufacturing managers must decide whether their profits can be maximized by producing more of product A and less of product B, or vice versa. Linear programming is a technique for solving these kinds of problems.[18]

Linear programming is a mathematical technique that allocates resources so as to optimize a predefined objective. Moreover, linear programming assumes that the decision maker has limited resources with which to attain the objective.

linear programming
A quantitative technique that allocates resources so as to optimize a predefined organizational objective.

The nontechnical manager needs to understand only the three basic steps in formulating a linear programming problem:

EXHIBIT 8.6
Resource Requirements for Wicker Classics

	Soaking Time (Hours)	Weaving Time (Hours)	Drying Time (Hours)	Profit
Per basket	0.2	0.4	0.3	$3.25
Per seat	0.4	0.4	0.8	5.00
Available hours	60.0	90.0	108.0	

- **Step 1:** Define the relevant decision variables. These variables must be controllable by the manager.
- **Step 2:** Define the objective in terms of the decision variables. There can be only one objective; thus, it must be chosen carefully.
- **Step 3:** Define the resource restrictions or constraints *first* as word statements and then as mathematical statements.

The following example demonstrates the three steps used in formulating a linear programming model.

WICKER CLASSICS

• Wicker Classics makes wicker baskets and seats. Both products must be processed by soaking, weaving, and drying. A basket has a profit margin of $3.25 and a seat a profit margin of $5. Exhibit 8.6 summarizes the number of hours available for soaking, weaving, and drying and the number of hours required to complete each task. The question confronting Wicker Classics' managers is: How many baskets and seats should Wicker make per day to maximize profits?

Step 1 is to define the decision variables. What can Wicker managers control in the production process? Two readily controllable variables are the number of baskets and seats to be produced. Thus, we can let X_1 = number of baskets to produce and X_2 = number of seats to produce.

Step 2 is to define an objective function. The objective is clear: Maximize profits. This objective can be described mathematically by using the two decision variables. The profit for each basket is $3.25, or 3.25X_1$. Similarly, the profit for each seat produced is $5, or 5X_2$. Total profits for the firm will be the sum of these two components:

$$\text{Maximize profits} = \$3.25X_1 + \$5.00X_2.$$

Step 3 is to define resource constraints. This is the most difficult step in formulating a linear programming model. Wicker is constrained by three scarce resources, expressed in words as follows:

1. Soaking time cannot exceed 60 hours.
2. Weaving time cannot exceed 90 hours.
3. Drying time cannot exceed 108 hours.

These constraints enable us to state in mathematical terms that total soaking time must be less than or equal to 60 hours. Every basket takes 0.2 hours of soaking time and every seat 0.4 hours. The total production of baskets and seats cannot exceed 60 hours; therefore, our mathematical statement can be:

$$0.2X_1 + 0.4X_2 \leq 60.$$

The remaining constraints can be described in similar fashion. Weaving time cannot exceed 90 hours, which is expressed as

$$0.4X_1 + 0.4X_2 \leq 90.$$

Drying time cannot exceed 108 hours, which is expressed mathematically as

$$0.3X_1 + 0.8X_2 \leq 108.$$

A final constraint for keeping the mathematical calculations in the correct range is that neither seats nor baskets can be produced in a volume of less than zero. This is expressed mathematically as

$$X_1 \geq 0$$
$$X_2 \geq 0.$$

The completed problem formulation looks like this:

- Maximize profits = $3.25X_1 + 5X_2$
- Subject to
  Soaking time: $0.2X_1 + 0.4X_2 \leq 60$
  Weaving time: $0.4X_1 + 0.4X_2 \leq 90$
  Drying time: $0.3X_1 + 0.8X_2 \leq 108$
  Nonnegativity: $X_1 \geq 0$, $X_2 \geq 0$

Exhibit 8.7 graphs the constraints for Wicker Classics. Each constraint defines a boundary called the *feasibility region*, which is that region bounded by a resource restriction. The optimal solution for maximizing profits is found at the intersection of two or more constraints at the edge of the feasibility region. Those intersections are at point A, B, C, or D.

Management science specialists use computers and sophisticated software to solve linear programming problems. For a simple problem such as Wicker Classics', the solution can be defined on the graph in Exhibit 8.7. Profit maximization is formally defined as the point (A, B, C, or D) that lies furthest from the origin (0) and through which a line can be drawn that has only one point in common with the feasibility region. In Exhibit 8.7 this is point C, because it is furthest from the origin and the green line drawn through point C touches the feasibility region at only one point. Thus, the production mix to maximize profits is 150 baskets and 75 seats.[19]

PERSONAL COMPUTERS. Linear programming may seem complicated, but it has many applications in small business. With the advent of personal computers and new software such as "What's Best!," small businesses can use this powerful tool for planning and decision making. A user simply sets up the information on costs and other constraints on the Lotus 1-2-3 spreadsheet, and the computer will calculate what should be optimized. The cost for software is inexpensive, ranging from $200 to $1,000 depending on complexity. Hawley

EXHIBIT 8.7
Graphical Solution to Wicker Classics Linear Programming Problem

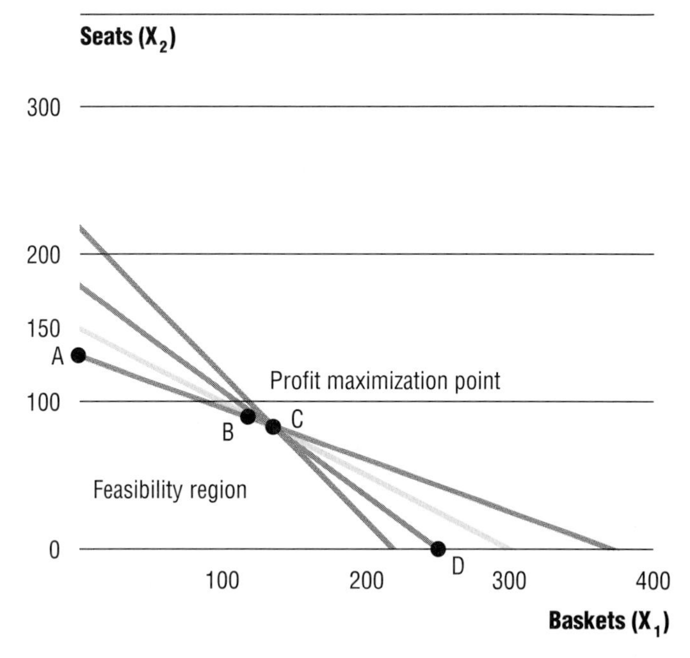

Fuel Corporation, for example, uses a personal computer to make the cheapest blend of coal that meets utility customers' demands for a particular sulfur content, ash content, and heating value. Even small-business managers who do not understand the underlying mathematics can use PCs and linear programming software for decision making.[20]

PERT

Organizations often confront a situation in which they have a large project to complete for which a complicated, single-use plan is developed. A large project may consist of many interrelated activities. In 1958, the U.S. Navy was confronted with the enormous task of coordinating thousands of contractors to build the Polaris nuclear submarine. The Program Evaluation and Review Technique (PERT) was developed to manage the building of submarines.

PERT The Program Evaluation and Review Technique; consists of breaking down a project into a network of specific activities and mapping out their sequence and necessary completion dates.

PERT allows managers to decompose a project into specific activities and to plan far in advance when it is to be completed. PERT can pinpoint bottlenecks and indicate whether resources should be reallocated. It also provides a map of the project and allows managers to control its execution by determining whether activities are completed on time and in the correct sequence.

There are four basic steps required in the use of PERT:

1. Identify all major activities (tasks) to be performed in the project.
2. Determine the sequence in which the tasks must be completed and whether tasks can be performed simultaneously.

3. Determine the amount of time required to complete each task.
4. Draw a PERT network for controlling the project.

A PERT network is a graphical representation of a large project. *Activities* are the tasks that must be completed in order to finish the project. Each activity must have a discrete beginning and ending. Activities are illustrated as solid lines on a PERT network. *Events* represent the beginning and ending of specific activities. Events are represented on the PERT network as circled numbers. *Paths* are strings of activities and events on a network diagram. Project managers determine the sequence of activities that must be performed in order to complete the entire project. A *critical activity* is one that if delayed will cause a slowdown in the entire project. The path with the longest total time is called the **critical path** and represents the total time required for the project.[21]

The application of PERT can best be seen through an illustration.

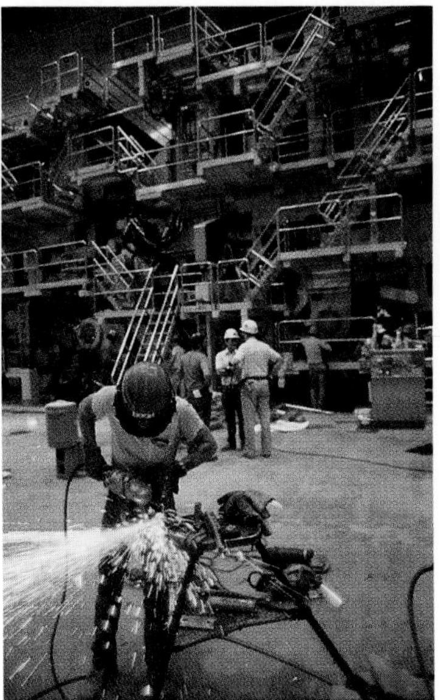

Pulp and papermills are large, technologically advanced, one-of-a-kind complexes of structural elements, vessels, moving parts, drives, piping, valves, wiring, energy components, and electronics. *PERT* network techniques are used to manage and control the construction of the mill shown here by Bowater, Inc. This is the dryer section, which uses just part of the cavernous building that houses the paper machine, coater, and finishing departments. This was the largest single investment ever undertaken by the company, requiring two years to build and involving 90 subcontractors, 1,500 vendors, and 6.6 million worker hours to complete. Computers monitored 6,000 control points to minimize disruption and maintain schedule.

CAREER RESOURCES, INC. • Career Resources, Inc., is a consulting firm that provides training seminars for companies all around the country. Planning these seminars can be a difficult project, because each company's requirements are different and a number of factors must be brought together in a timely fashion. Doug Black is director of Executive Training Programs, and he decided to develop a PERT network for the next training seminar. He began by listing all activities to be completed and determined whether each had to be done before or after other activities, as illustrated in Exhibit 8.8.

Doug's next step was to determine the length of time required for each activity. To do this, he and two other managers decided on an optimistic, most likely, and pessimistic estimate of how long each activity would take. The optimistic time indicates how quickly the activity will be completed if there are no problems or obstacles. The pessimistic time indicates the amount of time required if everything goes wrong. The most likely time is the estimate assuming that only a few routine problems will occur.

The expected time is a weighted average of the three estimates. The most likely time is weighted by four. The estimated time is calculated by the following formula:

$$\text{Estimated time} = \frac{\text{Optimistic} + (4)\ \text{Most likely} + \text{Pessimistic}}{6}$$

critical path The path with the longest total time; represents the total time required for the project.

The expected time for completing each activity is shown in the right-hand column of Exhibit 8.8.

Based on the information listed in Exhibit 8.8, Doug drew the PERT network illustrated in Exhibit 8.9. This network shows when activities must be completed in order to move on to the next activity. The critical path is the longest path through the network, which for Doug's project is A-B-G-H-I-J. Thus, the project is expected to take 4 + 6 + 5 + 3 + 8 + 4 = 30 weeks to complete.

EXHIBIT 8.8
Activities Required for Designing a Training Program

Activity	Description	Immediate Predecessor(s)	Estimated Time (Weeks) Optimistic	Most Likely	Pessimistic	Expected
A	Determine topic	—	3.0	4.0	5.0	4.0
B	Locate speakers	A	4.0	5.0	12.0	6.0
C	Find potential meeting sites	—	2.0	4.0	6.0	4.0
D	Select location	C	3.0	4.0	5.0	4.0
E	Arrange speaker travel plans	B, D	1.0	2.0	3.0	2.0
F	Finalize speaker plans	E	2.0	4.0	6.0	4.0
G	Prepare announcements	B, D	2.0	4.0	12.0	5.0
H	Distribute announcements	G	2.0	3.0	4.0	3.0
I	Take reservations	H	6.0	8.0	10.0	8.0
J	Attend to last-minute details	F, I	3.0	4.0	5.0	4.0

PERSONAL COMPUTERS. Doug Black of Career Resources, Inc., drew the PERT chart by hand, but microcomputers have made PERT charting much easier. More than two dozen project-planning software packages are now on the market. These packages provide an easy method of charting and following any kind of task. For example, Rick Gehrig, production coordinator at Westuff Tool & Die, St. Louis, can coordinate 80 different projects at once, printing out charts and schedules for each one, on his IBM PC. He even links the projects together in one big schedule to show resource needs for the whole plant. Nuvatec, Inc., located in Downers Grove, Illinois, manages 50 consulting projects with a microcomputer. The tasks and times required for each step in a consulting project are plugged into the computer, which provides a nice method for reporting the status of consulting projects to customers as well as forestalling unpleasant surprises.[22]

QUANTITATIVE APPROACHES TO DECISION MAKING

Now we turn to quantitative techniques that help managers make choices under conditions of risk and uncertainty. Recall from Chapter 7 that managerial decision making follows six steps: problem definition, diagnosis, development of alternatives, selection of an alternative, implementation, and evaluation/feedback. Decision aids focus on the fourth step — selecting an alternative. First we will examine two quantitative decision approaches: the payoff matrix and the decision tree. Then we will discuss simulation models, an extension of the two decision approaches.

EXHIBIT 8.9
PERT Network for Designing a Training Program

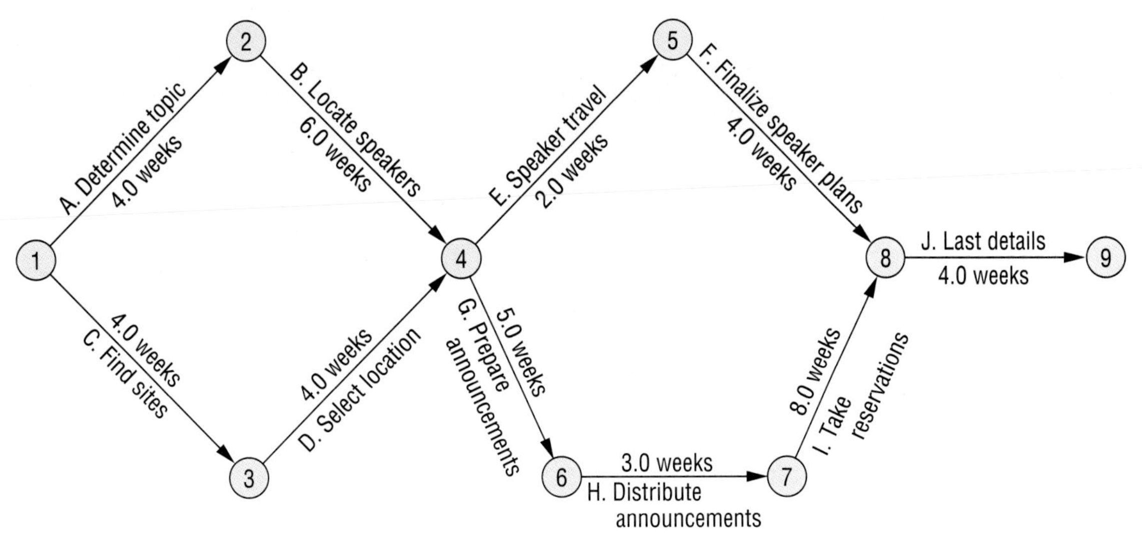

PAYOFF MATRIX

To use the **payoff matrix** as an aid to decision making, a manager must be able to define four variables.

payoff matrix A decision-making aid comprised of relevant strategies, states of nature, probability of occurrence of states of nature, and expected outcome(s).

STRATEGIES. *Strategies* are the decision alternatives. There can be two strategies or ten depending on the number of alternatives available. For example, a manager wanting to open a new store might consider four different locations, or a university considering an expansion of its football stadium might consider three expansion alternatives of 8,000, 15,000, and 20,000 seats.

STATES OF NATURE. Future events or conditions that are relevant to decision outcomes are called **states of nature.** For example, the states of nature for a new store location could be the anticipated sales volume at each site, and those for expanding the football stadium could be the number of additional paying fans at football games.

state of nature A future event or condition that is relevant to a decision outcome.

PROBABILITY. *Probability* represents the likelihood, expressed as a percentage, that a given state of nature will occur. Thus, the store owner may calculate the probability of making a profit in location 1 as 20 percent, in location 2 as 30 percent, and in location 3 as 50 percent. A probability of 50 percent would be listed in the payoff matrix as 0.5. University administrators would estimate the probability of filling the stadium under each condition of 8,000, 15,000, and 20,000 additional seats. The probabilities associated with the states of nature must add up to 100 percent.

This rig drills in the Gulf of Mexico for Amoco Corporation. Amoco uses decision models to estimate probabilities and evaluate future oil drilling projects. Using *payoff matrix*–type computations, Amoco has defined low-, medium-, and high-risk projects. The last are in frontier basins such as those in Africa or its coastal waters. Computations indicate that although the probability of success is small, the potential financial payoff is huge; thus, the expected value is high. Amoco undertakes both high- and low-risk projects to obtain multiple opportunities for finding oil and natural gas.

expected value The weighted average of each possible outcome for a decision alternative.

OUTCOME. The outcome is the payoff calculated for each strategy given the probabilities associated with each state of nature. The outcome is called the **expected value,** which is the weighted average of each possible outcome for a decision alternative. For example, the store owner could calculate the expected profit from each store location, and the university administrators could calculate the expected returns associated with each construction alternative of 8,000, 15,000, and 20,000 seats.

To illustrate the payoff matrix in action, let us consider the problem facing Sanders Industries' managers, who are trying to decide how to finance the construction of a new plant and its equipment.

SANDERS INDUSTRIES

• The senior managers at Sanders Industries wish to raise funds to finance the construction and new machinery for a new plant to be located in Alberta, Canada. They have determined that they have three alternative funding sources: to issue common stock, bonds, or preferred stock. The desired decision outcome is the net dollars that can be raised through each financing vehicle. The state of nature that affects the decision is the interest rate at the time the securities are issued, because interest rates influence the firm's ability to attract investment dollars. If interest rates are high, investors prefer bonds; if interest rates are low, they prefer stocks. Sanders' financial experts have advised that if interest rates are high, a common stock issue will bring $1 million, bonds $5 million, and preferred stock $3 million. If interest rates are moderate, common stocks will yield $3.5 million, bonds $3.5 million, preferred stock $3 million. If interest rates are low, common stock will return $7.5 million, bonds $2.5 million, and preferred stock $4 million. The financial experts also have estimated the likelihood of low interest rates at 10 percent, of moderate interest rates at 40 percent, and of high interest rates at 50 percent.

EXHIBIT 8.10
Payoff Matrix for Sanders Industries

	Event (Interest Rate Level/ State of Nature)		
Strategy (Decision Alternative)	**Low (0.1)**	**Moderate (0.4)**	**High (0.5)**
Common stock	$7,500,000	$3,500,000	$1,000,000
Bonds	2,500,000	3,500,000	5,000,000
Preferred stock	4,000,000	3,000,000	3,000,000

Sanders' senior managers want to use a logical structure to make this decision, and the payoff matrix is appropriate. The three decision alternatives of stock, bonds, and preferred stock are shown in Exhibit 8.10. The three states of nature — low, moderate, and high interest rates — are listed across the top of the exhibit. The listing of strategy on one side and of states of nature on the other side composes the payoff matrix. The probability associated with each interest rate is also included in the exhibit.

The decision outcome as defined by the managers is to gain the highest expected monetary value from issuing a security. Thus, the managers must calculate the expected monetary return associated with each decision alternative. The calculation of expected value for each decision alternative is performed by multiplying each dollar amount by the probability of occurrence. For the figures in Exhibit 8.10, the expected value of each strategy is calculated as follows:

$$\begin{aligned}
\text{Expected value of common stock} &= (0.1)(7.5 \text{ million}) \\
&\quad + (0.4)(3.5 \text{ million}) \\
&\quad + (0.5)(1 \text{ million}) \\
&= \$2{,}650{,}000 \\
\text{Expected value of bonds} &= (0.1)(2.5 \text{ million}) \\
&\quad + (0.4)(3.5 \text{ million}) \\
&\quad + (0.5)(5 \text{ million}) \\
&= \$4{,}150{,}000 \\
\text{Expected value of preferred stock} &= (0.1)(4 \text{ million}) \\
&\quad + (0.4)(3 \text{ million}) \\
&\quad + (0.5)(3 \text{ million}) \\
&= \$3{,}100{,}000
\end{aligned}$$

From this analysis, the best decision clearly is to issue bonds, which have an expected value of $4,150,000. Although managers cannot be certain about which state of nature will actually occur, the expected value calculation weights each possibility and indicates the choice with the highest likelihood of success.

DECISION TREE

Management problems often require that several decisions be made in sequence. As the outcome of one decision becomes obvious or as additional information becomes available, another decision is required to correct past mistakes or take advantage of new information. For instance, a production manager analyzing the company's product line may decide to add a new product on a trial basis. If customers buy the product, the manager must then decide how to increase production to meet demand. Conversely, if the new product fails to generate sufficient demand, the manager must then decide whether to drop the product.

decision tree A decision-making aid used for decision situations that occur in sequence; consists of a pictorial representation of decision alternatives, states of nature, and outcomes of each course of action.

This type of decision is difficult to structure into a payoff matrix because of the decision sequence. **Decision trees** are an alternative to payoff tables for decision situations that occur in sequence. The objective of decision tree analysis is the same as for payoff tables: to select the decision that will provide the greatest return to the company. The decision tree approach requires the following variables:

1. The decision tree, which is a pictorial representation of decision alternatives, states of nature, and the outcomes of each course of action
2. The estimated probabilities of each outcome occurring
3. The payoff (profit or loss) associated with each outcome
4. The expected value, which is calculated based on the probabilities and conditional payoffs along each branch of the decision tree

The decision tree consists of a series of nodes and connecting lines. A square node, called a *decision fork,* represents the alternative strategies available to the decision maker *at that time.* From a decision fork the decision maker must choose one branch to follow. A numbered node, called a *chance fork,* represents states of nature over which the decision maker has no control. For branches emanating from a chance fork, the decision maker cannot choose which path to follow and must wait until after the decision has been made to see which state of nature occurred.

The use of a decision tree for decision making can be illustrated by the risks and uncertainties associated with the decision to use fire in contemporary forest management.

NATIONAL FOREST SERVICE • Forest management personnel often use fires under controlled conditions to reduce natural fire hazards and enhance the wildlife habitat. However, decision uncertainties are inherent in the use of fire. For example, the decisions to commit personnel and equipment to the burn site and to actually initiate the burn must be made before weather conditions and fire behavior can be determined with certainty.

A specific burn has two basic alternatives, as illustrated in Exhibit 8.11. Decision fork 1 shows that forest managers can either (1) commit resources to the burn or (2) postpone the burn. Two uncertainties are central to this decision. The first is the actual weather conditions on the day of the burn, illustrated in chance fork A. There is a 50 percent likelihood that the weather will be poor, in which case the burn will have to be canceled. The second results from the decision to carry out the burn: Will the objectives be met, or will the burn be only marginally successful? This decision is illustrated by chance fork B in Exhibit 8.11. The experts have estimated a 60 percent probability of a successful burn and a 40 percent probability of a marginal burn in that situation.

EXHIBIT 8.11
Decision Tree for Controlled Forest Fire

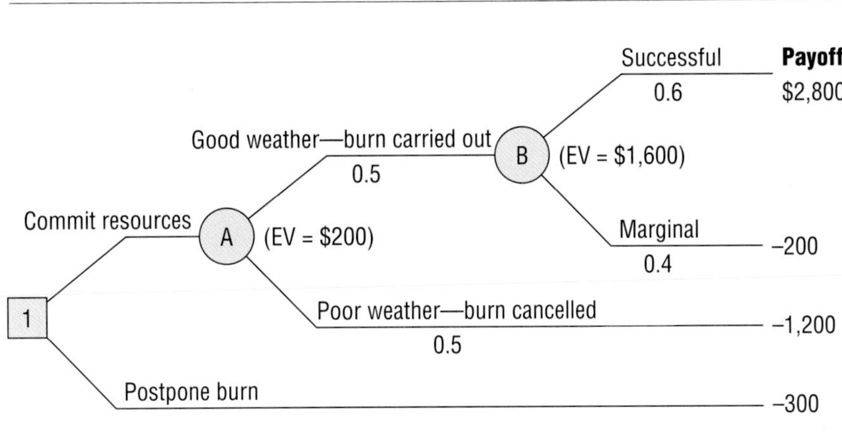

Source: David Cohan, Stephen M. Haas, David L. Radloff, and Richard F. Yancik, "Using Fire in Forest Management: Decision Making under Uncertainty," *Interfaces* 14 (September/October 1984), 8–19. © 1984 The Institute of Management Sciences. Reprinted with permission.

Given the uncertainties facing National Forest Service managers, should they decide to commit the resources or postpone the burn to await better information? The payoff value of each outcome is listed on the far right in Exhibit 8.11. If everything is successful, the benefit to the forest service will be $2,800. If a marginal burn occurs, there will be a loss of $200. If the burn is canceled after resources have been committed, there will be a loss of $1,200. If the burn is postponed indefinitely, there will be a loss of $300 in management costs.

The way to choose the best decision is through a procedure known as rollback. The *rollback* procedure begins with the end branches and works backward through the tree by assigning a value to each decision fork and chance fork. A fork's value is the expected return from the branches emanating from the fork. Applying the rollback procedure to the data in Exhibit 8.11 produces the following outcomes: The expected value (EV) of chance fork B is $(0.6)(2{,}800) + 0.4(-200) = \$1{,}600$; the expected value of chance fork A is $(0.5)(1{,}600) + 0.5(-1{,}200) = \$200$.

These figures provide the information needed for the decision. If the managers decide to commit resources, there is a positive expected value of $200. If they postpone the burn, there is a certain loss of $300. Thus, it is worthwhile to go ahead with the planned burn despite management's uncertainty about the weather and possible outcomes.[23]

Decision tree analysis is one of the most widely used decision analysis techniques.[24] As with linear programming and PERT charting described earlier, excellent software programs are available. General managers and small-business managers can use decision tree analysis without hiring a staff specialist. This technique can be used for any decision situation in which probabilities can be estimated and decisions occur in sequence, such as those concerning new-product introduction, pricing, plant expansion, advertising campaigns, or even acquiring another firm.

SIMULATION MODELS

Another useful tool for management decision makers is a simulation model. **Simulation models** are mathematical representations of the relationships among variables in real-life organizational situations.[25] For example, simulations are popular for the risky business of new-product innovations. For, say, a new bar of soap, managers can feed data into a computer about where the soap will be introduced, how much money will be spent on advertising, and what kind of promotion will be done. Data from past new products are in the computer, providing comparisons. The simulation model can predict the new soap's yearly sales. Simulation would take no more than 90 days and cost around $50,000, compared with a minimum 9 months and $1 million dollars to test a real product. Simulations will not always be accurate, however, especially for highly innovative products that have no historical base, but simulations have become very accurate where firms have compiled new-product case histories.[26]

A unique computerized ship deployment simulator model, developed by American President Companies (APC), makes possible the flexible deployment of APC's vessels. Logistics specialists can pinpoint and resolve possible scheduling problems before they occur. *Simulation models* help the company arrange the fastest and most efficient container transportation on ships, such as this one sailing from Sri Lanka to Taiwan. Simulation models also improve the scheduling of train and truck departures and arrivals.

simulation model
A mathematical representation of the relationships among variables in real-world organizational situations.

Simulations have many applications, and because they typically are done by computer, many options can be tried. For example, Monsanto Corporation has one ocean-going chemical tanker, and managers wished to have a model that would help them determine the number of trips per year that would provide the most income. A simulation model provided the answer. The model included nine ports, fuel prices, operating charges for the tanker, voyage time, amount of fuel used, time in port, time steaming, and voyage itinerary. The simulation model gave operating managers an ongoing decision tool. If vessel managers needed to evaluate the impact of taking on an additional load, they simply simulated the current trip using the model. By inserting the data for the additional load and expenses for the extra stop, they could also ask the model if the steaming speed for the voyage could be increased so that the additional stop would not increase total voyage time. They could also calculate the cost increase from making the additional stop and simply charge the additional cost plus a reasonable profit to the customer. Using the simulation model to assist management decisions on scheduling the tanker has saved Monsanto an estimated $20,000 per year.[27]

STRENGTHS AND LIMITATIONS OF MANAGEMENT SCIENCE AIDS

When selectively applied, management science techniques provide information for improving both planning and decision making. Many businesses have operations research departments in which experts apply management science techniques to organizational problems. And with the use of microcomputers and the many available software programs, management science aids can also be used by small-business managers. Whether using these techniques in small businesses or large businesses, however, managers should be aware of their basic strengths and limitations, which are summarized in Exhibit 8.12.

EXHIBIT 8.12
Strengths and Limitations of Management Science Techniques

Strengths	Limitations
• Enhance decision effectiveness in many situations	• Do not fit many situations
• Provide a framework for handling complex problems	• May not reflect reality
• Promote rationality	• Overhead costs
• Inexpensive compared with alternatives	• Are given too much legitimacy

STRENGTHS

The primary strength of management science aids is their ability to enhance decision effectiveness in many situations. For example, time series forecasting helps predict seasonal sales variations. Causal models help managers understand the reasons for future sales increases or decreases. Decision trees, payoff matrices, and PERT networks are valuable when data can be organized into the framework the model requires.

Another strength of management science techniques is that they provide a systematic way of thinking about and organizing complex problems. Managers may use these models intuitively, perhaps sketching things out to clarify their thinking. Moreover, new software packages ask all the right questions so managers will provide the correct data. The computer helps managers organize their thinking and reach the best decision.

Still another strength is that the models promote management rationality when fully applied. They help managers define a problem, select alternatives, gauge probabilities of alternatives' success, and understand the trade-offs and potential payoffs. Managers need not rely on hunch or intuition to make a complicated, multidimensional decision.

Finally, management science aids are inexpensive compared with alternatives such as organizational experiments. If an organization actually had to build a new plant to learn whether it would increase profits, a failure would be enormously expensive. Management science models provide a way to experiment with the decision without having to build the plant.

LIMITATIONS

The growth of management science has led to some problems. First—and perhaps most important—management science techniques do not yet fit many decision situations. Many management decisions are too ambiguous and subjective. For example, management science techniques have little impact on the poorly structured strategic problems at the top levels of corporations.

A second limitation is that they may not reflect the reality of the organizational situation. The management science model is a simplification, and the outcome can be no better than the numbers and assumptions fed into the model. If these numbers are not good or important variables are left out, the outcome will be unrealistic.

A third limitation is overhead costs. The organization may hire management science specialists and provide computer facilities. If these specialists are not frequently used to help solve real problems, they will add to the organization's overhead costs while providing little return.[28]

Finally, management science techniques can be given too much legitimacy. When managers are trying to make a decision under uncertainty, they may be desperate for a clear and precise answer. A management science model may produce an answer that is taken as fact even though the model is only a simplification of reality and the decision needs the interpretation and judgment of experienced managers.

SUMMARY

This chapter described several important points about management science aids for managerial planning and decision making. Forecasting is the attempt to predict behavior in the future. Forecasting techniques can be either quantitative or qualitative. Quantitative techniques include time series analysis and causal modeling. Qualitative techniques include the Delphi method, sales force composite, and jury of opinion.

Quantitative aids to management planning include breakeven analysis, linear programming, and PERT. Breakeven analysis indicates the volume at which a new product will earn enough revenues to cover costs. Linear programming helps managers decide which product mix will maximize profits or minimize costs. PERT helps managers plan, monitor, and control project progress.

Management science aids to decision choices also were described. The payoff matrix helps managers determine the expected value of various alternatives. The decision tree is a similar procedure that is used for decisions made in sequence. Simulation models use mathematics to evaluate the impact of management decisions. Microcomputers and new software make all of these techniques accessible to managers, but managers should remember that management science aids have limitations as well as strengths.

MANAGEMENT SOLUTION

New York City's Department of Sanitation faced a seemingly impossible problem keeping city streets clean. Management science specialists attacked the problem with management science techniques. The first job was to obtain basic data; thus, they commissioned studies to determine the rate at which litter accumulated in streets, the point at which a street appeared unacceptably dirty, the dirtiest districts, and the effect of additional street cleaners and equipment on street cleanliness. Through these data, the specialists analyzed the impact of having litter baskets on sidewalks, alternative-side-of-the-street parking regulations, and using motorized street sweepers. Next they used a regression model to determine how the number of employees assigned to a district influenced street cleanliness. Simulation models indicated the effects of changes in litter basket placement, human resources, vehicles, and parades. As a result of these management science aids, employees were reallocated, litter baskets were strategically placed, and machines were allocated to the neediest districts. The net effect was a reduction of 400 cleaners, a financial saving of $12 million a year, and street cleanliness ratings near record levels.[29]

DISCUSSION QUESTIONS

1. In 1989, the Texas Department of Corrections predicted an increase of 20,000 prisoners in five years. What forecasting approach do you think was used to arrive at this figure? What approach would you recommend?
2. Think back to a decision you had to make that was difficult because you were uncertain about the outcomes of each alternative. Attempt to analyze that decision using a payoff matrix or a decision tree. Would either procedure have helped your decision?
3. What is the difference between time series analysis and causal model forecasting?
4. What is the correct relationship between a nontechnical manager and management science decision tools? Can management science thinking be delegated to staff specialists?
5. If the objective of a business is to maximize profit, what value will break-even analysis have for a manager?
6. What is the critical path? Why is it especially important for a manager to know which activities lie along the critical path?
7. In linear programming, all inputs to the production process are assumed to be known with certainty and constant. Is this a realistic assumption? If not, why do you suppose linear programming is one of the most frequently used management science techniques?
8. Will future managers have an advantage over today's managers if they are familiar with management science tools and their applications? Explain.
9. Discuss the pros and cons of using management science techniques in organizations.

MANAGEMENT IN PRACTICE: ETHICAL DILEMMA

Freelance Follies

Eric owns a small business that provides freelance production of videotapes for use by corporations. Compensation is typically a percentage of the total cost of the videotape. Completed videotapes typically costs $3,000 to $5,000 per minute of tape.

A large industrial company approaches Eric requesting a 15-minute videotape for an executive presentation to the local city government. Before signing a contract, the company requests a tentative budget proposal. Eric can do a simple, straightforward videotape to meet the company's need for about $50,000. However, he is tempted to propose a budget of $70,000 so he can incorporate special effects that will impress his client. He believes that an interesting tape will probably result in future contracts with the company. Eric believes the company does not really need a fancy videotape so he proposes the $50,000 project, which is accepted.

In the middle of completing the project, Eric faces a dilemma. A technician discovers technical software that dramatically reduces the time required to assemble final videotapes. The savings is sufficient that special effects could be added to the tape without additional cost to the client. Eric has to make a decision, balancing factors of profit, client needs, and his contract agreement.

What Do You Do?

1. Make the simple videotape as agreed and charge the company $20,000 less. The client saves money, but because Eric receives a percentage, he will earn less money.
2. Provide the simple videotape, but do not tell the company about the savings. After all, a contract is a contract and Eric deserves the profit from his improved efficiency.
3. Insert the special effects using the new software while staying within the original budget. Eric would still get a percentage of the full $50,000, and the client may do future business because of the videotape's quality and interest.

CASES FOR ANALYSIS

SECOND NATIONAL BANK

You are a member of a notorious bank-robbing gang. The secret of your success is that your robberies are always well planned. For your next caper, you have selected a rural branch of the Second National Bank. From your surveillance, you have discovered that it will take the police 7.5 minutes to reach the bank once the alarm has sounded. You now want to determine if the robbery can be completed successfully in that amount of time.

To complete the robbery, two members of your gang (one gunperson and a safecracker) will be dropped off behind the bank and be responsible for picking the lock on the rear door. The rest of the gang will be driven to the front of the bank to wait. Once the alarm has sounded, the entire gang will enter the bank. The gunpeople will point their weapons at the guards and customers, the counter leaper will leap over the counter and empty the teller's drawers, and the safecracker will crack or blow open the safe and empty it. Once these things have been accomplished, the gang will leave.

The details are as follows:

Activities

1. Drop off one gunperson and the safecracker in the alley behind the bank.
2. Drop off the other gang members in front of the bank.
3. Everyone enters the bank at the same time.
4. The gunpeople take up their positions and point their weapons at everyone in the bank.
5. The counter leaper leaps over the counter and empties the tellers' drawers.
6. The safecracker cracks open the safe and empties it.
7. All gang members leave the bank at the same time.
8. The driver meets the rest of the gang in front of the bank when the robbery is completed.

Timing

1. 2 minutes to pick the lock on the rear door.
2. The alarm goes off when the back door is picked; the police arrive in 7.5 minutes.
3. 45 seconds to drive from the alley to the front of the bank.
4. 30 seconds for the gunpeople to enter the bank and take up their positions.
5. 60 seconds for the safecracker to reach the safe from the back door.
6. 30 seconds for the counter leaper to leap over the counter and start to empty the drawers.
7. 3 minutes to empty the tellers' drawers.
8. 2 minutes to open the safe.
9. 2 minutes to empty the safe.
10. 45 seconds to exit from the bank and reach the car at the front curb.

Questions

1. Draw a PERT network for the bank robbery scenario.
2. Can the robbery be accomplished in the 7.5 minutes before the police arrive?
3. How quickly can it be accomplished — in other words, what is the critical path?

Source: Adapted from Mark P. Sharfman and Timothy R. Walters, "Robbery: Planning with PERT," J. William Pfeiffer and Leonard D. Goodstein (Eds.), *The 1983 Annual for Facilitators, Trainers, and Consultants*, San Diego, CA: University Associates, Inc., 1983, pp. 40–44. Used with permission.

GIBSON GLASS COMPANY

Gibson Glass Company opened its doors for business in April 1972. From its small beginnings, the company grew into a large operation. However, the glassmaking technology installed in 1972 has remained essentially unchanged. Because technological innovations adopted by competitors have begun to make Gibson's equipment and processes obsolete, management is considering whether to modernize or to continue operations as is. The choice between these two alternatives depends on anticipated future demand for Gibson's glass bottles and jars. The market forecasters have estimated two possible states of nature to consider. One is high demand for the company's output, which has a 45 percent chance of occurring. The other is moderate demand for the company's products, which has a 55 percent change of occurring.

According to Gibson's financial analysts, if the company modernizes and demand is high, there will be a positive return of $4 million, and if demand is low, the return will be only $1.5 million. However, if management decides not to modernize, the payoff will be $3 million in the case of high demand and $2.5 million in the case of low demand. With these data, Gibson's managers are trying to determine which choice — to modernize or not — would be the better.

Questions

1. Using a payoff matrix, determine the correct decision.
2. What factors not included in the model might the decision makers want to consider? Are these factors strong enough to overrule the decision from the payoff matrix?
3. Is this an appropriate problem for which to use management science decision aids? Discuss.

Source: Excerpts from *The Managerial Experience: Cases, Exercises, and Readings*, Fourth Edition, p. 102, by Lawrence R. Jauch, Sally A. Coltrin, Arthur G. Bedeian, and William F. Glueck.

VIDEO CASE

KIRK STIEFF COMPANY

Baltimore-based Kirk Stieff Company is one of the oldest and largest makers and marketers of silver and pewter products in the United States. It has survived through a long history of environmental fluctuations. Prior to 1900, small silversmiths produced pieces that were valued by many in the upper class who appreciated quality and skilled craftwork. The market crash in 1929 caused problems in the silver business, and silversmiths had to merge to survive. The national economic recovery during World War II did not greatly benefit silversmiths because of silver shortages. The period after World War II was perhaps the best ever. An enormous pent up demand for silver flatware was turned loose, and it took years for silversmiths to catch up. Demand tapered off by 1960, and by 1980, silver and pewter products were considered a mature market with only gradual growth possibilities.

The 1960s saw a change in lifestyles as consumers developed a taste for products other than traditional silver. In 1979, the Stieff Company acquired the Kirk Company in an effort to consolidate and survive in a declining market. The new Kirk Stieff Company had several strengths, with 215 skilled employees, a tradition of quality, and numerous dealerships. Shortly thereafter, instability in the external environment became the major problem, with silver prices skyrocketing to $50 an ounce, plummeting to $10 an ounce, rising to $25, and then plummeting again. The silver business became unprofitable. Kirk Stieff sales dropped 25 percent, and valued employees were laid off. The entire sterling flatware market was off by 45 percent. Kirk Stieff lost one-third of its net worth in 1983 alone.

In 1984, a new president, Pierce Dunn, was hired from outside the company. His job was to develop a strategy that would enable Kirk Stieff to survive in an environment considered both stable and volatile. It was stable in the sense that favorite flatware patterns had been in demand for 100 years or more, and a segment of the population always desired silver. But so many other changes were taking place in consumer taste, in silver prices, and in the labor market that volatility seemed normal, and Kirk Stieff Company had to learn to react more quickly.

Dunn's strategic plan was to innovate. He wanted the company to experiment with new products, weeding out those that did not work. A few new-product ideas were taken to a Tabletop Accessory Show, and retailers were delighted with the new upscale designs and sparkling jeweled flatware. This reaction reinforced Dunn's strategy to be market driven and market sensitive as Kirk Stieff diversified to become stronger.

Kirk Stieff's strengths were its size, its position in the industry, and its excellent reputation. Flatware made up 60 percent of its market and giftware 40 percent. These products were sold in four areas: traditional products, awards, classic contemporary, and bridal. The traditional area was competitive and slow growing, but was an area of Kirk Stieff strength. Awards was a growing market to which pewter lent itself well, because it is easy to engrave and it shows well. Classic contemporary was an emerging giftware market of young, upscale customers, which was important to the future of the business. The bridal market was traditional, but important for flatware, and every silversmith had to address it.

Johnna O'Kelly, director of marketing, was hired to help develop and market new products. Her initial efforts included cloissoné stainless flatware, silverplated vases, silverplated goblets, and silverplated gift items and perfume atomizers. Many of these products sold for less than $25. A box of stemware sold for $39.95 and champagne flutes for $69.95. Jeweled giftware went much higher, with top prices at $9,500. A new line of jeweled stainless flatware sold for $75 per five-piece setting, considered fashion jewelry for the table at a reasonable price.

Other innovations included the sourcing of raw materials from several new countries. A telemarketing program was started to assist retailers. Kirk Stieff employees would call brides who had registered with retailers to answer questions on flatware warranties and to help them work toward completing their table service.

Kirk Stieff gradually decided to invest heavily in the market for highly crafted specialty goods that were expensive but unique and to rely less heavily on tableware. It invested $200,000 in a New York showroom to attract retailers to its product line. It also built an on-site retail store to tap other customers. New giftware was also designed to appeal as corporation gifts, because corporations could afford elegant giftware.

Major changes internal to Kirk Stieff were the hiring of excellent outside people as members of the management team. A new financial officer helped revamp the company's cost accounting system. The new system allowed Kirk Stieff managers to identify the profitability of each product line, discovering that some 15 percent of products did not sell well. These product lines were dropped as innovative products were introduced to appeal to changing market demand.

Another change initiated by President Dunn decentralized decision making. He pushed authority down to the people making the products. He created teams that were solely responsible for producing a product and for insuring product quality. Each team performed all the functions of polishing, welding, stamping, and engraving that were previously performed by different departments. The system was more efficient in terms of time, labor, and inventory costs, and it also engaged the commitment of employees. If a problem arose, the whole group would solve it. Quality inspections were by team members only.

By late 1989, a new spirit was infused throughout Kirk Stieff. The company suddenly found itself paralleling the innovative spirit initiated by the founder more than 100 years ago.

Discussion Questions

1. Provide a situation analysis of Kirk Stieff Company. Does its current strategy fit its situation? Discuss.
2. Identify two decisions in the case or video (such as the decision to produce the kaleidoscope). Are these decisions programmed or nonprogrammed; are they characterized by risk, uncertainty, or ambiguity; and were the decisions made using the classical or administrative model of decision making?
3. What business-level strategy framework best describes the strategy of Kirk Stieff?
4. What techniques were used by Pierce Dunn to implement the new strategy? Was the resulting organizational design appropriate for a strategy of innovation? Explain.

Source: "Kirk Stieff Unveils Upscaled Designs," *HFD — The Weekly Home Furnishings Newspaper*, July 7, 1986, 60; "Group Launches Drive to Spur Pewter Demand," *American Metal Market*, February 1986, 4; and "Kirk Stieff Company" video produced for Growing a Business PBS series, copyright 1989 by Ambrose Video Publishing Inc.

PART 3

ORGANIZING

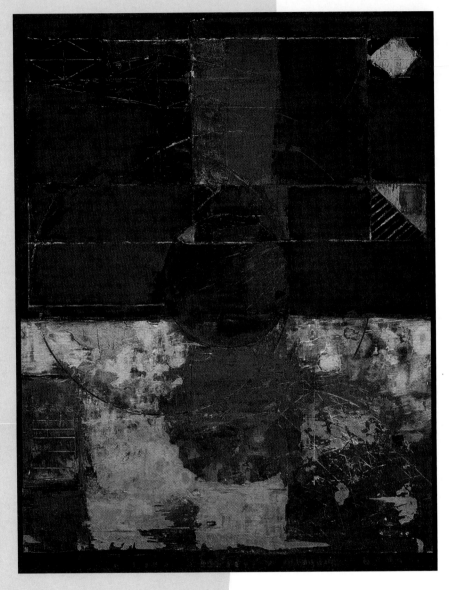

Source: Michael David, *Doppleganger II (Wings of Desire)*, 1988, and polymer medium on wood, 97 1/2″ × 72″. Collection of Standard Federal Bank, Troy, Michigan. Photograph courtesy of Knoedler and Company, New York, New York.

Standard Federal Bank began its corporate art collection when it formed plans for a new corporate headquarters. The founding principles of the collection were to focus on modern works that would reflect the bank's progressive nature and enhance the working environment for employees. Works are placed throughout the building's expansive six-story atrium as well as in common areas and private work spaces. The collection contains paintings, sculptures, and textiles by many well-known contemporary masters.

CHAPTER 9

FUNDAMENTALS OF ORGANIZING

CHAPTER OUTLINE

Organizing the Vertical Structure

Work Specialization
Chain of Command
Authority, Responsibility, and Delegation
Span of Management
Centralization and Decentralization
Administrative Overhead
Formalization

Departmentalization

Functional Approach
Divisional Approach
Matrix Approach
Team Approach
Network Approach

LEARNING OBJECTIVES

After studying this chapter, you should be able to:

- Explain the fundamental characteristics of organizing, including such concepts as work specialization, chain of command, line and staff, and task forces.
- Explain when specific structural characteristics such as centralization, span of management, and formalization should be used within organizations.
- Explain the functional approach to structure.
- Explain the divisional approach to structure.
- Explain the matrix approach to structure and its advantages and disadvantages compared with other structures.
- Explain the contemporary team and network structures and why they are being adopted by organizations.

MANAGEMENT PROBLEM

Assume you own a small business that sells and rents equipment to local construction contractors. Your credit manager is doing a great job minimizing risk, because bad-debt totals, bounced checks, and unpaid bills are low. But your marketing manager is angry, because new customers with marginal credit experience are turned away because they cannot pass a strict credit test. This happened to Lester Heath III, president of Albany Ladder Company, who wants local carpenters, plumbers, and masons to think of Albany Ladder first, even if they are new contractors and have no credit experience. The credit department slams the door on people who could be major customers in a few years.[1]

If you were Lester Heath, how might you restructure your business to gain cooperation between the credit and marketing departments?

The problem confronting Albany Ladder is one of organizing. President Lester Heath III wants to use structure to achieve greater cooperation between the credit and marketing departments. Every firm wrestles with the problem of how to organize. Reorganization often is necessary to reflect a new strategy, changing market conditions, or innovative production technology. For example, both Hewlett-Packard and Digital Equipment recently centralized research and other functions that had been delegated to far-flung managers, whereas IBM decentralized many top-management functions to newly independent divisions.[2] Greyhound Lines, Inc., recently restructured itself from one large company into four independent regional divisions.[3] International firms such as Unilever and U.S. Steel have taken steps to decentralize decision making and give middle managers more authority.[4] Brunswick Corporation restructured in a different way, chopping out many of its headquarters' staff departments and one layer of management to reduce administrative overhead.[5]

Each of these organizations is using fundamental concepts of organizing. **Organizing** is the deployment of organizational resources to achieve strategic objectives. The deployment of resources is reflected in the organization's division of labor into specific departments and jobs, formal lines of authority, and mechanisms for coordinating diverse organization tasks.

organizing The deployment of organizational resources to achieve strategic objectives.

JCPenney established its own television network as part of a recent *structural reorganization.* Four major business groups were created, each one focusing on a major merchandising category: women's, men's, children's, and home and leisure. This structure brings together the buying and marketing functions for each merchandise category into a single division, within which buyers and store associates jointly plan merchandise assortments for their customers. The new structure, supported by the television hookup, enables geographically separated employees to focus on their customers' interests and to achieve superb coordination between buying and merchandising for each business group.

Organizing is important because it follows from strategy—the topic of Part 2. Strategy defines *what* to do; organizing defines *how* to do it. Organization structure is a tool that managers use to harness resources for getting things done. Part 3 explains the variety of organizing principles and concepts used by managers. This chapter covers fundamental concepts that apply to all organizations and departments. These ideas are extended in Chapter 10, where we look at how structural designs are tailored to the organization's situation. Chapter 11 discusses how organizations can be structured to facilitate innovation and change. Chapter 12 examines how to utilize human resources to the best advantage within the organization's structure.

Organizing the Vertical Structure

The organizing process leads to the creation of organization structure, which defines how tasks are divided and resources deployed. **Organization structure** is defined as (1) the set of formal tasks assigned to individuals and departments; (2) formal reporting relationships, including lines of authority, decision responsibility, number of hierarchical levels, and span of managers' control; and (3) the design of systems to insure effective coordination of employees across departments.[6]

The set of formal tasks and formal reporting relationships provides a framework for vertical control of the organization. The characteristics of vertical structure are portrayed in the **organization chart,** which is the visual representation of an organization's structure.

A sample organization chart for a textile mill is illustrated in Exhibit 9.1. The mill has five major departments—accounting, personnel, manufacturing, marketing, and research and development. The organization chart delineates the chain of command, indicates departmental tasks and how they fit together, and provides order and logic for the organization. Every employee has an appointed task, line of authority, and decision responsibility. The following sections discuss several important features of vertical structure in more detail.

Work Specialization

organizational structure
The framework in which the organization defines how tasks are divided, resources are deployed, and departments are coordinated.

organization chart The visual representation of an organization's structure.

work specialization The degree to which organizational tasks are subdivided into individual jobs; also called *division of labor.*

Organizations perform a wide variety of tasks. A fundamental principle is that work can be performed more efficiently if employees are allowed to specialize.[7] **Work specialization,** sometimes called *division of labor,* is the degree to which organizational tasks are subdivided into separate jobs. Work specialization in Exhibit 9.1 is illustrated by the separation of manufacturing tasks into weaving, yarn, finishing, and needling. Employees within each department perform only the tasks relevant to their specialized function. When work specialization is extensive, employees specialize in a single task. Jobs tend to be small, but they can be performed efficiently. Work specialization is readily visible on an automobile assembly line, where each employee performs the same task over and over again. It would not be efficient to have a single em-

EXHIBIT 9.1
Organization Chart for a Textile Company

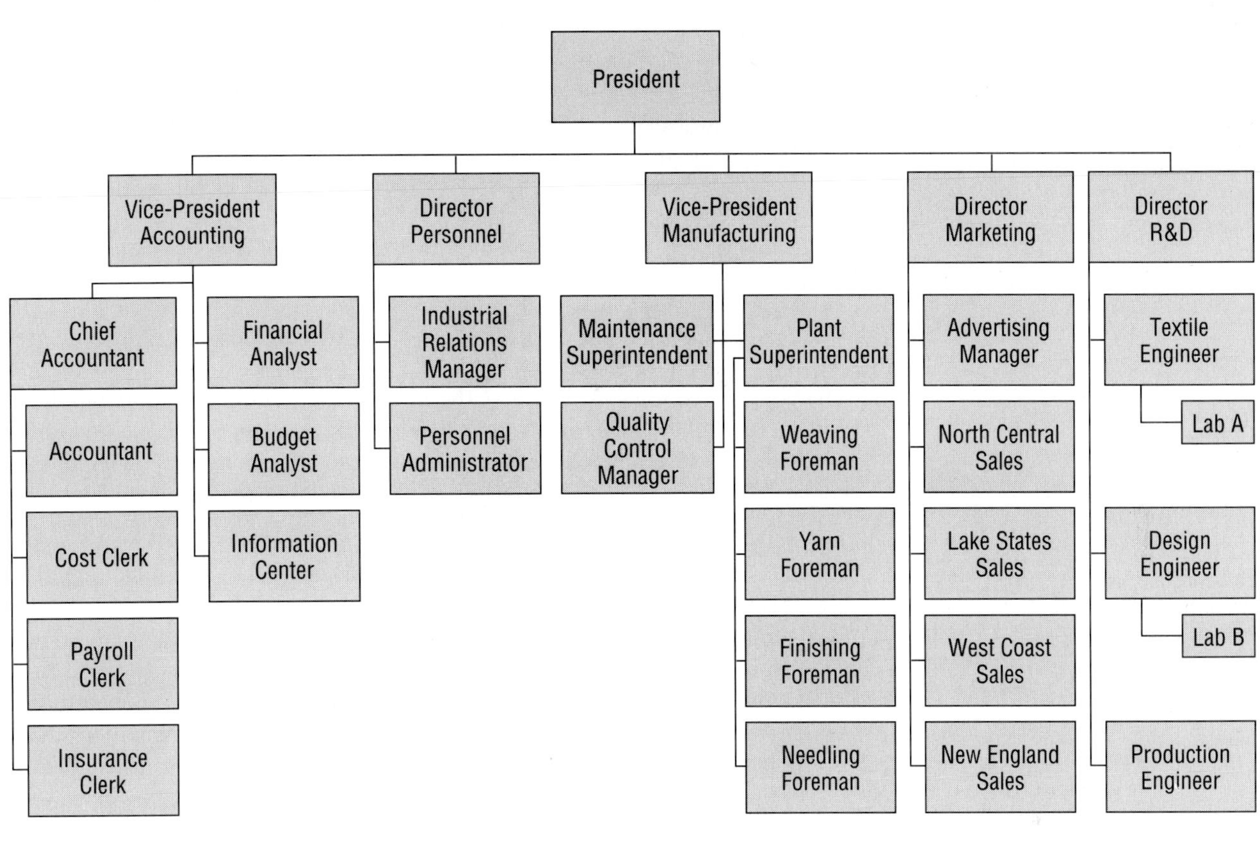

ployee build the entire automobile or even perform a large number of unrelated jobs.

Specialization is a fundamental principle of organizing for several reasons. First, production is efficient because employees perform small, well-defined tasks. Second, employees can acquire expertise in their tasks. Third, employees can be selected with the appropriate ability and attitude for the task to be performed. Fourth, the organization achieves standardization across tasks. Managers know what to expect and can easily detect task-related performance problems.

Despite the advantages, however, organizations can overdo work specialization. This leads to the design of tasks wherein employees do only a single, tiny, boring job. Once the task is mastered, it offers no challenge. Specialization, although necessary, should not be carried to such an extreme. If workers become bored and alienated, organizations can enlarge tasks to find the right fit between work specialization and employee motivation. Specific approaches to designing jobs to fit employee needs are described in Chapter 14.

Chain of Command

chain of command An unbroken line of authority that links all individuals in the organization and specifies who reports to whom.

The **chain of command** is an unbroken line of authority that links all persons in an organization and shows who reports to whom. It is associated with two underlying principles. *Unity of command* means that each employee is held accountable to only one supervisor. The *scalar principle* means a clearly defined line of authority in the organization that includes all employees. Authority and responsibility for different tasks should be distinct. All persons in the organization should know to whom they report as well as the successive management levels all the way to the top. In Exhibit 9.1, the payroll clerk reports to the chief accountant, who in turn reports to the vice-president, who in turn reports to the president.

Authority, Responsibility, and Delegation

authority The formal and legitimate right of a manager to make decisions, issue orders, and allocate resources to achieve organizationally desired outcomes.

The chain of command illustrates the authority structure of the organization. **Authority** is the formal and legitimate right of a manager to make decisions, issue orders, and allocate resources to achieve organizationally desired outcomes. Authority is distinguished by three characteristics:[8]

1. *Authority is vested in organizational positions, not people.* Managers have authority because of the positions they hold, and other people in the same positions would have the same authority.
2. *Authority is accepted by subordinates.* Although authority flows top down through the organization's hierarchy, subordinates comply because they believe that managers have a legitimate right to issue orders. The acceptance theory of authority argues that a manager has authority only if subordinates choose to accept his or her commands. If subordinates refuse to obey because the order is outside their zone of acceptance, a manager's authority disappears.[9] For example, Richard Ferris, the former chairman of United Airlines, resigned because few people accepted his strategy of acquiring hotels, a car rental company, and other organizations to build a travel empire. When key people refused to accept his direction, his authority was lost, and he resigned.
3. *Authority flows down the vertical hierarchy.* Positions at the top of the hierarchy are vested with more formal authority than are positions at the bottom.

responsibility The duty to perform the task or activity an employee has been assigned.

Responsibility is the flip side of the authority coin. **Responsibility** is the duty to perform the task or activity an employee has been assigned. Typically managers are assigned authority commensurate with responsibility. When managers have responsibility for task outcomes, but little authority, the job is possible but difficult. They rely on persuasion and luck. When managers have authority exceeding responsibility, they may become tyrants, using authority toward frivolous outcomes.[10]

accountability The fact that the people with authority and responsibility are subject to reporting and justifying task outcomes to those above them in the chain of command.

Accountability is the mechanism through which authority and responsibility are brought into alignment. **Accountability** means that the people with authority and responsibility are subject to reporting and justifying task outcomes to those above them in the chain of command. Subordinates must be aware that they are accountable for a task and accept the responsibility and authority for performing it. Accountability can be built into the organization

Chevron's new structural approach is to delegate *authority, responsibility,* and *accountability* to smaller business segments. The four puzzle pieces shown here represent four segments among Chevron's many worldwide activities. Within each segment, managers and employees are encouraged to function like operators of a small company — to make business decisions that enable their group to meet specific goals. Top executives believe that decentralization and delegation of authority are structural keys to Chevron's success.

structure. For example, at Whirlpool incentive programs provide strict accountability. Performance of all managers is monitored carefully and bonus payments are tied to successful outcomes.[11]

Another concept related to authority is delegation.[12] **Delegation** is the process managers use to transfer authority and responsibility to positions below them in the hierarchy. Most organizations today encourage managers to delegate authority to the lowest possible level to provide maximum flexibility to meet customer needs and adapt to the environment. Managers are encouraged to delegate authority, although they often find it difficult. Techniques for delegation are discussed in the Manager's Shoptalk box. The trend toward increased delegation begins in the chief executive's office in companies such as USX, PPG Industries, Johnsonville Foods, Ford, and General Electric. At Johnsonville, a committee of employees from the shop floor have been delegated authority to formulate the manufacturing budget.

delegation The process managers use to transfer authority and responsibility to positions below them in the hierarchy.

LINE AND STAFF AUTHORITY. An important distinction in many organizations is between line authority and staff authority, reflecting whether managers work in line or staff departments in the organization's structure. *Line departments* perform tasks that reflect the organization's primary goal and mission. In a manufacturing organization, line departments make and sell the product. *Staff departments* include all those that provide specialized skills in support of line departments. Staff departments have an advisory relationship with line departments and typically include strategic planning, labor relations, research, accounting, and personnel. Exhibit 9.2 shows a partial organization chart for an

EXHIBIT 9.2
Line and Staff Structure for an Automotive Company

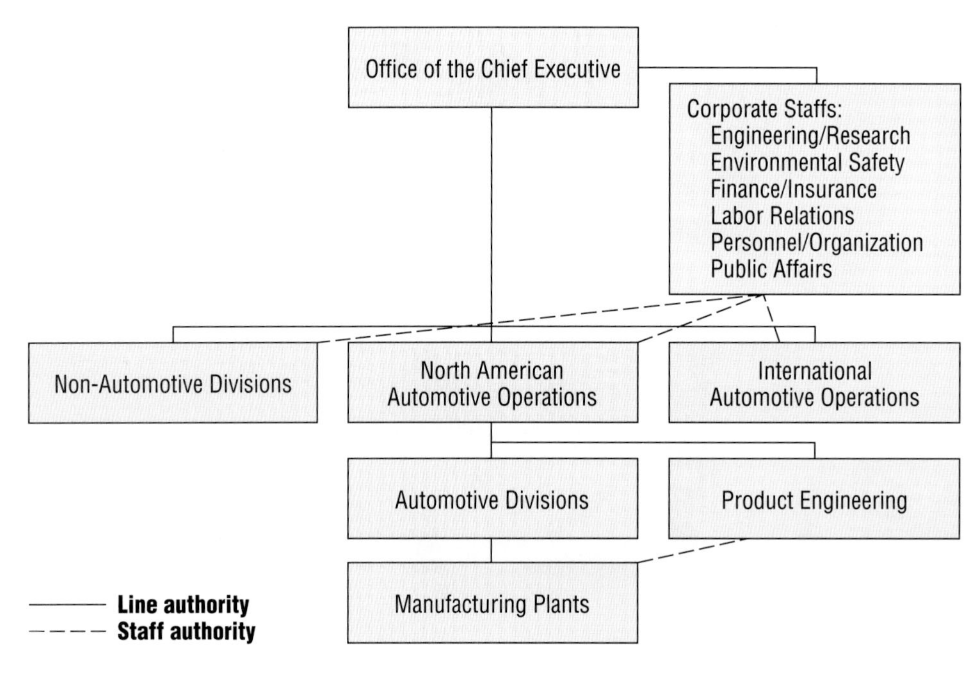

automotive manufacturing company such as General Motors or Ford. The line departments follow the line of authority from the office of the chief executive down to the manufacturing plants. Staff departments exist at the corporate and divisional levels and assist company managers in discharging their line responsibilities.

line authority A form of authority in which individuals in management positions have the formal power to direct and control immediate subordinates.

staff authority A form of authority granted to staff specialists in their areas of expertise.

Line authority means that people in management positions have formal authority to direct and control immediate subordinates. **Staff authority** is narrower and includes the right to advise, recommend, and counsel in the staff specialists' area of expertise. Staff authority often is a communication relationship; staff specialists advise managers in technical areas. Thus, an engineering manager may have authority to define acceptable tolerances for manufacturing machines based on engineering studies. Accounting specialists may tell line managers which accounting forms to complete so as to facilitate payroll services. Staff authority is confined to the area of staff expertise. Staff authority is represented by dashed lines, such as those in Exhibit 9.2, which imply that corporate staff members communicate with and advise senior line managers.

SPAN OF MANAGEMENT

span of management The number of employees who report to a supervisor; also called *span of control*.

The **span of management** is the number of employees reporting to a supervisor. Sometimes called the *span of control*, this characteristic of structure determines how closely a supervisor can monitor subordinates. Traditional views of

EXHIBIT 9.3
Reorganization to Increase Span of Management for President of an International Metals Company

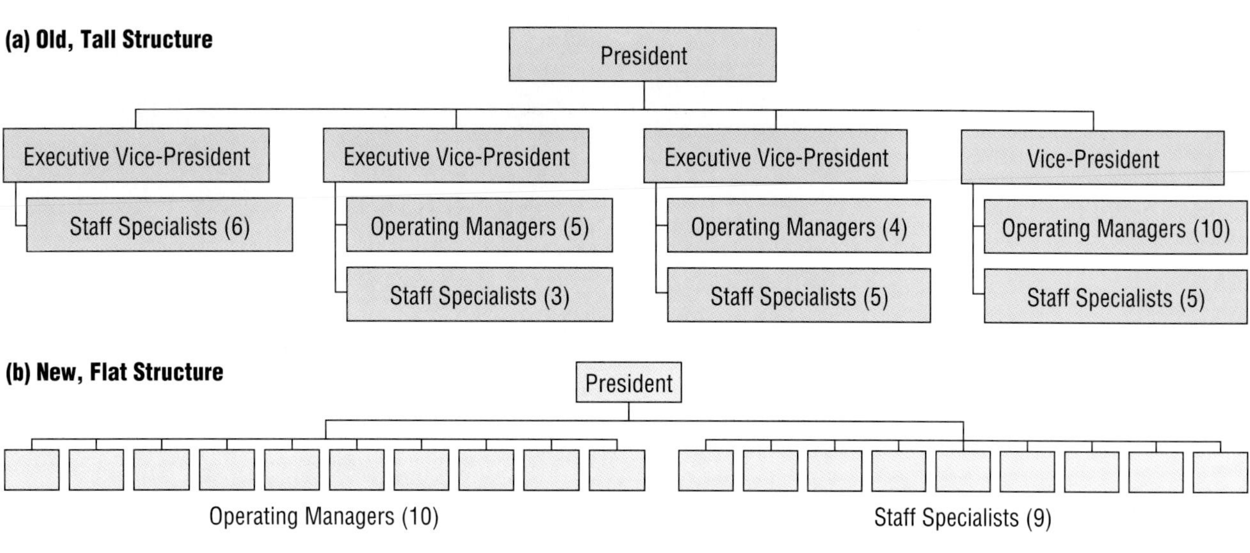

organization design recommend a span of management of from four to seven subordinates per manager. However, many organizations have been observed to have larger spans of management and a few smaller. Research on the Lockheed Missile and Space Company and other manufacturing companies has suggested that span of management can vary widely and that several factors influence the correct span.[13] Generally, when supervisors must be closely involved with subordinates the span should be small, and when supervisors need little involvement with subordinates it can be large. The following factors are associated with less supervisor involvement and thus larger spans of control:

1. Work performed by subordinates is stable and routine.
2. Subordinates perform similar work tasks.
3. Subordinates are concentrated in a single location.
4. Subordinates are highly trained and need little direction in performing tasks.
5. Rules and procedures defining task activities are available.
6. Support systems and personnel are available for the manager.
7. Little time is required in nonsupervisory activities such as coordination with other departments or planning.
8. Managers' personal preferences and styles favor a large span.

TALL VERSUS FLAT STRUCTURE. The average span of control used in an organization determines whether the structure is tall or flat. A **tall structure** has an overall narrow span and more hierarchical levels. A **flat structure** has a wide span, is horizontally dispersed, and has fewer hierarchical levels.

The trend in the 1980s and 1990s is toward larger spans of control as a way to facilitate delegation.[14] Exhibit 9.3 illustrates how an international metals

tall structure A management structure characterized by an overall narrow span of management and a relatively large number of hierarchical levels.

flat structure A management structure characterized by an overall broad span of control and relatively few hierarchical levels.

Thanks to Texaco's policy of *decentralizing* significant decision making to departmental and field operations levels, this 11,000-ton producing platform is being built ahead of schedule in Morgan City, Louisiana. Juice Martin (center) is in charge and works closely with project coordinator David Popp (left) and chief inspector Bob Conner. "Pushing decision responsibilities down to the department level," Martin says, "lets me run the project day-to-day, without waiting for approval from people in New Orleans."

company was reorganized. The multilevel set of managers shown in panel (a) was replaced with ten operating managers and nine staff specialists reporting directly to the CEO, as shown in panel (b). The CEO welcomed this wide span of 19 management subordinates because it fit his style, his management team was top quality and needed little supervision, and they were all located on the same floor of an office building.

CENTRALIZATION AND DECENTRALIZATION

centralization The location of decision authority near top organizational levels.

decentralization The location of decision authority near lower organizational levels.

Centralization and decentralization pertain to the hierarchical level at which decisions are made. **Centralization** means that decision authority is located near the top of the organization. With **decentralization,** decision authority is pushed downward to lower organization levels. Organizations may have to experiment to find the correct hierarchical level at which to make decisions.

In the United States and Canada, the trend over the last 30 years has been toward greater decentralization of organizations. Decentralization is believed to make greater use of human resources, unburden top managers, ensure that decisions are made close to the action by well-informed people, and permit more rapid response to external changes.

However, this trend does not mean that every organization should decentralize all decisions. Managers should diagnose the organizational situation and select the decision-making level that will best meet the organization's needs. Factors that typically influence centralization versus decentralization are as follows:

1. Greater change and uncertainty in the environment are usually associated with decentralization.

MANAGER'S SHOPTALK

HOW TO DELEGATE

The attempt by top management to decentralize decision making often gets bogged down because middle managers are unable to delegate. Managers may cling tightly to their decision-making and task responsibilities. Failure to delegate occurs for a number of reasons: Managers are most comfortable making familiar decisions; they feel they will lose personal status by delegating tasks; they believe they can do a better job themselves; or they have an aversion to risk—they will not take a chance on delegating because performance responsibility ultimately rests with them.

Yet decentralization offers an organization many advantages. Decisions are made at the right level, lower-level employees are motivated, and employees have the opportunity to develop decision-making skills. Overcoming barriers to delegation in order to gain these advantages is a major challenge. The following approach can help each manager delegate more effectively:

1. *Delegate the whole task.* A manager should delegate an entire task to one person rather than dividing it among several people. This gives the individual complete responsibility and increases his or her initiative while giving the manager some control over the results.
2. *Select the right person.* Not all employees have the same capabilities and degree of motivation. Managers must match talent to task if delegation is to be effective. They should identify subordinates who have made independent decisions in the past and have shown a desire for more responsibility.
3. *Delegate responsibility and authority.* Merely assigning a task is not effective delegation. The individual must have the responsibility for completing the task and the authority to perform the task as he or she thinks best.
4. *Give thorough instruction.* Successful delegation includes information on what, when, why, where, who, and how. The subordinate must clearly understand the task and the expected results. It is a good idea to write down all provisions discussed, including required resources and when and how the results will be reported.
5. *Maintain feedback.* Feedback means keeping open lines of communication with the subordinate to answer questions and provide advice, but without exerting too much control. Open lines of communication make it easier to trust subordinates. Feedback keeps the subordinate on the right track.
6. *Evaluate and reward performance.* Once the task is completed, the manager should evaluate results, not methods. When results do not meet expectations, the manager must assess the consequences. When they do meet expectations, the managers should reward employees for a job well done with praise, financial rewards when appropriate, and delegation of future assignments.

ARE YOU A POSITIVE DELEGATOR?

Positive delegation is the way an organization implements decentralization. Do you help or hinder the decentralization process? If you answer yes to more than three of the following questions, you may have a problem delegating:

- I tend to be a perfectionist.
- My boss expects me to know all the details of my job.
- I don't have the time to explain clearly and concisely how a task should be accomplished.
- I often end up doing tasks myself.
- My subordinates typically are not as committed as I am.
- I get upset when other people don't do the task right.
- I really enjoy doing the details of my job to the best of my ability.
- I like to be in control of task outcomes.

Source: Andrew E. Schwartz, "The Why, What, and to Whom of Delegation," *Management Solutions* (June 1987), 31–38, and "Delegation," *Small Business Report* (June 1986), 38–43.

2. Corporate history and culture socialize managers into a decision approach. The choice between centralization and decentralization often reflects the pattern of decisions made in the past.
3. As organizations increase in size, some decentralization is required. In a very small organization the top manager can make nearly all decisions, thus centralizing decision authority.
4. Greater cost of decision alternatives or greater risk of failure means that centralization is preferred. Top managers are reluctant to delegate decisions that put the entire organization at risk.

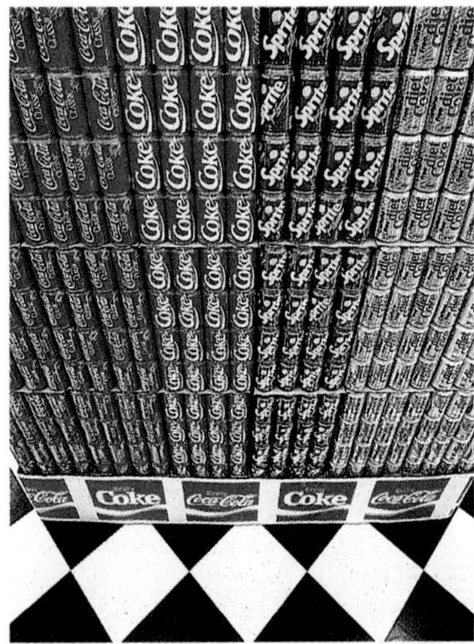

The benefits of *formalization* are illustrated by the operations of Coca-Cola Enterprises Inc. Uniform written standards provide continuity in retail display, merchandising, and promotion across each territory and promote clear understanding of company direction for employees. For example, written standards exist for the order and position of products on grocery shelves and in cooler displays. Moreover, managers can move around within the system, because skills learned in a small sales center transfer to a major operation such as Los Angeles.

5. Efficient communication and control systems often facilitate centralization. New information and computer technologies enable data to be sent to top management for evaluation and decision making.[15]
6. The amount of centralization or decentralization should fit the firm's strategy. For example, Hewlett-Packard has a strategy of cutting costs and standardizing research and manufacturing, so top management centralized these activities under top bosses. Digital Equipment Corporation did the same thing, because managers in far-flung divisions were going in separate directions, often conflicting with one another. By contrast, Pepsico's strategy is to place decision authority at the lowest possible level. Thus when Coke took Pepsi by surprise with an innovative advertisement during a Super Bowl broadcast, a rebuttal commercial was designed, shot, and aired within a dizzying three days. Normally such a decision would take a month or more, but decentralization fits Pepsi's strategy of fast competitive response.[16]

ADMINISTRATIVE OVERHEAD

Because organization structure is the deployment of resources so as to accomplish organizational goals, one characteristic of interest to many managers pertains to the percentage of resources deployed for line activities versus that for administrative and support activities. Two elements of **administrative overhead** can be measured by the following ratios:

1. *Indirect-to-direct-labor ratio.* Direct labor includes line employees who work directly on the organization's product or service. Indirect employees include all other employees — accountants, engineers, clerks — in the organization. This ratio is similar to a line-staff ratio.
2. *Top administrator ratio.* This ratio measures the percentage of total employment made up by top management. For a wide span of control in a flat organization, this percentage would be low.

In the highly competitive global environment managers face today, reducing administrative overhead is often a priority. For example, Sears is trying to reduce its high administrative cost, which runs 29.9 percent of sales compared with Wal-Mart's 15.3 percent. This difference amounts to millions of dollars in overhead. Many companies have made a religion of staying lean at the top. Nucor has only 17 headquarters administrators to manage an $800 million company with 3,700 employees. Borg-Warner uses only 175 headquarters employees to perform administrative functions for 8,200 employees in several divisions. General Foods recently announced it would eliminate most of its 2,000 headquarters jobs.[17]

administrative overhead The resources allocated to administrative and support activities.

formalization The written documentation used to direct and control employees.

FORMALIZATION

Formalization is the written documentation used to direct and control employees. Written documentation includes rule books, policies, procedures, job descriptions, and regulations. These documents complement the organization chart by providing descriptions of tasks, responsibilities, and decision authority. The use of rules, regulations, and written records of decisions is part of the bureaucratic model of organizations described in Chapter 2. As proposed by Max Weber, the bureaucratic model defines the basic organizational characteristics that enable the organization to operate in a logical and rational manner.

Although written documentation is intended to be rational and helpful to the organization, it often creates "red tape" that causes more problems than it solves. If an organization tries to do everything through the written word, rules and procedures become burdensome. Consider the government's attempt to define a rule concerning the size of scallops:

> A violation of the four-ounce standard occurs if the average of the aggregate weights of the 10 smallest scallops in all the one-pint samples taken fails to meet the four-ounce standard. If a violation of the four-ounce standard is found among those undeclared scallops from a particular vessel and being treated as a separate entity for the purpose of sampling, the entire amount of scallops in possession or control will be deemed in violation. If a violation of the four-ounce standard is found among scallops possessed by a dealer/processor, only those scallops being treated as a separate entity for the purpose of sampling (i.e., the total amount of scallops, up to 10% of which has been drawn as samples) will be deemed in violation.[18]

DEPARTMENTALIZATION

Another fundamental characteristic of organization structure is **departmentalization,** which is the basis for grouping positions into departments and departments into the total organization. Managers make choices about how to use the chain of command to group people together to perform their work. There are five approaches to structural design that reflect different uses of the chain of command in departmentalization. The functional, divisional, and matrix are traditional approaches that rely on the chain of command to define groupings and reporting relationships. Two contemporary approaches are the use of teams and networks. These newer approaches have engaged to meet organizational needs in a highly competitive global environment. A brief illustration of the five structural alternatives are in Exhibit 9.4.

departmentalization The basis on which individuals are grouped into departments and departments into total organizations.

1. *Functional approach.* People are grouped together in departments by common skills and work activities, such as in an engineering department and an accounting department.
2. *Divisional approach.* Departments are grouped together into separate, self-contained divisions based on a common product, program, or geographical region. Diverse skills rather than similar skills are the basis of departmentalization.
3. *Matrix approach.* Functional and divisional chains of command are implemented simultaneously and overlay one another in the same departments. Two chains of command exist, and some employees report to two bosses.
4. *Team approach.* The organization creates a series of teams or task forces to accomplish specific tasks and to coordinate major departments. Teams can exist from the office of the president all the way down to the shop floor.
5. *Network approach.* The organization becomes a small, central broker electronically connected to other organizations that perform vital functions. Departments are independent contracting services to the broker for a profit. Departments can be located anywhere in the world.[19]

EXHIBIT 9.4
Five Approaches to Structural Design

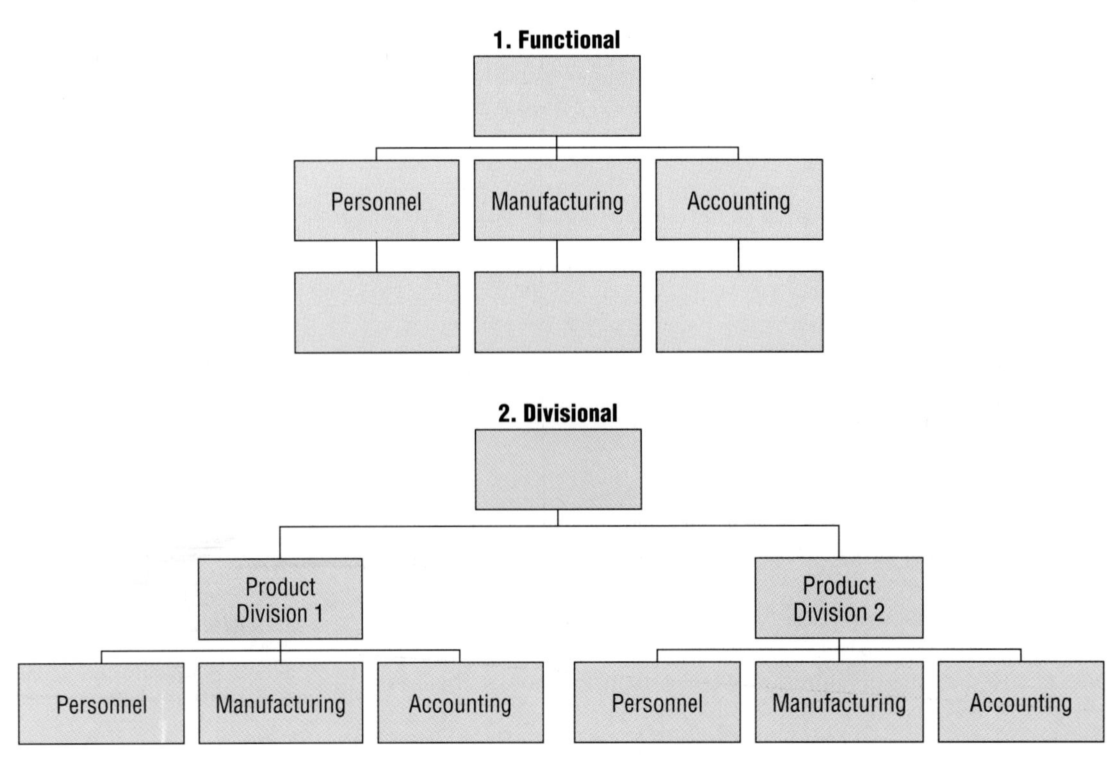

Each approach to structure serves a distinct purpose for the organization, and each has advantages and disadvantages. The basic difference among structures is the way in which employees are departmentalized and to whom they report. The differences in structure illustrated in Exhibit 9.4 have major consequences for employee goals and motivation. The ability of managers to know when and how to use each form of structure allows them to solve problems such as we saw in the Albany Ladder Company described at the beginning of this chapter. Let us now turn to each of the five structural designs and examine their implications for managers.[20]

Functional Approach

functional structure
An organizational structure in which positions are grouped into departments based on similar skills, expertise, and resource use.

Functional structure is the grouping of positions into departments based on similar skills, expertise, and resource use. A functional structure can be thought of as departmentalization by organizational resources, because each type of functional activity — personnel, engineering, manufacturing — represents

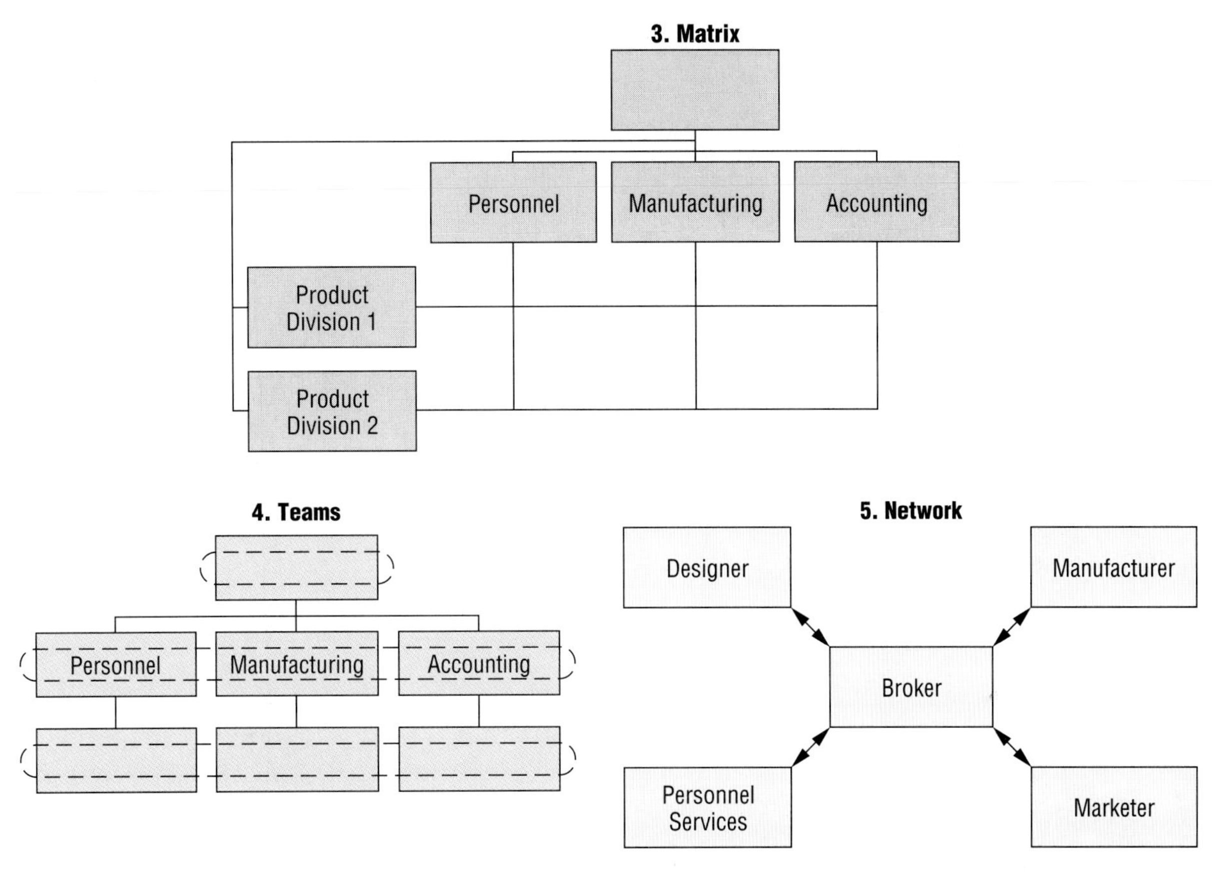

specific resources for performing the organization's task. People and facilities representing a common organizational resource are grouped together into a single department.

An example of a functional structure for American Airlines is presented in Exhibit 9.5. The major departments under Chairman Crandall are groupings of similar expertise and resources, such as employee relations, government affairs, operations, information systems, and marketing. Each of the functional departments at American Airlines is concerned with the airline as a whole. The employee relations vice-president is concerned with employees in all areas, and the marketing department is responsible for all sales and marketing.

ADVANTAGES AND DISADVANTAGES. Grouping employees into departments based on similar skills has many advantages for an organization. Employees who perform a common task are grouped together so as to permit economies of scale and efficient resource use. At American Airlines, as illustrated in Exhibit 9.5, all information systems people work in the same department. They have the expertise for handling almost any problem within a single, large

EXHIBIT 9.5
Functional Structure for American Airlines

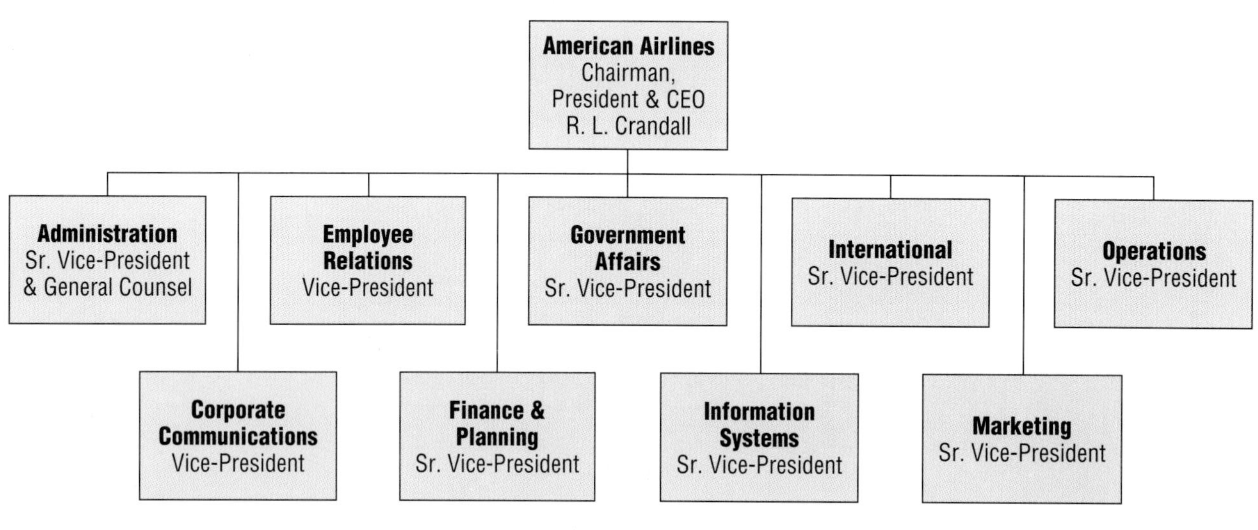

Source: Used with permission of American Airlines.

Arkansas Power & Light Company uses a *functional structure* to excel at important tasks. The four people shown here work in the public affairs function and as a team strengthen ties with regulatory officials. They work with both the Arkansas General Assembly and elected officials at the Washington level. These employees help the company to detect regulatory changes and to see and capitalize on new opportunities.

department. The large functional departments enhance the development of in-depth skills because people work on a variety of problems and are associated with other experts. Career progress is based on functional expertise; thus, employees are motivated to develop their skills. Managers and employees are compatible because of similar training and expertise.

The functional structure also offers a way to centralize decision making and provide unified direction from the top, because the chain of command converges at the top of the organization. Sometimes the functional structure is also associated with wider spans of control because of large departments and common expertise. Communication and coordination among employees within each department are excellent. Finally, functional structure promotes high-quality technical problem solving. The pool of well-trained experts, motivated toward functional expertise, gives the company an important resource, especially those that work with sophisticated technology.

The disadvantages of functional structure reflect the barriers that exist across departments and a slow response to environmental changes. Because people are separated into distinct departments, communication and coordination across functions are often poor. Poor coordination means a slow response to environmental changes, because innovation and change require involvement of several departments. Because the chains of command are separate beneath the top of the organization, decisions involving more than one department may pile up at the top of the organization and be delayed. The functional structure also stresses work specialization and division of labor, which may produce routine, nonmotivating employee tasks.

The functional structure also creates management problems, such as difficulty in pinpointing problems within departments. In the case of an insurance

EXHIBIT 9.6
Advantages and Disadvantages of Functional Structure

Advantages	Disadvantages
• Efficient use of resources, economies of scale	• Poor communication across functional departments
• In-depth skill specialization and development	• Slow response to external changes, lagging innovation
• Career progress within functional departments	• Decisions concentrated at top of hierarchy, creating delay
• Top manager direction and control	• Responsibility for problems difficult to pinpoint
• Excellent coordination within functions	• Limited view of organizational goals by employees
• High-quality technical problem solving	• Limited general management training for employees

company, for example, each function works on all products and performs only a part of the task for any product line. Hence, if one life insurance product is not performing well, there is no specific department or group that bears responsibility. In addition, employees tend to focus on the attainment of departmental goals, often to the exclusion of organizational goals. They see only their respective tasks and not the big picture. Because of this narrow task specialization, employees are trained to become experts in their fields and not to manage and coordinate diverse departments. Thus, they fail to become groomed for top management and general management positions.

The advantages and disadvantages of functional structure are summarized in Exhibit 9.6.

DIVISIONAL APPROACH

In contrast to the functional approach, in which people are grouped by common skills and resources, the **divisional structure** occurs when departments are grouped together based on organizational outputs. The difference between functional and divisional structure is illustrated in Exhibit 9.7. In the divisional structure, divisions are created as self-contained units for producing a single product. Each functional department resource needed to produce the product is assigned to one division. For example, in a functional structure, all engineers are grouped together and work on all products. In a divisional structure, separate engineering departments are established within each division. Each department is smaller and focuses on a single product line. Departments are duplicated across product lines.

divisional structure
An organizational structure in which departments are grouped based on similar organizational outputs.

The divisional structure is sometimes called a *product structure, program structure,* or *self-contained unit structure.* Each of these terms means essentially the same thing: Diverse departments are brought together to produce a single organizational output, whether it be a product, a program, or service to a single customer.

In very large companies, a divisional structure is essential. Most large corporations have separate business divisions that perform different tasks, serve different clients, or use different technologies. When a huge organization produces products for different markets, the divisional structure works because each division is an autonomous business. For example, PepsiCo uses a divisional structure. Frito-Lay, Pizza Hut, Taco Bell, North American Van Lines, and Wilson's Sporting Goods are stand-alone divisions within PepsiCo. Ten-

EXHIBIT 9.7
Functional versus Divisional Structures

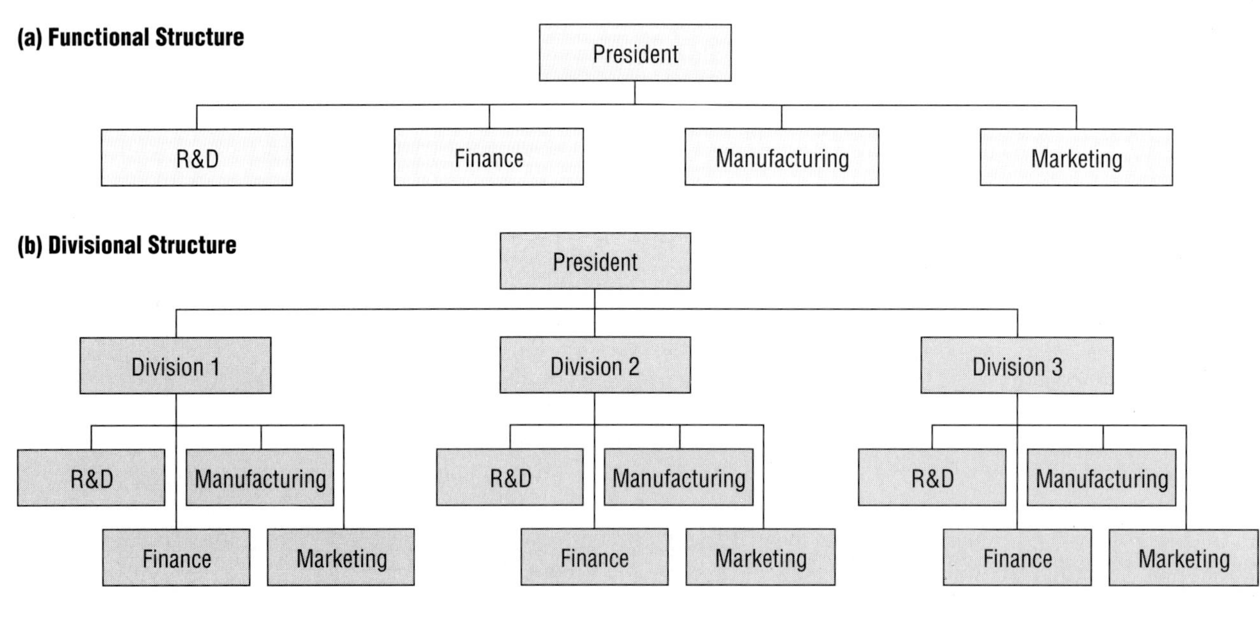

neco Inc. also uses a divisional structure. Divisions include J. I. Case, a manufacturer of farm implements, and Newport News Shipbuilding, which builds submarines and other ships for the Navy. Each of these companies is run as a separate division under the guidance of Tenneco corporate headquarters.

A major difference between divisional and functional structures is that the chain of command from each function converges lower in the hierarchy. In Exhibit 9.7, differences of opinion among R&D, marketing, manufacturing, and finance would be resolved at the divisional level rather than by the president. Thus, the divisional structure encourages decentralization. Decision making is pushed down at least one level in the hierarchy, freeing up the president and other top managers for strategic planning.

GEOGRAPHICALLY AND CUSTOMER-BASED DIVISIONS. Two variations of the divisional structure are the organization of divisions by geography and by customer. Departmentalization by customer simply means that all skills needed to service a specific customer are grouped together in a single division. A company may have a very large customer — say, the U.S. government — for a certain line of products. It can create a separate division to serve that customer full time. Another example is a supplier that manufactures parts for both General Motors autos and Boeing aircraft. It may create two divisions, one for each major customer. A divisional status provides a common employee focus on the customer's needs. A company such as Macmillan, which produces textbooks, is divided into divisions for the high school, grade school, and college markets. Although the manufacturing technology is the same for all divisions, the writing and selling of textbooks is different for each type of customer.

MagneTek transformers supply power to this 744-foot long neon sculpture in United Airlines' "Terminal of Tomorrow" at Chicago's O'Hare International Airport. MagneTek, Inc., is organized into four product *divisions,* one of which provides a clear focus on customers for transformers. Approximately half of all the neon signs in the nation utilize MagneTek transformers, reflecting the company's ability to respond to customer needs. Approximately 80 million travelers view O'Hare's neon sculpture each year.

Geographical divisions are created when an organization serves a national or international area and functional skills need to be located in each geographical region. Sears, Roebuck is organized into five regions, each with its own warehousing, inventory control, distribution systems, and stores. Recent changes in the economy forced Greyhound Lines Inc. to reorganize from a functional to a geographical structure with four regional divisions. The functional structure had worked when bus routes ran from city to city throughout the nation. But competition from low-cost airlines had reduced long-distance bus travel by half; the average bus trip is now less than 250 miles. Greyhound's management decided that four divisions, representing the eastern, central, southern, and western regions, would provide better service and more efficient control. The new geographical structure enables closer coordination of bus routes designed to meet the needs of the customer within the region served by each division.

ADVANTAGES AND DISADVANTAGES. For medium-size companies, the choice between functional and divisional structure is difficult because each represents different strengths and weaknesses. The advantages and disadvantages of the divisional structure are listed in Exhibit 9.8. By dividing employees and resources along divisional lines, the organization will be flexible and responsive to change because each unit is small and tuned in to its environment. By having employees working on a single product line, the concern for customers' needs is high. Coordination across functional departments is better because employees are grouped together in a single location and committed to one product line. Great coordination exists within divisions. The divisional structure also enables top management to pinpoint responsibility for performance problems in product lines. Because each division is a self-contained unit, poor performance can be assigned directly to the manager of that unit. Finally, employees' goals typically are directed toward product success rather than toward their own functional departments. Employees develop a broader goal orientation that can help them develop into general managers.

EXHIBIT 9.8
Advantages and Disadvantages of Divisional Structure

Advantages	Disadvantages
• Fast response, flexibility in an unstable environment	• Duplication of resources across divisions
• Fosters concern for customers' needs	• Less technical depth and specialization in divisions
• Excellent coordination across functional departments	• Poor coordination across divisions
• Easy pinpointing of responsibility for product problems	• Less top management control
• Emphasis on overall product and division goals	• Competition for corporate resources
• Development of general management skills	

The product structure also has well-defined disadvantages. The major disadvantage is duplication of resources and the high cost of running separate divisions. Instead of a single research department in which all research people use a single facility, there may be several. The organization loses efficiency and economies of scale. Because departments within each division are small, there is a lack of technical specialization, expertise, and training. The divisional structure fosters excellent coordination *within* divisions, but coordination *across* divisions is often poor. Companies such as Hewlett-Packard and Digital Equipment prided themselves on the divisional structure that gave autonomy to many small divisions. Problems occurred, however, when these divisions went in opposite directions. The software produced in one division did not fit the hardware produced in another. Thus, divisional structures were realigned to establish adequate coordination across divisions. Moreover, divisions may feel themselves in competition with one another, especially for resources from corporate headquarters. This can lead to political behavior that is unhealthy for the company as a whole. Because top management control is somewhat weaker under the divisional structure, top managers must assert themselves in order to get divisions to work together.

Many companies must carefully decide whether the divisional or functional structure better suits their needs. It is not uncommon for a company to try one structure and then switch to another as its needs change. One example is Apple Computer, which went to a divisional structure to insure excellent cooperation within divisions and a rapid response to the external environment. However, a declining market for personal computers made efficiency more important, and Apple reorganized back into a functional structure in 1985. Then in 1989 Apple reorganized into a product structure, with each division reporting to CEO John Sculley.[21]

MATRIX APPROACH

matrix structure
An organizational structure that utilizes functional and divisional chains of command simultaneously in the same part of the organization.

The **matrix approach** utilizes functional and divisional chains of command simultaneously in the same part of the organization.[22] The matrix actually has dual lines of authority. In Exhibit 9.9, the functional hierarchy of authority runs vertically and the divisional hierarchy of authority runs laterally. The lateral chain of command formalizes the divisional relationships. Thus, the lateral structure provides coordination across functional departments, while the vertical structure provides traditional control within functional departments. The

Exhibit 9.9
Dual-Authority Structure in a Matrix Organization

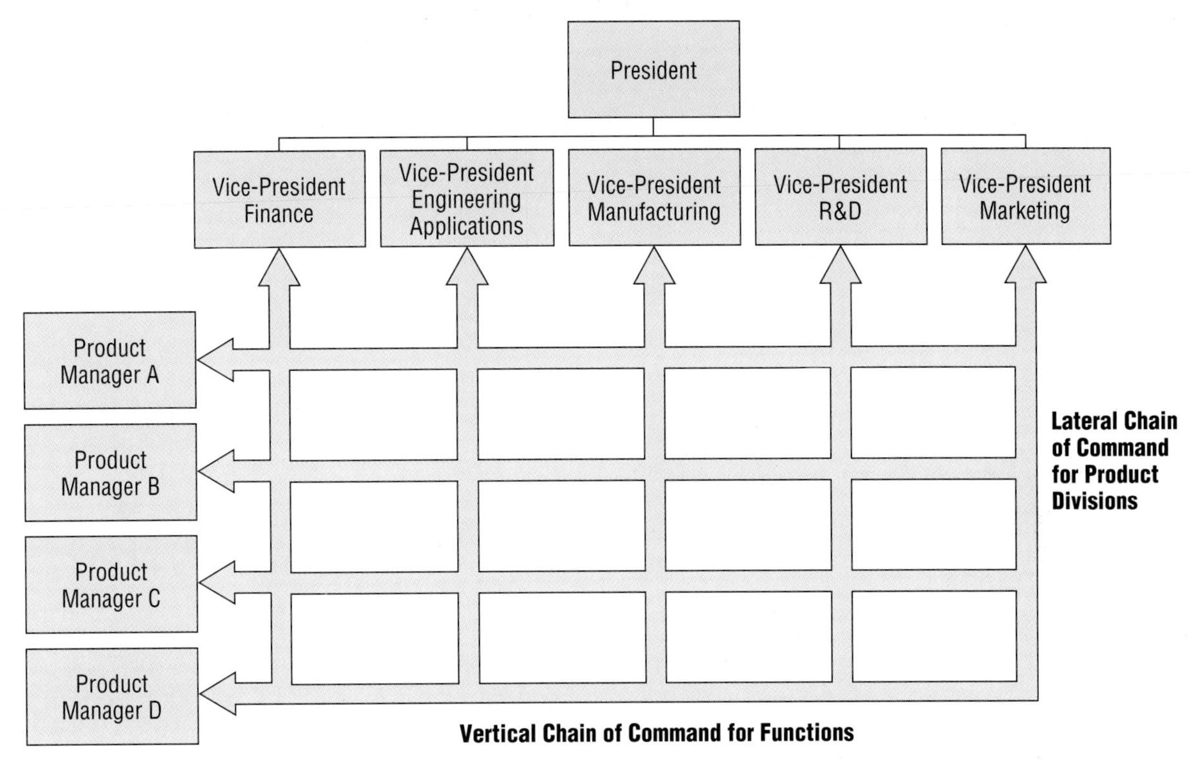

matrix approach to structure therefore provides a formal chain of command for both the functional and divisional relationships.

The matrix structure typically is used when the organization experiences environmental pressure for both a strong functional departmentalization and a divisional departmentalization. Thus, the organization may need to have in-depth skills in functional departments (engineering, research) and at the same time the ability to respond flexibly and adaptively to changing environmental demands. The matrix structure enables the organization to achieve greater economies of scale than does the divisional structure, because functional employees can be shared across several divisions. Resource duplication is minimized by having employees work for more than one division or by transferring employees among divisions as personnel requirements change. In Exhibit 9.9, the engineering vice-president can reassign engineers as the needs of each product line change.

Key Relationships. The success of the matrix structure depends on the abilities of people in key matrix roles. Exhibit 9.10 provides a close-up of the reporting relationships in the dual chain of command. The senior engineer in the medical products division reports to both the medical products vice-president and the engineering director. This violates the unity of command concept

EXHIBIT 9.10
Key Positions in a Matrix Structure

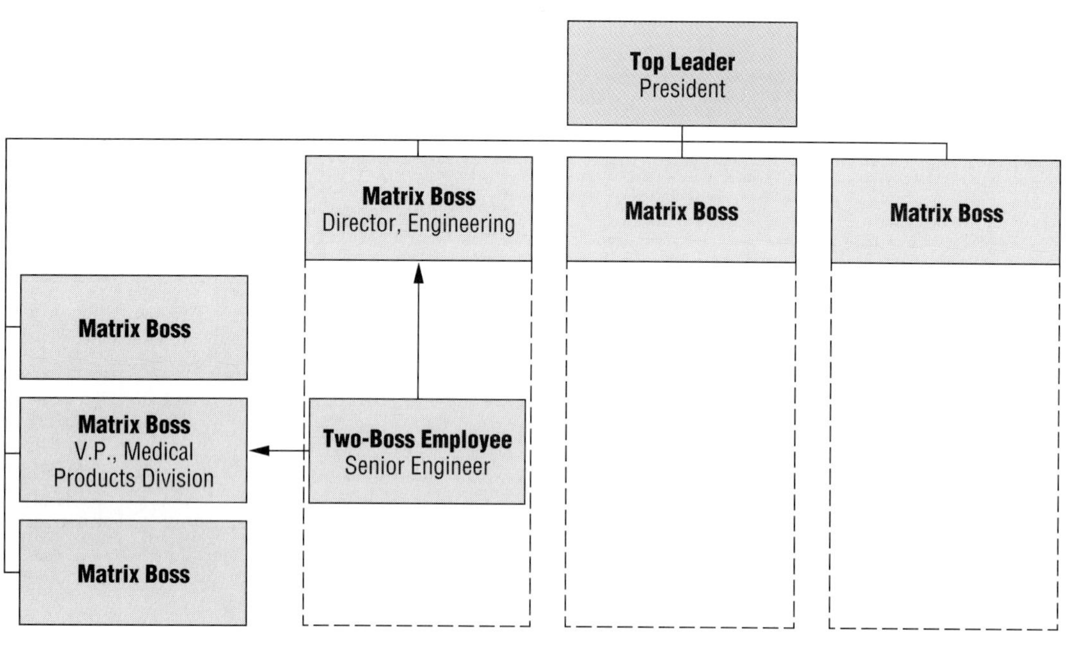

described earlier in this chapter, but is necessary to give equal emphasis to both functional and divisional lines of authority. Confusion is reduced by separating responsibilities for each chain of command. The functional boss is responsible for technical and personnel issues, such as quality standards, providing technical training, and assigning technical personnel to projects. The divisional boss is responsible for programwide issues, such as overall design decisions, schedule deadlines, and coordinating technical specialists from several functions.

two-boss employee An employee who reports to two supervisors simultaneously.

matrix boss A product or functional boss, responsible for one side of the matrix.

top leader The overseer of both the product and the functional chains of command, responsible for the entire matrix.

The senior engineer is called a **two-boss employee** because he or she reports to two supervisors simultaneously. Two-boss employees must resolve conflicting demands from the matrix bosses. They must confront senior managers and reach joint decisions. They need excellent human relations skills with which to confront managers and resolve conflicts. The **matrix boss** is the product or functional boss, who in Exhibit 9.10 is the engineering director and the medical products vice-president. The matrix boss is responsible for one side of the matrix. The top leader is responsible for the entire matrix. The **top leader** oversees both the product and functional chains of command. His or her responsibility is to maintain a power balance between the two sides of the matrix. If disputes arise between them, the problem will be kicked upstairs to the top leader.[23]

Matrix bosses and two-boss employees often find it difficult to adapt to the matrix. The matrix boss has only half of each employee. Without complete control over employees, bosses must consult with their counterparts on the other side of the matrix. This necessitates frequent meetings and discussions to coordinate matrix activities. The two-boss employee experiences problems of conflicting demands and expectations from the two supervisors.

Advantages and Disadvantages. The matrix structure is controversial because of the dual chain of command. However, it has been used successfully in companies such as Dow Chemical. Most important, it makes efficient use of human resources compared with the divisional structure, thus solving the duplication of resource problem. The functional boss can reassign specialists from one division to another, and people can be assigned half time to two divisions, thus fully utilizing personnel. Moreover, the matrix structure works well in a shifting environment, wherein the organization is expected to be adaptable and innovative. The conflict and frequent meetings generated by the matrix enable new issues to be raised and resolved. The matrix also provides training for both functional and general management skills. People within functional departments have access to in-depth training and specialization and at the same time coordinate with other specialists and programs, which helps them develop a general management perspective. Finally, the matrix structure engages the participation of employees in team meetings and in the achievement of divisional goals. Thus, it challenges and motivates employees, giving them a larger task than would be possible in a functional structure.

Tenneco Inc. has organized its many businesses into a divisional structure. Within the Newport News Shipbuilding division a *matrix structure* is used to coordinate the many functions and ships being built. The *Key West* was one of two attack submarines delivered in the late 1980s. Newport News also used the matrix structure to develop plans for a new class of submarines and coordinate the 18-month overhaul for the aircraft carrier *Theodore Roosevelt.* The matrix structure permits the coordination and sharing of resources needed for these difficult tasks.

The matrix structure also has several disadvantages. The major problem is the confusion and frustration caused by the dual chain of command. Matrix bosses and two-boss employees have difficulty with the dual reporting relationships. The matrix structure also generates high conflict because it pits divisional against functional goals. This leads to the third disadvantage: time lost to meetings and discussions devoted to resolving this conflict. Often the matrix structure leads to more discussion than action because different goals and points of view are being addressed. To survive and perform well in a matrix, employees need human relations training to learn to deal with two bosses, to get by with only "half" of each employee, and to confront and manage conflict. Finally, many organizations find it difficult to maintain the power balances essential for matrix success. The functional and divisional sides of the matrix must have equal power. If one side acquires greater formal authority, the advantages of the matrix structure will be lost. The organization will then operate like a functional structure with informal lateral relationships.

The advantages and disadvantages of the matrix structure are summarized in Exhibit 9.11.

One company in which the matrix structure works very well is Crane Plastics Inc. in Columbus, Ohio. There is only one matrix boss on the divisional side, but the approach has succeeded because of the skills of Howard Bennett.

Crane Plastics Inc.

• Gary Fulmer, executive vice-president of Crane Plastics, had not even heard of the matrix structure until he ran across some published articles. The matrix seemed a solution to the intense cooperation needed among departments during a product changeover. "Making the conversion in our large-volume custom products was driving me up a wall," said Fulmer. "Rarely had we done anything that cut across so many departments. It took compounding experts, toolmakers, extrusion people, quality control people — in all, it took about five

EXHIBIT 9.11
Advantages and Disadvantages of Matrix Structure

Advantages	Disadvantages
• More efficient use of resources than divisional structure	• Frustration and confusion from dual chain of command
• Flexibility, adaptability to changing environment	• High conflict between divisional and functional interests
• Development of both general and functional management skills	• Many meetings, more discussion than action
• Interdisciplinary cooperation, expertise available to all divisions	• Needed human relations training
• Enlarged tasks for employees	• Power dominance by one side of matrix

different disciplines to make this thing work. . . . But it wasn't working." He continued, "People would have a meeting. They'd come back after two or three weeks with all good intentions, but they just didn't get it done, because they had more important things to do in their own functional areas."

Managers resisted the matrix, because team members work for two bosses — team and function — at the same time. Crane Plastics implemented the matrix with one team boss, and it really began to click when Howard Bennett took that position. Bennett understood lateral relationships. He guarded against interdepartmental friction by having functional department heads sign an agreement allowing their subordinates' participation in a team. His style encouraged cooperation. But Bennett admits it took some practice: "When I assumed this position, I was totally engrossed in manufacturing. . . . I had no sympathy for marketing, accounting, or most of the other functions. This job gave me a broader outlook."

Bennett was responsible for coordinating all new products, several of which were developed simultaneously, as illustrated by the multiple lines emanating from his position in Exhibit 9.12. His full-time job was to manage these teams, and his rank equaled vice-presidents' of other departments. But it was Bennett's management skill as much as formal rank that made the matrix work. Said one team member, "With other companies, matrix management is reduced to shouting matches. . . . It's inevitable any time you have two bosses." But thanks to Howard Bennett, this did not happen at Crane Plastics.[24]

TEAM APPROACH

Probably the most widespread trend in departmentalization has been the effort by companies to implement team concepts. The vertical chain of command is a powerful means of control, but passing all decisions up the hierarchy takes too long and keeps responsibility at the top. Companies in the 1990s are trying to find ways to delegate authority, push responsibility to low levels, and create participative teams that engage the commitment of workers. This approach enables organizations to be more flexible and responsive in the harshly competitive global environment. The Winning Moves box indicates how Snap-on Tools combined teams with a divisional structure to respond to stiff competition.

cross-functional team A group of employees assigned to a functional department that meets as a team to resolve mutual problems.

Cross-functional teams consist of employees assigned to functional departments who are responsible to meet as a team and resolve mutual problems.

EXHIBIT 9.12
Matrix Structure for Crane Plastics Inc.

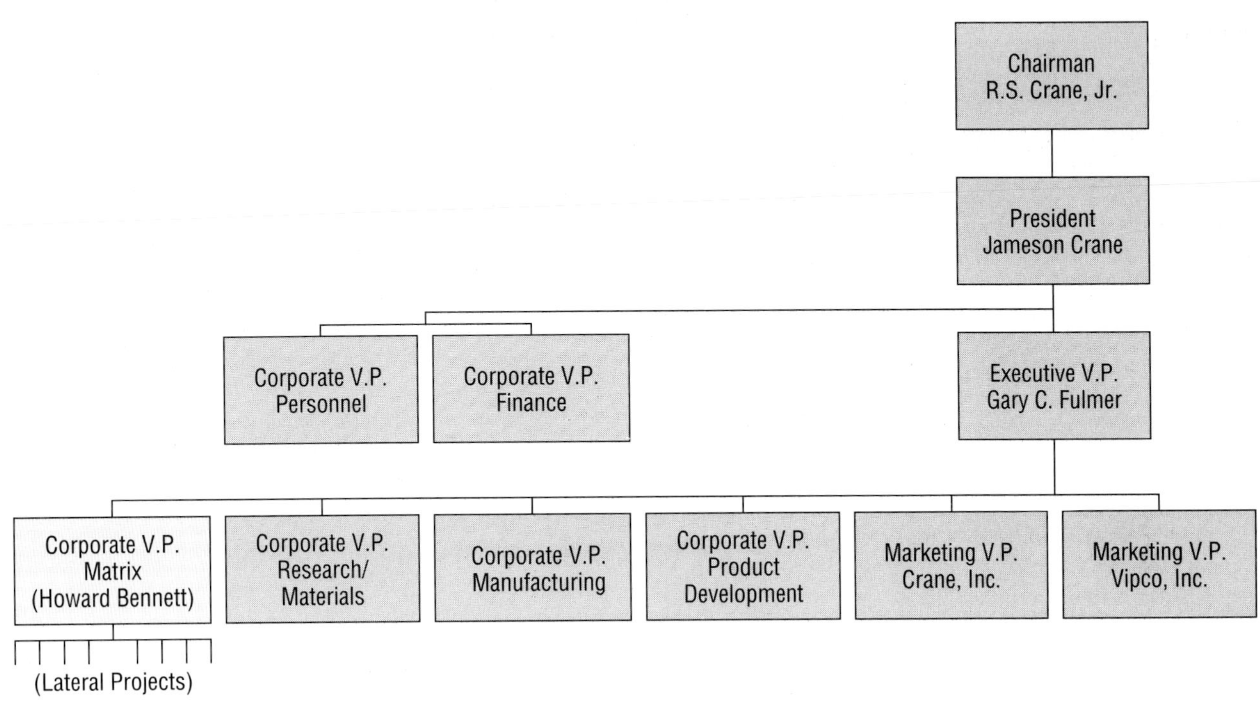

Source: Howard Bennett, Corporate Vice-President, Matrix, Crane Plastics Inc., 1985. Used with permission.

Team members formally report up the chain of command in their functional departments, but they also have a dotted-line relationship to the team, one member of whom may be the leader. Computer-based companies such as Lanier Technology Corporation, Compaq Computer Corporation, Quantum Corporation, and AST Research are obsessed with creating a team atmosphere using cross-functional teams.[25] At Compaq, lateral groups are called "smart teams," which represent an interdisciplinary approach to management. This structural approach assumes that people from the treasurer's office and engineering have ideas to contribute to decisions about marketing and manufacturing. The Deskpro 286 was created by a smart team in response to IBM's super PC. Kevin Ellington, who was in charge of the project, created his own smart team, drawing members from every department in the company. Team members worked in parallel: Marketing was positioning the Deskpro in the marketplace, finance was arranging to pay for it, and manufacturing was figuring out how to produce it. Team members communicated constantly. Within six months, Compaq was shipping its first models — indeed, it beat IBM to the punch because IBM was still suffering production problems. Ellington offers three reasons for the Deskpro 286's success: "The first, second, and third reason was teamwork."[26]

Ortho-Kinetics, which produces lift chairs and mobility vehicles for the handicapped, was struggling to correct a shipping problem with service parts.

WINNING MOVES

SNAP-ON TOOLS CORPORATION

For a long time, Snap-on Tools Corp. customers would buy everything it could produce. Suddenly, the market was swamped with competitive products that were clones of Snap-on's popular designs. To keep its lead, Snap-on Tools had to become more aggressive in developing new concepts and products, which called for innovative reorganization. Snap-on's desire was to eliminate the functional department structure, wherein each department performed its task in isolation, "throwing the project over the wall" to the next department when finished.

The first step was to restructure the Research and Engineering Division into four product groups — traditional hand tools, air tools, sheet-metal goods, and electronic products. Each was a self-contained unit with its own engineering function. Next, engineering teams were created to work with marketing and customer focus groups to discuss ideas and define new products. In the photograph shown here, team leader Jim Butzen demonstrates the new PS100 sander to several team members. Cross-divisional teams solve potential problems before they arise. Thanks to team cooperation, new-product projects now sail smoothly through the various phases of the new-product design cycle.

Thanks largely to an innovative use of team concepts, Snap-on Tools Corp. has regained its momentum with a higher percentage of sales coming from new products.

Source: Joyce Hoffman, editor, "Reflections," vol. 10, 1989, 12–15. Used by permission.

It normally took 3 days to ship parts, but customers needed them within 24 hours. The president decided to create a cross-functional team to tackle this problem. Within a month, the team had 90 percent of the parts going out in 24 hours, compared with 25 percent previously. In the third month, 100 percent of parts were going out within 24 hours. This success created the groundwork for using teams for other problems.[27]

permanent team A group of participants from several functions that are permanently assigned to solve ongoing problems of common interest.

Permanent teams are brought together as a formal department in the organization. Instead of just working together, employees are placed in the same location and report to the same supervisor. In some organizations, permanent teams start at the top with what is called the Office of the Chairman, or the Office of the President. For example, National City Corporation, a huge bank holding company headquartered in Cleveland, uses the concept called Office of the Chairman. The chairman, president, and two deputy chairmen brainstorm about problems and make decisions jointly, thereby incorporating a wide range of issues and opportunities. This approach at the top also signals the importance of teamwork to the rest of the organization.[28]

At lower organization levels, the permanent-team approach resembles the divisional approach described earlier, except that teams are much smaller. Teams may consist of only 20 to 30 members, each bringing a functional specialty to the team. For example, Kollmorgen Corporation, a manufacturer of electronic circuitry and other goods, divided its organization into teams that average 75 employees.[29] Even at this size employees think of themselves as a team. Performance jumped dramatically after Kollmorgen shifted to this con-

How does Colgate achieve flexibility and responsiveness to the competitive global environment? One answer is the *team approach,* as illustrated by this multi-country task force used to seek cooperation of European dishwasher manufacturers with the use of Colgate's new dishwasher liquids. Dishwasher liquids are a new product competing directly with traditional powders. Since the initial launch in the U.S. in mid-1986, Colgate's dishwasher liquids have become established in 8 countries, representing 90 percent of world demand. In each of these markets, Colgate holds leadership position within the growing liquid segment, thanks in large part to the cooperation achieved through multi-country, cross-functional teamwork.

cept. Union Carbide is shifting to a team approach within its plants. First-line supervisors have been replaced with an elected hourly worker who is the team leader.[30]

One dramatic example of reorganizing into permanent teams occurred at an old-line insurance company called Aid Association for Lutherans (AAL).

AID ASSOCIATION FOR LUTHERANS • AAL's traditional organization structure consisted of three functional departments with employees specialized to handle health insurance, life insurance, or support services as illustrated in part (a) of Exhibit 9.13. This structure seemed efficient, but policyholder inquiries often were passed among several departments and then back again. For example, a request to use the cash value of a life policy to pay the premiums for health insurance would bounce through all sections, taking at least 21 days. Coordination across sections took additional time when misunderstandings arose.

Top managers decided to risk everything on a team approach. At precisely 12 noon, nearly 500 clerks, technicians, and managers wheeled their chairs to new locations, becoming part of 25-person teams. The new structure is illustrated in part (b) of Exhibit 9.13. Each section consists of three to four teams that serve a region of the country. Each team has specialists who can do any of the 167 tasks required for policyholder sales and service. The request to pay health insurance premiums with life insurance cash value now is handled in five days. Productivity is up 20 percent and case-processing time has been reduced by as much as 75 percent. Administrative overhead is way down, because teams need little supervision. A total of 55 middle management jobs were eliminated as the teams took over self-management responsibility. AAL now handles 10 percent more transactions of all kinds, with 10 percent fewer employees thanks to the team concept.[31]

Ford Motor Company uses an *Office of the Chief Executive* to signal the team approach and the importance of teamwork to the rest of the organization. Ford's team at the top, which includes, from left, Philip E. Benton, Jr., Stanley A. Seneker, Harold A. Poling, and Allan D. Gilmour, is the starting point for excellent performance, respect, and communication throughout Ford's people-oriented culture. The spirit of involvement characterized by both permanent and temporary teams is the source of Ford's competitive strength.

ADVANTAGES AND DISADVANTAGES. Designing team relationships often helps overcome shortcomings in a functional top-down approach to organizing. With cross-functional teams, the organization is able to retain some advantages of a functional structure, such as economies of scale and in-depth training, while gaining the benefits of team relationships. The team concept breaks down barriers across departments. Team members know one another's problems and will compromise rather than blindly pursue their own goals. The team concept also allows the organization to more quickly adapt to customer requests and environmental changes, and speeds decision making because decisions need not go to the top of the hierarchy for approval. Another big advantage is the morale boost. Employees are enthusiastic about their involvement in bigger projects rather than narrow departmental tasks. Jobs are enriched. The final advantage is reduced administrative overhead. The creation of teams enables responsibility and authority to be pushed down the hierarchy, requiring fewer managers for supervision.

But the team approach also has disadvantages. Employees may be enthusiastic about team participation, but they may also experience conflicts and dual loyalties. A cross-functional team may make different demands on members than their department managers, and members who participate in more than one team must resolve these conflicts. A large amount of time is devoted to meetings, thus increasing coordination time. Unless the organization truly needs teams to coordinate complex projects and adapt to the environment, it

EXHIBIT 9.13
The Team Structure at AAL

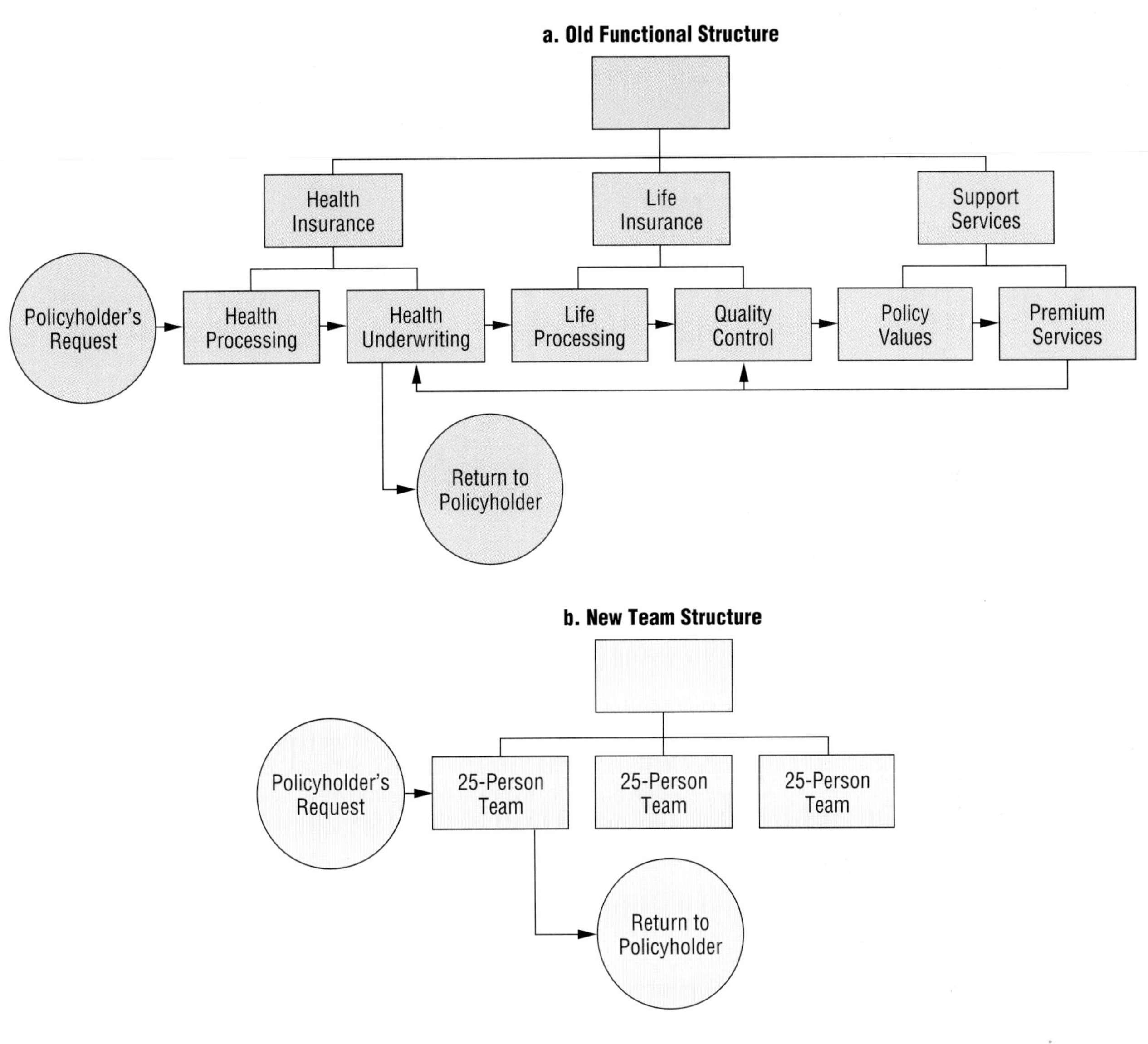

Source: Based on John Hoerr, "Work Teams Can Rev Up Paper-Pushers, Too," *Business Week*, November 28, 1988, 64–72.

will lose production efficiency. Finally, the team approach may cause too much decentralization. Senior department managers who traditionally made decisions may feel left out when a team moves ahead on its own. Team members often do not see the big picture of the corporation and may make decisions that are good for their group but bad for the organization as a whole. Top management can help keep the team in alignment with corporate goals.

EXHIBIT 9.14
Advantages and Disadvantages of Team Structure

Advantages	Disadvantages
• Some advantages of functional structure	• Dual loyalties and conflict
• Reduced barriers among departments, greater compromise	• Time and resources spent on meetings
• Less response time, quicker decisions	• Unplanned decentralization
• Better morale, enthusiasm from employee involvement	
• Reduced administrative overhead	

The advantages and disadvantages of the team structure are summarized in Exhibit 9.14.

NETWORK APPROACH

network structure
An organizational structure that disaggregates major functions into separate companies that are brokered by a small headquarters organization.

The newest approach to departmentalization has been called a "dynamic network" organization.[32] The **network structure** means that the organization disaggregates major functions into separate companies that are brokered by a small headquarters organization. Rather than manufacturing, engineering, sales, and accounting being housed under one roof, these services are provided by separate organizations working under contract and connected electronically to the central office.[33] An illustration of a hypothetical network organization is shown in Exhibit 9.15.

The network approach is revolutionary because it is difficult to answer the question, "Where is the organization?" in traditional terms. For example, a firm may contract for expensive services such as training, transportation, legal, and engineering, so these functions are no longer part of the organization. Or consider a piece of ice hockey equipment that is designed in Scandinavia, engineered in the U.S., manufactured in Korea, and distributed in Canada by a

EXHIBIT 9.15
Network Approach to Departmentalization

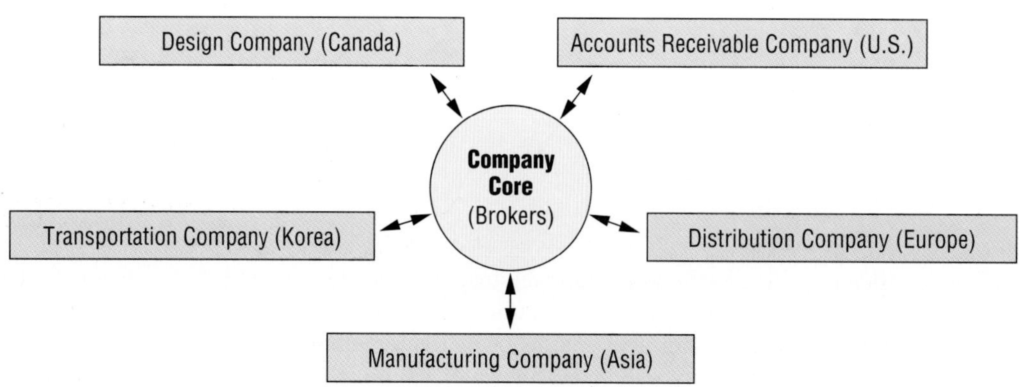

EXHIBIT 9.16
Advantages and Disadvantages of Network Structure

Advantages	Disadvantages
• Global competitiveness	• No hands-on control
• Work-force flexibility/challenge	• Can lose organizational part
• Reduced administrative overhead	• Employee loyalty weakened

Japanese sales organization. These pieces are drawn together contractually and coordinated electronically, creating a new form of organization.

This organizational approach is especially powerful for international operations. For example, Schwinn Bicycle Company went to a network structure, importing bicycles manufactured in Asia and distributing them through independent dealers who are coordinated electronically. Lewis Galoob Toys, Inc., sold $58 million worth of toys with only 115 employees. Galoob farms out manufacturing and packaging to contractors in Hong Kong, toy design to independent inventors, and sales to independent distribution representatives. Galoob never touches a product and does not even collect the money. The company is held together with phones, telexes, and other electronic technology.

ADVANTAGES AND DISADVANTAGES. The network approach to organizing is still new, but the biggest advantage to date seems to be competitiveness on a global scale. Network organizations, even small ones, can be truly global. A network organization can draw on resources worldwide to achieve the best quality and price and can sell its products and services worldwide. A second advantage is work-force flexibility and challenge. Flexibility comes from the ability to hire whatever services are needed, such as engineering design or maintenance, and to change a few months later without constraints from owning plant, equipment, and facilities. The organization can continually redefine itself to fit new products and market opportunities. For those employees who are a permanent part of the organization, the challenge comes from greater job variety and job satisfaction from working within the lean structure. Finally, this structure is perhaps the leanest of all organizational forms. Administrative overhead is small because little supervision is required. Large teams of staff specialists and administrators are not needed. A network organization may have only two or three levels of hierarchy compared with ten or more in traditional organizations.[34] These advantages, along with the disadvantages, of a network structure are summarized in Exhibit 9.16.

This computer-generated image illustrates the *network structure* through which Safeguard Scientifics Inc. achieves connections with and among its partnership companies. The network connections contribute to the sales and growth of each small company, with some serving as distribution channels for other partnership companies and others sharing new technologies and resources. Networking is what Safeguard is about. The network structure produces daily conversations among partnership companies that create innovations in software, graphics, laser communications, and computer furniture and systems.

One of the major disadvantages is lack of hands-on control. Managers do not have all operations under one roof and must rely on contracts, coordination, negotiation, and electronic messages to hold things together. A problem of equal importance is the possibility of losing an organizational part. If a subcontractor fails to deliver, goes out of business, or has a plant burn down, the headquarters organization can be put out of business. Uncertainty is higher because necessary services are not under one roof and under direct management control. Finally, in this type of organization employee loyalty can weaken. Employees may feel they can be replaced by contract services. A cohesive corporate culture is less likely to develop, and turnover tends to be higher because emotional commitment between organization and employee is weak. With changing products and markets, the organization may need to reshuffle employees at any time to acquire the correct mix of skills.

SUMMARY

This chapter introduced a number of important organizing concepts. Fundamental characteristics of organization structure include work specialization, chain of command, authority and responsibility, span of management, centralization and decentralization, administrative overhead, and formalization. These dimensions of organization represent the vertical hierarchy and indicate how authority and responsibility are distributed along the hierarchy.

The other major concept is departmentalization, which describes how organization employees are grouped. Three traditional approaches are functional, divisional, and matrix, and contemporary approaches are team and network structures. The functional approach groups employees by common skills and tasks. The opposite structure is divisional, which groups people by organizational output such that each division has a mix of functional skills and tasks. The matrix structure uses two chains of command simultaneously, one for functions and one for divisions, and some employees have two bosses. The team approach uses cross-functional teams and permanent teams to achieve better coordination and employee commitment than is possible with a pure functional structure. The network approach represents the newest form of organizational structure. Departmental tasks are subcontracted to other organizations, so the central organization is simply a broker that coordinates several independent organizations to accomplish its goal. Each organizational form has advantages and disadvantages and can be used by managers to meet the needs of the competitive situation.

MANAGEMENT SOLUTION

The Albany Ladder Company in Albany, New York, is a small supplier of equipment to local contractors. Credit and sales were separate functional departments that were in conflict because excellent credit performance meant reduced sales, and increased sales often meant accepting poor credit risks. President Lester J. Heath III attacked this problem by combining sales and credit into a single department, forming a permanent team of the credit and sales managers. The team's goal was to increase sales and market share without undue risk to the company.

The results have been quite extraordinary. Credit manager James Ullery *helps* make sales. Letters are mailed to new businesses inviting potential customers to come in and apply for credit. Albany Ladder makes many of its own loans, collecting a nice contribution to profits from its 24 percent lending rate. Bad debt is about 1.3 percent of sales, nearly double the industry average. But everyone is happy because the increased risk enables Albany Ladder to expand market share and profit. As part of a marketing team, the credit manager is concerned with sales and market share, not bad debt. The credit function works hard to help marginal customers pay their bills. Outstanding bills come up on the computer each month, and the credit team works the telephones to keep payments current. A few deadbeats get away without paying, but very few potential customers walk away without purchases because they cannot get credit. The new credit approach is to seek out creditworthy customers and to make loans to marginal customers that increase profits for Albany Ladder. The team approach to structure paid off.[35]

DISCUSSION QUESTIONS

1. Sonny Holt, manager of Electronics Assembly, asks Hector Cruz, his senior technician, to handle things in the department while Sonny worked on the budget. Sonny needed peace and quiet for at least a week to complete his figures. After ten days, Sonny discovered that Hector had hired a senior secretary, not realizing that Sonny had promised interviews to two other people. Evaluate Sonny's approach to delegation.
2. Many experts note that organizations have been making greater use of teams in recent years. What factors might account for this trend?
3. Contrast centralization with span of management. Would you expect these characteristics to affect one another in organizations? Why?
4. An organizational consultant was heard to say, "Some aspect of functional structure appears in every organization." Do you agree? Explain.
5. The divisional structure is often considered almost the opposite of a functional structure. Do you agree? Briefly explain the major differences in these two approaches to departmentalization.
6. What are important skills for matrix bosses and two-boss employees in a matrix organization?
7. Some people argue that the matrix structure should be adopted only as a last resort because the dual chains of command can create more problems than they solve. Do you agree or disagree? Why?
8. What is the network approach to structure? Is the use of authority and responsibility different compared with other forms of departmentalization? Explain.
9. Why are divisional structures frequently used in large corporations? Does it make sense for a huge corporation such as American Airlines to stay in a functional structure?
10. Crane Plastics Inc. was described in the chapter as having a matrix structure. One observer argued that this is a variation of the team approach. Are the matrix and team approaches to structure similar?

MANAGEMENT IN PRACTICE: ETHICAL DILEMMA

Quality Control Supervision

Jane was an engineer in the quality control department of a new manufacturing plant. She used to work under Ed, the head of quality control, who in turn reported to the vice-president of manufacturing. Jane is a college graduate and learned a lot from Ed, who has worked in manufacturing for 32 years.

One of Jane's responsibilities was to measure the chemical concentrations in the plant's waste water and sign the monthly reports sent to city officials certifying that the concentrations are below dangerous levels. She recently decided to switch to a newer test that is more reliable and less expensive and discovered that the actual concentrations of pollutants are above mandated levels.

Jane showed the new results to Ed, who agreed the situation was serious. However, the vice-president of manufacturing did not agree. After many arguments between Ed and the vice-president, Ed was found overqualified for his job and was transferred to another plant. The vice-president of manufacturing reinstituted the old test.

Jane is now head of quality control. The plant just received an exclusive contract that will cause production to double in two years. The chemical concentrations keep rising. The vice-president of manufacturing tells Jane that when concentrations become too high as measured by the old test, they will add more water to dilute the waste.

What Do You Do?

1. Obey the vice-president of manufacturing. He has ultimate authority and responsibility for this task.
2. Confront the vice-president of manufacturing and argue the case for better control of pollutants, being prepared to lose your job if necessary.
3. Blow the whistle on the company by taking test results to city officials and the press. This will protect you and force the company to adhere to the tests.

CASES FOR ANALYSIS

TENNESSEE MANUFACTURING

Norma Franklin has been with Tennessee Manufacturing for eight years. Norma is a graphics technician in the engineering drafting department, developing slides and other visual aids for company presentations. Tennessee Manufacturing is expanding at a rapid rate, and its new emphasis is on innovation. With the introduction of a matrix structure, Norma found herself working for two managers. In addition to working for Tim Hendricks, manager of drafting, she now also works for Rick Wilson, who is responsible for the development of a new line of plastic products. Norma is part of a plastic products team that meets twice weekly with Rick.

Norma noticed an immediate increase in her work load. Her new boss gave her frequent assignments at the last minute, needing excellent graphics for presentations to senior management and potential customers about the new plastics line. Meanwhile Tim Hendricks took it for granted that Norma would be able to complete her normal work load in the graphics department. After two months, the heavy work load began to wear on Norma. Her performance review was due, during which Tim explained he was giving her an average rating. "Your attitude has been poor, and you are not turning out the work the way you used to," he said.

Norma exploded. "You don't seem to realize my work load has doubled since this matrix structure thing started. Between you and Rick I have been run ragged, and you have the nerve to tell me I am only doing average work. I'm doing the work of two people. You seem to think the work I do for Rick shouldn't affect the work I do for you, but I've had to stay late almost every night for the past month."

"Norma," Tim said, "I'm sorry, but the work needs to go out, and we can't get another graphics technician. Your work has not been as good as before, and I have to rate you strictly on your performance."

Questions

1. Did Tim Hendricks handle this situation correctly? As a matrix boss, what is his responsibility toward Norma?
2. What should Norma do in this situation to manage her work load?
3. How would you evaluate the implementation of this matrix structure?

Source: Based on Grace Lander, "Double Duty," *Supervisory Management* (February 1989), 44–45.

TUCKER COMPANY

In 1978 the Tucker Company underwent an extensive reorganization that divided the company into three major divisions. These new divisions represented Tucker's three principal product lines. Mr. Harnett, Tucker's president, explained the basis for the new organization in a memo to the board of directors as follows:

> The diversity of our products requires that we reorganize along our major product lines. Toward this end I have established three new divisions: commercial jet engines, military jet engines, and utility turbines. Each division will be headed by a new vice-president who will report directly to me. I believe that this new approach will enhance our performance through the commitment of individual managers. It should also help us to identify unprofitable areas where the special attention of management may be required.
>
> For the most part, each division will be able to operate independently. That is, each will have its own engineering, manufacturing, accounting departments, etc. In some cases, however, it will be necessary for a division to utilize the services of other divisions or departments. This is necessary because the complete servicing with individual divisional staffs would result in unjustifiable additional staffing and facilities.

The old companywide laboratory was one such service department. Functionally it continued to support all of the major divisions. Administratively, however, the manager of the laboratory reported to the manager of manufacturing in the military jet engine division.

From the time the new organization was initiated until February of 1988, when the laboratory manager Mr. Garfield retired, there was little evidence of interdepartmental or interdivisional conflict. His replacement, Mr. Hodge, unlike Mr. Garfield, was always eager to gain the attention of management. Many of Hodge's peers perceived him as an empire builder who was interested in his own advancement rather than the company's well-being. After about six months in the new position, Hodge became involved in several interdepartmental conflicts over work that was being conducted in his laboratory.

Historically, the engineering departments had used the laboratory as a testing facility to determine the properties of materials selected by the design engineers. Hodge felt that the laboratory should be more involved in the selection of these materials and in the design of experiments and subsequent evaluations of the experimental data. Hodge discussed this with Mr. Franklin of the engineering department of the utility turbine division. Franklin offered to consult with Hodge but stated that the final responsibility for the selection of materials was charged to his department.

In the months that followed, Hodge and Franklin had several disagreements over the implementation of the results. Franklin told Hodge that, because of his position at the testing lab, he was unable to appreciate the detailed design considerations that affected the final decision on materials selection. Hodge claimed that Franklin lacked the materials expertise that he, as a metallurgist, had.

Franklin also noted that the prompt handling of his requests, which he had become accustomed to under Garfield's management, began to take longer and longer under Hodge's management. Hodge explained that military jet engine divisional problems had to be assigned first priority because of his administrative reporting structure. He also told Franklin that if he were more involved in Franklin's problems, he could perhaps appreciate when a true sense of urgency existed and he could revise priorities.

The tensions between Franklin and Hodge reached a peak when one of Franklin's critical projects failed to receive the scheduling that he considered necessary. Franklin phoned Hodge to discuss the need for a schedule change. Hodge suggested that they have a meeting to review the need for the work. Franklin then told Hodge that this was not a matter of his concern and that his function was merely to perform the tests as requested. He further stated that he was not satisfied with the low priority rating that his division's work received. Hodge reminded Franklin that when Hodge had suggested a means for resolving this problem, Franklin was not receptive. At this point, Franklin lost his temper and hung up on Hodge.

Questions

1. Sketch out a simple organization chart showing Tucker Company's three divisions, including the location of the laboratory. Why would the laboratory be located in the military jet engine division?
2. Analyze the conflict between Mr. Hodge and Mr. Franklin. Do you think the conflict is based on personalities or on the way in which the organization is structured?
3. Sketch out a new organization chart showing how you would restructure Tucker Company so that the laboratory would provide equal services to all divisions. What advantages and disadvantages do you see in the new structure compared with the previous one?

CHAPTER 10

USING STRUCTURAL DESIGN TO ACHIEVE STRATEGIC OBJECTIVES

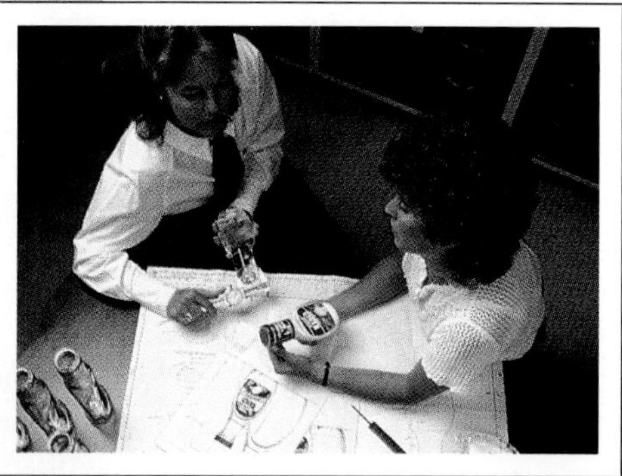

CHAPTER OUTLINE

Coordination

Information Systems
Task Forces and Teams
Integrating Managers

Loose versus Tight Organization Structure

Factors Affecting Structure

Contingency Factor: Strategic Objectives
Contingency Factor: The Environment
Contingency Factor: Size and Life Cycle
Contingency Factor: Manufacturing and Service Technologies
Contingency Factor: Departmental Interdependence

LEARNING OBJECTIVES

After studying this chapter, you should be able to:

- Explain why organizations need coordination across departments and hierarchical levels.
- Describe mechanisms for achieving coordination and when they may be applied.
- Describe how structure can be used to achieve an organization's strategic objectives.
- Describe how organization structure can be designed to fit environmental uncertainty.
- Describe four stages of the organizational life cycle and explain how size and life cycle influence the correct structure.
- Define production technology (manufacturing and service) and explain how it influences organization structure.
- Explain the types of departmental interdependence and how structure can be used to accommodate them.

Management Problem

For years Troxel Manufacturing Company was the world's largest manufacturer of bicycle seats. Then because of aggressive actions by competitors and reduced market share, the company diversified, adding tubular steel manufacturing and plastic molding operations in a separate division. The Tubing Division remained relatively independent of the Consumer Products Division, with its own purchasing, scheduling, and sales departments. Despite the new division, top management was dissatisfied with Troxel's financial performance. Overhead costs were mounting, and a psychological wall grew up between the two divisions. There was a lack of communication and teamwork, and employees seemed resistant to change.[1]

If you were a senior executive at Troxel Manufacturing, how would you respond? How would you redesign the organization to increase cooperation, reduce overhead, and facilitate change?

Managers in companies like Troxel frequently must rethink structure and may reorganize to meet new conditions in the environment, production technology, or size. In Chapter 9 we examined the fundamentals of structure that apply to all organizations. In this chapter we focus more precisely on structure as a tool, especially on how managers can use such concepts as departmentalization and chain of command to achieve specific goals. In recent years many corporations, including American Express, Apple, IBM, Amex Corporation, and Bausch & Lomb, have realigned departmental groupings, chains of command, and teams and task forces to attain new strategic goals. Structure is a powerful tool for reaching strategic goals, and a strategy's success often is determined by its fit with organization structure. By the end of this chapter, the problem at Troxel will be readily identifiable as a mismatch of structure and Troxel's competitive situation.

EXHIBIT 10.1
Example of a Position Created to Deal with Environment and Strategy

Source: Courtesy of Korbel Champagne Cellars.

DIRECTOR OF ROMANCE

Korbel Champagne Cellars, California-based producer of America's best-selling premium champagne, seeks dynamic individual for one-of-a-kind corporate position as Director of Romance for the winery's Department of Romance, Weddings & Entertaining. Position involves:

- reporting to media on lighthearted romance surveys commissioned by Korbel
- researching the latest news and information on the romance front
- writing articles on romance-related subjects
- appearing on television and radio programs to discuss the subject of romance

Ideal candidate will have published books or articles on the subject of romance, possess a degree in a related field such as psychology and/or personify romance in some highly visible or glamorous way. Previous media experience preferred. Individuals and spokesperson search firm applicants welcome. No phone calls please. An equal opportunity employer. Send resume to:

FRANK DE FALCO
KORBEL CHAMPAGNE CELLARS
13250 RIVER ROAD
GUERNEVILLE, CA 95446

COORDINATION

As organizations grow and evolve, two things happen. First, new positions and departments are added to deal with factors in the external environment or with new strategic needs.[2] For example, Raytheon established a new-products center to facilitate innovation in its various divisions. Korbel Champagne Cellars created a Department of Romance, Weddings, and Entertaining to enhance the linkage between romance and champagne consumption among potential customers. Exhibit 10.1 shows a recent ad for Korbel's Director of Romance that generated more than 800 applications.[3] Comerica created a position of corporate quality manager to form a department that would be responsible for Comerica's "Managing Total Quality" program. Employees in this new department help people understand and implement the quality process within their area. The Fiber Glass group of Manville Corporation created a "Growth Department." This department concentrates on activities that help the division grow, such as developing partnerships worldwide for applying the division's unique technology and production equipment. Over time, companies can become incredibly complex, with hundreds of positions and departments scattered around the world.

Second, senior managers have to find a way to tie all of these departments together. The formal chain of command and the supervision it provides is effective, but it is not enough. The organization needs systems to process information and enable communication among people in different departments and

Dyansen Corporation's rapid growth in number of galleries and art sales has led to *new positions and departments.* A vice-president of human resources, chief financial officer, MIS director, vice-president of sales, and an in-house marketing and advertising department all have been added to Dyansen's functional structure. These new tasks deal with needs both within the company and in the external environment. The new positions will provide better use of financial resources and selection of locations for its galleries. The gallery shown here recently opened in the spectacular Hyatt Regency Waikoloa in Hawaii. The expanding structure has helped Dyansen achieve a growth rate and a sales rate above the art retailing industry.

at different levels. **Coordination** refers to the quality of collaboration across departments. Without coordination, a company's left hand will not act in concert with the right hand, causing problems and conflicts. Coordination is required regardless of whether the organization has a functional, divisional, or team structure. Employees identify with their immediate department or team, taking its interest to heart, and may not want to compromise with other units for the good of the organization as a whole.

coordination The quality of collaboration across departments.

Without a major effort at coordination, an organization may act like Chrysler Corporation when Lee Iacocca took over:

> What I found at Chrysler were thirty-five vice presidents, each with his own turf. . . . I couldn't believe, for example, that the guy running engineering departments wasn't in constant touch with his counterpart in manufacturing. But that's how it was. Everybody worked independently. I took one look at that system and I almost threw up. That's when I knew I was in really deep trouble.
>
> I'd call in a guy from engineering, and he'd stand there dumbfounded when I'd explain to him that we had a design problem or some other hitch in the engineering-manufacturing relationship. He might have the ability to invent a brilliant piece of engineering that would save us a lot of money. He might come up with a terrific new design. There was only one problem: he didn't know that the manufacturing people couldn't build it. Why? Because he had never talked to them about it. Nobody at Chrysler seemed to understand that interaction among the different functions in a company is absolutely critical. People in engineering and manufacturing almost have to be sleeping together. These guys weren't even flirting![4]

How can managers ensure that coordination will take place? Coordination is the outcome of information and cooperation. Managers can design systems and structures to promote communication. The most important methods for achieving coordination are information systems, task forces and teams, and integrating managers.

Dow Corning's warehouse area in Mississauga, Canada, is operating more efficiently thanks to an Inter-America Area task force that recommends better inventory management methods. By consolidating individual efforts into teams and task forces, successful employee performances become great performances. This *cross-functional task force* saved $1 million by optimizing inventory storage methods, reinforcing Dow Corning's belief that ideas become solutions when committed employees team up for success.

INFORMATION SYSTEMS

Information systems are the written and electronically based internal systems for processing data and information among employees. Information systems include memos, bulletins, and written reports, as well as technological systems such as computers, electronic mail, electronic bulletin boards, and teleconferences. Electronic systems have the capacity to process enormous volumes of data across hierarchical levels and departments, thereby enabling greater coordination.

An effective use of information systems for vertical coordination is the customer attitude surveys performed by Ford and other auto manufacturers. All car buyers are surveyed about a month after purchase, and again a year later, to find out how they were treated by dealers. The compiled data is an information tool that helps the manufacturer and dealers pinpoint problems and ultimately win steady customers.[5] Another application of information systems for coordination was used in the Air Force. A base commander used a portable radio network to link all senior officers. Each officer could overhear conversations among other officers and thus was kept informed of ongoing events.

TASK FORCES AND TEAMS

A **task force** is a temporary team or committee designed to solve a short-run problem involving several departments.[6] Task force members represent their departments and share information that enables coordination.

For example, the Shawmat National Corporation created two task forces in the human resources department to consolidate all employment services into a single area. The task force looked at job banks, referral programs, employment procedures, and applicant tracking systems; found ways to perform these functions for all Shawmat's divisions in one human resource department; and then disbanded.[7] General Motors uses task forces to solve temporary problems in its manufacturing plants. When a shipment of car doors arrived from a fabricating plant with surface imperfections, the plant manager immediately created a task force to solve the problem: "I got the vice president of manufacturing — who is my boss — the plant manager of the stamping plant, the dye engineers, the quality engineers, the United Auto Workers representatives from both plants, the Olds guy from Lansing, a Cadillac guy, and the Fisher Body guy from the Tech Center. So I had everybody right out there on the floor looking at the exact part that is giving us the problem, and the problem was resolved in about two hours."[8]

In addition to creating task forces, companies also set up teams. As used for coordination, a **team** is a group of participants from several departments who meet regularly to solve ongoing problems of common interest.[9] The permanent team is similar to a task force except that it works with continuing rather than temporary problems and may exist for several years. Teams used for coordination are similar to the cross-functional teams described in Chapter 9. For example, PLY GEM, a national manufacturer of home improvement products, has eight operating divisions. To coordinate technology, marketing, and operations skills, an Executive Management Committee consisting of each division president was created. Chemical Bank created a team of consumer

information system A written or electronic internal system for processing data and information among employees.

task force A temporary team or committee formed to solve a specific short-run problem involving several departments.

team A group of participants from several departments who meet regularly to solve ongoing problems of common interest.

EXHIBIT 10.2
Example of Integrating Manager Relationships to Other Departments

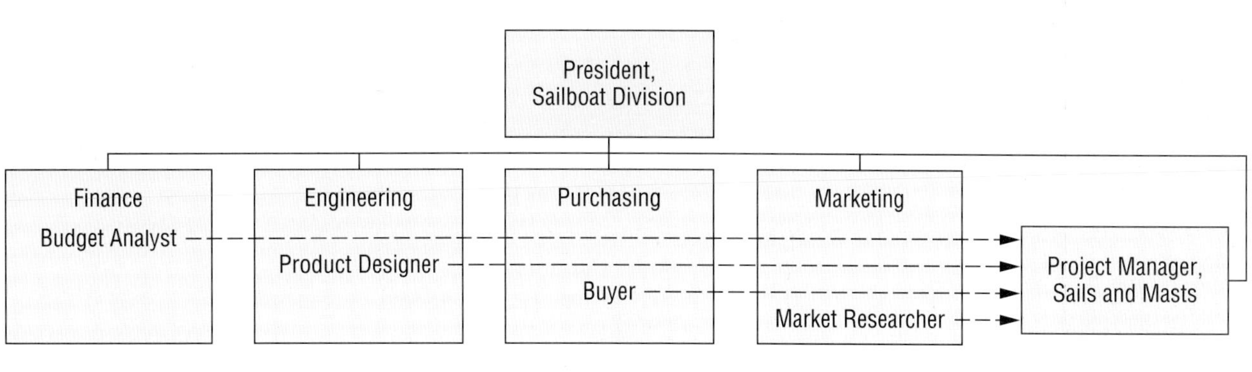

banking specialists to devise a unified management system for all of Chemical's suburban branches. The team develops and implements management techniques that involve customer flow management and teller scheduling that make all branches more efficient.[10]

INTEGRATING MANAGERS

An **integrating manager** is a person in a full-time position created for the purpose of coordinating the activities of several departments.[11] The distinctive feature of the integrating position is that the person is not a member of one of the departments being coordinated. These positions often have titles such as product manager, project manager, program manager, or branch manager. The coordinator is assigned to coordinate departments on a full-time basis to achieve desired project or product outcomes.

integrating manager
An individual responsible for coordinating the activities of several departments on a full-time basis to achieve specific project or product outcomes.

General Mills, Procter & Gamble, and General Foods all use product managers to coordinate their product lines. A manager is assigned to each line, such as Cheerios, Bisquick, and Hamburger Helper. Product managers set budget goals, marketing targets, and strategies and obtain the cooperation from advertising, production, and sales personnel needed for implementing product strategy.

In some organizations project managers are included on the organization chart, as illustrated in Exhibit 10.2. The project manager is drawn to one side of the chart to indicate authority over the project but not over the people assigned to it. Dashed lines to the project manager indicate responsibility for coordination and communication with assigned team members, but department managers retain line authority over functional employees.

An interesting variation of the integrator role was developed at Florida Power & Light Company. To keep the construction of a nuclear power plant on schedule, several project managers were assigned the role of "Mothers." The philosophy of the person in charge was, "If you want something to happen, it has to have a mother." The Mothers could nurture their projects to timely

EXHIBIT 10.3
Differences in Mechanistic versus Organic Organizations

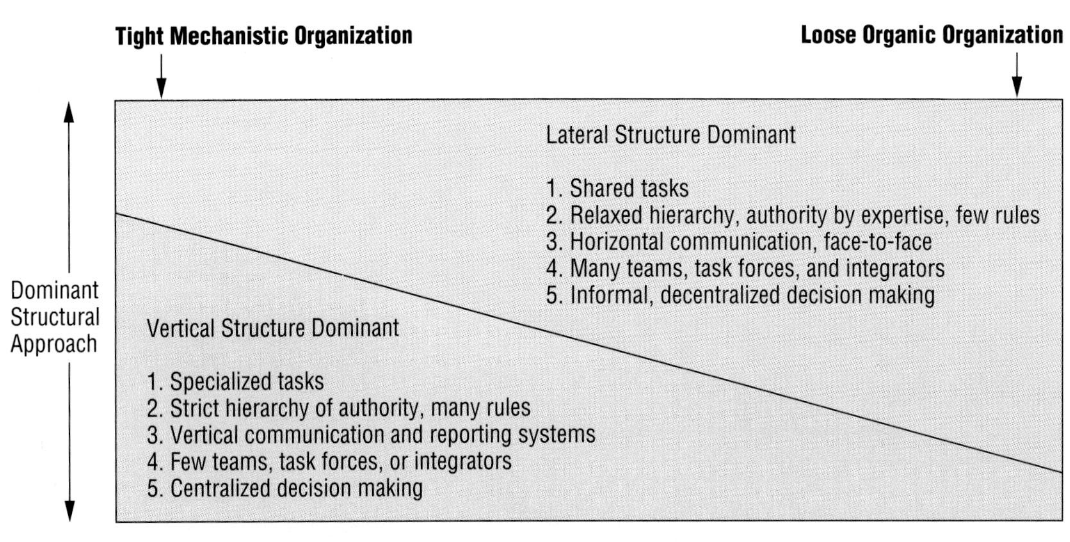

completion. This unusual label worked. Although departmental employees did not report directly to a Mother, the Mothers had a great deal of responsibility, which encouraged departmental managers to listen and cooperate.[12]

Loose versus Tight Organization Structure

Recall that the purpose of structure is to organize resources to accomplish organizational goals. Elements of structure such as chain of command, centralization/decentralization, formal authority, teams, and coordination devices fit together to form an overall structural approach. In some organizations the formal, vertical hierarchy is emphasized as the way to achieve control and coordination. In other organizations decision making is decentralized, cross-functional teams are implemented, and employees are given great freedom to pursue their tasks as they see fit. In many organizations a trade-off occurs, because an emphasis on vertical structure means less opportunity for horizontal coordination, and vice versa.

The balance between vertical and lateral structure is similar to the concepts of mechanistic and organic organizations introduced in Chapter 3.[13] When the vertical structure is very tight, the organization is *mechanistic*. The organization emphasizes vertical control. Tasks are broken into routine jobs and are rigidly defined. Voluminous rules exist, and the hierarchy of authority is the major form of control. Decision making is centralized, and communication

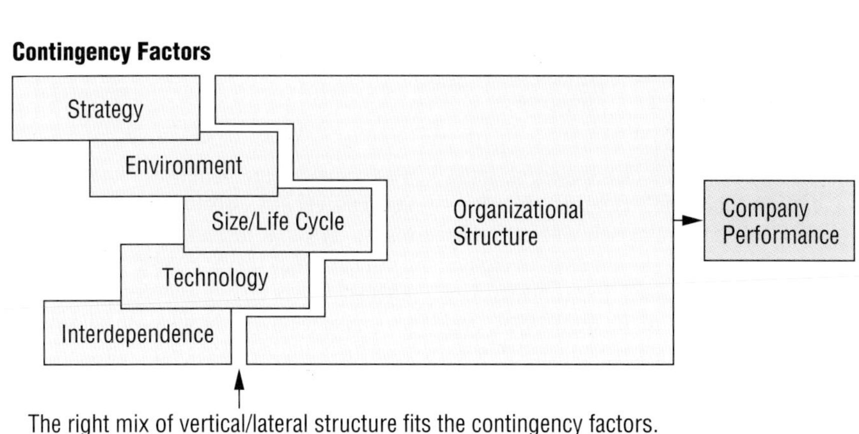

EXHIBIT 10.4
Contingency Factors That Influence Organization Structure

is vertical. When lateral structures dominate, the organization is *organic.* The organization is loosely structured. Tasks are frequently redefined to fit employee and environmental needs. There are few rules, and authority is based on expertise rather than the hierarchy. Decision making is decentralized. Communication is horizontal and is facilitated through the use of task forces, teams, and integrators. An organic organization may not have job descriptions or even an organization chart. The characteristics of mechanistic versus organic organizations are summarized in Exhibit 10.3.

FACTORS AFFECTING STRUCTURE

How do managers know whether to design a tight or loose structure? The answer lies in the contingency factors that influence organization structure. Recall from Chapter 2 that *contingency* pertains to those factors on which structure depends. Research on organization structure shows that the emphasis given to loose or tight structure depends on the contingency factors of strategy, environment, size/life cycle, production technology, and departmental interdependence. The right structure is designed to "fit" the contingency factors as illustrated in Exhibit 10.4. Let us look at the relationship between each contingency factor and organization structure in more detail to see how structure should be designed. When structure is incorrect, warning signs arise as described in the Manager's Shoptalk box.

Clorox Company's *contingency factor* is a strategy to develop new and differentiated household products to promote future growth and profit. This *differentiation strategy* utilizes Clorox's strength in research and development, manufacturing, and marketing. Teams of specialists from various company functions jointly uncover consumer needs and determine how to fill them. Clorox teams have produced 50 new products and improvements over the last five years. One of the most successful has been *Hidden Valley Ranch* bottled salad dressing. As they design the new packaging, Margi Mead (left) and Leanne Beatie consult frequently with other members of the new-product development team.

CONTINGENCY FACTOR: STRATEGIC OBJECTIVES

In Chapter 6, we discussed several strategies that business firms can adopt. Two strategies proposed by Porter are differentiation and cost leadership.[14] With a differentiation strategy, the organization attempts to develop innovative products unique to the market. With a cost leadership strategy, the organization strives for internal efficiency. The strategies of cost leadership versus

MANAGER'S SHOPTALK

STRUCTURAL WARNING SIGNS

Managers often have a difficult time knowing when to redesign the organization's structure. When structure is correct, it is hardly noticed. Structural approach, division of labor, reporting relationships, and teamwork are in alignment, and performance objectives are met. However, when organization structure is incorrect, certain symptoms appear. Some of the warning signals that a structural change may be needed are as follows:

1. *Changes are occurring in the contingency factors of strategy, production technology, environmental uncertainty, organization size, or interdependence.* These factors determine the correct structure. When they change, structure may need to be altered. A once-stable environment may suddenly shift, such as occurred when the fuel crisis hit airlines and deregulation struck banks. Adoption of a new production technology or major increases in growth also signal the need for a new structure. A new strategy, such as emphasis on production efficiency or innovation, also may require a structural change.
2. *The organization does not respond to the environment.* This occurs because coordination among departments fails to accommodate changes in products or services desired by customers, or departments for scanning, forecasting, and innovation planning may be lacking. Organizational responsiveness requires that departments have assigned responsibilities for dealing with the environment and respond as a coordinated whole.
3. *Too much conflict is evident.* Interdepartmental conflict means employees are identifying too closely with their own departments and do not see the organization's larger goals. Departments may be under pressure to reach their own goals and thus avoid cooperation with others. Departments may be out of step, and lateral relationships in the form of task forces and teams may need strengthening. Reorganization into divisional units may also help.
4. *Top management decision making is too slow and lacks quality.* Top managers may be overloaded with decisions because the hierarchy funnels too many problems to them. Structure may be too centralized. Moreover, information may not reach top managers, keeping them out of touch with operations. Likewise, if decision making is too decentralized, decisions will be fragmented and uncoordinated.
5. *Employee morale and motivation is low.* With the wrong structure, employees may have routine jobs and unclear expectations. They may perceive themselves as having little responsibility or involvement in important activities. Management decisions may appear inconsistent and arbitrary. A clearly defined structure and lateral relationships enabling employees to participate in broader activities will enhance morale.
6. *Personnel costs are too high.* Personnel costs increase when resources are duplicated across divisions or between divisions and headquarters. Perhaps several departments are hiring their own computer programmers rather than using the service available from the information systems department. Some departments may have excess personnel whereas others do not have enough people, equipment, or facilities to accomplish high-priority tasks. Personnel costs also are high when large professional staffs are created at headquarters to control divisions. If headquarters control is essential, a functional structure is more appropriate than a divisional structure.
7. *Managers are overloaded.* If managers are overloaded, responsibilities may need realignment. Spans of control may be too wide, responsibility may be too broad, and new positions or departments may be needed. Teams and task forces can also reduce overload. Support systems in the form of rules, procedures, and information systems may be needed. Decentralization also may help.
8. *Performance objectives are not being met.* Performance problems may have many causes, but structure is often a culprit. A performance deficiency may be seen in several ways: Specific targets are not being met, or managers feel the organization should be going better on a variety of dimensions. The perception of performance deficiency may be caused by employee dissatisfaction, too much conflict, slow response, low morale, or poor resource utilization. If structure is severely out of alignment with company needs, reduced performance will result.

Source: Based on John Childs, *Organization: A Guide to Problems and Practice,* 2d ed. (London: Harper & Row, 1984), Chapters 1, 10.

differentiation typically require different structural approaches, so managers try to pick strategies and structures that are congruent.

Exhibit 10.5 shows a simplified continuum that illustrates how structural approaches are associated with strategic objectives. The pure functional structure is appropriate for achieving internal efficiency goals. The functional structure uses task specialization and a strict chain of command to gain efficient use of scarce resources, but it does not enable the organization to be flexible or

EXHIBIT 10.5
Relationship of Strategic Objectives to Structural Approach

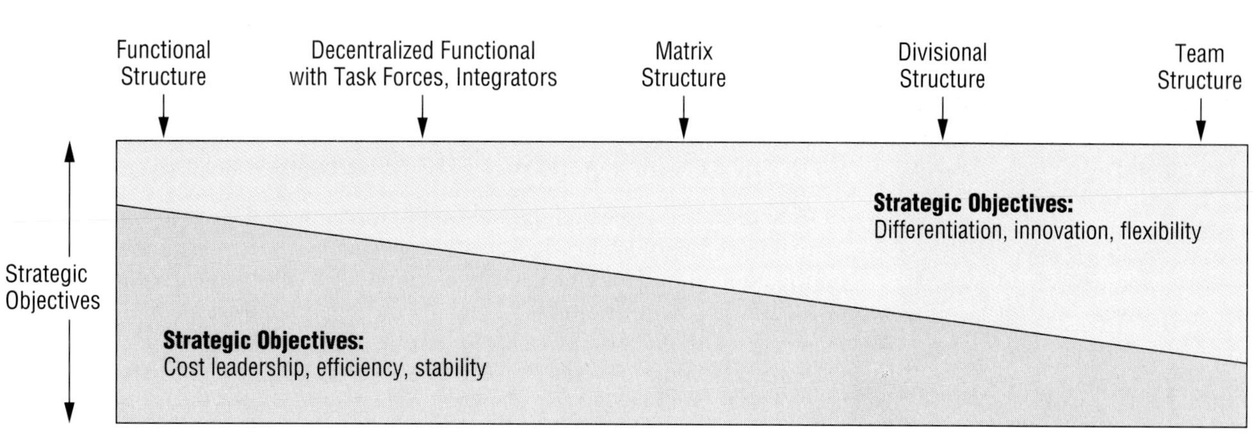

innovative. In contrast, the team structure described in Chapter 9 is appropriate when the primary goal is innovation and flexibility. Each team is small, able to be responsive, and has the people and resources necessary for performing its task. Team structure enables organizations to differentiate themselves and respond quickly to the demands of a shifting environment, but at the expense of efficient resource use.

Exhibit 10.5 also illustrates how the other forms of structure described in this chapter — decentralized with lateral coordination, matrix, and divisional — represent intermediate steps on the organization's path to efficiency and/or innovation. The functional structure with lateral teams and integrating managers provides greater coordination and flexibility than the pure functional structure. The matrix structure uses two chains of command, a functional hierarchy to promote efficiency and a product hierarchy to promote innovation and coordination. The divisional structure promotes differentiation because each division can focus on specific products and customers, although divisions tend to be larger and less flexible than small teams. Exhibit 10.5 does not include all possible structures, but it illustrates how structures can be used to facilitate the strategic objectives of cost leadership or differentiation. For example, Polaroid changed its structure as it changed its strategy.

POLAROID • Polaroid president I. M. Booth used a scale similar to Exhibit 10.5 to describe his efforts to tear down internal barriers, decentralize decisions, and achieve coordination across functional departments. He defined a structural scale of 1 to 10. A "10" is a structure made up of autonomous groups, each with its own marketing, engineering, and management departments working as a team. A "1" is a totally functional structure, with a single manufacturing division for the whole company, a single marketing division, and so on. Booth claims that Polaroid was a 1 for many years. Its departments were uncoordinated, and little things were

The vertical alignment of these Marines symbolizes the *mechanistic structure* that typifies military organizations. Military organizations emphasize vertical control. Tasks are broken into narrow, clearly defined jobs. Many rules exist, and the hierarchy of authority is a major form of control. Military organizations need a mechanistic structure because their mission is relatively stable, and they must have employee compliance when called into action.

being neglected. Booth has been trying to break up Polaroid's functional structure by creating separate divisions for three businesses: magnetics, consumer products, and industrial photography products. Booth feels that the right amount of flexibility and innovation would put Polaroid at a 6 or 7 on the structural scale but admits that it is still only a 2 or 3. He plans to continue pushing until he gets it near the high end of the scale.[15]

Contingency Factor: The Environment

In Chapter 3, we discussed the nature of environmental uncertainty. Environmental uncertainty means that decision makers have difficulty acquiring good information and predicting external changes. Uncertainty occurs when the external environment is rapidly changing and complex. An uncertain environment causes three things to happen within an organization:

1. *Greater differences occur among departments.* In an uncertain environment, each major department — marketing, manufacturing, R&D — focuses on the task and environmental sectors for which it is responsible and hence distinguishes itself from the others with respect to goals, task orientation, and time horizon.[16] Departments work autonomously. These factors create barriers among departments.
2. *The organization needs greater coordination to keep departments working together.* With greater differences, more emphasis on lateral coordination is required to link departments together and overcome differences in departmental goals and orientations.
3. *The organization must adapt to change.* The organization must maintain a flexible, responsive posture toward the environment. Changes in products and technology require cooperation among departments, which means a greater emphasis on coordination through the use of teams, task forces, and lateral information processing.[17]

The contingency relationship between environmental uncertainty and structural approach is illustrated in Exhibit 10.6. When the external environment is certain, the organization should have a mechanistic structure that emphasizes vertical control. There is little need for change, flexibility, or intense coordination. The structure can emphasize specialization, centralized decision making, wide spans of control, and low administrative overhead. When environmental uncertainty is high, an organic structure that emphasizes lateral relationships such as teams and task forces is appropriate. Vertical structure characteristics such as specialization, centralization, and formalized procedures should be downplayed. In an uncertain environment, the organization figures things out as it goes along, departments must cooperate, and decisions should be decentralized to the teams and task forces working on specific problems.

When managers use the wrong structure for the environment, reduced performance will result. A rigid, mechanistic structure in an uncertain environment prevents the organization from adapting to change. Likewise, a loose, organic structure in a stable environment is inefficient. Too many resources are devoted to meetings and discussions when employees could be more productively focused on specialized tasks.

Many companies are forced to alter their structures as the environment changes. Consider the recent reorganization at IBM.

EXHIBIT 10.6
Relationship between Environment and Structure

Environment \ Structure	Mechanistic	Organic
Uncertain (Unstable)	Incorrect Fit: Mechanistic structure in uncertain environment Structure too tight	Correct Fit: Organic structure in uncertain environment
Certain (Stable)	Correct Fit: Mechanistic structure in certain environment	Incorrect Fit: Organic structure in certain environment Structure too loose

IBM • CEO John Akers is introducing the most fundamental structural changes in the history of International Business Machines. Why? Because IBM lost sight of the customers' changing tastes. Computer users were shifting from big mainframe machines to powerful desktop models, which IBM was late to develop. Powerful new technologies eroded IBM's near-monopoly in the 1980s. Increased emphasis on software and microcomputers was also needed.

Akers's decision was to get away from the functional structure that brought most decisions to the corporate management board and replace it with seven autonomous business divisions. Within each division the new approach was to decentralize decision making and give people more freedom. Now general managers simply negotiate their annual business plans with corporate management and then are free to run their departments. The corporate management board spends two-thirds less time on monthly reports. Redefining the structure into a divisional setup has been a major step in adapting to the rapidly changing environment in the computer industry. The looser, organic structure gives IBM's 387,000 employees an opportunity to keep pace in an external market teeming with small, nimble competitors.[18]

CONTINGENCY FACTOR: SIZE AND LIFE CYCLE

The organization's **size** is its scope or magnitude and frequently is measured by number of employees. A large body of research findings has shown that large organizations are structured differently than small ones. Small organizations are informal, have little division of labor, few rules and regulations, ad hoc budgeting and performance systems, and small professional and clerical support staffs. Large organizations such as IBM necessarily have an extensive division of labor, large professional staffs, rules and regulations, and internal systems for control, rewards, and innovation.[19]

size The organization's scope or magnitude, typically measured by number of employees.

Organizations evolve from small to large by going through stages of a life cycle. Within the **organization life cycle,** organizations follow predictable

organization life cycle The organization's evolution through major developmental stages.

EXHIBIT 10.7
Structural Characteristics during Organization Life Cycle Stages

	Birth Stage	**Youth Stage**	**Midlife Stage**	**Maturity Stage**
Size	Small	Medium	Large	Very Large
Bureaucracy	Nonbureaucratic	Prebureaucratic	Bureaucratic	Very Bureaucratic
Structural characteristics:				
Division of labor	Overlapping tasks	Some departments	Many departments, well-defined tasks, organization chart	Extensive — small jobs, written job descriptions
Centralization	One-person rule	Top leaders rule	Decentralization to department heads	Enforced decentralization, top management overloaded
Formalization	No written rules	Few rules	Policy and procedures manuals	Extensive — most activities covered by written manuals
Administrative intensity	Secretary, no professional staff	Increasing clerical and maintenance, little professional staff	Increasing professional support staff	Large — multiple professional and clerical staff departments
Internal systems (information, budget, planning, performance)	Nonexistent	Crude budget and information system	Control systems in place — budget, performance, operational reports	Extensive — planning, financial, and personnel systems added
Lateral teams, task forces for coordination	None	Top leaders only	Some use of integrators and task forces	Frequent at lower levels to break down barriers of bureaucracy

Source: Based on Robert E. Quinn and Kim Cameron, "Organizational Life Cycles and Some Shifting Criteria of Effectiveness: Some Preliminary Evidence," *Management Science* 29 (1983), 31–51; Richard L. Daft and Richard M. Steers, *Organizations: A Micro/Macro Approach* (Glenview, Ill.: Scott, Foresman, 1986).

patterns through major developmental stages that are sequential in nature. This is similar to the product life cycle described in Chapter 6 except that it applies to the organization as a whole. Each stage involves changes in the range of organization activities and overall structure.[20] Every organization progresses through the life cycle at its own pace, but most encounter the four stages defined in Exhibit 10.7: birth, youth, midlife, and maturity.

birth stage The phase of the organization life cycle in which the company is created.

BIRTH STAGE. In the **birth stage,** the organization is created. The founder is an entrepreneur, who alone or with a handful of employees performs all tasks. The organization is very informal, and tasks are overlapping. There is no professional staff, no rules and regulations, and no internal systems for planning, rewards, or coordination. Decision authority is centralized with the owner. Apple Computer was in the birth stage when it was created by Steven Jobs and Stephen Wozniak in Wozniak's parents' garage. Jobs and Wozniak sold their own belongings to raise money to personally build 200 Apple computers. Kentucky Fried Chicken was in the birth stage when Colonel Harland Sanders was running a combination gas station/restaurant in Corbin, Kentucky, before the popularity of his restaurant began to spread.

The *contingency factor* of *size* and *life cycle* is illustrated by General Electric, which has about 300,000 employees. The company grew too bureaucratic, so CEO John F. Welch slashed out the second and third echelons of management and insisted on world-class businesses without bureaucratic hassle. The Lighting Division of General Electric is number one in its industry. The Lighting Division, which provided the 546 floodlights that finally made night baseball a reality at Chicago's Wrigley Field, has a distribution program called "Lighting Express" that reduces bureaucracy and speeds customer delivery.

Youth Stage. In the **youth stage,** the organization has more employees and a product that is succeeding in the marketplace. The organization is growing rapidly. The owner no longer has sole possession. A few trusted colleagues share in the decision making, although control is still relatively centralized. A division of labor is emerging, with some designation of task responsibility to newly created departments. Internal systems remain informal. A few formal rules and policies will appear, and there are few professional and administrative personnel. Apple Computer was in the youth stage during the years of rapid growth from 1978 to 1981, when the major product line was established and over 2,000 dealers signed on to sell Apple computers. Kentucky Fried Chicken was in the youth stage when Colonel Sanders convinced over 400 franchises in the United States and Canada to use his original recipe. Although both organizations were growing rapidly, they were still being run in a very informal fashion.

youth stage The phase of the organization life cycle in which the organization is growing rapidly and has a product enjoying some marketplace success.

Midlife Stage. By the **midlife stage,** the organization has prospered and grown quite large. At this point, the organization begins to look like a more formalized bureaucracy. An extensive division of labor appears, with statements of policies and responsibilities. Rules, regulations, and job descriptions are used to direct employee activities. Professional and clerical staff are hired to undertake specialized activities in support of manufacturing and marketing. Reward, budget, and accounting control systems are put in place. Top management decentralizes many responsibilities to functional departments, but flexibility and innovation may decline. Apple Computer is now well into the midlife stage because it has adopted a host of procedures, internal systems, and staff departments to provide greater control over the organization. Kentucky Fried Chicken moved into the midlife stage when Colonel Sanders sold his company to John Y. Brown, who took the company through a national promotion and building campaign.

midlife stage The phase of the organization life cycle in which the firm has reached prosperity and grown substantially large.

maturity stage The phase of the organization life cycle in which the organization has become exceedingly large and mechanistic.

MATURITY STAGE. In the **maturity stage,** the organization is large and mechanistic — indeed, the vertical structure often becomes too strong. Budgets, control systems, rules, policies, large staffs of engineering, accounting, and finance specialists, and a refined division of labor are in place. Decision making is centralized. At this point, the organization is in danger of stagnation. To offset the rigid vertical hierarchy, inspire innovation, and shrink barriers among departments, the organization may decentralize, as IBM did. To regain flexibility and innovation, managers may decentralize and design teams, task forces, and integrator positions. This is especially true for such mature organizations as Procter & Gamble, Sears, Westinghouse, Deere, and General Motors, which have experienced major changes in the external environment and found that the mature vertical structure inhibited flexible responses.

MOVING THROUGH THE LIFE CYCLE. Organizations do not progress through the four life cycle stages in a logical, orderly fashion. Stages may lead or lag in a given organization. The transition from one stage to the next is difficult and often promotes crises. Employees who were present at the organization's birth often long for the informal atmosphere and resist the formalized procedures, departmentalization, and staff departments required in maturing organizations. Organizations that prematurely emphasize a rigid vertical structure or that stay informal during later stages of the life cycle will have the wrong structure for their situation. Performance will suffer. The failure of People's Express occurred because the firm never grew up. Despite its being the fifth largest airline, top management ran it informally without a strong vertical structure. The structure fit neither People's Express' size nor life cycle stage.

CONTINGENCY FACTOR: MANUFACTURING AND SERVICE TECHNOLOGIES

technology The knowledge, tools, techniques, and activities used to transform the organization's inputs into outputs.

Technology includes the knowledge, tools, techniques, and activities used to transform organizational inputs into outputs.[21] Technology includes machinery, employee skills, and work procedures. A useful way to think about technology is as "work flow." The production work flow may be to produce steel castings, television programs, or computer software.

Production technology is significant because it has direct influence on the organization structure. Structure must be designed to fit the technology as well as to accommodate the external environment and organization size. Technologies vary between manufacturing and service organizations. In the following paragraphs, we will discuss each characteristic of technology and the structure that best fits it.

WOODWARD'S MANUFACTURING TECHNOLOGY. The most influential research into the relationship between manufacturing technology and organization structure was conducted by Joan Woodward, a British industrial sociologist.[22] She gathered data from 100 British firms to determine whether basic structural characteristics, such as administrative overhead, span of control, centralization, and formalization, were different across firms. She found that manufacturing firms could be categorized according to three basic types of work flow technology:

1. *Small batch and unit production.* **Small batch production** firms produce goods in batches of one or a few products designed to customer specification. Each customer orders a unique product. This technology also is used to make large, one-of-a-kind products, such as computer-controlled machines. Small batch manufacturing is close to traditional skilled-craft work, because human beings are a large part of the process; they run machines to make the product. Examples of small batch manufacturing include custom clothing, special-order machine tools, space capsules, satellites, and submarines.

small batch production A type of technology that involves the production of goods in batches of one or a few products designed to customer specifications.

2. *Large batch and mass production.* **Mass production** technology is distinguished by standardized production runs. A large volume of products is produced, and all customers receive the same product. Standard products go into inventory for sale as customers need them. This technology makes greater use of machines than does small batch production. Machines are designed to do most of the physical work, and employees complement the machinery. Examples of mass production are automobile assembly lines and the large batch techniques used to produce Macintosh computers, tobacco products, and textiles.

mass production A type of technology characterized by the production of a large volume of products with the same specifications.

3. *Continuous process production.* In **continuous process production,** the entire work flow is mechanized. This is the most sophisticated and complex form of production technology. Because the process runs continuously, there is no starting and stopping. Human operators are not part of actual production because machinery does all of the work. Human operators simply read dials, fix machines that break down, and manage the production process. Examples of continuous process technologies are chemical plants, distilleries, petroleum refineries, and nuclear power plants.

continuous process production A type of technology involving mechanization of the entire work flow and nonstop production.

The difference among the three manufacturing technologies is called technical complexity. **Technical complexity** means that machines are more complex and perform more of the work. With a complex technology, employees are hardly needed except to monitor the machines.

technical complexity The degree to which machinery is involved in the production process to the exclusion of people.

The structural characteristics associated with each type of manufacturing technology are illustrated in Exhibit 10.8. Note that formalization and centralization are high for mass production technology and low for continuous process. Unlike small batch and continuous process, standardized mass production machinery requires centralized decision making and well-defined rules and procedures. The administrative ratio and the percentage of indirect labor required also increase with technological complexity. Because the production process is nonroutine, closer supervision is needed. More indirect labor in the form of maintenance people is required because of the machinery's complexity; thus, the indirect–direct labor ratio is high. Span of control for first-line supervisors is greatest for mass production. On an assembly line, jobs are so routinized that a supervisor can handle an average of 48 employees. The number of employees per supervisor in small batch and continuous process production is lower because closer supervision is needed. Overall, small batch and continuous process firms have organic structures and mass production firms have mechanistic structures.

The important conclusion about manufacturing technology was described by Woodward as follows: "Different technologies impose different kinds of demands on individuals and organizations, and these demands have to be met

EXHIBIT 10.8
Relationship between Manufacturing Technology and Organization Structure

Source: Based on Joan Woodward, *Industrial Organizations: Theory and Practice* (London: Oxford University Press, 1965).

	Manufacturing Technology		
	Small Batch	**Mass Production**	**Continuous Process**
Technical complexity of production technology	Low	Medium	High
Organization structure:			
Formalization	Low	High	Low
Centralization	Low	High	Low
Top administrator ratio	Low	Medium	High
Indirect–direct labor ratio	1/9	1/4	1/1
Supervisor span of control	23	48	15
Communication:			
Written (vertical)	Low	High	Low
Verbal (lateral)	High	Low	High
Overall structure	Organic	Mechanistic	Organic

through an appropriate structure.[23] Woodward found that the relationship between structure and technology was directly related to company performance. Low-performing firms tended to deviate from the preferred structural form, often adopting a structure appropriate for another type of technology. High-performing organizations had characteristics very similar to those listed in Exhibit 10.8.

flexible manufacturing A manufacturing technology using computers to automate and integrate manufacturing components such as robots, machines, product design, and engineering analysis.

FLEXIBLE MANUFACTURING. The most recent development in manufacturing technology is called **flexible manufacturing,** which uses computers to automate and integrate manufacturing such components as robots, machines, product design, and engineering analysis. Companies such as Deere, General Motors, Intel, and Illinois Tool Works use flexible manufacturing in a single manufacturing plant to do small batch and mass production operations *at the same time.* Bar codes enable machines to make instantaneous changes — such as putting a larger screw in a different location — as different batches flow down the automated assembly line. Flexible manufacturing is considered at a higher level of technical complexity than the three manufacturing technologies studied by Woodward. The structures associated with the new technology tend to have few rules, decentralization, a small ratio of administrators to workers, face-to-face lateral communication, and a team-oriented, organic approach.[24]

service technology Technology characterized by intangible outputs and direct contact between employees and customers.

SERVICE TECHNOLOGY. Service organizations are becoming increasingly important in North America. Since 1982, more employees have been employed in service organizations than in manufacturing organizations. Thus, new research has been undertaken to understand the structural characteristics of service organizations. **Service technology** can be defined as follows:

1. *Intangibility.* The output of a service firm is intangible. Services are perishable and, unlike physical products, cannot be stored in inventory. The service is either consumed immediately or lost forever. Manufactured products are produced at one point in time and can be stored until sold at another time.

2. *Direct contact with customers.* Customers and employees interact directly to provide and purchase the service. Production and consumption are simultaneous. Service firm employees have direct contact with customers. In a manufacturing firm, technical employees are separated from customers, and hence no direct interactions occur.[25]

Service organizations work on people; manufacturing organizations work on things. Examples of service firms include consulting companies, law firms, brokerage houses, airlines, hotels, advertising firms, public relations, amusement parks, and educational organizations. Service technology also characterizes many departments in large corporations, even manufacturing firms. In a manufacturing organization such as Ford Motor Company, the legal, personnel, finance, and market research departments provide service. Thus, the structure and design of these departments reflect its own service technology rather than the manufacturing plant's technology. Service technology concepts therefore can be used to structure both service organizations and the many large service departments within manufacturing organizations.

Motorola's *flexible manufacturing system* in Boynton Beach, Florida, produces high-quality Bravo® pagers in minutes instead of several days. This system allows pagers to be built in mass production and to customer order. Motorola believes in decentralization and participative management, which is the right structure for this sophisticated technology. Motorola's structural and technical success was recognized by its recent receipt of the Malcolm Baldrige National Quality Award.

A useful way of characterizing service technology is the extent to which it is routine versus nonroutine.[26] The routine-nonroutine distinction can be used to describe differences across organizational technologies as well as those among various departments within a single organization. A **routine service technology** means that the work can be reduced to a series of explicit steps and employees can follow an objective procedure for serving customers and solving problems. The number of problems is low. There is little task variety because the service is provided in a repetitious manner. Day-to-day job requirements are similar, such as those for sales clerks in a discount store. In service organizations, routine technologies are used when services are not labor intensive because physical facilities standardize the services. Examples of routine services are sanitation, hotels, airline transportation, and ferry boats.

routine service technology
Service technology in which work can be broken down into explicit steps and employees can follow objective procedures for serving customers and solving problems.

nonroutine service technology
Service technology in which there are no specific procedures for directing employees, problem situations are varied, and employees must rely on personal resources for problem solving.

A **nonroutine service technology** means that new problems are encountered every day and variety is high. Moreover, when problems arise there is no specific procedure for telling people what to do. Employees must rely on education, experience, and trial and error, such as lawyers in a defense trial. Nonroutine services typically are labor intensive and provided entirely by individuals. For example, a tax accountant provides a complete tax service for a customer. Nonroutine services include doctors, lawyers, architects, and accountants.[27]

Selected characteristics of organization structure for service technologies are illustrated in Exhibit 10.9. The nonroutine, people-oriented services tend to be more organic.[28] They are informal and decentralized. These services are also dispersed, hence, each firm is typically small, as in the case of local video stores or doctors' offices. They must be located close to geographically dispersed customers. Routine services have a smaller people component. Organizations such as hotels, banks, and auto repair facilities can be designed with a more mechanistic structure. Formalization and division of labor are greater, and decision making can be centralized. As a general pattern, however, even routine service firms have greater variety in the production process than do assembly line manufacturing technologies, and structures tend to be more organic.

An example of how structure should fit technology in a more routine service firm is Marriott Corporation.

EXHIBIT 10.9
Relationship between Service Technology and Organization Structure

	Service Technology	
	Routine	**Nonroutine**
Labor intensity and complexity of service	Low	High
Structural characteristics:		
Division of labor	High	Low
Formalization	High	Low
Centralization	High	Low
Administrative ratio	Low	Moderate
Span of control	High	Moderate
Employee skill and training	Low	High
Geographical dispersion	High	Low
Overall structure	Mechanistic	Organic

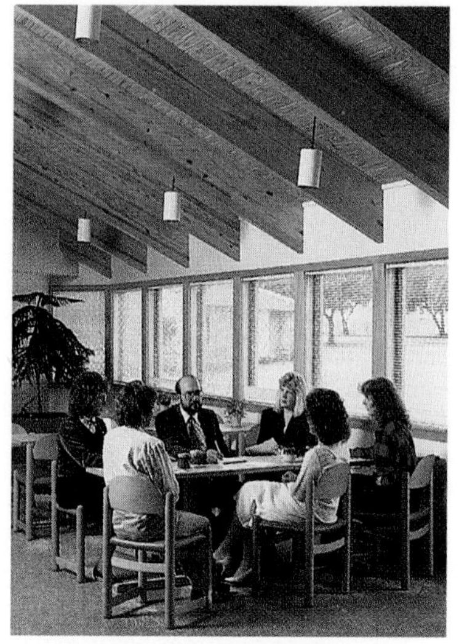
Universal Health Services' Meridell Achievement Center is an example of a *nonroutine service technology*. Residential treatment is provided to children by creating teams representing the full spectrum of psychiatric disciplines, including psychiatrists, clinical physiologists, social workers, occupational therapists, and teachers. The teams meet regularly to provide cohesive individualized treatment plans for each child. This organic structure approach is ideally suited to the contingency factor of nonroutine technology.

MARRIOTT CORP. •

Marriott Corporation is now the nation's largest hotel operator, and the president, Bill Marriott, plans to make it even bigger. Marriott's success has come from two strategies: Put hotels where the customers are and provide excellent service. Putting hotels where the customers are means building hotels downtown and at airports. Convention centers, such as Atlantic City, are another target. Marriott also searches for new niches. The Courtyard is a new type of garden apartment hotel aimed at the moderate-priced segment of the market. Courtyards will be scattered around major metropolitan areas.

At Marriott, the hotel itself is the main service, and a mind-boggling system is used to make the right impression every time. Top managers make no apologies for the tightly centralized system of policies, procedures, and controls for operational details. Room attendants have 66 things to do in cleaning a room, from dusting the tops of pictures (number 7) to keeping the telephone book and Bibles in a neat condition (number 37). Bill Marriott says, "The more the system works like the Army, the better." The cooks have 6,000 recipes available to them, and they are not allowed to deviate. One rule for chefs says, "Deviations from the standard written specifications may not be made without prior approval and written consent of the vice president of food and beverages."

Marriott Corporation plans to build 9,000 new rooms a year. It routinizes the service and builds luxury into the physical structure to ensure that guests are treated the same way every time. Marriott was rated as one of the five best-managed companies, and Bill Marriott and four executive vice-presidents spend half the year on the road visiting company facilities. The close, personal supervision and careful reading of customer suggestions help Bill Marriott give business travelers the service they expect and deserve.[29]

The managers at Marriott designed the structure and procedures to reflect a routine service technology. The many rules and procedures, centralized decision making, and refined division of labor provide a mechanistic structure that is suited to the underlying technology.

Putting their heads together, Kathy Lobene, Geri Jensen, and Leslie Lampert now provide super service to Boise Cascade Corporation's coated paper customers. Boise's customer service was spotty because the interdependence between customer service representatives and production planners was not recognized, with customer service reps located in New York City and production planners in Oregon. During a sweeping reorganization, these people were consolidated under one roof, reporting to the same supervisor at division headquarters. Recognizing the contingency factor of *reciprocal interdependence* provided an excellent fix, making Boise Cascade the best in customer service.

CONTINGENCY FACTOR: DEPARTMENTAL INTERDEPENDENCE

The final characteristic of the organization's situation that influences structure is called interdependence. **Interdependence** means the extent to which departments depend on each other for resources or materials to accomplish their tasks. A low level of interdependence means that departments do their work independently and have little need for interaction, coordination, or exchange of materials. A high level of interdependence means that departments must constantly exchange information and resources. Three types of interdependence that influence organization structure are illustrated in Exhibit 10.10.[30]

EXHIBIT 10.10
Types of Interdependence and Required Coordination

Form of Interdependence	Type of Coordination Required
1. Pooled (Bank) — Clients	Chain of Command, Standardization of Procedures, Rules and Regulations
2. Sequential (assembly line) — Client	Plans and Schedules, Scheduled Meetings, Liaison Roles
3. Reciprocal (hospital) — Client	Unscheduled Meetings, Teams, Task Forces, Project Manager

POOLED. Pooled interdependence means that each department is part of the organization and contributes to the common good, but each department is relatively independent because work does not flow between units. Citibank branch banks or Wendy's restaurants are examples of pooled interdependence. They share financial resources from a common pool but do not interact with each other.

SEQUENTIAL. Sequential interdependence means that parts or outputs of one department become inputs to another department in serial fashion. The first department must perform correctly for the second department to perform correctly. An example is assembly line technology, such as in the automobile industry. This is greater interdependence than pooled, because departments exchange resources and depend on others to perform well.

RECIPROCAL. The highest level is reciprocal interdependence, which means that the output of operation A is the input to operation B, and the output of operation B is the input back again to operation A. Departmental outputs influence other departments in reciprocal fashion. For example, hospitals must

EXHIBIT 10.11
Product Development, Product Delivery, and Customer Service Interdependencies

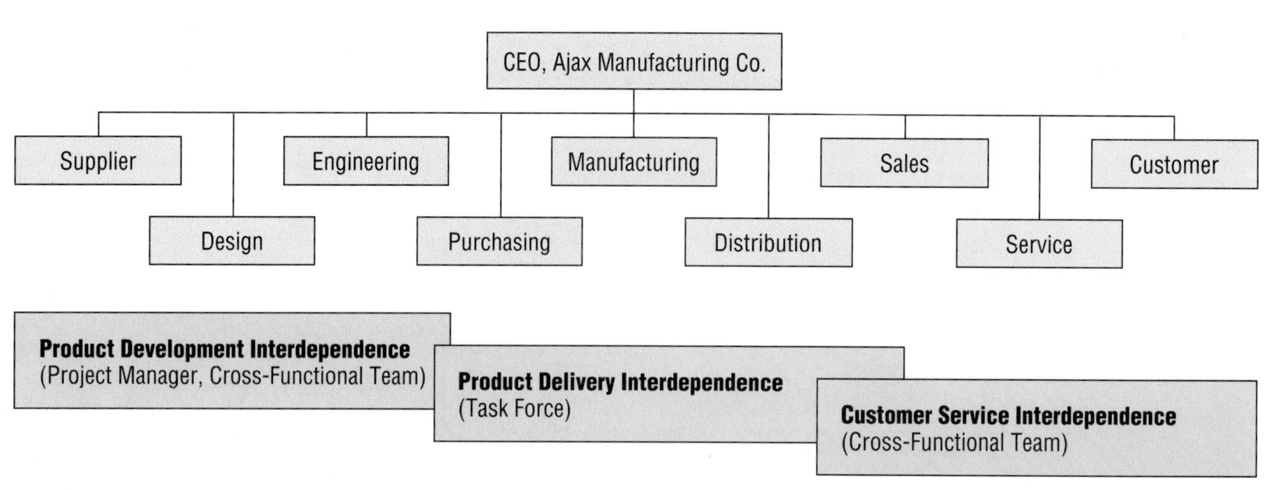

Source: Based on John F. Rockart and James E. Short, "IT in the 1990s: Managing Organizational Interdependence," *Sloan Management Review* (Winter 1989), 7–17.

interdependence The extent to which departments depend on each other for resources or materials to accomplish their tasks.

coordinate services to patients, such as when a patient moves back and forth between the surgery, physical therapy, and X-ray departments.

STRUCTURAL IMPLICATIONS. When interdependence among departments is pooled, coordination is relatively easy. Managers can develop standardized procedures, rules, and regulations that insure similar performance in all branches. For sequential interdependence, coordination is somewhat more difficult, requiring future planning and scheduling so that the flow of outputs and resources is coordinated to the benefit of all departments. Moreover, scheduled meetings and face-to-face discussions are used for day-to-day coordination between departments. Reciprocal interdependence is the most difficult. These departments should be located physically close together in the organization so that communication is facilitated. Structural mechanisms for coordination include teams, task forces, unscheduled meetings, and perhaps an integrating manager to ensure that departments are working out coordination problems on a daily basis.[31]

Within most organizations, interdependence will be high (reciprocal) for some departmental activities and low (pooled) for others. For example, Exhibit 10.11 illustrates how reciprocal interdependence among sets of departments exists for the tasks of product development, product delivery, and customer service. The design and purchasing departments can work independently on many tasks, but for product development they must be coordinated, perhaps with a team or task force. Purchasing must be coordinated with distribution for the delivery of products. Suppliers and customers are also a part of the interdependence and in some organizations may be included as part of a team.

When consultants analyzed NCR (formerly National Cash Register Company) to learn why new products were so slow in being developed, they found that the development and marketing of products took place in separate divisions with little communication. NCR broke up its traditional functional structure and created several stand-alone units of about 500 people each. Locating together all the people needed to develop a new product made coordination easier. When an organization has sufficient personnel, stand-alone units may be created, otherwise coordination is achieved through teams, task forces, and project managers.

SUMMARY

This chapter introduced a number of important organizing concepts. As organizations grow, they add new departments, functions, and hierarchical levels. A major problem confronting management is how to tie the whole organization together. Structural characteristics such as chain of command, work specialization, and departmentalization are valuable organization concepts, but often are not sufficient to coordinate far-flung departments. Lateral coordination mechanisms provide coordination across departments and include information systems, task forces, teams, and integrating managers.

Managers can design organizations to be organic or mechanistic. Mechanistic organizations rely heavily on vertical structure and are characterized by tight control, whereas organic organizations are loosely structured and rely heavily on lateral coordination mechanisms. Contingency factors of strategy, environment, size and life cycle, production technology, and departmental interdependence influence the correct structural approach. When a firm's strategy is to be the low-cost producer, a functional, mechanistic structure is best. If the strategy is to be innovative and to differentiate the firm's product from competitors, a more organic structural approach using teams, decentralization, and perhaps a divisional matrix structure is appropriate. When environmental uncertainty is high, lateral coordination is important and the organization should have an organic structure. For manufacturing firms, small batch, continuous process, and flexible manufacturing technologies tend to be structured organically, whereas a mechanistic structure is appropriate for mass production. Service technologies are people oriented, but services such as hotels and transportation are considered routine and can be controlled with a mechanistic structure. People-intensive services, such as universities and medical clinics, tend to be more organically structured.

As organizations increase in size, they require greater vertical control. Organizations in the birth and youth stages typically are loosely structured. In the midlife stage, a strong vertical structure emerges. In a mature organization the vertical structure may be too strong, necessitating the installation of teams, task forces, and other lateral devices to achieve greater cooperation across departments. Finally, departmental interdependence also determines the form of structure. An organization with a low level of interdependence, such as pooled, can be controlled mainly with the vertical chain of command and standardization of procedures, rules, and regulations. When interdependence is high, such as for new-product introductions, then lateral coordination mechanisms such as unscheduled meetings, teams, and project managers are required, or the organization may place the interdependent groups into separate, self-contained units.

MANAGEMENT SOLUTION

Troxel Manufacturing Company was suffering conflicts between its Consumer Products and Tubing Divisions, which contributed to declining profits and market share. A study of Troxel's structure was undertaken, which produced the following changes. The two divisions were consolidated into four major functions: operations, marketing, finance and accounting, and personnel. Because Troxel had grown quickly, job responsibilities had not been defined, so job descriptions were prepared clarifying authority and responsibility for each management position. More planning was undertaken with the help of a senior planning team to facilitate coordination among functions. Moreover, first-line managers were given broader spans of control, reducing supervisors by 30 percent. The clarification of responsibilities enabled Troxel to move to the next stage in the life cycle. The consolidation of the two divisions allowed duplicate functions to be eliminated and administrative overhead to be reduced. As a result of this restructuring, production capacity increased 10 percent with no increase in employees and cost of sales dropped 13 percent. Sales volume is up more than 30 percent. These improvements would have been impossible without the new organization structure.[32]

DISCUSSION QUESTIONS

1. Carnival Cruise Lines provides pleasure cruises to the masses. Carnival has several ships and works on high volume/low price rather than offering Cadillac cruises. Would this be a routine or nonroutine service technology, and what would you predict about the organization structure of a Carnival Cruise ship?
2. Why is structure different depending on whether a firm's strategy is low cost or differentiation?
3. The chapter suggested that structure should be designed to fit strategy. Some theorists argue that strategy should be designed to fit the organization's structure. Do you agree or disagree? Explain.
4. Explain the three levels of departmental interdependence and give an example of each.
5. Some experts argue that interdependence within organizations is greater now than 15 years ago because of rapid changes in the global environment. If so, what does this mean for the present structure of organizations compared with 15 years ago?
6. What is the difference between a task force and an integrating manager? Which would be more effective in achieving coordination?
7. Discuss why an organization in an uncertain environment requires more lateral relationships than one in a certain environment.
8. Explain the difference between assembly line and continuous process production. How do these two technologies influence structural characteristics such as indirect–direct labor ratio and span of control?
9. What is the difference between manufacturing and service technology? How would you classify a university, a local discount store, a nursery school? How would you expect the structure of a service organization to differ from that of a manufacturing organization?

10. Flexible manufacturing systems combine elements of both small batch and mass production. What effect might this new form of technology have on organization structure? Explain.

MANAGEMENT IN PRACTICE: EXPERIENTIAL EXERCISE

Family Business

You are the father/mother of ten children and have just used your inheritance to acquire a medium-sized pharmaceutical company. Last year's sales were down 18 percent from the previous year. In fact, the last three years have been real losers. You want to clean house of current managers over the next ten years and bring your children into the business. Being a loving parent, you agree to send your children to college to educate each of them in one functional specialty. The ten children are actually five sets of twins exactly one year apart. The first set will begin college this fall, followed by the remaining sets the next four years. The big decision is which specialty each child should study. You want to have the most important functions taken over by your children as soon as possible, so you will ask the older children to study the most important areas.

Your task right now is to rank in order of priority the functions to which your children will be assigned and develop reasons for your ranking.

The ten functions are:

_____ Distribution
_____ Manufacturing
_____ Market Research
_____ New-Product Development
_____ Personnel
_____ Product Promotion
_____ Quality Assurance
_____ Sales
_____ Legal and Governmental Affairs
_____ Office of the Controller

Analyze your reasons for how functional priority relates to the company's environmental/strategic needs. Now rank the functions as part of a group. Discuss the problem until group members agree on a single ranking. How does the group's reasoning and ranking differ from your original thinking?

CASES FOR ANALYSIS

REPUBLIC NATIONAL BANK

Republic National Bank was located in a well-to-do suburb in southern California. The population grew rapidly to 250,000, and growth stabilized by the late 1980s.

The bank began operations in 1965 under the guidance of its founder and president, Richard Johnson. After only five years, deposits grew to $15 million. During those years, the community grew rapidly and the bank grew with it. The organization structure was informal. The bank had no organization chart despite having some 30 employees and two branches. Richard Johnson believed in keeping things informal so that employees could enjoy a family atmosphere.

In 1968, the bank was purchased by Ted White. White immediately imposed a traditional management structure. He asked the personnel director to write job descriptions for all positions and to develop an up-to-date organization chart. He stressed centralized decision making and standard procedures. The two branches and the main bank were urged to offer the same services despite their proximity to different customer groups.

One branch was in an ethnic community, the other was near a junior college, and the main branch was in a residential area. Vertical communication and "following the rules" were deemed safe, responsible management approaches for a community bank.

This approach worked successfully for 15 years, but major changes in the early 1980s caused problems within the bank. The bank's assets had grown to over $500 million. Management trainees had been hired from universities and promoted to managerial positions. The new managers began to propose changes. One manager suggested that the bank establish an advisory board to involve residents in bank decisions and provide bank officials with good information about community needs. Another manager urged the creation of several committees to study the effects of government regulation. One committee could study asset/liability management to help the bank make the transition to variable-rate loans and to explore new investment opportunities. Another could work on cost control and the use of new electronic technology to reduce the cost of fund transfers. Yet another could investigate service pricing and the generation of noninterest income, including fees for returned checks, overdrafts, and checking account services.

Ted White resisted these changes. He did not want to create task forces that would decentralize decision making to a lower level. White believed that banks had to have tight control to insure depositors' safety. Within a year, three of the new managers quit in frustration. White also noticed that the bank was not growing and even had lost market share to competitors, some of which were newly created banks run in an informal fashion.

Questions

1. Was it appropriate to develop a stronger vertical structure as the bank grew larger?
2. What are the advantages and disadvantages of implementing lateral relationships in the form of task forces? Do you feel the bank should place greater emphasis on lateral relationships? Why or why not?
3. Would you characterize Republic National Bank's structure as organic or mechanistic? What is the correct structure for the bank's contingency factors of technology, environment, and size/life cycle?

Source: Based on Richard L. Daft and Richard M. Steers, *Organizations: A Micro/Macro Approach* (Glenview, Ill.: Scott, Foresman and Company, 1986), 314–316.

MALARD MANUFACTURING COMPANY

Malard Manufacturing Company produces control valves that regulate flows through natural gas pipelines. Malard has approximately 1,400 employees and has successfully produced a standard line of control valves that are price competitive in the industry. However, whenever the production of a new control valve is required, problems arise. Developments in electronics, metallurgy, and flow control theory required the introduction of new products every year or two. These new products have been associated with interdepartmental conflict and disagreement.

Consider the CV305. As usual, the research and development group developed the basic design and the engineering department converted the designs into a prototype control valve. Now the materials department must acquire parts for the prototype and make plans for obtaining parts needed for production runs. The production department is to manufacture and assemble the product, and marketing is responsible for sales.

Department heads feel that work on the CV305 should be done simultaneously instead of sequentially. Marketing wants to provide input to research and development so that the design will meet customer needs. Production insists that the design fit machine limitations and be cost efficient to manufacture — indeed, it wants to speed up development of the final plans so that it can acquire tooling and be ready for standard production. Engineering, on the other hand, wants to slow down development to ensure that specifications are correct and have been thoroughly tested.

All of these controversies with the CV305 exist right now. Department managers are frustrated and becoming uncommunicative. The R&D and engineering departments are keeping their developmental plans secret, causing frustration for the other departments. Moreover, several department managers are new and inexperienced in new-product development. Mr. Crandell, the executive vice-president, likes to keep tight control over the organization. Department managers must check with him before making major decisions. However, with the CV305 he has been unable to keep things running smoothly. The span of control is so large that Crandell has no time to personally shepherd the CV305 through the system.

On November 1, Crandell received a memo from the marketing department head. It said, in part,

> The CV305 must go to market immediately. This is urgent. It is needed now because it provides the precision control our competitors' products already have. Three of our salespeople reported that loyal customers are about to place orders with competitors. We can keep this business if we have the CV305 ready for production in 30 days.

Questions

1. What is the balance between vertical and lateral structure in Malard Manufacturing? Is it appropriate that department managers always turn to the executive vice-president for help rather than to one another?
2. If you were Mr. Crandell, how would you resolve this problem? What could you do to facilitate production of the CV305 over the next 30 days?
3. What structural changes would you recommend to prevent these problems in future new-product developments? Would a smaller span of control help? An integrating manager with responsibility for coordinating the CV305? A task force?

CHAPTER 11

INNOVATION AND CHANGE

CHAPTER OUTLINE

Managing Organizational Change

Forces for Change
Need for Change

Initiating Change

Search
Creativity
Idea Champions
New-Venture Teams

Implementing Change

Resistance to Change
Force Field Analysis
Implementation Tactics

Types of Planned Change

Technology Changes
New-Product Changes
Structural Changes
Culture/People Changes

Organizational Development

OD Activities
OD Steps

LEARNING OBJECTIVES

After studying this chapter, you should be able to:

- Define organizational change and explain the forces for change.
- Describe the sequence of four change activities that must be performed in order for change to be successful.
- Explain the techniques managers can use to facilitate the initiation of change in organizations, including idea champions and new-venture teams.
- Define sources of resistance to change.
- Explain force field analysis and other implementation tactics that can be used to overcome resistance to change.
- Explain the difference among technology, product, structure and culture/people changes.
- Explain the change process — bottom up, top down, horizontal — associated with each type of change.
- Define organizational development and organizational revitalization.

Management Problem

Several years ago, top management at Maryland-based Preston Trucking Company started to fear for the future of its organization. Deregulation was making the trucking industry more competitive, and a survey of employees uncovered 40 negative comments for every positive comment about the company. Rather than help the company become more efficient, employees were unhappy and often hostile. One truck driver stayed parked on a customer's lot for two hours to show Preston managers who ran the company. Top managers at Preston were frustrated because creating a culture that fostered innovation and commitment seemed so difficult.[1]

If you were a manager at Preston Trucking Company, how would you engage employees in innovative behavior to help the company be more efficient? How would you improve employee attitudes?

Managers at Preston are not alone. Every organization experiences stress and difficulty coping with change. Innovation from within is widely recognized as one of the critical problems facing business today in the United States and Canada. To be successful, organizations must embrace many types of changes. Businesses must develop improved production technologies, create new products desired in the marketplace, implement new administrative systems, and upgrade employees' skills. Companies such as Westinghouse, Intel, Black & Decker, Herman Miller, and Merck implement all of these changes and more.

How important is organizational change? Consider this: The parents of today's college students grew up without cable television, crease-resistant clothing, personal computers, detergents, VCRs, electronic games, compact disks, frozen entrees, video stores, or laser checkout systems in supermarkets. Companies that produce the new products have prospered, while many of those caught in the transition with outdated products and technologies have failed. Organizations that change and innovate successfully, such as IBM, Hewlett-Packard, Raychem, 3M, Citicorp, and Frito-Lay, are both profitable and admired.

EXHIBIT 11.1
Model of Change Sequence of Events

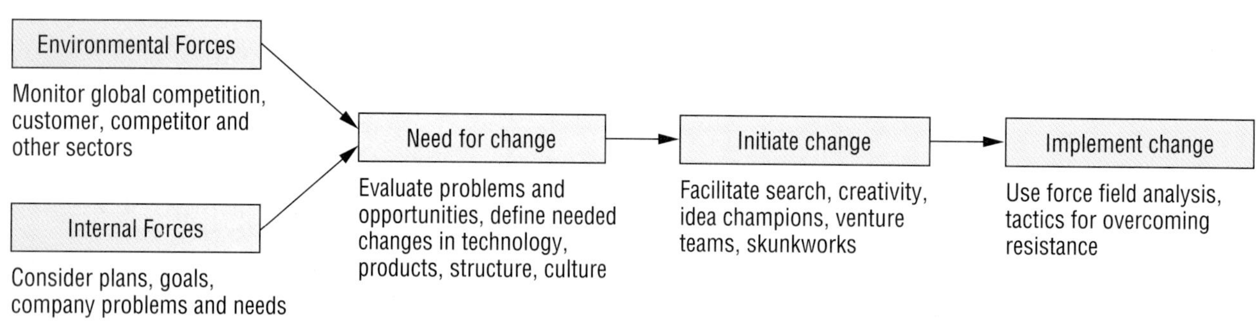
Environmental Forces
Monitor global competition, customer, competitor and other sectors
Internal Forces
Consider plans, goals, company problems and needs
Need for change
Evaluate problems and opportunities, define needed changes in technology, products, structure, culture
Initiate change
Facilitate search, creativity, idea champions, venture teams, skunkworks
Implement change
Use force field analysis, tactics for overcoming resistance

organizational change The adoption of a new idea or behavior by an organization.

Organizational change is defined as the adoption of a new idea or behavior by an organization.[2] In this chapter, we will look at how organizations can be designed to respond to the environment through internal innovation and change. First we will examine the basic forces for organizational change. Then we will look closely at how managers facilitate two change requirements: initiation and implementation. Finally, we will discuss the four major types of change — technology, new product, structure, and culture/people — and how the organization can be designed to facilitate each.

PURCHASE PROTECTION

American Express Travel Related Services (TRS) is a leading *innovator* in the financial services industry. This unique bag illustrates the benefits of the Purchase Protection Plan, which insures most items bought on an American Express card. This is one of several new products and product enhancements developed by TRS in recent years. Another visible and successful new product is the Optima Card. TRS also is adopting new technology for data processing and communication requirements. Innovations in the area of human resources include flexible work schedules, elder care, and special support for disabled employees.

MANAGING ORGANIZATIONAL CHANGE

Change can be managed. By observing external trends, patterns, and needs, managers use planned change to help the organization adapt to external problems and opportunities.[3] When organizations are caught flat-footed, failing to anticipate or respond to new needs, management is at fault.

An overall model for planned change is presented in Exhibit 11.1. Four events make up the change sequence: (1) Internal and external forces for change exist; (2) organization managers monitor these forces and become aware of a need for change; (3) the perceived need triggers the initiation of change, which (4) is then implemented. How each of these activities is handled depends on the organization and managers' styles.

We now turn to a brief discussion of the specific activities associated with the first two events — forces for change and the perceived need for the organization to respond.

FORCES FOR CHANGE

Forces for organizational change exist both in the external environment and within the organization.

ENVIRONMENTAL FORCES. As described in Chapter 3, external forces originate in all environmental sectors, including customers, competitors, technology, economic, and international. For example, many North American compa-

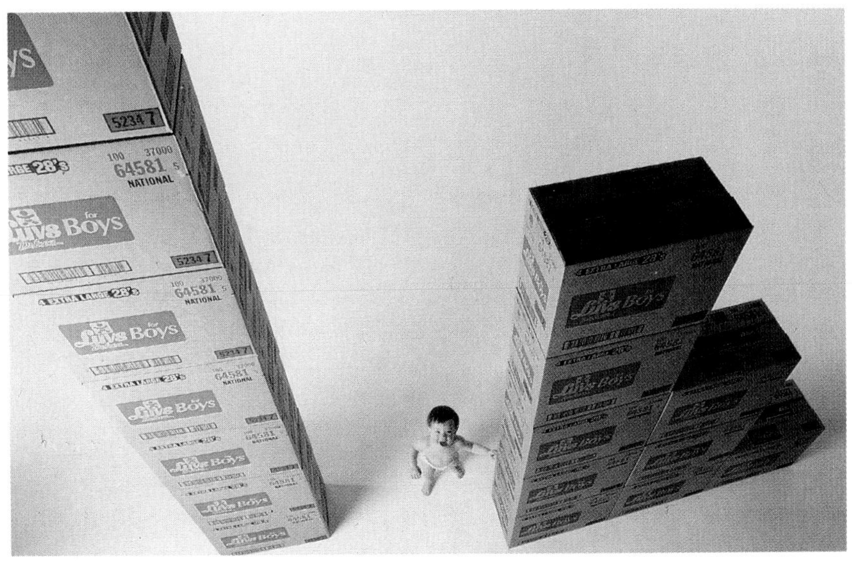

The major *force for change* at Stone Container Corporation is the customer, in this case Procter & Gamble. P&G needed a stronger container for shipping and storing its popular Pampers® and Luvs® disposable diapers. The boxes shown here are made with Stackor®, a new high-performance grade of paper that provides greater stacking strength without additional cost or weight from heavier corrugated board. More than 500 of Stone Container's customers have converted to Stackor boxes. The Luvs boxes shown here can support more than 1,200 pounds, hence can be stacked more than 20 feet high.

nies have been blindsided by global competition. Consider General Electric, which built a new factory to produce microwave ovens. As plans were being made, Yun Soo Chu was working 80 hours per week for Samsung in Korea perfecting a microwave oven. About the time the GE plant came on stream, Samsung started exporting thousands of microwaves to the United States at one-third the cost of General Electric's microwaves. Today, Samsung has 25 percent of the U.S. market, and GE is one of its best customers. GE closed its microwave plant, preferring to buy cheaper Samsung ovens to sell under the GE label.[4] As another example, McDonald's experienced an external force from the customer sector. Customers were tired of eating hamburgers in their cars, to which top managers responded by incorporating sit-down facilities in McDonald's restaurants. The Manager's Shoptalk box describes how Johnson Wax stays abreast of and responds to external forces from around the globe.

INTERNAL FORCES. Internal forces for change arise from internal activities and decisions. If top managers select a goal of rapid company growth, internal actions will have to be changed to meet that growth. New departments or technologies will be created. General Motors' senior management, frustrated by poor internal efficiency, designed the Saturn manufacturing plant to solve this internal need. Demands by employees, labor unions, and production inefficiencies can all generate a force to which management must respond with change.

NEED FOR CHANGE

As indicated in Exhibit 11.1, external or internal forces translate into a perceived need for change within the organization.[5] Managers sense a need for change when there is a **performance gap** — a disparity between existing and desired performance levels. The performance gap may occur because current procedures are not up to standard or because a new idea or technology could

performance gap A disparity between existing and desired performance levels.

MANAGER'S SHOPTALK

AN INTERVIEW WITH SAMUEL C. JOHNSON

S. C. Johnson & Sons, known widely as Johnson Wax, is an extremely successful consumer products company with sales that top $2 billion annually. Its many well-known products include Pledge, Raid, Glade, Future floor polish, and OFF! bug repellent. Some of the ways a company such as Johnson & Sons keeps in touch with environmental forces are through global research, efficient use of available technology, and strong communications. In the following excerpt, Samuel C. Johnson, great-grandson of the company's founder, discusses his strategies with *New York Times Business Forum* editor Joel Kurtzman.

Question: How do you conduct your research? Is it concentrated in the United States or distributed throughout the globe?

Mr. Johnson: Racine is where we have our largest lab. We also have one in Britain that concentrates on products for Europe. A lab in Japan basically works on Japan and the Pacific Rim. And we have a lab in Argentina, which is small. We usually have at least a small lab in every country working on new products.

We have research going on around the world because many of the raw materials that we use are manufactured by others. For example, the strongest chemicals companies are in Europe. By having chemists in Europe it gives us close proximity to these companies so when they come up with new materials we find out about them early. That's the main reason for not concentrating all our research in one location. If the Germans are developing the best new products, we want to be there.

Question: What are the major obstacles you encounter to innovation?

Mr. Johnson: Bureaucratization of research is our biggest problem. Everybody worries about their bureaucracies. Every sensible chief executive worries about good communications between people working on technology, marketing, manufacturing, and sales to put to use the best of ideas people have.

Every company goes through periods of very high innovation and new-product success, and then it somehow hits a new-products dry hole for a year or two. Usually it isn't a matter of strategy but of jacking up your communication to make sure your people stand up for what they believe are good ideas. Every once in a while a chief executive has to do something to bring out latent good ideas. We had a little bit of a dry hole a couple of years ago.

Question: What are you doing to promote innovation?

Mr. Johnson: We now have a structure that is somewhat similar to what they have at the 3M Company. That company amazes me. If I would like our company to be like any other company, I would like it to be like 3M. They have a culture that promotes new ideas coming to surface.

We are also using what we call "sponsor groups," which get together people from different disciplines who sponsor an idea and then see it through to implementation. These groups meet regularly. The person who has the idea is in charge. Each person brings his own discipline to the table.

Questions: Why is the group led by the researchers?

Mr. Johnson: If you have a sponsor group made up of vice-presidents, it won't work as well. That's because vice-presidents bring management to the equation, not ideas.

Question: What else are you doing to be innovative?

Mr. Johnson: We are trying to listen to the marketplace. We do this through market research. We do extensive market research both here and abroad. We have our ears open.

I just set up a new product and technology department that reports to the president. It is like having a set of eyes and ears looking outside the company. It looks at the work of other companies and is headed by my No. 2 son who is a Ph.D. chemist and physicist. He has marketing people, chemists, general management, and finance types working with him. It's a small think tank and it comes up with thoughts by looking outside our company. It will help get us out of the "not invented here syndrome."

Source: Joel Kurtzman, "Managing When It's All in the Family," *The New York Times,* April 9, 1989, sec. 3, 2.

improve current performance. Recall from Chapter 6 that management's responsibility is to monitor threats and opportunities in the external environment as well as strengths and weaknesses within the organization to determine whether a need for change exists. One striking need for change occurred when executives at General Electric's Louisville refrigerator plant realized that the Japanese, Brazilians, and Italians were building cheaper compressors of better quality than theirs. GE could not compete because of high wages. Thanks to visionary engineers and managers, GE chose to innovate with a rotary compressor manufactured in a new automated plant.[6]

Managers must detect problems and opportunities, because the perceived need for change is what sets the stage for subsequent actions that create a new product or technology. Big problems are easy to spot. Sensitive monitoring systems are needed to detect gradual changes that can fool managers into thinking their company is doing fine. An organization may be in greater danger when the environment changes slowly, because managers may fail to trigger an organizational response. Failing to use planned change to meet small needs can place the organization in hot water, as illustrated in the following passage:

> When frogs are placed in a boiling pail of water, they jump out — they don't want to boil to death. However, when frogs are placed in a cold pail of water, and the pail is placed on a stove with the heat turned very low, over time the frogs will boil to death.[7]

Initiating Change

After perceiving the need for change, the next part of the change process is initiating change, a truly critical aspect of change management. This is where the ideas that solve perceived needs are developed. Responses an organization can make are to search for or create a change to adopt.

Search

Search is the process of learning about current developments inside or outside the organization that can be used to meet the perceived need for change. Search typically uncovers existing knowledge that can be applied or adopted within the organization. Managers talk to friends and colleagues, read professional reports, or hire consultants to learn about ideas used elsewhere. For example, an internal consulting program was developed for the Office of Employee Relations for New York State, creating teams of 10 to 20 managers from a cross-section of agencies to provide information to managers experiencing problems. The consulting team provided a quick way for managers to search out new ideas used in other departments.

search The process of learning about current developments inside or outside the organization that can be used to meet a perceived need for change.

Many needs, however, cannot be resolved through existing knowledge but require that the organization develop a new response. Initiating a new response means that managers must design the organization so as to facilitate creativity of both individuals and departments, encourage innovative people to initiate new ideas, or create new-venture departments. These techniques have been adopted by such corporations as IBM and Apple with great success.

Creativity

Creativity is the development of novel solutions to perceived problems.[8] Creative individuals develop ideas that can be adopted by the organization. People noted for their creativity include Edwin Land, who invented the Polaroid camera; Frederick Smith, who came up with the idea for Federal Express's

creativity The development of novel solutions to perceived organizational problems.

EXHIBIT 11.2
Characteristics of Creative People and Organizations

Source: Based on Gary A. Steiner, ed., *The Creative Organization* (Chicago: University of Chicago Press, 1965), 16–18; Rosabeth Moss Kanter, "The Middle Manager as Innovator," *Harvard Business Review* (July/August 1982), 104–105; James Brian Quinn, "Managing Innovation: Controlled Chaos," *Harvard Business Review* 63 (May/June 1985), 73–84.

The Creative Individual	The Creative Organization or Department
1. Conceptual fluency Openmindedness	1. Open channels of communication Contact with outside sources Overlapping territories Suggestion systems, brainstorming, nominal group techniques
2. Originality	2. Assigns nonspecialists to problems Allows eccentricity Uses teams
3. Less authoritarian Independent	3. Decentralized; loosely defined positions; loose control Mistakes okay Risk-taking norms
4. Playfulness Undisciplined exploration Curiosity	4. Allows freedom to choose and pursue problems Not run as a tight ship; playful culture Freedom to discuss ideas; long time horizon
5. Persistent Committed Highly focused	5. Resources allocated to creative personnel and projects without immediate payoff Reward system encourages innovation Absolved of peripheral responsibilities

overnight delivery service during an undergraduate class at Yale; and Swiss engineer George de Mestral, who created Velcro after noticing the tiny hooks on the burrs caught on his wool socks. Each of these people saw unique and creative opportunities in a familiar situation.

One test of creativity is to imagine a block of ice sitting on your desk. What use could you make of it? A creative person might see that it could be used to quench someone's thirst, reduce a patient's fever, crack a victim's skull, or produce steam by boiling.[9] Or consider the person interviewing college graduates for job openings. "Show me a new use for this stapler," the interviewer said. Calmly picking up the scissors on the desk, one creative woman cut the interviewer's tie in half and then stapled it back together. Smiling, she asked, "Now that I've demonstrated my instant mender, how many will you take?"

Each of us has the capacity to be creative. Characteristics of highly creative people are illustrated in the left-hand column of Exhibit 11.2. Creative people often are known for originality, curiosity, openmindedness, a focused approach to problem solving, persistence, a relaxed and playful attitude, and receptiveness to new ideas.[10]

Creativity can also be designed into organizations. Companies or departments within companies can be organized to be creative and initiate changes. The characteristics of creative organizations correspond to those of individuals, as illustrated in the right-hand column of Exhibit 11.2. Creative organizations are loosely structured. People find themselves in a situation of ambiguity, assignments are vague, territories overlap, tasks are poorly defined, and much work is done through teams.[11] Creative organizations have an internal culture of playfulness, freedom, challenge, and grass-roots participation.[12] They harness all potential sources of new ideas from within. Many participative management programs are born out of the desire to enhance creativity for initiating changes. People are not stuck in the rhythm of routine jobs. Managers in an

Playful, life-size sculptures of working people, such as this one by Stephen Hansen, add to the creative culture at Herman Miller Inc., the innovative office furniture manufacturer. The sculptures add to an internal environment designed to nurture creativity and imagination, which is required for innovative furniture design. Organized as a *creative department,* Herman Miller executives seek participation of all employees in management decisions, and employees are urged to try new things and make mistakes.

insurance company that had been tightly controlled from the top remarked on the changes that enabled them to be more creative:

> We used to run by the book and now I don't even know where the book is.
>
> Yesterday's procedures are outdated today.
>
> If you don't like the organization chart, just wait until next week, we'll have a new one.[13]

The most creative companies encourage employees to make mistakes. Jim Read, president of the Read Corporation, says, "When my employees make mistakes trying to improve something, I give them a round of applause. No mistakes mean no new products. If they ever become afraid to make one, my company is doomed."[14] Ross Perot, founder of EDS, believed creative managers could not keep their noses clean: "We teach people that mistakes are like skinned knees for little children. . . . My people are covered with the scars of their mistakes. By the time they get to the top, their noses are pretty well broken."[15]

Open channels of communication, overlapping jobs, discretionary resources, decentralization, and employees' freedom to choose problems and make mistakes can generate unexpected benefits for companies. Creative organizational conditions such as those described in Exhibit 11.2 enable more than 200 new products a year to bubble up from 3M's research labs. The same conditions enabled brand manager Cal Blodgett at General Mills to propose a change for the 6-by-300-foot sheets of granola rolling out of the oven to be crumbled into cereal bits. "Let's cut that into bars," he thought, and Nature Valley Granola Bars were born. In another General Mills department, Craig Nalen responded to the frustration of developing a new snack food with the idea of turning the food into a product: "Why not peddle the snack food as a toy?" With that idea, Lickety Sticks were born and General Mills entered the toy market.[16]

EXHIBIT 11.3
Four Roles in Organizational Change

Inventor	Champion	Sponsor	Critic
Develops and understands technical aspects of idea Does not know how to win support for idea or make a business of it	Believes in idea Visualizes benefits Confronts organizational realities of costs, benefits Obtains financial and political support Overcomes obstacles	High-level manager who removes organizational barriers Approves and protects idea within organization	Provides reality test Looks for shortcomings Defines hard-nosed criteria that idea must pass

Source: Based on Harold L. Angle and Andrew H. Van De Ven, "Suggestions for Managing the Innovation Journey," in *Research in the Management of Innovation: The Minnesota Studies*, ed. A. H. Van de Ven, H. L. Angle, and Mabel S. Poole (Cambridge, Mass.: Ballinger/Harper & Row, 1989), and Jay R. Galbraith, "Designing the Innovating Organization," *Organizational Dynamics* (Winter 1982). 5–25.

IDEA CHAMPIONS

idea champion A person who sees the need for and champions productive change within the organization.

If creative conditions are successful, new ideas will be generated that must be carried forward for acceptance and implementation. This is where idea champions come in. The formal definition of an **idea champion** is a person who sees the need for and champions productive change within the organization. For example, Linda Clemens of Federal Express championed the idea of developing an internal hot line for employees to complain about red tape and excess paperwork, thereby cutting back corporate bureaucracy. Wendy Black of Best Western International championed the idea of coordinating the corporate mailings to the company's 2,800 hoteliers into a single packet every two weeks. Some hotels were receiving three special mailings a day from different departments. Her idea has saved $600,000 a year for five years in postage alone.[17] Remember: Change does not occur by itself. Personal energy and effort are required to successfully promote a new idea. Often a new idea is rejected by management. Champions are passionately committed to a new product or idea despite rejection by others.

Championing an idea successfully requires roles in organizations, as illustrated in Exhibit 11.3. Sometimes a single person may play two or more of these roles, but successful innovation in most companies involves an interplay of different people, each adopting one role. The *inventor* develops a new idea and understands its technical value but has neither the ability nor the interest to promote it for acceptance within the organization. The *champion* believes in the idea, confronts the organizational realities of costs and benefits, and gains the political and financial support needed to bring it to reality. The *sponsor* is a high-level manager who approves the idea, protects it, and removes major organizational barriers to acceptance. The *critic* counterbalances the zeal of the champion by challenging the concept and providing a reality test against hard-nosed criteria. The critic prevents people in the other roles from adopting a bad idea.[18]

Debby Rucco (standing), supervisor of the collections department of the United Telephone Company of the Northwest, has been an *idea champion* for administrative changes. She threw out the old rules, encouraging her group to make up procedures as they go along. In weekly brainstorming and discussion sessions, Rucco coaxes ideas from her staff. Her department was the first to try flex time, compile a district profile of customer information, and suggest new procedures for handling insufficient-funds checks. Rucco is a coach and a champion, not a rulemaker and disciplinarian, creating a department within which others can be champions, too.

Al Marzocchi was both an inventor and a champion at Owens-Corning Fiberglass. He invented ways to strengthen fiberglass, developed the fiberglass belted tire in conjunction with Armstrong Tire, and pioneered new ways of using asphalt. One reason Marzocchi thrived was that Owens-Corning's president, Harold Boeschenstein, sponsored his activities and held critics at bay. Once Marzocchi violated company rules by going directly to an outside firm, but the president protected him and his idea.[19]

Managers can directly influence whether champions will flourish. When Texas Instruments studied 50 of its new-product introductions, a surprising fact emerged: Without exception, every new product that had failed had lacked a zealous champion. In contrast, most of the new products that succeeded had a champion. Texas Instruments' managers made an immediate decision: No new product would be approved unless someone championed it.

New-Venture Teams

A recent idea for facilitating corporate innovation is called a new-venture team. A **new-venture team** is a unit separate from the rest of the organization and is responsible for developing and initiating a major innovation.[20] New-venture teams give free reign to members' creativity because their separate facilities and location free them from organizational rules and procedures. These teams typically are small, loosely structured, and organic, reflecting the characteristics of creative organizations described in Exhibit 11.2. Peter Drucker advises organizations that wish to innovate to use a separate team or department:

new-venture team A unit separate from the mainstream of the organization that is responsible for developing and initiating innovations.

> For the existing business to be capable of innovation, it has to create a structure that allows people to be entrepreneurial. . . . This means, first, that the entrepreneurial, the new, has to be organized separately from the old and the existing. Whenever we have tried to make an existing unit the carrier of the entrepreneurial project, we have failed.[21]

The new-venture team is quite different from the use of lateral relationships or the matrix structure described in Chapter 9. In those structures,

EXHIBIT 11.4
Location of New-Venture Team in an Organization

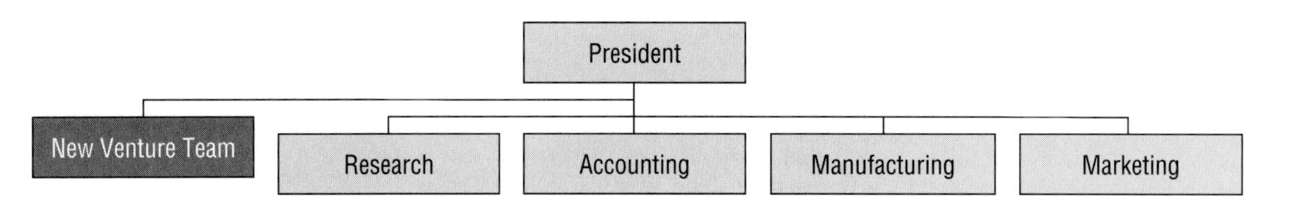

employees remain members of their everyday departments and simply work on a project part time while reporting to their regular boss. Under the new-venture team concept, employees no longer report through the normal structure.[22] The team exists as a separate departmental entity, as illustrated in Exhibit 11.4. New-venture teams are kept small and separate to ensure that no bureaucracy will intrude.

For a giant corporation such as IBM, new-venture teams free people from the constraints of the large organization. IBM was one of the first companies to use the new-venture team successfully, and its genius was to suspend normal product development practices. IBM has started 14 new-venture units. Each is a tiny company-within-a-company that explores areas of customized software, robots, and electrocardiographs. IBM's biggest success — the personal computer — was built by a new-venture group. The PC new-venture team was so appealing that 5,000 employees applied for the initial 50 positions.[23] Other companies that have created new-venture units are Monsanto, Levi Strauss, Exxon, Du Pont, Dow, and Motorola.

skunkworks Small, informal, and sometimes unauthorized groups that create innovations.

One variation of venture teams used by some companies is called skunkworks.[24] **Skunkworks** are small, informal, and sometimes unauthorized groups that create innovations. Companies such as Kollmorgen, IBM, Merck, Philip Morris, and Macy encourage employees to form informal groups, often working nights and weekends, to develop a new idea. If the new venture is successful, group members are rewarded and encouraged to run the new business.

new-venture fund A fund providing resources from which individuals and groups draw to develop new ideas, products, or businesses.

Another variation of new-venture teams is the **new-venture fund,** which provides resources from which individuals and groups can draw to develop new ideas, products, or businesses. For example, Teleflex, a producer of many technical and consumer products, allocates one-half of one percent of sales to a new-venture fund. More than $1 million dollars was allocated to employees in 1988 to explore new ideas.[25]

IMPLEMENTING CHANGE

A creative culture, idea champions, and new-venture teams are ways to facilitate the initiation of new ideas. The other step to be managed in the change process is implementation. A new, creative idea will not benefit the organization until it is in place and being fully utilized. One frustration for managers is that employees often seem to resist change for no apparent reason. To effectively manage the implementation process, managers should be aware of the reasons for employee resistance and be prepared to use techniques for obtaining employee cooperation.

Resistance to Change

Idea champions often discover that other employees are unenthusiastic about their new ideas. Members of a new-venture group may be surprised when managers in the regular organization do not support or approve their innovations. Managers and employees not involved in an innovation often seem to prefer the status quo. Employees appear to resist change for several reasons, and understanding them helps managers implement change more effectively.

Self-Interest. Employees typically resist a change they believe will take away something of value. A proposed change in job design, structure, or technology may lead to a perceived loss of power, prestige, pay, or company benefits. The fear of personal loss is perhaps the biggest obstacle to organizational change.[26] When Mesa Oil Corporation tried to buy Phillips Petroleum, Phillips employees started a campaign to prevent the takeover. Employees believed that Mesa would not treat them well and that they would lose financial benefits. Their resistance to change was so effective that the merger failed to take place.

Lack of Understanding and Trust. Employees often do not understand the intended purpose of a change or distrust the intentions behind it. If previous working relationships with an idea champion have been negative, resistance may occur. One manager had a habit of initiating a change in the financial reporting system about every 12 months, then losing interest and not following through. After the third time, employees no longer went along with the change because they did not trust the manager's intention to follow through to their benefit.

Uncertainty. *Uncertainty* is the lack of information about future events. It represents a fear of the unknown. Uncertainty is especially threatening for employees who have a low tolerance for change and fear the novel and unusual. They do not know how a change will affect them and worry about whether they will be able to meet the demands of a new procedure or technology.[27] Union leaders at General Motors' Steering Gear Division in Saginaw, Michigan, resisted the introduction of employee participation programs. They were uncertain about how the program would affect their status and thus initially opposed it.

Different Assessments and Goals. Another reason for resistance to change is that people who will be affected by innovation may assess the situation differently than an idea champion or new-venture group. Often critics voice legitimate disagreements over the proposed benefits of a change. Managers in each department pursue different goals, and an innovation may detract from performance and goal achievement for some departments. For example, if marketing gets the new product it wants for its customers, the cost of manu-

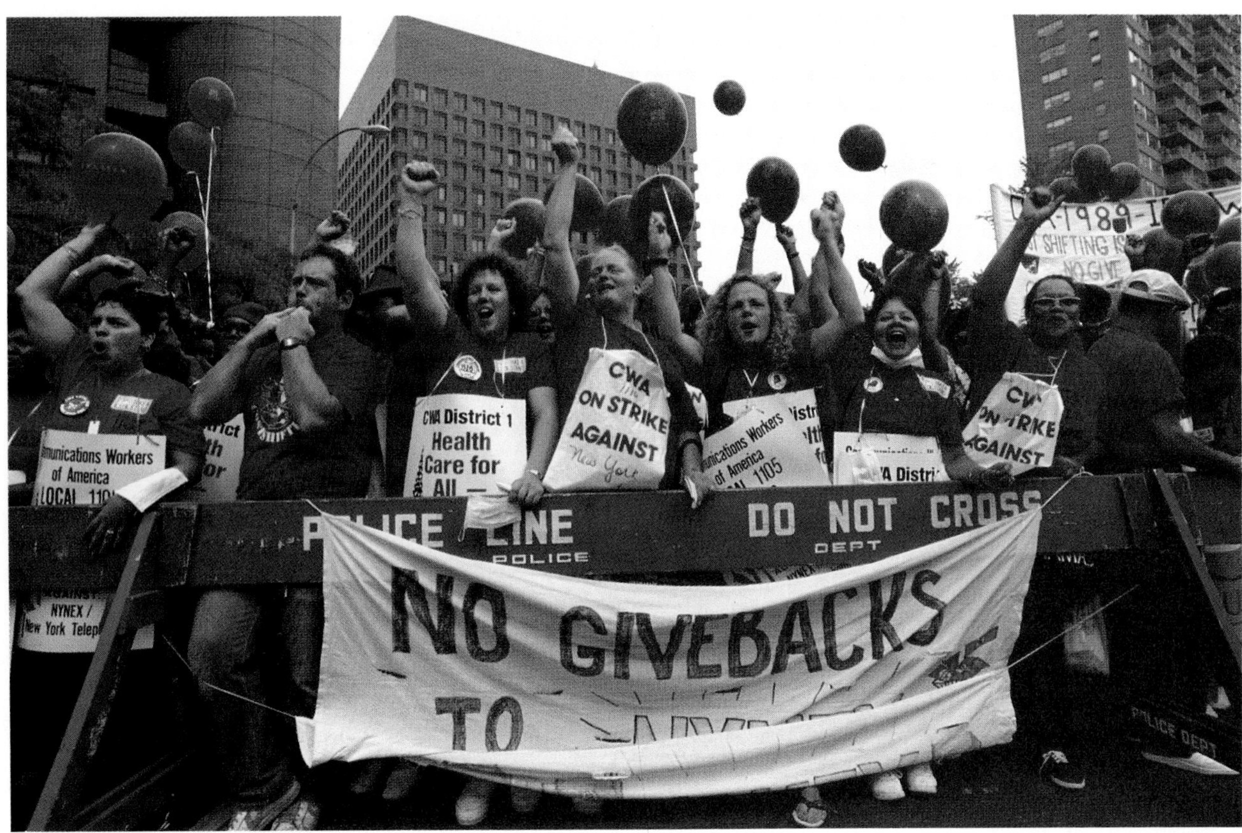

Resistance to change is often motivated by *self-interest* and *different assessments and goals.* When 200,000 telephone workers walked out on four Bell companies, their objective was to keep the companies from shifting health insurance costs to them. Increasing medical costs are a hot issue, with management complaining it cannot afford insurance premiums and workers fighting health cost sharing. The worker goal is to maintain full coverage, but some unions have compromised by helping contain costs with preferred provider networks of doctors who charge lower rates.

facturing may increase and the manufacturing superintendent thus will resist. Resistance may call attention to problems with the innovation. At a consumer products company in Racine, Wisconsin, middle managers resisted the introduction of a new employee program that turned out to be a bad idea. The managers truly believed that the program would do more harm than good. One manager bluntly told his boss, "I've been here longer than you, and I'll be here after you've gone, so don't tell me what really counts at this company."[28]

These reasons for resistance are legitimate in the eyes of employees affected by the change. The best procedure for managers is not to ignore resistance but to diagnose the reasons and design strategies to gain acceptance by users.[29] Strategies for overcoming resistance to change typically involve two approaches: the analysis of resistance through the force field technique and the use of selective implementation tactics to overcome resistance.

FORCE FIELD ANALYSIS

force field analysis The process of determining which forces drive and which resist a proposed change.

Force field analysis grew from the work of Kurt Lewin, who proposed that change was a result of the competition between *driving* and *restraining forces.*[30] When a change is introduced, some forces drive and other forces resist it. To implement a change, management should analyze the change forces. By selectively removing forces that restrain change, the driving forces will be strong enough to enable implementation, as illustrated by the move

EXHIBIT 11.5
Using Force Field Analysis to Change from Traditional to Just-in-Time Inventory System

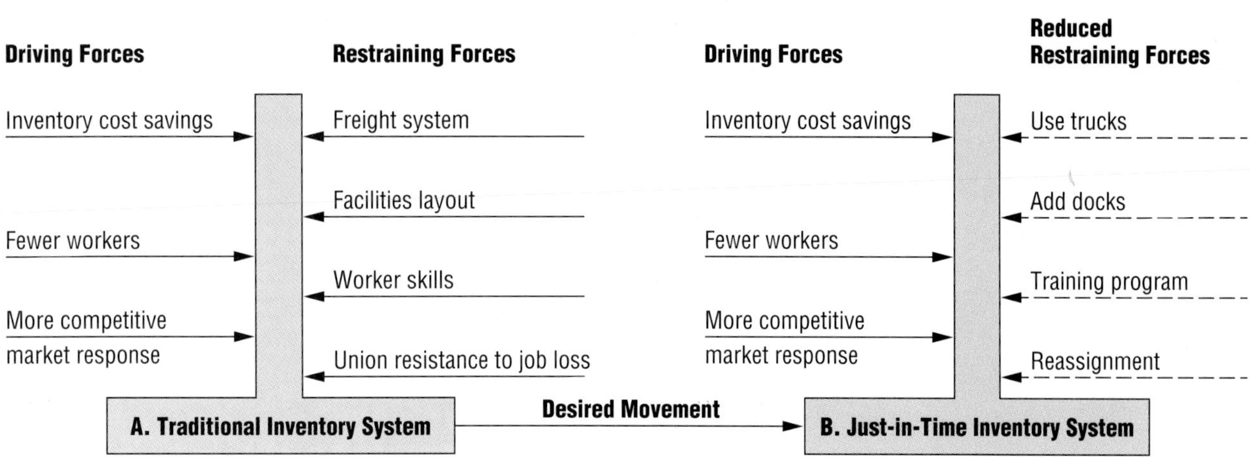

from A to B in Exhibit 11.5. As restraining forces are reduced or removed, behavior will shift to incorporate the desired changes.

Just-in-time (JIT) inventory control systems schedule materials to arrive at a company just as they are needed on the production line. In an Ohio manufacturing company, management's analysis showed that the driving forces associated with the implementation of JIT were (1) the large cost savings from reduced inventories, (2) savings from needing fewer workers to handle the inventory, and (3) a quicker, more competitive market response for the company. Restraining forces discovered by managers were (1) a freight system that was too slow to deliver inventory on time, (2) a facility layout that emphasized inventory maintenance over new deliveries, (3) worker skills inappropriate for handling rapid inventory deployment, and (4) union resistance to loss of jobs. The driving forces were not sufficient to overcome the restraining forces.

To shift the behavior to JIT, managers attacked the restraining forces. An analysis of the freight system showed that delivery by truck provided the flexibility and quickness needed to schedule inventory arrival at a specific time each day. The problem with facility layout was met by adding four new loading docks. Inappropriate worker skills were attacked with a training program to instruct workers in JIT methods and in assembling products with uninspected parts. Union resistance was overcome by agreeing to reassign workers no longer needed for maintaining inventory to jobs in another plant. With the restraining forces removed, the driving forces were sufficient to allow the JIT system to be implemented.

IMPLEMENTATION TACTICS

The other approach to managing implementation is to adopt specific tactics to overcome employee resistance. For example, resistance to change may be overcome by educating employees or inviting them to participate in

EXHIBIT 11.6
Tactics for Overcoming Resistance to Change

Approach	When to Use
Communication, education	When change is technical; when accurate information and analysis are needed by users to understand change.
Participation	When users need to feel involved; when design requires information from others; when users have power to resist.
Negotiation	When a group has power over implementation; when a group will lose out in the change.
Coercion	When there is a crisis; when initiators clearly have power; when other implementation techniques have failed.
Top management support	When change involves multiple departments or reallocation of resources; when legitimacy of change is doubted by users.

Source: Based on J. P. Kotter and L. A. Schlesinger, "Choosing Strategies for Change," *Harvard Business Review* 57 (March/April 1979), 106–114.

implementing the change. Methods for dealing with resistance to change have been studied by researchers. The following five tactics, summarized in Exhibit 11.6, have proven successful.[31]

COMMUNICATION AND EDUCATION. Communication and education are used when solid information about the change is needed by users and others who may resist implementation. Education is especially important when the change involves new technical knowledge or users are unfamiliar with the idea. Florida Power & Light Company instituted a change in company procedures that initially confused managers. Realizing it had implemented the change too quickly, the company stepped back and tailored special training sessions to educate managers. The training program resolved the difficulty, and implementation was a success.[32]

PARTICIPATION. *Participation* involves users and potential resisters in designing the change. This approach is time consuming, but it pays off because users understand and become committed to the change. When General Motors tried to implement a new management appraisal system for supervisors in its Adrian, Michigan, plant, it met with immediate resistance. Rebuffed by the lack of cooperation, top managers proceeded more slowly, involving supervisors in the design of the new appraisal system. Through participation in system design, managers understood what the new approach was all about and dropped their resistance to it.

NEGOTIATION. Negotiation is a more formal means of achieving cooperation. *Negotiation* uses formal bargaining to win acceptance and approval of a desired change. For example, if the marketing department fears losing power if a new management structure is implemented, top managers may negotiate with marketing to reach a resolution. General Motors, General Electric, and other companies that have strong unions frequently must formally negotiate change with the unions. The change may become part of the union contract reflecting the agreement of both parties.

President Mike Warren (in tie) visits Alabama Gas workers in the trenches to implement a culture/people change. He knows *top management support* is a critical component of successful change. Warren found relations with the company's union poor so he made a personal effort to support this change. He eats dinner regularly with union leaders, visits with workers, surveys employees, and solicits their suggestions. Thanks to Warren's effort, employees enjoy a new culture at Alabama Gas.

COERCION. *Coercion* means that managers use formal power to force employees to change. Resisters are told to accept the change or lose rewards or even their jobs. Coercion is necessary in crisis situations where a rapid response is urgent. When middle managers at TRW Inc.'s Valve Division in Cleveland refused to go along with a new employee involvement program, top management reassigned several first-line supervisors and managers. The new jobs did not involve supervisory responsibility. Further, other TRW managers were told that future pay increases depended on their adoption of the new procedures. The coercive techniques were used as a last resort because managers refused to go along with the change any other way.[33]

TOP MANAGEMENT SUPPORT. The visible support of top management also helps overcome resistance to change. Top management support symbolizes to all employees that the change is important for the organization. Top management support is especially important when a change involves multiple departments or when resources are being reallocated among departments. Without top management support, these changes can get bogged down in squabbling among departments. Moreover, when top managers fail to support a project, they can inadvertently undercut it by issuing contradictory orders. This happened at Flying Tiger Lines before it was acquired by Federal Express. The airborne freight hauler came up with a plan to eliminate excessive paperwork by changing the layout of offices so that two agents rather than four could handle each shipment. No sooner had part of the change been implemented than top management ordered another system; thus, the office layout was changed again. The new layout was not as efficient, but it was the one that top management supported. Had middle managers informed top managers and obtained their support earlier, the initial change would not have been defeated by a new priority.[34]

EXHIBIT 11.7
Four Types of Organizational Change

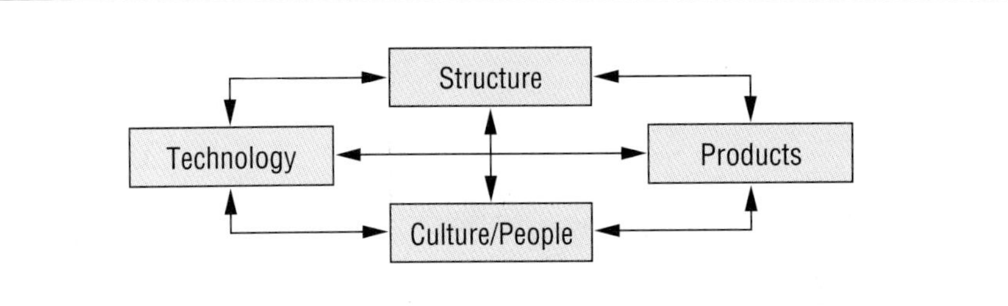

Source: Based on Harold J. Leavitt, "Applied Organizational Change in Industry: Structural, Technical, and Human Approaches," in *New Perspectives in Organization Research*, ed. W. W. Cooper, H. J. Leavitt, and M. W. Shelly II (New York: Wiley, 1964), 55–74.

In another example, Navistar managers saved a lot of money for the company by adopting smart implementation techniques.

NAVISTAR INTERNATIONAL • Managers at Navistar International—formerly International Harvester—successfully introduced a maintenance, repair, and operating (MRO) buying program. Purchasing costs were far too high, buyers were buried under an avalanche of 14,000 requisitions per year, hundreds of suppliers were used, inventory turnover was slow, and there was little coordination between warehousing and purchasing.

James Hall and Pierre Bodeau of the Construction Equipment Group in Melrose Park, Illinois, proposed a redesigned requisition process, including a computerized inventory control system and a new procedure for analyzing vendor capability. They also devised a plan for successful implementation.

Implementation involved several steps: Survey 120 industrial suppliers for accurate information; involve IH employees in discussions to further refine and improve the buying program; undertake internal training to teach employees the new procedures; and analyze other forces for resistance. After the program was fully developed, key employees were already on board because they had participated in program design. Training for other employees went smoothly. The program was launched in June, and by April of the next year 90 percent of the purchases had gone through the MRO system. Cost savings through price reductions amounted to $78,000 the first year, and MRO inventories dropped $1 million in eight months.[35]

TYPES OF PLANNED CHANGE

Now that we have explored how the initiation and implementation of change can be carried out, let us look at the different types of change that occur in organizations. We will address two issues: what parts of the organization can be changed and how managers can apply the initiation and implementation ideas to each type of change.

The four types of organizational change are technology, products, structure, and culture/people, as illustrated in Exhibit 11.7. Organizations may innovate in one or more areas depending on internal and external forces for change. In the rapidly changing toy industry, a manufacturer will have to introduce new products frequently. In a mature, competitive industry, production technology changes will be adopted to improve efficiency. The arrows connecting the four

Focus on Global Competition

MOTOROLA INC.

In the early and mid-1980s, foreign competitors — mostly Japanese — deluged the world with extremely high quality cellular phones, pagers, and memory chips. Because of this, Motorola temporarily withdrew from selected U.S. and foreign markets. But Motorola refused to be counted out. Under the leadership of Chairman Robert Galvin, the company decided to get in shape for a return bout. Innovation was to be the key.

Motorola spent, and continues to spend, billions of dollars in research and development. It invested ten years of R&D — an unheard of length of time for a U.S. company — in the MicroTac cellular phone (one-third lighter than the nearest foreign competitor). The MicroTac allowed Motorola to flex its muscles, regaining market share in the United States and foreign markets with this innovative cellular telephone.

Next Motorola came out with the first Dick Tracy-type wristwatch pager. The firm teamed up with Timex Corporation and miniaturized inner parts of the pager so they could add extra features, such as message time-stamping. Another success was achieved, with Motorola delivering a blow to foreign competitors in another market.

In 1988, Motorola introduced a new signal-processing chip capable of storing and transmitting images, sounds, and other analog signals. Future plans call for an even more powerful chip. In semiconductors, Motorola is increasing market share in Europe, Southeast Asia, and Japan in the face of withering competition.

How is Motorola pulling off all these innovations? By emphasizing R&D; adding American flair; changing culture, technology, and products at the same time; and applying Japanese-style management improvements. The new emphasis on quality has enabled Motorola to reach Six Sigma quality manufacturing, or 3.4 defects per million, on simple products like calculators. It expects to reach the same extraordinary quality on all products by 1992.

Another tactic has been to knock down barriers wherever they can be found. People from departments such as design, manufacturing, and marketing work together in the early stages of new projects. This also means that Motorola divisions are expected to collaborate with one another, with new products coming on stream that involve two, three, or four divisions. Horizontal linkages are even in place between Motorola and other companies. Motorola supports R&D consortiums through which companies develop and share new technology together.

These changes cannot be made without investments in overhauling culture and upgrading people. All 105,000 employees are being trained in topics such as decision making, global competitiveness, and statistical quality control to the tune of $60 million in 1989.

What's next? Cellular phones are the wave of the future, so expect more innovations here. Also, Motorola will be installing a nationwide network through which fleet operators can keep in touch with their drivers. Motorola is focused on anticipating customer needs and having solutions ready. Motorola is again the best in the global marketplace, thanks to the management of innovation.

Source: Based on Lois Therrien, "The Rival Japan Respects," *Business Week*, November 13, 1989, 108–118.

types of change in Exhibit 11.7 show that a change in one part may affect other parts of the organization: A new product may require changes in technology, and a new technology may require new people skills or a new structure. For example, when Shenandoah Life Insurance Company computerized processing and claims operations, the structure had to be decentralized, employees required intensive training, and a more participative culture was needed. Related changes were required for the new technology to increase efficiency. Motorola, discussed in the Focus on Global Competition box, underwent several types of changes to become competitive again.

Rubbermaid introduced a staggering 1,000 new products during the past five years. More than 30 percent of sales each year comes from newer products, and total sales have quadrupled since 1980. Rubbermaid is so good at *new-product innovation* that it's no wonder the company has been cited by *Fortune, Business Month,* and *Business Week* for its reputation and management excellence. Rubbermaid's proliferation of well-crafted and colorful housewares is illustrated in this upbeat avant-garde television commercial used in Canada. Drummers create music on Rubbermaid products, increasing brand awareness among Canadian consumers.

Technology Changes

technology change A change that pertains to the organization's production process.

A **technology change** pertains to the organization's production process—how the organization does its work. Technology changes are designed to make the production of a product or service more efficient. For example, the adoption of robotics to improve production efficiency at General Motors and Chrysler is a technology change, as is the adoption of laser-scanning checkout systems at supermarkets. At IBM's manufacturing plant in Charlotte, North Carolina, an automated miniload storage and retrieval system was installed to handle production parts. This change provided an efficient method for handling small-parts inventory and changed the technology of the IBM plant.

How can managers encourage technology change? The general rule is that technology change is bottom up.[36] The *bottom-up approach* means that ideas are developed at lower organization levels and channeled upward for approval. Lower-level technical experts act as idea champions—they invent and champion technological changes. Employees at lower levels understand the technology and have the expertise needed to propose changes. For example, at Kraft General Foods, employees have proposed several hundred cost-saving projects. One that can save $3.5 million a year is simply to improve the accuracy of machines that weigh product portions.[37]

Managers can facilitate the bottom-up approach by designing creative departments as described earlier in this chapter. A loose, flexible, decentralized structure provides employees with the freedom and opportunity to initiate changes. A rigid, centralized, standardized structure stifles technology innovation. Anything managers can do to involve the grass roots of the organization—the people who are experts in their parts of the production process—will increase technology change.

A *top-down approach* to technology change usually does not work.[38] Top managers are not close to the production process and lack expertise in technological developments. Mandating technology change from the top produces

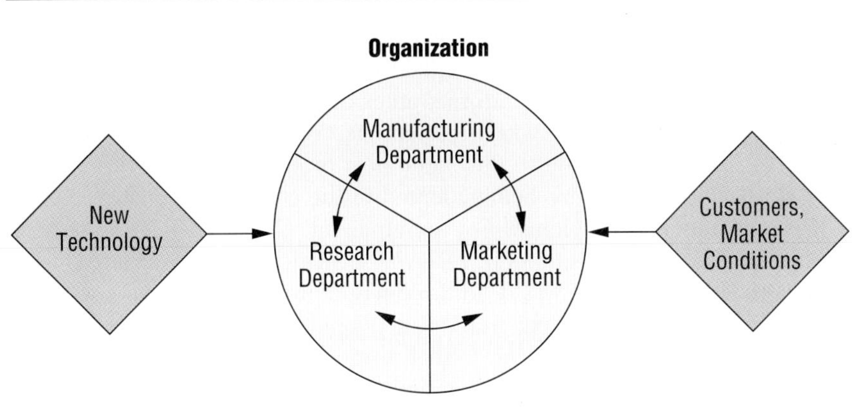

EXHIBIT 11.8
Horizontal Linkage Model for New-Product Innovation

fewer rather than more technology innovations. The spark for a creative new idea comes from people close to the technology. The rationale behind Motorola's "participative management program," Data General's "pride teams," and Honeywell's "positive action teams" is to extract new technology ideas from people at lower organization levels.

NEW-PRODUCT CHANGES

A **product change** is a change in the organization's product or service output. New-product innovations have major implications for an organization, because they often are an outcome of a new strategy and may define a new market.[39] Examples of new products are Frito-Lay's introduction of O'Grady's potato chips, Hewlett-Packard's introduction of a professional computer, and GE's development at its Medical Division of a device for monitoring patients' heart cycles.

product change A change in the organization's product or service output.

The introduction of a new product is difficult, because it not only involves a new technology but must meet customers' needs. In most industries, only about one in eight new-product ideas are successful.[40] Companies that successfully develop new products usually have the following characteristics:

1. People in marketing have a good understanding of customer needs.
2. Technical specialists are aware of recent technological developments and make effective use of new technology.
3. Members from key departments — research, manufacturing, marketing — cooperate in the development of the new product.[41]

These findings mean that the ideas for new products typically originate at the lower levels of the organization just as they do for technology changes. The difference is that new-product ideas flow horizontally among departments. Product innovation requires expertise from several departments simultaneously. A new-product failure is often the result of failed cooperation.[42]

One approach to successful new-product innovation is called the **horizontal linkage model,** which is illustrated in Exhibit 11.8.[43] The model shows that research, manufacturing, and marketing must simultaneously develop new products. People from these departments meet frequently in teams and task

horizontal linkage model An approach to product change that emphasizes shared development of innovations among several departments.

forces to share ideas and solve problems. Research people inform marketing of new technical developments to learn whether they will be useful to customers. Marketing people pass customer complaints to research to use in the design of new products. Manufacturing informs other departments whether a product idea can be manufactured within cost limits. When the horizontal linkage model is used, the decision to develop a new product is a joint one.

Horizontal linkages are being adopted in the computer industry to overcome new-product problems. For example, at Convergent Technologies, "Workslate," a portable computer, received accolades when it was introduced. One year later, Workslate was dead. Production problems with the new product had not been worked out. Marketing people had not fully analyzed customer needs. The idea had been pushed through without sufficient consultation among research, manufacturing, and marketing. At Lotus Development Corporation, the delays in new software ran on for months and years, earning the name "vaporware" because they never appeared. New senior vice-president Frank King enforced a regime of daily and weekly meetings involving programmers and code writers, and monthly gatherings of all employees to update one another. These enforced linkages are gradually reducing product development time.[44]

time-based competition A strategy of competition based on the ability to deliver products and services faster than competitors.

Innovation is becoming a major strategic weapon in the global marketplace. **Time-based competition** means delivering products and services faster than competitors, giving companies a significant strategic advantage. For example, Hewlett-Packard reduced the time to develop a new printer from 4.5 years to 22 months. Lenscrafters jumped from 3 to 300 stores based on its ability to provide quality eyeglasses in one hour. Dillard's department stores went to an automatic reorder system that replenishes stocks in 12 days rather than 30, providing retail goods to customers more quickly.[45] Sprinting to market with a new product requires a *parallel approach,* or *simultaneous linkage* among departments. This is similar to a rugby match wherein players run together, passing the ball back and forth as they move down field together. The teamwork required for the horizontal linkage model is a major component of using rapid innovation to beat the competition with speed.[46] The Winning Moves box tells how RCA quickly created a new product.

Structural Changes

structural change Any change in the way in which the organization is designed and managed.

Structural changes pertain to the hierarchy of authority, goals, structural characteristics, administrative procedures, and management systems.[47] Almost any change in how the organization is managed falls under the category of structural change. At General Telephone & Electronics Corporation, recent structural changes have included a structural reorganization, new pay incentives, a revised performance appraisal system, and affirmative action programs. IBM's change from a functional to a product structure was a structural change. The implementation of a no-smoking policy is usually considered a structural or administrative change.

Successful structural change is through a top-down approach, which is distinct from technology change (bottom up) and new products (horizontal).[48] Structural change is top down because the expertise for administrative improvements originates at the middle and upper levels of the organization. The champions for structural change are middle and top managers. Lower-level

Winning Moves

TIME-BASED COMPETITION AT RCA

RCA's Consumer Electronics Division, a division of Thomson Consumer Electronics, was in a horse race with its Japanese competition to build an electronic control system, called Color Television Chassis (CTC), that was virtually a self-contained computer for handling consumer electronics functions. To dominate the market, RCA had to be first with its new product innovation in the face of two Japanese competitive weapons: product development speed that was half that of U.S. firms and zero defect goals that produced almost perfect electronic components.

Beating the Japanese was impossible given RCA's corporate culture which enshrined traditional, sequential approaches to getting things done. The culture and structure positioned design engineering as the focal point for new product innovations. Engineering designed the innovation with some input from marketing, and then dumped it on manufacturing saying, "Here it is. Good luck." Design engineering then became the lightning rod for criticism about poor quality and clashed with manufacturing about design changes needed to produce the product.

Managers and line personnel from around the division were asked, "What would an ideal new product innovation process look like?" The consensus was to abandon the sequential approach in favor of a coordinated development process. Key managers in the functional structure also understood that they did not know how to do this and needed training in team building, problem solving, performance reviews, and conducting effective meetings. A consulting firm provided the training for managers — 110 in all — from every functional department. Ultimately, 14 Natural Work Teams were formed to handle a share of the 7,000 separate tasks needed to develop the CTC.

A database was developed to computerize activities so people could track their own and others' progress. Within a few months people stopped saying, "That's not my problem" and started saying, "What can I do to solve it?" They took responsibility for a previously unclear goal: improving RCA's competition position worldwide. The team-based horizontal coordination process produced spectacular results. All development milestones were achieved in less than half the typical time and innovative technology was designed and manufactured at substantially less cost than before. The quality of the CTC surpassed that of any previous new product. Failure rates were cut in half and consumer repair calls tumbled.

The difficult new product innovation goals of speed, cost, and quality were simultaneously exceeded in the Consumer Electronics Division, a nearly impossible feat. Horizontal teams, reflecting changes in both structure and culture, catapulted RCA to the forefront of world manufacturing.

Source: Based on Daniel Valentino and Bill Christ, "Teaming Up For Market: Cheaper, Better, Faster," *Management Review,* November 1989, 46–49.

technical specialists have little interest or expertise in administrative procedures. If organization structure causes negative consequences for lower employees, complaints and dissatisfaction alert managers to a problem. Employee dissatisfaction is an internal force for change. The need for change is perceived by higher managers, who then take the initiative to propose and implement it.

The top-down process does not mean that coercion is the best implementation tactic. Implementation tactics include education, participation, and negotiation with employees. Unless there is an emergency, managers should not force structural change on employees. They may hit a resistance wall, and the change will fail. This is exactly what happened at the company for which Mary Kay Ash worked before she started her own cosmetics business. The owner learned that even a top-down change in commission rate needs to incorporate education and participation to succeed:

Culture change at Xerox is symbolized by these senior managers spending less time in their offices. Xerox president Paul Allaire (second from left) realized the company needed to be more market-driven as a cultural value, which meant revamping and improving marketing processes. Company publications stressed the need for people to get out into the marketplace. Moreover, each executive spends one day a month answering complaints from customers. Marketing experts make presentations to Xerox scientists, and researchers' salary increases are tied to how well they understand customer requirements. Xerox's new culture has enabled it to move from being a copier company to becoming a true customer-driven systems company.

> I worked for a company whose owner decided to revise the commission schedule paid to his sales managers. All brochures and company literature were changed accordingly. He then made plans for personally announcing the changes during a series of regional sales conferences. I accompanied him to the first conference. I'll never forget it.
>
> To an audience of fifty sales managers he announced that the 2 percent override they were presently earning on their units' sales production was to be reduced to 1 percent. "However," he said, "in lieu of that 1 percent, you will receive a very nice gift for each new person you recruit and train."
>
> At that point a sales manager stood up and let him have it with both barrels. She was absolutely furious. "How dare you do this to us? Why, even 2 percent wasn't enough. But cutting our overrides in half and offering us a crummy gift for appeasement insults our intelligence." With that she stormed out of the room. And every other sales manager for that state followed her — all fifty of them. In one fell swoop the owner had lost his entire sales organization in that region — the best in the country. I had never seen such an overwhelming rejection of a change of this kind in my entire life![49]

Top-down change means that initiation of the idea occurs at upper levels and is implemented downward. It does not mean that lower-level employees are not educated about the change or allowed to participate in it.

Culture/People Changes

A **culture/people change** refers to a change in employees' values, norms, attitudes, beliefs, and behavior. Changes in culture and people pertain to how employees think; these are changes in mindset rather than technology, structure, or products. People change pertains to just a few employees, such as when a handful of middle managers are sent to a training course to improve their leadership skills. Culture change pertains to the organization as a whole, such as when Union Pacific Railroad changed its basic mindset by becoming less bureaucratic and focusing employees on customer service and quality through teamwork and employee participation.[50] Training is the most frequently used tool for changing the organization's mindset. A company may offer training programs to large blocks of employees on subjects such as teamwork, listening skills, quality circles, and participative management. Training programs will be discussed further in Chapter 12 on human resource management.

Another major approach to changing people and culture is organizational development. This has evolved as a separate field that is devoted to large-scale organization change.

culture/people change A change in employees' values, norms, attitudes, beliefs, and behavior.

Organizational Development

organizational development (OD) The application of behavioral science techniques to improve an organization's health and effectiveness through its ability to cope with environmental changes, improve internal relationships, and increase problem-solving capabilities.

Organizational development (OD) is the application of behavioral science knowledge to improve an organization's health and effectiveness through its ability to cope with environmental changes, improve internal relationships, and increase problem-solving capabilities.[51] Organizational development improves working relationships among employees.

The following are three types of current problems that OD can help managers address.[52]

1. *Mergers/Acquisitions.* The disappointing financial results of many mergers and acquisitions is caused by the failure of executives to determine whether the administrative style and corporate culture of the two companies "fit." Executives may concentrate on potential synergies in technology, products, marketing, and control systems, but fail to recognize that two firms may have widely different values, beliefs, and practices. These differences create stress and anxiety for employees, and these negative emotions affect future performance. Cultural differences should be evaluated in the acquisition process, and OD experts can be used to smooth the integration of two firms.
2. *Organizational Decline/Revitalization.* Organizations undergoing a period of decline and revitalization experience a variety of problems, including a low level of trust, lack of innovation, high turnover, and high levels of conflict and stress. The period of transition requires opposite behaviors, including confronting stress, open communication, and creative innovation to emerge with high levels of productivity. OD techniques can contribute greatly to cultural revitalization by managing conflicts, fostering commitment, and facilitating communication.
3. *Conflict Management.* Conflict can occur at any time and place within a healthy organization. For example, a product team for the introduction of a new software package was formed at a computer company. Made up of strong-willed individuals, the team made little progress because members would not agree on project goals. At a manufacturing firm, salespeople promised delivery dates to customers that were in conflict with shop supervisor priorities for assembling customer orders. In a publishing company, two managers disliked each other intensely. They argued at meetings, lobbied politically against each other, and hurt the achievement of both departments. Organizational development efforts can help solve these kinds of conflicts.

Organizational development can be used to treat the types of problems described above and many others. Specialized OD techniques have been developed for these applications.

OD Activities

A number of OD activities have emerged in recent years. Some of the most popular and effective are as follows.

1. *Team-Building Activities.* **Team building** enhances the cohesiveness and success of organizational groups and teams. For example, a series of OD exercises can be used with members of cross-departmental teams to help them learn to act and function as a team. An OD expert can work with team members to increase their communication skills, facilitate their ability to confront one another, and accept common goals.
2. *Survey-Feedback Activities.* **Survey feedback** begins with a questionnaire distributed to employees on values, climate, participation, leadership, and group cohesion within their organization.[53] After the survey is completed, an OD consultant meets with groups of employees to provide feedback about their responses and the problems identified.[54] Employees are engaged in problem solving based on the data.

team building A type of OD intervention that enhances the cohesiveness of departments by helping members to learn to function as a team.

survey feedback A type of OD intervention in which questionnaires on organizational climate and other factors are distributed among employees and the results reported back to them by a change agent.

Employees at General Motors of Canada experience a heart-stopping event when standing on a wobbly disc on top of the 25-foot "Pamper Pole" at New Mexico's Pecos River Conference Center. GM uses this *organizational development* program to help employees break old patterns and fears and to help open them up to new possibilities. Often groups are cross-functional teams, so the OD training enhances intergroup coordination and effectiveness.

3. *Intergroup Activities.* These activities include retreats and workshops to improve the effectiveness of groups or departments that must work together. The focus is on helping employees develop the skills to resolve conflicts, increase coordination, and develop better ways of working together.
4. *Process-Consultation Activities.* Organizational development consultants help managers understand the human processes within their organization and how to manage them. Managers learn to think in terms of culture values, leadership, communication, and intergroup cooperation.
5. *Symbolic Leadership Activities.* This approach helps managers learn to use the techniques for cultural change described in Chapter 3, including public statements, symbols, ceremonies, and slogans. For example, public statements that define a path-finding vision and cultural values account for the success of such companies as Disney, Dana, and Wal-mart. Managers can signal appropriate behavior through symbols and ceremonies, such as when Roy Ash had several of AM International's copying machines removed to signal the need for less paperwork. Harold Geneen, president of ITT, captured the new value for his corporation with the slogan: "Search for the Unshakeable Facts," which helped do away with smoke screens and political games.

OD Steps

Consider the cultural change at Westinghouse Canada's manufacturing facility at Airdrie, Alberta. Cycle time for made-to-order motor-controlled devices was reduced from 17 weeks to 1 week. One major requirement for reducing the time was to change the mindset of both managers and workers to give workers more discretion. Instead of waiting for approval from superiors, production employees now talk directly with customers and suppliers to solve their problems.[55]

Organization development experts acknowledge that corporate culture and human behavior are relatively stable and that companywide changes, such as at Westinghouse Canada, require major effort. The theory underlying organizational development proposes three distinct steps for achieving behavioral and attitudinal change: (1) unfreezing, (2) changing, and (3) refreezing.[56]

unfreezing A step in the diagnosis stage of organizational development in which participants are made aware of problems in order to increase their willingness to change their behavior.

change agent An OD specialist who contracts with an organization to facilitate change.

changing A step in the intervention stage of organizational development in which individuals experiment with new workplace behavior.

In the first step, **unfreezing,** participants must be made aware of problems and be willing to change. This step is often associated with *diagnosis,* which uses an outside expert called a change agent. The **change agent** is an OD specialist who performs a systematic diagnosis of the organization and identifies work-related problems. He or she gathers and analyzes data through personal interviews, questionnaires, and observations of meetings. The diagnosis helps determine the extent of organizational problems and helps unfreeze managers by making them aware of problems in their behavior.

The second step, **changing,** occurs when individuals experiment with new behavior and learn new skills to be used in the workplace. This is sometimes known as *intervention,* during which the change agent implements a specific plan for training managers and employees. This plan may include team-building, intergroup, process-consultation, and symbolic leadership activities as described above.

Employees of Continental Inc. participate in a two-day seminar on service and enthusiasm. Theodora M. Pierakos, the facilitator, helps *unfreeze* and encourage *movement* toward new behaviors. Pierakos works with the Quality Service Institute, a joint effort of Texas Air Corporation and Scandinavian Airlines System. Employees enjoy the seminar and are learning new attitudes and values that will be *refrozen* and used on the job.

The third step, **refreezing,** occurs when individuals acquire new attitudes or values and are rewarded for them by the organization. The impact of new behaviors is evaluated and reinforced. The change agent supplies new data that show positive changes in performance. Senior executives can reward positive behavioral changes by employees. Managers and employees also participate in refresher courses to maintain and reinforce the new behaviors.

refreezing A step in the reinforcement stage of organizational development in which individuals acquire a desired new skill or attitude and are rewarded for it by the organization.

The spirit of what OD tries to accomplish with culture/people change was illustrated in Honeywell's use of OD to change the corporate culture from an autocratic to a participative mindset.

HONEYWELL CORP.

• For many years a Honeywell division had been an authoritarian entity. Now top managers believed that individuals could contribute to effectiveness if middle- and lower-level managers would allow them to participate more fully:

> Many organizations today want to break out of the beat-'em-up school of management and move toward a more participative management style. But like abused children who grow up to become abusive parents, managers raised in a less enlightened manner may have difficulty operating under a new set of rules.
>
> At Honeywell, we have been working to change from what I call the Patton style of management to a more collaborative way of operating. The way we manage people is still less than perfect. But now our employees can have a real share of the action rather than feeling blocked or frustrated by a rigid bureaucracy.[57]

The implementation of this new way of thinking was not easy. Managers and employees alike had to think in a different way and approach one another with respect and a desire for a positive working relationship. The new values that Honeywell wished to inculcate included the following management principles, published and circulated among all employees:

1. Productivity is a responsibility shared by management and employees.
2. Broadened employee participation in decision making will be fostered.

3. Teamwork, mutual respect, and a sense of ownership will be promoted at all divisional levels.
4. A positive climate for career growth will be supported throughout the division.
5. Work life and personal life have interacting requirements that will be recognized.

Through OD Honeywell created a higher level of participation for employees. Managers learned to think of employees as whole people, not as instruments of production.[58]

SUMMARY

Change is inevitable in organizations. This chapter discussed the techniques available for managing the change process. Managers should think of change as having four elements — the forces for change, the perceived need for change, initiation of change, and implementation of change. Forces for change can originate either within or outside the firm, and managers are responsible for monitoring events that may require a planned organizational response. Techniques for initiating changes include designing the organization for creativity, encouraging change agents, and establishing new-venture teams or skunkworks. The final step is implementation. Force field analysis is one technique for diagnosing restraining forces, which often can be removed. Managers also should draw on the implementation tactics of communication, participation, negotiation, coercion, or top management support.

This chapter also discussed specific types of change. Technology changes are accomplished through a bottom-up approach that utilizes experts close to the technology. Successful new-product introduction requires horizontal linkage among marketing, research and development, manufacturing, and perhaps other departments. Structural changes tend to be initiated in a top-down fashion, because upper managers are the administrative experts and champion these ideas for approval and implementation. Culture/people change pertains to the skills, behaviors, and attitudes of employees. Organizational development is an important approach to changes in people's mindset and corporate culture. The OD process entails three steps — unfreezing (diagnosis of the problem), the actual change (intervention), and refreezing (reinforcement of new attitudes and behaviors). Popular OD techniques include team building, survey feedback, intergroup skills, and process consultation.

MANAGEMENT SOLUTION

Preston Trucking Company, hammered by deregulation and unhappy employees, decided to revise its corporate culture and encourage bottom-up change in its production process. The survey results indicating how bad things were unfroze management. Consultants were brought in, and meetings were held to determine the best way to proceed and to gain employee participation. A new mindset was introduced that made employees equal partners in the trucking business. Improved production efficiency occurred through weekly idea meetings from which suggestions flowed from lower-level employees. In one year, over

4,000 money-making ideas were proposed, worth about $1.5 million. One idea helped decrease truck service maintenance from 23 hours to 11 hours. With both a new corporate culture and a steady bottom-up flow of modifications in production technology, Preston has become the darling of the trucking industry. Growth is rapid, sales and profits are up, and grievances are way down. Preston is a model for how to change effectively.[59]

DISCUSSION QUESTIONS

1. A manager for an international chemical company said that very few new products in her company were successful. What would you advise the manager to do to help increase the company's success rate?
2. What are internal and external forces for change? Which force do you think is the major cause of organizational change?
3. Carefully planned change often is assumed to be effective. Do you think unplanned change can sometimes be beneficial to an organization? Discuss.
4. Why do organizations experience resistance to change? What techniques can managers use to overcome resistance?
5. Explain force field analysis. Analyze the driving and restraining forces for a change with which you have been associated.
6. Define the roles associated with an idea champion. Why are idea champions so essential to the initiation of change?
7. To what extent would changes in technology affect products, and vice versa? Compare the process for changing technology and that for product change.
8. Given that structure change is often made top down, should coercive implementation techniques be used?
9. Do the underlying values of organizational development differ from assumptions associated with other types of change? Discuss.
10. Compare and contrast team-building and survey-feedback techniques for OD intervention.

MANAGEMENT IN PRACTICE: EXPERIENTIAL EXERCISE

Is Your Company Creative?

An effective way to assess the creative climate of an organization for which you have worked is to fill out the questionnaire below. Answer each question based on your work experience in that firm. Discuss the results with members of your group and talk about whether changing the firm along the dimensions in the questions would make it more creative.

Instructions: Answer each of the following questions using the five-point scale. (*Note there is no rating of 4:* 0, we never do this; 1, we rarely do this; 2, we sometimes do this; 3, we frequently do this; 5, we always do this.

_______ We are encouraged to seek help anywhere inside or outside the organization with new ideas for our work unit.

_______ Assistance is provided to develop ideas into proposals for management review.

_______ Our performance reviews encourage risky, creative efforts, ideas, and actions.

_______ We are encouraged to fill our minds with new information by attending professional meetings, trade fairs, visiting customers, etc.

_______ Our meetings are designed to allow people to free-wheel, brainstorm, and generate ideas.

_______ All members contribute ideas during meetings.
_______ During meetings, there is much spontaneity and humor.
_______ We discuss how company structure and our actions help or spoil creativity within our work unit.
_______ During meetings, the chair is rotated among members.
_______ Everyone in the work unit receives training in creativity techniques and maintaining a creative climate.

To measure how effectively your organization fosters creativity, use the following scale:

Highly effective:	15–20
Moderately effective:	10–14
Moderately ineffective:	5–9
Ineffective:	0–4

Source: Adapted from Edward Glassman, *Creativity Handbook: Idea Triggers and Sparks That Work* published by LCS Press (Chapel Hill, NC: 1990). Used by permission. (919/967-2015)

CASES FOR ANALYSIS

DELL IMAGING SYSTEMS, INC.

Monica was angry and frustrated. "How do *they* expect me to run my department if I don't know what's going on?" She asked herself. The "they" she was angry with were Rudy Levine, her immediate supervisor, and Andy Shoreham, the vice-president of the division.

Monica's department was responsible for the production and assembly of high-performance terminals. Her team was experienced and knowledgeable about all phases of production. Production for the last quarter was down, the number of rejects was up, and the number of complaint calls for delayed deliveries was well above normal. But Monica did not blame her staffers. The problem was with upper management, namely Rudy and Andy.

For weeks, Rudy and Andy had discussed producing a newer, better type of terminal. Much research had been done on the new design, and an outside contractor had been hired to produce a dozen prototypes. These were tested and found to be superior to the former model. So Rudy and Andy decided to start production as soon as the new equipment had been ordered, delivered, and installed. Then Rudy told Monica about their plans. Monica was so flabbergasted that she at first couldn't speak.

"The new equipment will be coming in a couple of weeks," he said, "and we'd like you to start production as soon as everything is set up."

"This is a fine time to tell me about your plans," Monica finally said. "How am I supposed to have my staff ready for the new operation?"

"Well, there'll be a training period, of course," Rudy said, "but your team of experts should have no trouble picking up a new routine. The equipment isn't so different from what they're using now. We expect production to be up to your usual standards by the end of the quarter."

"That's not very much time, Rudy."

"Well, I'm sure your staff can handle it."

"I'm glad you're so sure," Monica said just before she left his office.

When Monica told her staffers the news, they were shocked. They wanted to know all about the change: why they weren't told about it sooner, what the new equipment was like, how much training would be needed, how much time they had to master the new procedures. Monica answered their questions as best she could but Rudy hadn't given her much information during their meeting that morning.

By the end of the quarter, Monica was not surprised that some of her staffers still had not mastered the equipment. She had attended the training sessions with her crew and had helped out wherever she could. But production was slow going, and Rudy was asking what the problems were with output.

Questions

1. What type of innovation is the new terminal, and what process was used for its introduction?
2. How could Rudy and Andy have better handled this situation?
3. What might Monica do to ease the situation for her staffers?

Source: Grace Lander, "Terminal Trouble," *Supervisory Management* (September 1989), 3–5. Used with permission.

SOUTHWESTERN BELL CORPORATION

Southwestern Bell was a conservative, stable company with a dedicated work force. Suddenly the environment shifted. Sweeping regulatory changes and a flood of new technology and market opportunities washed over the company. The telecommunications world was literally turned upside down.

How did SBC respond? CEO Zane Barnes decided to launch a program to encourage employees to be idea champions. He believed that the response to environmental changes had to come from individual employees: "Our people know this business, and they have good ideas. We want them to know those ideas will be appreciated and used."

Barnes started implementing the innovation values in several ways. He explained the idea to top managers at the annual corporate policy seminar. He also brought in experts to speak to management groups. A new quarterly, *Enterprise,* was devoted to articles celebrating company idea champions. SBC also created small, separate profit centers to give divisions more autonomy. Expenditure decisions were pushed down to low levels. A new management incentive program gave bonuses to exceptional performers.

The next problem concerned reinforcing employees who had helped make the company more efficient or responsive to customers. Barnes decided to create a series of awards. The Rider Service Award was given for creative employee contributions. One winner was a manager whose invention had trimmed average service restoration time from 4 hours to 15 minutes. New procedures were also established for helping employees get financial help and protoypes built.

The innovative culture is working. One subsidiary that publishes yellow pages directories has a hot new product — the Silver Pages discount directory for senior citizens. Another subsidiary, Telecom, radically changed its commission schedule for salespeople. An engineer at Southwestern Bell Mobile Systems devised an ingenious system for monitoring the mobile telephone network 24 hours a day. This saves the company money and is going to be developed and sold to other companies.

Questions

1. Do the changes taking place at Southwestern Bell Corporation follow four stages of forces, need, initiation, and implementation? Explain.
2. What type of change — technology, products, structure, or people — is the shift toward idea champions? To what extent does the primary change have secondary effects on other types of change at SBC?
3. What techniques were used for change implementation? Would you recommend additional techniques to further implement the new philosophy at SBC?

Source: Based on "'Intrapreneuring' after the Big Breakup," *Management Review* (July 1986), 8–9.

CHAPTER 12

HUMAN RESOURCE MANAGEMENT

CHAPTER OUTLINE

Goals of HRM

Environmental Influences on HRM

Competitive Strategy
Federal Legislation
Trends in Society

Attracting an Effective Work Force

Human Resource Planning
Recruiting
Selection

Developing an Effective Work Force

Training and Development
Performance Appraisal

Maintaining an Effective Work Force

Compensation
Wage and Salary Structure
Benefits
Terminations

LEARNING OBJECTIVES

After studying this chapter, you should be able to:

- Explain the role of human resource management in organizational strategic planning.
- Describe federal legislation and societal trends that influence human resource management.
- Describe how human resource professionals work with line managers to attract, develop, and maintain human resources in the organization.
- Explain how organizations determine their future staffing needs through human resource planning.
- Describe the tools managers use to recruit and select employees.
- Describe how organizations develop an effective work force through training and performance appraisal.
- Explain how organizations maintain a work force through the administration of wages and salaries, benefits, and terminations.

Management Problem

When Thomas Melohn acquired North American Tool & Die Inc., the company was in trouble. The metal-stamping and subassembly small business used older, labor-intensive machines, whereas its well-heeled, offshore competitors used highly automated technology to achieve efficiency and quality. Other domestic job-shops were going out of business left and right, so Melohn needed a strategy to regain his company's competitiveness. North American's profits were marginal, its work force unenthusiastic, and its prospects dim. Employee turnover was 27 percent annually. A full 7 percent of production output was rejected. CEO Melohn agonized over his top priority — how to find and keep good people.[1]

What should Thomas Melohn do to meet the need for high-quality employees? Can human resources be part of the strategy to restore North American's competitiveness?

North American Tool & Die's past performance illustrates the need for managing human resources. Thomas Melohn and his management team must develop the company's ability to recruit, train, and keep first-quality employees; otherwise, company growth will be restricted and performance will continue to suffer. The term **human resource management (HRM)** refers to activities undertaken to attract, develop, and maintain an effective work force within an organization. Companies such as IBM, General Electric, and Hewlett-Packard have become famous for their philosophy about human resource management, which is the foundation of their success.

human resource management (HRM) Activities undertaken to attract, develop, and maintain an effective work force within an organization.

Human resource management consists of three parts. First, all managers are human resource managers. For example, at IBM every manager is expected to pay attention to the development and satisfaction of subordinates. Line managers use surveys, career planning, performance appraisal, and compensation to encourage lifelong commitment to IBM.[2] Second, employees are viewed as assets. Employees, not buildings and machinery, give a company a competitive advantage, such as Tom Melohn is trying to accomplish with North American Tool & Die. Third, human resource management is a matching process, integrating the organization's goals with employees' needs. Employees should receive satisfaction equal to the company.

Enlightened firms such as Tenneco view employees as *assets* and are concerned about their personal as well as professional growth. These Tenneco employees are jogging on the indoor track at Tenneco's Employee Center. It also contains complete exercise facilities, saunas, whirlpools, and racquetball courts. Facilities are free to Tenneco employees. The benefits of counting healthy employees as assets include reduced turnover, less absenteeism, and higher morale and productivity.

GOALS OF HRM

In this chapter, we will examine the three primary goals of HRM as illustrated in Exhibit 12.1. These goals take place within the larger organizational environment, including competitive strategy, federal legislation, and societal trends. The three goals are to attract an effective work force to the organization, develop the work force to its potential, and maintain the work force over the longer term.[3] Achieving these goals requires skills in planning, forecasting, training, performance appraisal, wage and salary administration, benefit programs and even termination. Each of the activities in Exhibit 12.1 will be discussed in this chapter. Most organizations employ human resource professionals to perform these functions. *Human resource specialists* focus on one of the HRM areas, such as recruitment of employees or administration of wage or benefit programs. *Human resource generalists* have responsibility in more than one HRM area.

ENVIRONMENTAL INFLUENCE ON HRM

As the value of human resource management has been increasingly recognized in recent years, HRM departments have contributed to organizations in three ways. First, senior HRM executives participate directly in the formulation and implementation of a company's competitive strategy. Second, HRM professionals interpret federal legislation and implement corresponding procedures. Third, issues and trends in society are detected and changes implemented to meet the evolving needs of the work force.

COMPETITIVE STRATEGY

The human resource management function has changed enormously over the years. In the 1920s, HRM was a low-level position charged with ensuring that procedures were developed for hiring and firing employees and with implementing benefit plans. By the 1950s unions were a major force, and the HRM manager was elevated to a senior position as chief negotiator. During the 1980s, unions began to decline and top HRM managers became directly involved in corporate strategic management.[4]

Exhibit 12.2 illustrates the interdependence between organizational and human resource strategy. The organization's competitive strategy may include mergers and acquisitions, downsizing to increase efficiency, or the acquisition of automated production technology. These strategic decisions determine the demand for skills and employees. The human resource strategy, in turn, must include the correct employee makeup to enable the organization to take advantage of strategic opportunities. In the 1990s strategic decisions more than ever have to be based on human resource considerations. For example, **downsizing** is the systematic reduction in the number of managers and employees to make a company more cost efficient and competitive.[5] When IBM needed a leaner work force to remain competitive in the late 1980s, the HRM department

downsizing The systematic reduction in the number of managers and employees to make a company more cost efficient and competitive.

EXHIBIT 12.1
Human Resource Management Goals

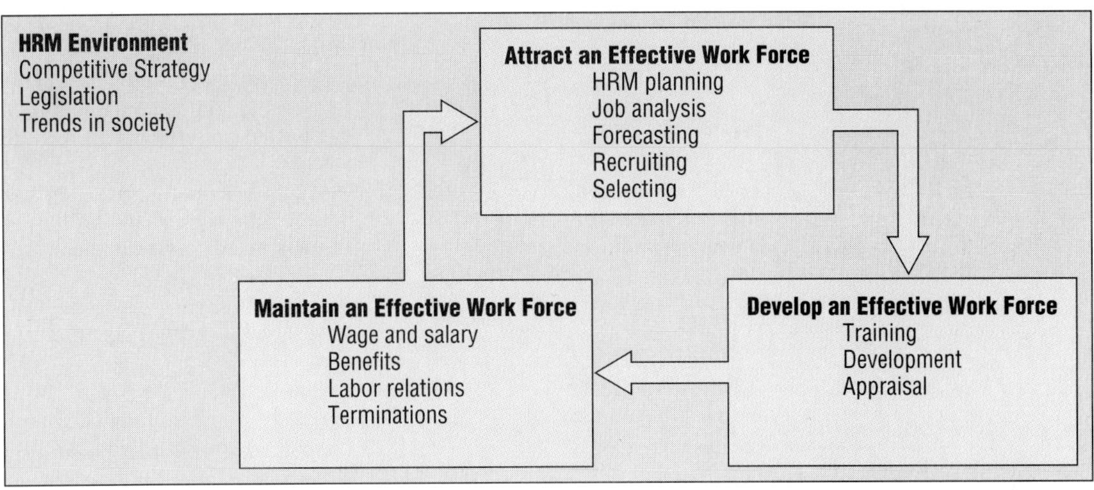

EXHIBIT 12.2
Interdependence of Organizational and Human Resource Strategy

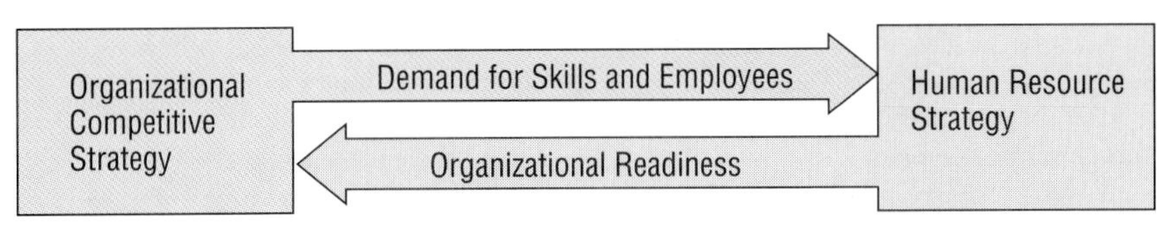

Source: Adapted from Cynthia A. Lengnick-Hall and Mark L. Lengnick-Hall, "Strategic Human Resources Management: A Review of the Literature and a Proposed Typology," *Academy of Management Review* 13 (1988), 454–470.

made it a morale-boosting rather than morale-busting exercise. An early retirement program was designed that was accepted by 15,000 employees. In addition, 9,400 people were retrained to move from declining to expanding divisions. Another 24,600 employees were lost through normal attrition. During this time, 23,400 new hires were added to high-growth businesses such as software. The net effect was the strategic reduction of IBM's employment by 16,200—without an ax—thanks to an effective human resource strategy.[6]

As another example, the introduction of flexible manufacturing systems such as those described in Chapter 10 have dramatically changed the need for work-force skill. These new machines require a highly skilled work force, including interpersonal skills and the ability to work as a team. To make the strategic change to automated technology, the HRM department must upgrade the quality of employees and recruit new employees who have human skills as well as technical skills. The HRM department must also develop new pay systems that provide group incentives and profit sharing, provide worker retraining and development, and facilitate new labor-management relationships.[7]

EXHIBIT 12.3
Major Federal Laws Related to Human Resource Management

Federal Law	Year	Provisions
Equal Pay Act	1963	Prohibits sex differences in pay for substantially equal work.
Civil Rights Act, Title VII	1964	Prohibits discrimination in employment on basis of race, religion, color, sex, or national origin.
Executive Orders 11246 and 11375	1965 1967	Requires federal contractors to eliminate employment discrimination through affirmative actions.
Age Discrimination in Employment Act (amended 1978 and 1986)	1967	Prohibits age discrimination against those between the ages of 40 and 65 years and restricts mandatory retirement.
Executive Order 11478	1969	Prohibits discrimination in the U.S. postal service and in various government agencies.
Occupational Safety and Health Act (OSHA)	1970	Establishes mandatory safety and health standards in organizations.
Vocational Rehabilitation Act	1973	Prohibits discrimination based on physical or mental handicap and requires that employees be informed about affirmative action plans.
Vietnam-Era Veterans Readjustment Act	1974	Prohibits discrimination against disabled veterans and Vietnam-era veterans and requires affirmative action.
Pregnancy Discrimination Act	1978	Requires that women affected by pregnancy, childbirth, or related medical conditions be treated as all other employees for employment-related purposes, including benefits.
Immigration Reform and Control Act	1986	Prohibits employers from knowingly hiring illegal aliens, and prohibits employment on the basis of national origin or citizenship.

FEDERAL LEGISLATION

Over the last 30 years, several federal laws have been passed to insure equal employment opportunity (EEO). A summary of key legislation and Executive orders is in Exhibit 12.3. The point of the laws is to stop discriminatory practices that are unfair to specific groups and to define enforcement agencies for these laws. EEO legislation attempts to balance the pay given to men and women; provide employment opportunities without regard to race, religion, national origin, and sex; insure fair treatment for employees of all ages; and avoid discrimination against handicapped individuals. More recent legislation pertains to Vietnam-era veterans, pregnant women, and illegal aliens.

discrimination The hiring or promoting of applicants based on criteria that are not job relevant.

The Equal Employment Opportunity Commission (EEOC) created by the Civil Rights Act of 1964 initiates investigations in response to complaints concerning discrimination. The EEOC is the major agency involved with employment discrimination. **Discrimination** occurs when some applicants are hired or promoted based on criteria that are not job relevant. For example, refusing

XEROX
A team that has no prejudice has no limits.
The strongest team, the strongest business, the strongest country, is one where there is freedom to be yourself without inequality or prejudice.
We have seen prejudice hurt all those who participate in it. And we've seen togetherness and equality give power and joy.
That's why, at Xerox, we are dedicated to working towards a world where there is only one race...the human race.
Starting in 1968 we began a major effort, both within Xerox and in the communities around us, to make the concept of equal opportunity a reality.
In a 1968 memo, Xerox president Joseph Wilson said: "We, like all other Americans, share the responsibility for a color-divided nation and, in all honesty, we need not look beyond our own doorstep to find out why. But we can and will change."
And we did. Xerox developed programs in every phase of its structure, from pre-entry training up through the top of upper management.
Over the years, our minority programs made so much progress that we were awarded the Department of Labor Exemplary Voluntary Effort Award for affirmative action.
We've created a team that we believe is the strongest possible, without the constraints of prejudice, to serve our clients proudly and productively.
But to us at Team Xerox, it's just the beginning. Until the whole world is a team that works together with respect, fairness and equality; until all of us are without prejudice, we have only just begun.
Team Xerox.
We document the world.

The spirit of *affirmative action* is alive at Xerox. For more than 20 years Xerox has developed programs to make equal opportunity a reality for everyone, from preentry through upper management. The company allows no prejudice against minority groups, the aging, or the handicapped. Xerox believes it can serve clients proudly and productively with its strongest possible team only without the constraints of prejudice.

to hire blacks or women for jobs they could readily handle or paying a woman a lower wage than a man for the same work are examples of discrimination. When discrimination is found, remedies include back pay and affirmative action. **Affirmative action** requires that an employer take positive steps to guarantee equal employment opportunities for people within protected groups. An affirmative action plan is a formal document that can be reviewed by employees and enforcement agencies. Organizational affirmative action reduces or eliminates internal inequities among affected employee groups.

Failure to comply with equal employment opportunity legislation can result in substantial fines and penalties for employers. For example, Wendy's was charged with failing to promote female managers. The food chain agreed to pay a total of $1.4 million to 700 women, fill 40 percent of upper-management and 50 percent of lower-management vacancies with women, and hold EEO seminars for all managerial employees. AT&T agreed to pay over $15 million in back wages to women and other minority groups whose pay was deemed to be arbitrarily low because of discriminatory practices. In another case, a policewoman was found to have been sexually harassed and then retaliated against by management for filing a discrimination complaint. She was awarded over $22,000 in back pay and $24,000 in lieu of being reinstated as a police officer.[8]

affirmative action A policy requiring employers to take positive steps to guarantee equal employment opportunities for people within protected groups.

One thing concerning human resource legislation is clear: The scope of equal employment opportunity legislation is increasing at federal, state, and municipal levels. The interest in the working rights and conditions of women, minorities, older employees, and the handicapped will all receive increasing attention in the future. Also, most cases in the past have concerned lower-level jobs, but the 1990s will see more attention given to equal employment opportunity in upper-level management positions.

TRENDS IN SOCIETY

The complexity of demands on human resource executives often seems overwhelming. Just as HR managers learn to insert themselves into corporate strategy making and learn the subtleties of such federal regulations as the Vietnam-Era Veterans Readjustment Act, other trends surface that raise new problems for staffing the firm. These trends include everything from court decisions that decide against companies that fire employees to dramatic changes in the makeup of the labor force. A few of the important current trends are as follows.

WORK-FORCE DIVERSITY. The people filling jobs in the year 2000 will have a different racial and gender makeup than current employees. Native white males made up 47 percent of employees in 1989 but will constitute only 15 percent of new entrants. By the year 2000 Hispanics will account for almost 28 percent of labor force growth and blacks about 17 percent. White women will provide about 42 percent of labor force growth. Innovative human resource managers will adapt to these changes with special recruiting programs targeted toward these groups and organizational changes to accommodate their needs. Day-care centers, special benefit packages, and language training may all become part of the inducements to employees.[9]

LABOR SCARCITY. The changing makeup of the labor force is partly explained by its slowing growth. The baby bust following the baby boom means that fewer workers are entering the work force compared with the explosive growth in the early 1980s. This shortage hits small businesses especially hard because two-thirds of new entrants to the work force begin their careers in a small business. These shortages are leading to creative responses on the part of many companies. One approach is to examine untapped human resources such as retired people and teenagers. Indeed, so many businesses are turning to teenagers that violations in child labor laws have skyrocketed.[10] Another approach is for businesses to provide basic education to dropouts so that they are prepared for the technical and social demands of a career in business. More concessions will be made to working women, and some efforts may even be undertaken to lower the requirements for immigration from other countries.[11]

EMPLOYMENT AT WILL. Employers no longer enjoy the undisputed right to fire employees. Many discharged employees are filing lawsuits with almost 80 percent of the verdicts favoring the employee and damage awards exceeding $100,000. The *employment-at-will* rule traditionally permitted an employer to fire an employee for just cause, or even no cause. Now 40 states have written employment laws to protect wrongful firing of employees who refuse to violate

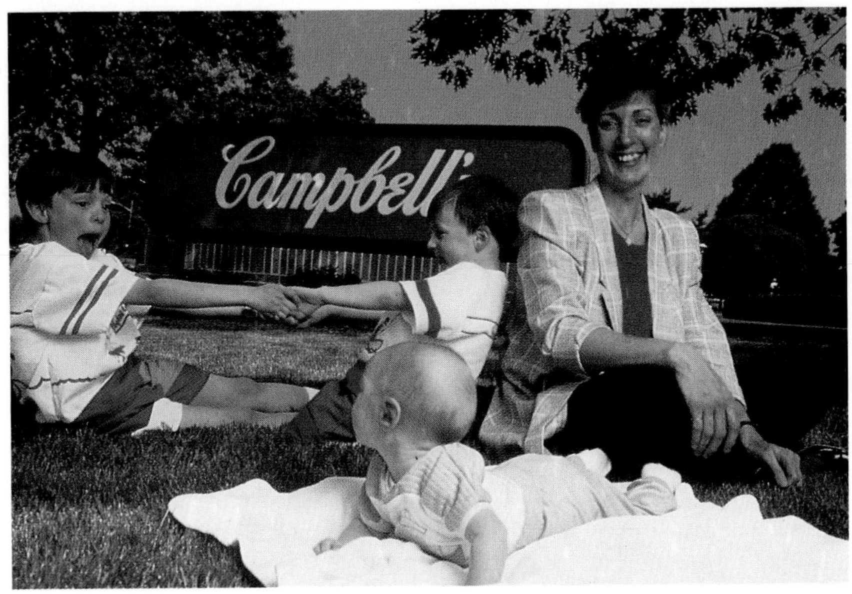

Susan Snyder remains a loyal employee of Campbell Soup Company, because it provides on-site day care and permits part-time work schedules. Susan Snyder reflects one aspect of *work-force diversity* wherein mothers make up a larger percentage of the labor force. Her days run nonstop, from six in the morning until ten at night with a part-time work schedule, errands, chores, and caring for three children with her husband. Campbell has adapted its human resource management policies to make room for employees like Snyder to the benefit of both employee and company.

a law or who expose an illegal action by their employers. Many employers are now spelling out their termination policy to employees, asking them to acknowledge that the employment agreement can be terminated at any time, thereby avoiding an implied long-term employment contract.[12]

EMPLOYEE FLEXIBILITY. One of the clearest trends is the increased effort to obtain quality employees and at the same time reduce excess employee costs so that firms can remain competitive in the global marketplace. This means employers will be making greater use of part-time employees, work schedules that allow employees to work other than the traditional hours during the day, employee leasing and temporary employees, as well as employees who work under contract only for specific hours and tasks, thereby allowing employers to get exactly what they need and avoiding the provision of offices and benefits on a full-time basis.

Companies such as Bowater, Digital Equipment, Hallmark, Pacific Bell, and Worthington Industries have turned to employee flexibility to reduce costs without laying off valued employees. For example, during slack times, Hallmark manufacturing workers may take a turn working in the kitchen of the company cafeteria. Hallmark also conducts classes in shorthand and typing, filling clerical positions with people formerly in factory jobs.

UNIONIZATION. The general trend in North America is away from unionization, but many employees belong to unions and unions continue to unionize new companies. The National Labor Relation Act of 1935 provides that employees may elect to be represented by unions in negotiations with employers over wages, hours, and other terms and conditions of employment. Currently about one-fourth of all workers are covered by collective bargaining agreements. In companies where unions represent workers, union officials research the needs of members, the elements of the pay package, and the employers'

EXHIBIT 12.4
Attracting an Effective Work Force

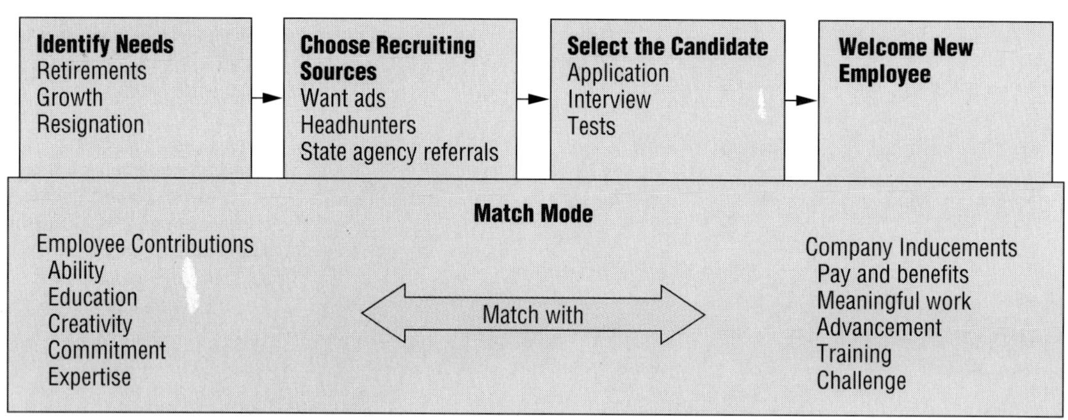

financial condition. When a contract expires, union officials negotiate on behalf of the members of the bargaining unit for desired pay components and other issues relevant to workers.[13]

Some companies find unionization a benefit; others try to avoid unionization. Indeed, just the threat of a union may cause an employer to adjust pay and benefits. At Cannon Mills Company, three mills had to be closed and as a result some employees tried to unionize. Cannon's management responded by persuading workers that the union would not improve benefits and would simply take part of the employees' paychecks in the form of union dues. The most promising trend in recent years has been the responsiveness of unions to new competitive conditions. The need for cross training, employee participation, and new compensation systems to meet global competition have brought unions into closer collaboration with management.

Within this context of changes in the larger society, human resource managers must achieve the three primary goals described earlier in this chapter: attracting, developing, and maintaining an effective work force for the organization. Let us now review some of the established techniques for accomplishing these goals.

ATTRACTING AN EFFECTIVE WORK FORCE

The first goal of HRM is to attract individuals who show signs of becoming valued, productive, and satisfied employees. The first step in attracting an effective work force involves human resource planning, in which managers or HRM professionals predict the need for new employees based on the types of vacancies that exist, as illustrated in Exhibit 12.4. The second step is to use recruiting procedures to communicate with potential applicants. The third step is to select from the applicants those persons believed to be the best potential contributors to the organization. Finally, the new employee is welcomed into the organization.

Underlying the organization's effort to attract employees is a matching model. With the **matching model,** the organization and the individual attempt to match the needs, interests, and values that they offer each other. The organization offers "inducements," and the employee offers "contributions."[14] HRM professionals attempt to identify a correct match. For example, a small software developer may require long hours from creative, technically skilled employees. In return, it can offer freedom from bureaucracy, tolerance of idiosyncrasies, and potentially high pay. A large manufacturer can offer employment security and stability, but it may have more rules and regulations and require greater skills for "getting approval from the higher-ups." The individual who would thrive working for the software developer might feel stymied and unhappy working for a large manufacturer. Both the company and the employee are interested in finding a good match.

matching model An employee selection approach in which the organization and the applicant attempt to match each other's needs, interests, and values.

human resource planning The forecasting of human resource needs and the projected matching of individuals with expected job vacancies.

Human Resource Planning

Human resource planning is the forecasting of human resource needs and the projected matching of individuals with expected vacancies. Human resource planning begins with several questions:

- What new technologies are emerging, and how will these affect the work system?
- What is the volume of the business likely to be in the next five to ten years?
- What is the turnover rate, and how much, if any, is avoidable?

The responses to these questions are used to formulate specific questions pertaining to HRM activities, such as the following:

- How many senior managers will we need during this time period?
- What types of engineers will we need, and how many?
- Are persons with adequate computer skills available for meeting our projected needs?
- How many administrative personnel — technicians, secretaries — will we need to support the additional managers and engineers?[15]

Answers to these questions help define the direction for the organization's HRM strategy. For example, if forecasting suggests that there will be a strong need for more technically trained individuals, the organization can (1) define the jobs and skills needed in some detail; (2) hire and train recruiters to look for the specified skills; and/or (3) provide new training for existing employees. By anticipating future HRM needs, the organization can prepare itself to meet competitive challenges more effectively than organizations who react to problems only as they arise.

One of the most successful applications of human resource planning occurred at EDS (Electronic Data Systems).

Human resource planning at McDonald's has helped the company grow with demographic changes. Most employees used to be between 16 and 24 years old, but that percentage is steadily dropping due to an aging population. The number of people age 55 and over has increased dramatically. Many older workers have re-entered the workforce or begin new work experiences at McDonald's later in life. To assist seniors, McDonald's created a program called McMasters that values life experiences and offers a variety of new experiences. In addition, handicapped people can become part of McDonald's through McJobs, a program that identifies and assists these workers.

EDS • EDS's mission is to assume responsibility for customers' computer information processing needs. Following the merger of EDS into General Motors, EDS's work force grew in one year from 14,000 to 40,000. The integration into General Motors more than doubled the demand for EDS services, because EDS took over the reshaping of all GM information systems. Specific projects included a computer-aided telemarketing center, a toll-free customer assistance network, and bringing together computers, robots, and other information technologies to improve information efficiencies.

The impact on human resources was dramatic. EDS had to recruit and hire more than 16,000 new employees and assimilate 9,000 of General Motors' information services employees. EDS's human resources nearly tripled in one year.

HRM professionals responded. EDS defined 7,000 new technical development positions and sought applications, which totaled 225,000. The HRM staff increased the number of full-time recruiters from 70 to over 220. EDS line managers provided backup support and shared the interviewing and selection tasks. One source of pride was that EDS standards were not lowered to meet the enormous hiring goals. Test results showed the new recruits to be among the best qualified ever. Without excellent human resource planning, EDS could not have hired and assimilated this large number of new employees. Human resource management was perhaps the year's single greatest achievement for EDS.[16]

job analysis The process of obtaining accurate and complete information about jobs through a systematic examination of job content.

JOB ANALYSIS. To determine the nature of jobs that are changing, HRM professionals often rely on job analysis. **Job analysis** is the process of obtaining accurate and complete information about jobs through a systematic examination of job content. Job analysis provides valuable data for personnel forecasting and other HRM activities. For example, the information collected during job analysis can be used to determine the qualifications applicants need to perform a job adequately, the performance dimensions on which employees should be evaluated, and the worth of jobs for compensation purposes.

Job analysis information can be gathered by observing incumbents as they work, through interviewing incumbents and/or their supervisors, or through the administration of questionnaires. An example of a job analysis questionnaire is presented in Exhibit 12.5. Observation, interviews, and questionnaires have their own advantages; thus, HRM specialists in job analysis often use more than one technique to obtain the most accurate information.[17]

HRM FORECASTING TECHNIQUES. A variety of HRM forecasting techniques are in use today. These can be classified as short-range and long-range.

Short-range forecasting frequently uses the following steps:

- The demand for the organization's product or service is predicted. Major expected external changes (such as increased demand for a new line of products) are accounted for in this estimation.
- The overall sales forecast is estimated; anticipated internal changes (for example, the conversion to word processors from typewriters) are considered.

EXHIBIT 12.5
Sample Job Analysis Questions

The following questions often are used in job analysis. Written answers are provided by the jobholder.

1. **Job purpose:** In one or two sentences, summarize the primary purpose of your job.
   Sample: Technician — Insures the accuracy of mechanical instruments by performing preventive maintenance, repair, and calibration of equipment. Modifies existing equipment and assists higher classified personnel in the development, construction, testing, and installation of new equipment.
2. **Work activities:** List the activities that you must perform to successfully complete your job assignments. It may be helpful to think of the things you do beginning with the start of your workday and list in normal sequence each activity you perform during the day.
3. **Review and approval of work:**
   (a) Other than your immediate supervisor, does anyone regularly provide guidance to you, review your work in progress, or approve your completed work? Explain who and types of approval.
   (b) Do you regularly provide guidance to anyone, assign, review, or approve work? Explain.
4. **Action/decision authority:** What authority do you have to make decisions on your own or to take personal initiative in fulfilling the activities of your job?
5. **Job requirements:** If you were interviewing someone to fill the position you now hold:
   (a) What kind of knowledge, prior experience, formal training, or certifications should that person possess *at a minimum* upon starting on the job?
   (b) What kind of knowledge, skills, and abilities would you expect the newly hired person to gain while *on the job?*

Source: Based on R. I. Henderson and M. N. Wolfe, *Workbook for Compensation Management: Rewarding Performance,* 4th ed. (Reston, Va.: Reston, 1985).

- Working budgets to reflect the expected work loads of every department are estimated.
- Personnel requirements are determined through conversion of dollars or units into numbers of people.
- Forecasts of labor market conditions or internal organization factors (such as turnover rate) that may affect the future labor supply are considered.

Long-range forecasting ranges from the intuitive to the sophisticated. As described in Chapter 8, some forecasting techniques are based on mathematical extrapolation from past trends. Others involve group decision-making techniques, such as the Delphi method, wherein groups of top managers or other experts use their judgment to make forecasts. Statistical data also are used to project the impact of future employment levels, sales activity, employee turnover, and other variables on the organization's future labor needs.

An example of short-range forecasting occurred when USAir introduced the first Boeing 737-300 into scheduled service. Introducing a new aircraft into an airline operation required careful planning and coordination, beginning with a forecast of the number of pilots needed. Then 737-300 flight simulators had to be obtained and set up in a classroom. Pilots had to be trained before the new aircraft was introduced. New pilots with qualifications fitting the 737-300 also had to be hired. The need for long-range planning was illustrated by General Electric when top executives realized that corporate human resources did not fit new products and technologies. General Electric's chairman said, "We were a company with 30,000 electromechanical engineers becoming a company that needed electronics engineers. We didn't plan for this change . . .

recruiting The activities or practices that define the desired characteristics of applicants for specific jobs.

realistic job preview (RJP) A recruiting approach that gives applicants all pertinent and realistic information about the job and the organization.

and it caused us big problems. . . ." Without planning, a company such as GE could be forced to drain engineers and managers from a stable division to support a growing division, which would propel people into positions above their competence and necessitate a costly rapid-hiring effort.[18]

RECRUITING

Recruiting is defined as "activities or practices that define the characteristics of applicants to whom selection procedures are ultimately applied."[19] Although we frequently think of campus recruiting as a typical recruiting activity, many organizations use *internal recruiting*, or "promote-from-within" policies, to fill their higher-level positions.[20] At Mellon Bank, for example, current employees are given preference when a position opens. Open positions are listed in Mellon's career opportunity bulletins, which are distributed to employees. Internal recruiting has several advantages: It is less costly than an external search, and it generates higher employee commitment, development, and satisfaction, because it offers opportunities for career advancement to employees rather than outsiders.

Frequently, however, *external recruiting* — recruiting newcomers from outside the organization — is advantageous. Applicants are provided by a variety of outside sources including newspaper advertising, state employment services, private employment agencies ("headhunters"), job fairs, and employee referrals. Some employers even provide cash awards for employees who submit names of people who subsequently accept employment, because referrals is one of the cheapest and most reliable methods for external recruiting.[21]

Price Waterhouse recruits people with intelligence, initiative, creativity, and enthusiasm. Beginning with an on-campus interview, Price Waterhouse interviewers learn about candidate qualifications, interests, career goals, and ability to communicate. During an office visit, shown here, candidates talk to Price Waterhouse people at all levels. Candidates are expected to ask questions about the nature of the work and the duties and responsibilities they are expected to perform, which is one form of a *realistic job preview*. Price Waterhouse wants candidates to have all the facts so they can make the right job decision.

REALISTIC JOB PREVIEWS. One approach to enhancing recruiting effectiveness is called a realistic job preview. A **realistic job preview (RJP)** gives applicants all pertinent and realistic information — positive and negative — about the job and the organization.[22] RJPs enhance employee satisfaction and reduce turnover, because they facilitate matching individuals, jobs, and organizations. Individuals have a better basis on which to determine their suitability to the organization and "self-select" into or out of positions based on full information. When employees choose positions without RJPs, unmet expectations may cause initial job dissatisfaction and increased turnover. For example, Linda McDermott left a good position in an accounting firm to become an executive vice-president of a new management consulting company. She was told she would have a major role in helping the business grow. As it turned out, her boss relegated her to administrative duties so she quit after a few months, causing the company to initiate another lengthy search and sidetracking her career for a year or two.[23]

LEGAL CONSIDERATIONS. Organizations must ensure that their recruiting practices conform to the law. As discussed earlier in this chapter, equal employment opportunity (EEO) laws stipulate that recruiting and hiring decisions cannot discriminate on the basis of race, national origin, religion, or sex. Affirmative action refers to the use of goals, timetables, or other methods in recruiting to promote the hiring, development, and retention of "protected groups" — persons historically underrepresented in the workplace. For exam-

Exhibit 12.6
Prudential's Corporate Recruiting Policy

An Equal Opportunity Employer

Prudential recruits, hires, trains, promotes, and compensates individuals without regard to race, color, religion or creed, age, sex, marital status, national origin, ancestry, liability for service in the armed forces of the United States, status as a special disabled veteran or veteran of the Vietnam era, or physical or mental handicap.

This is official company policy because:
- we believe it is right
- it makes good business sense
- it is the law

We are also committed to an ongoing program of affirmative action in which members of under-represented groups are actively sought out and employed for opportunities in all parts and at all levels of the company. In employing people from all walks of life, Prudential gains access to the full experience of our diverse society.

Source: Prudential Insurance Company.

ple, companies adopting an affirmative action policy may recruit at colleges with large enrollments of black students. A city may establish a goal of recruiting one black firefighter for every white firefighter until the proportion of black firefighters is commensurate with that in the community.

Most large companies try to comply with affirmative action and EEO guidelines. Prudential Insurance Company's policy is illustrated in Exhibit 12.6. Prudential actively recruits employees and takes affirmative action steps to recruit new ones from all walks of life.

Selection

The next step for managers is to select desired employees from the pool of recruited applicants. In the **selection** process, employers attempt to determine the skills, abilities, and other attributes needed to perform a particular job. Then they assess applicants' characteristics in an attempt to determine the "fit" between the job and applicant characteristics.

selection The process of determining the skills, abilities, and other attributes needed to perform a particular job.

Job Descriptions. A good place to start in making a selection decision is the job description. Human resource professionals or line managers who make selection decisions may have little direct experience with the job to be filled. If these persons are to make a good match between job and candidate, they should read the job description before they review applications.

A **job description** typically lists job duties as well as desirable qualifications for a particular job. An example of a job description for American Airlines appears in Exhibit 12.7.

job description A listing of duties as well as desirable qualifications for a particular job.

Selection Devices. Several devices are used for assessing applicant qualifications. The most frequently used are the

- Application form
- Interview
- Paper-and-pencil test
- Assessment center

EXHIBIT 12.7
A Sample Job Description

Source: Used with permission of American Airlines.

AmericanAirlines

JOB DESCRIPTION

Title: Associate - Corporate Development

Department: Corporate Development

Location: Corporate Headquarters
Dallas/Fort Worth Airport, Texas

Reports To: Managing Director - Corporate Development

American Airlines is seeking an Associate for its Corporate Development Department. This position supports the growing diversification activities of AMR Corporation, American Airlines and other subsidiaries.

Functional Description:

Responsibilities include identifying, analyzing and negotiating merger and acquisition transactions in a diverse group of industries. Position involves interaction with senior management as well as the Legal, Tax and operating departments.

Qualifications:

MBA degree required. The successful applicant will have excellent communication and analytical skills. Prior experience in mergers and acquisition and knowledge of PC financial modeling techniques are preferred.

P.O. BOX 619616, DALLAS/FORT WORTH AIRPORT, TEXAS 75261-9616, CABLE ADDRESS AMAIR

Many companies use a combination of these devices. Human resource professionals consider the extent to which each device produces a valid prediction of employee job performance. **Validity** refers to the relationship between one's score on a selection device and one's future job performance. A valid selection procedure will provide high scores that correspond to subsequent high job performance.

validity The relationship between an applicant's score on a selection device and his or her future job performance.

APPLICATION FORM. The **application form** is used to collect information about the applicant's education, previous job experience, and other background characteristics. Research in the life insurance industry shows biographical information inventories can predict future job success.[24]

application form A device for collecting information about an applicant's education, previous job experience, and other background characteristics.

One pitfall to be avoided is the inclusion of questions that are irrelevant to job success. In line with affirmative action, the application form should not ask questions that will create an adverse impact on "protected groups" unless the questions are clearly related to the job.[25] For example, employers should not ask whether the applicant rents or owns his or her own home because (1) an applicant's response might adversely affect his or her chances at the job,

(2) minorities and women may be less likely to own a home, and (3) homeownership is probably unrelated to job performance. On the other hand, the CPA exam is relevant to job performance in a CPA firm; thus, it is appropriate to ask whether an applicant for employment has passed the CPA exam even if only one-half of all women or minority applicants has done so versus nine-tenths of men applicants.

Interview.[26] The interview is used to hire persons in almost every job category in virtually every organization. The *interview* serves as a two-way communication channel that allows both the organization and the applicant to collect information that would otherwise be difficult to obtain.

Although widely used, the interview as generally practiced is a poor predictor of later job performance. Researchers have identified many reasons for this. Interviewers frequently are unfamiliar with the job. They tend to make decisions in the first few minutes of the interview before all relevant information has been gathered. They also may base decisions on personal biases (such as against minority groups or physically unattractive persons and in favor of those similar to themselves). The interviewer may talk too much and spend time discussing matters irrelevant to the job.[27]

Organizations will continue to use interviews in spite of the pitfalls. Thus, researchers have identified methods for increasing their validity. Advice for effective interviewing — as well as some examples of unsuitable applicants — is summarized in the Manager's Shoptalk box.

Paper-and-Pencil Test. Many companies use **paper-and-pencil tests** such as intelligence tests, aptitude and ability tests, and personality inventories, particularly those shown to be good predictors.[28] For example, a 109-question personality test has been used by independent insurance agents to hire clerical and customer service employees. The test is designed to measure such traits as "motivation to please others" and "people orientation." The insurance agencies feel they need something to accurately gauge applicants' strengths and weaknesses. The test has been successful, because candidates hired have displayed stronger tendencies to provide service to customers.[29]

paper-and-pencil test A written test designed to measure a particular attribute such as intelligence or aptitude.

Assessment Center. The assessment center was developed by psychologists at AT&T several decades ago. Now it is used to select individuals with high potential for managerial careers by such organizations as AT&T, IBM, General Electric, JCPenney, and Standard Oil (Ohio).[30] **Assessment centers** present a series of managerial situations to groups of applicants over, say, a two- or three-day period. One technique is the in-basket simulation, which requires the applicant to play the role of a manager who must decide how to respond to ten memos in his or her in-basket within a two-hour period. Panels of two or three trained judges observe the applicant's decisions and assess the extent to which they reflect interpersonal, communication, and problem-solving skills.

assessment center A technique for selecting individuals with high managerial potential based on their performance on a series of simulated managerial tasks.

Assessment centers have proven to be valid predictors of managerial success,[31] and some organizations now use them for hiring technical workers. At Kimberly-Clark's newest plants, for example, applicants for machine operator jobs are put through a simulation in which they are asked to play the role of a

MANAGER'S SHOPTALK

THE RIGHT WAY TO INTERVIEW A JOB APPLICANT

A so-so interview usually nets a so-so employee. Many hiring mistakes can be prevented during the interview. The following techniques will insure a successful interview:

1. *Know what you want.* Before the interview, prepare questions based on your knowledge of the job to be filled. If you do not have a thorough knowledge of the job, read a job description. If possible, call one or more jobholders and ask them about the job duties and what is required to succeed. Another idea is to make up a list of traits and qualifications for the ideal candidate. Be specific about what it will take to get the job done.
2. *Prepare a road map.* Develop questions that will reveal whether the candidate has the correct background and qualifications. The questions should focus on previous experiences that are relevant to the current job. If the job requires creativity and innovation, ask a question such as "What do you do differently from other sales reps?"
3. *Use open-ended questions in which the right answer is not obvious.* Ask the applicant to give specific examples of previous work experiences. For example, don't ask, "Are you a hard worker?" or "Tell me about yourself." Instead ask, "Can you give me examples from your previous work history that reflect your level of motivation?" or "How did you go about getting your current job?"
4. *Do not ask questions that are irrelevant to the job.* This is particularly important when the irrelevant questions might adversely affect minorities or women. Questions that are considered objectionable are the same as those considered objectionable on application blanks.
5. *Listen, don't talk.* You should spend most of the interview listening. If you talk too much, the focus will shift to you and you may miss important cues. Listen carefully to tone of voice as well as content. Body language also can be revealing; for example, failure to make eye contact is a danger signal.
6. *Allow enough time so that the interview will not be rushed.* Leave time for the candidate to ask questions about the job. The types of questions the candidate asks can be an important clue to his or her interest in the job. Try to delay forming an opinion about the applicant until after the entire interview has been completed.
7. *Avoid reliance on your memory.* Request the applicant's permission to take notes; then do so unobtrusively during the interview or immediately after. If several applicants are interviewed, notes are essential for remembering what they said and the impressions they made.

Even a well-planned interview may be disrupted by the unexpected. Last summer, Robert Half asked vice-presidents and personnel directors at 100 major American corporations to describe the most unusual thing that they were aware of ever happening during a job interview. Various applicants reportedly:

"Wore a Walkman and said she could listen to me and the music at the same time."

- "Announced she hadn't had lunch and proceeded to eat a hamburger and french fries in the interviewer's office."
- "Wore a jogging suit to interview for a position as a vice-president."
- "He said he was so well-qualified that if he didn't get the job, it would prove that the company's management was incompetent."
- "A balding candidate abruptly excused himself. He returned to the office a few minutes later wearing a hairpiece."
- "Not only did he ignore the 'No Smoking' sign in my office, he lit up the wrong ends of several filter-tip cigarettes."
- "She chewed bubble gum and constantly blew bubbles."
- "Job applicant challenged the interviewer to arm wrestle."
- "He stretched out on the floor to fill out the job application."
- "He interrupted to telephone his therapist for advice on answering specific interview questions."
- "He dozed off and started snoring during the interview."
- "He said that if he were hired, he would demonstrate his loyalty by having the corporate logo tattooed on his forearm."

Source: James M. Jenks and Brian L. P. Zevnik, "ABCs of Job Interviewing," *Harvard Business Review* (July–August 1989), 38–42; Martha H. Peak, "What Color is Your Bumbershoot?" Reprinted by permission of publisher from *Management Review* (October 1989), 63,

supervisor. The idea is to see whether candidates have sufficient "people skills" to fit into the participative work atmosphere.

Assessment center approaches are especially important because they measure interpersonal skills better than paper-and-pencil tests. Companies such as Toyota rely heavily on a combination of selection techniques to fill jobs at a greater than 90 percent success rate.

TOYOTA MOTOR CORP.

• To land one of the 3,000 production jobs at a new U.S. Toyota plant takes at least 18 hours. First, prospective employees must pass a literacy and general knowledge exam as well as a test of their attitudes toward work. Employees go in groups of 12 to an assessment center for a session of problem solving. Candidates go through a manufacturing exercise in which they are expected to improve the method of assembling plastic pipes. They are also told that a lawn mower manufacturer has production problems to see which employees ask the right questions and can work cooperatively to find a solution. Finally, intense interviews help weed out employees who have bad attitudes. Only 10 percent of applicants make it through the tests for reading, math, manual dexterity, job fitness, technical knowledge, hypothetical production problems, interpersonal skills, and attitude. The resulting Toyota team members are a spirited elite who love their jobs and are devoted to Toyota.[32]

DEVELOPING AN EFFECTIVE WORK FORCE

Following selection, the major goal of HRM is to develop employees into an effective work force. Development includes training and performance appraisal.

TRAINING AND DEVELOPMENT

Training and development represent a planned effort by an organization to facilitate employees' learning of job-related behaviors.[33] Some authors distinguish the two forms of intervention by noting that the term *training* usually refers to teaching lower-level or technical employees how to do their present jobs, whereas *development* refers to teaching managers and professionals the skills needed for both present and future jobs. For simplicity, we will refer to both interventions as training.

Organizations spend nearly $100 billion each year on training. IBM alone spends more than $750 million a year on corporate schooling, more than the entire budget of Harvard University.[34] Training may occur in a variety of forms. The most common method is on-the-job training. In **on-the-job training (OJT),** an experienced employee is asked to take a new employee "under his or her wing" and show the newcomer how to perform job duties. OJT has many advantages, such as few out-of-pocket costs for training facilities, materials, or instructor fees and easy transfer of learning back to the job. The learning site is the work site.

on-the-job training (OJT)
A type of training in which an experienced employee "adopts" a new employee to teach him or her how to perform job duties.

Other frequently used training methods include

- *Orientation training,* in which newcomers are introduced to the organization's "culture"
- *Classroom training,* including lectures, films, audiovisual techniques, and simulations
- *Programmed and computer-assisted instruction,* in which the employee works at his or her own pace to learn material from a text that includes exercises and quizzes to enhance learning

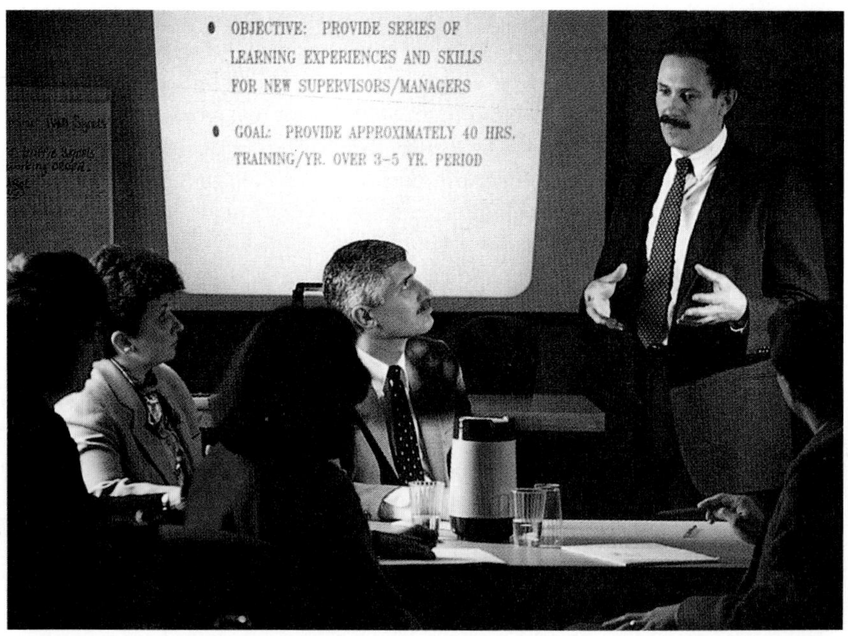

Merck & Company is one of the most admired corporations in the world, in large part because of its ability to attract, develop, and train top people. These managers are focusing on the design and implementation of core training programs to enhance the skills of supervisors and managers. This classroom training is supplemented by conferences and case discussion groups. Merck also uses new-employee *orientation training* to introduce people into its special culture.

- *Conference and case discussion groups*, in which participants analyze cases or discuss topics assisted by a training leader

Companies such as Toyota that spend heavily on selection also invest in employee training. The 10 percent of employees selected undergo several weeks of training for their specific jobs, often at the employees' own expense. At General Motors' new truck plant, each assembly line worker received 400 to 500 hours of paid training. Skilled workers got 1,000 hours apiece of training—the equivalent of almost six months. Motorola, Macy's, and Texas Instruments are examples of other companies that appreciate the importance of thorough training to remain competitive in the global marketplace. Companies such as Continental Airlines and Zack's Famous Frozen Yogurt used training to reinforce key values and corporate culture. As global competition has an impact on more companies, training budgets have increased.[35]

PROMOTION FROM WITHIN. Promotion from within helps companies retain and develop productive employees. It provides challenging assignments, prescribes new responsibilities, and helps employees grow by developing their abilities.

One approach to promotion from within is *job posting*, which means that positions are announced on bulletin boards or in company publications as openings occur. Interested employees notify the human resource department, which then helps make the fit between employees and positions.

Another approach is *employee resource charts*, which are designed to identify likely successors for each management position. The chart looks like a typical organization chart with every employee listed. Every key position includes the names of top candidates to move into that position when it becomes vacant. Candidates are rated on a five-point scale reflecting whether they are ready for immediate promotion or need additional experience. These charts show the potential flow of employees up through the hierarchy and provide motivation to employees who have an opportunity for promotion.

Performance Appraisal

Performance appraisal is another important technique for developing an effective work force. **Performance appraisal** comprises the steps of observing and assessing employee performance, recording the assessment, and providing feedback to the employee. Managers use performance appraisal to describe and evaluate the employees' performances. During performance appraisal, skillful managers give feedback and praise concerning the acceptable elements of the employee's performance. They also describe performance areas that need improvement. Employees can use this information to change their job performance. Performance appraisal can also reward high performers through merit pay, recognition, and other rewards.

performance appraisal The process of observing and evaluating an employee's performance, recording the assessment, and providing feedback to the employee.

For example, PepsiCo uses performance appraisal to weed out the weak and nurture the strong. First, each boss is required to sit down with subordinates once a year and discuss performance. This appraisal pertains to what the manager did to make a big difference in the business, not whether he or she is a nice person. Second, managers then get divided into four categories. Those at the top are promoted. Those in the second group get challenging jobs. Those in the third category continue to be evaluated and rotated. Those in the bottom category are out.[36]

Generally, HRM professionals concentrate on two things to make performance appraisal a positive force in their organization: (1) the accurate assessment of performance through the training of managers and the development of assessment systems such as rating scales, and (2) the performance appraisal interview, in which managers can provide feedback that will reinforce good performance and motivate employee development.

Assessing Performance Accurately. To obtain an accurate performance rating, managers must acknowledge that jobs are multidimensional and performance thus may be multidimensional as well. For example, a sports broadcaster may perform well on the job knowledge dimension; that is, she or he may be able to report facts and figures about the players and describe which rule applies when there is a questionable play on the field. But the same sports broadcaster may not perform as well on another dimension, such as communication. She or he may be unable to express the information in a colorful way that interests the audience or may interrupt the other broadcasters.

The dimensions of a job can be derived from job analysis information as described earlier. If performance is to be rated accurately, the performance appraisal form should require the rater — usually the supervisor — to assess each relevant performance dimension and not those that are inapplicable to a given job. A multidimensional form increases the usefulness of the performance appraisal for giving rewards and facilitates employee growth and development.

EXHIBIT 12.8
Example of a Behaviorally Anchored Rating Scale

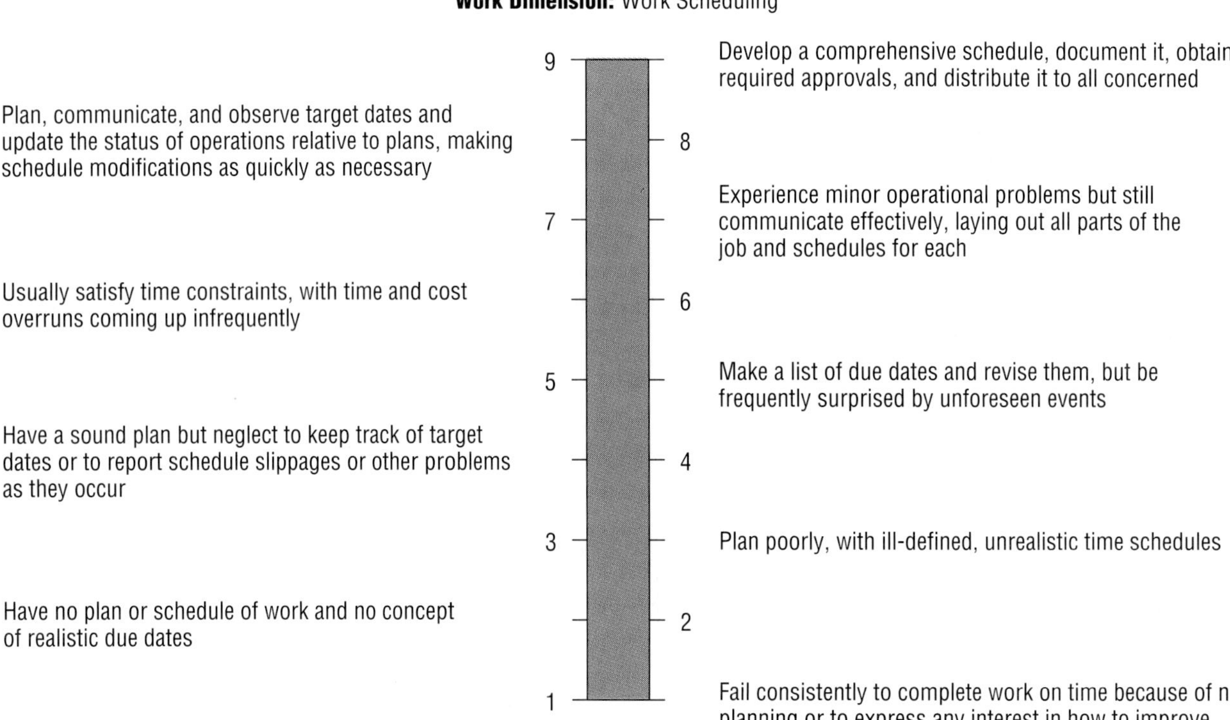
Job: Production Line Supervisor
Work Dimension: Work Scheduling
9
Develop a comprehensive schedule, document it, obtain required approvals, and distribute it to all concerned
Plan, communicate, and observe target dates and update the status of operations relative to plans, making schedule modifications as quickly as necessary
8
7
Experience minor operational problems but still communicate effectively, laying out all parts of the job and schedules for each
Usually satisfy time constraints, with time and cost overruns coming up infrequently
6
5
Make a list of due dates and revise them, but be frequently surprised by unforeseen events
Have a sound plan but neglect to keep track of target dates or to report schedule slippages or other problems as they occur
4
3
Plan poorly, with ill-defined, unrealistic time schedules
Have no plan or schedule of work and no concept of realistic due dates
2
1
Fail consistently to complete work on time because of no planning or to express any interest in how to improve

Source: Based on J. P. Campbell, M. D. Dunnette, R. D. Arvey, and L. V. Hellervik, "The Development and Evaluation of Behaviorally Based Rating Scales," *Journal of Applied Psychology* 57 (1973), 15–22, and Francine Alexander, "Performance Appraisals," *Small Business Reports* (March 1989), 20–29.

halo error A type of rating error that occurs when an employee receives the same rating on all dimensions regardless of his or her performance on individual ones.

homogeneity A type of rating error that occurs when a rater gives all employees a similar rating regardless of their individual performances.

behaviorally anchored rating scale (BARS) A rating technique that relates an employee's performance to specific job-related incidents.

Although we would like to believe that every manager carefully assesses employees' performances, researchers have identified several rating problems.[37] For example, **halo error** occurs when an employee receives the same rating on all dimensions even if his or her performance is good on some dimensions and poor on others. **Homogeneity** occurs when a rater gives all employees a similar rating even if their performances are not equally good.

One approach to overcome management performance evaluation errors is to use a behavior-based rating technique, such as the behaviorally anchored rating scale. The **behaviorally anchored rating scale (BARS)** is developed from critical incidents pertaining to job performance. Each job performance scale is anchored with specific behavioral statements that describe varying degrees of performance. By relating employee performance to specific incidents, raters can more accurately evaluate an employee's performance.[38]

Exhibit 12.8 illustrates the BARS method for evaluating a production line supervisor. The production supervisor's job can be broken down into several dimensions, such as equipment maintenance, employee training, or work scheduling. A behaviorally anchored rating scale should be developed for each dimension. The dimension in Exhibit 12.8 is work scheduling. Good performance is represented by a 7, 8, or 9 on the scale and unacceptable performance as a 1, 2, or 3. If a production supervisor's job has eight dimensions, the total performance evaluation will be the sum of the scores for each of eight scales.[39]

Performance Appraisal Interview. Most corporations provide formal feedback in the form of an annual **performance appraisal interview** with the employee. Too often, however, this meeting between boss and subordinate does not stimulate better job performance.[40] Managers may be unaware of the true causes of performance problems because they have not carefully observed employee job activities. They may have a number of useful ideas for subordinates but present them in a threatening manner. As a result, employees may feel defensive and reject suggestions for improvement.

performance appraisal interview A formal review of an employee's performance conducted between the superior and the subordinate.

Research into the performance appraisal interview suggests a number of steps that will increase its effectiveness:[41]

1. Raters (usually supervisors) should be knowledgeable about the subordinates' jobs and performance levels.
2. Raters should welcome employee participation during the interview rather than "tell and sell" their views by lecturing to subordinates. This is particularly true when the employee is knowledgeable and accustomed to participating with the supervisor.
3. A contingency approach to feedback based on the characteristics of the subordinate, the job, and his or her performance level is useful. For example:
   —With difficult, nonroutine jobs, high performers need feedback that is given at flexible time intervals and focused on development.
   —With routine jobs, satisfactory performers need infrequent feedback (positive or negative) that is focused only on deviations from acceptable performance.
   —Newer employees need more frequent feedback.
4. Training is needed to help supervisors devise interview strategies for different situations. This training should include the observation and rating of performance. Role playing that involves practice appraisal interviews is helpful for this purpose.

HRM researchers also have studied ways in which feedback itself can be effective. Giving specific examples of good and bad performance is more helpful than general statements. For example, "Your attendance record shows that you were here on time nearly every day this month, and this is a great improvement over last month" is more specific and helpful than "You seem to have a much better attitude these days about your work." Some experts suggest that managers keep diaries of employee performance so they will not have to rely on their memories to generate specific examples.

One of the most recent appraisal innovations is to involve peers in performance review. Companies such as General Electric, Allied-Signal, Public Service of New Mexico, and Raritan Steel have found that this *peer review* process dramatically increases openness, commitment, and trust within the organiza-

Performance appraisal is an excellent opportunity for communication between managers and employees. However, some managers find it difficult to provide negative feedback during a performance appraisal interview. In this role-play sequence designed to build supervisory skills for employees of Varian Associates Inc., managers practice performance appraisal interviewing. Employees take turns in roles of manager and subordinate. Managers learn to assess performance accurately and give the positive and negative feedback necessary for their subordinates' continued development.

tion and prevents problems that sometimes occur with a one-on-one interview. Managers learn that employees have good opinions about performance, and soliciting opinions from other employees provides a group approach to problem solving around important performance issues.[42]

MAINTAINING AN EFFECTIVE WORK FORCE

Now we turn to the topic of how managers and HRM professionals maintain a work force that has been recruited and developed. Maintenance of the current work force involves compensation, wage and salary structure, benefits, and occasional terminations.

COMPENSATION

compensation Monetary payments (wages, salaries) and nonmonetary goods/commodities (fringe benefits, vacations) used to reward employees.

The term **compensation** refers to (1) all monetary payments and (2) all goods or commodities used in lieu of money to reward employees.[43] An organization's compensation structure includes wages and/or salaries and fringe benefits such as health insurance, paid vacations, or employee fitness centers. A company's compensation structure does not just happen. It is designed to fit company strategy and to provide compensation equity.

COMPENSATION STRATEGY. Ideally, management's strategy for the organization should be a critical determinant of the features and operations of the pay system.[44] For example, managers may have the goal of maintaining or improving profitability or market share by stimulating employee performance. Thus, they should design and use a merit pay system rather than a system based on other criteria such as seniority. As another example, managers may have the

EXHIBIT 12.9
Steps in Building a Point-Based Wage and Salary Structure

1. Create or update job descriptions by performing a job analysis.
2. Choose a point-based job evaluation method and evaluate the job descriptions.
3. Select the key jobs and obtain a pay survey to determine their market pay rates.
4. Calculate the pay-trend line and assign average pay rates to the nonkey jobs.
5. Group jobs into classes and establish pay ranges within each class.

goal of attracting and retaining desirable employees. Here they can use a pay survey to determine competitive wages in comparable companies and adjust pay rates to meet or exceed the going rates.

Pay-for-performance systems are becoming extremely popular in both large and small businesses, including Caterpillar, Aluminum Company of America, and Hewlett-Packard. These systems are usually designed as a form of profit sharing to reward employees when profitability goals are met. At Alcoa, payouts to employees equal 7 percent of each worker's salary. Caterpillar employees each received an $800 bonus, and Ford employees received an average $3,700 per employee. Employees have an incentive to make the company more efficient and profitable, because if goals are not met no bonuses are paid. Jim Bernstein, CEO of General Health Inc., a small business, promised all 30 employees they would get an extra month's pay if the company hit the sales target. Sales shot up, going far beyond the target, showing how powerful the correct incentive can be.[45]

Why is Linda Fritch smiling? Manville Corporation recently installed *pay-for-performance* incentives that give employees a piece of the action. Linda Fritch is a papermill forklift operator, preparing to load a roll of paperboard for shipment. Manville has been setting production records, so employees like Linda Fritch are getting bonuses. Manville executives see a lot more smiles, and people are asking more questions to help cut costs. A new sense of teamwork has emerged, because employees do not want to let each other down.

COMPENSATION EQUITY. Managers often wish to maintain a sense of fairness and equity within the pay structure and thereby fortify employee morale. **Job evaluation** refers to the process of determining the value or worth of jobs within an organization through an examination of job content. Job evaluation techniques enable managers to compare similar and dissimilar jobs and to determine internally equitable pay rates—that is, pay rates that employees believe are fair compared with those for other jobs in the organization. Managers also may want to provide income security so that their employees need not be overly concerned with the financial consequences of disability or retirement.

WAGE AND SALARY STRUCTURE

Large organizations typically employ HRM compensation specialists to establish and maintain a pay structure. They may also hire outside consultants, such as the Hay Group or PAQ (Position Analysis Questionnaire) Associates, whose pay systems have been adopted by many companies and government organizations. The majority of large public- and private-sector U.S. employers use some formal process of job evaluation.[46]

The most commonly used job evaluation system is the **point system.**[47] The steps typically followed when using point systems are summarized in Exhibit 12.9.

job evaluation The process of determining the values of jobs within an organization through an examination of job content.

point system A job evaluation system that assigns a predetermined point value to each compensable job factor in order to determine the worth of a given job.

EXHIBIT 12.10
Pay-Trend Line

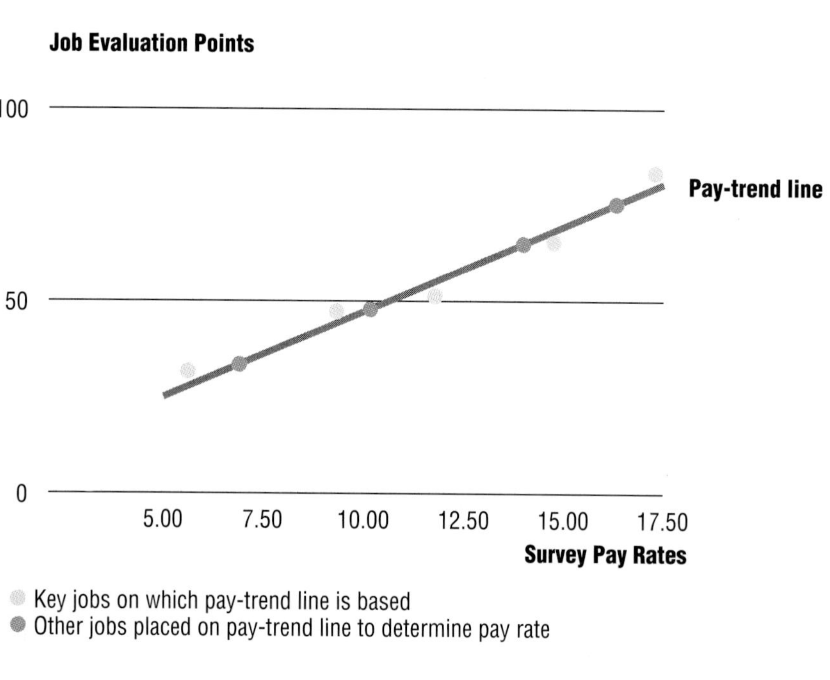

First, compensation specialists must ensure that job descriptions are complete, up to date, and accurate. If, for example, a computer programmer's duties have changed since the last update, a pay value based on the old job description will probably be too low or too high. The process of job analysis described earlier is used to maintain accurate job descriptions.

Next, a job evaluation system for assessing the job descriptions is chosen. The system should allow top managers to select compensable job factors (such as skill, effort, and responsibility) and decide how each factor will be weighed in establishing job worth. These factors are described in a point manual, which is used to assign point values to each job. For example, the characteristic of responsibility could receive from 0 to 5 points depending on whether job responsibility was "routine work performed under close supervision" (0 points) or "complete discretion with errors having extreme consequences to the organization and public safety" (5 points).

The compensation specialist then compares the extent of responsibility apparent in a given job description to that specified in the point manual. This process is repeated until the job has been evaluated on all factors. Then the compensation specialist evaluates a second job and repeats the process until all jobs have been evaluated.

The job evaluation process can establish an internal hierarchy of job worth. However, to determine competitive market pay rates, most organizations obtain one or more pay surveys. **Pay surveys** show what other organizations pay incumbents in jobs that match a sample of "key" jobs selected by the organization. Pay surveys are available from many sources, including consulting firms and the U.S. Bureau of Labor Statistics.

pay survey A study of what other companies pay employees in jobs that correspond to a sample of key positions selected by the organization.

The compensation specialist then compares the survey pay rates for key jobs with their job evaluation points by plotting them on a graph as illustrated in Exhibit 12.10. The **pay-trend line** shows the relationship between pay and total point values. The compensation specialist can use the pay-trend line to determine the pay values of all jobs for which point values have been calculated. Ranges of pay for each job class are established, enabling a newcomer or lower performer to be paid less than other people in the same job class. The organization must then specify how individuals in the same job class can advance from the low to the high end of the range. For example, the organization can reward merit, seniority, or a combination of both.

One innovation in *employee benefits* is the sabbatical leave offered by Tandem Computers Incorporated. Rosemarie Hall worked six weeks for the California Marine Mammal Center. The sabbatical program grants an employee on each fourth anniversary of employment a six-week, fully paid leave — in addition to vacation time. New benefit programs constantly are under development to help Tandem develop and retain outstanding people.

BENEFITS

The wage and salary structure is an important part of the compensation package that maintains a productive work force, but equally important are the benefits offered by the organization. Benefits were once called "fringe" benefits, but this term is no longer accurate because they are now a central rather than peripheral part of the pay structure. A U.S. Chamber of Commerce survey has revealed that benefits in general comprise more than one-third of labor costs and in some industries nearly two-thirds.[48]

A major reason benefits make up such a large portion of the compensation package is that health care costs have been increasing more quickly than the inflation rate. Because employers frequently provide health care insurance as an employee benefit, these costs are important in the management of benefits. One survey showed that more than 70 percent of responding employers plan to place a major emphasis on health care cost containment.[49]

pay-trend line A graph that shows the relationship between pay and total job point values for determining the worth of a given job.

Organizations that want to provide cost-effective benefits should be sensitive to changes in employee life-styles. Several years ago, benefits were based on the assumption that the typical worker was a married man with a dependent wife and two school-age children. The benefits packages provided life insurance coverage for the worker, health insurance coverage for all family members, and no assistance with child care expenses. But today fewer than 10 percent of American workers fit the description of the so-called typical worker.[50] Increasing work-force diversity means that far more workers are single, and both spouses in most families are working. These workers are not likely to value the traditional benefits package. In response, some companies are establishing cafeteria-style benefits packages that allow employees to select the benefits of greatest value to them. Other companies use surveys to determine which combination of fixed benefits is most desirable. The benefits packages provided by large companies attempt to meet the needs of all employees. One of the newest type of benefits is allowing employees paid leave of absences to perform social service work, as illustrated in the Focus on Ethics box.

TERMINATIONS

Despite the best efforts of line managers and HRM professionals, the organization will lose employees. Some will retire, others will depart voluntarily for other jobs, and still others will be forced out through mergers and cutbacks.

FOCUS ON ETHICS

XEROX CORPORATION

One day recently, Sarah Lampard carried paper bags full of bread, cereal, and vegetables up the steps into Denver's inner-city Agape Christian Church. That day, she was helping deliver a truckload of food to churches that would help feed over 1,200 poverty-stricken families for the next week. In days past, she has harvested spinach under the August sun, negotiated with food company executives to acquire surplus food, and unloaded thousands of pounds of potatoes from a semitrailer. No matter what the task, it's all in a day's work for this Xerox employee: She's a Social Service Leave-taker.

In 1988, through the Social Service Leave Program, Sarah took a six-month, fully-paid leave of absence from her job as a Xerox account manager in Denver, Colorado, to work for a nonprofit food bank cooperative called COMPA. COMPA acquires and purchases surplus food from supermarkets, restaurants, and farmers and gives it to 33 local churches that feed hundreds of Denver people who just cannot afford to eat every day.

Now back at her regular Xerox job, Sarah says: "Social Service Leave changed my personal values. Before, material things were important; now I use my money to help others. I also learned how to listen to people's problems and help them find solutions. This helps with my Xerox customers. They're very impressed that Xerox would invest so much money, time, and talent in such worthwhile community projects. In fact, some of my customers are thinking about modeling programs of their own after Xerox's program."

Since the program began in 1971, nearly 350 employees have taken sabbaticals of a month to a year from their Xerox jobs to pursue social-action projects of their own choosing within their communities. Leave-takers continue to receive full pay and benefits, and on their return to Xerox they get their old jobs back or new positions of equal responsibility.

Source: Xerox, 1988 Annual Report. Used by permission.

exit interview An interview conducted with departing employees to determine the reasons for their termination.

The value of terminations for maintaining an effective work force is twofold. First, employees who are poor performers can be dismissed. Productive employees often resent disruptive, low-performing employees who are allowed to stay with the company and receive pay and benefits comparable to theirs. Second, employers can use exit interviews. An **exit interview** is an interview conducted with departing employees to determine why they are leaving.[51] The exit interview is an excellent and inexpensive tool for learning about pockets of dissatisfaction within the organization and hence for reducing future turnover.

With so many companies experiencing downsizing through mergers or because of global competition, often a large number of managers and workers are terminated at the same time. In these cases, enlightened companies try to find a smooth transition for departing employees. For example, General Electric laid off 900 employees in three gradual steps. It also set up a reemployment center to assist employees in finding new jobs or in learning new skills. It provided counseling in how to write a resume and conduct a job search. An additional step General Electric took was to place an advertisement in local newspapers saying that these employees were available.

The need for companies to be lean and competitive will be a continuing trend over the next few years. Practically all major companies have been affected by this trend, including Apple Computers, Du Pont, CBS, Control Data, Eastman Kodak, and Exxon. By showing genuine concern in helping place these employees, the company communicates the value of human resources and helps maintain a positive corporate culture.[52]

Summary

This chapter described several important points about human resource management in organizations. All managers are responsible for human resources, and most organizations have a human resource department that works with line managers to insure a productive work force. The human resource department is responsible for interpreting and responding to the larger human resource environment. The HR department must be part of the organization's competitive strategy, implement procedures to reflect federal and state legislation, and respond to trends in the larger society. Within this context, the HR department tries to achieve three goals for the organization. The first goal of the human resource department is to attract an effective work force through human resource planning, recruiting, and employee selection. The second is to develop an effective work force. Newcomers are introduced to the organization and to their jobs through orientation and training programs. Moreover, employees are appraised through performance appraisal programs. The third goal is to maintain an effective work force. Human resource managers retain employees with wage and salary systems, benefits packages, and termination procedures.

Management Solution

Thomas Melohn, president of North American Tool & Die, was faced with low profits, an unenthusiastic work force, a 7 percent customer reject rate of production, and 27 percent employee turnover. He attacked this problem by setting up systems to recruit and hire the best possible employees. First, he got the word out to generate a large pool of applications, only 10 percent of whom made it to a formal interview. The interviews focused on finding people with the right values who could do quality work and fit the culture and strategy of North American. References were carefully checked, and a trial work period was used to see if the employee was compatible. These procedures took a great deal of time, but acquiring the right human resources has produced impressive results: employee turnover plummeted to less than 4 percent, the customer reject rate is below 0.1 percent, employees are enthusiastic, and profits have increased 100 percent a year for seven years. Human resources have enabled this small company to beat well-heeled foreign competitors at price, quality, and delivery.[53]

Discussion Questions

1. It is the year 2000. In your company, central planning has given way to front-line decision making and bureaucracy has given way to teamwork. Shop floor workers use computers and robots. There is a labor shortage for many job openings, and the few applicants lack skills to work in teams, make decisions, or use sophisticated technology. As vice-president of

human resource management since 1990, what did you do to prepare for this problem?

2. If you were asked to advise a private company about its equal employment opportunity responsibilities, what two points would you emphasize as most important?
3. How can the human resource activities of planning, recruiting, performance appraisal, and compensation be related to corporate strategy?
4. Think back to your own job experience. What human resource management activities described in this chapter were performed for the job you filled? Which ones were absent?
5. Why are planning and forecasting necessary for human resource management? Discuss.
6. Job analysis is a central HRM activity. How does job analysis contribute to (a) planning, (b) recruiting, (c) selection, (d) training, (e) performance appraisal, and (f) compensation?
7. What techniques can managers adopt to improve their recruiting and interviewing practices?
8. How does affirmative action differ from equal employment opportunity in recruiting and selection?
9. How can exit interviews be used to maintain an effective work force?
10. Describe the procedure used to build a wage and salary structure for an organization.

Management in Practice: Ethical Dilemma

Fraternization Policy

Previous complications prompted Aeronautical Associations to write a human resource policy prohibiting married couples from working in the company, even in different departments.

Tom and Ginny were secretly married two years after Ginny was hired by the company. Although they worked in separate departments, cross-functional projects sometimes required professional cooperation between them. Tom and Ginny always maintained a professional relationship at work, making sure their performance was not hampered by their personal life.

After completion of an especially important project, Tom and Ginny's departments met informally to celebrate at a local restaurant. During the gathering, one of Tom and Ginny's friends from outside the company entered the restaurant by chance and unknowingly revealed their secret in front of several coworkers.

Monday morning, Tom came to see you, his supervisor, about an appropriate course of action.

What Do You Do?

1. Do nothing. Things have worked out okay, so do not make an issue of it.
2. Work toward keeping Tom and Ginny with the company, but also seek mild punishment for them. Unpunished disregard of company policy would send a negative message to other employees.
3. Insist one of them leave the company. Tom and Ginny caused the problem by not being forthright.
4. Fight the policy. Champion Tom and Ginny's cause with upper management because the company has no right to limit personal relationships.

Cases for Analysis

MONY

Senior executives at Mutual of New York (MONY) decided to relocate its operations division from Manhattan to nearby Westchester County. Although MONY's headquarters remained in New York City, many economies could be achieved by moving the operations division to another location.

The human resource environment in Westchester County was different from Manhattan, and Sue Garbey, Director of Human Resources, had her work cut out for her. More than 50 percent of the needed 1,000 employees would relocate from Manhattan, thanks to a generous relocation package. However, MONY was the corporate newcomer in the area, and it was a small competitor compared with neighbors IBM, General Foods, PepsiCo, and Reader's Digest. To recruit and retain quality employees, members of the human resource department would have to be innovative. They realized they were facing a labor shortage due to the baby bust, made even more difficult by recruiting competition from MONY's corporate neighbors. Moreover, the pool of potential workers was affluent, had many choices, and was considered selective about employers.

In response, MONY's HR department decided to experiment with nontraditional programs such as flexible hours, summer hours, job sharing, variable work sites, and child care assistance. Flexible hours meant that each department must have coverage during the core business hours of 8:30 A.M. to 4:30 P.M., but individual staff members can work any time from 7:30 A.M. to 9:00 P.M. Some 25 employees are involved in job sharing, which means the position is filled by two people, each working less than 40 hours. Part-time employees receive prorated benefits. Variable work sites means that many people are allowed to work at home at least part of the time. These employees do computer work and can log on anytime of the day or night. Child care assistance includes six months of unpaid leave and guaranteed same job upon return. MONY also offers flexible spending accounts as part of the benefit package that can help reimburse for dependent care.

MONY's philosophy is "what's good for the individual is also good for business." Top management and HR professionals believe the nontraditional means to recruit and retain people will enable high productivity and a successful division.

Questions

1. Evaluate the extent to which the recruiting and retention policies reflect the environment within which the human resource department works.
2. Would you like to work for MONY's operations division? Why?
3. What suggestions would you make about additional programs MONY might undertake to recruit and retain employees in this environment?

Source: Based on Marlene C. Piturro, "HR Policies Give Companies New Direction," *Management Review* (April 1989), 16–18.

TRIANGLE EQUIPMENT

In 1989, Jane Foster joined Triangle Equipment, a Kansas manufacturer of farm equipment located in a rural area. Triangle employed 1,700 people, most of whom were welders, machine operators, and assemblers in the plant. The company was successful because of a loyal clientele, committed employees, and efficient production methods.

Jane was in charge of administrative services, but she had a problem. She had reviewed her first-level managers for merit pay. She had worked hard on the performance appraisal and kept records about employee performance. She believed in rewarding those who contributed the most to the organization. However, before holding the appraisal interview with each employee, she was required to get approval from her boss, Frank Galloway, before implementing the promised raises.

Frank was a vice-president, a close personal friend of the president, and was well liked by many employees.

Unfortunately, Frank wanted to change the recommended merit pay increases for each of Jane's managers. Frank told Jane that this year's performance was not as important as the individual's potential, attitude, years to retirement, age, and family situation. Because Jane was still new, Frank decided to overrule her in each case.

The following information reflects Jane's notes about the performance of three employees as well as Frank's response.

David Thompson had 18 years with Triangle but had never been an outstanding performer. His recent poor effort had held up the assembly operation, and Jane had sent several memos requesting improvement. David was a close personal friend of Frank Galloway and had several children, two of whom were in college. Jane recommended a salary increase from $30,000 to $31,000, but Frank believed David's salary should be increased to $35,000.

Dolores Rodriguez had shown remarkable improvement over the last year. She was a hard worker and had been coming to work early and staying late. She had spent many hours untangling problems created by others and had clearly found her position in the organization. Jane could always rely on Dolores to do whatever was needed and do it in an efficient manner. Dolores was unmarried and a high-school graduate. Jane's salary increase recommendation was from $22,000 to $26,500. Frank would approve only a $1,500 increase.

Ray Sanders had always been an outstanding employee. However, during the last year Ray had experienced family problems, including a divorce, followed by his former wife and children moving out of state. His performance had declined markedly; his misspecified equipment drawings had cost the company time and money. Jane recommended a small salary increase from $41,000 to $42,500. Frank believed that Ray's salary should be increased to $46,000.

Questions

1. Frank believed his recommended raises reflected the company's goals. Do you agree?
2. Do any of Frank's recommendations violate laws concerning equitable pay for employees?
3. If you were a personnel specialist consulting with Jane, what would you recommend that Jane do?

Video Case

Lakeway Resort & Conference Center

During the construction of their house along Lake Travis in Lakeway, Texas, a family discovered an indentation in the shoreline at the rear of their lot. Experts authenticated it as a dinosaur print. Many relics of a more recent age, beginning about 3,000 B.C., have been found, too. Charred rocks from campfires, flint, weapons, arrowheads, tools, bones, shells, and former permanent Indian campsites dot the area. The large, odd-shaped oaks on a golf course are the result of Indians tying down saplings so the trees pointed to the nearest watering place as they grew. The pleasant environment that attracted Indians, white settlers, and then vacationers has also attracted resort facilities.

Lakeway Resort & Conference Center, the most famous resort in Texas, is nestled in the famous Texas Hill Country along Lake Travis. Although Lakeway's recreational facilities were superb when it was built in the 1960s, over a 20-year span the accommodations, furnishings, and food, beverage, and meeting facilities became worn and tired. Lakeway was perceived as a middle-aged local Texas resort, with only 10 percent of its clientele coming from businesses or vacationers from outside of Texas. During the 1980s, Lakeway was further threatened by increasing competition from resorts that were targeting its traditional clientele.

Acquired by the Dolce Company in 1987, Lakeway has recently undergone a major renovation. Dolce's strategic plan is to have five world-class resort and conference centers strategically located in different geographical areas of the United States. Lakeway is located just 18 miles west of Austin, Texas. The 138-room facility is on a cliff overlooking 65-mile-long Lake Travis. Dolce has invested $15 million, and the result is a stunning facility to match the beautiful surroundings. One hundred twenty-five new guest rooms have been added in country villas. Other additions include a dining room, game room, and fitness facility. Plans to build a spa and an $800,000 corporate meeting room are ready to be announced. Recreation facilities include three 18-hole golf courses, one designed by Jack Nicklaus; 32 tennis courts; horseback riding; biking, jogging, and walking trails; three swimming pools; water sports such as fishing, sailing, skiing, paddle boats, and party boats; and a variety of banquet and meeting rooms.

Dolce's strategy is to upgrade the resort to distinguish it from the competition and create a nationally recognized conference center that will attract prestigious national corporate clients and vacationers. The mix of Texas versus national customers had been 90 percent/10 percent, and that is expected to become 60 percent/40 percent in 1990.

The resort is a service business, which means that employees are involved with customers. Lakeway is selling fun, enjoyment, hospitality, and friendliness; it is selling an "experience" rather than a tangible good.

Lakeway has about 250 employees organized into seven functional departments. The organization chart is shown in Exhibit 1. For two years the seven departments reported directly to Lawrence Barbir, general manager. Recently an assistant general manager was added to provide greater attention on those departments involved in day-to-day guests encounters. Department heads have been delegated authority and responsibility to run their departments as if president of their own companies. Each manager is held accountable for his or her actions and expenses.

Coordination among departments occurs primarily through executive committee meetings attended by department heads, the general manager, and the assistant general manager. The executive committee discusses whatever challenges are anticipated for the coming week, current business in-house, and progress on current projects. Information concerning problems in any department is shared. The goals from Dolce are also presented. Each manager has meetings with departmental staff to pass information down the line. The results of service evaluations completed by guests are also discussed in these meetings. Below the manager level, employee representatives meet monthly to discuss employee problem areas. For day-to-day coordination, employees make direct contact across departments as needed.

The major change to take place within Lakeway since it was acquired by Dolce is the corporate culture. The new attitude is one of aggressive hospitality, which means that employees actively make guests happy. Lawrence Barbir, general manager, implemented this change using various methods. One has been to tell stories that exemplify good service. These stories initially came from other organizations, but in the last few months the stories are about Lakeway heroes. One story initially told to illustrate aggressive hospitality is about a maid walking down the sidewalk toward a villa. Upon passing a guest, the maid said nothing, which is no hospitality at all. In a second incident, the guest said, "How are you?" The maid responded, "I'm fine, thank you." This is passive hospitality. In the third incident, the maid takes the initiative with, "Good morning. How are you?" The guest replied, "I'm fine, thank you. How are you?" This is aggressive hospitality.

Another approach to changing employee attitudes has been the publication of Lakeway's operational philosophy. It reads as follows:

> There are only a few great resorts that can "make the difference" between average and outstanding. We feel Lakeway is one of those resorts. The only way to become great is to understand and satisfy the needs of our guests better than anyone else. We are committed to doing whatever is necessary to achieve that goal. Aggressive hospitality makes the difference.

This philosophy is written on a large scroll that each employee signs once a year. Moreover, the operational philosophy is read and discussed at the monthly council meeting of employee representatives. Barbir and other managers also repeat the operational philosophy at meetings with employees and at training sessions for new hires. Moreover, Barbir and other managers aggressively reinforce the attitude with awards, including an employee of the month award, an aggressive hospitality award, and plaques in the dining room.

In a service organization, human resource management is especially important because employees interact directly with customers. Primary emphasis is given to selection — finding employees who will fit Lakeway's philosophy and who enjoy pleasing customers. Every position has a written job description clearly stating the title and scope of the job and also the specific responsibilities an employee will have. The human resource department tries to find people who fit the needs of the job. The most important thing to the human resource manager is to find people with enthusiasm — people who are confident, who maintain eye contact, and who are naturally outgoing. By being visible and a great place to work, Lakeway can attract good applicants. A supply of applicants is essential because of Lakeway's anticipated growth. Through interviews, employees are categorized as introverts or extroverts and by their ability to work with guests. If people enjoy working with the public, they are considered for front-of-the-house jobs. Other people work at the back of the house, but they interact with guests on occasion and are also trained in aggressive hospitality.

Training differs from department to department. In the food and beverage department, waiters and waitresses are trained to understand the wine list and how to sell that item. People at the front desk are trained to sell rooms and upgrades to suites. All employees are trained in the meaning of aggressive hospitality, including greetings, friendly smiles, and always asking if there is "anything I can do."

The major long-run problem facing Lakeway's human resource department is the staggering number of high-school dropouts. These students have neither technical nor social skills. Consequently, Lakeway's human resource pool is diminishing, and it may have to take an active role in providing fundamental skills to potential employees. Lakeway currently has a job pro-

EXHIBIT 1
Organization Chart for Lakeway Resort and Conference Center

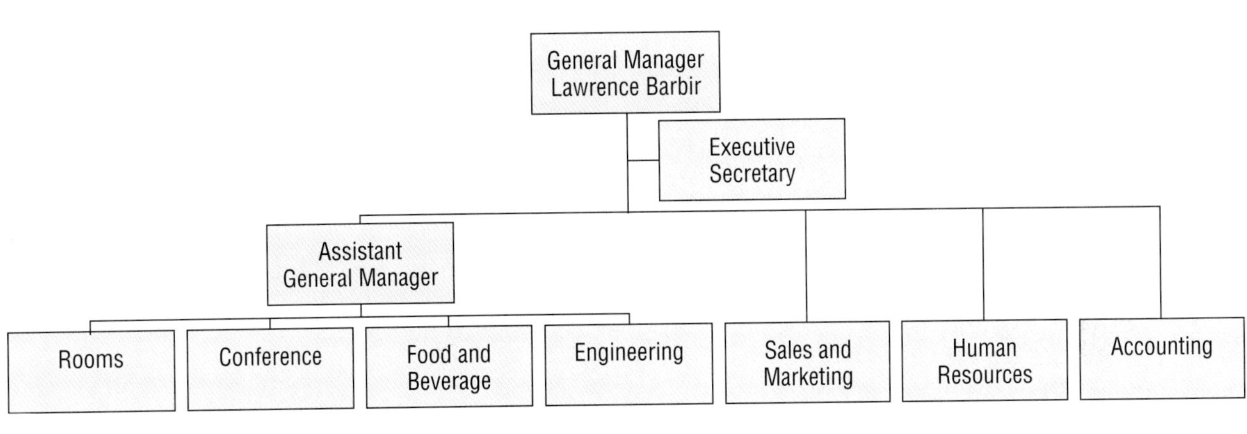

gram with a high school in which students are hired to work on the property and receive credits toward graduation. Lakeway is also preparing to face such issues as AIDS and drugs.

All new employees are given an Employee Handbook that outlines their responsibilities and benefits. It discusses such details as awards, holiday pay, insurance, uniforms, vacation, departmental meetings, the suggestion box, job descriptions, and employee responsibility for such things as cleanliness, attendance, performance, chewing gum, handling tips and gratuities, and disciplinary procedures.

To this point, the Lakeway revitalization is working. Dolce's goals are being met. Employees are happy and highly motivated. And the plan to make Lakeway a world-class facility and a nationally recognized center for meetings is being realized. No one can predict whether this will continue into the future, but the prospects are exciting.

DISCUSSION QUESTIONS

1. To what extent is Lakeway's organization structure and management approach appropriate for its service technology and competitive strategy?
2. What significant changes took place in this case? Were the changes implemented properly? What else might have been done?
3. Evaluate the human resource management approach used at Lakeway. Is it appropriate for Lakeway's strategy?
4. Changing a resort's national reputation is an elusive goal. Do you think Lakeway is on the right track? Explain.

PART 4

LEADING

Source: © 1984 Herb Comess, Untitled, 1,4-Cyclohexanediol, 99% +4,4′-Dimethoxydenzophenone. Cibachrome photograph of chemicals under a microscope. Collection of Bell & Howell Company.

In 1985, Bell & Howell moved its corporate headquarters to a new building in suburban Chicago. At that time, the company made substantial additions to its collection of art. The collection is displayed in both private offices and public areas of the building. It enhances the work environment and provides an opportunity for both employees and visitors to appreciate fine art. The Bell & Howell collection supports art in a variety of media including sculpture, painting, and photography.

C H A P T E R 1 3

Leadership in Organizations

Chapter Outline

Learning Objectives

After studying this chapter, you should be able to:

- Define leadership and explain its importance for organizations.
- Identify personal characteristics associated with effective leaders.
- Explain the five sources of leader influence and how each causes different subordinate behavior.
- Describe the leader behaviors of initiating structure and consideration and when they should be used.
- Describe Hersey and Blanchard's situational theory and its application to subordinate participation.
- Explain the path-goal model of leadership.
- Explain how leadership fits the organizational situation and how organizational characteristics can substitute for leadership behaviors.
- Describe inspirational leadership and when it should be used.

MANAGEMENT PROBLEM

When it was time to replace the head of United Technologies Corporation, Robert F. Daniell seemed an unlikely choice. He had rescued United Technologies' Sikorsky helicopter division, but had little headquarters experience and a style opposite his predecessor, Harry Gray. Gray ruled the conglomerate with an iron grip, creating an autocratic, impersonal, compartmentalized organization. Daniell's strength had been to inspire cooperation, see the big picture, and listen to problems from all levels. At Sikorsky he was known as a shop floor president, and some questioned whether this style would work to run a huge conglomerate.[1]

Will Robert Daniell's people-oriented style be a good thing for United Technologies? What leadership style would you recommend that he adopt for this situation?

Robert Daniell is the new leader of a giant corporation, and his style is different from the previous CEO. Many styles of leadership can be successful in organizations depending on the leader and the situation. Ron Canion, co-founder and chief executive officer of Compaq Computer, stresses that in his company "the casual — and often idiosyncratic — clothing seen at California personal computer makers is out, and employees are encouraged to work normal hours." Canion has no private parking space at his company and, like other employees, flies coach when he travels. Beth Pritchard successfully led Johnson Wax's insect control division by recognizing people's potential and delegating authority. She says, "My philosophy is that you can't do anything yourself. Your people have to do it." In another case, Steve Chen inspired 40 people to leave Cray Research with him because of his vision to build a super computer that Cray decided not to build.[2]

This chapter explores one of the most widely discussed and researched topics in management — leadership. Here we will define leadership and explore the sources of leadership influence. We will discuss trait, behavioral, and contingency theories of leadership effectiveness. We will also explore a new type of leader, called the *inspirational leader*, who creates a vision, inspires

President Ellen Gordon of Tootsie Roll Industries is a *leader,* because she influences people toward the attainment of goals. One of her goals was to diversify Tootsie Roll into multiple flavors, sizes, packages, and related products, as shown here. As a leader, Gordon influences people to contribute through empowerment. She draws out ideas and develops a consensus. Thanks to her leadership, a small family business has been transformed into a penny-candy giant that uses sophisticated technology, has a friendly, open-door policy, and is highly profitable.

loyalty, and leads corporate transformations. Chapters 14 through 16 deal with many of the functions of leadership, including employee motivation, communication, and leading groups.

THE NATURE OF LEADERSHIP

leadership The ability to influence people toward the attainment of organizational goals.

Among all the ideas and writings about leadership, three images stand out — people, influence, and goals. Leadership occurs between people, involves the use of influence, and is used to attain goals.[3] Influence means that the relationship among people is not passive. Moreover, influence is designed to achieve some end or goal. Thus, our formal definition of leadership is: **Leadership** is the ability to influence people toward the attainment of goals. This definition captures the idea that leaders are involved with other people in the achievement of objectives. Leadership is a "people" activity, distinct from administrative paper shuffling or problem-solving activities. Leadership is dynamic and involves the use of power. Power is important for influencing others, because it determines whether a leader is able to command compliance from followers.

SOURCES OF LEADER INFLUENCE

power The potential ability to influence others' behavior.

Power is the potential ability to influence the behavior of others.[4] Power represents the resources with which a leader effects changes in employee behavior. Leadership is the actual use of that power. Within organizations, leaders typically have five sources of power: legitimate, reward, coercive, expert, and referent.[5]

Legitimate Power. Power coming from a formal management position in an organization and the authority granted to it is called **legitimate power.** For example, once a person has been selected as a supervisor, most workers understand that they are obligated to follow his or her direction with respect to work activities. Subordinates accept this source of power as legitimate, which is why they comply.

Reward Power. Another kind of power, **reward power,** stems from the leader's authority to bestow rewards on other people. Leaders may have access to formal rewards, such as pay increases or promotions. They also have at their disposal rewards such as praise, attention, and recognition. Leaders can use rewards to influence subordinates' behavior.

Coercive power. The opposite of reward power is **coercive power:** It refers to the leader's authority to punish or recommend punishment. Leaders have coercive power when they have the right to fire or demote employees, criticize, or withdraw pay increases. For example, if Paul, a salesman, does not perform as expected, his supervisor has the coercive power to criticize him, reprimand him, put a negative letter in his file, and hurt his chance for a raise.

Expert Power. Power resulting from a leader's special knowledge or skill regarding the tasks performed by followers is referred to as **expert power.** When the leader is a true expert, subordinates go along with recommendations because of his or her superior knowledge. Leaders at supervisory levels often have experience in the production process that gains them promotion. At top management levels, however, leaders may lack expert power because subordinates know more about technical details than they do.

Referent Power. The last kind of power, **referent power,** comes from leader personality characteristics that command subordinates' identification, respect, and admiration so they wish to emulate the leader. When workers admire a supervisor because of the way she deals with them, the influence is based on referent power. Referent power depends on the leader's personal characteristics rather than formal title or position and is most visible in the area of inspirational leadership, which will be discussed later in this chapter.

Lee Iacocca uses three sources of leader influence: *legitimate, expert,* and *referent power*. He holds the formal position of CEO of Chrysler Corporation, and he knows the auto business profoundly well from his experience at both Ford and Chrysler. Iacocca stands out as a heroic leader who saved Chrysler. His referent power is so strong that it extends to the American public. He appears in Chrysler's new advertising campaign persuading Americans that U.S. cars are as good in quality as foreign-built cars.

legitimate power Power that stems from a formal management position in an organization and the authority granted to it.

reward power Power that results from the leader's authority to reward others.

coercive power Power that stems from the leader's authority to punish or recommend punishment.

expert power Power that stems from the leader's special knowledge of or skill in the tasks performed by subordinates.

referent power Power that results from leader characteristics that command subordinates' identification with, respect and admiration for, and desire to emulate the leader.

The Use of Power

Leaders use the above five sources of power to affect the behavior and performance of followers. But how do followers react to each source? Three reactions that have been studied are commitment, compliance, and resistance by followers.[6] *Commitment* means that workers will share the leader's point of view and enthusiastically carry out instructions. Expert power and referent power are the sources most likely to generate follower commitment. *Compliance* means that workers will obey orders and carry out instructions, although they may personally disagree with the instructions and will not necessarily be enthusiastic. Legitimate power and reward power are most likely to generate follower compliance. *Resistance* means that workers will deliberately try to avoid carrying out instructions and attempt to disobey orders. Coercive power most often generates resistance.

In General Foods' "Boat exercise," executives learn that it is hard to do a complex task when the top brass keeps meddling. This exercise teaches General Foods executives the importance of *empowering* lower employees to reach organizational goals. The task is to make rafts out of 50-gallon drums, two-by-fours, and rope. When the boss leaves the troops alone to produce their own solutions, they build a shipshape craft and win the prize. New-style leaders get the most from followers by giving them responsibility and winning their trust.

For example, Glenn Van Pelt, production supervisor at a steel fabrication plant, was respected by everyone for his knowledge of the production process and his pleasant attitude. One day Glenn asked John Simmons, one of his line managers, to reassign one of his people to help finish a project in another department. John felt he did not have enough people, but he knew the boss used good judgment and trusted his expertise. Thus, he agreed to lend one employee to Glenn and committed himself to making it work. However, had Glenn threatened John with punishment, John would have found a reason why he could not get along without the employee. Had Glenn used his formal position or reward power to force John's agreement, John would have complied, but without commitment.

A significant recent trend in corporate America is for top executives to *empower* lower employees. Fully 74 percent of executives in a survey claimed that they are more participatory, more concerned with consensus building, and rely more on communication than on command compared with the past. Executives are no longer keeping power themselves. For example, at Johnsonville Foods, the real power of top executives comes from giving it up to others who are in a better position to get things done. Empowering employees works because total power in the organization seems to increase. Everyone has more say and hence contributes more to organizational goals. The goal of senior executives in many corporations today is not simply to wield power, but to give it away to people who can get jobs done.[7]

LEADERSHIP TRAITS

traits The distinguishing personal characteristics of a leader, such as intelligence, values, and appearance.

Early efforts to understand leadership success focused on the leader's personal characteristics or traits. **Traits** are the distinguishing personal characteristics of a leader, such as intelligence, values, and appearance. The early research fo-

EXHIBIT 13.1
Personal Characteristics of Leaders

Physical characteristics:	Personality:	Social characteristics:
Activity	Alertness	Ability to enlist cooperation
Energy	Originality, creativity	Cooperativeness
	Personal integrity, ethical conduct	Popularity, prestige
Social background:	Self-confidence	Sociability, interpersonal skills
Mobility	Work-related characteristics	Social participation
	Achievement drive, desire to excel	Tact, diplomacy
Intelligence and ability:	Drive for responsibility	
Judgment, decisiveness	Responsible in pursuit of objectives	
Knowledge	Task orientation	
Fluency of speech		

Source: Adapted from *Stogdill's Handbook of Leadership*, Revised Edition, by Bernard M. Bass, pp. 75–76, The Free Press, 1981. This adaptation appeared in R. Albanese and D. D. Van Fleet, *Organizational Behavior: A Managerial Viewpoint.* Hinsdale, IL: The Dryden Press, 1983.

cused on leaders who had achieved a level of greatness and hence was referred to as the "great man" approach. The idea was relatively simple: Find out what made these people great, and select future leaders who already exhibited the same traits or could be trained to develop them. Generally, research found only a weak relationship between personal traits and leader success.[8] For example, Tom Osborne, football coach at Nebraska, and Johnny Majors, football coach at the University of Tennessee, have different personality traits, but both are successful leaders of their football programs.

In addition to personality traits, physical, social, and work-related characteristics of leaders have been studied. Exhibit 13.1 summarizes the physical, social, and personal leader characteristics that have received the greatest research support.[9] However, these characteristics do not stand alone. The appropriateness of a trait or set of traits depends on the leadership situation. The same traits do not apply to every organization.

For example, Sarah Brown is the manager of Far Eastern imports for a major steel corporation. There is an opening for a subordinate manager in her department who will supervise the field sales personnel. For this position, the personal characteristic of intelligence and a working knowledge of steel product marketing are important, as are desire for responsibility, a task orientation, and supervisory skills. Sarah Brown's ability to understand the situation and the type of leader who will succeed in it will help her select the appropriate person for the job.

AUTOCRATIC VERSUS DEMOCRATIC LEADERS

autocratic leader A leader who tends to centralize authority and rely on legitimate, reward, and coercive power to manage subordinates.

democratic leader A leader who delegates authority to others, encourages participation, and relies on expert and referent power to manage subordinates.

One way to approach leader characteristics is to examine autocratic and democratic leaders. An **autocratic leader** is one who tends to centralize authority and rely on legitimate, reward, and coercive power. A **democratic leader** delegates authority to others, encourages participation, and relies on expert and referent power to influence subordinates.

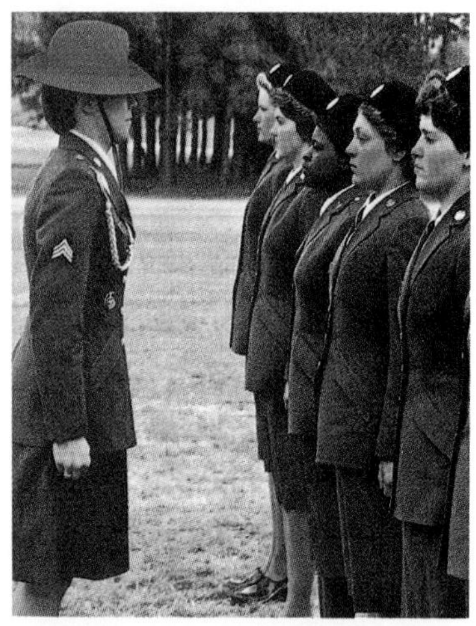

Recruits into the U.S. Army learn about *autocratic leadership*. The military has a well-defined leadership structure. Autocratic leaders tend to centralize authority and rely on legitimate, reward, and coercive power. The sergeant has the authority to bestow rewards such as recognition and to punish subordinates for failure to perform. Although military organizations also use democratic leadership, autocratic leadership remains important in many situations.

The first studies on these leadership characteristics were conducted at Iowa State University by Kurt Lewin and his associates.[10] These studies compared autocratic and democratic leaders and produced some interesting findings. The groups with autocratic leaders performed highly so long as the leader was present to supervise them. However, group members were displeased with the close, autocratic style of leadership, and feelings of hostility frequently arose. The performance of groups who were assigned democratic leaders was almost as good, and these were characterized by positive feelings rather than hostility. In addition, under the democratic style of leadership group members performed well even when the leader was absent and left the group on its own.[11] The participative techniques and majority rule decision making used by the democratic leader trained and involved group members such that they performed well with or without the leader present. These characteristics of democratic leadership explain why the empowerment of lower employees is a popular trend in companies today.

This early work suggested that leaders were either autocratic or democratic in their approach. However, further work by Tannenbaum and Schmidt indicated that leadership could be a continuum reflecting different amounts of employee participation.[12] Thus, one leader might be autocratic (boss centered), another democratic (subordinate centered), and a third a mix of the two styles. The leadership continuum is illustrated in Exhibit 13.2.

Tannenbaum and Schmidt suggested that the extent to which leadership is boss centered or subordinate centered depends on organizational circumstances. For example, if there is time pressure on a leader or if it takes too long for subordinates to learn how to make decisions, the leader will tend to use an autocratic style. When subordinates are able to learn decision-making skills readily, a participative style can be used. Another situational factor is the skill difference between subordinates and leader. The greater the skill difference, the more autocratic the leader approach, because it is difficult to bring subordinates up to the leader's expertise level.[13]

For example, Stephen Fleming uses an autocratic style as a marketing manager in an oil products company. He is being groomed for a higher position because his marketing department has performed so well. However, this has meant time spent at meetings away from his group, and their performance has declined because their subordinates have not learned to function independently. In contrast, Jan Carlzon, president and CEO of Scandinavian Airlines, believes that people are managed best by showing them respect and trust. They have to be given the freedom to do a job as they see fit in order to do the best for the company. Carlzon's success turned around SAS, which won the Airline of the Year award. This democratic approach enabled one flight attendant to purchase coffee and cookies with her own money to give to passengers on a flight delayed leaving the gate. She created many satisfied customers who would not have existed with an autocratic leadership style.[14]

Two-Dimensional Approaches

The autocratic and democratic styles suggest that it is the "behavior" of the leader rather than a personality trait that determines leadership effectiveness. Perhaps any leader can adopt the correct behavior with appropriate training.

EXHIBIT 13.2
Leadership Continuum

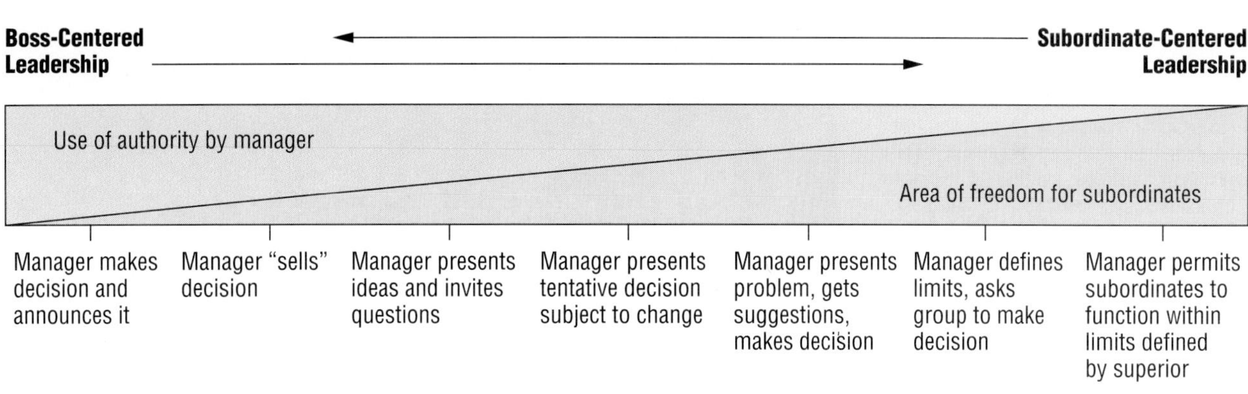
Boss-Centered Leadership
Subordinate-Centered Leadership
Use of authority by manager
Area of freedom for subordinates
Manager makes decision and announces it
Manager "sells" decision
Manager presents ideas and invites questions
Manager presents tentative decision subject to change
Manager presents problem, gets suggestions, makes decision
Manager defines limits, asks group to make decision
Manager permits subordinates to function within limits defined by superior

Source: Reprinted by permission of the *Harvard Business Review*. An exhibit from "How to Choose a Leadership Pattern" by Robert Tannenbaum and Warren Schmidt (May/June 1973). Copyright © 1973 by the President and Fellows of Harvard College; all rights reserved.

The focus of recent research has shifted from leader personality traits toward the behaviors successful leaders display. Important research programs on leadership behavior were conducted at Ohio State University, the University of Michigan, and the University of Texas.

OHIO STATE STUDIES

Researchers at Ohio State University surveyed leaders to study hundreds of dimensions of leader behavior.[15] They identified two major behaviors, called consideration and initiating structure.

Consideration is the extent to which the leader is mindful of subordinates, respects their ideas and feelings, and establishes mutual trust. Considerate leaders are friendly, provide open communication, develop teamwork, and are oriented toward their subordinates' welfare.

consideration A type of leader behavior that describes the extent to which a leader is sensitive to subordinates, respects their ideas and feelings, and establishes mutual trust.

Initiating structure is the extent to which the leader is task oriented and directs subordinate work activities toward goal attainment. Leaders with this style typically give instructions, spend time planning, emphasize deadlines, and provide explicit schedules of work activities.

initiating structure A type of leader behavior that describes the extent to which a leader is task oriented and directs subordinates' work activities toward goal achievement.

Consideration and initiating structure are independent of each other, which means that a leader with a high degree of consideration may be either high or low on initiating structure. A leader may have any of four styles: high initiating structure–low consideration, high initiating structure–high consideration, low initiating structure–low consideration, or low initiating structure–high consideration. The Ohio State research found that the high consideration–high initiating structure style achieved better performance and greater satisfaction than the other leader styles. However, new research has found that

Sam Walton, founder and chairman of Wal-Mart Stores, Inc., is a leader high in both *consideration* and *initiating structure.* For Sam Walton, the key to success is people and the way they are treated and feel about their company. Walton spends four days a week on the road, shown here speaking to associates in Conway, Arkansas. With direction from the top, state-of-the-art technology helps Wal-Mart employees do their job better. Inventory systems, reordering, and warehouse distribution systems provide an effective structure within which employees deliver superb products and services to customers.

effective leaders may be high on consideration and low on initiating structure or low on consideration and high on initiating structure depending on the situation. Thus, the "high-high" style is not always the best.[16]

Michigan Studies

Studies at the University of Michigan at about the same time took a different approach by comparing the behavior of effective and ineffective supervisors.[17] The most effective supervisors were those who focused on the subordinates' human needs in order to "build effective work groups with high performance goals." The Michigan researchers used the term *employee-centered leaders* for leaders who established high performance goals and displayed supportive behavior toward subordinates. The less effective leaders were called *job-centered leaders;* these tended to be less concerned with goal achievement and human needs in favor of meeting schedules, keeping costs low, and achieving production efficiency.

The Managerial Grid

managerial grid A two-dimensional leadership theory that measures a leader's concern for people and concern for production.

Blake and Mouton of the University of Texas proposed a two-dimensional leadership theory called **managerial grid** that builds on the work of the Ohio State and Michigan studies.[18] The two-dimensional model and its five major management styles are depicted in Exhibit 13.3. Each axis on the grid is a 9-point scale, with 1 meaning low concern and 9 high concern. Concern for production is the same as initiating structure in the Ohio State model and pertains to getting results and achieving objectives with little regard for the people involved. Concern for people is the same as consideration behavior described earlier and emphasizes healthy interpersonal relationships in the work group.

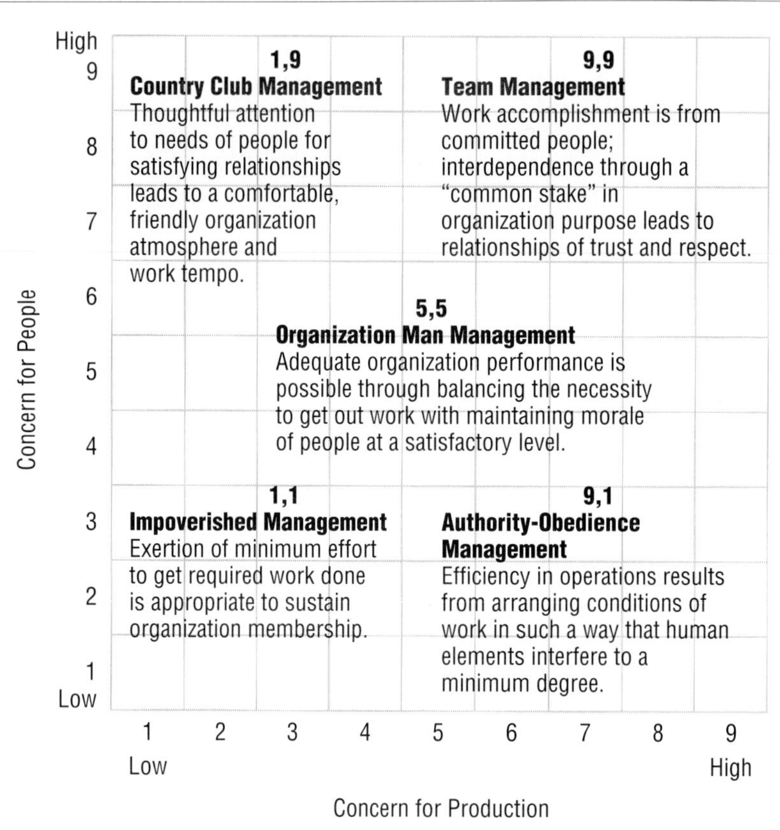

EXHIBIT 13.3
The Managerial Grid®

Source: Robert R. Blake and Jane S. Mouton, *The New Managerial Grid III* (Houston: Gulf, 1985), 12.

Team management (9,9) often is considered the most effective style and is recommended for managers because organization members work together to accomplish tasks. *Country club management* (1,9) occurs when primary emphasis is given to people rather than to work outputs. *Authority-obedience management* (9,1) occurs when efficiency in operations is the dominant orientation. *Organization Man management* (5,5) reflects a moderate amount of concern for both people and production. *Impoverished management* (1,1) means the absence of a management philosophy; managers exert little effort toward interpersonal relationships or work accomplishment.

Exhibit 13.3 is an interpretation of all three streams of research on leader behavior. The significance of the research is that each stream discovered similar dimensions of leadership style. The effectiveness of leaders depends on the types of behavior they display. The Ohio State, Michigan, and Texas research programs suggested that leader behavior is more complex than the simple autocratic versus democratic behavior described earlier. The two dimensions of leadership are illustrated in the following examples.

CHICK-FIL-A, INC. •

Samuel Truett Cathy is founder and president of Chick-fil-A, Inc. Cathy has been remarkably successful, and one of the keys is his people orientation. "Truett Cathy is probably the most person-oriented individual I've ever known," says a close friend. "He honestly believes his highest obligation is to help people reach their highest potential. . . . He's one of the most tolerant persons I've known." The executive vice-president of Chick-fil-A calls his boss "the most patient man I've ever encountered, and one totally committed to individual development. He delegates easily, lets people grow by trusting them."

Of course, to be successful Cathy also had to set goals and provide direction for his company. But the reason he succeeded was that he was an outstanding encourager of other people.[19]

Compare Cathy's leadership style with that of Dick Joseph Corr, who started in heavy manufacturing and recently took over Continental Airlines. He is a blunt talker who ferrets out waste and pushes his managers to save money. Not considered a people person, he told his operations managers to cut huge aircraft maintenance bills and reschedule flights to save costs and ease the work load for pilots. Corr's credentials as Mister Fix-it are important to Continental, which needs greater efficiency, but he probably will not inspire employees.[20]

Truett Cathy's leadership style is characterized by a high level of consideration and a moderate level of initiating structure. Joseph Corr, in contrast, is high on initiating structure and low on consideration. However, both managers are successful because of their situations.

Contingency Approaches

contingency approach A model of leadership that describes the relationship between leadership styles and specific organizational situations.

Several models of leadership that explain the relationship between leadership styles and specific situations have been developed. These are termed **contingency approaches** and include the leadership model developed by Fiedler and his associates, the situational theory of Hersey and Blanchard, the path-goal theory presented by Evans and House, and the substitutes-for-leadership concept.

Fiedler's Contingency Theory

An early, extensive effort to combine leadership style and organizational situation into a comprehensive theory of leadership was made by Fiedler and his associates.[21] The basic idea is simple: Match the leader's style with the situation most favorable for his or her success. By diagnosing leadership style and the organizational situation, the correct fit can be arranged.

LPC scale A questionnaire designed to measure relationship-oriented versus task-oriented leadership style according to the leader's choice of adjectives for describing the "least preferred coworker."

Leadership Style. The cornerstone of Fiedler's contingency theory is the extent to which the leader's style is relationship oriented or task oriented. A *relationship-oriented leader* is concerned with people, as in the consideration style described earlier. A *task-oriented leader* is primarily motivated by task accomplishment, which is similar to the initiating structure style described earlier.

Leadership style was measured with a questionnaire known as the least preferred coworker (LPC) scale. The **LPC scale** has a set of 16 bipolar adjectives along an 8-point scale. Examples of the bipolar adjectives used by Fiedler on the LPC scale are as follows:

open	—	—	—	—	—	—	—	—	guarded
quarrelsome	—	—	—	—	—	—	—	—	harmonious
efficient	—	—	—	—	—	—	—	—	inefficient
self-assured	—	—	—	—	—	—	—	—	hesitant
gloomy	—	—	—	—	—	—	—	—	cheerful

If the leader describes the least preferred coworker using positive concepts, he or she is considered relationship oriented, that is, cares about and is sensitive to other people's feelings. Conversely, if a leader uses negative concepts to describe the least preferred coworker, he or she is considered task oriented, that is, sees other people in negative terms and places greater value on task activities than on people.

SITUATION. Leadership situations can be analyzed in terms of three elements: the quality of leader-member relationships, task structure, and position power.[22] Each of these elements can be described as either favorable or unfavorable for the leader.

1. *Leader-member relations* refers to group atmosphere and members' attitude toward and acceptance of the leader. When subordinates trust, respect, and have confidence in the leader, leader-member relations are considered good. When subordinates distrust, do not respect, and have little confidence in the leader, leader-member relations are poor.
2. *Task structure* refers to the extent to which tasks performed by the group are defined, involve specific procedures, and have clear, explicit goals. Routine, well-defined tasks, such as those of assembly line workers, have a high degree of structure. Creative, ill-defined tasks, such as research and development or strategic planning, have a low degree of task structure. When task structure is high, the situation is considered favorable to the leader; when low, the situation is less favorable.
3. *Position power* is the extent to which the leader has formal authority over subordinates. Position power is high when the leader has the power to plan and direct the work of subordinates, evaluate it, and reward or punish them. Position power is low when the leader has little authority over subordinates and cannot evaluate their work or reward them. When position power is high, the situation is considered favorable for the leader; when low, the situation is unfavorable.

Combining the three situational characteristics yields a list of eight leadership situations, which are illustrated in Exhibit 13.4. Situation I is most favorable to the leader because leader-member relations are good, task structure is high, and leader position power is strong. Situation VIII is most unfavorable to the leader because leader-member relations are poor, task structure is low, and leader position power is weak. All other octants represent intermediate degrees of favorableness for the leader.

EXHIBIT 13.4
Fiedler's Classification of Situation Favorableness

	Very Favorable		Intermediate				Very Unfavorable	
Leader-Member Relations	Good	Good	Good	Good	Poor	Poor	Poor	Poor
Task Structure	High		Low		High		Low	
Leader Position Power	Strong	Weak	Strong	Weak	Strong	Weak	Strong	Weak
Situations	I	II	III	IV	V	VI	VII	VIII

Source: Fred E. Fiedler, "The Effects of Leadership Training and Experience: A Contingency Model Interpretation," *Administrative Science Quarterly* 17 (1972), 455. Reprinted by permission of *Administrative Science Quarterly*.

EXHIBIT 13.5
How Leader Style Fits the Situation

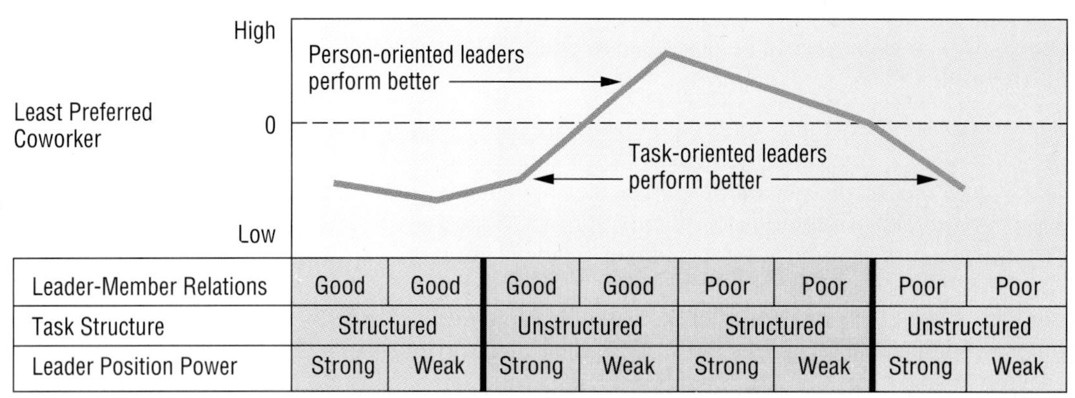

Source: Fred E. Fiedler, "The Effects of Leadership Training and Experience: A Contingency Model Interpretation," *Administrative Science Quarterly* 17 (1972), 455. Reprinted by permission of *Administrative Science Quarterly*.

CONTINGENCY THEORY. When Fiedler examined the relationships among leadership style, situational favorability, and group task performance, he found the pattern shown in Exhibit 13.5. Task-oriented leaders are more effective when the situation is either highly favorable or highly unfavorable. Relationship-oriented leaders are more effective in situations of moderate favorability.

The reason the task-oriented leader excels in the favorable situation is that when everyone gets along, the task is clear, and the leader has power, all that is needed is for someone to take charge and provide direction. Similarly, if the situation is highly unfavorable to the leader, a great deal of structure and task direction is needed. A strong leader defines task structure and can establish authority over subordinates. Because leader-member relations are poor anyway, a strong task orientation will make no difference in the leader's popularity.

F. Ross Johnson's tough, task-oriented leadership style has been just the thing to improve organizational effectiveness at RJR Nabisco, Inc. Quick to get rid of poor-performing people and divisions, Johnson illustrates *Fiedler's contingency theory*. He is quick to say no to proposals, respecting ideas over feelings, and prefers to invest in technology rather than staff. Johnson does not like to see RJR Nabisco's numerous brands in second place. The results are phenomenal, with creaky old corporate cultures now operating with zing and corporate profits zooming.

The reason the relationship-oriented leader performs better in situations of intermediate favorability is that human relations skills are important in achieving high group performance. In these situations the leader may be moderately well liked, and have some power, and supervise jobs that contain some ambiguity. A leader with good interpersonal skills can create a positive group atmosphere that will improve relationships, clarify task structure, and establish position power.

A leader, then, needs to know two things in order to use Fiedler's contingency theory. First, the leader should know whether he or she has a relationship- or task-oriented style. Second, the leader should diagnose the situation and determine whether leader-member relations, task structure, and position power are favorable or unfavorable. Fitting leader style to the situation can yield large dividends. Consider the situation that existed at Greyhound.[23]

GREYHOUND CORP. •

John Teets, chairman of Greyhound, found himself in a situation that fit his leadership style. Teets is a very tough, task-oriented leader. As one vice-president said, "He'd rather kick a door down than turn the handle." Teets fired questions at top executives to see whether they knew the details of their operations. He was known to shout during meetings and rip pages out of reports. He exhorted managers to work harder and to achieve a 15 percent return. When the union refused to cut wages, he shut down 29 plants in one day.

Because of Teets' fierce style, Greyhound shaped up. The company was a sleepy, poor performer and did not provide a good situation for any leader. Teets sold off some divisions, insisted on higher performance in others, and fought with managers and the union. His task-oriented style was just right for Greyhound Corp. and was responsible for whipping it back into shape.[24]

John Teet's experience at Greyhound illustrates Fiedler's model: A task-oriented style worked in an unfavorable situation.

An important contribution of Fiedler's research is that it goes beyond the notion of leadership styles to show how styles fit the situation to improve organizational effectiveness. On the other hand, the model has also been criticized.[25] Using the LPC score as a measure of relationship- or task-oriented behavior seems simplistic, and how the model works over time is unclear. For example, if a task-oriented leader is matched with an unfavorable situation and is successful, the organizational situation is likely to improve and become more favorable to the leader. In other words, as Greyhound's performance improved, the formal position power, leader-member relations, and task structure also improved and became more positive for the leader, and the hard-nosed style of John Teets might no longer be appropriate. Teets might have to change his style or go to a new situation to find the same challenge for his task-oriented leader style.

Hersey and Blanchard's Situational Theory

situational theory A contingency approach to leadership that links the leader's two-dimensional style with the task maturity of subordinates.

The **situational theory** of leadership is an interesting extension of the two-dimensional theories described earlier and summarized in the managerial grid (Exhibit 13.3). The point of Hersey and Blanchard is that subordinates vary in maturity level. People low in task maturity, because of little ability or training, or insecurity, need a different leadership style than those who are highly mature and have good ability, skills, confidence, and willingness to work.[26]

The relationships between leader style and task maturity are summarized in Exhibit 13.6. The upper part of Exhibit 13.6 indicates style of leader, which is based on a combination of relationship behavior and task behavior. The bell-shaped curve is called a prescriptive curve because it indicates when each leader style should be used. The four styles — telling (S1), selling (S2), participating (S3), and delegating (S4) — depend on the maturity of followers, indicated in the lower part of Exhibit 13.6. M1 is low maturity and M4 represents high maturity. The telling style is for low-maturity subordinates, because people are unable and unwilling to take responsibility for their own task behavior. The selling and participating styles work for followers with moderate maturity, and delegating is appropriate for employees with high maturity.

This contingency model is easier to understand than Fiedler's model, but it incorporates only the characteristics of followers and not those of the situation. The leader should evaluate subordinates and adopt whichever style is needed. If one or more followers are immature, the leader must be very specific, telling them exactly what to do, how to do it, and when. For followers high in maturity, the leader provides a general goal and sufficient authority to do the task as they see fit. Leaders must carefully diagnose the maturity level of followers and then tell, sell, participate, or delegate.

A recent public example of the wrong leadership style occurred at the Department of Housing and Urban Development (H.U.D.). Samuel Pierce, Jr., the secretary of H.U.D. during the Reagan administration, used a hands-off, delegating style. Yet employees within H.U.D. were not mature, using their positions to reportedly provide favors and contracts to friends and political supporters. The net result has been a charge of mismanagement against the leader of H.U.D., because the leadership style did not fit the situation.[27]

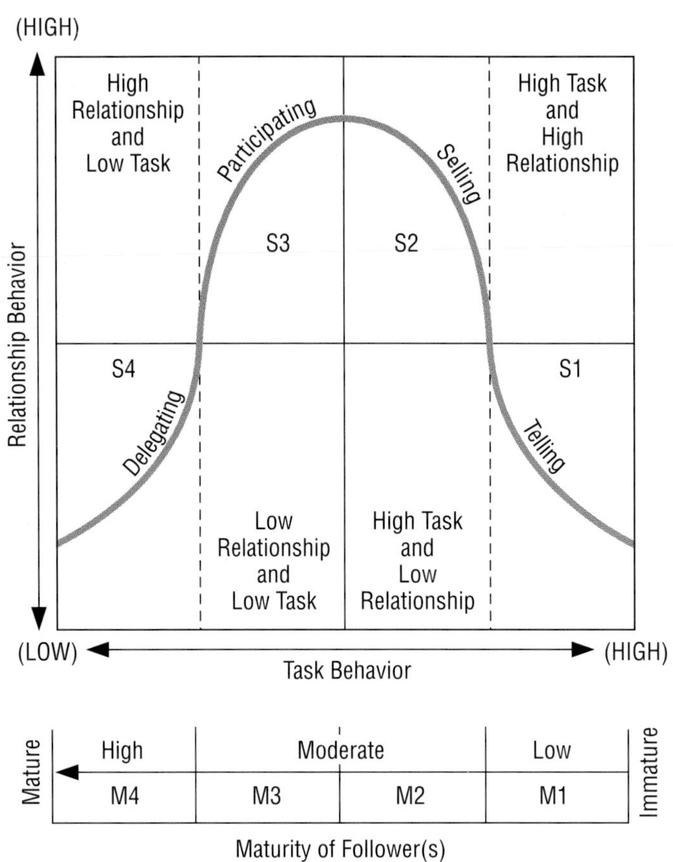

EXHIBIT 13.6
The Situational Theory of Leadership

Source: Paul Hersey and Kenneth H. Blanchard, *Management of Organizational Behavior: Utilizing Human Resources*, 4th ed. (Englewood Cliffs, N.J.: Prentice-Hall, 1982). Used with permission.

PATH-GOAL THEORY

Another contingency approach to leadership is called the path-goal theory.[28] According to the **path-goal theory,** the leader's responsibility is to increase subordinates' motivation to attain personal and organizational goals. As illustrated in Exhibit 13.7, the leader increases their motivation by either (1) clarifying the subordinates' path to the rewards that are available or (2) increasing the rewards that they value and desire. Path clarification means that the leader works with subordinates to help them identify and learn the behaviors that will lead to successful task accomplishment and organizational rewards. Increasing rewards means that the leader talks with subordinates to learn which rewards are important to them — that is, whether they desire intrinsic rewards from the work itself or extrinsic rewards such as raises or promotions. The leader's job is to increase personal payoffs to subordinates for goal attainment and to make the paths to these payoffs clear and easy to travel.[29]

path-goal theory A contingency approach to leadership specifying that the leader's responsibility is to increase subordinates' motivation by clarifying the behaviors necessary for task accomplishment and rewards.

This model is called a contingency theory because it consists of three sets of contingencies — leader behavior and style, situational contingencies, and the use of rewards to meet subordinates' needs.[30]

EXHIBIT 13.7
Leader Roles in the Path-Goal Model

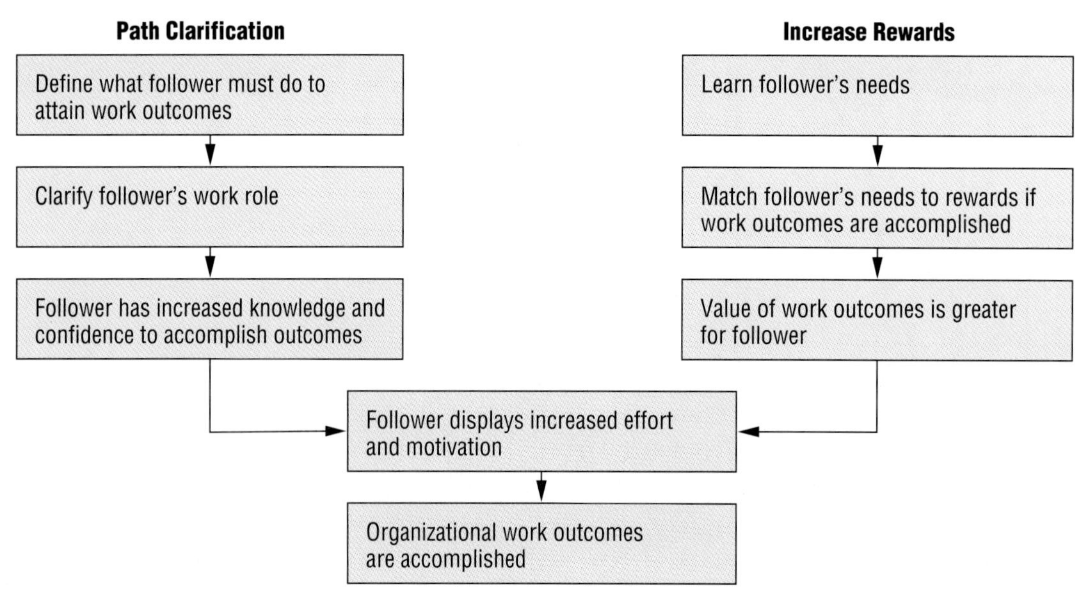

Source: Based on Bernard M. Bass, "Leadership: Good, Better, Best," *Organizational Dynamics* 13 (Winter 1985), 26–40.

LEADER BEHAVIOR. The path-goal theory suggests a fourfold classification of leader behaviors.[31] These classifications are the types of leader behavior the leader can adopt and include supportive, directive, achievement-oriented, and participative styles.

Supportive leadership involves leader behavior that shows concern for subordinates' well-being and personal needs. Leadership behavior is open, friendly, and approachable, and the leader creates a team climate and treats subordinates as equals. Supportive leadership is similar to the consideration leadership described earlier.

Directive leadership occurs when the leader tells subordinates exactly what they are supposed to do. Leader behavior includes planning, making schedules, setting performance goals and behavior standards, and stressing adherence to rules and regulations. Directive leadership behavior is similar to the initiating structure leadership style described earlier.

Participative leadership means that the leader consults with his or her subordinates about decisions. Leader behavior includes asking for opinions and suggestions, encouraging participation in decision making, and meeting with subordinates in their workplaces. The participative leader encourages group discussion and written suggestions.

Achievement-oriented leadership occurs when the leader sets clear and challenging objectives for subordinates. Leader behavior stresses high-quality performance and improvement over current performance. Achievement-

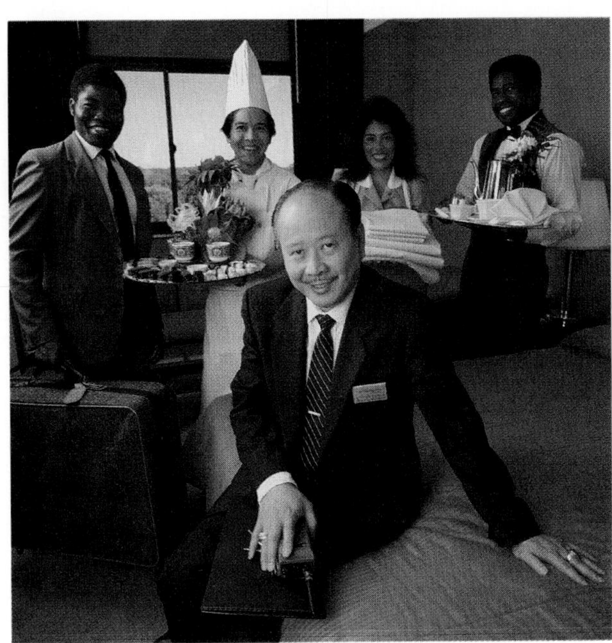

Victor Vongs used a *supportive leadership style* to turn around the floundering Holiday Inn Crowne Plaza in White Plains, New York. He slashed turnover from 83 percent to 11 percent and increased revenues sixfold. He does it by hiring immigrants and helping them find a home and sign up for English classes. Vongs encourages employees to think of the hotel as a second home. With their increased confidence comes effort and high performance.

oriented leaders also show confidence in subordinates and assist them in learning how to achieve high goals.

The four types of leader behavior are not considered ingrained personality traits; rather, they reflect types of behavior that every leader is able to adopt depending on the situation.

SITUATIONAL CONTINGENCIES. The two important situational contingencies in the path-goal theory are (1) the personal characteristics of group members and (2) the work environment. Personal characteristics of subordinates are similar to Hersey and Blanchard's maturity level and include such factors as ability, skills, needs, and motivations. For example, if an employee has a low level of ability or skill. the leader may need to provide additional training or coaching in order for the worker to improve performance. If a subordinate is self-centered, the leader must manipulate rewards to motivate him or her. Subordinates who want clear direction and authority require a directive leader who will tell them exactly what to do. Craftworkers and professionals, however, may want more freedom and autonomy and work best under a participative leadership style.

The work environment contingencies include the degree of task structure, the nature of the formal authority system, and the work group itself. The task structure is similar to the same concept described in Fiedler's contingency theory; it includes the extent to which tasks are defined and have explicit job descriptions and work procedures. The formal authority system includes the amount of legitimate power used by managers and the extent to which policies and rules constrain employees' behavior. Work group characteristics are the educational level of subordinates and the quality of relationships among them.

EXHIBIT 13.8
Path-Goal Situations and Preferred Leader Behaviors

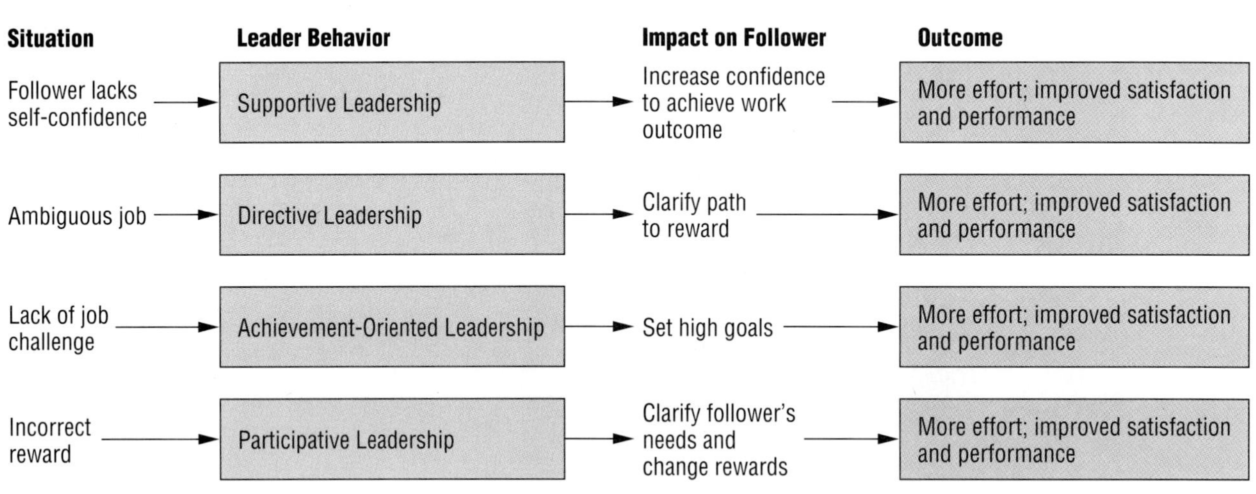

Source: Adapted from Gary A. Yukl, *Leadership in Organizations* (Englewood Cliffs, N.J.: Prentice-Hall, 1981), 146–152.

USE OF REWARDS. Recall that the leader's responsibility is to clarify the path to rewards for subordinates or to increase the amount of rewards to enhance satisfaction and job performance. In some situations, the leader works with subordinates to help them acquire the skills and confidence needed to perform tasks and achieve rewards already available. In others, the leader may develop new rewards to meet the specific needs of a subordinate.

Exhibit 13.8 illustrates four examples of how leadership behavior is tailored to the situation. In situation 1, the subordinate lacks confidence; thus, the supportive leadership style provides the social support with which to encourage the subordinate to undertake the behavior needed to do the work and receive the rewards. In situation 2, the job is ambiguous and the employee is not performing effectively. Directive leadership behavior is used to give instructions and clarify the task so that the follower will know how to accomplish it and receive rewards. In situation 3, the subordinate is unchallenged by the task; thus, an achievement-oriented behavior is used to set higher goals. This clarifies the path to rewards for the employee. In situation 4, an incorrect reward is given to a subordinate and the participative leadership style is used to change this. By discussing the subordinate's needs, the leader is able to identify the correct reward for task accomplishment. In all four cases, the outcome of fitting the leadership behavior to the situation produces greater employee effort by either clarifying how subordinates can receive rewards or changing the rewards to fit their needs.

In some organizations, such as Fireman's Fund Insurance Company, leaders display complementary leadership styles to meet subordinates' needs.

Fireman's Fund Insurance Co. • John Byrne and William McCormick have been called the "odd couple of insurance." McCormick is in charge of Fireman's Fund Insurance Company, and Byrne is his boss. McCormick is somewhat of an intellectual and repeats his vision for the company to employees at every opportunity. McCormick confronts employees when they are the cause of performance problems and rewards them when performance is high. He sets challenging goals and provides rewards accordingly. When he joined the company, the difference between the best and worst branch managers' bonus was only $3,000. Now it is $42,000.

Byrne, in contrast, is at home backslapping with employees. Byrne likes small talk, attends cocktail parties, and dislikes a stiff, memo-writing, policy-setting style. He is a people person and provides support whenever he can—indeed, as McCormick's boss, he gives McCormick the freedom to run Fireman's Fund as he likes.[32]

McCormick's leadership style is achievement oriented, but it also includes some elements of directive behavior. This is appropriate because of Fireman's Fund's difficulties in recent years. Strong direction and high goals are improving performance. Byrne's style is considered supportive leadership behavior, which gives McCormick the support to overcome obstacles and achieve higher performance.

Path-goal theorizing can be complex, but much of the research on it has been encouraging.[33] Using the model to specify precise relationships and make exact predictions about employee outcomes may be difficult, but the four types of leader behavior and the ideas for fitting them to situational contingencies provide a useful way for leaders to think about motivating subordinates.

Substitutes for Leadership

The contingency leadership approaches considered so far have focused on the leaders' style, the subordinates' nature, and the situation's characteristics. The final contingency approach suggests that situational variables can be so powerful that they actually substitute for or neutralize the need for leadership.[34] This approach outlines those organizational settings in which a leadership style is unimportant or unnecessary.

Exhibit 13.9 shows the situational variables that tend to substitute for or neutralize leadership characteristics. A **substitute** for leadership makes the leadership style unnecessary or redundant. For example, highly professional subordinates who know how to do their tasks do not need a leader who initiates structure for them and tells them what to do. A **neutralizer** counteracts the leadership style and prevents the leader from displaying certain behaviors. For example, if a leader has absolutely no position power or is physically removed from subordinates, the leader's ability to give directions to subordinates is greatly reduced.

substitute A situational variable that makes a leadership style redundant or unnecessary.

neutralizer A situational variable that counteracts a leadership style and prevents the leader from displaying certain behaviors.

Situational variables in Exhibit 13.9 include characteristics of the subordinate, the task, and the organization itself. For example, when subordinates are highly professional and experienced, both leadership styles are less important. The employees do not need as much direction or consideration. With respect

EXHIBIT 13.9
Substitutes and Neutralizers for Leadership

Variable		Task-Oriented Leadership	People-Oriented Leadership
Organizational variables:	Group cohesiveness	Substitutes	Substitutes
	Formalization	Substitutes	
	Inflexibility	Neutralizes	
	Low positional power	Neutralizes	Neutralizes
	Physical separation	Neutralizes	Neutralizes
Task characteristics:	Highly structured task	Substitutes	
	Automatic feedback	Substitutes	
	Intrinsically satisfying		Substitutes
Group characteristics:	Professionalism	Substitutes	Substitutes
	Trained/experienced	Substitutes	
	Low value of rewards	Neutralizes	Neutralizes

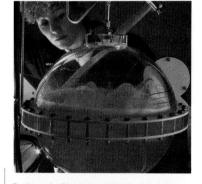

to task characteristics, highly structured tasks substitute for a task-oriented style and a satisfying task substitutes for a people-oriented style. With respect to the organization itself, group cohesiveness substitutes for both leader styles. Formalized rules and procedures substitute for leader task orientation. Physical separation of leader and subordinate neutralizes both leadership styles.

The value of the situations described in Exhibit 13.9 is that they help leaders avoid leadership overkill. Leaders should adopt a style with which to complement the organizational situation. For example, the work situation for bank tellers provides a high level of formalization, little flexibility, and a highly structured task. The head teller should not adopt a task-oriented style, because the organization already provides structure and direction. The head teller should concentrate on a people-oriented style. In other organizations, if group cohesiveness or previous training meet employees' social needs, the leader is free to concentrate on task-oriented behaviors. The leader can adopt a style complementary to the organizational situation to ensure that both task needs and people needs of the work group will be met.

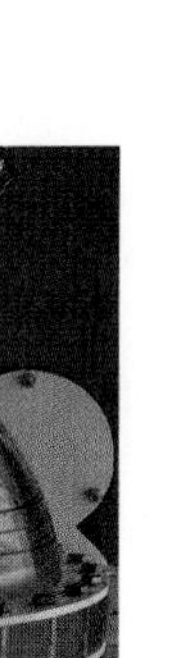

Barbara A. Bicknell, of Martin Marietta Space Systems, prepares an experiment to test how fluids behave in weightlessness to examine the possibility of refueling spacecraft in orbit. Bicknell and her team built their experiment in just three months. The leadership style used for her team differs from that used in other company areas because of the high level of employee training, professionalism, and autonomy that reduces the need for both task- and people-oriented leadership styles. The situation *substitutes* for leadership in research settings.

INSPIRATIONAL LEADERSHIP

In Chapter 1, we defined management to include the management functions of leading, planning, organizing, and controlling. But recent work on leadership has begun to distinguish leadership as something more: a quality that inspires and motivates people beyond their normal levels of performance. The difference between traditional management and inspirational leadership is illustrated in Exhibit 13.10.

LEADING VERSUS MANAGING

The traditional management function of leading has been called transactional leadership.[35] **Transactional leaders** clarify the role and task requirements of subordinates, initiate structure, provide appropriate rewards, and try to be

EXHIBIT 13.10
Leaders versus Managers

Let's Get Rid of Management

People
don't want
to be
managed.
They want
to be led.
Whoever heard
of a world
manager?
World leader,
yes.
Educational leader.
Political leader.
Religious leader.
Scout leader.
Community leader.
Labor leader.
Business leader.
They lead.
They don't manage.
The carrot
always wins
over the stick.
Ask your horse.
You can *lead* your
horse to water,
but you can't
manage him
to drink.
If you want to
manage somebody,
manage yourself.
Do that well
and you'll
be ready to
stop managing.
And start
leading.

Source: Courtesy of United Technologies Corporation, Hartford, CT 06101.

considerate to and meet the social needs of subordinates. Transactional leaders help satisfy subordinates to improve productivity. Transactional leaders excel at management functions. They are hardworking, tolerant, and fair-minded. They take pride in keeping things running smoothly and efficiently. Transactional leaders often stress the impersonal aspects of performance, such as plans, schedules, and budgets. They have a sense of commitment to the organization and conform to organizational norms and values.

transactional leader A leader who clarifies subordinates' role and task requirements, initiates structure, provides rewards, and displays consideration for subordinates.

INSPIRATIONAL LEADERS

Inspirational leadership goes beyond transactional leadership techniques. The **inspirational leader** has the capacity to motivate people to do more than normally expected. The impact of inspirational leaders is normally from (1) stating a lofty vision of an imagined future that employees identify with, (2) shaping a corporate value system for which everyone stands, and (3) trusting subordinates and earning their complete trust in return.[36] Inspirational leaders raise subordinates' consciousness about new outcomes and motivate them to transcend their own interests for the sake of the department or organization. Inspirational leaders tend to be less predictable than transactional leaders. They create an atmosphere of change, and they may be obsessed by visionary ideas that excite, stimulate, and drive other people to work hard. Inspirational leaders have an emotional impact on subordinates. They stand for

inspirational leader A leader who has the ability to motivate subordinates to transcend their expected performance.

Disney CEO Michael Eisner is considered an *inspirational leader*. Disney's uniqueness stems from having a creative executive in charge rather than a financier or lawyer. He shapes the corporate value system by inducing creativity in others and giving them free rein. Freewheeling and wildly creative brainstorming sessions are typical of what Eisner will do to get creative energy flowing. His vision of creativity extends the corporate culture founded by Walt Disney and fuels Disney's current growth and competitiveness.

something, have a vision of the future, are able to communicate that vision to subordinates, and motivate them to realize it.[37] The Manager's Shoptalk provides a short quiz to help you determine whether you have the potential to be an inspirational leader.

One example of an inspirational leader is Charles Bryan, who heads the International Association of Machinists at Eastern Airlines. His bulldog belief against settling with Eastern Airlines was based on a vision of high-paid union members and the belief that the union should not give back wages or benefits. His intensity worked for years, but ultimately caused difficulties when Eastern went bankrupt rather than cave in to the union.[38] At General Motors, the vision of Roger Smith is finally taking hold, but his vision did not have an immediate impact because communication failed. In Smith's own words:

> I sure wish I'd done a better job of communicating with GM people. I'd do that differently a second time around and make sure they understood and shared my vision for the company. Then they would have known why I was tearing the place up, taking out whole divisions, changing our whole production structure. If people understand the *why* they'll work at it. Like I say, I never got this across. There we were, charging up the hill right on schedule, and I looked behind me and saw that many people were still at the bottom, trying to decide whether to come along.
>
> I've had a vision for this company for a long time. It goes back to 1972. . . . But I've also known for a long time that if I was the only one who had that vision, it was no good.[39]

Inspirational leaders sometimes are called *charismatic leaders* because of their unique ability to influence others through speaking, writing, and personal actions.[40] Charismatic leaders include Mother Theresa, Martin Luther King, Adolf Hitler, and Jim Jones of Jonestown, Guyana. The true charismatic leader often does not fit within a traditional organization and may lead a social movement rather than a formal organization. The Winning Moves box on Anita Roddick shows how inspirational leadership can provide the foundation for a successful business.

MANAGER'S SHOPTALK

ARE YOU A LEADER?

If you were the head of a major department in a corporation, how important would each of the following activities be to you? Answer yes or no to indicate whether you would strive to perform each activity.

1. Help subordinates clarify goals and how to reach them.
2. Give people a sense of mission and overall purpose.
3. Help get jobs out on time.
4. Look for the new product or service opportunities.
5. Use policies and procedures as guides for problem solving.
6. Promote unconventional beliefs and values.
7. Give monetary rewards in exchange for high performance from subordinates.
8. Command respect from everyone in the department.
9. Work alone to accomplish important tasks.
10. Suggest new and unique ways of doing things.
11. Give credit to people who do their jobs well.
12. Inspire loyalty to yourself and to the organization.
13. Establish procedures to help the department operate smoothly.
14. Use ideas to motivate others.
15. Set reasonable limits on new approaches.
16. Demonstrate social nonconformity.

The even-numbered items represent behaviors and activities of inspirational leaders. Inspirational leaders are personally involved in shaping ideas, goals, and direction of change. They use an intuitive approach to develop fresh ideas for old problems and seek new directions for the department or organization. The odd-numbered items are considered more traditional management activities, or what would be called transactional leadership. Managers respond to organizational problems in an impersonal way, make rational decisions, and coordinate and facilitate the work of others. If you answered yes to more even-numbered than odd-numbered items, you may be a potential inspirational leader.

Source: Based on Bernard M. Bass, *Leadership and Performance Beyond Expectations* (New York: Free Press, 1985), and Lawton R. Burns and Selwyn W. Becker, "Leadership and Managership," in *Health Care Management*, ed. S. Shortell and A. Kaluzny (New York: Wiley, 1986).

When an organization goes through a major strategic change, it may need a different type of leader. A variation of the inspirational leader is called the *transformational leader.*[41] Transformational leaders emerge to take an organization through a major change, such as revitalization. They have the ability to make the necessary changes in the organization's mission, structure, and human resource management. Employees are persuaded to go along. In recent years a number of firms, such as General Electric, Campbell Soup, and Coca-Cola, have undergone transformation after appointing a new chief to act in the leadership role. John Welch of General Electric, Gordon McGovern of Campbell Soup, and Roberto Goizuta of Coca-Cola helped invigorate and revitalize their firms.

LEADERSHIP BY ORGANIZATIONAL LEVEL

Leadership is important throughout every organization. However, leader approaches depend on organizational level. A new college graduate in her first leadership position will use different approaches than a senior executive with 25 years of experience. The ideas described in this chapter often follow the pattern in Exhibit 13.11.

WINNING MOVES

INSPIRATIONAL LEADERSHIP DRIVES THE BODY SHOP

In the cosmetics industry, companies generally invest vast sums for slick advertising and promotional gimmicks. Employee training is geared toward making a sale and, like all big business, the bottom line counts. Anita Roddick has defied these standards by building a successful cosmetics company based on her personal vision of business making the world a better place. Founded 14 years ago in England with a $6,000 loan, this year The Body Shop will top sales of $141 million and continues to grow at a rate of 50 percent annually. Despite this phenomenal success, it is not profits that interest Roddick so much as people and the environment. "The idea of business, I'd agree, is not to lose money," she concedes, "but to focus all the time on profits, profits, profits — I have to say I think it's deeply boring."

So what does Roddick spend her time worrying about? The environment for one thing. From the beginning she has incorporated her passionate environmentalism into the business. The Body Shop's products are all biodegradable and in the United Kingdom shops offer to refill used containers. The company has an environmental projects department that monitors internal compliance with its own policies. It also helps organize campaigns for causes such as stopping the destruction of the Amazon rain forest. The Body Shop has contributed hundreds of thousands of dollars to this particular cause alone. Roddick regularly mobilizes employees for petition drives and fundraising carried out on company time.

Occasionally someone will berate Roddick for using her environmental activities as public relations merely to generate more profits. She bristles under such accusations saying that a poster to promote saving the rain forest "links us to the community but will not increase sales. What increases sales is an article saying Princess Diana uses Body Shop products. Then we get 7,000 phone calls asking for our catalog." Despite her clear sense that she is not using the campaigns to market her company, Roddick's causes do inspire customer loyalty.

In addition to the strong corporate focus on environmentalism, Roddick has built a corporate culture based on her passion for education. Customers benefit from brochures, videos, labels, and a well-trained shop staff for information about The Body Shop's products. Roddick's policy is to be sure that anyone can know where a product originally came from, how it is made, what it contains, how it has been tested, and what it is best used for. This atmosphere of consumer education establishes credibility for customers and helps employees feel that they are part of an enterprise that seeks to do something besides cater to fashion trends. In fact, The Body Shop's stated corporate mission is "to sell cosmetics with a minimum of hype and packaging . . . to promote health rather than glamor." Employees receive extensive training but it is all geared toward instruction on the nature and use of Body Shop products. Other companies "train for a sale," says Roddick, "we train for knowledge."

How does Roddick's leadership affect her employees? Like the best inspirational leaders, she has shaped a corporate value system that encourages excitement and commitment. "I want them to understand that this is no dress rehearsal. You've got one life, so just lead it. And try to be remarkable." Roddick's interest in her employees runs deep. She supervises the company newsletter which tends to focus on environmental issues such as the ozone problem rather than on company topics. She personally carries out company-wide educational programs. Her goal is to get employees to feel they are doing something important — not just selling shampoo or body lotion. "They're learning," she explains, "what it is to be a global citizen. And what it produces is a sense of passion you won't find in a Bloomingdale's department store." Roddick's style of leadership inspires employees with a dedication that is hard to find elsewhere.

Source: Based on Bo Burlingham, "This Woman Has Changed Business Forever," *INC.*, June, 1990, 34–46.

Lower-level leaders spend time training and coaching subordinates and seeing that they follow rules and procedures. Expert power is based on technical knowledge. Because the time horizon often is short, leaders must get quick results through the use of reward power and coercive power. The two-dimen-

EXHIBIT 13.11
Levels of Leadership in Organizations

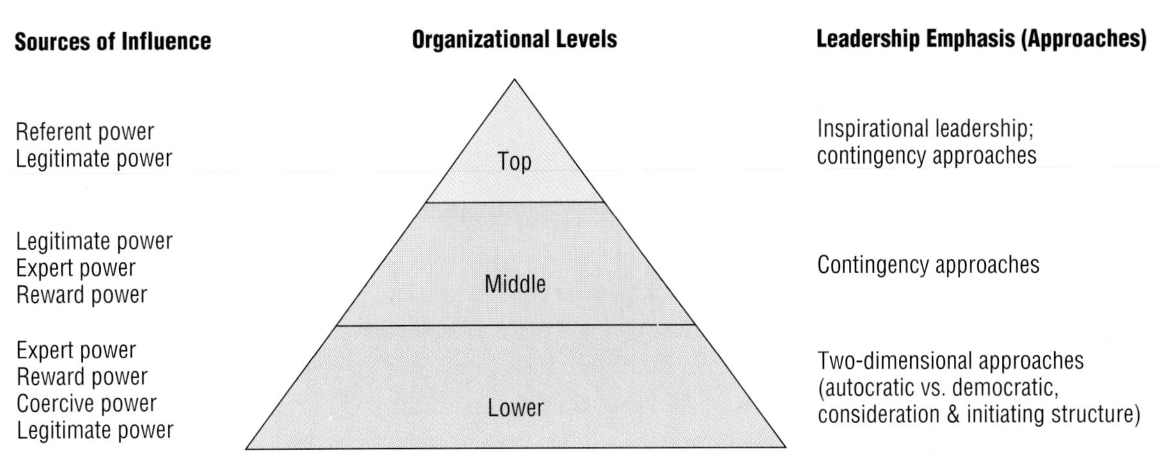

sional leadership approaches apply at this level. The supervisor can concentrate on being autocratic or democratic or on displaying task-oriented or people-oriented behaviors.

Middle-level leaders have a somewhat broader responsibility. They are responsible for larger groups and entire departments. Legitimate power is an important source of influence, as are expert power and reward power. Leadership tends to reflect the contingency approach, with the leader tailoring personal behavior and style to the needs of subordinates and the organizational situation. The key models at this level would be Hersey and Blanchard's situational theory, Fiedler's contingency theory, the path-goal model, and possible substitutes for leadership.

At the top level of the organization, the pattern changes once again. These leaders spend time on strategic activities. The important sources of influence are referent power and legitimate power. Top leaders develop a vision for their organizations. Leader approaches at this level incorporate inspirational leadership. Senior executives must articulate a vision, provide direction, and motivate the organization toward desired goals. Contingency approaches are also used at this level, depending on the leader's style and situation.

SUMMARY

This chapter covered several important ideas about leadership. The early research on leadership focused on personal traits such as intelligence, energy, and appearance. Since that time, research attention has shifted to leadership behaviors that are appropriate to the organizational situation. Two-dimensional approaches dominated the early work in this area; consideration and initiating structure were suggested as behaviors that lead work groups toward high performance. The Ohio State and Michigan approaches and the managerial grid are in this category. Contingency approaches include Fiedler's theory, Hersey and Blanchard's situational theory, the path-goal model, and the substitutes-for-leadership concept.

A recent concept is that of inspirational leadership, which is the ability to articulate a vision and motivate employees to make it a reality. Inspirational leadership is similar to charisma. Inspirational leaders are especially important during periods of organizational transformation.

MANAGEMENT SOLUTION

When Robert Daniell took over as CEO of United Technologies, the conglomerate had been used to a heavy-handed, autocratic leadership style. Daniell's approach was to promote teamwork and cooperation and to treat employees as family. His vision was to put the "United" back in United Technologies. He started Saturday morning meetings of managers from various divisions to share experiences. He confronted the operating managers with, "What are the bureaucratic issues that bother you . . . ?" "Let's cut the crap and get it right on the table." Things changed after that. At the Carrier division, for example, air-conditioning fans were too noisy. Five engineers from Hamilton's propeller operations were dispatched to the Carrier division, and a quieter fan was designed within a month. Scientists, engineers, and managers at all levels are cooperating across divisions and are becoming committed to the new United Technologies. Daniell's style reflects the inspirational leadership view and agrees with the Fiedler and Hersey and Blanchard theories. His vision inspires teamwork and commitment. A people-oriented leader works best in a moderately favorable situation, and a participating or delegating leadership style is best when subordinates are mature.[42]

DISCUSSION QUESTIONS

1. Rob Martin became manager of a forklift assembly plant and believed in participative management, even when one supervisor used Rob's delegation to replace two competent line managers with his own friends. What would you say to Rob about his leadership style in this situation?
2. Suggest some personal traits that you believe would be useful to a leader. Are these traits more valuable in some situations than in others?
3. What is the difference between trait theories and behavioral theories of leadership?
4. Suggest the sources of power that would be available to a leader of a student government organization. To be effective should student leaders keep power to themselves or delegate power to other students?
5. Would you prefer working for a leader who has a consideration or an initiating structure leadership style? Discuss the reasons for your answer.
6. What similarities do you see among the following contingency leadership theories: Hersey-Blanchard, Fiedler, and path-goal?
7. What is inspirational leadership? Differentiate between inspirational leadership and transactional leadership. Give an example of each.
8. One critic argued that the Jim Jones-Hitler syndrome can apply to inspirational leaders, meaning that they can run off the rails taking the organization with them. What is your evaluation of this criticism?

9. Do you think leadership style is fixed and unchangeable for a leader or flexible and adaptable? Discuss.
10. Consider the leadership position of a senior partner in a law firm. What task, subordinate, and organizational factors might serve as substitutes for leadership in this situation?

MANAGEMENT IN PRACTICE: EXPERIENTIAL EXERCISE

T–P Leadership Questionnaire: An Assessment of Style

Some leaders deal with general directions, leaving details to subordinates. Other leaders focus on specific details with the expectation that subordinates will carry out orders. Depending on the situation, both approaches may be effective. The important issue is the ability to identify relevant dimensions of the situation and behave accordingly. Through this questionnaire, you can identify your relative emphasis on two dimensions of leadership: task orientation and people orientation. These are not opposite approaches, and an individual can rate high or low on either or both.

Directions: The following items describe aspects of leadership behavior. Respond to each item according to the way you would most likely act if you were the leader of a work group. Circle whether you would most likely behave in the described way: always (A), frequently (F), occasionally (O), seldom (S), or never (N).

A F O S N 1. I would most likely act as the spokesperson of the group.
A F O S N 2. I would encourage overtime work.
A F O S N 3. I would allow members complete freedom in their work.
A F O S N 4. I would encourage the use of uniform procedures.
A F O S N 5. I would permit members to use their own judgment in solving problems.
A F O S N 6. I would stress being ahead of competing groups.
A F O S N 7. I would speak as a representative of the group.
A F O S N 8. I would needle members for greater effort.
A F O S N 9. I would try out my ideas in the group.
A F O S N 10. I would let members do their work the way they think best.
A F O S N 11. I would be working hard for a promotion.
A F O S N 12. I would tolerate postponement and uncertainty.
A F O S N 13. I would speak for the group if there were visitors present.
A F O S N 14. I would keep the work moving at a rapid pace.
A F O S N 15. I would turn the members loose on a job and let them go to it.
A F O S N 16. I would settle conflicts when they occur in the group.
A F O S N 17. I would get swamped by details.
A F O S N 18. I would represent the group at outside meetings.
A F O S N 19. I would be reluctant to allow the members any freedom of action.
A F O S N 20. I would decide what should be done and how it should be done.
A F O S N 21. I would push for increased production.
A F O S N 22. I would let some members have authority which I could keep.
A F O S N 23. Things would usually turn out as I had predicted.
A F O S N 24. I would allow the group a high degree of initiative.
A F O S N 25. I would assign group members to particular tasks.
A F O S N 26. I would be willing to make changes.
A F O S N 27. I would ask the members to work harder.
A F O S N 28. I would trust the group members to exercise good judgment.
A F O S N 29. I would schedule the work to be done.
A F O S N 30. I would refuse to explain my actions.
A F O S N 31. I would persuade others that my ideas are to their advantage.
A F O S N 32. I would permit the group to set its own pace.
A F O S N 33. I would urge the group to beat its previous record.
A F O S N 34. I would act without consulting the group.
A F O S N 35. I would ask that group members follow standard rules and regulations.

T_______ P _______

Source: The T–P Leadership Questionnaire was adapted by J. B. Ritchie and P. Thompson in *Organization and People* (New York: West, 1984). Copyright 1969 by the American Educational Research Association. Adapted by permission of the publisher.

The T–P Leadership Questionnaire is scored as follows:

a. Circle the item number for items 8, 12, 17, 18, 19, 30, 34, and 35.
b. Write the number 1 in front of a *circled item number* if you responded S (seldom) or N (never) to that item.
c. Also write a number 1 in front of *item numbers not circled* if you responded A (always) or F (frequently).
d. Circle the number 1s that you have written in front of the following items: 3, 5, 8, 10, 15, 18, 19, 22, 24, 26, 28, 30, 32, 34, and 35.
e. *Count the circled number 1s.* This is your score for concern for people. Record the score in the blank following the letter P at the end of the questionnaire.
f. *Count uncircled number 1s.* This is your score for concern for task. Record this number in the blank following the letter T.

CASES FOR ANALYSIS

SOUTHWEST AIRLINES

The zaniness of Herbert D. Kelleher, chairman and CEO of Southwest Airlines Company, permeates the airline. He loves people and wants employees' work to be fun filled. On a flight to Austin, Texas, last winter, flight attendants were dressed as reindeer and elves, and the pilot sang Christmas carols over the loudspeaker while gently rocking the plane. New employees watch a rap-music video that describes departmental functions. Kelleher has been described as "crazy," and "a real maniac." But these people underestimate his impact on Southwest. Kelleher's vision is to use fun to create the most efficient airline, and Southwest's operating costs per passenger-mile are the industry's lowest. His vision also includes aggressive expansion, opening new routes in California and the Midwest that will put him up against big carriers such as American Airlines and USAir. He plans to double the number of airplanes over the next ten years, expanding services while keeping costs low.

Kelleher's unique style did not emerge until he took over the CEO's job in 1981. He had set up a law firm in San Antonio and then founded Southwest with a group of investors, owning only a small stake himself. Now he is the airline's most visible property, and many of his 7,000 employees call him "Uncle Herb" or "Herbie." One former associate says that Kelleher holds power very tightly and makes all major decisions himself. But he has made few mistakes. His new route structures reflect controlled growth rather than reckless pursuit of a dream, which happened to Braniff several years ago. So far, Kelleher's style has been good medicine for Southwest.

Questions

1. How would you characterize Kelleher's leadership style using the models from this chapter? Include at least three models or concepts in your discussion.
2. What sources of power does Kelleher seem to rely on, and is the reaction of followers what you would predict? Explain.
3. If Kelleher were replaced tomorrow, what leadership style would you recommend for his successor?

Source: Based on Kevin Kelly, "Southwest Airlines: Flying High with 'Uncle Herb,'" *Business Week*, July 3, 1989, 53–55.

EDITORIAL DEPARTMENT

Toni Ramsey just learned that she was not getting a replacement for her editorial assistant, who had resigned. Her boss said, "With the salary and hiring freezes in effect, you'll have to give her work to others." Toni was disappointed, but was proud of her subordinates' commitment and knew they could do the extra work. She spent the afternoon deciding how to divide the work among her other subordinates in the editorial department.

The next morning, Toni announced to her seven staff members that Dianne had resigned and would not be replaced. Toni had divided Dianne's job into seven categories, with one person responsible for each. Toni informed each person of the additional work required from Dianne's resignation.

Toni noticed grumbling as she announced the assignments. The next day, she found Ed waiting in her office. "Why did you assign the press lunches to me?" he asked. "I hate listening to boring speeches. Can't you give this to someone else?"

The next person at her door was James. "Can't you reassign the traveling interviews to someone else? Just because my wife likes to travel on vacations doesn't mean I enjoy it."

Complaints came in all day. Toni attempted to juggle and switch assignments until it nearly drove her crazy. She called another staff meeting and said, "I've tried to accommodate you, but it can't be done. Take the assignments I've given you and do your best."

In the meantime, Ernest said to James, "I know you hate the traveling interviews, so I'll do them if you'll take the proofreading." Rose Marie told Ed, "I'll give you my research work if you'll do the copyediting." Other people started to trade jobs also, and the voices began to get loud. Toni came out of her office to see what the noise was about.

When Toni learned about the trading of assignments, she was upset. She went to her boss and said, "Several of the staff members seem happy with their trades, but the ones who didn't trade are unhappy. How should I have handled this?"

Questions

1. What leadership style did Toni Ramsey use? Was it appropriate for the situation?
2. Based on the Hersey-Blanchard theory, should Toni have been more participative? What style should she have adopted?
3. Because her approach did not work, what should Toni do now?

Source: Based on "The Case of the Missing Staffer," *Supervisory Management* (December 1985), 36–37.

CHAPTER 14

MOTIVATION IN ORGANIZATIONS

CHAPTER OUTLINE

The Concept of Motivation

Foundations of Motivation

Traditional Approach
Human Relations Approach
Human Resource Approach
Contemporary Approaches

Content Perspectives on Motivation

Hierarchy of Needs Theory
Two-Factor Theory
Acquired Needs Theory

Process Perspectives on Motivation

Equity Theory
Expectancy Theory

Reinforcement Perspective on Motivation

Reinforcement Tools
Schedules of Reinforcement

Job Design for Motivation

Job Simplification
Job Rotation
Job Enlargement
Job Enrichment
Job Characteristics Model

New Motivational Programs

Pay for Performance
Gain Sharing
ESOPs
Lump-Sum Bonuses
Pay for Knowledge
Flexible Work Schedules

LEARNING OBJECTIVES

After studying this chapter, you should be able to:

- Define motivation and explain the difference between current approaches and traditional approaches to motivation.
- Identify and describe content theories of motivation based on employee needs.
- Identify and explain process theories of motivation.
- Describe reinforcement theory and how it can be used to motivate employees.
- Discuss major approaches to job design and how job design influences motivation.
- Discuss new management applications of motivation theories.

Management Problem

At 30, Gary Aronson was frustrated, bored, and wondering why he was in the gourmet fast-food business. As manager of an Au Bon Pain store, he made a meager $26,000 a year and was known as a whiner and complainer. His heart was not in what he considered a dead-end job, and many of his employees seemed to feel the same. The best he could hope for after five more years was another $3,000 in annual income, so he put in his time trying to figure out what he was going to do next. Unfortunately, Gary Aronson was typical of managers in all 40 Au Bon Pain stores.[1]

If you were the president of Au Bon Pain, how would you motivate managers like Gary Aronson to give their all to the company? Is high motivation even possible in this kind of service business?

The problem for Au Bon Pain is that unmotivated managers mean unmotivated employees, all doing minimum work and causing the chain to lose its competitive edge. For example, one secret of success for small- and medium-size businesses is motivated and enthusiastic employees. The challenge facing Au Bon Pain and other companies is to keep employee motivation consistent with organizational objectives. Motivation is a challenge for managers because motivation arises from within employees and typically differs for each employee. For example, Janice Rennie makes a staggering $350,000 a year selling residential real estate in Toronto because she likes to listen carefully to clients and then find a house to meet their needs. Greg Storey is a skilled machinist who is challenged by writing programs for numerically controlled machines. After dropping out of college, he swept floors in a machine shop and was motivated to learn to run the machines. Frances Blais sells *World Book Encyclopedia.* She is a top salesperson, but she does not care about the $50,000-plus commissions: "I'm not even thinking money when I'm selling. I'm really on a crusade to help children read well." In stark contrast, Rob Michaels gets sick to his stomach before he goes to work. Rob is a telephone salesperson who spends all day trying to get people to buy products they do not need, and the rejections are

EXHIBIT 14.1
A Simple Model of Motivation

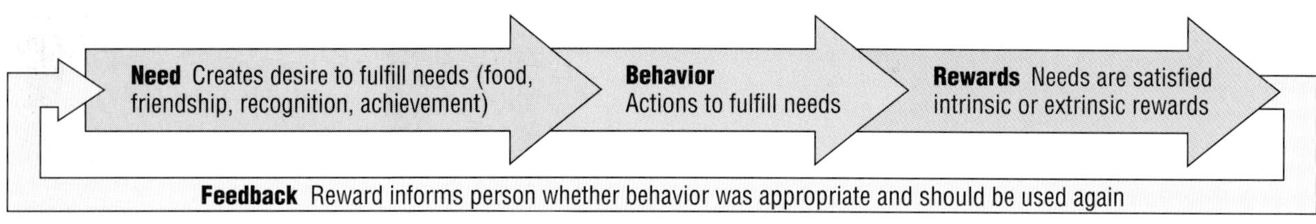

painful. His motivation is money, because he earned $120,000 in the past year and cannot make nearly that much doing anything else.[2]

Rob is motivated by money, Janice by her love of listening and problem solving, Frances by the desire to help children read, and Greg by the challenge of mastering numerically controlled machinery. Each person is motivated to perform, yet each has different reasons for performing. With such diverse motivations, it is a challenge for managers to motivate employees toward common organizational goals.

This chapter reviews theories and models of employee motivation. First we will review traditional approaches to motivation. Then we will cover models that describe the employee needs and processes associated with motivation. Finally, we will discuss the designing of jobs to increase employee motivation.

THE CONCEPT OF MOTIVATION

Most of us get up in the morning, go to school or work, and behave in ways that are predictably our own. We respond to our environment and the people in it with little thought as to why we work hard, enjoy certain classes, or find some recreational activities so much fun. Yet all of these behaviors are motivated by something. **Motivation** generally is defined as the arousal, direction, and persistence of behavior.[3] The study of motivation concerns what prompts people to initiate action, what influences their choice of action, and why they persist in doing it over time.

motivation The arousal, direction, and persistence of behavior.

A simple model of human motivation is illustrated in Exhibit 14.1. People have basic *needs*, such as for food, achievement, or monetary gain, that translate into an internal tension that motivates specific behaviors with which to fulfill the need. To the extent that the behavior is successful, the person is rewarded in the sense that the need is satisfied. The reward also informs the person that the behavior was appropriate and can be used again in the future.

Rewards are of two types: intrinsic and extrinsic. **Intrinsic rewards** are received as a direct consequence of a person's actions. The completion of a complex task may bestow a pleasant feeling of accomplishment. **Extrinsic rewards** are given by another person, typically a manager, and include promotions and pay increases. For example, Frances Blais sells encyclopedias for the

intrinsic reward A reward received as a direct consequence of a person's actions.

extrinsic reward A reward given by another person.

intrinsic reward of helping children read well. Rob Michaels, who hates his sales job, nevertheless is motivated by the extrinsic reward of high pay.

The importance of motivation as illustrated in Exhibit 14.1 is that it can lead to behaviors that reflect high performance within organizations.[4] Managers can use motivation theory to help satisfy employees' needs and simultaneously encourage high work performance.

Union Camp Corporation's motivational goal is to create a company environment within which employees can realize their potential as complete human beings. Reflecting the *human resource approach,* Union Camp's state-of-the-art mill in Eastover, South Carolina, is operated by a series of teams, with individuals interchanging responsibilities as the need arises. Union Camp believes that self-reliance, training, and enthusiastic involvement are vital to company performance. Team members are provided the opportunity to learn new skills, and all employees are believed capable of contributing solutions that improve company efficiency and competitiveness.

Foundations of Motivation

A manager's assumptions about employee motivation and use of rewards depend on his or her perspective on motivation. Three distinct perspectives on employee motivation that have evolved are the traditional approach, the human relations approach, and the human resources approach.[5] The most recent theories about motivation represent a fourth perspective called contemporary approaches.

Traditional Approach

The study of employee motivation really began with the work of Frederick W. Taylor on scientific management. Recall from Chapter 2 that scientific management pertains to the systematic analysis of an employee's job for the purpose of increasing efficiency. Economic rewards are provided to employees for high performance. The emphasis on pay evolved into the perception of workers as *economic men* — people who would work harder for higher pay. This approach led to the development of incentive pay systems, in which people were paid strictly on the quantity and quality of their work outputs.

Human Relations Approach

The economic man was gradually replaced by a more sociable employee in managers' minds. Beginning with the landmark Hawthorne studies at a Western Electric plant, noneconomic rewards, such as congenial work groups who met social needs, seemed more important than money as a motivator of work behavior.[6] For the first time workers were studied as people, and the concept of *social man* was born. Further study led researchers to conclude that simply paying attention to workers could change their behavior for the better; this was called the *Hawthorne effect.*

Human Resource Approach

The human resource approach carries the concepts of economic man and social man further to introduce the concept of the *whole person.* Human resource theory suggests that employees are complex and motivated by many factors. For example, the work by McGregor on Theory X and Theory Y described in Chapter 2 argued that people want to do a good job and that work is as natural and healthy as play. Proponents of the human resource approach felt that earlier approaches had tried to manipulate employees through economic or social rewards. By assuming that employees are competent and able to make major contributions, managers can enhance organizational performance. The human resource approach laid the groundwork for contemporary perspectives on employee motivation.

Contemporary Approaches

Contemporary approaches to employee motivation are dominated by three types of theories, each of which will be discussed in the remaining sections of this chapter. The first are *content theories*, which stress the analysis of underlying human needs. Content theories provide insight into the needs of people in organizations and help managers understand how needs can be satisfied in the workplace. *Process theories* concern the thought processes that influence behavior. They focus on how employees seek rewards in work circumstances. *Reinforcement theories* focus on employee learning of desired work behaviors. In Exhibit 14.1, content theories focus on the concepts in the first box, process theories on those in the second, and reinforcement theories on those in the third.

Content Perspectives on Motivation

content theories A group of theories that emphasize the needs that motivate people.

Content theories emphasize the needs that motivate people. At any point in time, people have basic needs such as those for food, achievement, or monetary reward. These needs translate into an internal drive that motivates specific behaviors in an attempt to fulfill the needs. An individual's needs are like a hidden catalog of the things he or she wants and will work to get. To the extent that managers understand worker needs, the organization's reward systems can be designed to meet them and reinforce employees for directing energies and priorities toward attainment of organizational goals.

Hierarchy of Needs Theory

hierarchy of needs theory A content theory that proposes that people are motivated by five categories of needs — physiological, safety, belongingness, esteem, and self-actualization — that exist in a hierarchical order.

Probably the most famous content theory was developed by Abraham Maslow.[7] Maslow's **hierarchy of needs theory** proposes that humans are motivated by multiple needs and that these needs exist in a hierarchical order as illustrated in Exhibit 14.2. Maslow identified five general types of motivating needs in order of ascendance:

1. *Physiological needs.* These are the most basic human physical needs, including food, water, and sex. In the organizational setting, these are reflected in the needs for adequate heat, air, and base salary to insure survival.
2. *Safety needs.* These are the needs for a safe and secure physical and emotional environment and freedom from threats, that is, for freedom from violence and for an orderly society. In an organizational workplace, safety needs reflect the needs for safe jobs, fringe benefits, and job security.
3. *Belongingness needs.* These needs reflect the desire to be accepted by one's peers, have friendships, be part of a group, and be loved. In the

EXHIBIT 14.2
Maslow's Hierarchy of Needs

Fulfillment Off the Job	Need Heirarchy	Fulfillment On the Job
Education, religion, hobbies, personal growth	Self-Actualization Needs	Opportunities for training, advancement, growth, and creativity
Approval of family, friends, community	Esteem Needs	Recognition, high status, increased responsibilities
Family, friends, community groups	Belongingness Needs	Work groups, clients, coworkers, supervisors
Freedom from war, pollution, violence	Safety Needs	Safe work, fringe benefits, job security
Food, water, sex	Physiological Needs	Heat, air, base salary

organization, these needs influence the desire for good relationships with coworkers, participation in a work group, and a positive relationship with supervisors.

4. *Esteem needs.* These needs relate to the desire for a positive self-image and to receive attention, recognition, and appreciation from others. Within organizations, esteem needs reflect a motivation for recognition, increases in responsibility, high status, and credit for contributions to the organization.
5. *Self-actualization needs.* These represent the need for self-fulfillment, which is the highest need category. They concern developing one's full potential, increasing one's competence, and becoming a better person. Self-actualization needs can be met in the organization by providing people with opportunities to grow, be creative, and acquire training for challenging assignments and advancement.

According to Maslow's theory, lower-order needs take priority — they must be satisfied before higher-order needs are activated. The needs are satisfied in sequence: Physiological needs come before safety needs, safety needs before social needs, and so on. A person desiring physical safety will devote his or her efforts to securing a safer environment and will not be concerned with esteem needs or self-actualization needs. Once a need is satisfied, it declines in importance and the next higher need is activated. When a union wins good pay and working conditions for its members, basic needs are met; union members may then desire to get belongingness and esteem needs met in the workplace.

ERG THEORY. Clayton Alderfer proposed a modification of Maslow's theory in an effort to simplify it and respond to criticisms of its lack of empirical verification.[8] His **ERG theory** identified three categories of needs:

ERG theory A modification of the needs hierarchy theory that proposes three categories of needs: existence, relatedness, and growth.

EXHIBIT 14.3
Herzberg's Two-Factor Theory

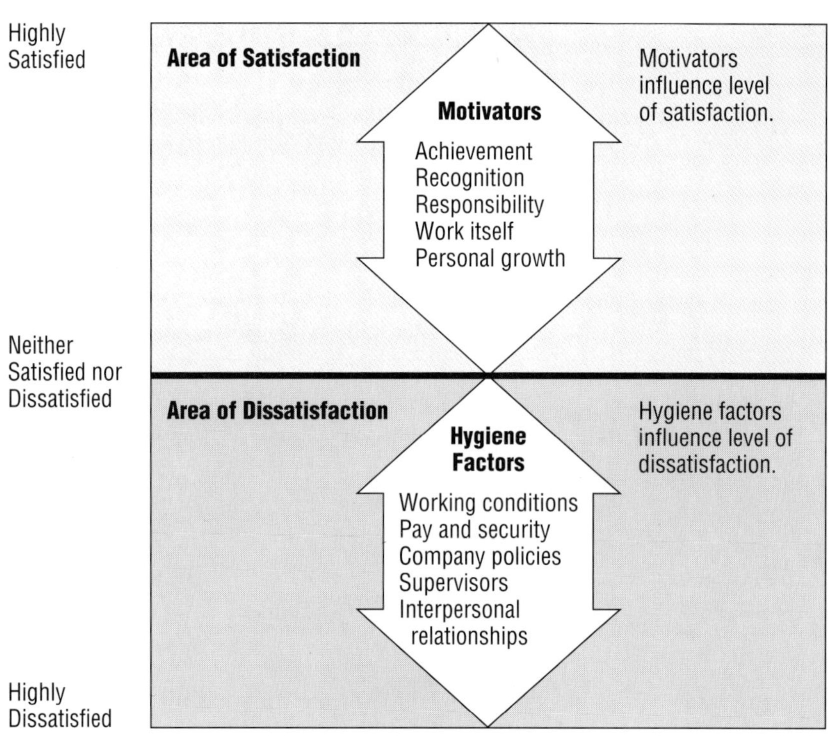

1. *Existence needs.* These are the needs for physical well-being.
2. *Relatedness needs.* These pertain to the need for satisfactory relationships with others.
3. *Growth needs.* These focus on the development of human potential and the desire for personal growth and increased competence.

frustration-regression principle
The idea that failure to meet a higher-order need may cause a regression to an already satisfied lower-order need.

The ERG model and Maslow's need hierarchy are similar because both are in hierarchical form and presume that individuals move up the hierarchy one step at a time. However, Alderfer reduced the number of need categories to three and proposed that movement up the hierarchy is more complex, reflecting a **frustration-regression principle,** namely, that failure to meet a higher-order need may trigger a regression to an already fulfilled lower-order need. Thus, a worker who cannot fulfill a need for personal growth may revert to a lower-order social need and redirect his or her efforts toward making a lot of money. The ERG model therefore is less rigid than Maslow's need hierarchy, suggesting that individuals may move down as well as up the hierarchy depending on their ability to satisfy needs.

For example, need hierarchy theory helps explain why organizations find ways to recognize employees and encourage their participation in decision making. Employees at Federal Express receive "Bravo Zulu" awards for outstanding performance, and the recognition letter is more important to recipients than the money. The importance of filling higher-level belongingness and esteem needs on the job was illustrated by a young manager who said, "If I had

Longs Drug Stores meets the higher-level needs of employees with opportunities for employee recognition and personal growth. This photo appeared in an ad entitled "Our Priceless Ingredient" that was mailed to thousands of customers. It recognizes employees and indicates how the company truly feels about its people. Purchasing, pricing, promotions, and training are decentralized to the store or district level, providing opportunities for employee responsibility, achievement, personal growth, and recognition. This policy reflects motivation principles inherent in *Maslow's hierarchy of needs theory* and *Herzberg's two-factor theory*.

to tell you in one sentence why I am motivated by my job, it is because when I know what is going on and how I fit into the overall picture it makes me feel important."[9]

Two-Factor Theory

Frederick Herzberg developed another popular theory of motivation called the *two-factor theory*.[10] Herzberg interviewed hundreds of workers about times when they were highly motivated to work and other times when they were dissatisfied and unmotivated at work. His findings suggested that the work characteristics associated with dissatisfaction were quite different from those pertaining to satisfaction, which prompted the notion that two factors influence work motivation.

The two-factor theory is illustrated in Exhibit 14.3. The center of the scale is neutral, meaning that workers are neither satisfied nor dissatisfied. Herzberg believed that two entirely separate dimensions contribute to an employee's behavior at work. The first, called **hygiene factors,** involves the presence or absence of job dissatisfiers, such as working conditions, pay, company policies, and interpersonal relationships. When hygiene factors are poor, work is dissatisfying. However, good hygiene factors simply remove the dissatisfaction; they do not in themselves cause people to become highly satisfied and motivated in their work.

hygiene factors Factors that involve the presence or absence of job dissatisfiers, including working conditions, pay, company policies, and interpersonal relationships.

The second set of factors does influence job satisfaction. **Motivators** are higher-level needs and include achievement, recognition, responsibility, and opportunity for growth. Herzberg believed that when motivators are absent workers are neutral toward work, but when motivators are present, workers are highly motivated and satisfied. Thus, hygiene factors and motivators represent two distinct factors that influence motivation. Hygiene factors work only in the

motivators Factors that influence job satisfaction based on fulfillment of higher-level needs such as achievement, recognition, responsibility, and opportunity for growth.

area of dissatisfaction. Unsafe working conditions or a noisy work environment will cause people to be dissatisfied; their correction will not lead to a high level of motivation and satisfaction. Motivators such as challenge, responsibility, and recognition must be in place before employees will be highly motivated to excel at their work.

The implication of the two-factor theory for managers is clear. Providing hygiene factors will eliminate employee dissatisfaction but will not motivate workers to high achievement levels. On the other hand, recognition, challenge, and opportunities for personal growth are powerful motivators and will promote high satisfaction and performance. The manager's role is to remove dissatisfiers — that is, provide hygiene factors sufficient to meet basic needs — and then use motivators to meet higher-level needs and propel employees toward greater achievement and satisfaction. Consider the manager's role at Marquette Electronics.

MARQUETTE ELECTRONICS • Michael Cudahy, president of Marquette Electronics, knows about motivation. Cudahy does not skimp on hygiene factors — 50 cents on top of every dollar in salary goes to benefits such as savings, insurance, and day care.

Higher-level needs also are given priority: "You can't put people in boxes, telling them what they can do, when they can do it and who's going to get rid of them if they don't do it. You've got to give people a voice in their jobs. You've got to give them a piece of the action, and a chance to excel." Cudahy works hard to ensure that employees have a chance for recognition, to belong to a group, and for personal growth, all of which meet the higher-level needs of Marquette employees.

Does it work? Marquette holds 80 percent of the market for centralized electrocardiograph management systems, 26 percent of the stress-testing market, and 20 percent of the market for patient monitoring devices. Marquette has been profitable since its third year of operations, and recent earnings were nearly $7 million.[11]

ACQUIRED NEEDS THEORY

The final content theory was developed by David McClelland. The *acquired needs theory* proposes that certain types of needs are acquired during the individual's lifetime. In other words, people are not born with these needs but may learn them through their life experiences.[12] The three needs most frequently studied are:

1. *Need for achievement:* the desire to accomplish something difficult, attain a high standard of success, master complex tasks, and surpass others.
2. *Need for affiliation:* the desire to form close personal relationships, avoid conflict, and establish warm friendships.
3. *Need for power:* the desire to influence or control others, be responsible for others, and have authority over others.

Early life experiences determine whether people acquire these needs. If children are encouraged to do things for themselves and receive reinforce-

Tammy Ackers, Taco Bell store manager in Ashland, Kentucky, enjoys her new Trans Am, first prize in Taco Bell's World Series of Speed, a contest among store teams. Tammy possesses both *need for achievement* and *affiliation,* which account for her store's astonishing success, with 45 percent real growth in an area with 30 percent unemployment, an outstanding store quality rating, and increases of over 30 percent in profitability. Her star quality comes partly from her desire to be recognized as the best. Ackers loves high achievement and is uncompromising about store standards, but at the same time loves to develop people and interact with them. She achieves because of her people — not in spite of them.

ment, they will acquire a need to achieve. If they are reinforced for forming warm human relationships, they will develop a need for affiliation. If they get satisfaction from controlling others, they will acquire a need for power.

For over 20 years, McClelland studied human needs and their implication for management. People with a high need for achievement tend to be entrepreneurs. They like to do something better than competitors and take sensible business risks. On the other hand, people who have a high need for affiliation are successful "integrators," whose job is to coordinate the work of several departments in an organization.[13] Integrators include brand managers and project managers who must have excellent people skills. People high in need for affiliation are able to establish positive working relationships with others.

A high need for power often is associated with successful attainment of top levels in the organizational hierarchy. For example, McClelland studied managers at AT&T for 16 years and found that those with a high need for power were more likely to follow a path of continued promotion over time. Over half of the employees at the top levels had a high need for power. In contrast, managers with a high need for achievement but a low need for power tended to peak earlier in their careers and at a lower level. The reason is that achievement needs can be met through the task itself, but power needs can be met only by ascending to a level at which a person has power over others.

In summary, content theories focus on people's underlying needs and label those that motivate people to behave. The hierarchy of needs theory, the ERG theory, the two-factor theory, and the acquired needs theory all help managers understand what motivates people. In this way, managers can design work to meet needs and hence elicit appropriate and successful work behaviors.

PROCESS PERSPECTIVES ON MOTIVATION

Process theories explain how workers select behavioral actions to meet their needs and determine whether their choices were successful. There are two basic process theories: equity theory and expectancy theory.

process theories A group of theories that explain how employees select behaviors with which to meet their needs and determine whether their choices were successful.

EQUITY THEORY

equity theory A process theory that focuses on individuals' perceptions of how fairly they are treated relative to others.

Equity theory focuses on individuals' perceptions of how fairly they are treated compared with others. Developed by J. Stacy Adams, equity theory proposes that people are motivated to seek social equity in the rewards they expect for performance.[14]

According to equity theory, if people perceive their compensation as equal to what others receive for similar contributions, they will believe that their treatment is fair and equitable. People evaluate equity by a ratio of inputs to outcomes. Inputs to a job include education, experience, effort, and ability. Outcomes from a job include pay, recognition, benefits, and promotions. The input to outcome ratio may be compared to another person in the work group or to a perceived group average. A state of **equity** exists whenever the ratio of one person's outcomes to inputs equals the ratio of another's outcomes to inputs.

equity A situation that exists when the ratio of one person's outcomes to inputs equals that of another's.

Inequity occurs when the input-outcome ratios are out of balance, such as when a person with a high level of education or experience receives the same salary as a new, lesser educated employee. Perceived inequity also occurs in the other direction. Thus, if an employee discovers she is making more money than other people who contribute the same inputs to the company, she may feel the need to correct the inequity by working harder, getting more education, or accepting lower pay. Perceived inequity creates tensions within individuals that motivate them to bring equity into balance.[15]

The most common methods for reducing a perceived inequity are:

- *Change inputs.* A person may choose to increase or decrease his or her inputs to the organization. For example, underpaid individuals may reduce their level of effort or increase their absenteeism. Overpaid people may increase effort on the job.
- *Change outcomes.* A person may change his or her outcomes. An underpaid person may request a salary increase or a bigger office. A union may try to improve wages and working conditions in order to be consistent with a comparable union whose members make more money.
- *Distort perceptions.* Research suggests that people may distort perceptions of equity if they are unable to change inputs or outcomes. They may artificially increase the status attached to their jobs or distort others' perceived rewards to bring equity into balance.
- *Leave the job.* People who feel inequitably treated may decide to leave their jobs rather than suffer the inequity of being under- or overpaid. In their new jobs, they expect to find a more favorable balance of rewards.

The implication of equity theory for managers is that employees indeed evaluate the perceived equity of their rewards compared to others'. An increase in salary or a promotion will have no motivational effect if it is perceived as inequitable relative to other employees. Some organizations, for example, have created a two-tier wage system to reduce wage rates. New employees make far less than experienced ones, which creates a basis for inequity. Flight attendants at American Airlines are determined to topple the two-tier structure under which they are paid. Chris Boschert, who sorts packages for United Parcel Service, was hired after the two-tier wage system took effect. "It makes me mad," Boschert said. "I get $9.68 an hour, and the guy working next to me

Nucor Corporation has a policy that employees must be treated fairly. This application of *equity theory* means that senior executives do not enjoy perquisites such as company cars and country club memberships that are denied to production workers. Moreover, production workers receive bonuses based directly on their productivity. Workers who are late and hence do not make a full contribution lose their bonus for the day. This approach to equity works. The average employee earns over $32,000 per year, and 1,300 applicants showed up to fill eight openings.

makes $13.99 doing exactly the same job."[16] Inequitable pay puts pressure on employees that is sometimes almost too great to bear. They attempt to change their work habits, try to change the system, or leave the job.[17]

Smart managers try to keep feelings of equity in balance in order to keep their work forces motivated. Consider Nucor Corporation.

NUCOR CORPORATION

• Ken Iverson, CEO at Nucor Corporation, goes one step beyond apparent equity to get the results he wants. Because of his commitment not to lay people off during hard times, everyone at Nucor Minimills feels the pain during bad times so that everyone can stay employed. In Iverson's "share-the-pain" program, the cuts get stiffer as they go *up* the corporate ladder. In order for everyone to remain employed, a worker might lose 25 percent of his or her salary; however, the worker's department head could lose 35 to 40 percent. The officers, whose compensation is tied to return on stockholders' equity, might lose 60 or 70 percent. These cuts are severe, but they are perceived as more than equitable by the work force. Iverson claims he heard no complaints from the production floor when workers were forced to go to a three-and-a-half-day week in order to avoid layoffs. Iverson correctly anticipated the workers' perception of relative inputs and outputs. As he put it, "Management should take the biggest drop in pay because they have the most responsibility."[18]

EXHIBIT 14.4
Major Elements of Expectancy Theory

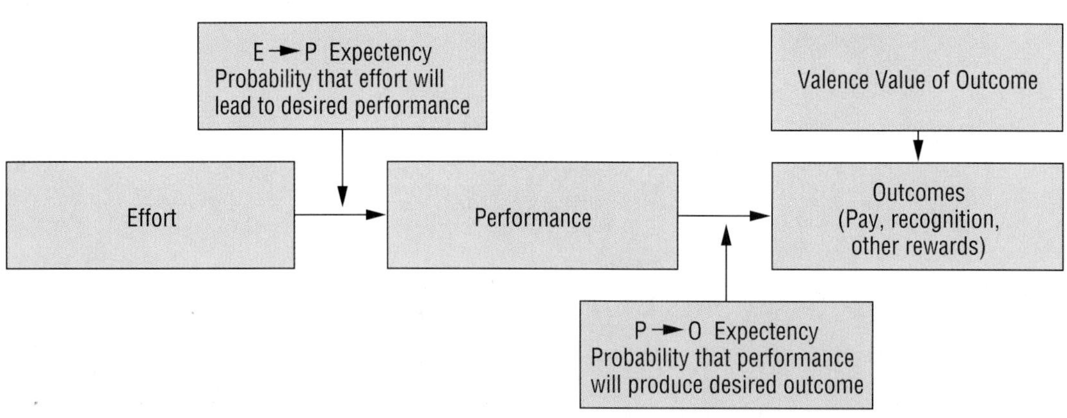

EXPECTANCY THEORY

expectancy theory A process theory that proposes that motivation depends on individuals' expectations about their ability to perform tasks and receive desired rewards.

Expectancy theory suggests that motivation depends on individuals' expectations about their ability to perform tasks and receive desired rewards. Expectancy theory is associated with the work of Victor Vroom, although a number of scholars have made contributions in this area.[19] Expectancy theory is concerned not with identifying types of needs but with the thinking process that individuals use to achieve rewards. Consider Bill Bradley, a university student with a strong desire for a B in his accounting course. Bill has a C+ average and one more exam to take. Bill's motivation to study for that last exam will be influenced by (1) the expectation that hard study will lead to an A on the exam and (2) the expectation that an A on the exam will result in a B for the course. If Bill believes he cannot get an A on the exam or that receiving an A will not lead to a B for the course, he will not be motivated to study extra hard.

Expectancy theory is based on the relationship among the individual's *effort*, the individual's *performance*, and the desirability of *outcomes* associated with high performance. These elements and the relationships among them are illustrated in Exhibit 14.4. The keys to expectancy theory are the expectancies for the relationships among effort, performance, and outcomes and the value of the outcomes to the individual.

E → P expectancy Expectancy that putting effort into a given task will lead to high performance.

E → P expectancy involves whether putting effort into a task will lead to high performance. For this expectancy to be high, the individual must have the ability, previous experience, and necessary machinery, tools, and opportunity to perform. For Bill Bradley's getting a B in the accounting course, the E → P expectancy is high if Bill truly believes that with hard work he can get an A on the final exam. If Bill believes he has neither the ability nor the opportunity to achieve high performance, the expectancy will be low, and so will his motivation.

P → O expectancy Expectancy that successful performance of a task will lead to the desired outcome.

P → O expectancy involves whether successful performance will lead to the desired outcome. In the case of a person who is motivated to win a job-related award, this expectancy concerns the belief that high performance will

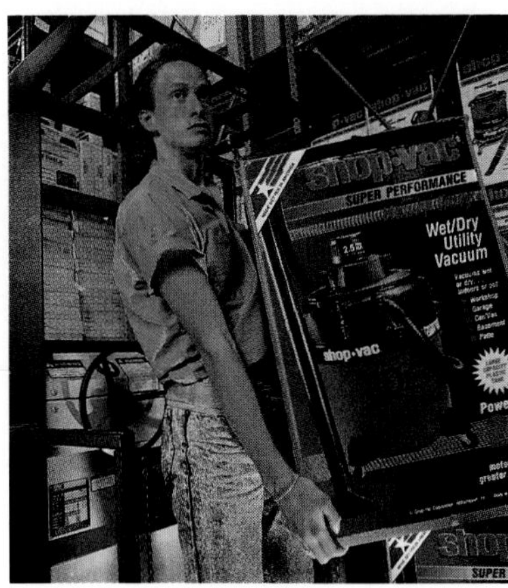

Lechmere Inc., a retail store chain, uses *expectancy theory* to motivate employees to learn multiple jobs. Employees like Brad Davis are given pay incentives to learn an increasing number of jobs. Davis and other employees know that expending additional effort will result in increased pay. Brad Davis can serve as stockperson, cashier, and salesperson, providing flexibility for Lechmere. With this incentive, employees learn more and the store is more productive than stores without pay incentives for job knowledge.

truly lead to the award. If the P → O expectancy is high, the individual will be more highly motivated. If the expectancy is that high performance will not produce the desired outcome, motivation will be lower. If an A on the final exam is likely to produce a B in the accounting course, Bill Bradley's P → O expectancy will be high. Bill may talk to the professor to see whether an A will be sufficient to earn him the B in the course. If not, he will be less motivated to study hard for the final exam.

Valence is the value of outcomes for the individual. If the outcomes that are available from high effort and good performance are not valued by employees, motivation will be low. Likewise, if outcomes have a high value, motivation will be higher.

valence The value of outcomes for the individual.

Expectancy theory attempts not to define specific types of needs or rewards but only to establish that they exist and may be different for every individual. One employee may want to be promoted to a position of increased responsibility, and another may have high valence for good relationships with peers. Consequently, the first person will be motivated to work hard for a promotion and the second for the opportunity for a team position that will keep him or her associated with a group.

A simple sales department example will explain how the expectancy model in Exhibit 14.5 works. If Jane Anderson, a salesperson at the Diamond Gift Shop, believes that increased selling effort will lead to higher personal sales, we can say that she has a high E → P expectancy. Moreover, if Jane also believes that higher personal sales will lead to a bonus or pay raise, we can say that she has a high P → O expectancy. Finally, if Jane places a high value on the bonus or pay raise, valence is high and Jane will have a high motivational force. On the other hand, if either the E → P or P → O expectancy is low, or if the money or promotion has low valence for Jane, the overall motivational force will be low. For an employee to be highly motivated, all three factors in the expectancy model must be high.[20]

Implications for Managers. The expectancy theory of motivation is similar to the path-goal theory of leadership described in Chapter 13. Both theories are personalized to subordinates' needs and goals. Managers' responsibility is to help subordinates meet their needs and at the same time attain

EXHIBIT 14.5
Changing Behavior with Reinforcement

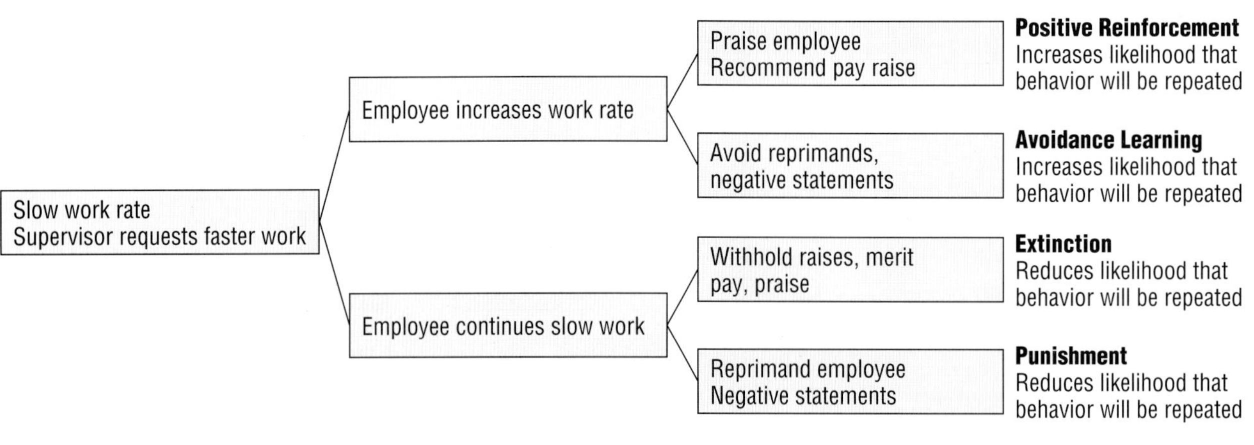

Source: Based on Richard L. Daft and Richard M. Steers, *Organizations: A Micro/Macro Approach* (Glenview, Ill.: Scott, Foresman, 1986), 109.

organizational goals. Managers must try to find a match between a subordinate's skills and abilities and the job demands. To increase motivation, managers can clarify individuals' needs, define the outcomes available from the organization, and ensure that each individual has the ability and support (namely, time and equipment) needed to attain outcomes.

Some companies use expectancy theory principles by designing incentive systems that identify desired organizational outcomes and give everyone the same shot at getting the rewards. The trick is to design a system that fits with employees' abilities and needs. Consider the changes made by Solar Press Inc.

SOLAR PRESS INC. • Back in the 1970s, when Solar Press was a small family-owned business, owner John Hudetz passed out checks most months for $20 to $60. Everybody got the same amount, but no one knew why they received it.

To tie bonuses more clearly to productivity, this direct-mail company divided employees into teams, giving each team a bonus based on whether it produced more than other teams. Production immediately jumped, but teams started competing with one another in an unhealthy way. Teams would not perform regular maintenance on equipment, for example, and hoarded ideas from fellow employees for fear of not winning their bonus. This competitiveness within Solar Press caused more problems than it solved.

In 1987 Solar Press adopted a new system. When individual employees did a good job, they were given a pay increase. Moreover, all employees were given bonuses from a pool based on company profits. Thus employees cooperated to help the company make more money. The system now in place works well, because people get a share when the company does well.[21]

In the initial system at Solar Press, the connections among effort, performance, and outcomes were unclear. In the group system, employees had the ability to keep the E → P expectancy high, and the P → O expectancy was also high, although it threw groups into competition. Expectancies under the most recent system are also high, and to achieve desired outcomes employees are motivated to cooperate for the benefit of the company.

Tyson has grown to be the world's largest poultry grower and marketer by rewarding employee contributions. It provides *positive reinforcement* in the form of cash for ideas that provide savings to the company. The top reward is $6,000, and any idea that provides a minimum savings of $1,000 can win up to $1,000. Reinforcement theory also is reflected in the policy of employee stock ownership, because employees share increased dividends based on their efforts to reduce costs and improve profits.

REINFORCEMENT PERSPECTIVE ON MOTIVATION

The reinforcement approach to employee motivation sidesteps the issues of employee needs and thinking processes described in the content and process theories. **Reinforcement theory** simply looks at the relationship between behavior and its consequences. It focuses on changing or modifying the employees' on-the-job behavior through the appropriate use of immediate rewards and punishments.

REINFORCEMENT TOOLS

Behavior modification is the name given to the set of techniques by which reinforcement theory is used to modify human behavior. The basic assumption underlying behavior modification is the **law of effect,** which states that behavior that is positively reinforced tends to be repeated, and behavior that is not reinforced tends not to be repeated. **Reinforcement** is defined as anything that causes a certain behavior to be repeated or inhibited. The four reinforcement tools are positive reinforcement, avoidance learning, punishment, and extinction.[22] Each type of reinforcement is a consequence of either a pleasant or unpleasant event being applied or withdrawn following a person's behavior. The four types of reinforcement are summarized in Exhibit 14.5.

POSITIVE REINFORCEMENT. *Positive reinforcement* is the administration of a pleasant and rewarding consequence following a desired behavior. A good example of positive reinforcement is immediate praise for an employee who arrives on time or does a little extra in his or her work. The pleasant consequence will increase the likelihood of the excellent work behavior occurring again.

AVOIDANCE LEARNING. *Avoidance learning* is the removal of an unpleasant consequence following a desired behavior. Avoidance learning is sometimes called *negative reinforcement.* Employees learn to do the right thing by avoiding unpleasant situations. Avoidance learning occurs when a supervisor stops harassing or reprimanding an employee once the incorrect behavior has stopped.

PUNISHMENT. *Punishment* is the imposition of unpleasant outcomes on an employee. Punishment typically occurs following undesirable behavior. For example, a supervisor may berate an employee for performing a task incorrectly. The supervisor expects that the negative outcome will serve as a punishment and reduce the likelihood of the behavior recurring. The use of

reinforcement theory
A motivation theory based on the relationship between a given behavior and its consequences.

behavior modification The set of techniques by which reinforcement theory is used to modify human behavior.

law of effect The assumption that positively reinforced behavior tends to be repeated and unreinforced or negatively reinforced behavior tends to be inhibited.

reinforcement Anything that causes a given behavior to be repeated or inhibited.

punishment in organizations is controversial and often criticized because it fails to indicate the correct behavior.

EXTINCTION. *Extinction* is the withdrawal of a positive reward, meaning that behavior is no longer reinforced and hence is less likely to occur in the future. If a perpetually tardy employee fails to receive praise and pay raises, he or she will begin to realize that the behavior is not producing desired outcomes. The behavior will gradually disappear if it is continually nonreinforced.

Some executives use reinforcement theory very effectively to shape employees' behavior. Jack Welch, chairman of General Electric, always made it a point to reinforce behavior. As an up-and-coming group executive, Welch reinforced purchasing agents by having someone telephone him whenever an agent got a price concession from a vendor. Welch would stop whatever he was doing and call the agent to say, "That's wonderful news; you just knocked a nickel a ton off the price of steel." He would also sit down and scribble out a congratulatory note to the agent. The effective use of positive reinforcement and the heightened motivation of purchasing employees marked Jack Welch as executive material in the organization.[23]

SCHEDULES OF REINFORCEMENT

schedule of reinforcement The frequency with and intervals over which reinforcement occurs.

A great deal of research into reinforcement theory suggests that the timing of reinforcement has an impact on the speed of employee learning. **Schedules of reinforcement** pertain to the frequency with and intervals over which reinforcement occurs. A reinforcement schedule can be selected to have maximum impact on employees' job behavior. There are five basic types of reinforcement schedules.

continuous reinforcement schedule A schedule in which every occurrence of the desired behavior is reinforced.

partial reinforcement schedule A schedule in which only some occurrences of the desired behavior are reinforced.

CONTINUOUS AND PARTIAL REINFORCEMENT. With a **continuous reinforcement schedule,** every occurrence of the desired behavior is reinforced. This schedule can be very effective in the early stages of learning new types of behavior, because every attempt has a pleasant consequence.

However, in the real world of organizations it is often impossible to reinforce every correct behavior. With a **partial reinforcement schedule,** the reinforcement is administered only after some occurrences of the correct behavior. There are four types of partial reinforcement schedules: fixed-interval, fixed-ratio, variable-interval, and variable-ratio.

FIXED-INTERVAL SCHEDULE. The *fixed-interval schedule* rewards employees at specified time intervals. If an employee displays the correct behavior each day, reinforcement may occur every week. Regular paychecks or quarterly bonuses are examples of a fixed-interval reinforcement.

FIXED-RATIO SCHEDULE. With a *fixed-ratio schedule,* reinforcement occurs after a specified number of desired responses, say, after every fifth. For example, paying a field hand $1.50 for picking 10 pounds of peppers is a fixed-ratio schedule. Most piece-rate pay systems are considered fixed-ratio schedules.

EXHIBIT 14.6
Schedules of Reinforcement

Schedule of Reinforcement	Nature of Reinforcement	Effect on Behavior When Applied	Effect on Behavior When Withdrawn	Example
Continuous	Reward given after each desired behavior	Leads to fast learning of new behavior	Rapid extinction	Praise
Fixed-interval	Reward given at fixed time intervals	Leads to average and irregular performance	Rapid extinction	Weekly paycheck
Fixed-ratio	Reward given at fixed amounts of output	Quickly leads to very high and stable performance	Rapid extinction	Piece-rate pay system
Variable-interval	Reward given at variable times	Leads to moderately high and stable performance	Slow extinction	Performance appraisal and awards given at random times each month
Variable-ratio	Reward given at variable amounts of output	Leads to very high performance	Slow extinction	Sales bonus tied to number of sales calls, with random checks

VARIABLE-INTERVAL SCHEDULE. With a *variable-interval schedule*, reinforcement is administered at random times that cannot be predicted by the employee. An example would be a random inspection by the manufacturing superintendent of the production floor, at which time he or she commends employees on their good behavior.

VARIABLE-RATIO SCHEDULE. The *variable-ratio schedule* is based on a random number of desired behaviors rather than on variable time periods. Reinforcement may occur after 5, 10, 15, or 20 displays of behavior. One example is the attraction of slot machines for gamblers. People anticipate that the machine will pay a jackpot after a certain number of plays, but the exact number of plays is variable.

The schedules of reinforcement available to managers are illustrated in Exhibit 14.6. Continuous reinforcement is most effective for establishing new learning, but behavior is vulnerable to extinction. Partial reinforcement schedules are more effective for maintaining behavior over extended time periods. The most powerful is the variable-ratio schedule, because employee behavior will persist for a long time due to the administration of reinforcement only after a long interval.[24]

One example of a small business that successfully uses reinforcement theory is Parsons Pine Products.

PARSONS PINE PRODUCTS • Parsons Pine Products has only 75 employees, but it is the world's largest manufacturer of slats for louvered doors and shutters. Managers have developed a positive reinforcement scheme for motivating and rewarding workers. The plan includes the following:

FOCUS ON GLOBAL COMPETITION

MOTIVATION IN A COMMUNIST COUNTRY

Many communist countries are shifting to market competition and individual incentives in an effort to increase worker productivity and to produce goods that are competitive in world markets. Psychologists have argued that human motivation is similar the world over, hence similar incentives should work in various countries.

In China, Tang Daqin is director of the Sichuan No. 1 Knitting Mill. Liberalized government policies have allowed the implementation of incentives to motivate both Tang and his workers. Tang's plant adopted the director responsibility system, giving him a stake in the factory's performance. If his knitting mill matches the previous year's profit of $540,000, Tang stands to earn a bonus of $300, worth about four months' salary. If the factory doesn't make it, he will forfeit $270 of his own money. Tang works hard to achieve his goal, despite government regulations that limit the selling price of the factory's garments and his ability to lay off or fire workers.

The workers are motivated in two ways. First, Tang introduced a piece-rate system last year. Hard-working employees can increase their pay according to the amount they produce. Although the pay variance is limited, it is better than the previous system — rigid Communism — under which all workers got a guaranteed wage. No workers got rich, but no one did much work.

Tang's second approach is to appeal to the workers' belief in the collective system. He has prepared a series of elaborate posters that hang in the building to illustrate losses due to worker inefficiency. He believes it is important to show workers how negative behavior costs everyone money.

Overall, the Chinese system is a mix of what Westerners call hierarchy of needs, expectancy theory, and reinforcement. So far productivity is improving in China, reinforcing the expectation that incentives are effective in all cultures.

Source: Based on Adi Ignatius, "For China's Managers, Keeping Plants Going is a Daily Struggle," *The Wall Street Journal,* April 13, 1990, pp. A1, A6.

1. *Safety pay.* Every employee who goes for a month without a lost-time accident receives a bonus equal to four hours' pay.
2. *Retro pay.* If the company saves money when its worker's compensation premiums go down because of a lower accident rate, the savings are distributed among employees.
3. *Well pay.* Employees receive monthly well pay equal to eight hours' wages if they have been neither absent nor tardy.
4. *Profit pay.* All company earnings above 4 percent after taxes go into a bonus pool, which is shared among employees.

The plan for reinforcing correct behaviors has been extraordinarily effective. Parsons's previous accident rate had been 86 percent above the state average; today it is 32 percent below it. Turnover and tardiness are minimal, and absenteeism has dropped to almost nothing. The plan works because the reinforcement schedules are strictly applied, with no exceptions. Owner James Parsons has said, "One woman called to say that a tree had fallen, and she couldn't get her car out. She wanted me to make an exception. If I did that, I'd be doing it all the time."[25]

Reinforcement also works at such organizations as Campbell Soup Co., Emery Air Freight, Michigan Bell, and General Electric because managers reward appropriate behavior. They tell employees what they can do to receive reinforcement, tell them what they are doing wrong, distribute rewards equitably, tailor rewards to behaviors, and keep in mind that failure to reward deserving behavior has an equally powerful impact on employees.

Indeed, reinforcement as well as the content and process perspectives of motivation described earlier are now being adopted in Eastern European countries as well as in Russia and China. The Focus on Global Competition box tells about the implementation of incentives in a Chinese factory where everyone used to earn the same pay.

EXHIBIT 14.7
Types of Job Design

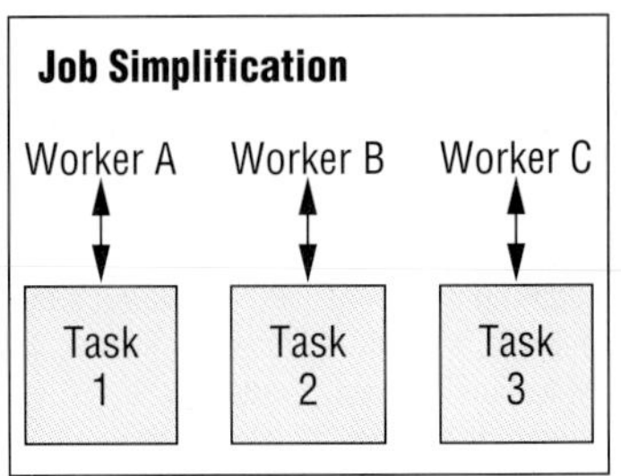

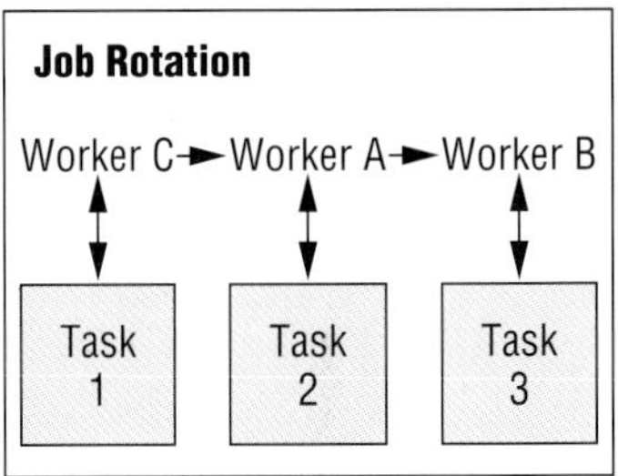

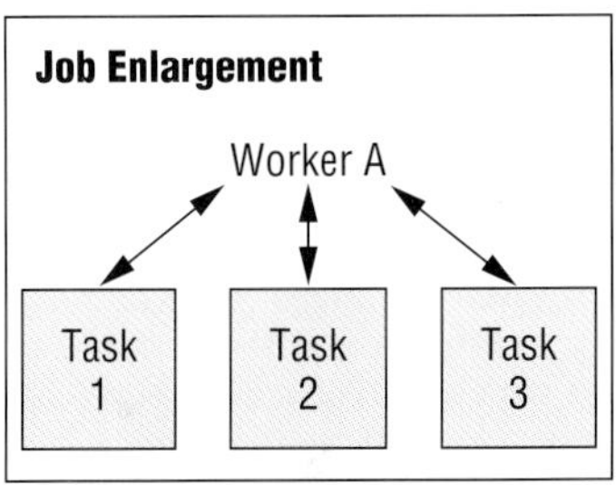

JOB DESIGN FOR MOTIVATION

A *job* in an organization is a unit of work that a single employee is responsible for performing. A job could include writing tickets for parking violators in New York City or doing long-range planning for ABC television. Jobs are important because their components may provide rewards that meet employees' needs. An assembly line worker may install the same bolt over and over, whereas an emergency room physician may provide each trauma victim with a unique treatment package. Managers need to know what aspects of a job provide motivation as well as how to compensate for routine tasks that have little inherent satisfaction. **Job design** is the application of motivational theories to the structure of work for improving productivity and satisfaction. Approaches to job design are generally classified as job simplification, job rotation, job enlargement, and job enrichment.

JOB SIMPLIFICATION

Job simplification pursues task efficiency by reducing the number of tasks one person must do. Job simplification is based on principles drawn from scientific management and industrial engineering. Tasks are designed to be simple, repetitive, and standardized. As complexity is stripped from a job, the worker has more time to concentrate on doing more of the same routine task. Workers with low skill requirements can perform the job, and the organization achieves a high level of efficiency. Indeed, workers are interchangeable, because they need little training or skill and exercise little judgment. As a motivational technique, however, job simplification has failed. People dislike routine and boring jobs and react in a number of negative ways, including sabotage, absenteeism, and unionization. Job simplification is compared with job rotation and job enlargement in Exhibit 14.7.

JOB ROTATION

Job rotation systematically moves employees from one job to another, thereby increasing the number of different tasks an employee performs without increasing the complexity of any one job. For example, an autoworker may install windshields one week and front bumpers the next. Job rotation still takes advantage of engineering efficiencies, but it provides variety and stimulation for employees. Although employees may find the new job interesting at first, the novelty soon wears off as the repetitive work is mastered.

Companies such as National Steel, Motorola, and Dayton Hudson have built on the notion of job rotation to train a flexible work force. As companies

job design The application of motivational theories to the structure of work for improving productivity and satisfaction.

job simplification A job design whose purpose is to improve task efficiency by reducing the number of tasks a single person must perform.

job rotation A job design that systematically moves employees from one job to another to provide them with variety and stimulation.

U.S. Shoe uses *job enlargement* to increase employee motivation and satisfaction. Modular work areas have been created as part of U.S. Shoe's quick-response manufacturing techniques. Greater quality and flexibility are achieved by cross training employees to perform two or three shoe-making steps instead of only one as in traditional production lines. Employees also are given training in communication skills and group dynamics to enhance the satisfaction and motivational impact of working in modular teams.

break away from ossified job categories, workers can perform several jobs, thereby reducing labor costs. One employee might shift between the jobs of millwright, welder, and pipe fitter, depending on the company's need at the moment. Some unions have resisted the idea, but many now go along, realizing that it helps the company be more competitive.[26]

Job Enlargement

job enlargement A job design that combines a series of tasks into one new, broader job to give employees variety and challenge.

Job enlargement combines a series of tasks into one new, broader job. This is a response to the dissatisfaction of employees with oversimplified jobs. Instead of only one job, an employee may be responsible for three or four and will have more time to do them. Job enlargement provides job variety and a greater challenge for employees. At Maytag, jobs were enlarged when work was redesigned such that workers assembled an entire water pump rather than doing each part as it reached them on the assembly line. In General Motors' new assembly plants, the assembly line is gone. In its place is a motorized carrier that transports a car through the assembly process. The carrier allows a vehicle to stop, and a group of workers perform logical blocks of work, such as installing an engine and its accessories. The workers get to perform an enlarged job on a stationary automobile rather than a single task on a large number of automobiles.

Job Enrichment

job enrichment A job design that incorporates achievement, recognition, and other high-level motivators into the work.

Recall the discussion of Maslow's need hierarchy and Herzberg's two-factor theory. Rather than just changing the number and frequency of tasks a worker performs, **job enrichment** incorporates high-level motivators into the work, including job responsibility, recognition, and opportunities for growth, learning, and achievement. In an enriched job, employees have control over the resources necessary for performing it, make decisions on how to do the work, experience personal growth, and set their own work pace. Many companies,

EXHIBIT 14.8
The Job Characteristics Model

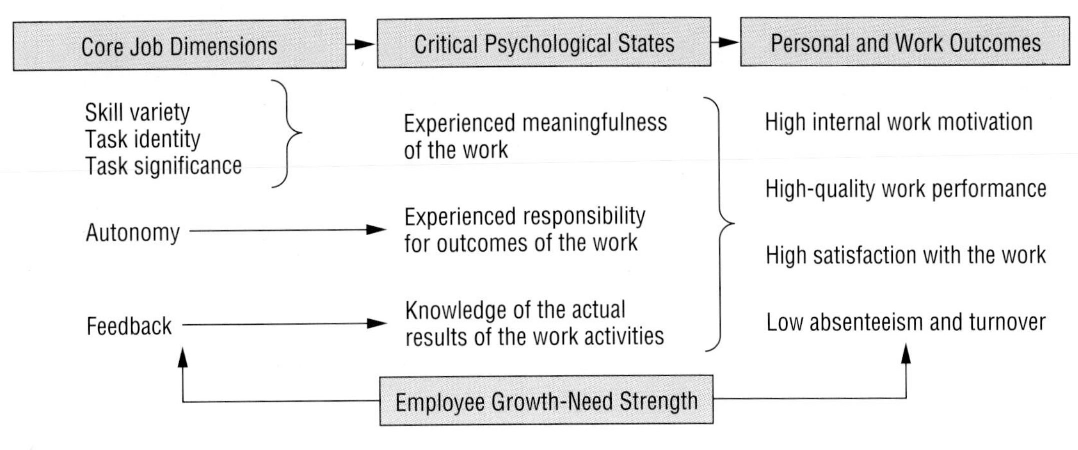

Source: Adapted from J. R. Hackman and G. R. Oldham, "Motivation through the Design of Work: Test of a Theory," *Organizational Behavior and Human Performance* 16 (1976), 256.

including AT&T, IBM, and General Foods, have undertaken job enrichment programs to increase employees' motivation and job satisfaction.

JOB CHARACTERISTICS MODEL

The most recent work on job design is the job characteristics model developed by Richard Hackman and Greg Oldham.[27] Hackman and Oldham's research concerned **work redesign,** which is defined as altering jobs to increase both the quality of employees' work experience and their productivity. Hackman and Oldham's research into the design of hundreds of jobs yielded the **job characteristics model,** which is illustrated in Exhibit 14.8. The model consists of three major parts: core job dimensions, critical psychological states, and employee growth-need strength.

work redesign The altering of jobs to increase both the quality of employees' work experience and their productivity.

job characteristics model A model of job design that comprises core job dimensions, critical psychological states, and employee growth-need strength.

CORE JOB DIMENSIONS. Hackman and Oldham identified five dimensions that determine a job's motivational potential:

1. *Skill variety* is the number of diverse activities that comprise a job and the number of skills used to perform it. A routine, repetitious assembly line job is low in variety, whereas an applied research position that entails working on new problems every day is high in variety.
2. *Task identity* is the degree to which an employee performs a total job with a recognizable beginning and ending. A chef who prepares an entire meal has more task identity than a worker on a cafeteria line who ladles mashed potatoes.
3. *Task significance* is the degree to which the job is perceived as important and having impact on the company or consumers. People who distribute

These motivated employees are working on the new MD-11 long-range tri-jets at McDonnell Douglas. Changes within McDonnell Douglas in core job dimensions and psychological states illustrate the *job characteristics model.* Development of self-managing work teams created *autonomy,* and empowering people with responsibility and job ownership increased *task significance. Skill variety* was increased by the reduction of job classifications to 3, allowing broad flexibility in work assignments. The new job characteristics have produced personal and work outcomes of high motivation, high satisfaction, and low turnover.

penicillin and other medical supplies during times of emergencies would feel they have significant jobs.

4. *Autonomy* is the degree to which the worker has freedom, discretion, and self-determination in planning and carrying out tasks. A house painter can determine how to paint the house; a paint sprayer on an assembly line has little autonomy.
5. *Feedback* is the extent to which doing the job provides information back to the employee about his or her performance. Jobs vary in their ability to let workers see the outcomes of their efforts. A football coach knows whether the team won or lost, but a basic research scientist may have to wait years to learn whether a research project was successful.

The job characteristics model says that the more these five core characteristics can be designed into the job, the more motivation employees will have and the higher will be performance quality and satisfaction.

Critical Psychological States. The model posits that core job dimensions are more rewarding when individuals experience three psychological states in response to job design. In Exhibit 14.8, skill variety, task identity, and task significance tend to influence the employee's psychological state of *experienced meaningfulness of work.* The work itself is satisfying and provides intrinsic rewards for the worker. The job characteristic of autonomy influences the worker's *experienced responsibility.* The job characteristic of feedback provides the worker with *knowledge of actual results.* The employee thus knows how he or she is doing and can change work performance to increase desired outcomes. The impact of the five job characteristics on the psychological states of experienced meaningfulness, responsibility, and knowledge of actual results leads to the personal and work outcomes of high work motivation, high work performance, high satisfaction, and low absenteeism and turnover.

EMPLOYEE GROWTH-NEED STRENGTH. The final component of the job characteristics model is called *employee growth-need strength,* which means that people have different needs for growth and development. If a person wants to satisfy lower-level needs, such as safety and belongingness, the job characteristics model has less effect. When a person has a high need for growth and development, including the desire for personal challenge, achievement, and challenging work, the model is especially effective. People with a high need to grow and expand their abilities respond very favorably to the application of the model and to improvements in core job dimensions.

One application of the job characteristics model that worked extremely well took place at Traveler's Insurance Company.

TRAVELER'S INSURANCE CO. • Traveler's Insurance Company executives wanted to increase the motivation and job satisfaction of keypunch operators. The company was experiencing absenteeism and turnover and felt that employees' needs were not being met. The keypunch operator's job consisted of a single skill — the ability to accurately punch data onto cards. Employees punched cards continuously and did not have identifiable, whole jobs. Once a batch was completed, it disappeared and the workers received no feedback on performance quality. Operators were isolated from the rest of the company and had little knowledge about how their work was used.

Researchers investigated the job and recommended several changes. First, instead of being assigned a random set of cards, each operator was given responsibility for a computer user account. In addition, each was given the opportunity for direct contact with clients when problems arose. The operators also were allowed to do planning and control in addition to keypunching. They were asked to correct obvious errors on their own and to set their own daily work schedules. Finally, all incorrectly punched cards were returned to operators for correction, along with weekly printouts of error rates.

These changes dramatically increased the motivating potential of the keypunch operator's job. The job now had greater variety, task identity, and perceived significance. Autonomy and task feedback also were increased.

What were the consequences of the work redesign? Productivity increased 39.6 percent. The error rate dropped from 1.53 to 0.99 percent. Absenteeism declined 24.1 percent. Reported job satisfaction increased 16.5 percent. Moreover, because operators had greater responsibility, supervision was reduced, providing more freedom for keypunch operators and even greater savings for Traveler's.[28]

NEW MOTIVATIONAL PROGRAMS

Organizations have adopted a number of new programs in recent years that apply motivational theory to improve employees' satisfaction and performance. These new forms of incentive pay and employee involvement include pay for performance, gain sharing, ESOPs, lump-sum bonuses, pay for knowledge, and

WINNING MOVES

SPRINGFIELD REMANUFACTURING EMPLOYEES ARE OWNERS TOO

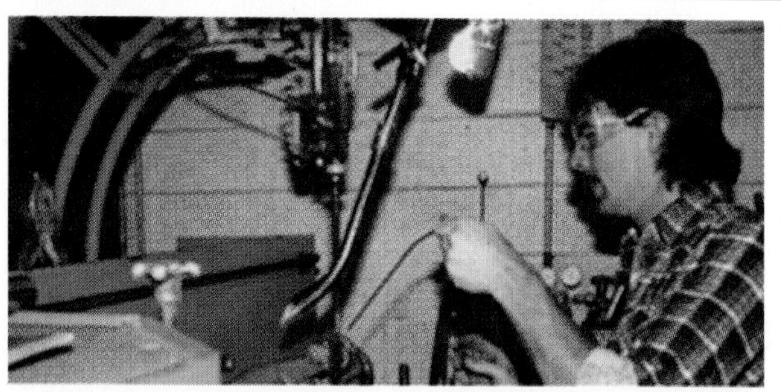

In 1983, Springfield Remanufacturing Corporation was a poorly performing division of International Harvester. In 1990, it is a phenomenally successful independent corporation that services clients such as Mercedes Benz and General Motors. With sales of over $58 million a year, SRC has grown 35 to 40 percent annually since its management team bought it seven years ago. When asked about this remarkable turnaround, the corporation's director of human resources says, "It's pretty simple. We make sure every employee understands how their work adds to or subtracts from every line on the financial statement . . . " Through strong job enrichment programs, as well as an ESOP plan, Springfield Remanufacturing motivates its workers to be full participants. The results of this approach have been improved morale, better career opportunities, and increased productivity.

CEO Jack Stack credits his approach to problems he saw at International Harvester: "There was a tremendous distinction between the working class and management. The only way we communicated was through a contract." So when he took over SRC, Stack was determined to make a strong investment in human capital. Motivating employees was his first priority. The foundation of his approach is perhaps best expressed by director of human resources, Gary Brown: "We're trying to create a working environment that involves ordinary, blue-collar workers in more than just day-to-day routines. We firmly believe employees are capable of more than coming to work just to grind crankcases."

The most important part of Stack's program is the employee stock ownership plan. Like many ESOPs, it is designed to reinforce full participation and instill a sense of pride in the corporation's success. SRC wants its employees to feel like business partners who will see increased financial benefits from improving performance. Currently over 30 percent of the outstanding stock is held in the ESOP trust, while the rest is held by the managers who originally bought SRC from International Harvester. The ESOP is managed by a committee of seven members. Three of these individuals are elected by the hourly and salaried employees. This gives the entire workforce a voice in the conduct of corporate affairs.

In fact, when an SRC employee is first hired, he or she is told that 70 percent of the job is rebuilding engines and 30 percent is learning how to make profits. As part of their basic training, all employees must learn how to evaluate weekly income statements, cash flow projections, debt-to-equity ratios, balance sheets, after-tax-profits, and net earnings. Everyone is expected to understand the bottom line effect of his or her job and to help SRC achieve maximum profitability.

This involvement in the corporation's financial standing is carried out through company-wide production information meetings held twice each month. Senior managers and supervisors begin each meeting with a status discussion that leads to a revised financial forecast. Supervisors then hold meetings on the shop floor. They pass out the revised forecast and conduct a question-and-answer session. In this way the entire work force, from telephone operators to top management, knows exactly how the company is doing.

As part of SRC's job enrichment policy, the company also offers regularly scheduled courses in topics such as accounting, warehousing, and remedial reading for those who need it. A career planning counselor helps workers outline career paths. Stack proudly claims, "We've got people knocking down the door of the HR manager's office asking how to run their own companies." Many well-prepared employees go on to manage one of SRC's many branches and have the opportunity to buy out a large percent of the particular company they run.

Stack claims the difference that makes SRC so successful is that employees "understand performance and productivity as equity." SRC has given its people the tools to improve their careers and a piece of the profits that their efforts build. Given the fact that the stock has gone from 10 cents to $13.80 a share, this is some of the best motivation possible.

Source: Based on Frank T. Adams, "Motivation and the Bottom Line," *Human Capital,* July 1990, 19–26.

flexible work schedules. Companies can combine these ideas with other ideas from this chapter to create their own motivational program.

Pay for Performance

Pay for performance means that employees are rewarded in proportion to their performance contributions. Typically called merit pay, this is a logical outgrowth of such motivational concepts as expectancy theory and reinforcement theory because pay raises are tied to work behavior. In many organizations, pay raises had become automatic and merit pay had no meaning.

pay for performance A motivational compensation program that rewards employees in proportion to their performance contributions.

This trend is illustrated at General Motors, which dropped annual cost-of-living raises for salaried employees and established a pay-for-performance system. A merit increase is going to be something employees have to earn. Bosses have to pick the top 10 percent of performers, the next 25 percent, the next 55 percent, and the bottom 10 percent and enforce pay differences among the groups.[29]

Gain Sharing

Gain sharing is an incentive program in which employees and managers within a designated unit receive bonuses when unit performance beats a predetermined performance target. These targets may specify productivity, costs, quality, customer service, or profits. Unlike pay for performance, gain sharing encourages coordination and teamwork because all employees are contributing to the benefit of the business unit. Most companies develop a precise formula that is calculated for, say, a six-month period, after which bonuses may be paid.[30]

gain sharing A motivational compensation program that rewards employees and managers when predetermined performance targets are met.

Gain sharing was a major factor in the turnaround of the Great Atlantic & Pacific Tea Company, considered the worst-run supermarket chain in the late 1970s and early 1980s. A&P used an experimental arrangement in an attempt to harness employee abilities: If a store's employees could keep labor costs at 10 percent of sales by working more efficiently, they would get a cash bonus equal to 1 percent of the store's sales. This was considered an enormous bonus in an industry in which profit seldom runs above 1 percent of sales. But it worked. Employees jumped in enthusiastically, and A&P operating profits have increased 81 percent. The bonus approach has spread to 281 stores, where workers are earning an average of 85 cents an hour in bonuses.[31]

ESOPs

Employee stock ownership plans (ESOPs) give employees partial ownership of the business, thereby allowing them to share in improved profit performance. ESOPs have been popular with small businesses, although a few large businesses such as Avis, Procter & Gamble, and JC Penney have also adopted ESOPs. The ESOP allows a company to boost productivity at the cost of ownership, which most business executives are finding to be a good trade. Employees work harder because they are owners and share in gains and losses. For

employee stock ownership plan (ESOP) A motivational compensation program that gives employees part ownership of the organization.

ESOPs to work, managers must provide complete financial information to employees, give employees the right to participate in major decisions, and give employees voting rights, which includes voting for the board of directors.

At Avis, employees take their ownership seriously. Each class of line worker, from mechanics to rental agents, meets in employee participation groups where they suggest ways of improving customer service and running the business more efficiently. Since start of the ESOP, Avis has recorded higher profit-sales ratios than Hertz and now aims to overtake Hertz in market share.[32] The Winning Moves box on Springfield Remanufacturing shows how an ESOP plan, in combination with job enrichment, helped initiate a dramatic turnaround in the company's success.

Lump-Sum Bonuses

lump-sum bonus A motivational compensation program that rewards employees with a one-time cash payment based on performance.

Often salary increases do not seem very large when spread over an entire year. **Lump-sum bonuses** are one-time cash payments based on performance. The single payment is designed to increase motivational value. For example, a 10 percent raise for an employee earning $20,000 would be a one-time $2,000 payment. This plan works when employees have a sense that their bonus truly mirrors the company's prosperity. It also lets the company control wage costs by not building increases into the permanent wage structure unless company performance is good.

Pay for Knowledge

pay for knowledge A motivational compensation program that links employee's salary with the number of tasks performed.

Pay for knowledge means that an employee's salary is increased with the number of tasks he or she can do. This is linked to the ideas of job rotation and job enrichment because employees learn the skills for many jobs. Pay for knowledge increases company flexibility and efficiency, because fewer employees are needed to perform all tasks. Workers achieve a broader perspective, making them more adept at problem solving. To implement this plan, a company must have a well-developed employee-assessment procedure, and jobs must be well identified so that pay can be increased as new job skills are acquired.

Flexible Work Schedules

Flexible work schedules drop the restriction that employees work the normal eight-hour workday from 8 a.m. to 5 p.m. These modifications include the four-day workweek, flex time, and job sharing.

With the *four-day workweek* employees work four days for ten hours each instead of five days for eight hours. The motivational factor is that of meeting the needs of workers who want more leisure time.

Flex time allows employees to determine their workday schedules. People can choose starting and quitting times. For example, a company may have core hours during which employees must be present, perhaps from 9 a.m. to 4 p.m. Employees then are free to start work anywhere from 7 a.m. to 9 a.m. and to

Marti O'Brien has chosen more home time with son Peter, thanks to Steelcase Inc.'s policy of *job sharing*. O'Brien shares her job with another employee, each working two and a half days a week recruiting employees for the marketing department. This innovative approach to job scheduling has reduced absenteeism among working mothers, and roughly 400 of Steelcase's 2,000 office workers are in the program. O'Brien remains a loyal and grateful employee and probably will return to full-time work later, saving Steelcase the cost of finding and training a new employee.

finish anywhere from 4 p.m. to 6 p.m., depending on their own needs and desires.

Job sharing involves two or more persons jointly covering one job over a forty-hour week. Job sharing allows part-time workers, such as a mother with small children, to work only part of a day without having to create a special job. Job sharing also relieves job fatigue if work is routine or monotonous.

SUMMARY

This chapter introduced a number of important ideas about the motivation of people in organizations. The content theories of motivation focus on the nature of underlying employee needs. Maslow's hierarchy of needs, Alderfer's ERG theory, Herzberg's two-factor theory, and McClelland's acquired needs theory all suggest that people are motivated to meet a range of needs. Process theories examine how people go about selecting rewards with which to meet needs. Equity theory says that people compare their contributions and outcomes with others' and are motivated to maintain a feeling of equity. Expectancy theory suggests that people calculate the probability of achieving certain outcomes. Managers can increase motivation by treating employees fairly and by clarifying employee paths toward meeting their needs. Still another motivational approach is reinforcement theory, which says that employees learn to behave in certain ways based on the availability of reinforcements.

The application of motivational ideas is illustrated in job design and other motivational programs. Job design approaches include job enrichment and work redesign, which provide an opportunity for employees to meet higher-level needs. Other motivational programs include pay for performance, gain sharing, ESOPs, lump-sum bonuses, pay for knowledge, and flexible work schedules.

MANAGEMENT SOLUTION

Gary Aronson was an unmotivated store manager at Au Bon Pain, making a mere $26,000 a year. Thanks to a new incentive system, Aronson will make at least $80,000 this year, and he throws his heart and soul into his work, putting in a minimum of 65 hours a week and loving it. The dramatic motivation began when top executives devised a plan to split controllable profits on a 50-50 basis with store managers. Controllable profits are ones store managers can do something about. Aronson got rid of one assistant manager to save on overhead, reorganized the store to increase seating capacity, and motivated his own staff more effectively to insure prompt service. Aronson and other store managers solved problems they had previously dumped on the company. Under the new system, stores ran 40 percent ahead of their profit goals, showing that incentives and a sense of ownership work.[33] Perhaps the best explanation for the sharply improved performance is expectancy theory, because managers saw how to link effort and performance to the outcomes they desired. They also received positive reinforcement, and their job responsibilities were enriched, thereby satisfying higher-level needs.

DISCUSSION QUESTIONS

1. Low-paid service workers represent a motivational problem for many companies. Consider the ill-trained and poorly motivated X-ray machine operators trying to detect weapons in airports. How might these people be motivated to reduce boredom and increase their vigilance?
2. One small company recognizes an employee of the month, who is given a parking spot next to the president's space near the front door. What theories would explain the positive motivation associated with this policy?
3. Campbell Soup Company reduces accidents with a lottery. Each worker who works 30 days or more without losing a day for a job-related accident is eligible to win prizes in a raffle drawing. Why has this program been successful?
4. One executive argues that managers have too much safety because of benefit and retirement plans. He rewards his managers for taking risks and has removed many guaranteed benefits. Would this approach motivate managers? Why?
5. If an experienced secretary discovered that she made less money than a newly hired janitor, how would she react? What inputs and outcomes might she evaluate to make this comparison?
6. Would you rather work for a supervisor high in need for achievement, need for affiliation, or need for power? Why? What are the advantages and disadvantages of each?
7. A survey of teachers found that two of the most important rewards were the belief that their work was important and a feeling of accomplishment. Is this consistent with Hackman and Oldham's job characteristics model?
8. The teachers in question 7 also reported that pay and fringe benefits were poor; yet they continued to teach. Use Herzberg's two-factor theory to explain this finding.

9. Many organizations use sales contests and motivational speakers to motivate salespeople to overcome frequent rejections and turndowns. How would these devices help motivate salespeople?
10. What characteristics of individuals determine the extent to which work redesign will have a positive impact on work satisfaction and work effectiveness?
11. Which of the new motivational programs would you be most comfortable with as a manager? Why?

MANAGEMENT IN PRACTICE: EXPERIENTIAL EXERCISE

Motivation Questionnaire

You are to indicate how important each characteristic is to you. Answer according to your feelings about the most recent job you had or about the job you currently hold. Circle the number on the scale that represents your feeling—1 (very unimportant) to 7 (very important).

When you have completed the questionnaire, score it as follows:

Rating for question 5 = ___. Divide by 1 = ___ security.
Rating for questions 9 and 13 = ___. Divide by 2 = ___ social.
Rating for questions 1, 3, and 7 = ___. Divide by 3 = ___ esteem.
Rating for questions 4, 10, 11, and 12 = ___. Divide by 4 = ___ autonomy.
Rating for questions 2, 6, and 8 = ___. Divide by 3 = ___ self-actualization.

The instructor has national norm scores for presidents, vice-presidents, and upper middle-level, lower middle-level, and lower-level managers with which you can compare your *mean* importance scores. How do your scores compare with the scores of managers working in organizations?

1. The feeling of self-esteem a person gets from being in that job	1	2	3	4	5	6	7
2. The opportunity for personal growth and development in that job	1	2	3	4	5	6	7
3. The prestige of the job inside the company (that is, regard received from others in the company)	1	2	3	4	5	6	7
4. The opportunity for independent thought and action in that job	1	2	3	4	5	6	7
5. The feeling of security in that job	1	2	3	4	5	6	7
6. The feeling of self-fulfillment a person gets from being in that position (that is, the feeling of being able to use one's own unique capabilities, realizing one's potential)	1	2	3	4	5	6	7
7. The prestige of the job outside the company (that is, the regard received from others not in the company)	1	2	3	4	5	6	7
8. The feeling of worthwhile accomplishment in that job	1	2	3	4	5	6	7
9. The opportunity in that job to give help to other people	1	2	3	4	5	6	7
10. The opportunity in that job for participation in the setting of goals	1	2	3	4	5	6	7
11. The opportunity in that job for participation in the determination of methods and procedures	1	2	3	4	5	6	7
12. The authority connected with the job	1	2	3	4	5	6	7
13. The opportunity to develop close friendships in the job	1	2	3	4	5	6	7

Source: Lyman W. Porter, *Organizational Patterns of Managerial Job Attitudes* (New York: American Foundation for Management Research, 1964), 17, 19.

CASES FOR ANALYSIS

BLOOMINGDALE'S

Bloomingdale's is at the forefront of a quiet revolution sweeping department store retailing. Thousands of hourly sales employees are being converted to commission pay. Bloomingdale's hopes to use commissions to motivate employees to work harder, to attract better salespeople, and to enable them to earn more money. For example, under the old plan a Bloomingdale's salesclerk in women's wear would earn about $16,000 a year, based on $7 per hour and 0.5 percent commission on $500,000 sales. Under the new plan the annual pay would be $25,000 based on 5 percent commission on $500,000 sales.

John Palmerio, who works in the men's shoe salon, is enthusiastic about the changeover. His pay has increased an average of $175 per week. But in women's lingerie, employees are less enthusiastic. A target of $1,600 in sales per week is difficult to achieve but is necessary for salespeople to earn previous salary and even to keep their jobs. In previous years the practice of commission pay has been limited to big-ticket items such as furniture, appliances, and men's suits, where extra sales skill pays off. The move into small-item purchases may not work as well, but Bloomingdale's and other stores are trying anyway.

One question is whether Bloomingdale's can create more customer-oriented salespeople when they work on commission. They may be reluctant to handle complaints, make returns, and clean shelves, preferring instead to chase customers. Moreover, it costs Bloomingdale's about $1 million per store to install the commission system because of training programs, computer changes, and increased pay in many departments. If the overall impact on service is negative, the increased efficiency may not seem worthwhile.

Questions

1. What theories about motivation underlie the switch from salary to commission pay?
2. Are higher-level needs met under the commission system?
3. As a customer, would you prefer to shop where employees are motivated to make commissions?

Source: Based on Amy Dunkin, "Now Salespeople Really Must Sell for Their Supper," *Business Week*, July 31, 1989, 50–52.

AUTOMOBILE CLAIMS DEPARTMENT

Ellen Richards supervised 30 stenographers in the automobile claims department of a large insurance company. She spent much of her time assigning dictation to the staffers who handled correspondence arising out of accident claims against the company. Some of this correspondence was fairly routine, but letters involving litigation were quite complicated. As a rule, Ellen gave the most difficult dictation to the most experienced stenographers.

She tried to remind herself of this as it became time to announce the annual merit raises. She used her records on attendance, lateness, and daily letter output to determine the size of each raise. After she had made her decisions, Ellen called each person to her desk individually to report the amount of the raise. The next day, Annette Simmons came up to Ellen's desk, obviously upset. "Ellen," she said, trying to control her voice, "could you please tell me why Jason got a bigger raise than I did? I have had very few absences and I'm never late. You often compliment me on my work, and you give me some of the hardest assignments." Ellen got out her records and looked at them. "You're a good worker, Annette," she said, "but your letter output is just a little below average. If you could raise your output, next time I'm sure you'll get a bigger raise."

"But I get the hardest dictation!" Annette said angrily. "And when Gene came into our section, you put him next to me and told me to help him until he got familiar with the work. I don't mind helping someone new, but he still interrupts me with questions about things he should know by now. Don't you take things like that into consideration before deciding how much of a raise I deserve?"

"In a section as large as ours," Ellen explained, "I have to use objective standards like output and attendance to determine each person's raise. Here productivity is everything. I'm sorry you're upset, because I know how helpful you are to the less experienced workers, and I know how much they appreciate your giving them a hand."

"Evidently they are the only ones who appreciate my giving them a hand. From now on, I'll just attend to my own work." With that, Annette turned away and went back to her desk before Ellen could reply.

Questions

1. Is Ellen Richards successfully motivating her staff? What mistake is she making?
2. Use expectancy theory to analyze Annette's motivation. What are the E → P and P → O expectancies?
3. If you were Ellen, what would you do now?

Source: Adapted by permission of the publisher, from "I Deserve a Bigger Raise," *Management Solutions,* June 1986, 43–44.

CHAPTER 15

COMMUNICATING IN ORGANIZATIONS

CHAPTER OUTLINE

LEARNING OBJECTIVES

After studying this chapter, you should be able to:

- Explain why communication is essential for effective management.
- Define the basic elements of the communication process.
- Describe how perception, nonverbal behavior, and listening affect communication among people.
- Describe the concept of channel richness and explain how communication channels influence the quality of communication among managers.
- Explain the difference between formal and informal organizational communications and the importance of each for organization management.
- Describe team communications and how structure influences communication outcomes.
- Describe barriers to organizational communications and suggest ways to avoid or overcome them.

Management Problem

CEO John Egan was given a simple mandate: Make Jaguar Cars profitable or shut it down. Customer surveys indicated that quality ratings for Jaguar autos and service were terrible. An already small market share was getting smaller. A major part of the problem was communication. Production employees did not appreciate top management's goal of high quality. Top managers did not understand the problems or concerns of supervisors and shop floor employees trying to produce cars. Dealers did not understand customers' wishes or how to communicate them back to the factory. John Egan faced the challenge of improving Jaguar quality and productivity, but to do so meant improving communication in all directions.[1]

If you were John Egan, what would you do to improve communications at Jaguar? How would you enhance the flow of information to pull the company together?

CEO John Egan believes in communication but sees a big problem breaking down communication barriers at Jaguar. In today's intensely competitive environment, senior executives at most companies are trying to improve communication. The president of Syntex Corporation, a pharmaceuticals maker, eats breakfast at 7:30 each morning in the employee cafeteria exchanging information with workers. Stephen M. Wolf, chairman of United Air Lines, meets regularly with rank-and-file employees in a series of chairman's lunches. John Scully, CEO of Apple Computer, insists that top executives listen to customer complaints on the toll-free number. Although Apple executives often lack the technical expertise to solve customers' problems, they quickly learn customers' concerns about Apple computers.[2]

These executives are interested in staying connected with employees and customers and with shaping company direction. To do so, they must be in touch, hence they excel at personal communications. Nonmanagers often are amazed at how much energy successful executives put into communication. Consider Robert Strauss, former chairman of the Democratic National Committee:

Chairman George Schaefer (right) and President Pete Donis of Caterpillar are being interviewed for a videotape to be distributed to employees. They can't visit all 55,000 employees personally, so they have redoubled efforts to communicate with the work force. Global competition during the 1980s forced several plant closings, hence increased communication within the company to inform employees was required. These two top managers also solicit information from employees, to learn about issues and concerns of the work force. Communication is a major part of a manager's job, and Caterpillar's top managers know how to facilitate it.

> One of his friends says, "His network is everywhere. It ranges from bookies to bank presidents. . . ."
>
> He seems to find time to make innumerable phone calls to "keep in touch;" he cultivates secretaries as well as senators; he will befriend a middle-level White House aide whom other important officials won't bother with. Every few months, he sends candy to the White House switchboard operators.[3]

This chapter explains why executives such as Robert Strauss, John Scully, and the presidents of United Air Lines and Syntex Corporation are effective communicators. First we will see how managers' jobs require communication. Next, we will define communication and describe a model of the communication process. Then we will consider the interpersonal aspects of communication, including perception, channels, and listening skills, that affect managers' ability to communicate. Next, we will look at the organization as a whole and consider formal upward and downward communications as well as informal communications. Finally, we will examine barriers to communication and how managers can overcome them.

Communication and the Manager's Job

How important is communication? Consider this: Managers spend at least 80 percent of every working day in direct communication with others. In other words, 48 minutes of every hour is spent in meetings, on the telephone, or talking informally while walking around. The other 20 percent of a typical manager's time is spent doing desk work, most of which is also communication in the form of reading and writing.[4]

Communication permeates every management function described in Chapter 1.[5] For example, when managers perform the planning function, they gather information; write letters, memos, and reports; and then meet with other managers to explain the plan. When managers lead, they communicate with subordinates to motivate them. When managers organize, they gather information about the state of the organization and communicate a new structure to others. Communication skills are a fundamental part of every managerial activity.

What Is Communication?

Before going further, let's determine what communication is. A professor at Harvard once asked a class to define communication by drawing pictures. Most students drew a manager speaking or writing. Some placed "speech balloons" next to their characters; others showed pages flying from a typewriter. "No," the professor told the class, "none of you have captured the essence of communication." He went on to explain that communication means "to share" — not "to speak" or "to write."

Communication thus can be defined as the process by which information is exchanged and understood by two or more people, usually with the intent to motivate or influence behavior. Communication is not just sending information. This distinction between *sharing* and *proclaiming* is crucial for successful management. A manager who does not listen is like a used-car salesperson who claims, "I sold a car — they just did not buy it." Management communication is a two-way street that includes listening and other forms of feedback. Effective communication, in the words of one expert, is as follows:

communication The process by which information is exchanged and understood by two or more people, usually with the intent to motivate or influence behavior.

> When two people interact, they put themselves into each other's shoes, try to perceive the world as the other person perceives it, try to predict how the other will respond. Interaction involves reciprocal role-taking, the mutual employment of empathetic skills. The goal of interaction is the merger of self and other, a complete ability to anticipate, predict, and behave in accordance with the joint needs of self and other.[6]

It is the desire to share understanding that motivates executives to visit employees on the shop floor or eat breakfast with them. The things managers learn from direct communication with employees shape their understanding of the corporation.

The Communication Process

Many people think communication is simple because they communicate without conscious thought or effort. However, communication is usually complex, and the opportunities for sending or receiving the wrong messages are innumerable. How often have you heard someone say, "But that's not what I meant"? Have you ever received directions you thought were clear and yet still got lost? How often have you wasted time on misunderstood instructions?

To more fully understand the complexity of the communication process, note the key elements outlined in Exhibit 15.1. Two common elements in every communication situation are the sender and the receiver. The *sender* is anyone who wishes to convey an idea or concept to others, to seek information, or to express a thought or emotion. The *receiver* is the person to whom the message is sent. The sender **encodes** the idea by selecting symbols with which to compose a message. The **message** is the tangible formulation of the idea that is

encode To select symbols with which to compose a message.

message The tangible formulation of an idea to be sent to a receiver.

EXHIBIT 15.1
A Model of the Communication Process

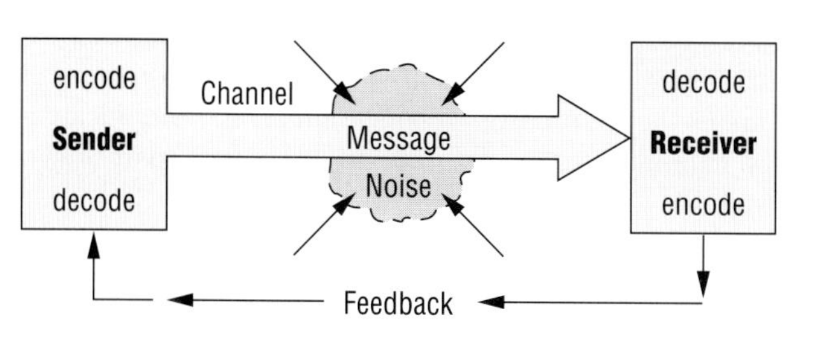

channel The carrier of a communication.

decode To translate the symbols used in a message for the purpose of interpreting its meaning.

feedback A response by the receiver to the sender's communication.

sent to the receiver. The message is sent through a **channel,** which is the communication carrier. The channel can be a formal report, a telephone call, or a face-to-face meeting. The receiver **decodes** the symbols to interpret the meaning of the message. Encoding and decoding are potential sources for communication errors, because knowledge, attitudes, and background act as filters and create "noise" when translating from symbols to meaning. Finally, **feedback** occurs when the receiver responds to the sender's communication with a return message. Without feedback, the communication is *one-way;* with feedback, it is *two-way.* Feedback is a powerful aid to communication effectiveness, because it enables the sender to determine whether the receiver correctly interpreted the message.

Managers who are effective communicators understand and use the circular nature of communication. For example, James Treybig of Tandem Computers Inc. has widened the open-door policy in order to communicate with employees. Treybig appears on a monthly television program broadcasted over the company's in-house television station. Employees around the world watch the show and call in their questions and comments. The television is the channel through which Treybig sends his encoded message. Employees decode and interpret the message and encode their feedback, which is sent through the channel of the telephone hookup. The communication circuit is complete. Similarly Tom Monaghan, president of Domino's Pizza, maintains communication channels with employees when he fields complaints for two hours during a monthly "call-in." Monaghan also maintains toll-free numbers with which employees call him directly. Treybig and Monaghan understand the elements of communication and have developed systems that work.[7]

COMMUNICATING AMONG PEOPLE

The communication model in Exhibit 15.1 illustrates the components that must be mastered for effective communication. Communications can break down if sender and receiver do not encode or decode language in the same way.[8] The selection of communication channels can determine whether the message is distorted by noise and interference. The listening skills of both parties can determine whether a message is truly shared. Thus, for managers to be effective communicators, they must understand how interpersonal factors such as perception, communication channels, nonverbal behavior, and listening all work to enhance or detract from communication.

Perception and Communication

The way we perceive people is the starting point for how we communicate. When one person wishes to share an idea with another, the message is formulated based on references constructed from past events, experiences, expectations, and current motivations. When a receiver hears a message, he or she relies on a particular frame of reference for decoding and understanding it. The more similar the frames of reference between people, the more easily they can communicate.

Perception is the process one uses to make sense out of the environment. However, perception in itself does not always lead to an accurate picture of the environment.[9] **Perceptual selectivity** means that various objects and stimuli that vie for our attention are screened and selected by individuals. Certain stimuli catch their attention, and others do not. Once a stimulus is recognized, individuals organize or categorize it according to their frame of reference, that is, **perceptual organization.** Only a partial cue is needed to enable perceptual organization to take place. For example, all of us have spotted an old friend from a long distance and, without seeing the face or other features, recognized the person from the body movement.

Things are not always what they seem. Although this picture suggests that the airplane is distorted, the phenomenon of *perceptual organization* tells us that this is not true. The mind interprets the cues and assumes that the airplane is intact. Perceptual organization helps people acquire an accurate picture of the world despite limited or inconsistent perceptual cues.

The most common form of perceptual organization is stereotyping. A **stereotype** is a widely held generalization about a group of people that assigns attributes to them solely on the basis of one or a few categories, such as age, race, or occupation. For example, young people may assume that older people are old-fashioned or conservative. Students may stereotype professors as absent-minded or as political liberals.

How do perceptual selectivity and organization affect manager behavior? Consider the following comment from Joe, a staff supervisor, on his expectations about the annual budget meeting with his boss, Charlie:

> About a month before the meetings are to begin, I find myself waking up around 4:00 a.m., thinking about Charlie and the arguments I'm going to have with him. I know he'll accuse me of trying to "pad" my requests and, in turn, I'll accuse him of failing to understand the nature of my department's needs. I'll be trying to anticipate every little snide remark he can generate and every argument that he's likely to propose, and I'll be getting ready with snide remarks and arguments of my own. This year, as always, I've got to be sure to get him before he gets me.[10]

Joe's selective perception will cause him to immediately recognize any cues that resemble snide remarks. He will also organize these remarks to fit his belief that Charlie's motivation is to reduce his budget. No matter what frame of mind Charlie brings to the communication, Joe is set to perceive in his own way, which will surely prevent open and honest communication.

Perceptual differences and perceptual mistakes also occur when people perceive simple objects in dissimilar ways. Typical examples are illustrated in Exhibit 15.2. In panel a, many people see a sad old woman, but others see a beautiful young lady with a large head covering. In panel b, the top airplane looks larger to most people because of perceptual organization. The background lines provide a frame of reference that distorts the actual size of the airplanes.

perception The process of making sense out of one's environment.

perceptual selectivity The screening and selection of objects and stimuli that compete for one's attention.

perceptual organization The categorization of an object or stimulus according to one's frame of reference.

stereotype A widely held generalization about a group of people that assigns attributes to them solely on the basis of a limited number of categories.

EXHIBIT 15.2
Perception: What Do You See?

(a)

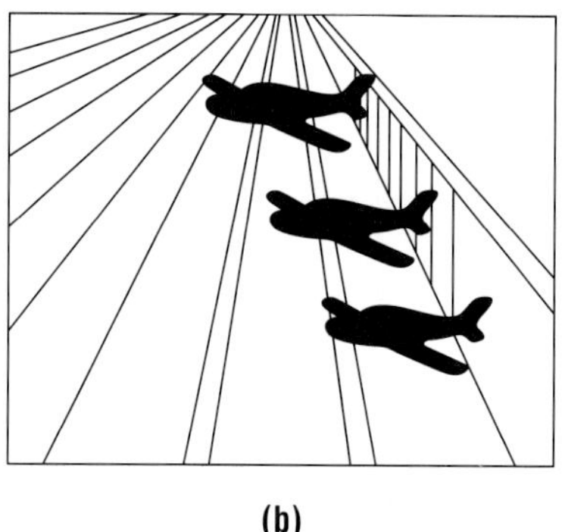

(b)

An important point for managers to understand is that perceptual differences are natural but can distort messages and create noise and interference for communications. Each person has a distinct personality and perceptual style, hence each interprets messages in a personal way. Managers should remember words can mean different things to different people and should not assume they already know what the other person or the communication is about.

COMMUNICATION CHANNELS

Managers have a choice of many channels through which to communicate to other managers or employees. A manager may discuss a problem face to face, use the telephone, write a memo or letter, or put an item in a newsletter, depending on the nature of the message. Recent research has attempted to explain how managers select communication channels to enhance communication effectiveness.[11] The research has found that channels differ in their capacity to convey information. Just as a pipeline's physical characteristics limit the kind and amount of liquid that can be pumped through it, a communication channel's physical characteristics limit the kind and amount of information that can be conveyed among managers. The channels available to managers can be classified into a hierarchy based on information richness. **Channel richness** is the amount of information that can be transmitted during a communication episode. The hierarchy of channel richness is illustrated in Exhibit 15.3.

channel richness The amount of information that can be transmitted during a communication episode.

The capacity of an information channel is influenced by three characteristics: (1) the ability to handle multiple cues simultaneously; (2) the ability to facilitate rapid, two-way feedback; and (3) the ability to establish a personal focus for the communication. Face-to-face discussion is the richest medium, because it permits direct experience, multiple information cues, immediate feedback, and personal focus. Face-to-face discussions facilitate the assimilation of broad cues and deep, emotional understanding of the situation. For example, Tony Burns, CEO of Rider Systems Inc. likes to handle things face to face: "You can look someone in the eyes, and you can tell by the look in his eyes or the inflection in his voice what the real problem or question or answer is."[12]

Exhibit 15.3
Hierarchy of Channel Richness and Application to Messages

Richest Channel ◄			► **Leanest Channel**
Physical presence (face to face talk)	Interactive channels (telephone, electronic media)	Personal static channels (memos, letters)	Impersonal static channels (fliers, bulletins, general reports)
Best for nonroutine, ambiguous, difficult messages ◄			► Best for routine, clear, simple messages

Telephone conversations and interactive electronic media, such as video conferencing and electronic mail, lack the element of "being there." Eye contact, gaze, blush, posture, and body language cues are eliminated. Written media that are personalized, such as memos, notes, and letters, can be personally focused, but they convey only the cues written on paper and are slow to provide feedback. Impersonal written media, including fliers, bulletins, and standard computer reports, are the lowest in richness. These channels are not focused on a single receiver, use limited information cues, and do not permit feedback.

Channel selection depends on whether the message is routine or nonroutine. *Nonroutine messages* typically are ambiguous, concern novel events, and impose great potential for misunderstanding. Nonroutine messages often are characterized by time pressure and surprise. Managers can communicate nonroutine messages effectively only by selecting rich channels. On the other hand, routine communications are simple and straightforward. *Routine messages* convey data or statistics or simply put into words what managers already agree on and understand. Routine messages can be efficiently communicated through a channel lower in richness. Written communications also should be used when the audience is widely dispersed or when the communication is "official" and a permanent record is required.[13]

Consider a CEO trying to work out a press release with public relations people about a plant explosion that injured 15 employees. If the press release must be ready in three hours, the communication is truly nonroutine and forces a rich information exchange. The group will meet face to face, brainstorm ideas, and provide rapid feedback to resolve disagreement and convey the correct information. If the CEO has three days to prepare the release, less information capacity is needed. The CEO and public relations people might begin developing the press release with an exchange of memos and telephone calls.

The key is to select a channel to fit the message. One successful manager who understood channel selection was Harold Geneen of ITT.

ITT • Harold Geneen was at the helm of ITT for 18 years. He strove to make ITT a unified organization despite its huge size. One of his first decisions was to create ITT-Europe, which would

Hewlett-Packard relies heavily on communication systems such as the in-house video teleconferencing facilities pictured here to meet the challenge of doing business on several continents. This *rich communication channel* lets employees worldwide reach mutual understanding of nonroutine issues such as new product designs, research lab activities, engineering modifications, and strategic plans.

serve as headquarters for European operations. ITT's strategy was to grow by acquisition, eventually increasing to more than 200 subsidiary companies around the world. One of Geneen's most difficult problems was how to get French, German, Italian, and American managers to go along with central decisions. Initial executive sessions sounded like a United Nations meeting. Gradually, Geneen solved the communication problem by relying on face-to-face channels:

> One of the first things I learned in those early days was that when I responded to a question or request from Europe while sitting in New York, my decision was often different from what it would have been had I been in Europe. In New York, I might read a request and say no. But in Europe, I could see the man's face, hear his voice, understand the intensity of his conviction, and the answer to the same question might be yes. So, early on, I decided that if I and my headquarters' team intended to monitor and oversee the European operations, I owed it to the European managers to be there on the spot. . . . It became our policy to deal with problems on the spot, face-to-face.[14]

Geneen discovered that the face-to-face channel was needed for handling difficult communications among managers from different countries. Thus, for 17 years Geneen and his senior staff went to Europe for one week every month to deal personally with the European managers' requests and needs. It worked: ITT went on to become one of the best-managed companies in the world.

Nonverbal Communication

nonverbal communication
A communication transmitted through actions and behaviors rather than through words.

Nonverbal communication refers to messages sent through human actions and behaviors rather than through words.[15] Although most nonverbal communication is unconscious or subconscious on our part, it represents a major portion of the messages we send and receive. Most managers are astonished to learn that words themselves carry little meaning. Major parts of the shared understanding from communication come from the nonverbal messages of facial expression, voice, mannerisms, posture, and dress.

Nonverbal communication occurs mostly face to face. One researcher found three sources of communication cues during face-to-face communication: the verbal, which are the actual spoken words; the vocal, which include the pitch, tone, and timber of a person's voice; and facial expressions. According to this study, the relative weights of these three factors in message interpretation are as follows: verbal impact, 7 percent; vocal impact, 38 percent; and facial impact, 55 percent.[16]

Can you tell what Mike Ditka, coach of the Chicago Bears, is feeling? *Nonverbal communication* refers to messages sent through human action and behavior and includes facial expression, poise, mannerisms, posture, and dress. Coach Ditka's body language indicates his frustration about the Bears' poor play much better than words could. Research on nonverbal communication suggests that body language communicates feelings quite accurately and accounts for 55 percent of message interpretation.

This research strongly implies that "it's not what you say, but how you say it." Nonverbal messages convey thoughts and feelings with greater force than do our most carefully selected words. Body language often communicates our real feelings eloquently. Thus, while the conscious mind may be formulating vocal messages such as "I'm happy" or "Congratulations on your promotion," the body language may be signaling true feelings through blushing, perspiring, glancing, crying, or avoiding eye contact. When the verbal and nonverbal messages are contradictory, the receiver may be confused and usually will give more weight to behavioral actions than to verbal messages.[17]

A manager's office also sends powerful nonverbal cues. For example, what do the following seating arrangements mean if used by your supervisor: (1) She stays behind her desk and you sit in a straight chair on the opposite side. (2) The two of you sit in straight chairs away from her desk, perhaps at a table. (3) The two of you sit in a seating arrangement consisting of a sofa and easy chair. To most people, the first arrangement indicates "I'm the boss here" or "I'm in authority." The second arrangement indicates "This is serious business." The third indicates a more casual and friendly, "Let's get to know each other."[18] Nonverbal messages can be a powerful asset to communication if they complement and support verbal messages. Managers should pay close attention to nonverbal behavior when communicating. They must learn to coordinate their verbal and nonverbal messages and at the same time be sensitive to what their peers, subordinates, and supervisors are saying nonverbally.

LISTENING

Managers who believe that giving orders is the important communication requirement are in for a surprise in the 1990s. The new skill is *listening*, both to customers and to employees. Most executives now believe that important information flows from the bottom up, not the top down, and managers had better be tuned in.[19] In the communication model in Exhibit 15.1, the listener is responsible for message reception, which is a vital link in the communication process. **Listening** involves the skill of receiving messages to accurately grasp facts and feelings to interpret the message's genuine meaning. Only then can the receiver provide the feedback with which to complete the communication circuit. Listening requires attention, energy, and skill.

listening The skill of receiving messages to accurately grasp facts and feelings to interpret the genuine meaning.

Many people do not listen effectively. They concentrate on formulating what they are going to say next rather than on what is being said to them. Our listening efficiency, as measured by the amount of material understood and remembered by subjects 48 hours after listening to a 10-minute message, is, on average, no better than 25 percent.[20]

EXHIBIT 15.4
Ten Keys to Effective Listening

Keys	Poor Listener	Good Listener
Listens actively	Passive, laid back	Asks questions, paraphrases what is said
Finds areas of interest	Tunes out dry subjects	Looks for opportunities, new learning
Resists distractions	Easily distracted	Fights or avoids distractions; tolerates bad habits; knows how to concentrate
Capitalizes on the fact that thought is faster than speech	Tends to daydream with slow speakers	Challenges, anticipates, mentally summarizes; weighs the evidence; listens between the lines to tone of voice
Is responsive	Little involvement	Nods; shows interest, give and take, positive feedback
Judges content, not delivery	Tunes out if delivery is poor	Judges content; skips over delivery errors
Holds one's fire	Preconceptions, starts to argue	Does not judge until comprehension is complete
Listens for ideas	Listens for facts	Listens for central themes
Works at listening	Shows no energy output; faked attention	Works hard, exhibits active body state, eye contact
Exercises one's mind	Resists difficult material in favor of light, recreational material	Uses heavier material as exercise for the mind

Source: Adapted from Sherman K. Okum, "How to Be a Better Listener," *Nation's Business* (August 1975), 62, and Philip Morgan and Kent Baker, "Building a Professional Image: Improving Listening Behavior," *Supervisory Management* (November 1985), 34–38.

What constitutes good listening? Exhibit 15.4 illustrates a number of ways to distinguish a bad from a good listener. A good listener finds areas of interest, is flexible, works hard at listening, and uses thought speed to mentally summarize, weigh, and anticipate what the speaker will say. Some companies, such as IBM and Delta, take listening very seriously. Managers know they are expected to *listen* to employees.

Norman Brinker, chairman of Chili's Inc., has a bedrock belief in listening. He says it is important to hear what employees have to say. They are not to be bullied. Tom Peters, the famous management author and consultant, says that executives can become good listeners by observing the following: Effective listening is engaged listening; ask dumb questions, break down barriers by participating with employees in casual get-togethers, force yourself to get out and about, provide listening forums, take notes, promise feedback — and deliver.[21] The Winning Moves box shows how Boise Cascade used listening as the foundation for a successful turnaround.

ORGANIZATIONAL COMMUNICATION

Another aspect of management communication concerns the organization as a whole. Organizationwide communications typically flow in three directions — downward, upward, and horizontally. Managers are responsible for establish-

WINNING MOVES

BOISE CASCADE MANAGERS LISTEN

In the southwestern Louisiana community of DeRidder, a Boise Cascade paper mill has transformed itself. Once a marginal operation, the DeRidder mill is now a jewel in the crown of Boise's network. By mid-1988, in just four years, a group of dedicated managers and staff had improved quality by 32 percent, increased productivity by 22 percent, and lowered costs by 22 percent. The mill also had won two awards for exceptional safety performance. The cornerstone of the DeRidder revitalization program has been good communication between management and staff.

Says Paul Parker, a veteran employee of the shipping department, "I used to hate to come to work, not because I didn't like my job but because of all the trouble we had here." Common problems included tension and infighting among departments, mistrust of management, minimal communication about key aspects of the mill's operation, and inconsistent management practices. Worst of all were supervisor–employee relations. Milton Cole, a supervisor since 1977, remembers, "In those days we were message carriers. A decision was made and we were told to carry the message. Employees asked a question and I had to tell them I'd get an answer from my boss." This style created an atmosphere of mistrust and low morale. Employees did what was required of them and no more.

Then, in 1982, Boise decided to bring in an entirely new management team. Headed by Dave Spence, they introduced a plan for managing that most employees today recognize as the key factor in the turnaround. The plan put emphasis on safety, listening, training, and employee involvement. Says Cole, Spence and his team began to push decisions down in the organization. Instead of carrying messages, I make the decisions I ought to be making and I allow my folks to make the decisions they ought to be making." For the first time, supervisors listened to employee ideas and worked with them to determine how their ideas could be implemented.

How did Spence accomplish this? One of the first things he did was to get DeRidder employees at all levels involved in listening sessions. "In those meetings," Spence says, "we talk about what employees want to talk about." Most importantly he notes, "If you tell people you want to hear what they have to say you'd better be ready to respond; you'd better be ready to do something about what they tell you." Since these meetings began in 1984, the focus on listening has spread throughout the mill. "Now," says supervisor Peter Pugh, "instead of fighting among ourselves, employees are working as a team to make a quality product in a safe manner."

The DeRidder management group believes that the actions that have grown out of people listening more to each other have driven the dramatic results in safety, quality, productivity, and costs. While many factors certainly play a role in any turnaround situation, the DeRidder story shows how healthy communication practices are essential to overall success.

Source: Andrew Drysdale, "Turnaround Time in the South," *Boise Cascade Insight,* November 1988, 1–4.

ing and maintaining formal channels of communication in these three directions. Managers also use informal channels, which means they get out of their offices and mingle with employees.

FORMAL COMMUNICATION CHANNELS

Formal communication channels are those that flow within the chain of command or task responsibility defined by the organization. The three formal channels and the types of information conveyed in each are illustrated in Exhibit 15.5.[22]

formal communication channel A communication channel that flows within the chain of command or task responsibility defined by the organization.

EXHIBIT 15.5
Downward, Upward, and Horizontal Communication in Organizations

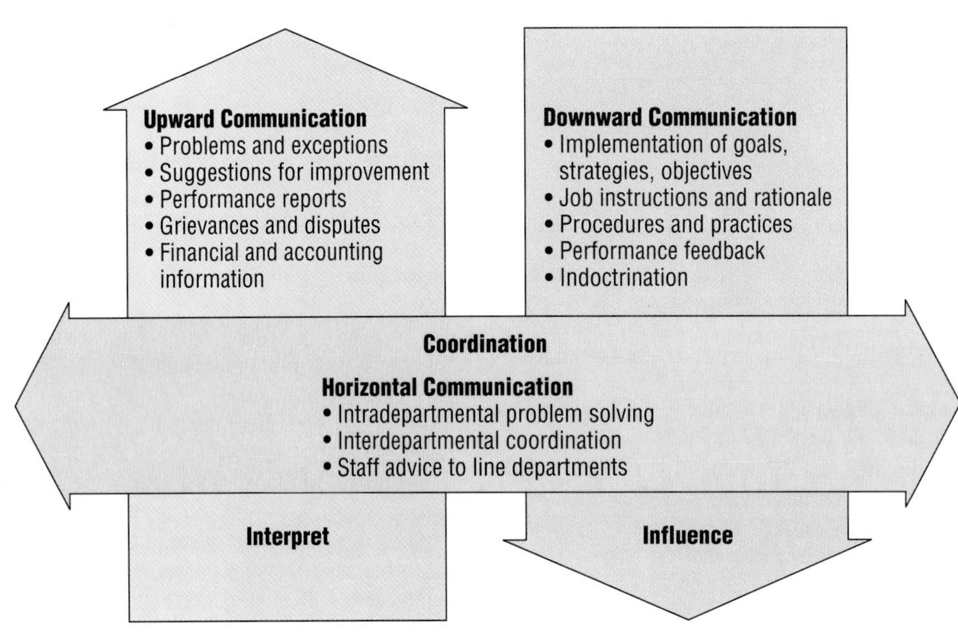

Source: Adapted from *Organizations: A Micro/Macro Approach* by Richard L. Daft and Richard M. Steers, p. 538. Copyright © 1986 by Scott, Foresman and Company. Used by permission.

downward communication Messages sent from top management down to subordinates.

DOWNWARD COMMUNICATION. The most familiar and obvious flow of formal communication, **downward communication,** is the messages and information sent from top management to subordinates in a downward direction. The president of Tenneco, for example, sends bulletins to his vice-presidents, who in turn send memos to their subordinates. Ronald Del Mauro, CEO of Saint Barnabas Medical Center in Livingston, New Jersey, launched a series of quarterly "state of the hospital" addresses to employees. Using astonishing candor, Del Mauro and other executives attract a standing-room-only audience to the Center's 500-seat auditorium.[23] Managers can communicate downward to employees through speeches, messages in company publications, information leaflets tucked into pay envelopes, material on bulletin boards, and policy and procedure manuals.

Downward communication in an organization usually encompasses the following topics:

1. *Implementation of goals, strategies, and objectives.* Communicating new strategies and goals provides information about specific targets and expected behaviors. It gives direction for lower levels of the organization. Example: "The new quality campaign is for real. We must improve product quality if we are to survive."

2. *Job instructions and rationale.* These are directives on how to do a specific task and how the job relates to other organizational activities. Example: "Purchasing should order the bricks now so the work crew can begin construction of the building in two weeks."
3. *Procedures and practices.* These are messages defining the organization's policies, rules, regulations, benefits, and structural arrangements. Example: "After your first 90 days of employment, you are eligible to enroll in our company-sponsored savings plan."
4. *Performance feedback.* These messages appraise how well individuals and departments are doing their jobs. Example: "Joe, your work on the computer network has greatly improved the efficiency of our ordering process."
5. *Indoctrination.* These messages are designed to motivate employees to adopt the company's mission and cultural values and to participate in special ceremonies, such as picnics and United Way campaigns. Example: "The company thinks of its employees as family and would like to invite everyone to attend the annual picnic and fair on March 3."

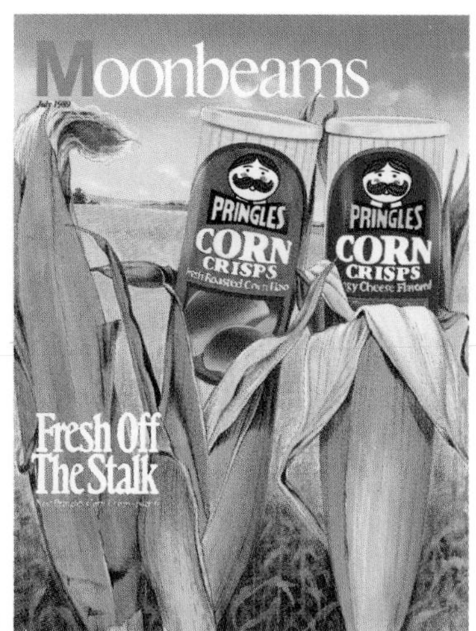

Moonbeams is the Proctor & Gamble employee magazine used to achieve *downward communication.* The magazine begins with the "CEO" column where the CEO shares his vision by interpreting company principles and showing how they guide top management thinking. Such topics have included current issues such as company restructuring, employee recruiting and career development, and improved manufacturing and distribution processes. The magazine also contains articles about employee achievements and awards, thereby signalling corporate values. *Moonbeams* provides a formal mechanism for strategy implementation, general performance feedback on company businesses, and broad-based company information sharing for P&G employees.

The major problem with downward communication is *drop off,* the distortion or loss of message content. Although formal downward communications are a powerful way to reach all employees, much information gets lost — 25 percent or so each time a message is passed from one person to the next. In addition, the message can be distorted if it travels a great distance from its originating source to the ultimate receiver. A tragic example is the following:

> A reporter was present at a hamlet burned down by the U.S. Army 1st Air Cavalry Division in 1967. Investigations showed that the order from the Division headquarters to the brigade was: "On no occasion must hamlets be burned down."
>
> The brigade radioed the battalion: "Do not burn down any hamlets unless you are absolutely convinced that the Viet Cong are in them."
>
> The battalion radioed the infantry company at the scene: "If you think there are any Viet Cong in the hamlet, burn it down."
>
> The company commander ordered his troops: "Burn down that hamlet."[24]

Information drop off cannot be completely avoided, but the techniques described in the previous sections can reduce it substantially. Using the right communication channel, consistency between verbal and nonverbal messages, active listening, and aligning messages with the perception of users can maintain communication accuracy as it moves down the organization.

UPWARD COMMUNICATION. Formal **upward communication** includes messages that flow from the lower to the higher levels in the organization's hierarchy. Most organizations take pains to build in healthy channels for upward communication. Employees need to air grievances, report progress, and provide feedback on management initiatives. Coupling a healthy flow of upward and downward communication ensures that the communication circuit between managers and employees is complete.[25] Five types of information communicated upward are:

upward communication
Messages transmitted from the lower to the higher level in the organization's hierarchy.

1. *Problems and exceptions.* These messages describe serious problems with and exceptions to routine performance in order to make senior managers aware of difficulties. Example: "The printer has been out of operation for two days, and it will be at least a week before a new one arrives."

The use of this all-terrain vehicle called the Marsh-Master resulted from effective *upward communication* at Florida Progress Corporation. Employee teams at the company's Florida Power electric utility, who have first-hand knowledge of work activities, identified areas for improvement and made recommendations to management. The Central Division Line team confronted the problem of reaching and servicing transmission lines in the wetlands of Florida Power's territory. The team researched and recommended the purchase of this vehicle, which is a cost-effective way to maintain rights-of-way while preserving the environment.

2. *Suggestions for improvement.* These messages are ideas for improving task-related procedures to increase quality or efficiency. Example: "I think we should eliminate step 2 in the audit procedure because it takes a lot of time and produces no results."
3. *Performance reports.* These messages include periodic reports that inform management how individuals and departments are performing. Example: "We completed the audit report for Smith & Smith on schedule but are one week behind on the Jackson report."
4. *Grievances and disputes.* These messages are employee complaints and conflicts that travel up the hierarchy for a hearing and possible resolution. Example: "The manager of operations research cannot get the cooperation of the Lincoln plant for the study of machine utilization."
5. *Financial and accounting information.* These messages pertain to costs, accounts receivable, sales volume, anticipated profits, return on investment, and other matters of interest to senior managers. Example: "Costs are 2 percent over budget, but sales are 10 percent ahead of target, so the profit picture for the third quarter is excellent."

Many organizations make a great effort to facilitate upward communication. Mechanisms include suggestion boxes, employee surveys, open-door policies, management information system reports, and face-to-face conversations between workers and executives. For example, Ronald Del Mauro of Saint Barnabas Medical Center introduced a series of monthly breakfast meetings between himself and employees. Long Island Lighting Company initiated a series of focus groups that provide employees an opportunity to comfortably express their deepest concerns about their jobs to upper managers. A group meets every six weeks and funnels information directly to senior managers.[26]

Despite these efforts, however, barriers to accurate upward communication exist. Managers may resist hearing about employee problems, or employees may not trust managers sufficiently to push information upward.[27] One of the most innovative ways to make sure information gets to top managers without distortion was developed by a small business, Smith & Hawken, a marketer of quality garden tools.

SMITH & HAWKEN

• Honest communication is so important that it is written down at Smith & Hawken. Cofounder Paul Hawken developed an upward communication technique called the "5-15 report," which requires no more than 15 minutes to write and 5 minutes to read. It is submitted every Friday by most employees to their supervisor. The report tells what the employee did, his or her morale, and at least one idea for improving the job. The owners get the reports of the department heads, who in turn receive reports from their people. The 5-15s are a powerful means of upward communication, knitting together the entire company.

Once a year, the 5-15s are suspended, and a new report is written by each person, called "Go for Broke." Each employee lists everything that is broken in his or her department or elsewhere in the company. Everything includes relationships as well as work procedures and facilities. In the past year, more than 1,000 changes were made based on the Go for Broke report, thoroughly improving the company.

These innovative upward-communication techniques put the responsibility for the company's success with employees, whom the owners trust completely. The top managers listen well and act on what they hear. At Smith & Hawken, upward communication really works.[28]

HORIZONTAL COMMUNICATION. **Horizontal communication** is the lateral or diagonal exchange of messages across peers or coworkers. It may occur within or across departments. The purpose of horizontal communication is not only to inform but also to request support and coordinate activities. Horizontal communication falls into one of three categories:

horizontal communication The lateral or diagonal exchange of messages across peers or coworkers.

1. *Intradepartmental problem solving.* These messages take place between members of the same department and concern task accomplishment. Example: "Betty, can you help us figure out how to complete this medical expense report form?"
2. *Interdepartmental coordination.* Interdepartmental messages facilitate the accomplishment of joint projects or tasks. Example: "Bob, please contact marketing and production and arrange a meeting to discuss the specifications for the new subassembly. It looks like we may not be able to meet their requirements."
3. *Staff advice to line departments.* These messages often go from specialists in operations research, finance, or computer services to line managers seeking help in these areas. Example: "Let's go talk to the manufacturing supervisor about the problem he's having interpreting the computer reports."

Recall from Chapters 9 and 10 that many organizations build in horizontal communications in the form of task forces, committees, or even a matrix structure to encourage coordination. For example, Carol Taber, publisher of *Working Woman,* was bothered by the separation of departments at her magazine. She instituted frequent meetings among department heads and a monthly report to keep everyone informed and involved on a horizontal basis.[29]

INFORMAL COMMUNICATION CHANNELS

Informal communication channels exist outside the formally authorized channels and do not adhere to the organization's hierarchy of authority. Informal communications coexist with formal communications but may skip hierarchical levels, cutting across vertical chains of command to connect virtually anyone in the organization. For example, Jim Treybig of Tandem Computers uses informal channels by letting any employee reach him through his computer terminal. Treybig also holds Friday afternoon beer busts at each of Tandem's 132 offices worldwide. The idea is to create an informal communication channel for employees. Treybig says, "Over beer and popcorn, employees are more willing to talk openly."[30] An illustration of both formal and informal communications is given in Exhibit 15.6. Note how formal communications can be vertical or horizontal depending on task assignments and coordination responsibilities.

informal communication channel A communication channel that exists outside formally authorized channels without regard for the organization's hierarchy of authority.

Two types of informal channels used in many organizations are "management by wandering around" and the "grapevine."

EXHIBIT 15.6
Formal and Informal Organizational Communication Channels

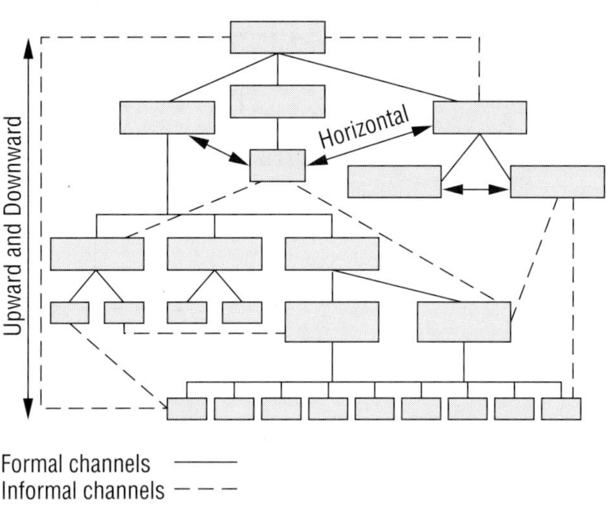

management by wandering around (MBWA) A communication technique in which managers interact directly with workers to exchange information.

MANAGEMENT BY WANDERING AROUND. The communication technique known as **management by wandering around (MBWA)** was made famous by the books *In Search of Excellence* and *A Passion for Excellence.*[31] These books describe executives who talk directly with employees to learn what is going on. MBWA works for managers at all levels. They mingle and develop positive relationships with employees, and learn directly from them about their department, division, or organization. For example, the president of ARCO had a habit of visiting a district field office. Rather than schedule a big strategic meeting with the district supervisor, he would come in unannounced and chat with the lowest-level employees. Andy Pearson of PepsiCo starts his tours from the bottom up: He goes directly to a junior assistant brand manager and asks, "What's up?" In any organization both upward and downward communication are enhanced with MBWA. Managers have a chance to describe key ideas and values to employees and in turn learn about the problems and issues confronting employees.

When managers fail to take advantage of MBWA, they become aloof and isolated from employees. For example, Peter Anderson, president of Ztel Inc., a maker of television switching systems, preferred not to personally communicate with employees. He managed at arm's length. As one manager said, "I don't know how many times I asked Peter to come to the lab, but he stayed in his office. He wasn't that visible to the troops." This formal management style contributed to Ztel's troubles and eventual bankruptcy.[32]

grapevine An informal, person-to-person communication network of employees that is not officially sanctioned by the organization.

THE GRAPEVINE. The **grapevine** is an informal, person-to-person communication network of employees that is not officially sanctioned by the organization.[33] The grapevine links employees in all directions, ranging from the president through middle management, support staff, and line employees. The grapevine will always exist in an organization, but it can become a dominant force when formal channels are closed. In such cases, the grapevine is actually

Management by wandering around is one of the most powerful communication devices available to executives. Here Chairman Charles Lazarus of Toys "R" Us pays serious attention to his expert consumer research. Lazarus, who founded the chain that now commands 25 percent of the $13 billion U.S. retail toy market, stays close to both employees and customers. It's risky to bet on kids' fantasies, but Toys "R" Us is the savviest trend-spotter in the industry. MBWA yields rich information about buyer preferences and trends. Effective companies like Toys "R" Us use informal communication channels to convey information.

a service because the information it provides helps make sense of an unclear or uncertain situation. Employees use grapevine rumors to fill in information gaps and clarify management decisions. The grapevine tends to be more active during periods of change, excitement, anxiety, and sagging economic conditions. For example, when Jel Inc., an auto supply firm, was under great pressure from Ford and GM to increase quality, rumors circulated on the shop floor about the company's possible demise. Management changes to improve quality — learning statistical process control, introducing a new compensation system, buying a fancy new screw machine from Germany — all started out as rumors, circulating days ahead of the actual announcements, and were generally accurate.[34]

Research suggests that a few people are primarily responsible for the grapevine's success. Exhibit 15.7 illustrates the two most typical grapevines.[35] In the *gossip chain*, a single individual conveys a piece of news to many other people. In a *cluster chain*, a few individuals each convey information to several others. Having only a few people conveying information may account for the accuracy of grapevines. If every person told one other person in sequence, distortions would be greater.

Surprising aspects of the grapevine are its accuracy and its relevance to the organization. About 80 percent of grapevine communications pertain to business-related topics rather than personal, vicious gossip. Moreover, from 70 to 90 percent of the details passed through a grapevine are accurate.[36] Many managers would like the grapevine to be destroyed because they consider its rumors to be untrue, malicious, and harmful to personnel. Typically this is not the case; however, managers should be aware that almost five of every six important messages are carried to some extent by the grapevine rather than through official channels. When official communication channels are closed, destructive rumors can occur.

EXHIBIT 15.7
Two Grapevine Chains in Organizations

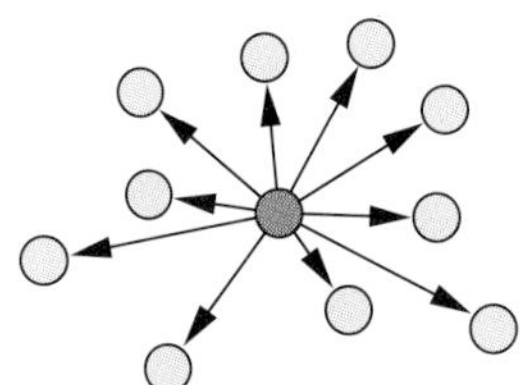

Gossip Chain
(One tells many)

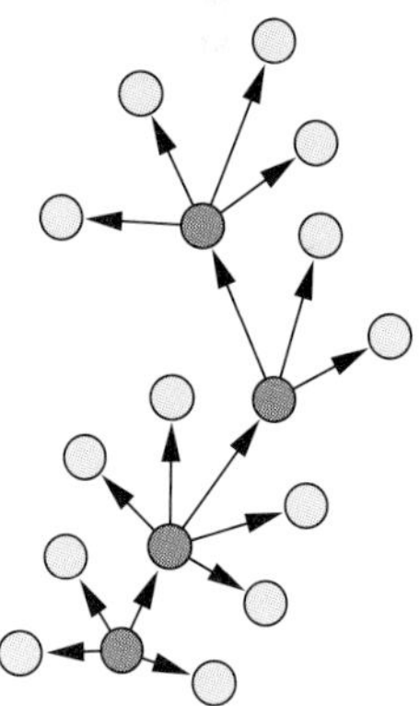

Cluster Chain
(A few tell selected others)

Source: Based on Keith Davis and John W. Newstrom, *Human Behavior at Work: Organizational Behavior*, 7th ed. (New York: McGraw-Hill, 1985).

EXHIBIT 15.8
Effectiveness of Team Communication Network

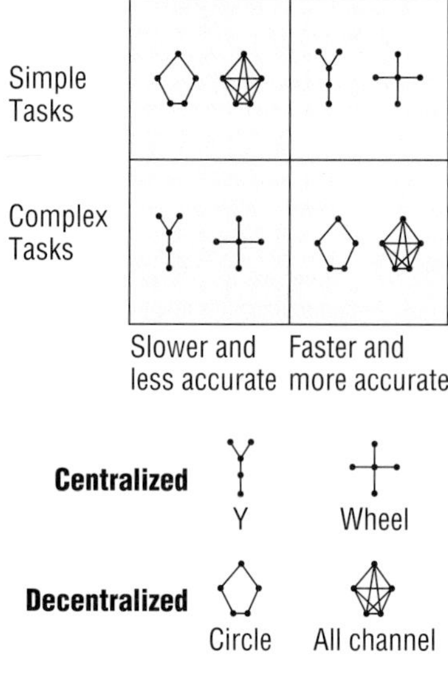

Source: Adapted from A. Bavelas and D. Barrett, "An Experimental Approach to Organization Communication," *Personnel* 27 (1951), pp. 366–371; M. E. Shaw, *Group Dynamics: The Psychology of Small Group Behavior* (New York: McGraw-Hill, 1976); E. M. Rogers and R. A. Rogers, *Communication in Organizations* (New York: Free Press, 1976).

COMMUNICATING IN TEAMS

The emphasis on teamwork in organizations, discussed in more detail in Chapter 16, emphasizes the need for team communication. Team members work together to accomplish tasks, and the team's communication structure influences both team performance and employee satisfaction. Research into team communication has focused on two characteristics: the extent to which team communications are centralized and the nature of the team's task.[37] The relationship between these characteristics is illustrated in Exhibit 15.8. In a **centralized network,** team members must communicate through one individual to solve problems or make decisions. In a **decentralized network,** individuals can communicate freely with other team members. Members process information equally among themselves until all agree on a decision.[38]

In laboratory experiments, centralized communication networks achieved faster solutions for simple problems. Members could simply pass relevant information to a central person for a decision. Decentralized communications were slower for simple problems because information was passed among individuals until someone finally put the pieces together and solved the problem. However, for more complex problems, the decentralized communication network was faster. Because all necessary information was not restricted to one person, a pooling of information through widespread communications provided greater input into the decision. Similarly, the accuracy of problem solving was related to problem complexity. The centralized networks made fewer errors on simple problems but more errors on complex ones. Decentralized networks were less accurate for simple problems but more accurate for complex ones.[39]

The implication for organizations is as follows: In a highly competitive global environment, organizations use groups and teams to deal with complex problems. When team activities are complex and difficult, all members should share information in a decentralized structure to solve problems. Teams need a free flow of communication in all directions.[40] Members should be encouraged to discuss problems with one another, and a large percentage of employee time should be devoted to information processing. However, groups who perform routine tasks spend less time processing information, and thus communications can be centralized. Data can be channeled to a supervisor for decisions, freeing workers to spend a greater percentage of time on task activities.

MANAGING ORGANIZATIONAL COMMUNICATION

centralized network A team communication structure in which team members communicate through a single individual to solve problems or make decisions.

decentralized network A team communication structure in which team members freely communicate with one another and arrive at decisions together.

Many of the ideas described in this chapter pertain to barriers to communication and how to overcome them. Barriers can be categorized as those that exist at the individual level and those that exist at the organizational level. First we will examine communication barriers; then we will look at techniques for overcoming them. These barriers and techniques are summarized in Exhibit 15.9.

BARRIERS TO COMMUNICATION

Barriers to communication can exist within the individual or as part of the organization.

Exhibit 15.9
Communication Barriers and Ways to Overcome Them

Barriers	How to Overcome
Individual	
1. Interpersonal dynamics	1. Active listening
2. Channels and media	2. Selection of appropriate channel
3. Semantics	3. Knowledge of other's perspective
4. Inconsistent cues	4. MBWA
Organizational	
1. Status and power differences	1. Climate of trust
2. Departmental needs and goals	2. Development and use of formal channels
3. Communication network unsuited to task	3. Encouragement of multiple channels, formal and informal
4. Lack of formal channels	4. Changing organization or group structure to fit communication needs

Individual Barriers. First, there are interpersonal barriers; these include problems with emotions and perceptions held by employees. For example, rigid perceptual labeling or categorizing of others prevents modification or alteration of opinions. If a person's mind is made up before the communication starts, communication will fail. Moreover, people with different backgrounds or knowledge may interpret a communication in different ways.

Second, selecting the wrong channel or medium for sending a communication can be a problem. For example, when a message is emotional, it is better to transmit it face to face rather than in writing. On the other hand, writing works best for routine messages but lacks the capacity for rapid feedback and multiple cues needed for difficult messages.

Third, semantics often causes communication problems. **Semantics** pertains to the meaning of words and the way they are used. A word such as "effectiveness" may mean achieving high production to a factory superintendent and employee satisfaction to a personnel staff specialist. Many common words have an average of 28 definitions; thus, communicators must take care to select the words that will accurately encode ideas.[41]

semantics The meaning of words and the way they are used.

Fourth, sending inconsistent cues between verbal and nonverbal communications will confuse the receiver. If one's facial expression does not match one's words, the communication will contain noise and uncertainty. The tone of voice and body language should be consistent with the words, and actions should not contradict words.

Organizational Barriers. Organizational barriers pertain to factors for the organization as a whole. First is the problem of status and power differences. Low-power people may be reluctant to pass bad news up the hierarchy, thus giving the wrong impression to upper levels.[42] High-power people may not pay attention or may feel that low-status people have little to contribute.

Second, differences across departments in terms of needs and goals interfere with communications. Each department perceives problems in its own terms. The production department is concerned with production efficiency and may not fully understand the marketing department's need to get the product to the customer in a hurry.

Over the years, managers at Ford Motor Company have worked hard to overcome organizational *barriers to communication*. Here Joe Kordick (right), head of the Parts and Service Division, gets input from employees over coffee on a regular basis. Supervisors and managers receive training in communicating with employees and building a culture of trust. Employee involvement encourages honest communication. Ford also uses a formal communication channel — the Ford Communications Network — which publishes an internal newspaper and operates a television system that delivers company and industry news in a timely fashion.

Third, the communication flow may not fit the group's or organization's task. If a centralized communication structure is used for nonroutine tasks, there will not be enough information circulated to solve problems. The organization, department, or group is most efficient when the amount of communication flowing among employees fits the task.

Fourth, the absence of formal channels reduces communication effectiveness. Organizations must provide adequate upward, downward, and horizontal communication in the form of employee surveys, open-door policies, newsletters, memos, task forces, and liaison personnel. Without these formal channels, the organization cannot communicate as a whole.

Overcoming Communication Barriers

Managers can design the organization so as to encourage positive, effective communication. Designing involves both individual skills and organizational actions.

Individual Skills. Perhaps the most important individual skill is active listening. Active listening means asking questions, showing interest, and occasionally paraphrasing what the speaker has said to ensure that one is interpreting accurately. Active listening also means providing feedback to the sender to complete the communication loop.

Second, individuals should select the appropriate channel for the message. A complicated message should be sent through a rich channel, such as face-to-face discussion or telephone. Routine messages and data can be sent through memos, letters, or electronic mail, because there is little chance of misunderstanding.

Third, senders and receivers should make a special effort to understand each other's perspective. Managers can sensitize themselves to the information receiver so that they will be better able to target the message, detect bias, and clarify missed interpretations. By understanding others' perspectives, semantics can be clarified, perceptions understood, and objectivity maintained.

The fourth individual skill is management by wandering around. Managers must be willing to get out of the office and check communications with others. For example, John McDonnell of McDonnell Douglas always eats in the employee cafeteria when he visits far-flung facilities. Through direct observation and face-to-face meetings, managers develop an understanding of the organization and are able to communicate important ideas and values directly to others.

ORGANIZATIONAL ACTIONS. Perhaps the most important thing managers can do for the organization is to create a climate of trust and openness. This will encourage people to communicate honestly with one another. Subordinates will feel free to transmit negative as well as positive messages without fear of retribution. Efforts to develop interpersonal skills among employees can be made to foster openness, honesty, and trust.

Second, managers should develop and use formal information channels in all directions. Scandinavian Design uses two newsletters to reach employees. GM's Packard Electric plant is designed to share all pertinent information — financial, future plans, quality, performance — with employees. Bank of America uses programs called "Innovate" and "Idea Tap" to get ideas and feedback from employees. Other techniques include direct mail, bulletin boards, and employee surveys.

Third, managers should encourage the use of multiple channels, including both formal and informal communications. Multiple communication channels include written directives, face-to-face discussions, MBWA, and the grapevine. For example, managers at GM's Packard Electric plant use multimedia, including a monthly newspaper, frequent meetings of employee teams, and an electronic news display in the cafeteria. Sending messages through multiple channels increases the likelihood that they will be properly received.

Fourth, the structure should fit communication needs. For example, Harrah's created a "Communication Team" as part of its structure at the Casino/Holiday Inn in Las Vegas. The team includes one member from each department. They deal with urgent company problems and help people think beyond the scope of their own departments to communicate with anyone and everyone to solve those problems. An organization can be designed to use teams, task forces, integrating managers, or a matrix structure as needed to facilitate the horizontal flow of information for coordination and problem solving. Structure should also reflect group information needs. Where group tasks are difficult, a decentralized structure should be implemented to encourage discussion and participation.

SUMMARY

This chapter described several important points about communicating in organizations. Communication takes up 80 percent of a manager's time. Communication is a process of encoding an idea into a message, which is sent through a channel and decoded by a receiver. Communication among people can be affected by perceptions, communication channels, nonverbal communication, and listening skills.

At the organizational level, managers are concerned with managing formal communications in a downward, upward, and horizontal direction. Informal communications also are important, especially management by wandering around and the grapevine. Moreover, research shows that communication structures in groups and departments should reflect the underlying tasks.

Finally, several barriers to communication were described. Individual barriers include interpersonal dynamics, the wrong communication channel, semantics, and inconsistent cues. Organizational barriers include status and power differences, different departmental needs, the wrong communication network, and lack of formal channels. These barriers can be overcome with elements such as active listening, selecting appropriate channels, MBWA, a climate of trust, use of formal channels, and designing the correct structure to fit communication needs.

Management Solution

Jaguar's quality problems were leading the company into bankruptcy despite having an attractive product with a venerable history. Led by president John Egan, communication was the key to a turnaround. To attack problems in production quality, senior executives met face to face with supervisors in task forces to discuss ways to reduce defects. Management also created a direct communication channel to employees — bypassing the union — by stopping the line each week to brief the troops. The most telling communication strategy was to record telephone conversations with several hundred buyers each month. Senior and middle managers listened to the intensity of customers' feelings about dirty waiting rooms, incompetent mechanics, indifferent dealers, and "service that stinks." Top management also sent an unambiguous message to dealers: "You'd better satisfy the customer, because we are not going to be content with anything else." Two years later, Jaguar made the biggest one-year leap in customer satisfaction in history: It moved into sixth place, between Honda and Mazda. Then Ford paid top dollar to acquire Jaguar, sensing an opportunity to greatly enhance its luxury car line.[43]

Discussion Questions

1. ATI Medical Inc. has a "no-memo" policy. The 300 employees must interact directly for all communications. What impact would this policy have on the organization?
2. Describe the elements of the communication process. Give an example of each part of the model as it exists in the classroom during communication between teacher and students.
3. How might perception influence communication accuracy? Is perception more important for ambiguous or unambiguous messages? Explain.
4. Should the grapevine be eliminated? How might managers control information that is processed through the grapevine?
5. What do you think are the major barriers to upward communication in organizations? Discuss.

6. What is the relationship between group communication and group task? For example, how should communications differ in a strategic planning group and a group of employees who stack shelves in a grocery store?
7. Some senior managers believe they should rely on written information and computer reports because these yield more accurate data than do face-to-face communications. Do you agree?
8. Why is management by wandering around considered effective communication? Consider channel richness and nonverbal communications in formulating your answer.
9. Is speaking accurately or listening actively the more important communication skill for managers? Discuss.
10. Assume you have been asked to design a training program to help managers become better communicators. What would you include in the program?

MANAGEMENT IN PRACTICE: EXPERIENTIAL EXERCISE

Listening Self-Inventory

INSTRUCTIONS: Go through the following questions, checking yes or no next to each question. Mark it as truthfully as you can in the light of your behavior in the last few meetings or gatherings you attended.

	Yes	No
1. I frequently attempt to listen to several conversations at the same time.	____	____
2. I like people to give me only the facts then let me make my own interpretation.	____	____
3. I sometimes pretend to pay attention to people.	____	____
4. I consider myself a good judge of nonverbal communications.	____	____
5. I usually know what another person is going to say before he or she says it.	____	____
6. I usually end conversations that don't interest me by diverting my attention from the speaker.	____	____
7. I frequently nod, frown, or whatever to let the speaker know how I feel about what he or she is saying.	____	____
8. I usually respond immediately when someone has finished talking.	____	____
9. I evaluate what is being said while it is being said.	____	____
10. I usually formulate a response while the other person is still talking.	____	____
11. The speaker's "delivery" style frequently keeps me from listening to content.	____	____
12. I usually ask people to clarify what they have said rather than guess at the meaning.	____	____
13. I make a concerted effort to understand other people's point of view.	____	____
14. I frequently hear what I expect to hear rather than what is said.	____	____
15. Most people feel that I have understood their point of view when we disagree.	____	____

The correct answers according to communication theory are as follows: No for questions 1, 2, 3, 5, 6, 7, 8, 9, 10, 11, 14. Yes for questions 4, 12, 13, 15. If you missed only one or two questions, you strongly approve of your own listening habits, and you are on the right track to becoming an effective listener in your role as manager. If you missed three or four questions, you have uncovered some doubts about your listening effectiveness, and your knowledge of how to listen has some gaps. If you missed five or more questions, you probably are not satisfied with the way you listen, and your friends and coworkers may not feel you are a good listener either. Work on improving your active listening skills.

Source: Ethel C. Glenn and Elliott A. Pood, "Listening Self-Inventory." Reprinted by permission of the publisher from *Supervisory Management* (January 1989), 12–15,

Cases for Analysis

ATLANTA TOOL AND DIE INC.

The president of Atlanta Tool and Die Inc., Rich Langston, wanted to facilitate upward communication. He believed an open-door policy was a good place to start. He announced that his own door was open to all employees and encouraged senior managers to do the same. He felt this would give him a way to get early warning signals that would not be filtered or redirected through the formal chain of command. Langston found that many employees who used the open-door policy had been with the company for years and were comfortable talking to the president. Sometimes messages came through about inadequate policies and procedures. Langston would raise these issues and explain any changes at the next senior managers' meeting.

The most difficult complaints to handle were those from people who were not getting along with their bosses. One employee, Leroy, complained bitterly that his manager had overcommitted the department and put everyone under too much pressure. Leroy argued that long hours and low morale were major problems. But he would not allow Rich Langston to bring the manager into the discussion nor to seek out other employees to confirm the complaint. Although Langston suspected that Leroy might be right, he could not let the matter sit and blurted out, "Have you considered leaving the company?" This made Leroy realize that a meeting with his immediate boss was unavoidable.

Before the three-party meeting, Langston contacted Leroy's manager and explained what was going on. He insisted that the manager come to the meeting willing to listen and without hostility toward Leroy. During the meeting, Leroy's manager listened actively and displayed no ill will. He learned the problem from Leroy's perspective and realized he was over his head in his new job. After the meeting, the manager said he was relieved. He had been promoted into the job from a technical position just a few months earlier and had no management or planning experience. He welcomed Rich Langston's offer to help him do a better job of planning.

Questions

1. What techniques increased Rich Langston's communication effectiveness? Discuss.
2. Do you think that an open-door policy was the right way to improve upward communications? What other techniques would you suggest?
3. What problems do you think an open-door policy creates? Do you think many employees are reluctant to use it? Why?

Source: Based on Everett T. Suters, "Hazards of an Open-Door Policy," *INC.*, January 1987, 99–102.

THE TRAVEL DEPARTMENT

Helen Wesley runs the travel department for a large Fortune 500 corporation. Helen is a devoted employee and prefers written communications because they are precise and accurate, which she feels is necessary for making travel arrangements. April Faulk is the new advertising department head. She has not had time to meet other department heads, but she travels extensively. April did not have the luxury of a travel department in her previous job, so she made all of her own flight and hotel reservations. When her bills arrived at accounting, they were forwarded to Helen for approval and explanation. Company policy states that travel requests are to be made in writing two weeks in advance and that all travel be scheduled through the travel department. Realizing that April had not read the travel policies given to her when she was hired, Helen wrote a terse memo: "I am enclosing another copy of the company's policy on travel. I'm sure this will help us handle your future travel needs more efficiently." Helen also sent a copy of the memo to April's boss.

For April's next trip, the travel department was contacted by her secretary, secured the best prices on air travel and hotels, and delivered the tickets to April's office. But on the morning of the trip, April's secretary called to request a different travel time, a different airline, a limo at the airport, and a different hotel. This caused last-minute work and doubled the price of the trip.

Helen asked one of her reservationists to talk to April's secretary and explain the policy again. This did little good. Last-minute requests from April's secretary continued to be phoned in, and written requests were incomplete and changed before the trip. Helen was truly upset about the complaints from her reservationists and the extra money these changes were costing the company.

Questions

1. What mistakes have Helen and April made with respect to their communications?
2. Are last-minute changes in travel arrangements to be expected in advertising work? If so, how might communications be structured differently between the advertising and travel departments?
3. If you were Helen, how would you handle this problem? Discuss.

Source: Based on "When a Peer Steps on Your Toes," *Savvy,* April 1986, 16–18.

CHAPTER 16

TEAMWORK IN ORGANIZATIONS

CHAPTER OUTLINE

LEARNING OBJECTIVES

After studying this chapter, you should be able to:

- Identify the types of teams in organizations.
- Discuss new applications of teams to facilitate employee involvement.
- Identify roles within teams and the type of role you could play to help a team be effective.
- Explain the general stages of team development.
- Explain the concepts of team cohesiveness and team norms and their relationship to team performance.
- Understand the causes of conflict within and among teams and how to reduce conflict.
- Discuss the assets and liabilities of organizational teams.

Management Problem

Tom Huber, president of Hearing Technology, Inc., founded his hearing-aid company to provide a flexible response to dealers. His six employees could provide a rapid three-day response to dealers for custom hearing aids. The sales, production, and credit people had the right attitude to make things happen. But when the company quickly grew to 80 employees, response times for orders stretched to eight days, enough to cause dealers to try other manufacturers. Moreover, dealers complained about the sluggish credit department, its poor coordination with production and sales, and the slowness with which suggestions were implemented. Huber tried to refocus everyone's efforts by one-on-one sessions and speeches, but sluggishness remained. Huber started to wonder if his company, at 80 employees, had grown so inflexible and unresponsive that it could not be competitive.[1]

What would you recommend to Tom Huber to recapture flexibility and responsiveness in his growing company? How might the formation of teams help solve this problem?

The problems facing a small business like Hearing Technology also confront large companies. How can they be more flexible and responsive in an increasingly competitive global environment? A quiet revolution is taking place in corporate America as more companies try using teams as a solution. The notion of teamwork is changing the look of organizations. Teams are replacing individuals as the basic building block of organizations. For example, the *Wall Street Journal* surveyed 200 Fortune 500 companies and found that teamwork was the most frequent topic to be taught in company training programs.[2] As another example, in an article called "The Team as Hero," the authors argue that

> If we are to compete in today's world, we must begin to celebrate collective entrepreneurship, endeavors in which the whole of the effort is greater than the sum of individual contributions. We need to honor our teams more, our aggressive leaders and maverick geniuses less.[3]

Teams are popping up in the most unexpected places. At AT&T, teams rather than individuals are used to create new telephones. Volvo uses teams of

Harvey Kinzelberg (center) and his *top management team* go overboard to pool their resources for strategic planning. Kinzelberg, chairman of the Meridian Group, an Illinois computer-leasing firm, leads his team of top managers in a five-day brainstorming session during which they scuba dive in pairs. Each executive is buddied at least once with every other executive during the five-day session, learning to depend on one another. This team-building exercise facilitates interaction to accomplish the team's strategic planning objective.

seven to ten hourly workers to assemble a complete car, abandoning the assembly line. Hecla Mining Company uses teams for company goal setting; a major telecommunications company uses teams of salespeople to deal with big customers with complex purchasing requirements; and Lassiter Middle School in Jefferson County, Kentucky, uses teams of teachers to prepare daily schedules and handle student discipline problems. Multinational corporations are now using international teams composed of managers from different countries. Ford uses teams to spot quality problems and improve efficiency, and other manufacturers use teams to master sophisticated new production technologies.[4] And as we saw in Chapter 7, teams are often used to make important decisions, and many organizations are now run by top management teams under the title of Office of the CEO.

As we will see in this chapter, teams have emerged as a powerful management tool, because they involve and empower employees. Teams can cut across organizations in unusual ways. Hence workers are more satisfied, and higher productivity and product quality typically result. Moreover, managers discover a more flexible organization where workers are not stuck in narrow jobs.

This chapter focuses on teams and their new applications within organizations. We will define various types of teams, explore their stages of development, and examine such characteristics as size, cohesiveness, and norms. We will discuss how individuals can make contributions to teams and review the benefits and costs associated with teamwork. Teams are an important aspect of organizational life, and the ability to manage them is an important component of manager and organization success.

TEAMS AT WORK

In this section, we will first define teams and then discuss a model of team effectiveness that summarizes important concepts.

EXHIBIT 16.1
Work Team Effectiveness Model

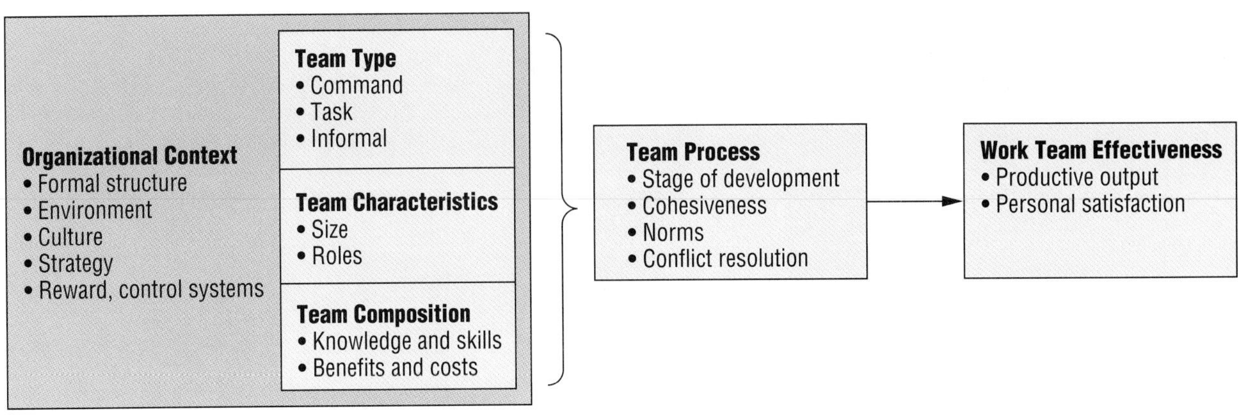

WHAT IS A TEAM?

A **team** is a unit of two or more people who interact and coordinate their work to accomplish a specific objective.[5] This definition has three components. First, two or more people are required. Teams can be quite large, running to as many as 75 people, although most have fewer than 15 people. Second, people in a team have regular interaction. People who do not interact, such as when standing in line at a lunch counter or riding in an elevator, do not comprise a team. Third, people in a team share a performance objective, whether it be to design a new type of hand calculator or write a textbook. Students often are assigned to teams to do classwork assignments, in which case the purpose is to perform the assignment and receive an acceptable grade. A "team" is similar to what is usually called a "group" in organizations, but "team" has become the popular word in the business community. The team concept implies a greater sense of mission and contest, although the words can be used interchangeably.

team A unit of two or more people who interact and coordinate their work to accomplish a specific objective.

MODEL OF WORK TEAM EFFECTIVENESS

Some of the factors associated with team effectiveness are illustrated in Exhibit 16.1. Work team effectiveness is based on two outcomes — productive output and personal satisfaction.[6] *Satisfaction* pertains to the team's ability to meet the personal needs of its members and hence maintain their membership and commitment. *Productive output* pertains to the quality and quantity of task outputs as defined by team goals.

The factors that influence team effectiveness begin with the organizational context.[7] The organizational context in which the group operates is described in other chapters and includes such factors as structure, strategy, environment, cultural, and reward systems. Within that context, managers define teams. Important team characteristics are the type of team, the team structure, and team composition. Managers must decide when to create permanent teams

EXHIBIT 16.2
Horizontal and Vertical Teams in an Organization

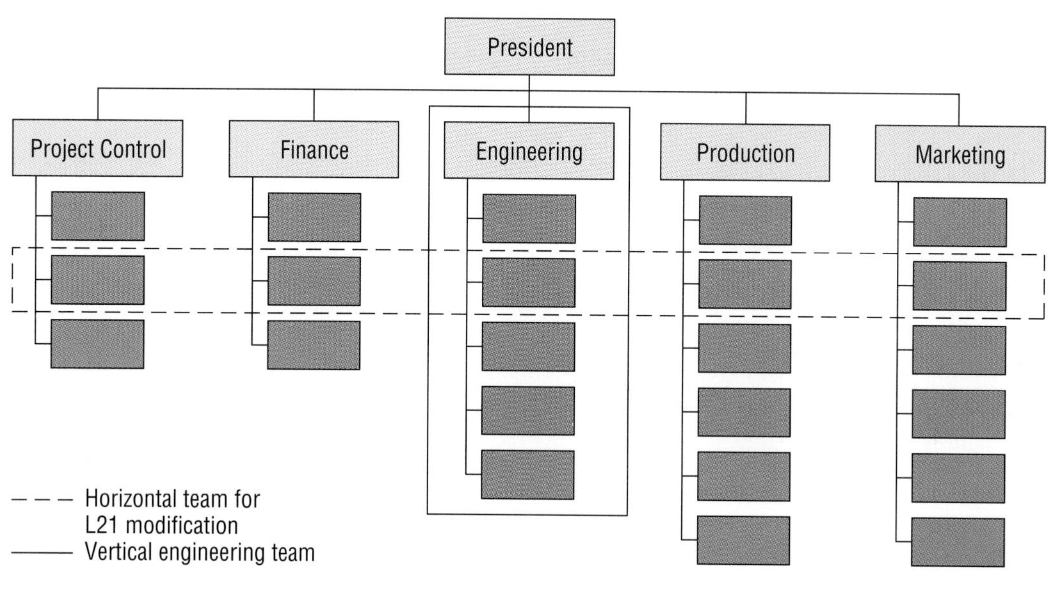

within the formal command structure and when to use a temporary task team. Team size and roles also are important. Managers must also consider whether a team is the best way to do a task. If costs outweigh benefits, managers may wish to assign an individual employee to the task.

These team characteristics influence processes internal to the team, which in turn affect output and satisfaction. Leaders must understand and manage stages of development, cohesiveness, norms, and conflict in order to establish an effective team. These processes are influenced by team and organizational characteristics and by the ability of members and leaders to direct these processes in a positive manner.

The model of team performance in Exhibit 16.1 is the basis for this chapter. In the following sections, we will examine types of organizational teams, team structure, internal processes, and team benefits and costs.

TYPES OF TEAMS

Many types of teams can exist within organizations. The easiest way to classify teams is in terms of those created as part of the organization's formal structure and those created to increase employee participation.

FORMAL TEAMS

formal team A team created by the organization as part of the formal organization structure.

Formal teams are created by the organization as part of the formal organization structure. Two common types of formal teams are vertical and horizontal, which typically represent vertical and horizontal structural relationships, as

Committees often are a permanent part of an organization's structure, and membership is usually based on organizational positions. J. P. Morgan's Credit Policy Committee meets weekly to review significant credit developments. The committee is responsible for seeing that credit quality is maintained and problems identified and dealt with immediately. Members include Morgan vice-presidents and senior vice-presidents.

described in Chapters 9 and 10. These two types of teams are illustrated in Exhibit 16.2. A third type of formal team is the special-purpose team.

A **vertical team** is composed of a manager and his or her subordinates in the formal chain of command. Sometimes called a *functional team* or a *command team,* the vertical team may in some cases include three or four levels of hierarchy within a functional department. Typically the vertical team includes a single department in an organization. The third-shift nursing team on the second floor of St. Luke's Hospital is a vertical team that includes nurses and a supervisor. A financial analysis department, a quality control department, an accounting department, and a personnel department are all command teams. Each is created by the organization to attain specific goals through members' joint activities and interactions.

A **horizontal team** is composed of employees from about the same hierarchical level but from different areas of expertise.[8] A horizontal team is drawn from several departments, given a specific task, and may be disbanded after the task is completed. The two most common types of horizontal teams are task forces and committees.

As described in Chapter 10, a *task force* is a group of employees from different departments formed to deal with a specific activity and existing only until the task is completed. Sometimes called a *cross-functional team,* the task force might be used to create a new product in a manufacturing organization or a new history curriculum in a university. Several departments are involved and many views have to be considered, so these tasks are best served with a horizontal team. IBM used a large task force to develop the System 360. Contact among team members was intense, and principal players met every day.

A **committee** is generally long-lived and may be a permanent part of the organizations' structure. Membership on a committee is usually decided by a person's title or position rather than by personal expertise. A committee often needs official representation, compared with selection for a task force, which is based on personal qualifications for solving a problem. Committees typically are formed to deal with tasks that recur regularly. For example, a grievance committee handles employee grievances; an advisory committee makes

vertical team A formal team composed of a manager and his or her subordinates in the organization's formal chain of command.

horizontal team A formal team composed of employees from about the same hierarchical level but from different areas of expertise.

committee A long-lasting, sometimes permanent team in the organization structure created to deal with tasks that recur regularly.

MANAGER'S SHOPTALK

HOW TO RUN A GREAT MEETING

Many executives believe that meetings are a waste of time. Busy executives may spend up to 70 percent of their time in meetings at which participants doodle, drink coffee, and think about what they could be doing back in their offices.

Meetings need not be unproductive. Most meetings are called to process important information or to solve a problem. The key to success is what the chairperson does. Most of the chairperson's contributions are made before the meeting begins. He or she should make sure discussion flows freely and follow up the meeting with agreed-upon actions. The success of a meeting depends on what is done in advance of, during, and after it.

Prepare in Advance. Advance preparation is the single most important tool for running an efficient, productive meeting. Advance preparation should include the following:

1. *Define the objective.* Is the objective to communicate critical information? To discuss a difficult problem? To reach a final decision? If the purpose of the meeting is to "discuss the reduction of the 1989 research and development budget," then say so explicitly in the memo sent out to members.
2. *Circulate background papers.* Any reading materials relevant to the discussion should be given to each member in advance. These can be circulated with the agenda or with the minutes of the previous meeting. Members as well as the chairperson must be prepared, so make sure members know their assignments and have background materials.
3. *Prepare an agenda.* The agenda is a simple list of the topics to be discussed. It's important because it keeps the meeting on track. The agenda provides order and logic and gives the chairperson a means of control during the meeting if the discussion starts to wander.
4. *Issue invitations selectively.* If the group gets too big, the meeting won't be productive. If members with little to learn or contribute are invited, they will be bored. If everyone is expected to participate, membership between four and seven is ideal. Twelve is the outside limit; above twelve, many people will just sit and listen.
5. *Set a time limit.* A formal meeting should have a specified amount of time. The ending time should be announced in advance, and the agenda should require the meeting to move along at a reasonable pace. Unexpected issues can be handled if they will take little time; otherwise, they should be postponed until another meeting.

During the Meeting. If the chairperson is prepared in advance, the meeting will go smoothly. Moreover, certain techniques will bring out the best in people and make the meeting even more productive:

6. *Start on time.* This sounds obvious — but do not keep busy people waiting. Some companies have a norm of waiting five minutes for everyone to arrive and then beginning the meeting even if some people are absent. Starting on time also has symbolic value, because it tells people that the topic is important.
7. *State the purpose.* The chairperson should start the meeting by stating the

recommendations in the areas of employee compensation and work practices; a worker-management committee may be concerned with work rules, job design changes, and suggestions for work improvement.[9]

As part of the horizontal structure of the organization, task forces and committees offer several advantages: (1) They allow organization members to exchange information; (2) they generate suggestions for coordinating the organizational units that are represented; (3) they develop new ideas and solutions for existing organizational problems; and (4) they assist in the development of new organizational practices and policies.

special-purpose team A team created outside the formal organization to undertake a project of special importance or creativity.

Special-purpose teams are created outside the formal organization structure to undertake a project of special importance or creativity. The new-venture team described in Chapter 11 for creating new products such as the IBM PC is an example of a special-purpose team. McDonald's created a special team to create the Chicken McNugget. E. J. (Bud) Sweeney was asked to head up a team to bring bits of batter-covered chicken to the marketplace. The McNugget team needed breathing room and was separated from the formal explicit purpose and clarifying what should be accomplished by the time the meeting is over. Members should already know the purpose, but this restatement helps refocus everyone's attention on the matter at hand.

8. *Encourage participation.* Good meetings contain lots of discussion. If the chairperson merely wants to present one-way information to members, he or she should send a memo. A few subtle techniques go a long way toward increasing participation:

a. *Draw out the silent.* This means saying "Bob, what do you think of Nancy's idea?"

b. *Control the talkative.* Some people overdo it and dominate the discussion. The chairperson's job is to redirect the discussion toward other people. This is more effectively done by drawing other people into the discussion than by trying to quiet the talkative people.

c. *Encourage the clash of ideas.* A good meeting is not a series of dialogues but a cross-current of discussion and debate. The chairperson guides, mediates, stimulates, and summarizes this discussion. Many effective chairpeople refuse to participate in the debate, preferring to orchestrate it instead.

d. *Call on the most senior people last.* Sometimes junior people are reluctant to disagree with senior people, so it is best to get the junior people's ideas on the table first. This will provide wider views and ideas.

e. *Give credit.* Make sure that people who suggest ideas get the credit, because people often make someone else's ideas their own. Giving due credit encourages continued participation.

f. *Listen.* The chairperson should not preach or engage in one-on-one dialogue with group members. The point is to listen and to facilitate discussion. If the chairperson really listens, he or she will be able to lead the meeting to a timely conclusion and summarize what has been accomplished.

After the Meeting. The actions following the meeting are designed to summarize and implement agreed-upon points. Post-meeting activities are set in motion by a call to action.

9. *End with a call to action.* The last item of the meeting's agenda is to summarize the main points and make sure everyone understands his or her assignments. Deadlines should be prescribed. The chairperson should also commit to sending out minutes, organizing the next meeting, and mailing other materials that participants may need.

10. *Follow-up.* Mail minutes of the meeting to members. Use this memorandum to summarize the key accomplishments of the meeting, suggest schedules for agreed-upon activities, and start the ball rolling in preparation for the next meeting.

Source: Based on Edward Michaels, "Business Meetings," *Small Business Reports* (February 1989), 82–88; Daniel Stoffman, "Waking Up to Great Meetings," *Canadian Business,* November 1986, 75–79; Antoney Jay, "How to Run a Meeting," *Harvard Business Review* (March/April 1976), 120–134.

corporate structure to give it the autonomy to perform successfully. A special-purpose team is still part of the formal organization and has its own reporting structure, but members perceive themselves as a separate entity.[10]

The formal teams described above must be skillfully managed to accomplish their purpose. One important skill, knowing how to run a team meeting, is described in the Manager's Shoptalk box.

Employee Involvement Teams

Employee involvement (EI) teams are designed to increase the participation of lower-level workers in decision making and the conduct of their jobs, with the goal of improving performance. Employee involvement teams represent a revolution in business prompted by the success of teamwork in Japanese companies. Hundreds of companies, large and small, are jumping aboard the EI bandwagon, including Boeing, Caterpillar, LTV Steel, Cummins Engine,

employee involvement team
A team designed to increase the participation of lower-level workers in decision making and the conduct of their jobs in order to improve performance.

FOCUS ON ENTREPRENEURSHIP

TEAMWORK AT WHOLE FOODS MARKET

Why would a wealthy Houston lawyer and his wife drive out of their way on a Sunday morning to shop at John Mackey's Whole Foods Market? Like many people, they have discovered that despite the higher prices, they prefer the quality and healthfulness of the foods his store offers. They recognize that the service is outstanding too. Mackey's first store started with a mission to get people to eat in a more healthy way. Now he has six stores throughout Texas and California as well as his own wholesale network that purchases produce. In 1989, the company brought in an estimated $45 million.

A typical Whole Foods Market can be 20,000 square feet and carry over 10,000 items. While many customers start out shopping at Whole Foods for gourmet products such as balsamic vinegar or radicchio, Mackey believes that they return because they become interested in healthier eating. In fact, the stores are geared toward providing educational information about the products. Organic produce is clearly marked, as are high fiber, low sodium, and low fat items. Each store has an information booth and clerks frequently lead shoppers on a tour of the store. A monthly newsletter keeps patrons up to date on new products. Mackey attributes a large measure of his success to the spirit of teamwork that is found throughout the organization.

John Mackey compares his Austin-based company to the United Federation of Planets in *Star Trek*. He uses this analogy because the key to his management style is teams. Each store department such as dairy, meats, or produce, has its own team of workers. Unlike the centralized buying of big food chains, each team at Whole Foods makes its own purchasing decisions. Mackey's belief is that team members will know their own customers best. He awards the team a bonus based on their gross margin so they have an incentive to purchase exactly the right amount of stock. To boost productivity, he sets a labor budget for each team but allows members to keep any savings as an additional bonus. While this scheme does not save wages, it does save on benefits that would be paid to additional workers and encourages strong team unity. Teams are even responsible for voting on whether a new employee may stay on the job after a six-week probation period.

Mackey's team system motivates employees to feel good about their work, serve their customers well, and help bring in profits. Some may balk when he says, "We're trying to build a company on trust and love," but as a successful entrepreneur with plans to keep growing, he has created the organization to do it.

Source: Based on Toni March, "Good Food, Great Margins," *Forbes*, October 17, 1988, 112–115.

and Tektronix. The two major types of EI teams in use are problem-solving teams and self-managing teams.[11]

problem-solving team Typically 5 to 12 hourly employees from the same department who meet to discuss ways of improving quality, efficiency, and the work environment.

Problem-solving teams typically consist of 5 to 12 volunteer hourly employees from the same department who meet two hours a week to discuss ways of improving quality, efficiency, and the work environment. Recommendations are proposed to management for approval. Problem-solving teams are usually the first step in a company's move toward greater employee participation. The most widely known application is quality circles, initiated by the Japanese, in which employees focus on ways to improve quality in the production process. USX has adopted this approach in several of its steel mills, recognizing that quality takes a team effort. Under the title All Product Excellence Program (APEX), USX has set up 40 APEX teams of up to 12 employees at its plant in West Mifflin, Pennsylvania. These teams meet several times a month to solve quality problems. The APEX teams have since spread to mills in Indiana, Ohio, and California.[12]

As a company matures, problem-solving teams can gradually evolve into self-managing teams, which represent a fundamental change in how employee work is organized. **Self-managing teams** consist of 5 to 12 multiskilled workers who rotate jobs and produce an entire product or service, and who take over managerial duties such as work and vacation scheduling, ordering materials, and hiring new members. Self-managing teams work with minimal supervision, often electing one of their own as supervisor, who may change each year. The Focus on Entrepreneurship box provides an example of a small company that successfully uses the concepts of self-managing teams.

self-managing team A team consisting of 5 to 12 multiskilled workers who rotate jobs to produce an entire product or service and perform managerial duties, often supervised by an elected member.

AT&T Credit Corporation set up teams of 10 to 15 new workers that are responsible for dealing with all customer requests. The credit teams establish a personal relationship with AT&T salespeople and customers and take responsibility for solving customers' problems. The teams are largely self-managing, making their own decisions about how to deal with customers, schedule their time off, reassign work when people are absent, and interview prospective employees. The result is that teams process up to 800 credit applications a day versus 400 previously, and they often reach a final answer within 24 hours, compared with several days previously.[13]

Giant corporations such as General Motors are trying to integrate team approaches into their production plants. When designing the new Saturn automobile, General Motors had a blank slate to design the plant structure as it wished and gave high priority to teams.

GM's Saturn Plant • In General Motors' new Saturn facility in Tennessee, work teams are being trained to operate without foremen. Teams are created at all levels to replace the old hierarchy of bosses. Higher-level teams consist of representatives from management and the union. Managers ask for union approval on all decisions. In its old-style assembly plants, GM had six levels of authority, from the plant manager down to the foremen. There were 90 foremen per shift, each responsible for several workers.

The new structure has four rather than six levels, as illustrated in Exhibit 16.3. At the bottom is the Work Unit of from 6 to 15 workers led by an elected counselor. No manager is assigned. The team decides who does which job. It is almost self-sufficient, because the team maintains equipment, orders supplies, and sets vacation schedules. It has a personal computer with which to keep tabs on production schedules and freight deliveries.

Management input comes at the next level up, which is called the Work Unit Module. Each consists of three to six work units and a management advisor. The advisor acts as a liaison to technical experts in engineering and personnel. The next level up is the Business Unit, which includes the plant manager, union representatives, and staff specialists. A fourth group, called the Manufacturing Advisory Committee, is responsible for the entire Saturn complex. It consists of UAW representatives, company officials, and staff specialists from the business units. This committee reaches consensus on decisions relevant to all Saturn employees, such as changes in salaries and benefits.

The new structure is a dramatic change in the direction of employee involvement. To get a job in this plant, people are interviewed by teams of workers. The workers must feel the right chemistry and see that candidates

EXHIBIT 16.3
Team Structure at GM's Saturn Plant

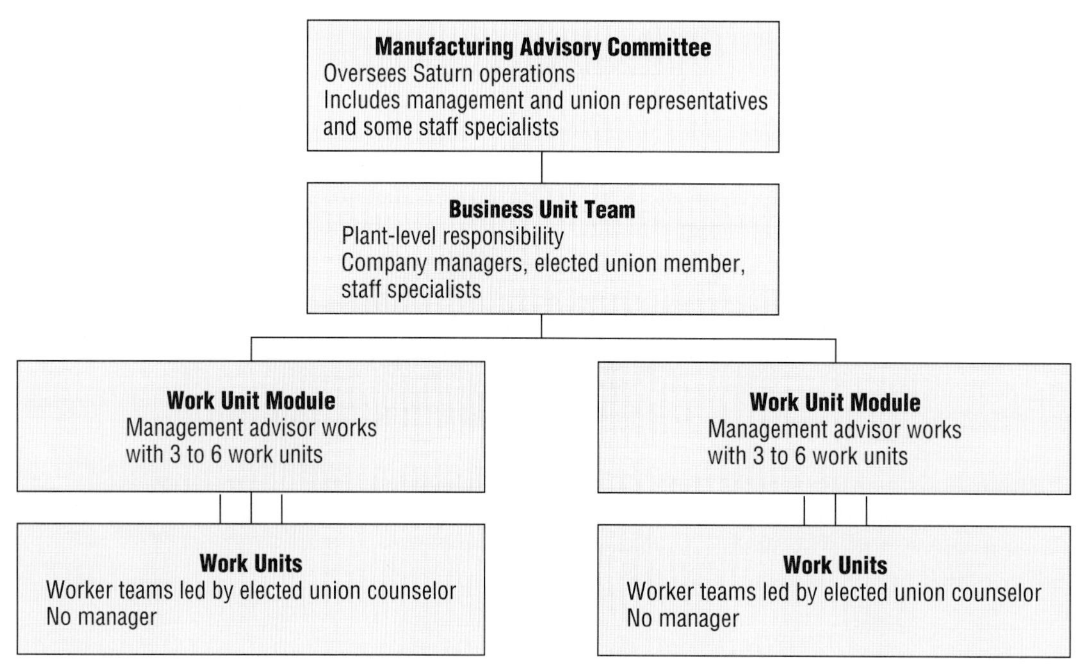

have skills relevant to the group's requirements. Everything is structured around teams, and although this involves risks, GM managers feel it is worth it.[14]

WORK TEAM CHARACTERISTICS

Teams in organizations take on characteristics that are important to internal processes and team performance. Two characteristics of concern to managers are team size and member roles.

SIZE

The ideal size of work teams is often thought to be 7, although variations of from 5 to 12 are typically associated with good team performance. These teams are large enough to take advantage of diverse skills, enable members to express good and bad feelings, and aggressively solve problems. They are also small enough to permit members to feel an intimate part of the group.

In general, as a team increases in size it becomes harder for each member to interact with and influence the others. A summary of research on group size suggests the following:

Teamwork is a way of life at MagneTek. Opportunity teams abound with increasing numbers of people participating as team leaders or members. As each team completes its task, it is immediately disbanded. So important is the team concept that supervisors participate in a coaching skills program, shown here. The program teaches team leaders how to be better communicators and how to help team members adopt roles to meet the team's *task* and *socioemotional* needs.

1. Small teams (two to four members) show more agreement, ask more questions, and exchange more opinions. Members want to get along with one another. Small teams report more satisfaction and enter into more personal discussions. They tend to be informal and make few demands on team leaders.
2. Large teams (12 or more) tend to have more disagreements and differences of opinion. Subgroups often form, and conflicts among them occur. Demands on leaders are greater because there is more centralized decision making and less member participation. Large teams also tend to be less friendly. Turnover and absenteeism are higher in a large team, especially for blue-collar workers. Because less satisfaction is associated with specialized tasks and poor communication, team members have fewer opportunities to participate and feel an intimate part of the group.[15]

As a general rule, large teams make need satisfaction for individuals more difficult; thus, there is less reason for people to remain committed to its goals. Teams of from 5 to 12 seem to work best. If a team grows larger than 20, managers should divide it into subgroups, each with its own members and goals.

Member Roles

For a team to be successful over the long run, it must be structured so as to both maintain its members' social well-being and accomplish the team's task. In successful teams, the requirements for task performance and social satisfaction are met by the emergence of two types of roles: task specialist and socioemotional.[16]

People who play the **task specialist role** spend time and energy helping the team reach its goal. They often display the following behaviors:

task specialist role A role in which the individual devotes personal time and energy to helping the team accomplish its task.

- *Initiation:* Propose new solutions to team problems.
- *Give opinions:* Offer opinions on task solutions; give candid feedback on others' suggestions.

EXHIBIT 16.4
Team Member Roles

Member Task Behavior	Low Member Social Behavior	High Member Social Behavior
High	**Task Specialist Role** Focuses on task accomplishment over human needs Important role, but if adopted by everyone, team's social needs won't be met	**Dual Role** Focuses on task and people May be a team leader Important role, but not essential if members adopt task specialist and socioemotional roles
Low	**Nonparticipator Role** Contributes little to either task or people needs of team Not an important role—if adopted by too many members, team will disband	**Socioemotional Role** Focuses on people needs of team over task Important role, but if adopted by everyone, team's task won't be accomplished

- *Seek information:* Ask for task-relevant facts.
- *Summarize:* Relate various ideas to the problem at hand; pull ideas together into a summary perspective.
- *Energize:* Stimulate the team into action when interest drops.[17]

socioemotional role A role in which the individual provides support for team members' emotional needs and social unity.

People who adopt a **socioemotional role** support team members' emotional needs and help strengthen the social entity. They display the following behaviors:

- *Encourage:* Are warm and receptive to others' ideas; praise and encourage others to draw forth their contributions.
- *Harmonize:* Reconcile group conflicts; help disagreeing parties reach agreement.
- *Reduce tension:* May tell jokes or in other ways draw off emotions when group atmosphere is tense.
- *Follow:* Go along with the team; agree to other team members' ideas.
- *Compromise:* Will shift own opinions to maintain team harmony.[18]

Exhibit 16.4 illustrates task specialist and socioemotional roles in teams. When most individuals in a team play a social role, the team is socially oriented. Members do not criticize or disagree with one another and do not forcefully offer opinions or try to accomplish team tasks, because their primary interest is to keep the team happy. Teams with mostly socioemotional roles can be very satisfying, but they also can be unproductive. At the other extreme, a team made up primarily of task specialists will tend to have a singular concern for task accomplishment. This team will be effective for a short period of time but will not be satisfying for members over the long run. Task specialists convey little emotional concern for one another, are unsupportive, and ignore team members' social and emotional needs. The task-oriented team can be humorless and unsatisfying.

As seen in Exhibit 16.4, some team members may play a dual role. People with **dual roles** both contribute to the task and meet members' emotional needs. Such people may become team leaders because they satisfy both types of needs and are looked up to by other members. Exhibit 16.4 also shows the final type of role, called the nonparticipator role. People in the **nonparticipator role** contribute little to either the task or the social needs of team members. They typically are held in low esteem by the team.

The important thing for managers to remember is that effective teams must have people in both task specialist and socioemotional roles. Humor and social concern are as important to team effectiveness as are facts and problem solving. Managers also should remember that some people perform better in one type of role; some are inclined toward social concerns and others toward task concerns. A well-balanced team will do best over the long term because it will be personally satisfying for team members and permit the accomplishment of team tasks.

dual role A role in which the individual both contributes to the team's task and supports members' emotional needs.

nonparticipator role A role in which the individual contributes little to either the task or members' socioemotional needs.

forming The stage of team development characterized by orientation and acquaintance.

TEAM PROCESSES

Now we turn our attention to internal team processes. Team processes pertain to those dynamics that change over time and can be influenced by team leaders. In this section, we will discuss the team processes of stages of development, cohesiveness, and norms. The fourth type of team process, conflict, will be covered in the next section.

STAGES OF TEAM DEVELOPMENT

After a team has been created, there are distinct stages through which it develops.[19] New teams are different from mature teams. Recall a time when you were a member of a new team, such as a fraternity or sorority pledge class, a committee, or a small team formed to do a class assignment. Over time the team changed. In the beginning, team members had to get to know one another, establish roles and norms, divide the labor, and clarify the team's task. In this way, members became parts of a smoothly operating team. The challenge for leaders is to understand the stage of the team's development and take action that will help the group improve its functioning.

Research findings suggest that team development is not random but evolves over definitive stages. Although several models describing these stages exist, one useful model is shown in Exhibit 16.5. The five stages typically occur in sequence. In teams that are under time pressure or that will exist for only a few days, the stages may occur rapidly. Each stage confronts team leaders and members with unique problems and challenges.[20]

FORMING. The **forming** stage of development is a period of orientation and getting acquainted. Members break the ice and test one another for friendship possibilities and task orientation. Team members find which behaviors are acceptable to others. Uncertainty is high during this stage, and members usually accept whatever power or authority is offered by either formal or informal leaders. Members are dependent on the team until they find out what the

EXHIBIT 16.5
Five Stages of Team Development

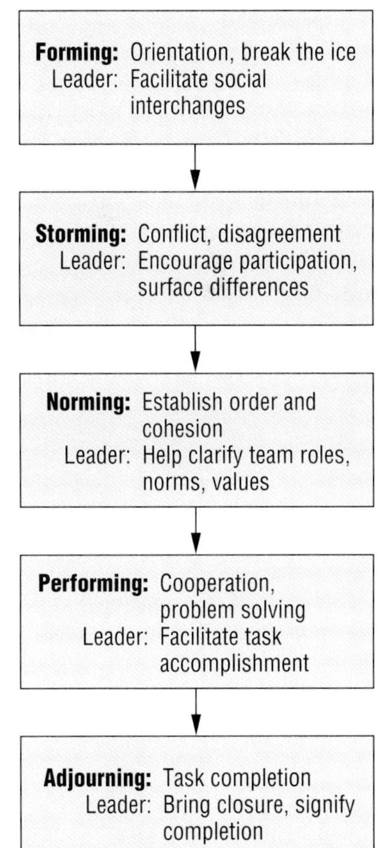
Forming: Orientation, break the ice
Leader: Facilitate social interchanges
Storming: Conflict, disagreement
Leader: Encourage participation, surface differences
Norming: Establish order and cohesion
Leader: Help clarify team roles, norms, values
Performing: Cooperation, problem solving
Leader: Facilitate task accomplishment
Adjourning: Task completion
Leader: Bring closure, signify completion

ground rules are and what is expected of them. During this initial stage, members are concerned about such things as "What is expected of me?" "What is acceptable?" "Will I fit in?" During the forming stage, the team leader should provide time for members to get acquainted with one another and encourage them to engage in informal social discussions.

storming The stage of team development in which individual personalities and roles, and resulting conflicts, emerge.

STORMING. During the **storming** stage, individual personalities emerge. People become more assertive in clarifying their roles and what is expected of them. This stage is marked by conflict and disagreement. People may disagree over their perceptions of the team's mission. Members may jockey for positions, and coalitions or subgroups based on common interests may form. One subgroup may disagree with another over the total team's goals or how to achieve them. The team is not yet cohesive and may be characterized by a general lack of unity. Unless teams can successfully move beyond this stage, they may get bogged down and never be high performing. During the storming stage, the team leader should encourage participation by each team member. Members should propose ideas, disagree with one another, and work through the uncertainties and conflicting perceptions about team tasks and goals.

norming The stage of team development in which conflicts developed during the storming stage are resolved and team harmony and unity emerge.

NORMING. During the **norming** stage, conflict is resolved and team harmony and unity emerge. Consensus develops on who has the power, who is the leader, and members' roles. Members come to accept and understand one another. Differences are resolved, and members develop a sense of team cohesion. This stage typically is of short duration. During the norming stage, the team leader should emphasize oneness within the team and help clarify team norms and values.

PERFORMING. During the **performing** stage, the major emphasis is on problem solving and accomplishing the assigned task. Members are committed to the team's mission. They are coordinated with one another and handle disagreements in a mature way. They confront and resolve problems in the interest of task accomplishment. They interact frequently and direct discussion and influence toward achieving team goals. During this stage, the leader should concentrate on managing high task performance. Both socioemotional and task specialists should contribute.

ADJOURNING. The **adjourning** stage occurs in committees, task forces, and teams that have a limited task to perform and are disbanded afterward. During this stage, the emphasis is on wrapping up and gearing down. Task performance is no longer a top priority. Members may feel heightened emotionality, strong cohesiveness, and depression or even regret over the team's disbandment. They may feel happy about mission accomplishment and sad about the loss of friendship and associations. At this point the leader may wish to signify the team's disbanding with a ritual or ceremony, perhaps giving out plaques and awards to signify closure and completeness.

performing The stage of team development in which members focus on problem solving and accomplishing the team's assigned task.

adjourning The stage of team development in which members prepare for the team's disbandment.

TEAM COHESIVENESS

team cohesiveness The extent to which team members are attracted to the team and motivated to remain in it.

Another important aspect of the team process is cohesiveness. Team **cohesiveness** is defined as the extent to which members are attracted to the team and motivated to remain in it.[21] Members of highly cohesive teams are committed

Illustrating the *adjourning stage* of team development, these tired but jubilant members of the Martin Marietta Magellan team in Florida celebrate after the Space Shuttle Atlantis reached orbit. This was the first American interplanetary mission in eleven years. The team spent ten years building and readying the spacecraft for launch.

to team activities, attend meetings, and are happy when the team succeeds. Members of less cohesive teams are less concerned about the team's welfare. High cohesiveness is normally considered an attractive feature of teams.

Determinants of Team Cohesiveness. Characteristics of team structure and context influence cohesiveness. First is team interaction. The greater the amount of contact among team members and the more time spent together, the more cohesive the team. Through frequent interactions members get to know one another and become more devoted to the team.[22] Second is the concept of shared goals. If team members agree on goals, they will be more cohesive. Agreeing on purpose and direction binds the team together. Third is personal attraction to the team, meaning that members have similar attitudes and values and enjoy being together.

Two factors in the team's context also influence group cohesiveness. The first is the presence of competition. When a team is in direct competition with other teams, its cohesiveness increases as it strives to win. Whether competition is among sales teams to attain the top sales volume or among manufacturing departments to reduce rejects, competition increases team solidarity and cohesiveness.[23] Finally, team success and favorable evaluation of the team by outsiders adds to cohesiveness. When a team succeeds in its task and others in the organization recognize the success, members feel good and their commitment to the team will be high.

For example, Compaq Computer, the astoundingly successful personal computer maker in Houston, encourages team cohesiveness. Compaq managers believe it is not individual superstars who make the company great but a bunch of bright people who are committed to the team. The team commitment

Bill's Banditos won First Security Corporation's SuperKnow III in Salt Lake City. First Security is committed to quality service and created the College Bowl-like contest to stimulate product-knowledge training. Over 100 teams, representing every office, vied in the competition. *Team cohesiveness* produced both high morale and productivity for members. The fiesta theme belies the months of exhaustive study and intense competition leading to this contest.

was put to the test when a senior manager first wanted to produce a laptop computer that would be small enough to fit inside a briefcase. Mary Dudley, a market researcher, surveyed the market and concluded that there were not enough customers to justify manufacturing a laptop computer. Dudley pushed her negative assessment because she was committed to the team. Compaq's history of frequent interactions, shared goals and values, and product success enabled Dudley to disagree with top management. Her point prevailed. And it was a good thing Compaq waited, because when its laptop came out two years later it swept the market. Early laptops by other companies were failures.[24]

Consequences of Team Cohesiveness. The outcome of team cohesiveness can fall into two categories — morale and productivity. As a general rule, morale is higher in cohesive teams because of increased communication among members, a friendly team climate, maintenance of membership because of commitment to the team, loyalty, and member participation in team decisions and activities. High cohesiveness has almost uniformly good effects on the satisfaction and morale of team members.[25]

With respect to team performance, research findings are mixed,[26] but cohesiveness may have several effects. First, in a cohesive team, members' productivity tends to be more uniform. Productivity differences among members is small because the team exerts pressure toward conformity. Noncohesive teams do not have this control over member behavior and hence tend to have wider variation in member productivity.

With respect to the productivity of the team as a whole, research findings suggest that cohesive teams have the potential to be productive, but the degree of productivity depends on the relationship between management and the working team. Thus, team cohesiveness does not necessarily lead to higher team productivity. One study surveyed over 200 work teams and correlated job performance with their cohesiveness.[27] Highly cohesive teams were more productive when team members felt management supported them and less productive when they sensed management hostility and negativism. Management hostility led to team norms and goals of low performance, and the highly cohesive teams performed poorly, in accordance with their norms and goals.

EXHIBIT 16.6
Relationship among Team Cohesiveness, Performance Norms, and Productivity

Team Performance Norms	Low Team Cohesiveness	High Team Cohesiveness
High	**Moderate Productivity** Weak norms in alignment with organization goals	**High Productivity** Strong norms in alignment with organization goals
Low	**Low/Moderate Productivity** Weak norms in opposition to organization goals	**Low Productivity** Strong norms in opposition to organization goals

The relationship between performance outcomes and cohesiveness is illustrated in Exhibit 16.6. The highest productivity occurs when the team is cohesive and also has a high performance norm, which is a result of its positive relationship with management. Moderate productivity occurs when cohesiveness is low, because team members are less committed to performance norms. The lowest productivity occurs when cohesiveness is high and the team's performance norm is low. Thus, cohesive teams are able to attain their goals and enforce their norms, which can lead to either very high or very low productivity.

norm A standard of conduct that is shared by team members and guides their behavior.

TEAM NORMS

A team **norm** is a standard of conduct that is shared by team members and guides their behavior.[28] Norms are informal. They are not written down as are rules and procedures. Norms are valuable because they define boundaries of acceptable behavior. They make life easier for team members by providing a frame of reference for what is right and wrong. Norms identify key values, clarify role expectations, and facilitate team survival. For example, union members may develop a norm of not cooperating with management because they do not trust management's motives. In this way, norms protect the group and express key values.

Norms begin to develop in the first interactions among members of a new team.[29] Norms that apply to both day-to-day behavior and employee output and performance gradually evolve. Norms thus tell members what is acceptable and direct members' actions toward acceptable productivity or performance. Four common ways in which norms develop for controlling and directing behavior are illustrated in Exhibit 16.7.[30]

Doug Villiers (white shirt) created a *team norm* of trust by leaving his department's tool cabinet unlocked. He trusts his team to do the right thing. Doug inspired confidence within his department, and his coworkers started taking calculated risks to improve performance. The result was a 41 percent reduction in wasted time in one year. Villiers' team works for Worcester's Bonded Abrasives Maintenance Department of Norton Company.

CRITICAL EVENTS. Often there are *critical events* in a team's history that establish an important precedent. One example occurred when Arthur Schlesinger, despite his serious reservations about the Bay of Pigs invasion, was pressured by Attorney General Robert Kennedy not to raise his objections to President Kennedy. This critical incident helped create a norm in which team members refrained from expressing disagreement with the President.

Any critical event can lead to the creation of a norm. In one organization, a department head invited the entire staff to his house for dinner. The next day

EXHIBIT 16.7
Four Sources of Team Norms

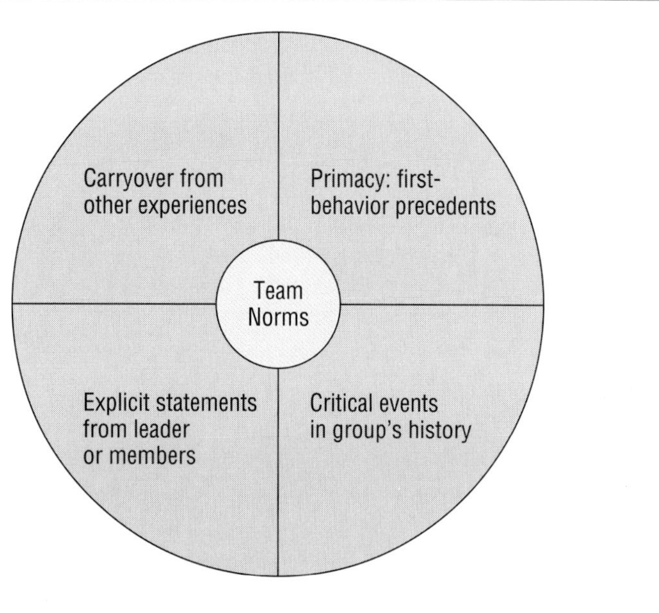

people discovered that no one had attended, and this resulted in a norm prohibiting outside entertaining.[31]

PRIMACY. *Primacy* means that the first behaviors that occur in a team often set a precedent for later team expectations. For example, when the president of Sun Company set up teams in the Dallas-based exploration division, top managers made sure the initial meetings involved solving genuine company problems. The initial success created a norm that team members carried into other work. "Suddenly we had two hundred evangelists," said Sun President McCormick.[32]

CARRYOVER BEHAVIORS. *Carryover behaviors* bring norms into the team from outside. One current example is the strong norm against smoking in many management teams. Some team members sneak around, gargling with mouthwash, and fear expulsion because the team culture believes everyone should kick the habit. At such companies as Johnson & Johnson, Dow Chemical, and Aetna Life & Casualty, the norm is, "If you want to advance, don't smoke."[33] Carryover behavior also influences small teams of college students assigned by instructors to do class work. Norms brought into the team from outside suggest that students should participate equally and help members get a reasonable grade.

EXPLICIT STATEMENTS. With *explicit statements,* leaders or team members can initiate norms by articulating them to the team. Explicit statements symbolize what counts and thus have considerable impact. Making explicit statements is probably the most effective way for managers to change norms in an established team. For example, Richard Boyle of Honeywell wrote a memo to create a new norm.

HONEYWELL • Honeywell undertook a major change program to relax the company's traditional militaristic style of management and substitute a more participative approach. One norm of the company was excessive formality. Richard Boyle, vice-president and group executive for Honeywell Defense and Marine Systems Group in Minneapolis, wrote a memo called "Loosening Up the Tie." The memo said in part:

> I wish to announce a relaxed wearing apparel policy, and loosen my tie for the summer. Let's try it starting on May 15th and tentatively ending on September 15th. Since departments vary in customer contact and, depending on location, may even vary slightly in temperature, Department Heads are hereby given authority to allow variations. . . .
>
> This change requires each of us to use good judgment. On the one extreme it means you do not have to wear a tie; on the other tennis shoes, shorts, and a t-shirt is too relaxed. Have a comfortable, enjoyable summer. I hope to.

The tie memo helped demonstrate management's interest in developing a relaxed, more casual atmosphere at Honeywell. Employee response suggested that the freedom to exercise common sense over arbitrary rules was healthy for the organization. When Mr. Boyle showed up at the office without a tie, people really began to believe that the new dress code was okay.[34]

MANAGING TEAM CONFLICT

The final characteristic of team process is conflict. Of all the skills required for effective team management, none is more important than handling the conflicts that inevitably arise among members. Whenever people work together in teams, some conflict is inevitable. Conflict can arise among members within a team or between one team and another. **Conflict** refers to antagonistic interaction in which one party attempts to block the intentions or goals of another.[35] Competition, which is rivalry between individuals or teams, can have a healthy impact because it energizes people toward higher performance.[36] However, too much conflict can be destructive, tear relationships apart, and interfere with the healthy exchange of ideas and information.[37]

conflict Antagonistic interaction in which one party attempts to thwart the intentions or goals of another.

CAUSES OF CONFLICT

Several factors can cause people to engage in conflict:[38]

SCARCE RESOURCES. Resources include money, information, and supplies. In their desire to achieve goals, individuals may wish to increase their resources, which throws them into conflict. Whenever individuals or teams must compete for scarce or declining resources, conflict is almost inevitable.

JURISDICTIONAL AMBIGUITIES. Conflicts also emerge when job boundaries and responsibilities are unclear. When task responsibilities are well defined and predictable, people know where they stand. When they are unclear, people may disagree about who has responsibility for specific tasks or who has a claim on resources. The conflict between owners' and players' associations in both professional football and baseball is often a struggle to see which organization has jurisdiction over such things as drug testing.[39]

COMMUNICATION BREAKDOWN. Communication, as described in Chapter 15, is sometimes faulty. Poor communications result in misperceptions and misunderstandings of other people and teams. In some cases information may be intentionally withheld, which can jeopardize trust among teams and lead to long-lasting conflict.

PERSONALITY CLASHES. A personality clash occurs when people simply do not get along with one another and do not see eye to eye on any issue. Personality clashes are caused by basic differences in personality, values, and attitudes. Often it's a good idea to simply separate the parties so that they need not interact with one another.

POWER AND STATUS DIFFERENCES. Power and status differences occur when one party has disputable influence over another. Low-prestige individuals or departments may resist their low status. People may engage in conflict to increase their power and influence in the team or organization.

GOAL DIFFERENCES. Conflict often occurs simply because people are pursuing conflicting goals. Goal differences are natural in organizations. Individual salespeople's targets may put them in conflict with one another or with the sales manager. Moreover, the sales department may have goals that conflict with those of manufacturing. One emerging conflict within the United Auto Workers is because one subgroup is against teamwork, believing that it exploits workers and does nothing but make them work harder. Other factions in the UAW believe it is beneficial for both workers and the organization. These opposing goals are causing major clashes between these UAW subgroups.[40]

An interesting example of conflict occurred within a product marketing team at Salvo, a designer of computer software programs.

SALVO INC. • Product marketing teams at Salvo developed demonstration tapes of their new games and programs for use in dealer stores. The tapes are filled with sound, color, and clever graphics that are successful sales tools. The marketing person on the team works up an outline for a tape based on product content. The outline is then submitted to the team member from the information systems department to work out displays and graphics.

Larry from marketing is energetic, has a good sense of humor, and has a high standard for excellence. He knows what a computer can do, but he is not a programmer. Larry submitted an outline of a new videotape to Eric in information systems for development. Eric, a new member of the team, is serious and somewhat introverted. He sent a highly technical memo to Larry explaining why the project wouldn't work as requested. Larry was upset because he didn't understand the memo or why Eric had written a memo instead of talking to him face to face.

Larry and Eric had a blowup at their first meeting because of their different goals and personalities. Miscommunication further aggravated the situation. Also, it was unclear who was responsible for each task in the development of the demonstration tapes, because Eric was new and unaccustomed to taking orders from another team member. Although both Eric and Larry supposedly had the same team goal, the problems with personality, communication, juris-

Inland Steel resolves potential conflicts between groups by using a *superordinate goal* and *facilitating communication*. These Inland employees are delivery champions, helping the steel company reach the goal of 90 percent on-time deliveries. The responsibility for shipping on time rests with team members from sales, manufacturing, and operations planning, so teamwork promotes communication across departments to reach the overall goal. Each department saw the delivery problem in a different light, but team members helped one another solve problems and reach the delivery goal.

dictional ambiguity, and individual goals caused an almost explosive conflict between them.[41]

Resolving Conflicts

What does a manager or team leader do when a conflict erupts within a team or among teams? Research suggests several helpful techniques for confronting and resolving conflicts.

Superordinate Goals. The larger mission that cannot be attained by a single party is identified as **superordinate goals.**[42] A superordinate goal requires the cooperation of the conflicting parties for achievement. People must pull together. To the extent that employees can be focused on team or organization goals, the conflict will decrease because they see the big picture and realize they must work together to achieve it.

superordinate goals A goal that cannot be reached by a single party.

Bargaining/Negotiation. Bargaining and negotiation mean that the parties engage one another in an attempt to systematically reach a solution. They attempt logical problem solving to identify and correct the conflict. This approach works well if the individuals can set aside personal animosities and deal with the conflict in a businesslike way.

Mediation. Using a third party to settle a dispute involves **mediation.** A mediator could be a supervisor, higher-level manager, or someone from the personnel department. The mediator can discuss the conflict with each party

mediation The process of using a third party to settle a dispute.

and work toward a solution. If a solution satisfactory to both sides cannot be reached, the parties may be willing to turn the conflict over to the mediator and abide by his or her solution.

PROVIDING WELL-DEFINED TASKS. When conflict is a result of ambiguity, managers can reduce it by clarifying responsibilities and tasks. In this way, all parties will know the tasks for which they are responsible and the limits of their authority.

FACILITATING COMMUNICATION. Managers can facilitate communication to ensure that conflicting parties hold accurate perceptions. Providing opportunities for the disputants to get together and exchange information reduces conflict. As they learn more about one another, suspicions diminish and improved teamwork becomes possible.

For example, the conflict between Larry and Eric and Salvo Inc. over the demonstration tape was eventually resolved by improved communication, clear definition of their respective tasks, and stronger commitment to the superordinate goal of finishing the tape. Larry went to see Eric and discussed the problem with him. The discussion revealed that they were pursuing different goals because Larry wanted the tape right away and Eric wanted to keep it until he could perfect it. Discussing each point of view was the key to their solution. Debbie, another team member, agreed to help them so that the tape could be of high quality and still be finished in two weeks. Larry and Eric also worked out a clear schedule that specified their respective responsibilities and tasks.

BENEFITS AND COSTS OF TEAMS

In deciding whether to use teams to perform specific tasks, managers must consider both benefits and costs. Teams may have positive impact on both the output productivity and satisfaction of members. On the other hand, teams may also create a situation in which motivation and performance are actually decreased.

POTENTIAL BENEFITS OF TEAMS

Teams come closest to achieving their full potential when they enhance individual productivity through increased member effort, members' personal satisfaction, integration of diverse abilities and skills, and increased organizational flexibility.

LEVEL OF EFFORT. Employee involvement teams often unleash enormous energy and creativity from workers who like the idea of using their brains as well as their bodies on the job. Companies such as Kimberly-Clark have noticed this change in effort among employees as they switched to team approaches.[43] One explanation for this motivation is the research finding that working in a team increases an individual's motivation and performance. **Social facilitation** refers to the tendency for the presence of others to enhance

social facilitation The tendency for the presence of others to influence an individual's motivation and performance.

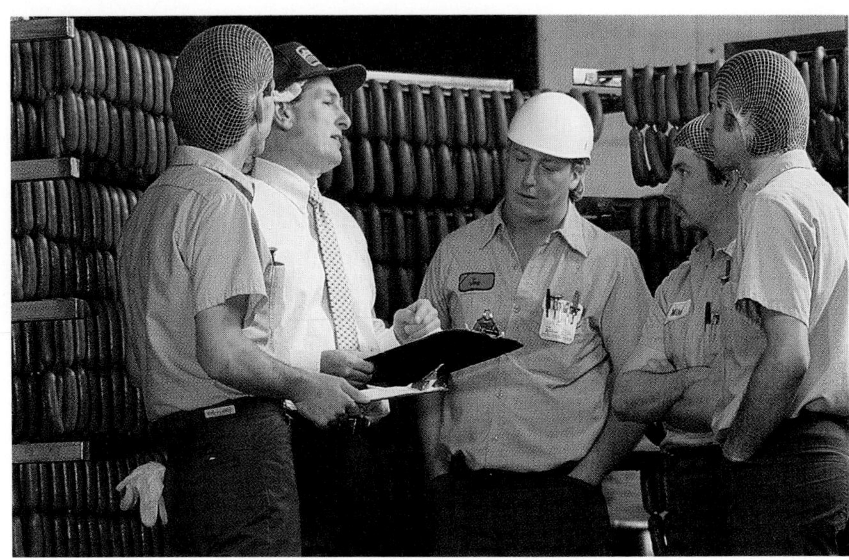

Teams of blue-collar workers at Johnsonville Foods of Sheboygan, Wisconsin, help CEO Ralph Stayer (second from left) make strategic decisions. Strayer turned over to production workers, organized in teams of five to twenty, the decision about whether to accept a contract to manufacture sausage under a private label. After 10 days of deliberations, the teams said yes. The teams then decided how much new machinery to buy and how many new people to hire. Productivity has risen over 50 percent in the factory, thanks to increased *level of effort, organizational flexibility,* and *satisfaction of team members.*

an individual's motivation and performance. Simply being in the presence of other people has an energizing effect.[44]

Satisfaction of Members. As described in Chapter 14, employees have needs for belongingness and affiliation. Working in teams can help meet these needs. Participative teams reduce boredom and often increase employees' feeling of dignity and self-worth because the whole person is employed. People who have a satisfying team environment cope better with stress and enjoy their jobs.

Expanded Job Knowledge and Skills. The third major benefit of using teams is that employees bring greater knowledge and ability to the task. For one thing, multiskilled employees learn all of the jobs that the team performs. Teams also have the intellectual resources of several members who can suggest shortcuts and offer alternative points of view for team decisions.

Organizational Flexibility. Traditional organizations are structured so that each worker does only one specific job. But when employee involvement teams are used, from 5 to 15 people work next to one another and are able to exchange jobs. Work can be reorganized and workers reallocated as needed to produce products and services with great flexibility. The organization is able to be responsive to rapidly changing customer needs.

Potential Costs of Teams

When managers decide whether to use teams, they must also assess certain costs or liabilities associated with teamwork. When teams do not work very well, the major reasons usually are power realignment, free riding, or coordination costs.

POWER REALIGNMENT. When companies form shop workers into teams, the major losers are lower- and middle-level managers. These managers are reluctant to give up power. Indeed, when teams are successful, fewer supervisors are needed. This is especially true for self-managing teams because workers take over supervisory responsibility. The adjustment is difficult for managers who fear the loss of status and who have to learn new, people-oriented skills to survive.[45]

free rider A person who benefits from team membership but does not make a proportionate contribution to the team's work.

FREE RIDING. The term **free rider** refers to a team member who attains benefit from team membership but does not do a proportionate share of the work.[46] Free riding is sometimes called *social loafing,* because members do not exert equal effort. In large teams, some people are likely to work less. For example, research found that the pull exerted on a rope was greater by individuals working alone than by individuals in a group. Similarly, people who were asked to clap and make noise made more noise on a per person basis when working alone or in small groups than they did in a large group.[47] The problem of free riding has been experienced by people who have participated in student project groups. Some students put more effort into the group project than others, and often it seems that no members work as hard for the group as they do for their individual grades.

coordination costs The time and energy needed to coordinate the activities of a team to enable it to perform its task.

COORDINATION COSTS. The time and energy required to coordinate the activities of a group to enable it to perform its task are called **coordination costs.** Groups must spend time getting ready to do work and lose productive time in deciding who is to do what and when.[48] Once again student project groups illustrate coordination costs. Members must meet after class just to decide when they can meet to perform the task. Schedules must be checked, telephone calls made, and meeting times arranged in order to get down to business. Hours may be devoted to the administration and coordination of the group. Students often feel they could do the same project by themselves in less time.

SUMMARY

Several important concepts about teams were described in this chapter. Organizations use teams both as part of the formal structure and to encourage employee involvement. Formal teams include vertical teams along the chain of command and horizontal teams such as cross-functional task forces and committees. Special-purpose teams are used for special, large-scale, creative organization projects. Employee involvement teams are designed to bring lower-level employees into decision processes to improve quality, efficiency, and satisfaction. Companies typically start with problem-solving teams, which may evolve into self-managing teams that take on responsibility for management activities.

Most teams go through systematic stages of development: forming, storming, norming, performing, and adjourning. Team characteristics that can influence organizational effectiveness are size, cohesiveness, norms, and members' roles. All teams experience some conflict because of scarce resources, ambiguous responsibility, communication breakdown, personality clashes, power and status differences, and goal conflicts. Techniques for resolving these conflicts include superordinate goals, bargaining, clear definition of task responsibilities, mediation, and communication. Advantages of using teams include increased motivation, diverse knowledge and skills, satisfaction of team members, and organizational flexibility. Potential costs of using teams are power realignment, free riding, and coordination costs.

Management Solution

Hearing Technology, Inc., grew rapidly to 80 employees and became sluggish in its response to hearing-aid dealers. President Tom Huber was frustrated because the three-day response time increased to eight days, provoking complaints from dealers. Huber's attempt to reenergize the company failed, and he tried a drastic restructuring along a team approach. Huber implemented three things that made the team approach work: Regular meetings of employee teams were held, usually every week; departments were encouraged to talk with one another and work together through cross-functional teams; and power was shared with employees. Four longtime employees jointly supervised manufacturing, reinforcing the team approach. The company is suddenly wide open to new ideas, which are heard and implemented. The response time for custom orders has been halved to four days, and dealers are happy again. Employees are enjoying themselves, too.[49]

Discussion Questions

1. Volvo went to self-managed teams to assemble cars because of the need to attract and keep workers in Sweden, where pay raises are not a motivator (high taxes) and many other jobs are available. Is this a good reason for using a team approach? Discuss.
2. During your own work experience, have you been part of a formal vertical team? A task force? A committee? An employee involvement team? How did your work experience differ in each type of team?
3. What are the five stages of team development? What happens during each stage?
4. How would you explain the emergence of problem-solving and self-managing teams in companies throughout North America? Do you think implementation of the team concept is difficult in these companies? Discuss.
5. Assume you are part of a student project team and one member is not doing his or her share. Which conflict resolution strategy would you use? Why?
6. Do you think a moderate level of conflict might be healthy for an organization? Discuss.
7. When you are a member of a team, do you adopt a task specialist or socioemotional role? Which role is more important for a team's effectiveness? Discuss.
8. What is the relationship between team cohesiveness and team performance?

9. Describe the advantages and disadvantages of teams. In what situations might the disadvantages outweigh the advantages?
10. What is a team norm? What norms have developed in teams to which you have belonged?

Management in Practice: Ethical Dilemma

Nancy was part of a pharmaceutical team developing a product called loperamide, a liquid treatment for diarrhea for people unable to take solid medicine, namely infants, children, and the elderly. Loperamide contained 44 times the amount of saccharin allowed by the FDA in a 12-ounce soft drink, but there were no regulations governing saccharin content in medication.

Nancy was the only medical member of the seven-person project team. The team made a unanimous decision to reduce the saccharin content before marketing loperamide, so the team initiated a three-month effort for reformulation. In the meantime management was pressuring the team to allow human testing with the original formula until the new formula became available. After a heated team debate, all the team members except Nancy voted to begin testing with the current formula.

Nancy believed it was unethical to test a drug she considered potentially dangerous on old people and children. As the only medical member of the team, she had to sign the forms allowing testing. She refused and was told that unless she signed she would be removed from the project, demoted, and seen as a poor team player, nonpromotable, lacking in judgment, and unable to work with marketing people. Nancy was aware that no proof existed that high saccharin would be directly harmful to potential users of loperamide.

What Do You Do?

1. Refuse to sign. As a medical doctor, Nancy must stand up for what she believes is right.
2. Resign. There is no reason to stay in this company and be punished for ethically correct behavior. Testing the drug will become someone else's responsibility.
3. Sign the form. The judgment of other team members cannot be all wrong. The loperamide testing is not illegal and will move ahead anyway, so it would preserve team unity and company effectiveness to sign.

Source: Based on Tom L. Beauchamp, *Ethical Theory and Business*, 2d ed. (Englewood Cliffs, N.J.: Prentice-Hall, 1983).

Cases for Analysis

A. O. Smith Corporation

A. O. Smith Corporation's Milwaukee plant had bored workers repeating the same robotlike task every 20 seconds, welding and riveting car and truck frames for supply to General Motors. Beginning in the early 1980s, General Motors shifted some of its business elsewhere. Later, GM and other automakers forced Smith and other suppliers to cut prices.

With resources getting tight, Smith tried a quality circle program as a way to introduce teamwork. Quality improved, but the union refused to be involved. As external threats became greater, union president Blackman began to support widespread application of the teamwork concept. The union pressed for five- to seven-member teams, letting workers rotate jobs and elect team leaders. Smith's management went along, turning the control of the shops over to employees. The ratio of supervisors to workers was reduced from one supervisor to ten workers to one supervisor to thirty-four workers.

Smith's executives moved slowly because a consultant argued that self-managed teams would not work until workers wanted them to happen; teams must evolve from their own experience. With the support of the union, Smith undertook the rare transformation from a traditional manufacturing plant with rigid work rules and labor-management warfare to a new culture with participation and equality. All the problems are not yet resolved, because the plant still has not reached its potential. However, observers believe an obsolete production system has been transformed into a competitive one.

Questions

1. What types of teams discussed in the chapter are represented in this case?
2. Do you agree that workers must want the teamwork concept before it can be imposed by management? Explain.
3. What might be a next step to further improve the employee involvement climate at A. O. Smith?

Source: Based on John Hoerr, "The Cultural Revolution at A. O. Smith," *Business Week*, May 29, 1989, 66–68.

SPECIAL TASK FORCE

Phil Douglas, supervisor of the Special Task Force, was proud of the amount and quality of work that the members of the force had done in the few weeks they had been working together. He remembered the time one of the task force members had an idea about one problem that was costing the company a lot of money. It was close to lunchtime, so the group decided to discuss the idea over lunch. They were so excited and optimistic over the chance of success that they had spent two-and-a-half hours at the restaurant discussing possible results, problems, and implementation. But the idea was a success, and no one on the task force complained about all the nights spent working on the project.

However, Ted Young, Phil's boss, told Phil that some of the engineers in Fred Jacobi's department were griping about unfair treatment. "I'm sorry that some of our brainstorming and other creative techniques are being misunderstood, Ted," Phil replied, "but look at what we've been able to accomplish — we've improved the production methods and quality of our products, bringing in many more orders." Phil started to suggest, "Perhaps if Fred tried some of our methods, his engineers would be more content . . ."

"Try to see this from another point of view, Phil," Ted interrupted. "You and I know that your people are actually working when they take a two-and-a-half-hour lunch to discuss some new idea, but it doesn't look that way. Fred's engineers see them laughing and talking in a restaurant at 12 and then see them coming back to the office at 2:30. How do you think that looks to them?

"In their department, keeping regular hours is crucial. I think the only fair solution is to insist that the Special Task Force people keep the same hours, lunch hours, and coffee breaks as everyone else," Ted concluded.

"But Ted, no one's here to see them when they work on past 5:00. It's their freedom from a rigid schedule that has brought such good results."

"I'm sorry to interrupt, Phil, but I have to make a management meeting at two."

Phil left Ted's office and stepped into an elevator with several workers from Fred Jacobi's department. "Must be nice to get back from coffee break in time to go home," one engineer commented. Phil laughed and replied, "It's none of your business, but I'm going to the library."

"Yeh. He's going to check out the new librarian," another man rejoined. The group laughed, and Phil left the elevator more troubled than before. He hadn't realized how much the other departments resented his group.

Questions

1. What accounts for the high level of motivation on the Special Task Force? Evaluate other benefits and costs of using the task force.
2. What norms seem to have evolved on this task force? Is the group cohesive? If so, does this help or hurt productivity?
3. If you were Ted, how would you handle Fred Jacobi's complaint?

Source: Adapted by permission of the publisher, from "'Special' Task Force," *Supervisory Management*, August 1983, 44–45,

Video Case

Quad/Graphics (A)

Harry V. Quadracci is a risk-taking leader who believes in people. In 1971, he purchased a small abandoned factory for $150,000, paying for it with what he called a "rubber $10,000 check" as the deposit, taking a second mortgage on his home to raise money. Today Quad/Graphics' client list includes *Time, Newsweek, People, U.S. News & World Report, Playboy,* and the *Journal of the American Medical Association.* Since 1978, Quad/Graphics has grown at the outrageous pace of 40 percent annually, in an industry where 10 percent growth is considered exceptional. Quad now has more than 3,500 employees and has reached $500 million in sales.

Employees are unbelievably motivated. There are no procedure manuals, time clocks, or budgets. Employees give all they have to Quad/Graphics. In return they receive personal growth, technical learning, day-care and fitness centers, and an opportunity to do their own thing. They also get responsibility and a sense of achievement. Although free to do their own thing, employees feel part of a team, including the people they work with and the company as a whole. In 1973, when the company started adding presses, Quadracci refused to put anyone in charge of the pressroom. "I said each pressman is going to run [his] own press." That is how the current management system was born. Quadracci would rather have 50 people out there thinking independently, being in conflict with ideas, than obediently doing what some manager dictates.

In 1974, a tradition called the annual Spring Fling began. That is when management exits to do strategic planning, leaving the rank and file to run the company. When some unexpected printing work came during the 1974 planning break, Quadracci decided to keep the plant open and let the workers handle on their own whatever needed to be done. This is a high stakes game, because a small mistake can cost hundreds of thousands of dollars. But leaving employees unsupervised also gives them responsibility and teaches them they can do things on their own. It is a challenge that employees have grown to love.

Within Quad/Graphics, employees are extraordinarily well informed. Openness is valued. Each employee shares his or her knowledge and insights with others coming up while learning from people who have been in the job longer.

The decentralized structure would seem perfect for a high-tech research firm employing highly educated scientists and engineers. Instead decentralization is used to run a large, fast-growing manufacturing company. Although Quad is very much a technology-based company, its average employee has a high-school diploma. Quad operates as if it has 3,500 engineers, but without the 3,500 engineers. Employees can learn and grow as fast as they wish, being promoted on knowledge rather than seniority. The time required to become a first press operator is typically from three to five years compared with ten years in other firms. Employees have been promoted to press operators at 22 years of age, becoming salaried managers with a say in all areas including running a major piece of equipment, scheduling, and hiring and training their own crews.

Employees as a group own about 22 percent of the company. Nonsalary benefits at Quad total 40 percent of direct compensation, which puts the firm among the top 2 percent of U.S. employers in company benefits.

Discussion Questions

1. Which leadership models describe Harry Quadracci? Which describe Bill Graushar, Manager Finishing R&D (video)?
2. How do you account for the extraordinary motivation of Quad/Graphics employees? Can this level of motivation be explained by the models in Chapter 14?
3. How can communication be so effective without paperwork? Is reliance on face-to-face communication appropriate in this environment? Why?
4. Quadracci seems to emphasize the individual over the team, yet the whole organization is a team. Discuss.
5. Can Quad/Graphics maintain the same level of motivation as it grows ever larger?

Source: Daniel M. Kehrer, "The Miracle of Theory Q," *Business Month,* September 1989, 44–49; Daniel M. Kehrer, "The P.T. Barnum of Printing," *Across the Board,* May 1989, 53–54; David Hill, "What's the Trouble with Harry?" *Business Month,* January 1990, 7; Ellen Wojan, "Management by Walking Away," *INC.,* October 1983, 68–76.

PART 5

CONTROLLING

Fred Gutzeit, *Glove Box,* 1982, asphalt siding, work gloves, spectral mylar and fluorescent paint, 41″ × 32″ × 4″. From the collection of John Hechinger, Chairman, Hechinger Company, Washington, D.C.

The John W. Hechinger Collection has a unique focus: Each piece in some way addresses products the company purveys. These include tools, hardware, and building materials. Works by established and newer artists show the great variety of expression that can be brought to a single subject. The collection reflects chairman Hechinger's belief that the products themselves have style and character. Because Hechinger employees can view these works of art daily, the collection helps reinforce the sense that the articles they deal with every day enable others to create their own visions.

CHAPTER 17

Control Concepts for Quality and Productivity

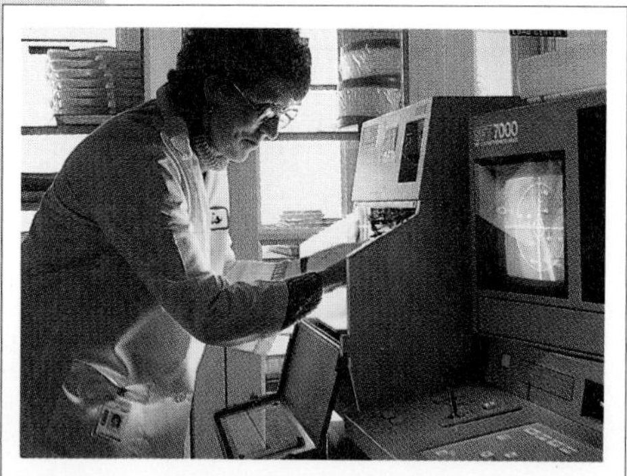

Chapter Outline

Learning Objectives

After studying this chapter, you should be able to:

- Define organizational control and explain why it is a key management function.
- Explain the four steps in the control process.
- Describe how organizational control relates to strategic planning.
- Describe differences in control focus, including feedforward, concurrent, and feedback control.
- Describe bureaucratic and clan control approaches and the methods used within the organization to implement each.
- Describe the concept of total quality control and explain how quality circles can be used to improve quality control in organizations.
- Describe statistical quality control and the procedures used to implement it.
- Describe the trends in effective organizational control.

Management Problem

Charles Stott was installed as president and Richard Packer as vice-president for manufacturing at Whistler, one of the biggest U.S. sellers of radar detectors. Why? To take control of quality. Demand for radar detectors grew so fast that two plants went out of control — 25 percent of the detectors failed inspection. Of Whistler's 250 production workers, more than 100 spent all their time fixing defective units. Against one plant wall stood $2 million of defective parts and other stocks. Production costs were far higher than for a sister plant in South Korea. Stott and Packer were told by Dynatech, the parent company, to get costs down and quality up or the U.S. plants would be closed.[1]

If you were a consultant to Stott and Packer, what would you recommend they do? How can they best go about getting control of Whistler's manufacturing plants?

Whistler had the luxury of a large demand for a great product, but poor quality was killing the company. In this typically well-run company, rejection rates went out of control. Whistler shows how vital control is to organizational success and how difficult it can be to achieve effective control.

Control is an issue facing every manager in every organization. Newspaper articles about the skyrocketing default rate and loans to political cronies at the Department of Housing & Urban Development are about control.[2] Or consider the problems on Wall Street during the explosive growth in the late 1980s. Security firms outgrew their management know-how to police large numbers of people, control costs, monitor and analyze risk, and plan for the future. Consequently, a string of highly publicized management failings hit the newspapers, including Merrill Lynch's and First Boston's huge losses from loosely supervised traders and Kidder-Peabody's securities-law violations.[3]

Organizational control is the process through which managers regulate company activities to make them consistent with plans, targets, and standards of performance. Waste Management uses space-age robotics and computerized analytical equipment as shown here to achieve its plan to protect groundwater. Up to 60,000 samples from thousands of monitoring points at Waste Management processing and disposal centers are analyzed yearly to assure the highest standards of environmental quality.

organizational control The systematic process through which managers regulate organizational activities to make them consistent with the expectations established in plans, targets, and performance standards.

THE IMPORTANCE OF CONTROL

Here is a true story: Ken Jones, president of the Ontario Centre for Advanced Manufacturing, said that a few years ago IBM Canada Ltd. ordered some parts from a new supplier in Japan. The company stated in its order that acceptable quality allowed for 1.5 percent defects — a high standard in North America at that time. The Japanese sent the order, with a few parts packaged separately in plastic. Their letter said: "We don't know why you want 1.5 percent defective parts, but for your convenience we have packaged them separately."[4]

This story crystalizes the problems with control in North America. First is complacency, the assumption that our management techniques are the best in the world. Second is a top-down, pyramidal control style that is almost feudal in nature. Top management expects to control everything, making all decisions, while middle and lower managers implement decisions, and production workers do only as they are told.

This philosophy is now being stood on its head as a new control philosophy emerges. As we saw in the chapters on leadership, structure, motivation, and teams, low-level employees are being included in management and control decisions. Top management no longer decides the "right" way to do something. More and more, the people who are in control of a particular work setting are those who work within 50 feet of it. Thus at IBM Canada Ltd., *all* 11,000 employees have now been organized into participation groups. A 1.5 percent defect standard is no longer tolerable.[5]

Organizational control is defined as the systematic process through which managers regulate organizational activities to make them consistent with the expectations established in plans, targets, and standards of performance.[6] To effectively control an organization, managers (or workers) must plan and set performance standards, implement an information system that will provide knowledge of actual performance, and take action to correct deviations from the standard. For example, Whistler's managers understood the standard of performance and had information that rejection rates were too high. They did not, however, have a way to implement corrections that would change behavior to meet the standard.

STEPS IN THE CONTROL PROCESS

Based on our definition of organizational control, a well-designed control system consists of four key steps, which are illustrated in Exhibit 17.1.

ESTABLISH STANDARDS OF PERFORMANCE. Within the organization's overall strategic plan, managers define goals for organizational departments in specific, operational terms that comprise a *standard of performance* against which to compare organizational activities. A standard of performance could include "reducing the reject rate from 15 to 3 percent," "increasing the corporation's return on investment to 7 percent," or "reducing the number of accidents to 1 per each 100,000 hours of labor." American Airlines sets standards for such activities as acquiring additional aircraft for its fleet, designing discount fares to attract price-conscious travelers, improving passenger load factors, and increasing freight business. Standards must be defined in a precise

Exhibit 17.1
Steps in the Control Process

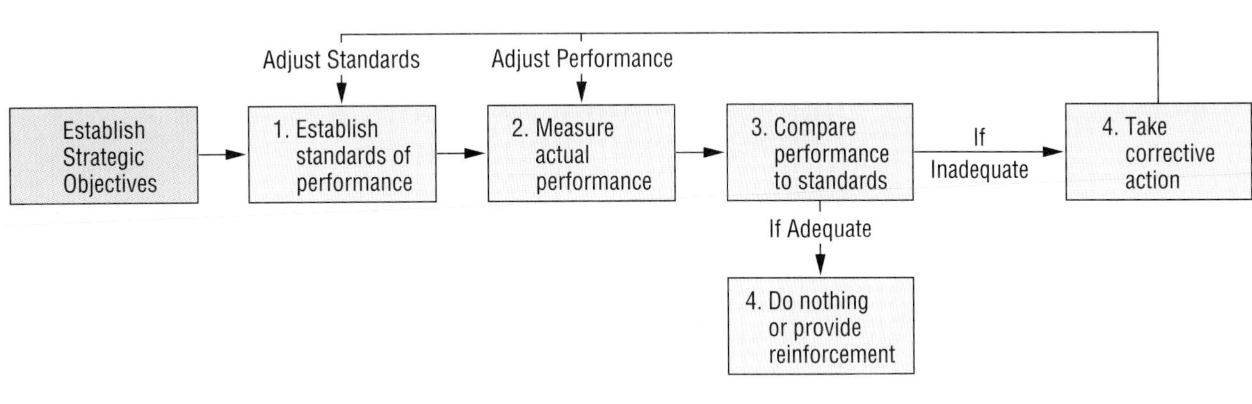

way so that managers and workers can determine whether activities are on target. Standards can then be understood by the people in the organization responsible for achieving them.

Measure Actual Performance. Many organizations develop quantitative measurements of performance that can be reviewed on a daily, weekly, or monthly basis. For example, Richard Simmons, chief executive of Allegheny Ludlum Steel Corporation, explained why his company has a fanatical system for measuring internal operations. "It's simple," says Simmons. "If you can't measure it, you can't manage it."[7] In most companies, however, managers do not rely exclusively on quantitative measures. They get out into the organization to see how things are going, especially for such goals as increasing employee participation and personal growth. Managers have to observe for themselves whether employees are participating in decision making and are being offered challenging opportunities for personal growth.

Compare Performance to Standards. The third step is the explicit comparison of actual activities to performance standards. Managers take time to read computer reports or walk through the plant and thereby compare actual performance to standards. At Alleghany Ludlum, targeted performance standards are right on the computer printout along with the actual performance for the previous week and year. This makes the comparison easy for managers. A. O. Smith manufactures heavy metal frames for automobiles. With changes in the design of automobiles, it adopted a goal of product diversification. Smith's managers obtained data revealing that 20 percent of sales were from products not made five years earlier, indicating they were on target for diversification.

However, when performance falls below standard, remember that interpreting the comparison between standards and actual performance is not always easy. Managers are expected to dig beneath the surface and find the cause of the problem. If the sales goal is to increase the number of sales calls by 10

Oklahoma Gas and Electric Company has taken *corrective action* to meet higher performance standards. In order to lower costs and be more responsive to customers, the company reorganized by changing from the traditional four-person line crew to the two-person crew as shown here. This action eliminates the need to send more personnel than are needed to any given project, although multiple crews can be assigned to large jobs.

percent and a salesperson achieved an increase of 8 percent, where did she fail to achieve her goal? Perhaps several businesses on her route closed, or additional salespeople were assigned to her area by competitors, or she needs training in making cold sales calls. Management should take an inquiring approach to deviations in order to gain a broad understanding of factors that influenced performance. Effective management control involves subjective judgment and employee discussions as well as objective analysis of performance data.

TAKE CORRECTIVE ACTION. *Corrective action* is follow up to change work activities in order to bring them back to acceptable performance standards. In a traditional top-down control approach, managers exercise their formal authority to make necessary changes. Managers may encourage employees to work harder, redesign the production process, or fire employees. One Friday night, the night shift at the Toledo, Ohio, AMC Jeep plant had a 15 percent no-show rate for workers, which is below the acceptable absenteeism standard of 10 percent. Management's corrective action was to shut the plant down and send the other 85 percent of workers home without pay. In the newer, participative control approach, managers and employees together would decide corrective action, perhaps through problem-solving teams or quality circles.

In some cases, corrective managers may change performance standards. They may realize that standards are too high or too low if departments continuously fail to meet or exceed standards. If contingency factors that influence organizational performance change, performance standards may need to be altered to be more realistic and provide positive motivation for employees.

Managers may wish to provide positive reinforcement when performance meets or exceeds targets. They may reward a department that has exceeded its planned goals or congratulate employees for a job well done. Managers should not ignore high-performing departments in favor of working on corrective actions elsewhere.

CONTROL AND STRATEGIC PLANNING

To exert effective control for the organization, management must integrate control with the strategic planning ideas described in Part 2. If control simply monitors internal activities, it may not help the organization achieve its strategic objectives. The linkage of strategy to control is important because strategy reflects changes in the problems and opportunities that appear in the external environment.

ENVIRONMENTAL CHANGE

environmental discontinuity
A large change in the organization's environment over a short period.

Environments create uncertainty for organizations because of change. As we discussed in Chapter 3, social, economic, technological, and political forces all influence an organization.[8] Sometimes environmental change is gradual, permitting organizations to shift internal controls in an incremental fashion. At other times changes are **environmental discontinuities,** which are large changes over a short time period. Organizations may need to respond almost

EXHIBIT 17.2
Relationship of Organizational Control to Strategic Planning

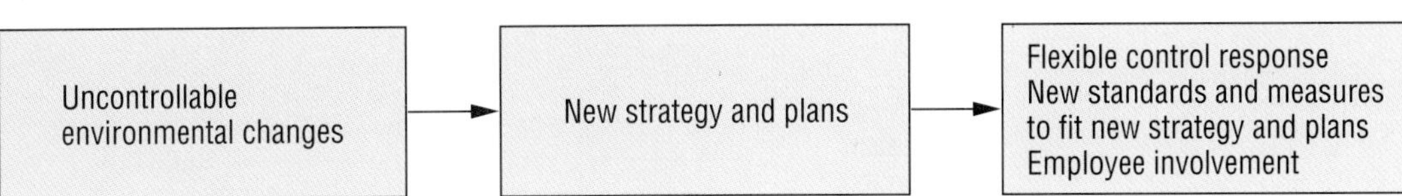

Source: Based on Peter Lorange, Michael F. Scott Morton, and Summantra Ghoshal, *Strategic Control* (St. Paul, Minn.: West, 1986), Chapter 1.

overnight. The banking business, for example, used to be straightforward. Interest rates and the number of banks were determined by the government. Suddenly—within a few months—the financial services industry spewed forth new organizations. Banks now compete with insurance companies and retailers such as Sears, Roebuck.

What do environmental discontinuities mean for organizational control? The firm adapts to these events through strategic planning. As described in the chapters on planning, the organization scans the environment and develops strategic plans that reflect opportunities and potential threats. Internal control systems must change to reflect new strategic objectives and new standards of performance. The internal control system should be flexible to accommodate factors considered uncontrollable.[9]

As illustrated in Exhibit 17.2 uncontrollable events lead to the creation of new strategic plans, which in turn lead to new standards of performance, activities, and feedback systems. Control flexibility usually requires employee involvement. Thus, the control cycle, which establishes standards, measures performance, and takes corrective action, is continuously changing. If managers do not carefully link control to strategy, the organization may exert tight control over current tasks—which are the wrong tasks for successful performance.

The Frito-Lay division of PepsiCo recently shortened its control cycle to meet strategic changes.

FRITO-LAY • In the past, highly centralized Frito-Lay had the leverage of massive purchasing power and efficient, large-scale production. But it was slow to react to market changes. If sales dropped in Cleveland or Dallas, it would take four or five months to find out why.

The control cycle had to be shortened, and the key was quick data on actual sales performance. With competition so intense in the snack-food industry, market share could be lost quickly to new products or price competition. The answer was 10,000 hand-held computers used by salespeople to report the day's sales to headquarters. The data on sales in every store in the country is ready to analyze within 24 hours. Salespeople no longer spend long hours filling out forms that languish in the pipeline for months. Instead computers do the donkey work, with salespeople having more time to spend on promotions

Exhibit 17.3
Organizational Control Focus

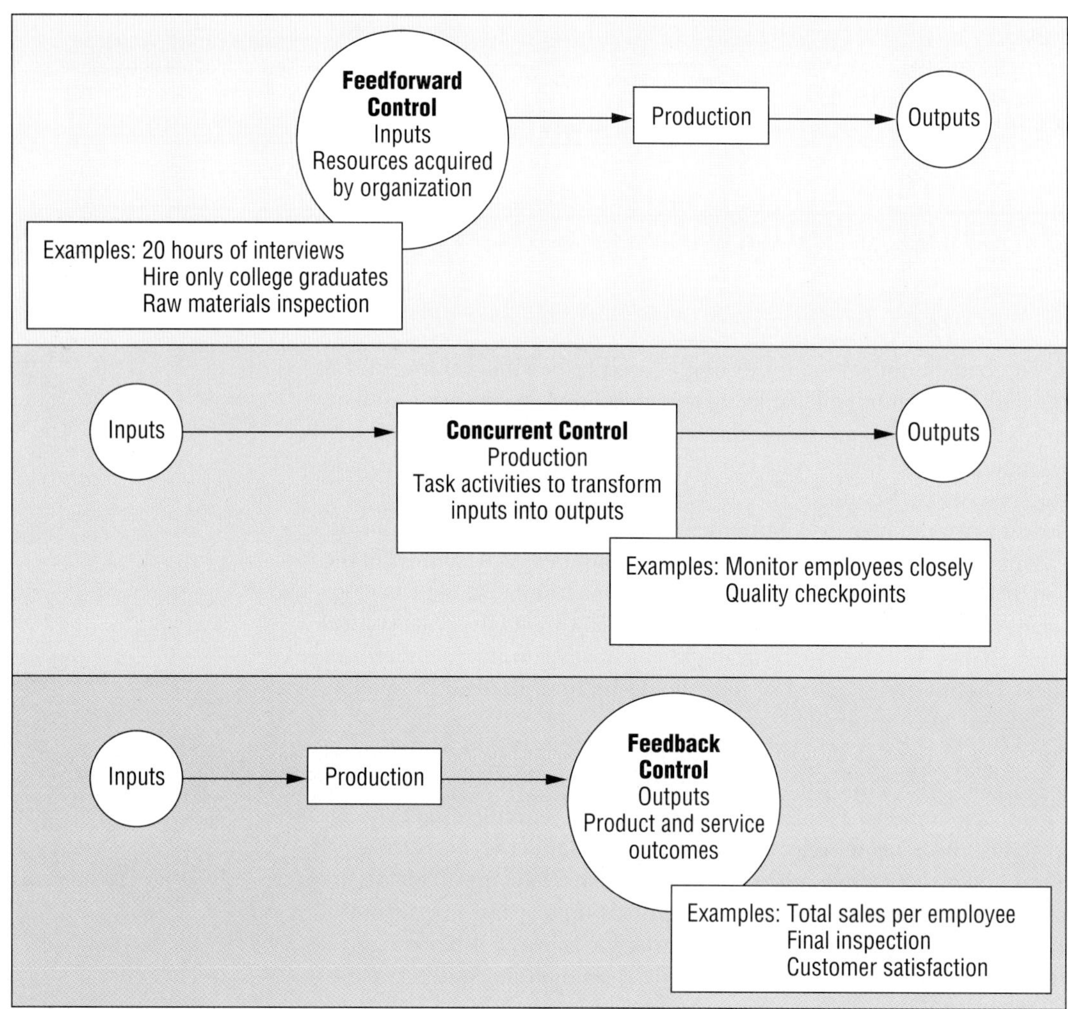

and exhortations. A minor decline in salty snacks is discovered immediately, and new promotions or price cuts are put in place. The flexible control response enables Frito-Lay to respond to sudden environmental changes.[10]

Organizational Control Focus

When managers design and implement the four steps of control described above, on which part of the organization should they focus? The organization is a production process, and control can focus on events before, during, or after this process.[11] For example, a local automobile dealer can focus control on activities before, during, or after sales of new cars. Careful inspection of new cars and cautious selection of sales employees are examples of control that occurs before sales take place. Monitoring how salespeople act with customers and providing rules and procedures for guiding the sales process would be considered control during the sales task. Counting the number of new cars sold during the month or telephoning buyers about their satisfaction with sales transactions would constitute control after sales have taken place. These three types of control are formally called feedforward, concurrent, and feedback and are illustrated in Exhibit 17.3.

feedforward control Control that focuses on human, material, and financial resources flowing into the organization; also called *preliminary* or *preventive control.*

concurrent control Control that consists of monitoring ongoing employee activities to ensure their consistency with established standards.

feedback control Control that focuses on the organization's outputs; also called *post-action* or *output control.*

Feedforward Control

Feedforward control focuses on human, material, and financial resources that flow into the organization. Sometimes called *preliminary* or *preventative control,* its purpose is to ensure that input quality is sufficiently high to prevent problems when the organization performs its tasks.[12] Feedforward control is anticipatory and attempts to identify and prevent deviations before they occur.

Feedforward controls are evident in the selection and hiring of new employees. Westinghouse selects only 5 percent of job applicants for its College Station plant, because only a certain type of person fits the plant's culture. Tandem Computer Company subjects potential middle managers to 20 grueling hours of interviews with both top-level managers and prospective peers to ensure that no problems will occur after hiring.[13] Before McDonald's could open its restaurant in Moscow, experts had to spend time in Russia helping farmers learn to grow high-quality potatoes and bakers to bake high-quality bread. These preventative control techniques enabled the Moscow restaurant to achieve world-class standards. The requirement that professional football, basketball, and baseball players pass a physical exam before their contracts are validated is still another form of feedforward control.

Hershey Chocolate U.S.A. procures fine cocoa beans from more than a dozen countries to use in chocolate production. Here employees practice *feedforward control* as they monitor the quality of cocoa beans entering production at the Hershey, PA, plant. Hershey also organizes plant employees into teams for *concurrent control* in each area of the candy-making operation.

Concurrent Control

Concurrent control monitors ongoing employee activities to ensure that they are consistent with planned standards. Concurrent control is a common form of control because it assesses current work activities. It relies on performance standards and includes rules and regulations for guiding employee tasks and behaviors. Concurrent control is designed to ensure that employee work activities produce the correct results.

At a construction company, the construction superintendent may hire laborers with little screening. Employees are given a chance to perform, and the superintendent monitors their behavior. If employees obey the rules and work effectively, they are allowed to stay; if they do not, they are let go. In a manufacturing firm, it is not unusual for production managers to have a series of quality checkpoints to see whether the production steps have been completed satisfactorily. Frito-Lay's use of hand-held computers to monitor daily sales activities is an example of concurrent control.

Feedback Control

Feedback control focuses on the organization's outputs. Sometimes called *post-action* or *output control,* it focuses on the end product or service after the

The Larsen Company, a subsidiary of Dean Foods Company, produces canned and frozen vegetables. These employees at Larsen's research lab in Green Bay, WI, use *feedback control* to test the company's output of canned vegetables during the weekly comparative product test. Several brands of vegetables are sampled as they would appear in stores.

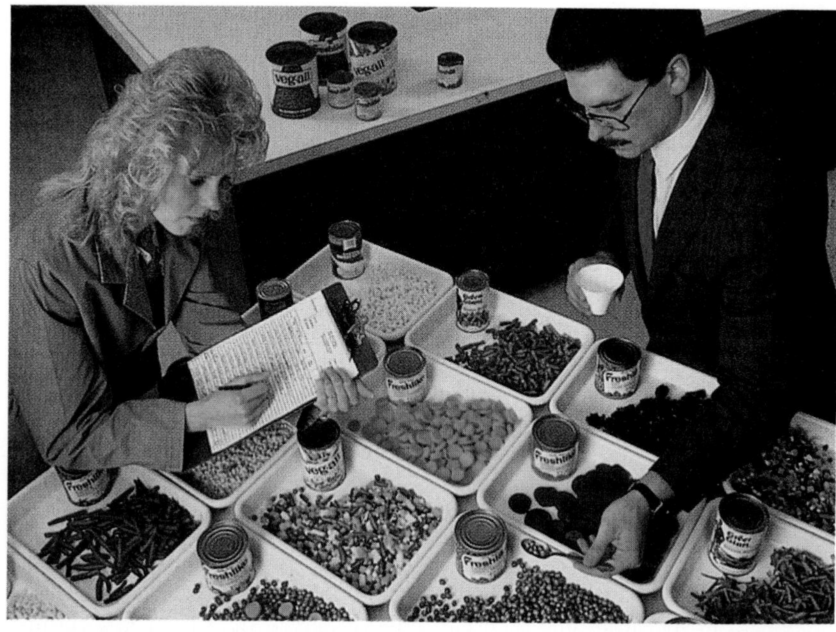

organization's task is completed. An intensive final inspection of a refrigerator at a General Electric assembly plant is an example of feedback control in the manufacturing department. Caterpillar Tractor Company uses feedback control when it surveys customers after 300 and 500 hours of product use. In the National Basketball Association, feedback control is used when team managers focus on games won or lost. If a basketball team wins the targeted number of games for the season, the organization is considered effective.

STRATEGIC CONTROL POINTS

multiple control system A control system involving the simultaneous use of feedforward, concurrent, and feedback control.

strategic control point An activity that is especially important for achieving the organization's strategic objectives.

Most organizations use **multiple control systems** simultaneously. Thus, managers are able to control resource inputs, ongoing task activities, and final outputs. Managers design control systems to define standards of performance and acquire information feedback at strategic control points. **Strategic control points** are those activities that are especially important for achieving strategic objectives. An organization may decide that 60 percent of its total success comes from its ability to control current activities. Thus, a strategic control point would be the monitoring of the production process. Another firm may feel that it can achieve 50 percent of its strategic objectives if it acquires the right people and materials. Thus, resource inputs would be a strategic control point.

An organization's transformation process can be thought of as a value-added chain in which each department performs work that adds value to the final product. A simple value-added chain for a manufacturing firm is illustrated in Exhibit 17.4.[14] This firm uses feedforward, concurrent, and feedback control simultaneously. The control linkage to inbound people and supplies establishes performance standards and monitors the rejection rate for raw materials inventory. No direct control is used for parts drilling and machining on

EXHIBIT 17.4
Strategic Control Points Using Multiple Control Systems

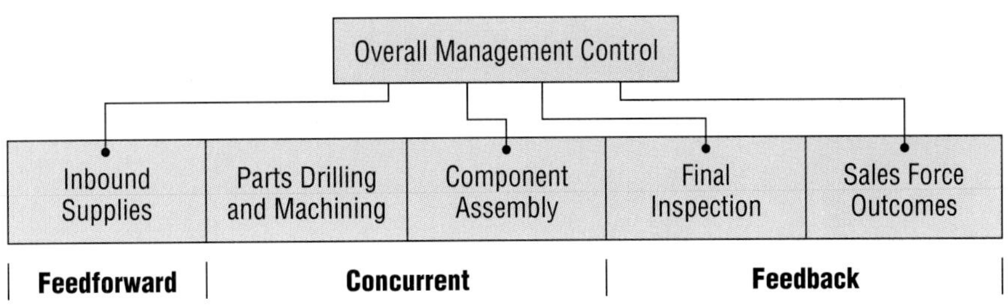

Source: Based on Peter Lorange, Michael F. Scott Morton, and Sumantra Ghoshal, *Strategic Control* (St. Paul, Minn.: West, 1986), Chapter 5.

the shop floor, because employees and supervisors monitor their own quality performance. Component assembly, however, is monitored. Standards can be set for the number and quality of components to be assembled on a daily basis. This is concurrent control. Feedback control is provided at the strategic points of final inspection and by the sales force. Final inspection reveals rejection rates and provides feedback regarding needed changes in either raw materials acquisition or the production process. Sales force control indicates success rates in selling products.

The implementation of multiple controls in organizations can be complex, but each control system plays a logical part. The system can be designed to anticipate problems through feedforward control, monitor ongoing activities through concurrent control, or inspect final output for feedback control. Moreover, employees can be involved in the selection and implementation of control systems that affect them.

CORPORATE CULTURE AND CONTROL

Regardless of whether the organization focuses control on inputs, production, or outputs, another choice must be made between bureaucratic and clan control approaches. These two control approaches represent different philosophies of corporate culture, which was discussed in Chapter 3. Most organizations display some aspects of both bureaucratic and clan control, but many managers emphasize one or the other depending on the culture within their organization.

BUREAUCRATIC CONTROL

bureaucratic control The use of rules, policies, hierarchy of authority, reward systems, and other formal devices to influence employee behavior and assess performance.

Bureaucratic control is the use of rules, policies, hierarchy of authority, written documentation, reward systems, and other formal mechanisms to influence employee behavior and assess performance.[15] Bureaucratic control relies

As UPS expands its package delivery service around the world, it maintains *bureaucratic control* over nearly every aspect of its operation. Each task is carefully calibrated in this top-down control culture. No matter where they are located around the world, UPS drivers must keep their hair trimmed short and a sharp crease on their brown pants.

on the cultural value of traditional top-down control and is implemented through the organization's administrative system. It assumes that targets can be defined and that employees' work behavior will conform to those targets if formal rules and regulations are provided. The following control elements are typically associated with bureaucratic control.

RULES AND PROCEDURES. Rules and procedures include the standard operating procedures and policies that prescribe correct employee behavior. Rules are based on organizational experience and newly defined strategies. They indicate acceptable behaviors and standards for employee performance.

MANAGEMENT CONTROL SYSTEMS. Management control systems include those internal organization systems, such as budgeting, financial reporting, reward systems, operations management, and management by objectives, that monitor and evaluate performance. These systems are normally quantitative in nature and sometimes measure performance on a daily or even hourly basis. Control systems will be discussed in detail in Chapters 18 through 20.

HIERARCHY OF AUTHORITY. Hierarchy of authority relies on central authority and personal supervision for control. Managers are responsible for the control of subordinates through direct surveillance. The supervisor has formal authority for control purposes. Lower-level employees are not expected to participate in the control process.

SELECTION AND TRAINING. Under bureaucratic control methods, selection and training are highly formalized. Objective written tests are administered to see if employees meet hiring criteria. Demographic characteristics, such as education and work experience, are quantified to see whether applicants qualify. Formalized selection procedures are intended to allow broad opportunities for employment, but they are associated with extensive paperwork.

TECHNOLOGY. Technology extends bureaucratic control in two ways. First, it can control the flow and pace of work. In an assembly line manufacturing plant, for example, the technology defines the speed and standards at which workers must perform. Second, computer-based technology can be used to monitor employees. This occurs frequently in service firms. AT&T has a monitoring system that counts the number of seconds that elapse prior to operators answering each call and the number of seconds spent on each call. American Express uses electronic techniques to monitor data entry personnel who record account payments as well as operators who answer phone queries from credit cardholders. The system reports daily productivity data for each operator and each department. New systems available to organizations enable supervisors to eavesdrop on employees and count the times they call home.[16]

Although many managers effectively use bureaucratic control, too much control can backfire. Employees resent being watched too closely, and they may try to sabotage the control system. However, too little bureaucratic control also can backfire. Finding the right level is the challenge. Bureaucratic control methods can be implemented and used in many kinds of organizations, even elementary schools.

FRANKLIN ELEMENTARY SCHOOL • In response to the public's demand for improved student performance scores, Franklin Elementary School has adopted bureaucratic control techniques. First, precise educational objectives are set forth for both teachers and students. One objective for first-grade students is to "write complete sentences, using periods correctly." The principal also visits each teacher's classroom and monitors what each child actually does minute by minute.

The school principal also provides a rigid disciplinary code. Rules define the response to violations. On the third cafeteria violation, the rule is: "Student stands against wall . . . if lunch completed, otherwise at recess." Rules even extend to the homework regimen. Teachers no longer accept excuses, and missed homework must be made up during the lunch hour or a free period.

Bureaucratic control programs have improved student achievement, attendance, and discipline. Barbara Martin, Franklin's principal, does not want the school to become too impersonal and rule bound. She stresses a nurturing, warm environment between teachers and students. With the rules to define appropriate behavior, teachers are free to create a positive working relationship with students.[17]

CLAN CONTROL

Clan control represents cultural values almost the opposite of bureaucratic control. **Clan control** relies on social values, traditions, shared beliefs, and trust to foster compliance with organizational goals. Employees are trusted, and managers believe employees are willing to perform correctly without extensive rules or supervision. Given minimal direction and standards, employees are assumed to perform well — indeed, they participate in setting standards and designing the control system. Clan control is usually implemented through the following techniques.

clan control The use of social values, traditions, common beliefs, and trust to generate compliance with organizational goals.

CORPORATE CULTURE. Corporate culture was described in Chapter 3 as the norms and values shared by organization members. If the organization has a strong corporate culture and the established values are consistent with its goals, corporate culture will be a powerful control device. The organization is like a large family, and each employee is committed to activities that will best serve it. Corporate traditions such as IBM's 100% Club and Mary Kay's pink Cadillac awards instill values in employees that are consistent with the goals and behaviors needed for corporate success.

AT&T has caught the new wave of *clan control*. These workers at the Denver factory can bring circuit board assembly to a halt with the push of a button. Workers are organized into product teams that have a responsibility to improve efficiency and satisfy customers. Managers also share the findings from customer surveys with plant workers, and any employee can call a quality circle meeting to solve a problem.

PEER GROUP. In Chapter 16, we saw that norms evolve in working teams and that cohesive teams influence employee behavior. If peer control is established, less top-down bureaucratic control is needed. Employees are likely to pressure coworkers into adhering to team norms and achieving departmental goals.

SELF-CONTROL. No organization can control employees 100 percent of the time. Self-discipline and self-control are what keep employees performing their tasks up to standard. Most employees bring to the job a belief in doing a fair day's work and a desire to contribute to the organization's success in return

EXHIBIT 17.5
Bureaucratic and Clan Methods of Control

	Bureaucratic	Clan
Purpose	Employee compliance	Employee commitment
Techniques	Rules, formal control systems, hierarchy, selection and training, technology	Corporate culture, peer group, self-control, selection, and socialization
Performance expectations	Measurable standards define minimum performance; fixed indicators	Emphasis on higher performance and oriented toward dynamic marketplace
Organization structure	Tall structure, top-down controls	Flat structure, mutual influence
	Rules and procedures for coordination and control	Shared goals, values, traditions for coordination and control
	Authority of position	Authority of knowledge and expertise
Rewards	Based on employee's achievement in own job	Based on group achievements and equity across employees
Participation	Formalized and narrow (e.g., grievance procedures)	Informal and broad, including control systems design and organizational governance

Source: Based on Richard E. Walton, "From Control to Commitment in the Workplace," *Harvard Business Review* (March/April 1985), 76–84.

for rewards and fair treatment. To the extent that managers can take greater advantage of employee self-control, bureaucratic controls can be reduced. Employees high in self-control often are those who have had several years of experience and training and hence have internal standards of performance. It is common to see departments of attorneys, researchers, or doctors at large corporations such as General Motors, Reynolds Metals, Phillips Petroleum, and Penn Central. The experience, training, and socialization of professionals provide internal standards of performance that allow for self-control.[18]

EMPLOYEE SELECTION AND SOCIALIZATION. Clan methods of selection use personal evaluations rather than formal testing procedures. For example, companies that use clan control methods often subject employment candidates to a rigorous selection process. We mentioned earlier that Tandem Computer subjects managers to 20 grueling hours of interviews. For an entry-level position at Procter & Gamble, the person is interviewed at length by a line manager; people from the personnel department are not involved. The line managers have been trained to probe deeply into the applicant's qualities. The candidate also goes through a second interview of similar depth and takes a test of general knowledge. Then there is a full day of one-on-one interviews at corporate headquarters and a group interview over lunch.[19] After candidates are hired, they are subjected to intensive training in company values, standards, and traditions. Rigorous selection and socialization activities are an effective way to ensure that candidates buy into the company's values, goals, and traditions and hence need few rules and little supervision for control.

In summary, clan control utilizes methods different from those of bureaucratic control. The important point is that both methods provide organizational control. It is a mistake to assume that clan control is weak or represents the absence of control simply because visible rules, procedures, and supervision are absent. Indeed, some people believe that clan control is the stronger form of control because it engages employees' commitment and involvement. Clan control is the wave of the future, with more companies adopting it as part of a strong corporate culture that encourages employee involvement.

Exhibit 17.5 compares bureaucratic and clan control methods. Bureaucratic control is concerned with compliance and clan control with employee commitment.[20] Bureaucratic methods define explicit standards that translate into minimum performance and use top-down control. Compensation is based on individual performance. Employees rarely participate in the control process. With clan methods, employees strive to achieve standards beyond explicitly stated objectives. Influence is mutual, with employees having a say in how tasks are performed and even in determining standards of performance and design of control systems. Shared goals and values replace rules and procedures. Compensation is based on group, departmental, and organizational success rather than on individual performance. This induces individuals to help rather than compete against one another. Employees participate in a wide range of issues, including company governance, objective setting, and performance standards.

An example of how far clan control can go is Marquette Electronics.

MARQUETTE ELECTRONICS • Marquette Electronics makes sophisticated medical devices that doctors use to make life-or-death decisions. Considering the seriousness of its task, it is surprising to see the company characterized by disorder. Some employees wear Hawaiian shirts and have a boom box playing in the background. In the company cafeteria, employees may enjoy a beer. The day care center takes care of employees' children, and employees can take time off to play with them. Managers at Marquette Electronics do not overcontrol. "The truth is, we're all quite bad managers," says the engineering vice-president. "Maybe we're not managers at all."

The company is well managed, but management consciously delegates important responsibilities to employees. Marquette's approach scorns policies and procedures and eschews memos and directives. The guiding philosophy, as expressed by Mike Cudahy, is: "People want to love their job, their boss, and their company. They want to perform. You've got to give people a voice in their jobs. You've got to give them a piece of the action and a chance to excel."

The Marquette culture is fluid and informal, but that does not mean a lack of control. People are not bound by traditional rules, but the group norms and the company culture demand a high standard of performance. Everyone shares a simple but strong expectation: Make good products, give good customer service, and do it all fast. This may seem an unusual approach to management, but as one former employee has said, "Boy, does it work."[21]

TOTAL QUALITY CONTROL

A recent Gallup survey of top executives showed that executives viewed the task of improving service quality and product quality as the most critical challenge facing their companies. Executives believe that quality has been the dominate factor in the success of the Japanese in world markets and that improved quality is a major weapon to restore North America's competitive position in the global marketplace.[22] To achieve high quality, more and more companies are finding it necessary to make an organizationwide commitment to quality and to include quality as a major strategic objective.

The term used to describe this approach is called *total quality control.* This approach was successfully implemented by Japanese companies that earned an international reputation for quality. Some Japanese companies prefer the term *companywide quality control* to convey the idea of total employee involvement. Ironically, this approach to quality was introduced in an American book by A. V. Feigenbaum called *Total Quality Control.*[23] The Japanese snapped up the ideas that Americans ignored for years. Recent books, such as *Quality Is Free: The Art of Making Quality Certain* by Philip Crosby and *The Deming Management Method* by Mary Walton, have helped reawaken and extend quality ideas throughout North America.[24]

total quality control A control concept that gives workers rather than managers the responsibility for achieving standards of quality.

The theme of **total quality control** is simple: "The burden of quality proof rests . . . with the makers of the part."[25] In other words, workers, not managers, are responsible for achieving standards of quality. This is a revolution in management thinking, because quality control departments and formal control systems no longer have primary control responsibility. Companies that really want to improve quality are urged to stop inspecting every part and to get rid of their quality control departments. These companies are then told to train the workers and trust them to take care of quality.

This approach can give traditional executives several sleepless nights as their traditional means of control vanish. Total quality control essentially means a shift from a bureaucratic to a clan method of control. Total quality uses clan methods to gain employees' commitment as was described in Exhibit 17.5.

American Airlines is the airline cited most frequently by customers for the high quality of its service. Chairman Robert L. Crandall explains how it goes back to a policy decision to improve the traditionally adversarial relationship between labor and management.

> The airline business has historically had a strong military bent and developed as a rather rigid, procedures-based and confrontational workplace. On top of that, the industry became heavily unionized. Very early in the deregulation process, we made the decision to make a sustained, long-term effort to change that confrontational, non-cooperative, non-participative environment into an environment based on trust and mutual respect.[26]

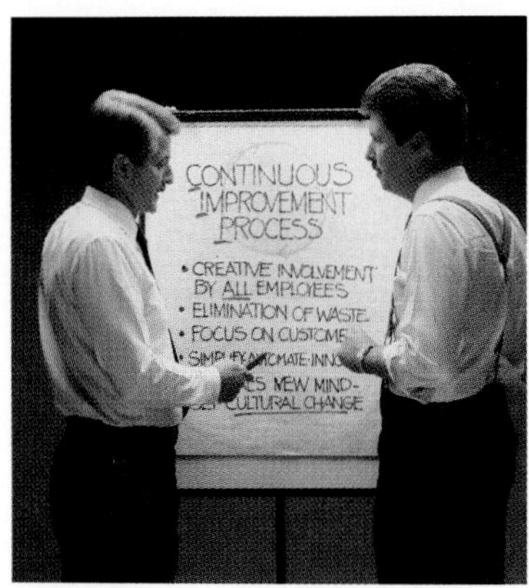

Brush Wellman Inc. is a leading international producer of high-performance engineered materials. The company introduced a continuous improvement process to improve quality companywide. This approach to *total quality control* helps Brush provide its customers with the highest quality products and service. Jim Dudziak (left), Vice President–Operations Services, and Dan Skoch, Corporate Director of Personnel, discuss implementation of the program.

Companywide participation in quality control requires quite a change in corporate culture values as described in Chapter 11. The mindset of both managers and employees must shift. Companies traditionally have practiced the Western notion of achieving an "acceptable quality level." This allows a certain percentage of defects and engenders a mentality that imperfections are okay. Only defects caught by a quality control department need be corrected. Total quality control not only engages the participation of all employees but has a target of zero defects. Everyone strives for perfection. A rejection rate of 2 percent will lead to a new quality target of 1 percent. This approach instills a habit of continuous improvement rather than the traditional Western approach of attempting to meet the minimum acceptable standard of performance.

Two recent books that advocate a systematic quality effort suggest the following precepts for successful companywide quality control programs.[27]

1. Management is obsessed with quality. Top management places quality at the top of every agenda.
2. The system for creating quality is prevention, not appraisal. The motto is, "Do it right the first time."
3. Overall quality is measured. For example, data are gathered from customer complaints or from customer satisfaction surveys and are then published widely.
4. Quality is rewarded. Executive pay includes quality incentives. Suppliers are penalized if quality declines.
5. Everyone from the president down is trained in the basics of quality assessment.
6. Teams comprising members from different departments cooperate to identify and solve quality problems.
7. Small improvements are highly valued.
8. *Everybody*, every employee plus suppliers and customers, participates in the quality improvement program.
9. The performance standard must be zero defects, not "that's close enough."
10. Cost savings from quality improvements are calculated and reported. The cost of poor quality accounts for 25 to 40 percent of a company's operating costs due to reprocessing data, field service for repairs, excess inventory, remachining products, hot lines for disgruntled customers, and extra shipping costs.

Quality control thus becomes part of the day-to-day business of every employee. Management needs to evaluate quality in terms of lost sales and total company performance rather than as some percentage indicator from a management control system. Each employee must internalize the value of preventing defects. When handled properly, the total quality approach really works. Standout companies using these techniques are Eastman Kodak, Ford Motor Company, Motorola, Westinghouse, CIGNA, Federal Express, and Florida Power & Light. The Focus on Entrepreneurship box tells how one small company successfully implemented the total quality approach.

The implementation of total quality control is similar to that of other control methods. Targets must be set for employee involvement and for new quality standards. Employees must be trained to think in terms of prevention, not detection, and they must be given the responsibility of correcting their own errors and exposing any quality problems they discover. In the Kawasaki plant in Lincoln, Nebraska, the implementation of the new approach caused a sharp decrease in the size of the quality control department and its role in inspections. Kawasaki shifted from feedback to feedforward control. Quality control inspectors were assigned to the receiving dock to inspect items to be used by Kawasaki workers. If workers had good materials to work with, the final output would be of high quality.[28]

quality circle A group of six to twelve volunteer employees who meet regularly to discuss and solve problems that affect their common work activities.

Campbell Soup Company has 50 separate business units with nearly 500 *quality circles* throughout the company. These teams help build in quality at every step of the manufacturing process. Involving the people who make the soup is the heart of the quality process.

QUALITY CIRCLES

Another approach to implementing a total quality philosophy and engaging the work force in a clan approach is that of quality circles (QCs). A **quality circle** is a group of from six to twelve volunteer employees who meet regularly to discuss and solve problems affecting their common work activities.[29] Time is

FOCUS ON ENTREPRENEURSHIP

DUCANE INDUSTRIES MAKES BARBECUES WORRY FREE

When you flip hamburgers at a summer barbecue, you probably don't worry about how well the grill is functioning. But to John Ducate, Jr., president of Ducane Industries, the quality of the gas grills he manufactures is his primary concern. This Columbia, South Carolina, entrepreneur has developed a unique quality control program that involves all 700 members of his firm.

When he first began production, quality control was considered the sole responsibility of the final inspector. If a defective product slipped through, only the inspector would be considered responsible. But Ducate recognized that if he could get all of his employees to accept responsibility for the quality of their work he would have an overall quality improvement. So he began active quality checks during production. Now, in each of the factory's assembly areas traffic lights notify workers of their quality check status. When an area is under inspection, the light changes from green to amber. As many as five amber lights may be on at one time. A red light indicates that a product in that part of the assembly process failed the audit.

When there is a failure, the plant deals with it constructively. Assembly line operations are halted while inspectors and supervisors determine what the problem might be. Once it is solved, photographs and descriptions of the defect are posted throughout the facility so that employees can know what happened and how to avoid the problem in the future.

Employee training has also helped Ducane improve the quality control of its product. Workers in each department are asked to put together an entire grill without any help. Through this exercise, they learn how mistakes in their production step can slow down the line, and they come to understand the problems that workers face in other parts of manufacturing.

The traffic light program has produced very positive results. Quality and sales are at an all-time high. Because the company does not do a lot of active marketing, Ducate attributes this new success to his improved quality control. "The fact that most of our sales originate as word-of-mouth referrals," says Ducate, "indicates to us that the program is working."

Source: "Giving Quality the Green Light," *Small Business Report* (March 1988), 60–61. Used with permission.

set aside during the workweek for these groups to meet, raise problems, and try to find solutions. The key idea is that people who do the job know the job better than anyone else and can make recommendations for improved performance. QCs also push control decision making to a lower organizational level. Circle members are free to collect data and take surveys. In many companies, team members are given training in team building, problem solving, and statistical quality control to enable them to confront problems and solutions more readily. The groups do not focus on personal gripes and problems. Often a facilitator is present to help guide the discussion. Quality circles use many of the teamwork concepts described in Chapter 16. The quality circle process as used in most American companies is illustrated in Exhibit 17.6.

The quality circle concept has spread to the United States and Canada from Japan. Originally quality circles were a way for Japanese companies to gain employees' commitment to high standards. They spread to the United States when executives from Lockheed visited Japan and were impressed by how well quality circles worked. The Manager's Shoptalk box lists ten important ways to ensure that quality circles are successful. Such North American

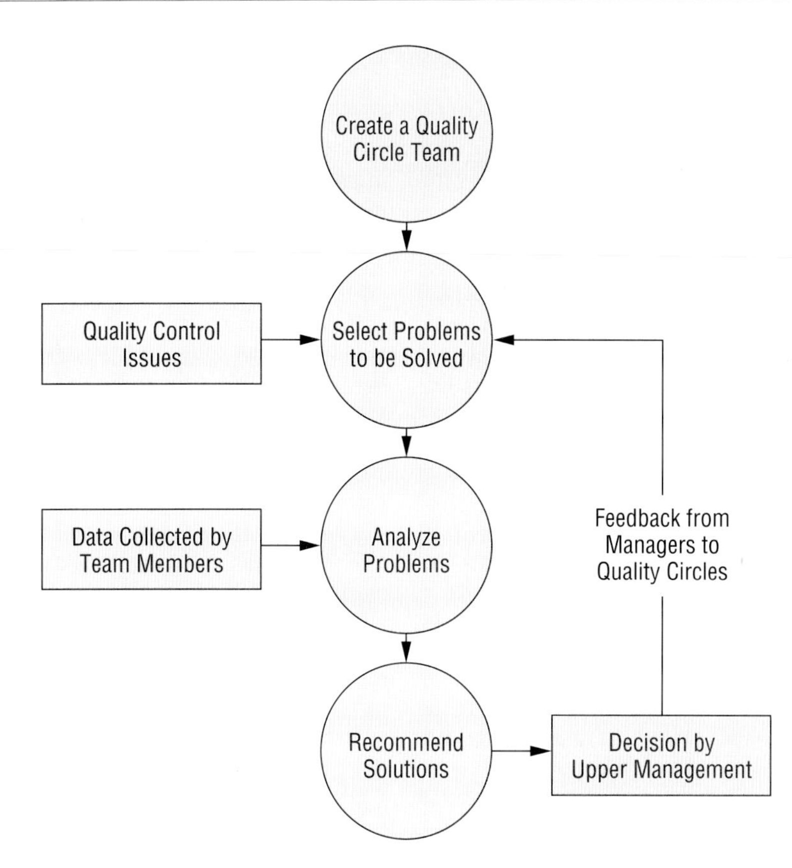

EXHIBIT 17.6
The Quality Circle Process

Source: Adapted from Burlington Industries, Inc., *1985 Annual Report*, 9.

companies as Westinghouse, Digital Equipment, Martin Marietta Corporation, and Baltimore Gas & Electric Company have adopted quality circles. In several of these companies, managers attest to the improved performance and cost savings. Westinghouse has over 100 quality circles; a single innovation proposed by one group saved the company $2.4 million. To build on these successes, Westinghouse created the Productivity and Quality Center that assists departments throughout the company. It acts as a SWAT team of sorts to help divisions do the same work in half the time with better quality results.[30]

QC CONTINGENCY FACTORS

Recall from Chapter 2 that contingencies are situational factors that affect the success of management programs. Despite their promise, quality circles do not always work. A few firms have had disappointing results. Generally, the organizational contingency factors in Exhibit 17.7 will influence the chance for QC success.[31] A positive contingency factor is the task skill demands on employees in the QC. When skill demands are great, the quality circle can further enhance productivity. When tasks are simple and require low skills, improved

MANAGER'S SHOPTALK

TEN KEYS TO SUCCESSFUL QUALITY CIRCLES

1. *Explain the quality control (QC) concept to managers and supervisors, and solicit volunteers.* Assert that quality is a primary objective rather than a side issue. Before any circles are formed, all employees must thoroughly understand what QCs are and what they can do.
2. *Train management volunteers in the QC philosophy so that they can set up circles, train circle members, and maintain the program.* Companies with unions will find it important to treat the QC program as a cooperative venture between the company and the union.
3. *Trained managers present the idea to their work groups and solicit volunteers.* Initial meetings teach employees basic QC techniques. Circle leaders must be skilled in the techniques of team building, motivation, and problem solving.
4. *Trained facilitators coordinate the program's overall structure and provide support to groups.* Facilitators should be people oriented, good communicators, and willing to engage in challenging discussions with individuals from all company levels.
5. *Established circles meet regularly to identify, analyze, and solve work-related problems.* Meetings should be scheduled for one hour to ensure a problem focus. Problem areas are easy to identify, but deciding which problem to address first is difficult.
6. *Quality is defined and measured in concrete terms so that positive steps to improve quality control can be taken.* Both statistical (for example, scrap rate) and general (such as consumer response) measurements can be taken.
7. *As circles acquire problem-solving skills, they split, disband, and reform, with experienced members serving as group leaders.* Group leaders may be provided training in motivation, team building, and problem solving.
8. *Responsibility for coordinating QCs may be assigned to a single person or department, and standard operating procedures are developed to avoid overlaps in QC responsibilities.* The responsible manager or department should also monitor QCs to ensure that they are properly motivated and producing results.
9. *Top management supplies the reinforcement and feedback necessary to keep enthusiasm and participation high.* Recognition in the form of management acknowledgment, trophies, T-shirts, or a special luncheon is appropriate.
10. *A committee composed of top managers studies the proposals from the circles and takes action to implement favorable suggestions.* An explanation is provided for the rejection of a recommendation. Some companies award circle members 10 percent of the money saved from QC suggestions. Others pay participants overtime for the time spent in meetings.

Source: Based on Joel Dreyfuss, "Victories in the Quality Crusade," *Fortune,* October 10, 1988, 80–88; "Quality Circles," *Business Update,* vol. 1, no. 8, 12–18; Gerald R. Ferris and John A. Wagner III, "Quality Circles in the United States: A Conceptual Reevaluation," *Journal of Applied Behavioral Science* 21 (1985), 155–167.

skills from QC meetings will have little impact on output. Quality circle success also increases when the circle serves to enrich jobs and improve employee motivation. In addition, when the quality circle improves workers' problem-solving skills, productivity is likely to increase. Finally, when the participation and teamwork aspects of QCs are used to tackle significant, nonprogrammed problems, such as how to keep metal parts free of oil film, the outcome is better. QCs should not be used to tackle simple, routine problems, such as where to locate the water cooler.

Quality circles often have trouble when senior management's expectations are too high. Managers quickly become disaffected if they are expecting immediate jumps in quality. QC success comes through a series of small, incremental gains. Moreover, middle- and upper-level managers sometimes are dissatisfied because problem-solving opportunities are taken from them and given to employees on the shop floor. Also, when workers are dissatisfied with their organizational lives outside the quality circle, the QC will have a smaller chance of success. Union leaders can also upset the quality circle program if they feel left

EXHIBIT 17.7
Quality Circle Contingency Factors

Positive Factors	Negative Factors
Tasks make high skill demands on employees.	Management expectations are unrealistically high.
The QC serves to enrich jobs and motivate employees.	Middle managers frequently are dissatisfied about loss of authority.
Problem-solving skills are improved for team participants.	Workers are dissatisfied with other aspects of organizational life.
Participation and teamwork are used to tackle significant, nonprogrammed problems.	Union leaders are left out of QC discussions.
	Highly automated plants limit improvements in personal productivity.

out of the discussions between workers and management. Finally, in highly automated plants where machines do most of the work, quality circles have less impact because worker improvements add little to productivity.

When correctly applied, quality circles generate enormous savings. At Lockheed, savings of $3 million were documented. At the Norfolk Naval Shipyard, savings of $3.41 for every dollar invested in a QC program were reported over an 18-month period. Another company that succeeded with quality circles as a way of implementing a total quality control program is Florida Power & Light Company, the first company outside Japan to win a Deming Prize—Japan's prestigious award for quality.

FLORIDA POWER & LIGHT

• Who would believe that a regulated monopoly with little pressure to excel would become a benchmark of business excellence? The judges for the Deming Prize believed it after spending 18 months scrutinizing Florida Power & Light's management techniques and delivery of services.

How does FPL do it? This is a story of quality management beginning with quality circles. Thousands of employees serve on about 1,900 volunteer teams. It is not unusual for a team of meter readers or lineworkers to pause from their daily work to diagram and analyze a particular service problem. But employees love the challenge, and they have produced startling results. A power-line team devised a plastic pipe to make line installation faster and easier. Meter readers were the most injury-prone employees because of dog bites, so a team devised a way to program hand-held computers to beep a warning at residences with a dog on the premise. One team even devised a way to reduce power outages caused by lightning strikes.

What does all this employee involvement mean? The hundreds of team suggestions have produced dramatic payoffs. The best quality indicator is customer satisfaction. Customers are delighted because FPL has not sought a rate increase in five years. The number of complaints to the Public Service Commission dropped 75 percent and is the best record of any utility in Florida. Another measure is service outages, which used to average 100 minutes per customer per year, similar to the national average; not a bad record. Outages have been driven down to an average of 43 minutes, and it keeps declining.

EXHIBIT 17.8
A Process Control Chart

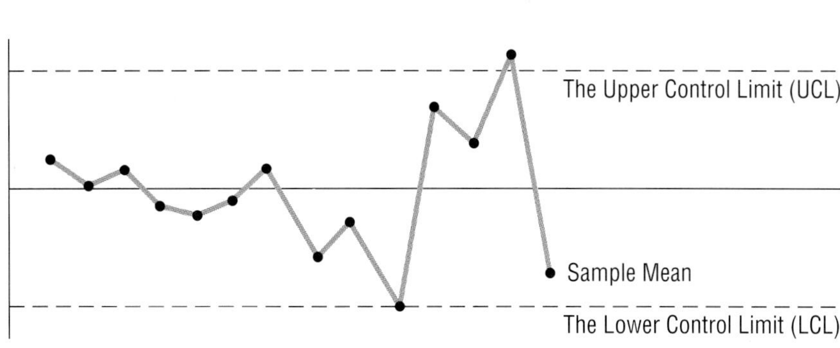

Source: Ross Johnson and William O. Winchell, "Management and Quality," American Society for Quality Control, Milwaukee, Wis., 7. Used with permission.

Today, FPL is a laboratory. Nearly 1,000 companies have made pilgrimages to FPL, which had to develop a how-we-do-it seminar to spread the word.[32]

STATISTICAL QUALITY CONTROL

Quality is not just an abstract concept. It must be measured. But measurement is by workers, not top managers or formal control systems. Workers must be given the training and tools to use statistical techniques to evaluate their tasks and make improvements as needed. The use of statistical measurements is a powerful weapon in the drive to improved quality.

statistical quality control The application of statistical techniques to the control of quality.

statistical process control (SPC) A type of managerial control that employs carefully gathered data and statistical analysis to evaluate the quality and productivity of employee activities.

Statistical quality control refers to the application of statistical techniques to the control of quality. The best known is called **statistical process control (SPC),** the application of statistical techniques to the control of work processes to detect production of defective items.[33] In addition, workers are often trained in traditional statistical concepts such as frequency distributions, regression and correlation, acceptance sampling, and tests of significance. These techniques are widely used in manufacturing departments, because production activities can be measured and analyzed.

For example, employees can be trained to use charts as graphic representations of work processes. A statistical process control chart measures a specific characteristic, as illustrated in Exhibit 17.8. In this particular chart, workers take a sample of five parts each hour, where the production rate is approximately 100 per hour. The diameters of the five parts are measured, and the sample mean is calculated and plotted on the chart. If the upper control limit or lower control limit is exceeded, the variation is too great and is not due to chance alone. If either limit is exceeded, the operation is stopped and the cause determined. In the case illustrated in Exhibit 17.8, the tool had become loose, so it was reset.

Procedures have been developed for implementing statistical quality control, which include the following steps.

Varian Associates is a diversified international electronics company. As part of its quality improvement process, the Eimac San Carlos Division uses *statistical process control* (SPC) techniques to monitor the acceptance of critical tube components. SPC testing, shown here, alerts employees to problems before they affect multiple parts. Thanks to quality improvement, the rejection rate for ceramics dropped from 20 percent to 1.5 percent, hence tubes reach customers quicker and with better results.

1. *Define the characteristics of a high-quality output.* The output can be a hamburger produced by a Wendy's restaurant, a job description written by an employee in the personnel department, or a radial tire produced at a Firestone plant. The supervisor must provide an exact definition of a high-quality output or service.
2. *Decompose the work activities into the discrete elements required for producing a high-quality output.* For making a hamburger, one discrete element is forming the raw hamburger patty, a second is cooking it, and a third is garnishing it. The quality associated with each discrete element must be defined.
3. *Each work element must have a standard that is current and reasonable.* If standards for work elements are not already available, they must be developed. The standard is the basis for comparison of worker performance.
4. *Specific performance expectations for every job must be discussed with workers.* Each worker must understand what is expected with respect to his or her work elements and quality outputs. Workers should participate in decisions about how their performances will be measured.
5. *Make checksheets and collect data for each task element.* Written documents must be developed that reflect performance, and machine operators must be taught to collect data and assess whether their performances are up to standard. Likewise, supervisors can monitor departmental performance by gathering data on team outputs.
6. *Employee progress must be evaluated against standards at frequent intervals.* In some manufacturing situations, the output records should be checked for every worker several times during the day. If employees are involved in running several different batches of material, different standards will apply. If planned quality standards are not met, adjustments can be made before the end of the work period.

Bell Atlantic has implemented an *effective control* approach that is flexible, linked to its strategy of innovation, and widely accepted by employees. Jack Coppley was the product champion for THINX software. Bell Atlantic's system encourages behavior such as Coppley's, which is consistent with strategic objectives and meets employee needs for creativity and involvement.

For example, Tridon Ltd., an Oakville, Ontario, manufacturer of windshield wiper blades, implemented an SPC program. It discovered that 25 percent of the output from the rubber extrusion line was defective. The rubber could not be reworked and thus was lost. To set up its program, Tridon conducted a feasibility study to identify the dimensions of high-quality parts. After defining standards for performance, it taught operators how the production line functioned and how to collect data that would indicate whether quality standards were being met. Setting up the SPC program cost almost $30,000 for studies, analysis, and training. Since implementing the SPC program, Tridon's scrap rate has decreased 10 percent. Now each part is higher quality but actually costs less to produce. Customers are happy and owners are, too.[34]

Statistical techniques go hand in hand with quality circles in developing a total quality program for a company. At Florida Power & Light, the quality circle teams work with checksheets, scatter diagrams, regression lines, histograms, and other statistical tools. Teams use these techniques on their own in the field. Employee training in statistics is as important as training in effective communication and other teamwork skills.

Trends in Effective Control

Whether organizational control focuses on feedforward or feedback activities, or emphasizes the bureaucratic or clan methods, or stresses total quality control, certain characteristics should be present. For organizational controls to be effective, they should be tailored to the organization's needs and facilitate the accomplishment of its task. Effective controls share the following traits:[35]

1. *Be linked to strategy.* The control system should not simply measure what was important in the past or be tailored to current operations. It should reflect where the organization is going and adapt to new strategies. Moreover, the organization should focus on strategic control points that are most relevant for strategic objectives. If the dominant competitive issue facing a company is to develop innovative products, the control system should not emphasize raw materials cost, which is unrelated to innovation.
2. *Use all control steps.* The control steps consist of setting standards of performance, gathering information about actual performance, comparing standards to real performance, and taking corrective action. The control system will not be effective unless it involves each step. Assuming that people know what standard is expected, for example, is a mistake. Managers should make standards explicit and then identify and obtain relevant information on performance. With valid information on performance, managers or workers can take action to redirect activities to correct deficiencies.
3. *Be accepted by members.* The total quality control approach is effective because managers concentrate first on involving the entire organization membership in the control process. The more committed employees are to control standards, the more successful the control system will be. The control system should motivate rather than demotivate. It should set standards and provide information feedback that is meaningful to employees.

4. *Balance objective and subjective data.* Managers can be misled when control system data are either completely numeric or based solely on subjective opinion. Control should be perceived as objective, but quantitative information tells only part of the story. Easily measured activities will receive more weight unless managers balance quantitative and qualitative performance indicators. Good control systems are objective and unbiased and incorporate both hard and soft data to provide a well-rounded picture of performance.
5. *Be accurate.* Upward communication, especially about performance, often is influenced by what employees feel management wants to hear. Subordinates may distort communications to present a positive image of themselves. Junior managers tend to filter upward communications to highlight positive messages and downplay negative ones.[36] The control system must encourage accurate information in order to detect deviations. If the system is too rigid or oppressive, inaccurate information will be fed into it. The senior management of the Boy Scouts of America learned that membership figures had been exaggerated in response to the pressures of a national membership drive. This campaign led people to feed inaccurate data into the system, and top managers mistakenly believed that the drive was successful.
6. *Be flexible.* Organizations exist in changing environments. Internal goals and strategies change over time in response to the environment. The control system must be flexible enough to make adaptations from one year to the next. Managers who rely too heavily on existing controls will find themselves out of synchronization with changing events. The control system should allow for changing objectives and standards.
7. *Be timely.* The control system should provide information soon enough to permit a management response. Corrective action is of no value if performed too late. A study of air conditioner manufacturers in Japan and the United States found that control data were received twice as fast in Japanese companies and management's responses were quicker.[37] Organizations such as Campbell Taggart in the United States use computer-based control systems to get performance reports to managers on the same day the information is obtained.

SUMMARY

This chapter introduced a number of important concepts about organizational control. Organizational control is the systematic process through which managers regulate organizational activities to meet planned standards of performance. The implementation of control includes four steps: establishing standards of performance, measuring actual performance, comparing performance to standards, and taking corrective action. Control should be linked to strategic planning. Changes in the environment require that internal control systems adapt to strategic changes; control systems must not continue measuring what was important in the past.

The focus of organizational control can be on resource input, the production process, or product and service outputs. These forms of control are called, respectively, feedforward, concurrent, and feedback control. Most organizations use all three types simultaneously but emphasize the form that most closely corresponds to their strategic objectives.

Organizational control techniques used by managers can emphasize either bureaucratic or clan methods. Bureaucratic control uses the organization's formal rules, procedures, and systems. Clan control involves employee commitment and relies on trust, shared values, and traditions of high performance.

Total quality control is a new approach to control being widely adopted in Canada and the United States that reflects clan control ideas. Everyone in the organization is involved and committed to the control function. Quality circles, which are teams of six to twelve employees who raise quality problems and discuss solutions, are one means of implementing a total quality control philosophy in an organization. Statistical quality control represents an additional set of tools important to achieving high quality in organizations.

Finally, effective organizational control consists of several characteristics, including a link to strategy, using all four control steps, acceptance by members, balancing objective and subjective data, and the qualities of accuracy, flexibility, and timeliness.

MANAGEMENT SOLUTION

Whistler, the maker of radar detectors, had two plants out of control with 25 percent of detectors failing inspection. Charles Stott and Richard Packer were challenged to turn things around. "We were fat, dumb, and happy," said one manager. Now Whistler is lean and smart, because it created a new control structure. A consulting firm specializing in quality control was asked to help. Then a team of 25 employees from planning, testing, manufacturing, and engineering joined forces with the consultants to design a new production line. Employees, not managers, started making decisions. Circuit boards costing $5 previously were piled up carelessly, but now were stored as if they cost $100. The quality team redefined every job and helped train workers in quality techniques. The most controversial move was to eliminate the quality control department, but the team felt is was necessary to make quality everyone's responsibility.

The results? The defect rate has dropped to 1 percent, and that will be cut in half in a few months. The production work force has been reduced from 250 to 120 without lowering output or quality. Recall that 100 workers previously spent all their time fixing defective units. Manufacturing costs are now almost as low as the sister plant in Korea.[38]

DISCUSSION QUESTIONS

1. Federal policy is to take blood tests of operators after a train crash. Would it be more effective to take regular tests of operators on a random basis? What types of control do these different tests represent?
2. Why is control an important management function? How does it relate to the other management functions of planning, organizing, and leading?
3. Briefly describe the four steps of control. Give an example of each step from your own organizational work experience.

4. What does it mean to say that organizational control should be linked to strategic planning?
5. How do organizations that use multiple control systems decide which control elements are most important?
6. What is the difference between bureaucratic and clan control? Which do you think is the stronger form?
7. Which three precepts associated with successful total quality programs do you consider most essential? Explain.
8. Because statistical quality control uses exact measurements of employee behavior, do you think it will thwart clan control in an organization? Explain.
9. The theme of total quality control is "The burden of quality proof rests . . . with the makers of the part." How does this differ from traditional North American approaches to quality?
10. What is a quality circle? How can it be used to improve organizational quality control?

MANAGEMENT IN PRACTICE: EXPERIENTIAL EXERCISE

Quality Improvement Questionnaire

For each item circle the number that best describes your attitude or behavior on the job or at school.

	Disagree				Agree
1. I recognize the practical constraints of existing conditions when someone proposes an improvement idea.	5	4	3	2	1
2. I like to support change efforts, even when the idea may not work.	1	2	3	4	5
3. I believe that many small improvements are usually better than a few big improvements.	1	2	3	4	5
4. I encourage other people to express improvement ideas, even if they differ from mine.	1	2	3	4	5
5. There is truth to the statement, "If it isn't broke, don't fix it."	5	4	3	2	1
6. I work at the politics of change to build agreement for my improvement ideas.	1	2	3	4	5
7. I study suggestions carefully to avoid change just for the sake of change.	5	4	3	2	1
8. I like to have clear objectives that support improvement, even if changes upset my efficiency.	1	2	3	4	5
9. I constantly talk about ways to improve what I'm doing.	1	2	3	4	5
10. I am able to get higher-ups to support my ideas for improvement.	1	2	3	4	5

Total Score ______

Your score indicates the extent to which you are a positive force for quality improvement. The questions represent behaviors associated with the Japanese approach to companywide continuous improvement of quality.

- 40–50: Great. A dynamo for quality improvement.
- 30–40: Good. A positive force.
- 20–30: Adequate. You have a typical North American attitude.
- 10–20: Poor. You may be dragging down quality efforts.

Go back over the questions on which you scored lowest and develop a plan to improve your approach toward quality. Discuss your ideas with other students.

CASES FOR ANALYSIS

LIGHTHOUSE ELECTRIC COMPANY

Jerry Dean was recently hired as director of Lighthouse Electric's quality control department. Lighthouse had once been a top-ranked manufacturer of electrical heaters and small electric motors, but its reputation had fallen in recent years along with market share. Jerry was expected to turn things around with an improved quality control program.

This morning Jerry went to see his boss, Andy Whitmore, vice-president of manufacturing, about a problem on the shop floor. Several fan blades on a shipment of 1021 electric heaters were too tight, and one of Jerry's inspectors red tagged them. Sheila Jackson, manufacturing director, felt it would take too long to fix the fans, so she turned all the electric heaters on high speed, burning the washers down to the right clearance. Marketing shipped the fans that afternoon. Andy listened to the story and Jerry's frustrations about not having the last word on whether items were shipped. Andy said, "We are all under pressure to make a good product, but we don't want to lose money doing it. There's no time to rework all these heaters."

Jerry investigated further, learning that Sheila was always under pressure from sales to deliver products immediately. One reason the fan blades were too tight was the poor training of new employees. People barely learned where to hang their coats before they started on the assembly line. No trainers were available from personnel. Moreover, Sheila reported wide variation in washers. Putting five washers on a fan shaft could leave a clearance of between five-thousandths and twenty-five-thousandths of an inch.

Jerry recommended that assemblers adjust for the variation when they assemble the electric heater. Sheila would have none of that, saying, "They can't use a micrometer every time they put a few washers on a shaft." However, she implied that if Jerry had enough people, his inspectors could measure those washers. "Besides," Sheila said, "95 percent of our orders are shipped on time, which is a great record. It's our delivery performance that gets us business. I'm not going to change that."

Questions

1. What is the problem here? Is there a problem here?
2. What steps should Jerry Dean take to improve quality?
3. Is Lighthouse Electric likely to succeed in its desire to improve quality? Explain.

Source: Based on Frank S. Leonard, "The Case of the Quality Crusader," *Harvard Business Review* (May/June 1988), 12–20.

USING PRIVATE EYES AT GM

Recently at General Motors' Mansfield, Ohio, plant, drug abuse went too far. Marijuana and cocaine were being used on the plant floor, in the parking lot, and near the cafeteria. Supposedly at least one out of every ten workers was using drugs or alcohol on the job. A community resident complained that narcotics were flooding the community. One worker received a death threat. Another worker's son died of an opium overdose.

GM's action was extreme: It hired undercover agents to work on the assembly line. The agents worked with law enforcement officials to identify and arrest drug pushers. Users were given disciplinary action or treatment.

How do companies such as General Motors control this problem? Some of the tactics used by Fortune 500 companies include compulsory urinalysis, lie detectors, drug-sniffing dogs, counseling and treatment programs, and undercover detectives. GM chose the last option in an effort to destroy the drug culture at the Mansfield and eight other plants.

The detectives were astonished at what they found. They purchased "dime bags" of marijuana easily and pretended to snort cocaine through dollar bills behind machinery on the plant floor. Drug use was difficult to control because the Mansfield plant is huge and employs 4,000 workers. Traditional control techniques did not work. Security guards were supposed to monitor illegal activities, but one worker attempted to sell cocaine to an undercover agent while security guards were less than 20 feet away. A $4,000 cocaine purchase took place as unsuspecting security guards cruised by.

GM's approach was partially successful. Nearly 200 people were arrested, most of them employees. One arrest of 21 people on the plant floor was applauded by other employees.

Questions

1. Which of the four steps in the control process—setting standards, gathering information on performance, comparing performance to the standard, and taking corrective action—is the most difficult to implement in the case of drug use by employees?
2. Would companies such as General Motors be better off using feedforward rather than concurrent or feedback control to control drugs? Explain. Would clan control work if a drug culture existed in a company?
3. What would be the advantages and disadvantages of other control techniques such as lie detectors, compulsory urinalysis, or drug counseling? Which of these techniques would you consider unethical with respect to employees' rights?

Source: Based on Bryan Burrough, "How GM Began Using Private Eyes to Fight Drugs, Crime," *The Wall Street Journal*, February 27, 1986, 1, 17.

C H A P T E R 1 8

Management Control Systems

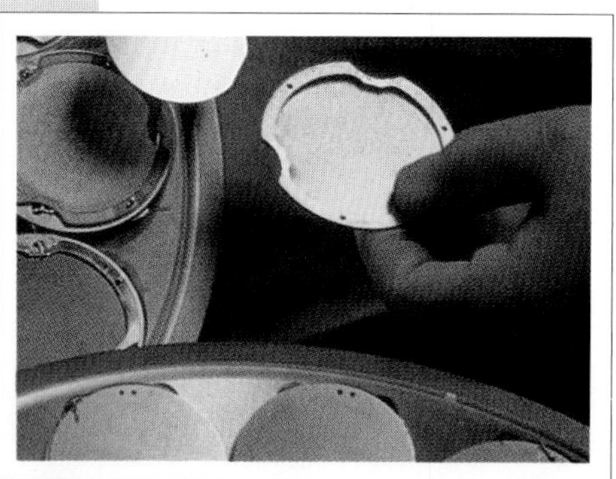

Chapter Outline

Learning Objectives

After studying this chapter, you should be able to:

- Identify the components of the core management control system.
- Describe financial statements, financial analysis, and financial audits used for top management controls.
- Explain the concept of responsibility centers and their relationship to operating and financial budgets.
- Explain the advantages of top-down, bottom-up, zero-based budgeting.
- Define the four essential steps in the MBO process.
- Explain the advantages and disadvantages of using MBO for management control.
- Describe organizational indicators of inadequate control systems.

MANAGEMENT PROBLEM

R. S. Bacon Veneer Company, an entrepreneurial company, was doing nicely selling about $4 million worth of wood veneer products to furniture manufacturers. Then its Big Eight accounting firm designed an elaborate financial report containing about 100 pages of items such as "operating income theoreticals" and "yield variances." Then sales stagnated just after Bacon invested in a new production facility. President Jim McCracken and Chief Executive George Wilhelm could not get a handle on cash flow or appropriate inventory levels. The crisis exploded when the accounting firm warned that the company needed an infusion of capital, and a few months later it urged Bacon to liquidate because bankruptcy was imminent.[1]

Do you think the problem here is with the report or with management's inability to understand financial numbers? What would you recommend McCracken and Wilhelm do?

The crisis at R. S. Bacon Veneer illustrates a problem of control — the managers are unsure of where they are going and do not have the numbers to tell whether they are on target. The Bacon example also suggests that numbers can be a problem as well as a solution. Financial management techniques have been criticized as inadequate and out of date in this era of rapid change and global competition. Concepts such as discounted cash flow analysis for plant and equipment purchases, for example, are abstract and theoretical. Many managers are learning that they are better off asking workers which piece of equipment they need to be more efficient.[2] And cost accounting systems, which are supposed to tell managers the cost and profitability of each product line, were designed 70 years ago to evaluate inventory. Today inventories are minimized, and the cost system assigns numbers that prices some products too high and some too low, thereby weakening strategic competitiveness.[3] Knowing accurate costs would let managers know which product lines to expand and where to reduce prices.

Despite the criticisms, managers need management control systems, including financial analyses, budgets, management by objectives, and other statistical reports. These control systems provide formal data and reports for management problem identification and corrective action. And these control systems can be used with the clan approach to control described in Chapter 17. The Japanese pioneered quality circles and other clan approaches, and one study showed that managers in Japanese firms had more quantitative information available from formal control systems than did managers in American firms.[4]

Every organization needs basic systems for allocating financial resources, approving and developing human resources, analyzing financial performance, and evaluating operational productivity. In long-established organizations such as Cummins Engine, Lever Brothers, and Mack Trucks, the challenge for managers is to know how to use these control systems and improve them. In new, entrepreneurial firms — especially those that have grown rapidly, such as Culver Personnel Agency and Record Exchange of Roanoke — managers must design and implement new control systems.

We will begin by explaining how multiple control systems fit together to provide overall control for top managers and then examine control systems used by middle managers.

CORE MANAGEMENT CONTROL SYSTEM

core control system The strategic plans, financial forecasts, budgets, management by objectives, operations management techniques, and MIS reports that form an integrated system for directing and monitoring organizational activities.

Research into the design of control systems across organizations has revealed the existence of a core management control system. The **core control system** consists of the strategic plans, financial forecasts, budgets, management by objectives, operations management techniques, and MIS reports that together provide an integrated system for directing and monitoring organizational activities.[5] The elements of the core control system and their relationship to one another are illustrated in Exhibit 18.1. The strategic plan and financial forecast provide guidance for the budget, management by objectives (MBO), and operations management systems used at middle management levels. The definition of each element in the core control system is as follows:[6]

1. *Strategic plan.* The strategic plan consists of the organization's strategic objectives, as discussed in Chapters 5 and 6. It is based on in-depth analysis of the organization's industry position, internal strengths and weaknesses, and environmental opportunities and threats. The written plan typically discusses company products, competition, economic trends, and new business opportunities.
2. *Financial forecast.* The financial forecast is based on a one- to five-year projection of company sales and revenues. This forecast is used to project income statements, balance sheets, and departmental expenditures. This is the company's financial projection based on the overall strategic plan. Companies such as W. R. Grace, Teledyne, and Union Carbide use projected financial statements to estimate their future financial positions.
3. *Operating budget.* The operating budget is an annual projection of estimated espenses, revenues, assets, and related financial figures for each operating department for the coming year. Budget reports typically are

EXHIBIT 18.1
Core Control System Components

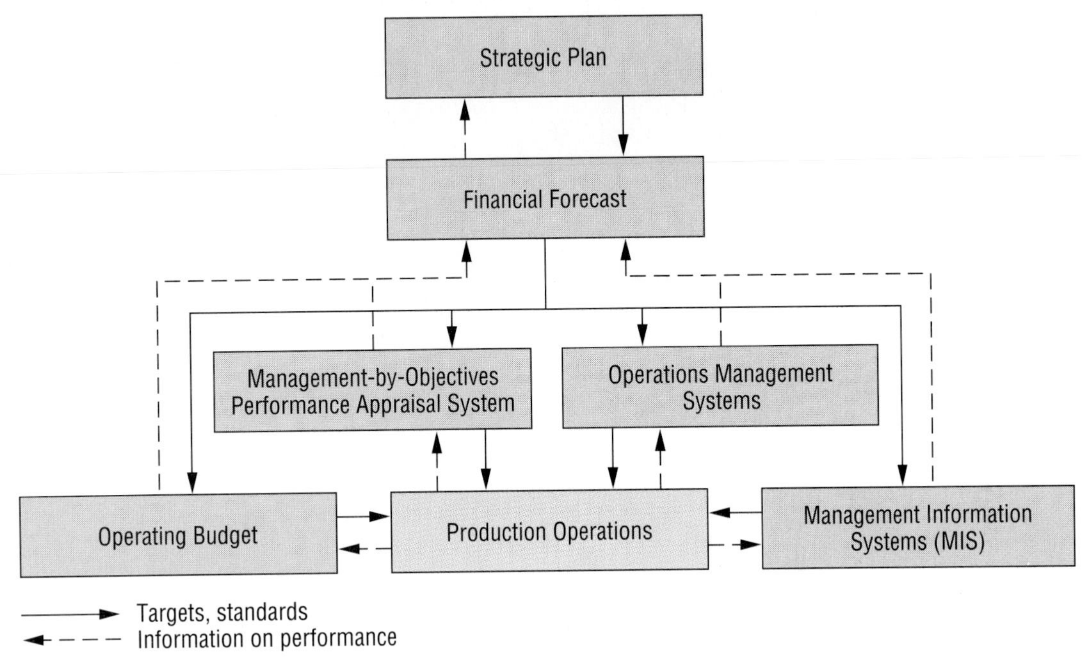

issued monthly and include comparisons of expenditures with budget targets. Budget reports are developed for all divisions and departments.

4. *Management by objectives.* Recall from Chapter 12 that performance appraisal is the formal method of evaluating and recording the performances of managers and employees. It typically includes standard forms and rating scales that evaluate employee skills and abilities. Many companies also use management by objectives to direct employee activities toward corporate objectives. MBO is integrated into the performance appraisal system and enhances management control.
5. *Operations management systems and reports.* Operations management systems pertain to inventory (economic order quantity, just-in-time), purchasing and distribution systems, and project management (PERT charts). Using operations management systems for control is the topic of Chapter 20.
6. *Management information system (MIS) reports.* MIS reports are composed of statistical data, such as personnel complements, volume of orders received, delinquent account ratios, percentage sales returns, and other statistical data relevant to the performance of a department or division. MIS reports typically contain nonfinancial data, whereas operating budgets contain financial data. MIS reports are issued weekly and monthly, and their exact content depends on the nature of tasks and available measures. A sales department MIS report may describe the number of new

As part of Whirlpool Corporation's overall *management control system,* its strategic plan is to become the leader in the worldwide appliance industry through product redesign and production efficiency. The operating budget has been used to acquire sophisticated manufacturing technologies such as the robots at the Clyde, Ohio plant, shown here, that have improved production efficiency and cost effectiveness. Effective control systems are helping position Whirlpool to win in the global marketplace.

sales, whereas an assembly department report may record the number of parts assembled per hour. Management information systems will be discussed in Chapter 19.

Each control system component is separate and distinct from the others. The overall strategic plan is top management's responsibility and the financial forecast the controller's. The budget is concerned with the financial figures and is also the controller's responsibility. The management by objectives system is usually the responsibility of the personnel department. Operations management techniques are the responsibility of the production department. MIS reports are produced and distributed by the information system department. Although each control system element is distinct, a successful core control system combines them into an integrated package of controls.

In this chapter, we discuss control systems as they are used by top and middle management levels, as illustrated in Exhibit 18.2. Top management control systems concern financial performance for the organization as a whole and include financial statements, financial analyses, and audits. Middle managers are responsible for departments and rely heavily on budgets and MBO systems for control. The other components of the core control system — MIS reports and operations management techniques — will be discussed in Chapters 19 and 20, respectively.

TOP MANAGEMENT FINANCIAL CONTROL

Based on the overall strategic plan, top management must define a financial forecast for the organization, perform financial analyses of selected ratios to reveal business performance, and use financial audits to evaluate internal oper-

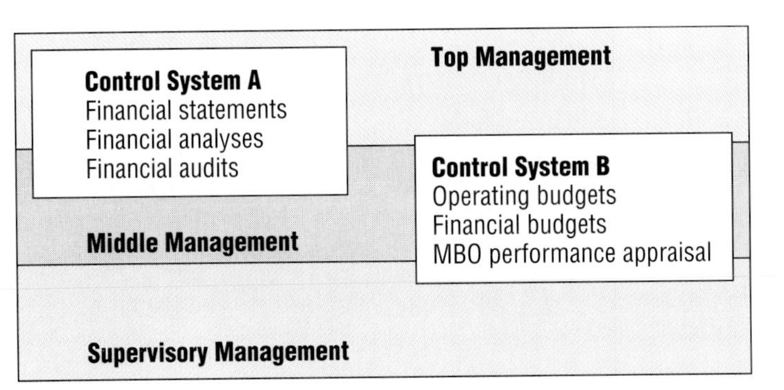

EXHIBIT 18.2
Application of Control Systems to Management Levels

ations. Each of these controls is based on financial statements — the building blocks of financial control.

FINANCIAL STATEMENTS: THE BASIC NUMBERS

Financial statements provide the basic information used for financial control of a company. Two major financial statements — the balance sheet and the income statement — are the starting points for financial control.

balance sheet A financial statement showing the firm's financial position with respect to assets and liabilities at a specific point in time.

The **balance sheet** shows the firm's financial position with respect to assets and liabilities at a specific point in time. An example of a balance sheet is presented in Exhibit 18.3. The balance sheet provides three types of information: assets, liabilities, and owners' equity. *Assets* are what the company owns and include *current assets* (assets that can be converted into cash in a short time period) and *fixed assets* (assets such as buildings and equipment that are long term in nature). *Liabilities* are the firm's debts. Liabilities include both *current debt* (obligations that will be paid by the company in the near future) and *long-term debt* (obligations payable over a long period). *Owners' equity* is the difference between assets and liabilities and is the company's net worth in stock and retained earnings.

income statement A financial statement that summarizes a company's financial performance over a given time interval.

The **income statement,** sometimes called a *profit-and-loss statement,* summarizes the firm's financial performance for a given time interval, usually one year. A sample income statement is given in Exhibit 18.4. Some firms calculate the income statement at three-month intervals during the year to see if they are on target for sales and profits. The income statement shows revenues coming into the organization from all sources and subtracts all expenses, including cost of goods sold, interest, taxes, and depreciation. The bottom line indicates the net income — profit or loss — for the given time period.

For example, Jim Greenwood, founder of Aahs!, a specialty retailing chain in California, used the income statement to detect that sales and profits were dropping during the summer months. He immediately evaluated company activities and closed two money-losing stores. He also began a new education program to teach employees how to increase sales and decrease costs to improve net income. During the last three months of the year, the Aahs! gross

EXHIBIT 18.3
Balance Sheet

Lester's Clothiers
Consolidated Balance Sheet
December 31, 1991

Assets			**Liabilities and Owners' Equity**		
Current assets:			Current liabilities:		
Cash	$ 25,000		Accounts payable	$200,000	
Accounts receivable	75,000		Accrued expenses	20,000	
Inventory	500,000		Income taxes payable	30,000	
Total current assets		$ 600,000	Total current liabilities		$ 250,000
Fixed assets:			Long-term liabilities:		
Land	250,000		Mortgages payable	350,000	
Buildings and fixtures	1,000,000		Bonds outstanding	250,000	
Less depreciation	200,000		Total long-term liabilities		$ 600,000
Total fixed assets		1,050,000	Owners' equity:		
			Common stock	540,000	
			Retained earnings	260,000	
			Total owners' equity		800,000
Total assets		$1,650,000	Total liabilities and net worth		$1,650,000

EXHIBIT 18.4
Income Statement

Lester's Clothiers
Statement of Income
For the Year Ended December 31, 1988

Gross sales	$3,100,000	
Less sales returns	200,000	
Net sales		$2,900,000
Less expenses and cost of goods sold:		
Cost of goods sold	2,110,000	
Depreciation	60,000	
Sales expenses	200,000	
Administrative expenses	90,000	2,460,000
Operating profit		440,000
Other income		20,000
Gross income		460,000
Less interest expense	80,000	
Income before taxes		380,000
Less taxes	165,000	
Net income		$ 215,000

profit margin was 3 percent ahead of target.[7] This use of the income statement follows the control cycle described in Chapter 17, beginning with the measurement of actual performance and then taking corrective action to improve performance to meet targets.

FINANCIAL ANALYSIS: INTERPRETING THE NUMBERS

The most important numbers typically are not actual dollars spent or earned, but ratios. Any business is a set of hundreds of relationships among people, things, and events.[8] Key relationships are typically revealed in ratios that provide insight into some aspect of company behavior. These insights make manager decision making possible.

A *financial ratio* is the comparison of two financial numbers. To understand their business, managers have to understand financial ratios. For example, a small corner grocery store had plenty of customers but was losing money. The store's financial numbers looked okay, so the owners sought help. The consultant said the books looked good, except for the labor cost ratio, indicating labor costs were 18 percent of revenues. The owners did not know that a specialty food retailer typically cannot make a profit if labor exceeds 10 percent of sales. They cut labor and the store has been profitable ever since. When Paul Hawken started Smith & Hawken, he learned an absolutely vital ratio. In the catalog business, the cost of goods, the catalog, and any advertising, must not exceed 70 percent of revenue. Monitoring this single ratio tells him how things are going on a weekly basis and whether to add or reduce labor.[9]

Several financial ratios can be studied to interpret company performance. Managers must decide which ratios reveal the most important relationships for their business. Frequently calculated ratios typically pertain to liquidity, activity, and profitability. Many companies compare their performance with those of other firms in the same industry as well as with their own budget targets.

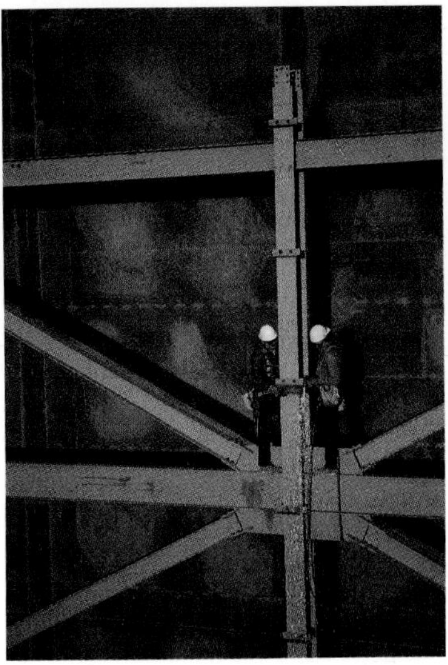

Consolidated Papers, Inc.'s *liquidity ratio* of 4.05 to 1 is so good that the company can finance expansion without borrowing money. These employees are working on an $8 million expansion of chemical pulping capacity at the Kraft Division. The high liquidity ratio allows Consolidated's managers to control the quality and pace of reinvestment to meet customer needs and to build projects at below typical industry costs.

LIQUIDITY RATIO. A **liquidity ratio** indicates the organization's ability to meet its current debt obligations. For example, the *current ratio* tells whether there are sufficient assets to convert into cash to pay off debts if needed. If a hypothetical company, Oceanographics Inc., had current assets of $600,000 and current liabilities of $250,000, the current ratio is 2.4, meaning it has sufficient funds to pay off immediate debts 2.4 times. This is normally considered a satisfactory margin of safety.

liquidity ratio A financial ratio that indicates the company's ability to meet its current debt obligations.

ACTIVITY RATIO. An **activity ratio** measures internal performance with respect to key activities defined by management. For example, *inventory turnover* is calculated by dividing total sales by average inventory. This ratio tells how many times the inventory is turned over to meet the total sales figure. If inventory sits too long, money is wasted. For Oceanographics Inc., inventory turnover is 10, which compares favorably to industry standards. The *conversion ratio* is purchase orders divided by customer inquiries, which measures company effectiveness in converting inquiries into sales. For Oceanographics Inc., this ratio is 50 percent, which is low compared with 60 percent for the industry. A sharp manager will infer that the number of inquiries is low or the sales force is doing a poor job closing sales. After investigation, improvements will be made either in promotional advertising or sales force training.

activity ratio A ratio that measures the firm's internal performance with respect to key activities defined by management.

PROFITABILITY. **Profitability ratios** describe the organization's profits. One important profitability ratio is the *profit margin on sales*, which is calculated as net income divided by sales. For Oceanographics Inc., the profit margin on sales is 8 percent. Another profitability measure is *return on total assets (ROA)*, which is the percentage return to investors on assets. It is a valuable

profitability ratio A financial ratio that describes the firm's profits.

yardstick of the return on investment compared with other investment opportunities. Return on total assets for Oceanographics is 13 percent, which means senior managers are making good use of assets to earn profits; thus, the owners are unlikely to sell the company and invest their money elsewhere.

Analyzing these various financial ratios can help managers of U.S. companies understand their business more clearly, especially with the increase in global competition.

Financial Audits: Verifying the Numbers

financial audit An independent appraisal of the organization's financial records, conducted by external or internal experts.

Financial audits are independent appraisals of the organization's financial records. Audits are of two types — external and internal.[10] An *external audit* is conducted by experts from outside the organization, typically certified public accountants (CPAs) or CPA firms. An *internal audit* is handled by experts within the organization. Large companies such as Allis-Chalmers, American Can, Boise Cascade, and Boeing have an accounting staff assigned to the internal audit function. The internal auditors evaluate departments and divisions throughout the corporation to ensure that operations are efficient and conducted according to prescribed company financial practices.

Both external and internal audits should be thorough. Their purpose is to examine every nook and cranny to verify that the financial statement represents actual company operations. Some of the areas examined by auditors are:

- *Cash:* Go to banks and confirm bank balances; review cash management procedures.
- *Receivables:* Obtain guarantees from customers concerning amounts owed and anticipated payments; confirm balances.
- *Inventory:* Conduct physical count of inventory and compare with financial statement; review for obsolescence.
- *Fixed assets:* Make physical observation, evaluate depreciation; determine whether insurance is adequate.
- *Loans:* Review loan agreements; summarize obligations.
- *Revenues and expenses:* Evaluate timing, propriety, and amount.[11]

Brunswick Corporation uses *financial controls* to make decisions about new product development. The flotilla shown here is a sampling of new boats introduced by the Fishing Boats Division. Brunswick redesigned almost 50 percent of its boat product lines for 1990, despite declining sales in 1989. Using financial analysis to dig beneath the numbers indicated increasing future demand, major opportunities in international markets, and ways to help dealers eliminate inventory. Moreover, corrective actions to reduce costs have been put in place.

Using Financial Controls

Remember that the point of financial numbers is to gain insight into company relationships to identify areas out of control and take corrective action. Managers must use numbers wisely and see beneath the surface to decide exactly what is causing the problem and devise a solution. A financial performance shortfall often has several causes, and managers must be familiar with company operations and activities in order to make an accurate diagnosis. Managers can use numbers creatively and dig beneath the figures to find the causes of problems. After defining the causes, they can initiate programs that will rectify the problem and bring the financial figures back into line.

Lee Iacocca is best known for his turnaround of Chrysler Corporation. But Iacocca learned to analyze financial statements, dig beneath the figures, and initiate corrective programs while he was president of Ford. In Iacocca's own words, here is how he used financial statements as the starting point for solving a number of deeply rooted problems at Ford.

Ford Motor Company

• When I became president, the Ford Motor Company had approximately 432,000 employees. In North America alone, we were building close to 2.5 million cars a year and 750,000 trucks. Our total sales for 1970 added up to $14.9 billion, on which we made a profit of $515 million.

Now, while $515 million was certainly nothing to sneeze at, it represented only 3.5 percent of total sales. In the early 1960s, our return on sales had never dipped below 5 percent. I was determined to get it back up.

One of the first moves I made as president was to convene a meeting of top managers to establish a cost-cutting program. I called it "four fifties," as its purpose was to cut operating expenses by $50 million in each of four areas — timing foul-ups, product complexity, design costs, and outmoded ways of doing business. If we could reach our goal within three years, we could improve our profits by $200 million — a gain of almost 40 percent — even before selling a single additional car.

There was plenty of room for improvement. For example, it took us two weeks out of each year to prepare our factories for the production of the next year's models. Through more vigorous computer programming and more sophisticated scheduling, it was possible to reduce the changeover period from two weeks to two days.

Another area where we cut costs was shipping. We began packing the freight cars much more tightly. At one point, I recall, we trimmed a fender design by two inches to allow a few more cars to fit onto each train. With huge sums of money at stake, the last thing I wanted was to be shipping air. When you're dealing with figures like $500 million for freight, even a minuscule saving of half of one percent came to $2.5 million.[12]

Middle Management Budget Control

Budgets are a primary control device for middle management. Of course, top managers too are involved with budgets for the company as a whole, but middle managers are responsible for the budget performance of their departments or divisions. Budgets identify both planned and actual expenditures for cash, assets, raw materials, salaries, and other resources departments need. Budgets are the most widely used control system, because they plan and control resources and revenues essential to the firm's health and survival.[13]

A budget is created for every division or department within the organization, no matter how small, so long as it performs a distinct project, program, or function. In order for budgets to be used, the organization must define each department as a responsibility center.

Responsibility Centers

A responsibility center is the fundamental unit of analysis of a budget control system. A **responsibility center** is defined as any organizational department under the supervision of a single person who is responsible for its activity.[14] A three-person appliance sales office in Watertown, New York, is a responsibility

responsibility center Any organizational department under the supervision of a single individual who is responsible for its activity.

EXHIBIT 18.5
Types of Responsibility Centers

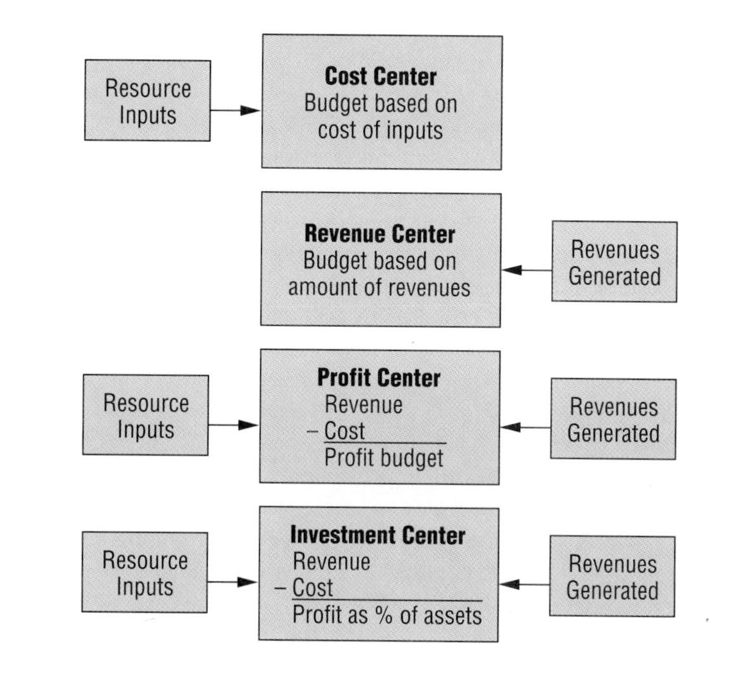

center, as is General Electric's entire refrigerator manufacturing plant. The manager of each unit has budget "responsibility."

There are four major types of responsibility centers — cost centers, revenue centers, profit centers, and investment centers. The budget focus for each type of cost center is illustrated in Exhibit 18.5.

COST CENTER. A *cost center* is a responsibility center in which the manager is held responsible for controlling cost inputs. The manager is responsible for salaries, supplies, and other costs relevant to the department's operation. Staff departments such as personnel, legal, and research typically are organized as cost centers, and budgets reflect the cost to run the department.

REVENUE CENTER. In a *revenue center,* the budget is based on generated revenues or income. Sales and marketing departments frequently are revenue centers. The department has a revenue goal, such as $3,500,000. Assuming each salesperson can generate $250,000 of revenue per year, the department can be allocated 14 salespeople. Revenue budgets can also be calculated as the number of items to be sold rather than as total revenues. For example, the revenue budget for an appliance shop might include 50 refrigerators, 75 washers, 60 dryers, and 40 microwaves to be sold for 1991.

PROFIT CENTER. In a *profit center,* the budget measures the difference between revenues and costs. For budget purposes, the profit center is defined as a self-contained unit to enable a profit to be calculated. In Kollmorgen Corporation, each division is a profit center. Control is based on profit targets rather than on cost or revenue targets.

INVESTMENT CENTER. An *investment center* is based on the value of assets employed to produce a given level of profit. Profits are calculated in the same way as in a profit center, but for control purposes managers are concerned with return on the investment in assets for the division. For example, Exxon may acquire a gasoline refinery for a price of $40 million. If Exxon managers target a 10 percent return on investment, the gasoline refinery will be expected to generate profits of $4 million a year. Exxon managers are not concerned with the absolute dollar value of costs, revenues, or profits so long as the budgeted return on assets reaches 10 percent.

RELATIONSHIP TO STRUCTURE. Responsibility centers are closely related to the types of organization structure described in Chapter 9. Cost centers and revenue centers typically exist in a functional structure. The production, assembly, finance, accounting, and personnel departments control expenditures through cost budgets. Marketing or sales departments, however, often are controlled as revenue centers. Profit centers typically exist in a divisional structure. Each self-contained division can be evaluated on the basis of total revenues minus total costs, which equals profits. Finally, very large companies in which each division is an autonomous business use investment centers. Frito-Lay and Taco Bell are investment centers for PepsiCo. PepsiCo managers are concerned with the return on investment from these companies, and each business is left alone so long as investment goals are met.

OPERATING BUDGETS

An **operating budget** is the financial plan for each organizational responsibility center for the budget period. The operating budget outlines the financial resources allocated to each responsibility center in dollar terms, typically calculated for a year in advance. The most common types of operating budgets are expense, revenue, and profit budgets.

operating budget The plan for the allocation of financial resources to each organizational responsibility center for the budget period under consideration.

EXPENSE BUDGET. An **expense budget** outlines the anticipated expenses for each responsibility center and for the total organization. Expense budgets apply to cost centers, as described above. The department of management at the University of Illinois may have a travel budget of $24,000; thus, the department head knows that the expense budget can be spent at approximately $2,000 per month. Three different kinds of expenses normally are evaluated in the expense budget — fixed, variable, and discretionary.

expense budget An operating budget that outlines the anticipated expenses for each responsibility center and for the organization as a whole.

Fixed costs are based on a commitment from a prior budget period and cannot be changed. Expensive machinery purchased three years ago that is paid over a period of 10 years is a fixed cost. The same is true for the annual mortgage payments on a building amortized over 15 years.

fixed costs Costs that are based on a commitment from a previous budget period and cannot be altered.

Variable costs, often called *engineered costs,* are based on an explicit physical relationship with the volume of departmental activity. Variable costs are calculated in manufacturing departments when a separate cost can be assigned for each product produced. A variable cost budget might allocate two hours of machine time for each turbine blade or $3 in supplies for each integrated circuit board. The greater the volume of production, the greater the expense budget the department will have.

variable costs Costs that are based on an explicit physical relationship with the volume of department activity; also called *engineered costs.*

American Airlines watches its operating expense budget closely to allocate resources and control costs. *Fixed costs* are for airplanes, as shown here, and new terminals. *Variable costs* are for expenditures such as crew training and employee hiring. *Discretionary costs* include fuel price variations. Managers must react to the price of fuel and allocate necessary resources. When fuel prices decline, managers have the discretion to allocate these savings elsewhere. American Airlines believes that controlling costs is a key to profitability in the airline business.

discretionary costs Costs based on management decisions and not on fixed commitments or volume of output.

Discretionary costs are based on management decisions. They are not based on a fixed, long-term commitment or on volume of items produced, because discretionary costs cannot be calculated with precision. In the judgment of top management, an expense budget of $120,000 might be assigned to the inspection department to pay the salaries of four inspectors, one assistant, and one secretary. This budget could be increased or decreased the following year depending on whether management feels more inspectors are needed.

revenue budget An operating budget that identifies the revenues required by the organization.

REVENUE BUDGET. A **revenue budget** identifies the revenues required by the organization. The revenue budget is the responsibility of a revenue center, such as marketing or sales. The revenue budget for a small manufacturing firm could be $3 million, based on sales of 600,000 items at $5 each. The revenue budget of $6 million for a local school district would be calculated not on sales to customers but on the community's current tax rate and property values.

profit budget An operating budget that combines both expense and revenue budgets into one statement showing gross and net profits.

PROFIT BUDGET. A **profit budget** combines both expense and revenue budgets into one statement to show gross and net profits. Profit budgets apply to profit and investment centers. If a bank has budgeted income of $2 million and budgeted expenses of $1,800,000, the estimated profit will be $200,000. If the budget profit is unacceptable, managers must develop a plan for increasing revenues or decreasing costs to achieve an acceptable profit return.

financial budget A budget that defines where the organization will receive its cash and how it will spend it.

FINANCIAL BUDGETS

Financial budgets define where the organization will receive its cash and how it intends to spend it. Three important financial budgets are the cash, capital expenditure, and balance sheet budgets.

cash budget A financial budget that estimates cash flows on a daily or weekly basis to ensure that the company has sufficient cash to meet its obligations.

CASH BUDGET. The **cash budget** estimates cash flows on a daily or weekly basis to ensure that the organization has sufficient cash to meet its obligations.

EXHIBIT 18.6
Relationships among Budgets

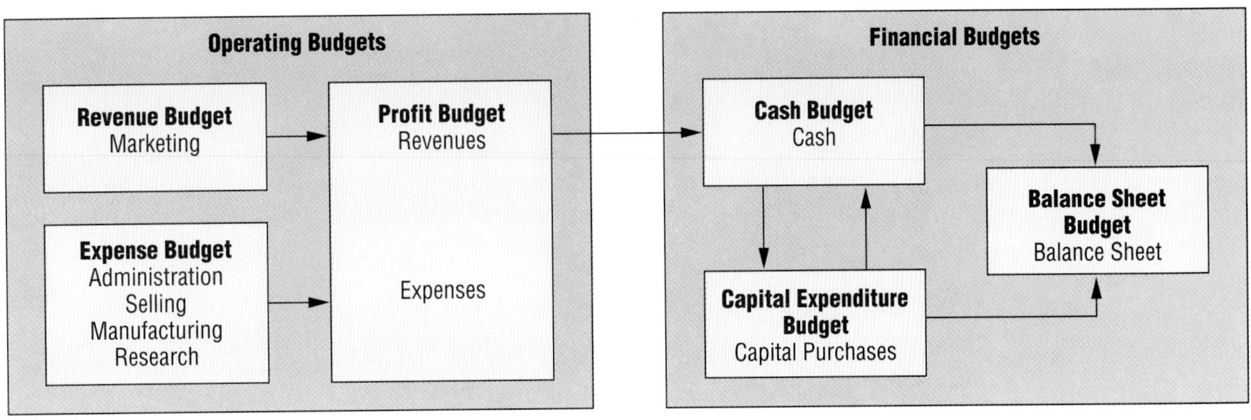

The cash budget shows the level of funds flowing through the organization and the nature of cash disbursements. If the cash budget shows that the firm has more cash than necessary, the company can arrange to invest the excess cash in Treasury bills to earn interest income. If the cash budget shows a payroll expenditure of $20,000 coming at the end of the week but only $10,000 in the bank, the controller must borrow cash to meet the payroll.

CAPITAL EXPENDITURE BUDGET. The **capital expenditure budget** plans future investments in major assets such as buildings, trucks, and heavy machinery. *Capital expenditures* are major purchases that are paid for over several years. Capital expenditures must be budgeted to determine their impact on cash flow and whether revenues are sufficient to cover capital expenditures and annual operating expenditures. Large corporations such as Navistar, Scott Paper, and Joseph E. Seagram & Sons assign financial analysts to work exclusively on the development of a capital expenditure budget. The analysts also monitor whether actual capital expenditures are being made according to plan.

capital expenditure budget
A financial budget that plans future investments in major assets to be paid for over several years.

BALANCE SHEET BUDGET. The **balance sheet budget** plans the amount of assets and liabilities for the end of the time period under consideration. It indicates whether the capital expenditures and cash management, revenues, and operating expenses will mesh into the financial results desired by senior management. The balance sheet budget shows where future financial problems may exist. Financial ratio analysis can be performed on the balance sheet and profit budgets to see whether important ratio targets, such as debt to total assets, and ROA will be met.

balance sheet budget
A financial budget that plans the amount of assets and liabilities for the end of the time period under consideration.

The relationships among the operating and financial budgets are illustrated in Exhibit 18.6. All company budgets are interconnected. The revenue budget combined with the cost budget leads to the profit budget. The profit

top-down budgeting
A budgeting process in which middle- and lower-level managers set departmental budget targets in accordance with overall company revenues and expenditures specified by top management.

bottom-up budgeting
A budgeting process in which lower-level managers budget their departments' resource needs and pass them up to top management for approval.

budget influences the amount of cash available, which in turn determines the amount of capital purchases the company can afford. The data from these budgets enable calculation of the balance sheet budget.

THE BUDGETING PROCESS

The budgeting process is concerned with how budgets are actually formulated and implemented in an organization. In this section, we will briefly describe the procedure many companies use to develop the budget for the coming year.

TOP-DOWN OR BOTTOM-UP BUDGETING

Many traditional companies use **top-down budgeting,** which is consistent with the bureaucratic control approach discussed in Chapter 17. The budgeted amounts for the coming year are literally imposed on middle- and lower-level managers.[15] The top-down process has certain advantages: Top managers have information on overall economic projections; they know the financial goals and forecasts; and they have reliable information about the amount of resources available in the coming year. Thus, the top-down process enables managers to set budget targets for each department to meet the needs of overall company revenues and expenditures.

The problem with the top-down budgeting process is that lower managers often are not committed to achieving budget targets. They are excluded from the budgeting process and resent their lack of involvement in deciding the resources available to their departments in the coming year.[16]

Quaker Oats Company employs a *top-down, bottom-up approach* to planning and budgeting. Its overall financial objectives, including earnings, dividends, growth rates, and profits, are established at the top and passed down to divisions. Specific budget plans and operating strategies within divisions, such as Quaker-Canada, are defined bottom-up. The two sets of plans are reviewed by senior management and integrated to meet the needs of divisions and the overall corporation.

In response to these negative outcomes, many organizations adopt **bottom-up budgeting,** which is in line with the clan approach to control. Lower managers anticipate their departments' resource needs, which are passed up the hierarchy and approved by top management. The advantage of the bottom-up process is that lower managers are able to identify resource requirements about which top managers are uninformed, have information on efficiencies and opportunities in their specialized areas, and are motivated to meet the budget because the budget plan is their responsibility.[17]

However, the bottom-up approach also has problems. Managers' estimates of future expenditures may be inconsistent with realistic economic projections for the industry or with company financial forecasts and objectives. A university accounting department may plan to increase the number of professors by 20 percent, which is too much if the university plans to increase accounting student enrollment by only 10 percent.

The result of these advantages and disadvantages is that many companies use a joint process. Top managers and the controller define economic projections and financial goals and forecasts and then inform lower managers of the anticipated resources available to them. Once these overall targets (for example, a resource increase of 4 to 7 percent) are made available, department managers can develop their budgets within them. Each department can take advantage of special information, resource requirements, and opportunities. The budget is then passed up to the next management level, where inconsistencies across departments can be removed.

EXHIBIT 18.7
Top-down and Bottom-up Budgeting

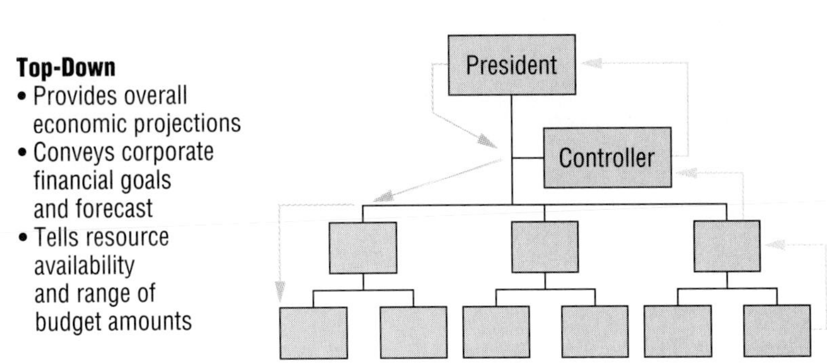
Top-Down
• Provides overall economic projections
• Conveys corporate financial goals and forecast
• Tells resource availability and range of budget amounts
President
Controller
Bottom-Up
• Identifies specific resource requirements
• Includes economies and opportunities in specialized areas
• Resolves resource inconsistencies among departments
• Increases employee commitment

Source: Based on Neil C. Churchill, "Budget Choice: Planning vs. Control," *Harvard Business Review* (July/August 1984), 150–164.

The combined top-down and bottom-up process is illustrated in Exhibit 18.7. Top managers begin the cycle. They also end it by giving final approval to all departmental budgets. Departmental budgets fall within the guidelines provided by top management, and the overall company budget reflects the specific knowledge, needs, and opportunities within each department.

ZERO-BASED BUDGETING

In most organizations, the budgeting process begins with the previous year's expenditures; that is, managers plan future expenditures as an increase or decrease over the previous year. This procedure tends to lock departments into a stable spending pattern that lacks flexibility to meet environmental changes. **Zero-based budgeting (ZBB)** was designed to overcome this rigidity by having each department start from zero in calculating resource needs for the new budget period.[18] ZBB assumes that the previous year's budget is not a valid base from which to work. Rather, based on next year's strategic plans, each responsibility center justifies its work activities and needed personnel, supplies, and facilities for the next budget period. Responsibility centers that cannot justify expenditures for the coming year will receive fewer resources or be disbanded altogether. In zero-based budgeting, each year is viewed as bringing a new set of goals. It forces department managers to thoroughly examine their operations and justify their departments' activities based on their direct contribution to the achievement of organizational goals.[19]

zero-based budgeting (ZBB)
A budgeting process in which each responsibility center calculates its resource needs based on the coming year's priorities rather than on the previous year's budget.

The zero-based budgeting technique was originally developed for use in government organizations as a way to justify cost requests for the succeeding year. The U.S. Department of Agriculture was the first to use zero-based budgeting in the 1960s. ZBB was adopted by Texas Instruments in 1970 and by many government and business corporations during the 1970s and 1980s. Companies such as Ford, Westinghouse, Owens-Illinois, and New York Telephone, as well as government agencies at both the federal and state levels, use zero-based budgeting.

EXHIBIT 18.8
Advantages and Disadvantages of Budgets

Advantages	Disadvantages
• Facilitate coordination across departments	• Can be used mechanically
• Translate strategic plans into departmental actions	• Can demotivate employees because of lack of participation
• Record organizational activities	• Can cause perceptions of unfairness
• Improve communication with employees	• Can create competition for resources and politics
• Improve resource allocation	• Can limit opportunities for innovation and adaptation
• Provide a tool for corrective action through reallocations	

The specific steps used in zero-based budgeting are as follows:

1. Managers develop a *decision package* for their responsibility centers. The decision package includes written statements of the department's objectives, activities, costs, and benefits; alternative ways of achieving objectives; consequences of not performing each activity; and personnel, equipment, and resources required during the coming year. Managers then assign a rank order to the activities in their department for the coming year.
2. The decision package is then forwarded to top management for review. Senior managers rank the decision packages from the responsibility centers according to their degree of benefit to the organization. These rankings involve widespread management discussions and may culminate in a voting process in which managers rate activities from "essential" to "would be nice to have" to "not needed."
3. Top management allocates organizational resources based on activity rankings. Budget resources are distributed according to the activities rated as essential to meeting organizational goals. Some departments may receive large budgets and others nothing at all.

Zero-based budgeting demands more time and energy than conventional budgeting. Because it forces management to abandon traditional budget practices, top management should develop a consensus among participants that ZBB will have a positive influence on both the company and its employees.

ADVANTAGES AND DISADVANTAGES OF BUDGET CONTROL

Budgeting is the most widely used control system in North American organizations. It offers several advantages to managers but can also create problems. The advantages and disadvantages of budgets are summarized in Exhibit 18.8.

The first major strength of budgeting is that it coordinates activities across departments. The budget ties together resource requirements from each responsibility center into a financial blueprint for the entire firm. Second, budgets translate strategic plans into action. They specify the resources, revenues, and activities required to carry out the strategic plan for the coming year.

Third, budgets provide an excellent record of organizational activities. Fourth, budgets improve communication, because they provide information to employees. Budgets let people see where the organization is going and their role in that mission. Fifth, budgets improve resource allocation, because all requests are clarified and justified. Senior managers get a chance to compare budget requests across departments and set priorities for resource allocation. Finally, budgets provide a way of implementing corrective action. For example, when personal computer sales declined in 1989, IBM used a budget to reduce expenditures for PC manufacturing and increase budgeted resources for other computer lines. The Manager's Shoptalk box describes how Harold Geneen used budget numbers to run ITT.

Budgets can also cause headaches for managers when improperly used. The major problem occurs when budgets are applied mechanically and rigidly. The budgeting process is then only an exercise in filling out paperwork, with each department getting the same percentage increase or decrease as the others. Second, when managers and employees are not allowed to participate in the budget-setting process, budgeting is demotivating. If budgets are arbitrarily imposed top down, employees will not understand the reason for budgeted expenditures and will not be committed to them. A third weakness occurs when budget perceptions differ across hierarchical levels. Supervisors also may feel they did not receive a fair share of resources if top managers do not explain corporate priorities and budget decisions. Fourth, budgets may pit departments against one another. Managers may feel their own activities are essential and even resort to politics to get more resources. Finally, a rigid budget structure reduces initiative and innovation at lower levels, making it impossible to obtain money for new ideas. Some companies, such as 3M, set discretionary resources aside to prevent this problem.

Skilled managers who understand budgets and how to use them have a powerful control tool with which to attain departmental and organizational goals. One manager who knows how to use budgets to achieve goals is the CEO of a grocery store chain in Orlando, Florida.

A major advantage of budget control for Hilton Hotels Corporation is *coordination* of high-quality service to guests from city to city around the world. The Hilton Hawaiian Village, shown here, provides the same quality service as Hilton's other 270 properties representing 95,000 rooms. Once budgets are set, managers in individual hotels have the authority to control costs to provide first-class service without needless waste. Moreover, each department head knows the budget forecast and learns how it matches actual performance.

THRIFTY SCOTT WAREHOUSE FOOD • Bob Popaditch, CEO of Thrifty Scott Warehouse Food, likes to talk about cost control and profit margins. He understands budget matters and has learned how to use them to motivate managers.

In a talk to several of his store managers, he reviewed budget performance. "Let's talk about the last 36 weeks," he began. "You could say that things looked pretty good. Sales were just 2.9 percent off budget. Not bad. Payroll was over budget a bit, but only by 0.24 percent. Pretty close."

Popaditch knows that overall budget figures are abstract and boring for his managers. He has learned that budgets motivate people when "spoken" in their language. Thus, the 2 percent shortfall in sales amounts to $244,000 for the 36 weeks. Popaditch went on breaking down the sales shortfall. That comes down to $26.85 in sales per hour. The average number of customers per hour is 87, which is just $0.31 more sales per customer. Store managers understand this. They simply need to get each customer to buy $0.31 more while in the store.

MANAGER'S SHOPTALK

THE NUMBERS

Harold Geneen, trained as an accountant, used accounting and budget numbers to understand ITT when he was president. In his view, numbers were essential to diagnosing problems. Here is what he said:

"Too many people mistakenly believe that large American corporations, like ITT, are run (heartlessly) by the numbers. They make that mistake because most people read words better than they do numbers. They may understand the complex novels of Henry James or James Joyce or Marcel Proust, but they read columns of numbers as they would a vocabulary list of strange, esoteric words. As symbols of what is going on in business, numbers represent measurements, not the business activity itself. René Magritte, the surrealist artist, painted a picture of a man's pipe and on the canvas he wrote, "This is not a pipe." It wasn't. It was a picture of a pipe. So I say: The numbers are not the business; they are only pictures of the business.

"Nevertheless, no business could run without them. Numbers serve as a sort of thermometer which measures the health and well-being of the enterprise. They serve as the first line of communication which informs management what is going on, and the more precise the numbers are, the more they are based upon "unshakable facts," the clearer the line of communication.

"When a manager makes up a budget for the coming year, he is putting down on paper a series of expectations, expressed in numbers. They include the whole gamut of costs of the product or products — design, engineering, supplies, production, labor, plants, marketing, sales, distribution — and also anticipated income from sales based upon market share, back orders, and what have you. . . . When all the figures are pulled together for one company or one division, you have its budget. At ITT we had 250 of these profit centers and their annual budgets, replete with numbers, when lined up side by side, occupied thirty-odd feet of shelf space.

"Any significant variation between your expectations and what is actually happening in the marketplace, as expressed in those numbers, is a signal for action. The sooner you see the numbers, the sooner you can take action, if needed. However — and this is most important — the numbers themselves will not tell you what to do. They are only a signal for action, a trigger to thinking. It is akin to the man with the divining rod who points to the spot where there is water underground. But to get the water, you have to dig for it. The key issue in business is to find out what is happening behind those numbers.

"Once you start digging into the areas which the numbers represent, then you get into the guts of your business. If sales are off, is it because of the design of your product? Its cost? Marketing? Distribution? Financing? What? The search goes on not only at the top of the company but also at the operating levels. . . . You don't want to manage the numbers; you don't want to push sales or receivables from one quarter to another, for the truth will always catch up with you. That is like treating the thermometer instead of the patient. If a thermometer registers above 98.6 degrees, it is telling you the patient has a fever; he is sick. It is not telling you what is wrong, only that something is wrong. You can put the thermometer in a glass of ice water or dunk the whole patient into a bathtub of cold water, and that will bring the number down. But it won't cure him. In business, you want to manage and control the elements of the business itself, not the numbers on your profit-and-loss statement."

Source: Excerpts from *Managing* by Harold Geneen with Alvin Moscow, pp. 182–184, copyright © 1984 by Harold S. Geneen and Alvin Moscow. Reprinted by permission of Doubleday & Company, Inc.

What about payroll? Over budget by 0.24 percent is pretty close, but it amounts to $9,163 per store, or $254 per week for each store. That's about 52 hours of labor. Since each store has about 50 employees, that's one hour per employee per week.

So that's how Bob Popaditch gets his managers to look at the problem: "$0.30 per customer, 60 minutes per employee." A small increase in income and an easily manageable decrease in costs will lead to 100 percent attainment of budget targets and a tidy increase of $65,804 in net profit. Budget figures are not abstract numbers drawn out of the air. When used by effective managers, they translate into action that produces better performance.[20]

THE MBO PROCESS

In addition to budgets, middle managers can use performance appraisal systems to control their departments. As discussed in Chapter 12, the performance appraisal system provides a basis for rewarding and developing employees in all departments — marketing, advertising, finance, quality control, and industrial engineering.

The performance appraisal system has the potential to be a control device for management. Management by objectives (MBO) was developed to strengthen the control aspect of performance appraisal. With MBO, the performance appraisal system is a means with which to set targets for employees, monitor their performance, compare performance to targets, and take corrective action — the four steps in the organizational control process.

MANAGEMENT BY OBJECTIVES

Management by objectives (MBO) is related to goal- and objective-setting ideas described in Chapter 5. The management by objectives concept is credited to Peter Drucker and has been widely adopted in American and Canadian corporations. Traditional performance appraisal systems focus on employee characteristics, such as strengths and weaknesses, but MBO focuses on the achievement of explicit objectives.[21] **Management by objectives** is a method whereby managers and employees define objectives for every department, project, and person and use them to control subsequent performance.

management by objectives (MBO) A method whereby managers and employees define objectives for each department, project, and employee and use them to control subsequent performance.

A model of the essential steps of the MBO process is presented in Exhibit 18.9. The four major activities that must occur in order for MBO to be successful are setting objectives, developing action plans, reviewing progress, and appraising overall performance.[22]

SETTING OBJECTIVES. Setting objectives is the most difficult step in MBO. Objective setting looks beyond day-to-day activities to answer the question "What are we trying to accomplish?" Objective setting involves employees at all levels. Top managers set overall corporate objectives that define priorities for middle managers. Middle managers define objectives for the departments and divisions for which they are responsible. Corporate and departmental objectives are used to set objectives for individual employees.

A good objective should be concrete and realistic, provide a specific target and a time frame, and assign responsibility. Objectives may be quantitative or qualitative depending on whether outcomes are measurable. Quantitative objectives typically are described in numerical terms, such as "Salesperson Jones will obtain 16 new sales accounts in December," or "the Finance Department will hire three financial analysts from among university graduates this spring."

EXHIBIT 18.9
Model of the MBO Process

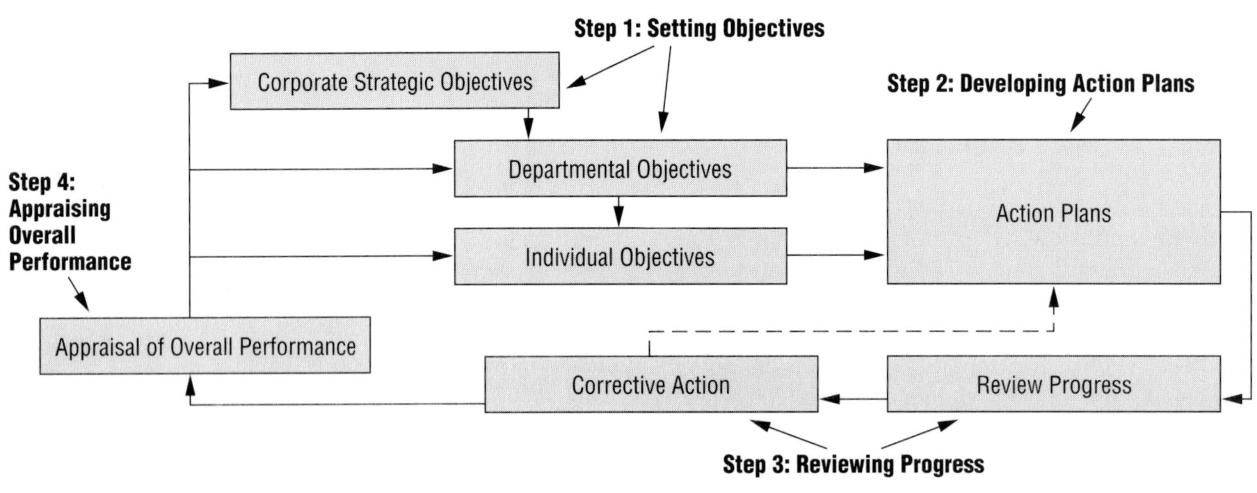

Qualitative objectives use terms such as "Marketing will improve customer service by reducing complaints next year," or "the Personnel Department will write a plan to increase minority hiring within 90 days." The qualitative statements must be sufficiently precise to permit realistic appraisal and evaluation.

Objectives should be jointly derived. Mutual agreement between subordinate and supervisor results in the strongest commitment to achieving objectives. In the case of teams, all team members may participate in setting objectives. If employees have no voice in objective setting, they will resist MBO control and be unmotivated to achieve their objectives. Mutual agreement is crucial for obtaining total commitment and a shared responsibility for achieving results.

action plan A step in MBO that defines the course of action needed to achieve stated objectives.

DEVELOPING ACTION PLANS. An **action plan** defines the course of action needed to achieve the stated objectives. Action plans are made for both individuals and for departments. A department may undertake an entirely new work activity because of a new corporate objective. If a university decides to raise $5 million in donations, the college of arts and sciences will have to start fund-raising activities. The action plan would define exactly how fund raising should be performed to achieve the objective. Likewise, each employee must develop an action plan for achieving his or her personal objectives. If a marketing manager is given the objective of increasing the sales volume by 6 percent, the following action plan might be undertaken: (1) Start a sales discount program for high-volume buyers; (2) work with salespeople to increase sales performance by 5 percent; (3) seek a 10 percent increase in the advertising budget; and (4) hire one additional salesperson.

REVIEWING PROGRESS. A periodic progress review is important to ensure that action plans are working. These reviews can occur informally between managers and subordinates, or the organization may wish to conduct three-,

EXHIBIT 18.10
Progress Report for Departmental Objectives

Department	Objective	Progress
Inventory Control	Maintain finished goods at 2.5 months average sales.	Finished goods inventory now at 3 months average sales due to unexpected mild sales slump for Product A. Special report to be forwarded from Marketing by end of week.
Accounting	Limit accounts receivable to 1.5 months sales.	Accounts receivable at 1.4 months sales.
Sales	Improve Product Y sales by 20% over previous year.	New marketing program launched March 1 is paying off. Year-to-date sales now 12% higher than last year. Present-month sales 22% above same month last year. Should hit target.
Production	Decrease scrap rates — target 25% reduction.	Scrap rates down 30% year-to-date primarily due to scrap incentive program.

Source: Based on "Staying in Control: The Key to Better Reports," *Small Business Reports* (May 1987), 30–34.

six-, and nine-month reviews during the year. This periodic checkup allows managers and employees to see whether they are on target and whether corrective action is necessary. Exhibit 18.10 illustrates progress reports for one important objective for each of four departments. Sales reports on the progress toward achieving the 20 percent increase for Product Y. In the case of production, the action plan for scrap incentives is successfully decreasing scrap rates. The progress report also may indicate that the action plan is not working. Managers and employees should not be locked into predefined behavior and must be willing to undertake whatever actions are necessary to produce meaningful results. The point of MBO is to achieve objectives. The action plan can be changed whenever objectives are not being met.

APPRAISING OVERALL PERFORMANCE. The final step in MBO is to evaluate whether annual objectives have been achieved for both individuals and departments. This appraisal carefully evaluates whether finished goods inventory was maintained at 2.5 months average sales, scrap rates were reduced 25 percent, and Product Y sales increased 20 percent during the year. Qualitative objectives, such as increasing minority hiring, also are carefully appraised. Success or failure to achieve objectives can become part of the performance appraisal system and the designation of salary increases and other rewards.

The appraisal of departmental and overall corporate performance shapes objectives for the next year. The MBO cycle repeats itself on an annual basis. The specific application of MBO must fit the needs of each company. An example of how one company used MBO to solve a safety problem follows.

PRODUCERS GAS AND TRANSMISSION • Producers Gas and Transmission Company is a medium-size refinery and distributor of gasoline and other refinery products. A major concern of top management was an unusually high employee accident rate during the previous year. Ten employees had minor injuries, four were severely injured, and one was killed. The company lost 112 employee days of work due to accidents. Top management discussed the accident rate with department heads and decided on a corporate objective of a 50 percent reduction in all accidents for 1991.

Middle managers developed an action plan that included (1) the establishment of an employee safety training program, (2) the creation of a companywide safety committee, and (3) a new system of safety recognition. Also, (4) line supervisors were asked to develop safety training sessions for their departments within 60 days, and (5) middle managers were given 30 days to nominate supervisors to the safety committee. Finally, (6) the safety committee had 30 days in which to design a safety recognition program, including awards.

Progress was reviewed through the compilation of quarterly safety reports measuring percentage of accidents compared to the previous year. The action plan could be revised if obstacles were discovered. The safety committee appraised the safety performance of each department every 90 days and posted the results for all employees to see. Letters of commendation were given to departments that met or exceeded the 50 percent reduction objective.

At the end of the year, an overall performance appraisal was held for individuals, departments, and the corporation as a whole. Departments that had successfully reduced accidents by 50 percent were given awards (wall plaques). Information about safety procedures and accident rates was used to set a new safety objective for 1992. Delinquent departments were given stringent objectives. Most important, the company achieved its 1991 objective of reducing accidents by 50 percent. The MBO system energized employee actions companywide toward a goal deemed critical by top management. MBO got all employees working toward the same end.[23]

ASSESSING MBO EFFECTIVENESS

Research findings have reported no dramatic increases in performance by organizations that use MBO.[24] However, many companies, such as Intel, Tenneco, Black and Decker, and DuPont, have adopted MBO, and most managers feel that MBO is effective.[25] Managers believe they are better oriented toward goal achievement when MBO is used. Like any system, MBO has many benefits when used properly and is associated with management problems when used improperly.

BENEFITS OF MBO. Major benefits to companies that use MBO include the following:

1. Corporate objectives are achieved by focusing manager and employee efforts on those activities that will lead to their attainment.
2. Performance can be improved at all company levels because employees are committed to attaining objectives.
3. Employees are motivated because they help decide what is expected and are free to be resourceful in accomplishing their objectives.
4. Departmental and individual objectives are aligned with company objectives. Objectives at lower levels enable the attainment of objectives at top management levels.

Hewlett-Packard practices *management by objectives*. These objectives include technical innovation and a commitment to customer satisfaction. HP has achieved status as the leader in cost effective manufacturing of advanced light-emitting diodes, shown here, that are 50 times brighter than devices HP created in 1968. Through technical innovation, this product has a wider range of possible uses, including outdoor applications. HP's MBO system contributes to the openness and informality of the HP culture by fostering individual dignity and pride in accomplishment.

5. Relationships between managers and subordinates are improved by having explicit discussions about objectives, defining activities that will help achieve them, and assigning responsibility.
6. Control procedures are improved because systems for reporting on progress toward objective achievement are developed and used. Managerial attention is focused on a few activities critical for goal attainment rather than on every activity within their departments.[26]

PROBLEMS WITH MBO. MBO does not work in every situation. Some of the problems that can occur with MBO are as follows:

1. Constant change prevents MBO from taking hold. The environment and internal activities must have some stability in order for performance to be measured and compared against goals. If new objectives are defined every few months, the implementation of action plans and appraisal will have no time to take effect before the objectives are abandoned and new ones established.
2. An environment of poor employer-employee relations reduces MBO effectiveness. If management lacks confidence in subordinates or feels that they will not be committed to objectives, the objective-setting process will be ineffective.
3. Organizational values that discourage participation can harm the MBO process. Managers may lack the training or ability to jointly set objectives with employees. Training must be undertaken to help employees at all levels learn participative MBO skills.
4. Lack of top management support will undercut MBO efforts. The initiative for MBO must come from the top of the organization as a clear statement of corporate objectives. If top managers take no steps to define corporate goals and appraise whether they are being reached, the MBO program will not work.

5. Too much paperwork saps MBO energy. If MBO becomes a process of routinely filling out annual forms rather than energizing employees to achieve explicit goals, MBO will be an empty exercise. Once the routine paperwork is completed, employees will forget about the objectives and go about their daily activities — only to have to fill out paperwork again the following year.

SIGNS OF INADEQUATE CONTROL SYSTEMS

Financial statements, financial analysis, budgets, and management by objectives are designed to provide adequate control for the organization. Often, however, management control systems are not working properly. Then they must be examined for possible clarification, revision, or overhaul. Indicators of the need for a more effective control approach or revised management control systems are as follows:[27]

- Deadlines missed frequently.
- Poor quality of goods and services.
- Declining or stagnant sales or profits.
- Loss of leadership position or market share within the industry.
- Inability to obtain data necessary to evaluate employee or departmental performance.
- Low employee morale and high absenteeism.
- Insufficient employee involvement and management-employee communications.
- Excessive company debts or unpredictable borrowing requirements.
- Inefficient use of human and material resources, equipment, and facilities.

Management control systems help achieve overall company objectives. They help ensure that operations progress satisfactorily by identifying deviations and correcting problems. Properly used, controls help management respond to unforeseen developments and achieve strategic plans. Improperly designed and used, management control systems can lead a company into bankruptcy.

SUMMARY

This chapter introduced a number of important concepts about management control systems and techniques. Organizations have a core management control system consisting of the strategic plan, financial forecast, operating budget, management by objectives, operations management system, and management information system. Top management financial control uses the balance sheet, income statement, and financial analyses of these documents.

At the middle levels of the organization, budgets are an important control system. Departments are responsibility centers, each with a specific type of operating budget — expense, revenue, or profit. Financial budgets are also used for organizational control and include the cash, capital expenditure, and balance sheet budgets. The budget process can be either top down or bottom up, but a budget system that incorporates both seems most effective. Zero-based budgeting is a variation of the budget process and requires that managers start from zero to justify budget needs for the coming year. Management by objectives is another important control device used by middle managers. MBO involves four steps: setting objectives, developing action plans, reviewing progress, and appraising overall performance. Finally, indicators of inadequate control systems were discussed.

MANAGEMENT SOLUTION

R. S. Bacon Veneer Company was about to go bankrupt, despite 100 pages of accounting information. President McCracken and Chief Executive Wilhelm sought another opinion, throwing the Big Eight accounting firm out the door. The new accountant from a Chicago firm began by quizzing Wilhelm and McCracken about the numbers they felt they could best benefit from knowing. Would it be helpful to know inventory levels to manage the company effectively? Did they want to know the profit margin of each veneer line? The goal was to find key financial items for control that would make up one monthly report of no more than ten pages. The new financial reports worked like a shot of penicillin to revive the company. Knowing the cost of each product spurred Wilhelm and McCracken to diversify to high-profit items. Low-margin lines were eventually dropped. Today, business is better than ever. Sales have increased 300 percent, and the new reports still give McCracken and Wilhelm superb control.[28]

DISCUSSION QUESTIONS

1. What is the core control system? How do its components relate to one another for control of the organization?
2. What are the four types of responsibility centers, and how do they relate to organization structure?
3. What types of analyses can be performed on financial statements to help managers diagnose a company's financial condition?
4. Which do you think is a more important use of financial analyses: diagnosing organizational problems or taking corrective action to solve them? Discuss.
5. Explain the difference among fixed costs, variable costs, and discretionary costs. In which situation would each be used?
6. What are the advantages of top-down versus bottom-up budgeting? Why is it better to combine the two approaches?
7. According to zero-based budgeting, a department that cannot justify a budget will cease to exist. Do you think this actually happens under zero-based budgeting? Discuss.
8. If you were a top manager of a medium-size real estate sales agency, would you use MBO? What types of objectives would you set for managers and sales agents?
9. What are action plans? Why are they so important for MBO effectiveness?
10. Why might low employee morale or insufficient employee involvement be indicators of inadequate controls in an organization?

MANAGEMENT IN PRACTICE: ETHICAL DILEMMA

Computer Screwup

Ken and Barbara are coworkers in the telecommunications department of a large firm. One weekend, Ken asked Barbara and several other coworkers to help him move to a new apartment. While placing Ken's computer into its original packing, Barbara noticed that the address on the box was for their telecom office. When Barbara questioned Ken about it, he replied, "Oh yeah, we ordered ten terminals from the manufacturer a year ago, but they accidently shipped eleven. We didn't get charged for it." When Barbara expressed disapproval, Ken became defensive and said the boss, Dave, knew about it. "Besides, I was the one who pushed that we buy from that manufacturer, and I do a lot of work on my home computer, so our company owes me something anyway."

What Do You Do?

1. Nothing. This is not your responsibility. The fault is with the two companies' control systems that let the computer slip through.
2. Try to persuade Ken to offer to pay for it. This would be the right thing for him to do even if his offer is refused.
3. Bring it up with your boss, Dave. If it's okay for your company to accept the extra computer, it should be shared with coworkers.

CASES FOR ANALYSIS

BATTERY & TIRE WAREHOUSE INC.

When Charles Bodenstab took over Battery & Tire Warehouse in St. Paul, Minnesota, it was doing $7 million in sales, but was losing money fast. Bodenstab gradually discovered inadequate financial controls in several areas.

One problem area was accounts receivable, about which Bodenstab knew nothing. In his experience in large companies, other managers handled the credit details. As manager of an entrepreneurial company, he needed to be involved in everything.

When Bodenstab asked his credit manager basic questions such as why the percentage of past due accounts was up, he heard a different answer each month. Yet the negative trends continued. Bodenstab had to act, and his first move was to replace the credit manager.

Next, he looked into the reports and was dissatisfied with the aggregate data. Some 3,000 accounts were listed on 120 pages. The report disguised problems rather than identified them.

After careful thought, Bodenstab decided he had to know two things each month. First, which accounts were deteriorating? Second, which customers were chronic deadbeats? Bodenstab decided to create two monthly reports — one on adverse change, the other on chronic problems. The adverse-change report would list all accounts that exhibited a pattern of deterioration, such as an increase in an overdue account. The chronic-problem report would include accounts that were consistently past due. He hired a local software firm to program his computer to provide this data.

Suddenly, the problem is under control. A recent adverse-change report listed 77 accounts that had deteriorated for one reason or another. Bodenstab could skim the report in 30 minutes. The new credit manager then takes necessary action. The chronic-problems report lists over 100 companies, and he and the credit manager developed a system for motivating them to pay. Moreover, new credit is not extended when customers are not paying. Compared with the previous aggregate credit report, the new system is a dream. The trick, says Bodenstab, is to choose the criteria. The management skill is knowing which data identify and solve the problems. Then management's responsibility is to design control systems to provide those answers.

Questions

1. Which signs of inadequate controls described in the text alerted Bodenstab to the credit control problem?
2. Would an MBO system apply here? Discuss.
3. Was it proper for Bodenstab to become personally involved in the credit reporting systems? Should he delegate more responsibility to the credit manager?

Source: Based on Bruce G. Posner, "Hitting Your Numbers," *INC.*, April 1987, 106–108.

METALLIC FINISHES INC.

Metallic Finishes Inc. is a producer of chrome finishes and specialty metals. In 1990 the new executive vice-president, Stuart Galante, was committed to using the latest management techniques. His first step was to install a new management-by-objectives system for middle and senior managers. The plan was to appraise managers on goal achievement rather than on general activities. Each manager met with his or her superior to set objectives through mutual discussion.

One day Galante had lunch with Dr. Hank Gilman, vice-president for research and development. One of the topics discussed was whether the MBO system was working in the R&D department. Galante was concerned that Metallic Finishes would fail to achieve its long-term goal of having 25 percent of all sales come from new products by 1990.

Gilman reassured Galante that there was no problem. He explained that it took several years to produce a new product and top management should have confidence in the research team. To illustrate, Gilman said they had data showing an increase in the number of technical papers written and conferences attended and that equipment purchases were down 5 percent. Moreover, the waste rate on experimental materials had dropped 12 percent. The R&D department also was employing one less researcher and one less lab technician than in the previous year. "All in all," said Gilman, "we are running a very efficient operation, and I don't see how we can do much more under this new MBO system of yours."

Questions

1. Do you agree with Gilman's conclusions about the successful performance of the research and development department?
2. How does this MBO system fit the MBO model as summarized in Exhibit 18.9? What improvements would you make? Which aspects seem satisfactory?
3. Do you think the executive vice-president, Stuart Galante, did a good job of implementing the MBO system? Explain.

Source: Based on "Metallic Finishes, Inc.," in Richard L. Daft, *Organization Theory and Design* (St. Paul, Minn.: West, 1986), 320–321, and "Goals and Gripes," in Richard N. Farmer, Barry M. Richman, and William G. Ryan, *Incidents for Studying Management and Organization* (Belmont, Cal.: Wadsworth, 1970), 83.

CHAPTER 19

INFORMATION SYSTEMS FOR MANAGEMENT

CHAPTER OUTLINE

LEARNING OBJECTIVES

After studying this chapter, you should be able to:

- Describe the importance of information systems for management and the characteristics of useful information.
- Explain how computer-based information systems are designed to meet the needs of managers at different levels in the organizational hierarchy.
- Explain transaction processing, MIS, and EIS and the role of each in organizations.
- Describe other new information technologies being used in organizations.
- Discuss the impact of information technology on operational efficiency and business strategy.
- Discuss the implementation of computer-based information systems.

MANAGEMENT PROBLEM

When Daddy's Junky Music Stores, headquartered in Salem, New Hampshire, opened its sixth outlet, the lack of information and control became apparent. Customers often wanted to trade in a guitar and amplifier on more expensive equipment. This transaction involved finding the new equipment in inventory, estimating trade-in value, handling the financing, and inserting the used equipment into stock. The recordkeeping entailed phone calls back and forth among stores, filling out paperwork, reviewing sales slips, searching for inventory, and being a good guesser. Hiring more bookkeepers to keep track of things did not help. A computer seemed like the right idea, but that had been tried and failed. Daddy's entrepreneurial business, growing rapidly until now, may have peaked.[1]

What suggestions do you have for improving information and control at Daddy's? Would a computer system help Daddy's give better service to customers?

The problem confronting Daddy's Junky Music Stores is to develop internal data bases and information systems to help salespeople and store managers keep track of inventory, customers, and sales activities. Two issues face all managers, whether running an entrepreneurial business or a large corporation: getting access to disorganized data and turning the data into useful information.[2] Useful information can have remarkable benefits, in both improved control and improved competitiveness.

These two benefits — information for improved control and information as a competitive weapon — are the themes in this chapter. As described in Chapters 17 and 18, information systems provide a management control system in organizations. Yet the introduction of computers does not necessarily mean centralized, top-down control. Information can be shared widely and can be a tool for decentralizing decision making to employees at lower levels. Information systems can also serve as a competitive weapon by shortening the control cycle and response time of the organization.

The proliferation of new information technology can be overwhelming, causing managers to lose sight of the control and competitive purposes of

FOCUS ON GLOBAL COMPETITION

KOMPYUTERS IN THE SOVIET UNION

Sell U.S.-made computers in the Soviet Union? It's a genuine possibility with the advent of two joint ventures now under way. The Soviets have only about 100,000 personal computers in use, compared with some 30 million in the United States. One Soviet goal is to place 1 million personal computers in secondary schools. For *perestrioika* to succeed, there has to be significant expansion of information technology.

Why are the Soviets 10 to 15 years behind? One reason is the decision made in the late 1960s to copy western computer designs rather than develop their own computer industry. This allowed the Soviets to copy huge amounts of western hardware and software, but it provided no Soviet infrastructure for computer design and manufacturing. The Soviet bureaucracy also inhibits development, because many ministries try to control computer technology, and each must approve computer-related decisions. Yet another reason is alleged "psychological barriers." For example, a plant manager may receive an expensive computer system but leave it in the warehouse for fear of losing more control to a central authority. Managers want to process their own financial data so that they can fudge plans if they have to.

A few computer devotees are getting hold of personal computers, but they must construct their own keyboards and wiring harnesses and use television screens for monitors. Moreover, Soviet personal computers will never be able to talk to one another as they do in the United States, because the telephone lines are of insufficient quality to support data channels. However, the Soviet Union already has one similarity with the United States: a phenomenon known as "hackers," who in the Soviet Union are called "khakers." Parents often call the computer center to find out why their children are not home for dinner.

One reason for the computer lethargy is the Soviet's penchant for control. Because xeroxing carries a seven-year prison sentence, the government bureaucracy is not about to start giving away printing presses.

Perestroika is changing this, but low-quality Soviet manufacturing is a major problem. Joint ventures can do something about that. One joint venture is designed to manufacture Soviet-designed IBM PC clones for sale in the Soviet Union and for export. It links six Soviet partners and a consulting group from Chicago. The second joint venture links the Soviet Trade Agency with three U.S. partners. IBM PC–compatible kits will be shipped to the Soviet Union, where they will be assembled and sold.

More important than selling computers, these joint ventures will promote computer adoption, which means *Soviet society may have to change.*

The revolution in information technology taking place in the United States may yet occur in the Soviet Union. The two important questions about the future of computer technology in the Soviet Union are: Can computerization in the Soviet Union simply be decreed by the government like everything else? If computerization does take place, will it change the structure of a closed society?

Source: Based on Michael Rogers, "Red Hackers Arise!" *Newsweek,* March 20, 1989, 58–59, and Peter Galuszka, "The Soviets Start Learning Their Bits and Bytes," *Business Week,* February 29, 1988, 40–41.

information. Had the automobile industry experienced a similar rate of development, you could buy a Rolls Royce for $280 and drive it 1 million miles on a gallon of gas. Managers must try to understand the technology of the Information Age and how it can be used. Management of information is even more important with the increase of competition in the global marketplace. And, as the Focus on Global Competition box shows, the information revolution that is taking place in the United States may also hold in the Soviet Union.

INFORMATION AND MANAGEMENT

In a very realistic sense, information is the lifeblood of organizations. To appreciate how managers use information in control and decision making, let's first distinguish data from information and then look at the characteristics of useful information.

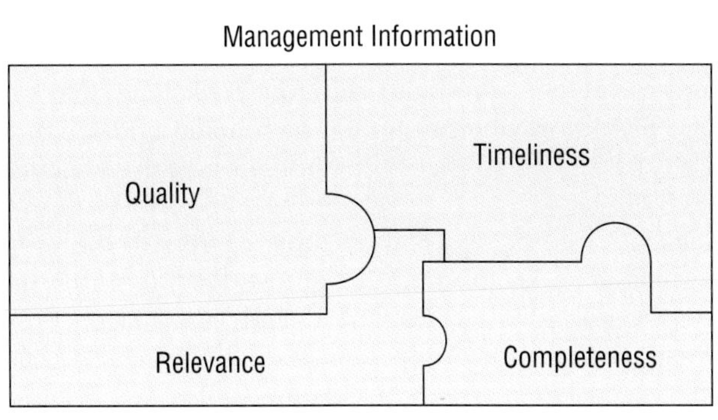

EXHIBIT 19.1
Characteristics of Useful Management Information

DATA VERSUS INFORMATION

The terms *data* and *information* often are used interchangeably. Yet there is an important difference. **Data** are raw, unsummarized, and unanalyzed facts. **Information** is data that are meaningful and alter the receiver's understanding.[3] Information is the data that managers actually use to interpret and understand events in the organization and the environment. For example, the Boddie brothers have an information system for controlling their 200 Hardee's restaurants. Thousands of data transactions are fed into the information system, including food sales, sales tax, water and electricity usage, and movement of inventory items. However, these raw data have no meaning, and in unsummarized form are worthless. Data require proper organization to produce meaningful information, such as total sales for the 200 Hardee restaurants, sales by store and by region, and key activity and profitability ratios.[4]

data Raw, unsummarized, and unanalyzed facts.

information Data that are meaningful and alter the receiver's understanding.

CHARACTERISTICS OF USEFUL INFORMATION

What makes information valuable? Information has many attributes, such as verifiability, accessibility, clarity, precision, and cost. Four factors that are especially important for management information are quality, timeliness, completeness, and relevance, as illustrated in Exhibit 19.1.[5]

QUALITY. Information that accurately portrays reality is said to have **quality.** The data are accurate and reliable. If the data say that a valve in a nuclear power plant is open, such quality is important to management decision making. A police officer in San Jose, California, runs a license plate check by tapping into the state license plate records system. If the data were inaccurate, an innocent person could be stopped or a guilty one let go.[6] Quality is what makes any information system work. Once a system is known to have errors, managers will no longer use it and its value for decision making will disappear.

quality The degree to which information accurately portrays reality.

TIMELINESS. Information that is available soon after events occur has **timeliness.** Managers work at a fast pace, and things change quickly. The most immediate benefit of computerized management is quick response time. Companies can shorten new-product development time, respond immediately to

timeliness The degree to which information is available soon after events occur.

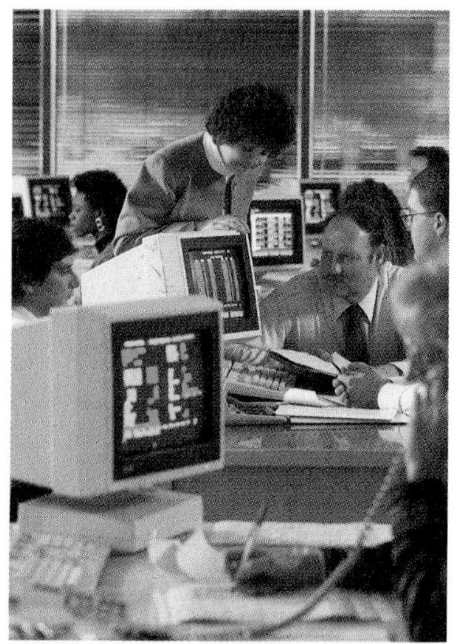

The value of *information quality* and *timeliness* is demonstrated at Chrysler Credit Corporation. Elaine Carpenter, credit supervisor, and John Hussey, branch operation supervisor, use a new branch information system to review a customer's account. The system links all 114 branch offices to provide instant access to dealer inventory records, retail and lease account histories, payoff quotations, and automated credit applications. The quality and speed of credit data are helping Chrysler Credit win new customers across the industry.

competitive changes, and shrink the control and feedback cycle within organizations. At Oxford Industries, an Atlanta clothing company, workers' activities are clocked to a thousandth of a minute. Oxford has figured, for instance, that a stitcher should spend 3.4 seconds on each front pocket and may work on 5,000 pockets a day. The information system gives running updates throughout the day of each worker's pace so that problems can be solved immediately.[7]

COMPLETENESS. Information **completeness** refers to the proper quantity of data. Too much data lead to information overload; too little fail to tell the complete story. As described in Chapters 17 and 18, managers exercise control by recognizing deviations from targets and instituting necessary changes. Managers often devise *exception reports* that contain only a few pages of deviations from target rather than hundreds of pages of raw data. These reports are complete because they contain key information, but in an amount managers can digest.

RELEVANCE. Information **relevance** means that the information must pertain to the problems, decisions, and tasks for which a manager is responsible. Information relevance is a difficult problem for an information system to solve, because every manager's situation is unique. Production managers need data on scrap rates, production volume, and employee productivity. Personnel managers need data on employee background, work experience, insurance programs, employee demographics, and position descriptions. Marketing managers need data on customer accounts, sales forecasts, sales activity, and individual salespeople's commissions.

INFORMATION SYSTEMS

Now that we understand the characteristics of useful information, we will discuss systems for providing information to managers. An **information system** is a mechanism that collects, organizes, and distributes data to organizational personnel. Most information systems are manual, which means people perform the information activities by hand. For example, Northrop Corporation generates 400,000 pieces of paper when building each fuselage for the F/A-18 jet fighter. A **computer-based information system (CBIS)** is a system that uses electronic computing technology to create the information system. Thus, a CBIS differs from a manual system only in the physical components that perform the functions. Input into a CBIS may be done through a terminal or automatic scanning systems. The computer manipulates data according to defined procedures. Data storage is electronic in the form of magnetic tapes and disks that can store huge volumes of data. Control over the system is provided by a software program that contains specific instructions for organizing data needed by users. Outputs are computer reports of data provided on a terminal screen.

For example, Northrop computerized the paper flow for building jet fighters. The 10-foot pile of paper (400,000 pieces) for each fuselage is put on one laser disk. Employees now consult a computer for instructions. Supervisors can make instant changes in procedures across the factory, avoiding the mess of paper changes. Computerizing the information provided a remarkable im-

completeness The extent to which information contains the appropriate amount of data.

relevance The degree to which information pertains to the problems, decisions, and tasks for which a manager is responsible.

information system A mechanism for collecting, organizing, and distributing data to organizational employees.

computer-based information system (CBIS) An information system that uses electronic computing technology to create the information system.

provement in timeliness, while maintaining high quality, completeness, and relevance. The new system helped Northrop save $20 million on the fuselage project.[8]

Hardware and Software

Hardware is the name given to the physical equipment used in a computer-based information system. The growth in computer use by business has emphasized different hardware. In the early 1970s, most businesses used mainframe computers, which are large machines that centralized all business computing in one location. Minicomputers became the rage by the late 1970s. These smaller, yet powerful computers allowed data processing to be decentralized to departments and divisions. The next hardware wave was personal computers in the mid 1980s. These small computers decentralized computing even further, allowing individuals to achieve high efficiency. Right now network computers are popular. New hardware links PC workstations into networks by groups of scientists, engineers, or business and finance professionals. The network allows information sharing and coordination.[9]

Software is the set of instructions that control and direct computer processing. It is the primary device used for controlling an information system. Software transforms raw data into usable information. New software had to be developed for each wave of computer hardware. Software for linking computers into networks is especially complex. Some of the popular software programs managers use for minicomputer and PC applications include *VisiCalc* and *Lotus 1-2-3* (electronic spreadsheets) and *dBASE IV* (data base management system). As the Manager's Shoptalk box shows, designing new software is fairly complex and therefore needs especially good management.

Information Systems and the Management Hierarchy

Recall from Chapter 1 that management activities differ according to top, middle, and first-line management levels in the hierarchy as illustrated in Exhibit 19.2. Hierarchical differences mean that managers need different kinds of information. For example, strategic planning is a primary responsibility at the top level, whereas operational control is a primary responsibility of first-line supervisors. Top managers work on nonprogrammable problems, such as new-product development, marketing plans, and acquisition of other companies. First-line managers, in contrast, deal with programmable decisions arising from well-defined problems, such as inventory control, production scheduling, and sales analysis.

The information top managers use pertains mostly to the external environment. It is broad in scope to cover unanticipated problems that may arise and is oriented toward the future, including trends and forecasts. First-line managers need information on internal operations that is narrowly focused on specific activities and deals with past performance.

MANAGER'S SHOPTALK

SOFT ON SOFTWARE

Most businesses cannot operate without computers. Computers cannot operate without software. And as companies are discovering, software cannot operate without sound management. Computer software, not hardware, is the cause of major problems in business computing.

The Board of Water & Light in Lansing, Michigan, is working on a seemingly simply task, consolidating the monthly bills for water and electricity. So far the programmers have spent more than 40 person-years and $2 million on the project. Why? The software required a fundamental change in company philosophy, needing coordination and new procedures for departments used to working alone. Businesses are discovering that software projects require hours of debate to revise procedures and policies.

Why is software such a tar pit? Because software is "pure thought," abstract, conceptual, artistic. By comparison, designing and developing computer hardware is a cinch, because explicit diagrams can be drawn and capacities precisely calculated.

When acquiring a new computer system, be aware that software can cause big implementation problems. Software design will uncover organizational rivalries, unrealistic scheduling, and the inability of programmers to understand business problems. To reduce problems and increase the quality of software applications, consider these guidelines.

- **Give data-processing departments the same clout as everybody else.** Having a chief information officer, for example, gives software projects credibility, which is essential to force major changes in business procedures.

- **Make data-processing managers periodically work side by side with software users.** This keeps everyone involved in software development. It gives data managers an insider's view of business problems.

- **Break up big projects to keep programming teams small.** The best size for teams is 5 to 10 members. This makes communication and management problems easier.

- **Give programmers elbow room.** This means both physically and intellectually. Programmers working in 100 square feet of office space are twice as productive as those working in 40 square feet. Programmers who can own a problem and use their full creativity can produce better software, so long as they understand the business problem.

Executives have to realize that hardware is not a silver bullet to correct business problems. Software is the most complex and difficult activity. To get the most from a new computer system, good old-fashioned management is the answer.

Source: Based on Brenton R. Schlender, "How to Break the Software Logjam," *Fortune*, September 25, 1989, 100–112.

To meet the different information needs along the hierarchy, three types of computer-based information systems have evolved. At the lower organization level, transaction processing systems (TPSs) assist first-line supervisors with recordkeeping, routine calculations, and data sorting. Middle-managers use management information systems (MISs). Top managers use executive information systems (EISs) to provide information for strategic and nonprogrammable decisions.

TRANSACTION PROCESSING SYSTEMS

transaction processing system (TPS) A type of CBIS that performs the organization's routinely occurring transactions.

The initial purpose of business computing in the 1960s was to reduce clerical costs by computerizing the flow of day-to-day business transactions. The **transaction processing system (TPS)** performs the organization's routine, recurring transactions. Examples of transactions include sending bills to customers,

EXHIBIT 19.2
Information Requirements by Management Level

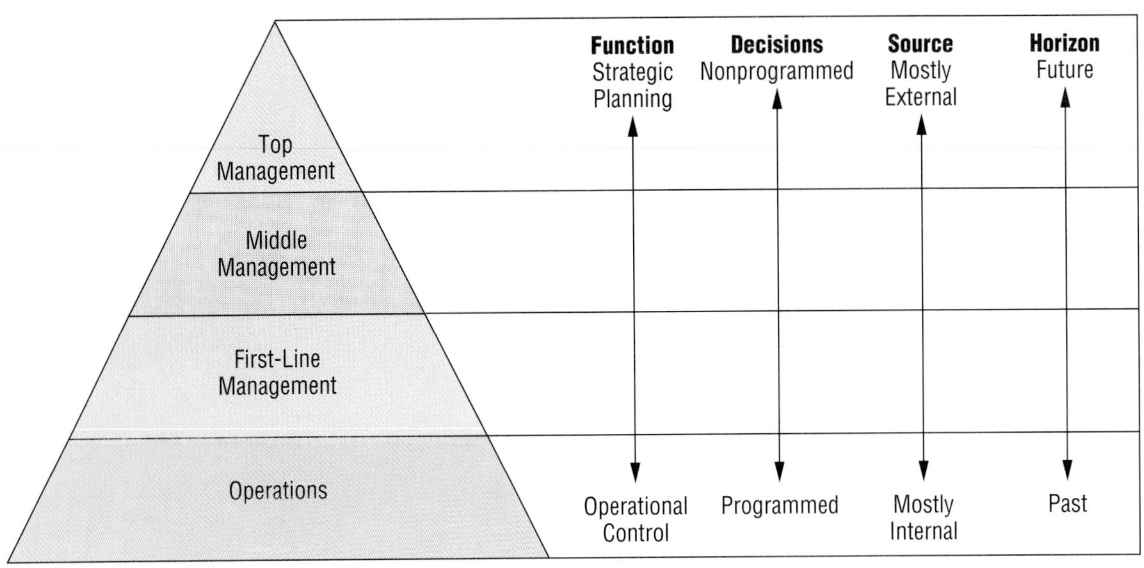

Source: Adapted from Rolland Hurtubise, *Managing Information Systems: Concept and Tools* (West Hartford, Conn.: Kumarian Press, 1984), 57, and G. Anthony Gorry and Michael S. Scott Morton, "A Framework for Management Information Systems," *Sloan Management Review* 13 (1971), 55–70.

depositing checks in the bank, placing orders, recording receipts and payments, and paying invoices. Large companies such as American Airlines, AT&T, and American Express could not account for their operations, control their assets, or manage projects without huge transaction processing systems. American Express has 16 major information-processing centers, 10 worldwide data networks, 90 mainframe computer systems, 400 minicomputer systems, and 30,000 individual workstations to support its transaction processing requirements. The TPS typically is not the concern of general managers, because specialists in information technology manage these systems.

MANAGEMENT INFORMATION SYSTEMS

A **management information system (MIS)** is a mechanism that collects, organizes, and distributes data used by managers in performing their management functions. As information systems evolved, management information systems were the next stage of evolution beyond transaction processing systems. As data bases accumulated, managers began visualizing ways in which the computer could help them make important decisions. Managers needed informa-

management information system (MIS) A form of CBIS that collects, organizes, and distributes the data managers use in performing their management functions.

A unique *transactions processing system* provides the parents of these boys at a nursery school in Toyama, Japan, with a report on their activities, including how much they ate for lunch and when they were picked up at the end of the day. The system enables the school to keep detailed records on its 100 youngsters, handles accounting functions and salary records for the staff, and tracks nutritional content of school meals. Developed by IBM, the software can also provide MIS data to nursery school managers for making decisions about school activities.

tion in summary form that pertained to specific management problems. The lists of thousands of daily organizational transactions were useless for planning, controlling, or decision making.

MISs provided information reports designed to help managers make decisions. For example, when a production manager needs to make decisions about production scheduling, he or she may need data on the anticipated number of orders in the coming month based on trends, current inventory levels, and availability of equipment and personnel. The MIS can provide these data. At Visible Changes hair salons, managers use the MIS to learn about customer age and sex, repeat business, and productivity by salon and haircutter.[10]

The MIS required more complex software that would instruct computers to translate data into useful reports. Computer hardware also became more complex and sophisticated because it needed greater capacity and the ability to integrate diverse data bases. For example, thousands of transactions take place daily in supermarkets. One leader in developing management information systems is Gromer Supermarket Inc.

GROMER SUPERMARKET INC. • Gromer's is a huge superstore in Elgin, Illinois. The laser scanners at Gromer's ten checkout counters speed shoppers through the checkout lines, but more important, they provide tons of information. Millions of transactions are recorded, and a quarter of a million dollars' worth of computer hardware and software are used to provide management reports on everything from checker efficiency, bagging speed, and food turnover. Take cereal, for example. The MIS data showed that Rice Krispies had six size categories, but two were slow movers and thus were eliminated.

executive information system (EIS) An interactive CBIS that retrieves, manipulates, and displays information serving the needs of top managers; also called *decision support system.*

In the meat department, MIS reports tell the meat manager how much gross margin a side of beef will produce. The system also describes the cuts from a pork loin that will maximize gross profits. Labor cost decisions are made efficiently because the number of baggers scheduled to work is chosen to fit

EXHIBIT 19.3
EIS Components and Data Sources

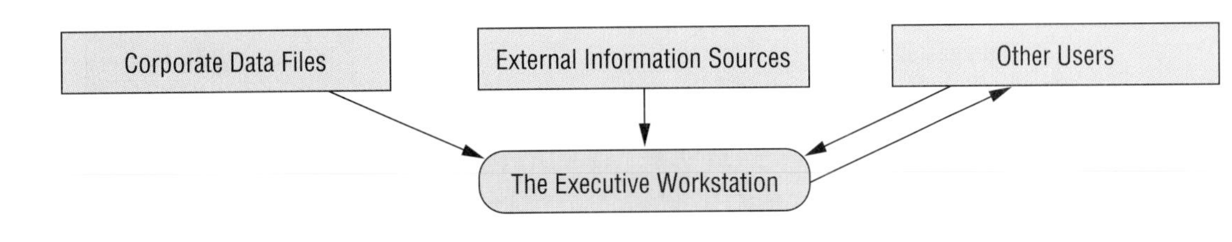

Source: *CA-Insight, The Computer Associates Software Magazine*, vol. 2, no. 2, 7.

the number of customers coming through the store and the known rate at which a bagger can bag. The millions of numbers crunched through the MIS system help managers decide how to display products, which products to stock, and how to make storage and delivery more efficient.[11]

EXECUTIVE INFORMATION SYSTEMS

Until recently, information systems have not possessed the sophistication and simplicity that senior executives needed. Executive information systems were developed because managers needed help with unanticipated and unstructured problems that MISs were not flexible enough to provide.

An **executive information system (EIS)** is the use of computer technology to support the information needs of senior managers.[12] EISs were formed from powerful PCs that could shape masses of numbers into simple, colorful charts and from networks that can weave together a company's different hardware and data bases.[13] EISs are also called *decision support systems*, because they allow an executive to interact with the information system to retrieve, manipulate, and display data needed to make specific decisions. For example, the CEO of Duracell asked for data comparing the performance of hourly and salaried work forces in the United States and overseas. Within seconds, he had a crisp table in color showing that U.S. workers produced more sales. Asking for more data, he discovered that too many overseas salespeople were wasting time calling on small stores. As a result, executives made the decision to sign up distributors to cover small stores, improving foreign profits.[14] EISs give managers access to multiple data bases depending on their immediate information needs, as illustrated in Exhibit 19.3.

Executive information systems deal with nonprogrammed decisions such as strategic planning. Consequently, the hardware and software technologies are very sophisticated. Indeed, to be accessible to top managers who are not computer experts, up to 75 percent of the computer system's capacity may be used for software that permits managers to "talk" to the system in everyday English. This frees the remaining 25 percent to handle multiple data bases, translate inquiries into simple graphs and charts, and provide an instant answer to almost any question. Initial research indicates that EISs help people make

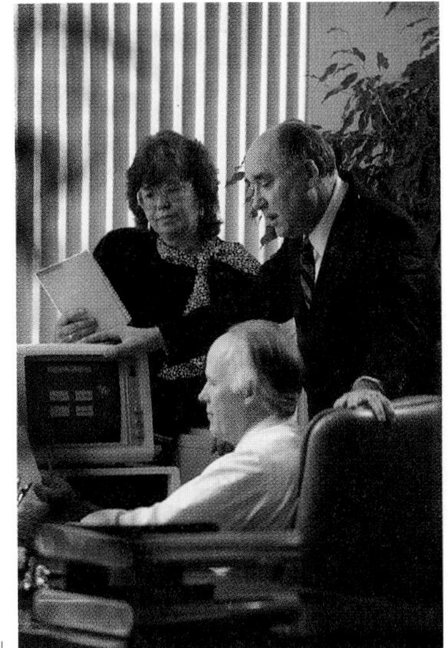

UNUM Corporation is a specialty insurance company headquartered in Portland, Maine, with approximately 4,000 employees. Technology gives UNUM a competitive edge thanks to advances such as the *executive information system* (EIS) shown here. The EIS provides important data on claims, sales, reserves, and employment so that senior managers can easily spot emerging trends and take appropriate action. Pat Walsh, manager of the EIS development group, and John Alexander, senior VP and chief information officer, review the EIS with Gwain Gillespie, Executive VP of Finance and Administration.

EXHIBIT 19.4
Evolution of Management Applications of Computer Technology

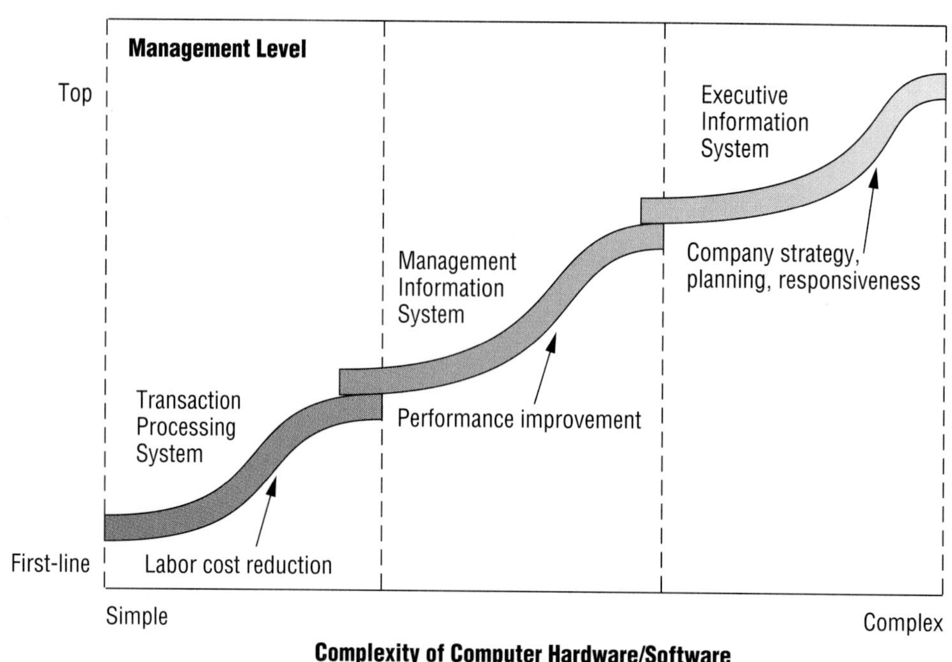

faster and more effective decisions, an important consideration in today's global marketplace.[15]

EISs are being adopted widely. Some examples are as follows:[16]

- At California Federal, an EIS is used to track CD maturity projections and both consumer and mortgage loan growth to develop a strategy to ensure that managers are on top of opportunities and problems.
- The president of Pratt & Whitney uses an EIS nearly every day to monitor and act on new engine development and manufacturing status information.
- The treasurer of General Motors uses an EIS to get immediate access to international currency information so he can direct currency moves and get instant answers when other GM executives call.

Exhibit 19.4 summarizes the evolution of computer-based information systems used in organizations. Transaction processing came first; it used simple hardware and software to reduce costs and improve efficiency at lower organization levels. Management information systems represented a higher level of complexity and allowed managers to make decisions to improve the performance of departments and divisions. Executive information systems represent the latest and most complex technology that is applicable to top management's nonprogrammed decisions. EISs can address broad strategic issues, help managers formulate strategic plans, and respond to rapid external changes.[17]

Emerging Information Technologies

Developments in MISs and EISs have paralleled advances in other computer-based information technologies. The computerization of organizations has enabled the widespread use of electronic mail, computer conferencing, and electronic bulletin boards.[18] More recent advances are group decision support systems, artificial intelligence, and interorganizational networks. Each harnesses computer power to facilitate organizational work.

Group Decision Support Systems

A **group decision support system (GDSS)** is an interactive computer-based system that facilitates group decision making.[19] Also called *collaborative work systems*, GDSSs are designed to allow team members to interact and at the same time take advantage of computer-based support data. Participating managers sit around a conference table equipped with a computer terminal at each position. Each participant can create displays on his or her own screen, and a large public display screen is also available.[20] More sophisticated versions of GDSS allow for team conferences of spatially separated participants. Members can use a live television hookup to see one another during their conference, and computer screens in each location allow participants to share data displays. Collaborative systems are especially helpful for contributing diverse data bases to team decision making and removing interpersonal communication barriers. These systems also facilitate brainstorming during problem solving by the team.

group decision support system (GDSS) An interactive CBIS that facilitates group communication and decision making; also called *collaborative work system.*

Artificial Intelligence

Artificial intelligence (AI) is information technology whose ultimate goal is to make computers think, see, talk, and listen like humans. Concepts from psychology, linguistics, and computer science have been combined to create programs that can perform tasks never before done by machines. For example, Hal, the supercomputer in the movies *2001* and *2010*, was the ideal result of AI technology; it could think, talk, and make decisions like a human being.

artificial intelligence (AI) Information technology that attempts to make computers think, talk, see, and listen like people.

The area of AI that has had the greatest impact on organizations is called the expert system. An **expert system** duplicates the thinking process that professionals and managers use when making decisions. An expert system is developed by codifying a specialist's knowledge into decision rules that are written into a computer program to mimic the expert's problem-solving strategy.[21] For example, Campbell was about to experience a serious loss when Aldo Cimino retired. He knew more than anyone about maintaining the seven-story soup sterilizers and kettles used in Campbell's kitchens. Campbell's solution was to develop an expert system that could duplicate Cimino's thought processes. Developing the expert system was painstaking and difficult. A programmer from Texas Instruments interviewed Cimino day after day to obtain the minutest details on what he thought and why he took every step. It took seven months to boil Cimino's experience down to 151 "if-then" rules that a computer could understand. Now whenever a problem comes up with a huge

expert system An area of AI that attempts to program a computer to duplicate an expert's decision-making and problem-solving strategies.

At Corning Glass Works, a compaq personal *computer network* assists hundreds of engineers in every phase of new product development, from designing and testing prototypes to laying out factory floor plans for production. The network PCs allow professionals like these at the W.C. Decker engineering facility to quickly share new information with engineers at research labs located elsewhere. By using this network, Corning has shortened product development time and improved product quality.

networking The linking together of people and departments within or among organizations for the purpose of sharing information resources.

electronic data interchange (EDI) An interorganizational computer network used by trading partners to exchange business data.

kettle, the expert system tells managers how Cimino would have responded.[22] Companies such as General Electric, Schlumberger, Digital Equipment Corporation, and Arthur D. Little have developed artificial intelligence to assist in activities such as analyzing oil-drilling logs, diagnosing diesel locomotives, and telling managers what machinery is needed to manufacture a new product.[23]

NETWORKING

Networking is the linking together of people and departments within or among organizations to share information resources such as data bases. Linking together stand-alone computers has the same potential for coordination that the telephone has for individuals. The problem is that computers in each part of the organization must use the same programs, formats, and computer languages. Once compatibility is achieved, managers across the network have access to the data bases and resources of all participants. For example, a credit union in Richmond, British Columbia, was drowning in bad loans. Top managers attacked the problem by trying to increase business through discounts to high-volume customers. A personal computer network was acquired that connected 250 tellers in 6 offices. New pricing information was shared immediately throughout the network, and revenues increased by $429,000 annually. Networks are powerful because they make it easier for employees to communicate by computer, cut down on meeting time, handle large amounts of information, and eliminate duplicate software purchases.[24]

Interorganizational networks are now being created to link the information systems of two or more organizations. The technology for this is called **electronic data interchange (EDI),** the computer-to-computer exchange of business data between trading partners.[25] EDI eliminates paperwork and dramatically speeds purchases, reordering, and invoicing. For example, JCPenney linked up with Lanier Clothes, an apparel supplier. The supplier is linked directly to Penney's cash register sales. Automatic reordering lets Penney replenish supplies of popular suits fast enough to meet that season's demand. Although sales increased, and it carried more sizes of suits, Penney cut inventory 20 percent with EDI.

An example of a more complex EDI network is illustrated in Exhibit 19.5. This network is similar to those used by Japanese automakers.[26] The computer at the auto company headquarters electronically receives a car order specifying model, color, and options. It automatically orders the required parts from suppliers. The computer issues instructions for building a car at the assembly plant. The computer at company headquarters can electronically invoice the dealer and pay suppliers through the network linkage to the bank.

STRATEGIC USE OF INFORMATION TECHNOLOGY

The adoption of MISs, EISs, GDSSs, or artificial intelligence has strategic consequences for organizations. One desired consequence is improved operational efficiency, especially in the management functions of decision making and controlling. Operational efficiency enables a company to lower costs, mak-

EXHIBIT 19.5
An Interorganizational Computer Network

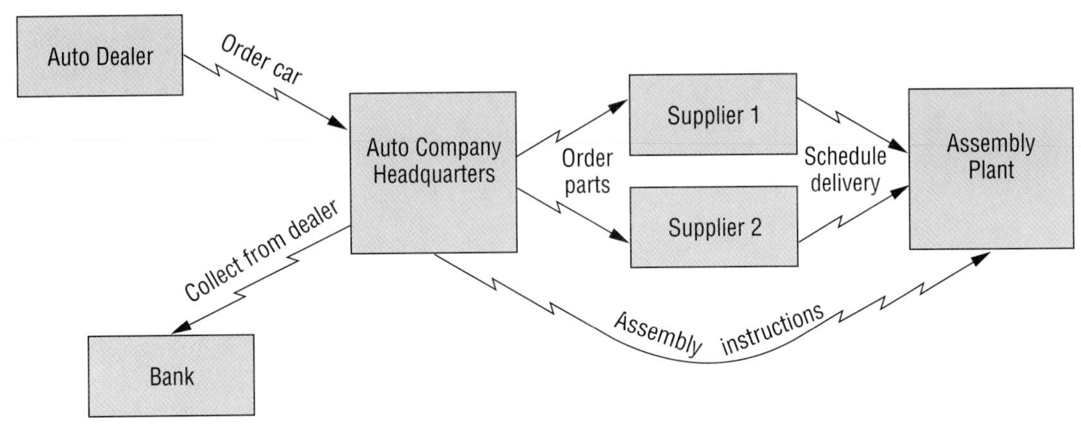

Source: Based on Joel Dreyfuss, "Networking: Japan's Latest Computer Craze," *Fortune*, July 7, 1986, 95.

ing it more competitive. Another desired consequence is to present new strategic options to senior managers. Information technology enables the organization to lock in customers and broaden market reach. These options differentiate the firm strategically, giving it advantage in the marketplace.

OPERATIONAL EFFICIENCY AND CONTROL

MANAGEMENT EFFICIENCY. The impact of information technology on management falls primarily on the functions of decision making and control. Information technology is easily adapted to first-line management activities such as production, scheduling, inventory management, and office procedures. At middle management levels desktop terminals give managers access to more information than ever before, and electronic mail and computer conferencing enable coordination and rapid communication. With electronic mail, managers can avoid telephone tag. Just the reduction in paperwork can improve management efficiency at all levels. Recall how Northrop saved 400,000 pieces of paper on each fuselage it built. The American Automobile Society puts its documents on optical disks, giving employees immediate access to documents and saving tons of paperwork.[27]

The efficiency of information technology is realized in many companies by the appointment of a *chief information officer* (CIO) who is responsible for managing organizational data bases and implementing new information technology. Technology can be selected and implemented to fit the strategic needs of the organization. For example, at Primerica, a vice-president of information services spent 75 percent of his time using information technology to cut costs, the key need for Primerica to stay competitive.

Computer-based technologies have had less impact on top management. However, when senior people do use EISs, their efficiency often increases. One senior bank executive commented, "Everything I do on the computer I do ten times faster than I used to." An executive at Mobil's New York headquarters remarked on his increased efficiency: "When I shave in the morning, I find myself contemplating all the ways I can solve a problem using the computer instead of worrying if there's a solution at all."[28]

Airborne Express provides door-to-door express delivery throughout the United States and many foreign countries. The implementation of computer technology has improved *operational efficiency* to the point where Airborne now has one of the lowest costs per shipment of any carrier in the industry. The computer technology includes a positive tracking system that allows Airborne to immediately trace a package anywhere in the system. Accounting data is also computer automated, resulting in more efficiency and fewer errors. In some centers, productivity has improved approximately 72 percent. This operational efficiency enables Airborne Express to win business in its primary niche, large volume corporate shippers.

IMPROVED COORDINATION, FLEXIBILITY. Another efficiency of information technology is to break down barriers among departments and across hierarchical levels. Managers who are wired into a computer system communicate with anyone who can help solve a problem. Citicorp managers around the globe seek advice from one another thanks to a computer conferencing system.

A new organizational form is developing called the cluster organization. In a **cluster organization,** groups of people work together to solve business problems and then disband when the job is done.[29] At Digital Equipment Corporation, new teams are brought together face-to-face for a week or more to develop closeness and friendship. Then managers return to their regular locations around the world and communicate by electronic mail and group decision support systems. Teams can be clustered together in infinite combinations to solve problems that arise. When a problem is solved, the team disbands and individuals are reformed into new teams.

cluster organization An organizational form in which team members from different company locations use electronic mail and GDSSs to solve problems.

SMALLER MANAGEMENT STRUCTURE. The general outcome of information technology has been to reverse the trend of hiring new managers. By speeding up information routing, the number of managers in many organizations has been reduced. This reduction has been felt through an increased span of control and a decrease in the number of levels in the management hierarchy.[30] Technology allows managers to increase their spans of control.

For example, one organization that has gone heavily into information technology is Hercules Inc., where a sophisticated combination of electronic and voice mail, computer conferencing, word processing, and high-speed communications have led to a leaner management structure. Hercules started with a satellite dish on the roof and five computer conferencing rooms on different floors. It then introduced a network of more than 400 word processing terminals and 205 personal computers. Under the system memos and text can be routed electronically through any company office worldwide. This has led to a 40 percent reduction in secretarial hours.

Hercules' electronic mail and conferencing technology has saved the company over $4 million a year in time and travel expenses. These improvements have enabled Hercules to trim 1,800 jobs, including assistant department managers, assistant plant managers, and a level of vice-presidents.[31]

COMPETITIVE STRATEGY

LOCK IN CUSTOMERS. One of the most significant influences of computer-based information technology is to give a competitive advantage with customers.

Mercantile Stores Company operates 78 department and two specialty stores, and has adopted computer technology as part of its *competitive strategy.* A major component of this strategy is electronic data interchange — the electronic transfer of business documents and data, including invoices, purchase orders, and shipping lists. At the point of sale, product information contained on merchandise tags, shown here, is transmitted directly to manufacturers, who in turn send it along to their suppliers. This electronic linkage reduces inventories and substantially increases sales. Buyers make merchandise decisions with immediate, accurate data about what customers want, and replacement goods arrive in stores while demand is still high.

Consider American Hospital Supply Corporation, a health goods manufacturer. In a smart strategic move, senior executives decided to give computer terminals free to hospitals around the country. These terminals linked hospital purchasers with American Hospital Supply and enabled them to directly place orders for any of more than 100,000 products. This corporate strategy linked the company directly to its customers, and it was a strategic breakthrough. AHS gained sales and market share at competitors' expense. Hospitals had the advantage of lowered inventory carrying costs, because they were confident that orders with AHS would be processed quickly. AHS was one of the first companies to use information technology in corporate strategy. Customers were locked in because they could not switch to another supplier without losing efficiency and convenience.[32] Interorganizational linkages can link a company with suppliers and bankers as well as customers to gain speedy transactions, providing further competitive advantage.

BROADEN MARKET REACH. Information technology can be used to tap into market intelligence data bases on competitors, demographics, customers, and census factors to spot unused niches and needs for new products. By having salespeople use laptop computers in the field, a quick call can confirm inventory availability and instantly close a deal. Speed and timely service give an advantage over competitors. For example, Red Lion Inns uses a computer network to target messages to customer groups, give salespeople methods for entering orders directly through portable computers, and stimulate new product features.

IMPLEMENTATION OF INFORMATION TECHNOLOGY

Although information technology has undergone a revolution and can enhance corporate strategy as well as improve manager efficiency and control, it still suffers barriers to implementation. Some of these barriers pertain to the technology and others pertain to its lack of acceptance and use within organizations.

Barriers to Utilization

Unsuitable for Many Tasks. CBISs have not yet become the primary source of management information. Recall from Chapter 1 that a manager's job is characterized by variety and fragmentation. Managers do not spend time analyzing data. Managers — especially top managers — work in an informal, reactive manner that is unsuited to the design of MISs or even of EISs. Moreover, as described in Chapter 15, managers need rich, face-to-face communications in order to interpret ambiguous events, establish personal relationships, and build coalitions for important decisions, none of which can be accomplished through a CBIS.

Unrealistic Expectations. Most organizations adopt new information technology with high expectations. Yet new information systems merely work within the organization's current information structure. If an information system suddenly provides data ten times as fast or provides ten times the volume of data, the improvement in manager performance may be only modest — say, 10 percent — because all that additional data and speed are unnecessary. Further, if the previous manual system did not provide useful data, the same worthless data will come through the computer system.

Underused or Sabotaged Systems. The implementation of a new, computer-based information system has consequences for power and control — indeed, one motivation for adopting a new system is to increase management's control over the organization. The new system has the potential to provide data that will measure and monitor the performances of both individuals and departments. In response, operating personnel in some organizations have deliberately distorted or destroyed input data such as time cards and production control information. In one case, corporate accountants took the initiative of introducing the new system as a way of tightening control over organizational divisions. Division managers fought cooperation with the new system, attacking it for design, technical, and feasibility limitations. The most frequent problem is not sabotage but employees who avoid or bypass the new system.

Working in the area of *artificial intelligence,* Ed Wilson of Chevron is building an *expert system* that provides data on hazardous material regulations and handling advice. Chevron supports several projects that use computers this way, which is like putting expertise in a box. Wilson uses effective *implementation techniques* by meeting with shift supervisors and other experts to gain their participation and cooperation. He will also develop a *prototype,* testing the system before it goes into broader application.

Implementation Techniques

The implementation of information technology has generated many horror stories. For instance, Allstate Insurance Company designed a computer system to run its office operations and shorten the period needed to introduce new policies. The target cost was $8 million. One year after the expected date of completion, the project cost $15 million, and the new cost estimate for completing the project was many months and $100 million.[33]

As discussed in Chapter 11 on change, any new technology must be implemented properly in order for it to be successful. An effective strategy for developing and implementing a CBIS is called the **systems development life cycle,** which is the sequence of events that system designers should use to bring a new system to reality.[34] The life cycle starts with a feasibility study that ascertains user needs. Then the technology requirements are determined, followed by the system's design and physical construction. Physical construction consists of the design of appropriate software and acquisition of hardware. Next, the system is implemented. Implementation requires user participation, education, and communication. The more users are involved in the system's design, the more they will understand, accept, and use it.

systems development life cycle The sequence of events that CBIS designers follow in developing and implementing a new system.

Another variation for implementation used by some system designers is prototyping. A **prototype** is a working version of an information system developed to test the system's features.[35] The prototype provides samples of output to users and gives managers a chance to work with the output. A good implementation strategy is to ensure that management users are involved throughout all stages of development.[36]

prototype A working model of an information system developed to test the system's features.

TAILOR INFORMATION TO USER NEEDS. One of the biggest problems for both new and ongoing computer-based information systems is that information may not precisely fit what managers need to make decisions or control a large corporation. This is a continuing dilemma because as management problems change, the data provided by information systems also must change. Too often data end up being designed to satisfy machine requirements or design specialists rather than the managers who will use it. Specialists may be enamored with the volume of data a system can produce and overlook the need to provide small amounts of data in a timely and useful format for decision making.

Three techniques that help bridge the gap between information system specialists and managers' needs have been identified:

1. *Key indicator system.* A **key indicator system** is based on the selection of key business indicators, exception reporting, and the use of graphics packages. The key indicator system emphasizes managers' control needs and provides specific data rapidly and selectively.
2. *Total study.* The **total study** is a process of assessing information needs at all levels of the management hierarchy. Managers are interviewed about their information requirements. Interview results are compared with available data bases, and priorities for information reports are set. The difficulty with this system is that it is time consuming and tries to meet all managers' needs from the same information system, which may mean that no information needs are fully satisfied.
3. *Critical success factors.* **Critical success factors (CSFs)** are the "limited number of areas in which results, if they are satisfactory, will ensure successful and competitive performance for the organization."[37] CSFs are obtained through lengthy interviews with individual managers, which define the managers' goals and methods for assessing goal attainment. Then the interviews are used to define which information will keep the managers apprised of key performance areas. CSFs differ from company to company and among managers within a firm. They force managers to consider only important information needs, thus eliminating useless data.

key indicator system A technique for determining managers' information needs based on key business indicators, exception reporting, and the use of graphics packages.

total study A process that attempts to assess information requirements at all management levels.

critical success factors (CSFs) The particular areas in which satisfactory results will enhance the organization's overall performance.

ADDITIONAL IMPLEMENTATION TECHNIQUES. The first technique found to work in business organizations is to make technology believers of top management. This engages their support for the new technology and persuades employees to go along. Second, identifying technology champions also helps. Champions believe in the technology and persuade peers to try it. Third, a prototype can also be used in the sense that the first encounter with the new technology must be successful for employees. If they try the new technology in a way that is enjoyable and challenging, they will embrace the technology as part of their work.[38] Finally, measure the benefits. When technology alters behavior in a positive way or shows other tangible payoffs, report it widely to gain support. These techniques, along with the implementation techniques described in Chapter 11, can make new information technology a success.[39]

SUMMARY

This chapter discussed several important points about management information systems. Nontechnical managers need not understand hardware and software, but they should be aware of how information technology can enhance organizational efficiency and effectiveness. We are becoming an information society, and computer-based information systems are an important part of most organizations today.

Information systems process huge amounts of data and transform them into useful information for managers. Useful management information has the characteristics of quality, timeliness, completeness, and relevance. Computer-based information systems include three types: transaction processing, management information systems, and executive information systems. Transaction processing is used at lower organizational levels; MISs provide information for middle managers; and EISs help senior managers answer strategic questions. Other new technologies being adopted by organizations include group decision support systems, artificial intelligence, and networking.

Information technology has an impact on operational efficiency and business strategy. Information systems should be adopted and implemented in congruence with the organization's strategic objectives. Finally, computer-based information systems have some barriers to utilization, including unsuitability for many tasks, unrealistic expectations, and underused or sabotaged output. Implementation can be enhanced by tailoring systems to managers' specific needs.

MANAGEMENT SOLUTION

Daddy's Junky Music Stores found it difficult to control new and used inventories, accounting records, taxes, customer profiles, and the like. The solution was a computer, but store managers would not tolerate printouts they could not believe. Two senior managers took responsibility for acquiring a computer and developing appropriate procedures. Implementation took time, but was carefully done. Soon, monthly reports were ready within three days. The data identified high-profit items so that they could be quickly restocked. It also eliminated mass purchases of low-priced items that failed to sell well. Suddenly salespeople had orderly orders — the records on available stock were accurate and item location was correct. They also could see what to pay for trade-in equipment. The computer system allowed everyone more control, causing managers to ask how they ever survived without it.[40]

DISCUSSION QUESTIONS

1. Randy Fields of Mrs. Fields Cookies argues that managers must have a vision of what they want to accomplish with information technology. They must imagine which data they need and which functions they want to control, and not be constrained by the technology. Does this philosophy make sense to you? Explain.
2. What are four characteristics of useful information? How can information systems be designed to include these characteristics?
3. How do information needs for control and decision making differ by hierarchical level?
4. What are barriers to the use of computer-based information systems? Are they due to characteristics of technology or human behavior?
5. If you were asked to help design and implement an information system for a department at your university, how would you proceed? How would you overcome possible resistance?
6. What is an executive information system? How does an EIS differ from an MIS?
7. Describe artificial intelligence and expert systems. How do these systems differ from other computer-based information systems?
8. What are the possible effects of information technologies on organization structure? Discuss.
9. Recent thinking suggests that CBISs should be adopted to further competitive strategy. How might information systems be used in this way?

MANAGEMENT IN PRACTICE: ETHICAL DILEMMA

Buying a Network

Purchasing agent Mike Stevens sat down with chief information officer George Sterns with supplier bids for 30 PC workstations that would be linked into a network. The system also would require cables and software that would interconnect with the current computer system.

Mike reported, "The companies are close with respect to quality and reputation. The only difference is price, with Kentucky Electronics on the low end and Quanton Inc. on the high end. I think we should go with Kentucky."

Sterns responded, "Are you sure that's the best choice? After all, the plant is over 300 miles away, which could mean problems with delivery and service. I'd prefer Quanton, who we've used once before. They provided good service. Besides Frank Johns (one of their top people) and I go way back; we were fraternity brothers in college. I can count on him to smooth out any rough spots."

"But the extra 4 percent would put us over budget," said Mike. "The president won't like that."

"Don't worry. It's not such a big overrun. I'll explain the situation."

"But the purchasing regulations require us to accept the lowest bidder, unless there is a difference in quality or some other factor. I've also heard that Kentucky is hungry and has a staff of good programmers."

"A few extra pennies won't kill the budget. Hey, Johns is giving a barbecue next weekend. I'll give him a call and squeeze you in. He's a great guy, and you'll enjoy meeting him."

What Do You Do?

1. Select Quantron Inc. Personal contacts are better for the company than formal bids and company regulations. Enjoy the party.
2. Pass the bids to the head of purchasing. Selecting Quantron Inc. violates regulations, and Kentucky Electronics should be given a chance to compete.
3. Try to persuade the CIO to change his mind. Point out that he is using personal favoritism as his decision criterion. It's your responsibility to do the right thing, because you are the purchasing agent responsible for this project.

CASES FOR ANALYSIS

MEMORIAL COUNTY HOSPITAL

In 1984, Memorial County Hospital was hit by the same changes in Medicare reimbursement as all other hospitals. For years, the longer patients were hospitalized, the more Memorial County got paid. Now the government uses a fixed-fee system, under which hospitals are paid a specific amount for each disease. If the hospital's cost is less than the amount paid, the hospital keeps the profit; if too high, it takes the loss.

Memorial County is scrambling to implement a series of new information systems. An information systems department has been created, and an MIS expert, Jack Grant, has been hired to run it. The challenge facing Grant is awesome: Memorial County must be able to track costs patient by patient, doctor by doctor, and disease by disease. Memorial County never needed this information before because it simply did a rough approximation of overhead costs for each patient before billing Medicare.

The system Grant wants to design will have several characteristics. When a pharmacist fills a prescription, the data will also go into the patient's computer file so that the hospital will know the cost immediately. Similarly, doctors will be expected to file information on patient treatments directly into the computer through terminals in their offices. The hospital has a strong incentive to treat patients as quickly and inexpensively as possible and expects doctors to help in the process. Grant also envisions a cost-tracking system that will follow each doctor's use of the X-ray department, laboratory tests, and other hospital resources. The information system also will report the consumption of all hospital resources per each patient and each disease. Weekly and monthly reports will reveal the different patterns among attending physicians and give Memorial County's senior managers a chance to buttonhole doctors to be aware of costs.

Another change Grant envisions is to integrate financial and medical records. These records were always kept separately, but now the medical record has financial implications, and both medical and financial data will be accessible from a patient's file.

The new technologies will cost Memorial County Hospital several hundred thousand dollars over the next three years. Administrators hope the new computer-based information systems will make the hospital more efficient. Managers will be able to determine, for example, if a cataract treatment costs $2,356 when reimbursement is only $2,128. With such information, administrators can concentrate on shortening hospital stays, reducing the number of tests, or treating some cases as outpatient.

Questions

1. Has the change in Medicare reimbursement altered Memorial County Hospital's competitive strategy? Will information systems help implement that strategy?
2. What impact do you think the increase in information systems will have on structure, social relationships, and operational efficiency within Memorial County Hospital? Discuss.
3. Would you characterize the new information systems as transaction processing, MIS, or EIS? Explain.

UNITED WAY

In September 1986, Mark Mechanic, the director of a university computer center in upstate New York, was working at his desk when the phone rang. On the other end was Paul Powers, an executive in charge of evaluation at the local United Way. Paul wondered if Mark would help design a consolidated information system that would help center directors cut paperwork and also give the United Way more objective performance data for agency evaluation and control. Mark Mechanic indicated that he was very interested. A week later, he had his first meeting with the directors of eight neighborhood centers and executives from three funding agencies. The directors all had similar problems. Most of the centers had evolved from local settlement houses to neighborhood centers that provided a number of services to local residents. Services varied widely but usually included housing, employment, recreation, food, clothing, child care, health services, and referrals and transportation to other agencies. Each had its own unique variety of funding sources, and each was inundated with paperwork.

During the discussion of a potential information system, Mechanic explained what might be done to reduce the paperwork. He pointed out that the current narrative reports written by the caseworkers and the wide variety of forms could be reduced to several standardized forms. From the information on the standardized forms, the computer could produce summaries that would eliminate 80 percent of the paperwork that the directors were doing. The presentation generated considerable enthusiasm, and it was agreed that Mechanic's staff would begin to wade through the numerous forms used in each of the agencies.

After three months, the computer staff had conducted over 100 interviews with people from all levels of the eight agencies and had gathered 190 forms that were currently in use. By the end of five months, the computer staff members felt that they had a rough understanding of information needs, and . . . they scheduled interviews with each of the eight center directors. Shortly thereafter, Mechanic met with the members of his staff. At one point in the meeting, the following discussion took place.

> Mechanic: *Up until now you have all been enthusiastic. All of a sudden you seem discouraged. What happened?*
> Bill Meadows (project director): *Mark, the directors of the centers are idiots. They don't understand the first thing about information systems.*
> Mechanic: *Idiots! What do you mean?*
> Meadows: *We go in and ask them what information they need. They get a shocked look on their face, like they never had thought of such a question. They hem and haw. They have no vision of what an information system is or what it might do for them. No matter how many times we go back, they still cannot deal with the questions we need answered. Whenever we are around the directors disappear.*
> Mechanic: *If they disappear, what do you do?*
> Meadows: *Well, it is sort of a tacit agreement. We don't bother them with questions and they don't bother us with objections. We show them the forms and they look at them and say O.K.*

Questions

1. What type of information system — transaction processing, MIS, or EIS — will be most appropriate for the United Way agency?
2. Do the United Way agencies truly need a computer-based information system? What limitations do you see in the ability of a CBIS to meet its information needs?
3. How would you characterize the procedure being used to design and implement the information system? What techniques should Bill Meadows use to help managers define their information needs and overcome their resistance?

Source: Robert E. Quinn, "Computers, People, and the Delivery of Services: How to Manage the Management Information System," in John E. Diettrich and Robert A. Zawacki, *People & Organizations*, 2d ed. (Plano, Tex.: Business Publications, 1985), 226–232. Used with permission of Robert Quinn.

CHAPTER 20

OPERATIONS AND SERVICE MANAGEMENT

CHAPTER OUTLINE

LEARNING OBJECTIVES

After studying this chapter, you should be able to:

- Define operations management and describe its area of application within manufacturing and service organizations.
- Explain the role of operations management strategy in the company's overall competitive strategy.
- Discuss product, process, and fixed-position layouts and their relative advantages.
- Explain why small inventories are preferred by most organizations.
- Discuss the differences among EOQ, MRP, and JIT for the management of material and inventory.
- Define productivity and explain its relationship to total quality management.
- Describe alternative structural arrangements for the operations management function.

Management Problem

Tom Blount, head of advanced manufacturing for refrigerators of GE's Major Appliance Business Group (MABG), had to do something about Building 4. That's where compressors for GE's refrigerators were made, a loud, dirty operation built with 1950s technology. It costs MABG over $48 to make a compressor. Japanese and Italian manufacturers were producing quality compressors for under $30, and a Singapore plant was aiming at $24. GE took 65 minutes of labor to make a compressor, compared with 25 minutes in Japan and Italy. Blount was faced with two options. One was to buy quality compressors from foreign manufacturers at a cheap price to keep the cost of GE refrigerators down. The other option was to invest in a new, more effective manufacturing facility.[1]

Should Tom Blount buy inexpensive, high-quality compressors from overseas, or take the risk of investing in a new plant? If you were an advisor, would you give MABG any chance of competing with foreign companies?

The choice facing GE's refrigerator division is not unusual. Many companies have discovered that strategic success is contingent on efficient manufacturing operations. In the 1990s, the manufacturing function is held in high esteem in the corporate world and is considered a key to corporate success.

- The Timken Company gambled $500 million on an ultramodern steel plant when the roller bearing industry was in decline. In the face of whithering foreign competition, it invested in new technology and won changes from the steel union on staffing and work rules.[2]
- Fireplace Manufacturers Inc. (FMI), an entrepreneurial company, hired a Japanese manufacturing expert to redesign its factory, adopting just-in-time production techniques. Hardworking immigrants were hired and given substantial say over their jobs. As a result, scrap from the manufacturing process fell nearly 60 percent, inventory cost dropped, and overall

Operations management is concerned with the operation and control of the organization's *technical core.* At Home Shopping Network (HSN), the technical core includes 1,500 telephone operators, automated voice response units, and computers to create an order processing network that can handle over one million calls per day. Through its telephone and electronic network, HSN provides personal service right in the customer's home. HSN's excellent service has enabled it to capture 50 percent of sales in the electronic retailing industry.

productivity jumped more than 30 percent. The average price of FMI's stoves was cut 25 percent.[3]

- Corning Inc. revamped its manufacturing process, relying heavily on restructuring to gain flexibility on work hours and job duties. Its quality was so high that it won a supply contract with Honda Motor Company beating out a leading Japanese competitor.[4]

Manufacturing operations such as these are important because they represent the company's basic purpose — indeed, its reason for existence. Without the ability to produce products and services that are competitive in the global marketplace, companies cannot expect to succeed.[5]

This chapter describes techniques for the planning and control of manufacturing and service operations. The three preceding chapters described overall control concepts, including management information systems. In this chapter, we will consider the management and control of production operations. First we define operations management. Then we look at how some companies bring operations into strategic decision making. Finally, we consider specific operational design issues such as plant layout, location planning, inventory management, manufacturing productivity, and structure of the operations management function.

Organizations as Production Systems

In Chapter 1, the organization was described as a system used for transforming inputs into outputs. At the center of this transformation process is the **technical core,** which is the heart of the organization's production of its product or service.[6] In an automobile company, the technical core includes the plants that manufacture automobiles. In a university, the technical core includes the academic activities of teaching and research. Inputs into the technical core include human resources, land, equipment, buildings, and technology. Outputs from the technical core include the goods and services that are provided for customers and clients. Operations strategy and control feedback shape the quality of outputs and the efficiency of operations within the technical core.

technical core The heart of the organization's production of its product or service.

The topic of operations management pertains to the day-to-day management of the technical core, as illustrated in Exhibit 20.1. **Operations management** is formally defined as the application of special tools and techniques to the physical production of goods and services. In essence, operating managers are concerned with all production activities within the organization.

operations management The field of management that specializes in the physical production of goods or services and uses quantitative techniques for solving manufacturing problems.

Manufacturing and Service Operations

Although terms such as *production* and *operations* seem to imply manufacturing organizations, operations management applies to all organizations. The service sector has increased three times as fast as the manufacturing sector in the North American economy. Today more than one-half of all businesses are service organizations. Operations management tools and techniques apply to services as well as manufacturing.

manufacturing organization An organization that produces physical goods.

Manufacturing organizations are those that produce physical goods. Ford Motor Company, which produces automobiles, and Levi Strauss, which

EXHIBIT 20.1
The Organization as an Operations Management System

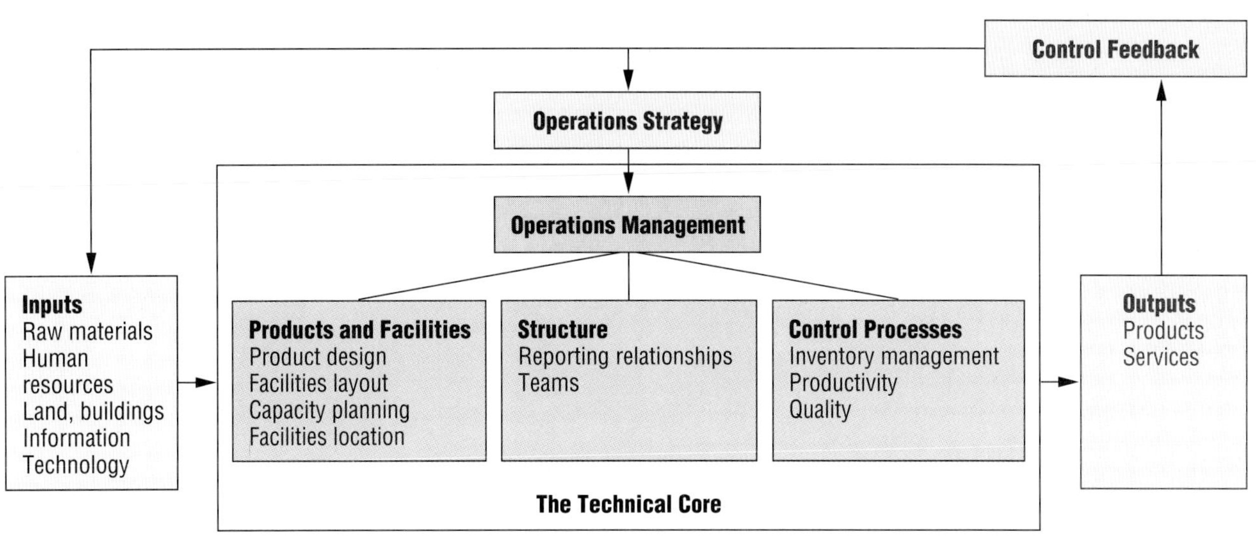

makes clothing, are both manufacturing companies. In contrast, **service organizations** produce nonphysical outputs, such as medical, educational, or transportation services provided for customers. Airlines, doctors, lawyers, and the local barber all provide services. Services also include the sale of merchandise. Although merchandise is a physical good, the service company does not manufacture it but merely sells it as a service to the customer. Retail stores such as Sears and McDonald's are service organizations.

service organization
An organization that produces nonphysical goods that require customer involvement and cannot be stored in inventory.

Services differ from manufactured products in two ways. First, the service customer is involved in the actual production process.[7] The patient actually visits the doctor to receive the service, and it's difficult to imagine a barber or a beautician providing services without direct customer contact. The same is true for hospitals, restaurants, and banks. Second, manufactured goods can be placed in inventory whereas service outputs, being intangible, cannot be stored. Manufactured products such as clothes, food, cars, and VCRs can all be put in warehouses and sold at a later date. However, a beautician cannot wash, cut, and set hair in advance and leave it on the shelf for the customer's arrival, nor can a doctor place examinations in inventory. The service must be created and provided for the customer exactly when he or she wants it.

Despite the differences between manufacturing and service firms, they face similar operational problems. First, each kind of organization needs to be concerned with scheduling. A medical clinic must schedule appointments so that doctors' and patients' times will be used efficiently. Second, both manufacturing and service organizations must obtain materials and supplies. Third, both types of organizations should be concerned with quality and productivity. Because many operational problems are similar, operations management tools and techniques can and should be applied to service organizations as readily as they are to manufacturing.

EXHIBIT 20.2
Four Stages of Operations Strategy

Stage 1
No Involvement
Operations management provides no positive contribution to strategy formulation. Concerned with costs and labor efficiency.

Stage 2
Industry Current
Operations management sets objectives according to industry practice. Concerned with capital investment, quality control, inventory management, capacity.

Stage 3
Organizationally Supportive
Operations management closely follows and supports organization's competitive strategy. Concerned with advanced process technologies, new plants, what to make the U.S. buy.

Stage 4
Initiates Competitive Advantage
Operations management develops advanced capabilities and provides significant input to strategic process. Concerned with new products, new services, new technologies.

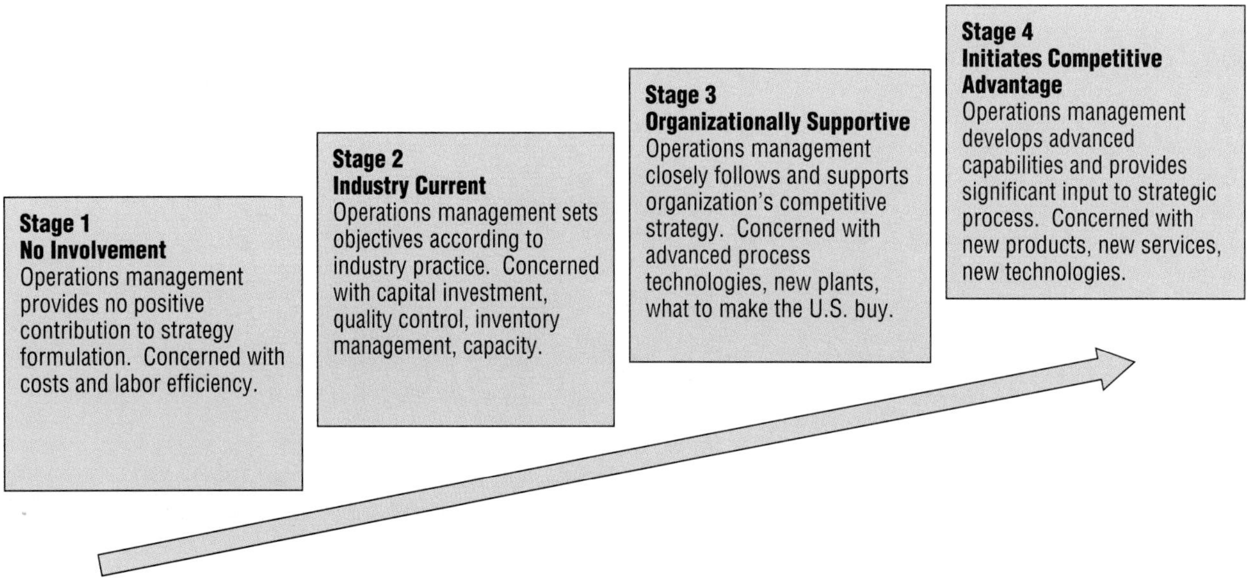

Source: Based on R. H. Hayes and S. C. Wheelwright, *Restoring Our Competitive Edge: Competing Through Manufacturing* (New York: Wiley, 1984).

OPERATIONS STRATEGY

Many operations managers are involved in day-to-day problem solving and lose sight of the fact that the best way to control operations is through strategic planning. The more operations managers become enmeshed in operational details, the less likely they are to see the big picture with respect to inventory buildups, parts shortages, and seasonal fluctuations.[8] Indeed, one reason suggested for the Japanese' success is their direct involvement of operations in strategic management. To manage operations effectively, managers must understand operations strategy.

operations strategy The recognition of the importance of operations to the firm's success and the involvement of operations managers in the organization's strategic planning.

Operations strategy is the recognition of the important role of operations in organizational success and the involvement of operations managers in the organization's strategic planning.[9] Exhibit 20.2 illustrates four stages in the evolution of operations strategy.

Many companies are at stage 1, where business strategy is set without considering the capability of operations. The operations department is concerned only with labor costs and operational efficiency. For example, a major electronics instrument producer experienced a serious mismatch between strategy and the ability of operations to manufacture products. Because of fast-paced technological changes, the company was changing its products and developing new ones. However, the manufacturer had installed a materials-handling system in the operations department that was efficient, but could not handle diversity and change of this magnitude. Operations managers were blamed for the company's failure to achieve strategic objectives even though the operations department's capacity had never been considered during strategy formulation.

At stage 2, the operations department sets objectives according to industry practice.[10] The organization tries to be current with respect to operations management techniques and views capital investment in plant and equipment, quality control, or inventory management as ways to be competitive.

At stage 3, operations managers are more strategically active. Operations strategy is in concert with company strategy, and the operations department will seek new operational techniques and technologies to enhance strategy.

At the highest level of operations strategy, stage 4, operations managers may pursue new technologies on their own in order to do the best possible job of delivering the product or service. At stage 4, operations can be a genuine competitive weapon.[11] Operations departments develop new strategic concepts themselves. With the use of new technologies, operations management becomes a major force in overall company strategic planning. Operations can originate new products and processes that will add to or change company strategy.

Why will a company that operates at stage 3 or 4 be more competitive than those that rely on marketing and financial strategies? The reason is that customer orders are won through better price, quality, performance, delivery, or responsiveness to customer demand. These factors are affected by operations, which help the company win orders in the marketplace.[12]

Clark Equipment Company has a *stage 4 operations strategy*. These robots in the Melroe division lead the industry, with one robot for every 45 employees. Grouped into cells, a welding robot and other machines require only three employees to produce axles for the popular Bobcat loaders, saving 50 percent of *manufacturing costs* compared to earlier manufacturing methods. Clark's worldwide redesign of manufacturing simultaneously increased sales and reduced costs, improving profits by $62.7 million.

One example of operations strategy is the shift at General Electric's headquarters from profit growth through massive acquisitions to squeezing more profits from existing businesses. The operations strategy is to increase manufacturing productivity, which is aligned with overall corporate strategy. General Electric created the post of productivity czar to help implement the strategy change. For example, in the electrical distribution business, new products are developed with the operational goals of reducing number of parts, assembly time, and total cost of materials, thereby producing new circuit breakers that are cheaper and more profitable. Production was consolidated from six plants into one, and the number of parts needed to produce various circuit breaker models plunged from 280,000 to fewer than 100. Structure was also changed, with shop floor teams given responsibility for scheduling inventory and production rates. This strategic approach to operations management has provided the big productivity gains General Electric desired.[13]

DESIGNING OPERATIONS MANAGEMENT SYSTEMS

Every organization must design its production system. This starts with the design of the product or service to be produced. A restaurant designs the food items on the menu. An automobile manufacturer designs the cars it produces. Once products and services have been designed, the organization turns to other design considerations, including facilities layout, production technology, facilities location, and capacity planning.

Golden Valley used *product design* to develop the first microwave french fry that is golden brown, crisp, and tasty. Starting from scratch, Golden Valley researchers started with the basic potato and studied various ways french-fried potato products are grown, processed, and packaged. The simplicity of design of every Golden Valley product enables the company to be the low-cost producer in the industry, while also providing first-quality products.

PRODUCT AND SERVICE DESIGN

The big discovery in the business world is called design for manufacturability and assembly (DFMA).[14] Engineering designers have long fashioned products with disdain for how they would be produced. Elegant designs nearly always had too many parts. One study showed that simply eliminating screws and other fasteners from products saves up to 75 percent of assembly costs. Thus the watchword is *simplicity*, making the product easy and inexpensive to manufacture.[15]

Using DFMA is ridiculously inexpensive. IBM cut assembly time for a printer from 30 minutes to only 3 minutes, achieving efficiency better than the Japanese. DFMA often requires restructuring operations, creating teams of designers, manufacturers, and assemblers to work together. For example, Hewlett-Packard got designers to work with manufacturing to develop a new low-cost terminal. It uses 40 percent fewer parts and can be assembled in hours versus three days previously. The new model saves 55 percent on materials and 75 percent on labor. Breakthroughs in design simplicity are making U.S. manufacturers competitive again.[16]

The notions of simplicity and DFMA translate into four concerns for product design: producibility, cost, quality, and reliability. *Producibility* is the degree to which a product or service can actually be produced for the customer within the firm's existing operational capacity.

The issue of *cost* simply means the sum of the materials, labor, design, transportation, and overhead expense associated with a product or service. Striving for simplicity and few parts keeps product and service designs within reasonable costs.

The third issue is *quality*, which is the excellence of the product or service. Quality represents the serviceability and value that customers gain by purchasing the product.

Reliability, the fourth issue, is the degree to which the customer can count on the product or service to fulfill its intended function. The product should function as designed for a reasonable length of time. Highly complex products often have lower reliability because more things can go wrong.

IBM achieves these design attributes on its typewriters by putting as many of the same parts as possible in different products. Sharing parts allows IBM to maximize quality, reliability, and producibility by focusing on keeping parts count to a minimum. Its current typewriters have only one-fifth as many parts as the old Selectrics did. Screws and bolts are not allowed.[17]

The design of services also should reflect producibility, cost, quality, and reliability. However, services have one additional design requirement: timing. *Timing* is the degree to which the provision of a service meets the customer's delivery requirements. Recall that a service cannot be stored in inventory and must be provided when the customer is present. If you take your friend or spouse to a restaurant for dinner, you expect the meal to be served in a timely manner. The powerful push for self-service reflects the need to provide service when the customer wants and needs it. Banking by machine, pumping your own gas, and trying on your own shoes are all ways that organizations provide timely service, which is important in today's time-pressure world.[18]

For example, when Pizza Hut announced a special lunch menu that could be served in five minutes or less, the timing required that operations — the kitchen — develop a small list of special items that could consistently be made in five minutes or less. Indeed, pizzas had to be redesigned to accommodate the five-minute requirement. Each step in the delivery of pizza items to customers had to be streamlined to ensure that the timing promise was kept.

FACILITIES LAYOUT

Once a product or service has been designed, the organization must plan for the actual production. The four most common types of layout are process, product, cellular, and fixed-position.[19] Exhibit 20.3 illustrates these four layouts.

PROCESS LAYOUT. As illustrated in panel (a) of Exhibit 20.3, a **process layout** is one in which all machines that perform a similar function or task are grouped together. In a machine shop, the lathes perform a similar function and are located together in one section. The grinders are in another section of the shop. Equipment that performs a similar "process" is grouped together. Service organizations also use process layouts. In a bank, the loan officers are in one area, the tellers in another, and managers in a third.

process layout A facilities layout in which machines that perform the same function are grouped together in one location.

The advantage of the process layout is that it has the potential for economies of scale and reduced costs. For example, having all painting done in one spray-painting area means that fewer machines and people are required to paint all products for the organization. In a bank, having all tellers located together in one carefully controlled area provides increased security. Placing all operating rooms together in a hospital makes it possible to control the environment for all rooms simultaneously.

The drawback to the process layout, as illustrated in Exhibit 20.3(a), is that the actual path a product or service takes can be long and complicated. A product may need several different processes performed on it and thus must travel through many different areas before production is complete.

PRODUCT LAYOUT. Panel (b) of Exhibit 20.3 illustrates a **product layout** — one in which machines and tasks are arranged according to the progressive steps in producing a single product. The automobile assembly line is a classic example, because it produces a single product starting from the raw materials to the finished output. The product layout at Ford is so carefully tailored to each product line that Ford can make Mustangs only on the Mustang assembly line and cannot use it to make Thunderbirds. Many fast-food restaurants also use the product layout, with activities arranged in sequence to produce hamburgers or chicken depending on the products available.

product layout A facilities layout in which machines and tasks are arranged according to the sequence of steps in the production of a single product.

The product layout is efficient when the organization produces huge volumes of identical products. Note in Exhibit 20.3(b) that two lines have paint areas. This duplication of functions can be economical only if the volume is high enough to keep each paint area busy working on specialized products.

CELLULAR LAYOUT. Illustrated in panel (c) of Exhibit 20.3 is an innovative layout, called **cellular layout,** based on group-technology principles in which machines dedicated to sequences of operations are grouped into cells. Grouping technology into cells provides some of the efficiencies of both process and

cellular layout A facilities layout in which machines dedicated to sequences of production are grouped into cells in accordance with group-technology principles.

EXHIBIT 20.3
Basic Production Layouts

Source: Based on J. T. Black, "Cellular Manufacturing Systems Reduce Setup Time, Make Small Lot Production Economical," *Industrial Engineering* (November 1983), 36–48, and Richard J. Schonberger, "Plant Layout Becomes Product-Oriented With Cellular, Just-in-Time Production Concepts," *Industrial Engineering* (November 1983), 66–77.

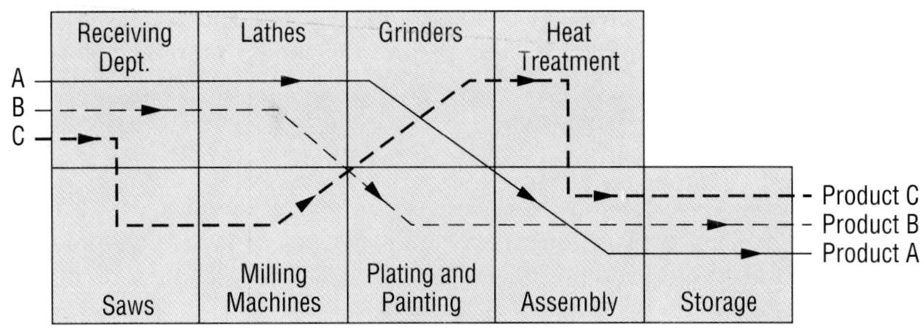

(a) Process Layout

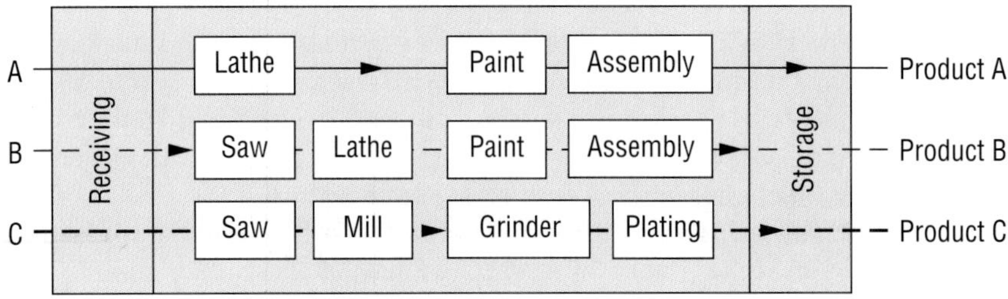

(b) Product Layout

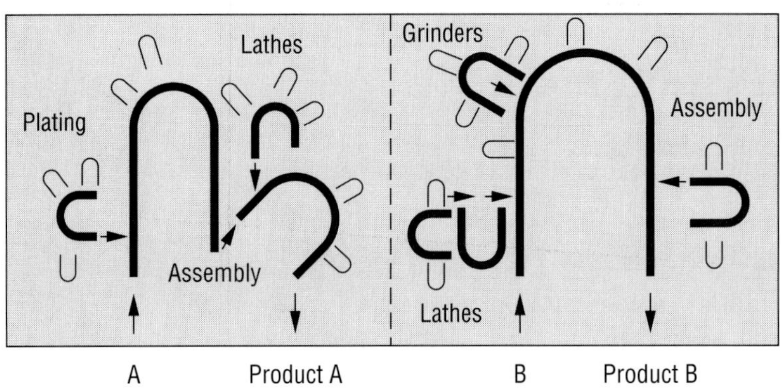

(c) Cellular Layout

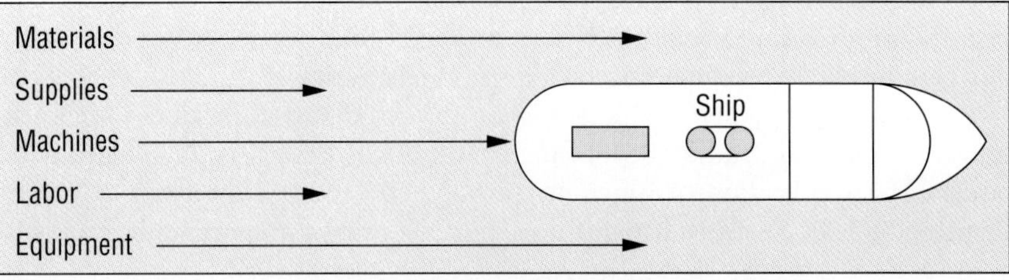

(d) Fixed-Position Layout

product layouts. Even more important, the U-shaped cells in Exhibit 20.3(c) provide efficiencies in material and tool handling and inventory movement. One great advantage is for the workers, who work in clusters that facilitate teamwork and joint problem solving. Staffing flexibility is enhanced because one person can operate all the machines in the cell and walking distance is small.

FIXED-POSITION LAYOUT. As shown in panel (d) of Exhibit 20.3, the **fixed-position layout** is one in which the product remains in one location, and tasks and equipment are brought to it. The fixed-position layout is used to create a product or service that is either very large or one of a kind, such as aircraft, ships, and buildings. The product cannot be moved from function to function or along an assembly line; rather, the people, materials, and machines all come to the fixed-position site for assembly and processing. This layout is not good for high volume but it is necessary for large, bulky products and custom orders.

fixed-position layout A facilities layout in which the product remains in one location and the required tasks and equipment are brought to it.

PRODUCTION TECHNOLOGY

One goal of many operations management departments is to move toward more sophisticated technologies for producing products and services. New technology is sometimes called the "factory of the future." Extremely sophisticated systems that can work almost unaided by employees are being designed. For example, General Motors invested $52 million in the Vanguard plant in Saginaw, Michigan, to produce front-wheel drive axles. Only 42 hourly workers are needed because the work is done by robots. The product was designed to be made with supersophisticated technology. GM wants to learn whether robot technology is the most efficient way to proceed with manufacturing operations.[20]

Two other types of production technologies that are becoming widely used in operations management are flexible manufacturing systems and CAD/CAM.

FLEXIBLE MANUFACTURING SYSTEMS. A small or medium-size automated production line is called a **flexible manufacturing system.**[21] The machinery uses computers to coordinate and integrate the automated machines. Functions such as loading, unloading, storing parts, changing tools, and machining are done automatically. Moreover, the computer can instruct the machines to change parts, machining, and tools when a new product must be produced. This is a breakthrough compared with the product layout, in which a single line is restricted to a single product. With a flexible manufacturing system, a single line can be readily readapted to small batches of different products based on computer instructions. Cummins Engine, Chrysler, Caterpillar, and Rockwell have acquired FMSs.

flexible manufacturing system (FMS) A small or medium-size automated production line that can be adapted to produce more than one product line.

CAD/CAM. CAD (computer-aided design) and CAM (computer-aided manufacturing) represent new uses of computers in operations management.

CAD enables engineers to develop new-product designs in about half the time required with traditional methods. Computers provide a visual display for the engineer and illustrate the implications of any design change. For example,

CAD A production technology in which computers perform new-product design.

Autodie is the world's leading independent maker of large-scale dies and molds for the automobile industry. Autodie's engineers, using state-of-the-art *CAD/CAM technology* shown here, design a tool with three-dimensional imaging. Transferred to the shop floor by computer, machine tools fabricate molds and dies with digital precision. This technology enables Autodie to respond with new products more quickly and at less cost than ever before.

CAD systems have helped a sportswear manufacturer adjust to rapidly changing product lines. Products change five times a year, and each new season's line requires new production standards, new bills of material for use on the shop floor, and new cutting patterns. Engineers can use the CAD system to design the pattern layouts and then determine the manufacturing changes needed to produce new sizes and styles, expected labor standards, and bills of material.[22]

CAM A production technology in which computers help guide and control the manufacturing system.

CAM is similar to the use of computers in flexible manufacturing systems. The computer is harnessed to help guide and control the manufacturing system. For example, for the above sportswear manufacturer, the entire sequence of manufacturing operations — pattern scaling, layout, and printing — has now been mechanized through the use of computers. Computer-controlled cutting tables have been installed. Once the computer has mathematically defined the geometry, it guides the cutting blade, eliminating the need for paper patterns. Fabric requisitions, production orders for cutting and sewing operations, and sewing line work can also be directed by computer programs.

Facility Location

At some point, almost every organization must make a decision concerning the location of facilities. A bank may need to open a new branch office, Wendy's needs to find locations for some of the 100 or so new stores opened each year, or a manufacturer needs to build a warehouse. When these decisions are made unwisely, they are expensive and troublesome for the organization. For example, Modulate Corporation moved its head office six times in seven years because it had incorrectly anticipated its building requirements.

The most common approach to selecting a site for a new location is to do a cost-benefit analysis.[23] For example, a bank may identify four possible locations. The costs associated with each location are the land (purchase or lease), transportation from the current facility, and construction, including zoning laws, building codes, land features, and size of the parking lot. Taxes, utilities, rents, and maintenance are other cost factors to be considered in advance. Each possible bank location also will have certain benefits. Benefits to be evaluated are accessibility of customers, location of major competitors, general quality of working conditions, and nearness to restaurants and shops, which would be desirable for both employees and customers.

Once the bank managers have evaluated the worth of each benefit, total benefits can be divided by total costs for each location, and managers can select the location with the highest ratio. Sophisticated techniques that can aid in location decisions were described in Chapter 8. These include linear programming, the payoff matrix, and decision tree analysis, each of which provides a useful framework for making a location decision.

Facility location is a major concern of McDonald's executives. One innovation was to locate restaurants on tollways. The cost-benefit analysis revealed that greater construction costs for tollway locations were more than offset by increased sales. Tollway restaurants such as this one on the Illinois tollway at Des Plaines have sales of from two to ten times greater than those of previous food service operations on the same sites. McDonald's has targeted more nontraditional sites — tollways, hospitals, airports — for the future.

Capacity Planning

Capacity planning is the determination and adjustment of the organization's ability to produce products or services to match demand. For example, if a bank anticipates a customer increase of 20 percent over the next year, capacity planning is the procedure whereby it will ensure that it has sufficient capacity to service that demand.

Organizations can do several things to increase capacity. One is to create additional shifts and hire people to work on them. A second is to ask existing people to work overtime to add to capacity. A third is to subcontract extra work to other firms. A fourth is to expand a plant and add more equipment. Each of these techniques will increase the organization's ability to meet demand without risk of major excess capacity.

For example, Cooper Tire & Rubber Company produces 531,000 tires a day. When expansion is necessary, Cooper refits existing plants instead of building new ones allowing for gradual growth to fit capacity requirements. Gradual growth has increased production 40 percent over five years. Building new plants would only be undertaken with major study and certainty of the demand for its products. Normally, adding people to a second shift or for overtime work increases capacity without long-term risk. Plant expansions are riskier but solve long-term capacity requirements.

The biggest problem for most organizations, however, is excess capacity. When misjudgments occur, transportation companies have oil tankers sitting empty in the harbor, oil companies have refineries sitting idle, semiconductor companies have plants shuttered, developers have office buildings half full, and the service industry may have hotels or amusement parks operating at partial capacity.[24] The challenge is for managers to add capacity as needed without excess.

Inventory Management

A large portion of the operations manager's job consists of inventory management. **Inventory** is the goods the organization keeps on hand for use in the production process. Most organizations have three types of inventory — finished goods, work-in-process, and raw materials.

capacity planning The determination and adjustment of the organization's ability to produce products and services to match customer demand.

inventory The goods that the organization keeps on hand for use in the production process.

Tasty Baking's donut manufacturing plant is a direct result of the company's strategic plan to *increase capacity* for making and selling donuts. Because the new donut line was successful, executives planned an addition to the existing bakery building. The additional capacity will produce a full line of mini-, powered, honey wheat, and chocolate-covered donuts as well as the regular line of full-size premium donuts.

finished-goods inventory Inventory consisting of items that have passed through the complete production process but have yet to be sold.

work-in-process inventory Inventory composed of the materials that are still moving through the stages of the production process.

raw materials inventory Inventory consisting of the basic inputs to the organization's production process.

Finished-goods inventory includes items that have passed through the entire production process but have not been sold. This is highly visible inventory. The new cars sitting in the storage lot of an automobile factory are finished-goods inventory, as are the hamburgers and french fries waiting under the lamps at a McDonald's restaurant. Finished-goods inventory is expensive, because the organization has invested labor and other costs to make the finished product.

Work-in-process inventory includes the materials moving through the stages of the production process that are not yet a completed product. Work-in-process inventory in an automobile plant includes engines, wheel and tire assemblies, and dashboards waiting to be installed. In a fast-food restaurant, the french fries in the fryer and hamburgers on the grill are work-in-process inventory.

Raw materials inventory includes the basic inputs to the organization's production process. This inventory is cheapest because the organization has not yet invested labor in it. Steel, wire, glass, and paint are raw materials inventory for an auto plant. Meat patties, buns, and raw potatoes are the raw materials inventory in a fast-food restaurant.

THE IMPORTANCE OF INVENTORY

Why is inventory management so important to organizations? Because inventory costs money. Many years ago a firm's wealth was measured by its inventory. Today inventory is recognized as an unproductive asset. Dollars not tied up in inventory can be used in other productive ventures. For example, Corky Johnson is responsible for keeping inventories down for Sun Company's refining and marketing unit. Poor planning on his part produces excess inventory that adds up to 10 cents a gallon to the wholesale price of gasoline. Inventory management determines whether Sun has a competitive price in the marketplace.[25]

The Japanese analogy of rocks and water describes the current management attitude toward the importance of inventory.[26] As illustrated in Exhibit 20.4, the water in the stream is the inventory in the organization. The higher the water, the less managers have to worry about the rocks, which represent problems. In operations management, these problems apply to scheduling, plant layout, product design, and quality. When the water level goes down, managers see the rocks and must deal with them. When inventories are reduced, the problems of a poorly designed and managed production process also are revealed. The problems then must be solved. When inventory can be kept at an absolute minimum, operations management is considered excellent.

Ed Heard, a consultant who specializes in inventory management, has the following message:

> The best criterion for gauging the effectiveness of a manufacturing operation is inventory. If you have a lot of it sitting on the floor, you are probably not doing as good a job as you could be. Inventory is simply the best indicator of manufacturing performance that we have. There is no problem, no screw-up, that doesn't show up in the inventory number. Both raw materials and work-in-process are supposed to be where they are needed in the right quantity at the right time. Too much too soon and money invested in inventory is wasted. Too little too late and the production process is held up waiting for more inventory.[27]

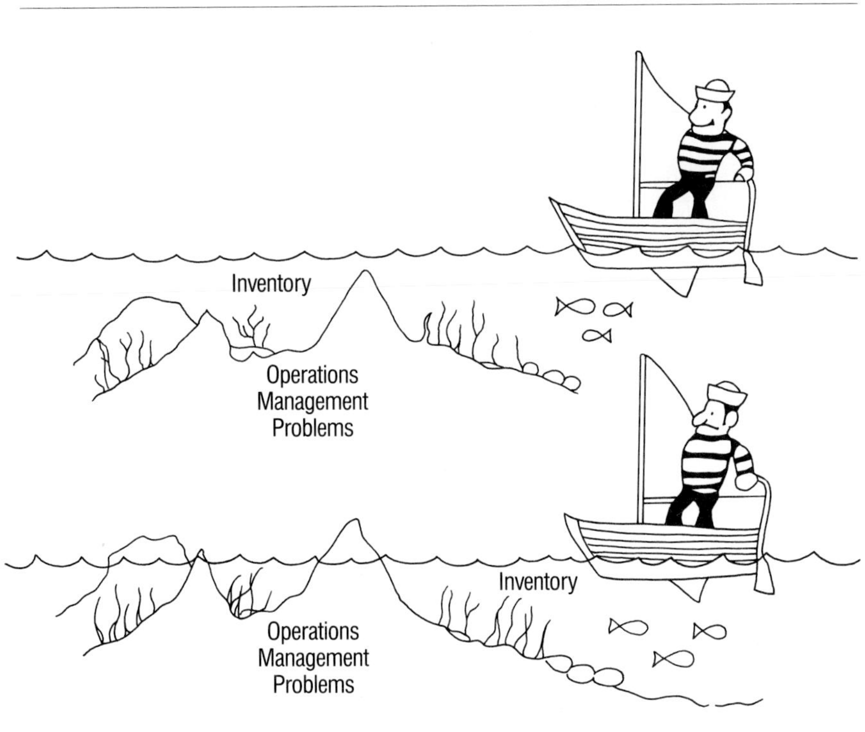

EXHIBIT 20.4
Large Inventories Hide Operations Management Problems

Source: R. J. Schonberger, *Japanese Manufacturing Techniques: Nine Hidden Lessons in Simplicity* (New York: The Free Press, 1982).

Let's now consider specific techniques for inventory management. Four important ones are economic order quantity, materials requirement planning, manufacturing resource planning, and just-in-time inventory systems.

ECONOMIC ORDER QUANTITY

Two basic decisions that can help minimize inventory are how much raw material to order and when to order from outside suppliers.[28] Ordering the minimum amounts at the right time keeps the raw materials, work-in-process, and finished-goods inventories at low levels. One popular technique is **economic order quantity (EOQ),** which is designed to minimize the total of ordering costs and holding costs for inventory items. *Ordering costs* are the costs associated with actually placing the order, such as postage, receiving, and inspection. *Holding costs* are costs associated with keeping the item on hand, such as storage space charges, finance charges, and materials-handling expenses.

economic order quantity (EOQ) An inventory management technique designed to minimize the total of ordering and holding costs for inventory items.

The EOQ calculation indicates the order quantity size that will minimize holding and ordering costs based on the organization's use of inventory. The EOQ formula includes ordering costs (C), holding costs (H), and annual demand (D). For example, consider a hospital's need to order surgical dressings. Based on hospital records, the ordering costs for surgical dressings are $15, the annual holding cost is $6, and the annual demand for dressings is 605. The formula for the economic order quantity is:

EXHIBIT 20.5
Inventory Control of Surgical Dressings by EOQ

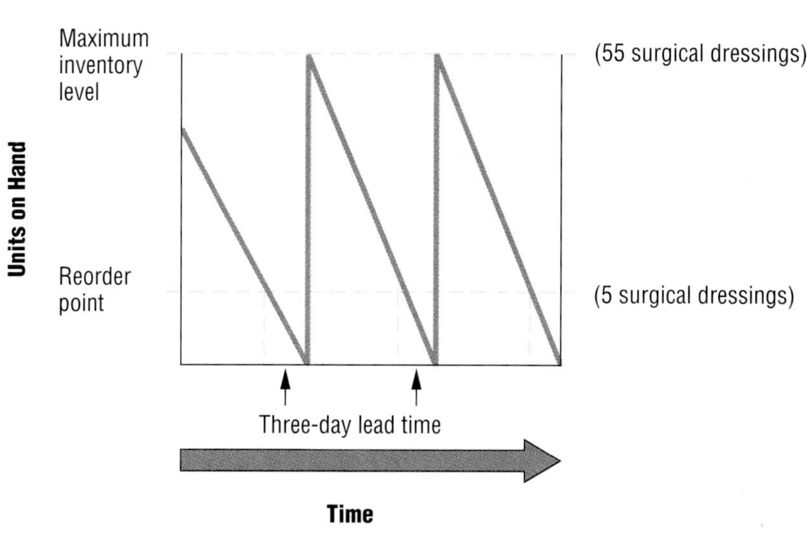

$$EOQ = \sqrt{\frac{2DC}{H}} = \sqrt{\frac{2(605)(15)}{6}} = 55.$$

The EOQ formula tells us that the best quantity to order is 55.

reorder point (ROP) The most economical level at which an inventory item should be reordered.

The next question is when to make the order. For this decision a different formula, called **reorder point (ROP),** is used. ROP is calculated by the following formula, which assumes that it takes three days to receive the order after the hospital has placed it:

$$ROP = \frac{D}{Time}(\text{Lead time}) = \frac{605}{365}(3) = 4.97, \text{ or } 5.$$

The reorder point tells us that because it takes three days to receive the order, at least five dressings should be on hand when the order is placed. As nurses use surgical dressings, operations managers will know that when the level reaches the point of 5, the new order should be placed for a quantity of 55.

This relationship is illustrated in Exhibit 20.5. Whenever the reorder point of 5 dressings is reached, the new order is initiated, and the 55 arrive just as the inventory is depleted. In a typical hospital, however, some variability in lead time and use of surgical dressings will occur. Thus, a few extra items of inventory, called *safety stock,* are used to ensure that the hospital does not run out of surgical dressings.

MATERIALS REQUIREMENT PLANNING

The EOQ formula works well when inventory items are not dependent on one another. For example, in a restaurant the demand for hamburgers is independent of the demand for milkshakes; thus, an economic order quantity is calculated for each item. A more complicated inventory problem occurs with **dependent demand inventory,** meaning that item demand is related to the demand for other inventory items. For example, if Ford Motor Company decides to make 100,000 cars, it will also need 400,000 tires, 400,000 rims, and 400,000 hubcaps. The demand for tires is dependent on the demand for cars.

dependent demand inventory Inventory in which item demand is related to the demand for other inventory items.

The most common inventory control system used for handling dependent demand inventory is **materials requirement planning (MRP).** MRP is a dependent demand inventory planning and control system that schedules the exact amount of all materials required to support the desired end product. MRP is computer based and requires sophisticated calculations to coordinate information on inventory location, bill of materials, purchasing, production planning, invoicing, and order entry. Unlike with EOQ, inventory levels are not based on past consumption; rather, they are based on precise estimates of future orders. With MRP, inventory costs can be cut dramatically.[29]

materials requirement planning (MRP) A dependent demand inventory planning and control system that schedules the precise amount of all materials required to support the production of desired end products.

For example, consider the hospital described earlier using an MRP approach. The hospital would set up the surgical schedule for the coming week—the equivalent of a master production schedule. For each scheduled surgery, a bill of materials would be issued listing the dressings and other needed items. The inventory status file would show how many surgical dressings the hospital has on hand. Now assume that the master production schedule shows that 20 surgeries will be performed next week and the inventory status file shows 5 surgical dressings on hand. MRP would then calculate that the hospital needs 20 surgical dressings, less the 5 on hand; thus, 15 would be ordered. They arrive, are used in the 20 operations, and the entire inventory is used up. There are no extra inventory carrying costs and no risk of needing to scrap excess or obsolete inventory. In the meantime, the schedule of surgeries for the following week has been fed into the MRP system, the need for surgical dressings identified, and the inventory ordered. Inventory flows into the hospital as it is needed, thereby minimizing inventory storage and handling costs.

Manufacturing Resource Planning

Manufacturing resource planning, called **MRP II,** represents a major development beyond MRP. MRP is a technique for managing inventory, while MRP II reaches into every company operation to control all resources. MRP II creates a model of the overall business that allows senior managers to control production scheduling, cash flow, human resource planning, capacity planning, inventory, distribution, and materials purchasing. MRP II also supports marketing and engineering and provides financial information. It unites business functions by translating all operations into financial data and provides the entire company with access to the same set of numbers. In the ideal application, it is a computer-based model of the company's operations.

manufacturing resource planning (MRP II) An extension of MRP to include the control of resources pertaining to all operations of the organization.

Although MRP II evolved from MRP, it plays more of a strategic planning role for senior managers. The hardware and software for MRP II are sophisticated and complex and typically are used only in larger companies. Under MRP II, the entire company's efforts are analyzed and the computer produces corporate plans and solves corporate problems. MRP II starts with the company's business plan, which is translated into sales objectives by product line. Sales objectives, in turn, are translated into forecasts of materials requirements, inventory needs, and production schedules.[30]

Boeing uses *MRP II* to coordinate resources for manufacturing the 757. Called the Manufacturing Inventory Planning System at Boeing Aerospace Company, computer technology helps coordinate inventory, manufacturing, engineering, materials control, and accounting. Factory employees work with accurate data that saves time, reduces part shortages on the shop floor, and cuts back on inventory.

JUST-IN-TIME INVENTORY

just-in-time (JIT) inventory systems An inventory control system that schedules materials to arrive precisely when they are needed on a production line.

Just-in-time (JIT) inventory systems are designed to reduce the level of an organization's inventory to zero. Sometimes these systems are referred to as *stockless systems, zero inventory systems,* or *Kanban systems.* Each system centers on the concept that suppliers deliver materials only at the exact moment needed, thereby reducing raw material inventories to zero. Moreover, work-in-process inventories are kept to a minimum because goods are produced only as needed to service the next stage of production. Finished-goods inventories are minimized by matching them exactly to sales demand.

Just-in-time inventory requires that the production system be simple and well coordinated, as illustrated in Exhibit 20.6.[31] Each part of the production process produces and moves goods forward only when the next stage requires them. JIT is called a *demand-pull* system because each work station produces its product only when the next work station says it is ready to receive more input. This is in contrast to the traditional *batch-push system,* in which parts are made in large, supposedly efficient batches and pushed to the next operation on a fixed schedule, where they sit until used. In a push system, each work station produces at a constant rate regardless of the actual requirement of the next work station. The demand-pull system can result in reduced inventories, improved quality, and better responsiveness, but it requires excellent coordination among all parts of the production sequence.

Recall the Japanese analogy of the rocks and the water. To reduce inventory levels to zero means that all management and coordination problems will surface and must be resolved. Scheduling must be scrupulously precise. For example, Johnson Controls makes automobile seats two hours before they are to be installed in an automobile on Chrysler's assembly line. After production,

EXHIBIT 20.6
Just-in-Time Inventory System

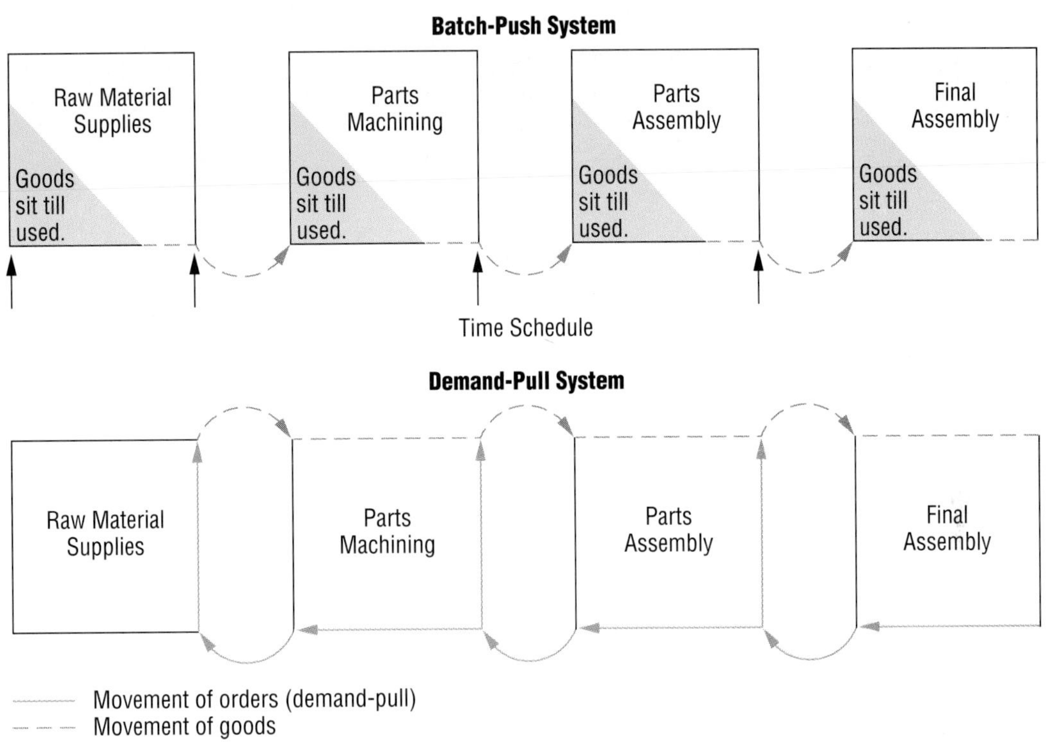

the seats are driven to the Chrysler plant 75 miles away and taken directly to the moving assembly line for installation.[32]

Just-in-time inventory systems also require excellent employee motivation and cooperation. Workers are expected to perform at their best because they are entrusted with the responsibility and authority to make the zero inventory system work. Employees must help one another when they fall behind and must be capable of doing different jobs. Workers experience the satisfaction of being in charge of the system and making useful improvements in the company's operations.[33]

Just-in-time systems have tremendous advantages. The reduced inventory level frees productive capital for other company uses. For example, Omark Industries, a $300 million corporation in Oregon, saved an estimated $7 million in inventory carrying costs. It calls its version the Zero Inventory Production System (ZIPS). General Motors has used just-in-time since 1980, slashing inventory-related costs from $8 billion to $2 billion dollars. In a dramatic case, Polycom Huntsman, Inc., built its newest plant just 1,500 feet from General Motors' Harrison Radiator Division in Lockport, New York, and then connected the two factories by a pneumatic conveying system. Now when the GM plant starts to run low on plastic compounds, a computer-controlled system

In an AT&T factory several football fields long, the speediest way to get parts to the assembly line is on wheels. AT&T has increased productivity in its factories with a *just-in-time inventory system* that delivers parts to the production line as they are needed. Working closely with suppliers, stocks are replenished just before they run out, and parts are pulled from stockrooms only when needed. The Denver factory has saved $150 million with better methods for carrying, storing, and managing inventory.

automatically begins shipping material from Polycom. "It's probably the best just-in-time system you've ever seen," said a GM purchasing manager.[34]

Another illustration of cost savings from inventory flexibility occurred in a Kawasaki motorcycle plant.

KAWASAKI • The Kawasaki plant in Lincoln, Nebraska, installed a JIT system and found that scheduling had to be absolutely precise. Workers on the line needed to know that every KZ100 motorcycle would be followed by two KZ750 motorcycles and thus have the necessary parts available for assembly. With such precise scheduling, there was little need to have inventory sitting on the floor or in bins.

After the system was successfully implemented, Kawasaki managers found that the most important benefit was the increased flexiblity and responsiveness to the marketplace. For example, at one point the Kawasaki plant had planned for and was making both blue and red motorcycles. However, the blue motorcycles were not selling well. The marketing people investigated and found out that black was the hot new color and that Kawasaki should be making black rather than blue motorcycles. In a plant with lots of work-in-process and finished-goods inventory, it could have taken weeks or even months to work off the inventory of blue tanks and other parts. During those weeks, Kawasaki would be shipping blue motorcycles to stores that did not want and could not sell them. However, with the JIT system in place, the change in color took Kawasaki less than one day. By nightfall they were shipping new, black motorcycles to customers. The change in color caused sharply increased sales.[35]

MANAGING PRODUCTIVITY

People have argued that the United States is in the midst of a productivity crisis because U.S. growth and productivity have declined while sharp productivity increases have been reported in Japan, West Germany, Canada, and other countries.[36] Productivity is significant because it influences the well-being of the entire society as well as of individual companies. The only way to increase the output of goods and services to society is to increase organizational productivity.

MEASURING PRODUCTIVITY

What is productivity, and how is it measured? In simple terms, **productivity** is the organization's output of goods and services divided by its inputs. This means that productivity can be improved by either increasing the amount of output using the same level of inputs or reducing the number of inputs required to produce the output. For example, May Department Stores gauges productivity as sales per square foot. Sales is the measure of output, and floor space is a summary of inputs. During a recent year, sales per square foot were $123, up 35 percent in three years, which means productivity is improving. May executives are designing new stores to have twice the productivity of old stores.

productivity The organization's output of products and services divided by its inputs.

Typically, the accurate measure of productivity is more complex than dividing sales by square feet, which is a single measure of outputs and inputs. Two approaches for measuring productivity are total factor productivity and partial productivity.[37] **Total factor productivity** is the ratio of total outputs to the inputs from labor, capital, materials, and energy:

total factor productivity The ratio of total outputs to the inputs from labor, capital, materials, and energy.

$$\text{Total factor productivity} = \frac{\text{Output}}{\text{Labor} + \text{Capital} + \text{Materials} + \text{Energy}}.$$

Total factor productivity represents the best measure of how the organization is doing. Often, however, managers need to know about productivity with respect to certain inputs. **Partial productivity** is the ratio of total outputs to a major category of inputs. For example, many organizations are interested in labor productivity, which would be measured as follows:

partial productivity The ratio of total outputs to the inputs from a single major input category.

$$\text{Productivity} = \frac{\text{Output}}{\text{Labor dollars}}.$$

Calculating this formula for labor, capital, or materials provides information on whether improvements in each element are occurring. However, managers are often criticized for relying too heavily on partial productivity measures, especially direct labor.[38] Measuring direct labor misses the valuable improvements in materials, manufacturing processes, and work quality. Labor productivity is easily measured, but may show an increase as a result of capital improvements. Thus managers will misinterpret the reason for productivity increases.

Frito-Lay, a division of PepsiCo, improves both *productivity* and *quality* through workers, management, and technology. Productivity improvements saved more than $50 million in one year. One measurement of factory productivity is manufacturing cost per pound, which is expected to stay flat despite increased wages. Workers upgrade their work methods with 14,000 employee-suggested improvements each year. Management gains productivity by reducing ingredient costs and administrative costs. Quality is continuously improved, contributing significantly to Frito-Lay's leadership in the snack food industry, with the production of Ruffles and other snack foods that even pets love.

Total Quality Management

Total quality management (TQM) improves quality and productivity by striving to perfect the entire manufacturing process. Total quality management is to manufacturing what *total quality control,* described in Chapter 17, is to the entire firm. Under TQM, employees are encouraged to participate in the improvement of quality. Quality and productivity teams are created. Training budgets are increased. Statistical techniques are used to assist in spotting defects and correcting them. Moreover, TQM stresses coordination with other departments, especially product design, purchasing, sales, and service, so that all groups are working together to enhance manufacturing quality and productivity.

total quality management (TQM) Operations management that strives to perfect the entire manufacturing process through improvements in quality and productivity.

In the United States, operations managers traditionally have resisted spending money to improve quality, believing that productivity would suffer. In the new way of thinking, also discussed in the Manager's Shoptalk, improvements in quality have a positive impact on productivity. One reason is that dollars spent on improved quality dramatically reduce waste. Poor quality causes huge delayed costs, such as the cost to rework defective products, the cost of maintenance, the cost of dissatisfied customers who do not buy additional products, and the time involved in dealing with dissatisfied customers and returned products.[39] One example of a company successfully using total quality management is Heinz.

H. J. Heinz Company

• In 1987, Heinz Chairman Anthony J. F. O'Reilly warned his top executives of a looming crisis. Several of Heinz's big brands were losing marketshare. After a stem-to-stern review of the company, Heinz decided to redirect itself from the fanatical cost cutting of the 1980s to a quality focus in the 1990s.

Quality consultants helped Heinz implement a total quality management (TQM) approach. Instead of simply reducing costs, Heinz focused on quality, assuming improved quality would improve productivity. At the Ore-Ida division, training budgets were tripled and quality teams of hourly and salaried employees brainstormed to solve product problems. They actually slowed production to restore the chunky texture and crispy flavor of Tater-Tots. The quality improvement was immediately reflected in sales, which jumped 18 percent. At Star-Kist tuna, adding more workers actually saved money. Cleaning tuna is so labor intensive that it is all done by hand, and overworked employees were inadvertently throwing away choice meat. Heinz has learned that the cheapest way to do business is to produce quality products from its manufacturing operations.[40]

Improving Productivity

Quality problems plague many firms. One Ford engine plant had so much variation in pistons for the same engine that they were classified into 13 sizes. Quality improvements over five years reduced the sizes to three and then to one. Now any piston fits any engine block, as in Japan.[41]

When an organization decides that improving productivity is important, there are three places to look: technological productivity, worker productivity, and managerial productivity.

MANAGER'S SHOPTALK

PRODUCTIVITY OR CUSTOMER SERVICE?

William H. Davidow and Bro Uttal, coauthors of *Total Customer Service: The Ultimate Weapon,* classify firms into two groups. The first group includes firms who promote quality and customer service regardless of the cost, such as IBM. Big Blue's machines are designed so they are easy for hardware and software designers to work with, and the company has invested in a reputation for service.

The second group includes firms that cut costs in an effort to maximize profits. For example, past chairman Ray McDonald of the now defunct Burroughs Corporation considered customer service "A skirmish between Burroughs and its customers." Cost-cutting efforts saved Burroughs money, but savings from omitting special hardware to diagnose machine failures were offset by lost sales, hundreds of lawsuits, and a damaged reputation.

Davidow and Uttal suggest that firms can increase productivity, quality, and customer service at the same time by looking hard at six components.

1. Develop a strategy for customer service. Determine customer expectations, and develop a plan to provide products and services they desire.
2. Executive leadership is essential to provide an example of service. Leaders must both communicate the importance of the service strategy and make personal visits to customers.
3. Real customer service occurs where customers interface with frontline employees. Push authority and responsibility down to those employees so they can respond to customer demands quickly.
4. Design products and services with customer service in mind. Poor service often can be traced back to an engineer who failed to listen to customer demands or field technicians when designing the product.
5. Restructure to create special teams devoted to a product or service for the sole purpose of looking after customer needs and wants.
6. Measure company performance on customer service. Involve employees in developing goals for customer service and analyze customer service records for feedback.

In an environment of complex manufacturing technology, investing in quality enhances both productivity and customer service. Investing wisely in operations management is the key to company survival.

Source: Based on Christopher Elias, "Putting the Customer First Again," *Insight,* October 16, 1989, 40–41.

Technological productivity means the use of more efficient machines, robots, computers, and other technologies to increase outputs. The flexible manufacturing and CAD/CAM systems described earlier in this chapter are technological improvements that enhance productivity. Robots are another example.[42]

Worker productivity means having workers produce more output in the same time period. Improving worker productivity is a real challenge for American companies, because too often workers have an antagonistic relationship with management. At Corning Glass, workers are formed into temporary "corrective action teams" to solve specific problems. Employees also fill out "method improvement requests," which are promptly reviewed. Zebco got its workers involved by taking them to a trade show to see how good the Japanese fishing reels were. With workers' efforts, Zebco's productivity doubled in four years.[43]

Managerial productivity simply means that managers do a better job of running the business. Leading experts in productivity and quality have often stated that the real reason for productivity problems in the United States is poor management.[44] One of these authorities went so far as to propose specific points for telling management how to improve productivity. These points are listed in Exhibit 20.7.

Management productivity improves when managers emphasize quality over quantity, break down barriers and empower their employees, and do not

EXHIBIT 20.7
Deming's 14 Points for Management Productivity

Source: Reprinted from *Quality, Productivity and Competitive Position* by W. Edwards Deming by permission of MIT and W. Edwards Deming. Published by MIT, Center for Advanced Engineering Study, Cambridge, MA 02139. Copyright 1982 by W. E. Deming.

1. Create constancy of purpose toward improved product and service.
2. Adopt a new philosophy, because the old ones no longer work.
3. Cease dependence on mass inspection and require statistical evidence of design quality.
4. End the practice of awarding business on price alone. Quality must also be recognized.
5. Find problems by monitoring the system continually.
6. Institute modern methods of on-the-job training.
7. Institute modern methods of supervision.
8. Drive out fear so that everyone is working for the company.
9. Break down barriers between parts of the organization.
10. Eliminate numerical goals and slogans asking for higher levels of output without providing methods.
11. Eliminate standards that prescribe numerical quotas.
12. Remove the barriers between the worker and pride in the job.
13. Institute vigorous programs of education and retraining.
14. Create a management structure that will work on the above 13 points every day.

overmanage using numbers. Managers must learn to use reward systems, management by objectives, employee involvement, teamwork, and other management techniques that have been described throughout this book. For example, in a recent look at Honda and Jeep automobile assembly plants in Ohio, a dramatic difference in quality and productivity was found. The Honda plant produced 870 cars a day with 2,423 workers, and the Jeep plant produced 750 cars with 5,400 workers. The greater productivity in the Honda plant was attributed to better management.[45]

ORGANIZING THE OPERATIONS MANAGEMENT FUNCTION

Our final topic concerns the organization of operations management activities to achieve the greatest impact on the firm's productivity and effectiveness. Operations management includes many departmental activities, such as inventory management, purchasing, materials handling, distribution, traffic, receiving, scheduling, and plant layout. In many organizations, these departments are widely disbursed. Inventory management and materials handling may report to a production control manager. Distribution and traffic may be part of the marketing department. Receiving may be part of quality control.

Departmental separation leads to poor communication and coordination, higher than necessary inventories, and lower productivity. Thus, the choice of organization structure should consider two factors: whether to group all materials management activities together into a single department and to whom this department should report.

EXHIBIT 20.8
Two Reporting Levels for Materials Management Department

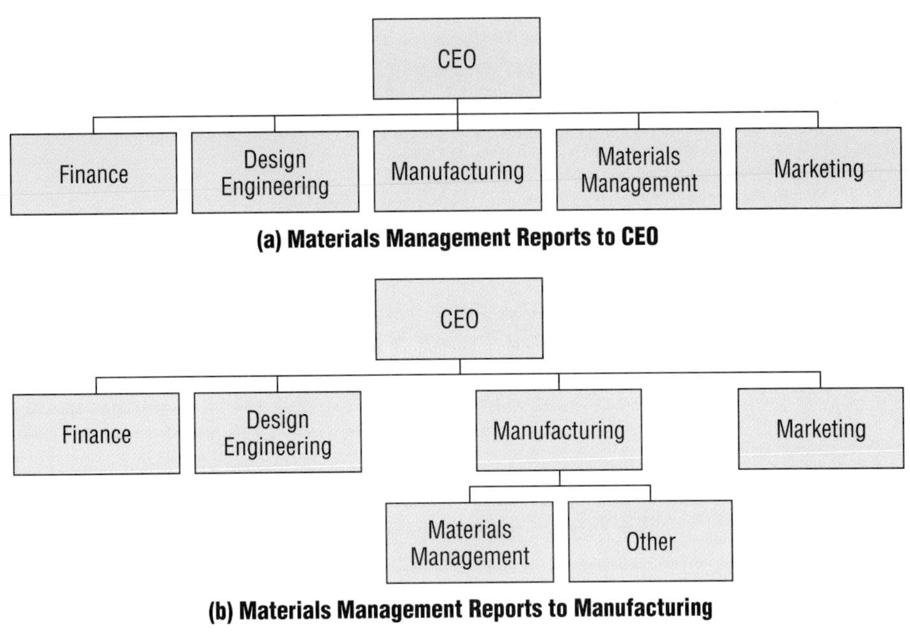

MATERIALS MANAGEMENT APPROACH

The first step is to group the materials management departments together into a single function, which is called the materials management concept. **Materials management** is the total integration under one manager of all organizational departments and activities that contribute to the cost of materials.[46] The materials management concept suggests that it is in the organization's interest to effectively coordinate and control the acquisition and use of materials. Grouping all materials-handling activities together under one senior materials manager heightens the emphasis given to achieving operations management objectives and improves communication among departments.

materials management The complete integration under one manager of all organizational departments and activities that contribute to the costs of materials.

REPORTING RELATIONSHIPS

The second aspect of structure pertains to whom the materials manager should report. One alternative is for the materials manager to report to the CEO just like the head of marketing, finance, engineering, and manufacturing, as illustrated in panel (a) of Exhibit 20.8. Having the materials manager report to such a high level has the advantage of infusing operations into the organization's strategic planning.

The second alternative is for the materials manager to report to the head of manufacturing, as illustrated in panel (b). As a practical matter, this structure typically is easier to achieve. Some of the materials management activities probably already report to manufacturing; thus, the changes necessary for bringing all materials management activities together are not great. Also, because the structural changes are occurring at a lower level, the power and political dynamics will be easier to handle. The drawback to reporting to the manufacturing manager is the reduced visibility and impact of materials management on top management. Many ideas described in this chapter — layout, capacity, new technology, MRP, JIT, and FMS — are less likely to be infused into the organization's overall strategic planning.

TEAMS

Another use of structure, as described in Chapters 9 and 16, is to create cross-functional teams and task forces to achieve integration. Teams can be formed within materials management departments that include members from purchasing, materials handling, scheduling, and plant layout. Teams also can exist between materials management and other departments to coordinate with manufacturing, design engineering, and marketing for the development of new products. Teamwork for product design ensures that new products are producible at low cost and still meet customer needs. Finally, employee involvement teams can be used to encourage the participation of lower-level employees in the improvement of quality and productivity. Quality circles provide an outlet for the creative ideas of all employees.

SUMMARY

This chapter described several points about operations management. Operations management pertains to the tools and techniques used to manage the organization's core production process. These techniques apply to both manufacturing and service organizations. Operations management has a great impact when it influences competitive strategy. Areas of operations management described in the chapter include product and service design, location of facilities, facilities layout, capacity planning, and the use of new technologies.

The chapter also discussed inventory management. Three types of inventory are raw materials, work-in-process, and finished goods. Economic order quantity, materials requirement planning, and just-in-time inventory are techniques for minimizing inventory levels.

Another important concept is that operations management can enhance organizational productivity. Total factor productivity is the best measurement of organizational productivity. Total quality management is an approach to improving quality and productivity of operations. Managers can improve both quality and productivity through technology, management, and work-force improvements.

Finally, operations management's effectiveness can be enhanced through organization structure. The materials management concept suggests that all departments that contribute to the cost of materials be grouped together under a single materials manager. The materials manager can report either to the manufacturing manager or to the president of the organization. Teams enhance coordination within materials management and with other departments.

MANAGEMENT SOLUTION

Tom Blount had to decide whether GE's Major Appliance Business Group (MABG) should buy inexpensive, high-quality refrigerator compressors from overseas or invest in a new plant to manufacture its own. After extensive study, the decision was made to introduce a new product design in the form of a rotary compressor that was simpler and more effective than the reciprocating unit. The new design shrunk the number of parts from 51 to 29. The decision was made to invest $120 million in a new plant to compete head-to-head with already efficient plants in Japan and Italy. The decision seemed crazy, but Blount and his team pulled it off. GE's compressors are 20 percent cheaper than those of its dollar-an-hour competitors from overseas. One reason for the plant's productivity is worker involvement. Some contributed 400 hours for their training without receiving a paycheck. The plant has achieved precision that the suppliers of the automated technology did not believe possible. Miracles can happen with good product design and committed employees.[47]

DISCUSSION QUESTIONS

1. What is the difference between manufacturing and service organizations? Which has the greater need for operations management techniques?
2. Briefly explain the difference between process and product layout. What do you see as the advantages and disadvantages of each?
3. If you were asked by a local video store owner to help identify a location for a second video store, how would you proceed? How might you help the owner plan for the new store's capacity?
4. What are the three types of inventory? Which of these is most likely to be affected by the just-in-time inventory system? Explain.
5. What is materials requirement planning? How does it differ from using economic order quantity to reduce inventory?
6. Many managers believe that improvements in product quality reduce plant productivity. Why do you think managers feel this way? Are they correct?
7. Assume that a local manufacturing manager asks you about ways to improve productivity. What would you advise the manager?
8. What is the appropriate strategic role for operations management? Should operations management take the initiative in influencing competitive strategy?
9. What are the structural issues relevant to operations management? How might the solution to these issues influence operations strategy?

MANAGEMENT IN PRACTICE: ETHICAL DILEMMA

A Stinky Situation

At 3:30 A.M., Jacob Schilden, industrial relations manager, walked into the fuel tank assembly plant four hours earlier than usual. Jacob was called in because Sam Harding, a skilled welder, was threatening to walk off the job. Schilden was responsible for resolving conflicts between the managers, workers, and union representatives.

The problem was a new process of dipping two metal halves of fuel tanks into an anti-corrosion agent before welding them together. The design engineers said the agent was known to be highly toxic as a liquid, but was safe after drying on the metal. Unfortunately, it created horrible fumes during welding, which was Sam's job.

The ventilation system installed by the engineers did not decrease the smell. Sam threatened to walk off the job unless the fumes were corrected. Union representatives questioned whether safety standards were in jeopardy, saying perhaps the agent was toxic in gaseous form.

Management was trying to maintain high quality, which Schilden supports. Employee involvement teams had made a real difference and Schilden did not want to alienate them. However, manufacturing management refused to stop the line to deal with this problem, because the gas tanks went to a car assembly plant ten miles away. The auto plant had no tanks in inventory, depending on just-in-time delivery from this assembly plant. Shutting down the tank assembly line would also shut down the car assembly plant. As of this moment, union representatives and management are in a heated argument about whether Sam should continue working.

What Do You Do?

1. Support Sam Harding and ask that the line be stopped. It is unethical to endanger Sam's health, and supporting the workers will enhance quality over the long term.
2. Support management's position of keeping the line going. Explain to Sam and the union representatives that the engineers studied the anti-corrosion agent carefully. Management will work on improving ventilation first thing in the morning.
3. Propose an intermediate solution. Perhaps give Sam longer breaks than usual, set up fans in the area, or encourage worker rotation until the fumes can be removed.

CASES FOR ANALYSIS

XALOY INC.

Xaloy Inc., located in the Blue Ridge Mountains of Southwest Virginia, manufactures steel and alloy cylinders used to extrude plastics and other materials. The cylinders begin as logs of steel that are bored out, filled with a special metal alloy, and then heated to 2,000°F. After cooling, the cylinders are straightened, ground smooth, and machined so that they can be connected to an extrusion machine. The cylinders are used to produce food products such as puffed rice and puffed wheat.

Plant manager Kelley Nunley and materials manager Danny Porter were concerned about a number of problems on the shop floor that indicate materials management inefficiencies. There were huge piles of cylinders stacked among the boring machines and latches; other giant cylinders hung from cranes above the shop floor. In all, some 2,000 cylinders were waiting to be worked on. One reason was that the bandsaw that cut the cylinders was the fastest machine in the place, so cylinders were stacked everywhere waiting to go on to other production stages.

A related problem was that workers liked to have lots of inventory sitting around. They associated accumulated cylinders with good times and no awaiting stacks of work with bad times. Workers thus had achieved comfort with high work-in-process inventory.

Another problem was plant layout. Xaloy made several cylinder sizes, each of which had to travel around the 96,000-square-foot plant because the machines that performed similar operations were located together. This created the potential for accidents and damage. Sometimes a cylinder would go back and forth in the plant several times in one week.

Still another problem was purchasing. A salesperson had offered a quantity discount, at which one of the senior managers jumped. Nearly 400,000 pounds of steel—a five- or six-month supply—arrived at the back door, overwhelming the raw materials inventory storage area. The manager believed that buying material cheaply in huge amounts was a smart way to save money.

The final problem that concerned Nunley and Porter was the cylinder-straightening process. They could not understand why the steel came into the plant straight and was precisely machined, yet was getting bent and necessitating later straightening. Something must have been happening to the steel during the production process.

Questions

1. To what extent can the problems faced by Nunley and Porter be solved with operations management techniques?
2. Which operations management ideas described in this chapter are most appropriate to the Xaloy situation?
3. What suggestions would you make to help Xaloy improve productivity and quality?

Source: Craig R. Waters, "Profit and Loss," *INC.*, April 1985, 103–112.

BLUE BELL INC.

Blue Bell Inc. is one of the world's largest manufacturers of wearing apparel. Blue Bell is headquartered in Greensboro, North Carolina, and employs over 27,000 people worldwide. In the United States, Blue Bell has 80 plants and 32 distribution centers. Blue Bell is organized into three major businesses: the Wrangler Group, which manufactures denim and corduroy jeans; Red Kap, which makes durable garments for on-the-job wear; and Jantzen, which manufactures sportswear.

Apparel manufacturing is a working capital-intensive business. Inventory and accounts receivable comprise three-fourths of Blue Bell's asset base. A few years ago, Blue Bell's management became concerned about the high investment in working capital. These concerns were legitimate. Over the previous 12 months, inventory had averaged over $371 million, or more than 50 percent of Blue Bell's assets. Annual charges for maintaining inventory, including warehousing, short-term borrowing, and product obsolescence, totaled at least 25 percent of the investment in inventory. Moreover, short-term interest rates were near 20 percent. Thus, the cost of carrying inventory had become acute. The interest expense alone for Blue Bell had ballooned from $1.1 million to $21.9 million three years later. Simply financing the inventory had pushed up Blue Bell's cost of doing business and sharply increased retail prices.

Accompanying these inventory and working capital problems were changing customer expectations. Blue Bell's major customers included national and regional chain stores, mass merchandisers, and catalog houses. These customers were making new demands on apparel manufacturers:

1. Lead time on orders was decreasing. Retailers were sensitive to the high cost of financing their own inventory and thus ordering products closer to the time of actual sale. This meant Blue Bell had a shorter lead time and less opportunity to plan production. This led some managers to believe they should produce more apparel for finished-goods inventory to meet the uncertainties regarding customer orders.
2. Service demands were increasing. Retailers were becoming increasingly concentrated as major chains and discounters took a larger share of the business. These powerful retailers exerted pressure on Blue Bell for immediate product availability, on-time shipments, and delivery of complete orders. Recognizing the competitive advantage of superior customer service, Blue Bell was reluctant to reduce inventory at its expense.
3. The pressures on Blue Bell's management caused them to consider a new planning process. Managers saw the need to coordinate sales, marketing, manufacturing, operations, and finance. One manager proposed that a task force be created to include representatives of each function to develop a plan for reducing inventories yet maintaining customer service.

Questions

1. At what stage is Blue Bell in its operations strategy? At what stage is it striving to be?
2. Which techniques described in this chapter would help Blue Bell manage its huge inventories?
3. What could Blue Bell do to reduce inventory without impairing customer relations? Will lower inventories require better management? Discuss.

Source: Jerry R. Edwards, Harvey M. Wagner, and William P. Wood, "Blue Bell Trims Its Inventory," *Interfaces* 15 (January/February 1985), 34–52.

VIDEO CASE

R. R. DONNELLEY & SONS

R. R. Donnelley & Sons began in 1864, while the United States was still involved in the Civil War. Today it is the number-one printing company in the United States, with about $3 billion in 1990 sales.

Donnelley is composed of eight business units, covering such areas as books, magazines, catalogs, financial printing, computer and technical documentation, and information services. Each division uses a different technology. The book business is different from the magazine business, and the magazine business is different from financial printing. In the book business, the strategy is to provide quality books as publishers need them. In financial printing, speed is everything. Donnelley has its own satellite communication service to speed data around the world for daily printing.

As a technology-based manufacturing company, Donnelley knows how to be competitive. Location is one way to be responsive to customers. In documentation services, for example, Donnelley built facilities next to key customers. It literally finds the ten best customers and builds the facility in the geographical middle to service every one effectively.

Moreover, Donnelley always touts the industry's latest technology. In magazine publishing, Donnelley developed selective binding, which enables magazines to put out multiple editions in the same press run with advertising in each edition targeted to a specific group of subscribers. One issue of *Farm Journal,* with a circulation of 850,000, came out in 2,500 separate editions. Advertising and editorial content differed depending on the subscriber's farming specialty. The technology that allows the mixing of editions in a single run maintains low costs while providing better customer service, creating a competitive advantage.

In book printing, Donnelley is designing a just-in-time inventory system of sorts for its customers. A direct computer linkage with publishers will let them order books as needed. A customer could place an electronic order for 700 copies of a title and receive the books in 36 hours — less than the time to receive an order through the mail. This on-line system will provide another competitive advantage.

An important trend for a manufacturing company is the recent emphasis on decentralized structure and control. Dividing the company into eight business units was the first step. Within each unit, accountability and responsibility are pushed down to the people who operate the equipment. Increasing these people's commitment through involvement teams keeps quality high. Moreover, a customer representative is assigned to each account who coordinates horizontally across respective functions.

Donnelley's 25,000 employees are considered a key resource. The decentralized environment emphasizes the entrepreneur, the individual who makes things happen. In 1988 employees suggested 5,400 changes of which 40 percent were implemented, saving hundreds of thousands of dollars and improving quality and customer satisfaction. In the future, Donnelley plans to become more decentralized and to continue promoting change as a way of life.

One area in which Donnelley has not excelled is just-in-time management of its own inventory. The reason is the absence of standard items used in its manufacturing process. Orders cannot be predicted in advance, and supplies such as paper require a two-month lead time. Thus paper and other items must be kept on hand as a necessary cost of doing business.

DISCUSSION QUESTIONS

1. At what stage of operations strategy is Donnelley & Sons? How important is computer technology to this strategy? Discuss.
2. To what extent is a clan control or bureaucratic control philosophy used at Donnelley? How would Donnelley rate on each of the items in Exhibit 17.5?
3. To what extent would financial control likely be important at a company such as Donnelley?
4. How important are such concepts as plant location, plant layout, productivity, quality, and the transformation process to the success of Donnelley? Explain.

Source: Jill Roth, "A Conversation with John R. Walter," *American Printer,* July 1989, 32–34; Sharon Nelton, "Values with a Long Reach," *Nation's Business,* February 1990, 32; Jagannath Dubashi, "Power Printing," *Financial World,* June 13, 1989, 56–57.

In 1970, Great Western Savings and Loan acquired Lytton Savings and Loan. With this acquisition came the corporate art collection the founder, Bart Lytton, had built. A friend of Picasso and lover of fine art, Lytton began his corporate collection to improve the visual quality of his bank's working environment. Because he wanted to encourage local artists, the collection focused exclusively on pieces by California artists. Now containing over 450 works, the collection is on display throughout branch offices in California.

PART 6

EMERGING MANAGEMENT ISSUES

Source: Stanton MacDonald-Wright, *Du Nord,* 1958, oil on canvas, 33″ × 41″. Collection of Great Western Bank, Northridge, CA. Photograph by Scott Streble, Scott Streble Photography, Pasadena, CA.

C H A P T E R 2 1

MANAGING IN A GLOBAL ENVIRONMENT

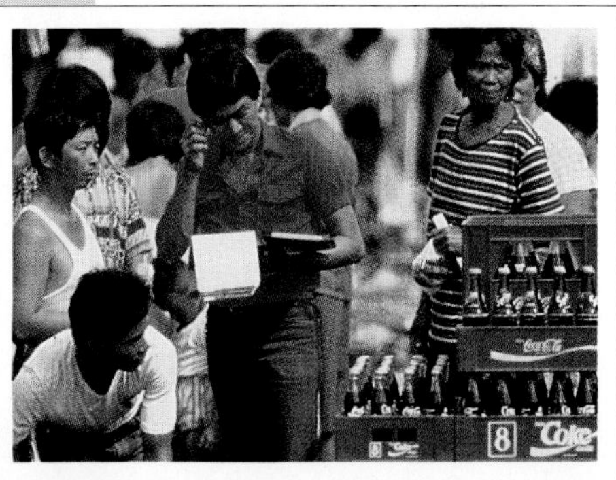

CHAPTER OUTLINE

The International Business Environment

The Economic Environment
The Legal-Political Environment
The Sociocultural Environment
Summary of the International Environment

Getting Started Internationally

Outsourcing
Exporting
Licensing
Direct Investment

The Multinational Corporation

Characteristics of Multinational Corporations

Multinational Corporate Strategy

Grand Strategies
Strategic Planning

Multinational Organization Structure

International Division
Product-Based Structure
Geographic-Based Structure
Functional-Based Structure
Matrix Structure

Tailoring Management Style to Cultural Values

Leadership
Decision Making
Motivation
Control

LEARNING OBJECTIVES

After studying this chapter, you should be able to:

- Define international management and explain how it differs from the management of domestic business operations.
- Indicate how dissimilarities in the economic, sociocultural, and legal-political environments throughout the world can affect business operations.
- Describe market entry strategies that business firms use to develop foreign markets.
- Describe the characteristics of a multinational corporation and the generic strategies available to them.
- Explain the steps in the strategic planning process for multinational corporations.
- Identify the organizational structures that multinationals use and factors that determine the appropriate structure.

Management Problem

For five straight years Black & Decker lost market share to the likes of Makita of Japan and Borsh of West Germany. Black & Decker's strategy had been to create geographical fiefdoms around the world, each with its own product design and marketing departments to serve its markets. The British subsidiary made tools for Britons, the Italian subsidiary made tools for Italians, and so on. This sounds fine, except for some problems. Dustbuster, the cordless vacuum cleaner, was a runaway best seller in the United States, but the Australians refused to introduce it in their market. The European managers refused to sell Black & Decker housewares, maintaining that the products were strictly for Americans. Each fiefdom seemed successful, but there were no savings or synergy among them. The decision facing Black & Decker's managers was whether to centralize control and develop standard products for sale around the globe or continue with autonomous operations in each country.[1]

If you were a consultant to CEO Nolan Archibald, would you recommend selling standard products worldwide? What structural changes would you recommend to achieve better coordination across foreign operations?

Black & Decker is a well-established, international competitor facing changes in strategy and structure. Companies such as McDonald's, IBM, Coca-Cola, Kellogg, Boeing, General Motors, and Caterpillar Tractor all rely on international business for a substantial portion of sales and profits. These companies face special problems in trying to tailor their products to the unique needs of foreign countries — but if they succeed, the whole world is their marketplace.

How important is international business to the study of management? *If you are not thinking international, you are not thinking business management.* It's that serious. As you read this page, ideas, takeover plans, capital investments, business strategies, Reeboks, services, and T-shirts are traveling around the planet by telephone, fax, and overnight mail.

Typical of managers of the future, Michel Rabanal is fluent in French, English, and Spanish. Rabanal, Prime Computer's manager of international marketing, moved to Massachusetts from France in late 1988. Prime Computer has a *global vision,* with over half of its business coming from outside North America. Prime's success comes from bringing together people from different continents and cultures to serve clients worldwide with quality products.

If you think you are isolated from global influence, think again. Even if you will not budge from your hometown, your company may be purchased by the English, Japanese, or Germans tomorrow. People who work for Standard Oil, any of the Federated Department Stores, Pillsbury, Shell Oil, Chesebrough-Pond's, Carnation, Celanese, Firestone, or CBS Records are already working for foreign bosses. The Japanese alone purchased 174 mostly small- and medium-size American companies in 1989.

Or consider this: You arrive at work tomorrow and your CEO puts globalization in the company's mission statement and says to promote employees who have international experience and foreign-language ability. Or worse yet, a foreign competitor may be launching a competitive assault on your industry. A few years ago U.S. firms made 85 percent of the world's memory chips and were unassailable, or so they thought. Soon Japan had a 75 percent share of the world market, with the U.S. share shrunk to 15 percent. No one is immune. A small entrepreneurial company, Florod Corporation, made a laser eraser that had a small market of no more than 40 companies. Giant NEC from Japan pushed its way in with a better product, practically destroying Florod, which had to find other products to survive. With this kind of competition, is it any surprise that foreign-born people with international experience have been appointed to run such companies as Du Pont, Coca-Cola, Revlon, Gerber, NCR, and Heinz?[2]

This chapter introduces some basic concepts about international management. First we consider the difficulties of operating in foreign environments. We then discuss multinational corporations and the types of strategies and structures they use to compete effectively on a global scale. Finally, we examine international management issues associated with leadership, decision making, motivation, and control.

THE INTERNATIONAL BUSINESS ENVIRONMENT

International management is the management of business operations conducted in more than one country. The fundamental tasks of business management, including the financing, production, and distribution of products and services, do not change in any substantive way when a firm is transacting business across international borders. The basic management functions of planning, organizing, leading, and controlling are the same whether a company operates domestically or internationally. However, managers will experience greater difficulties and risks when performing these management functions on an international scale. For example:

international management The management of business operations conducted in more than one country.

- Managers at one American company were shaken when they discovered that the brand name of the cooking oil they had introduced in Latin America translated into Spanish as "jackass oil."
- Still another company tried to sell its toothpaste in Southeast Asia by stressing that it whitens teeth. Managers were chagrined to discover that local people chew betel nut to blacken their teeth because they find the result attractive.[3]
- One company stamped "OK" on each page of its catalog. In many parts of South America, OK is a vulgar gesture. Six months were lost because the company had to reprint the catalogs.

Environmental factors that affect international business are similar to the task and general environmental sectors described in Chapter 3. However, when comparing one country with another, the economic, legal-political, and sociocultural sectors present the greatest difficulties. Key factors to understand in the international environment are summarized in Exhibit 21.1.

THE ECONOMIC ENVIRONMENT

The economic environment represents the economic conditions in the country where the international organization operates. This part of the environment includes such factors as economic development; resource and product markets; infrastructure; exchange rates; and inflation, interest rates, and economic growth.

ECONOMIC DEVELOPMENT. Economic development differs widely among the countries and regions of the world. Countries can be categorized as either "developing" or "developed." The developing countries are referred to as *less-developed countries (LDCs).* The criterion traditionally used to classify countries as developed or developing is *per capita income*, which is the income generated by the nation's production of goods and services divided by total population. The developing countries have low per capita incomes. LDCs generally are in the Southern Hemisphere, including Africa, Asia, and South America, whereas developed countries tend to be in the Northern Hemisphere, including North America, Europe, and Japan.[4]

Most international business firms are based in the developed countries. They show a preference for confining their operations to the wealthier and economically advanced nations. However, based on the number of prospective

Exhibit 21.1
Key Factors in the International Environment

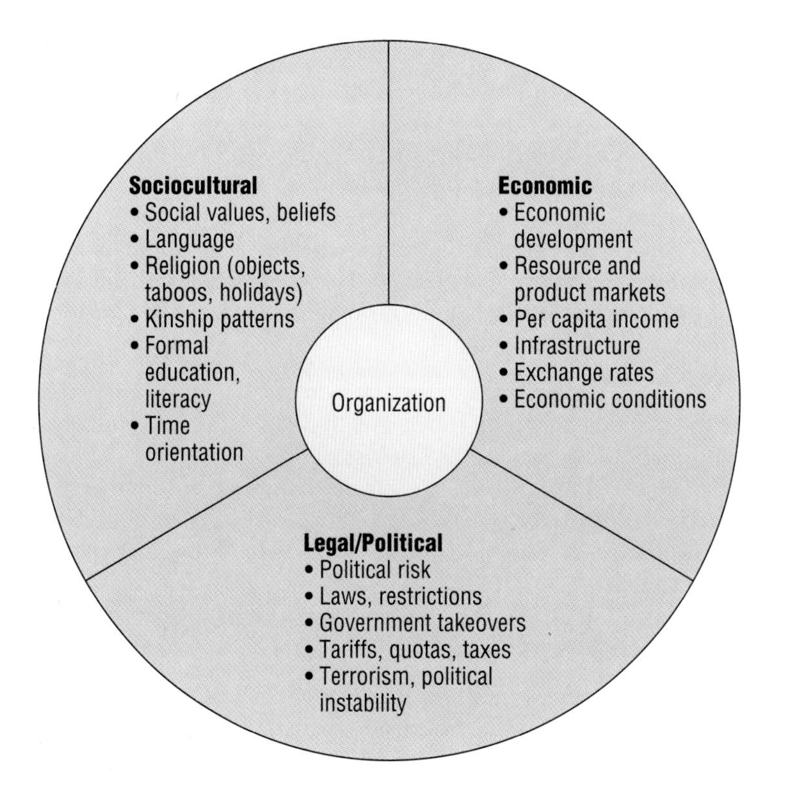

customers, developing countries constitute an immense and largely untapped market.

infrastructure A country's physical facilities that support economic activities.

Infrastructure. A country's physical facilities that support economic activities is called its **infrastructure** and includes transportation facilities such as airports, highways, and railroads; energy-producing facilities such as utilities and power plants; and communication facilities such as telephone lines and radio stations. Companies operating in LDCs must contend with lower levels of technology and perplexing logistical, distribution, and communication problems.

Resource and Product Markets. When operating in another country, managers must evaluate the market demand for its products. If market demand is high, it may choose to export products to that country. To develop manufacturing plants, however, resource markets for providing needed raw materials and labor must also be available. For example, the greatest challenge for McDonald's restaurants overseas is to obtain supplies of everything from potatoes to hamburger buns to plastic straws. Often supplies that meet McDonald's exacting standards are unavailable. The hamburger bun was the most difficult item to procure in Britain because local bakeries would not meet their standards. In Thailand, McDonald's actually helped farmers cultivate Idaho Russet potatoes of sufficient quality to produce their golden french fries.[5]

Coca-Cola's strategy includes both growth and globalization based on three factors: increasing availability, enhancing affordability, and broadening acceptability of its soft-drink products. Coca-Cola uses railcarts in the Manilla market, as shown here, to fit the transportation *infrastructure*. Coke's global strategy has been extraordinarily successful, with its international market share growing to 47 percent. Coke is available, affordable, and acceptable to consumers because it adapts to the infrastructure of both high and low per capita consumption countries.

EXCHANGE RATES. *Exchange rates* are the rate at which one country's currency is exchanged for another country's. Changes in the exchange rate can have major implications for the profitability of international operations.[6] For example, assume that the American dollar is exchanged for 8 French francs. If the dollar increases in value to 10 francs, U.S. goods will be more expensive in France because it will take more francs to buy a dollar's worth of U.S. goods. It will be more difficult to export American goods to France, and profits will be slim. If the dollar drops to a value of 6 francs, on the other hand, U.S. goods will be cheaper in France and can be exported at a profit.

THE LEGAL-POLITICAL ENVIRONMENT

Businesses must deal with unfamiliar political systems when they go international, as well as with more government supervision and regulation. Government officials and the general public often view foreign companies as outsiders or even intruders and are suspicious of their impact on economic independence and political sovereignty. Some of the major legal-political concerns affecting international business are political risk, political instability, and laws and restrictions.

POLITICAL RISK. A company's **political risk** is defined as its risk of loss of assets, earning power, or managerial control due to events or actions by host governments that are politically based.[7] Political risk includes government takeovers of property and acts of violence directed against a firm's properties or employees. Because such acts are not uncommon, companies must formulate special plans and programs to guard against unexpected losses. For example, Hercules Inc., a large chemical company, has increased the number of security guards at several of its European plants. Monsanto Corporation canceled a ceremony to celebrate the opening of a new plant in England.[8]

political risk A company's risk of loss of assets, earning power, or managerial control due to politically motivated events or actions by host governments.

Chiquita Brands International, Inc. markets high-quality Chiquita brand food products around the world. The company's earnings are heavily dependent upon the *legal-political environment,* because of risk, political instability, and strict laws in countries where food products are grown. Risks faced by Chiquita Brands include government regulation, currency restrictions, risk of expropriation, and burdensome taxes. Governmental regulations where it markets bananas include import quotas and foreign exchange controls. Chiquita Brands leases its agricultural lands in Panama from the Republic of Panama, which recently experienced a disruption of government when the Noreiga government was toppled.

POLITICAL INSTABILITY. Another frequently cited problem for international companies is political instability, which includes riots, revolutions, civil disorders, and frequent changes in government. Political instability increases uncertainty. For example, companies rushing into Eastern European countries such as Hungary and Poland will face instability because of changing government personnel and political philosophies. Two Germanys are becoming one.[9] Deals made today may be revoked tomorrow. International firms can operate under almost any political system so long as it is stable. Drastic changes in the political system, however, make operations risky.

LAWS AND REGULATIONS. Government laws and regulations differ from country to country and make manufacturing and sales a true challenge for international firms. Host governments have myriad laws concerning libel statutes, consumer protection, information and labeling, employment and safety, and wages. International companies must learn these rules and regulations and abide by them. The most striking changes in laws and regulations that affect global companies are occurring in Europe. Consider the impact of Europe 1992.

EUROPE 1992 • The European Economic Community (EEC) was formed in 1958 to improve economic and social conditions within its member nations. The EEC has grown to 12 European countries, which are shown in Exhibit 21.2. In the early 1980s Europeans became concerned that Europe would become a second-rate world power because of economic stagnation. This caused a push for a truly free internal market by the end of 1992.

The free market will be achieved when member nations adopt a series of 300 directives to reduce barriers to trade that are being pushed by the EEC Commission. Perhaps 200 of these directives will be passed by the end of 1992, and additional directives will be passed in later years to make a true common market in Europe.

The impact of Europe 1992 is to create a huge market for companies within the EEC. The market will contain 320 million people, compared with 240 million in the United States and 120 million in Japan. The increased competition and economies of scale within the EEC will enable European companies to grow large and efficient. The program will result in larger, better organized, and more competitive European companies attacking the U.S. and other world markets.

Another possible outcome is a trade barrier around the EEC protecting it from international competition. This is not the intended goal, but many observers believe that 1992 will introduce "Fortress Europe" that will be difficult to penetrate by U.S. exports. This threat has generated something of a rush by U.S. companies to become established within European borders before the 1992 program begins.

North American firms must prepare for 1992 and beyond, readying for heightened competitive battles both here and abroad. The eventual outcome cannot be predicted precisely, because the international trade environment continues to change at a dizzying pace. The revolutionary U.S.-Canada Trade Agreement is being implemented during 1990 and beyond. Before the ink was dry on the Europe 1992 agreement, changes in Eastern Europe enabled the

EXHIBIT 21.2
The Twelve Nations within the EEC

beginning of economic integration of East and West Germany. The eventual economic resurgence of Eastern Europe will create even more competition problems for the United States, Japan, and Canada.[10]

THE SOCIOCULTURAL ENVIRONMENT

A nation's **culture** includes the shared knowledge, beliefs, and values, as well as the common modes of behavior and ways of thinking, among members of a society. Cultural factors are more perplexing than political and economic

culture The shared knowledge, beliefs, values, behaviors, and ways of thinking among members of a society.

factors in foreign countries. Culture is intangible, pervasive, and difficult to learn. It is absolutely imperative that international businesses comprehend the significance of local cultures and deal with them effectively.

SOCIAL VALUES. Research by Geert Hofstede on 116,000 IBM employees in 40 countries identified four dimensions of national value systems that influence organizational and employee working relationships:[11]

power distance The degree to which people accept inequality in power among institutions, organizations, and people.

uncertainty avoidance A value characterized by people's intolerance for uncertainty and ambiguity and resulting support for beliefs that promise certainty and conformity.

individualism A preference for a loosely knit social framework in which individuals are expected to take care of themselves.

collectivism A preference for a tightly knit social framework in which individuals look after one another and organizations protect their members' interests.

masculinity A cultural preference for achievement, heroism, assertiveness, and material success.

femininity A cultural preference for modesty, tending to the weak, and quality of life.

1. *Power distance.* High **power distance** means that people accept inequality in power among institutions, organizations, and people. Low power distance means that people expect equality in power. Countries that value high power distance are Malaysia, the Philippines, and Panama. Countries that value low power distance are Denmark, Austria, and Israel.
2. *Uncertainty avoidance.* High **uncertainty avoidance** means that members of a society feel uncomfortable with uncertainty and ambiguity and thus support beliefs that promise certainty and conformity. Low uncertainty avoidance means that people have high tolerance for the unstructured, the unclear, and the unpredictable. High uncertainty avoidance countries include Greece, Portugal, and Uruguay. Countries with low uncertainty avoidance values are Singapore and Jamaica.
3. *Individualism and collectivism.* **Individualism** reflects a value for a loosely knit social framework in which individuals are expected to take care of themselves. **Collectivism** means a preference for a tightly knit social framework in which individuals look after one another and organizations protect their members' interests. Countries with individualist values include the United States, Canada, Great Britain, and Australia. Countries with collectivist values are Guatemala, Ecuador, and Panama.
4. *Masculinity/femininity.* **Masculinity** stands for preference for achievement, heroism, assertiveness, and material success. **Femininity** reflects the values of relationships, modesty, caring for the weak, and quality of life. Societies with strong masculine values are Japan, Austria, Mexico, and Germany. Countries with feminine values are Sweden, Norway, Denmark, and Yugoslavia. Both men and women subscribe to the dominant value in masculine and feminine cultures.

Social values influence organizational functioning and management styles. For example, organizations in France and Latin and Mediterranean countries tend to be hierarchical bureaucracies. Germany and other central European countries have organizations that strive to be impersonal, well-oiled machines. In India, Asia, and Africa, organizations are viewed as large families. Effective management styles differ in each country, depending on cultural characteristics.[12]

ethnocentrism A cultural attitude marked by the tendency to regard one's own culture as superior to others.

OTHER CULTURAL CHARACTERISTICS. Other cultural characteristics that influence international organizations are language, religion, attitudes, social organization, and education. Some countries, such as India, are characterized by *linguistic pluralism,* meaning that several languages exist there. Other countries rely heavily on spoken versus written language. Religion includes sacred objects, philosophical attitudes toward life, taboos, and rituals. Attitudes toward achievement, work, and time can all affect organizational productivity. An attitude called **ethnocentrism** means that people have a tendency to regard their own culture as superior and to downgrade other cultures. Ethnocentrism within a country makes it difficult for foreign firms to operate there. Social organization includes status systems, kinship and families, social institutions, and opportunities for social mobility. Education influences the literacy level, the availability of qualified employees, and the predominance of primary or secondary degrees.

Managers in international companies have found that cultural differences cannot be ignored if international operations are to succeed. For example, Procter & Gamble ran into unanticipated cultural barriers when marketing its Cheer laundry soap in Japan. Cheer initially prospered by discounting its price, but that alienated wholesalers who were not used to having reduced margins.[13] On the other hand, organizations that manage cultural differences report major successes. Kellogg introduced breakfast cereals into Brazil, where the traditional breakfast is coffee and a roll. Through carefully chosen advertising, many Brazilians were won over to the American breakfast. Many families now start the day with Kellogg's Sucrilhos (Frosted Flakes) and Crokinhos (Cocoa Krispies).[14]

Citibank's Consumer Services Group-International spent several years learning international consumer banking. Corporate banking is similar around the world, but consumer banking is not, because of differences in the *sociocultural environment*. The English accept credit cards but only carry one or two. The Saudis complain of teller machine limits of $1,000 per day and don't want interest on their deposits. Citibank's typical Brazilian customer is male, has accounts at six or seven banks, and copes with hyperinflation by managing money on a daily basis. Germans feel guilty about debt, preferring cash to credit. Focusing on consumer needs in each unique culture has enabled Citibank to develop a coherent overseas consumer business.

Summary of the International Environment

Some of the complexities of operating in diverse countries are illustrated in Exhibit 21.3. The upper portion of the exhibit shows a firm operating in its domestic market and native culture. The lower portion shows how complicated business operations can become when operating in several countries simultaneously. Through its foreign affiliates, the organization must carry on the same basic types of relationships in other countries, but to do so it must adapt to their cultures and legal-political systems. Moreover, the organization must transcend the boundaries of separate cultures to transfer resources and products between the firm and foreign affiliates. The organization must also coordinate technological know-how, advertising, and managerial directives across cultural boundaries.

One company that has transcended foreign boundaries and thrives internationally is American Express.

American Express •

For years, American Express cards were carried by Americans. Then the company realized that credit card services can be global in nature and adopted an international mindset. So how does American Express market a credit card to consumers in countries with clashing values and tastes? The trick is to think in terms of local environments. The strategy is global, but the advertising is local. Themes such as "Don't leave home without it" are sent around the world with subtle tailoring. Local advertising agencies also create ads for specific countries. In Japan, a popular ad depicts a young couple who can stay two days longer at a favorite vacation spot. In Australia, an exuberant young couple has a weekend blast on their American Express card.

Today, about 25 percent of American Express's cardholders are non-U.S. citizens. Foreign cardholders bring in 31 percent more revenue per card than Americans, and the company's international business will generate 40 percent of the growth in profits over the next few years.[15]

EXHIBIT 21.3
Environmental Influences on an International Firm

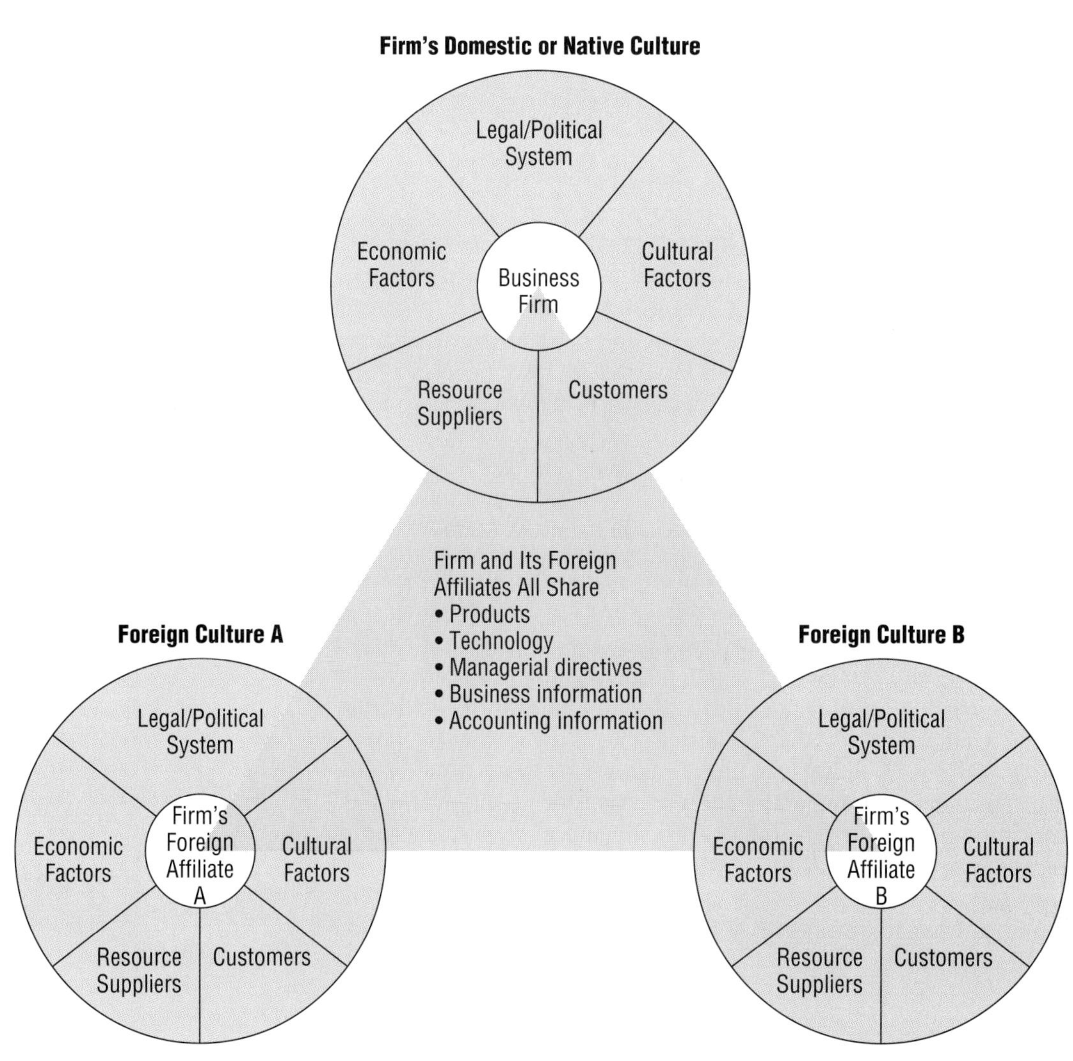

GETTING STARTED INTERNATIONALLY

market entry strategy
An organizational strategy for entering a foreign market.

Small- and medium-size companies have a couple of ways to become involved internationally. One is to seek cheaper sources of supply offshore, which is called *outsourcing.* Another is to develop markets for finished products outside their home country, which may include exporting, licensing, and direct investment. These are called **market entry strategies,** because they represent alternative ways to sell products and services in foreign markets. Most firms

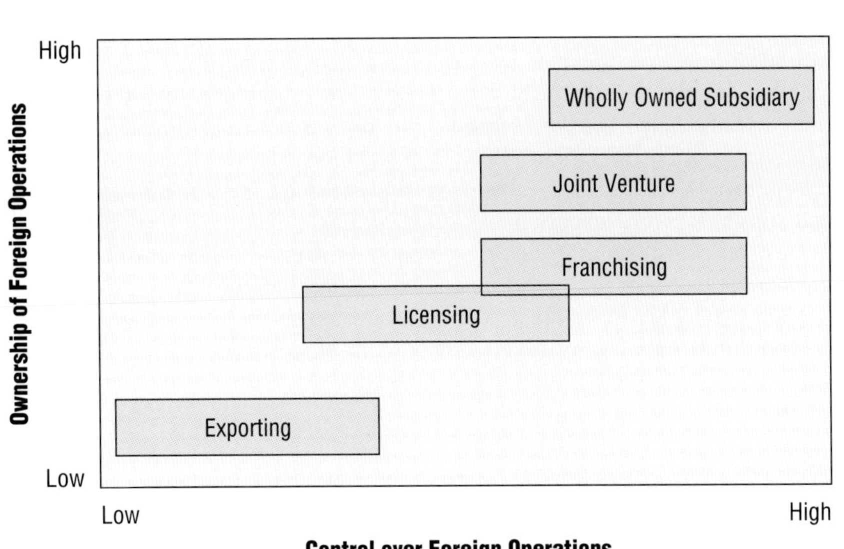

EXHIBIT 21.4
Strategies for Entering International Markets

begin with exporting and work up to direct investment. Exhibit 21.4 shows the strategies companies can use to enter foreign markets.

OUTSOURCING

outsourcing Engaging in the international division of labor so as to obtain the cheapest sources of labor and supplies regardless of country; also called *global sourcing*.

Outsourcing, sometimes called *global sourcing,* means engaging in the international division of labor so that manufacturing can be done in countries with the cheapest sources of labor and supplies. A company may take away a contract from a domestic supplier and place it with a company in the Far East, 8,000 miles away. For example, Seagate Technology sells low-cost hard disk drives for personal computers. Its enormous success has been based on using low-cost Asian labor to crank out products cheaply. These products are then finished off and sold in the United States.[16]

A unique variation is the Maquiladora industry along the Texas-Mexico border. In the beginning, twin plants were set up with the U.S. plant manufacturing components with sophisticated machinery and the Mexican plant assembling components using cheap labor. This helped combat Mexico's high unemployment. With increasing sophistication in Mexico, new factories with sophisticated equipment are being built further south of the border. Manufactured products are then imported into the United States at highly competitive prices.[17]

EXPORTING

exporting An entry strategy in which the organization maintains its production facilities within its home country and transfers its products for sale in foreign markets.

With **exporting,** the corporation maintains its production facilities within the home nation and transfers its products for sale in foreign countries.[18] Exporting enables a country to market its products in other countries at small resource cost and with limited risk. Exporting does entail numerous problems based on physical distances, government regulations, foreign currencies, and cultural differences, but it is less expensive than committing the firm's own capital to building plants in host countries. For example, a high-tech equipment supplier called Gerber Scientific Inc. prefers not to get involved directly in foreign country operations. Because machinery and machine tools are hot areas of export, executives are happy to ship overseas. Indeed, more and more small businesses are experiencing great success in international markets.[19]

countertrade The barter of products for other products rather than their sale for currency.

A form of exporting to less-developed countries is called **countertrade,** which is the barter of products for products rather than the sale of products for currency. Many less-developed countries have products to exchange but have no foreign currency. An estimated 20 percent of world trade is countertrade.

Licensing

licensing An entry strategy in which an organization in one country makes certain resources available to companies in another in order to participate in the production and sale of its products abroad.

With **licensing,** a corporation (the licensor) in one country makes certain resources available to companies in another country (the licensee). These resources include technology, managerial skills, and/or patent and trademark rights. They enable the licensee to produce and market a product similar to what the licensor has been producing. This arrangement gives the licensor an opportunity to participate in the production and sale of products outside its home country. Hasbro has licensing agreements with companies in several Latin American countries and Japan. Hasbro builds brand identity and consumer awareness by contracting with toy companies to manufacture products locally. Glidden has licensing arrangements for its paint manufacturing technology with manufacturers in over 25 countries.

franchising A form of licensing in which an organization provides its foreign franchisees with a complete assortment of materials and services.

Franchising is a form of licensing in which the franchisor provides foreign franchisees with a complete package of material and services, including equipment, products, product ingredients, trademark and trade name rights, managerial advice, and a standardized operating system. Some of the best known international franchisers are the fast-food chains. Kentucky Fried Chicken, Burger King, Wendy's, and McDonald's outlets are found in almost every large city in the world. The story is often told of the Japanese child visiting Los Angeles who excitedly pointed out to his parents, "They have McDonald's in America

Licensing and franchising offer a business firm relatively easy access to international markets, but they limit its participation in and control over the development of those markets.

Direct Investment

direct investment An entry strategy in which the organization is involved in managing its production facilities in a foreign country.

joint venture A variation of direct investment in which an organization shares costs and risks with another firm to build a manufacturing facility, develop new products, or set up a sales and distribution network.

A higher level of involvement in international trade is direct investment in manufacturing facilities in a foreign country. **Direct investment** means that the company is involved in managing the productive assets, which distinguishes it from other entry strategies that permit less managerial control.

Currently the most popular type of direct investment is to engage in strategic alliances and partnerships. In a **joint venture,** a company shares costs and risks with another firm, typically in the host country, to develop new products,

The I.M. Pei entryway pyramid houses 16 Otis escalators that carry thousands of daily visitors to the Louvre in Paris. Otis, a division of United Technologies, is the world's largest elevator company, selling in 163 countries. Otis has not relied on exports, preferring to invest in foreign production. Through *wholly owned foreign affiliates* and *joint ventures,* Otis manufactures elevators in every country in Europe, and employs more than 16,000 people in Asia-Pacific countries.

build a manufacturing facility, or set up a sales and distribution network.[20] A partnership is often the fastest, cheapest, and least risky way to get into the global game. Entrepreneurial companies such as Molex, a manufacturer of connectors, and Nypro, a maker of industrial components, both used partnerships to gain overseas access to several countries. Giants such as AT&T and Japan's NEC Corporation joined forces to share design technology and microchip manufacturing. Other giant partnerships include Texas Instruments and Kobe Steel (Japan) and Mitsubishi of Japan and Daimler-Benz AG of West Germany.[21] International joint ventures are expected to be the hallmark of business in the 1990s. As shown in the Focus on Entrepreneurship box, joint ventures are also being undertaken between the Soviet Union and the United States.

The other choice is to have a **wholly owned foreign affiliate,** over which the company has complete control. Direct investment provides cost savings over exporting by shortening distribution channels and reducing storage and transportation costs. Local managers also have heightened awareness of economic, cultural, and political conditions. The company must expend capital funds and human resources to acquire productive assets that will be exposed to risks from the host country's economic, legal-political, and sociocultural environments.

wholly owned foreign affiliate
A foreign subsidiary over which an organization has complete control.

For example, companies in the advertising industry have recently become involved in direct investment by buying agencies around the globe to provide advertising services for global companies. Foote Cone & Belding acquired advertising agencies in Europe, South America, and Asia. Saatchi & Saatchi, based in London, has taken over 12 agencies in Europe and the United States. Such mergers create wholly owned subsidiaries that enable advertising agencies to coordinate the advertising for multinational clients. Direct investment gives them complete control over agencies in host countries.[22]

FOCUS ON ENTREPRENEURSHIP

THE AMERICAN TRADE CONSORTIUM

Jim Giffen became interested in conducting business with the USSR as a law student at UCLA. He even wrote a textbook on the subject. After joining Armco in 1973, he helped sell oil-drilling equipment to the Soviets. His signature was on a letter of intent for Armco and Phillips Petroleum to develop oil in the Soviet Union, and he also arranged for Armco to build a steel plant for electrical transformers. Unfortunately, these two deals broke down under political pressure caused by the Afganistan conflict. But Giffen's recent entrepreneurial efforts at U.S.-Soviet business relations appear to have great promise under *perestroika.*

In 1984 Giffen set up the private merchant bank, Mercator Corporation, and became president of the nonprofit U.S.-USSR Trade and Economic Council. This position allowed him access to Soviet policymakers during the onset of *perestroika.* Giffen claims that even Gorbachev, before becoming the Soviet leader, encouraged his efforts to arrange joint ventures.

Gorbachev's encouragement sparked an idea for a consortium of U.S. companies wishing to conduct business in the USSR, for which the initial agreement was signed in April 1988. The American Trade Consortium consists of five major companies — Chevron, RJR Nabisco, Eastman Kodak, Johnson & Johnson, and Archer Daniels Midland — which have proposals for at least 25 joint ventures totaling between $5 and $10 billion in American investment. The U.S. companies stand to increase their profits in a large country full of people wanting to spend pocketfuls of rubles on items ranging from computers to basic consumer products. After all, they have little else on which to spend their rubles.

The Soviets stand to increase their own business through joint ventures to produce tomato products, cigarettes, crackers, and cereal (RJR); blood analyzers, computer floppy disks, and retail outlets for film and processing (Kodak); and wheat products such as fructose sweeteners and gluten for bread (Archer Daniels Midland). Johnson & Johnson is secretive concerning its intentions, but many of their products such as baby shampoo, Q-Tips, toilet paper, and other personal products will probably appear on Soviet shelves. Coincidently, entrepreneur Jim Giffen stands to gain millions of dollars in fees if the joint ventures succeed.

Source: Based on Louis Kraar, "Top U.S. Companies Move Into Russia," *Fortune,* July 31, 1989, 165–172.

THE MULTINATIONAL CORPORATION

The size and volume of international business are so large that it is hard to comprehend. The value of the annual output of U.S. overseas affiliates has exceeded the gross national product of every world nation except the United States and Soviet Union.[23]

A large volume of international business has largely been carried out by a rather small number of very large business firms called *multinational corporations (MNCs).* Also called *global corporations*, or *transnational corporations*, MNCs have been the subject of tremendous attention and concern.[24] MNCs can move assets from country to country and influence nations' economies, politics, and cultures. A large multinational can have sales revenues exceeding $10 billion per year — more than most countries' gross national products.

multinational corporation (MNC) An organization that receives more than 25 percent of its total sales revenues from operations outside the parent company's home country; also called *global corporation* or *transnational corporation.*

CHARACTERISTICS OF MULTINATIONAL CORPORATIONS

Although there is no precise definition, a **multinational corporation (MNC)** typically receives more than 25 percent of its total sales revenues from operations outside the parent's home country. MNCs also have the following distinctive managerial characteristics:

1. An MNC is managed as an integrated worldwide business system. This means that foreign affiliates act in close alliance and cooperation with one another. Capital, technology, and people are transferred among country affiliates. The MNC can acquire materials and manufacture parts wherever in the world it is most advantageous to do so.
2. An MNC is ultimately controlled by a single management authority that makes key, strategic decisions relating to the parent and all affiliates. Some centralization of management is imperative for maintaining worldwide integration and profit maximization for the enterprise as a whole.
3. MNC top managers are presumed to exercise a global perspective. They regard the entire world as one market for strategic decisions, resource acquisition, location of production, and marketing efficiency.

In a few cases, the MNC management philosophy may differ from that described above. For example, some researchers have distinguished among *ethnocentric companies,* which place emphasis on their home countries, *polycentric companies,* which are oriented toward the markets of individual foreign host countries, and *geocentric companies,* which are truly world oriented and favor no specific country.[25] In general, a multinational corporation can be thought of as a business enterprise that is composed of affiliates located in different countries and whose top managers make decisions primarily on the basis of global business opportunities and objectives.

MULTINATIONAL CORPORATE STRATEGY

In today's global corporations, senior executives try to formulate coherent strategies to provide synergy among worldwide operations for the purpose of fulfilling common objectives. A systematic strategic planning process for deciding on the appropriate strategic alternative should be used.

GRAND STRATEGIES

Recall from Chapter 6 that growth and retrenchment are two grand strategies available to large corporations. Growth is a major motivation for both small and large businesses going international. Each country or region represents a new market with the promise of increased sales and profits. Grand strategies and other strategy concepts, such as situation analyses, portfolio strategy, and product life cycle, also apply to international firms, but implementation is more complex because the whole world is the market. In the international arena, MNCs face an additional strategic dilemma between global integration and national responsiveness. Organizations must decide whether they want each affiliate to act autonomously or whether activities should be standardized and centralized across countries. This choice leads managers to select basic strategic alternatives such as globalization versus multidomestic strategy.[26]

GLOBALIZATION. When an organization chooses a strategy of **globalization,** it means that its product design and advertising strategies are standardized throughout the world.[27] This approach is based on the assumption that a

globalization The standardization of product design and advertising strategies throughout the world.

Procter & Gamble has gradually shifted from a strategy of *globalization* to a *multidomestic strategy.* P&G once believed its marketing prowess could ignore cultural differences, but its overseas success stems from going native — investing in painstaking research to learn what consumers want around the world. These laundresses test P&G's detergents in waters and washing machines from such countries as Japan, Peru, Mexico, and Venezuela. Edwin Artzt, who is responsible for P&G's international success, was rewarded with promotion to CEO.

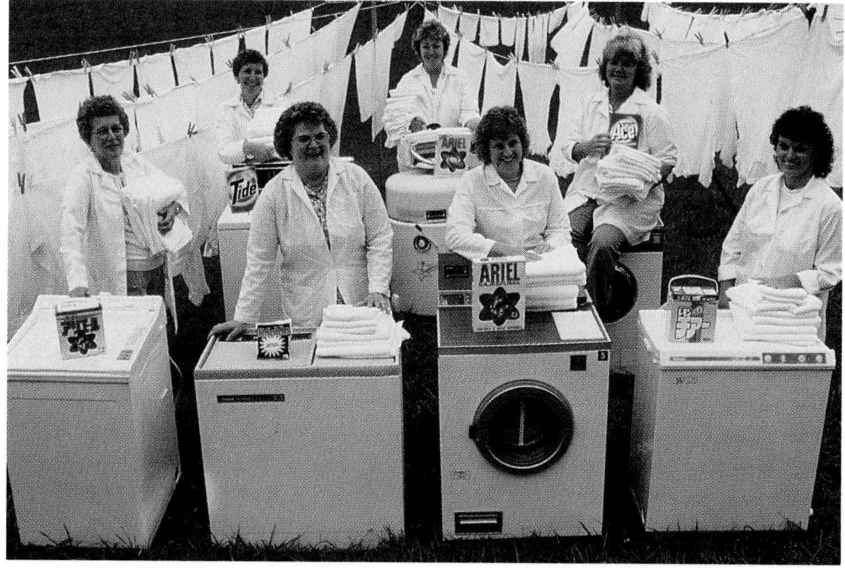

single global market exists for most consumer and industrial products. The theory is that people everywhere want to buy the same products and live the same way. People everywhere want to drink Coca-Cola and wear Levi blue jeans.[28] For example, the planned dropping of European customs barriers in 1992 will help make Europe one unified market for standardized manufacturing, packaging, and ads. Ford Motor Company treats the world as one market by selling the same Escort in all markets. Assembly plants around the world all use standard products, saving millions of dollars compared with designing a unique car for each country or region.

Globalization enables marketing departments alone to save millions of dollars. For example, Colgate-Palmolive Company sells Colgate toothpaste in over 40 countries. For every country where the same commercial runs, it saves $1 to $2 million in production costs alone. More millions have been saved by standardizing the look and packaging of brands.[29] International Playtex developed a single advertising campaign for selling its Wow bra in 12 countries. It avoided the more expensive approach of assigning ad agencies in each country the job of developing a marketing campaign.[30]

multidomestic strategy The modification of product design and advertising strategies to suit the specific needs of individual countries.

MULTIDOMESTIC STRATEGY. When an organization chooses a **multidomestic strategy,** it means that competition in each country is handled independently of industry competition in other countries. Thus, the MNC is present in many countries, but it encourages marketing, advertising, and product design to be modified and adapted to the specific needs of each country.[31] Many companies reject the idea of a single global market. They have found that the French do not drink orange juice for breakfast, that laundry detergent is used to wash dishes in parts of Mexico, and that people in the Middle East prefer toothpaste that tastes spicy. Parker Pen launched a single international ad campaign and reduced pen styles from 500 to 100, causing a strategic disaster. New pens and advertising campaigns have now been developed for each market.[32] Du Pont produces customized herbicides for problems with weeds that are unique to countries such as Brazil and Japan. Avon found that its door-to-door sales strategy would not work in Japan and thus customized a soft-sell approach.[33]

STRATEGIC PLANNING

Intense global competition has increased MNCs' requirement for strategic planning. Management must systematically assess political risks and fashion overall corporate strategies with which to counter them. The strategic planning process should enable MNC affiliates to support one another and achieve economies of scale for the whole enterprise.[34] Combined top-down and bottom-up strategy making provides strategic flexibility for the MNC and insures the availability of appropriate information for making the best strategic decisions.

Multinational strategic planning is similar to the processes described in Chapters 6 and 7, although its horizon is broader. Strategic planning in most MNCs contains the elements outlined in Exhibit 21.5.[35]

ENVIRONMENTAL ANALYSIS. The first step in environmental analysis is a global screening procedure in which the firm scans the entire world and selects or rules out countries on the basis of broad criteria. A firm might establish some minimum standards in terms of population size, per capita income, political stability, or stage of industrialization essential for successful operations. Additional analysis would encompass economic, legal-political, and cultural environments within the target country or region.

Environmental analysis is used to target potential new markets and to determine whether to expand or contract existing marketing or production facilities. Environmental analysis also provides valuable guidance for deciding whether exporting, licensing, a joint venture, or a wholly owned subsidiary would be the best approach in a specific country. Political instability and competitive intensity, for example, might indicate that exporting is preferable to building a new plant.

INTERNAL ANALYSIS The second requirement for strategic planning is to look inward and evaluate strengths and weaknesses of the organization itself. This analysis should consider the multinational corporation as a complete entity and extend to individual divisions and affiliates. Internal analysis appraises the quality of the firm's products, production capability and efficiency, management competence, financial resources, and managers' commitment to international operations.

OVERALL STRATEGY DEVELOPMENT. The next step is to decide on an overall mission and strategy. The organization can consider its own strengths as well as international opportunities. This decision pertains to overall opportunities and risks and may extend to a portfolio of business opportunities as well as the generic approaches of growth, retrenchment, globalization, or multidomestic strategies.

Exhibit 21.5
Multinational Strategic Planning Process

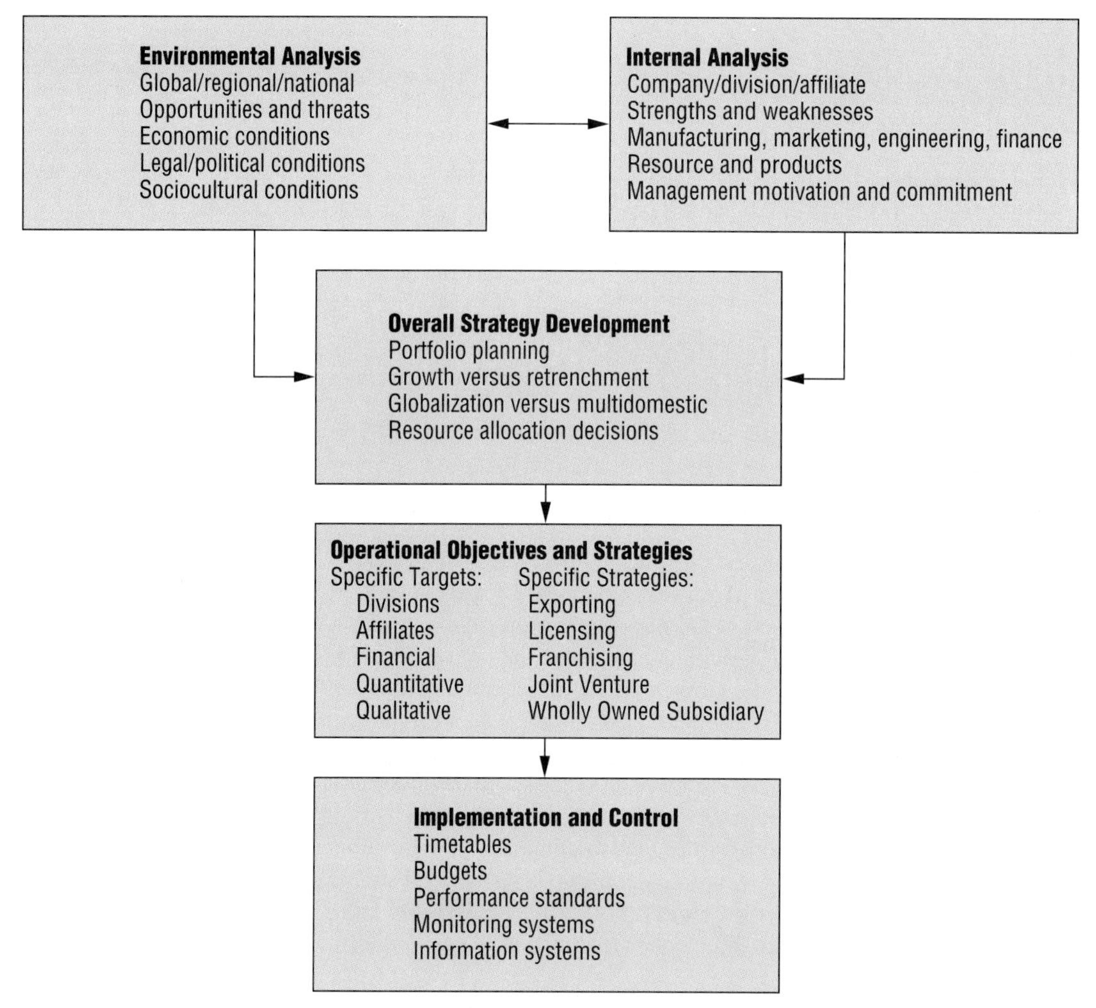

Operational Objectives and Strategies. The next step is to focus in on strategies that can be operationalized. This step involves setting objectives for each MNC affiliate and making decisions on whether to export, license, or directly invest in other countries. The operational statement of objectives will include expected financial targets, such as rate of return on assets or sales, or the expected year-to-year rate of growth. Specific targets may also be qualitative, such as to establish goodwill in a new country. PepsiCo did this in China by distributing cases of Pepsi to officials in cities where it was to conduct business.

Based on *environmental analysis,* Alcoa tailors strategic objectives to country needs. In a highly-developed country like the United Kingdom, an Alcoa recycling center is helping change consumer preferences to aluminum beverage cans (left). In Brazil, products such as electric cable serve the increasing need for aluminum and help build the country's industrial infrastructure (right). Industrialized nations have greater demand for aluminum, but less developed nations represent new markets with increasing potential as they industrialize.

Implementation and Control. The final step is implementation and control. Specific timetables are set, courses of action defined, and resources allocated. Budgets and timetables may be drawn up for each affiliate as well as for regional organization groupings. In addition, control systems are created to monitor progress toward desired objectives. Because each affiliate is geographically distant from top management, monitoring and information systems are valuable tools for determining whether performance standards are being met.

For example, Best Western International has over 1,000 hotels located outside the United States and Canada. To maintain control, Best Western uses a 1,000-point inspection list and employs 14 full-time inspectors to check every Best Western property twice a year for cleanliness and quality. Best Western also uses a computerized reservation and control system. This helps coordinate hotels worldwide and also provides information for headquarters on each affiliate's activities.

The strategic planning process is difficult and time consuming, but many MNCs use it to enhance strategic effectiveness. Companies such as Bausch & Lomb Inc., Borden, Mobil Oil, Kellogg, Signa, Upjohn, and Chase Manhattan try to use some elements of formal planning for their international operations. Corning Glass Works has developed a formal strategy for dealing with Europe 1992 and the rest of the world.

Corning Glass • Corning's environmental and internal analysis revealed the following problems. It had 28 separate business entities scattered throughout Europe, in a business where duplication of facilities is expensive and potentially deadly. The Corning name meant little or nothing to the average European. Moreover, market presence was out of balance, with a strong position in France and England, but a weak position in West Germany. Based on its ratio analysis of sales to country gross domestic product, the $10 million sales in Germany should have been $50 million to $80 million.

EXHIBIT 21.6
International Division Structure

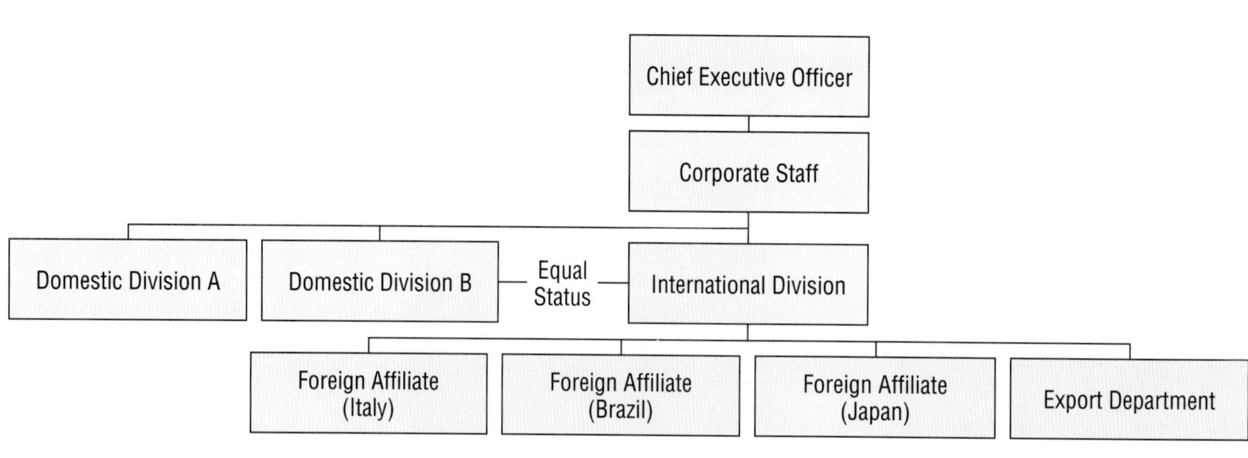

Corning executives designed a strategy to solve these problems. First, Corning reduced the number of business entities, and it attached the Corning name to most remaining operations. Next, it brought more nationals into its management ranks, bringing home 15 high-ranking Americans. These changes reduced costs, simplified operations, and boosted Corning's name. Next, it purchased a subsidiary in Germany, using it to increase sales in the German industrial market for electronic components. The German consumer market has taken longer to develop, but retail products such as Pyrex are established and growing.

The final step was implementation by reorganizing each of its major businesses, so that the French company is responsible for technical glass products for all Europe, the English company for consumer products, and so on. Corning is ready for Europe 1992 and in other world markets.[36]

MULTINATIONAL ORGANIZATION STRUCTURE

Multinational strategy is closely linked to MNCs' organization structure.[37] Organization structure typically falls into two general categories. The first is a separate *export department,* which may grow into an international division. The second is a *global management structure* that combines domestic and foreign operations. Global management structures include product-based, geographic-based, functional-based, and matrix structures.[38]

INTERNATIONAL DIVISION

Entrepreneurial companies typically start international operations by appointing an individual to coordinate exports. As the volume of foreign sales increases, the MNC establishes a separate export department. This department

EXHIBIT 21.7
Product-Based Global Organization Structure

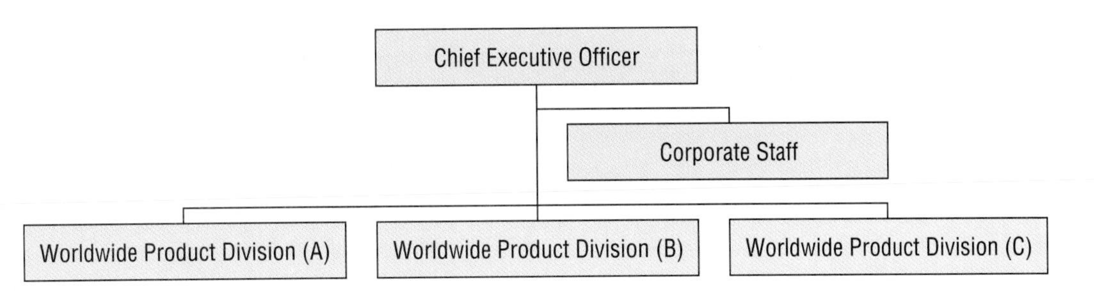

has specialists who are responsible for the export portion of the firm's manufacturing and sales. When the organization's strategy moves to foreign production or foreign licensing, more complex structures are required because a greater commitment of organizational resources and management attention is needed.

Historically, firms that have gone beyond exporting have established an international division, which is illustrated in Exhibit 21.6. An **international division** is set up alongside one or more domestic divisions and has equal status in the management hierarchy. The international division supervises and coordinates all business operations outside the company's home country. For example, Coca-Cola got started in international business around 1900 by exporting soft drinks to Cuba, Puerto Rico, and England because managers knew of potential customers there. Exports were handled by an export department, which in 1930 was replaced by a "foreign department."

international division
An organizational division that is established alongside one or more domestic divisions and has equal status in the management hierarchy.

An international division provides a clear focus for the company's strategy of increasing foreign operations. It consolidates management of overseas activities and establishes clear lines of authority between foreign affiliates and the parent company. On the negative side, however, an international division splits the company into rival segments and perpetuates the separation of domestic and foreign operations. This may cause duplication of functions and personnel and may interfere with the smooth coordination and exchange of resources among domestic and foreign divisions. To overcome these problems, some organizations have moved to one of the global management structures.

PRODUCT-BASED STRUCTURE

Many multinational companies assign managerial responsibility on the basis of worldwide products or product groups, as illustrated in Exhibit 21.7. Under a **product-based structure,** the firm sets up product divisions and each division manager plans, organizes, and controls all functions that produce and distribute its products domestically and around the world. The product approach is appropriate for firms that make products that are technologically similar within a product group but technologically distinct across groups. Moreover, this structure works well when opportunities exist for product

product-based structure
A global organization structure in which an MNC establishes product divisions whose managers plan, organize, and control all functions for producing and distributing their products at home and worldwide.

EXHIBIT 21.8
Geographic-Based Global Organization Structure

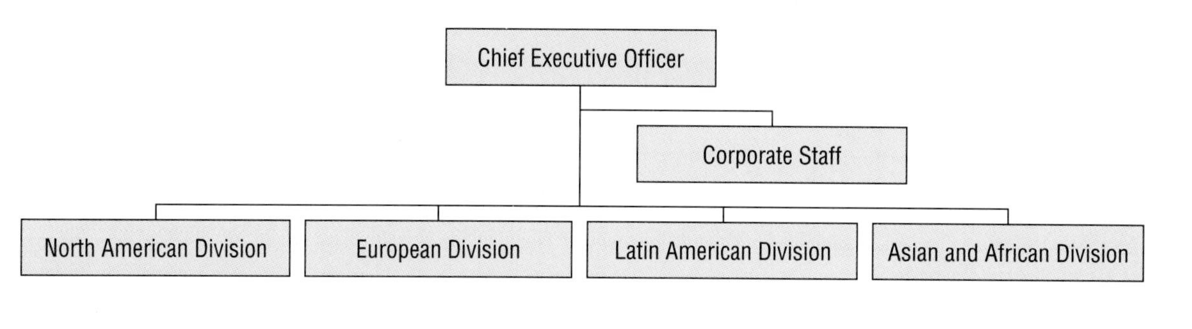

EXHIBIT 21.9
Functional-Based Global Organization Structure

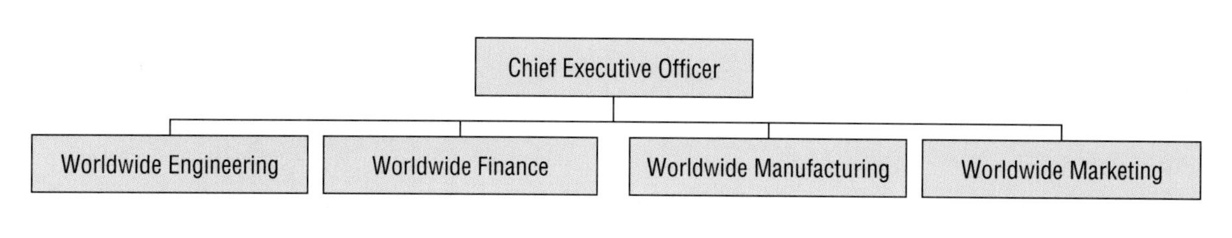

globalization strategies, that is, standard manufacturing, packaging, sourcing, and advertising throughout the world. Each product group champions global efficiency and competitiveness for its product line.[39]

GEOGRAPHIC-BASED STRUCTURE

geographic-based structure
A global organization structure in which all of an MNC's products and functions in a particular country or region report to the same division manager.

An alternative for assigning management responsibility is to group the MNC's activities by geographic region, as illustrated in Exhibit 21.8. Under a **geographic-based structure,** all products and functions in a specific country or region report to the same division manager. The geographic approach is ideal for companies with a line of products that are sensitive to local market conditions. This structure typically is used when few opportunities exist for worldwide globalization and standardization of products, but there are opportunities for locally based competitive advantages. The advantage comes from the production or sale of the product adapted to a given country or region. Organizations that produce foods, beverages, cosmetics, and other consumer staples often use the geographic structure. For example, at LSI Logic Corporation, a semiconductor company based in California, management's strategy is to divide the world into three geographical markets — Japan, the United States, and Europe — with autonomous operations in each division. This way each division is able to focus on the fierce competition in its part of the world.[40]

EXHIBIT 21.10
Global Matrix Structure

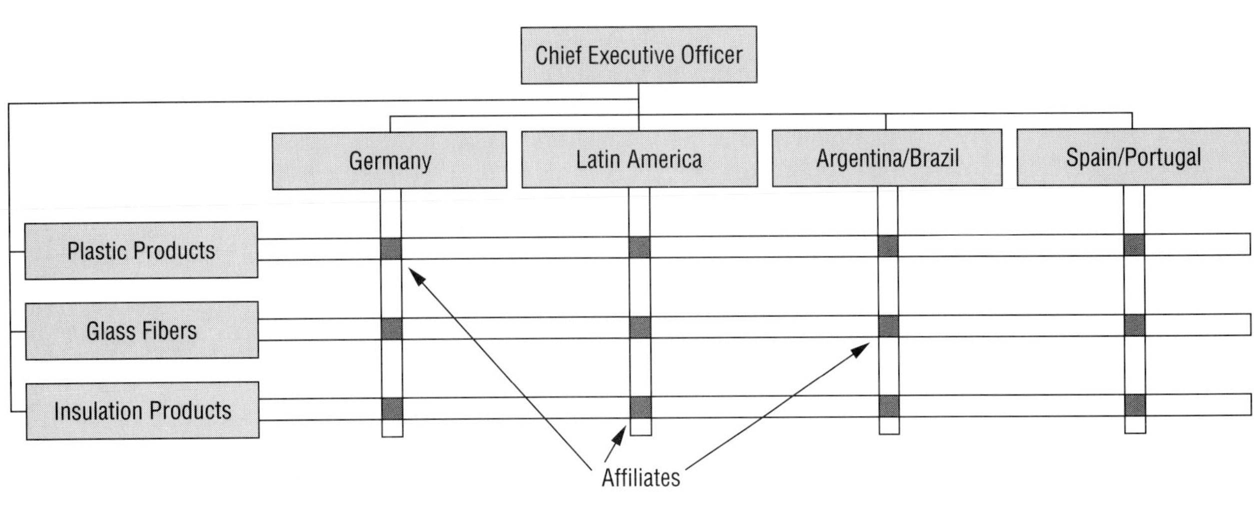

Functional-Based Structure

The worldwide **functional-based structure** divides management responsibility and authority along functional lines. A senior executive at the parent corporation is responsible for worldwide manufacturing operations. Another executive is responsible for worldwide marketing of the firm's product. Still another is in charge of engineering, finance, and so on, as illustrated in Exhibit 21.9. The functional structure has been criticized for being rigid and inflexible, but it allows an organization to build and transfer its core competencies worldwide, whether in manufacturing, marketing, or engineering. This structure overcomes duplication of resources and provides a clear chain of command. However, the international firm must develop linkages between functions so, for example, manufacturing and marketing are coordinated in each country.

functional-based structure A global organization structure in which managers' responsibility and authority are assigned along functional lines.

Matrix Structure

The problems that occur when a structure emphasizes a single dimension, such as functional or product, may be overcome with a matrix structure. Designing a multinational corporation is a difficult task, and a **matrix structure** provides a way to achieve vertical control and horizontal coordination simultaneously. Matrix structures used by MNCs are similar to those described in Chapter 9 except that geographical distances for communication and coordination are greater.

matrix structure A global organization structure that permits an MNC to achieve vertical control and horizontal coordination simultaneously.

The most typical matrix structure has two lines of authority — geographic and product — as illustrated in Exhibit 21.10. The product executives and regional executives all report to the MNC president. Managers of affiliates report to two superiors. In Exhibit 21.10, the general manager of a plant producing plastic containers in Venezuela reports to both the head of the plastic products division and the head of Latin American operations.

The matrix structure creates the potential for confusion because of the dual lines of authority, but it also encourages both product and regional concerns to be considered in production and marketing decisions. For example, Westinghouse disbanded its product division structure because of poor coordination across divisions and product managers' insensitivity to the needs of individual nations. A matrix structure was put in place that gave regional managers authority equal to product managers'. The matrix structure helped Westinghouse overcome the one-dimensional bias built into the global product structure and respond to national differences while simultaneously coordinating its worldwide businesses.[41]

The various structural approaches offer advantages and disadvantages similar to those described in Chapter 9. As companies grow and evolve in their international operations, they often reorganize into a new structure, as illustrated by Boston's Gillette Company.

Gillette Co.

• Anticipating the growth in the European market and believing it could easily advertise its products across borders, Gillette switched from 15 country-based subsidiaries to a product-line structure. The implementation of the new structure required that product-line managers be multilingual and sensitive to culture differences for their products. Consolidating a single product line under one authority has produced cost savings of up to 30 percent on production runs and advertising campaigns. This structure works well because each of Gillette's products is accepted in consumer markets around the world without major variations. However, Gillette's managers found the change a wrenching experience. They must learn foreign languages, and they have to think in terms of worldwide marketing rather than marketing in a single country.[42]

Tailoring Management Style to Cultural Values

Managers in the global arena deal with employees from different cultures. What one culture sees as participative management another sees as incompetence. Before undertaking an assignment in a foreign country, managers must understand the subtleties of culture and how to provide proper leadership, decision making, motivation, and control.[43]

Leadership

In relationship-oriented societies, leaders should take a strong personal interest in employees. In Asia, the Arab world, and Latin America, managers should use a warm, personalized approach, appearing at soccer games and birthday parties. In Latin America and China, managers should have periodic social visits with workers, inquiring about morale and health.

Leaders should be especially careful about criticizing others. To Asians, Africans, Arabs, and Latin Americans, the loss of self-respect brings dishonor to themselves and their families. Public criticism is intolerable. In a moment of exasperation, an American supervisor on an oil rig in Indonesia shouted at his timekeeper to take the next boat to shore. A mob of outraged Indonesians grabbed fire axes and went after the supervisor. He escaped and barricaded himself in his quarters. The moral: One simply never berates an Indonesian in public.

The Upjohn Company has learned to tailor *management style* to local culture as it expands its pharmaceutical business worldwide. Employees in Upjohn manufacturing plants increased productivity 20 percent when Upjohn went from a six- to a five-day week, fitting the local culture. Since 70 percent of Korean patients get their medical advice from pharmacists, highly-trained company representatives increase respect for Upjohn in the Korean health-care industry. Here, a representative provides information to a pharmacist in Seoul. Drawers in the background contain traditional (herbal) medicine.

DECISION MAKING

European managers frequently use centralized decision making. American employees might discuss a problem and give the boss a recommendation, but German managers expect the boss to issue specific instructions. East Indian and Latin American employees typically do not understand participatory decision making. Deeply ingrained social customs suggest that a supervisor's effort toward participation signifies ignorance and weakness.

In Arab and African nations, managers are expected to use consultative decision making in the extreme. Arabs prefer one-on-one consultation and make decisions in an informal and unstructured manner.

The Japanese prefer a bottom-up style of decision making, which is consistent with Far Eastern cultures that emphasize group harmony. In Taiwan, Hong Kong, and South Korea, managers are paternalistic figures who guide and help employees.

MOTIVATION

Motivation must fit the incentives within the culture. In Japan, employees are motivated to satisfy the company. A financial bonus for star performance would be humiliating for Japanese, Chinese, or Yugoslav employees. An American executive in Japan offered a holiday trip to the top salesperson, but employees were not interested. After he realized that Japanese are motivated in groups, he changed the reward to a trip for everyone if together they achieved the sales target. They did.

In Latin America, employees work for an individual rather than for a company. Among Turks and Arabs the individual is supreme, and employees are evaluated on their loyalties to superiors more so than on job performance.

CONTROL

When things go wrong, managers in foreign countries often are unable to get rid of employees who do not work out. In Europe, Mexico, and Indonesia, to hire and fire on performance seems unnaturally brutal. Workers are protected by strong labor laws and union rules. In Mexico, employees are considered permanent after a 30-day work period. British and Belgian labor laws dramatically favor employees, and in the USSR workers are guaranteed jobs. Managers must find creative ways of dealing with unproductive employees.

In foreign cultures, managers also should not control the wrong things. A Sears manager in Hong Kong insisted that employees come to work on time instead of 15 minutes late. The employees did exactly as they were told, but they also left on time instead of working into the evening as they had previously. A lot of work was left unfinished. The manager eventually told the employees to go back to their old ways. His attempt at control had a negative effect.

In another case, a Japanese manager was told to criticize an American employee's performance. It took the manager five tries before he could be direct enough to confront the American on his poor performance. Japanese managers are unused to confrontations.

Summary

This chapter has stressed the growing importance of an international perspective on management. Successful companies are preparing to expand their business overseas and to withstand domestic competition from foreign competitors. Business in the global arena involves special risks and difficulties because of complicated economic, legal-political, and sociocultural forces. Moreover, the global environment changes rapidly, as illustrated by the emergence of Europe 1992 and the shift in Eastern Europe to democratic forms of government.

Companies wishing to develop and serve foreign markets can do so in several ways. The major alternatives are exporting, licensing, franchising, and direct investment through joint ventures or wholly owned subsidiaries.

Much of the growth in international business has been carried out by large businesses called MNCs. Generic strategies for MNCs are globalization versus multidomestic strategy. Organization structure of MNCs should be selected to reflect strategic objectives. Major structures include an international division, product-based structure, geographic-based structure, functional-based structure, and matrix structure.

Finally, we discussed several key points for management success in foreign cultures. Successful leadership, decision making, motivation, and control depend on understanding the specific culture and tailoring management style to its values.

Management Solution

Black & Decker faced increasing worldwide competition in power tools. Its solution was globalization. Similar products were designed and sold in all countries, providing enormous savings in manufacturing and marketing. However, breaking up the geographical fiefdoms around the world was not easy. The number of plants was reduced from 25 to 19, and uncooperative managers were fired. Closer linkages were established with distributors and customers, who provided new product ideas for world markets. Black & Decker soon unveiled 50 new power tool models, each standardized for world production and marketing. Next, the home appliance business purchased from General Electric was streamlined for globalization. Black & Decker used its worldwide distribution system for standard toasters, can openers, and coffee makers.[44]

DISCUSSION QUESTIONS

1. Why do you think international businesses traditionally prefer to operate in industrialized "First World" countries? Discuss.
2. What considerations in recent years have led international businesses to expand their activities into less-developed Third World countries?
3. What policies or actions would you recommend to an entrepreneurial business wanting to do business in Europe?
4. What steps could a company take to avoid making product design and marketing mistakes when introducing new products into a foreign country?
5. Compare the advantages associated with the foreign market entry strategies of exporting, licensing, and wholly owned subsidiaries.
6. Should a multinational corporation operate as an integrated, worldwide business system, or would it be more effective to let each subsidiary operate autonomously?
7. Are formulation and implementation of corporate strategies likely to be different in a multinational firm than in a domestic firm? Explain.
8. Compare a product-based organization structure with a geographic-based structure. When would each be more appropriate for a multinational corporation?
9. What might managers do to avoid making mistakes concerning leadership, motivation, control, and decision making when operating in a foreign culture?
10. What is meant by the cultural values of individualism and masculinity/femininity? How might these values affect organization design and management processes?

MANAGEMENT IN PRACTICE: EXPERIENTIAL EXERCISE

A global environment requires that American managers learn to deal effectively with people in other countries. The assumption that foreign business leaders behave and negotiate in the same manner as Americans is false. How well prepared are you to live with globalization? Consider the following.

Are you guilty of:	**Definitely No**				**Definitely Yes**
1. Impatience? Do you think "Time is money" or "Let's get straight to the point"?	1	2	3	4	5
2. Having a short attention span, bad listening habits, or being uncomfortable with silence?	1	2	3	4	5
3. Being somewhat argumentative, sometimes to the point of belligerence?	1	2	3	4	5
4. Ignorance about the world beyond your borders?	1	2	3	4	5
5. Weakness in foreign languages?	1	2	3	4	5

6. Placing emphasis on short-term success?	1	2	3	4	5
7. Believing that advance preparations are less important than negotiations themselves?	1	2	3	4	5
8. Being legalistic? Of believing "A deal is a deal," regardless of changing circumstances?	1	2	3	4	5
9. Having little interest in seminars on the subject of globalization, failing to browse through libraries or magazines on international topics, not interacting with foreign students or employees?	1	2	3	4	5
Total Score	______				

If you scored less than 27, congratulations. You have the temperament and interest to do well in a global company. If you scored more than 27, it's time to consider a change. Regardless of your score, go back over each item and make a plan of action to correct deficiencies indicated by answers to any question of 4 or 5.

Source: Reprinted by permission of the publisher from Cynthia Barmun and Netasha Wolninsky, "Why Americans Fail at Overseas Negotiations," *Management Review* (October 1989), 55–57,

Cases for Analysis

NESTLÉ

A few years ago, the outlook for Nestlé, the lethargic Swiss chocolate maker, was not favorable. Unprofitable, bloated by corporate staff, and fighting a storm of controversy about marketing infant formula to Third World mothers, it was time for a change. Chief Executive Helmut Maucher has since turned Nestlé into a powerhouse. How? Great strategy. He ended the boycott of infant formula by meeting with church leaders, halting Third World consumer advertising, and created a commission to monitor Nestlé compliance. Then he drastically cut staff at headquarters and gave authority to operating units.

Maucher also emphasized marketing Nestlé's food lines — ranging from Friskies pet food to Kit Kat candy bars — around the world. The food business is capital intensive. Developing new prepared foods requires expensive research and development. To get maximum mileage from the investment, selling similar brands worldwide is the key.

Here is an example of how the strategy works. Lean Cuisine is a hit in the U.S. market. At great expense, this product was exported to Britain, where it was a success despite high shipping costs and customs duties. Manufacturing plants then were built in Britain, and Nestlé now holds 33 percent of the British market for frozen dinners. Another component of strategy is to acquire related companies, such as Carnation in the United States, the chocolate maker Rowntree in Britain, and the Italian pasta maker Buitoni. These companies provide marketing and distribution systems for foods manufactured in Nestlé's 60 plants around the globe. The acquisition of the British and Italian companies also provides a wedge to the unified market created by Europe 1992. Nestlé is using Carnation to break into the huge infant formula market in the United States with products developed elsewhere.

What's next? The Third World and the food of tomorrow, pasta. Chairman Maucher does not believe the world can be fed on beefsteak, so noodles are the pathway into less-developed countries. With his success so far, observers believe he can do it, further solidifying Nestlé as the number-one food company in the world.

Questions

1. Evaluate Nestlé's overall international strategy. Would you characterize it as primarily a globalization strategy or a multidomestic strategy? Discuss.
2. What type of international organization structure do you think Nestlé should use? Explain.

Source: Based on Shawn Tully, "Nestlé Shows How to Gobble Markets," *Fortune,* January 16, 1989, 74–78.

OK TEDI MINING LTD.

Ok Tedi (pronounced "Owk teddy") is a joint venture headed by Standard Oil Company of Indiana and Broken Hill Proprietary Company of Australia that was formed in the early 1980s to mine gold and copper in Papua New Guinea. Papua New Guinea is a newly independent "developing" country that needed advanced foreign technology for extracting its mineral ores. The Ok Tedi mine was expected to help develop a remote and poor region of the country that is rich in natural resources. The minerals were expected to be easily mined, since all that Ok Tedi had to do was bulldoze Mount Fublian, a 6,000-foot mountain of copper ore capped by a crown of gold-bearing ore. The joint venture was put together quickly during a period of rapidly rising metal prices. There was no time to conduct detailed engineering studies or to purchase insurance against political risk.

Local tribes believe that Mount Fublian is the haunt of evil spirits, and the western engineers working on the project no longer laugh at this belief. The region surrounding the mine is one of the wettest on earth; yet as soon as Ok Tedi began bringing heavy equipment up river by barge, the rains stopped for five months and equipment had to be airlifted to the mine site. When the rains returned, they did so with a vengeance, washing away roads and equipment. Just after work on a tailings dam was started, 50 million tons of soft, black mud slid down the mountainside and covered the dam site. The estimated cost of building the dam jumped from $50 million to $350 million. To start mining gold, Ok Tedi tried a chemical method of neutralizing wastes. Two accidents released untreated cyanide into nearby streams. Alarmed villagers found dead fish and crocodiles, and the government became concerned about the villagers' health.

Ok Tedi managers believe that local unhappiness has caused additional problems with the government. Because of simultaneous cost overruns and falling metal prices, the company decided to concentrate on producing gold, which has higher profit potential. The government of Papua New Guinea regarded this as a violation of its agreement with Ok Tedi, which called for both copper and gold production. The government insisted that Ok Tedi build processing lines for copper ore, hydroelectric facilities, and a permanent dam to contain the mine tailings, despite an additional cost of $800 million, which managers could not afford.

In February 1985, the government ordered the mine closed. The company can resume gold production if it agrees to proceed with the construction of the waste dam and one copper processing line.

Questions

1. Did senior managers at Ok Tedi do insufficient strategic planning, or can the project's problems be attributed to uncontrollable circumstances?
2. Discuss the interplay among economic, political, and cultural factors in this situation. Do you think that unanticipated problems such as these could occur in any less-developed country?
3. What do you think Ok Tedi's managers should do now?

Source: "Ok Tedi Can Stay Open If Foreign Owners Guarantee Completion of Copper-Gold Mine," *The Wall Street Journal,* February 13, 1985, 34; "Government of Papua New Guinea Orders Ok Tedi Mine Closed," *The Asian Wall Street Journal,* February 4, 1985, 2; "Ok Tedi Will Start Up Its Gold and Copper Mine in Papua New Guinea in May, 1984," *American Metal Markets,* January 1, 1984, 2; "Papua New Guinea Goes for the Gold," *Business Asia,* February 10, 1984, 46.

CHAPTER 22

Entrepreneurship and Small-Business Management

Chapter Outline

What Is Entrepreneurship?

Entrepreneurship and the Economy

- Definition of Small Business
- Impact of Entrepreneurial Companies

Who Are Entrepreneurs?

Starting an Entrepreneurial Firm

- New Business Idea
- The Business Plan
- Legal Form
- Financial Resources
- Tactics
- Getting Help

Managing a Growing Business

- Stages of Growth
- Planning
- Organizing
- Leading
- Controlling

Intrapreneurship in a Growing Business

Learning Objectives

After studying this chapter, you should be able to:

- Describe the importance of entrepreneurship to the U.S. economy.
- Define personality characteristics of a typical entrepreneur.
- Describe the planning necessary to undertake a new business venture.
- Discuss decision tactics and sources of help that increase chances for new business success.
- Describe the five stages of growth for an entrepreneurial company.
- Explain how the management functions of planning, organizing, leading, and controlling apply to a growing entrepreneurial company.
- Discuss how to facilitate intrapreneurship in established organizations.

Management Problem

Melinda and Robert Blanchard were unhappy with their jobs and wanted to start a business. They started one business, which they sold after it became moderately successful. Then they tried a second business, which failed. With a $2,000 tax refund from the failed business, they purchased jars for salad dressings, dessert toppings, and mustards Melinda had concocted. The products went over great with neighbors, so they set up a display at a gourmet products show in San Francisco. Thrilled, the Blanchards returned with 75 orders averaging $300 apiece. Then reality sank in. How were they going to fill all those orders? How were they going to generate additional business? What did they do next? Their nine-year-old son and six neighbors volunteered to help.[1]

If you were a neighbor, what advice would you give the Blanchards? Have they started correctly in order to have a successful business?

The Blanchards represent a significant fact in American life. Most people dream of having their own business. In the local bookstore, titles such as *Entrepreneurship Guide; Entrepreneurial Life: How to Go for it and Get it,* and *How to Run a Small Business* outnumber books on how to get rich in stocks or real estate. Americans embrace entrepreneurship. Seventy-five percent of second-year MBA students at Harvard and Stanford signed up for courses on entrepreneurship. The enormous growth of franchising gives beginners an escorted route into a new business. Some 300 incubators for new companies have sprung up. So have self-help clubs through which entrepreneurs aid one another. Computers have given big-business power to little companies. The environment in the United States is favorable for enterpreneurs because of an expanding economy and the hero status of entrepreneurial successes.[2]

Don Shipe, owner of Entrees On Trays, is an *entrepreneur.* He initiated his business venture in Fort Worth, Texas, to capitalize on the desire of many people to eat gourmet meals even though they don't have time to prepare them. Shipe got the idea after seeing a Domino's Pizza delivery car drive by. His firm delivers food to local residents from more than 48 of the finest restaurants in the Fort Worth area. Shipe recognized a viable idea and acted on it.

What Is Entrepreneurship?

entrepreneurship The process of initiating a business venture, organizing the necessary resources, and assuming the associated risks and rewards.

entrepreneur Someone who recognizes a viable idea for a business product or service and carries it out.

Entrepreneurship is the process of initiating a business venture, organizing the necessary resources, and assuming the associated risks and rewards.[3] An **entrepreneur** is someone who engages in entrepreneurship. An entrepreneur recognizes a viable idea for a business product or service and carries it out. This means finding and assembling necessary resources — money, people, machinery, location — to undertake the business venture. The entrepreneur also assumes the risks and reaps the rewards of the business. He or she assumes the financial and legal risks of ownership and receives the business's profits.

For example, Marc Friedland creates artistic, handmade invitations and stationary for such celebrities as Ivana Trump, Melanie Griffith, and Pee Wee Herman. He stumbled upon a market of clients who need extravagant invitations to attract attention and get important people to attend their parties. He took the risk and is now reaping rewards.[4] Practically everyone has heard of Frederick Smith, who started Federal Express after he got a C on a term paper spelling out the idea for a nationwide overnight parcel delivery service. He borrowed money, acquired an initial fleet of 14 French-built Falcon jets, and on the first night delivered 16 packages. After two years of losses, the company took off like a rocket, and spawned a new industry.[5]

Entrepreneurship and the Economy

Definition of Small Business

Entrepreneurial businesses typically start small and hence fall within the definition of "small business" used by the Small Business Administration (SBA). The full definition of small business is detailed and complex, taking up 37

EXHIBIT 22.1
Examples of SBA Definitions of a Small Business

Industry	A Business Is Defined as Small if:
Manufacturing	
Meat packing	Its number of employees does not exceed 500.
Household laundry equipment	Its number of employees does not exceed 1,000.
Retail	
Hardware store	Average annual receipts for its preceding 3 fiscal years do not exceed $3.5 million.
Variety store	Average annual receipts for its preceding 3 fiscal years do not exceed $5.5 million.
Grocery store	Average annual receipts for its preceding 3 fiscal years do not exceed $13.5 million.
Service	
Carpet and upholstery cleaners	Average annual receipts for its preceding 3 fiscal years do not exceed $2.5 million.
Computer programmers	Average annual receipts for its preceding 3 fiscal years do not exceed $7.0 million.
Motion picture theaters	Average annual receipts for its preceding 3 fiscal years do not exceed $14.5 million.
Miscellaneous	
Banks	It has no more than $100 million in assets.

pages of SBA regulations. Most people think of a business as small if it has fewer than 500 employees. This general definition works fine, but the SBA further refines it by industry. Exhibit 22.1 gives a few examples of how the SBA defines small business for a sample of industries. It also illustrates the types of businesses most entrepreneurs start — retail, manufacturing, and service. Additional types of new small businesses are construction, agriculture, and wholesaling.

IMPACT OF ENTREPRENEURIAL COMPANIES

The U.S. economy is fertile soil for entrepreneurs. The economy changes constantly, providing opportunities for new businesses. For example, the demand for services is booming, and 97 percent of service firms are small, with fewer than 100 employees. Since government deregulation in 1980 removed restrictions that inhibited small-business formation, more than 13,000 trucking companies have been started. Small commuter airlines were created to fill gaps when air travel was deregulated. Technological change often helps small businesses. Using new technology in the steel industry, minimills with fewer than 100 workers can underprice giant steel manufacturers. Intense global competition and rapid environmental change also give competitive advantage to flexibility and fast response rather than to huge companies with economies of scale. Large, inflexible businesses often subcontract portions of their work to entrepreneurial companies.

Understanding these environmental forces helps entrepreneurs understand the types of businesses that will survive. The impact of entrepreneurial companies on our economy is underscored by the latest figures: approximately

EXHIBIT 22.2
Statistics on New Business Start-Ups

Most Frequently Started Businesses		Businesses Most Likely to Survive		Businesses Most Likely to Grow Significantly	
Rank	**Type of Industry**	**Rank**	**Type of Industry**	**Rank**	**Type of Industry**
1	Misc. business services	1	Veterinary services	1	Commercial savings banks
2	Eating & drinking places	2	Funeral services	2	Electronic component mfr.
3	Misc. shopping goods	3	Dentists' offices	3	Paperboard container mfr.
4	Automotive repair shops	4	Commercial savings banks	4	Computer & office machine mfr.
5	Residential construction	5	Hotels & motels	5	Misc. paper product mfr.
6	Machinery & equipment wholesalers	6	Campground & trailer parks	6	Misc. plastic product mfr.
7	Real-estate operators	7	Physicians' offices	7	Basic steel mfr.
8	Misc. retail stores	8	Barbershops	8	Pharmaceutical mfr.
9	Furniture & furnishings retailers	9	Bowling & billiards places	9	Communication equipment mfr.
10	Computer & data-processing services	10	Cash grain crops	10	Partition & fixture mfr.

Source: David L. Birch, "The Truth About Start-Ups," *INC.*, January 1988, 14–15.

700,000 businesses are incorporated in the United States each year, along with another 600,000 unincorporated start-ups — about 1.3 million new enterprises.[6] By comparison, only 90,000 new incorporations took place in 1950. Also, new data show that most new businesses survive for the first three to five years.

Exhibit 22.2 shows findings from a survey of over 980,000 companies during the period 1982 to 1987. The data included 236 industries that had at least 300 start-ups. The first column indicates that the most frequently started businesses are those that are easy to start and in which people have interest. The second column suggests that businesses most likely to survive are difficult to begin because high education and assets are barriers to entry. In the third column, those most likely to grow tend to be manufacturing firms, indicating there is still a huge demand for quality manufactured products despite the growth of the service sector in the economy.[7]

The entrepreneurship miracle in the United States is an engine for job creation, innovation, and opportunities for women and minorities.

JOB CREATION. Although estimates vary, small entrepreneurial companies are responsible for the creation each year of from 40 percent to 80 percent of all new jobs in the United States.[8] Over 65 percent of all initial jobs for Americans are in a small business. Some 5 million jobs a year are created just from start-ups of new establishments.[9] The jobs created by new businesses give the United States an economic vitality that no other country can claim.

INNOVATION. Entrepreneurial companies create a disproportionate number of new products and services. Of the notable products for which small businesses can be credited are cellophane, the jet engine, and the ball-point pen. Virtually every new business represents an innovation of some sort, whether a

Chairman Richard Nicotra helps *minorities* discover the promise of entrepreneurship. His company, Everything Yogurt's, tries to make sure that at least ten percent of its franchises are owned by minority-group members. He says this results in loyalty, appreciation, and motivation from franchisees such as Vicky Frazer, shown here.

new product or service, how the product is delivered, or how it is made.[10] Entrepreneurial innovation often spurs larger companies to try new things. Lamaur Inc. created a new shampoo for permanent-waved hair. Soon, three giant competitors launched similar products. Small-business innovation keeps U.S. companies competitive, which is especially important in today's global marketplace.

WOMEN AND MINORITIES. Entrepreneurship offers opportunities for individuals who may feel blocked in established corporations. Women and minorities are also discovering the promise of entrepreneurship. Large firms such as McDonald's and Wendy's make special efforts to recruit and provide financing for minorities. Derrick and Dorian Malloy, twin brothers, believed that being poor, black, and from a housing project would not be barriers to entrepreneurship. They acquired experience working at McDonald's, and now they own two Wendy's restaurants.[11] There are nearly 4 million women business owners in the United States, and the growth is spectacular. One projection is that by the year 2000 half of all business owners will be women.

WHO ARE ENTREPRENEURS?

The heroes of American business — Ray Kroc, Spike Lee, Henry Ford, Mary Kay Ashe, Steve Jobs, Ross Perot — are almost always entrepreneurs. Entrepreneurs start with a vision. Often they are unhappy with their present job and

EXHIBIT 22.3
Characteristics of Entrepreneurs

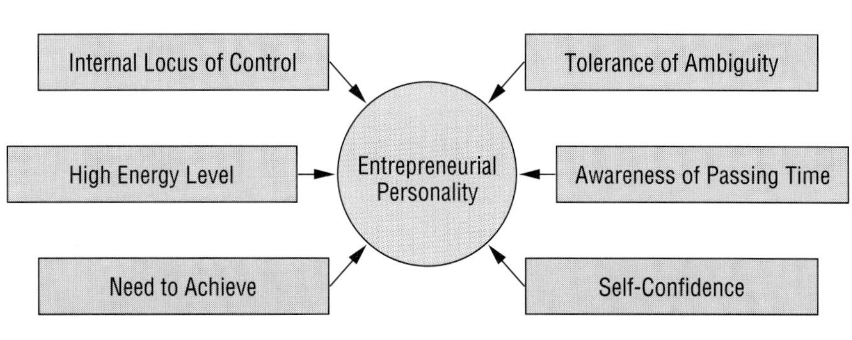

Source: Adapted from Charles R. Kuehl and Peggy A. Lambing, *Small Business: Planning and Management* (Chicago: The Dryden Press, 1990), 39.

see an opportunity to bring together the resources needed for a new venture. However, the image of entrepreneurs as bold pioneers is probably overly romantic. A survey of the CEOs of the nation's fastest-growing small firms found that these entrepreneurs could be best characterized as hardworking and practical, with great familiarity with their market and industry.[12] For example, Bobby Frost worked 22 years in the mirror-manufacturing industry before leaving his employer. He started a business to use technology that his former employer refused to try and that Frost believed would work. It did. Tom Scholl left Young & Rubicam ad agency after 13 years to set up his own agency serving clients he believed Y&R overlooked.

A number of studies have investigated the personality characteristics of entrepreneurs and how they differ from successful managers in established organizations. Some 40 traits have been identified as associated with entrepreneurship, but six have special importance.[13] These characteristics are illustrated in Exhibit 22.3.

internal locus of control The belief by individuals that their future is within their control and that other external forces will have little influence.

external locus of control The belief by individuals that their future is not within their control but rather is influenced by external forces.

LOCUS OF CONTROL. The task of starting and running a new business requires the belief that you can make things come out the way you want. The entrepreneur not only has a vision, but also must be able to plan to achieve that vision and believe it will happen. An **internal locus of control** is the belief by individuals that their future is within their control and that other external forces will have little influence. For entrepreneurs, reaching the future is seen as being in the hands of the individual. Many people, however, feel that the world is highly uncertain and that they are unable to make things come out the way they want. An **external locus of control** is the belief by individuals that their future is not within their control but rather is influenced by external forces. Entrepreneurs are individuals who are convinced they can make the difference between success and failure, hence they are motivated to take the steps needed to achieve the goal of setting up and running a new business.

ENERGY LEVEL. A business start-up requires great effort. Most entrepreneurs report struggle and hardship. They persist and work incredibly hard despite traumas and obstacles.[14] A survey of business owners reported that half worked 60 hours or more per week. Another reported that entrepreneurs

EXHIBIT 22.4
Reported Hours per Week Worked by Owners of New Businesses

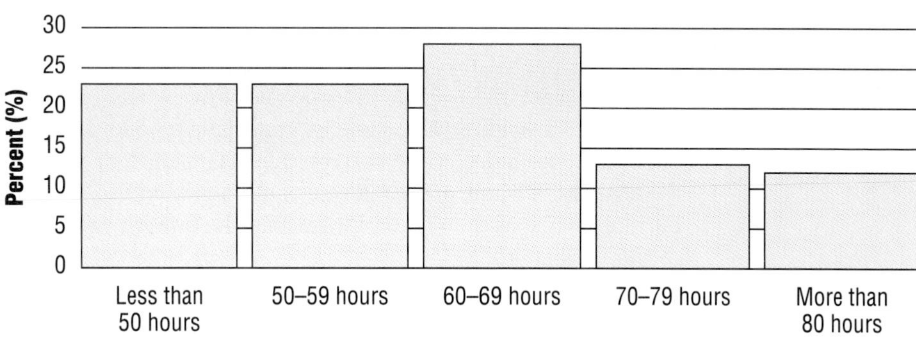

Source: National Federation of Independent Business. Reported in Mark Robichaux, "Business First, Family Second," *The Wall Street Journal*, May 12, 1989, BI.

worked long hours, but that beyond 70 hours little benefit was gained. The data in Exhibit 22.4 show findings from a survey conducted by the National Confederation of Independent Business. New business owners work long hours, with only 23 percent working fewer than 50 hours, which is close to a normal workweek for managers in established businesses.

NEED TO ACHIEVE. Another human quality closely linked to entrepreneurship is the **need to achieve,** which means that people are motivated to excel and pick situations in which success is likely.[15] People with high achievement needs like to set their own goals. They also select goals that are moderately difficult. Very easy goals present no challenge, and unrealistically difficult goals cannot be achieved. Intermediate goals are challenging and provide great satisfaction when achieved. High achievers also like to pursue goals for which they can obtain feedback about their success.

need to achieve A human quality linked to entrepreneurship in which people are motivated to excel and pick situations in which success is likely.

SELF-CONFIDENCE. People who start and run a business must act decisively. They need confidence about their ability to master the day-to-day tasks of the business. They must feel sure about their ability to win customers, handle the technical details, and keep the business moving. Entrepreneurs also have a general feeling of confidence that they can deal with anything in the future; complex, unanticipated problems can be handled as they arise.

AWARENESS OF PASSING TIME. Entrepreneurs tend to be impatient; they feel a sense of urgency. They want things to progress as if there is no tomorrow. They want things moving immediately and seldom procrastinate. Entrepreneurs "seize the moment."

TOLERANCE FOR AMBIGUITY. Many people need work situations characterized by clear structure, specific instructions, and complete information. **Tolerance for ambiguity** is the psychological characteristic that allows a person to be untroubled by disorder and uncertainty. This is an important trait, because

tolerance for ambiguity The psychological characteristic that allows a person to be untroubled by disorder and uncertainty.

MicroFridge Inc. sells this novel kitchen device, a combination refrigerator-freezer-microwave oven, that students have gone crazy over for their dorm rooms. Robert Bennett worked long hours, thought about the company constantly, persisted in raising money and finding customers— all activities requiring enormous energy and self confidence—while believing he could control the outcomes. These *characteristics of entrepreneurs* are vital in new businesses like MicroFridge to get them off the ground and established before competitors launch similar products.

few situations present more uncertainty than starting a new business. Decisions are made without clear understanding of options or certainty about which option will succeed.

Demographic Factors. In addition to the six personality traits described above, entrepreneurs often have background and demographic characteristics that distinguish them from other people. Entrepreneurs are more likely to be the first born within their families, and their parents are more likely to have been entrepreneurs. Most entrepreneurs launch their new business between the ages of 25 and 40. Children of immigrants also are more likely to be entrepreneurs, as are children for whom the father was absent for at least part of the childhood.[16]

A successful entrepreneur may have any combination of traits, and no one should be discouraged from starting a business because personality traits do not fit a specific profile. Sometime entrepreneurial traits do not emerge until a person is in the right situation. Consider Rosemary Garbett.

Los Tios • Middle-aged Rosemary Garbett is indefatigable. Running up the steps with the energy of a teenager, she is planning restaurants eight and nine of her Tex-Mex chain in Houston, called Los Tios. Her husband started the chain in 1973, but died in 1976 with only three restaurants running. Rosemary's advisors urged her to sell because she did not have the ability to run them.

From somewhere came the self-confidence and belief that she could control things. After having the head chef and top administrator quit, office employees telling her they would not work for "a housewife," and a landlord who sneered, "No way you're going to pay the rent, I'll be stuck with enchiladas," Garbett plunged into the business anyway. She had a dream of providing consistent quality, with value for the dollar. She soon learned she could manage budgets, juggle schedules, and make the tax payment on time.

Next she took control of the business by keeping the kitchen doors locked and by tallying checks against receipts each night, thereby reducing theft and pilferage. She adopted a style the opposite of her husband's, preferring to listen to employees and delegating responsibility. She soon saw the result of her long hours in her daily bank deposits.

The next challenge was to obtain financing to build additional restaurants, but the banks would not deal with an unproven entrepreneur. Ultimately, one banker was impressed with what she had done in difficult circumstances, and the rest is history. Rosemary Garbett, once a shy housewife, is now an outstanding entrepreneur.[17]

Starting an Entrepreneurial Firm

For people who decide that the benefits of entrepreneurship are worth pursuing, the first step is to start with a viable idea for the new venture. With the new idea in mind, a business plan must be drawn and decisions made about legal structure, financing, and basic tactics, such as whether to start the business from scratch and whether to pursue international opportunities from the start.

EXHIBIT 22.5
Where Entrepreneurial Ideas Come From

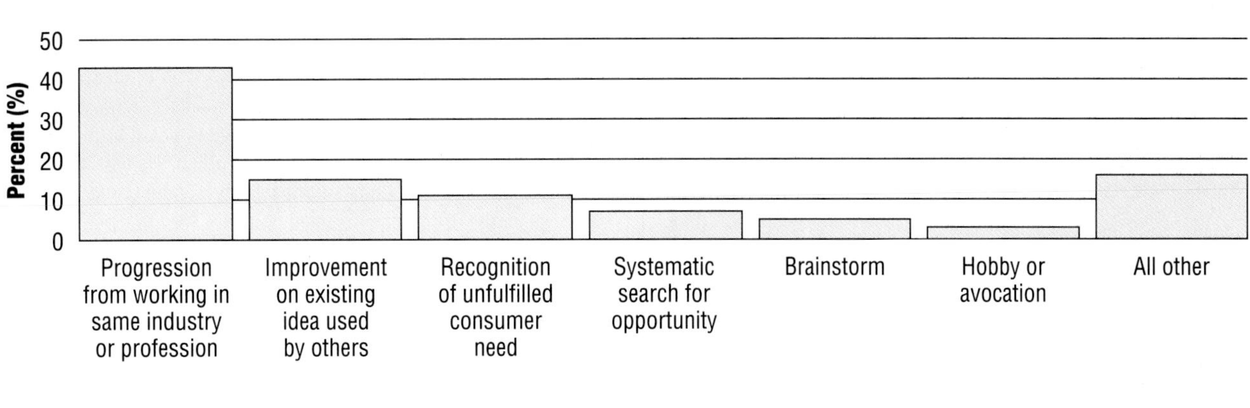

Source: Based on John Case, "The Origins of Entrepreneurship," *INC.*, June 1989, 51–63.

NEW BUSINESS IDEA

To some people, the idea for a new business is the easy part. They do not even consider entrepreneurship until they are inspired by an exciting idea. Other people decide they want to run their own business and set about looking for an idea or opportunity. Exhibit 22.5 shows the source of ideas based on a survey of 500 fast-growing firms in the United States. Note that 43 percent of business founders got the idea from work experience in the industry or profession. A few entrepreneurs believed they could do something better, and 11 percent saw an unfilled niche in the marketplace.[18]

The trick for entrepreneurs is to blend their own skills and experience with a need in the marketplace. Acting strictly on one's own skills may produce something no one wants to buy. On the other hand, finding a market niche that you do not have the ability to fill does not work either. Both personal skill and market need typically must be present. For example, single-parent and two-earner households have lead some entrepreneurs to use their skills to provide services that meet a need for people short of time. Reunion Time Inc. arranges high-school reunions, contracting to track down alumni. Moment's Notice Cuisine delivers meals to the homes of its customers, who are willing to pay 20 percent over the restaurant price.[19] Jean Griswold, a minister's wife, tried to find volunteers to help elderly parishioners. She had little luck, until she realized the old folks would pay for help. She created Special Care Inc. to hire students to do the work. It is now a $10 million business. She saw the need and had the skill to fill it.[20] The Winning Moves box describes how entrepreneur Frieda Caplan pioneered the U.S. market for exotic produce.

THE BUSINESS PLAN

Once an entrepreneur is inspired by a new-business idea, careful planning is crucial. A **business plan** is a document specifying the business details prepared by an entrepreneur in preparation for opening a new business. Planning

business plan A document specifying the business details prepared by an entrepreneur in preparation for opening a new business.

WINNING MOVES

FRIEDA'S FINEST BRINGS EXOTIC FARE TO U.S. GROCERIES

You may never have heard of the Chinese gooseberry, but thanks to California produce entrepreneur Frieda Caplan, many Americans have tasted a Kiwifruit. The transformation of the unknown Chinese gooseberry into the trendy Kiwifruit is just one of specialty produce wholesaler Caplan's many successes. What began as a new mother's part-time career has grown into a $20 million business. Frieda Caplan's story is similar to that of many entrepreneurs. She saw an opportunity in an unfilled market niche and pursued it despite standard industry practices that contradicted her plans.

Caplan launched Frieda's Finest/Produce Specialties in 1962 with a $10,000 loan from her father. In a field that was dominated by men, this native Californian broke all the rules. Traditionally, grocers have told the produce wholesalers what varieties they should carry. Caplan preferred to discover unusual produce that she thought should sell and then push it to the retailers until it did. "Our advantage has always been that we recognized that consumers were interested in what's new and unusual . . . right from the start we've never had a problem marketing an unusual produce item if we had a receptive retailer."

She began with fresh mushrooms. Now a common sight on the produce shelves, they were not readily available when Caplan set up her first stall in Los Angeles' Seventh Street Market. But Caplan's idea that cooks might prefer fresh mushrooms to canned proved to be correct. Soon her company was selling over $10,000 in fresh mushrooms each week. Caplan acquired a reputation as a wholesaler who was interested in unusual items.

In the mid-1960s Caplan's interest in the unusual brought a produce broker from New Zealand to her office. He was offering something called a Chinese gooseberry. While Caplan had never seen the fruit, she recalled that six months before a produce buyer from a major grocery chain had asked her if she knew anything about it. Caplan purchased 2,400 pounds of the hairy brown gooseberries, but sales lagged and she had to warehouse them. When she realized that the name might be hindering sales, she convinced New Zealand growers to try "Kiwifruit" instead. With the name change, sales soared. By 1967, Caplan had encouraged enough California growers to plant the fruit to establish a strong domestic industry as well.

Caplan took another risk when she began labeling her produce. Today the purple "Frieda" sticker is a symbol of quality. But in 1964, when she first proposed bagging and labeling some produce, she was told that it wouldn't work. When a major Chicago retail grocery chain agreed to carry packaged Sunchokes® (Jerusalem artichokes), sales of the item rose 600 percent in two months. Now Frieda uses labels as a method of conveying information about her unusual fruits and vegetables. The labels on squash have proven most useful. They contain descriptions and cooking instructions which have helped to popularize many new varieties.

Frieda Caplan continues to explore new items. The year 1990 will see the introduction of the Habanero Chile, the hottest chile in the world, cactus pears, coquito nuts from Chile, and jackfruit from Thailand. She is also working with Noel Vietmeyer of the National Academy of Sciences to develop Philippine winged beans for the U.S. and Canadian markets. Vietmeyer calls Caplan the entrepreneur's entrepreneur. "By breaking open markets for exotic or unusual crops she provides an important impetus for scientists and growers to explore and develop fruits and vegetables that were previously unexplored." While Frieda's Finest/Produce Specialties is now an 85-person operation, it hasn't lost its entrepreneurial spirit.

Source: Based on Dennis Rodkin, "Produce Pro," *Entrepreneur,* May, 1990, 138–144.

forces the entrepreneur to carefully think through all of the issues and problems associated with starting and developing the business. Most entrepreneurs have to borrow money, and a business plan is absolutely critical to persuading lenders and investors to participate in the business.

The details of business plans may vary, but a typical business plan contains much of the following.

Mary Anne Jackson dishes up My Own Meals to her own children from the company she started. Jackson spent 18 months studying the market, conceptualizing and developing the product, and crafting distribution and marketing strategies before introducing her line of microwave foods. The *business plan* produced a hit. Jackson blended her skills from working at Beatrice in finance and strategic planning with a need she identified in the marketplace for nutritious, microwaveable meals for kids.

- Information about the industry and market.
- Information about suppliers.
- Information about the number and types of personnel needed.
- Financial information spelling out the sources and uses of start-up funds and operating funds.
- Plans for production of the product or service, including layout of the physical plant and production schedules.
- The business's policy for extending credit to customers.
- Legal considerations, such as information about licenses, patents, taxes, and compliance with government regulations.
- Critical risks that may threaten business success.

More detailed suggestions for writing a business plan are illustrated in the Manager's Shoptalk. Many of the concepts described in earlier chapters, such as the breakeven point (Chapter 8), income statements, and balance sheets (Chapter 18) are helpful to developing the business plan.

LEGAL FORM

When entrepreneurs have founded a business, and perhaps again as it expands, they must then choose an appropriate legal structure for the company. The three basic choices are proprietorship, partnership, or corporation.

proprietorship An unincorporated business owned by an individual for profit.

PROPRIETORSHIP. A **proprietorship** is defined as an unincorporated business owned by an individual for profit. Proprietorships make up 70 percent of

This giant phone is a prop created by Jonathan Katz, Tom Field, and Dave Park, for a Federal Express TV commercial. The company, Cinnabar, is a *partnership* that builds sets and creates special effects for television programs and commercials. It was easy to start, requiring only the skills of its partners. With sales of $7 million dollars, Cinnabar employs about 75 people.

the 16 million businesses in the United States. The popularity of this form is that it is easy to start and has few legal requirements. A proprietor has total ownership and control of the company and can make all decisions without consulting anyone. However, this type of organization also has drawbacks. The owner has unlimited liability for the business, meaning that if someone sues, the owner's personal as well as business assets are at risk. Also, financing can be harder to obtain because business success rests on one person's shoulders.

partnership An unincorporated business owned by two or more people.

Partnership. A **partnership** is an unincorporated business owned by two or more people. Partnerships, like proprietorships, are relatively easy to start. Two friends may reach an agreement to start a pet store. To avoid misunderstandings and to make sure the business is well planned, it is wise to draw up and sign a formal partnership agreement with the help of an attorney. The agreement specifies how partners are to share responsibility and resources and how they will contribute their expertise. The disadvantages of partnerships are the unlimited liability of the partners and the disagreements that almost always occur between strong-minded people. Arguments often develop over such issues as money, contributions, and control. For these reasons, partnerships often dissolve within five years.

corporation An artificial entity created by the state and existing apart from its owners.

Corporation. A **corporation** is an artificial entity created by the state and existing apart from its owners. As a separate legal entity, the corporation is liable for its actions and must pay taxes on its income. Unlike other forms of ownership, the corporation has a legal life of its own; it continues to exist regardless of whether the owners live or die. And the corporation, not the owners, is sued in the case of liable. Thus continuity and limits on owners' liability are two principal advantages of forming a corporation. For example, a physician can form a corporation so that liability for malpractice will not affect his or her personal assets. The major disadvantage of the corporation is that it

MANAGER'S SHOPTALK

HINTS FOR WRITING THE BUSINESS PLAN

The Summary

- No more than three pages.
- This is the most crucial part of your plan because it must capture the reader's interest.
- What, How, Why, Where, etc. must be summarized.
- Complete this part *after* the finished business plan has been written.

The Business Description Segment

- The name of the business.
- A background of the industry with history of the company (if any) should be covered here.
- The potential of the new venture should be described clearly.
- Any unique or distinctive features of the venture should be spelled out.

The Marketing Segment

- Convince investors that sales projections and competition can be met.
- Market studies should be used and disclosed.
- Identify target market, market position, and market share.
- Evaluate *all* competition and specifically cover "why" and "how" you will be better than the competitors.
- Identity all market sources and assistance used for this segment.
- Demonstrate pricing strategy since your price must penetrate and maintain a market share to *produce profits*. Thus "lowest" price is *not* necessarily the "best" price.
- Identify your advertising plans with cost estimates to validate the proposed strategy.

The Research, Design, and Development Segment

- Cover the *extent* and *costs* involved in needed research, testing, or development.
- Explain carefully what has been accomplished *already* (prototype, lab testing, early development).
- Mention any research or technical assistance that has been provided for you.

The Manufacturing Segment

- Provide the advantages of your location (zoning, tax laws, wage rates).
- List the production needs in terms of facilities (plant, storage, office space) and equipment (machinery, furnishings, supplies).
- Describe the access to transportation (for shipping and receiving).
- Explain proximity to your suppliers.
- Mention the availability of labor in your location.
- Provide estimates of manufacturing costs — be careful, too many entrepreneurs "underestimate" their costs.

The Management Segment

- Provide resumes of all key people in the management of the venture.
- Carefully describe the legal structure of the venture (sole proprietorship, partnership, or corporation).
- Cover the added assistance (if any) of advisers, consultants, and directors.
- Provide information on how everyone is to be compensated. (How much, also.)

The Critical Risks Segment

- Discuss potential risks *before* investors point them out. Some examples include:
- Price cutting by competitors.
- Potentially unfavorable industry-wide trends.
- Design or manufacturing costs in excess of estimates.
- Sales projections not achieved.
- Product development schedule not met.
- Difficulties or long lead times encountered in the procurement of parts or raw materials.
- Larger than expected innovation and development costs to stay competitive.
- Alternative courses of action.

The Financial Segment

- Provide statements.
- Describe the needed sources for your funds and the uses you intend for the money.
- Provide a budget.
- Create stages of financing for purposes of allowing evaluation by investors as various points.

The Milestone Schedule Segment

- Provide a timetable or chart to demonstrate when each phase of the venture is to be completed. This shows the relationship of events and provides a deadline for accomplishment.

Source: Donald F. Kuratko and Ray V. Montagno, *The Entrepreneur's Guide to Venture Formation* (Center for Entrepreneurial Resources, Ball State University, 1986), 33–34. Reprinted with permission.

is expensive and complex to do the paperwork required to incorporate the business and to keep the records required by law. When proprietorships and partnerships are successful and grow large, they often incorporate to limit liability and to raise funds through the sale of stocks to investors.

Robin DeGraff, a secretary who wanted to get into business by buying the company she worked for, almost failed to obtain *debt financing.* Five banks turned down her applications, but she learned from each rejection. She upgraded her business plan and finally was allowed to borrow almost $100,000. Today she owns the firm Extol of Ohio, an insulation-fabricating company in Sandusky, Ohio.

FINANCIAL RESOURCES

A crucial concern for entrepreneurs is the financing of the business. An investment is usually required to acquire labor and raw materials and perhaps a building and equipment. The financing decision initially involves two options — whether to obtain loans that must be repaid (debt financing) or whether to share ownership (equity financing). A survey of successful growth businesses asked "How much money was needed to launch the company?" Approximately one-third were started on less than $10,000, one-third needed from $10,000 to $50,000, and one-third needed more than $50,000. The primary source of this money was the entrepreneurs' own resources, but they often had to mortgage their home, borrow money from the bank, or give part of the business to a venture capitalist.[21]

debt financing Borrowing money that has to be repaid in order to start a busines.

DEBT FINANCING. Borrowing money that has to be repaid to start a business is **debt financing.** One common source of debt financing for a start-up is to borrow from family and friends. Another common source is a bank loan. Banks provide some 25 percent of all financing for small business. Sometimes entrepreneurs can obtain money from a finance company, wealthy individuals, or potential customers.

Another form of loan financing is provided by the Small Business Administration (SBA). The SBA supplies direct loans to some entrepreneurs who are unable to get bank financing because they are considered high risk. The SBA's guaranteed loan program promises to repay the bank loan if the entrepreneur defaults. Bruce Burdick owns six Computer Land franchises in Kansas City and would not have gotten started without the guaranteed loan program. The SBA is especially helpful for people without substantial assets, providing an opportunity for single parents, minority group members, and others with a good idea.

equity financing Financing that consists of funds that are invested in exchange for ownership in the company.

EQUITY FINANCING. Any money invested by owners or by those who purchase stock in a corporation are considered equity funds. **Equity financing** consists of funds that are invested in exchange for ownership in the company.

EXHIBIT 22.6
New Business Criteria Rated Essential by Venture Capitalists

Criteria	Level of Importance
Capable of sustained intense effort	64%
Thoroughly familiar with market	62
At least ten times return in 5–10 years	50
Demonstrated leadership in the past	50
Evaluates and reacts to risk well	48
Investment can be made liquid	44
Significant market growth	43
Track record relevant to venture	37
Articulates venture well	31
Proprietary protection	29

Source: From the Center for Entrepreneurial Studies, NYU Graduate School of Business, as reported in "Venture Capitalists' Criteria," *Management Review* (November 1985), 7–8.

When a corporation's stock is sold only to friends and relatives, this is called a *private stock sale.* When the stock is available for sale to the general public, it is known as a *public sale.* For new businesses, a public sale is not a viable option because the company is not yet profitable. Once the business prospers, the company can sell stock publicly, providing a large financial windfall for the owner.

A **venture capital firm** is a group of companies or individuals that invest money in new or expanding businesses for ownership and potential profits. This is a potential form of capital for businesses with high earning and growth possibilities. Venture capital firms want new businesses with an extremely high rate of return, but in return the venture capitalist will provide help, advice, and information to help the entrepreneur prosper. A venture capital firm often has tens or hundreds of millions of dollars available for investment. Venture capitalists learn to spot promising businesses. A survey of venture capital firms indicated the criteria they use to evaluate entrepreneurial firms, which are listed in Exhibit 22.6. Of the top five items ranked, four pertain to characteristics of the entrepreneur. Venture capitalists bet on the person as well as the business.

venture capital firm A group of companies or individuals that invest money in new or expanding businesses for ownership and potential profits.

TACTICS

There are several ways an aspiring entrepreneur can become a business owner. These include starting a new business from scratch, buying an existing business, or starting a franchise. In addition, an entrepreneur may want to participate in a business incubator, consider being a spin-off of a large corporation, or seek international markets from the beginning.

START A NEW BUSINESS. One of the most common ways to become an entrepreneur is to start a new business from scratch. This is exciting because the entrepreneur sees a need for a product or service that has not been filled before and then sees the idea or dream become a reality. The advantage of this approach is the ability to develop and design the business in the entrepreneur's own way. The entrepreneur is solely responsible for its success. A potential disadvantage is the long time it can take to get the business off the ground and

Mini Maid Services Inc. is a *franchise* that operates in 24 states. A team can clean a house in only 55 minutes. Buying this franchise requires a cash investment of $12,500 and working capital from $18,000 to $20,000. Franchisees receive three weeks of intensive training, management assistance, advertising support, and continuous follow-up. CEO Leone Ackerly reports annual growth of 20 percent and extremely favorable customer response.

make it profitable. The uphill battle is caused by the lack of established clientele and the many mistakes made by someone new to the business. Moreover, no matter how much planning is done, a start-up is risky; there is no guarantee that the new idea will work.

BUY AN EXISTING BUSINESS. Because of the long start-up time and many mistakes, some entrepreneurs prefer to reduce risk by purchasing an existing business. This offers the advantage of a shorter time to get started and an existing track record. Moreover, the entrepreneur may get a bargain price if the owner wishes to retire or has other family considerations. Moreover, a new business may overwhelm an entrepreneur with the amount of work to be done and procedures to be established. An established business already has filing systems, a payroll tax system, and other operating procedures. Potential disadvantages are the need to pay for goodwill that the owner believes exists and the possible existence of ill will toward the business. In addition, the company may have bad habits and procedures or outdated technology, which may be why the business is for sale.

franchising An arrangement by which the owner of a product or service allows others to purchase the right to distribute the product or service with help from the owner.

BUY A FRANCHISE. Franchising is perhaps the most rapidly growing path to entrepreneurship. Over 500,000 franchisees exist in the United States. **Franchising** is an arrangement by which the owner of a product or service allows others to purchase the right to distribute the product or service with help from the owner. The franchisee invests his or her money and owns the business, but does not have to develop a new product, create a new company, or test the market. The franchisee typically pays a flat fee plus a percentage of gross sales. Franchises exist for weight-loss clinics, beauty shops, computer stores, real estate offices, rental cars, and auto tune-up shops.[22] The powerful advantage of a franchise is that management help is provided by the owner. For example, Burger King does not want a franchisee to fail and will provide the studies necessary to find a good location. The franchisor also provides an established name and national advertising to stimulate demand for the product or service. Potential disadvantages are the lack of control that occurs when franchisors want every business managed in exactly the same way. In addition, franchises can be very expensive, running as high as several hundred thousand dollars for a McDonald's restaurant. High costs are followed with monthly payments to the franchisor that can run from 2 percent to 12 percent of sales.

PARTICIPATE IN A BUSINESS INCUBATOR. An attractive innovation for entrepreneurs who want to start a business from scratch is to join a business incubator. Most incubators are sponsored by government organizations to spark job creation and business development. The **business incubator** provides shared office space, management support services, and management advice to entrepreneurs. By sharing office space with other entrepreneurs, managers share information about local business, financial aid, and market opportunities. Although this innovation has only been in existence a few years, more than 300 incubators are available in the United States and Canada. What gives incubators an edge is the expertise of the in-house mentor, who serves as advisor, role model, and cheerleader for entrepreneurs. For Sales Technologies, an Atlanta Company that develops software, access to the professional community—law firms, banks, accounting firms—was what the entrepreneurs needed to get the business up and running. Professional connections through the incubator allowed the owners to succeed where they might otherwise have failed.[23]

business incubator An innovation that provides shared office space, management support services, and management advice to entrepreneurs.

BE A SPIN-OFF. Spin-offs are a unique form of entrepreneurial company that is associated with another organization. A **spin-off** is an independent company producing a product or service similar to that produced by the entrepreneur's former employer.[24] Spin-offs occur when entrepreneurs quit their employers with a desire to produce a similar product, or in some cases produce a related product that is purchased by the former employer. The former employer may recognize that it can profit from the idea by selling patents to the spin-off and by investing in it. Employer approval is often the basis for a spin-off, although in some cases entrepreneurs start a new business because they disagree with former employers. Disagreement usually revolves around the failure of the employer to try a new idea that the entrepreneur believes in. A frustrated employee should discuss the possibility of starting a spin-off company with the support of his or her current employer. In this way the spin-off reduces risk and has a source of management advice. The entrepreneur may also have a guaranteed customer for the spin-off's initial output.

spin-off An independent company producing a product or service similar to that produced by the entrepreneur's former employer.

SEEK INTERNATIONAL MARKETS. It may seem hard to believe, but in today's global marketplace, many new firms start out with the idea of going international immediately. Other countries often provide the best market for American-made products and services. In fact, many businesses fail because the entrepreneur thinks provincially, being unaware of overseas markets. But if the entrepreneur has patience and commitment and is willing to do simple things such as write brochures in the local language, there is an excellent chance for success. For example, Beauty Products International, a cosmetics firm, was capitalized with just $25,000 in 1987. One year later it penetrated markets in Australia, Nigeria, Greece, Japan, and several other countries, and has large deals pending in Mexico, France, and Taiwan. The owner of regional car washes in Portland, Oregon, launched his car wash system as an international business and is now selling in 71 countries and earning $100 million a year. With the rapid globalization of the U.S. economy, it makes sense for new companies to target foreign markets. They must learn about the international marketplace and take the time to build effective relationships. With a little patience, Richard Becker found that he could sell his Blue Sky soda in Japan. It worked because he was willing to try and he took the time to develop a good sense for the market.[25]

GETTING HELP

The advice given to most entrepreneurs is to find a good accountant and attorney. They can help with the financial and legal aspects of the business. For a business that is incorporated, another great source of help is a board of directors. The entrepreneur can bring together for several meetings a year people who have needed expertise. These people may be recruited from local businesses and universities or be retired executives. Major problems can be discussed with the board. The board receives a small monthly stipend, gets a chance to help a business grow, and in some cases is given part ownership.[26]

Other sources of help are available for new entrepreneurs. For example, the Small Business Administration provides a loan program, described earlier. The government also provides financial assistance for specialized needs:[27]

- Loans for disadvantaged small businesses.
- Loans for physical disasters, such as loss of property due to floods.
- Small-business energy loans for implementing specific energy measures.
- Small-business pollution-control loans to meet pollution-control requirements.

The federal government also provides assistance in exporting. The U.S. Department of Commerce publishes *A Basic Guide to Exporting*, which provides specific information on trade opportunities abroad, foreign markets, financial aid to exporters, tax advantages of exporting, and international trade exhibitions.

In addition, four major management-assistance programs are sponsored by the SBA. The *Service Corp of Retired Executives* (SCORE) provides retired experts to help new businesses. The *Active Corp of Executives* (ACE) is a program in which active executives volunteer service to small business. *Small Business Development Centers* (SBDCs) are typically located on college campuses and keep consulting staff available to provide assistance and research services. The *Small Business Institutes* (SBI) is also operated in conjunction with university business schools and provides student teams to work on planning and analysis with entrepreneurs under a professor's guidance.

MANAGING A GROWING BUSINESS

Once an entrepreneurial business is up and running, how does the owner manage it? Often the traits of self-confidence, creativity, and internal locus of control lead to financial and personal grief as the enterprise grows. A hands-on

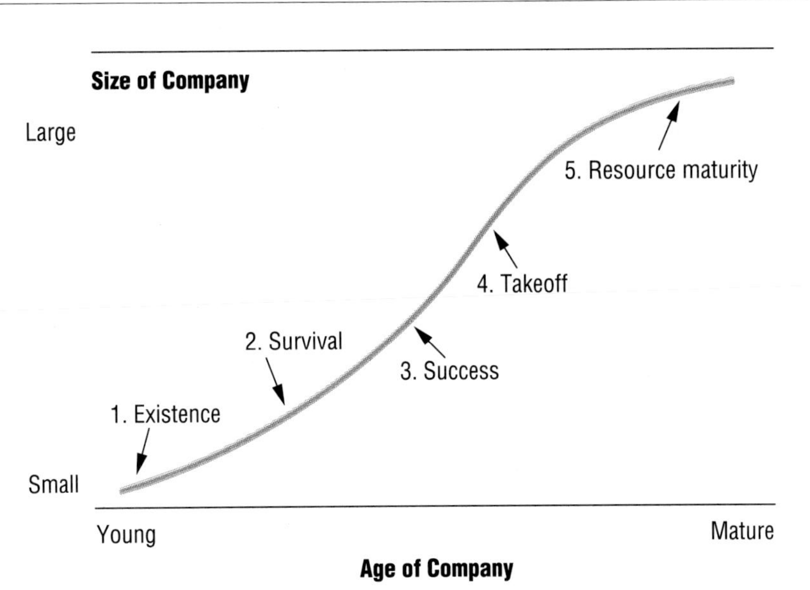

EXHIBIT 22.7
Five Stages of Growth for an Entrepreneurial Company

Source: Based on Neil C. Churchhill and Virginia L. Lewis, "The Five Stages of Small Business Growth, *Harvard Business Review* (May/June 1983), 30–50.

entrepreneur who gave birth to the organization loves perfecting every detail. But after the start-up, continued growth requires a shift in management style. Those who fail to adjust to a growing business can be the cause of the problems rather than the solution.[28] In this section we will look at the stages through which entrepreneurial companies move and then consider how managers should carry out their planning, organizing, leading, and controlling.

STAGES OF GROWTH

Entrepreneurial businesses go through distinct stages of growth. Recall from Chapter 10 that organizations go through a life cycle. During the early part of that life cycle, specific growth stages require different management skills. The five stages are illustrated in Exhibit 22.7.

1. *Existence.* In this stage the main problems are producing the product or service and obtaining customers. Key issues facing managers are: Can we get enough customers? Will we survive? Do we have enough money?
2. *Survival.* At this stage the business has demonstrated that it is a workable business entity. It is producing a product or service and has sufficient customers. Concerns here have to do with finances — generating sufficient cash flow to run the business and making sure revenues exceed expenses. The organization will grow in size and profitability during this period.
3. *Success.* At this point the company is solidly based and profitable. Systems and procedures are in place to allow the owner to slow down if desired. The owner can stay involved or consider turning the business over to professional managers.

Founder and CEO Barbara Lamont of WCCL-TV has positioned herself as the *low-cost producer* in New Orleans. She concentrates on controlling fixed and operating expenses so that her budget is one-third that of other independent TV stations. She is slowly building an audience for her bargain-basement programming and is also attracting ad revenues.

4. *Takeoff.* Here the key problem is how to grow rapidly and finance that growth. The owner must learn to delegate, and the company must find sufficient capital to invest in major growth. This is a pivotal period in an entrepreneurial company's life. Properly managed, the company can become a big business.
5. *Resource maturity.* At this stage the company has made substantial financial gains, but it may start to lose the advantages of small size, including flexibility and the entrepreneurial spirit. A company in this stage has the staff and financial resources to begin acting like a mature company with detailed planning and control systems.

Planning

In the early stage of existence, formal planning tends to be nonexistent. The primary goal is simply to remain alive. As the organization grows, formal planning is instituted generally around the success stage. The firm may adopt a strategic plan similar to those described in Chapter 6.

Recall that Porter proposed three types of strategy that can be used by entrepreneurial businesses.[29] The *differentiation strategy* means the firm competes on the basis of its ability to do things differently than other firms. For example, the Sock Shop invaded New York from Britain and was instantly successful because of its convenience and colorful products.[30] An entrepreneurial firm that uses a *low-cost strategy* builds competitive advantage by producing goods or services at the lowest possible cost. For example, a small advertising agency in Philadelphia called Harris Edward Communications received a lot of attention when it standardized prices for more than 100 different types of advertising projects. These prices were below the competition, and the one-woman firm was so successful that it rapidly grew to a 35-person agency with $18 million in billings.[31] An entrepreneurial firm using a *niche strategy* is a specialist that serves a narrow market segment. For example, Richard Melman created the restaurant called Café Ba-Ba-Reeba! in Chicago. The restaurant gained favor for its unique menu and outstanding service. Melman has created several restaurants, each with a distinctive niche.[32]

Organizing

In the first two stages of growth, the organization's structure is very informal with all employees reporting to the owner. At about stage three, success, functional managers are hired to take over duties performed by the owner. A functional organization structure will begin to evolve with managers in charge of finance, manufacturing, and marketing. During the latter stages of entrepreneurial growth, the manager must learn to delegate and decentralize authority. If the business has multiple product lines, the owner may consider creating teams or divisions responsible for each line. The organization must hire competent managers and have sufficient management talent to handle fast growth and eliminate problems caused by increasing size. The latter growth stages are also characterized by greater use of rules, procedures, and written job descriptions.

Leading

The driving force in the early stages of development is the leader's vision. This vision combined with the leader's personality shapes corporate culture. The leader can signal cultural values of service, efficiency, quality, or ethics. Often entrepreneurs do not have good people skills, but do have excellent task skills in either manufacturing or marketing. By the success stage of growth, the manager must either learn to motivate employees or bring in managers who can. Rapid takeoff is not likely to happen without employee cooperation.

For example, the president of Foreign Candy Company of Hull, Iowa, saw his company increase rapidly when he concentrated more on employee needs and less on financial growth. He made an effort to communicate with employees, conducted surveys to learn how they were feeling about the company, and found ways to involve them in decision making. His leadership style allowed the company to enter the takeoff stage with the right corporate culture and employee attitudes to sustain rapid growth.

Another reason leadership is important is that many small firms are having a hard time hiring qualified employees. Labor shortages often hurt small firms that grow rapidly. A healthy corporate culture can help attract and retain good people.[33]

Controlling

Financial control is important in each stage of the entrepreneurial firm's growth. In the initial stages, control is exercised by simple accounting records and by personal supervision. By stage three, success, operational budgets are in place and the owner should start implementing management by objectives or a similar goal-setting system. During the take-off stage, the company will need to make greater use of budgets, standard cost systems, and perhaps acquire computers to provide statistical reports. These control techniques will become more sophisticated during the resource maturity stage. However, managers should not rely exclusively on bureaucratic control as described in Chapter 17. A strong corporate culture is a form of clan control in entrepreneurial firms.

The Sock Shop, which made such a hit in New York City with its differentiated product, eventually failed due to lack of control. Although sales progressed nicely, costs zoomed out of sight. Lack of control encouraged theft and poor decision making such as putting stores in the wrong locations. Indeed, the chain expanded so fast that the debt-to-equity ratio shot up to three to one. With poor financial control systems, losses led to abrupt store closings and the loss of the retailer's good name.

Intrapreneurship in a Growing Business

As the entrepreneurial firm grows large, it has a tendency to lose its innovative spirit with the implementation of formal control systems and bureaucratic procedures. Established firms often lose innovative ideas to entrepreneurial spin-offs from frustrated employees. The way to keep innovation within the organization is to create conditions in which intrapreneurs can flourish.

3M manufactures more than 60,000 products with 87,000 employees in 52 countries and is known for its *intrapreneurship.* Post-it Notes were initiated by intrapreneur Art Frey, a 3M scientist who was frustrated when his page markers kept falling out of his church hymnal. The journey from that problem to the quality product of today involved years of hard work in an atmosphere that *encouraged action, tolerated failure,* and *rewarded innovation.* The self-stick removable notes now celebrate their tenth anniversary with more than 350 varieties for use in the home and office.

intrapreneurship The process whereby an individual sees the need for innovation and promotes it within the organization.

Intrapreneurship is the process whereby an individual sees the need for innovation and promotes it within the organization. Intrapreneurship is similar to the idea champion described in Chapter 11. The goal for managers, who at one time were innovators themselves, is to create an intrapreneurship climate. The rules below provide an approach for developing the necessary atmosphere:

1. Encourage action.
2. Use informal meetings whenever possible.
3 Tolerate failure and use it as a learning experience.
4. Be persistent in getting an idea to market.
5. Reward innovation for innovation's sake.
6. Plan the physical layout of the firm to encourage informal communication.
7. Encourage clever bootlegging of ideas.
8. Organize people into small teams for future-oriented projects.
9. Strip away rigid procedures and encourage personnel to go around red tape when they find it.
10. Reward and/or promote innovative personnel.[34]

One company that maintains the innovative spirit is Hewlett-Packard.

HEWLETT-PACKARD

• Charles House is an intrapreneur in Hewlett-Packard's innovative culture. He was assigned to develop a Federal Aviation Agency monitor similar to a television picture tube but with greatly enhanced capacity. It failed to meet government specifications, but House was more interested in other applications. He took a prototype to customers to learn whether it would solve their problems — in violation of HP's rules. He fought for money to support the technology despite no proven market. Finally, the project was ordered killed by Dave Packard himself. House's immediate superiors still supported him, how-

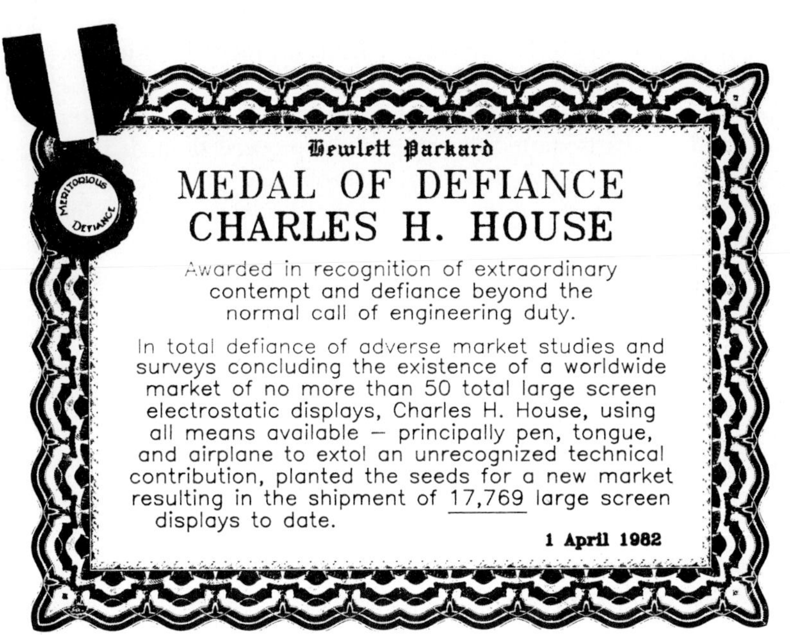

EXHIBIT 22.8
Reward for Intrapreneurship at Hewlett-Packard

Source: Reprinted with permission of Charles House.

ever, and gave him one more year. House and his team succeeded, generating $10 million in annual sales simply because House persisted and would not give up. House was awarded the Medal of Defiance, shown in Exhibit 22.8. This reward signals Hewlett-Packard's fundamental values in favor of innovation.[35]

In his book on *Entrepreneuring,* Gifford Pinchot argues that people like Charles House are needed in organizations. When spotted, intrapreneurs should be encouraged. Characteristics of intrapreneurs include: will circumvent orders aimed at stopping their dream; will do any job needed to make the project work; will work underground as long as they can; will be true to their goals; and will remember it is easier to ask for forgiveness than for permission.[36]

SUMMARY

This chapter explored entrepreneurship and small-business management. Entrepreneurs start new businesses, and entrepreneurship plays an important role in the economy by stimulating job creation, innovation, and opportunities for minorities and women. An entrepreneurial personality includes the traits of internal locus of control, high energy level, need to achieve, tolerance for ambiguity, awareness of passing time, and self-confidence.

Starting an entrepreneurial firm requires a new business idea. At that point a comprehensive business plan should be developed and decisions made about legal structure and financing. Tactical decisions for the new venture include whether to start, buy, or franchise, whether to participate in a business incubator, whether to be a company spin-off, and whether to go international. After the business is started, it will typically proceed through five stages of growth — existence, survival, success, takeoff, and resource maturity. The management functions of planning, organizing, leading, and controlling should be tailored to each stage of growth. Finally, intrapreneurship, a variation of entrepreneurship, is a mechanism for encouraging innovation within a larger firm.

MANAGEMENT SOLUTION

Robert and Melinda Blanchard had 75 orders for Melinda's salad dressing, dessert toppings, and mustards, but they had no way to fill the orders. Six neighbors pitched in to help fill and label jars and pack them for shipping. Other neighbors offered working cash, leaving two $5,000 checks. Son Jesse, 9, became the premier jar labeler. With the first order filled, new problems arose. Corporate suppliers would not extend credit. Neither would the banks. Luckily, product quality was superb, and the Blanchard's received $45,000 in new orders from a New York gift show. The president of a local family-owned firm decided to provide supplies and help get the business going. The Blanchards put together a business plan, and with their home as security, received a $75,000 bank loan. They purchased a computer to keep track of inventory, cost, and profits. They also concentrated on quality and service. Department stores love working with them because of their energy and can-do attitude. They received $500,000 from a venture capitalist, and the company has grown to over $10 million in sales.[37]

DISCUSSION QUESTIONS

1. Dan McKinnon started an airline with one airplane. To do so required filing over 10,000 pages of manuals, ordering 50,000 luggage tags, buying more than $500 million in insurance, and spending over $300,000 to train employees. A single inspection test cost $18,000. Evaluate whether you think this is a good entrepreneurial opportunity and discuss why you think Dan McKinnon undertook it.
2. What do you think are the most important contributions of small business to our economy?
3. Why would small-business ownership have great appeal to immigrants, women, and minorities?
4. Consider the six personality characteristics of entrepreneurs. Which two traits do you think are most like managers in large companies? Which two are least like managers in large companies?
5. Why is purchasing an existing business or franchise less risky than starting a new business?

6. If you were to start a new business, would you have to search for an idea or do you already have an idea to try? Explain.
7. Many entrepreneurs say they did little planning, perhaps scratching notes on a legal pad. How is it possible for them to succeed?
8. What is the difference between debt financing and equity financing? What are common sources of each type?
9. How does an entrepreneurial firm in the existence stage differ from one in the success stage?
10. How do the management functions of organizing and controlling differ for the existence and success stages?
11. Explain the difference between entrepreneurship and intrapreneurship. Why would entrepreneurs want intrapreneurship within their companies? Would an entrepreneur's personality tend to inhibit intrapreneurship? Discuss.

MANAGEMENT IN PRACTICE: EXPERIENTIAL EXERCISE

What Is Your Entrepreneurial Quotient?

The following questions are from a test developed by John R. Braun, psychology professor at the University of Bridgeport in Connecticut, and the Northwestern Mutual Life Insurance Company, based in Milwaukee. Simply answer yes or no to each question.

1. Are you a first-generation American?
2. Were you an honor student?
3. Did you enjoy group functions in school—clubs, team sports, even double dates?
4. As a youngster, did you prefer to be alone frequently?
5. As a child, did you have a paper route, a lemonade stand, or some other small enterprise?
6. Were you a stubborn child?
7. Were you a cautious youngster, the last in the neighborhood to try diving off the highboard?
8. Do you worry about what others think of you?
9. Are you in a rut, tired of the same routine day in and day out?
10. Would you be willing to dip deeply into your "nest egg"—and possibly lose all you invested—to go it alone?
11. If your new business should fail, would you get to work immediately on another?
12. Are you an optimist?

Answers:

1. Yes = 1, No = minus 1.
2. Yes = minus 4, No = 4.
3. Yes = minus 1, No = 1.
4. Yes = 1, No = minus 1.
5. Yes = 2, No = minus 2.
6. Yes = 1, No = minus 1.
7. Yes = minus 4, No = 4. If you were a particularly daring child, add another 4 points.
8. Yes = minus 1, No = 1.
9. Yes = 2, No = minus 2.
10. Yes = 2, No = minus 2.
11. Yes = 4, No = minus 4.
12. Yes = 2, No = minus 2.

Now calculate your total score. If you tallied 20 or more points, you have a strong entrepreneurial quotient. The score of 0 to 19 suggests that you have entrepreneurial possibilities. If you scored between 0 and minus 10, your chance of successfully starting an entrepreneurial business is marginal. A score below minus 11 suggests you are not the entrepreneurial type.

Go back over each question, thinking about changes you might make to become more or less entrepreneurial, depending on your career interests.

Source: Peter Lohr, "Should You Be in Business for Yourself?" *Readers Digest*, July 1989, 49–52.

Cases for Analysis

T. J. CINNAMONS

Ted and Joyce Rice started their business as a sideline. During a long vacation, they decided they would like to start a part-time business that would supplement their income. They were more interested in early retirement than a new career. They weighed many possibilities, finally deciding to sell cinnamon rolls. They believed that with showmanship they could make a go of it.

Joyce experimented at home until she developed a tasty recipe. They bought a custom-made trailer fitted as a mobile bakery and were soon selling rolls at cattle shows and state fairs. The response was incredibly positive.

They opened a permanent bakery in a Kansas City mall between two escalators. Ted wanted to catch shoppers coming and going. They put a glass roof on the bakery so shoppers could see the rolls being made.

They also noticed their T. J. Cinnamons bakery being observed by "a lot of people with yellow pads and stopwatches." They believed their idea was going to be copied quickly. They decided to team up with two businessmen and sell franchises for the bakery. To keep sales increasing in each store, a bakery menu of 50 items was developed.

At this point, their part-time business has grown into 200 gourmet bakeries with total sales of $56 million.

Questions

1. To what extent was this start-up typical of entrepreneurial companies?
2. Evaluate the Rices' decision to franchise their business concept.
3. In what stage of growth is T. J. Cinnamons now? Explain.

Source: Based on Michael Barrier, "Rolling in Dough," *Nation's Business*, February 1990, 15–17.

MR. BUILD INTERNATIONAL

Skip Kelley began his home remodeling business, Kustom House Company, with a Skill saw and a pick-up truck. For the first seven years, Kelley ran the business out of his basement and then converted an old railroad station into a showroom. The company, north of Boston, had gross sales of more than $330,000 after ten years.

Mr. Build International, a franchising system for home remodelers, approached Kelley about a deal. If he bought a franchise, Mr. Build offered advantages, including a brand name; a professional reputation; discount prices on materials; guaranteed work to customers; training in accounting, sales and marketing; national advertising; and a chance to be part of the biggest organization in the remodeling industry. The cost was $7,900 for a franchise fee, a monthly royalty of 6 percent of sales, and $300 a month for national advertising.

Kelley attended the training seminars and found the classes did not teach him anything new, but reminded him of everything he had forgotten to implement. Mr. Build provided him with a weekly time table, order forms, new stationery, letters for direct-mail advertising, accounting procedures, and the like. Emotionally, though, the changes were not easy. Changing Kustom House to Mr. Build meant giving up everything he had worked for. Kustom House had been his idea, his business, his life. When it changed to Mr. Build, Kelley lost part of himself.

Initial results were promising. Marketing costs dropped from 8 percent to 4.5 percent of sales while revenues jumped in the first year to $500,000. The size of jobs increased also, resulting in greater profits.

One unexpected result was that Mr. Kelley became a business manager rather than a craftsman. Instead of pounding nails, he subcontracted the work to other craftspeople. Because he learned to delegate responsibility, he found time for himself and his family. He has time for lunch, and for the first time in ten years went on a vacation.

Kelley now has concerns about the franchise. The promise of being part of a large organization with thousands of franchises, national advertising, and national recognition has not been realized. The parent corporation lost $3.3 million. Only 500 franchises exist. The name was changed to Mr. Build Total Property Services to include specialty contractors such as plumbing, landscaping, and heating and air conditioning to try to increase business.

Questions

1. Compare Mr. Kelley's management style before and after he purchased the franchise. Is this change consistent with changes in the stages of growth of a small company?
2. Identify the risks and rewards of buying into a franchise that is not fully established.

Source: Based on Curtis Hartman, "The Conversion of Skip Kelley," *INC.*, February 1984, 41–48.

Video Case

Moscow McDonald's

Imagine yourself standing in the waiting line to the Pushkin Square McDonald's restaurant in Moscow. First you notice that the line extends over 500 yards, eclipsing the procession of visitors to Lenin's tomb. Perhaps you wonder how Lenin would react to the site of the golden arches within walking distance of the Kremlin. Would he be outraged that a beacon of capitalism and freedom of choice would shine across the globe from the capital of communism? Could he have ever imagined that an icon of free enterprise would transfer innovative agricultural technology, effective management training and development, and philosophies of product quality and customer service to the receptive arms of his comrades? You may also wonder if Ray Kroc, the founder of McDonald's, ever imagined that his golden arches would serve as a gateway in Moscow to Western technology and management principles.

As you approach the largest McDonald's in the world, you may wonder if the anxious and hungry Soviets, who wait in line for 45 minutes to spend about one-fourth of a day's pay for a Big Mac, appreciate the significance of this joint venture and the factors that have led to its success.

The January 31, 1990, grand opening of McDonald's in the center of Moscow represents an important milestone for McDonald's Corporation and for the food service industry in the Soviet Union. The state-of-the-art renovated building, formerly a cafe and a cultural gathering place, seats over 700 people inside the building, has outside seating for 200, and is fully accessible to the handicapped. It currently employs over 1,000 people, the largest McDonald's crew in the world, and has served over 30,000 people per day. The original plans were to serve between 10,000 and 15,000 customers per day.

The Soviet Union has become the 52nd country to host the world's largest quick-service food restaurant company and the Russian language is the 28th working language in which the company operates. McDonald's Corporation, based in Oak Brook, Illinois, serves over 22 million people daily in 11,000 restaurants in 52 countries. The Soviet population of over 291 million represents the largest potential market of new customers for McDonald's.

In recent years, responding to Gorbachev's call for *perestroika* (restructuring), a number of joint ventures have been formed with the Soviet Union with varying degrees of success. The McDonald's venture is a success story for Gorbachev's policies and for the McDonald's organization because of several factors: entrepreneurial leadership with a long-term perspective, international cooperation, the transfer of innovative production technology, a focus on quality control and customer service, effective management and employee training, and a commitment to the community.

George A. Cohon, Vice Chairman of Moscow McDonald's and President and Chief Executive Officer of McDonald's Restaurants of Canada, Limited, provided the leadership for the company's successful venture. Much of the success of the venture can be attributed to Cohon's intrapreneurial spirit nurtured by the McDonald's organization. Cohon opened his first McDonald's restaurant in 1968 after leaving his hometown of Chicago to move to Canada as the McDonald's licensee for eastern Canada. In 1971, McDonald's restaurants throughout Canada were reorganized under ownership as McDonald's Restaurants of Canada, Limited; Cohon was named president. Under his leadership the organization has grown to become Canada's seventh largest employer with over 600 restaurants across the country.

Cohon's personal commitment and energy were irreplaceable during the long period of negotiations on the joint venture with the Soviet Union. Cohon's Canadian team spent over 12 years negotiating the agreement for McDonald's to enter into the Soviet market. In April 1988 McDonald's Canada completed negotiations for the largest joint venture ever made between a food company and the Soviet Union. This concluded the longest new-territory negotiations by the company since it was founded in 1955. Cohon and his Canadian team spent thousands of hours in Moscow making presentations to hundreds of senior trade officials, staff at various ministries, and countless other groups within the Soviet Union. Despite numerous setbacks and requests for endless submissions and revisions to their proposals, Cohon persisted because many Soviets appeared to genuinely want to establish closer ties with the West. According to Cohon, McDonald's negotiations "outlived three Soviet premiers."

Cohon stated that what ultimately sold the Soviets on McDonald's was the food technology it had to offer. In addition, the company's emphasis on quality, service, cleanliness, and value (QSC&V) convinced the Moscow city officials that McDonald's could work in their city. Vladimir Malyshkov, Chairman of the Board of Moscow McDonald's, stated that McDonald's "created a restaurant experience like no other in the Soviet Union. It demonstrates what can be achieved when people work together."

The historic joint venture contract provides for an initial 20 McDonald's restaurants in Moscow and a state-of-the-art food production and distribution center to supply the restaurants. The first McDonald's accepts only rubles; the next restaurant is scheduled to open at the end of 1990 and will accept only hard currency. McDonald's Canada is managing the new venture in partnership with the Food Service Administration of the Moscow City Council in a 51 to 49 percent Soviet-Canadian partnership.

Moscow McDonald's was clearly an international venture. McDonald's personnel from around the world helped prepare for the opening. Dutch agricultural consultants assisted in improving agricultural production. For example, they helped plant and harvest a variety of potato needed to make french fries that met McDonald's quality standards. Other international consultants assisted in negotiating contracts with farmers throughout the country to provide quality beef and other food supplies, including onions, lettuce, pickles, milk, flour, and butter. Once the Soviet farmers learned to trust the consultants, they became eager to learn about the new Western production technologies. Working together with Soviet farmers, McDonald's doubled the average potato yield on 60 hectares of land in 1989.

The development of the 10,000-square-meter food production and distribution center, located in the Moscow suburb of Solntsevo, was also an international effort with equipment and furnishings from Austria, Canada, Denmark, Finland, Holland, Italy, Japan, Spain, Sweden, Switzerland, Taiwan, Turkey, the United Kingdom, the United States, West Germany, and Yugoslavia. The center provides a state-of-the-art food processing environment that meets McDonald's rigid standards.

At full capacity the center will employ over 250 workers from the Soviet Union. Also, at full capacity the meat line will produce 10,000 patties per hour from locally acquired beef. Milk will be delivered in McDonald's refrigerated dairy trucks from a local Soviet farm and will be pasteurized and processed at the center. Flour, yeast, sugar, and shortening from sources in the Soviet Union will be used to produce over 14,000 buns per hour on the center's bakery line. Storage space at the center will hold 3,000 tons of potatoes and the pie line will produce 5,000 apple pies per hour, made from fruit from local farmers.

Training for the McDonald's crew and managers is essential to the customer service that the company provides. According to Bob Hissink, Vice President of Operations, Moscow McDonald's, hiring was just the beginning of assembling the largest McDonald's crew in the world. Over 25,000 applications were sorted and 5,000 of the most qualified candidates were interviewed. Finally, the 630 new members of the first Moscow McDonald's team were selected. Initial training sessions were compressed into a four-week period with four or five shifts 12 hours a day. Seasoned McDonald's staff from around the world assisted the Soviet managers with crew training. The new crew of 353 women and 277 men were trained to work in several different capacities at the restaurant and had accumulated over 15,000 hours of skills development by opening day. During restaurant operating hours, about 200 crew members at a time will be on duty.

The training requirements were more extensive for McDonald's managers. Four Soviets selected as managers of Moscow McDonald's spent more than nine months in

North American training programs that must be completed by any McDonald's manager in the world. The Soviets graduated from the Canadian Institute of Hamburgerology after completing over 1,000 hours of training. Their studies included classroom instruction, equipment maintenance techniques, and on-the-job restaurant management.

Their training also included a two-week, in-depth study program at Hamburger University, McDonald's international training center in Oak Brook, Illinois. With more than 200 other managers from around the world, they completed advanced restaurant operations studies in senior management techniques and operating procedures. The Soviet managers are qualified to manage any McDonald's restaurant in the world.

Another factor contributing to the success of the Moscow McDonald's venture was Cohon's personal and corporate commitment to the community. As the first non-Soviet citizen appointed as North American President and Director of the Soviet Children's Fund, the largest children's charity in the Soviet Union, George Cohon pledged to support the Fund. Advertising revenues from the Soviet broadcast of the 84th Annual Santa Claus parade in Toronto were donated to provide needed medical equipment and treatment for a number of Soviet children. In addition to the proceeds from an international gala celebrating the opening day of the first McDonald's restaurant in Moscow, half of the opening-day sales of the new restaurant were donated to the Soviet Children's Fund.

Other examples of McDonald's commitment to the community included "parents' night," where all the new employees of the Moscow restaurant were invited to bring their families for a meal and tour of the new restaurant. The three-hour event, a tradition wherever a McDonald's opens, helped foster an understanding for the company values among the families of its employees.

In addition, technology transfer provided important long-term benefits to the Soviet citizenry. For example, through the transfer of agricultural technology and equipment, the Soviet potato farm, Kishira, increased its yield by 100 percent. According to the Kishira Chairman, farmers from all over the Soviet Union have requested technical training in production methods to increase their crop yields. Also, since the Soviet machinery lagged 15 to 20 years behind Western technology, new machinery from Holland was used to harvest the potatoes used to make french fries. However, according to a Dutch agricultural consultant, because of the McDonald's venture it may not take the Soviets 20 years to catch up to Western production methods.

According to one Soviet official, the greatest impact of the McDonald's venture are the changes in the attitudes of the Soviet people. According to Vladimir Malyshkov, Chairman of Moscow McDonald's, the joint venture was formed to fill the needs of its citizens, but the Soviets acquired more than they first imagined from their McDonald's partners, including jobs, technology, and management expertise about motivation and organization. The impact on agricultural and production methods has established a foundation for a revolution in the food production system in the Soviet Union and has magnified the vivid imagination and entrepreneurial spirit of the Soviets.

According to Cohon, "McDonald's is a business, but also is a responsible member of the communities it serves. The joint venture with the Soviet Union should help foster cooperation between nations and a better understanding among people. When individuals from around the world work shoulder-to-shoulder, they learn to communicate, to get along, and to be part of a team. That's what we call burger diplomacy." There is a Soviet expression that says that you must eat many meals with a person before you come to know him. At 30,000 meals per day, it may not take long for the Soviets to better understand the West through its corporate ambassador, McDonald's.

Discussion Questions

1. What type of multinational corporate strategy did McDonald's choose to enter the Soviet market? What important environmental factors are evident in this case? Discuss.
2. What were the key strategy implementation factors for success of the Moscow McDonald's venture? Explain.
3. What elements of intrapreneurship contributed to the success of the venture? What is the impact of this entrepreneurial venture on the Soviet economy? Discuss.
4. How should Mr. Cohon measure the success of Moscow McDonald's? What factors should be considered when measuring the performance of the venture? Discuss.

Sources: "A Month Later, Moscow McDonald's Is Still Drawing Long and Hungry Lines," *Houston Post,* March 1, 1990; background information from McDonald's Restaurants of Canada, Ltd.; Tannenbaum, Jeffrey A., "Franchisers See a Future in East Bloc," *The Wall Street Journal,* June 5, 1990, B-1; Maney, Kevin, and Diane Rinehart, "McDonald's in Moscow Opens Today," *USA Today,* January 31, 1990, B-1; "McDonald's on the Volga," *Employment Review,* Vol. 3, No. 10, 1990; Moscow McDonald's videotape produced for Dryden Press, 1990; Wates, Oliver, "Crowds Still Gather at Lenin's Tomb But Lineups Are Longer at McDonald's," *The London Free Press,* June 9, 1990.

APPENDIX

Career Management

Everyone who works must make decisions about jobs and careers. These decisions determine whether their work lives will be satisfying, rewarding, and productive. Roger Smith started as an accounting clerk for GM, making $3,540 a year, and became chairman of General Motors. Hamish Maxwell, CEO of Phillip Morris, started as a $2,000-a-year travel agent for Thomas Cook in Paris. Michael Dickens started out as a $2.30-an-hour lifeguard for a Guest Quarters hotel; he progressed through 9 jobs over 16 years, including maintenance man and hotel general manager, and is now president of Guest Quarters.[1]

The topic of careers is important to both individuals striving to succeed in organizations and organizations that want to assist the careers of their employees. The right fit between person and career makes a difference. For example, a survey of vice-presidents found that the most important criterion for career success is love of work: "People don't get to the top unless they really love what they are doing and are willing to work very, very hard."[2] Sometimes a career causes problems. Suzanne is so obsessed with career success that she blocks out all aspects of her life other than work. She is cool, impersonal, aloof, attractive, and has easily reached the upper middle management of a major corporation, but she is really not happy.[3] Media coverage of career problems highlights career burnout and mid-career crisis.

This appendix explores the topic of career management in organizations. First we examine the scope of career issues in today's organizations. Then we discuss individuals' career planning, including steps for self-analysis and career selection, stages in a successful career, how to cope with stress, and the use of mentors. We also examine career management strategies from the organization's perspective, including career development systems, job matching, career paths, and succession planning. Finally, we will examine the special career problems of women, minorities, dual-career couples, and plateaued employees.

Changing Scope of Careers

Career versus Job

What does it mean to have a career? Most people do not want to just "go to work"; they want to "pursue a career." To some people having a career requires successful movement up the corporate ladder, marked by boosts in salary and status. To others, a career means having a profession — doctors and professors have careers, whereas secretaries and blue-collar workers have jobs. Still others will tell you that no matter what the occupation, the difference between a career and a job is about 20 hours a week — that is, people who have careers are so involved in their work that they extend beyond its requirements. For these people, it is psychological involvement in their work that defines a career.

A **job** is a specific task performed for an organization. A **career** is the sequence of jobs a person holds over a life span and the person's attitudes toward involvement in those job experiences.[4] A career has a long-term perspective and includes a series of jobs. Moreover, to understand careers, we must look not only at people's work histories or resumes but also at their attitudes toward their work. People may have more or less money or power, be professional or blue collar, and vary in the importance they place on the work in relation to the rest of their lives — yet all may have careers.

job A unit of work that a single employee is responsible for performing.

career A sequence of work-related activities and behaviors over a person's life span viewed as movement through various job experiences and the individual's attitudes toward involvement in those experiences.

A Career Development Perspective

Career development refers to employee progress or growth over time as a career unfolds. Career development is the result of two important activities: career planning and career management. *Career planning* emphasizes individual activities helpful in making career-related decisions. *Career management* focuses on organizational activities that foster employees' career growth.[5]

career development Employee progress or growth over time as a career unfolds.

A career management perspective means adopting a "big picture" of work in the total context of people's lives and recognizing that each person's work experiences add up to a career. More importantly, as long as people are employed with an organization, they have an *organizational career*, which is the sequence of work-related activities and experiences they accumulate during their time with the organization.

A Career in Management

Managers are responsible for developing people and helping manage their careers. But what about a career in management? What steps can a person take to become a manager? Recall from Chapter 1 that employees typically start out in organizations with a *technical skill* in an area such as finance, accounting, advertising, personnel, or computers. Most people get promoted into management positions after they become proficient in a technical skill area.

At some point, individuals will face the choice of whether to remain a technical specialist or take on supervisory and management responsibility. Examples of people who may choose to remain technical specialists are securities traders, lawyers, teachers, and investment bankers. More typically, at a company such as Sears, recent college graduates start out without management responsibilities. The first jobs provide basic training in store sales, merchandising, or catalog sales. Successful employees then are given the opportunity to move into first-level management positions such as sales supervisor, visual sales manager, convenience center manager, or sales support supervisor. From there a person's career may lead to higher-level positions such as regional merchandise manager, store operating manager, store manager, or general merchandise manager or operating manager for geographical area.

Those people who choose to move into management must be willing to shift away from reliance on technical skills toward reliance on *human skills.* As described in Chapter 1, human skill is the person's ability to work with and through other people and to participate effectively as a team member. This skill is demonstrated by the ability to motivate, facilitate, coordinate, lead, communicate, get along with others, and resolve conflicts. Human skills can be developed through practice, by taking courses and seminars, and by entering jobs that require superb human skills. For example, product manager or brand manager jobs at a consumer products company require excellent human skills.

Brand managers were called integrating managers in Chapter 10. Recall that an integrating manager has the responsibility to coordinate across several functions, but without formal authority. A brand manager for Fritos, Tide, or M&Ms coordinates all functions necessary to produce the product, which is a lot like running his or her own small company. The brand manager uses human skills to persuade people to perform activities necessary for product success. The brand manager also practices *conceptual skills* such as planning the advertising, retail, and trade promotions; developing a new product or packaging; and developing ways to increase sales. Companies such as Procter & Gamble, General Mills, General Foods, Ralston Purina, and M&M-Mars use brand management systems. Some 18 percent to 20 percent of graduating classes from some universities go into brand management to acquire experience useful to management careers.[6]

INDIVIDUAL CAREER PLANNING

"Work hard and you will be rewarded." When it comes to your career, the advice to work hard makes sense, but it is not enough. Although many organizations take great interest in the management of their employees' careers, you cannot expect to work hard and let the organization take care of your career. The responsibility for your career is yours alone. People who plan their careers improve their chance of having successful ones.

career planning The self-assessment, exploration of opportunities, goal setting, and other activities necessary to make informed career-related decisions.

Career planning is the self-assessment, exploration of opportunities, goal setting, and other activities necessary for making informed career-related choices. It is a crucial step in linking your personal needs and capabilities with career opportunities. Career planning involves systematic thinking and attention to short-term and long-term career goals. Career planning is an ongoing

EXHIBIT A.1
Self-Assessment Exercises

1. Write an autobiographical summary including a general scenario of your life, the people in your life, feelings about the future, the major changes that have occurred, the turning points, and the pros and cons of various career-related decisions and different jobs you have held.
2. Develop an inventory of your functional/transferable skills along such dimensions as machine or manual, athletic/outdoor/traveling, detail/follow-through, numerical/financial/accounting, influencing/persuading, leadership, developing/planning, language/reading, instructing/interpreting, serving/helping, intuitional and innovating, artistic, and so forth. Use data from your autobiographical summary.
3. Complete the Allport, Vernon, and Lindsey (AVL) *Study of Values*. The values indexed are theoretical, economic, aesthetic, social, political, and religious.[a]
4. Maintain a 24-hour dairy of what you do over one (or more) 24-hour periods.
5. Complete the *Strong-Campbell Interest Inventory* or the *Self-Directed Search*.
6. Develop a representation of your life-style (i.e., a pictorial, graphic, or written representation of your current life-style).
7. Write down your memories about the past and your feelings about the present. Stimulate visions about the future. Review themes and images in your writing for clues to your true interests and abilities.
8. Examine your life space concerns — activities, thoughts, and feelings that shape how you are relating to work, family, community, outside activities, and self.

[a]See M. London and S. A. Stumpf, *Managing Careers* (Reading, Mass.: Addison-Wesley, 1982) or your college counseling office for information on obtaining these instruments.

Source: Adapted from M. London and S. A. Stumpf, *Managing Careers* (Reading, Mass.: Addison-Wesley, 1982); J. G. Clawson, J. P. Kotter, V. A. Faux, and C. C. McArthur, *Self-Assessment and Career Development* (Englewood Cliffs, N.J.: Prentice-Hall, 1985); R. M. Bolles, *What Color Is Your Parachute?* (Berkeley, Cal.: Ten Speed Press, 1986).

activity, not something limited to high school and college graduates making an initial job choice. Because the world and organizations change, a periodic review of your career plans and progress is a must.[7]

Steps in Career Planning

There are five steps involved in career planning.

1. **Self-Assessment.** The first step is gathering data on yourself — your values, interests, skills, abilities, and preferred activities. You must learn to see yourself clearly and objectively. Consider what makes you happy in work, how closely your self-image is tied to your occupation, and rewards that are important to you. Self-assessment exercises designed to clarify abilities and interests are provided in Exhibit A.1. The questionnaire inventories for values and interests can be compared to those of people with similar interests who have successful careers. Richard K. Bernstein, a corporate vice-president for a housewares company, answered the following question as part of a self-assessment: "If you had two million dollars, how would you spend it?" Bernstein immediately pictured himself in medical school. Despite being 45 years old, he knew what he wanted and went on to study medicine and specialize in research and teaching on diabetes.[8]
2. **Explore Opportunities.** Step 2 involves gathering data on your opportunities and potential choices both within and outside your organization. Evaluate the job market and economic conditions. Also, find out about training and development opportunities offered by your organization, including chances to move into different jobs and departments. For example, when Sharon Burklund wanted to move from communications research into sales, her superiors were not interested. Thus, she used an

industry directory and called possible employers directly. Through direct contact, she discovered some opportunities. Sharon got her big break when she talked to the head of a trade paper who was about to launch a new publication and needed help in sales.

3. **Make Decisions and Set Goals.** Once you have evaluated yourself and available opportunities, you must make decisions about short-term and long-term goals. What do you want to accomplish in the next year? To which areas of the organization do you desire exposure? What skills do you want to acquire? Decide which target jobs or departments will help you get the necessary exposure and accomplish your goals. Define projects and work assignments that will provide growth opportunities.
4. **Action Planning.** This is the "how-do-I-get-there" part of career planning. It involves setting deadline dates, defining needed resources, and making plans to get around barriers. For example, when Sharon Burklund could not get the sales job in her own organization, she made action plans to find out about opportunities in other companies.
5. **Follow Up.** Once your plan is in place, periodic review and updating are needed. Take it out every six months and ask yourself, "How am I doing? Am I growing? Did I accomplish what I wanted? Are there new target jobs or work assignments that would be better for me?"

For example, Cindy Johnson, general manager of the Hotel Sofitel in Chicago, credits planning with helping her career. After deciding on the hotel business, she worked part-time in every department of the Holiday Inn while attending the University of Minnesota. She gained technical skills in everything from housekeeping and reservations to banquets and catering. After rising through the ranks of the Holiday Inn after graduation, she reassessed herself and adopted new action plans. Her plan was to move to a larger hotel and broaden her experience even more. After two years, she became director of catering for Jumer's Castle Lodge in Davenport, Iowa. At that point she had the human, technical, and conceptual skills to become a general manager and began looking for openings in other hotels. Hotel Sofitel recognized her years of experience and appointed her general manager of the Hotel Sofitel in Houston. From there she moved on to become general manager of the new hotel in Chicago, where she is responsible for the entire operation and a staff of 300. Understanding her own strengths and weaknesses, seeking opportunities, making decisions, and adopting action plans provided a valuable assist to Cindy Johnson's career.[9]

Avoiding Overplanning

Career planning should not be rigid, narrow one's options, or chart a single course at the expense of unexpected opportunities. No one can see 10 to 15 years into the future. The point of the plan is to assess yourself and chart a course consistent with your strengths.

Walter B. Wriston, who served 14 years as CEO of CitiBank, calls life a series of accidents. People must be prepared for opportunities. A big part of having a successful career is the corner you are standing on when the bus comes. If an organization is so static and employees so rigid that they know where they will be in five years, their jobs are not worth much. Every job

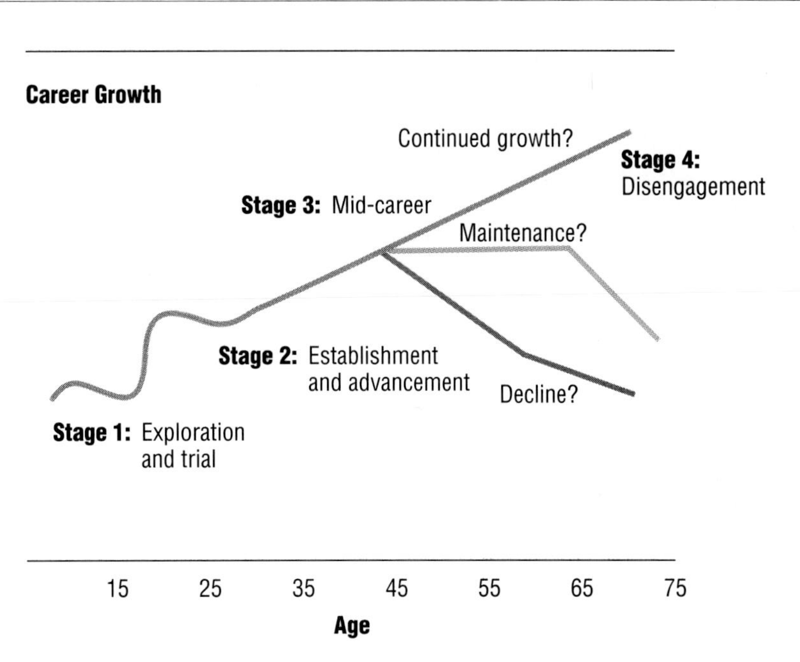

EXHIBIT A.2
Stages of Career Development

Source: Adapted from *Careers in Organizations* by Douglas Hall, p. 57. Copyright © 1976 by Scott, Foresman and Company. Used by permission.

Wriston had at the bank before becoming CEO did not exist when he joined it.[10] Likewise, the student newspaper of a large midwestern university ran the headline "Students Shouldn't Plan Their Careers" based on an interview with the university president. The president cautioned students against deciding too early on just one interest area and closing off other options.

The policy of paying careful attention to career planning is intended to do just the opposite. Career planning enables you to consider a broad range of options, identify several that will be satisfying, and choose the path that seems best at the time. Career planning provides you with self-insight to help you adjust your plans as you go along. Career planning gives you a criterion against which to evaluate unplanned opportunities so that you will know which ones to accept.

Stages of Career Development

As their careers unfold, people pass through stages that signify the course of career development over time. Most careers go through four distinct stages, each associated with different issues and tasks. Dealing successfully with these stages leads to career satisfaction and growth. The four stages are illustrated in Exhibit A.2[11]

Stage 1: Exploration and Trial. The **exploration and trial stage** usually occurs between the ages of 15 and 25. A person accepts his or her first job and may try several jobs, some part-time. People must decide whether to stay with an organization or try a job with another company. Job training,

exploration and trial stage The stage of career development during which a person accepts his or her first job and perhaps tries several jobs.

developing an image of a preferred occupation, job interviews, and early job challenges and feedback are all part of the learning process associated with this stage.

establishment and advancement stage The stage of career development during which the individual experiences progress with the organization in the form of transfers, promotions, and/or high visibility.

Stage 2: Establishment and Advancement. During the **establishment and advancement stage** — typically from age 25 to 45 — people experience progress within the organization. They are transferred and promoted, establish their worth to the organization, and become visible to those at higher levels. Many people form a specific career strategy, decide on a field of specialization, and find a mentor to support them. A person may receive offers from other organizations.

mid-career stage The stage of career development characterized by growth, maintenance, or decline.

Stage 3: Mid-Career. The **mid-career stage** often occurs from ages 45 to 65. Mid-career may move in three directions. If characterized by *growth,* the individual continues to progress, receiving promotions and increasing responsibility. The person may have a feeling of "making it" but fear stagnation and thus seek new challenges. If mid-career is characterized by *maintenance,* the person tends to remain in the same job or be transferred at the same level. The individual has job security and is loyal to the organization but stops progressing up the hierarchy. He or she enjoys professional accomplishments and may become a mentor. The person may also consider a second career. If the mid-career stage is characterized by *decline,* the individual is not valued by the organization. As a "surplus" employee, demotion is possible. Decline is characterized by insecurity, crisis, a feeling of failure, and possible early retirement.

disengagement state The stage of career development during which the person prepares for retirement and begins to disengage from both the organization and the occupation.

Stage 4: Disengagement. The **disengagement stage** comes toward the end of every career. The person prepares for retirement and begins to disengage from both the organization and the occupation. During this stage, a person may feel a need to mentor or teach others, find new interests, and prepare for retirement and a reduced role.

For example, Ellen Marram, 43, has done well in the establishment and advancement stage of her career and is now moving toward mid-career. She progressed rapidly at RJR Nabisco Inc., where she heads the $1.2 billion grocery products division. She commands 4,000 employees and has grown with the success of her product lines. Marram is on track for continued growth into mid-career and is considered a candidate for chief executive, either at Nabisco or elsewhere.[12]

Mentor Relationships

mentor A senior employee who acts as a sponsor and teacher to a younger, less experienced employee.

A **mentor** is a senior employee who acts as a sponsor and teacher to a younger, less experienced protégé.[13] The concept of mentor is derived from Greek mythology. Odysseus trusted the education of his son Telemachus to Mentor, a trusted counselor and friend. In today's organizations, mentors are senior, experienced employees who help younger, newer ones navigate the organization. A mentor relationship typically lasts from two to five years and goes through periods of initiation, cultivation, and separation.[14] The *initiation stage* is a period of six months or so during which mentor and protégé get to know each other. *Cultivation* is the major period, during which the mentor "supports,

EXHIBIT A.3
Characteristics of a Mentor Role

- Trusted counselor, guide, role model, and teacher
- Press agent/parent
- Respect with affection/caring
- Use of power on protégé behalf
- Taking protégé along when moving to new position
- Sharing of value system, personal feelings, and political strategies
- Enduring relationship

guides and counsels the young adult." During this period, the mentor-protégé relationship can be described by terms such as "master-apprentice" and "teacher-student." During the *separation* period, which lasts six months or so, the protégé may no longer want guidance and the mentor is likely to move on to other junior employees.

Mentoring has career and social implications.[15] Some of the characteristics of a mentor relationship are listed in Exhibit A.3. The relationship often goes beyond coaching and training to become a close, personal friendship that includes mutual respect and affection, helping the protégé understand organizational norms, using power on the protégé's behalf, and taking the protégé along when the mentor moves to a new position. The mentor is a friend, counselor, and source of support.

A survey of the top executives found that nearly two-thirds had a mentor at some point in their careers. The benefits of a mentoring relationship to an aspiring manager are substantial. Executives who had mentors received higher salaries, bonuses, and total compensation than did those who had not.[16] Mentors can be an important source of career development because they help new managers learn the ropes and benefit from their experience.[17]

Although it seems as though senior managers generally initiate mentoring relationships, there are steps that young managers can take to develop a mentoring relationship with experienced managers:

1. Determine who is successful and well thought of, and get to know him or her professionally and socially.
2. Seek out opportunities for exposure and visibility — committees and special projects — that will provide opportunities to work with experienced, successful people.
3. Inform experienced colleagues of your interests and goals; let your activities and successes be known to these people; seek specific feedback on your performance from experienced colleagues other than your boss.
4. Keep in mind that it may not be necessary to find a single, powerful senior manager to fulfill the mentor role. You may be able to develop mentoring relationships with a variety of experienced managers, including peers, during your career.[18]

Acquiring a mentor has made a difference in many careers. For example, Nancy Lane, executive producer at CNN News, was fortunate to have Mary Alice Williams, now NBC news anchor, as her mentor. Senator Bill Bradley saw special ability and skills in Betty Sapoch and took the time to help her gain confidence and skill. She has since become executive director of his campaigns and helps him win elections.[19]

Exhibit A.4
Sources of Management Stress

- Work overload, excessive time demands, and "rush" deadlines
- Erratic work schedules and take-home work
- Ambiguity regarding work tasks, territory, and role
- Constant change and daily variability
- Role conflict (e.g., with immediate supervisor)
- Job instability and fear of unemployment
- Negative competition (e.g., "cutthroat," "one-upmanship," "zero-sum game," and "hidden aggression")
- Type of vigilance required in work assignments
- Ongoing contact with "stress carriers" (e.g., workaholics, passive-aggressive subordinates, anxious and indecisive individuals)
- Sexual harassment
- Accelerated recognition for achievement (e.g., the Peter Principle)
- Detrimental environmental conditions of lighting, ventilation, noise, and personal privacy

Source: Based on K. R. Pelletier, *Healthy People in Unhealthy Places: Stress and Fitness at Work* (New York: Dell, 1984).

Managing Career Stress

Recall from Chapter 1 that managerial work is characterized by brevity, variety, and discontinuity. In other chapters we have seen that managers are responsible for organizing, controlling, and leading the organization. Successful managers are action oriented and responsible for high performance. Considering the nature of managerial work, stress is part of the job — indeed, many people have a stereotype of executives as harried, stressed-out, coronary-prone individuals.

stress The physiological and emotional response to demands, constraints, and opportunities that create uncertainty when important outcomes are at stake.

Stress is defined as the physiological and emotional response to demands, constraints, and opportunities that create uncertainty when important outcomes are at stake.[20] A key notion concerning stress is that people perceive the situation as taxing or as beyond their resources for responding appropriately.[21] Thus, you experience stress if your workload is too heavy for the available time, a deadline is rapidly approaching and you need more information to make a decision, or your boss is dragging his feet on approving a project important to your career. Many life events, such as a promotion, a death in the family, marriage, divorce, or a new baby, can induce stress because of the adjustments they require.[22]

Sources of Stress. There are many sources of stress for managers. Some common ones are listed in Exhibit A.4. Factors such as work overload, erratic schedules, job instability, and cutthroat competition influence the level of stress.[23] Managers also feel stress in the transition from one career stage to the next. Turbulence and uncertainty associated with the establishment and midcareer stages can be great, especially if the career is perceived as not going well or if there is no mentor relationship.

In recent years, a key source of stress for middle managers has been turbulence in the external environment, such as the threat of termination brought about by cutbacks, shifts in corporate strategy based on global competition, and mergers and acquisitions. The fear and uncertainty surrounding possible job

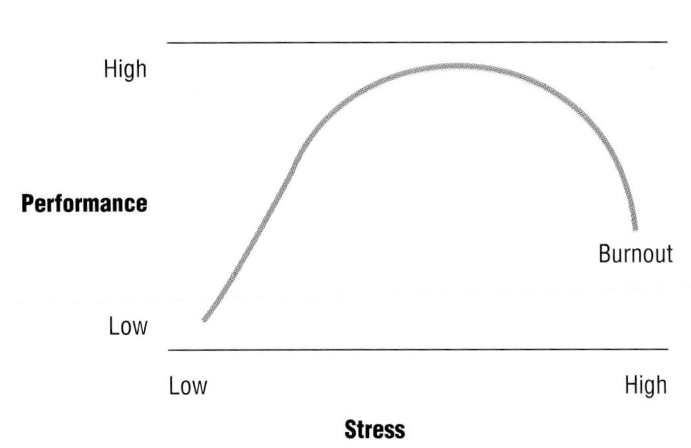

Exhibit A.5
Relationship of Stress Level to Performance

loss often create stress as great as that from actual job loss. Job insecurity and job loss due to rapid environmental changes and global competition will be major sources of manager stress in the 1990s.

One example of externally caused stress occurred at Phillips Petroleum Company. Due to a takeover attempt and a decline in the oil industry, 6,800 employees were laid off over several years in Bartlesville, Oklahoma, the company headquarters. The stress from job loss produced negative family consequences. Requests for assistance from a local shelter and counseling center for abused families shot up 69 percent. Women attending support groups for battered wives increased 41 percent. The number of children in counseling groups rose 74 percent. Emotional consequences were also felt by Phillips employees who did not lose their jobs.[24]

However, despite the negative consequences of severe stress, not all stress is bad. Hans Selye, one of the originators of stress research, observed that the only people who have no stress are dead![25] As illustrated in Exhibit A.5, a moderate amount of stress has a positive effect on performance, but extremely high stress contributes to performance decline. Extended periods of high stress can lead to **burnout,** which is the emotional exhaustion arising from overexposure to stress.[26] Moderate job stress is a natural part of managerial work. Although executives may complain of stress, few want lower-pressure jobs.

burnout The emotional exhaustion resulting from extended periods of stress.

Symptoms of Stress. How do managers manifest too much stress? Common stress systems are anxiety and tension, depression, and physical disorders such as headache, low back pain, hypertension, and gastrointestinal problems. Behavioral symptoms include difficulty sleeping, loss of creativity, compulsive eating, and alcohol or drug abuse.[27] For example, after General Motors took over Hughes Aircraft, Robert Hearsch experienced a stress nightmare. A successful manager at Hughes, he was put in charge of buying pens and pencils. He worked hard, but under the new system received constant criticism. He lost 20 pounds, his marriage hit the skids, and he suffered a minor nervous breakdown. A coworker handled his stress in another way, showing up at the office brandishing a handgun.[28]

COPING WITH STRESS. Research on effective ways of coping with managerial stress is just now emerging, but some trends have been identified. For example, ways to cope include learning to relax through meditation or regular exercise. Managers can learn to say no to unacceptable work overloads, stand up to the boss, and delegate responsibility to subordinates. Requesting resources needed to remove the cause of stress often helps.[29] Other effective behaviors are building resistance to stress through regular sleep, good eating and health habits, and discussing the stressful situation with coworkers, family, and friends.

Recent data indicate that factors under managerial control, such as performance feedback and clear job expectations, job decision latitude, and social support, are key factors in helping subordinates cope effectively with job stress.[30] In the end, however, each person must find his or her own strategies for coping with stress. For example, a survey of senior executives revealed a variety of techniques, including having other interests, maintaining a sense of humor, keeping in shape, keeping a balance in their lives, deciding not to let things bother them, and not taking matters too seriously.

ORGANIZATIONAL POLICIES FOR CAREER MANAGEMENT

Up to this point, we have been dealing with career planning from the viewpoint of the individual employee. Now we turn to career management policies and strategies that organizations can use to promote effective employee career development.

career management
Organizational activities designed to promote employees' career development.

Career management refers to organizational activities designed to promote employees' career development. These activities should function as a system designed to meet individual needs for job advancement, extension of skill, or the enhancement of human experience on the job, and to relate these needs to the future requirements of the organization.[31] A career development system is created by coordinating various personnel functions, such as recruiting, performance appraisal, and staffing, while providing a variety of special policies and programs focusing specifically on employee career development.

Exhibit A.6 illustrates the key components and functions of a career development system. The formal responsibility for career development is usually housed in the human resource management/personnel department. As with most human resource management programs, however, the success of career development depends on line managers' adoption of a career development perspective on a cooperative relationship with the human resource staff. The two dimensions in Exhibit A.6 are career planning and career management. As described earlier, career planning emphasizes individual actions, whereas career management emphasizes organizational initiatives. Moreover, as the arrows in Exhibit A.6 indicate, individual and organizational activities should jointly influence career development. Employees are more likely to do systematic career planning if the organization provides opportunities and structure for this purpose. Organizationally prescribed performance feedback and discussion of career potential are an important impetus to individual efforts. Organi-

EXHIBIT A.6
A Model for an Organizational Career Development System

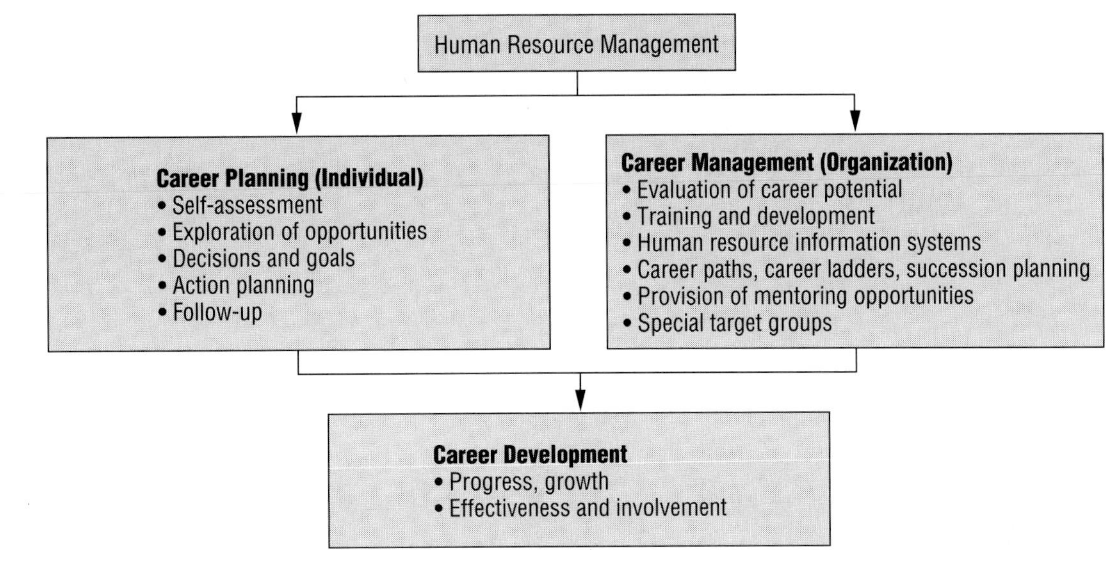

zations can provide career planning programs such as workshops and counseling, but individuals must choose to invest energy and time in action planning and follow-up if career development is to take place.

The major components of the organization's career management system are an evaluation of potential, training and development, human resource information systems, career paths, career planning programs, and providing mentoring opportunities.

Evaluation of Career Potential

A critical input into career development is the performance appraisal process described in Chapter 12. Feedback on job performance is important in all aspects of individual career planning, providing valuable data on skills and strengths and assisting employees in identifying realistic future goals.

The appraisal process also helps the organization assess future potential—the individual's probability of moving upward in the organization. Organizations may use a variety of tools to assess potential, such as commercially prepared tests and inventories, internally developed questionnaires, succession planning, or an assessment center. Often, however, it is the manager's role to determine future career potential using personal judgment. A section of the formal performance appraisal rating form can ask the manager to rate the employee's "future potential" or "promotability."

Training and Management Development

The backbone of a career management program is organizational commitment to training and employee development. *Training* programs focus on the immediately applicable, technically oriented skills required for the next level of job. *Management development* suggests a longer-term view of expanding a person's confidence and growth. Many organizations have a wide range of training and development programs that employees can attend. Some new managers attend management training programs sponsored by universities and the American Management Association to develop their human and conceptual skills.

Another important aspect of training and development is internal job moves. The most frequently used job moves for broadening and increasing an employee's potential for advancement are vertical and horizontal:

- *Vertical:* Moving up and down the organizational pyramid; job moves in this category involve changes in rank or organizational level.
- *Horizontal:* Lateral movement to a different function, division, or product line in the organization, such as from sales to marketing or from personnel to public relations.

Human Resource Information Systems

Effective career development systems depend on information. Data on organizational human resource planning and individual career planning must be available to managers and employees. These data usually come from job analysis and job matching systems.

Job Analysis. *Job analysis* was referred to in Chapter 12 as the systematic collection of information about the purpose, responsibilities, tasks, knowledge, and abilities needed for a job. Data are collected by the personnel staff through interviews with job incumbents and supervisors.

human resource inventory A data base that summarizes individuals' skills, abilities, work experiences, and career interests.

Human Resource Inventory. The **human resource inventory** is a database that summarizes individuals' skills, abilities, work experiences, and career interests. These data are made available to both managers and personnel specialists.

job matching system A method that links qualified individuals with career opportunities within the organization.

Job Matching Systems. The component for bringing together both job data and human resource interests is a **job matching system,** which links individuals with career opportunities within the organization. The job matching system brings together the human resources inventory as well as the job characteristics, descriptions, and profiles derived from the job analysis. The job matching system searches through all potentially qualified or interested employees and matches them with present or future openings.

One type of matching system developed by Gannett Company Inc. is called the Talent Tracking System. The system is a computerized job matching network managed by the corporate news staff in Arlington, Virginia, for all of the company's newspapers. Over 1,500 names have been logged into the system, and top editors from around the country use a computer to review the

EXHIBIT A.7
Career Ladder for Engineers at the Link Flight Simulation Division of The Singer Company

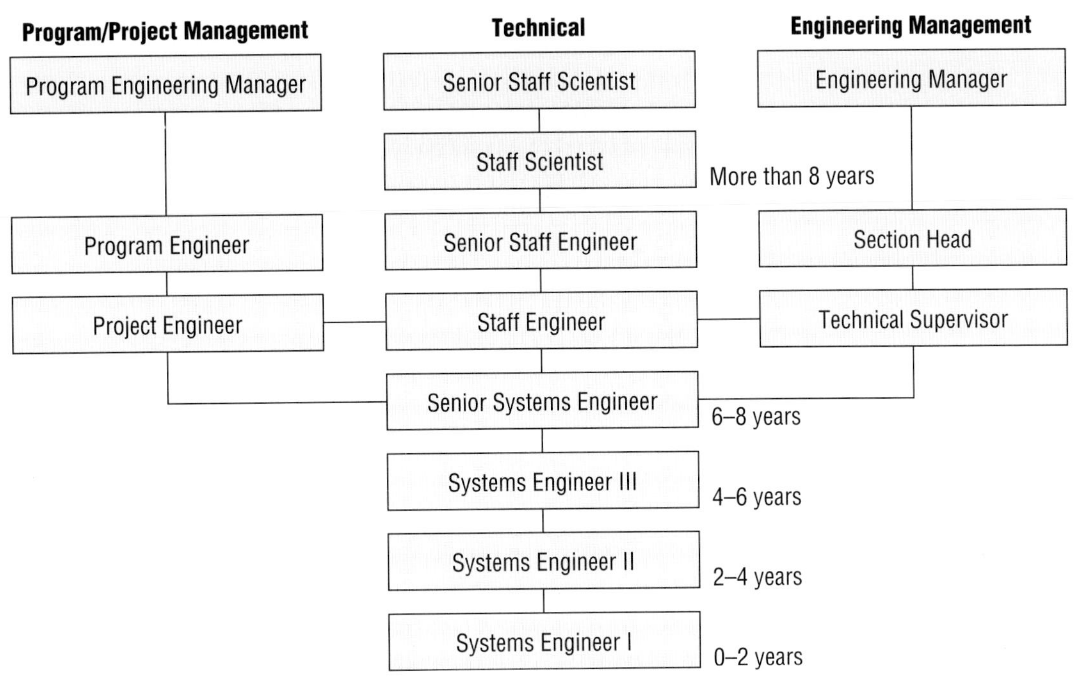

Source: Courtesy of Link Flight Simulation Division, The Singer Company.

credentials of job prospects. The system works like a giant cookie jar, with top managers able to select and recruit employees from around the Gannett system.[32]

Career Paths, Career Ladders, and Succession Planning

career path A job progression route along which an employee can advance through the organization.

Career paths are job progression routes along which employees can advance through the organization. Career paths typically are developed for specific employees, or they may be drawn up by the organization as general routes for employee advancement. They consist of a series of target jobs or functional areas that indicate future job moves appropriate for the individual's career. Career paths may include horizontal moves and an occasional downward move in order to obtain needed experience.

career ladder A formalized job progression route based on logically connected jobs.

Career ladders are formalized job progression routes based on jobs that are logically connected. Career ladders tend to be more precisely and objectively determined than career paths. Career ladders are based on data collected through job analysis and examination of personnel records showing historical patterns of employee job moves. An example of a career ladder for Link Flight Simulator Division of the Singer Company is illustrated in Exhibit A.7. This career ladder charts the normal progression for engineers. After an engineer advances through the first four stages, a decision must be made. The person can concentrate on technical challenges and remain in the staff engineering track, or he or she may decide to pursue a management track.

There are two ladders associated with management — functional management within the engineering department and program management that involves the coordination of entire projects. The decision to pursue a specific track will be based on the individual's self-assessment and interest in becoming either a staff scientist or a manager.

succession planning The process of creating a plan for moving people into higher organizational levels.

Succession planning is the process used to create a plan for moving people into the higher levels of the organization. Succession planning applies to a specific group of employees who have the development potential to become top-level managers. "Top level" usually is defined as two to four levels below the CEO. Organizations with progressive career development systems have extended succession planning for all professional and managerial positions.

Succession planning defines both present and future job requirements and determines the availability of candidates and their readiness to move into top jobs.[33] It also uses *employee resource charts* discussed in Chapter 12 to identify likely successors for each management position. This system suggests possible career paths and career ladders for a set of managers and managerial jobs. The succession planning time horizon is usually 12 to 36 months and is periodically updated. The appropriate emphasis in succession planning is on developing a pool of talent rather than selecting a "crown prince" to assume a top position.

Career Planning Programs

Career planning programs offered by the organization can take the form of career planning workshops and individual career counseling sessions. Group workshops can be conducted by personnel department staff or outside consultants. The workshops take employees through the systematic steps of individual career planning by using individual assessment exercises, holding small-group discussions, and providing information on organizational opportunities.

Individual career counseling may be provided by the personnel department, but a major part takes place during career planning discussions with supervisors. Supervisors must be trained and knowledgeable about career planning and opportunities. Career counseling requires that a manager assume the role of coach and counselor. Sometimes it is difficult to do career planning during a performance appraisal session because employees become defensive. Some organizations resolve this problem by asking supervisors to hold separate sessions — the first for performance evaluation and the second for creating a career plan.[34]

Provide Mentoring Opportunities

As we discussed earlier, mentoring provides many advantages to the career development of junior managers. Although mentoring is something that junior managers can undertake on their own, mentor relationships can be an important organizational tool for career development.

One approach organizations can use to encourage and facilitate mentoring is education.[35] Educational programs help senior managers understand mentoring and its importance in career management and help establish norms and cultural values in support of mentoring. Other changes that facilitate mentoring include adjusting the reward system to place greater emphasis on mentoring, modifying the work design, adapting performance management systems, and even introducing a formal mentoring program. In this way, senior managers can be encouraged and rewarded for mentoring and may even be assigned junior managers to support and assist. Organizational efforts to facilitate mentoring are important because informally developed, one-to-one relationships may not be available to all promising junior managers. One outcome of mentoring programs is to foster multiple developmental relationships between junior managers and more experienced senior people. Companies that have formal mentor systems include Ortho Pharmaceutical Corporation, Eastman Kodak Company, Pacific Bell, and Clairol.

Small entrepreneurial companies often have a difficult time developing managers because they cannot afford formal training programs. General Alum & Chemical Corporation invented their own in-house mentoring system to solve this problem. To socialize new managers and train them into the corporate culture, senior executives were assigned to a handful of developing managers. The junior managers had great potential but lacked experience. The mentor relationship enabled these young men and women to learn about subtle aspects of management, including human and conceptual skills. Formally assigning mentors made sure that all potential managers had this positive experience.[36]

Special Career Management Problems

Because of current social, economic, and legal pressures, organizational career management strategies may be focused on the unique needs of special target groups. Concerns about career development for women and minorities is a direct outgrowth of equal employment opportunity legislation. Although women and minorities are advancing within corporations, they are still underrepresented in middle- and top-level management.[37] The increasing number of dual-career couples has pressured organizations to solve the problems unique to this group of employees. Further, as organizations face increasing competition and are forced to streamline management structures, many management employees find they have plateaued because there are fewer opportunities to move up the hierarchy.

Women and Minorities

Because of common issues faced by women and minorities, recommended career development management strategies often consider these two target groups together. Organizations must confront issues related to assimilating and developing these two groups. For example, because minorities and women have only recently entered management ranks, they may have difficulty developing the social networking and mentoring helpful to career development.

Recall from Chapter 1 that work-force diversity is a major issue facing organizations in the 1990s. White males will make up a smaller proportion of the management work force in future years.

Women. Issues that women face include balancing multiple roles of career and family and sexual harassment.[38] A recent survey found that nearly one out of three women who received MBAs from the nation's top business schools ten years ago have left the managerial work force.[39] Because many of these women left to devote more time to their families, some companies are experimenting with innovative programs that respond to family pressures and offer more flexibility for both men and women.

The pressures are so great that some women must make difficult choices. Linda Searl, a managing partner in her own architectural firm, made the decision not to marry. She was afraid of being distracted and wanted to be able to focus completely on her job. She has succeeded but feels some regret about having no husband and children. Sarah Nesper Brewster, a divorced mother with two daughters, has made a conscious decision not to travel. This has hurt her career progress, but she feels it is essential for her children. She feels guilty because she is always pulled between her children and her job.[40]

Because only women have babies and often are responsible for child care, some female managers and professionals are leaving the fast track for what has been called the *mommy track*. These women devote time to raising a young family rather than devoting all their energies to career advancement. Some women dislike the notion of a mommy track, believing it identifies female employees as separate and unequal and may permanently derail women's careers, making them second-class citizens. Taking time to raise a family as well as work may confirm prejudices of male executives. So-called mommy trackers are less likely to be considered for promotion to highly responsible positions.[41]

Many companies encourage women to take time for their children because it allows the company to retain valued employees. These employees may be given extended leave, flexible scheduling, or opportunities for job sharing and telecommuting that enable them to raise a family. These managers come back to regular work when the children are older. For example, Mellon Bank allows women to work flexible hours, work at home, and engage in job sharing. At Peat Marwick Mitchell, women can opt for a lighter client load and a less than 40-hour workweek for two to three years. Procter & Gamble gives women eight weeks' paid maternity leave and six months' unpaid child care leave to either parent.[42]

Minorities. Despite a large and growing black middle class, the progress of blacks in U.S. corporations has been disappointing to blacks and whites alike. One survey of 400 large companies in 1986 found that less than 9 percent of all managers were minorities. One discouraged manager said, "The U.S. is in a global trade war and we're trying to fight without all our troops."[43]

The biggest barrier facing minorities, especially black managers, is advancement into upper management. Minorities must learn the "difficult, lonely and threatening way to navigate in a basically white environment." This environment is characterized by white executives' discomfort with nonwhites as well as the tendency to promote managers with backgrounds similar to their own. A recent survey of black managers revealed that many of them perceived the organizational climate for black managers in their organization as indifferent, patronizing, and reluctant to accept blacks. On the positive side, some organizational climates were seen as encouraging, supportive, and trusting.[44] Although the percentage is small, some blacks have triumphed in corporate careers, becoming successful managers in major companies.

Recommendations for addressing the unique needs of women and minorities include providing them with access to information, allowing nontraditional career moves, enforcing affirmative action, and providing better assessment and coaching skills for potential managers. Organizations should pay particular attention to assisting women and minorities in identifying and examining career paths and the requirements for advancement. Training programs should emphasize the job skills women and minorities need as well as the unique problems they face when advancing within the corporation.

Dual-Career Couples

The growing number of dual-career couples has prompted organizational career management programs to focus on the corporate problems posed by this expanding group of employees.[45] Traditionally it was assumed that if a wife worked, her own career took second place to her husband's. Today women are increasingly likely to place equal importance on their career involvement and are no longer expected to fit their careers to their husbands' career needs. As a result, more couples face the issue of having both a committed personal relationship and careers that are central to each spouse.

Dual-career relationships involve trade-offs, and both employees and managers are realizing that most people cannot "have it all"—happy marriage, children, charming home, many friends, and intense commitment to a career. Organizations are concerned because the pressures experienced by dual-career couples may harm productivity or morale and can pose difficulties when recruiting new employees or transferring current employees to new locations.[46]

There is a strong link between the career problems facing women and the problems of dual-career couples. Women MBAs who left the work force did so because of work-family conflicts. In the final analysis, in most families the responsibility for balancing work and family responsibilities falls disproportionately on the woman.[47]

These issues are difficult to resolve. Suppose, for example, that you have just been promoted to manager of market development for a fast-growing computer software firm in Chicago. Your spouse is offered a big promotion that requires a move to Dallas. What criteria would you use to decide whether to give up your new position or make your spouse pass up the promotion? Will you consider a commuting relationship? If so, for how long?

Ted Koppel resolved a dual-career dilemma by taking ten months off from his newscasting job at ABC to be at home with the children so that his wife, Grace Anne, could start law school at Georgetown University. Many lesser known couples make similar compromises. Others take turns promoting each other's careers. For example, Peter Briggs left a challenging job as data-processing manager in a Minneapolis bank to move with his family to Burlington, Vermont, so that his wife, Barbara Grant, could become an assistant professor of medicine at the University of Vermont. Following his spouse to a new city was an excruciating experience, because he had no job to look forward to. He found a new job at a bank in Burlington, but at a lower level.[48] Some couples end up taking jobs in separate locations and having a "commuter marriage." Robert and Marina Whitman live in Princeton, New Jersey. He commutes to Pittsburgh three days a week, where he teaches English at the University of Pittsburgh, and she commutes to New York and Detroit, where she is chief economist and vice-president for General Motors. Whenever they are in the same city, they always have dinner together.[49]

Organizations try to help dual-career couples in order to maintain productivity, alleviate stress, and retain competent people. Career management programs directed at these people include flexible work schedules, transfer policies, career planning assistance, and local support services such as day care for children. For example, at General Motors when one spouse is hired by the company and relocated, the other gets counseling and referral help in finding a new job. Sometimes the spouse is hired too. At Lotus Development, more than 70 percent of the married people are part of two-career families; thus, generous parental leave benefits are available.[50]

Plateaued Employees

career plateau A point in a career from which the opportunities for further promotion are scarce.

A **career plateau** is "a point in a career from which the likelihood of additional hierarchical promotion, in the judgment of the organization, is very low."[51] Due to the high value most people place on upward mobility, plateauing has come to be viewed by organizations as a problem and may lead to the employee being written off or ignored with respect to career development opportunities. As a practical matter, there is nothing inherently negative about reaching a career plateau. It is a natural consequence of the narrowing pyramid shape of organizations, and many employees experience a career plateau somewhere during mid-career.

Plateaued employees can fall into one of two categories. "Solid citizens" are plateaued employees rated as performing satisfactorily. "Deadwood" are plateaued employees whose performance has fallen below the satisfactory level.[52] Many plateaued employees are effective performers, and they should not be stereotyped as unmotivated or performing inadequately. Indeed, many companies want to keep plateaued employees and their accumulated knowledge. Many people have spent their entire careers in excellent organizations such as IBM, GE, Eastman Kodak, Westinghouse, and Hewlett-Packard, even after they had no prospect of further advancement.[53]

Many organizations anticipate a larger number of plateaued employees in the future. Fewer promotional opportunities will be available because of leaner management staffs. This may also mean that plateauing will occur earlier than in mid-career for some employees. Most managers will have plateaued employees on their staffs and will need to devote attention to developing and maintaining these people's competence.

One study found that plateaued managers performed better when they and their bosses agreed on clear performance objectives and when the managers received feedback on specific tasks and overall performance. Other factors that helped plateaued employees' performances were whether they knew the basis on which their performances were being evaluated and whether they had challenging, satisfying, and clearly defined jobs that were important to the company.[54]

Exhibit A.8
Techniques for Renewing Plateaued Managers

Source: Based on J. M. Bardwick, "Plateauing and Productivity," *Sloan Management Review* (Spring 1983), 67–73.

- Rotate people laterally among existing jobs.
- Use lateral or downward transfers to other departments.
- Increase job scope to require new knowledge and skills.
- Create temporary work units to solve specific problems.
- Provide training in current technical or administrative skills.
- Encourage development of mentoring, counseling, and advisory skills.
- Reward supplemental contributions such as mentoring and community or government relations.
- Use individuals as internal consultants in different parts of the organization.

A number of career management techniques organizations can use to help plateaued employees are listed in Exhibit A.8. One is to enhance job challenge and task accomplishment opportunities. This can be done through transfers or by changing the scope of the present job. Other techniques include job changes, training programs that provide mentoring and career counseling, and managerial and technical updating.[55]

Focus Career Development on Career Stages

To make career development more effective, the organization can focus on employee career stages. Rather than provide one program for all employees, each program can match the needs of specific employee groups. Examples of career management strategies associated with each of the four career stages described earlier are illustrated in Exhibit A.9.

In the exploration/trial stage, one concern is how to deal with *reality shock*, which is the upsetting experience and stress brought about by unmet expectations of organizational newcomers.[56] Reality shock can lead to early career dissatisfaction and high turnover. Thus, one career management strategy is to give new recruits *realistic job previews* that present job interviewees with the full picture of the organization without selling or "sugar coating" job opportunities. Other strategies during the early career stage are to provide varied job activities, opportunities for self-exploration, and opportunities to gain organizational knowledge.

For employees in the establishment/advancement stage, career management should focus on helping them gain competence in a specialty and develop personal creativity and innovation skills. People at this level should be encouraged to gain familiarity with different organizational areas, possibly through horizontal transfers. They should also be given an opportunity to develop and display their skills and expertise for potential mentor relationships and promotability.

For employees in mid-career, the organization should provide **mid-career renewal strategies,** which are designed to provide upward mobility for those who merit it while maximizing the contributions of plateaued employees who continue to perform satisfactorily. For employees who experience mid-career crises, planning workshops and support groups can help redirect career goals. The organization also can help managers combat obsolescence by providing technical and managerial skill training programs.

mid-career renewal strategies
A strategy designed to provide advancement opportunities for deserving mid-career employees while maximizing the contributions of plateaued employees who continue to perform satisfactorily.

Exhibit A.9
Stage-Related Career Development Focus

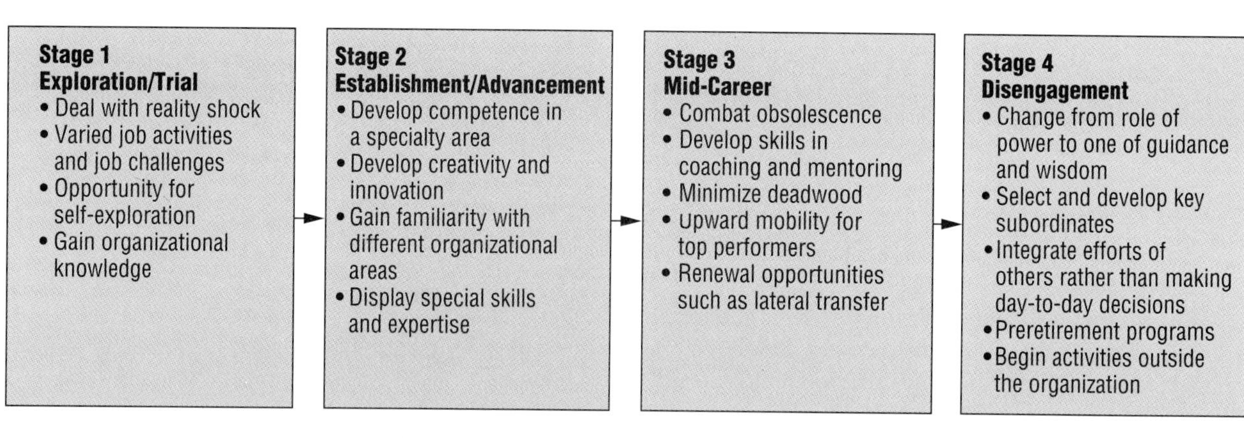

Source: Adapted from T. Gutteridge, *Career Planning and Management* (New York: Little, Brown, 1987); Douglas T. Hall and Marilyn A. Morgan, "Career Development and Planning," in *Contemporary Problems in Personnel*, rev. ed., ed. W. Clay Hammer and Frank Schmidt (Chicago: St. Clair Press, 1977), 205–225; Edgar H. Seatin, *Career Dynamics* (Reading, Mass.: Addison-Wesley, 1978), 40–46.

preretirement program A strategy designed to assist employees in coping with the stress of the transition from work to retirement.

For employees in the disengagement stage of their careers, an increasingly popular career management strategy is to provide preretirement programs. **Preretirement programs** assist employees in managing the stress of transition from work to retirement. Some educational areas that facilitate the transition are financial planning, leisure activities, work/career alternatives, and health.[57] Other ways to keep disengaging managers contributing to the organization are to help them shift from a role of power and decision making to one of consultation, guidance, and development of key subordinates. The organization can also help disengaging people find meaningful activities outside the organization.

Focusing on employees' needs relative to their career stages coordinates the organization's career management strategies with the varied needs of all personnel. The potential bottom-line payoffs to the organization for effective career management are substantial. Productivity, satisfaction, retention, and commitment of valued employees, stress reduction, and a flexible work force will help the organization remain competitive in our global economy.

Summary

This appendix covered several important issues about the management of careers. Career management was discussed from two perspectives: the individual who wants to have a successful career and the organization that wishes to provide career opportunities for its employees.

Individual career planning normally entails five steps — self-assessment, exploring opportunities, making decisions and setting goals, action planning, and follow-up. Individual careers follow predictable stages that include exploration and trial, establishment and advancement, mid-career, and disengagement. Other issues of concern to individual career planning are mentors and coping with stress.

Career management from the organization's viewpoint involves several systems and techniques. These include evaluation of career potential, training and development programs, human resource information systems, career paths and succession planning, career planning programs, and facilitation of mentoring. Other organizational concerns pertain to women and minorities, dual-career couples, and plateaued employees. Dealing effectively with these target groups can enhance the organization's human resource base. Finally, effective career management programs target individuals' needs at each stage in their career.

References

CHAPTER 1

1. Patrick Houston, "She Worked Magic in a Dead-End Job," *Business Week,* November 10, 1986, 94–95.
2. Wendy Zellner, "Chrysler's Next Generation," *Business Week,* December 19, 1988, 52–55.
3. Tom Peters and Nancy Austin, *A Passion for Excellence: The Leadership Difference* (New York: Random House, 1985).
4. Byron Harris, "The Man Who Killed Braniff," *Texas Monthly,* July 1982, 116–120, 183–189.
5. Brett Duval Fromson, "The Slow Death of E. F. Hutton," *Fortune,* February 29, 1988, 82–88.
6. Gary Hector, *Breaking the Bank: The Decline of BankAmerica* (Boston: Little, Brown, 1988).
7. James A. F. Stoner and R. Edward Freeman, *Management,* 4th ed. (Englewood Cliffs, N.J.: Prentice-Hall, 1989).
8. Peter F. Drucker, *Management: Tasks, Responsibilities, Practices* (New York: Harper & Row, 1974).
9. Hector, *Breaking the Bank.*
10. Peters and Austin, *A Passion for Excellence,* 11–12.
11. John Bussey and Douglas R. Sease, "Manufacturers Strive to Slice Time Needed to Develop Products," *The Wall Street Journal,* February 23, 1988, 1, 13.
12. Harris, "The Man Who Killed Braniff."
13. Peters and Austin, *A Passion for Excellence.*
14. Harris, "The Man Who Killed Braniff," 118–120.
15. Ibid.
16. Fromson, "The Slow Death of E. F. Hutton."
17. Alex Taylor III, "Lee Iacocca's Production Whiz," *Fortune,* June 22, 1987, 36–44.
18. David Wessell, "With Labor Scarce, Service Firms Strive to Raise Productivity," *The Wall Street Journal,* June 1, 1989, A1, A8.
19. Harold Geneen with Alvin Moscow, *Managing* (Garden City, N.Y.: Doubleday, 1984), 285.
20. John A. Byrne, Wendy Zellner, and Scott Ticer, "Caught in the Middle," *Business Week,* September 12, 1988, 80–88.
21. Robert L. Katz, "Skills of an Effective Administrator," *Harvard Business Review* 52 (September/October 1974), 90–102.
22. Alex Taylor III, "How a Top Boss Manages His Day," *Fortune,* June 19, 1989, 95–100.
23. Morgan W. McCall, Jr., and Michael M. Lombardo, "Off the Track: Why and How Successful Executives Get Derailed" (Technical Report No. 21, Center for Creative Leadership, Greensboro, N.C., January 1983).
24. Russell Mitchell, "After Harry Gray: Reshaping United Technologies," *Business Week,* January 18, 1988, 46–48.
25. Henry Mintzberg, *The Nature of Managerial Work* (New York: Harper & Row, 1973).
26. Robert E. Kaplan, "Trade Routes: The Manager's Network of Relationships," *Organizational Dynamics* (Spring 1984), 37–52; Rosemary Stewart, "The Nature of Management: A Problem for Management Education," *Journal of Management Studies* 21 (1984), 323–330; John P. Kotter, "What Effective General Managers Really Do," *Harvard Business Review* (November/December 1982), 156–167; Morgan W. McCall, Jr., Ann M. Morrison, and Robert L. Hannan, "Studies of Managerial Work: Results and Methods" (Technical Report No. 9, Center for Creative Leadership, Greensboro, N.C., 1978).
27. Henry Mintzberg, "Managerial Work: Analysis from Observation," *Management Science* 18 (1971), B97–B110.
28. Based on John P. Kotter, "What Effective General Managers Really Do," *Harvard Business Review* (November/December 1982), 156–167; Mintzberg, "Managerial Work"; and Ford S. Worthy, "How CEOs Manage Their Time," *Fortune,* January 18, 1988, 88–97.
29. Mintzberg, "Managerial Work."
30. Sloan Wilson, "What Do Successful Men Have in Common? Raw Energy," *Houston Chronicle,* March 30, 1980, section 6, 11.
31. Lance B. Kurke and Howard E. Aldrich, "Mintzberg was Right!: A Replication and Extension of *The Nature of Managerial Work,*" *Management Science* 29 (1983), 975–984; Cynthia M. Pavett and Alan W. Lau, "Managerial Work: The Influence of Hierarchical Level and Functional Specialty," *Academy of Management Journal* 26 (1983), 170–177; Colin P. Hales, "What Do Managers Do? A Critical Review of the Evidence," *Journal of Management Studies* 23 (1986), 88–115.
32. Francis C. Brown III, "American Airlines Blossoms as Champion of the Poor Passenger," *The Wall Street Journal,* March 4, 1988, 1, 11.
33. Martha E. Mengelsdorf, "Big vs. Small," *INC.,* May 1989, 22; Joseph G. P. Paolillo, "The Manager's Self-Assessment of Managerial Roles: Small vs. Large Firms," *American Journal of Small Business* (January/March 1984), 61–62.
34. McCall and Lombardo, "Off the Track," and Carol Hymowitz, "Five Main Reasons Why Managers Fail," *The Wall Street Journal,* May 2, 1988, 21.
35. Carol Hymowitz, "Day in the Life of Tomorrow's Manager," *The Wall Street Journal,* March 20, 1989, B1.
36. Andrew Kupfer, "Managing Now for the 1990s," *Fortune,* September 26, 1988, 44–47.
37. Jeremy Main, "The Winning Organization," *Fortune,* September 26, 1988, 50–60.
38. Rosabeth Moss Kanter, "The Contingent and the Post-Entrepreneurial Career," *Management Review* (April 1989), 22–27.
39. Arnoldo C. Hax, "Building the Firm of the Future," *Sloan Management Review* (Spring 1989), 75–82.
40. "Readying for the Global Bazaar," *Management Review,* September 1989, 18–19.
41. Houston, "She Worked Magic in a Dead-End Job."

CHAPTER 2

1. Ronald Grover, "High Drama from the Folks Who Brought You *Godzilla '85,*" *Business Week,* September 7, 1987, 30, and Peter Nulty, "New World's Boffo B Movie Script," *Fortune,* February 17, 1986, 48–50.
2. Alan M. Kantro, ed., "Why History Matters to Managers," *Harvard Business Review* 64 (January/February 1986), 81–88.
3. Susan Dentzer, "Profiting from the Past," *Newsweek,* May 10, 1982, 73–74.
4. Kim Heron, "Randy Travis: Making Country Music Hot Again," *The New York Times Magazine,* June 25, 1989, 28–58.
5. Daniel A. Wren, *The Evolution of Management Thought,* 2d ed. (New York: Wiley, 1979), 6–8. Much of the discussion of these forces comes from Arthur M. Schlesinger, *Political and Social History of the United States, 1829–1925* (New York: Macmillan, 1925), and Homer C. Hockett, *Political and Social History of the United States, 1492–1828* (New York: Macmillan, 1925).
6. Daniel A. Wren, "Management History: Issues and Ideas for Teaching and Research," *Journal of Management* 13 (1987), 339–350.
7. The following is based on Wren, *Evolution of Management Thought,* Chapters 4, 5, and Claude S. George, Jr., *The History of Management Thought* (Englewood Cliffs, N.J.: Prentice-Hall, 1968), Chapter 4.
8. Charles D. Wrege and Ann Marie Stoka, "Cooke Creates a Classic: The Story behind F. W. Taylor's Principles of Scientific Management," *Academy of Management Review* (October 1978), 736–749.

9. John F. Mee, "Pioneers of Management," *Advanced Management — Office Executive* (October 1962), 26–29, and W. J. Arnold and the editors of *Business Week, Milestones in Management* (New York: McGraw-Hill, vol. I, 1965; vol. II, 1966).
10. Wren, *Evolution of Management Thought,* 171; George, *History of Management Thought,* 103–104.
11. Henri Fayol, *Industrial and General Administration,* trans. J. A. Coubrough (Geneva: International Management Institute, 1930); Henri Fayol, *General and Industrial Management,* trans. Constance Storrs (London: Pitman and Sons, 1949); Arnold, "Milestones in Management."
12. Mary Parker Follett, *The New State: Group Organization: The Solution of Popular Government* (London: Longmans, Green, 1918), and Mary Parker Follett, *Creative Experience* (London: Longmans, Green, 1924).
13. Henry C. Metcalf and Lyndall Urwick, eds., *Dynamic Administration: The Collected Papers of Mary Parker Follett* (New York: Harper & Row, 1940), and Arnold, "Milestones in Management."
14. William B. Wolf, *How to Understand Management: An Introduction to Chester I. Barnard* (Los Angeles: Lucas Brothers, 1968), and David D. Van Fleet, "The Need-Hierarchy and Theories of Authority," *Human Relations* 9 (Spring 1982), 111–118.
15. Max Weber, *General Economic History,* trans. Frank H. Knight (London: Allen & Unwin, 1927); Max Weber, *The Protestant Ethic and the Spirit of Capitalism,* trans. Talcott Parsons (New York: Scribner, 1930); and Max Weber, *The Theory of Social and Economic Organizations,* eds. and trans. A. M. Henderson and Talcott Parsons (New York: Free Press, 1947).
16. Richard L. Daft, *Organization Theory and Design,* 3d ed. (St. Paul, Minn.: West, 1989), 181–182; Kathy Goode, Betty Hahn, and Cindy Seibert, "United Parcel Service: The Brown Giant" (Unpublished manuscript, Texas A&M University, 1981).
17. Charles D. Wrege, "Solving Mayo's Mystery: The First Complete Account of the Origin of the Hawthorne Studies — The Forgotten Contributions of Charles E. Snow and Homer Hibarger" (Paper presented to the Management History Division of the Academy of Management, August 1976).
18. Ronald G. Greenwood, Alfred A. Bolton, and Regina A. Greenwood, "Hawthorne a Half Century Later: Relay Assembly Participants Remember," *Journal of Management* 9 (Fall/Winter 1983), 217–231.
19. F. J. Roethlisberger, W. J. Dickson, and H. A. Wright, *Management and the Worker* (Cambridge, Mass.: Harvard University Press, 1939).
20. H. M. Parson, "What Happened at Hawthorne?" *Science* 183 (1974), 922–932.
21. Greenwood, Bolton, and Greenwood, "Hawthorne a Half Century Later," 219–221.
22. Douglas McGregor, *The Human Side of Enterprise* (New York: McGraw-Hill, 1960), 16–18.
23. Mark Ivey, "How Compaq Gets There Firstest with the Mostest," *Business Week,* June 26, 1989, 146–150, and Edward Prewitt, "America's 50 Biggest Exporters," *Fortune,* July 17, 1989, 50–51.
24. Mansel G. Blackford and K. Austin Kerr, *Business Enterprise in American History* (Boston: Houghton Mifflin, 1986), Chapters 10, 11, and Alex Groner and the editors of *American Heritage* and *Business Week, The American Heritage History of American Business and Industry* (New York: American Heritage Publishing, 1972), Chapter 9.
25. Larry M. Austin and James R. Burns, *Management Science* (New York: Macmillan, 1985).
26. Tom Scott and William A. Hailey, "Queue Modeling Aids Economic Analysis at Health Center," *Industrial Engineering* (February 1981), 56–61.
27. Ludwig von Bertalanffy, Carl G. Hempel, Robert E. Bass, and Hans Jonas, "General Systems Theory: A New Approach to Unity of Science," *Human Biology* 23 (December 1951), 302–361, and Kenneth E. Boulding, "General Systems Theory — The Skeleton of Science," *Management Science* 2 (April 1956), 197–208.
28. Fremont E. Kast and James E. Rosenzweig, "General Systems Theory: Applications for Organization and Management," *Academy of Management Journal* (December 1972), 447–465.
29. Daft, *Organization Theory,* 16–17.
30. Fred Luthans, "The Contingency Theory of Management: A Path Out of the Jungle," *Business Horizons* 16 (June 1973), 62–72, and Fremont E. Kast and James E. Rosenzweig, *Contingency Views of Organization and Management* (Chicago: Science Research Associates, 1973).
31. Robert Gunther, "Major Banks' Increases in Loan-Loss Reserves May Cramp Expansion," *The Wall Street Journal,* July 29, 1987, 1, 10.
32. B. Joseph White, "The Internationalization of Business: One Company's Response," *Academy of Management Executive* 2 (1988), 29–32.
33. Arnoldo C. Hax, "Building the Firm of the Future," *Sloan Management Review* (Spring 1989), 75–82.
34. Ibid.
35. Brian Dumaine, "What the Leaders of Tomorrow See," *Fortune,* July 3, 1989, 48–62.
36. William Ouchi, *Theory Z: How American Business Can Meet the Japanese Challenge* (Reading, Mass.: Addison-Wesley, 1981).
37. Ouchi, *Theory Z,* and R. Pascale and A. Athos, *The Art of Japanese Management: Applications for American Executives* (New York: Simon and Schuster, 1981).
38. William G. Ouchi and Alfred M. Jaeger, "Type Z Organizations: Stability in the Midst of Mobility," *Academy of Management Review* 3 (1978), 305–314.
39. Ibid.
40. Thomas J. Peters and Robert H. Waterman, Jr., *In Search of Excellence: Lessons from America's Best-Run Companies* (New York: Harper & Row, 1982); Tom Peters and Nancy Austin, *A Passion for Excellence: The Leadership Difference* (New York: Random House, 1985); and Tom Peters, "Putting Excellence into Management," *Business Week,* July 21, 1980, 196–201.
41. Tom Peters, "An Excellent Question," *INC.,* December 1984, 155–162.
42. "Ross Perot's Crusade," *Business Week,* October 6, 1986, 60–65.
43. "A Slimmed-Down Brunswick Is Proving Wall Street Wrong," *Business Week,* May 28, 1984, 90–98.
44. "Pepsi's Marketing Magic: Why Nobody Does It Better," *Business Week,* February 10, 1986, 52–57.
45. "Who's Excellent Now?", *Business Week,* November 5, 1984, 76+; Daniel T. Carroll, "A Disappointing Search for Excellence," *Harvard Business Review* 61 (November/December 1983), 78–79+; Jeremiah J. Sullivan, "A Critique of Theory Z," *Academy of Management Review* (January 1983), 132–142; William Bowen, "Lessons from Behind the Kimono," *Fortune,* June 15, 1981, 247–250.
46. Grover, "High Drama from the Folks Who Brought You *Godzilla* '85."

CHAPTER 3

1. Lucien Rhodes, "Kachajian's Rebellion," *INC.,* October 1986, 92–98.
2. Arthur M. Louis, "America's New Economy: How to Manage in It," *Fortune,* June 23, 1986, 21–25.
3. Jeremy Main, "Hot to Go Global — and Why," *Fortune,* August 28, 1989, 70–76.
4. Marc Beauchamp, "We're All Rejuvenated," *Forbes,* March 19, 1990, 124–126; Jonathan P. Hicks, "The Takeover of American Industry," *The New York Times,* May 28, 1989, Section 3, pp. 1, 8.
5. Based on Marc Beauchamp, "Toilets with Chips," *Forbes,* January 22, 1990, 100–104.

6. Richard L. Daft, *Organization Theory and Design,* 3d ed. (St. Paul, Minn.: West, 1989).
7. L. J. Bourgeois, "Strategy and Environment: A Conceptual Integration," *Academy of Management Review* 5 (1980), 25–39.
8. Walecia Konrad and Gail DeGeorge, "U.S. Companies Go for the Gray," *Business Week,* April 3, 1989, 64–67.
9. Mark Ivey and Geoff Lewis, "Compaq vs. IBM: Peace Comes to Shove," *Business Week,* May 1, 1989, 132.
10. John Bussey, "P & G's New Disposable Diaper Intensifies Marketing Battle with Kimberly-Clark," *The Wall Street Journal,* January 4, 1985, 13.
11. Bruce Nussbaum, "Needed: Human Capital," *Business Week,* September 19, 1988, 100–103; Aaron Bernstein and Zach Schiller, "Union Members Say: Thanks, But No Thanks," *Business Week,* July 18, 1988, 103.
12. William B. Marbach, "Super Television," *Business Week,* January 30, 1989, 56–63; Otis Port, "Materials that Think for Themselves," *Business Week,* December 5, 1988, 166–167.
13. David Lieverman, "Keeping Up with the Murdochs," *Business Week,* March 20, 1989, 32–34; Don Lee Bohl, ed., *Tying the Corporate Knot* (New York: American Management Association, 1989).
14. "State Regulators Rush in Where Washington No Longer Treads," *Business Week,* September 19, 1983, 124–131.
15. Susan B. Garland, "This Safety Ruling Could Be Hazardous to Employers' Health," *Business Week,* February 20, 1989, 34.
16. Joel Dreyfus, "Reinventing IBM," *Fortune,* August 14, 1989, 30–39, and Robert Durand, Teri Fogle, and Matt Stump, "International Business Machines" (Unpublished manuscript, Texas A&M University, December 1985).
17. David B. Jemison, "The Importance of Boundary Spanning Roles in Strategic Decision-Making," *Journal of Management Studies* 21 (1984), 131–152, and Marc J. Dollinger, "Environmental Boundary Spanning and Information Processing Effects on Organizational Performance," *Academy of Management Journal* 27 (1984), 351–368.
18. Brian Dumaine, "Corporate Spies Snoop to Conquer," *Fortune,* November 7, 1988, 68–76; Dodui Tsiantar and John Schwartz, "George Smiley Joins the Firm," *Newsweek,* May 2, 1988, 46–47; James E. Svatko, "Analyzing the Competition," *Small Business Reports,* January 1989, 21–28.
19. R. T. Lenz and Jack L. Engledow, "Environmental Analysis Units and Strategic Decision-Making: A Field Study of Selected 'Leading Edge' Corporations," *Strategic Management Journal* 7 (1986), 69–89; Mansour Javidan, "The Impact of Environmental Uncertainty on Long-Range Planning Practices of the U.S. Savings and Loan Industry," *Strategic Management Journal* 5 (1984), 381–392.
20. Tom Burns and G. M. Stalker, *The Management of Innovation* (London: Tavistock, 1961).
21. James E. Svatko, "Joint Ventures," *Small Business Reports,* December 1988, 65–70; Joshua Hyatt, "The Partnership Route," *INC.,* December 1988, 145–148.
22. Carol Davenport, "America's Most Admired Corporations," *Fortune,* January 30, 1989, 68–76.
23. "Dow Chemical: From Napalm to Nice Guy," *Fortune,* May 12, 1986, 75–78.
24. David B. Yoffie, "How an Industry Builds Political Advantage," *Harvard Business Review* (May/June 1988), 82–89; Douglas Harbrecht, "How to Win Friends and Influence Lawmakers," *Business Week,* November 7, 1988, 36.
25. Monica Langley, "Thrifts' Trade Group and Their Regulators Get Along Just Fine," *The Wall Street Journal,* July 16, 1986, 1, 14.
26. Yoash Wiener, "Forms of Value Systems: A Focus on Organizational Effectiveness and Culture Change and Maintenance," *Academy of Management Review* 13 (1988), 534–545; V. Lynne Meek, "Organizational Culture: Origins and Weaknesses," *Organization Studies* 9 (1988), 453–473; John J. Sherwood, "Creating Work Cultures with Competitive Advantage," *Organizational Dynamics* (Winter 1988), 5–27.
27. Ralph H. Kilmann, Mary J. Saxton, and Roy Serpa, "Issues in Understanding and Changing Culture," *California Management Review* 28 (Winter 1986), 87–94, and Linda Smircich, "Concepts of Culture and Organizational Analysis," *Administrative Science Quarterly* 28 (1983), 339–358.
28. Edgar H. Schein, "Coming to a New Awareness of Organizational Culture," *Sloan Management Review* (Winter 1984), 3–16, and Vijay Sathe, "Implications of Corporate Culture: A Manager's Guide to Actions," *Organizational Dynamics* (Autumn 1983), 5–23.
29. William Taylor, "The Gray Area," *Harvard Business Review* (May/June 1988), 178–182, and "Corporate Culture," *Business Week,* October 27, 1980, 148–160.
30. Russell Mitchell, "Masters of Innovation," *Business Week,* April 10, 1989, 58–63.
31. Taylor, "The Gray Area."
32. "Make No Mistake," *INC.,* June 1989, 115.
33. Susan Benner, "Culture Shock," *INC.,* August 1985, 73–82.
34. Joan O'C. Hamilton, "Why Rivals Are Quaking as Nordstrom Heads East," *Business Week,* June 15, 1987, 99–100, and Charlotte B. Sutton, "Richness Hierarchy of the Cultural Network: The Communication of Corporate Values" (Unpublished manuscript, Texas A&M University, 1985).
35. Terrence E. Deal and Allan A. Kennedy, *Corporate Cultures: The Rites and Rituals of Corporate Life* (Reading, Mass.: Addison-Wesley, 1982).
36. Brian Dumaine, "Those Highflying PepsiCo Managers," *Fortune,* April 10, 1989, 78–86, and Stew Leonard, "Love that Customer!" *Management Review* (October 1987), 36–39.
37. Harrison M. Trice and Janice M. Beyer, "Studying Organizational Cultures Through Rites and Ceremonials," *Academy of Management Review* 9 (1984), 653–669.
38. Thomas J. Peters and Robert H. Waterman, Jr., *In Search of Excellence* (New York: Harper & Row, 1982).
39. This discussion is based on Deal and Kennedy, *Corporate Cultures,* Chapter 6.
40. Carey Quan Jelernter, "Corporate Culture," *The Seattle Times,* June 5, 1986, sec. D, 1, 8.
41. Carey Quan Jelernter, "Safeco: Success Depends Partly on Fitting the Mold," *The Seattle Times,* June 5, 1986, sec. D, 8.
42. Ralph H. Kilmann, Mary J. Saxton, Roy Serpa, and Associates, *Gaining Control of the Coporate Culture* (San Francisco: Jossey-Bass, 1985).
43. Ralph Kilmann, "Corporate Culture," *Psychology Today,* April 1985, 62–68.
44. Morty Lefkoe, "Why So Many Mergers Fail," *Fortune,* June 20, 1987, 113–114.
45. Ibid., and Afsaneh Nahavandi and Ali R. Malekzadeh, "Aculturation in Mergers and Acquisitions," *Academy of Management Review* 13 (1988), 79–90.
46. Bohl, *Tying the Corporate Knot.*
47. Peters and Waterman, *In Search of Excellence.*
48. Gregory L. Miles, "Forging the New Bethlehem," *Business Week,* June 5, 1989, 108–110.
49. Russell Mitchell, "Jack Welch: How Good a Manager?" *Business Week,* December 14, 1987, 92–103.
50. Louis Kraar, "Roy Ash Is Having Fun at Addressogrief-Multigrief," *Fortune,* February 27, 1978, 47–52, and Thomas J. Peters, "Symbols, Patterns, and Settings: An Optimistic Case for Getting Things Done," *Organizational Dynamics* (Autumn 1978), 3–23.
51. Tom Peters and Nancy Austin, *A Passion for Excellence: The Leadership Difference* (New York: Random House, 1985), 278.
52. Karl E. Weick, "Cognitive Processes in Organizations," in *Research in Organizations,* vol. 1, ed. B. M. Staw (Greenwich, Conn.: JAI Press, 1979).
53. Rhodes, "Kachajian's Rebellion."

CHAPTER 4

1. Johnny I. Murdock and John S. Leipzig, "Case Studies of the Responses of Two Corporate Giants to Public Perception of Unethicality," paper presented at Association for Business Communication International Convention, October, 1988, and Philip Gold, "Virtue is Becoming a Capital Idea," *Insight*, October 31, 1988, 46–47.
2. Gregory Stricharchuk, "Bolar Recalls Antibiotic After U.S. Says it Switched Drugs to Get FDA Approval," *The Wall Street Journal*, October 10, 1989, A4, and John A. Byrne, "Businesses Are Signing Up for Ethics 101," *Business Week*, February 15, 1988, 56–57.
3. David Kirkpatrick, "Environmentalism: The New Crusade," *Fortune*, February 12, 1990, 44–54; Brian Bremner, "A New Sales Pitch: The Environment," *Business Week*, July 24, 1989, 50; Zachary Schiller, "Doing Well By Doing Good," *Business Week*, December 5, 1988, 53–57.
4. Gordon F. Shea, *Practical Ethics* (New York: American Management Association, 1988), and Linda K. Trevino, "Ethical Decision Making in Organizations; A Person-Situation Interactionist Model," *Academy of Management Review* 11 (1986), 601–617.
5. Rushworth M. Kidder, "The Three Great Domains of Human Action," *Christian Science Monitor*, January 30, 1990.
6. This discussion is based on Gerald F. Cavanagh, Dennis J. Moberg, and Manuel Velasquez, "The Ethics of Organizational Politics," *Academy of Management Review* 6 (1981), 363–374, and Justin G. Longenecker, Joseph A. McKinney, and Carlos W. Moore, "Egoism and Independence: Entrepreneurial Ethics," *Organizational Dynamics* (Winter 1988), 64–72.
7. Ron Winslow, "Rationing Care," *The Wall Street Journal*, November 13, 1989, R24.
8. Tad Tulega, *Beyond the Bottom Line* (New York: Penguin Books, 1987).
9. James Drummond, "Hazardous to Who's Health?" *Forbes*, December 11, 1989, 89–92.
10. This discussion is based on Trevino, "Ethical Decision Making in Organizations."
11. L. Kohlberg, "Moral Stages and Moralization: The Cognitive-Developmental Approach," in *Moral Development and Behavior: Theory, Research, and Social Issues*, ed. T. Lickona (New York: Holt, Rinehart & Winston, 1976), and L. Kohlberg, "Stage and Sequence: The Cognitive-Developmental Approach to Socialization," in *Handbook of Socialization Theory and Research*, ed. D. A. Goslin (Chicago: Rand McNally, 1969).
12. This discussion is based on Linda Klebe Trevino, "A Cultural Perspective on Changing and Developing Organizational Ethics," in *Research and Organizational Change and Development*, eds. R. Woodman and W. Pasmore (Greenwich, Conn.: JAI Press, 1990), 4: in press.
13. Ibid.; John B. Cullen, Bart Victor, and Carroll Stephens, "An Ethical Weather Report: Assessing the Organization's Ethical Climate," *Organizational Dynamics* (Autumn 1989), 50–62; Bart Victor and John B. Cullen, "The Organizational Bases of Ethical Work Climates," *Administrative Science Quarterly* 33 (1988), 101–125.
14. Eugene W. Szwajkowski, "The Myths and Realities of Research on Organizational Misconduct," in *Research in Corporate Social Performance and Policy*, ed. James E. Post (Greenwich, Conn.: JAI Press, 1986), 9:103–122; and Keith Davis, William C. Frederick, and Robert L. Blostrom, *Business and Society: Concepts and Policy Issues* (New York: McGraw-Hill, 1979).
15. Douglas S. Sherwin, "The Ethical Roots of the Business System," *Harvard Business Review* 61 (November/December, 1983), 183–192.
16. Nancy C. Roberts and Paula J. King, "The Stakeholder Audit Goes Public," *Organizational Dynamics* (Winter 1989), 63–79.
17. James E. Ellis, "Steve Wolf's Class Act: Straight Talk in the Schoolroom," *Business Week*, February 6, 1989, 57.
18. Jane Salodof, "Public Schools and the Business Community: An Uneasy Marriage," *Management Review* (January 1989), 31–37.
19. Gail DeGeorge, "A Sweet Deal for Disney is Souring its Neighbors," *Business Week*, August 8, 1988, 48–49.
20. Archie B. Carroll, "A Three-Dimensional Conceptual Model of Corporate Performance," *Academy of Management Review* 4 (1979), 497–505.
21. Milton Friedman, *Capitalism and Freedom* (Chicago: University of Chicago Press, 1962), 133, and Milton Friedman and Rose Friedman, *Free to Choose* (New York: Harcourt Brace Jovanovich, 1979).
22. Roy Rowan, "E. F. Hutton's New Man on the Hot Seat," *Fortune*, November 11, 1985, 130–136.
23. Eugene W. Szwajkowski, "Organizational Illegality: Theoretical Integration and Illustrative Application," *Academy of Management Review* 10 (1985), 558–567.
24. David J. Fritzsche and Helmut Becker, "Linking Management Behavior to Ethical Philosophy—An Empirical Investigation," *Academy of Management Journal* 27 (1984), 165–175.
25. James J. Chrisman and Archie B. Carroll, "Corporate Responsibility—Reconciling Economic and Social Goals," *Sloan Management Review* 25 (Winter 1984), 59–65.
26. Elizabeth Gatewood and Archie B. Carroll, "The Anatomy of Corporate Social Response: The Rely, Firestone 500, and Pinto Cases," *Business Horizons* 24 (September/October 1981), 9–16.
27. John Kenneth Galbraith, "Behind the Wall," *New York Review of Books*, April 10, 1986, 11–13.
28. Milton R. Moskowitz, "Company Performance Roundup," *Business and Society Review* 53 (Spring 1985), 74–77.
29. Chris Welles, "What Lead Beech-Nut Down the Road to Disgrace," *Business Week*, February 22, 1988, 124–128.
30. Saul W. Gellerman, "Managing Ethics from the Top Down," *Sloan Management Review* (Winter 1989), 73–79.
31. "Corporate Ethics: A Prime Business Asset," The Business Roundtable, 200 Park Avenue, Suite 2222, New York, New York, 10166, February 1988.
32. Ibid.
33. Ibid.
34. "A Code of Worldwide Business Conduct and Operating Principles," Caterpillar Inc., Revised May 1, 1985. Used by permission.
35. Patrick E. Murphy, "Creating Ethical Corporate Structures," *Sloan Management Review* (Winter 1989), 81–87.
36. Marcia Parmarlee Miceli and Janet P. Near, "The Relationship among Beliefs, Organizational Positions, and Whistle-Blowing Status: A Discriminant Analysis," *Academy of Management Journal* 27 (1984), 687–705.
37. Clair Safran, "Women Who Blew the Whistle," *Good Housekeeping*, April 1985, 25, 216–219.
38. Philip L. Cochran and Robert A. Wood, "Corporate Social Responsibility and Financial Performance," *Academy of Management Journal* 27 (1984), 42–56.
39. Jean B. McGuire, Alison Sundgren, and Thomas Schneeweis, "Corporate Social Responsibility and Firm Financial Performance," *Academy of Management Journal* 31 (1988), 854–872.
40. Roger Ricklefs, "Christian-Based Firms Find Following Principles Pays," *The Wall Street Journal*, December 8, 1989, B1, and Jo David and Karen File, "Saintly Companies that Make Heavenly Profits," *Working Woman*, October 1989, 122–126, 169–175.
41. Murdock and Leipzig, "Case Studies," and Gold, "Virtue is Becoming a Capital Idea."

CHAPTER 5

1. Arie P. de Geus, "Planning as Learning," *Harvard Business Review* (March/April 1988), 70–74.
2. Russell L. Ackoff, "On the Use of Models in Corporate Planning," *Strategic Management Journal* 2 (1981), 353–359.

3. Amitai Etzioni, *Modern Organizations* (Englewood Cliffs, N.J.: Prentice-Hall, 1984), 6.
4. "Vincent Sarni is Shattering the Old PPG," *Business Week*, August 17, 1987, 74–75.
5. Max D. Richards, *Setting Strategic Goals and Objectives*, 2d ed. (St. Paul, Minn.: West, 1986).
6. This discussion is based on Richard L. Daft and Richard M. Steers, *Organizations: A Micro/Macro Approach* (Glenview, Ill.: Scott, Foresman, 1986), 319–321; Herbert A. Simon, "On the Concept of Organizational Goals," *Administrative Science Quarterly* 9 (1964), 1–22; Charles B. Saunders and Francis D. Tuggel, "Corporate Goals," *Journal of General Management* 5 (1980), 3–13.
7. "Building Better Transit," *Metropolitan Transportation Authority Annual Report*, 1984.
8. John A. Pearce II and Fred David, "Corporate Mission Statements: The Bottom Line," *Academy of Management Executive* (1987), 109–116; Jerome H. Want, "Corporate Mission: The Intangible Contributor to Performance," *Management Review* (August 1986), 46–50; John A. Pearce II, "The Company Mission as a Strategic Tool," *Sloan Management Review* (Spring 1982), 15.
9. "Preparing for the Unexpected," *Columbia Today* (Winter 1985/1986), 2–4.
10. Richards, *Setting Strategic Goals*, and Charles Perrow, "Analysis of Goals in Complex Organizations," *American Sociological Review* 26 (1961), 854–866.
11. Peter F. Drucker, *The Practice of Management* (New York: Harper & Brothers, 1954), 65–83.
12. "Preparing for the Unexpected," 2.
13. Sarah Bartlett, "John Reed's Citicorp," *Business Week*, December 8, 1986, 90–96.
14. John O. Alexander, "Toward Real Performance: The Circuit-Breaker Technique," *Supervisory Management* (April 1989), 5–12.
15. Tom Richman, "What Business Are You Really In?" *INC.*, August 1983, 77–86.
16. "Positioning for the 1990s," *Intercom: A Monthly Publication for ALLTEL Employees and Friends*, September 1988, 1–2.
17. Edwin A. Locke, Garp P. Latham, and Miriam Erez, "The Determinants of Goal Commitment," *Academy of Management Review* 13 (1988), 23–39; Carl R. Anderson, *Management* (Dubuque, Iowa: Wm. C. Brown, 1984), 262.
18. Locke, Latham, and Erez, "The Determinants of Goal Commitment."
19. "ABC News," special news telecast, April 14, 1986, 9:30 P.M. EST.
20. William B. Stevenson, Jon L. Pearce, and Lyman W. Porter, "The Concept of 'Coalition' in Organization Theory and Research," *Academy of Management Review* 10 (1985), 256–268.
21. "Presidential Forum: Formulating Goals and Objectives," *Small Business Report* (August 1987), 18–19.
22. Miriam Erez, P. Christopher Early, and Charles L. Hulin, "The Impact of Participation on Goal Acceptance and Performance: A Two-Step Model," *Academy of Management Journal* 28 (1985), 50–66, and Miriam Erez and Frederick H. Kanfer, "The Role of Goal Acceptance in Goal Setting and Past Performance," *Academy of Management Review* 8 (1983), 454–463.
23. "Presidential Forum."
24. Daniel H. Gray, "Uses and Misuses of Strategic Planning," *Harvard Business Review* 64 (January/February 1986), 89–97.
25. Ibid.
26. James R. Norman, "Bob Wright's Surprising Script for NBC: Grow, Grow, Grow," *Business Week*, March 9, 1987, 70–72.
27. "Strategic Planning: Part 2," *Small Business Report* (March 1983), 28–32.
28. Paul Meising and Joseph Wolfe, "The Art and Science of Planning at the Business Unit Level," *Management Science* 31 (1985), 773–781.
29. "Jolt Cola Has It All — Sugar, Caffeine, and Strategy," *The Orlando Sentinel*, June 15, 1986, D3.
30. Kenneth Libich, "Making Over Middle Managers," *Fortune*, May 8, 1989, 58–64.
31. Jac Fitz-Eng, "White-Collar Effectiveness," *Management Review* (June 1986), 52–56.
32. Nancy L. Merritt, "Bank of America's Blueprint for a Policy on AIDS," *Business Week*, May 23, 1987, 127.
33. Bruce G. Posner, "The Best Little Handbook in Texas," *INC.*, February 1989, 84–85.
34. "Corporate Planning: Drafting a Blueprint for Success," *Small Business Report* (August 1987), 40–44.
35. Andrew Tanzer, "We Do Not Take a Short-Term View," *Forbes*, July 13, 1987, 372–374.
36. James B. Treece, "Can Ford Stay on Top?" *Business Week*, September 28, 1987, 78–86.
37. "Preparing for the Unexpected," 2–4.
38. "The New Breed of Strategic Planner," *Business Week*, September 17, 1984, 62–68.
39. Ibid.
40. Daniel H. Gray, "Uses and Misuses of Strategic Planning," *Harvard Business Review* 64 (January/February 1986), 89–97.
41. "The New Breed."
42. de Geus, "Planning as Learning."

CHAPTER 6

1. Douglas C. McGill, "Making Mashed Peas Pay Off," *The New York Times*, April 9, 1989, sec. 3, 4.
2. Steve Lawrence, "Bar Wars: Hershey Bites Mars," *Fortune*, July 8, 1985, 52–57.
3. Christopher Power, "Why National Distillers Went on the Wagon," *Business Week*, September 14, 1987, 78–82; Robert L. Rose, "Major U.S. Airlines Rapidly Gain Control Over Regional Lines," *The Wall Street Journal*, January 17, 1988, 1, 14; "New? Improved? The Brand-Name Mergers," *Business Week*, October 21, 1985, 108–110.
4. John E. Prescott, "Environments as Moderators of the Relationship between Strategy and Performance," *Academy of Management Journal* 29 (1986), 329–346; John A. Pearce II and Richard B. Robinson, Jr., *Strategic Management: Strategy, Formulation, and Implementation*, 2d ed. (Homewood, Ill.: Irwin, 1985); David J. Teece, "Economic Analysis and Strategic Management," *California Management Review* 26 (Spring 1984), 87–110.
5. Charles W. Hofer and Dan Schendel, *Strategy Formulation: Analytical Concepts* (St. Paul, Minn.: West, 1979), 25.
6. David Lieberman, "Guccione's Unlikely New Conquest," *Business Week*, November 23, 1987, 40, and Monci Jo Williams, "Synergy Works at American Express," *Fortune*, February 16, 1987, 79–80.
7. Milton Leontiades, *Strategies for Diversification and Change* (Boston: Little, Brown, 1980), 63, and Dan E. Schendel and Charles W. Hofer, eds., *Strategic Management: A New View of Business Policy and Planning* (Boston: Little, Brown, 1979), 11–14.
8. Joseph Weber, "Black & Decker Cuts a Neat Dovetail Joint," *Business Week*, July 31, 1989, 52–53.
9. Richard W. Anderson, "That Roar You Hear is Food Lion," *Business Week*, August 24, 1987, 65–66, and Jaclyn Fierman, "How to Make Money in Mature Markets," *Fortune*, November 25, 1985, 47–53.
10. Milton Leontiades, "The Confusing Words of Business Policy," *Academy of Management Review* 7 (1982), 45–48.
11. Lawrence G. Hrebiniak and William F. Joyce, *Implementing Strategy* (New York: Macmillan, 1984).
12. James E. Svatko, "Analyzing the Competition," *Small Business Reports* (January 1989), 21–28, and Brian Dumaine, "Corporate Spies Snoop to Conquer," *Fortune*, November 7, 1988, 68–76.
13. Pamela Sherrid, "Fighting Back at Breakfast," *Forbes*, October 7, 1985, 126–130.

14. Steve Swartz, "Basic Bedrooms: How Marriott Changes Hotel Design to Tap Mid-Priced Market," *The Wall Street Journal*, September 18, 1985, 1.
15. Larry Reibstein, "Federal Express Faces Challenges to Its Grip on Overnight Delivery," *The Wall Street Journal*, January 8, 1988, 1, 8, and Dean Foust, "Why Federal Express has Overnight Anxiety," *Business Week*, November 9, 1987, 62–66.
16. Frederick W. Gluck, "A Fresh Look at Strategic Management," *Journal of Business Strategy* 6 (Fall 1985), 4–19.
17. Kotha Suresh and Daniel Orna, "Generic Manufacturing Strategies: A Conceptual Synthesis," *Strategic Management Journal* 10 (1989), 211–231, and John A. Pearce II, "Selecting among Alternative Grand Strategies," *California Management Review* (Spring 1982), 23–31.
18. William L. Shanklin and John K. Ryans, Jr., "Is the International Cash Cow Really a Prize Heifer?" *Business Horizons* 24 (1981), 10–16.
19. Keith H. Hammonds, "At Gillette, Disposable is a Dirty Word," *Business Week*, May 29, 1989, 54–58, and Bobbie Holbrook, Sondra Rodgers, and Greg Lock, "Gillette Company" (Unpublished manuscript, Texas A&M University, 1986).
20. Ken G. Smith, James P. Guthrie, and Ming-Jer Chin," Strategy, Size and Performance," *Organization Studies* 10 (1989), 63–81, and Raymond E. Miles and Charles C. Snow, *Organizational Strategy, Structure, and Process* (New York: McGraw-Hill, 1978).
21. Donald C. Hambrick, "Some Tests of the Effectiveness and Functional Attributes of Miles and Snow's Strategic Types," *Academy of Management Journal* 26 (1983), 5–26.
22. "How Adversity Is Reshaping Madison Avenue," *Business Week*, September 15, 1986, 142–147.
23. Bill Hale and Paula Boudreaux, "Frito Lay Inc.: A Case Study" (Unpublished manuscript, Texas A&M University, 1986).
24. Michael E. Porter, *Competitive Strategy* (New York: Free Press, 1980), 36–46; Danny Miller, "Relating Porter's Business Strategies to Environment and Structure: Analysis and Performance Implementations," *Academy of Management Journal* 31 (1988), 280–308; Michael E. Porter, "From Competitive Advantage to Corporate Strategy," *Harvard Business Review* (May/June 1987), 43–59.
25. Thomas L. Wheelen and J. David Hunger, *Strategic Management and Business Policy* (Reading, Mass.: Addison-Wesley, 1989).
26. Anderson, "That Roar You Hear is Food Lion."
27. Nathaniel Gilbert, "John W. Bachmann: Securities Well In Hand," *Management Review* (January 1988), 17–19.
28. George W. Potts, "Exploit Your Product's Service Life Cycle," *Harvard Business Review* (September/October 1988), 32–36, and C. R. Wasson, *Dynamic Competitive Strategy and Product Life Cycles*, 3d ed. (Austin, Tex.: Austin Press, 1978).
29. Carl R. Anderson and Carl P. Zeithaml, "Stage of the Product Life Cycle, Business Strategy, and Business Performance," *Academy of Management Journal* 27 (1984), 5–24.
30. Walter G. Schmid, "Heinz Covers the Globe," *The Journal of Business Strategy* (March/April 1989), 17–20, and Bill Saporito, "Heinz Pushes to be the Low-Cost Producer," *Fortune*, June 24, 1985, 44–54.
31. Harold W. Fox, "A Framework for Functional Coordination," *Atlanta Economic Review* (now *Business Magazine*) (November/December 1973).
32. L. J. Bourgeois III and David R. Brodwin, "Strategic Implementation: Five Approaches to an Elusive Phenomenon," *Strategic Management Journal* 5 (1984), 241–264, and Anil K. Gupta and V. Govindarajan, "Business Unit Strategy, Managerial Characteristics, and Business Unit Effectiveness at Strategy Implementation," *Academy of Management Journal* (1984), 25–41.
33. Jay R. Galbraith and Robert K. Kazanjian, *Strategy Implementation: Structure, Systems and Process*, 2d ed. (St. Paul, Minn.: West, 1986); Paul C. Nutt, "Selecting Tactics to Implement Strategic Plans," *Strategic Management Journal* 10 (1989), 145–161.
34. Francine Schwadel, "Christmas Sales' Lack of Momentum Tests Store Managers' Mettle," *The Wall Street Journal*, December 16, 1987, 1, 13.
35. "Company Doctor: Q. T. Wiles," *INC.*, February 1988, 27–38, and Michael W. Miller, "Q. T. Wiles Revives Sick High-Tech Firms with Strong Medicine," *The Wall Street Journal*, June 23, 1986, 1, 12.
36. Miller, "Q. T. Wiles."
37. Zachary Schiller, "What's Deflating Uniroyal Goodrich," *Business Week*, November 30, 1987, 35.
38. Gupta and Govindarajan, "Business Unit Strategy," and Bourgeois and Brodwin, "Strategic Implementation."
39. Alex Beam, "Can the Boston Brahmin of Insurance Shake Off the Cobwebs?" *Business Week*, August 26, 1985, 51.
40. James E. Skivington and Richard L. Daft, "A Study of Organizational 'Framework' and 'Process' Modalities for the Implementation of Business-Level Strategies" (Unpublished manuscript, Texas A&M University, 1987).
41. Barry Meier, "Under Public Pressure, Chemical Firms Push Plant Safety Programs," *The Wall Street Journal*, November 11, 1985, 1, 17.
42. McGill, "Making Mashed Peas Pay Off."

CHAPTER 7

1. Kerry Hannon, "Two Doughnuts and a Martini, Please," *Forbes*, March 9, 1987, 128–130.
2. Mark Maremont, "Waterford is Showing a Few Cracks," *Business Week*, February 20, 1989, 60–65; John Markoff, "John Sculley's Biggest Test," *The New York Times*, February 26, 1989, sec. 3, 1, 26; Dyan Machan, "Never Look Down," *Forbes*, July 24, 1989, 270–272.
3. Ronald A. Howard, "Decision Analysis: Practice and Promise," *Management Science* 34 (1988), 679–695.
4. Herbert A. Simon, *The New Science of Management* (Englewood Cliffs, N.J.: Prentice-Hall, 1977), 47.
5. Samuel Eilon, "Structuring Unstructured Decisions," *Omega* 13 (1985), 369–377, and Max H. Bazerman, *Judgment in Managerial Decision Making* (New York: Wiley, 1986).
6. James G. March and Zur Shapira, "Managerial Perspectives on Risk and Risk Taking," *Management Science* 33 (1987), 1404–1418, and Inga Skromme Baird and Howard Thomas, "Toward a Contingency Model of Strategic Risk Taking," *Academy of Management Review* 10 (1985), 230–243.
7. Eilon, "Structuring Unstructured Decisions," and Philip A. Roussel, "Cutting Down the Guesswork in R&D," *Harvard Business Review* 61 (September/October 1983), 154–160.
8. Mark N. Vamos, "Time Inc.'s $47 Million Belly Flop," *Business Week*, February 17, 1986, 14–15.
9. Michael Masuch and Perry LaPotin, "Beyond Garbage Cans: An AI Model of Organizational Choice," *Administrative Science Quarterly* 34 (1989), 38–67, and Richard L. Daft and Robert H. Lengel, "Organizational Information Requirements, Media Richness and Structural Design," *Management Science* 32 (1986), 554–571.
10. David M. Schweiger, William R. Sandberg, and James W. Ragan, "Group Approaches for Improving Strategic Decision Making: A Comparative Analysis of Dialectical Inquiry, Devil's Advocacy, and Consensus," *Academy of Management Journal* 29 (1986), 51–71, and Richard O. Mason and Ian I. Mitroff, *Challenging Strategic Planning Assumptions* (New York: Wiley Interscience, 1981).
11. Ronald Grover, "Fat Times for Studios, Fatter Times for Stars," *Business Week*, July 24, 1989, 48, and Christopher Knolton, "Lessons from Hollywood Hitmen," *Fortune*, August 29, 1988, 78–82.
12. Boris Blai, Jr., "Eight Steps to Successful Problem Solving," *Supervisory Management* (January 1986), 7–9, and Earnest R. Acher, "How to Make a Business Decision: An Analysis of Theory and Practice," *Management Review* 69 (February 1980), 54–61.

13. Douglas A. Hay and Paul N. Dahl, "Strategic and Midterm Planning of Forest-to-Product Flows," *Interfaces* 14 (September/October 1984), 33–43.
14. Herbert A. Simon, *The New Science of Management Decision* (New York: Harper & Row, 1960), 5–6, and Amitai Etzioni, "Humble Decision Making," *Harvard Business Review* (July/August 1989), 122–126.
15. James G. March and Herbert A. Simon, *Organizations* (New York: Wiley, 1958).
16. Herbert A. Simon, *Models of Man* (New York: Wiley, 1957), 196–205, and Herbert A. Simon, *Administrative Behavior*, 2d ed. (New York: Free Press, 1957).
17. John Taylor, "Project Fantasy: A Behind-the-Scenes Account of Disney's Desperate Battle against the Raiders," *Manhattan* (November 1984).
18. Weston H. Agor, "The Logic of Intuition: How Top Executives Make Important Decisions," *Organizational Dynamics* 14 (Winter 1986), 5–18, and Herbert A. Simon, "Making Management Decisions: The Role of Intuition and Emotion," *Academy of Management Executive* 1 (1987), 57–64.
19. Daniel J. Isenberg, "How Senior Managers Think," *Harvard Business Review* 62 (November/December 1984), 80–90.
20. Annetta Miller and Dody Tsiantar, "A Test for Market Research," *Newsweek*, December 28, 1987, 32–33, and David Frost and Michael Deakin, *David Frost's Book of the World's Worst Decisions* (New York: Crown, 1983), 60–61.
21. James W. Fredrickson, "Effects of Decision Motive and Organizational Performance Level on Strategic Decision Processes," *Academy of Management Journal* 28 (1985), 821–843, and James W. Fredrickson, "The Comprehensiveness of Strategic Decision Processes: Extension, Observations, Future Directions," *Academy of Management Journal* 27 (1984), 445–466.
22. Marjorie A. Lyles and Howard Thomas, "Strategic Problem Formulation: Biases and Assumptions Embedded in Alternative Decision-Making Models," *Journal of Management Studies* 25 (1988), 131–145, and Susan E. Jackson and Jane E. Dutton, "Discerning Threats and Opportunities," *Administrative Science Quarterly* 33 (1988), 370–387.
23. Larry Reibstein, "A Finger on the Pulse: Companies Expand Use of Employee Surveys," *The Wall Street Journal*, October 27, 1986, 27.
24. Richard L. Daft, Juhani Sormumen, and Don Parks, "Chief Executive Scanning, Environmental Characteristics, and Company Performance: An Empirical Study" (Unpublished manuscript, Texas A&M University, 1988).
25. Jerry Jakuvovics, "Rising Stars in Toys and Togs," *Management Review* (May 1987), 19–20.
26. C. Kepner and B. Tregoe, *The Rational Manager* (New York: McGraw-Hill, 1965).
27. Alex Taylor III, "Here Comes Japan's New Luxury Cars," *Fortune*, August 14, 1989, 62–66.
28. William J. Hampton, "The Next Act at Chrysler," *Business Week*, November 3, 1986, 66.
29. Todd Mason, "Tandy Finds a Cold, Hard World Outside the Radio Shack," *Business Week*, August 31, 1987, 68–70.
30. Ann B. Fisher, "Coke's Brand-Loyalty Lesson," *Fortune*, August 5, 1985, 44–46; "How Coke Decided a New Taste Was It," *Fortune*, May 27, 1985, 80; Betsy D. Gelb and Gabriel M. Gelb, "New Coke's Fizzle — Lessons for the Rest of Us," *Sloan Management Review* (Fall 1986), 71–76.
31. V. H. Vroom and P. W. Yetton, *Leadership and Decision-Making* (Pittsburgh: University of Pittsburgh Press, 1973).
32. R. H. G. Field, "A Test of the Vroom-Yetton Normative Model of Leadership," *Journal of Applied Psychology* (October 1982), 523–532, and R. H. G. Field, "A Critique of the Vroom-Yetton Contingency Model of Leadership Behavior," *Academy of Management Review* 4 (1979), 249–257.
33. Jennifer T. Ettling and Arthur G. Jago, "Participation Under Conditions of Conflict: More on the Validity of the Vroom-Yetton Model," *Journal of Management Studies* 25 (1988), 73–83; Madeline E. Heilman, Harvey A. Hornstein, Jack H. Cage, and Judith K. Herschlag, "Reactions to Prescribed Leader Behavior as a Function of Role Perspective: The Case of the Vroom-Yetton Model," *Journal of Applied Psychology* (February 1984), 50–60; Arthur G. Jago and Victor H. Vroom, "Some Differences in the Incidence and Evaluation of Participative Leader Behavior," *Journal of Applied Psychology* (December 1982), 776–783.
34. Tom Richman, "One Man's Family," *INC.*, November 1983, 151–156.
35. Ettling and Jago, "Participation Under Conditions of Conflict."
36. Andre Delbecq, Andrew Van de Ven, and D. Gustafson, *Group Techniques for Program Planning* (Glenview, Ill.: Scott, Foresman, 1975), and William M. Fox, "Anonymity and Other Keys to Successful Problem-Solving Meetings," *National Productivity Review* 8 (Spring 1989), 145–156.
37. "Group Decision Making: Approaches to Problem Solving," *Small Business Reports* (July 1988), 30–33; N. Delkey, *The Delphi Method: An Experimental Study of Group Opinion* (Santa Monica, Cal.: Rand Corporation, 1969).
38. John L. Cotton, David A. Vollarth, Kirk L. Froggatt, Mark L. Lengnick-Hall, Kenneth R. Jennings, "Employee Participation: Diverse Forms and Different Outcomes," *Academy of Management Review* 13 (1988), 8–22, and Walter C. Swap, "Destructive Effects of Groups on Individuals" in *Group Decision Making*, ed. Walter C. Swap and Associates (Beverly Hills, Cal.: Sage, 1984).
39. Irving L. Janis, *Group Think*, 2d ed. (Boston: Houghton Mifflin, 1982), 9, and Glen Whyte, "Groupthink Reconsidered," *Academy of Management Review* 14 (1989), 40–56.
40. Roy Rowan, "The Maverick Who Yelled Foul at Citibank," *Fortune*, January 10, 1983, 46–56.
41. David M. Schweiger and William R. Sandberg, "The Utilization of Individual Capabilities in Group Approaches to Strategic Decision-Making," *Strategic Management Journal* 10 (1989), 31–43, and "The Devil's Advocate," *Small Business Report* (December 1987), 38–41.
42. Michael Duffy, "Mr. Consensus," *Time*, August 21, 1989, 16–22.
43. "Group Decision-Making," *Small Business Report* (July 1988), 30–33.
44. A. Osborn, *Applied Imagination* (New York: Scribner, 1957).
45. Hannon, "Two Doughnuts and a Martini, Please."

CHAPTER 8

1. Lucius J. Riccio, "Sweeping Changes at NYC Sanitation," *Management Review* (May 1987), 46–50.
2. David R. Anderson, Dennis J. Sweeney, and Thomas A. Williams, *Quantitative Methods for Business*, 4th ed., (St. Paul, Minn.: West, 1989), and H. Watson and P. Marett, "A Survey of Management Science Implementation Problems," *Interfaces* 9 (August 1979), 124–128.
3. For further explanation of management science techniques, see B. Render and R. Stair, *Quantitative Analysis for Management*, 2d ed. (Boston: Allyn & Bacon, 1985), and S. Lee, L. Moore, and B. Taylor, *Management Science* (Dubuque, Iowa: W. C. Brown, 1981).
4. William M. Bulkeley, "The Right Mix: New Software Makes the Choice Much Easier," *The Wall Street Journal*, March 27, 1987, 25.
5. Thomas H. Stone and Jack Fiorito, "A Perceived Uncertainty Model of Human Resource Forecasting Technique Use," *Academy of Management Review* 11 (1986), 635–642.
6. S. C. Wheelwright and S. Makridakis, *Forecasting Methods for Management* (New York: Wiley, 1973).
7. Ibid.

8. Robert F. Reilly, "Developing a Sales Forecasting System," *Managerial Planning* (July/August 1981), 24–30.
9. Dexter Hutchins, "And Now, the Home-Brewed Forecast," *Fortune,* January 20, 1986, 53–54.
10. N. Dalkey, *The Delphi Method: An Experimental Study of Group Opinion* (Santa Monica, Cal.: Rand Corporation, 1969).
11. Bruce Blaylock and L. Reese, "Cognitive Style and the Usefulness of Information," *Decision Sciences* 15 (Winter 1984), 74–91.
12. J. Duncan, "Businessmen Are Good Sales Forecasters," *Dun's Review* (July 1986).
13. Alex Taylor III, "Who's Ahead in the World Auto War," *Fortune,* November 9, 1987, 74–88.
14. M. Moriarty, "Design Features of Forecasting Systems Involving Management Judgments," *Journal of Marketing Research* 22 (November 1985), 353–364, and D. Kahneman, B. Slovic, and A. Tversky, eds., *Judgment under Uncertainty: Heuristics and Biases* (Cambridge, Mass.: Cambridge Press, 1982).
15. M. Anderson and R. Lievano, *Quantitative Management: An Introduction,* 2d ed. (Boston: Kent, 1986).
16. "Break-even Analysis: Analyzing the Relationship Between Costs and Revenues," *Small Business Report* (August 1986), 22–24.
17. Kevin McManus, "The Cookie Wars," *Forbes,* November 7, 1983, 150–152.
18. Anderson and Lievano, *Quantitative Management;* J. Byrd and L. Moore, "The Application of a Product Mix Linear Programming Model in Corporate Policy Making," *Management Science* 24 (September 1978), 1342–1350; D. Darnell and C. Lofflin, "National Airlines Fuel Management and Allocation Model," *Interfaces* 7 (February 1977), 1–16.
19. P. Williams, "A Linear Programming Approach to Production Scheduling," *Production and Inventory Management* 11 (3d Quarter, 1970), 39–49.
20. Bulkeley, "The Right Mix."
21. W. J. Erikson and O. P. Hall, *Computer Models for Management Science* (Reading, Mass.: Addison-Wesley, 1986).
22. Nancy Madlin, "Streamlining the PERT Chart," *Management Review* (September 1986), 67–68.
23. David Cohan, Stephen M. Haas, David L. Radloff, and Richard F. Yancik, "Using Fire in Forest Management: Decision Making under Uncertainty," *Interfaces* 14 (September/October 1984), 8–19.
24. J. W. Ulvila and R. V. Brown, "Decision Analysis Comes of Age," *Harvard Business Review* (September/October 1982), 130–141.
25. Render and Stair, *Quantitative Analysis for Management.*
26. Toni Mack, "Let the Computer Do It," *Forbes,* August 10, 1987, 94.
27. Raymond F. Boykin and Reuven R. Levary, "An Interactive Decision Support System for Analyzing Ship Voyage Alternatives," *Interfaces* 15 (March/April 1985), 81–84.
28. T. Naylor and H. Schauland, "A Survey of Users of Corporate Planning Models," *Management Science* 22 (1976), 927–937.
29. Riccio, "Sweeping Changes at NYC Sanitation," and Lucius J. Riccio, "Management Science in New York's Department of Sanitation," *Interfaces* 14 (March/April 1984), 1–13.

CHAPTER 9

1. Paul B. Brown, "Bad Debt Can Be Good for Business," *INC.,* March 1988, 119–122.
2. Geoff Lewis, "Big Changes at Big Blue," *Business Week,* February 15, 1988, 92–98, and Jonathan B. Levine, "Mild-Mannered Hewlett-Packard is Making Like Superman," *Business Week,* March 7, 1988, 110–114.
3. "Greyhound Splitting into Four to Go After Short-Haul Trade," *Chicago Tribune,* April 30, 1986, sec. 3, 8.
4. Andrew C. Brown, "Unilever Fights Back in the U.S.," *Fortune,* May 26, 1986, 32–38, and "The Toughest Job in Business: How They're Remaking U.S. Steel," *Business Week,* February 25, 1985, 50–55.
5. "A Slimmed-Down Brunswick Is Proving Wall Street Wrong," *Business Week,* May 28, 1984, 90–98, and J. Vettner, "Bowling for Dollars," *Forbes,* September 12, 1983, 138.
6. John Child, *Organization: A Guide to Problems and Practice,* 2d ed. (London: Harper & Row, 1984).
7. Adam Smith, *The Wealth of Nations* (New York: Modern Library, 1937).
8. This discussion is based on Richard L. Daft, *Organization Theory and Design,* 3d ed. (St. Paul, Minn., West, 1989), 400–401.
9. C. I. Barnard, *The Functions of the Executive* (Cambridge, Mass.: Harvard University Press, 1938).
10. Thomas A. Stewart, "CEOs See Clout Shifting," *Fortune,* November 6, 1989, 66.
11. Ibid.
12. Carrie R. Leana, "Predictors and Consequences of Delegation," *Academy of Management Journal* 29 (1986), 754–774.
13. Paul D. Collins and Frank Hull, "Technology and Span of Control: Woodward Revisited," *Journal of Management Studies* 23 (March 1986), 143–164; David D. Van Fleet and Arthur G. Bedeian, "A History of the Span of Management," *Academy of Management Review* 2 (1977), 356–372; C. W. Barkdull, "Span of Control — A Method of Evaluation," *Michigan Business Review* 15 (May 1963), 25–32.
14. Brian Dumaine, "What the Leaders of Tomorrow See," *Fortune,* July 3, 1989, 48–62.
15. Ernest Dale, *Organization* (New York: American Management Association, 1967).
16. Brian Dumaine, "Those Highflying PepsiCo Managers," *Fortune,* April 10, 1989, 78–86, and Levine, "Mild-Mannered Hewlett-Packard."
17. Thomas Moore, "Goodbye, Corporate Staff," *Fortune,* December 21, 1987, 65–76.
18. From the final rule published by the U.S. Department of Commerce, effective January 1, 1986.
19. Raymond E. Miles, "Adapting to Technology and Competition: A New Industrial Relation System for the 21st Century," *California Management Review* (Winter 1989), 9–28.
20. The following discussion of structural alternatives draws heavily on Jay R. Galbraith, *Designing Complex Organizations* (Reading, Mass.: Addison-Wesley, 1973); Jay R. Galbraith, *Oranization Design* (Reading, Mass.: Addison-Wesley, 1977); Robert Duncan, "What Is the Right Organization Structure?" *Organizational Dynamics* (Winter 1979), 59–80; J. McCann and Jay R. Galbraith, "Interdepartmental Relations," in *Handbook of Organizational Design,* eds. P. Nystrom and W. Starbuck (New York: Oxford University Press, 1981), 60–84.
21. John Markoff, "John Sculley's Biggest Test," *The New York Times,* February 26, 1989, sec. 3, 1, 26.
22. Lawton R. Burns, "Matrix Management in Hospitals: Testing Theories of Matrix Structure and Development," *Administrative Science Quarterly* 34 (1989), 349–368.
23. Stanley M. Davis and Paul R. Lawrence, *Matrix* (Reading, Mass.: Addison-Wesley, 1977).
24. Ellen Kolton, "Team Players," *INC.,* September 1984, 140–144, and personal communication from Howard Bennett, matrix vice-president.
25. Joel Kotkin, "The 'Smart-Team' at Compaq Computer," *INC.,* February 1986, 48–56.
26. Ibid., 56.
27. Susan Benner, "Three Companies in Search of an Author," *INC.,* August 1984, 49–55.
28. "National City Corporation 1988 Annual Report," National City Corporation, Cleveland, Ohio.

29. Lucien Rhodes, "The Passion of Robert Swiggett," *INC.*, April 1984, 121–140.
30. James R. Norman, "A New Union Carbide Is Slowly Starting to Gel," *Business Week*, April 18, 1988, 68–69.
31. John Hoerr, "Work Teams Can Rev Up Paper-Pushers, Too," *Business Week*, November 28, 1988, 64–72.
32. Miles, "Adapting to Technology and Competition."
33. Raymond E. Miles and Charles C. Snow, "Organizations: New Concepts for New Forms," *California Management Review* 28 (Spring 1986), 62–73, and "Now, The Post-Industrial Corporation," *Business Week*, March 3, 1986, 64–74.
34. Miles, "Adapting to Technology and Competition."
35. Brown, "Bad Debt Can be Good for Business."

CHAPTER 10

1. Robert W. Harrison and William G. Layton, "How Troxel Manufacturing Restructured Itself," *Management Review* (March 1988), 43–46.
2. Richard L. Daft, *Organization Theory and Design*, 3d ed. (St. Paul, Minn.: West, 1989).
3. Bruce Buursma, "Wanted: Romance Executive," *Chicago Tribune*, July 19, 1989.
4. Lee Iacocca with William Novak, *Iacocca: An Autobiography* (New York: Phantom Books, 1984), 152–153.
5. Thomas Moore, "Would You Buy a Car from This Man?" *Fortune*, April 11, 1988, 72–74.
6. William J. Altier, "Tasks Forces: An Effective Management Tool," *Management Review* (February 1987), 52–57.
7. "Tasks Forces Tackle Consolidation of Employment Services," *Shawmut News*, Shawmut National Corporation, May 3, 1989, 2.
8. Michael Brody, "Can GM Manage It All?" *Fortune*, July 8, 1985, 22–28.
9. Henry Mintzberg, *The Structuring of Organizations* (Englewood Cliffs, N.J.: Prentice-Hall, 1979).
10. Vicki Moss, "BUMP: The Consumer Bank's New Program Helps the Branches Run More Efficiently and Effectively," *Chemical Chronicle*, Chemical Banking Corporation, June/July 1989, 14–15.
11. Paul R. Lawrence and Jay W. Lorsch, "New Managerial Job: The Integrator," *Harvard Business Review* (November/December 1967), 142–151.
12. Ron Winslow, "Utility Cuts Red Tape, Builds Nuclear Plant Almost on Schedule," *The Wall Street Journal*, February 22, 1984, 1, 18.
13. Tom Burns and G. M. Stalker, *The Management of Innovation* (London: Tavistock, 1961).
14. Michael E. Porter, *Competitive Strategy* (New York: Free Press, 1980), 36–46.
15. Clem Morgello, "Booth: Creating a New Polaroid," *Dun's Business Month*, August 1985, 51–52.
16. Paul R. Lawrence and Jay W. Lorsch, *Organization and Environment* (Homewood, Ill.: Irwin, 1969).
17. Robert B. Duncan, "Characteristics of Organizational Environments and Perceived Environmental Uncertainty," *Administrative Science Quarterly* 17 (1972), 313–327; W. Alan Randolph and Gregory G. Dess, "The Congruence Perspective of Organization Design: A Conceptual Model and Multivariate Research Approach," *Academy of Management Review* 9 (1984), 114–127; Masoud Yasai-Ardekani, "Structural Adaptations to Environments," *Academy of Management Review* 11 (1986), 9–21.
18. Joel Dreyfuss, "Reinventing IBM," *Fortune*, August 14, 1989, 30–39, and Geoff Lewis, "Big Changes at Big Blue," *Business Week*, February 15, 1988, 92–98.
19. W. Graham Astley, "Organization Size and Bureaucratic Structure," *Organization Studies* 6 (1985), 201–228; John B. Cullen, Kenneth S. Anderson, and Douglas D. Baker, "Blau's Theory of Structural Differentiation Revisited: A Theory of Structural Change or Scale?" *Academy of Management Journal* 29 (1986), 203–229; Daft, *Organization Theory and Design*.
20. Robert E. Quinn and Kim Cameron, "Organizational Life Cycles and Shifting Criteria of Effectiveness: Some Preliminary Evidence," *Management Science* 29 (1983), 33–51, and John R. Kimberly, Robert H. Miles, and associates, *The Organizational Life Cycle* (San Francisco: Jossey-Bass, 1980).
21. Denise M. Rousseau and Robert A. Cooke, "Technology and Structure: The Concrete, Abstract, and Activity Systems of Organizations," *Journal of Management* 10 (1984), 345–361; Charles Perrow, "A Framework for the Comparative Analysis of Organizations," *American Sociological Review* 32 (1967), 194–208; Denise M. Rousseau, "Assessment of Technology in Organizations: Closed versus Open Systems Approaches," *Academy of Management Review* 4 (1979), 531–542.
22. Joan Woodward, *Industrial Organizations: Theory and Practice* (London: Oxford University Press, 1965), and Joan Woodward, *Management and Technology* (London: Her Majesty's Stationary Office, 1958).
23. Woodward, *Industrial Organizations*, vi.
24. Patricia L. Nemetz and Louis W. Fry, "Flexible Manufacturing Organizations: Implementation for Strategy Formulation and Organization Design," *Academy of Management Review* 13 (1988), 627–638, and Paul S. Adler, "Managing Flexible Automation," *California Management Review* (Spring 1988), 34–56.
25. Peter K. Mills and Thomas Kurk, "A Preliminary Investigation into the Influence of Customer-Firm Interface on Information Processing and Task Activity in Service Organizations," *Journal of Management* 12 (1986), 91–104; Peter K. Mills and Dennis J. Moberg, "Perspectives on the Technology of Service Operations," *Academy of Management Review* 7 (1982), 467–478; Roger W. Schmenner, "How Can Service Businesses Survive and Prosper?" *Sloan Management Review* 27 (Spring 1986), 21–32.
26. Michael Withey, Richard L. Daft, and William C. Cooper, "Measures of Perrow's Work Unit Technology: An Empirical Assessment and a New Scale," *Academy of Management Journal* 25 (1983), 45–63.
27. Schmenner, "How Can Service Businesses Survive?"
28. Richard B. Chase and David A. Tansik, "The Customer Contact Model for Organization Design," *Management Science* 29 (1983), 1037–1050, and Gregory B. Northcraft and Richard B. Chase, "Managing Service Demand at the Point of Delivery," *Academy of Management Review* 10 (1985), 66–75.
29. "Marriott: The Fearless Host," *Dun's Business Month*, December 1984, 36–37, and Thomas Moore, "Marriott Grabs for More Rooms," *Fortune*, October 31, 1983, 107–122.
30. James Thompson, *Organizations in Action* (New York: McGraw-Hill, 1967).
31. Jack K. Ito and Richard B. Peterson, "Effects of Task Difficulty and Interdependence on Information Processing Systems," *Academy of Management Journal* 29 (1986), 139–149, and Andrew H. Van de Ven, Andre Delbecq, and Richard Koenig, "Determinents of Coordination Modes Within Organizations," *American Sociological Review* 41 (1976), 322–338.
32. Harrison and Layton, "How Troxel Manufacturing Restructured Itself."

CHAPTER 11

1. Patty Watts, "Preston and the Teamsters Keep on Trucking," *Management Review* (March 1988), 22–24, and Alan Farnham, "The Trust Gap," *Fortune*, December 4, 1989, 56–78.
2. Richard L. Daft, "Bureaucratic vs. Nonbureaucratic Structure in the Process of Innovation and Change," in *Perspectives in Organi-*

zational Sociology: Theory and Research, ed. Samuel B. Bacharach (Greenwich, Conn.: JAI Press, 1982), 129–166.

3. Andre L. Delbecq and Peter K. Mills, "Managerial Practices That Enhance Innovation," *Organizational Dynamics* 14 (Summer 1985), 24–34.
4. Ira Magaziner and Mark Tatinkin, *The Silent War: Inside the Global Business Battles Shaping America's Future* (New York: Random House, 1989).
5. Andrew H. Van de Ven, Harold Angle, and Marshall Scott Poole, *Research on the Management of Innovation* (Cambridge, Mass.: Ballinger, 1989).
6. Magaziner and Tatinkin, *The Silent War.*
7. Attributed to Gregory Bateson in Andrew H. Van de Ven, "Central Problems in the Management of Innovation," *Management Science* 32 (1986), 595.
8. Charles Pearlman, "A Theoretical Model for Creativity," *Education* 103 (1983), 294–305, and Robert R. Godfrey, "Tapping Employees' Creativity," *Supervisory Management* (February 1986), 16–20.
9. Craig R. Hickman and Michael A. Silva, "How to Tap Your Creative Powers," *Working Woman,* September 1985, 26–30.
10. Gordon Vessels, "The Creative Process: An Open-Systems Conceptualization," *Journal of Creative Behavior* 16 (1982), 185–196, and Pearlman, "A Theoretical Model."
11. James Brian Quinn, "Managing Innovation: Controlled Chaos," *Harvard Business Review* 63 (May/June 1985), 73–84; Howard H. Stevenson and David E. Gumpert, "The Heart of Entrepreneurship," *Harvard Business Review* 63 (March/April 1985), 85–94; Marsha Sinetar, "Entrepreneurs, Chaos, and Creativity — Can Creative People Really Survive Large Company Structure?" *Sloan Management Review* 6 (Winter 1985), 57–62.
12. Cynthia Browne, "Jest for Success," *Moonbeams,* August 1989, 3–5, and Rosabeth Moss Kanter, *The Change Masters* (New York: Simon and Schuster, 1983).
13. Kanter, *The Change Masters.*
14. "Hands On: A Manager's Notebook," *INC.,* January 1989, 106.
15. Bo Burlingham and Curtis Hartman, "Cowboy Capitalist," *INC.,* January 1989, 60.
16. "Keeping the Fires Lit Under the Innovators," *Fortune,* March 28, 1988, 45; Paula Doody, Pat Hall, and Mike Nelson, "General Mills" (Unpublished paper, Texas A&M University, 1983); "Look Who's Playing with Toys!" *Forbes,* December 15, 1981, 22.
17. Katy Koontz, "How to Stand Out From the Crowd," *Working Woman,* January 1988, 74–76.
18. Harold L. Angle and Andrew H. Van de Ven, "Suggestions for Managing the Innovation Journey," in *Research in the Management of Innovation: The Minnesota Studies,* ed. A. H. Van de Ven, H. L. Angle, and Mabel S. Poole (Cambridge, Mass.: Ballinger/Harper & Row, 1989).
19. Gifford Pinchot III, *Intrapreneuring* (New York: Harper & Row, 1985).
20. Christopher K. Bart, "New Venture Units: Use Them Wisely to Manage Innovation," *Sloan Management Review* (Summer 1988), 35–43.
21. Peter F. Drucker, *Innovation and Entrepreneurship* (New York: Harper & Row, 1985).
22. Michael Tushman and David Nadler, "Organizing for Innovation," *California Management Review* 28 (Spring 1986), 74–92.
23. Carl E. Larson and Frank M. J. LaFasto, *TeamWork* (Newbury Park, CA: Sage, 1989; "How the PC Changed the Way IBM Thinks," *Business Week,* October 3, 1983, 86–90.
24. Tom Peters and Nancy Austin, *A Passion for Excellence: The Leadership Difference* (New York: Random House, 1985).
25. "Teleflex Incorporated Annual Report," 1988, Limerick, Penn.
26. John P. Kotter and Leonard A. Schlesinger, "Choosing Strategies for Change," *Harvard Business Review* 57 (March/April 1979), 106–114.
27. G. Zaltman and R. Duncan, *Strategies for Planned Change* (New York: Wiley Interscience, 1977).
28. Leonard M. Apcar, "Middle Managers and Supervisors Resist Moves to More Participatory Management," *The Wall Street Journal,* September 16, 1985, 25.
29. Dorothy Leonard-Barton and Isabelle Deschamps, "Managerial Influence in the Implementation of New Technology," *Management Science* 34 (1988), 1252–1265.
30. Kurt Lewin, *Field Theory in Social Science: Selected Theoretical Papers* (New York: Harper & Brothers, 1951).
31. Paul C. Nutt, "Tactics of Implementation," *Academy of Management Journal* 29 (1986), 230–261; Kotter and Schlesinger, "Choosing Strategies"; Richard L. Daft and Selwyn Becker, *Innovation in Organizations: Innovation Adoption in School Organizations* (New York: Elsevier, 1978); Richard Beckhard, *Organization Development: Strategies and Models* (Reading, Mass.: Addison-Wesley, 1969).
32. Patricia J. Paden-Bost, "Making Money Control a Management Issue," *Management Accounting* (November 1982), 48–56, and Apcar, "Middle Managers."
33. Apcar, "Middle Managers."
34. Jeremy Main, "The Trouble with Managing Japanese-Style," *Fortune,* April 2, 1984, 50–56.
35. Jabby Lowe, Greg Millsap, and Bill Breedlove, "International Harvester" (Unpublished manuscript, Texas A&M University, 1982), and Barbara Marsh, *A Corporate Tragedy: The Agony of International Harvester Company* (Garden City, N.Y.: Doubleday, 1985).
36. Richard L. Daft, *Organization Theory and Design* (St. Paul, Minn.: West, 1989), and Tom Burns and G. M. Stalker, *The Management of Innovation* (London: Tavistock Publications, 1961).
37. Stratford P. Sherman, "How Philip Morris Diversified Right," *Fortune,* October 23, 1989, 120–129.
38. Richard L. Daft, "A Dual-Core Model of Organizational Innovation," *Academy of Management Journal* 21 (1978), 193–210, and Kanter, *The Change Masters.*
39. Harold J. Leavitt, "Applied Organizational Change in Industry: Structural, Technical, and Human Approaches," in *New Perspectives in Organization Research,* ed. W. W. Cooper, H. J. Leavitt, and M. W. Shelly II (New York: Wiley, 1964), 55–74.
40. Edwin Mansfield, J. Rapoport, J. Schnee, S. Wagner, and M. Hamburger, *Research and Innovation in Modern Corporations* (New York: Norton, 1971).
41. Andrew H. Van de Ven, "Central Problems in the Management of Innovation," *Management Science* 32 (1986), 590–607; Daft, *Organization Theory;* Science Policy Research Unit, University of Sussex, *Success and Failure in Industrial Innovation* (London: Centre for the Study of Industrial Innovation, 1972).
42. William L. Shanklin and John K. Ryans, Jr., "Organizing for High-Tech Marketing," *Harvard Business Review* 62 (November/December 1984), 164–171; Arnold O. Putnam, "A Redesign for Engineering," *Harvard Business Review* 63 (May/June 1985), 139–144.
43. Daft, *Organization Theory.*
44. Keith H. Hammonds, "Teaching Discipline to Six-Year-Old Lotus," *Business Week,* July 4, 1988, 100–102.
45. Susan Caminiti, "A Quiet Superstar Rises in Retailing," *Fortune,* October 23, 1989, 167–174.
46. Brian Dumaine, "How Managers Can Succeed Through Speed," *Fortune,* February 13, 1989, 54–59, and George Stalk, Jr., "Time — The Next Source of Competitive Advantage," *Harvard Business Review* (July/August 1988), 41–51.
47. Fariborz Damanpour, "The Adoption of Technological, Administrative, and Ancillary Innovations: Impact of Organizational Factors," *Journal of Management* 13 (1987), 675–688.
48. Daft, "Bureaucratic vs. Nonbureaucratic Structure," and Daft, "A Dual-Core Model.".

49. Mary Kay Ash, *Mary Kay on People Management* (New York: Warner, 1984), 75.
50. Edgar H. Schein, "Organizational Culture," *American Psychologist* 45 (February 1990), 109–119; Andrew Kupfer, "An Outsider Fires Up a Railroad," *Fortune,* December 18, 1989, 133–146.
51. Marshall Sashkin and W. Warner Burke, "Organization Development in the 1980s," *General Management* 13 (1987), 393–417, and Edgar F. Huse and Thomas G. Cummings, *Organization Development and Change,* 3d ed. (St. Paul, Minn.: West, 1985).
52. Paul F. Buller, "For Successful Strategic Change: Bland OD Practices with Strategic Management," *Organizational Dynamics* (Winter 1988), 42–55, and Robert M. Fulmer and Roderick Gilkey, "Blending Corporate Families: Management and Organization Development in a Postmerger Environment," *The Academy of Management Executive* 2 (1988), 275–283.
53. David A. Nadler, *Feedback and Organizational Development: Using Data-Based Methods* (Reading, Mass.: Addison-Wesley, 1977).
54. Wendell L. French and Cecil H. Bell, Jr., *Organization Development: Behavioral Science Interventions for Organization Improvement,* 3d ed. (Englewood Cliffs, N.J.: Prentice-Hall, 1984).
55. Buller, "For Successful Strategic Change."
56. Kurt Lewin, "Frontiers in Group Dynamics: Concepts, Method, and Reality in Social Science," *Human Relations* 1 (1947), 5–41, and Huse and Cummings, *Organization Development.*
57. Richard J. Boyle, "Wrestling with Jelly Fish," *Harvard Business Review* (January/February 1984), 74–83.
58. Ibid.
59. Farnham, "The Trust Gap," and Watts, "Preston and the Teamsters Keep on Trucking."

CHAPTER 12

1. Thomas Melohn, "Screening for the Best Employees," *INC.*, January 1987, 104–106.
2. D. Kneale, "Working at IBM: Intense Loyalty in a Rigid Culture," *The Wall Street Journal,* April 7, 1986, 17.
3. Cynthia D. Fisher, "Current and Recurrent Challenges in HRM," *Journal of Management* 15 (1989), 157–180.
4. Cynthia A. Lengnick-Hall and Mark L. Lengnick-Hall, "Strategic Human Resources Management: A Review of the Literature and a Proposed Typology," *Academy of Management Review* 13 (1988), 454–470, and "Human Resources Managers Aren't Corporate Nobodies Any More," *Business Week,* December 2, 1985, 58–59.
5. Steven H. Appelbaun, Roger Simpson, and Barbara T. Shapiro, "The Tough Test of Downsizing," *Organizational Dynamics* (Autumn 1987), 68–79.
6. Aaron Bernstein, "How IBM Cut 16,200 Employees — Without an Ax," *Business Week,* February 15, 1988, 98.
7. Richard E. Walton and Gerald I. Susman, "People Policies for the New Machines," *Harvard Business Review* 87 (March/April 1987), 98–106, and Randall S. Schuler and Susan E. Jackson, "Linking Competitive Strategies with Human Resource Management Practices," *The Academy of Management Executive* 1 (1987), 207–219.
8. Robert L. Mathis and John H. Jackson, *Personnel/Human Resource Management* (St. Paul, Minn.: West, 1988), and Terry L. Leap and Michael D. Crino, *Personnel/Human Resource Management* (New York: Macmillan, 1989).
9. Joan C. Szabo, "Learning at Work," *Nation's Business,* February 1990, 27–28; "The Workforce of the Year 2000," *Management Review* (August 1989), 5–6; Carol Milano, "Re-evaluating Recruitment to Better Target Top Minority Talent," *Management Review* (August 1989), 29–32.
10. Froma Joselop, "Why Business Turns to Teen-Agers," *The New York Times,* March 26, 1989, sec. 3, 1, 6.
11. Udayan Gupta and Jeffrey A. Tannenbaum, "Labor Shortages Force Changes at Small Firms," *The Wall Street Journal,* May 22, 1989, B1, B2, and Elizabeth Ehrlich and Susan B. Garland, "Needed: Human Capital," *Business Week,* September 19, 1988, 100–120.
12. Aaron Bernstein, "More Dismissed Workers Are Telling it to the Judge," *Business Week,* October 17, 1988, 68–69, and Michael Goldblatt, "Perserving the Right to Fire," *Small Business Report* (December 1986), 87.
13. Rod Willis, "Can American Unions Transform Themselves?" *Management Review* (February 1988), 12–21.
14. James G. March and Herbert A. Simon, *Organizations* (New York: Wiley, 1958).
15. Dennis J. Kravetz, *The Human Resources Revolution* (San Francisco, Calif.: Jossey-Bass, 1989).
16. Electronic Data Systems Corporation, *1985 Annual Report,* 4–12.
17. Richard I. Henderson, *Compensation Management: Rewarding Performance,* 4th ed. (Reston, Va.: Reston, 1985).
18. D. Quinn Mills, "Planning with People in Mind," *Harvard Business Review* 63 (July/August 1985), 97–105, and USAir, *1985 Annual Report,* 5.
19. J. W. Boudreau and S. L. Rynes, "Role of Recruitment in Staffing Utility Analysis," *Journal of Applied Psychology* 70 (1985), 354–366.
20. Brian Dumaine, "The New Art of Hiring Smart," *Fortune,* August 17, 1987, 78–81.
21. P. Farish, "HRM Update: Referral Results," *Personnel Administrator* 31 (1986), 22.
22. J. P. Wanous, *Organizational Entry* (Reading, Mass.: Addison-Wesley, 1980).
23. Larry Reibstein, "Crushed Hopes: When a New Job Proves To Be Something Different," *The Wall Street Journal,* June 10, 1987, 25.
24. P. W. Thayer, "Somethings Old, Somethings New," *Personnel Psychology* 30 (1977), 513–524.
25. J. Ledvinka, *Federal Regulation of Personnel and Human Resource Management* (Boston: Kent, 1982); Civil Rights Act, Title VII, 42 U.S.C. Section 2000e *et seq.* (1964).
26. The material in this section is largely drawn from R. D. Arvey and J. E. Campion, "The Employment Interview: A Summary and Review of Recent Research," *Personnel Psychology* 35 (1982), 281–322.
27. James M. Jenks and Brian L. B. Zevnik, "ABCs of Job Interviewing," *Harvard Business Review* (July/August 1989), 38–42.
28. A. Brown, "Employment Tests: Issues without Clear Answers," *Personnel Administrator* 30 (1985), 43–56.
29. Larry Reibstein, "More Firms Use Personality Tests for Entry-Level, Blue-Collar Jobs," *The Wall Street Journal,* January 16, 1986, 25.
30. "Assessment Centers: Identifying Leadership Through Testing," *Small Business Report* (June 1987), 22–24, and W. C. Byham, "Assessment Centers for Spotting Future Managers," *Harvard Business Review* (July/August 1970), 150–167.
31. G. F. Dreher and P. R. Sackett, "Commentary: A Critical Look at Some Beliefs about Assessment Centers," in *Perspectives on Employee Staffing and Selection,* ed. G. F. Dreher and P. R. Sackett (Homewood, Ill.: Irwin, 1983), 258–265.
32. Louis Kraar, "Japan's Gun-Ho U.S. Car Plants," *Fortune,* January 30, 1989, 98–108, and Richard Koenig, "Toyota Takes Pains, and Time, Filling Jobs at Its Kentucky Plant," *The Wall Street Journal,* December 1, 1987, 129.
33. Bernard Keys and Joseph Wolfe, "Management Education and Development: Current Issues and Emerging Trends," *Journal of Management* 14 (1988), 205–229.
34. Michael Brody, "Helping Workers to Work Smarter," *Fortune,* June 8, 1987, 86–88.
35. Christopher Power, "Coffee, Tea, and the Power of Positive Thinking," *Business Week,* July 31, 1989, 36.

36. Brian Dumaine, "Those Highflying PepsiCo Managers," *Fortune*, April 10, 1989, 78–86.
37. V. R. Buzzotta, "Improve Your Performance Appraisals," *Management Review* (August 1988), 40–43, and H. J. Bernardin and R. W. Beatty, *Performance Appraisal: Assessing Human Behavior at Work* (Boston: Kent, 1984).
38. Ibid.
39. Francine Alexander, "Performance Appraisals," *Small Business Reports* (March 1989), 20–29.
40. D. Cederblom, "The Performance Appraisal Interview: A Review, Implications, and Suggestions," *Academy of Management Review* 7 (1982), 219–227.
41. Buzzotta, "Improve Your Performance Appraisals," and Alexander, "Performance Appraisals."
42. Steve Ventura and Eric Harvey, "Peer Review: Trusting Employees to Solve Problems," *Management Review* (January 1988), 48–51.
43. Henderson, *Compensation Management*.
44. Renée F. Broderick and George T. Milkovich, "Pay Planning, Organization Strategy, Structure and 'Fit': A Prescriptive Model of Pay" (Paper presented at the 45th Annual Meeting of the Academy of Management, San Diego, August 1985).
45. Michael Schroeder, "Watching the Bottom Line Instead of the Clock," *Business Week*, November 7, 1988, 134–136, and Bruce G. Posner, "You Get What You Pay For," *INC.*, September 1988, 91–92.
46. L. R. Burgess, *Wage and Salary Administration* (Columbus, Ohio: Merrill, 1984), and E. J. McCormick, *Job Analysis: Methods and Applications* (New York: AMACOM, 1979).
47. B. M. Bass and G. V. Barrett, *People, Work, and Organizations: An Introduction to Industrial and Organizational Psychology*, 2d ed. (Boston: Allyn & Bacon, 1981), and D. Doverspike, A. M. Carlisi, G. V. Barrett, and R. A. Alexander, "Generalizability Analysis of a Point-Method Job Evaluation Instrument," *Journal of Applied Psychology* 68 (1983), 476–483.
48. U.S. Chamber of Commerce, *Employee Benefits 1983* (Washington, D.C.: U.S. Chamber of Commerce, 1984).
49. D. C. Stone and E. G. S. Reitz, "Health Care Cost Containment and Employee Relations," *Personnel Administrator* 29 (1984), 27–33.
50. J. A. Haslinger, "Flexible Compensation: Getting a Return on Benefit Dollars," *Personnel Administrator* 30 (1985), 39–46, 224.
51. "Exit Interviews: An Overlooked Information Source," *Small Business Report* (July 1986), 52–55.
52. Rod Willis, "What's Happening to America's Middle Managers," *Management Review* (January 1987), 23–26, and Yvette Debow, "GE: Easing the Pain of Layoffs," *Management Review* (September 1987), 15–18.
53. Melohn, "Screening for the Best Employees."

CHAPTER 13

1. Russell Mitchell, "After Harry Gray: Reshaping United Technologies," *Business Week*, January 18, 1988, 46–48.
2. Kenneth Labich, "The Seven Keys to Business Leadership," *Fortune*, October 24, 1988, 58–66, and "The Newsmakers," *Business Week*, April 18, 1986, 194.
3. Gary Yukl, "Managerial Leadership: A Review of Theory and Research," *Journal of Management* 15 (1989), 251–289.
4. Henry Mintzberg, *Power in and around Organizations* (Englewood Cliffs, N.J.: Prentice-Hall, 1983), and Jeffrey Pfeffer, *Power in Organizations* (Marshfield, Mass.: Pitman, 1981).
5. J. R. P. French, Jr., and B. Raven, "The Bases of Social Power," in *Group Dynamics*, ed. D. Cartwright and A. F. Zander (Evanston, Ill.: Row, Peterson, 1960), 607–623.
6. G. A. Yukl and T. Taber, "The Effective Use of Managerial Power," *Personnel* (March/April 1983), 37–44.
7. Thomas A. Stewart, "New Ways to Exercise Power," *Fortune*, November 6, 1989, 52–64, and Thomas A. Stewart, "CEOs See Clout Shifting," *Fortune*, November 6, 1989, 66.
8. G. A. Yukl, *Leadership in Organizations* (Englewood Cliffs, N.J.: Prentice-Hall, 1981), and S. C. Kohs and K. W. Irle, "Prophesying Army Promotion," *Journal of Applied Psychology* 4 (1920), 73–87.
9. R. Albanese and D. D. Van Fleet, *Organizational Behavior: A Managerial Viewpoint* (Hinsdale, Ill.: Dryden Press, 1983).
10. K. Lewin, "Field Theory and Experiment in Social Psychology: Concepts and Methods," *American Journal of Sociology* 44 (1939), 868–896; K. Lewin and R. Lippitt, "An Experimental Approach to the Study of Autocracy and Democracy: A Preliminary Note," *Sociometry* 1 (1938), 292–300; K. Lewin, R. Lippitt, and R. K. White, "Patterns of Aggressive Behavior in Experimentally Created Social Climates," *Journal of Social Psychology* 10 (1939), 271–301.
11. R. K. White and R. Lippitt, *Autocracy and Democracy: An Experimental Inquiry* (New York: Harper, 1960).
12. R. Tannenbaum and W. H. Schmidt, "How to Choose a Leadership Pattern," *Harvard Business Review* 36 (1958), 95–101.
13. F. A. Heller and G. A. Yukl, "Participation, Managerial Decision-Making and Situational Variables," *Organizational Behavior and Human Performance* 4 (1969), 227–241.
14. "The Art of Loving," *INC.*, May 1989, 35–46.
15. C. A. Schriesheim and B. J. Bird, "Contributions of the Ohio State Studies to the Field of Leadership," *Journal of Management* 5 (1979), 135–145, and C. L. Shartle, "Early Years of the Ohio State University Leadership Studies," *Journal of Management* 5 (1979), 126–134.
16. P. C. Nystrom, "Managers and the High-High Leader Myth," *Academy of Management Journal* 21 (1978), 325–331, and L. L. Larson, J. G. Hunt, and R. N. Osborn, "The Great High-High Leader Behavior Myth: A Lesson from Occam's Razor," *Academy of Management Journal* 19 (1976), 628–641.
17. R. Likert, "From Production- and Employee-Centeredness to Systems 1-4," *Journal of Management* 5 (1979), 147–156.
18. Robert R. Blake and Jane S. Mouton, *The Managerial Grid III* (Houston: Gulf, 1985).
19. Jasper Dorsey, "S. Truett Cathy," *SKY*, February 1985, 45–50.
20. Todd Fogel, "A Mr. Fix-It Goes to Work on Lorenzo's Continental," *Business Week*, May 22, 1989, 133–136.
21. F. E. Fiedler, "Assumed Similarity Measures as Predictors of Team Effectiveness," *Journal of Abnormal and Social Psychology* 49 (1954), 381–388; F. E. Fiedler, *Leader Attitudes and Group Effectiveness* (Urbana, Ill.: University of Illinois Press, 1958); F. E. Fiedler, *A Theory of Leadership Effectiveness* (New York: McGraw-Hill, 1967).
22. F. E. Fiedler and M. M. Chemers, *Leadership and Effective Management* (Glenview, Ill.: Scott, Foresman, 1974).
23. F. E. Fiedler, "Engineer the Job to Fit the Manager," *Harvard Business Review* 43 (1965), 115–122, and F. E. Fiedler, M. M. Chemers, and L. Mahar, *Improving Leadership Effectiveness: The Leader Match Concept* (New York: Wiley, 1976).
24. Brian O'Reilly, "A Body Builder Lifts Greyhound," *Fortune*, October 28, 1985, 124–134.
25. R. Singh, "Leadership Style and Reward Allocation: Does Least Preferred Co-worker Scale Measure Taks and Relation Orientation?" *Organizational Behavior and Human Performance* 27 (1983), 178–197, and D. Hosking, "A Critical Evaluation of Fiedler's Contingency Hypotheses," *Progress in Applied Psychology* 1 (1981), 103–154.
26. Paul Hersey and Kenneth H. Blanchard, *Management of Organizational Behavior: Utilizing Human Resources*, 4th ed. (Englewood Cliffs, N.J.: Prentice-Hall, 1982).
27. E. J. Dionne, Jr., "Pierce at H.U.D.: Eight Years of Hands-Off Management," *The New York Times*, June 18, 1989, 1.
28. M. G. Evans, "The Effects of Supervisory Behavior on the Path-Goal Relationship," *Organizational Behavior and Human Perfor-*

mance 5 (1970), 277–298; M. G. Evans, "Leadership and Motivation: A Core Concept," *Academy of Management Journal* 13 (1970), 91–102; B. S. Georgopoulos, G. M. Mahoney, and N. W. Jones, "A Path-Goal Approach to Productivity," *Journal of Applied Psychology* 41 (1957), 345–353.

29. Robert J. House, "A Path-Goal Theory of Leader Effectiveness," *Administrative Science Quarterly* 16 (1971), 321–338.
30. M. G. Evans, "Leadership," in *Organizational Behavior*, ed. S. Kerr (Columbus, Ohio: Grid, 1974), 230–233.
31. Robert J. House and Terrence R. Mitchell, "Path-Goal Theory of Leadership," *Journal of Contemporary Business* (Autumn 1974), 81–97.
32. "The Team Pushing Fireman's Up the Ladder," *Business Week*, August 4, 1986, 50–51.
33. Charles Greene, "Questions of Causation in the Path-Goal Theory of Leadership," *Academy of Management Journal* 22 (March 1979), 22–41, and C. A. Schriesheim and M. A. von Glinow, "The Path-Goal Theory of Leadership: A Theoretical and Empirical Analysis," *Academy of Management Journal* 20 (1977), 398–405.
34. S. Kerr and J. M. Jermier, "Substitutes for Leadership: Their Meaning and Measurement," *Organizational Behavior and Human Performance* 22 (1978), 375–403, and Jon P. Howell and Peter W. Dorfman, "Leadership and Substitutes for Leadership among Professional and Nonprofessional Workers," *Journal of Applied Behavioral Science* 22 (1986), 29–46.
35. The terms *transactional* and *transformational* come from James M. Burns, *Leadership* (New York: Harper & Row, 1978), and Bernard M. Bass, "Leadership: Good, Better, Best," *Organizational Dynamics* 13 (Winter 1985), 26–40.
36. Walter Kiechel III, "A Hard Look at Executive Vision," *Fortune*, October 23, 1989, 207–211, and Allan Cox, "Focus on Teamwork, Vision, and Values," *The New York Times*, February 26, 1989, sec. F, 3.
37. Robert J. House, "Research Contrasting the Behavior and Effects of Reputed Charismatic vs. Reputed Non-Charismatic Leaders" (Paper presented as part of a symposium, "Charismatic Leadership: Theory and Evidence," Academy of Management, San Diego, 1985).
38. Pete Engardio, "Charlie Bryan Has Ideas — And Lorenzo Is Listening," *Business Week*, November 21, 1988, 88–93.
39. Roger Smith, "The U.S. Must Do as GM Has Done," *Fortune*, February 13, 1989, 70–73.
40. Jay A. Conger and Rabindra N. Kanungo, "Toward a Behavioral Theory of Charismatic Leadership in Organizational Settings," *Academy of Management Review* 12 (1987), 637–647.
41. Noel M. Tichy and David O. Ulrich, "The Leadership Challenge — A Call for the Transformational Leader," *Sloan Management Review* 26 (Fall 1984), 59–68.
42. Mitchell, "After Harry Gray: Reshaping United Technologies."

CHAPTER 14

1. Bruce G. Posner, "May the Force Be With You," *INC.*, July 1987, 70–75.
2. David Silburt, "Secrets of the Super Sellers," *Canadian Business*, January 1987, 54–59; "Meet the Savvy Supersalesmen," *Fortune*, February 4, 1985, 56–62; Michael Brody, "Meet Today's Young American Worker," *Fortune*, November 11, 1985, 90–98; Tom Richman, "Meet the Masters. They Could Sell You Anything . . . ," *INC.*, March 1985, 79–86.
3. Richard M. Steers and Lyman W. Porter, eds., *Motivation and Work Behavior*, 3d ed. (New York: McGraw-Hill, 1983).
4. Kenneth A. Kovach, "What Motivates Employees? Workers and Supervisors Give Different Answers," *Business Horizon* 30 (September/October), 58–65.
5. Steers and Porter, *Motivation*.
6. J. F. Rothlisberger and W. J. Dickson, *Management and the Worker* (Cambridge, Mass.: Harvard University Press, 1939).
7. Abraham F. Maslow, "A Theory of Human Motivation," *Psychological Review* 50 (1943), 370–396.
8. Clayton Alderfer, *Existence, Relatedness and Growth* (New York: Free Press, 1972).
9. Everett T. Suters, "Show and Tell," *INC.*, April 1987, 111–112.
10. Frederick Herzberg, "One More Time: How Do You Motivate Employees?" *Harvard Business Review* (January/February 1968), 53–62.
11. Ellen Wojan, "Will the Company Please Come to Order," *INC.*, March 1986, 78–86.
12. David C. McClelland, *Human Motivation* (Glenview, Ill.: Scott, Foresman, 1985).
13. David C. McClelland, "The Two Faces of Power," in *Organizational Psychology*, ed. D. A. Colb, I. M. Rubin, and J. M. McIntyre (Englewood Cliffs, N.J.: Prentice-Hall, 1971), 73–86.
14. J. Stacy Adams, "Injustice in Social Exchange," in *Advances in Experimental Social Psychology*, 2d ed., ed. L. Berkowitz (New York: Academic Press, 1965), and J. Stacy Adams, "Toward an Understanding of Inequity," *Journal of Abnormal and Social Psychology* (November 1963), 422–436.
15. Ray V. Montagno, "The Effects of Comparison to Others and Primary Experience on Responses to Task Design," *Academy of Management Journal* 28 (1985), 491–498, and Robert P. Vecchio, "Predicting Worker Performance in Inequitable Settings," *Academy of Management Review* 7 (1982), 103–110.
16. "The Double Standard That's Setting Worker against Worker," *Business Week*, April 8, 1985, 70–71.
17. James E. Martin and Melanie M. Peterson, "Two-Tier Wage Structures: Implications for Equity Theory," *Academy of Management Journal* 30 (1987), 297–315.
18. George Gendron, "Steel Man Ken Iverson," *INC.*, April 1986, 41–48.
19. Victor H. Vroom, *Work and Motivation* (New York: Wiley, 1964); B. S. Gorgopoulos, G. M. Mahoney, and N. Jones, "A Path-Goal Approach to Productivity," *Journal of Applied Psychology* 41 (1957), 345–353; E. E. Lawler III, *Pay and Organizational Effectiveness: A Psychological View* (New York: McGraw-Hill, 1981).
20. Richard L. Daft and Richard M. Steers, *Organizations: A Micro/Macro Approach* (Glenview, Ill.: Scott, Foresman, 1986).
21. Bruce G. Posner, "If At First You Don't Succeed," *INC.*, May 1989, 132–134.
22. H. Richlin, *Modern Behaviorism* (San Francisco: Freeman, 1970), and B. F. Skinner, *Science and Human Behavior* (New York: Macmillan, 1953).
23. Tom Peters and Nancy Austin, *A Passion for Excellence: The Leadership Difference* (New York: Random House, 1985), 267.
24. L. M. Sarri and G. P. Latham, "Employee Reaction to Continuous and Variable Ratio Reinforcement Schedules Involving a Monetary Incentive," *Journal of Applied Psychology* 67 (1982), 506–508, and R. D. Pritchard, J. Hollenback, and P. J. DeLeo, "The Effects of Continuous and Partial Schedules of Reinforcement on Effort, Performance, and Satisfaction," *Organizational Behavior and Human Performance* 25 (1980), 336–353.
25. "Creating Incentives for Hourly Workers," *INC.*, July 1986, 89–90.
26. Norm Alster, "What Flexible Workers Can Do," *Fortune*, February 13, 1989, 62–66.
27. J. Richard Hackman and Greg R. Oldham, *Work Redesign* (Reading, Mass.: Addison-Wesley, 1980), and J. Richard Hackman and Greg Oldham, "Motivation through the Design of Work: Test of a Theory," *Organizational Behavior and Human Performance* 16 (1976), 250–279.
28. J. Richard Hackman, Greg R. Oldham, R. Janson, and K. Purdy, "A New Strategy for Job Enrichment," *California Management Review* 17 (1975), 57–71, and Daft and Steers, *Organizations*, 173–174.

29. Jacob M. Schleslinger, "GM's New Compensation Plan Reflects General Trend Tying Pay to Performance," *The Wall Street Journal,* January 26, 1988, 31.
30. Timothy L. Ross, Larry Hatcher, and Ruth Ann Ross, "From Piecework to Companywide Gainsharing," *Management Review* (May 1989), 22–26, and Nancy J. Perry, "Here Come Richer, Riskier Pay Plans," *Fortune,* December 19, 1988, 50–58.
31. Christopher S. Eklund, "How A&P Fattens Profits by Sharing Them," *Business Week,* December 22, 1986, 44.
32. Christopher Farrell and John Hoerr, "ESOPs: Are They Good for You?" *Business Week,* May 15, 1989, 116–123, and John Case, "ESOPs: Dead or Alive?" *INC.,* June 1988, 94–100.
33. Posner, "May the Force Be With You."

CHAPTER 15

1. Michael H. Dale, "How We Rebuilt Jaguar in the U.S.," *Fortune,* April 28, 1986, 110–120, and Minda Zetlin, "John Egan: Tough Leadership Turns Jaguar Around," *Management Review* (May 1986), 20–22.
2. James E. Ellis, "Will the Carrot and Stick Work at United?" *Business Week,* February 6, 1989, 56–57, and Thomas F. O'Boyle and Carol Hymowitz, "More Corporate Chiefs Seek Direct Contact with Staff, Customers," *The Wall Street Journal,* February 27, 1985, 1, 12.
3. Elizabeth B. Drew, "Profile: Robert Strauss," *The New Yorker,* May 7, 1979, 55–70.
4. Henry Mintzberg, *The Nature of Managerial Work* (New York: Harper & Row, 1973).
5. Fred Luthans and Janet K. Larsen, "How Managers Really Communicate," *Human Relations* 39 (1986), 161–178, and Larry E. Penley and Brian Hawkins, "Studying Interpersonal Communication in Organizations: A Leadership Application," *Academy of Management Journal* 28 (1985), 309–326.
6. D. K. Berlo, *The Process of Communication* (New York: Holt, Rinehart and Winston, 1960), 24.
7. Nelson W. Aldrich, Jr., "Lines of Communication," *INC.,* June 1986, 140–144.
8. Bruce K. Blaylock, "Cognitive Style and the Usefulness of Information," *Decision Sciences* 15 (Winter 1984), 74–91.
9. Richard L. Daft and Richard M. Steers, *Organizations: A Micro/Macro Approach* (Glenview, Ill.: Scott, Foresman, 1986).
10. James R. Wilcox, Ethel M. Wilcox, and Karen M. Cowan, "Communicating Creatively in Conflict Situations," *Management Solutions* (October 1986), 18–24.
11. Robert H. Lengel and Richard L. Daft, "The Selection of Communication Media as an Executive Skill," *Academy of Management Executive* 2 (August 1988), 225–232, and Richard L. Daft and Robert H. Lengel, "Organizational Information Requirements, Media Richness and Structural Design," *Management Science* 32 (May 1986), 554–572.
12. Ford S. Worthy, "How CEOs Manage Their Time," *Fortune,* January 18, 1988, 88–97.
13. Richard L. Daft, Robert H. Lengel, and Linda Klebe Trevino, "Message Equivocality, Media Selection and Manager Performance: Implication for Information Systems," *MIS Quarterly* 11 (1987), 355–368.
14. Harold Geneen with Alvin Moscow, *Managing* (New York: Doubleday, 1984), 46–47.
15. I. Thomas Sheppard, "Silent Signals," *Supervisory Management* (March 1986), 31–33.
16. Albert Mehrabian, *Silent Messages* (Belmont, Cal.: Wadsworth, 1971), and Albert Mehrabian, "Communicating without Words," *Psychology Today,* September 1968, 53–55.
17. Sheppard, "Silent Signals."
18. Arthur H. Bell, *The Complete Manager's Guide to Interviewing* (Homewood, Ill.: Richard D. Irwin, 1989).
19. C. Glenn Pearce, "Doing Something About Your Listening Ability," *Supervisory Management* (March 1989), 29–34, and Tom Peters, "Learning to Listen," *Hyatt Magazine* (Spring 1988), 16–21.
20. Gerald M. Goldhaber, *Organizational Communication,* 4th ed. (Dubuque, Iowa: Wm. C. Brown, 1980), 189.
21. Peters, "Learning to Listen."
22. Daft and Steers, *Organizations,* and Daniel Katz and Robert Kahn, *The Social Psychology of Organizations,* 2d ed. (New York: Wiley, 1978).
23. Jack Cashill, "Creating an Environment for Success," *Management Review* (April 1989), 18–19.
24. J. G. Miller, "Living Systems: The Organization," *Behavioral Science* 17 (1972), 69.
25. Michael J. Glauser, "Upward Information Flow in Organizations: Review and Conceptual Analysis," *Human Relations* 37 (1984), 613–643, and "Upward/Downward Communication: Critical Information Channels," *Small Business Report* (October 1985), 85–88.
26. Sharon Y. Lopez, "Let's Talk," *On Call,* June 1989, 4–5. (Published by Long Island Lighting Company.)
27. Mary P. Rowe and Michael Baker, "Are You Hearing Enough Employee Concerns?" *Harvard Business Review* 62 (May/June 1984), 127–135; W. H. Read, "Upward Communication in Industrial Hierarchies," *Human Relations* 15 (February 1962), 3–15; Daft and Steers, *Organizations.*
28. Paul Hawken, *Growing a Business* (New York: Simon & Schuster, 1987).
29. Jacqueline Kaufman, "Carol Taber, Working Woman," *Management Review* (October 1986), 60–61.
30. Thomas F. O'Boyle and Carol Hymowitz, "More Corporate Chiefs Seek Direct Contact with Staff, Customers," *The Wall Street Journal,* February 27, 1985, 1, 12.
31. Peters and Waterman, *In Search of Excellence,* and Tom Peters and Nancy Austin, *A Passion for Excellence: The Leadership Difference* (New York: Random House, 1985).
32. Lois Therrien, "How Ztel Went from Riches to Rags," *Business Week,* June 17, 1985, 97–100.
33. Keith Davis and John W. Newstrom, *Human Behavior at Work: Organizational Behavior,* 7th ed. (New York: McGraw-Hill, 1985).
34. Joshua Hyatt, "The Last Shift," *INC.,* February 1989, 74–80.
35. Goldhaber, *Organizational Communication,* and Philip V. Louis, *Organizational Communication,* 3d ed. (New York: Wiley, 1987).
36. Donald B. Simmons, "The Nature of the Organizational Grapevine," *Supervisory Management* (November 1985), 39–42, and Davis and Newstrom, *Human Behavior.*
37. E. M. Rogers and R. A. Rogers, *Communication in Organizations* (New York: Free Press, 1976), and A. Bavelas and D. Barrett, "An Experimental Approach to Organization Communication," *Personnel* 27 (1951), 366–371.
38. This discussion is based on Daft and Steers, *Organizations.*
39. Bavelas and Barrett, "An Experimental Approach," and M. E. Shaw, *Group Dynamics: The Psychology of Small Group Behavior* (New York: McGraw-Hill, 1976).
40. Richard L. Daft and Norman B. Macintosh, "A Tentative Exploration into the Amount and Equivocality of Information Processing in Organizational Work Units," *Administrative Science Quarterly* 26 (1981), 207–224.
41. James A. F. Stoner and R. Edward Freeman, *Management,* 4th ed. (Englewood Cliffs, N.J.: Prentice-Hall, 1989).
42. Janet Fulk and Sirish Mani, "Distortion of Communication in Hierarchical Relationships," in *Communication Yearbook,* vol. 9, ed. M. L. McLaughlin (Beverly Hills, Cal.: Sage, 1986), 483–510.
43. "Would You Pay $2 Billion for a Sick Cat," *Business Week,* October 23, 1989, 58; Dale, "How We Rebuilt Jaguar," and Zetlin, "John Egan."

CHAPTER 16

1. Bruce G. Posner, "Divided We Fall," *INC.*, July 1989, 105–106.
2. "Training in the 1990s," *The Wall Street Journal,* March 1, 1990, B1.
3. Robert B. Reich, "Entrepreneurship Reconsidered: The Team as Hero," *Harvard Business Review* (May/June 1987), 77–83.
4. Frank V. Cespedes, Stephen X. Dole, and Robert J. Freedman, "Teamwork for Today's Selling," *Harvard Business Review* (March/April 1989), 44–55; Victoria J. Marsick, Ernie Turner, and Lars Cederholm, "International Managers as Team Leaders," *Management Review* (March 1989), 46–49; "Team Goal-Setting," *Small Business Report* (January 1988), 76–77.
5. Carl E. Larson and Frank M. J. LaFasto, *TeamWork* (Newbury Park, Cal.: Sage, 1989).
6. Eric Sundstrom, Kenneth P. De Meuse, and David Futrell, "Work Teams," *American Psychologist* 45 (February 1990), 120–133.
7. Deborah L. Gladstein, "Groups in Context: A Model of Task Group Effectiveness," *Administrative Science Quarterly* 29 (1984), 499–517.
8. Thomas Owens, "Business Teams," *Small Business Report* (January 1989), 50–58.
9. "Participation Teams," *Small Business Report* (September 1987), 38–41.
10. Larson and LaFasto, *TeamWork.*
11. John Hoerr, "The Payoff from Teamwork," *Business Week,* July 10, 1989, 56–62.
12. Gregory L. Miles, "Suddenly, USX is Playing Mr. Nice Guy," *Business Week,* June 26, 1989, 151–152.
13. John Hoerr, "Benefits for the Back Office, Too," *Business Week,* July 10, 1989, 59.
14. John Hoerr, "Is Teamwork a Management Plot? Mostly Not," *Business Week,* February 20, 1989, 70, and "How Power Will Be Balanced on Saturn's Shop Floor," *Business Week,* August 5, 1985, 65–66.
15. For research findings on group size, see M. E. Shaw, *Group Dynamics,* 3d ed. (New York: McGraw-Hill, 1981), and G. Manners, "Another Look at Group Size, Group Problem-Solving and Member Consensus," *Academy of Management Journal* 18 (1975), 715–724.
16. George Prince, "Recognizing Genuine Teamwork," *Supervisory Management* (April 1989), 25–36; K. D. Benne and P. Sheats, "Functional Roles of Group Members," *Journal of Social Issues* 4 (1948), 41–49; R. F. Bales, *SYMOLOG Case Study Kit* (New York: Free Press, 1980).
17. Robert A. Baron, *Behavior in Organizations,* 2d ed. (Boston: Allyn & Bacon, 1986).
18. Ibid.
19. Kenneth G. Koehler, "Effective Team Management," *Small Business Report,* July 19, 1989, 14–16, and Connie J. G. Gersick, "Time and Transition in Work Teams: Toward a New Model of Group Development," *Academy of Management Journal* 31 (1988), 9–41.
20. Bruce W. Tuckman and Mary Ann C. Jensen, "Stages of Small-Group Development Revisited," *Group and Organizational Studies* 2 (1977), 419–427, and Bruce W. Tuckman, "Developmental Sequences in Small Groups," *Psychological Bulletin* 63 (1965), 384–399. See also Linda N. Jewell and H. Joseph Reitz, *Group Effectiveness in Organizations* (Glenview, Ill.: Scott, Foresman, 1981).
21. Shaw, *Group Dynamics.*
22. Daniel C. Feldman and Hugh J. Arnold, *Managing Individual and Group Behavior in Organizations* (New York: McGraw-Hill, 1983).
23. Ricky W. Griffin, *Management* (Boston: Houghton Mifflin, 1984).
24. Joel Kotkin, "The 'Smart Team' at Compaq Computer," *INC.*, February 1986, 48–56.
25. Dorwin Cartwright and Alvin Zander, *Group Dynamics: Research and Theory,* 3d ed. (New York: Harper & Row, 1968), and Elliot Aronson, *The Social Animal* (San Francisco: W. H. Freeman, 1976).
26. Peter E. Mudrack, "Group Cohesiveness and Productivity: A Closer Look," *Human Relations* 42 (1989), 771–785.
27. Stanley E. Seashore, *Group Cohesiveness in the Industrial Work Group* (Ann Arbor, Mich.: Institute for Social Research, 1954).
28. J. Richard Hackman, "Group Influences on Individuals," in *Handbook of Industrial and Organizational Psychology,* ed. M. Dunnette (Chicago: Rand McNally, 1976).
29. Kenneth Bettenhausen and J. Keith Murnighan, "The Emergence of Norms in Competitive Decision-Making Groups," *Administrative Science Quarterly* 30 (1985), 350–372.
30. The following discussion is based on Daniel C. Feldman, "The Development and Enforcement of Group Norms," *Academy of Management Review* 9 (1984), 47–53.
31. Hugh J. Arnold and Daniel C. Feldman, *Organizational Behavior* (New York: McGraw-Hill, 1986).
32. Kenneth Libich, "Making Over Middle Managers," *Fortune,* May 8, 1989, 58–64.
33. Alix M. Freedman, "Cigarette Smoking is Growing Hazardous to Career in Business," *The Wall Street Journal,* April 23, 1987, 1, 14.
34. Reprinted by permission of the *Harvard Business Review.* Excerpts from "Wrestling with Jellyfish" by Richard J. Boyle (January/February 1984). Copyright © 1984 by the President and Fellows of Harvard College; all rights reserved.
35. Stephen P. Robbins, *Managing Organizational Conflict: A Nontraditional Approach* (Englewood Cliffs, N.J.: Prentice-Hall, 1974).
36. Daniel Robey, Dana L. Farrow, and Charles R. Franz, "Group Process and Conflict in System Development," *Management Science* 35 (1989), 1172–1191.
37. Koehler, "Effective Team Management," and Dean Tjosvold, "Making Conflict Productive," *Personnel Administrator* 29 (June 1984), 121.
38. This discussion is based in part on Richard L. Daft, *Organization Theory and Design* (St. Paul, Minn.: West, 1989), Chapter 11.
39. Brian Bremner, "That Head-Banging You Hear is the NFL Owners," *Business Week,* September 4, 1989, 36.
40. Wendy Zeller, "The UAW Rebels Teaming Up Against Teamwork," *Business Week,* March 27, 1989, 110–114, and Wendy Zeller, "Suddenly, The UAW is Raising its Voice at GM," *Business Week,* November 6, 1989, 96–100.
41. Based on Mary Jean Parson, "The Peer Conflict," *Supervisory Management* (May 1986), 25–31.
42. Robbins, *Managing Organizational Conflict.*
43. Gary Jacobson, "A Teamwork Ultimatum Puts Kimberly-Clark's Mill Back on the Map," *Management Review* (July 1989), 28–31.
44. R. B. Zajonc, "Social Facilitation," *Science* 149 (1965), 269–274.
45. Aaron Bernstein, "Detroit vs. the UAW: At Odds Over Teamwork," *Business Week,* August 24, 1987, 54–55.
46. Robert Albanese and David D. Van Fleet, "Rational Behavior in Groups: The Free-Riding Tendency," *Academy of Management Review* 10 (1985), 244–255.
47. Baron, *Behavior in Organizations.*
48. Harvey J. Brightman, *Group Problem Solving: An Improved Managerial Approach* (Atlanta: Georgia State University, 1988).
49. Posner, "Divided We Fall."

CHAPTER 17

1. Joel Dreyfuss, "Victories in the Quality Crusade," *Fortune,* October 10, 1988, 80–88.
2. Matthew Schifrin, "Who Checks the Checkers?" *Forbes,* August 7, 1989, 64.
3. Steve Swartz, "Wall Street's Growth is Seriously Outpacing Management Systems," *The Wall Street Journal,* July 27, 1987, 1.
4. "Quality: The Soul of Productivity, the Key to Future Business Growth," *Interview,* Inter-City Gas Corporation, vol. 3, Autumn

1988, 3–5. The story was originally related by Patrick Lush in *The Globe & Mail*, Toronto, June 15, 1988.
5. Ibid., and T. K. Das, "Organizational Control: An Evolutionary Perspective," *Journal of Management Studies* 26 (1989), 459–475.
6. Stephen G. Green and M. Ann Welsh, "Cybernetics and Dependence: Reframing the Control Concept," *Academy of Management Review* 13 (1988), 287–301, and Kenneth A. Merchant, *Control in Business Organizations* (Marshfield, Mass.: Pitman, 1985).
7. Bill Saporito, "Allegheny Ludlum Has Steel Figured Out," *Fortune*, June 25, 1984, 40–44.
8. Peter Lorange, Michael F. Scott Morton, and Sumantra Ghoshal, *Strategic Control* (St. Paul, Minn.: West, 1986), Chapter 1.
9. Ibid.
10. "Frito-Lay Shortens Its Business Cycle," *Fortune*, January 19, 1990, 11.
11. William H. Newman, *Constructive Control* (Englewood Cliffs, N.J.: Prentice-Hall, 1975).
12. Edward P. Gardner, "A Systems Approach to Bank Credential Management and Supervision: The Utilization of Feed Forward Control," *Journal of Management Studies* 22 (1985), 1–24.
13. Myron Magnet, "Managing by Mystique at Tandem Computers," *Fortune*, June 28, 1982, 84–91.
14. Lorange, Scott Morton, and Ghoshal, *Strategic Control*, 105–107.
15. William G. Ouchi, "Markets, Bureaucracies, and Clans," *Administrative Science Quarterly* 25 (1980), 129–141, and B. R. Baligia and Alfred M. Jaeger, "Multinational Corporations: Control Systems and Delegation Issues," *Journal of International Business Studies* (Fall 1984), 25–40.
16. Jeffrey Rothfeder and Michele Galen, "Is Your Boss Spying On You?" *Business Week*, January 15, 1990, 74–75, and Marlene C. Piturro, "Employee Performance Monitoring . . . or Meddling?" *Management Review*, May 19, 1989, 31–33.
17. Burt Schorr, "Schools Use New Ways to Be More Efficient and Enforce Discipline," *The Wall Street Journal*, December 15, 1983, 1, 16.
18. Beverly H. Burris, "Technocratic Organization and Control," *Organization Studies* 10 (1989), 1–22.
19. Richard Pascale, "Fitting New Employees into the Company Culture," *Fortune*, May 28, 1984, 28–40.
20. Richard E. Walton, "From Control to Commitment in the Workplace," *Harvard Business Review* (March/April 1985), 76–84.
21. Ellen Wojahn, "Will the Company Please Come to Order," *INC.*, March 1986, 78–86.
22. Ross Johnson and William O. Winchell, "Management and Quality," American Society for Quality Control, 1989.
23. A. V. Feigenbaum, *Total Quality Control: Engineering and Management* (New York: McGraw-Hill, 1961).
24. Philip B. Crosby, *Quality Is Free: The Art of Making Quality Certain* (New York: McGraw-Hill, 1979), and Mary Walton, *The Deming Management Method* (Dodd-Meade & Co., 1986).
25. Richard J. Schonberger, "Production Workers Bear Major Quality Responsibility in Japanese Industry," *Industrial Engineering* (December 1982), 34–40.
26. Jerry G. Bowles, "Beyond Customer Satisfaction Through Quality Improvement," *Fortune*, September 26, 1988, special insert.
27. Tom Peters, *Thriving on Chaos* (New York: Alfred A. Knopf, 1987), and Crosby, *Quality Is Free*.
28. Schonberger, "Production Workers."
29. Johnson and Winchell, "Management and Quality," and Edward E. Lawler III and Susan A. Mohrman, "Quality Circles after the Fad," *Harvard Business Review* (January/February 1985), 65–71.
30. Thomas A. Stewart, "Westinghouse Gets Respect At Last," *Fortune*, July 3, 1989, 92–98.
31. Robert Wood, Frank Hull, and Koya Azumi, "Evaluating Quality Circles: The American Application," *California Management Review* 26 (Fall 1983), 37–53, and Gregory P. Shea, "Quality Circles: The Danger of Bottled Change," *Sloan Management Review* 27 (Spring 1986), 33–46.
32. Donald C. Bacon, "A Pursuit of Excellence," *Nation's Business*, January 1990, 27–28.
33. Johnson and Winchell, "Management and Quality."
34. Sherrie Posesorski, "Here's How to Put Statistical Process Control to Work for You," *Canadian Business* (December 1985), 163.
35. James A. F. Stoner and R. Edward Freeman, *Management* (Englewood Cliffs, N.J.: Prentice-Hall, 1989), and Peter Lorange and Declan Murphy, "Considerations in Implementing Strategic Control," *Journal of Business Strategy* 4 (Spring 1984), 27–35.
36. W. H. Read, "Upward Communication in Industrial Hierarchies," *Human Relations* 15 (February 1962), 3–15, and Michelle J. Glauser, "Factors Which Facilitate or Impede Upward Communication in Organizations" (Paper presented at the Academy of Management meeting, New York, August 1982).
37. David A. Garbin, "Quality on the Line," *Harvard Business Review* 61 (September/October 1983), 65–75.
38. Dreyfuss, "Victories in the Quality Crusade."

CHAPTER 18

1. Jill Andresky Fraser, "Straight Talk," *INC.*, March 19, 1990, 97–98.
2. Kate Ballen, "The New Look of Capital Spending," *Fortune*, March 13, 1989, 115–120.
3. Ford S. Worthy, "Accounting Bores You? Wake Up," *Fortune*, October 12, 1987, 43–52.
4. David A. Garvin, "Quality on the Line," *Harvard Business Review* (September/October 1983), 65–75.
5. E. G. Flamholtz, "Accounting, Budgeting and Control Systems in Their Organizational Context: Theoretical and Empirical Perspectives," *Accounting, Organizations and Society* 8 (1983), 153–169.
6. Richard L. Daft and Norman B. Macintosh, "The Nature and Use of Formal Control Systems for Management Control and Strategy Implementation," *Journal of Management* 10 (1984), 43–66.
7. Bruce G. Posner, "How to Stop Worrying and Love the Next Recession," *INC.*, April 1986, 89–95.
8. Tom Richman, "The Language of Business," *INC.*, February 1990, 41–50, and Paul Hawken, "Mastering the Numbers," *INC.*, October 1987, 19–20.
9. Hawken, "Mastering the Numbers."
10. Arthur W. Holmes and Wayne S. Overmeyer, *Basic Auditing*, 5th ed. (Homewood, Ill.: Irwin, 1976).
11. John J. Welsh, "Pre-Acquisition Audit: Verifying the Bottom Line," *Management Accounting* (January 1983), 32–37.
12. Lee Iacocca with William Novak, *Iacocca: An Autobiography* (New York: Bantam Books, 1984), 92–94. Used with permission.
13. Daft and Macintosh, "Formal Control Systems," and Robert N. Anthony, John Dearden, and Norton M. Bedford, *Management Control Systems*, 5th ed. (Homewood, Ill.: Irwin, 1984).
14. This discussion is based on Peter Lorange, Michael F. Scott Morton, and Sumantra Ghoshal, *Strategic Control* (St. Paul, Minn.: West, 1986), Chapter 4; Anthony, Dearden, and Bedford, *Management Control Systems;* Richard F. Vancil, "What Kind of Management Control Do You Need?" *Harvard Business Review* (March/April 1973), 75–85.
15. Anthony, Dearden, and Bedford, *Management Control Systems.*
16. Participation in budget setting has been described in a number of studies, including Peter Brownell, "Leadership Style, Budgetary Participation and Managerial Behavior," *Accounting, Organizations and Society* 8 (1983), 307–321, and Paul J. Carruth and Thurrell O. McClandon, "How Supervisors React to 'Meeting the Budget' Pressure," *Management Accounting* 66 (November 1984), 50–54.
17. Neil C. Churchill, "Budget Choice: Planning vs. Control," *Harvard Business Review* (July/August 1984), 150–164.

18. "Zero-based Budgeting," *Small Business Report* (April 1988), 52–57, and Peter A. Pyhrr, *Zero-Based Budgeting: A Practical Mangement Tool for Evaluating Expense* (New York: Wiley, 1973).
19. "Zero-Based Budgeting: Justifying All Business Activity from the Ground Up," *Small Business Report* (November 1983), 20–25, and M. Dirsmith and S. Jablonsky, "Zero-Based Budgeting as a Management Technique and Political Strategy," *Academy of Management Review* 4 (1979), 555–565.
20. Based on Tom Richman, "Talking Cost," *INC.*, February 1986, 105–108.
21. George S. Odiorne, "MBO: A Backward Glance," *Business Horizons* 21 (October 1978), 14–24.
22. Jan P. Muczyk and Bernard C. Reimann, "MBO as a Complement to Effective Leadership," *The Academy of Management Executive* 3 (1989), 131–138, and W. Giegold, *Volume II: Objective Setting and the MBO Process* (New York: McGraw-Hill, 1978).
23. "Delegation," *Small Business Report* (July 1986), 71–75.
24. Jack N. Kondrasuk, "Studies in MBO Effectiveness," *Academy of Management Review* 6 (1981), 419–430, and Jan P. Muczyk, "Dynamics and Hazards of MBO Applications," *Personnel Administrator* 24 (May 1979), 52.
25. John Ivancevich, J. Timothy McMahon, J. William Streidl, and Andrew D. Szilagyi, "Goal Setting: The Tenneco Approach to Personnel Development and Management Effectiveness," *Organizational Dynamics* (Winter 1978), 48–80.
26. "Delegation," *Small Business Report* (July 1986), 71–75, and Robert C. Ford and Frank S. McLaughlin, "Avoiding Disappointment in MBO Programs," *Human Resource Management* 21 (Summer 1982), 44–49.
27. Based on "Controlling with Standards," *Small Business Report* (August 1987), 62–65.
28. Andresky Fraser, "Straight Talk."

CHAPTER 19

1. Robert A. Mamis, "Taking Control," *INC.*, February 1987, 82–88.
2. Joel Dreyfuss, "Catching the Computer Wave," *Fortune*, September 26, 1988, 78–82.
3. Steven L. Mandell, *Computers and Data Processing* (St. Paul, Minn.: West, 1985), and Richard L. Daft and Norman B. Macintosh, "A Tentative Exploration into the Amount and Equivocality of Information Processing in Organizational Work Units," *Administrative Science Quarterly* 26 (1981), 207–224.
4. Craig R. Waters, "Franchise Capital of America," *INC.*, September 1984, 99–108.
5. Charles A. O'Reilly III, "Variations in Decision Makers' Use of Information Sources: The Impact of Quality and Accessibility of Information," *Academy of Management Journal* 25 (1982), 756–771, and Niv Ahituv and Seev Neumann, *Principles of Information Systems for Management*, 2d ed. (Dubuque, Iowa: Wm. C. Brown, 1986).
6. Bob Davis, "As Government Keeps More Tabs on People, False Accusations Arise," *The Wall Street Journal*, August 20, 1987, 1, 10.
7. Michael W. Miller, "Computers Keep Eye on Workers and See If They Perform Well," *The Wall Street Journal*, June 3, 1985, 1, 12.
8. Frances Seghres, "A Search and Destroy Mission — Against Paper," *Business Week*, February 6, 1989, 91–95.
9. Stuart Gannes, "IBM and DEC Take On the Little Guys," *Fortune*, October 10, 1988, 108–114.
10. Bruce G. Posner and Bo Burlingham, "The Hottest Entrepreneur in America," *INC.*, January 1988, 44–58.
11. Gary Geipel, "At Today's Supermarket, the Computer Is Doing It All," *Business Week*, August 11, 1986, 64–65, and Tom Richman, "Supermarket," *INC.*, October 1985, 115–120.
12. Alan Paller, "A Guide to EIS for MIS Directors," *CA-Insight: The Computer Associates Software Magazine*, 1989, no. 2, 5–9.
13. Jeremy Main, "At Last, Software CEOs Can Use," *Fortune*, March 13, 1989, 77–81.
14. Ibid.
15. Ramesh Sharda, Steve H. Barr, and James C. McDonald, "Decision Support System Effectiveness: A Review and an Empirical Test," *Management Science* 34 (1988), 139–159.
16. Paller, "A Guide to EIS for MIS Directors."
17. David Churbuck, "Next Time, Think Big," *Forbes*, June 12, 1989, 155–156.
18. Robert Reark, "Electronic Mail Speeds Business Communication," *Small Business Reports* (February 1989), 73–77, and David Churbuck, "Prepare for E-Mail Attack," *Forbes*, January 23, 1989, 82–87.
19. Richard C. Huseman and Edward W. Miles, "Organizational Communication in the Information Age: Implications of Computer-Based Systems," *Journal of Management* 14 (1988), 181–204.
20. George P. Huber, "Issues in the Design of Group Decision Support Systems," *MIS Quarterly* 8 (1984), 195–204.
21. G. Michael Ashmore, "Applying Expert Systems to Business Strategy," *The Journal of Business Strategy* (September/October 1989), 46–49.
22. Emily T. Smith, "Turning an Expert's Skills into Computer Software," *Business Week*, October 7, 1985, 104–108; David E. Whiteside, "Artificial Intelligence Finally Hits the Desktop," *Business Week*, June 9, 1986, 68–70; Mary A. C. Fallon, "Losing an Expert? Hire an Expert System," Bryan-College Station *Eagle*, September 7, 1986, E1.
23. Karl W. Wiig, "AI: Management's Newest Tool," *Management Review* (August 1986), 24–28.
24. Richard Brandt and Deidre A. Depke, "The Personal Computer Finds Its Missing Link," *Business Week*, June 5, 1989, 120–128.
25. Anne E. Skagen, "Nurturing Relationships, Enhancing Quality with Electronic Data Interchange," *Management Review* (February 1989), 28–32.
26. Joel Dreyfuss, "Networking: Japan's Latest Computer Craze," *Fortune*, July 7, 1986, 94–96.
27. Pam Carroll, "The Paperless Office Comes True," *Working Woman*, October 1989, 73–76.
28. Peter Nulty, "How Personal Computers Change Managers' Lives," *Fortune*, September 3, 1984, 38–48, and John Dearden, "Will the Computer Change the Job of Top Management?" *Sloan Management Review* (Fall 1983), 57–60.
29. Lynda M. Applegate, James I. Cash, Jr., and D. Quinn Mills, "Information Technology and Tomorrow's Management," *Harvard Business Review* (November/December 1988), 128–136.
30. E. B. Swanson, "Information in Organization Theory: A Review" (*Information Systems* working paper, UCLA, 1986); John F. Magee, "What Information Technology Has in Store for Managers," *Sloan Management Review* (Winter 1985), 45–49; John Child, "New Technology and Developments in Management Organization," *OMEGA* 12 (1984), 211–223.
31. "Office Automation Restructures Business," *Business Week*, October 8, 1984, 118–125.
32. Laton McCartney, "Companies Get a Competitive Edge Using Strategic Computer Systems," *Dun's Business Month*, December 1985, 13–14, and Robert I. Benjamin, John F. Rockart, Michael S. Scott Morton, and John Wyman, "Information Technology: A Strategic Opportunity," *Sloan Management Review* 25 (Spring 1984), 3–10.
33. Jeffrey Rothfeder, "It's Late, Costly, Incompetent — But Try Firing a Computer System," *Business Week*, November 7, 1988, 164–165.
34. David R. Hampton, *Management*, 3d ed. (New York: McGraw-Hill, 1986), 723–725.

35. Ibid., 725.
36. John F. Rockart and Adam D. Crescenzi, "Engaging Top Management in Information Technology," *Sloan Management Review* 25 (Summer 1984), 3–16.
37. Andrew C. Boynton and Robert W. Zmud, "An Assessment of Critical Success Factors," *Sloan Management Review* 25 (Summer 1984), 17–27, and John F. Rockart, "Chief Executives Define Their Own Data Needs," *Harvard Business Review* 57 (March/April 1979), 81–93.
38. Tom Richman, "Break It To Me Gently," *INC.*, July 1989, 108–110.
39. Catherine L. Harris, "Office Automation: Making It Pay Off," *Business Week*, October 12, 1987, 134–146.
40. Mamis, "Taking Control."

CHAPTER 20

1. Ira C. Magaziner and Mark Patinkin, "Cold Competition: GE Wages the Refrigerator War," *Harvard Business Review* (March/April 1989), 114–124.
2. John Holusha, "Beating Japan at Its Own Game," *The New York Times*, July 16, 1989, sec. 3, 1, 7.
3. Joel Kotkin, "The Great American Revival," *INC.*, February 1988, 52–63.
4. Holusha, "Beating Japan at Its Own Game."
5. Everett E. Adam, "Towards a Typology of Production and Operations Management Systems," *Academy of Management Review* 8 (1983), 365–375.
6. James D. Thompson, *Organizations in Action* (New York: McGraw-Hill, 1967).
7. Gregory B. Northcraft and Richard B. Chase, "Managing Service Demand at the Point of Delivery," *Academy of Management Review* 10 (1985), 66–75, and Richard B. Chase and David A. Tansik, "The Customer Contact Model for Organization Design," *Management Science* 29 (1983), 1037–1050.
8. Harlan C. Meal, "Putting Production Decisions Where They Belong," *Harvard Business Review* (March/April 1984), 102–111.
9. Everett E. Adam, Jr., and Paul M. Swamidass, "Assessing Operations Management from a Strategic Perspective," *Journal of Management* 15 (1989), 181–203.
10. W. Skinner, "Manufacturing: The Missing Link in Corporate Strategy," *Harvard Business Review* (May/June 1969), 136–145.
11. R. H. Hayes and S. C. Wheelwright, *Restoring Our Competitive Edge: Competing Through Manufacturing* (New York: Wiley, 1984).
12. T. Hill, *Manufacturing Strategy: The Strategic Management of the Manufacturing Function* (London: Macmillan, 1985).
13. Todd Vogel, "Big Changes Are Galvanizing General Electric," *Business Week*, December 18, 1989, 100–102.
14. Otis Port, "Pssst! Want a Secret for Making Superproducts?" *Business Week*, October 2, 1989, 106–110.
15. Otis Port, "The Best-Engineered Part Is No Part at All," *Business Week*, May 8, 1989, 150.
16. Jonathan B. Levine, "How HP Built a Better Terminal," *Business Week*, March 7, 1988, 114, and Bruce Nussbaum, "Smart Design," *Business Week*, April 11, 1988, 102–108.
17. Zachary Schiller, "Big Blue's Overhaul," *Business Week*, Special Issue on Innovation, 1989, 147.
18. Claudia H. Deutsch, "The Powerful Push for Self-Service," *The New York Times*, April 9, 1989, sec. 3, 1, 15.
19. Barbara B. Flynn and F. Robert Jacobs, "An Experimental Comparison of Cellular (Group Technology) Layout with Process Layout," *Decision Sciences* 18 (1987), 562–581; Richard J. Schonberger, "Plant Layout Becomes Product-Oriented with Cellular, Just-in-Time Production Concepts," *Industrial Engineering*, November 1983, 66–77; Jack R. Meredith and Marianne M. Hill, "Justifying New Manufacturing Systems: A Managerial Approach," *Sloan Management Review* (Summer 1987), 49–61.
20. William J. Hampton, "GM Bets an Arm and a Leg on a People-Free Plant," *Business Week*, September 12, 1988, 72–73.
21. Sumer C. Aggarwal, "MRP, JIT, OPT, FMS?" *Harvard Business Review* 63 (September/October 1985), 8–16, and Paul Ranky, *The Design and Operation of Flexible Manufacturing Systems* (New York: Elsevier, 1983).
22. Kurt H. Schaffir, "Information Technology for the Manufacturer," *Management Review* (November 1985), 61–62.
23. Suren S. Singhvi, "A Quantitative Approach to Site Selection," *Management Review* (April 1987), 47–52.
24. Marvin B. Lieberman, "Strategies for Capacity Expansion," *Sloan Management Review* (Summer 1987), 19–27.
25. Bill Paul, "Corky Johnson's Job Is Trimming Inventory to Help Sun Co. Shine," *The Wall Street Journal*, April 20, 1987, 1, 7.
26. R. J. Schonberger, *Japanese Manufacturing Techniques: Nine Hidden Lessons in Simplicity* (New York: Free Press, 1982).
27. Craig R. Waters, "Profit and Loss," *INC.*, April 1985, 103–112.
28. Henry C. Ekstein, "Better Materials Control with Inventory Cardiograms," *Small Business Reports* (March 1989), 76–79.
29. "Inventory Management: Controlling Costs to Maximize Profits," *Small Business Report* (August 1987), 50–53.
30. Joel C. Polakoff, "Inventory Accuracy: Getting Back to Basics," *Management Review* (November 1987), 44–46.
31. R. W. Hall, *Zero Inventories* (Homewood, Ill.: Dow Jones-Irwin, 1983).
32. Dexter Hutchins, "Having a Hard Time with Just-in-Time," *Fortune*, June 9, 1986, 64–66.
33. "Kanban: The Just-in-Time Japanese Inventory System," *Small Business Report* (February 1984), 69–71, and Richard C. Walleigh, "What's Your Excuse For Not Using JIT?" *Harvard Business Review* 64 (March/April 1986), 38–54.
34. Martha E. Mangelsdorf, "Beyond Just-in-Time," *INC.*, February 1989, 21.
35. J. Claunch, "Implementing JIT" (Paper presented at the Spring Seminar of the Purchasing Management Association of Denver, Denver, 1985).
36. *Benchmarks* (American Productivity Center, 1982).
37. E. E. Adam, Jr., J. C. Hershauer, and W. A. Ruch, *Productivity and Quality: Measurement as a Basis for Improvement*, 2d ed. (Columbia, Mo.: Research Center, College of Business and Public Administration, University of Missouri — Columbia, 1986).
38. W. Bouce Chew, "No-Nonsense Guide to Measuring Productivity," *Harvard Business Review* (January/February 1988), 110–118.
39. Hank Johansson and Dan McArther, "Rediscovering the Fundamentals of Quality," *Management Review* (January 1988), 34–37.
40. Gregory L. Miles, "Heinz Ain't Broke, but It's Doing a Lot of Fixing," *Business Week*, December 11, 1989, 84–88.
41. Jeremy Main, "Detroit's Cars Really Are Getting Better," *Fortune*, February 2, 1987, 90–98.
42. Kimberly J. Studer and Mark D. Dibner, "Robots Invade Small Businesses," *Management Review* (November 1988), 26–31.
43. Maggie McComas, "Cutting Costs without Killing the Business," *Fortune*, October 13, 1986, 70–78.
44. W. E. Deming, *Quality, Productivity, and Competitive Position* (Cambridge, Mass.: Center for Advanced Engineering Study, MIT, 1982), and P. B. Crosby, *Quality Is Free* (New York: McGraw-Hill, 1979).
45. J. Merwin, "A Tale of Two Worlds," *Forbes*, June 16, 1986.
46. D. W. Dobler, L. Lee, Jr., and D. N. Burt, *Purchasing and Materials Management: Text and Cases* (New York: McGraw-Hill, 1984).
47. Magaziner and Patinkin, "Cold Competition," and Zachary Schiller, "The Refrigerator That Has GE Feeling the Heat," *Business Week*, April 25, 1988, 65–66.

CHAPTER 21

1. John Huey, "The New Power in Black & Decker," *Fortune,* January 2, 1989, 89–92; "Winning Turnaround Strategies at Black & Decker: An Interview with Marketing Executive Gary T. DiCamillo," *The Journal of Business Strategy* (March/April 1988), 30–33; Bill Saporito, "Black & Decker's Gamble on 'Globalization'," *Fortune,* May 14, 1984, 40–48.
2. Jonathan P. Hicks, "Foreign Owners are Shaking Up the Competition," *The New York Times,* May 28, 1989, sec. 3, 9; Cynthia Barnun and Natasha Wolniansky, "Moving a Step Beyond the International Firm," *Management Review* (September 1989), 30–34; Ira C. Magaziner and Mark Patinkin, *The Silent War* (New York: Random House, 1989).
3. John S. Hill and Richard R. Still, "Adapting Products to LDC Tastes," *Harvard Business Review* 62 (March/April 1984), 92–101, and David A. Ricks, *Big Business Blunders: Mistakes in Multinational Marketing* (Homewood, Ill.: Dow Jones-Irwin, 1983).
4. Karen Paul and Robert Barbarto, "The Multinational Corporation in the Less Developed Country: The Economic Development Model versus the North-South Model," *Academy of Management Review* 10 (1985), 8–14.
5. Kathleen Deveny, "McWorld?" *Business Week,* October 13, 1986, 78–86.
6. Bruce Kogut, "Designing Global Strategies: Profiting from Operational Flexibility," *Sloan Management Review* 27 (Fall 1985), 27–38.
7. Mark Fitzpatrick, "The Definition and Assessment of Political Risk in International Business: A Review of the Literature," *Academy of Management Review* 8 (1983), 249–254.
8. "Multinational Firms Act to Protect Overseas Workers from Terrorism," *The Wall Street Journal,* April 29, 1986, 31.
9. Bill Javetski and John Templeman, "One Germany: The Whole European Equation Has Changed," *Business Week,* April 2, 1990, 47–49.
10. Robert M. Bryan, "Europe 1992," *Small Business Reports* (January 1990), 30–38; "Readying for the Global Bazaar," *Management Review* (September 1989), 18–19; Thomas F. Gross, "Europe 1992: A Global Fulcrum for European Companies," *Management Review* (September 1989), 20–23.
11. Geert Hofstede, "The Interaction between National and Organizational Value Systems," *Journal of Management Studies* 22 (1985), 347–357, and Geert Hofstede, "The Cultural Relativity of the Quality of Life Concept," *Academy of Management Review* 9 (1984), 389–398.
12. Ellen F. Jackofsky, John W. Slocum, Jr., and Sara J. McQuaid, "Cultural Values and the CEO: Alluring Companions?" *Academy of Management Executive* 2 (1988), 39–49.
13. Jeffrey A. Trachtenberg, "They Didn't Listen to Anybody," *Forbes,* December 15, 1986, 168–169.
14. Kenneth Labich, "America's International Winners," *Fortune,* April 14, 1986, 34–46.
15. Jeremy Main, "How To Go Global — and Why," *Fortune,* August 28, 1989, 70–76.
16. Frank T. Curtin, "Global Sourcing: Is It Right for Your Company?" *Management Review* (August 1987), 47–49, and Richard Brandt, "Seagate Goes East — and Comes Back a Winner," *Business Week,* March 16, 1987, 94.
17. Gary Jacobson, "The Boom on Mexico's Border," *Management Review* (July 1988), 21–25.
18. Jen Kerr, "Export Strategies," *Small Business Reports* (May 1989), 20–25.
19. William J. Holstein and Brian Bremmer, "The Little Guys Are Making It Big Overseas," *Business Week,* February 27, 1989, 94–96, and Iris Lorenz-Fife, "Resource Guide: Small-Business Help from the Government," *Entrepreneur,* December 1989, 168–174.
20. Kathryn Rudie Harrigan, "Managing Joint Ventures," *Management Review* (February 1987), 24–41, and Therese R. Revesz and Mimi Cauley de Da La Sierra, "Competitive Alliances: Forging Ties Abroad," *Management Review* (March 1987), 57–59.
21. Bernard Wysocki, Jr., "Cross-Border Alliances Become Favorite Way to Crack New Markets," *The Wall Street Journal,* March 26, 1990, A1, A12.
22. Janice Castro, "Heavy-Duty Mergers," *Time,* May 12, 1986, 72–73.
23. Bureau of Economic Analysis, U.S. Department of Commerce, "1977 Benchmark Survey of U.S. Direct Investment Abroad," *Survey of Current Business* (April 1981), 29–37.
24. Main, "How To Go Global — and Why."
25. Howard V. Perlmutter, "The Torturous Evolution of the Multinational Corporation," *Columbia Journal of World Business* (January/February 1969), 9–18, and Youram Wind, Susan P. Douglas, and Howard V. Perlmutter, "Guidelines for Developing International Marketing Strategies," *Journal of Marketing* (April 1973), 14–23.
26. George Rabstejnek, "Let's Get Back to the Basics of Global Strategy," *The Journal of Business Strategy* (September/October 1989), 32–35.
27. Kenichi Ohmae, "Managing in a Borderless World," *Harvard Business Review* (May/June 1989), 152–161.
28. Theodore Levitt, "The Globalization of Markets," *Harvard Business Review* 61 (May/June 1983), 92–102.
29. Joanne Lipman, "Marketers Turn Sour on Global Sales Pitch Harvard Guru Makes," *The Wall Street Journal,* May 12, 1988, 1, 8.
30. Christine Dugas, "Playtex Kicks Off a One-Ad Fits All Campaign," *Business Week,* December 16, 1985, 48–49.
31. Michael E. Porter, "Changing Patterns of International Competition," *California Management Review* 28 (Winter 1986), 40.
32. Lipman, "Marketers Turn Sour On Global Sales Pitch."
33. Labich, "America's International Winners."
34. Sumantra Ghoshal, "Global Strategy: An Organizing Framework," *Strategic Management Journal* 8 (1987), 425–440.
35. The following discussion is based on William A. Dymsza, "Global Strategic Planning: A Model and Recent Developments," *Journal of International Business Studies* (Fall 1984), 169–183; Arvand P. Phatak, *International Dimensions of Management* (Boston: Kent, 1983), 39–62; S. B. Prasad and Y. Kirshna Shetty, *An Introduction to Multinational Management* (Englewood Cliffs, N.J.: Prentice-Hall, 1976), 67–82.
36. Richard Dulude, "Poised for Unification: Corning Crystallizes Its Global Strategy," *The Journal of European Business* (September/October 1989), 17–19.
37. Roderick E. White and Thomas A. Pointer, "Organizing for Worldwide Advantage," *Business Quarterly* (Summer 1989), 84–89, and William G. Egelhoff, "Strategy and Structure in Multinational Corporations: An Information Processing Approach," *Administrative Science Quarterly* 27 (1982), 435–458.
38. John D. Daniels, Robert A. Pitts, and Marietta J. Tretter, "Strategy and Structure of U.S. Multinationals: An Exploratory Study," *Academy of Management Journal* 27 (1984), 292–307, and Theodore T. Herbert, "Strategy and Multinational Organization Structure: An Interorganizational Relationships Perspective," *Academy of Management Review* 9 (1984), 259–271.
39. Christopher A. Bartlett and Sumantra Ghoshal, "Managing Across Borders: New Organizational Responses," *Sloan Management Review* (Fall 1987), 43–53.
40. Mike Tharp, "LSI Logic Corp. Does as the Japanese Do," *The Wall Street Journal,* April 17, 1986, 6.
41. Christopher A. Bartlett, "MNCs: Get Off the Organization Merry-Go-Round," *Harvard Business Review* 61 (March/April 1983), 138–146.
42. Joyce Heard and Jonathan Kapstein, "How Business Is Creating Europe Inc.," *Business Week,* September 7, 1987, 40–41.
43. The following discussion is based on Lennie Copeland and Lewis Griggs, "Getting the Best from Foreign Employees," *Management*

Review (June 1986), 19–26, and Amanda Bennett, "American Culture Is Often a Puzzle for Foreign Managers in the U.S.," *The Wall Street Journal,* February 12, 1986, 29.
44. Huey, "The New Power in Black & Decker"; "Winning Turnaround Strategies"; Saporito, "Black & Decker's Gamble."

CHAPTER 22

1. Stanley W. Angrist, "Family Affair," *Forbes,* October 5, 1987, 184–187.
2. Jeremy Main, "A Golden Age for Entrepreneurs," *Fortune,* February 12, 1990, 120–125, and Keith H. Hammonds, "What B-School Doesn't Teach You About Startups," *Business Week,* July 24, 1989, 40–41.
3. Donald F. Kuratko and Richard M. Hodgetts, *Entrepreneurship: A Contemporary Approach* (Chicago: The Dryden Press, 1989).
4. David J. Jefferson, "Creativity Isn't All That's Needed by a Creative Business," *The Wall Street Journal,* March 19, 1990, B2.
5. Eugene Carlson, "Federal Express Wasn't an Overnight Success," *The Wall Street Journal,* June 6, 1989, B2.
6. David L. Birch, "The Truth About Start-Ups," *INC.*, January 1988, 14–15, and Carl H. Vesper, *Entrepreneurship and National Policy* (Chicago: Heller Institute, 1983).
7. Birch, "The Truth About Start-Ups."
8. John Case, "The Disciples of David Birch," *INC.*, January 1989, 39–45.
9. Charles R. Kuehl and Peggy A. Lambing, *Small Business: Planning and Management,* 2d ed. (Chicago: The Dryden Press, 1990).
10. "100 Ideas for New Businesses," *Venture,* November 1988, 35–74.
11. Leon E. Wynter, "How Two Black Franchisees Owe Success to McDonald's," *The Wall Street Journal,* July 25, 1989, B1–B2.
12. John Case, "The Origins of Entrepreneurship," *INC.*, June 1989, 51–63.
13. This discussion is based on Kuehl and Lambing, *Small Business.*
14. Roger Ricklefs and Udayan Gupta, "Traumas of a New Entrepreneur," *The Wall Street Journal,* May 10, 1989, B1.
15. David C. McClelland, *The Achieving Society* (New York: Van Nostrand, 1961).
16. Robert D. Hisrich, "Entrepreneurship-Intrapreneurship," *American Psychologist,* February 1990, 209–222.
17. Curtis Hartman, "A Rose Blooms in Houston," *INC.*, October 1987, 38–42.
18. Case, "The Origins of Entrepreneurship."
19. Roger Ricklefs, "Pros Dare To Go Where Amateurs No Longer Bother," *The Wall Street Journal,* March 31, 1989, B2.
20. Case, "The Origins of Entrepreneurship."
21. "Venture Capitalists' Criteria," *Management Review* (November 1985), 7–8.
22. Meg Whittemore, "Four Paths to Franchising," *Nation's Business,* October 1989, 75–85, and Nancy Croft Baker, "Franchising into the 90s," *Nation's Business,* March 1990, 61–68.
23. Suzanne Woolley, "Feathered Nests for Your Fledgling Business," *Business Week,* February 19, 1990, 139–140, and Bruce Dobler, "Right from the Start," *Savvy,* November 1989, 86–88.
24. Thomas S. Bateman and Carl P. Zeithaml, *Management: Function and Strategy* (Homewood, Ill.: Irwin, 1990).
25. William J. Holstein and Brian Bremmer, "The Little Guys Are Making It Big Overseas," *Business Week,* February 27, 1989, 94–96; Paul B. Brown, "Over There," *INC.*, April 1990, 105–106; Harold Plotkin, "Multinational Start-Up," *INC.'s Guide to International Business,* 1988, 15–17.
26. Elizabeth Conlin, "Unlimited Partners," *INC.*, April 1990, 71–79.
27. Kuehl and Lambing, *Small Business.*
28. Carrie Dolan, "Entrepreneurs Often Fail as Managers," *The Wall Street Journal,* May 15, 1989, B1.
29. Michael Porter, *Competitive Strategies* (New York: Free Press, 1980).
30. Mark Maremont, "Did Sock Shop Get Too Big for Its Britches?" *Business Week,* January 15, 1990, 39–40.
31. "Revolution for the HEC of It," *INC.*, September 1988, 22.
32. Erik Larson, "The Man with the Golden Touch," *INC.*, October 1988, 67–77.
33. Udayan Gupta and Jeffrey A. Tannenbaum, "Labor Shortages Force Changes at Small Firms," *The Wall Street Journal,* May 22, 1989, B1, B2, and "Harnessing Employee Productivity," *Small Business Report* (November 1987), 46–49.
34. Kuratko and Hodgetts, *Entrepreneurship.*
35. Gifford Pinchot III, *Entrepreneuring* (New York: Harper & Row, 1985).
36. Ibid.
37. Angrist, "Family Affair."

APPENDIX

1. Janet Bamford, "Everyone Has to Start Somewhere," *Forbes,* July 14, 1986, 98–100.
2. R. Ricklafs, "Many Executives Complain of Stress, But Few Want Less-Pressure Jobs," *The Wall Street Journal,* September 29, 1982, 1.
3. William G. Flannigan, "What Makes Suzanne Run?" *Forbes,* October 7, 1985, 152.
4. Daniel C. Feldman, "Careers in Organizations: Recent Trends and Future Directions," *Journal of Management* 15 (1989), 135–156.
5. T. Gutteridge, *Career Planning and Management* (Boston: Little, Brown, 1987).
6. Janet Bamford, "Climb Quickly or Get Out Fast," *Forbes,* November 3, 1986, 224–226.
7. Mona Melanson, "Career Self-Assessment," *National Business Employment Weekly,* June 25, 1989, 9.
8. Scott Bronestein, "Past Forty and Back to Square One," *The New York Times,* October 20, 1985, 6F.
9. Edie Gibson, "Fast Track Often Starts at Bottom," *Chicago Tribune,* December 15, 1986, sec. 4, 15.
10. "Expert View," *Working Woman,* October 1985, 154.
11. The discussion of career stages is based on M. London and S. A. Stumpf, "Individual and Organizational Development in Changing Times," in Douglas T. Hall and associates, *Career Development in Organizations* (San Francisco: Jossey-Bass, 1986).
12. Laurie Baun, "Corporate Women," *Business Week,* June 22, 1987, 72–77.
13. Kathy E. Kram, *Mentoring at Work: Developmental Relationships in Organizational Life* (Glenview, Ill.: Scott, Foresman, 1985).
14. Kathy E. Kram, "Phases of the Mentor Relationship," *Academy of Management Journal* 26 (1983), 608–625.
15. David Marshall Hunt and Carol Michael, "Mentorship: A Career Training and Development Tool," *Academy of Management Review* 8 (1983), 475–485.
16. G. R. Roche, "Much Ado about Mentors," *Harvard Business Review* (January/February 1979), 14–28.
17. Kathy E. Kram and L. Isabella, "Mentoring Alternatives: The Role of Peer Relationships in Career Development," *Academy of Management Journal* 28 (1985), 110–132.
18. Rosabeth Moss Kanter, *Men and Women of the Corporation* (New York: Basic Books, 1977).
19. Aimee Lee Ball, "Mentors & Protégés," *Working Woman,* October 1989, 134–142.
20. T. A. Beehr and R. S. Bhagat, *Human Stress and Cognition in Organizations: An Integrated Perspective* (New York: Wiley, 1985).
21. R. S. Lazarus and S. Folkman, *Stress, Appraisal and Coping* (New York: Springer, 1984).

22. T. Homes and R. Rahe, "The Social Readjustment Rating Scale," *Journal of Psychosomatic Research* 11 (1967), 213–218.
23. K. R. Pelletier, *Healthy People in Unhealthy Places: Stress and Fitness at Work* (New York: Dell, 1984).
24. Emily T. Smith, "Stress: The Test Americans Are Failing," *Business Week,* April 18, 1988, 74–76.
25. Hans Selye, *The Stress of Life* (New York: McGraw-Hill, 1956).
26. Brian Dumaine, "Cool Cures for Burnout," *Fortune,* June 20, 1988, 78–84, and Jeannie Gaines and John M. Jermier, "Emotional Exhaustion in a High Stress Organization," *Academy of Management Journal* 26 (1983), 567–586.
27. Sana Siwolop, "The Crippling Ills That Stress Can Trigger," *Business Week,* April 18, 1988, 77–78.
28. Annetta Miller, "Stress on the Job," *Newsweek,* April 25, 1988, 40–45.
29. Ibid.
30. J. C. Latack, R. J. Aldag, and B. Joseph, "Job Stress: Determinants and Consequences of Coping Behaviors" (Working paper, Ohio State University, 1986), and R. A. Karasek, Jr., "Job Demands, Job Decision Latitude, and Mental Strain: Implications for Job Redesign," *Administrative Science Quarterly* 24 (1979), 285–308.
31. Jeffrey A. Sonnenfeld and Maury A. Peiperl," Staffing Policy as a Strategic Response: A Topology of Career Systems," *Academy of Management Review* 13 (1988), 588–600; "Career Development Programs," *Small Business Report* (November 1987), 30–35; E. H. Burack, *Career Planning and Management: A Managerial Summary* (Lake Forest, Ill.: Brace-Park Press, 1983).
32. Molly Badgett, "Computerized Talent Files Broaden Editors' Reach for New Employees," *Gannetteer,* published by Gannett Company, Inc. (June 1989), 4–5.
33. M. London, *Developing Managers* (San Francisco: Jossey-Bass, 1985).
34. D. T. Wight, "The Split Role in Performance Appraisal," *Personnel Administrator* (May 1985), 83–87, and A. H. Soerwine, "The Manager as Career Counselor: Some Issues and Approaches," in D. H. Montross and C. J. Shinkman, (eds.), *Career Development in the 1980s* (Springfield, Ill.: Charles C. Thomas, 1981).
35. Kram, *Mentoring at Work.*
36. Lisa R. Sheeran and Donna Fenn, "The Mentor System," *INC.,* June 1987, 136–142.
37. Anne B. Fisher, "Where Women Are Succeeding," *Fortune,* August 3, 1987, 78–86.
38. Felice N. Schwartz, "Management Women and the New Facts of Life," *Harvard Business Review* (January/February 1989), 65–76.
39. A. Taylor, "Why Women Managers Are Bailing Out," *Fortune,* August 18, 1986, 16–23.
40. Rochelle Distelheim, "The New Shoot-out at Generation Gap," *Working Woman,* March 1986, 113–117.
41. Elizabeth Ehrlich, "The Mommy Track," *Business Week,* March 20, 1989, 126–134.
42. Taylor, "Women Managers."
43. Colin Lolinster, "Black Executives: How They're Doing," *Fortune,* January 18, 1988, 109–120.
44. L. Riebstein, "Many Hurdles, Old and New, Keep Black Managers Out of Top Jobs," *The Wall Street Journal,* July 10, 1986, 1.
45. U. Sekaran, *Dual Career Families: Implications for Organizations and Counselors* (San Francisco: Jossey-Bass, 1986).
46. Colin Lolinster, "The Young Exec as Superdad," *Fortune,* April 25, 1988, 233–242.
47. D. T. Hall, "Career Development in Organizations: Where Do We Go from Here?" in Douglas T. Hall and associates, *Career Development in Organizations* (San Francisco: Jossey-Bass, 1986).
48. Denise Weil, "Husbands Who Star in Supporting Roles," *Working Woman,* June 1986, 114–116.
49. "The Uneasy Life of the Corporate Spouse," *Fortune,* August 20, 1984, 26–32.
50. Taylor, "Why Women Managers Are Bailing Out."
51. J. A. F. Stoner, T. P. Ference, E. K. Warren, and H. K. Christensen, *Managerial Career Plateaus: An Exploratory Study* (New York: Center for Research and Career Development, Columbia University, 1980).
52. Ibid.
53. Judith M. Bardwick, "How Executives Can Help Plateaued Employees," *Management Review* (January 1987), 40–46.
54. J. P. Carnazza, A. K. Korman, T. P. Ference, and J. A. F. Stoner, "Plateaued and Non-Plateaued Managers: Factors in Job Performance," *Journal of Management* 7 (1981), 7–25.
55. J. M. Bardwick, "Plateauing and Productivity," *Sloan Management Review* (Spring 1983), 67–73.
56. J. P. Wanous, *Organizational Entry: Recruitment, Selection, and Socialization of Newcomers* (Reading, Mass.: Addison-Wesley, 1980).
57. W. Arnone, "Preretirement Planning: An Employee Benefit That Has Come of Age," *Personnel* 61 (1982), 760–763.

Glossary

accommodative response A response to social demands in which the organization accepts — often under pressure — social responsibility for its actions to comply with the public interest.

accountability The fact that the people with authority and responsibility are subject to reporting and justifying task outcomes to those about them in the chain of command.

action plan A step in MBO that defines the course of action needed to achieve stated objectives.

activity ratio A ratio that measures the firm's internal performance with respect to key activities defined by management.

adjourning The stage of team development in which members prepare for the team's disbandment.

administrative model A decision-making model that describes how managers actually make decisions in situations characterized by nonprogrammed decisions, uncertainty, and ambiguity.

administrative overhead The resources allocated to administrative and support activities.

administrative principles A subfield of the classical management perspective that focused on the total organization rather than the individual worker, delineating the management functions of planning, organizing, commanding, coordinating, and controlling.

application form A device for collecting information about an applicant's education, previous job experience, and other background characteristics.

artificial intelligence (AI) Information technology that attempts to make computers think, talk, see, and listen like people.

assessment center A technique for selecting individuals with high managerial potential based on their performance on a series of simulated managerial tasks.

authority The formal and legitimate right of a manager to make decisions, issue orders, and allocate resources to achieve organizationally desired outcomes.

autocratic leader A leader who tends to centralize authority and rely on legitimate, reward, and coercive power to manage subordinates.

balance sheet A financial statement showing the firm's financial position with respect to assets and liabilities at a specific point in time.

balance sheet budget A financial budget that plans the amount of assets and liabilities for the end of the time period under consideration.

BCG matrix A concept developed by the Boston Consulting Group that evaluates SBUs with respect to the dimensions of business growth rate and market share.

behaviorally anchored rating scale (BARS) A rating technique that relates an employee's performance to specific job-related incidents.

behavioral sciences approach A subfield of the human resource management perspective that applied social science in an organizational context, drawing from economics, psychology, sociology, and other disciplines.

behavior modification The set of techniques by which reinforcement theory is used to modify human behavior.

bet-your-company culture A form of corporate culture characterized by a high-risk, high-stake, slow-feedback environment.

birth stage The phase of the organization life cycle in which the company is created.

bottom-up budgeting A budgeting process in which lower-level managers budget their departments' resource needs and pass them up to top management for approval.

boundary-spanning roles Roles assumed by people and/or departments that link and coordinate the organization with key elements in the external environment.

bounded rationality The concept that people have the time and cognitive ability to process only a limited amount of information on which to base decisions.

brainstorming A decision-making technique in which group members present spontaneous suggestions for problem solution, regardless of their likelihood of implementation, in order to promote freer, more creative thinking within the group.

breakeven analysis A quantitative technique that helps managers determine the level of sales at which total revenues equal total costs.

bureaucratic control The use of rules, policies, hierarchy of authority, reward systems, and other formal devices to influence employee behavior and assess performance.

bureaucratic organizations A subfield of the classical management perspective that emphasized management on an impersonal, rational basis through elements such as clearly defined authority and responsibility, formal recordkeeping, and separation of management and ownership.

burnout The emotional exhaustion resulting from extended periods of stress.

business incubator An innovation that provides shared office space, management support services, and management advice to entrepreneurs.

business-level strategy The level of strategy concerned with the question: "How do we compete?" Pertains to each business unit or product line within the organization.

business plan A document specifying the business details prepared by an entrepreneur in preparation for opening a new business.

CAD A production technology in which computers perform new-product design.

CAM A production technology in which computers help guide and control the manufacturing system.

capacity planning The determination and adjustment of the organization's ability to produce products and services to match customer demand.

capital expenditure budget A financial budget that plans future investments in major assets to be paid for over several years.

career A sequence of work-related activities and behaviors over a person's life span viewed as movement through various job experiences and the individual's attitudes toward involvement in those experiences.

career development Employee progress or growth over time as a career unfolds.

career ladder A formalized job progression route based on logically connected jobs.

career management Organizational activities designed to promote employees' career development.

career path A job progression route along which an employee can advance through the organization.

career planning The self-assessment, exploration of opportunities, goal setting, and other activities necessary to make informed career-related decisions.

career plateau A point in a career from which the opportunities for further promotion are scarce.

cash budget A financial budget that estimates cash flows on a daily or weekly basis to ensure that the company has sufficient cash to meet its obligations.

causal modeling A forecasting technique that attempts to predict behavior (the dependent variable) by analyzing its causes (independent variables).

cellular layout A facilities layout in which machines dedicated to sequences of production are grouped into cells in accordance with group-technology principles.

centralization The location of decision authority near top organizational levels.

centralized network A team communication structure in which team members communicate through a single individual to solve problems or make decisions.

central planning department A group of planning specialists who develop plans for the organization as a whole and its major divisions and departments and typically report to the president or CEO.

ceremony A planned activity that makes up a special event and is conducted for the benefit of an audience.

chain of command An unbroken line of authority that links all individuals in the organization and specifies who reports to whom.

change agent An OD specialist who contracts with an organization to facilitate change.

changing A step in the intervention stage of organizational development in which individuals experiment with new workplace behavior.

channel The carrier of a communication.

channel richness The amount of information that can be transmitted during a communication episode.

clan control The use of social values, traditions, common beliefs, and trust to generate compliance with organizational goals.

classical model A decision-making model based on the assumption that managers should make logical decisions that will be in the organization's best economic interests.

classical perspective A management perspective that emerged during the nineteenth and early twentieth centuries that emphasized a rational, scientific approach to the study of management and sought to make organizations efficient operating machines.

closed system A system that does not interact with the external environment.

cluster organization An organizational form in which team members from different company locations use electronic mail and GDSSs to solve problems.

coalition An informal alliance among managers who support a specific goal.

code of ethics A formal statement of the organization's values regarding ethics and social issues.

coercive power Power that stems from the leader's authority to punish or recommend punishment.

collectivism A preference for a tightly knit social framework in which individuals look after one another and organizations protect their members' interests.

committee A long-lasting, sometimes permanent team in the organization structure created to deal with tasks that recur regularly.

communication The process by which information is exchanged and understood by two or more people, usually with the intent to motivate or influence behavior.

compensation Monetary payments (wages, salaries) and nonmonetary goods/commodities (fringe benefits, vacations) used to reward employees.

compensatory justice The concept that individuals should be compensated for the cost of their injuries by the party responsible and also that individuals should not be held responsible for matters over which they have no control.

competitors Other organizations in the same industry or type of business that provide goods or services to the same set of customers.

completeness The extent to which information contains the appropriate amount of data.

computer-based information system (CBIS) An information system that uses electronic computing technology to create the information system.

conceptual skill The cognitive ability to see the organization as a whole and the relationship among its parts.

concurrent control Control that consists of monitoring ongoing employee activities to ensure their consistency with established standards.

conflict Antagonistic interaction in which one party attempts to thwart the intentions or goals of another.

consideration A type of leader behavior that describes the extent to which a leader is sensitive to subordinates, respects their ideas and feelings, and establishes mutual trust.

content theories A group of theories that emphasize the needs that motivate people.

contingency approach A model of leadership that describes the relationship between leadership styles and specific organizational situations.

contingency view An extension of the human resource perspective in which the successful resolution of organizational problems is thought to depend on managers' identification of key variables in the situation at hand.

continuous process production A type of technology involving mechanization of the entire work flow and nonstop production.

continuous reinforcement schedule A schedule in which every occurrence of the desired behavior is reinforced.

controlling The management function concerned with monitoring employees' activities, keeping the organization on track toward its goals, and making corrections as needed.

coordination The quality of collaboration across departments.

coordination costs The time and energy needed to coordinate the activities of a team to enable it to perform its task.

core control system The strategic plans, financial forecasts, budgets, management by objectives, operations management techniques, and MIS reports that form an integrated system for directing and monitoring organizational activities.

corporate-level strategy The level of strategy concerned with the question: "What business are we in?" Pertains to the organization as a whole and the combination of business units and product lines that make it up.

corporation An artificial entity created by the state and existing apart from its owners.

cost leadership A type of competitive strategy with which the organization aggressively seeks efficient facilities, cuts costs, and employs tight cost controls to be more efficient than competitors.

countertrade The barter of products for other products rather than their sale for currency.

creativity The development of novel solutions to perceived organizational problems.

critical path The path with the longest total time; represents the total time required for the project.

critical success factors (CSFs) The particular areas in which satisfactory results will enhance the organization's overall performance.

cross-functional team A group of employees assigned to a functional department that meets as a team to resolve mutual problems.

culture The set of key values, beliefs, understandings, and norms that members of an organization share; the shared knowledge, beliefs, values, behaviors, and ways of thinking among members of a society.

culture gap The difference between an organization's desired cultural norms and values and actual norms and values.

culture/people change A change in employees' values, norms, attitudes, beliefs, and behavior.

customers People and organizations in the environment who acquire goods or services from the organization.

data Raw, unsummarized, and unanalyzed facts.

debt financing Borrowing money that has to be repaid in order to start a business.

decentralization The location of decision authority near lower organizational levels.

decentralized network A team communication structure in which team members freely communicate with one another and arrive at decisions together.

decentralized planning staff A group of planning specialists assigned to major departments and divisions to help managers develop their own strategic plans.

decision A choice made from available alternatives.

decision making The process of identifying problems and opportunities and then resolving them.

decision tree A decision-making aid used for decision situations that occur in sequence; consists of a pictorial representation of decision alternatives, states of nature, and outcomes of each course of action.

decode To translate the symbols used in a message for the purpose of interpreting its meaning.

defensive response A response to social demands in which the organization admits to some errors of commission or omission but does not act obtrusively.

delegation The process managers use to transfer authority and responsibility to positions below them in the hierarchy.

Delphi group A group decision-making format that involves the circulation among participants of questionnaires on the selected problem, sharing of answers, and continuous recirculation/refinement of questionnaires until a consensus has been obtained.

Delphi technique A qualitative forecasting method in which experts reach consensus about future events through a series of continuously refined questionnaires rather than through face-to-face discussion.

democratic leader A leader who delegates authority to others, encourages participation, and relies on expert and referent power to manage subordinates.

demographic forecast A forecast of societal characteristics such as birthrates, educational levels, marriage rates, and diseases.

departmentalization The basis on which individuals are grouped into departments and departments into total organizations.

dependent demand inventory Inventory in which item demand is related to the demand for other inventory items.

descriptive An approach that describes how managers actually make decisions rather than how they should.

devil's advocate A decision-making technique in which an individual is assigned the role of challenging the assumptions and assertions made by the group to prevent premature consensus.

diagnosis The step in the decision-making process in which managers analyze underlying causal factors associated with the decision situation.

differentiation A type of competitive strategy with which the organization seeks to distinguish its products or services from competitors'.

direct investment An entry strategy in which the organization is involved in managing its production facilities in a foreign country.

discretionary costs Costs based on management decisions and not on fixed commitments or volume of output.

discretionary responsibility Organizational responsibility that is voluntary and guided by the organization's desire to make social contributions not mandated by economics, law, or ethics.

disengagement state The stage of career development during which the person prepares for retirement and begins to disengage from both the organization and the occupation.

distinctive competence The unique position the organization achieves with respect to competitors through its decisions concerning resource deployments, scope, and synergy.

distributive justice The concept that differential treatment of people should not be based on arbitrary characteristics. In the case of substantive differences, people should be treated differently in proportion to the differences between them.

divisional structure An organizational structure in which departments are grouped based on similar organizational outputs.

downward communication Messages sent from top management down to subordinates.

dual role A role in which the individual both contributes to the team's task and supports members' emotional needs.

econometric model A system of regression equations that are solved simultaneously to capture the interaction between economic conditions and the organization's activities.

economic dimension The dimension of the general environment representing the overall economic health of the country or region in which the organization functions.

economic forces Forces that affect the availability, production, and distribution of a society's resources among competing users.

economic order quantity (EOQ) An inventory management technique designed to minimize the total of ordering and holding costs for inventory items.

effectiveness The degree to which the organization achieves a stated objective.

efficiency The use of minimal resources — raw materials, money, and people — to produce a desired volume of output.

electronic data interchange (EDI) An interorganizational computer network used by trading partners to exchange business data.

employee involvement team A team designed to increase the participation of lower-level workers in decision making and the conduct of their jobs in order to improve performance.

employee stock ownership plan (ESOP) A motivational compensation program that gives employees part ownership of the organization.

encode To select symbols with which to compose a message.

entrepreneur Someone who recognizes a viable idea for a business product or service and carries it out.

entrepreneurship The process of initiating a business venture, organizing the necessary resources, and assuming the associated risks and rewards.

entropy The tendency for a system to run down and die.

environmental discontinuity A large change in the organization's environment over a short period.

E → P expectancy Expectancy that putting effort into a given task will lead to high performance.

equity A situation that exists when the ratio of one person's outcomes to inputs equals that of another's.

equity financing Financing that consists of funds that are invested in exchange for ownership in the company.

equity theory A process theory that focuses on individuals' perceptions of how fairly they are treated relative to others.

ERG theory A modification of the needs hierarchy theory that proposes three categories of needs: existence, relatedness, and growth.

establishment and advancement stage The stage of career development during which the individual experiences progress with the organization in the form of transfers, promotions, and/or high visibility.

ethical dilemma A situation that arises when all alternative choices or behaviors have been deemed undesirable because of potentially negative ethical consequences, making it difficult to distinguish right from wrong.

ethical ombudsman An official given the responsibility of corporate conscience who hears and investigates ethical complaints and points out potential ethical failures to top management.

ethics The code of moral principles and values that govern the behaviors of a person or group with respect to what is right or wrong.

ethics committee A group of executives assigned to oversee the organization's ethics by ruling on questionable issues and disciplining violators.

ethnocentrism A cultural attitude marked by the tendency to regard one's own culture as superior to others.

excellence characteristics A group of eight features found to typify the highest-performing U.S. companies.

executive information system (EIS) An interactive CBIS that retrieves, manipulates, and displays information serving the needs of top managers; also called *decision support system.*

exit interview An interview conducted with departing employees to determine the reasons for their termination.

expectancy theory A process theory that proposes that motivation depends on individuals' expectations about their ability to perform tasks and receive desired rewards.

expected value The weighted average of each possible outcome for a decision alternative.

expense budget An operating budget that outlines the anticipated expenses for each responsibility center and for the organization as a whole.

expert power Power that stems from the leader's special knowledge of or skill in the tasks performed by subordinates.

expert system An area of AI that attempts to program a computer to duplicate an expert's decision-making and problem-solving strategies.

exploration and trial stage The stage of career development during which a person accepts his or her first job and perhaps tries several jobs.

exporting An entry strategy in which

the organization maintains its production facilities within its home country and transfers its products for sale in foreign markets.

external locus of control The belief by individuals that their future is not within their control but rather is influenced by external forces.

extrinsic reward A reward given by another person.

feedback The degree to which doing the job provides information back to the employee regarding his or her performance; a response by the receiver to the sender's communication.

feedback control Control that focuses on the organization's outputs; also called *post-action* or *output control*.

feedforward control Control that focuses on human, material, and financial resources flowing into the organization; also called *preliminary* or *preventive control*.

femininity A cultural preference for modesty, tending to the weak, and quality of life.

financial audit An independent appraisal of the organization's financial records, conducted by external or internal experts.

financial budget A budget that defines where the organization will receive its cash and how it will spend it.

finished-goods inventory Inventory consisting of items that have passed through the complete production process but have yet to be sold.

first-line manager A manager who is at the first or second management level and directly responsible for the production of goods and services.

fixed costs Costs that are based on a commitment from a previous budget period and cannot be altered.

fixed-position layout A facilities layout in which the product remains in one location and the required tasks and equipment are brought to it.

flat structure A management structure characterized by an overall broad span of control and relatively few hierarchical levels.

flexible manufacturing A manufacturing technology using computers to automate and integrate manufacturing components such as robots, machines, product design, and engineering analysis.

flexible manufacturing system (FMS) A small or medium-size automated production line that can be adapted to produce more than one product line.

focus A type of competitive strategy that emphasizes concentration on a specific regional market or buyer group.

force field analysis The process of determining which forces drive and which resist a proposed change.

formal communication channel A communication channel that flows within the chain of command or task responsibility defined by the organization.

formalization The written documentation used to direct and control employees.

formal team A team created by the organization as part of the formal organization structure.

forming The stage of team development characterized by orientation and acquaintance.

franchising A form of licensing in which an organization provides its foreign franchisees with a complete assortment of materials and services; an arrangement by which the owner of a product or service allows others to purchase the right to distribute the product or service with help from the owner.

free rider A person who benefits from team membership but does not make a proportionate contribution to the team's work.

frustration-regression principle The idea that failure to meet a higher-order need may cause a regression to an already satisfied lower-order need.

functional-based structure A global organization structure in which managers' responsibility and authority are assigned along functional lines.

functional-level strategy The level of strategy concerned with the question: "How do we support the business-level strategy?" Pertains to all of the organization's major departments.

functional manager A manager who is responsible for a department that performs a single functional task and has employees with similar training and skills.

functional structure An organizational structure in which positions are grouped into departments based on similar skills, expertise, and resource use.

gain sharing A motivational compensation program that rewards employees and managers when predetermined performance targets are met.

general environment The layer of the external environment that affects the organization indirectly.

general manager A manager who is responsible for several departments that perform different functions.

geographic-based structure A global organization structure in which all of an MNC's products and functions in a particular country or region report to the same division manager.

GE screen A portfolio matrix developed by General Electric Company that evaluates business units along the dimensions of industry attractiveness and business strength.

globalization The standardization of product design and advertising strategies throughout the world.

goal A desired future state that the organization attempts to realize.

grand strategy The general plan or major action by which an organization intends to achieve its long-term objectives.

grapevine An informal, person-to-person communication network of employees that is not officially sanctioned by the organization.

group decision support system (GDSS) An interactive CBIS that facilitates group decision making; also called *collaborative work system*.

groupthink A phenomenon in which group members are so committed to the group that they are reluctant to express contrary opinions.

halo error A type of rating error that occurs when an employee receives the same rating on all dimensions regardless of his or her performance on individual ones.

Hawthorne studies A series of experiments on worker productivity begun in 1924 at the Hawthorne plant of Western

Electric Company in Illinois; attributed employees' increased output to managers' better treatment of them during the study.

hero A figure who exemplifies the deeds, character, and attributes of a corporate culture.

hierarchy of needs theory A content theory that proposes that people are motivated by five categories of needs — physiological, safety, belongingness, esteem, and self-actualization — that exist in a hierarchical order.

homogeneity A type of rating error that occurs when a rater gives all employees a similar rating regardless of their individual performances.

horizontal communication The lateral or diagonal exchange of messages across peers or coworkers.

horizontal linkage model An approach to product change that emphasizes shared development of innovations among several departments.

horizontal team A formal team composed of employees from about the same hierarchical level but from different areas of expertise.

human relations movement A movement in management thinking and practice that emphasized satisfaction of employees' basic needs as the key to increased worker productivity.

human resource inventory A data base that summarizes individuals' skills, abilities, work experiences, and career interests.

human resource management (HRM) Activities undertaken to attract, develop, and maintain an effective work force within an organization.

human resource perspective A management perspective that emerged during the mid-nineteenth century that emphasized enlightened treatment of workers and power sharing between managers and employees.

human resource planning The forecasting of human resource needs and the projected matching of individuals with expected job vacancies.

human resources forecast A forecast of the organization's future personnel needs.

human skill The ability to work with and through other people and to work effectively as a group member.

hygiene factors Factors that involve the presence or absence of job dissatisfiers, including working conditions, pay, company policies, and interpersonal relationships.

idea champion A person who sees the need for and champions productive change within the organization.

implementation The step in the decision-making process that involves the employment of managerial, administrative, and persuasive abilities to translate the chosen alternative into action.

income statement A financial statement that summarizes a company's financial performance over a given time interval.

individualism A preference for a loosely knit social framework in which individuals are expected to take care of themselves.

individualism approach The ethical concept that acts are moral when they promote the individual's best long-term interests, which ultimately leads to the greater good.

informal communication channel A communication channel that exists outside formally authorized channels without regard for the organization's hierarchy of authority.

information Data that are meaningful and alter the receiver's understanding.

information system A written or electronic internal system for processing data and information among employees; a mechanism for collecting, organizing, and distributing data to organizational employees.

infrastructure A country's physical facilities that support economic activities.

initiating structure A type of leader behavior that describes the extent to which a leader is task oriented and directs subordinates' work activities toward goal achievement.

inspirational leader A leader who has the ability to motivate subordinates to transcend their expected performance.

integrating manager An individual responsible for coordinating the activities of several departments on a full-time basis to achieve specific project or product outcomes.

interactive group A group decision-making format in which group members are brought together face to face and have a specific agenda and decision objectives.

interdependence The extent to which departments depend on each other for resources or materials to accomplish their tasks.

internal environment The environment within the organization's boundaries.

internal locus of control The belief by individuals that their future is within their control and that other external forces will have little influence.

international dimension The dimension of the general environment representing events that originate in foreign countries and opportunities for American firms abroad.

international division An organizational division that is established alongside one or more domestic divisions and has equal status in the management hierarchy.

international management The management of business operations conducted in more than one country.

intrapreneurship The process whereby an individual sees the need for innovation and promotes it within the organization.

intrinsic reward A reward received as a direct consequence of a person's actions.

intuition The immediate comprehension of a decision situation based on past experience but without conscious thought.

inventory The goods that the organization keeps on hand for use in the production process.

job A unit of work that a single employee is responsible for performing.

job analysis The process of obtaining accurate and complete information about jobs through a systematic examination of job content.

job characteristics model A model of job design that comprises core job dimensions, critical psychological states, and employee growth-need strength.

job description A listing of duties as well as desirable qualifications for a particular job.

job design The application of motivational theories to the structure of work for improving productivity and satisfaction.

job enlargement A job design that combines a series of tasks into one new, broader job to give employees variety and challenge.

job enrichment A job design that incorporates achievement, recognition, and other high-level motivators into the work.

job evaluation The process of determining the values of jobs within an organization through an examination of job content.

job matching system A method that links qualified individuals with career opportunities within the organization.

job rotation A job design that systematically moves employees from one job to another to provide them with variety and stimulation.

job simplification A job design whose purpose is to improve task efficiency by reducing the number of tasks a single person must perform.

joint venture A strategic alliance or program by two or more organizations; a variation of direct investment in which an organization shares costs and risks with another firm to build a manufacturing facility, develop new products, or set up a sales and distribution network.

jury of opinion A method of qualitative forecasting based on the average opinions of managers from various company divisions and departments.

justice approach The ethical concept that moral decisions must be based on standards of equity, fairness, and impartiality.

just-in-time (JIT) inventory systems An inventory control system that schedules materials to arrive precisely when they are needed on a production line.

key indicator system A technique for determining managers' information needs based on key business indicators, exception reporting, and the use of graphics packages.

labor supply The people available for hire by the organization.

law of effect The assumption that positively reinforced behavior tends to be repeated and unreinforced or negatively reinforced behavior tends to be inhibited.

leadership The ability to influence people toward the attainment of organizational goals.

leading The management function that involves the use of influence to motivate employees to achieve the organization's goals.

legal-political dimension The dimension of the general environment that includes federal, state, and local government regulations and political activities designed to control company behavior.

legitimate power Power that stems from a formal management position in an organization and the authority granted to it.

licensing An entry strategy in which an organization in one country makes certain resources available to companies in another in order to participate in the production and sale of its products abroad.

linear programming A quantitative technique that allocates resources so as to optimize a predefined organizational objective.

liquidity ratio A financial ratio that indicates the company's ability to meet its current debt obligations.

listening The skill of receiving messages to accurately grasp facts and feelings to interpret the genuine meaning.

LPC scale A questionnaire designed to measure relationship-oriented versus task-oriented leadership style according to the leader's choice of adjectives for describing the "least preferred coworker."

lump-sum bonus A motivational compensation program that rewards employees with a one-time cash payment based on performance.

management The attainment of organizational goals in an effective and efficient manner through planning, organizing, leading, and controlling organizational resources.

management by objectives (MBO) A method whereby managers and employees define objectives for each department, project, and employee and use them to control subsequent performance.

management by wandering around (MBWA) A communication technique in which managers interact directly with workers to exchange information.

management information system (MIS) A form of CBIS that collects, organizes, and distributes the data managers use in performing their management functions.

management science A set of quantitatively based decision models used to assist management decision makers.

management science perspective A management perspective that emerged after World War II and applied mathematics, statistics, and other quantitative techniques to managerial problems.

managerial grid A two-dimensional leadership theory that measures a leader's concern for people and concern for production.

manufacturing organization An organization that produces physical goods.

manufacturing resource planning (MRP II) An extension of MRP to include the control of resources pertaining to all operations of the organization.

market entry strategy An organizational strategy for entering a foreign market.

masculinity A cultural preference for achievement, heroism, assertiveness, and material success.

mass production A type of technology characterized by the production of a large volume of products with the same specifications.

matching model An employee selection approach in which the organization and the applicant attempt to match each other's needs, interests, and values.

materials management The complete integration under one manager of all organizational departments and activities that contribute to the costs of materials.

materials requirement planning (MRP) A dependent demand inventory planning and control system that schedules the precise amount of all materials required to support the production of desired end products.

matrix boss A product or functional boss, responsible for one side of the matrix.

matrix structure An organizational structure that utilizes functional and divisional chains of command simultaneously in the same part of the organization; a global organization structure that permits an MNC to achieve vertical control and horizontal coordination simultaneously.

maturity stage The phase of the organization life cycle in which the organization has become exceedingly large and mechanistic.

mechanistic structure An organizational structure characterized by rigidly defined tasks, many rules and regulations, little teamwork, and centralized decision making.

mediation The process of using a third party to settle a dispute.

mentor A senior employee who acts as a sponsor and teacher to a younger, less experienced employee.

merger The combination of two or more organizations into one.

message The tangible formulation of an idea to be sent to a receiver.

mid-career renewal strategies A strategy designed to provide advancement opportunities for deserving mid-career employees while maximizing the contributions of plateaued employees who continue to perform satisfactorily.

mid-career stage The stage of career development characterized by growth, maintenance, or decline.

middle manager A manager who works at the middle levels of the organization and is responsible for major departments.

midlife stage The phase of the organization life cycle in which the firm has reached prosperity and grown substantially large.

mission The organization's reason for existence.

mission statement A broadly stated definition of the organization's basic business scope and operations that distinguish it from similar types of organizations.

moral-rights approach The ethical concept that moral decisions are those that best maintain the rights of those people affected by them.

motivation The arousal, direction, and persistence of behavior.

motivators Factors that influence job satisfaction based on fulfillment of higher-level needs such as achievement, recognition, responsibility, and opportunity for growth.

multidomestic strategy The modification of product design and advertising strategies to suit the specific needs of individual countries.

multinational corporation (MNC) An organization that receives more than 25 percent of its total sales revenues from operations outside the parent company's home country; also called *global corporation* or *transnational corporation*.

multiple advocacy A decision-making technique that involves several advocates and presentation of multiple points of view, including minority and unpopular opinions.

multiple control system A control system involving the simultaneous use of feedforward, concurrent, and feedback control.

need to achieve A human quality linked to entrepreneurship in which people are motivated to excel and pick situations in which success is likely.

networking The linking together of people and departments within or among organizations for the purpose of sharing information resources.

network structure An organizational structure that disaggregates major functions into separate companies that are brokered by a small headquarters organization.

neutralizer A situational variable that counteracts a leadership style and prevents the leader from displaying certain behaviors.

new-venture fund A fund providing resources from which individuals and groups draw to develop new ideas, products, or businesses.

new-venture team A unit separate from the mainstream of the organization that is responsible for developing and initiating innovations.

nominal group A group decision-making format that emphasizes equal participation in the decision process by all group members.

nonparticipator role A role in which the individual contributes little to either the task or members' socioemotional needs.

nonprogrammed decision A decision made in response to a situation that is unique, is poorly defined and largely unstructured, and has important consequences for the organization.

nonroutine service technology Service technology in which there are no specific procedures for directing employees, problem situations are varied, and employees must rely on personal resources for problem solving.

nonverbal communication A communication transmitted through actions and behaviors rather than through words.

norm A standard of conduct that is shared by team members and guides their behavior.

normative An approach that defines how a decision maker should make decisions and provides guidelines for reaching an ideal outcome for the organization.

norming The stage of team development in which conflicts developed during the storming stage are resolved and team harmony and unity emerge.

objective A specific short-term target for which measurable results can be obtained.

obstructive response A response to social demands in which the organization denies responsibility, claims that evidence of misconduct is misleading or distorted, and attempts to obstruct investigation.

on-the-job training (OJT) A type of training in which an experienced employee "adopts" a new employee to teach him or her how to perform job duties.

open system A system that interacts with the external environment.

operating budget The plan for the allocation of financial resources to each organizational responsibility center for the budget period under consideration.

operational objectives Specific, measurable results expected from departments, work groups, and individuals within the organization.

operational plans Plans developed at the organization's lower levels that specify action steps toward achieving operational goals and support tactical planning activities.

operations management The field of management that specializes in the physical production of goods or services and uses quantitative techniques for solving manufacturing problems.

operations strategy The recognition of the importance of operations to the firm's success and the involvement of operations managers in the organization's strategic planning.

opportunity A situation in which managers see potential organizational accomplishments that exceed current objectives.

organic structure An organizational structure that is free flowing, has few rules and regulations, encourages employee teamwork, and decentralizes decision making to employees doing the job.

organization A social entity that is goal directed and deliberately structured.

organizational change The adoption of a new idea or behavior by an organization.

organizational control The systematic process through which managers regulate organizational activities to make them consistent with the expectations established in plans, targets, and performance standards.

organizational development (OD) The application of behavioral science techniques to improve an organization's health and effectiveness through its ability to cope with environmental changes, improve internal relationships, and increase problem-solving capabilities.

organizational environment All elements existing outside the organization's boundaries that have the potential to affect the organization.

organizational structure The framework in which the organization defines how tasks are divided, resources are deployed, and departments are coordinated.

organization chart The visual representation of an organization's structure.

organization life cycle The organization's evolution through major developmental stages.

organizing The management function concerned with assigning tasks, grouping tasks into departments, and allocating resources to departments; the deployment of organizational resources to achieve strategic objectives.

outsourcing Engaging in the international division of labor so as to obtain the cheapest sources of labor and supplies regardless of country; also called *global sourcing*.

paper-and-pencil test A written test designed to measure a particular attribute such as intelligence or aptitude.

partial productivity The ratio of total outputs to the inputs from a single major input category.

partial reinforcement schedule A schedule in which only some occurrences of the desired behavior are reinforced.

partnership An unincorporated business owned by two or more people.

path-goal theory A contingency approach to leadership specifying that the leader's responsibility is to increase subordinates' motivation by clarifying the behaviors necessary for task accomplishment and rewards.

pay for knowledge A motivational compensation program that links employee's salary with the number of tasks performed.

pay for performance A motivational compensation program that rewards employees in proportion to their performance contributions.

payoff matrix A decision-making aid comprised of relevant strategies, states of nature, probability of occurrence of states of nature, and expected outcome(s).

pay survey A study of what other companies pay employees in jobs that correspond to a sample of key positions selected by the organization.

pay-trend line A graph that shows the relationship between pay and total job point values for determining the worth of a given job.

perception The process of making sense out of one's environment.

perceptual organization The categorization of an object or stimulus according to one's frame of reference.

perceptual selectivity The screening and selection of objects and stimuli that compete for one's attention.

performance The organization's ability to attain its goals by using resources in an efficient and effective manner.

performance appraisal The process of observing and evaluating an employee's performance, recording the assessment, and providing feedback to the employee.

performance appraisal interview A formal review of an employee's performance conducted between the superior and the subordinate.

performance gap A disparity between existing and desired performance levels.

performing The stage of team development in which members focus on problem solving and accomplishing the team's assigned task.

permanent team A group of participants from several departments that meets regularly to solve ongoing problems of common interest.

PERT The Program Evaluation and Review Technique; consists of breaking down a project into a network of specific activities and mapping out their sequence and necessary completion dates.

plan A blueprint specifying the resource allocations, schedules, and other actions necessary for attaining goals.

planning The management function concerned with defining goals for future organizational performance and deciding on the tasks and resource use needed to attain them; the act of determining the organization's goals and the means for achieving them.

planning task force A temporary group consisting of line managers responsible for developing strategic plans.

P → O expectancy Expectancy that successful performance of a task will lead to the desired outcome.

point system A job evaluation system that assigns a predetermined point value to each compensable job factor in order to determine the worth of a given job.

policy A general statement based on the organization's overall goals and strategic plans that provides directions for individuals within the company.

political activity Organizational attempts, such as lobbying, to influence government legislation and regulation.

political forces The influence of political and legal institutions on people and organizations.

political risk A company's risk of loss of assets, earning power, or managerial control due to politically motivated events or actions by host governments.

portfolio strategy A type of corporate-level strategy that pertains to the organization's mix of SBUs and product lines that fit together in such a way as to provide the corporation with synergy and competitive advantage.

power The potential ability to influence others' behavior.

power distance The degree to which people accept inequality in power among institutions, organizations, and people.

preretirement program A strategy designed to assist employees in coping with the stress of the transition from work to retirement.

proactive response A response to social demands in which the organization seeks to learn what is in its constituencies' interest and to respond without pressure from them.

problem A situation in which organizational accomplishments have failed to meet established objectives.

problem-solving team Typically 5 to 12 hourly employees from the same department who meet to discuss ways of improving quality, efficiency, and the work environment.

procedural justice The concept that rules should be clearly stated and consistently and impartially enforced.

procedure A specific series of steps to be used in achieving certain objectives; usually applies to individual jobs.

process culture A type of corporate culture characterized by low-risk decision making, little or no feedback, and low-stake decisions.

process layout A facilities layout in which machines that perform the same function are grouped together in one location.

process theories A group of theories that explain how employees select behaviors with which to meet their needs and determine whether their choices were successful.

product-based structure A global organization structure in which an MNC establishes product divisions whose managers plan, organize, and control all functions for producing and distributing their products at home and worldwide.

product change A change in the organization's product or service output.

productivity The organization's output of products and services divided by its inputs.

product layout A facilities layout in which machines and tasks are arranged according to the sequence of steps in the production of a single product.

product life cycle The stages through which a product or service goes: (1) development and introduction into the marketplace, (2) growth, (3) maturity, and (4) decline.

profitability ratio A financial ratio that describes the firm's profits.

profit budget An operating budget that combines both expense and revenue budgets into one statement showing gross and net profits.

program A complex set of objectives and plans for achieving an important, one-time organizational goal.

programmed decision A decision made in response to a situation that has occurred often enough to enable decision rules to be developed and applied in the future.

project A set of relatively short-term, narrow objectives and plans for achieving a major, one-time organizational goal.

project manager A manager who coordinates people across several departments to accomplish a specific project.

proprietorship An unincorporated business owned by an individual for profit.

prototype A working model of an information system developed to test the system's features.

qualitative forecast A forecast based on the opinions of experts in the absence of precise historical data.

quality The degree to which information accurately portrays reality.

quality circle A group of six to twelve volunteer employees who meet regularly to discuss and solve problems that affect their common work activities.

quantitative forecast A forecast that begins with a series of past data values and then applies a set of mathematical rules with which to predict future values.

raw materials inventory Inventory consisting of the basic inputs to the organization's production process.

realistic job preview (RJP) A recruiting approach that gives applicants all pertinent and realistic information about the job and the organization.

recruiting The activities or practices that define the desired characteristics of applicants for specific jobs.

referent power Power that results from leader characteristics that command subordinates' identification with, respect and admiration for, and desire to emulate the leader.

refreezing A step in the reinforcement stage of organizational development in which individuals acquire a desired new skill or attitude and are rewarded for it by the organization.

regression analysis A statistical tool for predicting the value of a dependent variable based on the known values of independent variables.

reinforcement Anything that causes a given behavior to be repeated or inhibited.

reinforcement theory A motivation theory based on the relationship between a given behavior and its consequences.

relevance The degree to which information pertains to the problems, decisions, and tasks for which a manager is responsible.

reorder point (ROP) The most economical level at which an inventory item should be reordered.

resource deployment The level and pattern of the organization's distribution of physical, financial, and human resources for achieving its strategic goals.

responsibility The duty to perform the task or activity an employee has been assigned.

responsibility center Any organizational department under the supervision of a single individual who is responsible for its activity.

revenue budget An operating budget that identifies the revenues required by the organization.

reward power Power that results from the leader's authority to reward others.

risk propensity The willingness to undertake risk with the opportunity of gaining an increased payoff.

role A set of expectations for one's behavior.

routine service technology Service technology in which work can be broken down into explicit steps and employees can follow objective procedures for serving customers and solving problems.

rule A statement describing how a specific action is to be performed.

sales force composite A type of qualitative forecasting that relies on the combined expert opinions of field sales personnel.

sales forecast A forecast of future company sales based on projected customer demand for products or services.

satisfice To choose the first solution alternative that satisfies minimal decision criteria regardless of whether better solutions are presumed to exist.

schedule of reinforcement The frequency with and intervals over which reinforcement occurs.

scientific management A subfield of the classical management perspective that emphasized scientifically determined changes in management practices as the solution to improving labor productivity.

scope The number of businesses, products, or services that defines the size of the domain within which the organization deals with the environment.

search The process of learning about current developments inside or outside the organization that can be used to meet a perceived need for change.

selection The process of determining the skills, abilities, and other attributes needed to perform a particular job.

self-managing team A team consisting of 5 to 12 multiskilled workers who rotate jobs to produce an entire product or service and perform managerial duties, often supervised by an elected member.

semantics The meaning of words and the way they are used.

service organization An organization that produces nonphysical goods that require customer involvement and cannot be stored in inventory.

service technology Technology characterized by intangible outputs and direct contact between employees and customers.

simulation model A mathematical representation of the relationships among variables in real-world organizational situations.

single-use plans Plans that are developed to achieve a set of objectives that are unlikely to be repeated in the future.

situation analysis Analysis of the strengths, weaknesses, opportunities, and threats (SWOT) that affect organizational performance.

size The organization's scope or magnitude, typically measured by number of employees.

skunkworks Small, informal, and sometimes unauthorized groups that create innovations.

slogan A phrase or sentence that succinctly expresses a key corporate value.

small batch production A type of technology that involves the production of goods in batches of one or a few products designed to customer specifications.

social facilitation The tendency for the presence of others to influence an individual's motivation and performance.

social forces The aspects of a culture that guide and influence relationships among people — their values, needs, and standards of behavior.

social responsibility The obligation of organization management to make decisions and take actions that will enhance the welfare and interests of society as well as the organization's.

sociocultural dimension The dimension of the general environment representing the demographic characteristics, norms, customs, and values of the population within which the organization operates.

socioemotional role A role in which the individual provides support for team members' emotional needs and social unity.

span of management The number of employees who report to a supervisor; also called *span of control.*

special-purpose team A team created outside the formal organization to undertake a project of special importance or creativity.

spin-off An independent company producing a product or service similar to that produced by the entrepreneur's former employer.

stakeholder Any group within or outside the organization that has a stake in the organization's performance.

standing plans Ongoing plans that are used as guidance for tasks performed repeatedly within the organization.

state of nature A future event or condition that is relevant to a decision outcome.

statistical process control (SPC) A type of managerial control that employs carefully gathered data and statistical analysis to evaluate the quality and productivity of employee activities.

statistical quality control The application of statistical techniques to the control of quality.

stereotype A widely held generalization about a group of people that assigns attributes to them solely on the basis of a limited number of categories.

storming The stage of team development in which individual personalities and roles, and resulting conflicts, emerge.

story A narrative based on true events that is repeated frequently and shared by organizational employees.

strategic business unit (SBU) A division of the organization that has a unique business mission, product line, competitors, and markets relative to other SBUs in the same corporation.

strategic control point An activity that is especially important for achieving the organization's strategic objectives.

strategic goals Broad statements of where the organization wants to be in the future; pertain to the organization as a whole rather than to specific divisions or departments.

strategic management The set of decisions and actions used to formulate and implement strategies that will provide a competitively superior fit between the organization and its environment so as to achieve organizational objectives.

strategic plans The action steps by which an organization intends to attain its strategic goals.

strategy The plan of action that prescribes resource allocation and other activities for dealing with the environment and helping the organization attain its goals.

strategy formulation The stage of strategic management that involves the planning and decision making that lead to the establishment of the organization's goals and of a specific strategic plan.

strategy implementation The stage of strategic management that involves the use of managerial and organizational tools to direct resources toward achieving strategic outcomes.

stress The physiological and emotional response to demands, constraints, and opportunities that create uncertainty when important outcomes are at stake.

structural change Any change in the way in which the organization is designed and managed.

substitute A situational variable that makes a leadership style redundant or unnecessary.

subsystems Parts of a system that depend on one another for their functioning.

succession planning The process of creating a plan for moving people into higher organizational levels.

superordinate goals A goal that cannot be reached by a single party.

suppliers People and organizations who provide the raw materials the organization uses to produce its output.

survey feedback A type of OD intervention in which questionnaires on organizational climate and other factors are distributed among employees and the results reported back to them by a change agent.

symbol An object, act, or event that conveys meaning to others.

symbolic manager A manager who defines and uses signals and symbols to influence corporate culture.

synergy The concept that the whole is greater than the sum of its parts; the condition that exists when the organization's parts interact to produce a joint effect that is greater than the sum of the parts acting alone.

system A set of interrelated parts that function as a whole to achieve a common purpose.

systems development life cycle The sequence of events that CBIS designers follow in developing and implementing a new system.

systems theory An extension of the human resources perspective that describes organizations as open systems that are characterized by entropy, synergy, and subsystem interdependence.

tactical objectives Objectives that define the outcomes that major divisions and departments must achieve in order for the organization to reach its overall goals.

tactical plans Plans designed to help execute major strategic plans and to accomplish a specific part of the organization's strategy.

tall structure A management structure characterized by an overall narrow span of management and a relatively large number of hierarchical levels.

task environment The layer of the external environment that directly influences the organization's operations and performance.

task force A temporary team or committee formed to solve a specific short-run problem involving several departments.

task specialist role A role in which the individual devotes personal time and energy to helping the team accomplish its task.

team A group of participants from several departments who meet regularly to solve ongoing problems of common interest; a unit of two or more people who interact and coordinate their work to accomplish a specific objective.

team building A type of OD intervention that enhances the cohesiveness of departments by helping members to learn to function as a team.

team cohesiveness The extent to which team members are attracted to the team and motivated to remain in it.

technical complexity The degree to which machinery is involved in the production process to the exclusion of people.

technical core The heart of the organization's production of its product or service.

technical skill The understanding of and proficiency in the performance of specific tasks.

technological dimension The dimension of the general environment that includes scientific and technological advancements in the industry and society at large.

technological forecast A forecast of the occurrence of technological changes that could effect an organization's way of doing business.

technology The knowledge, tools, techniques, and activities used to transform the organization's inputs into outputs.

technology change A change that pertains to the organization's production process.

Theory Z A management perspective that incorporates techniques from both Japanese and North American management practices.

time-based competition A strategy of competition based on the ability to deliver products and services faster than competitors.

timeliness The degree to which information is available soon after events occur.

time series analysis A forecasting technique that examines the patterns of movement in historical data.

tolerance for ambiguity The psychological characteristic that allows a person to be untroubled by disorder and uncertainty.

top-down budgeting A budgeting process in which middle- and lower-level managers set departmental budget targets in accordance with overall company revenues and expenditures specified by top management.

top leader The overseer of both the product and the functional chains of command, responsible for the entire matrix.

top manager A manager who is at the top of the organizational hierarchy and responsible for the entire organization.

total factor productivity The ratio of total outputs to the inputs from labor, capital, materials, and energy.

total quality control A control concept that gives workers rather than managers the responsibility for achieving standards of quality.

total quality management (TQM) Operations management that strives to perfect the entire manufacturing process through improvements in quality and productivity.

total study A process that attempts to assess information requirements at all management levels.

tough-guy, macho culture A type of corporate culture that emerges in an environmental situation characterized by high-risk decision making, rapid feedback, and large-scale projects.

trade association An association made up of organizations with similar interests for the purpose of influencing the environment.

traits The distinguishing personal characteristics of a leader, such as intelligence, values, and appearance.

transactional leader A leader who clarifies subordinates' role and task requirements, initiates structure, provides rewards, and displays consideration for subordinates.

transaction processing system (TPS) A type of CBIS that performs the organization's routinely occurring transactions.

two-boss employee An employee who reports to two supervisors simultaneously.

uncertainty avoidance A value characterized by people's intolerance for uncertainty and ambiguity and resulting support for beliefs that promise certainty and conformity.

unfreezing A step in the diagnosis stage of organizational development in which participants are made aware of problems in order to increase their willingness to change their behavior.

upward communication Messages transmitted from the lower to the higher level in the organization's hierarchy.

utilitarian approach The ethical concept that moral behaviors produce the greatest good for the greatest number.

valence The value of outcomes for the individual.

validity The relationship between an applicant's score on a selection device and his or her future job performance.

variable costs Costs that are based on an explicit physical relationship with the volume of department activity; also called *engineered costs*.

venture capital firm A group of companies or individuals that invest money in new or expanding businesses for ownership and potential profits.

vertical team A formal team composed of a manager and his or her subordinates in the organization's formal chain of command.

Vroom-Yetton model A model designed to help managers gauge the amount of subordinate participation in decision making.

whistle-blowing The disclosure by an employee of illegal, immoral, or illegitimate practices by the organization.

wholly owned foreign affiliate A foreign subsidiary over which an organization has complete control.

work hard/play hard culture A form of corporate culture characterized by low-risk decision making, rapid feedback, and many small-scale decisions.

work-in-process inventory Inventory composed of the materials that are still moving through the stages of the production process.

work redesign The altering of jobs to increase both the quality of employees' work experience and their productivity.

work specialization The degree to which organizational tasks are subdivided into individual jobs; also called *division of labor.*

youth stage The phase of the organization life cycle in which the organization is growing rapidly and has a product enjoying some marketplace success.

zero-based budgeting (ZBB) A budgeting process in which each responsibility center calculates its resource needs based on the coming year's priorities rather than on the previous year's budget.

Photo Credits

Chapter 1

Page 2: © 1988 Michael C. Abramson. Page 4: Courtesy of The Promus Companies Incorporated. Page 8: Copyright 1988, Bob Gomel. Page 11: © Ovak Arslanian. Page 16: Courtesy of Stouffer Restaurant Company. Page 18: © 1988 Michael C. Abramson. Page 21: Courtesy of Figgie International Inc. Page 22: © 1989 Karen R. Preuss. Page 23: Courtesy of Banc One Corporation. Page 24: Courtesy of Gannett Co. Inc.

Chapter 2

Page 34: General Motors' Electro-Motive Division, La Grange, Illinois. Page 35: From the collection of Walter and Naomi Rosenblum. Used with permission. Page 37: Frederick W. Taylor Collection, S.C. Williams Library, Stevens Insititute of Technology. Page 38: (top) Courtesy of Ford Motor Company; (bottom) From the Collections of Henry Ford Museum and Greenfield Village. Page 39: Courtesy of Ronald G. Greenwood. Page 40: (top) Courtesy of Ronald G. Greenwood; (bottom) National Archives. Page 41: Courtesy of German Information Center. Page 43: Courtesy of Western Electric Photographic Services. Page 47: Courtesy of WestMarc Communications, Inc. Page 51: © 1989 George J. Riley Photography for GTE.

Chapter 3

Pages 60 and 64: Chuck Fox 1988 for *Southern Pacific Bulletin*. Page 66: Courtesy of Arby's Incorporated. Page 67: Courtesy of Compaq Computer Corporation. Page 68: Courtesy of Sara Lee Corporation. Page 72: Courtesy of The Stanley Works. Page 74: © The Procter & Gamble Company. Used with permission. Page 77: Courtesy of Southwest Airlines. Page 78: Courtesy of Stew Leonard's. Page 79: Courtesy of Quaker State Corporation. Page 82: Courtesy of Quad/Graphics, Inc. Page 84: Larry Phillips Photography, Inc. for Banc One Corporation.

Chapter 4

Page 92: Courtesy of Chevron U.S.A. Inc. Page 94: Courtesy of Union Carbide Corporation. Page 95: © 1990 by Seth Resnick. Page 97: © Chris Jones. Page 98: Courtesy of ServiceMaster. Page 102: © Ann States/SABA. Page 105: Courtesy of Merck & Co., Inc. Page 107: Courtesy of Xerox Corporation.

Chapter 5

Pages 120 and 124: Courtesy of Northrop Corporation. Page 128: Courtesy of Texaco Inc. Page 130: Reprint permission granted by Timex Corporation. Page 131: © 1990 Dick Spahr. Page 133: © Henry Yu. Page 134: Courtesy of Campbell Soup Company. Page 136: Courtesy of New England Telephone Company. Page 138: Ray Tyler for *Southern Pacific Bulletin*. Page 140: Art Direction: Mraz Design, Teresa Zimmerman Mraz. Photography: Carlos Alejandro. Page 144: Courtesy of PSE&G. Photo by T.J. Miller.

Chapter 6

Page 150: Courtesy of Air Products and Chemicals, Inc. Page 153: Tonka Corporation 1987 Annual Report. Used with permission. Page 155: Picture is of Norm Nickin, inventor of product and Director of Corporate Licensing. Courtesy of Domino's Pizza, Inc. Page 157: Courtesy of Air Products and Chemicals, Inc. Page 161: Courtesy of the BFGoodrich Company. Page 162: © Playskool Baby Inc., a subsidiary of Hasbro, Inc. Page 164: © Ted Kawalerski for Bausch & Lomb. Page 166: Courtesy of Wendy's International, Inc. Page 171: Courtesy of Caterpillar Inc.

Chapter 7

Page 178: © 1988 Bud Hunter, photographer. Page 181: Courtesy of Welch's, Concord, MA. Page 182: © 1989 John Abbott. Page 185: Courtesy of American Restaurants Corporation. Page 187: © Neil Selkirk for Monsanto Company. Page 190: Reprinted with permission of Federal Express Corporation. Page 191: Courtesy of Amoco Corporation. Page 194: Courtesy of Wetterau Incorporated. Page 197: © 1988 Bud Hunter, photographer. Page 200: Courtesy of NWNL Companies, Inc.

Chapter 8

Page 208: Courtesy of Amoco Corporation. Page 210: Courtesy of Church & Dwight Co., Inc. Page 213: Courtesy of Pier I Imports. Page 216: © Arthur Montes-De-Oca 1988. All Rights Reserved. Page 217: Courtesy of The Glidden Company. Page 219: Courtesy of Bristol-Myers Squibb Company. Page 223: Courtesy of Delta Air Lines, Inc. Page 227: Courtesy of Bowater Incorporated. Page 230: Courtesy of Amoco Corporation. Page 234: Courtesy of American President Companies.

Chapter 9

Page 244: Courtesy of Colgate-Palmolive Company. Page 246: Courtesy of J.C. Penney Publications. Page 249: Courtesy of Chevron Corporation, Ward Schumaker, Illustrator. Page 252: © Ovark Arslanian. Page 254: © Joe Baraban, photographer for Coca-Cola Enterprises Inc. Page 258: Bill Parsons Commercial Photography, Inc., Little Rock, AR, for Arkansas Power & Light Company. Page 261: Courtesy of MagneTek, Inc. Page 265: Courtesy of Tenneco, Inc. Page 268: © John Nienhuis 1989 for *Reflections*, Snap-on Tools Corporation. Page 269: Courtesy of Colgate-Palmolive Company. Page 270: Courtesy of Ford Motor Company. Page 273: Courtesy of Safeguard Scientifics, Inc.

Chapter 10

Page 278: Chuck Nacke/Picture Group. Page 281: Courtesy of Dyansen Corporation. Page 282: Courtesy of Dow Corning Corporation. Page 285: Chuck Nacke/Picture Group. Page 288: U.S. Marines. Page 291: © Stephen Green. Page 295: Courtesy of Motorola, Inc. Page 296: Courtesy of Universal Health Services, Inc. Page 297: Courtesy Boise Cascade Corporation.

Chapter 11

Page 304: Nina Berman/SIPA. Page 306: Courtesy of American Express Company. Page 307: Courtesy of Stone Container Corporation. Page 311: Courtesy of Herman Miller, Incorporated. Page 313: Tom Manning Photos, Courtesy of United Telecommunications, Inc. Page 316: Nina Berman/SIPA. Page 319: © Mike Clemmer 1989/Picture Group. Page 321: Ted Morrison © 1990. Page 322: Courtesy of Rubbermind Canada Inc. Page 325: Photographer: Pete Johnsen, Midwest Studios, Inc. Page 326: Courtesy of Xerox Corporation, Benchmark Magazine, Paul Prosise, Photography. Page 328: © Jill Fineberg. Page 329: Copyrighted by Ken Kerbs, 1990.

Chapter 12

Page 334: Courtesy of Xerox Corporation. Page 336: Courtesy of Tenneco Gas—Carlos Carpenter. Page 339: Courtesy of Xerox Corporation. Page 341: © Brad Trent/Outline Press Syndicate Inc. Page 343: Used with permission from McDonald's Corporation. Page 346: © 1986 Gary Gladstone. Page 352: Courtesy of Merck & Co., Inc. Page 356: Courtesy of Varian Associates, Incorporated. Page 357: Courtesy of Manville Corporation. Page 359: © Larry Keenan.

Chapter 13

Page 370: © Harry Benson. Page 372: © 1989 David Carter. Page 373: © James Schnepf 1987/Woodfin Camp & Associates. Page 374: © Taro Yamasaki. Page 376: U.S. Army Recruitment Brochure. Page 378: © Jim Knowles/Picture Group. Page 383: © Harry Benson. Page 387: © 1990 John S. Abbott Photography. Page 390: Courtesy of Martin Marietta Corporation. Page 392: Courtesy of The Walt Disney Company. Page 394: © Dudley Reed/Onyx.

Chapter 14

Page 400: © James Schnepf/Woodfin Camp & Associates. Page 403: Courtesy of Union Camp Corporation. Page 407: Courtesy of Longs Drugs. Page 409: Courtesy of *Frontline Magazine* published by Taco Bell Public Affairs Department. Page 411: © Jackson Hill 1988/Southern Lights. Page 413: © Andy Freeberg. Page 415: Courtesy of Tyson Foods, Inc. Page 420: Courtesy of the United States Shoe Corporation. Page 422: Courtesy of McDonnell Douglas Corporation. Page 424: Courtesy of Gary Brown. Page 427: © James Schnepf/Woodfin Camp & Associates.

Chapter 15

Page 434: Courtesy of Caterpillar Inc. Page 437: Courtesy of Southwest Airlines. Page 440: Courtesy of Hewlett-Packard Company. Page 441: © Duomo/Mitchell Layton. All Rights Reserved. Page 443: Courtesy of Boise Cascade Corporation. Page 445: Courtesy of Procter & Gamble Company. Page 446: Photo by Dick Dickinson for Florida Progress Corporation. Page 449: © 1989 by Jonathan Levine. All Rights Reserved. Page 452: Courtesy of Ford Motor Company.

Chapter 16

Page 460: © 1987 Lee Balterman. Page 463: Courtesy of J.P. Morgan & Company, Incorporated. Page 464: Zigy Kaluzny/Gamma Liaison. Page 469: Courtesy of MagneTek, Inc. Page 473: Courtesy of Martin Marietta Corporation. Page 474: *Winning Ways,* March 1989. *Winning Ways* is a sales publication produced for the employees of First Security Corporation. Editor: Patricia E. Pace. Used with permission. Page 475: © Alen MacWeeney for Norton Company. Page 479: Used with permission of Inland Steel Industries. Page 481: © Steve Woit.

Chapter 17

Page 492: Courtesy of Waste Management, Inc. Page 494: Courtesy of Oklahoma Gas and Electric Co. Page 497: Courtesy of Hershey Foods Corporation. Page 498: Courtesy of The Larson Company, a subsidiary of Dean Foods Company. Page 500: Lincoln Potter/Gamma Liaison. Page 501: Courtesy of AT&T. Page 504: Courtesy of Brush Wellman Inc. Page 505: Courtesy of Campbell Soup Company. Page 506: © George Fulton. Page 511: Courtesy of Varian Associates, Inc., James Karageorge, Photographer. Page 512: BURK UZZLE/Lee Gross Associates.

Chapter 18

Page 522: Courtesy of Whirlpool Corporation. Page 525: © Dick Durrance II. Page 526: Courtesy of Brunswick Corporation. Page 530: Courtesy of American Airlines, a subsidiary of AMR Corporation. Page 532: Courtesy of The Quaker Oats Company. Page 535: Courtesy of Hilton Hawaiian Village in Honolulu. Page 541: Courtesy of Hewlett-Packard Company.

Chapter 19

Page 550: Courtesy of Chrysler Financial Corporation. Page 554: Courtesy of International Business Machines Corporation. Page 555: John Earle Photography. Page 558: Courtesy of Compaq Computer Corporation. Page 560: Steve Firebaugh, photographer for Airborne Express. Page 561: Courtesy of Mercantile Stores Company, Inc. Page 562: Courtesy of Chevron Corporation.

Chapter 20

Page 570: Courtesy of Home Shopping Network, Inc. Page 573: Courtesy of Clark Equipment Company. Page 574: Courtesy of Golden Valley Microwave Foods, Inc. Page 578: Courtesy of Autodie Corporation. Page 579: Courtesy of McDonald's Corporation. Page 580: Courtesy of Tasty Baking Company. Page 584: Courtesy of Boeing Commercial Airplane Group. Page 586: Courtesy of AT&T. Page 588: Reproduced with permission, © PepsiCo, Inc. 1989.

Chapter 21

Page 602: © Walter Bibikow. Page 605: © 1990 Arthur Meyerson for The Coca-Cola Company. Page 606: Courtesy of Chiquita Brands International, Inc. Page 609: Courtesy of Citibank. Page 613: © 1989 Gabe Palmer: Palmer/Kane Inc. Page 616: © 1990 Louis Psihoyos/Matrix. Page 619: Courtesy of Aluminum Company of America. Page 625: Mark Tuschman/The UpJohn Company.

Chapter 22

Page 632: Courtesy of Entrees On-Trays Inc. Page 635: T. Michael Keza/*Nation's Business*. Page 638: © 1989 Brian Smith. Page 640: Courtesy of Frieda's Finest/Produce Specialties, Inc. Page 641: © Steve Leonard. Page 642: © 1989 Mark Richards. Page 644: © Mike Steinberg/Black Star 1990./Black Star. All rights reserved. Page 646: Courtesy of MiniMaid Services, Inc., Leone Ackerly founder and CEO. Page 650: © 1990 Ann States. Page 652: © Steve Niedorf 1989. All rights reserved. Reprinted with permission.

Name Index

Company Index

SUBJECT INDEX